ADMINISTRATIVE LAW

ADMINISTRATIVE LAW

BY

SIR WILLIAM WADE

QC, LL D, FBA

An Honorary Bencher of Lincoln's Inn
Formerly Master of Gonville and Caius College, Cambridge,
Rouse Ball Professor of English Law
in the University of Cambridge and Professor of
English Law in the University of Oxford

Sixth Edition

CLARENDON PRESS · OXFORD
1988

Oxford University Press, Walton Street, Oxford OX2 6DP

Oxford New York Toronto
Delhi Bombay Calcutta Madras Karachi
Kuala Lumpur Singapore Hong Kong Tokyo
Nairobi Dar es Salaam Cape Town
Melbourne Auckland

and associated companies in
Berlin Ibadan

Published in the United States by
Oxford University Press, New York

First Edition 1961   Reprinted 1978, 1980
Second Edition 1967   Fifth Edition 1982
Third Edition 1971   Reprinted 1984, 1985
Fourth Edition 1977   Sixth Edition 1988

Translations
Italian, of 2nd Edition, published by
Giuffrè Editore, Milan, 1969
with Introduction by Massimo Severo Giannini

Spanish of 2nd Edition, published by
Instituto de Estudios Politicos, Madrid, 1971
with Introduction by Manuel Peréz Olea

British Library Cataloguing in Publication Data
Wade, H. W. R. (Henry William Rawson), 1918–
Administrative law
1. England. Administrative law
I. Title
344.202'6
ISBN 0-19-876220-8
ISBN 019-876219-4 (pbk)

Library of Congress Cataloging in Publication Data
Wade, H. W. R. (Henry William Rawson), 1918–
Includes bibliographical references and index.
1. Administrative law—Great Britain. I. Title.
KD4879.W3 1988 342.41'06—dc19 [344.1026] 88-10286
ISBN 0-19-876220-8
ISBN 0-19-876219-4 (pbk)

Typeset by Cotswold Typesetting Ltd, Gloucester and
Printed in Great Britain
at the University Printing House, Oxford
by David Stanford
Printer to the University

This Book is Dedicated
to Marjorie, my Wife

PREFACE

Six years ago I was rash enough to say in my preface that administrative law was settling down into a relatively steady state. Within a fortnight of that edition's appearance the House of Lords created the most seismic disturbance that the subject had suffered in many years. By proclaiming a rigid dichotomy between public and private law, but without explaining how the line was to be drawn, the House of Lords created a host of new problems for litigants which have by no means yet been resolved. These problems were accentuated by the rapid growth of public law litigation, itself a product of the ever-increasing range of judicial review. As is pointed out in the Justice-All Souls Review, the number of judges nominated to hear cases in the Crown Office list has risen from four in 1981 to fourteen in 1988.

There is no sign that the ferment in the subject will abate. To Lord Diplock's testimonial previously cited (now at p. 703) may be added that of Lord Justice Woolf: 'I find it difficult to believe that there has been any other period of our legal history where a sphere of law has developed in such a rapid and exciting manner as administrative law over the period since I started practice.'[1] Although this edition contains more examples than before of the withholding of remedies in judicial discretion and occasional comments on the over-employment of judicial review, these are no more than were to be expected in a subject seething with new ideas. They do not suggest that the judges are disposed to retreat from the high ground which they have invaded so vigorously in recent years. In defiance of theoretical obstacles they have extended their empire by reviewing the exercise of the royal prerogative, the rulings of non-legal bodies such as the Take-Over Panel, decisions which conflict with published policies or undertakings, and discretionary decisions which an earlier generation of lawyers would have considered impregnable. It might have been supposed from the previous edition that judicial intervention had been carried virtually to the limit, but the courts have continued to spring surprises and they doubtless have plenty more in store.

At the same time there has appeared, in some areas at least, a welcome tendency towards simplification of doctrine and the upholding of wide general principles. This has benefited members of disadvantaged groups, such as immigrants and prisoners, where the House of Lords has swept away exceptions formerly made in their disfavour for inadequate reasons. Some of the complicated rules about error of fact and law are, as noted in chapter 9, giving way to simpler and broader rules, which may already

---

[1] 'Public Law – Private Law: Why the Divide?' (the Harry Street Lecture) [1986] PL 220.

justify the comment of Sir Robin Cooke, that 'the substantive principles of judicial review are simply that the decision-maker must act in accordance with law, fairly and reasonably.'[2] These fundamentals now look so secure that explanations of their past vicissitudes, when the courts were vacillating, may seem redundant. But just as I was thinking of removing some of the early material on audi alteram partem I found it quoted in a High Court judgment and decided that it had better stay.

The appearance of *Administrative Justice* (the Justice-All Souls Review) is an event of first-rate importance. A summary of a few of its salient recommendations will be found in the Appendix. When a Royal Commission was first proposed in 1969 I was not in favour of it, since it seemed that it might be aimed at a radical reorganisation of the courts and might check the judicial revolution, then in full swing. But the unofficial Justice-All Souls Committee was not set up until 1978 and not until a decade after that (an interval hardly to be equalled even by a Royal Commission) did its report appear. By this time there was a different case for reform, new defects being revealed and old ones being thrown into prominence by the improvements in administrative justice generally. The Committee is to be commended for concentrating on these. Its work raises hopes that the Neill Report, as it may be called, will prove as effective in stimulating reform as was the Franks Report of 1957. Since that time it has been left to the judges to make nearly all the running, but many of the improvements which are now needed will require the aid of Parliament. That is true, also, of Lord Justice Woolf's proposal that there should be a Director of Civil Proceedings who could represent the public interest and initiate or intervene in litigation where necessary, so as to relax the strictness of adversarial procedure.[3]

No subject calls out more loudly for reform than the unfortunate procedural dichotomy enforced by *O'Reilly* v. *Mackman*, criticised alike in the Review and in this volume (chapter 18). Every admirer of the late Lord Diplock would agree that his speech in that case was a brilliant virtuoso performance. But the misfortune resulting from it is that procedural technicality, always the bugbear of this subject, has become more dominant and more troublesome than ever. A solitary judgment in a single case is not an ideal instrument for proclaiming radical and sweeping changes. In his later years Lord Diplock was inclined to yield to the temptation to restate whole branches of the law in his own terms. His mastery of administrative law and his outstanding contributions to it entitle these ex cathedra statements to great respect; but it may not, I hope, be impertinent to point out their drawbacks as a technique either of codification or of law reform. A feat of Lord Diplock's, however, which as

[2] In Taggart (ed.), *Judicial Review of Administrative Action in the 1980s*, 5.
[3] See [1986] PL 220 at 236.

a mere academic I can only envy is his ability to put forward a novel theory in a lecture and then to enshrine it canonically in a speech in the House of Lords (see p. 301).

A central proposal of the Justice-All Souls Review is that there should be an independent Administrative Review Commission comparable to the Administrative Review Council which has existed in Australia since 1975. The Australian Administrative Appeals Tribunal Act 1975, under which the Council is constituted, and the Administrative Decisions (Judicial Review) Act 1977, which sets out the grounds for judicial review (with improvements) and confers a right to a reasoned decision on request, are models of enlightened legislation which Britain could follow if and when Parliament enacts, as surely it ought, a measure which will rescue litigants from the traps and pitfalls of the procedural dichotomy. That is now the most urgent problem, and a possible line of attack on it is suggested at pp. 680–1.

It will be noticed in this edition that many cases are cited from newspaper reports. The flow of material has become so great that the regular reports are unable to cope with it all. Much as any author of law books would deplore the appearance of yet another series, it does seem that administrative law is no less in need of specialised reports than, for example, local government, industrial relations, housing and road traffic. Australia and New Zealand already have administrative law reports.

My friend and colleague Professor D. G. T. Williams, President of Wolfson College, Cambridge, generously offered to read the proofs of this edition and gave me valuable suggestions as well as corrections. The Secretariat of the Council on Tribunals were most helpful to me in revising chapters 23 and 24. The services of the Clarendon Press have been as admirable as ever. For all this help I am most grateful.

I hope that I have succeeded in incorporating all important domestic material published before the date of this preface, though sometimes with difficulty where it demanded alteration of proofs. With overseas material there is a time-lag, sometimes a long one, in its arrival, so that I must plead this excuse if there are omissions of the most recent events.

20 June 1988   H.W.R.W.

CONTENTS

PART III   POWERS AND JURISDICTION

PART IV   DISCRETIONARY POWER

PART V   NATURAL JUSTICE

PART VI   REMEDIES AND LIABILITY

TABLE OF STATUTES

A chronological list of statutes will be found after this alphabetical table

CHRONOLOGICAL LIST OF STATUTES

For page references see the preceding alphabetical table

1215 (1225) Magna Carta
1427 Statute of Sewers
1461 Statute 1 Edw. 4, c. 1
1531 Statute of Sewers
1539 Statute of Proclamations
1601 Poor Relief Act
1660 Statute 12 Charles 2, c. 23
1679 Habeas Corpus Act
1689 Bill of Rights
1694 Bank of England Act
1700 Act of Settlement
1729 Licensing Act
1740 13 Geo. 2, c. 18
1742 Justices Jurisdiction Act
1751 Constables Protection Act
1816 Habeas Corpus Act
1829 Metropolitan Police Act
1831 Vestries Act
1832 Reform Act
1834 Poor Law Act
1834 Poor Law Amendment Act
1834–1930 Poor Law Acts
1834 Highway Act
1835 Municipal Corporations Act
1838 Small Tenements Recovery Act
1842 Defence Act
1843 Scientific Societies Act
1845 Companies Clauses Consolidation Act
1845 General Inclosure Act
1845 Lands Clauses Consolidation Act
1845 Railways Clauses Consolidation Act
1847 Markets and Fairs Clauses Act
1847 Towns Improvement Clauses Act
1848 Justices Protection Act
1848 Metropolitan Sewers Act
1848 Public Health Act
1848 Summary Jurisdiction Act
1849 Quarter Sessions Act
1850 Court of Chancery, England, Act
1851 Evidence Act
1851 Labouring Classes Lodging Houses Act
1852 Court of Chancery Procedure Act
1853 Charitable Trusts Act
1854 Common Law Procedure Act

1855 Metropolis Management Act
1857 Summary Jurisdiction Act
1860 Petitions of Right Act
1862 Habeas Corpus Act
1863 Telegraph Act
1864 Union Assessment Committee Amendment Act
1868 Promissory Oaths Act
1870 Education Act
1870 Naturalisation Act
1870–1935 Extradition Acts
1871 Railway Regulation Act
1872 Ballot Act
1872 Board of Trade Inquiries Act
1872 Public Health Act
1873–1875 Judicature Acts
1875 Public Health Act
1876 Appellate Jurisdiction Act
1881 Fugitive Offenders Act
1882 Electric Lighting Act
1882 Municipal Corporations Act
1883 Municipal Corporations Act
1884 Reform Act
1886 Local Government Act
1887–1943 British Settlements Acts
1888 Local Government Act
1888 Statute Law Revision Act
1890–1913 Foreign Jurisdiction Acts
1890 Housing of the Working Classes Act
1892 Foreign Marriage Act
1893 Public Authorities Protection Act
1893 Rules Publication Act
1894 Local Government Act
1894 Merchant Shipping Act
1897–1945 Workmen's Compensation Acts
1889 London Government Act
1902 Education Act
1904 Wireless Telegraphy Act
1905 Aliens Act
1907 Patents and Designs Act
1908 Old Age Pensions Act
1908 Smallholdings and Allotments Act
1909 Housing and Town Planning Act
1910 Finance (1909–1910) Act
1911 National Insurance Act

TABLE OF CASES

Principal references are shown in bold type

PART I
INTRODUCTION

1

INTRODUCTION

GOVERNMENT, LAW AND JUSTICE

The administrative state

'Until August 1914,' it has been said, 'a sensible law-abiding Englishman could pass through life and hardly notice the existence of the state, beyond the post office and the policeman.'[1] This worthy person could not, however, claim to be a very observant citizen. For by 1914 there were already abundant signs of the profound change in the conception of government which was to mark the twentieth century. The state schoolteacher, the national insurance officer, the labour exchange, the sanitary and factory inspectors, with their necessary companion the tax collector, were among the outward and visible signs of this change. The modern administrative state was already taking shape, reflecting the feeling that it was the duty of government to provide remedies for social and economic evils of many kinds. This feeling was the natural consequence of the great constitutional reforms of the nineteenth century. The enfranchised population could now make its wants known, and through the ballot box it had acquired the power to make the political system respond.

The advent of the welfare state might be dated from the National Insurance Act 1911, though the Education Act 1902, the Old Age Pensions Act 1908 and the Housing and Town Planning Act 1909 also have claims to consideration. But long before that period Parliament had imposed controls and regulations by such statutes as the Factories Acts, the Public Health Acts, and the railway legislation.[2] By 1854 there were already sixteen central government inspectorates.[3] The period 1865–1900 had been called 'the period of collectivism'[4] because of the outburst of regulatory legislation and the tendency to entrust more and more power to the state.[5]

---

[1] A. J. P. Taylor, *English History, 1914–1945*, 1.

[2] For the growth of the central government's powers and machinery in the nineteenth century see Holdsworth, *History of English Law*, xiv. 90–204.

[3] Parris, *Constitutional Bureaucracy*, 200.

[4] Dicey, *Law and Opinion in England in the Nineteenth Century*, 64.

[5] In 1888 Maitland wrote (*Constitutional History of England*, 1955 reprint, 501): 'We are becoming a much governed nation, governed by all manners of councils and boards and officers, central and local, high and low, exercising the powers which have been committed to them by modern statutes.'

The author of that remark would have been hard put to it to find words for the period since the second world war, which is as different from his own as his own was different from that of the Stuart kings. As his generation came to recognise the need for the administrative state, they had also to devise more efficient machinery. The Northcote–Trevelyan Report (1854) on the civil service was one milestone; another was the opening of the civil service to competitive examination in 1870. Meanwhile the modern type of ministerial department was replacing the older commissions and boards. The doctrine of ministerial responsibility was crystallising, with its correlative principles of civil service anonymity and detachment from politics. Thus were laid the foundations of the vast and powerful bureaucracy which is the principal instrument of administration today. Scarcely less striking has been the expansion of the sphere of local government, extending to education, town and country planning, and a great many other services and controls.

If the state is to care for its citizens from the cradle to the grave, to protect their environment, to educate them at all stages, to provide them with employment, training, houses, medical services, pensions, and, in the last resort, food, clothing, and shelter, it needs a huge administrative apparatus. Relatively little can be done merely by passing Acts of Parliament and leaving it to the courts to enforce them. There are far too many problems of detail, and far too many matters which cannot be decided in advance. No one may erect a building without planning permission, but no system of general rules can prescribe for every case. There must be discretionary power. If discretionary power is to be tolerable, it must be kept under two kinds of control: political control through Parliament, and legal control through the courts. Equally there must be control over the boundaries of legal power, as to which there is normally no discretion. If a water authority may levy sewerage rates only upon properties connected to public sewers, there must be means of preventing it from rating unsewered properties unlawfully.[6] The legal aspects of all such matters are the concern of administrative law.

Administrative law

A first approximation to a definition of administrative law is to say that it is the law relating to the control of governmental power. This, at any rate, is the heart of the subject. The governmental power in question is not that of Parliament: Parliament as the legislature is sovereign and beyond legal control. But the powers of all other public authorities are subordinated to the law, just as much in the case of the Crown and ministers as in the case of

---

[6] See *Daymond* v. *Plymouth City Council* [1976] AC 609; below, p. 852.

local authorities and other public bodies. All such subordinate powers have two inherent characteristics. First, they are all subject to legal limitations; there is no such thing as absolute or unfettered administrative power. Secondly, and consequentially, it is always possible for any power to be abused. Even where Parliament enacts that a minister may make such order as he thinks fit for a certain purpose, the court may still invalidate the order if it infringes one of the many judge-made rules. And the court will invalidate it, *a fortiori*, if it infringes the limits which Parliament itself has ordained.

The primary purpose of administrative law, therefore, is to keep the powers of government within their legal bounds, so as to protect the citizen against their abuse. The powerful engines of authority must be prevented from running amok. 'Abuse', it should be made clear, carries no necessary innuendo of malice or bad faith. Government departments may misunderstand their legal position as easily as may other people, and the law which they have to administer is frequently complex and uncertain. Abuse is therefore inevitable, and it is all the more necessary that the law should provide means to check it. It is a common occurrence that a minister's order is set aside by the court as unlawful, that a compulsory purchase order has to be quashed or that the decision of a planning authority is declared to be irregular and void. The courts are constantly occupied with cases of this kind which are nothing more than the practical application of the rule of law, meaning that the government must have legal warrant for what it does and that if it acts unlawfully the citizen has an effective legal remedy. On this elementary foundation the courts have erected an intricate and sophisticated structure of rules.

As well as power there is duty. It is also the concern of administrative law to see that public authorities can be compelled to perform their duties if they make default. The Inland Revenue may have a duty to repay tax, a licensing authority may have a duty to grant a licence, the Home Secretary may have a duty to admit an immigrant. The law provides compulsory remedies for such situations, thus dealing with the negative as well as the positive side of maladministration.

Function distinguished from structure

As a second approximation to a definition, administrative law may be said to be the body of general principles which govern the exercise of powers and duties by public authorities. This is only one part of the mass of law to which public authorities are subject. All the detailed law about their composition and structure, though clearly related to administrative law, lies beyond the proper scope of the subject. So it is not necessary to investigate how local councillors are elected or what are the qualifications for service on various tribunals. Nor is it necessary to enumerate all the powers which governmental authorities possess, which by itself would require a book. A great deal must be taken for granted in order to clear the field.

What has to be isolated is the law about the *manner* in which public authorities must exercise their functions, distinguishing function from structure and looking always for general principles. If it appears that some unwritten law requires that a man should be given a fair hearing before his house can be pulled down, before his trading licence can be revoked, and before he can be dismissed from a public office, a general principle of administrative law can be observed. If likewise a variety of ministers and local authorities are required by unwritten law to exercise their various statutory powers reasonably and only upon relevant grounds, there too is a general principle. Although this book supplies some particulars about the structure of public authorities and about some of their more notable powers, this is done for the sake of information merely. The essence of administrative law lies in judge-made doctrines which apply right across the board and which therefore set legal standards of conduct for public authorities generally.

There are, however, some areas in which more attention must be paid to structure. This is particularly the case with special tribunals and statutory inquiries, and to some extent also with delegated legislation. It is not by coincidence that these are the last three chapters of the book. They stand apart for the reason that the problems which need discussion relate as much to the organisation of the machinery for dispensing justice, and in the case of delegated legislation to the machinery of government, as to the role of the courts of law. In these final chapters, accordingly, there is a shift of emphasis towards what might be called constitutional questions.

The whole of administrative law, indeed, may be treated as a branch of constitutional law, since it flows directly from the constitutional principles of the rule of law, the sovereignty of Parliament and the independence of the judiciary; and it does much to determine the balance of power between the state and the citizen. The constitutional foundations of the subject are discussed later. It is, however, so distinct in character and so developed in detail that it needs to be studied independently.

Administrative justice

What gives unity to the subjects mentioned above, and further epitomised below, is the quest for administrative justice. Diverse as some of them are, this is the connecting thread which runs throughout. At every point the question is, how can the profession of the law contribute to the improvement of the technique of government? It is because all the various topics offer scope for this missionary spirit that they form a harmonious whole. Subject as it is to the vast empires of executive power that have been created, the public must be able to rely on the law to ensure that all this power may be used in a way conformable to its ideas of fair dealing and good administration. As liberty is subtracted, justice must be added. The more power the government wields, the more sensitive is public opinion to any kind of abuse or unfairness. While the greater part of this book is concerned with the standards required by the courts, the last two chapters (on tribunals and inquiries) are concerned also with standards required by Act of Parliament and by good administration. Taken together, the work of judiciary and legislature amounts to an extensive system of protection. It has its weaknesses, but it also has great strengths.

A continual danger is the tight control exercised over Parliament by the government of the day. The party system gives the government such dominance that the traditional parliamentary control over the executive has been progressively weakened. Legislation is drafted by government departments in their own interests and Parliament often has little influence upon it. The machinery of administrative justice, e.g. provisions for appeals, tribunals, and inquiries, receives little effective parliamentary scrutiny. But occasionally a new safeguard is provided, as by the constitution of the Council on Tribunals in 1958.[7] The legal system of administrative justice has received valuable supplementation from the Parliamentary Commissioner for Administration, otherwise known as the ombudsman, who since 1967 has been able to criticise, and often to remedy, injustice caused by maladministration lying beyond the reach of the law.[8]

ADMINISTRATIVE LAW EPITOMISED

A synopsis

A short epitome of the topics which make up administrative law, in the order in which they are treated in this book, will probably give a clearer idea of its subject-matter than further preliminary discussion. They may be catalogued as follows.

1. *Administrative authorities.* Chapters 3–6 describe in outline the legal framework of government, comprising central and local government, the police, and public corporations. Two features of the central government need detailed explanation: the peculiar law governing service under the

---

[7] Below, p. 914.
[8] Below, p. 79.

Crown, which makes civil servants liable to dismissal at will but gives them some of the benefits of modern labour law; and the Parliamentary Commissioner for Administration, alias the ombudsman, who since 1967 has investigated complaints against acts of maladministration by the central government. The outstanding feature of local government is the reorganisation into fewer and stronger local authorities effected by the Local Government Act 1972. Though stronger in one sense, local authorities have become weaker in another as the central government has increased its dominance. There is much more detailed law about local government than about the central government. The police have a special position regulated both by statute and by common law and their administration, status, and powers need explanation; in their case also there is legislation about the handling of complaints. Public corporations are a highly miscellaneous class but they include one more or less uniform, though dwindling, group, nationalised industries. The latter are not governmental authorities and strictly speaking do not fall within administrative law. The line dividing governmental bodies from others must be drawn at some point along the range of public corporations, which runs from mere government departments at one extreme to mere commercial enterprises at the other. The boundaries of administrative law are conterminous with the boundaries of government.

2. *Administrative functions.* Chapter 7 is necessarily selective. An attempt to describe all the various powers and duties of government would fill hundreds of pages without teaching much about administrative law as a system of legal principles. But there are certain fields of public administration which are particularly prominent in the case-law of the subject, and an outline of these will make later discussion more intelligible. The topics selected are compulsory purchase of land, town and country planning, new towns and town development, community land (despite repealing legislation), housing, health, social security, immigration, and prison discipline. The sketches here given are designed merely to supply background information. Nevertheless this group, taken together, illustrate the close collaboration between central government and local authorities which social administration demands.

3. *Judicial control—general principles.* Here we reach the essence of the subject itself. Its rules are derived from some basic constitutional principles noted in chapter 2; the rule of law, the sovereignty of Parliament and the power of the independent judiciary combine to produce the doctrine of ultra vires, which is the main principle on which almost all the courts' interventions are founded. This doctrine merely states that public authorities must act within the powers given to them by Act of Parliament. But there is much detailed law as to how such Acts should be interpreted, as is seen in chapters 8 and 9. Failure to fulfil some condition may or may not

be fatal. The word 'may' may turn out to mean 'must'. The authority may or may not be bound by some undertaking it has given. Then there are problems of jurisdiction over questions of fact and questions of law. The authority may be empowered to act if certain facts exist, or if it thinks that they exist, but what if they do not exist? And what if the authority makes some mistake as to the law? Here the courts must grapple with fundamental questions of jurisdiction, which basically means simply power. There is also a group of related problems about invalidity and nullity; an administrative act may be valid for some purposes but void for others. Chapters 8–10 cover an area of considerable technicality, in which courts have laid down important rules for keeping governmental authorities within the bounds of the law and in which they are still developing new restraints. But this is not the whole domain of judicial control. Two very important fields, which can be treated by themselves, remain to be dealt with.

4. *Discretionary power*. Most of the things that administrative authorities are empowered to do involve the exercise of discretion: decisions have to be made in the public interest, based on policy. Licensing powers are a good example. The rules about judicial review of discretion fall into two classes, the subjects of chapters 11 and 12 respectively. First, the discretion given by Parliament must be protected. It must be exercised by the proper authority only and not by some agent or delegate. It must be exercised without restraint and as the public interest may from time to time require. It must not be fettered or hampered by contracts or other bargains or by self-imposed rules of thumb. So a distinction must be made between following a consistent policy and blindly applying some rigid rule. Secondly, discretion must not be abused. A minister, for instance, may act within the apparent limits of his statutory powers, but still he may act for wrong motives or on irrelevant grounds or arbitrarily or unreasonably. The Act may say that he may revoke any television licence, but the court will not allow him to do so unreasonably or oppressively.[9] It may say that he may make such order as he thinks fit, but he will not be allowed to pass beyond the bounds of reasonableness. Here the judges become involved with the merits of discretionary action, finding their warrant in the implied intentions of Parliament and reading between the lines of the empowering Act. If the minister's order is not in line with the implicit policy of Parliament, it is outside the powers of the Act and ultra vires. The hypothesis that powers must be exercised reasonably is assumed to underlie the Act. In this way the law can restrain the abuse of the widely expressed powers which Parliament hands out to ministers, at their own instance,

[9] *Congreve* v. *Home Office* [1976] QB 629: below, p. 406.

with too free a hand. It is by invoking the principle of reasonableness that the courts have performed some of their boldest feats, particularly in recent years.

5. *Natural justice.* Just as the principle of reasonableness and its corollaries can be used to control the substance of an administrative decision, so the principles of natural justice can be used to enforce fair procedure. The concept of natural justice has existed for many centuries and it has crystallised into two rules: that no man should be judge in his own cause; and that no man should suffer without first being given a fair hearing. Chapters 14 and 15 explain these rules in detail. Under the first rule the decision of a tribunal or other collective body will be invalid if any person has participated in it who might be thought to be prejudiced or biased. Under the second rule any act of administrative power is likely to be invalid if the person adversely affected has not first been given a fair opportunity to object. This second rule is a particularly wide one, applying to the taking of property, refusal or revocation of licences, dismissal from public offices, and many other matters. It has come to play a very active role in administrative litigation and its revival since 1963 has been one of the most conspicuous signs of the progressive policy of the courts. They have been developing and extending the principles of natural justice so as to build up a kind of code of fair administrative procedure, to be obeyed by authorities of all kinds. They have done this, once again, by assuming that Parliament always intends power to be exercised fairly. However drastic the powers of government, therefore, the courts can see fair play.

6. *Remedies and liability.* A group of chapters (16–19) now deals with remedies. English administrative law has a system of powerful remedies, which bite as hard upon ministers of the Crown and other public authorities as they do upon private persons. They fall into two main groups, ordinary remedies and prerogative remedies, the latter being almost entirely confined to the sphere of public law. Ample mechanisms are thus supplied for quashing or forbidding unlawful acts, for awarding damages if appropriate, and for enforcing the performance of public duties. In theory the remedy should follow automatically from the right; but in administrative law, as elsewhere, the courts have developed their jurisdiction by extending remedies, sometimes preferring to disguise a new principle under some procedural technicality. The different remedies also have their own peculiarities. This has led to difficulties, some of which have been remedied by procedural reforms; and those reforms have themselves produced difficulties, in particular an excessively rigid division between public and private law. Problems also arise from legislation which attempts to restrict or remove legal remedies, so as to make administrative action of some kinds unchallengeable, or challengeable only within a short time. Unchallengeability is stoutly resisted by the courts, even to the extent of

refusing to enforce statutory clauses which deny remedies, so as to preserve the courts' protective role at all costs. Closely connected with remedies is the law of liability in damages for tort and breach of contract (chapters 20 and 21). Governmental bodies are legally liable for wrongs which they commit, such as damage caused by their vehicles on the road or other acts of negligence. Recent decisions have notably extended their liability for negligence both in deed and word. There are also certain special governmental torts, such as malicious revocation of a licence and deliberate abuse of authority. Although in principle the Crown bears the same liabilities, the peculiarities of the Crown's legal position demand separate explanation (chapter 21).

7. *Legislative and adjudicative procedures.* Under this head are grouped two disparate subjects: delegated legislation (chapter 22); and tribunals and inquiries (chapters 23 and 24). Delegated legislation means department rules and regulations, local authorities' byelaws, and other rules which are made administratively under the authority of Acts of Parliament. These are also subject to the doctrine of ultra vires, including even the principle of reasonableness, so the courts can invalidate them if necessary. They are required by law to be published, and the system of laying them before Parliament offers certain opportunities for political scrutiny. Tribunals and inquiries are statutory mechanisms which are in constant use for adjudicating disputes and hearing objections. Generally speaking, tribunals determine facts and apply law much as does a court. Examples are a national insurance tribunal deciding a claim to unemployment benefit and an industrial tribunal adjudicating a case of unfair dismissal. Inquiries, on the other hand, are usually held as a preliminary to some decision of policy by a minister, for example by confirming a compulsory purchase order or deciding a planning appeal. Tribunals play a most important part in the administration of the welfare state; inquiries are an indispensable part of the system for preventing the anti-social use of land. Both these procedures were at one time allowed to drift too far away from the legal system, so that there was a loss of public confidence in their fairness. Remedial measures were taken in 1958, when the Council on Tribunals was established to watch over the standard of justice in both tribunals and inquiries. Procedures have now been improved and contacts with the courts of law are closer. As well as discussing the law about tribunals and inquiries, these final chapters consider the problems of legal policy and organisation which the use of these special procedures raises. Inquiries involve an awkward amalgam of quasi-judicial procedure and political decision; and as well as being concerned with private rights they provide a system of public participation in decisions about planning, roads, reservoirs, power stations, airports, and other projects affecting the environment. This mixture of functions produces some dilemmas.

CHARACTERISTICS OF THE LAW

The Anglo-American system

The foregoing synopsis of the content of administrative law needs to be supplemented by pointing out some of the subject's salient characteristics, several of which mark it off sharply from the administrative law of other European countries. The British system is followed throughout the English-speaking world. Although in the United States of America it has naturally followed its own line of evolution, it is recognisably the same system.[10] This is true also of Scotland, although it must never be forgotten that Scots law may differ materially from English. It may be said of Scots administrative law that its foundations are the same as in England, but that there are important differences in detail.[11] This book does not deal with Scots law in general, but it points in several places to Scots law as an example of enlightenment in matters where English law has shown itself defective;[12] and useful Scots decisions can often be cited. Occasionally also a deficiency in Scots law is to be observed.[13]

The outstanding characteristic of the Anglo-American system is that the ordinary courts, and not special administrative courts, decide cases involving the validity of governmental action. There is no formal distinction between public law and private law. The ordinary law of the land, as modified by Acts of Parliament, applies to ministers, local authorities, and other agencies of government, and the ordinary courts dispense it. This is part of the traditional concept of the rule of law, as explained in the next chapter. This has both advantages and disadvantages. The advantages are that the citizen can turn to courts of high standing in the public esteem, whose independence is beyond question; that highly efficient remedies are available; that there are none of the demarcation problems of division of jurisdictions; and that the government is seen to be subject to the ordinary law of the land. Its disadvantages are that the judges are not experts in administrative law; that neglect of the subject in the past has seriously weakened it at certain times; and that its principles have sometimes been submerged in the mass of miscellaneous law which the ordinary courts administer. These disadvantages have recently become less

[10] The British and American systems are compared in Schwartz and Wade, *Legal Control of Government.*

[11] For the Scots system see Mitchell, *Constitutional Law*, 2nd edn., Pt. 3; Scottish Law Commission's Memorandum No. 14 (1971, A. W. Bradley); *The Laws of Scotland* (Stair Memorial Encyclopaedia), vol. i (A. W. Bradley).

[12] As in the case of default powers (below, p. 747) and of Crown privilege (below, p. 833).

[13] As the lack of prerogative remedies and review for error on the face of the record (below, p. 305).

menacing as the judiciary have become more conscious of the need to strengthen and extend the legal control of government.

Suggestions for improvement

It was often suggested that all administrative cases should be dealt with by one division of the High Court, so that its judges would acquire expertise and the dangers of diffusion would be minimised.[14] Under the arrangement of court business which obtained until 1977, applications for prerogative remedies would usually come before a Queen's Bench Divisional Court, actions for damages and declarations before a single Queen's Bench judge, and actions for injunctions would be heard in the Chancery Division. The practice reflected the division between the old courts of common law and chancery, which had been obsolete for a century; and it might have been devised for producing the maximum divergence of judicial opinion and the minimum consistency of principle. In 1977, however, procedural reforms were introduced which concentrated cases concerned with administrative law in the Queen's Bench Divisional Court, so that the court in effect became an administrative division of the High Court.[15] These reforms were pioneered by legislation in Ontario and New Zealand, and adopted in this country as the result of a report of the Law Commission made in 1976.[16] New Zealand had already established an administrative division of the High Court in 1968.[17]

Much wider proposals had been contemplated by the Law Commission in 1969, when they recommended that a royal commission or comparable body should conduct an inquiry into the whole system of administrative law in Britain, covering not only the scope of judicial control and remedies, but also the organisation and personnel of the courts dealing with proceedings against the administration.[18] This would have called in question the whole basis of the Anglo-American system and consideration would have to have been given to the possibility of replacing it with a hierarchy of special administrative courts of the Continental type.[19] It was just at this time, however, that the English courts were showing strong

[14] See e.g. *Administration Under Law* (a JUSTICE booklet), p. 26; (1968) 21 *Current Legal Problems* 75 at 90 (Wade); *Administrative Justice* (JUSTICE—All Souls Review), ch. 7.

[15] See below, p. 671. Since 1980, however, these cases normally come before a single judge under SI 1980 No. 2000, so that the expert character of the court may be diminished.

[16] Cmnd. 6407 (1976).

[17] Judicature Amendment Act 1968. For a commentary see (1972) 22 UTLJ 258 (Sir R. Wild, CJNZ).

[18] Law Com. No. 20, Cmnd. 4059 (1969).

[19] As advocated by Professor W. A. Robson to the Committee on Ministers' Powers (see Cmd. 4060 (1932), p. 110 and Robson, *Justice and Administrative Law*, 3rd edn., ch. 6); and in [1965] PL 95, [1967] CLJ 46 (J. D. B. Mitchell).

signs of throwing off the defeatism of the previous period, when it had certainly seemed that radical reforms might be necessary. The Lord Chancellor declined to authorise the proposed inquiry, and instead asked the Law Commission to undertake a review of the system of remedies only.[20] For that was a more evident need; and as a result of the Commission's above-mentioned report of 1976 the procedure for obtaining the various remedies was reformed—though with results which were less felicitous than had been hoped.[21]

The Continental system

In France, Italy, West Germany, and a number of other countries there is a separate system of administrative courts which deal with administrative cases exclusively. As a natural consequence, administrative law develops on its own independent lines, and is not enmeshed with ordinary private law as it is in the Anglo-American system. In France droit administratif is a highly specialised science, administered by the judicial wing of the Conseil d'État, which is staffed by judges of great professional expertise, and by a network of local tribunals of first instance.[22] Courts of this kind, whose work is confined to administrative law, may have a clearer view of the developments needed to keep pace with the powers of the state than have courts which are maids of all work. Certainly the Conseil d'État has shown itself more aware of the demands of justice in respect of financial compensation,[23] in contrast to the English reluctance—as Lord Wilberforce has observed.[24] But the French system is not without its disadvantages. Its remedies are narrow in scope and not always effective, and the division of jurisdictions between civil and administrative courts is the subject of rules of great intricacy.

Although the structure of the courts is so different, many of the cases that come before the Conseil d'État are easily recognisable as the counterparts of familiar English situations. Review of administrative findings of fact and determinations of law, abuse of discretion, ultra vires—all of these and many other English rubrics can be illustrated from the administrative law of France. There is also the similarity that both English and French systems are contained in case-law rather than in any statutory code. French authorities are by no means out of place when precedents are being sought for guidance on some novel issue.

---

[20] 306 HL Deb col. 190 (4 December 1969).

[21] See below, p. 676. For the JUSTICE—All Souls Review see Appendix.

[22] For an account in English see Brown and Garner, *French Administrative Law*, 3rd edn.

[23] As noted below, p. 386.

[24] In *Hoffman–La Roche & Co.* v. *Secretary of State for Trade and Industry* [1975] AC 295 at 358, contrasting 'more developed legal systems'.

Some French doctrines, such as those based upon the principle of equality, are without English equivalents: the French state broadcasting authority may not discriminate against an orchestra on unreasonable grounds;[25] but the British Broadcasting Corporation and the Independent Broadcasting Authority, which provide for their programmes by contract, probably enjoy the ordinary commercial freedom to give or deny their business to whom they wish on any grounds whatever.[26] And the French courts, unlike the British, are much occupied with litigation about employment in the civil service. On the other hand, French administrative law is weak in preventive and compulsory remedies, and largely lacks the system of public inquiries in connection with decisions of policy. Despite these differences, there is a general similarity of subject-matter, since all democratic countries face similar problems in attempting to impose legal control on ever-expanding state power.

In addition to the administrative jurisdictions of the various European countries there are the European Communities. Community law, which claims precedence over the laws of the member states, is in the course of rapid development by the European Court of Justice in Luxemburg, in accordance with the Treaties of Rome and Paris and the legislation made under them by the Community authorities. Community law contains its own administrative law, under which the Court of Justice can annul unlawful acts of the community authorities and award compensation against them 'in accordance with the general principles common to the laws of the member states'.[27] The Court also adjudicates, like the French administrative courts, disputes between the Community authorities and their employees. Its constitution and powers are in fact modelled on those of the Conseil d'État. Community law as laid down by the Court has to be applied by the courts of the United Kingdom and has overriding effect over Acts of Parliament.[28] Although the administrative law of the Communities at present operates directly only in its own separate sphere, it is showing signs of influencing our own administrative law[29] and will doubtless do so more and more as the interaction of the two legal systems proceeds.

Historical development

Administrative law in England has a long history, but the subject in its modern form did not begin to emerge until the second half of the

---

[25] CE 9 mars 1951, *Société des Concerts du Conservatoire*, Rec. 151.
[26] See below, p. 164.
[27] See Treaty of Paris, arts. 33–41; Treaty of Rome, arts. 173, 174, 215.
[28] European Communities Act 1972, s. 2(4).
[29] See the *Bourgoin* case, below, p. 776.

seventeenth century. A considerable number of its basic rules can be dated
back to that period, and some, such as the principles of natural justice, are
even older. In earlier times the justices of the peace, who were used as all-
purpose administrative authorities, were superintended by the judges of
assize, who on their circuits conveyed instructions from the Crown, dealt
with defaults and malpractices, and reported back to London on the affairs
of the country. Under the Tudor monarchy this system was tightened up
under the authority of the Privy Council and of the provincial Councils in
the North and in Wales.[30] This was a long step towards the centralisation of
power in a state of the modern type. The Privy Council's superintendence
was exercised through the Star Chamber, which could punish those who
disobeyed the justices of the peace, and reprove or replace the justices
themselves. But the powers of the state were not often challenged at the
administrative level. A freeman of a borough might resist unlawful
expulsion by obtaining a writ of mandamus[31] and writs of certiorari might
lie against the Commissioners of Sewers if they usurped authority.[32] But it
was on the constitutional rather than on the administrative plane, and
notably on the battlefields of the civil war, that the issues between the
Crown and its subjects were fought out.

After the abolition of the Star Chamber in 1642, and the destruction of
most of the Privy Council's executive power by the Revolution of 1688, a
new situation arose. The old machinery of central political control had
been broken, and nothing was put in its place. Instead, the Court of King's
Bench stepped into the breach and there began the era of the control of
administration through the courts of law. The King's Bench made its writs
of mandamus, certiorari, and prohibition, as well as its ordinary remedy of
damages, available to any one who wished to dispute the legality of
administrative acts of the justices and of such other authorities as there
were. The political dangers of doing so had ceased to exist, and the field was
clear for the development of administrative law. The chapter on local
government explains the part played by the justices in the eighteenth
century, and how in the course of the nineteenth century most of their
administrative functions were transferred to elected local authorities. All
through this time the courts were steadily extending the doctrine of ultra
vires and the principles of judicial review. These rules were applied without
distinction to all the new statutory authorities, such as county councils,
boards of works, school boards, and commissioners, just as they had been to
the justices of the peace. As the administrative state began to emerge later in

---

[30] Holdsworth, *History of English Law*, iv. 71.
[31] As in *Bagg's Case* (1616) 11 Co. Rep. 93; below, p. 500.
[32] As in *Hetley* v. *Boyer* (1614) Cro. Jac. 336; *Smith's Case* (1670) 1 Vent. 66; below, p. 395.

the nineteenth century, exactly the same rules were applied to central government departments. This is the same body of law which is still being developed today. The history of many of the detailed doctrines, such as the rules for review of jurisdictional questions, the principles of natural justice, and the scope of certiorari, will be seen in the treatment of them later in this book.

Administrative law, as it now exists, has therefore a continuous history from the later part of the seventeenth century. The eighteenth century was the period *par excellence* of the rule of law,[33] and it provided highly congenial conditions in which the foundations of judicial control could be consolidated. It is remarkable how little alteration has proved necessary in the law laid down two centuries ago in a different age. The spread of the tree still increases and it throws out new branches, but its roots remain where they have been for centuries.

Twentieth-century failings

Up to about the end of the nineteenth century administrative law kept pace with the expanding powers of the state. But in the twentieth century it began to fall behind. The courts showed signs of losing confidence in their constitutional function and they hesitated to develop new rules in step with the mass of new regulatory legislation. In 1914 the House of Lords missed an important opportunity to apply the principles of natural justice to statutory inquiries,[34] a new form of administrative procedure which ought to have been made to conform to the ordinary man's sense of fairness, for example by allowing him to know the reasons for the minister's decision and to see the inspector's report on which the decision was based. Not until 1958 were these mistakes corrected, and even then the remedy was provided by legislation and administrative concession rather than by the courts themselves. Meanwhile the executive took full advantage of the weak judicial policy, and inevitably there were loud complaints about bureaucracy. Eminent lawyers, including a Lord Chief Justice, published books under such titles as *The New Despotism*[35] and *Bureaucracy Triumphant*.[36] At the same time, Parliament was losing its control over ministers, so making it all the more obvious that the law was failing in its task of enforcing standards of fairness in the exercise of statutory powers.

The report of the Committee on Ministers' Powers of 1932[37] was

---

[33] See below, p. 104.
[34] *Local Government Board* v. *Arlidge* [1915] AC 120; below, p. 508.
[35] By Lord Hewart CJ (1929).
[36] By Sir Carleton Allen (1931).
[37] Cmd. 4060 (1932).

intended to appease the complaints about bureaucracy. It covered ministerial powers of delegated legislation and of judicial or quasi-judicial decision. By a quasi-judicial decision was meant a decision based on government policy, such as a decision to confirm a compulsory purchase order or a slum-clearance scheme; the quasi-judicial element was the preliminary procedure for investigating facts and hearing objections at an inquiry. This was opposed to a judicial decision, where after the facts are found the case is decided according to some rule or principle already laid down, or deduced objectively by reasoning into which executive policy does not enter, as happens in a court of law. Having made this elementary analysis, the Committee made some sound criticisms of the system of public inquiries which had come into use. But their recommendations for making it fairer and more impartial were not entirely realistic and they proved unacceptable to the strongly entrenched administration.[38] The report led to certain improvements in delegated legislation, but in other respects it was little more than an academic exercise. It did not discuss the scope of judicial control, and although it called for the vigilant observance of the principles of natural justice, it did not consider how widely they should be applied.

Discontent with administrative procedures therefore continued to accumulate. The practical reforms that were needed were not made until 1958, when the Report of the Committee on Administrative Tribunals and Enquiries (the Franks Committee)[39] led to the Tribunals and Inquiries Act 1958 and to a programme of procedural improvements, all to be supervised by a new body, the Council on Tribunals. The story of these reforms is told in later chapters.[40] They were of great importance in administrative law, but they were in no way due to the work of the courts.

The relapse and the revival

During and after the second world war a deep gloom settled upon administrative law, which reduced it to the lowest ebb at which it had stood for centuries. The courts and the legal profession seemed to have forgotten the achievements of their predecessors and they showed little stomach for continuing their centuries-old work of imposing law upon

---

[38] 'Few reports have assembled so much wisdom whilst proving so completely useless . . . its recommendations are forgotten, even by lawyers and administrators, and in no important respect did the report influence, much less delay, the onrush of administrative power, and the supersession of the ordinary forms of law which is taking place to-day.' Professor G. W. Keeton in *The Nineteenth Century and After* (1949), 230.

[39] Cmnd. 218 (1957). The Act of 1958 has been replaced by the Tribunals and Inquiries Act 1971.

[40] Below, pp. 915, 964.

government. It was understandable that executive power was paramount in wartime, but it was hard to understand why, in the flood of new powers and jurisdictions that came with the welfare state, administrative law should not have been vigorously revived, just when the need for it was greatest.

Instead, the subject relapsed into an impotent condition, marked by neglect of principles and literal verbal interpretation of the blank-cheque powers which Parliament showered upon ministers. The leading cases made a dreary catalogue of abdication and error. Eminent judges said that the common law must be given a death certificate, having lost the power to control the executive;[41] that certiorari was not available against an administrative act;[42] that there was no such thing in Britain as droit administratif;[43] and that there was no developed system of administrative law.[44] The following are some of the aberrations of what might be called 'the great depression'.

The court's power to quash for error on the face of the record was denied.[45]

The principles of natural justice were held not to apply to the cancellation of a licence depriving a man of his livelihood.[46]

Statutory phrases like 'if the minister is satisfied' were held to confer unfettered and uncontrollable discretion.[47]

Statutory restrictions on legal remedies were literally interpreted, contrary to long-settled principles.[48]

The Crown was allowed an unrestricted power to suppress evidence needed by litigants on grounds of Crown privilege.[49]

It was not even as if these were matters of first impression where the court had to consider questions of legal policy. Plentiful materials, in some cases going back for centuries, were available in the law, but they were ignored.

In the 1960s the judicial mood completely changed. It began to be understood how much ground had been lost and what damage had been done to the only defences against abuse of power which still remained. Already in the 1950s the courts had reinstated judicial review for error on the face of the record;[50] and there had been the statutory and administrative reforms of tribunal and inquiry procedures,[51] which helped to give a lead.

---

[41] Lord Devlin in 8 *Current Legal Problems* (1956) at p. 14.
[42] Lord MacDermott, *Protection from Power under English Law* (1957), 88.
[43] Below, p. 26.
[44] Lord Reid in *Ridge* v. *Baldwin* [1964] AC 40 at 72, quoted below, p. 519.
[45] Below, p. 306.
[46] Below, p. 514.
[47] Below, p. 447.
[48] Below, p. 735.
[49] Below, p. 833.
[50] Below, p. 306.
[51] Below, p. 915.

Soon the courts began to send out a stream of decisions which reinvigorated administrative law and re-established continuity with the past. The principles of natural justice were given their proper application, providing a broad foundation for a kind of code of administrative due process.[52] The notion of unfettered administrative discretion was totally rejected.[53] Restrictions on remedies were brushed aside where there was excess of jurisdiction, in accordance with 200 years of precedent;[54] and the law was widened so as to make an excess of jurisdiction out of almost every error.[55] The citadel of Crown privilege was overturned and unjustifiable claims were disallowed.[56] In all these matters the rules for the protection of the citizen had been repudiated by the courts. All were now reactivated. Lord Reid's remark of 1963 that 'we do not have a developed system of administrative law' was countered in 1971 by Lord Denning's, that 'it may truly now be said that we have a developed system of administrative law'.[57] Both Lord Reid and Lord Denning had made conspicuous contributions to its development, but they had done so more by steering the law back onto its old course than by making new deviations.

In retrospect it can be seen that the turning-point of the judicial attitude came in 1963 with the decision of the House of Lords which revived the principles of natural justice.[58] From then on a new mood pervaded the courts. It was given still further impetus by a group of striking decisions in 1968–9, one of which, Lord Diplock has said,[59]

made possible the rapid development in England of a rational and comprehensive system of administrative law on the foundation of the concept of ultra vires.

Since then the judges have shown no reluctance to reformulate principles and consolidate their gains. They have pressed on with what Lord Diplock in a case of 1981 described as[60]

that progress towards a comprehensive system of administrative law that I regard as having been the greatest achievement of the English courts in my judicial lifetime.

So conspicuous has that progress been that he said in the same case that

---

[52] Below, p. 517.
[53] Below, p. 399.
[54] Below, p. 724.
[55] Below, p. 299.
[56] Below, p. 837.
[57] *Breen* v. *Amalgamated Engineering Union* [1971] 2 QB 175 at 189.
[58] *Ridge* v. *Baldwin* (above).
[59] In the *Racal* case (below, p. 300), referring to the *Anisminic* case (below, p. 725).
[60] In the *Inland Revenue Commissioners Case* (below, p. 701). See likewise Lord Diplock's remarks in *O'Reilly* v. *Mackman* [1983] 2 AC 237 at 279 and in *Mahon* v. *Air New Zealand* [1984] AC 808 at 816.

judicial statements on matters of public law if made before 1950 were likely
to be a misleading guide to what the law is today.

A developed system?

Had the materials not been neglected, a developed system could have been
recognised long beforehand. In 1888 Maitland had percipiently
remarked:[61]

If you take up a modern volume of the reports of the Queen's Bench Division, you
will find that about half the cases reported have to do with rules of administrative
law; I mean such matters as local rating, the powers of local boards, the granting of
licences for various trades and professions, the Public Health Acts, the Education
Acts, and so forth.

And he added a caution against neglecting these matters, since otherwise a
false and antiquated notion of the constitution would be formed. But his
advice was not taken. Far too little study was given to the general principles
which could be seen working throughout the area. No systematic treatises
were published.[62] The decisions on housing, education, rating, and so on
were looked upon merely as technicalities arising on some isolated statute,
and not as sources of general rules. Tennyson's description of the law as a
'wilderness of single instances'[63] exactly fitted the profession's attitude. So
far from undertaking systematic study, generations of lawyers were being
brought up to believe, as Dicey had supposedly maintained, that
administrative law was wholly repugnant to the British constitution.[64] This
belief was misconceived, as explained below,[65] but it blighted the study of
the law in what should have been a formative period. The 'false and
antiquated notion of the constitution', against which Maitland warned,
was precisely what was inculcated. Even Lord Hewart, despite his protests
in *The New Despotism* and elsewhere against bureaucracy and its devices for
evading judicial control, referred disparagingly to 'what is called, in
Continental jargon, "administrative law" '.[66]

    Whether a developed system or not, administrative law is a highly

---

[61] *Constitutional History of England* (1955 reprint), 505.

[62] Port, *Administrative Law*, appeared in 1929. But there was no full-scale treatment of
judicial review until Professor de Smith's pioneering work, *Judicial Review of Administrative
Action*, was first published in 1959. The treatment in *Halsbury's Laws of England* was
fragmentary and inadequate until a title on Administrative Law, by Professor de Smith and
others, appeared in the 4th edition, 1973.

[63] Aylmer's Field, line 441.

[64] In 1915 Dicey published a short article on the *Rice* and *Arlidge* cases (below, p. 506)
entitled 'The Development of Administrative Law in England', 31 LQR 495. But this did
not remove the misconceptions which he had caused.

[65] Below, p. 26.

[66] *Not Without Prejudice*, 96.

insecure science so long as it is subject to such extreme vacillations in judicial policy as have taken place since the second world war. One of the arguments for a written constitution and a new Bill of Rights is that they should give the judiciary more confidence in their constitutional position and more determination to resist misuse of governmental power, even in the face of the most sweeping legislation. At the present time the courts are displaying enterprise and vigour and there seems to be no danger of another period of relapse. But the recent past is a solemn warning.

Alliance of law and administration

It is a mistake to suppose that a developed system of administrative law is necessarily antagonistic to efficient government. Intensive government will be more tolerable to the citizen, and the government's path will therefore be smoother, where the law can enforce high standards of legality, reasonableness, and fairness. Nor should it be supposed that the continuous intervention by the courts, which is now so conspicuous, means that the standard of administration is low. This has been well observed recently by Sir John Donaldson MR.[67]

Notwithstanding that the courts have for centuries exercised a limited supervisory jurisdiction by means of the prerogative writs, the wider remedy of judicial review and the evolution of what is, in effect, a specialist administrative or public law court is a post-war development. This development has created a new relationship between the courts and those who derive their authority from the public law, one of partnership based on a common aim, namely the maintenance of the highest standards of public administration.

With very few exceptions, all public authorities conscientiously seek to discharge their duties strictly in accordance with public law and in general they succeed. But it must be recognised that complete success by all authorities at all times is a quite unattainable goal. Errors will occur despite the best of endeavours. The courts, for their part, must and do respect the fact that it is not for them to intervene in the administrative field, unless there is a reason to inquire whether a particular authority has been successful in its endeavours. The courts must and do recognise that, where errors have, or are alleged to have, occurred, it by no means follows that the authority is to be criticised. In proceedings for judicial review, the applicant no doubt has an axe to grind. This should not be true of the authority.

Provided that the judges observe the proper boundaries of their office, administrative law and administrative power should be friends and not enemies. The contribution that the law can and should make is creative rather than destructive.

[67] *R. v. Lancashire CC ex p. Huddleston* [1986] 2 All ER 941 at 945.

2

CONSTITUTIONAL FOUNDATIONS OF THE POWERS OF THE COURTS

THE RULE OF LAW

Legality and discretionary power

The British Constitution is founded on the rule of law,[1] and administrative law is the area where this principle is to be seen in especially active operation. The rule of law has a number of different meanings and corollaries. Its primary meaning is that everything must be done according to law. Applied to the powers of government, this requires that every government authority which does some act which would otherwise be a wrong (such as taking a man's land), or which infringes a man's liberty (as by refusing him planning permission), must be able to justify its action as authorised by law—and in nearly every case this will mean authorised by Act of Parliament. Every act of governmental power, i.e. every act which affects the legal rights, duties, or liberties of any person, must be shown to have a strictly legal pedigree. The affected person may always resort to the courts of law, and if the legal pedigree is not found to be perfectly in order the court will invalidate the act, which he can then safely disregard.

That is the principle of legality. But the rule of law demands something more, since otherwise it would be satisfied by giving the government unrestricted discretionary powers, so that everything that they did was within the law. *Quod principi placuit legis habet vigorem* (the sovereign's will has the force of law) is a perfectly legal principle, but it expresses rule by arbitrary power rather than rule according to ascertainable law. The secondary meaning of the rule of law, therefore, is that government should be conducted within a framework of recognised rules and principles which restrict discretionary power. Coke spoke in picturesque language of 'the golden and straight metwand' of law, as opposed to 'the uncertain and crooked cord of discretion'.[2] Many of the rules of administrative law are rules for restricting the wide powers which Acts of Parliament confer very freely on ministers and other authorities. Thus the Home Secretary has a nominally unlimited power to revoke any television licence and a local planning authority may make planning permission subject to such

---

[1] The classic exposition is that of Dicey, *The Law of the Constitution*, ch. IV.
[2] 4 Inst. 41.

conditions as it thinks fit, but the courts will not allow these powers to be used in ways which Parliament is not thought to have intended.[3] An essential part of the rule of law, accordingly, is a system of rules for preventing the abuse of discretionary power. Intensive government of the modern kind cannot be carried on without a great deal of discretionary power; and since the terms of Acts of Parliament are in practice dictated by the government of the day, this power is often conferred in excessively sweeping language. The rule of law requires that the courts should prevent its abuse, and for this purpose they have performed many notable exploits, reading between the lines of the statutes and developing general doctrines for keeping executive power within proper guidelines, both as to substance and as to procedure.[4]

The principle of legality is a clear-cut concept, but the restrictions to be put upon discretionary power are a matter of degree. Faced with the fact that Parliament freely confers discretionary powers with little regard to the dangers of abuse, the courts must attempt to strike a balance between the needs of fair and efficient administration and the need to protect the citizen against arbitrary government. Here they must rely on their own judgment, sensing what is required by the interplay of forces in the constitution. The fact that this involves questions of degree has sometimes led critics to disparage the rule of law, treating it as a merely political phenomenon which reflects one particular philosophy of government.[5] But this is true only in the sense that every system of law must have its own standards for judging questions of abuse of discretionary power. As will be seen from chapter 12, the rules of law which our own system has devised for this purpose are objective and non-political, expressing indeed a particular judicial attitude but one that can be applied impartially to any kind of legislation irrespective of its political content. Without these rules all kinds of abuses would be possible and the rule of law would be replaced by the rule of arbitrary power. Their existence is therefore essential to the rule of law, and they themselves are principles of law, not politics.

Equality before the law

A third meaning of the rule of law, though it is a corollary of the first meaning, is that disputes as to the legality of acts of government are to be

---

[3] See below, pp. 406 and 431 respectively.

[4] See especially chs. 12, 15.

[5] The best-known criticism is that of Sir I. Jennings, *The Law and the Constitution*, 5th edn., 42–62, attacking Dicey's exposition (above). An effective reply was made by Sir W. Holdsworth in (1939) 55 LQR at 586 and in his *History of English Law*, xiv. 202.

decided by judges who are wholly independent of the executive. In Britain, as in the principal countries of the Commonwealth and in the United States of America, such disputes are adjudicated by the ordinary courts of law. Although many disputes must be taken before special tribunals ('administrative tribunals'), these tribunals are themselves subject to control by the ordinary courts[6] and so the rule of law is preserved. In countries such as France, Italy, and Germany, on the other hand, there are separate administrative courts organised in a separate hierarchy—though it does not follow that they are less independent of the government. The right to carry a dispute with the government before the ordinary courts, manned by judges of the highest independence, is an important element in the Anglo-American concept of the rule of law.

A fourth meaning is that the law should be even-handed between government and citizen. Clearly it cannot be the same for both, since every government must necessarily have many special powers. What the rule of law requires is that the government should not enjoy unnecessary privileges or exemptions from ordinary law. It was a 'lacuna in the rule of law'[7] that until 1947 the Crown was in law exempt from the ordinary law of employer's liability for wrongs done by its employees, since there was no necessity for this immunity and in practice the Crown did not claim it.[8] The Post Office still enjoys legal immunities which violate the rule of law.[9] The Crown also is not required to obey Acts of Parliament unless they contain some indication to that effect.[10] In principle all public authorities should be subject to all normal legal duties and liabilities which are not inconsistent with their governmental functions.

The rule of law has other important meanings outside the sphere of public administration, for example in the principle that no one should be punished except for some legally defined crime. It is made a rallying-cry when any inroad is threatened upon certain ideals which underlie the legal system. These ideals were perhaps most nearly translated into reality in the eighteenth century, when the central government had very little discretionary power and administration, such as it was, was mostly in the hands of judicial bodies, the justices of the peace. Even then it was visionary to hope that 'it may be a government of laws and not of men'.[11] Far though we have retreated from that aspiration today, the rule of law remains none the less a vital necessity to fair and proper government. The enormous

---

[6] Below, p. 307.
[7] Report of the Committee on Ministers' Powers, Cmd. 4060 (1932), p. 112.
[8] See below, p. 812.
[9] Below, p. 166.
[10] Below, p. 827.
[11] Constitution of Massachusetts (1780), Pt. I, art. 30.

growth in the powers of government makes it all the more necessary to preserve it. In one sense, the whole of this book is devoted to explaining how that is being done.

Fallacious comparisons

Although the concept of the rule of law might be called the mainspring of administrative law, Dicey's famous formulation of it in *The Law of the Constitution*[12] cast a prolonged blight over administrative law in Britain. At the root of this paradox was a verbal misunderstanding. Dicey maintained that 'administrative law' was utterly foreign to our constitution, that it was incompatible with the rule of law, with the common law, and with constitutional liberty as we understand it. But Dicey's 'administrative law' was a translation of the French droit administratif, and it was this, rather than any British conception, that Dicey denounced. He regarded it as a prime virtue of the rule of law that all cases came before the ordinary courts, and that the same general rules applied to an action against a government official as applied to an action against a private individual. Under the French system, with its special administrative courts, actions against officials or the state are in many cases subject to a separate system of judicature. What Dicey meant by 'administrative law' was a special system of courts for administrative cases. Even in Dicey's generation this was an unusual sense of the expression. But once that sense is appreciated, the paradox disappears.

Dicey's denunciation of the French system was based on his mistaken conclusion that the administrative courts of France, culminating in the Conseil d'État, must exist for the purpose of giving to officials 'a whole body of special rights, privileges, or prerogatives as against private citizens',[13] so as to make them a law unto themselves. It has long been realised that this picture was wrong, but it has become a traditional caricature. Even today English judges can speak as if droit administratif was a system for putting the executive above the law. Thus Lord Denning MR has said:[14]

Our English law does not allow a public officer to shelter behind a droit administratif.

---

[12] Ch. IV, first published in 1885.

[13] *The Law of the Constitution*, 10th edn., 336.

[14] *Ministry of Housing and Local Government* v. *Sharp* [1970] 2 QB 223 at 226. For similar remarks by Salmon LJ see the same case at 275 and *Re Grosvenor Hotel, London* (No. 2) [1965] Ch. 1210 at 1261 ('There is no droit administratif in this country').

But in fact French administrative law has a system of compensation for the acts of public officers which is in some respects more generous than that of English law.

The reality is that the French Conseil d'État is widely admired and has served as a model for other countries.[15] At the time when our own administrative law was in a state of relapse there were those who advocated importing the French system in Britain. Undoubtedly the French administrative courts have succeeded in imposing a genuinely judicial control upon the executive and in raising the standard of administration. They are impartial and objective courts of law in the fullest sense. Many of the legal doctrines which they have developed have their counterparts in English law, since the demands of fair and lawful administration are similar in both countries. Though their judges are government employees, they are no less critical of the administration than is the British Parliamentary Commissioner for Administration. The popularity of the Conseil d'État is such that at one time it was in danger of being overwhelmed by the number of cases brought before it; but in 1953 the work was devolved and distributed through a system of local tribunals of first instance. The Conseil itself, forming a wing of an administrative college of great power and prestige, can develop its own principles of law and keep them in step with the prevailing philosophy of the respective rights of government and governed. An English judge, trained basically in private law and administering a more legalistic control, may feel less free to break new ground where new problems of public law call for new solutions.

The most interesting aspect of the French system is that the administration has succeeded in developing, from within itself, its own machinery of self-discipline, administrative in its origins but yet fully imbued with legal technique. In Britain, on the other hand, the civil service works in an atmosphere far removed from legal influence, and legal control lies with entirely different organs, which by nature are unaccustomed to administrative work.[16] This exaggerates the cleavage between the legal and administrative worlds, and impedes the great objective—the improvement of administration by transfusion of the legal standards of justice. Both countries can claim great advantages for their methods. In Britain the standing of the courts is high, and few would wish to see them abandon their historic function of protecting the subject against unlawful acts of government. But no one should suppose that administrative courts necessarily weaken administrative law. The natural result ought to be the opposite.

---

[15] See Brown and Garner, *French Administrative Law*, 3rd edn., for a good general account in English.
[16] See below, p. 59.

THE SOVEREIGNTY OF PARLIAMENT

Legislative sovereignty

The sovereignty of Parliament is a peculiar feature of the British constitution which exerts a constant and powerful influence.[17] In particular, it is an ever-present threat to the position of the courts; and it naturally inclines the judges towards caution in their attitude to the executive, since Parliament is effectively under the executive's control. It is also responsible for the prominence in administrative law of the doctrine of ultra vires, as will shortly appear.

The sovereign legal power in the United Kingdom lies in the Queen in Parliament, acting by Act of Parliament. An Act of Parliament requires the assent of the Queen, the House of Lords, and the House of Commons, and the assent of each House is given upon a simple majority of the votes of members present. This is the one and only form of sovereign legislation, and there is no limit to its legal efficacy. It is true that Acts may be passed without the assent of the House of Lords under the procedures provided by the Parliament Acts 1911 and 1949; but these confer delegated, not sovereign, powers, for legislation passed under them owes its validity to their superior authority, and this is the hallmark of delegated legislation.[18] Sovereign legislation owes its validity to no superior authority: the courts accept it in its own right. Furthermore, no Act passed under the Parliament Acts can prolong the life of Parliament beyond five years,[19] whereas the power of a sovereign Act is boundless.

Any previous Act of Parliament can always be repealed by a later Act, either expressly or, in case of conflict, impliedly. Acts of the most fundamental kind, such as the Habeas Corpus Act 1679, the Bill of Rights 1689, the Act of Settlement 1700, the Statute of Westminster 1931 and (though subject to argument) the European Communities Act 1972 are just as easy to repeal, legally speaking, as is the Antarctic Treaty Act 1967. No special majorities or procedure are needed. The ordinary, everyday form of Act of Parliament is sovereign, and can effect any legal consequences whatsoever. Once an Act of Parliament is shown, the court cannot question it: it can only apply it. The courts give their entire obedience to Parliament as it exists for the time being.

But this legal paramountcy can be exercised only by an Act of the

---

[17] Here also Dicey's is the classic exposition: *The Law of the Constitution*, ch. 1. For an excellent discussion see de Smith, *Constitutional and Administrative Law*, 5th edn., ch. 4. See also below, p. 469.

[18] See Hood Phillips, *Constitutional and Administrative Law*, 7th edn., 90; [1954] CLJ at 265, [1955] CLJ at 193; Wade, *Constitutional Fundamentals*, 27.

[19] Parliament Act 1911, s. 2(1).

sovereign Parliament, assented to by Queen, Lords, and Commons. The two Houses of Parliament by themselves dispose of no such power, either jointly or severally. A resolution of either House, or of both Houses, has no legislative or legal effect whatever unless an Act of Parliament so provides.[20] There are many cases where some administrative order or regulation is required by statute to be approved by resolutions of the Houses.[21] But this procedure in no way protects the order or regulation from being condemned by the court, under the doctrine of ultra vires, if it is not strictly in accordance with the Act.[22] Whether the challenge is made before[23] or after [24] the Houses have given their approval is immaterial.

Lack of constitutional protection

One consequence of parliamentary sovereignty is that this country has no constitutional guarantees. We have nothing like the Constitution of the United States (including the so-called Bill of Rights) or the 'entrenched clauses' in South Africa, which can be changed only by special procedures. In other countries, the normal thing is to have a written constitution, embodied in a formal document, and protected, as a kind of fundamental law, against amendment by simple majorities in the legislature. In Britain, however, we have never made a fresh start with a new constitution, although in the seventeenth century the courts bowed to several revolutionary changes of sovereign. Not only do we have no constitutional guarantees: we cannot, it seems, create them. Since an ordinary Act of Parliament can repeal any law whatever, it is impossible for Parliament to render any statute unrepealable, or repealable only subject to conditions. Parliament cannot, in other words, modify or destroy its own continuing sovereignty, for the courts will always obey its commands. This situation could, indeed, be changed by a revolution of some kind. But while it lasts, the whole of our law and our liberties are at the mercy of the parliamentary majority of the moment.

There is now much dissatisfaction with this state of affairs, since the control of legislation has effectively passed into the hands of the executive. Parliament's independent control has been progressively weakened by the party system and it is called upon to pass many more Acts in each session

---

[20] *Stockdale* v. *Hansard* (1839) 9 Ad & E 1.

[21] Below, p. 887.

[22] See below, pp. 863, 870.

[23] As in *R.* v. *Electricity Commissioners ex p. London Electricity Joint Committee Co. (1920) Ltd.* [1924] 1 KB 171; *R.* v. *HM Treasury ex p. Smedley* [1985] QB 657.

[24] As in *Hoffman–La Roche & Co.* v. *Secretary of State for Trade and Industry* [1975] AC 295 at 354, 365, 372; *Laker Airways Ltd.* v. *Dept. of Trade* [1977] QB 643; and see *R.* v. *Secretary of State for the Environment ex p. Nottinghamshire CC* [1986] AC 240, explained below, p. 411.

than it can scrutinise properly. Dicey extolled judge-made law as a better protection for the liberty of the citizen than constitutional guarantees. But it is now beginning to be understood that a written constitution which is respected, as it is for example in the United States, provides valuable safeguards which in Britain are wholly lacking. Consequently there are many advocates of a new Bill of Rights or some written constitution such as is possessed by almost every other democratic country.[25] Further stimulus was provided when Britain became a founding member of the European Convention on Human Rights and Fundamental Freedoms of 1950 and when she acceded to the European Communities in 1973.[26] As yet it has not been necessary to determine how fundamental rights can be given a special constitutional status and made proof against repeal by legislation of the ordinary kind.[27]

Parliamentary sovereignty, as it now exists, profoundly affects the position of the judges. They are not the appointed guardians of constitutional rights, with power to declare statutes unconstitutional, like the Supreme Court of the United States. They cannot insist, for example, that power should be subject to 'due process of law' and similar guarantees, if a statute should attempt to infringe them. They can only obey the latest expression of the will of Parliament. Nor is their own jurisdiction sacrosanct. If they fly too high, Parliament may clip their wings. They entirely lack the impregnable constitutional status of their American counterparts. Nevertheless they have built up for themselves a position which is a good deal stronger than constitutional theory by itself might suggest. Feeling their way, case by case, they define their powers for themselves. In doing so they draw upon strong traditions of long standing and upon their own prestige, and with these resources they can do much. Some of their bold decisions discussed in this book, particularly those of recent years, show that they need not be deterred by the weakness of their constitutional status. Even under the British system of undiluted sovereignty, the last word on any question of law rests with the courts. When in the *Anisminic* case the House of Lords interpreted an Act of

[25] Arguments for and against are discussed in *Legislation on Human Rights* (1976), a 'discussion document' published by the Government, in Zander, *A Bill of Rights?* (3rd edn., 1985) and in Wallington and McBride, *Civil Liberties and a Bill of Rights* (1976).

[26] For the importance of these international obligations in administrative law see below, p. 497. For the question whether s. 2(4) of the European Communities Act 1972, by providing that Community law shall prevail over future Acts of Parliament, has effectively entrenched it, see Wade, *Constitutional Fundamentals*, 25, 31.

[27] Too much heavy weather has been made over this supposed problem. The simple solution, as in the United States and other countries with written constitutions, is that the judges should take an oath to uphold the constitution as the supreme law. For discussion see Wade (as above), 37.

Parliament to mean the exact opposite of what it appeared to say, Parliament, so far from retaliating, made important concessions to the legal point of view.[28] So long as the courts move in step with public opinion, their constitutional subservience need not prevent them from developing the principles of administrative law imaginatively.

Ministerial responsibility

One aspect of the supremacy of Parliament is that ministers are responsible to it, both individually and collectively, through the Cabinet. Parliament is the body before which ministers are called to account, and without the confidence of which they cannot continue. But here again the theory is far from the reality. The party system means in practice that, in anything but the last resort, the government controls Parliament. This is especially evident in the process of legislation. Bills are drafted by the government departments themselves and are often driven through Parliament by the party whips and with inadequate time for many of their clauses to be properly considered. Many matters of importance in administrative law, such as restrictions on legal remedies and the proliferation of statutory tribunals, are enacted without comment in either House and without attention to their legal consequences. Ministerial responsibility fails in practice to control legislation effectively, most statutes being enacted in almost exactly the form on which the government decided in advance.

The traditional methods of calling ministers to account for errors in administration are parliamentary questions, debates on the adjournment, and occasional debates such as those on Supply days in the House of Commons. But by these relatively cumbersome processes Parliament cannot possibly control the ordinary run of daily governmental acts except by taking up occasional cases which have political appeal. Administrative justice demands some regular, efficient, and non-political machinery for investigating individual complaints against governmental action of all kinds, including the action of subordinate officials. Ministerial responsibility is an erratic and defective instrument for this purpose. Every so often a Member of Parliament achieves spectacular success with a constituent's grievance by a parliamentary question or a motion on the adjournment. But this is the safety-valve, not the control mechanism, of the administrative system. Parliament works in a highly charged atmosphere, in which the doctrine of ministerial responsibility may make it politically suicidal for a minister to admit a mistake. This is exactly what is not required.

The deficiencies of ministerial responsibility as a system of protection

---

[28] *Anisminic Ltd.* v. *Foreign Compensation Commission* [1969] 2 AC 147. For this case and its sequel see below, p. 725.

against administrative wrongdoing led an eminent judge to say bitterly, as long ago as 1910,[29]

If ministerial responsibility were more than the mere shadow of a name, the matter would be less important, but as it is, the Courts are the only defence of the liberty of the subject against departmental aggression.

Dicey expressed similar views in 1915, criticising judicial reliance on 'so-called ministerial responsibility'.[30] And in 1981 Lord Diplock said:[31]

It is not, in my view, a sufficient answer to say that judicial review of the actions of officers or departments of central government is unnecessary because they are accountable to Parliament for the way in which they carry out their functions. They are accountable to Parliament for what they do so far as regards efficiency and policy, and of that Parliament is the only judge; they are responsible to a court of justice for the lawfulness of what they do, and of that the court is the only judge.

In fact the courts often acknowledge the importance of ministerial responsibility to Parliament, without in any way regarding it as a substitute for effective judicial review.

A constitutional improvement was introduced in 1967 in the person of the Parliamentary Commissioner for Administration. His method of investigating complaints against administration has all the advantages which the parliamentary process lacks: it is impartial, non-political and it can penetrate behind the screen which ministerial responsibility otherwise interposes between Parliament and government departments. As related later, the Parliamentary Commissioner Bill was opposed on the ground that it was inconsistent with ministerial responsibility, but the truth was that it remedied some of its defects.[32]

The high degree of detachment and anonymity in which the civil service works is largely a consequence of the principle of ministerial responsibility. Where civil servants carry out the minister's orders, or act in accordance with his policy, it is for him and not for them to take any blame. He also takes responsibility for ordinary administrative mistakes or miscarriages. But he has no duty to endorse unauthorised action of which he disapproves, though he has general responsibility for the conduct of his department and for the taking of any necessary disciplinary action.[33]

---

[29] *Dyson* v. *A.-G.* [1911] 1 KB 410 at 424 (Farwell LJ). The 'departmental aggression' was an unjustified demand for information by the Commissioners of Inland Revenue.

[30] (1915) 31 LQR 148 at 152.

[31] *R.* v. *Inland Revenue Commissioners ex p. National Federation of Self-Employed and Small Businesses Ltd.* [1982] AC 617.

[32] Below, p. 80.

[33] This paragraph is based on the Home Secretary's statement in Parliament in the debate on the *Crichel Down* case (below, p. 912: 530 HC Deb col. 1286 (20 July 1954).

GOVERNMENT SUBJECT TO LAW

Application of ordinary law

It is now necessary to explain in general terms some of the elements of judicial control, the details of which occupy so much of this book. The rules which govern disputes involving the government and public authorities come before the ordinary courts, and the courts so far as possible apply 'ordinary law', treating public authorities as if they were private individuals with all the normal legal duties and liabilities, except so far as modified by statute. Thus a local authority or a nationalised industry is legally liable for the negligence of its employees in exactly the same way as any other employer. The one serious obstacle was the legal immunity of the Crown, partly owing to the survival of the feudal idea that it was not subject to the jurisdiction of its own courts, and partly because it was thought to be incapable of being responsible for wrongs. But the obstacle was overcome first by the acceptance of liability in practice and secondly by the enactment of the Crown Proceedings Act 1947.[34] Furthermore, the non-availability of compulsory remedies against the Crown was evaded by the habit of conferring powers upon designated ministers, as mentioned below.[35] Ministers as such, though acting as ministers of the Crown, have none of the Crown's prerogatives or immunities in law, and are therefore in the same position as private individuals. The great majority of proceedings by and against public authorities, therefore, can be adjudicated without making any distinction between private and official capacities. As already explained in the context of the rule of law, the aim is to subordinate the government to the ordinary law of the land.

This principle is best illustrated by examples of the remedies which the courts may grant. Rights and remedies cannot be kept in separate compartments, and it is the nature of the remedy which determines the nature of the right. If a man is wrongfully arrested by the police, he may bring an ordinary action in tort for damages for assault and false imprisonment against any police officer who arrested or detained him, or on whose orders this was done, just as if the police were private individuals. Habeas corpus is available for his release, if necessary, without any distinction as to who is the person responsible. In one of the most famous of eighteenth-century cases, where a publisher's house and papers were ransacked by king's messengers sent by the Secretary of State, Lord Halifax, the remedy was an ordinary action of trespass, in which £300

---

[34] As explained below, p. 813.
[35] Below, p. 51.

damages were awarded.[36] In just the same way, if a man's land is compulsorily acquired under an order which for some reason is illegal, he can bring an action of trespass against any person who disturbs his possession in attempting to execute the order. Or, if execution is merely threatened, he can obtain an injunction to forbid it.

When acting outside their powers, therefore, public authorities are as liable for injury that they do as is any one else. So, as a general rule, are the Crown and all its various agencies, including ministers.[37] The liability of statutory bodies for the misdeeds of their servants was settled by the House of Lords in a case of 1866, in which the Mersey Docks and Harbour Board were held liable for not removing a mudbank at the entrance to one of their docks, on which a ship was damaged.[38] The House refused to extend to bodies of this kind the rule that applies to ministers of the Crown, namely, that they and their subordinates are all alike holders of public offices, and that the relationship of master and servant does not exist between them. That principle may well apply to relieve one subordinate from liability for another's wrongful act. But it does not protect the body which is the employer of them all. Thus statutory authorities such as the National Coal Board, the British Railways Board, and the British Airports Authority have the same legal liabilities as commercial companies, subject only to the provisions of their constituent statutes.

Some immunity is given to persons executing the orders of courts of law, such as sheriffs, police officers, and prison wardens;[39] and the police have a narrow statutory immunity in executing warrants for arrest.[40] But administrative authorities have virtually no immunity. A few statutes exempt the members and servants of local authorities from personal liability for things done bona fide, but in those cases the authority itself can be made liable.[41] Occasionally also special exemptions are given for special reasons.[42] In any case, a plaintiff is more likely to sue the authority who gave the orders than the servant who executed them, because the authority will be best able to pay the damages. All who participate in a wrongful act are jointly and equally liable. It is a fundamental rule that every minister, official, or other agent who commits an actionable wrong is fully liable personally and that superior orders are no defence.[43]

---

[36] *Entick* v. *Carrington* (1765) 19 St. Tr. 1030.

[37] Below, p. 751.

[38] *Mersey Docks & Harbour Board Trustees* v. *Gibbs* (1866) LR 1 HL 93.

[39] *Marshalsea Case* (1613) 10 Co. Rep. 76a; *Sirros* v. *Moore* [1975] QB 118, below, p. 785.

[40] Constables Protection Act 1751.

[41] e.g. Public Health Act 1875, s. 265, extended by National Health Service Act 1946, s. 72.

[42] e.g. Mental Health Act 1983, s. 139; see below, p. 775.

[43] Below, p. 812.

Remedies of public law

Extensive as is the range of the ordinary law, there are many administrative wrongs that it cannot reach. Public authorities may often act unlawfully without rendering themselves liable in trespass, nuisance, and so forth. If an application for a licence is wrongly refused, or if a licence is wrongly revoked, or if a claim to national insurance benefit is wrongly rejected, there will usually be no remedy in private law.[44] It is true that almost any kind of wrong can be brought before the court by an action for a declaration, in which the court can declare the claimant's rights. But this remedy has only recently come to the fore. Long before it did so, the courts had developed the nucleus of a system of public law out of the special 'prerogative' remedies of certiorari, prohibition, and mandamus, together also with habeas corpus.[45] These remedies are still of the greatest importance for the purpose of compelling ministers, tribunals, and other governmental bodies to act lawfully and to perform their duties. They cover the area where the remedies of private law are weak or ineffective. This in no way alters the fact that legality is enforced through the ordinary courts, applying principles of ordinary law.

These prerogative remedies are so called because they were originally used by the Crown and by the royal courts for the purpose of preventing inferior tribunals and other bodies from meddling in matters that did not concern them. They were designed to enforce order in the complex network of jurisdictions, both central and local, which was a feature of the legal system. Certiorari would issue from the Court of King's Bench to quash a decision, for example of justices of the peace, which was outside their jurisdiction or patently contrary to law. Prohibition would prevent them from proceeding in any matter outside their jurisdiction. Mandamus would command them to carry out their legal duties, if they were failing to do so. Habeas corpus would release any person wrongfully detained. But it was private individuals who usually called the attention of the court to these wrongs, and in time the prerogative remedies ceased to be a royal monopoly and became available to any subject. Nevertheless the Crown remained the nominal plaintiff and the remedies retained their character of remedies devised for upholding public order rather than private right. This character, as will be seen later, makes them especially valuable for correcting administrative illegalities which do not directly injure any particular person, for example a failure by a cinema licensing authority to prevent the exhibition of indecent films.[46]

[44] Below, p. 779.
[45] Below, p. 616.
[46] Below, p. 694.

Although there is no distinct system of public law, therefore, there are elements of such a system in some of the remedies. The courts draw upon a mixed collection of remedies, some belonging to private and some to public law, in order to cover as many cases as possible. Recent reforms have removed the procedural obstacles which formerly prevented the two groups of remedies from combining smoothly. They are now more freely interchangeable, but on the debit side the courts have established an awkward dichotomy between public and private law which did not exist before.[47]

Review and appeal contrasted

The system of judicial review is radically different from the system of appeals.[48] When hearing an appeal the court is concerned with the merits of the decision under appeal. When subjecting some administrative act or order to judicial review, the court is concerned with its legality. On an appeal the question is 'right or wrong?' On review the question is 'lawful or unlawful?'[49]

Rights of appeal are always statutory.[50] Judicial review, on the other hand, is the exercise of the court's inherent power to determine whether action is lawful or not and to award suitable relief. For this no statutory authority is necessary: the court is simply performing its ordinary functions in order to uphold the rule of law. The basis of judicial review, therefore, is common law. This is none the less true because nearly all cases in administrative law arise under some Act of Parliament. Where the court quashes an order made by a minister under some Act, it typically uses its common law power to declare that the Act did not entitle the minister to do what he did.[51]

Where the proceeding is an appeal, some superior court or authority will reconsider the decision of some lower court or authority on its merits. Sometimes any aspects of the lower decision is open to appeal, but sometimes statute will allow only an appeal on a point of law, as opposed to a question of fact. Since rights of appeal exist only where conferred by

---

[47] Below, p. 676.

[48] Sometimes the courts use 'review' in the opposite sense to make the same contrast, describing judicial review as 'supervision' and the appellate function as 'review'. See *R. v. Nat Bell Liquors* [1922] 2 AC 128 at 156; *Anisminic Ltd. v. Foreign Compensation Commission* [1969] 2 AC 147 at 195.

[49] The difference is shown by the rule that the existence of a right of appeal does not normally prejudice the right to review: below, p. 712.

[50] Below, p. 906.

[51] A number of Acts substitute a statutory power for the common law power (below, p. 733); but this does not alter the principle.

statute, in modern law there is no inherent appellate jurisdiction in the courts. Thus appeals from the High Court to the Court of Appeal now lie under the Supreme Court Act 1981, and appeals to the House of Lords lie under the Appellate Jurisdiction Act 1876 and the Administration of Justice Act 1969. Statutes have created many special appeal tribunals, such as the Social Security Commissioners, Social Security Tribunals, Industrial Tribunals, and the Lands Tribunal. There are also many statutory rights of appeal from one administrative authority to another, for example from a local planning authority to the Secretary of State for the Environment and from a police disciplinary authority to the Home Secretary. The complex system of statutory tribunals, explained later, has its own network of appeals. There is no automatic right of appeal from them to any court, but the policy of recent legislation has been to allow any question of law to be taken to the High Court on appeal, save in a few exceptional cases.

Judicial review is a fundamentally different operation. Instead of substituting its own decision for that of some other body, as happens when an appeal is allowed, the court on review is concerned only with the question whether the act or order under attack should be allowed to stand or not. If the Home Secretary revokes a television licence unlawfully, the court may simply declare that the revocation is null and void.[52] Should the case be one involving breach of duty rather than excess of power, the question will be whether the public authority should be ordered to make good a default. Refusal to issue a television licence to someone entitled to have one would be remedied by an order of the court requiring the issue of the licence. Action unauthorised by law and inaction contrary to law are equally subject to the court's control. In the case of unauthorised action the court's principal weapon is the doctrine of ultra vires, which as will be seen is the foundation of a large part of administrative law. If administrative action is in excess of power (ultra vires), the court has only to quash it or declare it unlawful (these are in effect the same thing) and then no one need pay any attention to it.

It is an inevitable consequence of our concept of the separation of powers, and of our lack of administrative courts, that there is a sharp distinction between appeal and review. It means that fine points of law, alleged to 'go to jurisdiction', are sometimes put forward in support of what is a thinly disguised appeal on the merits.[53] But the court's duty is to confine itself strictly to the question of legality. If the administrative authority has acted within its powers and according to law, it is no business

---

[52] See below, p. 406.
[53] Examples are *Woollett* v. *Minister of Agriculture and Fisheries* [1955] 1 QB 103 (below, p. 736), *Anisminic Ltd.* v. *Foreign Compensation Commission* [1969] 2 AC 147 (below, p. 725) and *R.* v. *Home Secretary ex p. Khawaja* [1984] AC 74 (below, p. 460).

of the court to interfere. The law draws the boundaries within which the administration is a free agent.

Judicial control, therefore, primarily means review, and is based on a fundamental principle, inherent throughout the legal system, that powers can be validly exercised only within their true limits. The doctrines by which those limits are ascertained and enforced form the very marrow of administrative law. Rights of appeal, on the other hand, have no such central place. They may or may not exist in any given case, and although it is in general most important that they should exist, this is a question of policy which can be reserved for the chapter on Statutory Tribunals.

Legality, merits and discretion

The distinction between 'merits' and 'legality' is not in fact so rigid as the previous section would suggest. Partly this is because there are various forms of error which can be remedied either on appeal or on review, so that the two systems overlap.[54] Partly also it is because there are many situations in which the courts interpret Acts of Parliament as authorising only action which is reasonable or which has some particular purpose, so that its merits determine its legality. Sometimes the Act itself will expressly limit the power in this way, but even if it does not it is common for the court to infer that some limitation is intended. The judges have been deeply drawn into this area, so that their own opinion of the reasonableness or motives of some government action may be the factor which determines whether or not it is to be condemned on judicial review. Although in principle the dichotomy between legality and merits is still observed, the dividing line becomes blurred. The further the courts are drawn into passing judgment on the merits of the actions of public authorities, the more they are exposed to the charge that they are exceeding their constitutional function.

But unless the courts are prepared to act boldly in this direction, they can give but feeble protection against administrative wrongdoing. The whole problem is centred on the question of discretionary power, which lies at the heart of administrative law. When Parliament grants power to public authorities, it inevitably also gives them discretion. Each authority has to decide for itself whether to act or not to act, and how it wishes to act. If this discretion is not conferred, the authority has not a power but a duty. Many of the most difficult problems of judicial review are concerned with the question where power stops and duty begins. Even if the authority has undoubted power to do something, there may be duties as to how it is to be done.

---

[54] See below, p. 712.

The ultra vires doctrine is therefore not confined to cases of plain excess of power; it also governs abuse of power, as where something is done unjustifiably, for the wrong reasons or by the wrong procedure. In law the consequences are exactly the same: an improper motive, or a false step in procedure, makes an administrative act just as illegal as does a flagrant excess of authority. Unless the courts are able to develop doctrines of this kind, and to apply them energetically, they cannot impose limits on the administrative powers which Parliament confers so freely, often in almost unrestricted language. If merely because an Act says that a minister may 'make such order as he thinks fit', or may do something 'if he is satisfied' as to some fact, the court were to allow him to act as he liked, a wide door would be opened to abuse of power and the rule of law would cease to operate.

It is a cardinal axiom, accordingly, that every power has legal limits, however wide the language of the empowering Act. If the court finds that the power has been exercised oppressively or unreasonably, or if there has been some procedural failing, such as not allowing a person affected to put forward his case, the act may be condemned as unlawful. Although lawyers appearing for government departments often argue that some Act confers unfettered discretion, they are guilty of constitutional blasphemy. Unfettered discretion cannot exist where the rule of law reigns. The notion of unlimited power can have no place in the system. The same truth can be expressed by saying that all power is capable of abuse, and that the power to prevent abuse is the acid test of effective judicial review.

The purpose of these generalisations is to emphasise that, despite the legalistic appearance of the doctrine of ultra vires, it need not prevent the development of wide-ranging judicial review. Many decisions of the courts have vividly illustrated the possibilities, especially in recent years.

THE DOCTRINE OF ULTRA VIRES

The central principle

The simple proposition that a public authority may not act outside its powers (ultra vires) might fitly be called the central principle of administrative law. To a large extent the courts have developed the subject by extending and refining this principle, which has many ramifications and which in some of its aspects attains a high degree of artificiality. The vital question is, to what lengths should it be carried?

Where the empowering Act lays down limits expressly, their application is merely an exercise in construing the statutory language and applying it to the facts. Thus if land may be taken by compulsory purchase provided that it is not part of a park, the court must determine in case of dispute whether the land is part of a park and decide accordingly.[55] If the Act says 'provided that in the opinion of the minister it is not a park', the question is not so simple. Reading the language literally, the court would be confined to ascertaining that the minister in fact held the opinion required. But then the minister might make an order for the acquisition of land in Hyde Park, certifying his opinion that it was not part of a park. It is essential to invalidate any malpractice of this kind, and therefore the court will hold the order to be ultra vires if the minister acted in bad faith or unreasonably or on no proper evidence.[56] Results such as these are attained by the art of statutory construction. It is presumed that Parliament did not intend to authorise abuses, and that certain safeguards against abuse must be implied in the Act. These are matters of general principle, embodied in the rules of law which govern the interpretation of statutes. Parliament is not expected to incorporate them expressly in every Act that is passed. They may be taken for granted as part of the implied conditions to which every Act is subject and which the courts extract by reading between the lines, or (it may be truer to say) insert by writing between the lines. These implied conditions are taken to be part and parcel of the Act, just as much as express conditions. Any violation of them, therefore, renders the offending act ultra vires.

As with substance, so with procedure. One of the law's notable achievements has been the development of the principles of natural justice, one of which is the right to be given a fair hearing before being penalised in any way. These principles are similarly based upon implied statutory conditions: it is assumed that Parliament, when conferring power, intends that power to be used fairly and with due consideration of rights and interests adversely affected. In effect, Parliament legislates against a background of judge-made rules of interpretation, which place the necessary restrictions on governmental powers so as to ensure that they are exercised not arbitrarily but fairly and properly.

The branches of the doctrine of ultra vires are thus extended to cover the numerous heads of judicial review of powers and duties explained in this book. Their extension is stimulated by the fact that legislation is drafted in government departments in terms designed to confer the widest possible powers and is subject to little effective control by Parliament. The harder draftsmen strive to devise judge-proof legislation, the more judges show determination and ingenuity in extending and refining the grounds of judicial review. Legislation deliberately designed to cut down the powers of the courts tends, paradoxically, to lead to their expansion.[57]

[55] For this case see below, p. 284.
[56] See below, pp. 442, 395, 319.
[57] The *Anisminic* case (below, p. 725) is a good example.

Jurisdiction and nullity

An act which is for any reason in excess of power (ultra vires) is often described as being 'outside jurisdiction'. 'Jurisdiction', in this context, means simply 'power', though sometimes it bears the slightly narrower sense of 'power to decide', e.g. as applied to statutory tribunals. It is a word to which the courts have given different meanings in different contexts, and with which they have created a certain amount of confusion. But this cannot be explained intelligibly except in the particular contexts where difficulties have been made. Nor should the difficulties be exaggerated. For general purposes 'jurisdiction' may be translated as 'power' with very little risk of inaccuracy.

Any administrative act or order which is ultra vires or outside jurisdiction is void in law, i.e. deprived of legal effect. This is because in order to be valid it needs statutory authorisation, and if it is not within the powers given by the Act, it has no legal leg to stand on. The court will then quash it or declare it to be unlawful or prohibit any action to enforce it. The terminology here depends to some extent on the remedy granted. 'Quashing' is used in connection with the remedy of certiorari, but in effect it is simply a declaration of nullity. A declaratory judgment is an alternative remedy with similar effect: it declares the offending act to be a nullity in law. Prohibition of execution may be an order of prohibition (a prerogative remedy) or an injunction. But these technicalities make no difference to the legal result: an act found to be outside jurisdiction (ultra vires) is void and a nullity, being destitute of the statutory authority without which it is nothing.

Once the court has declared that some administrative act is legally a nullity, the situation is as if nothing had happened. In this way the unlawful act or decision may be replaced by a lawful one. If a compulsory purchase order is quashed as being ultra vires, there is nothing to prevent another order being made in respect of the same land, provided that it is done lawfully. Thus a public authority or tribunal is often given *locus poenitentiae* and is able to correct an error by starting afresh—something which it might otherwise be unable to do.

Necessary artificialities

The technique by which the courts have constructed their system for the judicial control of powers is that of stretching the doctrine of ultra vires. As already observed, they can make the doctrine mean almost anything they wish by finding implied limitations in Acts of Parliament, as they do when they hold that the exercise of a statutory power to revoke a licence is void unless done in accordance with the principles of natural justice.

Realising that their task is to protect the citizen against unfairness and abuse of power, they build up a body of rules of administrative law which they presume that Parliament wishes them to enforce. But for this purpose, and subject to one exception,[58] they have only one weapon, the doctrine of ultra vires. This is because they have no constitutional right to interfere with action which is within the powers granted (intra vires): if it is within jurisdiction, and therefore authorised by Parliament, the court has no right to treat it as unlawful.

It is for constitutional reasons of this kind that the doctrine of ultra vires has become so artificial in some of its applications. There is no paramount Bill of Rights or written constitution on which the judge can fall back: in every case he must be able to demonstrate that he is carrying out the will of Parliament as expressed in the statute conferring the power. He is on safe ground only where he can show that the offending act is outside the power. The only way in which he can do this, in the absence of an express provision, is by finding an implied term or condition in the Act, violation of which then entails the condemnation of ultra vires.

Into this bed of Procrustes, accordingly, must be fitted not only the more obvious cases of inconsistency with statute, such as failure to follow expressly prescribed procedure, irregular delegation, and breach of jurisdictional conditions: but also the more sophisticated types of malpractice, such as unreasonableness, irrelevant considerations, improper motives, and breach of natural justice. If an Act empowers a minister to act as he thinks fit in some matter, the court will read into the Act conditions requiring him to act within the bounds of reasonableness, to take account of relevant but not of irrelevant considerations, to conform to the implicit policy of the Act, and to give a fair hearing to any one prejudicially affected. These are examples of the many grounds on which the court will invalidate improper action. Somehow they must be forced into the mould of the ultra vires doctrine, for unless that can be done the court will have no basis for its intervention.

'Jurisdiction'

It is at this point that artificiality becomes a problem. From time to time the judicial mind rebels against the misuse of language which is seemingly involved in saying that, for example, a minister who acts on wrong considerations or without giving some one a fair hearing is acting outside his jurisdiction. It is tempting to call this, in words which will be quoted later,[59] 'a wrong exercise of a jurisdiction which he has, and not a usurpation of a jurisdiction which he has not'. Sometimes, therefore, judges

---

[58] Error on the face of the record, explained below.
[59] Below, p. 321.

will say that errors such as improper motives or breach of natural justice do not involve excess of jurisdiction. But then they forget that, if this were correct, they would have no title to condemn them. Every administrative act is either intra vires or ultra vires; and (subject to the one exception) the court can condemn it only if it is ultra vires.

Judicial unfamiliarity with the 'basic English' of administrative law has been the cause of some confusion.[60] Relatively seldom do the courts feel it necessary to expound the analysis of ultra vires in its more subtle applications. But the House of Lords has done so in several important modern decisions, which put the matter beyond doubt. In *Ridge* v. *Baldwin*,[61] a leading case on natural justice, the House held that the dismissal of a chief constable, being vitiated by failure to give him a fair hearing, was void, and from that it follows inexorably that it was outside jurisdiction, i.e. ultra vires.[62] In the *Anisminic* case,[63] one of the high-water marks of judicial control, the House similarly held that a tribunal's decision was a nullity if it misunderstood the law and so took account of wrong factors. The connection between these various elements was clearly expressed in the same case by Lord Pearce:[64]

Lack of jurisdiction may arise in many ways. There may be an absence of those formalities or things which are conditions precedent to the tribunal having any jurisdiction to embark on an inquiry. Or the tribunal may at the end make an order that it has no jurisdiction to make. Or in the intervening stage, while engaged on a proper inquiry, the tribunal may depart from the rules of natural justice; or it may ask itself the wrong questions; or it may take into account matters which it was not directed to take into account. Thereby it would step outside its jurisdiction. It would turn its inquiry into something not directed by Parliament and fail to make the inquiry which Parliament did direct. Any of these things would cause its purported decision to be a nullity.

There is nothing new in this analysis.[65] The courts have in fact been using it

[60] As regards jurisdiction, it may be dated from the confusion over 'void or voidable' introduced by the dissenting speeches in *Ridge* v. *Baldwin* (below).

[61] [1964] AC 40; below, p. 517. A statement by the Privy Council that this was not the decision of the majority is erroneous: below, p. 527.

[62] Expressly confirmed by the Privy Council (Lord Diplock) in *A.-G.* v. *Ryan* [1980] AC 718 at 730.

[63] *Anisminic Ltd.* v. *Foreign Compensation Commission* [1969] 2 AC 147; below, p. 725.

[64] At 195. Lord Reid at 171 in substance says the same thing, but he gives an unusually narrow meaning to 'jurisdiction', thus holding that a decision can be a nullity without being in excess of jurisdiction. In the normal sense of these words, this is a contradiction in terms: see below, p. 294.

[65] See e.g. *Short* v. *Poole Cpn.* [1926] Ch. 66, a much cited case, where Warrington LJ observes (at 90) that no public body can have statutory authority to act in bad faith or on irrelevant grounds, and any such act is unauthorised and ultra vires. Similarly in *R.* v. *North ex p. Oakey* [1927] 1 KB 491 at 503, 505. Scrutton and Atkin L JJ hold that a breach of natural justice is an excess of jurisdiction. The reports are full of similar statements.

for centuries, for example when awarding damages for trespass when a public authority demolished a building under an order which was void for violation of natural justice.[66] If the order is void, it cannot be within jurisdiction; for if it is within jurisdiction, it must be valid.

There is therefore no escape (save in the one exceptional case) from the principle of ultra vires. But the notion that so many kinds of error all involve excess of jurisdiction is highly sophisticated and puts a strain upon the language conventionally used. Even with the House of Lords' words before them, judges may doubt whether the exercise of a discretion on wrong principles, or a breach of natural justice, can amount to an excess of jurisdiction.[67] It is the word 'jurisdiction' which is the stumbling-block here: if 'power' were substituted, there would be less difficulty. Judges sometimes think of 'jurisdiction' as meaning merely the authority to inquire into and determine a case, as opposed to what is done in the course of the proceedings. This narrower sense of the term has caused trouble in another context, as will appear later.[68]

In general, however, the courts adhere firmly to the wide meaning of 'jurisdiction', since this is the sheet-anchor of their power to correct abuses. They appear to be willing to stretch the doctrine of ultra vires to cover virtually all situations where statutory power is exercised contrary to some legal principle. This is the classic mode of progress in administrative law. But until the principle is uniformly understood, confusion will be prone to recur. In 1977 it recurred in the Court of Appeal, which held that bad faith or breach of natural justice did not amount to excess of jurisdiction,[69] despite the express rulings of the House of Lords to the contrary. A merely verbal confusion would not be serious; but, as explained later,[70] there are dangers.

The exception: error on the face of the record

Before the doctrine of ultra vires had been stretched to cover all the categories of abuse of power that must now be brought within it, the Court of King's Bench had established its power to quash the decisions of inferior tribunals and administrative agencies for error on the face of the record.

[66] *Cooper* v. *Wandsworth Board of Works* (1863) 14 CBNS 180; below, p. 503.

[67] See e.g. Browne J in the *Anisminic* case (above) at 244 and in *R.* v. *Southampton Justices ex p. Green* [1976] QB 11 at 22.

[68] Below, p. 293.

[69] *R.* v. *Secretary of State for the Environment ex p. Ostler* [1977] QB 122 (below, p. 738); but in *The Discipline of Law*, 108, Lord Denning MR has recanted these 'unguarded statements'.

[70] Below, pp. 354, 527.

The rise, decline, revival, and now perhaps the eclipse of this jurisdiction form a separate strand in the history of the subject, and this story will be told in a later chapter. What must be emphasised here is that the High Court's power to quash a decision merely because it displays some mistake in the record of its proceedings is an altogether exceptional power. It is exceptional because it is not a form of 'jurisdictional' control, i.e. it is not a branch of the doctrine of ultra vires. A decision which is erroneous on its face, perhaps because it reveals some misinterpretation of the law, can be quashed even on the assumption that it is within jurisdiction and therefore involves no excess of power. All jurisdiction involves the power to make mistakes, provided they are made within the area of jurisdiction conferred. A mistake which appears on the face of the record, if it is held to involve no excess of jurisdiction, does not render a decision a nullity. The decision is intra vires, yet paradoxically the court has power to quash it.

The explanation of the paradox must be sought in history rather than in logic. The Court of King's Bench succeeded in establishing this special jurisdiction by means of its power to issue the writ of certiorari to lower courts and judicial bodies for the purpose of calling up their decisions for review. The foundations of this system of control were laid before the ascendancy of the ultra vires doctrine, and the two different systems survived side by side. As will be seen, the older doctrine has made an important contribution to modern administrative law, although the latest extensions of the doctrine of ultra vires threaten to render it superfluous.

There is therefore one long-established category of judicial review which rests on an independent historical footing, outside the otherwise comprehensive principle of ultra vires. It might be asked, why should there not be more exceptions? Why should not categories like irrelevant considerations and breach of natural justice, which are brought within the principle of ultra vires only by reasoning of such artificiality that it bewilders judges, also stand on their own independent footing, as recognised exceptions? This would certainly involve no logical impossibility. But the courts have preferred to reduce rather than increase the exceptions because of their exposed constitutional position, as already explained.[71] So long as they work within the ultra vires principle, they can claim to be carrying out the mandates of Parliament, and to be using their powers only in accordance with the implications of the Act in question. This defensive instinct probably explains the judicial preference for squeezing everything possible into the jurisdictional framework. It may be seen at work in the developing subject of 'no evidence';[72]

[71] Above, p. 30.
[72] Below, p. 319.

and it reaches high-water mark in the new but controversial doctrine that any error of law, whether on the face of the record or not, renders a determination ultra vires, i.e. outside jurisdiction.[73] If this new doctrine becomes accepted, the old law about error on the record will be redundant. If room can be found within the principle of ultra vires for every element of judicial review, there is no need to supplement it with exceptions.

The general tendency, accordingly, is towards a unified theoretical basis for all the numerous grounds on which the courts may assert their control over the exercise of powers by public authorities.

Legislative, administrative, judicial and quasi-judicial functions

Administrative law needs consistent working definitions of the three primary constitutional functions, legislative, administrative, and judicial; and also of the hybrid 'quasi-judicial' function which has a part of its own to play. Some analysis of the distinctions between them is a help to clarity of thought, but the reader must be warned that the courts themselves are addicted to distinctions which are more superficial and more confusing than those discussed here, and which by no means always help to clarify. Nor is it very profitable to take concepts out of their particular contexts and analyse them in the abstract. A few pointers only will therefore be given here, with references to other parts of the book where the concepts can be seen in actual use.

The one distinction which would seem to be workable is that between judicial and administrative functions. A judicial decision is made according to law. An administrative decision is made according to administrative policy. A judge attempts to find what is the correct solution according to legal rules and principles. An administrator attempts to find what is the most expedient and desirable solution in the public interest. It is true, of course, that many decisions of the courts can be said to be made on grounds of legal policy and that the courts sometimes have to choose between alternative solutions with little else than the public interest to guide them. There will always be grey areas. Nevertheless the mental exercises of judge and administrator are fundamentally different. The judge's approach is objective, guided by his idea of the law. The administrator's approach is empirical, guided merely by expediency. Under this analysis, based on the nature of the functions, many so-called administrative tribunals, such as social security and industrial tribunals, have judicial rather than administrative functions,

---

[73] Below, p. 299.

since their sole task is to find facts and apply law objectively. Yet in the case of a local valuation court, whose task is similar, the House of Lords has held exactly the opposite.[74]

A quasi-judicial function is an administrative function which the law requires to be exercised in some respects as if it were judicial. A standard example is a minister deciding whether or not to confirm a compulsory purchase order or to allow a planning appeal after a public inquiry. The decision itself is administrative, dictated by policy and expediency. But the procedure is subject to the principles of natural justice, which require the minister to act fairly towards the objectors and not (for example) to take fresh evidence without disclosing it to them. A quasi-judicial decision is therefore an administrative decision which is subject to some measure of judicial procedure, such as the principles of natural justice. Since the great majority of administrative decisions which affect the rights or legal position of individuals are subject to the principles of natural justice, most of the administrative decisions with which this book is concerned are quasi-judicial. This is explained in detail in chapter 15, with comment on erratic judicial opinions.

In 1932 the Committee on Ministers' Powers formulated contrasting definitions of judicial and quasi-judicial decisions.[75] The important difference was that a judicial decision 'disposes of the whole matter by a finding upon the facts in dispute and an application of the law of the land to the facts so found', whereas in an administrative decision this is replaced by 'administrative action, the character of which is determined by the minister's free choice'.

To distinguish cleanly between legislative and administrative functions, on the other hand, is, as the Committee said, 'difficult in theory and impossible in practice'.[76] They are easy enough to distinguish at the extremities of the spectrum: an Act of Parliament is legislative and a deportation order is administrative. But in between is a wide area where

[74] *A.-G.* v. *British Broadcasting Corporation* [1981] AC 303, for which see below, p. 929. The House discussed numerous 'non-tests' (as Lord Edmund-Davies aptly called them) for determining what is a 'court' for purposes of contempt of court, and the majority held that the function of a local valuation court is administrative and not judicial. Tests used for interpreting the constitutions of other countries, as in *Shell Co. of Australia Ltd.* v. *Federal Commissioner of Taxation* [1931] AC 275 and *Ranaweera* v. *Ramachandran* [1970] AC 962, have quite different purposes and are of little help for the basic analysis needed in administrative law.

[75] Cmd. 4060 (1932), p. 73. For a helpful analysis see (1933) 49 LQR 94, 419 (D. M. Gordon). His views, together with the criticisms of the Committee's definitions made by Professors Jennings and Robson, are discussed in (1949) 10 CLJ 216 (Wade).

[76] As above, p. 17.

either label could be used according to taste, for example where ministers make orders or regulations affecting large numbers of people. For legislative and administrative action is alike governed by expediency. This is further explained at the outset of chapter 22.

PART II
AUTHORITIES AND FUNCTIONS

3

THE CENTRAL GOVERNMENT

This and the following chapters aim to supply information about public authorities of various kinds and some of their more important and characteristic functions. An exhaustive account of the structure and functions of government would require a large book by itself, nor is it necessary in order to explain the rules of administrative law. But some of the more prominent features of the system are here sketched in outline, so as to illustrate the machinery by which executive power is conferred and exercised, and so as to fill in the administrative background to situations which will be analysed in later chapters. Taking first the central government, we may start at the apex of the pyramid with the Crown and ministers.

THE CROWN AND MINISTERS

Allocation of powers

The Crown's legal powers, whether prerogative or statutory, must be exercised by the sovereign personally as a matter of law, e.g. by Order in Council or letters patent or royal warrant. In practice these powers are controlled by ministers, since convention requires that the Crown should act as its ministers advise in all constitutional affairs. The one case where the Crown may have to act of its own volition is in the appointment of a Prime Minister, the initial act of impetus which sets the machinery of cabinet government in motion; but even that is normally governed by settled conventions. The Crown has therefore no political will of its own. Politically speaking, its powers are exercised by its ministers who must answer for their actions in Parliament.

The Crown itself, however, has relatively few important legal powers, except in the capacity of employer.[1] In almost all other areas administrative powers are statutory, and it has long been the practice for Parliament to confer them upon the proper minister in his own name. The Act will say 'The minister may take regulations' or 'the minister may appoint' or 'the minister may approve'. The minister will of course be acting as a minister

---

[1] See below, p. 240.

of the Crown and on behalf of the Crown. But his powers and duties under the Act will in law be his alone.[2] This is of great legal importance, since the minister as such has none of the Crown's prerogatives and immunities. His unlawful actions may be invalidated, or he may be compelled to perform his duties, by remedies which do not lie against the Crown; and judgments may be enforced against him personally in ways which are impossible in the case of the Crown. If on the other hand the Act had conferred the powers upon the Crown itself, as by saying 'Her Majesty may (etc.)', the minister would in law be merely the servant or agent of the sovereign. The settled practice of conferring powers upon designated ministers therefore greatly assists the operation of legal remedies. The minister is treated in law as a private person, with no special privileges. If for example he neglects a statutory duty, the court may grant an order of mandamus against him which he can disobey only on pain of fine or imprisonment.[3] If the duty had been imposed upon the Crown directly, that remedy would not be available.

Powers are frequently conferred upon 'the Secretary of State' without naming his department, and they are then exercisable by any Secretary of State,[4] though only the appropriate one will normally act. The one minister upon whom they are not normally conferred is the Prime Minister. There is no legal reason why they should not be, and the convention is no more than a long-standing practice. It results from this curious taboo that the Prime Minister's name appears only rarely in the statutes,[5] and that the most powerful of all ministers has in law less power than his colleagues. Therefore when orders have to be made on matters which fall within no particular department's field, and for which the Prime

---

[2] In *Town Investments Ltd.* v. *Department of the Environment* [1978] AC 359 the House of Lords held by a majority, reversing a unanimous Court of Appeal, that principles of public law required ministers and officials acting for the Crown (i.e. the government) to be treated as the Crown in law, so that a lease granted to a minister made the Crown the tenant. Lord Diplock said: 'Executive acts of government that are done by any of them are acts done by "the Crown" in the fictional sense in which that expression is now used in English public law.' These propositions are unsound in both constitutional and administrative law. But the case did not concern statutory powers or duties and it should presumably not be taken to alter the rule that powers and duties conferred upon ministers belong to them personally and not to the Crown. Otherwise the system of remedies would be gravely weakened: see below, p. 808. In later cases judges have found ways round this decision: see *Linden* v. *Department of Health and Social Security* [1986] 1 WLR 164, holding that a lease to the Secretary of State made him and not the Crown the tenant; *Pearce* v. *Secretary of State for Defence* [1988] 2 WLR 144 (below, p. 819).

[3] See below, p. 654.

[4] Interpretation Act 1978, 1st sched.

[5] It appears in the trust deeds scheduled to the Chequers Estate Act 1917 and the Chevening Estate Act 1959; also in legislation about ministerial salaries and pensions: Ministers of the Crown Act 1937; Ministerial and Other Salaries Act 1972.

Minister is responsible, the practice is to confer the power upon the Crown itself, thus avoiding mention of the unmentionable. For example, the power to bring the Statutory Instruments Act 1946 into operation, which in departmental legislation would be given to the minister in charge of the department, was made exercisable by Order in Council.[6] Likewise under the Parliamentary Commissioner Act 1967 an Order in Council is required in order to alter the schedule of departments subject to investigation.[7] But the latter Act, exceptionally, mentions the Prime Minister as the authority to approve certificates protecting cabinet proceedings from disclosure;[8] and this may be the first instance of the Prime Minister being given a statutory power.

Departmental organisation

The titles and functions of ministers and their departments are constantly being changed under the schemes of reorganisation required by successive governments. Recently there has been a tendency to create very large departments by grouping together what were formerly separate departments. In 1968 the Department of Social Security was created out of the former ministries of Health and of Social Security.[9] In 1970 the Board of Trade and the Ministry of Technology were amalgamated in the Department of Trade and Industry,[10] and the Department of the Environment was formed out of the former ministries of Housing and Local Government, Transport and Public Buildings and Works.[11] The technique in such cases is to confer all the powers of the former ministries upon the Secretary of State in charge of the new department: the former ministries are dissolved and therefore disappear as separate legal entities, though some or all of their organisation may continue to exist administratively. The Secretary of State for the Environment now possesses powers and functions under sixty-eight different heads.[12] Like the heads of the other mammoth departments, he is assisted by a number of non-cabinet ministers with particular responsibilities, though none of them is invested with legal powers.

Departmental reorganisation is effected under the Ministers of the Crown Act 1975. Orders in Council may be made under this Act both for the transfer of functions from one department to another and for the

---

[6] s. 10.
[7] s. 4(2).
[8] s. 8(4).
[9] SI 1968 No. 1699.
[10] SI 1970 No. 1537.
[11] SI 1970 No. 1681.
[12] *Index to the Statutes*, 1235–1985, p. 716.

dissolution of departments no longer required. If it merely transfers functions the order need only be laid before Parliament and is then subject to annulment if either House so resolves; but if it dissolves an existing department, the order may not be made until each House has presented an address to the Crown in its favour.[13] Functions may also be made exercisable concurrently by two or more ministers.[14] The Act contains supplementary powers to deal with the transfer of property and the adaptation of enactments, but the number of ministers who may sit in the House of Commons may not be increased.[15]

These orders often confer corporate personality on the newly created department, so that it can hold property, make contracts, etc., in its own name and not merely as agent for the Crown. The usual form is to make the minister a corporation sole, so that he and his successors have continuous corporate personality. This was done, for example, when the Department of the Environment was created,[16] and when the Department of Transport was detached from it,[17] and when the Department of Trade and Industry was divided into four new departments.[18] But no corporate personality was conferred upon the Minister for the Civil Service when he took over the civil service functions of the Treasury,[19] nor upon the Secretary of State for Foreign and Commonwealth Affairs when he took charge of the amalgamated Foreign and Commonwealth Offices.[20]

THE CIVIL SERVICE

General aspects

The civil service comprises all the permanent and non-political offices and employments held under the Crown, with the exception of the armed forces. All these officers and employees form the permanent administrative staff of the central government. The legal test of a civil servant is that he should be in the non-military service of the Crown, i.e. there must be a legal relationship of master and servant. This test excludes nationalised industries and their employees, and it excludes the great majority of public corporations. The legal nature of Crown service is investigated in a later

---

[13] s. 5.
[14] Ministers of the Crown Act 1975, s. 1.
[15] s. 1(3).
[16] SI 1970 No. 1681.
[17] SI 1976 No. 1775.
[18] SI 1974 No. 692 (creating Departments of Energy, Industry, Trade, and Prices and Consumer Protection).
[19] SI 1968 No. 1656, transferring both statutory and non-statutory functions.
[20] SI 1968 No. 1657.

section, where stress is laid on the remarkable feature which differentiates the British civil service from that of other countries: the basically non-legal character of its organisation, management, and discipline. Meanwhile some broader features may be indicated here.[21]

The grand total of civil servants, if all clerical and industrial employees are included, is about 585,000. But the number of those who occupy positions of any constitutional importance and who have authority to take decisions is very much smaller, probably less than 10,000. Perhaps half this number are the true governors of the great administrative machine, formerly known as the administrative class, below whom there used formerly to be the executive class. This system of classes was criticised as over-rigid by the Fulton Committee in 1968[22] and was thereupon abolished by the government, since when it has not been so easy to estimate the precise size of the more important classes within the civil service, though the figures for numerous different grades are published annually. In addition there are great numbers in the clerical and industrial grades employed in work which is similar to other civilian work outside the service of the Crown. Their number is no longer swollen by all the employees of the Post Office, since that has since 1969 been reorganised as a public corporation and its staff are no longer civil servants.[23]

Although administrative law is constantly concerned with the acts of government departments, decided upon in the majority of cases by civil servants rather than by ministers personally, the departments do not have many legal powers conferred upon them in their own names. The powers of the central government are normally conferred upon ministers themselves, as already explained, and are exercised by their departments in the ministers' names. But there are certain exceptions, principally in the field of public revenue; thus powers are conferred directly upon inspectors of taxes and upon the Commissioners of Customs and Excise. Powers are of course conferred directly upon civil servants who have adjudicatory functions such as social security officers and inspectors of taxes.

Machinery of control

Until 1968 the general control of the civil service was the responsibility of the Treasury. The Treasury was accustomed to dealing with all

---

[21] For general information and history see the Fulton Report (below); Holdsworth, *History of English Law*, xiv. 106–40; Parris, *Constitutional Bureaucracy*. The word 'bureaucracy' came into use in the 1830s. In 1838 Lord Palmerston had to explain it to the young Queen Victoria: Carr, *Concerning English Administrative Law*, 1.

[22] Report of the Committee on the Civil Service, Cmnd. 3638 (1968), para. 215. The Report will be referred to as the Fulton Report. For the government's decision to abolish the former classes see 767 HC Deb. col. 456 (26 June 1968).

[23] See below, p. 165.

government departments in its supervision of their expenditure, and thus it came to control personnel administration throughout the civil service, regulating pay and conditions of service, and issuing instructions to other departments in Treasury circulars and minutes. But the responsible minister was the Prime Minister, not the Chancellor of the Exchequer, and it was therefore to the Prime Minister that the Permanent Secretary to the Treasury, as head of the civil service, used to report on civil service affairs.

Treasury control was brought to an end in 1968, in implementation of the Fulton Report. General control of the service was transferred to a new Civil Service Department, headed by a Minister for the Civil Service.[24] It was in this minister that the powers of control were vested, as already noted, but in fact the office was held by the Prime Minister. The senior permanent official of the department became the titular head of the home civil service. By the Civil Service Order in Council 1969 the Minister was empowered to make regulations and give instructions for controlling the home civil service and for the classification, remuneration, and other conditions of service of its staff, whether permanent or temporary.

In 1981, however, the scheme of the Fulton Report was abandoned.[25] The Treasury regained control over civil service manpower, pay, allowances, etc., and the Civil Service Department was abolished. The Prime Minister remained the minister for the civil service, assisted by a new 'management and personnel office' under the Secretary to the Cabinet, which was concerned in particular with organisation, overall efficiency, recruitment, training, and personnel management.[26] The Secretary to the Cabinet has since been the head of the home civil service.

The legal sanction behind these powers of control is nothing more than the Crown's power to dismiss its servants at pleasure, so that the Crown can prescribe or vary their conditions of employment as it wishes.[27] The civil service is regulated under Orders in Council[28] which have no statutory basis and are held by the courts to be made under the royal prerogative.[29] This is the authority by which the service formulates its disciplinary procedures.

---

[24] See 767 HC Deb col. 455 (26 June 1968): SI 1968 No. 1656; Civil Service Order in Council 1969 (22 October).

[25] See 12 HC Deb 658 (12 November 1981); SI 1981 No. 1670.

[26] SI 1987 No. 2039 transfers policy on recruitment, retirement, redundancy, and some other matters to the Treasury. The office now becomes 'the office of the Minister for the Civil Service'.

[27] See *Council of Civil Service Unions* v. *Minister for the Civil Service* [1985] AC 374 at 409 (Lord Diplock).

[28] Notably the Civil Service Order in Council 1982, under which regulations are made and the code on pay and conditions of service is issued.

[29] But note the alternative basis suggested by Lord Diplock (as cited above), namely a special rule of constitutional law.

Until 1972 a civil servant threatened with dismissal or premature retirement could merely appeal to the head of his department. Since then a Civil Service Appeal Board has been set up to hear all appeals of this kind by civil servants of at least two years' standing;[30] and civil servants have been given the benefit of the statutory law about unfair dismissal as well as of other statutes benefiting employees. The legal details of these changes, and the legal rules which underlie the management of the civil service, are explained below in the section on the law of Crown service. So is the wide exemption which protects the control of the civil service from investigation by the Parliamentary Commissioner for Administration. What may be emphasised here is that the civil service, though it has grown into an enormous industry, still retains a kind of legal extraterritoriality in its internal affairs, in marked contrast to the liability of officials to obey the ordinary law of the land in their dealings with other people. Although it is possible, as will be seen, that civil service regulations may in theory be legally enforceable as terms of a contract of employment, and although civil servants have now been brought within much of the legislation on labour relations, and in some respects within the scope of judicial review, the fact is that disputes over employment in the civil service do not often reach the courts of law.

Disputes over rates of pay and conditions of service, except for the highest grades and except in individual cases, are resolved through the machinery of the Whitley councils, so called from the report of the Whitley Committee of 1917. There are both national and departmental Whitley councils, which are analogous to the machinery of industrial negotiation, and on which the official side (i.e. the government) and the staff side (i.e. the staff associations) are represented. If agreement cannot be reached, arbitration is available before the Civil Service Arbitration Tribunal. There are various staff associations to which different grades and classes belong, and there is now no restriction on these associations being affiliated to outside bodies, even though they support political parties.[31] Civil servants enjoy the general rights of employees to join trade unions and engage in their activities,[32] except where there are overriding dangers to national security.[33]

[30] See [1972] PL 149; R. v. Civil Service Appeal Board ex p. Bruce [1987] The Times, 22 June. For matters affecting national security see Security Procedures in the Public Service, Cmnd 1681 (1962); 1963 PL 51 M.R. Joelson).

[31] The Trade Disputes and Trade Unions Act 1927, which imposed restrictions, was repealed by the Trade Disputes and Trade Unions Act 1946.

[32] Employment Protection (Consolidation) Act 1978, ss. 23, 58, 138.

[33] See Council of Civil Service Unions v. Minister for the Civil Service [1985] AC 374, explained below, p. 521.

Recruitment and character

The ideals of the modern civil service were proclaimed by the Northcote–Trevelyan Report of 1853,[34] much of which was put into force by Order in Council in 1870. The report called for entry by competitive examination instead of patronage, promotion by merit rather than by seniority, clear distinction between intellectual and manual work, an unified control of the service as a single organisation. This last principle was put into effect through Treasury control, remained in force until 1968 and was partially reinstated in 1981, as already noted. Standards of entry into the service were prescribed by the Civil Service Commission, an independent body established in 1855. The Civil Service Commission has to approve and certify the qualifications for all permanent appointments.[35] Formerly the Commission arranged for the stringent examinations which candidates had to sit, but selection is now based primarily on school and university examination results supplemented by interviews and certain special examinations and tests. The methods of selection have been broadened so as to secure a flow of entrants of the highest calibre destined for the top positions. There are also possibilities of entry at a senior level from industry and elsewhere. A civil service college, as recommended by the Fulton Committee, has been established for the training of those already in the service.

There is a certain constitutional significance in the method of recruitment for the highest class of administrative posts. The principal requirement is a good education, not technical or professional qualifications. Many technicians are of course employed for specialised work, but for administration generally what is sought is the ability to learn rather than expertise. Qualified lawyers, in particular, are very rarely found in the administrative ranks, save only in the Lord Chancellor's department: elsewhere they are employed almost exclusively as technicians, i.e. as legal advisers, draftsmen, and so forth. The administrators who hold the key positions in Whitehall therefore contrast markedly with their counterparts in many European countries, where the passport to an official career is a degree in law or a highly specialised training.

This 'philosophy of the amateur' was made a primary point of criticism by the Fulton Committee:[36]

The ideal administrator is still too often seen as the gifted layman who, moving frequently from job to job within the service, can take a practical view of any

---

[34] Reprinted in the Fulton Report, Cmnd. 3638 (1968), Appendix B; and see Holdsworth, *History of English Law*, xiv. 135.

[35] Civil Service Order in Council 1969 (22 October).

[36] Cmnd. 3638 (1968), para. 15.

problem, irrespective of its subject-matter, in the light of his knowledge and experience of the government machine.

The Committee found that this 'cult of the generalist' was 'obsolete at all levels' and had 'most damaging consequences'. They called for a move towards greater professionalism both among specialists (such as scientists and engineers) and administrators. The former should have more training in management and opportunities for wider careers. The latter should be able to specialise in one or other of different groups, e.g. as experts in economic and financial affairs or as social administrators. This policy is now accepted. At the same time a unified grading structure, with interchangeability between grades and posts, has replaced the former system of classes (administrative class, executive class, etc.) which the Fulton Committee condemned.

When the modern method of recruitment was first advocated by the reformers of 1853 it was said that high intellectual qualifications were unnecessary for administrative staff, and that they would produce 'statesmen in disguise'. Experience has proved exactly the opposite, for the British system has produced in a high degree the combination of executive ability with political neutrality. If men such as John Milton, Matthew Prior, Matthew Arnold, and Anthony Trollope are no longer found in government offices, it is because of the professionalisation of the service rather than because of any fall in the level of ability. The conventions and the rigours of government employment today mean that its Miltons are relatively mute and inglorious.

A most important feature of the civil service is that it contains no political appointees. Apart from the ministers themselves, who come and go with the fluctuating tides of politics, government departments consist wholly of permanent career officials with the addition sometimes of certain temporary staff appointed for special and non-political reasons. Ministers who have felt a need for advice and assistance of a politically sympathetic kind have brought a small number of personal advisers with them into their departments, but these are not civil servants and it is recognised that, as merely personal assistants to their ministers, they will leave the departments when their ministers go.

Attitude to law and lawyers

The absence of trained lawyers from the corps of higher administrative officials concerned with policy-making has a certain effect upon the character of the civil service. On many matters of policy and administration there is a distinct legal point of view. But in the British central administrative system, as opposed to that of other countries, this point of view is largely unrepresented except by lawyers whose function is that of technicians. The position is just the opposite in local government, where traditionally the chief executive officials were town or county clerks who were trained as solicitors; and many still are, despite the recent tendency to appoint chief executives without professional qualifications.[37] Throughout the central government, accordingly, there is a marked lack of legal influence on the style and technique of administration—a deficiency which may be observed in some of the cases discussed later. As has been rightly observed:[38]

Public administrators in Britain, wielding extensive statutory powers and duties which have increasingly come under judicial scrutiny, have remained largely an élitist group, separate and distinct from those professionally versed in the legal framework of those very same statutory powers and duties. Lawyers in government service have failed to attain anything more than formal equality of status within the hierarchy of the Civil Service, while retaining a professional pre-eminence restricted to traditional legal advice and assistance.

It seems, furthermore, that the operation of judicial review, now so greatly intensified, has led to little change in the traditional attitudes and arrangements.[39]

A result of this peculiarity is a certain antagonism, if that is not too strong a word, between the official and legal mentalities. The civil service, with its non-legal character and its autonomous internal management, tends to develop attitudes which are distinctly different from those of lawyers. The legal profession, by contrast, is exceptionally independent in status compared with the legal professions of other countries, especially in the fact that judges are recruited from the practising bar; there is no distinct judicial career in which a man's promotion may depend throughout his working life on a minister of justice. This polarisation of attitudes accentuates the feeling of tension between government and governed which runs through administrative law and suggests an exaggerated notion of the separation of powers. It has produced, for example, two radically different views of the character of statutory tribunals.[40] It also contributed to the unwillingness to interfere with executive action which the courts displayed at one time.[41] There can be no doubt that it has acted as an impediment to the development of administrative law. It might also be blamed for the

[37] See below, p. 122.
[38] See *Lawyers and Public Administrators: Separate and Unequal* (L. Blom-Cooper QC) [1984] PL 215 at 234.
[39] See (1986) 64 *Public Administration* 163 (Sir M. Kerry, formerly Treasury Solicitor), with headnote suggesting that the position may at last be changing.
[40] See below, p. 913.
[41] See above, p. 18.

technical and formal character of some of the decisions. On the other hand, it has helped to strengthen the rule of law and to preserve the independence of the judiciary and the legal profession. The balance-sheet is not an easy one to settle.

Political activities

Restrictions on the political activities of civil servants are incorporated in the (non-statutory) code of conditions of service. They were formulated in 1953 and were reviewed by a committee in 1978.[42] The restrictions are stringent for the higher administrative and professional grades, and for some of the executive and clerical grades who work with them and come into contact with the public. These classes may not take part in national politics, but may take part in local politics with the permission of their own departments. The rest of the executive and clerical grades may take part both in national and in local politics, subject to departmental permission, and subject also to a code of rules enjoining discretion on matters of government policy. The other minor grades are free from restriction except when on duty or on official premises or when wearing uniform.

By 1977, when the civil service had grown to 746,000, the restricted categories had greatly increased. The committee recommended relaxations which would tranfer some 175,000 civil servants, mainly in the executive grades, from the most restricted to the intermediate category, with an appeal body to hear appeals against refusal of permission and other complaints. Finally in 1984 these changes were agreed with the staff unions and incorporated in the conditions of service.[43]

A civil servant is disqualified by statute from membership of Parliament.[44] But if he belongs to the unrestricted class, he may stand for Parliament but resume his employment if not elected.[45]

Detachment and anonymity

The high degree of detachment from party politics and publicity attained in the British civil service is due in a large degree to the strict doctrine of ministerial responsibility to Parliament. Ministers must be answerable to Parliament for all that is done in their departments, and, except in cases where orders have been disobeyed or some unauthorised wrong has been

---

[42] White Paper, Cmd. 8783 (1953); Committee's Report, Cmnd. 7057 (1978).
[43] 64 HC Deb (WA) 272 (19 July 1984). Appeals go to the Civil Service Appeal Board.
[44] House of Commons Disqualification Act 1976.
[45] Servants of the Crown (Parliamentary Candidature) Order 1960 (11 May).

done, they cannot throw the blame onto their officials.[46] The cabinet system with its parliamentary majority provides a firm front against which the tides of public criticism surge and break, and behind which the civil service shelters. The whole shock of any major political attack is taken by political office-holders, and convention forbids any inquiry as to who has advised ministers or what advice has been given. The ministerial screen can now be penetrated by the Parliamentary Commissioner for Administration, as explained later; but his detailed reports on acts of maladministration committed in government departments stop short of identifying officials in person. Officials are identified only in the rare cases where an independent public inquiry is set up in some exceptional situation.[47]

By a natural corollary it is improper for civil servants in the higher ranks to take part in political controversies, to write letters to the newspapers on political topics, or to publish their replies to attacks made on them or their departments—although the practice of employing departmental public relations officers has led to some relaxation of the rule against self-defence in recent years. As a general rule, it is in Parliament that any defence must be made, and attacks made in other quarters are ignored. The civil servant thus achieves a very high degree of self-effacement, and although he is bound to be much concerned with questions of policy as well as with administration, he is insulated from the effects of political controversy. Working in this atmosphere of detachment, he can give his services to a government of any complexion with impartiality—or at least with the greatest degree of impartiality that it is reasonable to ask of a human being.

Official secrecy

A counterpart of the virtues of impartiality and anonymity is the occupational vice of secrecy, of which the civil service is continually accused despite the vast number of informative publications which it issues. The official reluctance to allow the public to see departmental papers of any kind had serious consequences for the law as to the production of documents in court,[48] and it retarded the valuable reform of publishing the reports of inspectors after public inquiries.[49] It is only on very exceptional occasions that there is any public inquiry into the actions of named officials, as happened in the Crichel Down affair of 1954[50] and in the inquiry into the

---

[46] For the classic statement of the minister's responsibility for mistakes made by his officials see 530 HC Deb col. 1286 (20 July 1954). This was made by the Home Secretary, Sir D. Maxwell-Fyfe, in the debate on the *Crichel Down* case (below). It is summarised in Wade (E.C.S.) and Bradley, *Constitutional Law*, 10th edn., 114.

[47] As in the cases of *Crichel Down* and the *Vehicle and General Insurance Co.* (below).

[48] Below, p. 833.

[49] Below, p. 972.

[50] Cmd. 9176 (1954); below, p. 912.

Vehicle and General Insurance Company's collapse in 1971.[51] Such
inquiries, which necessarily involve breaking the normal rules of
anonymity, can only act as a further spur to official reticence.

The Fulton Committee's criticisms of departmental secretiveness led the
government to publish a white paper explaining how much information is
already provided and encouraging the provision of more.[52] But it was
complacent about the Official Secrets Acts 1911–39, which are a serious
impediment to openness in government.[53] The principal Act of 1911 was a
hasty piece of catch-all legislation which passed through the House of
Commons in one day without debate at the time of the Agadir crisis.
Section 2 of the Act makes a criminal offence of all unauthorised[54]
disclosure of information from official sources, regardless of the question
whether the public interest really demands secrecy.[55] Prosecutions require
the consent of the Attorney-General, and it is only by executive control
that the law has been rendered tolerable. An indiscriminate law of this kind
is a breeding-ground of abuse, as was so clearly shown by the former law
about Crown privilege under which the government could refuse to
produce official documents in court.[56] In the United States, by contrast, the
Freedom of Information Act of 1966 entitles any one to have access to any
identifiable document of the federal government, subject only to specific
exceptions relating to national defence, foreign policy, commercial secrets,
etc.[57] The American citizen interested in the government of the country is
thus given a legal right to a great deal of information which it would be a
criminal offence to disclose or receive in Britain. In Sweden also the right of
public access to government documents is recognised in principle.[58]

Continuous complaint about the law in Britain, and the difficulty of
obtaining convictions under it,[59] led to a committee of inquiry which

[51] HC 133, 15 February 1972.
[52] Cmnd. 4089 (1969).
[53] For their history and defects see David Williams, *Not in the Public Interest*.
[54] Authorisation may be implied from release of the information to other people: *R. v. Galvin* [1987] QB 862.
[55] The Franks Committee (as below) at p. 112 epitomised the primary provision as making it an offence 'for a Crown servant or government contractor to make an unauthorised disclosure of information which he has learnt in the course of his job'. It also covers communication of information obtained in contravention of the Act or entrusted in confidence by an official, including the police (see below, p. 146).
[56] Below, p. 833.
[57] 5 USC s. 552. See Schwartz and Wade, *Legal Control of Government*, 77 and Appendix II (containing text of the Act); Cmnd. 5104 (1972), p. 128. The Act was strengthened in 1974 and 1976, the latter statute being given the short title 'The Government in the Sunshine Act'.
[58] See [1958] PL 50 (N. Herlitz); Cmnd. 5104 (1972), p. 127.
[59] In 1986 the House of Commons Select Committee on the Treasury and Civil Service reported that Section 2 was now unenforceable (7th Report, HC 1985–6 No. 92–1). For the government's comments see Cmnd. 9841.

vigorously condemned the main provision of the Act of 1911 and recommended much less indiscriminate legislation.[60] The committee advocated an Official Information Act to protect information contained in documents classified (as by being marked 'secret') for purposes of defence, public order, maintenance of essential supplies and services in contingencies short of war, foreign relations, and currency and financial reserves; to protect all official information likely to help the commission or concealment of crime, the escape or misconduct of prisoners, and the apprehension or prosecution of offenders; to protect cabinet documents;[61] and to protect information given to the government, whether or not in confidence and whether or not under compulsion, by private persons or concerns.

The government received the report favourably[62] and in 1979 put forward a Protection of Official Information Bill specifying six categories of protected information but not including cabinet secrets or information about economic affairs. Criminal penalties were not confined to classified information, but it was to be a defence that the information was publicly available, and prosecutions were to require a ministerial certificate of the likelihood of serious injury to the national interest or to some person's safety. The Bill was criticised in many respects, but its major flaw was that it appeared to make an offence of unauthorised disclosure of any protected information which was or had been held by a Crown servant or contractor, even though the person disclosing it had not himself obtained it from official sources. In this respect it was more severe than the Act of 1911. While it was before Parliament a book was published revealing grave security offences, using information about this country unobtainable here but obtained in the United States under the Freedom of Information Act.[63] Had the Bill been law it seems that this publication might have been an offence although the secret information was not obtained from British sources. In the general furore the government withdrew the Bill. Nothing has been heard of it since. Subsequently the government procured the

[60] Departmental Committee on Section 2 of the Official Secrets Act 1911 (chairman, Lord Franks), Cmnd. 5104 (1972).

[61] The court has inherent power on grounds of public policy, apart from the Official Secrets Acts, to prohibit by injunction the disclosure of cabinet proceedings, like certain other breaches of confidence: *A.-G.* v. *Jonathan Cape Ltd.* [1976] QB 752 (the Crossman Diaries case); but in this case an injunction was refused on the ground that the events disclosed had taken place ten years previously and no harm would result. In 1986 the Attorney-General obtained interim injunctions prohibiting newspapers from publishing extracts from P. M. Wright, *Spycatcher*, which contained confidential information about the security services: *Attorney-General* v. *Guardian Newspapers Ltd.* [1987] 1 WLR 1248.

[62] See Cmnd. 7285 (White Paper, 1978); *Disclosure of Official Information: A Report on Overseas Practice* (HMSO, 1979).

[63] A. Boyle, *The Climate of Treason.*

defeat of two private member's Bills. In 1987—fifteen years after the Committee's report—it was once again announced that the government would propose reforming legislation, and it must be hoped that this will be better drawn and more resolutely supported than in 1979.

THE LAW OF CROWN SERVICE

Nature of Crown service

Crown service is one of the most curious departments of public law. In most other democratic countries the position and rights of state employees form an important branch of administrative law, and the tenure of posts in the civil service gives rise to many questions for the courts, whether they be ordinary courts of law or special administrative courts. In England the position is just the opposite. The civil service, despite its great size and importance, is largely staffed and regulated under arrangements which are not legally enforceable. This accords, perhaps, with the way in which the civil service works, withdrawn as much as possible from the public gaze, and screened from scrutiny by the doctrine of ministerial responsibility.[64] But legally it is anomalous. It has generally been held that at common law civil servants of the Crown, and military servants also, have no legal right to their salaries and no legal protection against wrongful dismissal. Although recently the picture has begun to change, the law has long regarded the civil service as if it consisted of a handful of secretaries working behind the scenes in a royal palace. Although it has lost its domestic character in every other respect, it is still in a primitive state of legal evolution. It is also curious that the legal situation did not reveal itself clearly until late in the nineteenth century.

Another paradox is that in practice the situation is just the opposite of what these legal rules would suggest. The courts have to a large extent abrogated jurisdiction over contracts of service under the Crown. But Crown service, though legally the most precarious of all employments, is in reality the most secure. This is merely convention, but in the civil service the convention is deeply ingrained, so that there are probably better grounds for complaining that civil servants are excessively protected than for criticising their defencelessness in law.[65] The Crichel Down affair of 1954 provides a good example. This was one of the rare cases where serious

[64] Above, p. 31.

[65] The Fulton Committee found it hard to believe that the rate of dismissals for misconduct and inefficiency should not have been higher: Cmnd. 3638 (1968), para. 123. At that time dismissals in the grades of executive officer and above totalled twenty to twenty-five annually.

complaints against the conduct of officials were investigated in a public proceeding.[66] The charge was that they had not given proper attention to a landowner's claims for the restoration of land taken under compulsory powers before the war. There was no infringement of legal rights, but clearly there had been bad administration. A public inquiry was ordered by the Minister of Agriculture and all the correspondence was published[67]—a most unusual opportunity for the public to see the contents of official files. But despite the strong criticism which the report contained, there were no dismissals, and in the civil service the result of all the upheaval was no more than some rearrangement of duties. The Minister of Agriculture, however, resigned—although he personally was entirely free from blame, and had shown magnanimity in ordering the inquiry. There could hardly be a better illustration of the rock-like solidity of the civil service and, in contrast, of the irrational vicissitudes of politics. The doctrine of ministerial responsibility does not, indeed, require a minister to resign if his officials have done something which is not in accordance with his orders or his policy, and of which he does not approve.[68] But, when the choice had to be made, it was in fact the Minister who elected to pay the penalty.

There is a close connection between the responsibility of the minister and the security of tenure of the civil servant. There is no real need for this connection to produce such results as it did in the Crichel Down case; but since the public is accustomed to frequent changes of ministers and to complete stability in the administrative machine, there is a natural tendency for the sacrosanctity of tenure of official posts to be exaggerated. It is this which gives an atmosphere of unreality to the subject of Crown service. In the Crichel Down case itself the Home Secretary said of the position of a civil servant:[69]

It is worth stating again that he holds his office 'at pleasure' and can be dismissed at any time by the Minister; and that power is none the less real because it is seldom used.

The power of arbitrary dismissal is now to some extent restrained by statute, as will be seen, so that the gulf between theory and reality may have been narrowed.

Crown servants of all ranks are in law the servants of the Crown and not of one another.[70] A civil servant therefore has no contractual rights against

---

[66] This may also occur, though also rarely, when there is a Tribunal of Inquiry, for example the inquiry into the collapse of the Vehicle and General Insurance Company, in which officials were criticised (1972, HC 133).

[67] Cmd. 9176 (1954).

[68] See above, p. 32.

[69] 530 HC Deb. Col. 1286 (20 July 1954).

[70] *Bainbridge* v. *Postmaster-General* [1906] 1 KB 178; *Secretary of State for the Environment* v. *Hooper* [1981] RTR 169.

his department, his minister, or any superior officer. Whoever engages him acts merely as the Crown's agent, and if there is any contract of employment it is directly between the servant and the Crown. Any remedy must therefore be sought against the Crown alone. This is equally true where, as in the national health service,[71] statutory duties are laid upon a designated minister and other statutory authorities administer the service on his behalf: all are then servants of the Crown rather than of the minister or of any subordinate authority.[72]

How far state corporations and their staff count as servants of the Crown is explained later.[73]

Tenure: no protection at common law

The best-known decision on the legal insecurity of civil service tenure concerned the dismissal of a consular agent in Nigeria. He had been engaged for a term (as he said) of three years certain, but was prematurely dismissed. He sued the Crown by petition of right, but the Court of Appeal refused him any relief.[74] The court substantially accepted the Crown's argument reported in the following words:

... servants of the Crown hold office only during the pleasure of the Crown, except in cases where it is otherwise provided by statute. . . . The action of a civil servant of the Crown might, if he could not be dismissed, in some cases bring about a war. A contract to employ a servant of the Crown for a fixed period would be against the public interest and unconstitutional. It is not competent for the Crown to tie its hands by such a contract.

The basis of the rule that Crown servants are dismissible at pleasure, therefore, is the principle that the public interest requires that the government should be able to disembarrass itself of any employee at any moment. All the emphasis was on public policy. There was no suggestion that the rule had any connection with the royal prerogative.[75]

This case had a sequel, for having failed against the Crown the consular

[71] National Health Service Act 1977, Pt. I.
[72] *Wood* v. *Leeds Area Health Authority* [1974] ICR 535, applying *Pfizer Corporation* v. *Ministry of Health* [1965] AC 512. See also *Marshall* v. *Southampton Health Authority* [1986] QB 401 at 414 (European Court of Justice, opinion of Sir Gordon Slynn).
[73] Below, p. 169.
[74] *Dunn* v. *The Queen* [1896] 1 QB 116; similarly *Hales* v. *The King* (1918) 34 TLR 589; *Denning* v. *Secretary of State for India* (1920) 37 TLR 138. But see *Cameron* v. *Lord Advocate* 1952 SC 165, distinguishing *Dunn's* case where it was alleged that a promised post in Nigeria was never provided at all. See also Hogg, *Liability of the Crown*, 150; (1975) 34 CLJ 253 (G. Nettheim).
[75] It is ascribed to the prerogative in *R.* v. *Civil Service Appeal Board ex p. Bruce* [1987] The Times, 22 June, but presumably in the loose sense noted below, p. 242.

agent sued the officer who had engaged him.[76] It was plain that this officer had no authority to promise a certain period of tenure, for the law as laid down by the court was that any such term was unenforceable. He was therefore sued personally for breach of warranty of authority, on the principle explained later.[77] But here again he failed: first, because it was held that public policy excludes any remedy for breach of warranty of authority against a public servant who is acting purely in his public capacity; and secondly, because in fact the agent had been duly authorised in this instance, and the complaint was really that the law gave no remedy against the Crown's breach of the agreed terms of service rather than that any misrepresentation had been made by the agent. The first of these grounds will be criticised later, there being no evident reason why civil servants should not be as responsible for misrepresenting their authority as anyone else. An alternative way of escape is to say that the misunderstanding was one of law, as to which one person cannot in theory mislead another, for all are supposed to know it. Artificial as this is,[78] it avoids the greater evil of inventing new official immunities.

The rule that the Crown can always dismiss a public servant at pleasure, despite any engagement to the contrary, was followed in a number of later decisions,[79] and the general policy of the judges has clearly been to treat Crown service as no concern of the ordinary law. Yet the reasons put forward for this policy will not really bear examination. It is said that the public interest demands that public servants should be subject to summary dismissal because of the damage that it may be in their capacity to do. But any employer can always dismiss a servant: the only question is whether, if he does so, he should pay damages for breach of contract.[80] No master can be compelled to employ a servant, any more than a servant can be compelled to serve a master. The argument that the Crown could not otherwise relieve the public of an undesirable servant therefore falls to the ground. The question is merely one of monetary compensation. It may be said that the Crown should not be put in the dilemma of ignoring the public interest or else committing a breach of contract—for a breach of contract, despite Mr Justice Holmes' famous theory to the contrary,[81] is a wrongful act. But to that it can be answered that it is of even greater importance that engagements expressly entered into should at least be

---

[76] Dunn v. Macdonald [1897] 1 QB 401, 555.
[77] Below, p. 823.
[78] It was expressly rejected at first instance in Dunn v. Macdonald (above) at 406.
[79] e.g. Rodwell v. Thomas [1944] KB 596; Riordan v. War Office [1959] 1 WLR 1046, affirmed [1961] 1 WLR 210.
[80] See below, p. 562.
[81] Holmes held that a contract was a promise to perform or to pay damages at the promisor's option: The Common Law, 301.

honoured in the breach, if not in the observance. The Crown should be an honest man, and if driven to break its contract ought to pay damages, as it does for breach of other contracts.

In the armed forces the lack of any legal remedy for wrongful dismissal has been made clear in a parallel line of decisions which are, if anything, more categorical than those dealing with civil servants.[82] It was in fact the decisions about military service which provided persuasive precedents for the decisions about civil service. Although it has occasionally been suggested that there is no necessary reason why the rules should be the same in both cases, there are no very convincing reasons for differentiation. On the whole, however, the military cases tend more to the conclusion that this type of Crown service is not contractual at all. This was flatly stated by Lord Esher MR in 1890:[83]

The law is as clear as it can be . . . that all engagements between those in the military service of the Crown and the Crown are voluntary only on the part of the Crown and give no occasion for an action in respect of any alleged contract. . . . The courts of law have nothing to do with such a matter.

Remuneration: confusion at common law

The judicial reluctance to give even a money judgment against the Crown on a contract of service led to a decision in 1943 that a Crown employee has not even a contractual right to arrears of pay.[84] An Indian civil servant had made default in payments of alimony to his wife under a separation order, and the wife attempted to attach, by a garnishee order, arrears of pay due to her husband. But debts can be attached only if legally due, and the Crown took the point that since the husband could not sue for the pay, it was not legally due to him and so not attachable by his creditors. This contention was upheld, following a very similar Scots case in which the Court of Session had decided that contracts of service under the Crown were subject to an implied condition that the right to salary should not be legally enforceable.[85]

[82] Re Tufnell (1876) 3 Ch D 164; Grant v. Secretary of State for India (1877) 2 CPD 445; De Dohse v. R. (unreported, House of Lords), cited in Dunn v. The Queen (above).
[83] Mitchell v. R. (1890) [1896] 1 QB 121, note. The mention of the royal prerogative in the headnote appears to be a mistake, although military (as opposed to civil) service may have a prerogative basis. The law has been altered in Australia: see (1950) 66 LQR at 480 (Z. Cowen).
[84] Lucas v. Lucas [1943] P. 68. See similarly High Commissioner for India v. Lall (1948) LR 75 IA 225 (Privy Council); but contrast Picton v. Cullen [1900] 2 IR 612. As to military pay see Gibson v. East India Co. (1839) 5 Bing. NC 262; Mitchell v. R (above). For criticism and discussion see (1945) 61 LQR 263 (D. W. Logan).
[85] Mulvenna v. The Admiralty 1926 SC 842 (dockyard telephone attendant).

In decisions such as these, as in the cases on dismissal, the courts seemed determined to reduce the contractual element in Crown service almost to vanishing point, tending to the conclusion that it was not contractual at all. In some provocative *obiter dicta* Lord Goddard CJ took this ultimate step, saying that 'an established civil servant is appointed to an office and is a public officer, remunerated by moneys provided by Parliament, so that his employment depends not on a contract with the Crown but on appointment by the Crown . . .'.[86] This analysis was adopted recently when a Divisional Court held that an inland revenue employee held office by virtue of his appointment and not under any contract, though there was nothing unconstitutional about such contracts if the Crown wished to make them.[87] Lord Goddard's suggestion of a legal divorce between the Crown and its servants was a new idea, which seemed to run counter to the long accepted principle that there is a true relationship of master and servant between them. Lord Goddard nevertheless also suggested that a civil servant should have a legal right to arrears of pay by claiming on a *quantum meruit*, i.e. for the value of the services rendered. But against whom this claim would lie, if not against the Crown, he did not say, nor did he consider the authorities which expressly decided that arrears of pay were not legally recoverable.

It is not surprising that other judges have preferred to lay down more reasonable law. On two occasions the Privy Council more than hinted that there might be some contractual remedy for wrongful dismissal.[88] More recently, in holding that the law of Ceylon allowed a civil servant to sue the Crown for increments of salary, the Privy Council rejected the English and Scots decisions as being based on reasoning which was defective, contrary to authority and wrong.[89] The Privy Council stigmatised as a *non sequitur* the idea that the Crown's right to terminate a contract of service at will could affect the employee's 'right to salary already earned under the terms of his existing contract before its termination'.

The House of Lords, moreover, has allowed a Crown servant to recover arrears of pay by petition of right.[90] But this case is a mystery in which the

---

[86] *Inland Revenue Commissioners* v. *Hambrook* [1956] 2 QB 641 at 654.

[87] *R.* v. *Civil Service Appeal Board ex p. Bruce* [1987] The Times, 22 June. Conditions of service were treated as if legally enforceable in *Cresswell* v. *Inland Revenue Board* [1984] 2 All ER 713 (civil servants' objections to operating computers failed).

[88] *Shenton* v. *Smith* [1895] AC 229; *Reilly* v. *The King* [1934] AC 176. See also *Robertson* v. *Minister of Pensions* [1949] 1 KB 227 at 231; *Terrell* v. *Secretary of State for the Colonies* [1953] 2 QB 482 at 449 (below, p. 76).

[89] *Kodeeswaran* v. *A.-G. of Ceylon* [1970] AC 1111 at 1123. The Court of Appeal of New South Wales did the same in *Suttling* v. *Director General of Education* [1985] 3 NSWLR 427 (2-year appointment held binding and arrears of salary awarded).

[90] *Sutton* v. *A.-G.* (1923) 39 TLR 294.

House displayed an Olympian detachment from the usual problems. A Post Office telegraphist had enlisted in the armed forces in 1915 on the strength of a Post Office circular which promised 'full civil pay in addition to military pay'. The House of Lords held that he was legally entitled to increments of civil pay granted in the Post Office during his period of military service. Nothing however was said about the possible legal objections to such a claim, presumably because the Crown wished to obtain a ruling in a test case affecting many of its servants. Similar rulings were later given in other such cases in the Court of Appeal.[91]

The state of the decisions illustrates case-law at its worst, and Crown counsel have had to implore judges not to add to the confusion by propounding more doctrine.[92] Nevertheless it seems a fair prediction that judges will in future follow the Privy Council's lead in holding that Crown service is contractual and that arrears of pay can be recovered. The supposed rule to the contrary would be thoroughly anomalous as well as unjust, now that the Crown bears ordinary legal liabilities for most purposes under the Crown Proceedings Act 1947 and now that Crown employment is governed by much regulatory and social legislation. But it must be noted that the Crown Proceedings Act itself made no attempt to modify the law in this respect. Indeed, it did something to confirm the much criticised decision of 1943, since in the provision for machinery corresponding to a garnishee order, under which moneys due from the Crown may be attached like other debts, an express exception was made in respect of any wages or salary payable to an officer of the Crown as such.[93]

It must also be remembered that the non-legal character of the public service is in some ways in keeping with its whole constitutional position.[94] Extensive inroads into this traditional system have however been made by the legislation considered next.

Statutory regulation of Crown employment

The Crown, as the largest employer of labour in the country, could not remain unaffected by the far-reaching laws on employment, labour relations, and social security enacted in recent years. These statutes may be said without exaggeration to have transformed the legal character of Crown service, changing it from a relationship which was almost ignored by the law into one in which the employee has many legal rights and in

---

[91] *Pidduck* v. *A.-G.* (1924) 41 TLR 51.
[92] *Riordan* v. *War Office* [1959] 1 WLR 1046 at 1052.
[93] s. 27.
[94] See above, p. 61.

which the relationship is in some important ways minutely regulated by legal rules. The application of social legislation to Crown employment is not however a contemporary innovation entirely. For example, the national insurance system has covered employees of the Crown from its inception.[95] The Race Relations Act 1976, prohibiting racial discrimination in employment, was made binding on the Crown.[96] The redundancy payments scheme of 1965, now contained in the Employment Protection (Consolidation) Act 1978, is not made binding on the Crown directly, but it provides for the inclusion in the statutory scheme of such corresponding arrangements as the Crown may make,[97] as it has in fact done. On the other hand the provisions of the same Act, dating from 1972, which entitled employees to minimum periods of notice and to a written statement of their terms of employment, have no application to Crown service at all.[98]

The most radical alteration of the position of the Crown's employees at common law is that which brings them within the provisions against unfair dismissal first enacted in 1971 and now contained in the Employment Protection (Consolidation) Act 1978.[99] Under this Act Crown employees are entitled to financial compensation for unfair dismissal, as defined in the Act,[1] whether or not the dismissal is also a breach of contract. One example of lawful but unfair dismissal is compulsory retirement before the normal retiring age.[2] Another is dismissal after due notice because the employee took part in the activity of an independent trade union.[3] The compensation is assessed according to complex provisions, primarily based on the employee's age, length of employment, and weekly wage, but subject to supplementation for expenses and loss incurred and for discriminatory failure to obey a reinstatement order.[4] An average award for a senior employee may amount to something between one and two years' pay. Claims are made to an industrial tribunal, from which appeal lies to the Employment Appeal Tribunal,[5] a mixed tribunal of Supreme Court judges and others, from which appeal lies with leave to the Court of Appeal on a

[95] National Insurance Act 1911, ss. 53(1), 107(3). See now Social Security Act 1975, s. 127.
[96] s. 75, replacing Act of 1968, s. 27.
[97] Act of 1978, s. 111.
[98] Act of 1978, s. 138; *Woods* v. *Leeds Area Health Authority* [1974] ICR 535 (health service officer held to be Crown servant and not entitled to written record of terms of service).
[99] Pt. V, as amended by Employment Act 1980.
[1] ss. 55–62; Employment Act 1980, ss. 6–8.
[2] Claims on this ground failed in *Waite* v. *Government Communications Headquarters* [1983] 2 AC 714 and *Hughes* v. *Department of Health and Social Security* [1985] AC 776 (department held entitled to change normal retiring age).
[3] s. 58.
[4] ss. 73–6.
[5] Pt. VIII.

question of law, and thence to the House of Lords. In some circumstances the tribunal may make an order for reinstatement or reengagement, but the only effect of such an order is to make compensation payable if it is not obeyed.[6] These provisions are applied generally to the civil service of the Crown but not to the armed forces.[7] A civil servant who is dismissed, therefore, may be able to obtain compensation if the dismissal is unfair, even though it may not be a breach of contract. This gives him the protection of the principles of natural justice, including the right to be heard in his own defence, since it has been held that dismissal in violation of natural justice is unfair dismissal.[8] It would also seem right to assume that dismissal in breach of agreed terms of engagement would be unfair dismissal, even if not technically a breach of contract. The statutes are careful not to prejudice the question whether the service of the Crown is or is not contractual, translating the ordinary language of contracts of employment into that of 'Crown employment'.[9]

Employers and trade unions may, alternatively, make a 'dismissal procedures agreement', which the Secretary of State may approve if he is satisfied that it provides remedies for unfair dismissal which are on the whole as beneficial as those of the Act.[10] In that case the employee's rights under the agreement are substituted for those under the Act. A Civil Service Appeal Board was established in 1972 to deal with complaints of unfair dismissal or premature retirement and the Secretary of State approved it for the purposes of the Act.[11] It has been held that the Appeal Board is subject to judicial review, as is explained later.[12]

Civil servants may claim the benefit of many other provisions of these statutes, such as those relating to the code of practice for good industrial relations,[13] 'guarantee payments' for time when the employee is not provided with work,[14] payments when suspended from work on medical grounds,[15] 'maternity pay' and reinstatement,[16] time off work for trade union duties and activities and for public duties such as membership of local

---

[6] s. 71.
[7] s. 138.
[8] *Earl* v. *Slater & Wheeler (Airlyne) Ltd.* [1973] 1 WLR 51 (dismissal unfair but justified, so no compensation awarded).
[9] s. 138. The expression 'contractual retiring age' used by Lord Fraser in the *Waite* case (above) appears to have no significance for this purpose.
[10] s. 65.
[11] See [1972] PL 149.
[12] Below, p. 640.
[13] Employment Protection Act 1975, s. 6.
[14] Act of 1978, s. 12.
[15] Act of 1978, s. 19.
[16] Act of 1978, ss. 34, 45; Employment Act 1980, s. 12.

authorities and tribunals.[17] Two other Acts which confer important rights on Crown employees are the Equal Pay Act 1970[18] and the Sex Discrimination Act 1975,[19] both of which apply to the civil service but not to the armed forces.

Continuing anomalies

Now that employment under the Crown is so intensively regulated by social and labour legislation, it is all the more anomalous that its legal fundamentals remain obscure. A civil servant may now claim statutory compensation for unfair dismissal, but he still appears to have no clear rights at common law. The most that can be said is that several courts of high authority have called the older decisions into question and have refused to follow them. The civil servant's basic legal rights to enforce the terms of his employment, such as his right to tenure and his right to pay, remain in doubt. His terms of service are a strange amalgam of certainties and uncertainties.

Another anomaly, at least in the opinion of the Select Committee of the House of Commons on the Parliamentary Commissioner for Administration, is that Crown employment is excluded from the Parliamentary Commissioner's jurisdiction, so that he cannot investigate complaints of maladministration if the complaint arises out of the employment of a Crown servant. The Parliamentary Commissioner Act 1967 excludes from the Commissioner's purview any action in respect of appointments, removals, pay, discipline, superannuation, or other personnel matters both in the armed forces and in 'any office or employment under the Crown', including any office, employment, or contract for services under any of the government departments which are subject to the Commissioner's investigations,[20] or where the Crown, a minister or any such department has power to take action or approve action to be taken. Having found that the Commissioner had to reject substantial numbers of complaints in such matters, the Select Committee put forward a reasoned case against the continuance of the ban; but their proposals were summarily rejected by the government.[21]

[17] Act of 1978, ss. 27–30.
[18] See s. 1(8).
[19] See s. 85.
[20] 3rd sched., para. 10. See below, p. 82.
[21] In Cmnd. 4661 (1971), commenting on HC 1969–70 No. 127 and stating the procedures available for redress of grievances within the civil service and the armed forces. The Select Committee reiterated their views several times but in HC 593 (1979–80), paras. 8, 15, they recognised that it was justifiable to exclude matters of discipline, pay, promotion, and terms of service.

The judiciary

Judges may be regarded as servants of the Crown in the sense that they are 'Her Majesty's judges', holding offices granted by the Crown and bound by oath well and truly to serve the sovereign in those offices.[22] On the other hand it is axiomatic that judges are independent: the Crown has no legal right to give them instructions,[23] and one of the strongest constitutional conventions makes it improper for any sort of influence to be brought to bear upon them by the executive.[24] They do not therefore satisfy the test of the relationship of master and servant at common law, which is that the master must have power to control the servant. Consequently, as explained later on, the Crown bears no liability for acts of the judiciary, and the judiciary themselves have an extensive immunity.[25]

In a constitutional sense it is nevertheless evident that the judges in administering justice supply one of the most important services of the Crown. As has been pointed out in a Privy Council judgment, 'servant' may have a different meaning in public law from that which it has in private law: the test of 'control' is inappropriate; and 'servants of the Crown' most aptly means 'persons by whom the functions of government of a state are carried out'.[26] In the context of public law, as when a Commonwealth constitution is being interpreted, judges and others performing judicial functions may well fall within the meaning of 'servants of the Crown' or of similar expressions. Accordingly they were treated as 'persons in His Majesty's service' under the National Economy Act 1931.[27]

It is a cardinal principle that the superior judges, unlike others in the service of the Crown, should enjoy security of tenure. In the case of the judges of the High Court and the Court of Appeal their tenure is protected by the Supreme Court Act 1981,[28] replacing the Act of Settlement 1700, under which they hold office 'during good behaviour subject to a power of removal by Her Majesty on an address presented to Her by both Houses of Parliament'. The salaried judges in the House of Lords (Lords of Appeal in Ordinary) are protected in similar terms by the Appellate Jurisdiction Act

[22] Promissory Oaths Act 1868, s. 4; Supreme Court Act 1981, s. 10(4).
[23] Above, p. 25.
[24] For a remarkable ministerial attempt to influence the High Court to release the imprisoned Poplar councillors (below, p. 425) see [1962] PL 62 (B. Keith-Lucas).
[25] Below, p. 783.
[26] Ranaweera v. Ramachandran [1970] AC 962 at 972 (Lord Diplock, dissenting); R. v. Barrett [1976] 1 WLR 946 (registrar of births 'serving under the Crown').
[27] See below, p. 817.
[28] s. 11(3). Although the Crown Court is part of the Supreme Court (s. 1), Circuit judges and Recorders, who are judges of the Crown Court, are not judges of the Supreme Court (s. 151(4)).

1876.[29] Only once has a judge been removed on an address from both Houses.[30] The judges of the High Court, Court of Appeal and the House of Lords are subject to a retiring age of seventy-five if appointed after 1959.[31]

The lower ranks of the judiciary, on the other hand, have scarcely more legal protection against dismissal than have other holders of office under the Crown. Circuit judges, county court judges, recorders, and magistrates are by statute subject to removal by the Lord Chancellor for incapacity or misbehaviour.[32] Nor is there any legal principle to safeguard the tenure of judges in the absence of statute. This was decided in the case of a judge of the Supreme Court of Malaya who had been appointed in 1930 on the understanding that the retiring age should be sixty-two. When Malaya was overrun by the Japanese in 1942 he was retired on a pension, some time before he had reached sixty-two, on the footing that his office had been abolished. He claimed that he was protected by the Act of Settlement or alternatively by a contract that the Crown should employ him until the retiring age. Both claims were rejected, the first on the construction of the Act, and the second because the Crown could not (just as in the case of civil servants) be fettered by contract.[33]

The tenure of the judiciary of all ranks, however, is as firmly protected in practice as it could be by positive law. Any undue interference with it would raise a political storm. Fearless judicial impartiality is the indispensable basis of the rule of law, and has been respected as a constitutional principle since the revolution of 1688 put an end to the abuses of the Stuart kings.

Loss of services

Occasionally the Crown has brought actions to recover damages for the loss of services of an employee. At common law a master had an action against one who injured his servant and so deprived him of his services. Where a public servant is injured by a private person's negligence, so that

---

[29] s. 6.

[30] Sir Jonah Barrington, an Irish judge (removed in 1830).

[31] Judicial Pensions Act 1959, s. 2.

[32] Courts Act 1971, ss. 17, 21; County Courts Act 1959, s. 8(2); justices of the peace are removable from the commission of the peace on the order of the Lord Chancellor, under prerogative power except in certain statutory cases, e.g. under Justices of the Peace Act 1949, s. 1. Circuit judges, county court judges, and recorders retire at seventy-two, magistrates at seventy (being then transferred to the supplemental list). Members of certain statutory tribunals may not be removed by ministers without the consent of the Lord Chancellor, the President of the Court of Session, or the Lord Chief Justice of Northern Ireland, as the case may be: Tribunals and Inquiries Act 1971, s. 8.

[33] *Terrell* v. *Secretary of State for the Colonies* [1953] 2 QB 482.

the public loses the benefit of his services, the government may feel that damages should be recovered for the public purse. But, although a claim of this kind was once allowed against a motorist who injured members of the Royal Air Force,[34] the door has now been closed by a decision of the Court of Appeal in a similar case where an Inland Revenue official was injured in a road accident.[35] The action for loss of services (known as the action *per quod servitium amisit*) is now held to be confined to cases of 'menial' servants, meaning servants working *intra moenia* in a domestic establishment. It is therefore out of place where the injured servant is the holder of a public post, deriving as it does from times when a master was thought to have almost proprietary rights to his servants.[36] Rejecting the Crown's claim, Denning LJ said:

But, in my opinion, the action does not lie whenever the relationship of the master and servant exists. It only lies when the servant can properly be regarded as a member of the master's household, that is, as part of the family.

He then repudiated the notion that a servant should in law be looked upon as a chattel—'and not less so when he is a civil servant'.

COMPLAINTS AGAINST ADMINISTRATION

Non-legal remedies

Much of this book is devoted to explaining the legal remedies which may be invoked against governmental action which is irregular or improper. But there are other, non-legal remedies which are also important, even though strictly speaking they lie beyond the boundaries of the law; and without some knowledge of them the picture cannot be seen in true perspective. Major developments have taken place in the non-legal area since 1967, supplementing the aggrieved citizen's classical constitutional remedy of complaining to his Member of Parliament and getting him to put a parliamentary question to the minister responsible. The inadequacy of that remedy has been pointed out already.[37] An account of the system is

---

[34] *A.-G.* v. *Valle-Jones* [1953] 2 KB 209, disapproved in the case next cited.

[35] *Inland Revenue Commissioners* v. *Hambrook* [1956] 2 QB 641. See also *Taylor* v. *Neri* (1795) 1 Esp. 385; *A.-G. for New South Wales* v. *Perpetual Trustee Co. Ltd.* [1955] AC 457; *Commonwealth of Australia* v. *Quince* (1944) 68 CLR 227.

[36] The action was based on 'the property that every man has in the service of his domestics': Bl. Comm. 1, 429.

[37] Above, p. 31.

included here because it was first introduced to provide a remedy against maladministration by the central government. Since then it has been extended to local government, as to which details are given in the following chapter.

The administration of so many services and controls under the vast bureaucratic machinery of the central government inevitably causes many grievances and complaints. If something illegal is done, administrative law can supply a remedy, though the procedure of the courts is too formal and expensive to suit many complainants. But justified grievances may equally well arise from action which is legal, or at any rate not clearly illegal, when a government department has acted inconsiderately or unfairly or where it has misled the complainant or delayed his case excessively or treated him badly. Sometimes a statutory tribunal will be able to help him both cheaply and informally. But there is a large residue of grievances which fit into none of the regular legal moulds, but are none the less real. A humane system of government must provide some way of assuaging them, both for the sake of justice and because accumulating discontent is a serious clog on administrative efficiency in a democratic country.

The vital necessity is the impartial investigation of complaints. It has always been possible for the government to commission a special inquiry, as for instance in the case of Crichel Down,[38] but this is far too ponderous and expensive a process for the ordinary run of grievances. What every form of government needs is some regular and smooth-running mechanism for feeding back the reactions of its disgruntled customers, after impartial assessment, and for correcting whatever may have gone wrong. Nothing of this kind existed in our system before 1967, except in very limited spheres.[39] Yet it is a fundamental need in every system.[40] It was because it filled that need that the device of the ombudsman suddenly attained immense popularity, sweeping round the democratic world and taking root in Britain and in many other countries,[41] as well as inspiring a

---

[38] See below, p. 912.

[39] Complaints were investigated impartially, for example, by district auditors as regards certain local government expenditure and by the Council on Tribunals as regards tribunals and inquiries.

[40] The need for an ombudsman is not obviated by a system of separate administrative courts of the French type. France instituted an ombudsman with very wide jurisdiction under law 73–6 of 3 January 1973, calling him the Médiateur. See (1974) 90 LQR 211 (L. N. Brown and P. Lavirotte). Spain instituted an ombudsman (Defensor del Pueblo) in 1981.

[41] e.g. Australia (the federal government and all States), Canada (all the Provinces but not the federal government except for the Commissioner of Official Languages), New Zealand, India (several States), France, Italy (Regions of Liguria and Tuscany), United States (numerous States, cities and counties).

vast literature.[42] Over a hundred ombudsmen are now in office in various countries and localities.

The ombudsman: tribune of the people

Ombudsman is a Scandinavian word meaning officer or commissioner. In its special sense it means a commissioner who has the duty of investigating and reporting to Parliament on citizens' complaints against the government. An ombudsman requires no legal powers except powers of inquiry. In particular, he is in no sense a court of appeal and he cannot alter or reverse any government decision. His effectiveness derives entirely from his power to focus public and parliamentary attention upon citizens' grievances. But publicity based on impartial inquiry is a powerful lever. Where a complaint is found to be justified, an ombudsman can often persuade a government department to modify a decision or pay compensation in cases where the complainant unaided would get no satisfaction. For the department knows that a public report will be made and that it will be unable to conceal the facts from Parliament and the press. The consciousness of the ombudsman's vigilance has a healthy effect on the whole administration, making it more sensitive to public opinion and to the demands of fairness.

The essence of the ombudsman's technique is to receive the complaint informally, to enter the government department, to speak to the officials and read the files, and to find out exactly who did what and why. No formal procedure is involved at any stage, nor is any legal sanction in question. The system can be adopted with short and simple legislation, or even merely administratively, and countries with written constitutions have no need to amend them. This ready adaptability is another of the reasons for the ombudsman's world-wide appeal.

As his name implies, the ombudsman first appeared in Scandinavia. Sweden has had the institution, in a somewhat special form, for over a century and a half. But it was as established in Denmark after 1954 that it suddenly captured the attention of other countries, largely as a result of the missionary spirit of the first Danish ombudsman.[43] The first British country

---

[42] A few references are: for Britain: Gregory and Hutchesson, *The Parliamentary Ombudsman*; Stacey, *The British Ombudsman*; Wheare, *Maladministration and its Remedies*, ch. 5; for other countries: Gellhorn, *Ombudsmen and Others*; Gellhorn, *When Americans Complain*; Rowat, *The Ombudsman Plan*; Rowat (ed.), *The Ombudsman, Citizen's Defender*; *Il Difensore Civico* (Turin, 1974); D. W. Williams, *Maladministration, Remedies for Injustice*; [1958] PL 236 (Stephan Hurwitz); [1959] PL 115 (I. M. Pedersen); [1968] JSPTL 101 (Sir Edmund Compton, the first Parliamentary Commissioner); [1980] CLJ 304 (A. W. Bradley).

[43] Professor Stephan Hurwitz, whose visits to Britain aroused great interest and to whom a number of complaints were sent by hopeful Britons.

to adopt it was New Zealand, which established an ombudsman (under that name) in 1962.[44] His reports soon showed the success of the experiment, and a similar institution was proposed for Britain.[45] Despite doubts whether so personal an institution would be practicable in a large country, and despite doctrinal objections based on ministerial responsibility, an ombudsman for the United Kingdom was instituted by the Parliamentary Commissioner Act 1967.

Ministerial responsibility undermined?

The main opposition to a British ombudsman was founded, it need hardly be said, on the sacred principle of ministerial responsibility.[46] It was argued that it was fundamental to the constitution that, since the minister was responsible to Parliament for all that was done in his department and officials did not bear public responsibility, it would be wrong for an ombudsman to go behind the minister's back and pry into the workings of his department. But the truth was that some of the supposed corollaries of ministerial responsibility had become an abuse, sheltering mistakes and injustices and making it impossible for complainants and their members of Parliament to find out what had really happened. The minister would make a defensive answer in Parliament, where he would be most reluctant to admit any mistake, and nothing more could be done. This aspect of ministerial responsibility, therefore, was one that the constitution could do better without.[47] As one member of Parliament complained, 'ministerial responsibility is a cloak for a lot of murkiness, muddle and slipshoddery within the departments'.[48] Nor was the principle as inviolable as the critics supposed. The Comptroller and Auditor-General had acted as a kind of financial ombudsman since 1866, reporting to the House of Commons on wasteful government expenditure with the aid of several hundred inspectors working permanently in the departments and 'engaged in an internal and continuous, and to a large extent preventive, check on

[44] Parliamentary Commissioner (Ombudsman) Act 1962 (NZ).

[45] *The Citizen and the Administration* (a report by JUSTICE, 1961—the Whyatt Report). The recommendation was rejected by the Conservative government on grounds of incompatability with ministerial responsibility and undue interference with public administration: 666 HC Deb 1125 (8 November 1962). The report was substantially accepted by the Labour government and formed the basis of the Parliamentary Commissioner Act 1967. For the principal differences see 734 HC Deb col. 47 (second reading debate, 18 October 1966).

[46] See preceding note.

[47] For an illuminating discussion of the misconceptions surrounding ministerial responsibility in this context see Sir K. Wheare, *Maladministration and its Remedies*, ch. 3.

[48] 806 HC Deb col. 648 (12 November 1970, Mr F. Willey), quoted by Wheare (as above), 95.

maladministration'.[49] As if to underline this point, the government appointed as the first British ombudsman a former Comptroller and Auditor-General, a man of great experience in penetrating deeply into the departments behind the ministerial screen. Experience soon showed that his investigations, so far from conflicting with ministerial responsibility, helped it to work better by enabling both Parliament and ministers to correct faults in administration which would otherwise never have been brought to light.[50] Experience has now shown that minister and ombudsman operate for the most part[51] on different levels and with general constitutional compatibility.

The Act of 1967

The Parliamentary Commissioner Act 1967 established an ombudsman for the United Kingdom under the title of Parliamentary Commissioner for Administration. The first thing to emphasise is the word Parliamentary. The Commissioner may receive complaints only through members of the House of Commons,[52] and not as in many other countries from the public directly. He must report the result of his investigation to the member through whom the complaint came.[53] On his functions generally he reports to the two Houses of Parliament, and in particular he appears before the House of Commons' Select Committee on the Parliamentary Commissioner, which frequently examines both him and officials of the department which he criticises.[54] His case reports, issued quarterly, and his annual and special reports, together with the reports of the Select Committee, are the main sources of information about his work. The annual reports contain catalogues of injustices remedied, briefly summarised. In the quarterly reports selected cases are reported in full detail, but anonymously. The government department is necessarily indicated, but the identities of the officials concerned, of the complainant, and of the member of Parliament are concealed.

The Parliamentary Commissioner is thus in effect an agency of Parliament, helping to remedy grievances and check administrative errors and abuses. But, like the Comptroller and Auditor-General, he is appointed

[49] Wheare (as above), 110.
[50] As ministers now acknowledge: see 109 HC Deb 1056 (4 February 1987).
[51] Exceptions were the Sachsenhausen and Court Line cases, mentioned below.
[52] s. 5(1)(a).
[53] s. 10. A copy must go to the government department concerned.
[54] The government contended that ministerial responsibility required that the Select Committee should examine only heads of departments and such officials as they wished to accompany them, but the Committee asserted their right to examine subordinate officers: Second Report, Session 1967–8, HC 350, para. 24.

by the government;[55] and, like a High Court judge, he holds office during good behaviour, i.e. permanently, to the retiring age.[56] The first three commissioners were appointed from the civil service, though the first came via the office of Comptroller and Auditor-General; and, unlike most of the world's ombudsmen, none of them had legal training. Moreover, their staff consisted of civil servants who were not qualified lawyers either. The British-style ombudsman therefore began life strongly tinged with the 'philosophy of the amateur', so typical of the civil service.[57] Since 1978, however, an independent lawyer has been the Parliamentary Commissioner, and a number of non-civil servants are now on his staff.

Since it is vital that a Parliamentary Commissioner should understand the working of the civil service and should earn its respect, there was much to be said for the practice of appointing distinguished civil servants when the office was first instituted. Certainly there were no signs of any occupational reluctance to criticise former colleagues, or indeed ministers. The ex-civil servant Commissioners in fact proved very successful in establishing an office which was far from welcome to the civil service itself. This policy continued for ten years, until the government accepted that the time had come to appoint someone with substantially different experience. The Commissioner's staff, however, remains as before, and for legal advice he must go to the Treasury Solicitor, who may well be advising the government department under investigation.

The earlier appointments were made by the government without consulting Parliament, despite the parliamentary character of the office. The government ultimately agreed to consult the chairman of the Select Committee of the House of Commons, but declined to consult the House as a whole.[58]

The Commissioner charges no fees to complainants. He is one of the services of the welfare state.

Matters included and excluded

The Act of 1967 gave the Parliamentary Commissioner jurisdiction only over the central government, and only over the departments listed in a schedule.[59] This list comprised all the regular departments and offices,

---

[55] Nominally by the Crown: s. 1. The Act of 1987 (below), s. 6, allows an acting Commissioner to be appointed to fill a temporary vacancy.

[56] S. 1. This contrasts with many other countries which favour short-term appointments. Provision for his removal on grounds of ill health is made by the Parliamentary and Health Service Commissioners Act 1987, s. 2.

[57] See above, p. 58.

[58] See Cmnd. 6764, March 1977.

[59] s. 4 and sched. 2, now replaced by the Act of 1987.

including the Scottish departments.[60] But it did not include a large number of non-departmental public bodies[61] which in effect belong to the central government and whose activities may equally affect the citizen. Prompted by the Select Committee, Parliament has now brought many of these bodies into the Commissioner's jurisdiction by the Parliamentary and Health Service Commissioners Act 1987, which extends the schedule of departments, etc., from less than fifty to more than a hundred. Additions include the British Library, the Equal Opportunities Commission, the Commission for Racial Equality, the Research Councils, Industrial Training Boards, the Nature Conservancy Council, and the Red Deer Commission. The Commission for Local Administration, which is the ombudsman system for local government, is an entirely separate entity under the Local Government Act 1974, and is explained along with local government.

The list of departments may be amended by Order in Council and thus it is kept up to date as changes take place.[62] But the Act of 1987 restricts additions to bodies which are government departments or which act on behalf of the Crown, or official bodies financed as to half at least by Parliament or statutory fees or charges and wholly or partly appointed by the Crown or a government department; nor may bodies be added which are involved in education or non-industrial training, professional qualifications and conduct, or the investigation of complaints. The government's purpose, as explained to Parliament, is to confine the list to bodies 'subject to some degree of ultimate ministerial accountability to Parliament, in that they are dependent for their financing and continuing existence on government policy'.[63]

An important point is that the Act of 1967, unlike the corresponding New Zealand Act, expressly includes ministers along with their departments.[64] The Parliamentary Commissioner may therefore investigate and criticise decisions taken by ministers personally. Two notable cases in which he did so were the Sachsenhausen case, in which he criticised the Foreign Secretary's decision not to allow claims made against the German compensation fund by prisoners of war who had been held in a German concentration camp;[65] and the Court Line case, in which he criticised statements made by the Secretary of State for Industry which misled people

[60] For Northern Ireland see below, p. 99.
[61] Colloquially known as quangos (quasi-autonomous non-governmental organisations).
[62] s. 4(2) as amended by Act of 1987.
[63] 109 HC Deb 1057 (4 February 1987).
[64] s. 4(4).
[65] HC 1967–8 No. 54 (Commissioner's Special Report); No. 258 (Select Committee's comments).

to suppose that the firm with which they had booked holidays, and which defaulted on them, was financially sound.[66] Both ministers made speeches in Parliament rejecting the Commissioner's conclusions. In the Sachsenhausen case, however, the Foreign Secretary felt obliged to allow the claims.[67] In the Court Line case no satisfaction was given.[68]

A number of matters are excluded by the Act of 1967 and so are not subject to the Commissioner's investigation.[69] These are set out in a schedule which may be summarised as follows.

Action affecting foreign affairs.
Action taken outside the United Kingdom (except action by consular officers[70]).
Action taken in connection with territory overseas.
Extradition and fugitive offenders.
Investigation of crime.
Protection of state security (including passport matters).
Legal proceedings before any court of law in the United Kingdom or any international court or tribunal, and all disciplinary proceedings in the armed forces.
The prerogative of mercy and the reference of questions to certain courts.
The hospital service (see below).
Contractual and commercial transactions, other than the acquisition of land compulsorily or by agreement and the disposal of surplus land so acquired.
All personnel matters (including pay, discipline, removal) in the civil service and the armed forces, or where the government has power to take or determine or approve action.[71]
The grant by the Crown of honours, awards, privileges, or charters.

The hospital service was excluded because the other branches of the national health service were administered by local bodies, so that the service as a whole was not a service of the central government. But it has now become one under the reorganisation of 1973, and provision for Health Service Commissioners was made by the National Health Service Reorganisation Act 1973. The new arrangements are distinct from those of the Parliamentary Commissioner Act 1967, and are explained separately below.

Two controversial items in the list of exclusions are personnel administration in the civil service and contractual and commercial

[66] HC 498, 1974–5 (Commissioner's Special Report).
[67] 758 HC Deb col. 116 (5 February 1968).
[68] 897 HC Deb col. 575 (6 August 1975).
[69] s. 5(3) and 3rd sched. The notes to the 2nd sched. also make various exclusions.
[70] Parliamentary Commissioner (Consular Complaints) Act 1981, replacing SI 1979 No. 915.
[71] e.g. where the Home Secretary refuses approval of appointment of a chief constable.

transactions. The Select Committee has made repeated attempts to bring these into the Parliamentary Commissioner's jurisdiction, since he receives a flow of complaints about them, but so far without success.[72] The list of exclusions may also be criticised in other respects, e.g. as regards passports.[73]

Statistics and inferences

Britain was the first large country to adopt an ombudsman, and there were reasonable grounds for giving him a limited sphere of operation at the outset.[74] The volume and the productivity of his work can be seen from the table, which is derived from his annual reports.

The number of complaints within the Commissioner's jurisdiction has actually proved to be moderate. But it is extraordinary that Members of Parliament send him so many complaints (well over half the total) which under their own legislation he has no power to deal with. The theory behind the requirement that complaints must be submitted through MPs was that the MP would act as a filter and eliminate futile cases. In fact it seems that they prefer to let complaints be rejected by the Commissioner rather than to reject them themselves.

Another notable statistic is the rising percentage of cases where some degree of maladministration is found. To some extent this is attributable to the large number of complaints made good against the Department of Health and Social Security and the Inland Revenue, and to cases such as those of Court Line and television licences which bring in numerous complaints on the same subject. Nevertheless it seems fair to infer that the Commissioner's power of penetration has been growing. At the same time it should be emphasised that his investigations which discover no maladministration are by no means wasted. In explaining that the department's action was justified he is enabling the aggrieved citizen to understand what the department may have failed to make intelligible to him, or what he may have refused to recognise himself, and this alone helps to eliminate friction in the work of government.[75] More often than not the Commissioner justifies the civil service to the citizen, and on a

[72] See above, p. 74. The inclusion of commercial and contractual matters was recommended by the Royal Commission on Standards of Conduct in Public Life, Cmnd. 6524 (1976) and by the Commissioner himself: Annual Report for 1983, para. 9.

[73] See *Our Fettered Ombudsman* (JUSTICE, 1977), ch. IV; Commissioner's Annual Report for 1978, para. 13.

[74] For a general critique after the first ten years see *Our Fettered Ombudsman* (above).

[75] See the Health Service Commissioner's report, HC 161 (1974), paras. 35, 36; Parliamentary Commissioner's Annual Report for 1978, para. 49.

The Parliamentary Commissioner: Statistics for selected years

	1967 (7 months)	1968	1969	1970	1972	1974	1976	1978	1980	1982	1984	1986
1. Complaints received from MPs	1,069	1,120	761	645	573	704	815	1,259	1,031	838	837	719
2. Outside jurisdiction	561	727	445	362	318	374	505	927	686	574	658	549
3. Partially investigated and discontinued	100	80	43	30	17	27	29	35	16	8	9	2
4. Investigation completed[a]	188	374	302	259	261	252	320	343	225	202	183	168
5. Maladministration found[b]	19	38	48	59	79	94	139	57	142	145	170	166
6. 5 as a percentage of 4	10	10	16	23	30	37	43	55	63	72	93	99
7. Top departmental score in 5[c]	4	13	26	32	37	32	57	65	59	60	77	81

[a] Includes cases carried over from previous year.

[b] Includes cases where the complaint was not upheld but some element of maladministration was found.

[c] The top scoring departments are always Health and Social Security and the Inland Revenue.

broad view the civil service undoubtedly emerges with credit from its ordeal by inquisition.

Maladministration: discretionary decisions and rules

The key provision of the Act of 1967[76] is that the Commissioner may investigate action taken 'in the exercise of administrative functions' by or on behalf of any of the scheduled central government departments where

(a) a written complaint is duly made to a member of the House of Commons by a member of the public[77] who claims to have sustained injustice in consequence of maladministration in connection with the action so taken; and

(b) the complaint is referred to the Commissioner, with the consent of the person who made it, by a member of that House with a request to conduct an investigation thereon.

Maladministration is a new term in the law, though not in the language.[78] The Act does not explain or define it, as is perhaps natural since it requires only that the complainant should *claim* that maladministration has occurred. Parliament was told that the word would cover 'bias, neglect, inattention, delay, incompetence, ineptitude, arbitrariness and so on', and that 'it would be a long and interesting list'.[79] In fact no legal definition seems to be required. Once duly seized of a complaint, the Commissioner may investigate and report. He can be relied upon to criticise any lapse from the high standards expected of the public service.

But in one sole respect his freedom to criticise is restricted. The Act 'declares' that he is not authorised to 'question the merits of a decision taken without maladministration by a government department or other authority in the exercise of a discretion vested in that department or authority'.[80] For the purposes of this provision he may need to know what maladministration legally means. Yet, since the Act clearly implies that the Commissioner's task is to concern himself with maladministration, it would seem that he should in any case not be concerned with decisions taken without maladministration; so that the provision just quoted appears to be a tautology. It is in terms declaratory, and is perhaps a saving inserted

---

[76] s. 5(1).

[77] Not a very apt term, since it includes a corporation: s. 6(1).

[78] It has been in use at least since 1644: OED.

[79] 734 HC Deb col. 51 (18 October 1966). In ombudsman circles this became known as the 'Crossman catalogue'. But clearly it is open-ended, as stated by Lord Denning MR in R. v. *Local Commissioner for Administration ex p. Bradford MCC* [1979] QB 287.

[80] s. 12(3), 'drafted by the formidable pen of the Lord Chancellor himself' (Sir E. Compton, [1968] JSPTL at 110).

out of caution, so that the Commissioner is warned against interference where there is nothing substantially wrong.[81]

At first the Commissioner said that this saving clause prevented him from questioning the quality of discretionary decisions, even where they contained elements of bias or perversity. He distinguished between the procedure leading up to the decision (e.g. the collection of the evidence and the presentation of the case to the minister) and the quality of the decision itself, holding that he could not question the latter 'even if, in an extreme case, it has resulted in manifest hardship to the complainant'.[82] Under criticism from the Select Committee[83] the Commissioner undertook to change his interpretation of the Act; and it soon became clear from his case histories that he was prepared to criticise discretionary decisions which were simply bad on their merits. For example, where the Customs and Excise refused a discretionary refund of gaming licence duty 'on grounds which do not stand up to examination', he obtained a refund of £22,500 for the complainant company.[84] And he persuaded the Ministry of Housing and Local Government to reverse a discretionary decision not to award costs to a company which had successfully appealed against an enforcement notice.[85] Bad decisions are bad administration and bad administration is maladministration. In New Zealand the Ombudsman is expressly empowered to report on any decision which was unreasonable, unjust, based on mistake, or merely 'wrong'.[86]

Along with the 'bad decision' goes the 'bad rule'. The Commissioner was at first unwilling to criticise departmental rules and regulations,[87] so that what was maladministration if done once apparently ceased to be so if done repeatedly under a rule. Here again the Select Committee induced him to change his mind.[88] After some initial confusion with the fallacy that statutory regulations, because they are legislative, do not involve administrative action,[89] the Select Committee concluded that statutory

[81] See HC 350, 1967–8, para. 14 (Select Committee's interpretation). The interpretation of Lord Denning MR in the *Bradford* case (above) is more restrictive, distinguishing between 'manner' and 'merits'. Eveleigh LJ holds that 'inefficient or improper administration' or 'a faulty decision' may be maladministration.

[82] HC 6, 1967–8, para. 35.

[83] HC 350, 1967–8, para. 14.

[84] Annual Report for 1970 (HC 261), p. 36.

[85] Same, p. 96. See HC 513, 1970–1, p. 32, for discussion of these cases at the Select Committee.

[86] Parliamentary Commissioner (Ombudsman) Act 1962 (NZ), s. 19. See (1971) 4 NZULR 361 (K. J. Keith).

[87] HC 6, 1967–8, para. 36.

[88] HC 350, 1967–8, para. 16; HC 9, 1968–9; HC 129, 1968–9, para. 17. For an example of criticism of a bad rule see Annual Report for 1979, para. 55.

[89] The Attorney-General so contended in the case of statutory instruments but not in the case of other statutory orders: see HC 385, 1968–9, para. 10.

instruments and other statutory orders should fall within the Commissioner's field, at least as regards their effect and the action taken to review them.[90]

As the Commissioner has gained experience, he appears to have quietly disregarded these conceptual controversies. It seems that he now treats maladministration as meaning simply bad administration, i.e. any action or inaction by government departments which he feels ought to be criticised, including anything which is unreasonable, unjust or oppressive.[91] This is as it should be.

Cases where there are legal remedies

An ombudsman is not a substitute for the ordinary courts and tribunals. Consequently the Act of 1967 provides that the Commissioner shall not investigate cases where the person aggrieved has or had a remedy in any court of law, or a right of appeal, reference, or review in any statutory or prerogative tribunal.[92] But there is a significant proviso: the Commissioner may nevertheless investigate the complaint if he is satisfied that in the particular circumstances it is not reasonable to expect the remedy or right to be, or to have been, invoked. This proviso means that the line of demarcation between the Commissioner and the legal system is not a rigid one, and that much technicality and inconvenience can be eliminated by the Commissioner using his discretion. It may frequently happen that there is a possibility of a legal remedy but that the law is doubtful; in such cases the Commissioner may decide that it is not reasonable to insist on recourse to the law.[93] Where there is clearly a case for a court or tribunal, on the other hand, he will refuse to act.[94]

It is not easy to tell from the Commissioner's reports how often he has made use of the proviso.[95] But it seems probable that, with or without doing so, he has investigated many cases where there would have been legal remedies.[96] This cannot be stated with certainty except in rare cases where there is a subsequent and successful recourse to the law. But it was hardly conceivable that the Commissioner would apply the proviso accurately in the period 1967–78, when neither he nor his staff were qualified lawyers.

[90] HC 385, 1968–9, para. 11, suggesting however a wider jurisdiction in the case of statutory orders other than statutory instruments.
[91] See Annual Report for 1977, para. 18.
[92] s. 5(2).
[93] e.g. Annual Report for 1968, p. 19 (complaint against Customs and Excise investigated where legal remedy possible but doubtful).
[94] e.g. Annual Report for 1968, p. 148 (complaint of minister's dismissal of appeal against enforcement notice: right of appeal to High Court).
[95] Examples are given in (1971) 34 MLR 377 (D. Foulkes).
[96] See e.g. below, p. 982 n. 22; also HC 573 (1970–1), para. 13 (Select Committee).

From his most recent report it appears that he is willing to accept complaints in cases where the availability of a legal remedy is doubtful, as it must often be; and that he is inclined to apply the proviso generously.[97]

An example of a case where the Commissioner found maladminist-ration, but the law later provided a remedy, is that of the revocation of television licences in 1975.[98] The Home Office had threatened to revoke the licences of members of the public who had taken them out before their current licences expired, in order to renew them, as they were legally entitled to do, before a large increase of fee came into force. Many complaints were made to the Commissioner and, after full investigation, he found the Home Office seriously to blame for not giving the public proper warning, for inefficiency and lack of foresight, and for insufficient frankness with the public. But he was unable to criticise them for acting as their lawyers had advised was legal, and he therefore felt obliged to refrain from asking them to reconsider their threat to revoke some 36,000 licences. But shortly afterwards the Court of Appeal held that the Home Secretary's threat to use his power of revocation for this purpose was wholly unlawful, being an abuse of a power given to him for other purposes.[99] It then became clear that the complainants had a legal remedy from the start. The Commissioner, had he known this, might not have thought fit to invoke the proviso, since the situation was eminently one for a test case in a court of law.

Another case where the availability of a legal remedy was at least arguable was where the Department of Trade and Industry renewed a share-dealing company's licence in spite of evidence that the company was unsound. This might or might not have been actionable negligence, but the Commissioner obtained compensation in full for an investor who had lost £10,000.[1]

A certain overlap between the Commissioner and the legal system must be accepted as inevitable, and this, though untidy, is doubtless in the public interest.[2] The Commissioner provides a service which is free from both the expense and the uncertainty of the law. Although, unlike courts and tribunals, he has no decisive power, he has facilities for investigation and access to evidence which are not available to litigants. His probing into the television licence case revealed serious maladministration which it was salutary to bring to light. An ombudsman is a valuable adjunct to any system of administrative law, however comprehensive and efficient. In

[97] Annual Report for 1980, p. 1.
[98] HC 680, 1974–5 (special report, 19 pp.).
[99] *Congreve* v. *Home Office* [1976] QB 629; see below, p. 406. The Home Office refunded the fees paid under threat of revocation.
[1] Annual Report for 1986, p. 17.
[2] See [1980] CLJ 304 at 320 (A. W. Bradley) for comment on this question.

Britain he can also make good some of the system's failings, as the next section will illustrate.

Misleading statements and advice

A common form of maladministration is the giving of wrong information or advice by officials dealing with the public. The Commissioner has investigated many cases where the complainant had thus been misled and suffered loss, and in many of them he has persuaded the department to make compensation in money. This is a particularly interesting branch of his activities, since one of the defects of English administrative law, as will appear later,[3] is that it has failed to develop remedies for that situation. Although there may now be a right of action for negligent misstatement, the Commissioner's policy seems once again to be to disregard any possible legal remedy.

The following are some examples of such cases. Where customs officials had apparently advised that a car could be temporarily imported into the United Kingdom without payment of purchase tax, but on arrival the owner was made to pay £167 purchase tax which was in reality legally due, the Commissioner persuaded the department, which had refused any concession, to refund the full amount.[4] Where an official at an employment exchange wrongly told a director of a coal mine that he would not qualify for a redundancy payment, so that he did not claim one within the time allowed, the Commissioner's investigation procured a compensatory payment of £1,700 from the department.[5] Where a complainant was encouraged by the Board of Trade to suppose that his company would be eligible for investment grant if it installed a grain-processing plant, but the plant was ruled ineligible after the expenditure had been incurred, the Board agreed to pay compensation of £950.[6] Where the Customs and Excise department wrongly advised a company that its product would not be liable to purchase tax, and exaction of the tax drove the company into liquidation, the department agreed to pay £6,000 in compensation;[7] and in a similar case about excise duty on a mixture of beer and cider compensation of £30,000 was paid.[8] All these compensation payments

---

[3] Below, p. 386.
[4] Annual Report for 1969 (HC 138), p. 17.
[5] Same, p. 28.
[6] Same, p. 137.
[7] Annual Report for 1973 (HC 106), p. 7. For other examples, see Annual Report for 1979, para. 55 (misleading advice from 'jobcentre': £990 recovered); Select Cases 1981, ii. 32 (misleading advice about pension: £500 compensation paid); Annual Report for 1986, p. 7 (tax cases).
[8] Annual Report for 1986, p. 11.

were technically made ex gratia, on the assumption that there was no legal liability but that injustice and loss were suffered because of misleading official advice. It is probably a safe guess that without the Commissioner's intervention none of them would have been made.

As distinct from positive advice, a mere failure to warn may have a similar effect. Objections to many proposed orders affecting land, such as compulsory purchase orders, must be heard by a representative of the minister either at a public local inquiry or at a less formal hearing.[9] In one case a successful objector at a hearing asked for an award of costs, but the ministry had failed to warn him that costs could be awarded only after a formal inquiry. The Commissioner found maladministration and the department agreed to pay the complainant's costs on the inquiry basis.[10] In another case where the department had not given adequate publicity to the statutory time limit for claims under the Land Compensation Act 1973 the government introduced legislation to allow late claims in such circumstances.[11]

Complaints, investigations, reports

A complaint to the Commissioner may be made by any 'member of the public'[12]—an expression wide enough to include prisoners and immigrants, two classes who have both had success with various complaints.[13] Every complaint must be made through a member of the House of Commons, as emphasised already; but the member need not be the complainant's own member, and a peer must likewise complain through an MP.

It has often been suggested that complainants should have direct access to the Commissioner, particularly since this is allowed in the case of the Health Service and Local Commissioners, and the expectation that MPs would weed out ineligible complaints has not been fulfilled. Instead of rejecting every complaint made to him directly, however, the Commissioner now offers to forward suitable cases to the appropriate MP, so that the MP may then refer back to him. The Select Committee has decided that this roundabout procedure is an adequate substitute for direct access, but the Commissioner himself would prefer a uniform right of direct access to all Commissioners alike.[14]

[9] See below, p. 955.
[10] Annual Report for 1974 (HC 126), p. 7.
[11] Local Government, Planning and Land Act 1980, s. 113.
[12] Parliamentary Commissioner Act 1967, s. 5(1).
[13] See e.g. Annual Reports for 1979 (HC 402), para. 35; for 1983 (HC 322), para. 51; for 1984, paras. 33, 34; for 1986 (HC 248), paras. 50, 51.
[14] Annual Report for 1978, para. 10; for 1983, para. 7.

The complainant may be an individual or a body corporate, provided it is not a local authority, public service body, nationalised industry, or a body which is appointed or financed by the government.[15] The complaint must be made by the person actually aggrieved, except that a suitable representative may make it after his death.[16] He need not be a British subject or a parliamentary elector, provided that he was resident in the United Kingdom or else present there when the impugned action was taken.[17] By a recent concession a British subject resident abroad may complain about consular matters, provided that he has the right of abode in the United Kingdom.[18] Prisoners serving sentences are entitled to complain and the Commissioner is concerned to assist them in proper cases.[19]

The complaint must be made to the MP not later than twelve months from the day on which the person aggrieved first had notice of the matters alleged. But the Commissioner may dispense with this time limit if he considers it proper on account of special circumstances.[20]

The Commissioner has complete discretion in deciding whether to hold or pursue an investigation.[21] There is therefore no legal means of compelling him to act if he declines to do so.[22] It is also for him to determine whether a complaint is duly made.[23] But these powers do not allow him to extend his jurisdiction, e.g. by receiving complaints direct from members of the public, or by investigating authorities not permitted by the Act, or by acting on his own initiative.[24]

An investigation must be private, and the head of the department and any other official complained of must be given an opportunity to comment. In other respects the Commissioner may determine his own procedure.[25] He will normally examine both the department's files and the officials personally.[26] He may make contact with the complainant direct, sometimes by sending one of his staff to interview him in his home. He may call for information and documents from any one, including ministers and

---

[15] s. 6(1).

[16] s. 6(2).

[17] s. 6(4).

[18] Parliamentary Commissioner (Consular Complaints) Act 1981.

[19] Annual Report for 1978, para. 31; for 1979, para. 30. See *Our Fettered Ombudsman* (JUSTICE, 1977), ch. VI.

[20] s. 6(3).

[21] s. 5(5).

[22] *Re Fletcher's Application* [1970] 2 All ER 527 (leave to apply for mandamus refused).

[23] s. 5(5).

[24] He has regretted this last restriction, which does not apply elsewhere in the world: Annual Report for 1983, para. 8.

[25] s. 7.

[26] In both the 'Duccio' and Court Line cases he interviewed the minister personally: HC 316, 1968–9, para. 16; HC 498, 1974–5, para. 7.

officials, save only where they relate to the Cabinet.[27] For obtaining evidence he has all the compulsory powers of the High Court, including the power to administer oaths, and he can call upon the High Court to deal with obstruction or contempt.[28] No minister can veto his investigations. No plea of secrecy or Crown privilege can be put in his way,[29] for he is himself subject to the Official Secrets Acts.[30] But he can be prevented from disclosing secret information in his reports, if a minister certifies that this would be contrary to the public interest; and this may be certified for any class of documents and information generally as well as in particular cases.[31] Information obtained in the Commissioner's investigations may not be disclosed except in his reports and certain legal and consultative proceedings.[32]

Reports on investigations must be made by the Commissioner both to the member of Parliament through whom the complaint came and also to the head of the government department and any of his officials who were complained against.[33] The Commissioner must also make a general report annually, to be laid before each House of Parliament; and he may make other reports from time to time, and in particular special reports where there has been a failure to remedy injustice caused by maladministration.[34] His present practice is to make quarterly reports containing selected case histories, often in full detail but always without naming complainants or officials, and to make annual reports with general comments and statistics. He has made a number of independent reports on important cases.[35] His reports are in general no less detailed and elaborate than the judgments of courts of law, and in some cases more so.

Remedies and effectiveness

The Commissioner's reports show that he has been able to remedy a great many cases of injustice where, almost certainly, no remedy would

[27] s. 8(4). A certificate issued by The Secretary of State of the Cabinet with the approval of the Prime Minister is conclusive. Such a certificate was issued in the Court Line case: HC 498, 1974–5, para. 9.

[28] ss. 8, 9.

[29] s. 8(3).

[30] s. 11.

[31] s. 11(3).

[32] s. 11(2) as amended by Act of 1987, s. 4, allowing disclosure to Health Service Commissioners and vice versa.

[33] s. 10.

[34] s. 10(3). For the occasion of the first such special report see Annual Report for 1978, para. 56.

[35] e.g. Sachsenhausen (above, p. 83; Duccio (above); War Pensions (HC 587, 1970–1); Court Line (above, p. 83); Television Licences (above, p. 90).

otherwise have been obtained. In general he has found that government departments are willing to pay compensation or otherwise make reasonable amends when he has exposed maladministration, though in some cases he has had to press hard for it. In 1972 the Select Committee observed with satisfaction that 'Government departments are very ready to accept the views of the Commissioner and to afford a remedy for injustice.'[36] A share of the credit is due to the Select Committee itself, which has kept up a steady pressure on the departments, using the Commissioner's findings as a lever. Another influential factor is the department's knowledge that every case of maladministration will be reported to an MP. The results obtained seem to justify the verdict that the Commissioner 'has been remarkably effective'.[37] A notable improvement in administrative justice has thus been achieved.

In addition, a number of general reforms have resulted from the exposure of bad practices, as the Commissioner now reports annually.[38] As the result of a special report criticising the Department of Health and Social Security for not duly back-dating an officer's disability pension, some £12,000 was paid out in over forty other cases and over thirty were reviewed.[39] When the same department refused to back-date another allowance due to disabled war pensioners, the Commissioner's reports not only secured awards of £2,500 for one complainant and £4,000 for another, but also caused the review of 16,000 other cases.[40] A class of war pensioners was compensated after investigation of an exceptionally bad case where the Commissioner found that disabled officers had been deliberately and deceitfully refused part of their entitlement.[41] After this the Civil Service Department undertook a wide review of practices which might infringe the rights of individuals.[42] Where the Department of Transport's car-licensing reminder forms misled licensees into overpayment of licence duty and three complaints were upheld, the Department arranged for small refunds in over 100,000 similar cases at a cost of over £1m.[43]

The Commissioner has not always had success, and from time to time he has reported that a department has refused to make amends.[44] Most of the

---

[36] HC 334 (1971–2), para. 33.

[37] Wheare, *Maladministration and its Remedies*, 125.

[38] A first list was given in his annual report for 1972 (HC 72), para. 19.

[39] HC 587 (1970–1) (special report); HC 334 (1971–2), para. 28 (Select Committee).

[40] Annual Report for 1974 (HC 126), para. 20; for 1975 (HC 141), para. 28; HC 454 (1974–5), para. 28 (Select Committee).

[41] HC 312 (1977–8).

[42] Annual Report for 1979, para. 14.

[43] HC 247 (1978–9).

[44] See e.g. Annual Report for 1974 (HC 126), paras. 25, 35; for 1978 (HC 205), para. 56.

cases concern the Inland Revenue and the Customs and Excise, since in the sphere of taxation the administrative mind is stubborn. Successive Commissioners have expressed their concern at the number of serious injustices.[45] Two matters which have frequently been commented on by the Select Committee are the hardship caused by demands for arrears of tax which have accumulated owing to the department's own errors; and the failure to pay interest on overdue refunds of tax wrongly demanded. After being told that there were insurmountable difficulties, the Select Committee ultimately succeeded in obtaining a concession on the first matter[46] and a degree of statutory reform on the second.[47]

Although the head of the Inland Revenue testified that the Commissioner's investigations were 'gradually sapping morale and having a very bad effect indeed', the Select Committee found that they were not causing as much dislocation as had been feared.[48] In the long run the Commissioner should prove to be an ally of the civil service, since so many of his reports justify the department rather than the complainant.

Relations with the Council on Tribunals

The Commissioner is an ex officio member of the Council on Tribunals,[49] a body whose duties are explained elsewhere.[50] When he took office it was stated officially that he would not pursue issues covered by the Council on Tribunals, which include administrative procedures involving statutory inquiries, such as planning appeals and compulsory purchase procedures.[51] In these matters the Council itself had been handling complaints since its foundation in 1958. But the Commissioner has not adhered to this plan. He has investigated and reported on a great many matters which are squarely within the concerns of the Council on Tribunals, such as delays in planning appeals and the award of costs to successful objectors at inquiries.[52] These cases are so common that there is now a wide overlap between the Commissioner and the Council.

---

[45] Annual Report for 1979, para. 43.
[46] HC 334 (1971–2), para. 20.
[47] HC 454 (1974–5), para. 1: but see para. 21 as to other departments.
[48] HC 334 (1971–2), para. 13 (the quotation is from p. 37).
[49] Parliamentary Commissioner Act 1967, s. 1(5).
[50] Below, p. 915.
[51] Cmnd. 2767 (1965), para. 8 (white paper).
[52] e.g. HC 2 (1974), p. 22 (ministry's policy, based on Council on Tribunals' recommendations, wrongly applied; ex gratia payment of successful appellant's costs in planning appeal). Among many other examples are Annual Report for 1974 (HC 126), p. 7; HC 334 (1972) para. 34; HC 454 (1975), para. 41 (delays in planning appeals); HC 529 (1974–5), pp. 38, 41, 43, 49, 53, 55.

In fact the present position appears to be better than the original plan for exclusive spheres of operation. In probing the workings of government departments the Commissioner is strong and the Council is weak. The Council has none of the Commissioner's investigatory powers and it has not the facilities for handling numerous complaints; nor, most important of all, has it a committee of Parliament to back up its recommendations.[53] The Commissioner is therefore more likely to obtain satisfaction for the complainant, if his complaint is justified, and this matters more than a neat separation of functions.

The Health Service Commissioners

When the national health service was brought wholly under the central government by the National Health Service Reorganisation Act 1973, there was no longer any reason for excluding it from the system for investigating complaints. But separate provision was made in that Act[54] which, while generally on the model of the Parliamentary Commissioner Act 1967, contained some important differences. The legislation is now consolidated in the National Health Service Act 1977 and has been amended by the Parliamentary and Health Service Commissioners Act 1987.

The Act of 1973 constituted the new and separate offices of Health Service Commissioner for England and Health Service Commissioner for Wales. For Scotland there is separate but similar legislation.[55] In fact the existing Parliamentary Commissioner for Administration was appointed to all three of the new health service offices (for England, Wales and Scotland), so that there is a single administration for health service complaints along with others. In law, however, his functions are distinct, and he makes separate reports on health service complaints in his capacity as Health Service Commissioner for all three countries.

The powers of holding investigations and making reports conferred upon the Health Service Commissioner are in general the same as those of the Parliamentary Commissioner. But there are certain notable differences. In the first place, he is not 'Parliamentary' in the same sense as the Parliamentary Commissioner. His reports on investigations must be sent to the Secretary of State for Social Services (or for Wales or Scotland) or in certain cases to the regional or area health authority; and his annual and special reports must be made to the Secretary of State rather than to

[53] See below, p. 920.
[54] Pt. III. The Health Service Commissioner became effective on 1 October 1973, in advance of the reorganisation which took effect on 1 April 1974.
[55] National Health Service (Scotland) Act 1972.

Parliament. But the Secretary of State must himself lay them before both Houses,[56] and the same Select Committee of the House of Commons examines the work of the Commissioner in all his various capacities. In the second place, though to the same effect, the complainant has direct access to the Commissioner and need not make his complaint through an MP,[57] though any MP known to have assisted in the making of the complaint must be sent a copy of the report on it.[58] In the health service, therefore, the complaints system is integrated more with the administrative system and less with Parliament. Thirdly, a relative or other suitable person may complain on behalf of a person who has died or is unable to act for himself;[59] and a health service authority may itself refer to the Commissioner a complaint made to it about some matter within its own responsibility, so as to obtain an independent investigation.[60]

A number of matters are excluded from the Commissioner's powers of investigation.[61] These are the following.

Action taken by doctors, dentists, and others providing the basic services.
Diagnosis, care, or treatment, being action which in the Commissioner's opinion was taken solely in the exercise of some person's clinical judgment.
Acts of a Family Practitioner Committee in its capacity as a tribunal.
Employment, pay, discipline or other personnel matters.
Contractual or commercial transactions, except when made for providing services for patients.
Matters subject to inquiry under the Act.[62]

There is also a saving clause to exclude cases where there is a legal remedy, subject to the same power to make exceptions as under the Parliamentary Commissioner Act 1967.[63] Subject to these limitations, the Commissioner may investigate any failure in the services provided by the various health service authorities listed in the Act, or any other action taken by them or on their behalf.[64] The complaint must allege 'injustice or hardship in consequence of the failure or in consequence of maladministration connected with the other action.'[65]

The Health Service Commissioner's reports follow much the same

[56] National Health Service Act 1977, s. 119, distinguishing between different classes of reports.
[57] s. 114.
[58] Parliamentary and Health Service Commissioners Act 1987, s. 5.
[59] s. 111(2).
[60] s. 117. The Act of 1987 extends the time limit for this to 12 months.
[61] s. 116 and 13th sched.
[62] i.e. where an inquiry is held under s. 84.
[63] s. 116(1).
[64] ss. 109, 115.
[65] s. 115.

pattern as the Parliamentary Commissioner's. Generally speaking the results are similar. In the year 1986–7 he received 883 complaints, of which 386 were rejected as outside jurisdiction or otherwise unsuitable. He issued reports in 131 cases, in 60 per cent of which the complaint proved wholly or partly justified.[66] Within the 131 reports there were 483 separate grievances. The largest groups of complaints concerned nurses, medical staff and the handling of complaints by health authorities. In many such cases the complaint is of inconsiderate or rude behaviour, and an adequate remedy is an apology. The health service appears to generate a large volume of complaints about matters which are difficult to remedy, such as long waiting lists, postponement of operations, and inadequate nursing care.[67]

Every health authority is required to ensure that all its hospitals have a regular complaints procedure in accordance with directions given by the Secretary of State, but no right of appeal or review conferred by that procedure can prevent an investigation by the Health Service Commissioner.[68]

Northern Ireland

In Northern Ireland the Parliamentary Commissioner for Administration deals in the normal way with complaints about action for which the United Kingdom government is responsible.[69] For complaints against the government of Northern Ireland, while it existed, a separate Parliamentary Commissioner was established by the Parliamentary Commissioner Act (Northern Ireland) 1969. In addition, an ombudsman system covering local authorities and other public bodies was introduced by the Commissioner for Complaints Act (Northern Ireland) 1969.[70] Northern Ireland then enjoyed the services of three ombudsmen with mutually exclusive jurisdictions. When in 1974 the Northern Ireland Assembly was suspended, prior to being dissolved, the Northern Ireland Parliamentary Commissioner became the ombudsman for the central government, now administered from London, and his reports in that capacity were required to be laid before each House of Parliament of the United Kingdom, in the same way as reports of the UK Commissioner;[71] and in the same way, also, they are examined by the Select Committee of the House of Commons.

Since 1973 the two Northern Ireland offices have been held by the same

[66] Annual Report for 1986–7 (HC 31), ch. 2.

[67] See Annual Report for 1986–7, Appendix E. For two cases of loss of life see Selected Investigations, April–October 1987, pp. 1, 9.

[68] Hospital Complaints Procedure Act 1985.

[69] Parliamentary Commissioner Act 1967, s. 13.

[70] See [1972] PL 131 (K. P. Poole).

[71] Northern Ireland Act 1974, 1st sched., para. 4.

Commissioner. Complaints to him as Parliamentary Commissioner must be made through Members of Parliament, the Northern Ireland Assembly having again been dissolved in 1986. As Commissioner for Complaints he may receive complaints direct. Unlike the UK Commissioner he may deal with personnel matters in both capacities, and as Commissioner for Complaints he may deal also with commercial and contractual matters.

One unusual provision is to be noticed in the Commissioner for Complaints Act of 1969. On a finding by the Commissioner of injustice caused by maladministration, the person aggrieved may apply to the county court, which may award him such damages as it thinks just, or grant a mandatory or other injunction giving him specific relief; and where persistent maladministration seems likely, the Attorney-General may apply to the High Court for an injunction or other suitable order.[72] Little use appears to have been made of this remedy at first, but in 1974 the Commissioner reported two cases of maladministration in which the county court awarded substantial damages.[73] Since ombudsmen normally work entirely by persuasion, backed with the force of publicity and parliamentary criticism, it is interesting to note this instance of the harnessing of legal remedies to the Commissioner's investigations.

Spread of the ombudsman principle

One of the many proofs of the success of the ombudsman principle is its continual extension into new areas. Having been instituted in Britain for the central government, it has now been extended to the national health service and also, as explained later, to local government.[74] There has been legislation, as also mentioned later, introducing an independent element in connection with complaints against the police.[75] One feature of the proposals for separate Scottish and Welsh Assemblies, which proved abortive, was that there should be Assembly Commissioners to report on maladministration in the proposed Scottish and Welsh administrations.[76] Every year there are new extensions of the principle in other countries. Few indeed are the constitutional innovations for which such widespread success can be claimed.

The principle has spread outside the sphere of government into that of business and finance. Voluntary ombudsman systems have been established

---

[72] s. 7.

[73] Northern Ireland Commissioner for Complaints, Annual Report for 1973 (Assembly paper 9, 1974), para. 14.

[74] Below, p. 135.

[75] Below, p. 150.

[76] The Scotland Act 1978 and the Wales Act 1978 were repealed by SI 1979 Nos. 928 and 933 respectively.

successfully in the insurance and banking industries. Building Societies are obliged by statute to join a recognised scheme for the investigation of complaints by an adjudicator.[77] There is a similar scheme for adjudicating complaints against the Securities and Investments Board.[78] The statutory 'lay observer',[79] who examines complaints about the handling by the Law Society of complaints against solicitors, must also be counted among the ever-increasing varieties of ombudsmen.

[77] Building Societies Act 1986, ss. 83–4, making decisions binding but subject to appeal to the High Court on a question of law.

[78] This body is non-statutory but has delegated functions under the Financial Services Act 1986.

[79] Solicitors Act 1974, s. 45.

4

LOCAL GOVERNMENT

Local administration

Local authorities are organised in a hierarchy of geographical units by counties, districts, and parishes, with special arrangements for London.[1] Nearly all local authorities are directly elected by the inhabitants of their areas, but there are also certain bodies such as water authorities and the Inner London Education Authority which cut across county and district boundaries and have constitutions of their own. All local authorities work in more or less close conjunction with the central government, and they generally enjoy less autonomy than the bare legal framework would suggest. The social services and controls which in the aggregate make up the welfare state are administered partly centrally and partly locally. National insurance, income support (formerly the poor law), and the national health service are the province of the central government, whereas housing, public health and sanitation, welfare services for the handicapped, provision of accommodation for those in need, and the care of children are entrusted to local authorities. The provision of schools is another local responsibility, though subject to detailed central control. An efficient working partnership between central and local governments is therefore essential. In law, however, local authorities have their own independent existence and their own legal duties and liabilities. They are not part of the services of the Crown and they have no special privileges or immunities at common law.[2]

---

[1] The primary sources for modern local government law in England and Wales are the Local Government Acts 1972 and 1974, the Report of the Royal Commission on Local Government in England, 1969, Cmnd. 4040, and the Report of the Committee on the Management of Local Government, 1967. Sir John Maud was chairman of both the Commission and the Committee. Other important reports are those of the Layfield Committee (Local Government Finance, 1976, Cmnd. 6453) and the Widdicombe Committee (Conduct of Local Authority Business, 1986, Cmnd. 9797 with 4 volumes of research papers, Cmnd. 9798–801). General works are Hart, *Local Government and Administration*, 9th edn., 1973, by Hart and Garner; Cross, *Principles of Local Government Law*, 6th edn., 1981; Buxton, *Local Government*, 2nd edn., 1973; Loughlin, *Local Government in the Modern State*, 1986. For history see Holdsworth, *History of English Law*, x. 126; xiv. 204; Redlich and Hirst, *Local Government in England*.

[2] Below, p. 808.

A radical reorganisation was made in England and Wales by the Local Government Act 1972, and in Scotland by the Local Government (Scotland) Act 1973. An account of the law of local government (here confined to England and Wales) is therefore best divided into two eras, those before and after 1974, the year when the new system came into effect.

The reign of the justices

From the late fifteenth century onwards local government passed into the hands of the justices of the peace, who replaced the obsolete medieval system of county and hundred courts supervised by the sheriff.[3] The justices were not, however, the only administrative authorities. Commissioners of sewers had been appointed by the Crown for maritime and inland counties from early times under a succession of statutes, with power to make and maintain sea-walls and dykes, to carry out works for the control of rivers and the improvement of navigation, to organise land drainage, and for these purposes to make rules and orders with legal effect and to levy rates.[4] The powers possessed by these commissioners were a prominent feature of administrative law in the seventeenth century.[5] They were one of the earliest administrative authorities, comparable to the commissioners of customs whom the Crown appointed for the collection of import and export duties. They were comparable also to the justices of the peace in that they were technically a court,[6] thus illustrating the traditional system of putting administrative and judicial powers into the same hands, which is illustrated more notably still by the justices themselves.

The justices were given new administrative tasks by numerous Acts of Parliament of the Tudor period and later, which made use of them as general purpose local authorities. They exercised their powers in county quarter sessions, where they were responsible for the poor law, the upkeep of roads and bridges, the building of gaols, and many miscellaneous matters; and in 'brewster sessions' they sat for the licensing of alehouses.[7] Originally the justices were under close control by the Crown through the Privy Council and the Star Chamber, and their appointments were at the

[3] Holdsworth, *History of English Law*, iv. 134.

[4] Holdsworth (as above), x. 199. The principal Statute of Sewers was that of 1531 (23 Hen. 8, c. 5). The first statute to authorise commissions was that of 1427 (6 Hen. 6, c. 5), but the system was much older: see Callis, *Reading on the Statute of Sewers*, 25. The statute of 1531 (ss. 4, 12, 14) empowered the commissioners to make 'laws, ordinances and decrees' with full legal effect, though some of them required royal assent. It was repealed by the Land Drainage Act 1930.

[5] See below, p. 395; and see Bacon's Abridgment, ii. 539.

[6] Callis (as above), 164.

[7] Separate licensing sessions were required by an Act of 1729 (2 Geo. 2 c. 28); see now Licensing Act 1964, s. 2.

Crown's mercy: it was for this reason that so much power was conferred upon them. But the abuses of the Stuart kings led to the abolition of the Star Chamber in 1642 and to the Revolution of 1688, after which it was accepted that local government should be independent of political control. There then began the golden age of the justices, the uncrowned kings of every county, who wielded extensive powers, including the power to levy rates, and who could be called to account only by the cumbrous legal procedures of the prerogative writs of mandamus, certiorari and prohibition.[8] In this way there was established a 'rule of law' of almost theoretical perfection, with administration conducted locally under judicial forms and subject to no discretionary control from the centre. The repair of highways, for example, was enforced by 'presenting' the inhabitants of the county on indictment before the justices.[9] 'National policy', by which local government is so strictly confined today, was conspicuous by its absence. The justices were free to govern in a 'spirit of autocratic dilettantism'.[10] A celebrated illustration is the adoption of the 'Speenhamland system' by the justices of Berkshire in 1795—a radically new policy for the relief of the poor which spread to other counties and led to problems with which the nineteenth-century reformers had to grapple.

By degrees the justices separated their administrative from their judicial business, and came to conduct the former in private meetings rather than in public sessions. At the same time a rudimentary bureaucracy came into existence in the persons of county treasurers, surveyors, and other officials; and the employment of paid labour, financed by rates, replaced the inefficient medieval system of compulsory unpaid offices and compulsory work by the inhabitants. Undemocratic as they were, the justices inevitably lost ground in the nineteenth-century campaigns for reform. They were stripped of an important function when in 1834 the poor law was transferred to the Poor Law Commissioners,[11] a powerful centralised body working through 'unions' of parishes administered by elected 'guardians'. Long before that date there had set in a tendency to establish special commissioners or trustees for new undertakings requiring administrative enterprise, such as the improvement of towns by paving and lighting and the building of the turnpike roads. A multitude of statutory authorities, often equipped with rating powers, continued to proliferate through the nineteenth century: highway boards, school boards, boards of health, and burial boards worked alongside poor law guardians and improvement commissioners in a dense governmental jungle. Over this welter of

[8] See below, p. 630.
[9] As in the famous case of Cardiff Bridge, R v Inhabitants of Glamorganshire (1701) 1 Ld Raym. 580; below, p. 632.
[10] Redlich and Hirst, History of Local Government, i. 102.
[11] By the Poor Law Amendment Act 1834.

authorities the justices retained many powers until the situation was rationalised by the Local Government Act 1888. The reign of the county justices did not really close until that late date. They were given charge of the police when the county forces were constituted by Acts of 1839 and 1856, and even today they provide a third of the membership of local police authorities.[12] This together with their powers of liquor licensing (public houses etc.)[13] and a few other functions[14] are now the only surviving remnants of their administrative powers, which in their heyday were the principal agency of local government.

The mechanism through which the justices governed the counties was for many purposes the parish, where power traditionally resided in the 'vestry', i.e. the whole body of parishioners meeting in the church vestry.[15] From early times the vestry had power to levy a church rate for the repair and furnishing of the church and this system was used, subject to the control of the justices, for levying rates required for the poor law, highway maintenance, and other things.[16] After the poor law was transferred to the new authorities in 1834 vestries in rural areas declined in importance and their non-ecclesiastical powers were finally removed by the Local Government Act 1894. Urban vestries survived for longer, though with attenuated powers which were ultimately abolished only by the Local Government Act 1933. The most vigorous vestries were those of the London parishes, which were given new constitutions and powers by the Metropolis Management Act 1855, which also set up district boards of works; but both the vestries and the boards were in their turn abolished by the London Government Act 1899.

The boroughs

In addition there were the boroughs. Boroughs were corporations created by royal charter obtained (and commonly purchased) from the Crown. For a sufficient sum they could obtain grants of commercial and jurisdictional privileges, freedom from royal exactions, and representation in Parliament; and having corporate personality they could accumulate and administer their own property. A privilege which they often obtained

[12] Below, p. 142.

[13] Licensing Act 1964.

[14] Magistrates' courts exercise what are in substance administrative functions by way of appeal in certain licensing matters, e.g. as to street traders: see *R v Thames Magistrates' Court ex p Greenbaum* (1957) 55 LGR 129.

[15] In the interests of efficiency many parishes, especially in London, established 'select vestries' or combined 'district boards' under local Acts of Parliament or under the Vestries Act 1831. The House of Lords still raises the Select Vestries Bill (for reform of vestry abuses) before taking government business after the opening of Parliament.

[16] Notably by the Poor Relief Act 1601.

was the power to elect their own magistrates, thus escaping from the rule of the county justices. In granting charters the Crown came to favour small oligarchic corporations over which it could exert influence; but after the failure of James II's attempts to recall the older and more liberal charters, the boroughs were left in peace much as the county justices were, remaining for a century and a half in a state of stagnation commonly accompanied by corruption. Reform finally arrived with the Municipal Corporations Act 1835, which created town councils in a large number of specified boroughs, with an extended franchise similar to that introduced for Parliament by the Reform Act 1832. The Act put an end to the election of borough justices, thus recognising the objections to an elective judiciary. The town councils were made responsible for the police. At first they were not thought fit to become all-purpose authorities of the modern type, and many functions remained in the hands of the multifarious commissioners and other ad hoc bodies. But soon the town councils were enabled to take over such functions by adopting standardised powers under various Clauses Acts,[17] and many of them became sanitary authorities under the Public Health Act 1848, doing the work of local boards of health which the Act established throughout the country. The work of constitutional reform in the boroughs was completed by the Municipal Corporations Acts 1882 and 1883. They were then in a fit condition to shoulder their new responsibilities under the Local Government Act 1888.

Before this last Act there was only one municipal corporation in London: the ancient City, confined within its own small enclave and with its medieval guild-based constitution untouched by the reforming statutes. The City is a corporation by prescription, but many charters have granted it privileges and moulded its traditional institutions. The latter are complex and picturesque, but it suffices to mention the chief executive body, the Court of Common Council, which in 1888 acquired the functions of a London borough council. Outside the City the remainder of London, a vastly greater area, was administered by county justices, vestries, district boards, and numerous commissioners, with improvements effected by the Metropolitan Sewers Act 1848 and the Metropolis Management Act 1855. Ultimately this medley of authorities was replaced by the London County Council and the London Borough Councils under the Local Government Act 1886 and the London Government Act 1899 respectively.

The modern system

The watershed between the old and the new systems of local government may be said to be the two Local Government Acts of 1888 and 1894. These

---

[17]　e.g. Towns Improvement Clauses Act 1847; Markets and Fairs Clauses Act 1847.

Acts carried forward the policy of entrusting administrative functions to elected 'general purpose' authorities; and they established the 'two-tier' system which is still the basis of local government organisation to-day. The Act of 1888 established an elected county council for each county and transferred to it the administrative powers of the justices in quarter sessions. But the large cities[18] with populations in excess of 50,000 were made separate county boroughs. The Act of 1894 divided the counties, but not the county boroughs, into urban and rural districts which historically derived from the sanitary districts set up by the Public Health Acts of 1872 and 1875, and for each it established an elected urban or rural district council except where the district was a borough and already had a borough council. In the rural districts the Act of 1894 also instituted parish meetings and, for the larger parishes, parish councils. In country areas, therefore, there could be said to be a three-tier system; but the parish councils were given so little revenue that they could not make much contribution. The general scheme, therefore, was that powers were divided between the counties and the districts, except in the county boroughs where they were concentrated in a single authority. Of the former ad hoc authorities the only important survivors were the school boards and the poor law guardians; but their functions were assigned to the county and county borough councils by the Education Act 1902[19] and the Local Government Act 1929 respectively.

A greatly simplified structure of authorities thus emerged, keeping pace also with the extension of democracy. Just as the Reform Act of 1832 led to the reform of the municipal franchise by the Municipal Corporations Act 1835, so the enfranchisement of the agricultural population by the Reform Act of 1884 paved the way for the Act of 1888 which replaced the nominated justices by elected county councils. At the same time a framework of authorities had been created which could be used for the taking on of new tasks. And of these in the coming years there was no shortage. Housing and town planning powers were soon required, and were given by the Housing and Town Planning Act 1909. The rapid growth of population put ever-increasing pressure on the local authorities, and in order to make the most use of the two-tier structure the qualifying population for county borough status was raised to 75,000 in 1926[20] and to 100,000 in 1958.[21] The degree of uniformity thus achieved by the system

---

[18] 'City' has no legal meaning distinct from 'borough'. Some boroughs traditionally claim the title of city and others have obtained it by royal letters patent. It has no significance except as a title of honour, like 'lord mayor'. See Local Government Act 1972, s. 245(10).

[19] Certain district and borough councils also had responsibilities for primary schools, until these were transferred to county councils by the Education Act 1944.

[20] Local Government (County Boroughs and Adjustments) Act 1926.

[21] Local Government Act 1958, s. 34.

made it possible to consolidate and codify the law in a massive statute, the Local Government Act 1933, which stood as the basic enactment for forty years.

The district and non-county borough councils were primarily sanitary authorities, though they also acquired important responsibilities as housing authorities. They were also the rating authorities, levying rates both for themselves and for the counties in a single operation, after receiving the demand (precept) of the county council. County councils were responsible for education, town and country planning (though with some powers of delegation), the fire service, and some miscellaneous services connected with welfare and health. County boroughs administered all these services through the county borough council. Small boroughs which were too weak to undertake the responsibilities of districts, as sometimes happened when ancient boroughs were depopulated, were allowed to merge into rural districts and become, in effect, parishes under the Local Government Act 1958.[22] The precise constitutions of these various local authorities need not be described, since all have been replaced under the Local Government Act 1972.

Democratically elected as they were, the authorities of the new system were by no means independent, and by no means fully in command of their localities. The influence of the central government became ever more dominant. Partly this was exerted by ministerial powers of direction; partly through financial control, by the system of district audit, and by attaching conditions to government grants which the local authority could not afford to do without; and partly through statutory conditions requiring ministerial approval, as for the raising of money on loan and the compulsory purchase of land. Control by Whitehall became more and more pervasive, in complete contrast to the local liberty enjoyed in the eighteenth and early nineteenth centuries. This liberty was progressively lost as power gravitated to the centre: to the Poor Law Commissioners (1834), the Poor Law Board (1847), the General Board of Health (1848), the Local Government Board (1871), the Ministry of Health (1919), the Ministry of Town and Country Planning (1943), the Ministry of Housing and Local Government (1951), and the Department of the Environment (1970). In addition, the central government itself undertook local administration on an extensive scale. It managed the national insurance system set up by the National Insurance Act 1911. It took over a large area of the poor law under the Unemployment Act 1934 and the remainder under the National Assistance Act 1948. It took over major roads under the Trunk Roads Act 1936. After the war it undertook the direct administration of one of the most important social services under the

---

[22] s. 28. These were called rural boroughs.

National Health Service Act 1946 (taking over local authority hospitals) and continued another under the National Insurance Act 1946. Electricity, gas, and transport undertakings, which many municipalities had established, were transferred to the new nationalised industries. Valuation for rating was also transferred to the Inland Revenue by the Local Government Act 1948. Central and local government no longer occupied distinct spheres: their activities intermingled and became interdependent, introducing new sources of complication and friction.

The need for reform

Although the reorganisation made at the end of the nineteenth century produced a symmetrical and logical system of authorities covering the whole country, it came to reveal serious deficiencies with the constant growth of the population and the no less constant growth of governmental responsibilities. The forty-five administrative counties ranged from Lancashire with 2.4m. people to Rutland with less than 30,000. The seventy-nine county boroughs ranged from Birmingham with 1m. to Canterbury with 33,000. The 1,086 county districts, including boroughs, ranged from 100,000 to 1,500 including 103 with less than 5,000. It was natural that the smaller authorities found difficulty in discharging their functions as these became more exacting. Palliatives were found by setting up joint authorities for various purposes and by devolving powers from the county to the districts according to population scales (60,000 for education, health, and planning, 40,000 for libraries, 20,000 for certain roads, and so on). Since 1945 the Boundary Commission had tried to keep pace with demographic changes by adjusting the authorities' areas[23] and in 1958 the Local Government Commission was empowered both to review areas and to propose reorganisations.[24] But, as the Royal Commission of 1969 said, 'local government was torn by bitter fights between municipal and county councils, as county boroughs sought to expand and non-county boroughs struggled to acquire county borough status'.[25] The makeshift arrangements for joint authorities and devolution also produced what the Commission called 'a sort of pock-marked administrative pattern'.[26] Above all, it was clear that for modern social adminstration the day of the small local authority was over.

---

[23] Local Government (Boundary Commission) Act 1945. The Commission was dissolved by the Local Government (Boundary Commission) (Dissolution) Act 1949.

[24] Local Government Act 1958. There was a separate Commission for Wales. These Commissions were dissolved by the Local Government (Termination of Reviews) Act 1967.

[25] Cmnd. 4040 (1969), para. 84.

[26] Para. 72.

The Royal Commission pointed also to other serious failings. The existing system was based on a sharp division between town and country which was contrary to the realities of life in an era of immensely increased mobility. The fragmentation into counties and county boroughs made the proper planning of development and transportation impossible. In the counties the districts were too weak and the division of responsibilities was inconvenient. Relations with the public were injured by the confusion of authorities and powers: 'there is no correspondence between this welter of authorities and people's lives; and too often a local authority which is concerned with a particular problem does not have the power to settle it'.[27] There was too much domination by the central government.[28] Public apathy towards local government was aggravated by the fact that, except for county councils, elections for only a third of the council were held every year and on different days for different authorities.[29]

The plan produced in 1969 by the Royal Commission (which was not concerned with Scotland, Wales, or London) was for a much smaller number of more powerful authorities, organised for the most part in a one-tier system. It was recommended that the number of authorities be reduced from 1,210 (the total of counties, county boroughs, and districts) to eighty-one; and that the number of main areas should be sixty-one, fifty-eight of them under single all-purpose authorities and three of them (the conurbations of Birmingham, Liverpool, and Manchester) under metro-politan councils with twenty district councils as second-tier authorities.[30] The proposals for the metropolitan areas were modelled on the scheme introduced for London by the London Government Act 1963. With London included, England would then consist of four two-tier metropoli-tan areas and fifty-eight single-tier counties. This was the converse of the existing pattern, in which the two-tier system operated in the counties but not in the large cities other than London. It was also recommended that the sixty-one new areas should be grouped into eight provinces, each with its own provincial council indirectly elected by the main authorities and equipped with certain executive powers;[31] these provincial councils would replace the Regional Economic Planning Councils established in 1964, which were advisory only, and also the Regional Sports Councils. At the other end of the scale, to counteract the remoteness of the large authorities, there were to be local councils in the unitary areas, and if desired in the metropolitan areas, one to replace each existing county borough, borough,

27 Para. 96.
28 Para. 100.
29 Para. 98.
30 Paras. 287, 290.
31 Paras. 283, 411.

urban district, and parish council; their principal function would be to make known the views of the local community, but they should have certain powers in connection with housing, conservation, and minor improvements, with power to spend money.[32]

In 1970 the government proposed to put these revolutionary recommendations into effect, with relatively small modifications.[33] But a change of government then took place, and in the outcome the Royal Commission's scheme was abandoned in favour of a new scheme under which the two-tier principle was applied more comprehensively than ever.[34] The objection which prevailed was that the powerful main authorities would be too remote, and that the local councils would be too ineffective to fill the gap. The policy of creating fewer and stronger authorities was adopted nevertheless. The total of county and district authorities in England was reduced from 1,210 to 377.

Yet a further revolution took place in 1986, when London and the six big conurbations were reformed into a single-tier system, the upper-tier authorities being abolished by the Local Government Act 1985.

THE NEW SYSTEM OF LOCAL GOVERNMENT

The Local Government Act 1972

The new regime of local authorities were enacted by the Local Government Act 1972, which effectively came into operation on 1 April 1974. The extensive reorganisations of the national health service and of the water authorities were arranged to take effect simultaneously. This date was therefore a major milestone in administrative history.

The Act of 1972 not only provided for the new system of areas and authorities: it replaced the massive Act of 1933 which contained the general law regulating local authorities' elections, proceedings, powers, functions, and finance. It is an equally massive Act, with thirty schedules. It is further supplemented by the Local Government Act 1974, dealing mainly with finance, rating, and the new machinery for complaints against local authorities.

One of the most notable results of the new scheme is the disappearance of the single-tier county borough. The former county boroughs have been merged in the new districts, so that they are now second-tier authorities. This means that they have lost their responsibilities for education (except in the metropolitan areas), social services, highways, traffic, and (subject to

---

[32] Para. 371.
[33] Reform of Local Government in England, Cmnd. 4276 (1970).
[34] Local Government in England, Cmnd. 4584 (1971).

amalgamation schemes) the fire service and police. Even the strongest of the former authorities, therefore, have lost a great deal of power. Cities such as Southampton and Oxford, which used to be in full command of their areas, are now merely districts within the new counties, and their powers are much attenuated.

Also to be noted is the eclipse of the most ancient of the previous authorities, the borough. Boroughs were abolished by the Act of 1972;[35] but the Act also contained a detailed plan for preserving borough titles, ceremonials, privileges, and property, together with the rights of freemen of boroughs, since these were often a stimulus to local spirit. A new district council might petition the Crown for a charter conferring 'the status of a borough', entitling it to call itself a borough council and to call its chairman and vice-chairman mayor and deputy mayor, entitling it to appoint 'officers of dignity', and preserving other privileges.[36] Where the former borough became a mere parish its 'officers of dignity' could be appointed by the parish council;[37] and where it did not become a parish the Act provided for 'charter trustees' for the same purpose.[38] A parish may also resolve to call itself a town, with a mayor and deputy mayor.[39]

Both London and Wales come within the Act of 1972, but Scotland does not.[40]

Areas and authorities

In England the Act established six metropolitan counties, divided into thirty-six metropolitan districts, and thirty-nine non-metropolitan counties divided into 296 districts.[41] In Wales it established eight counties (non-metropolitan) divided into thirty-seven districts. The metropolitan counties, however, were abolished in 1986. They were the conurbations of Greater Manchester, Merseyside, West Midlands, West Yorkshire, South Yorkshire and Tyne and Wear. The districts within them are defined by the Act of 1972. The non-metropolitan counties are fewer and larger than the old counties, several of them being composite areas under new names:

[35] s. 1(9)–(11).
[36] ss. 245, 246.
[37] s. 246(3).
[38] s. 246(4).
[39] s. 245(6).
[40] Scotland is now divided into nine regions, containing fifty-three districts, and three island areas, replacing the former counties, districts, and burghs: Local Government (Scotland) Act 1973, s. 1 and 1st sched.
[41] 1st sched. In terms of population (1971 figures) the largest metropolitan county was Greater Manchester with 2.7m. and ten districts, the smallest was Tyne and Wear with 1.2m. and five districts; of the non-metropolitan counties the largest was Kent with 1.4m., the smallest was Isle of Wight with 109,000.

Avon, Cleveland, Cumbria, and Humberside.[42] The districts within the English counties are defined only by order.[43] Those in the Welsh counties are defined in the Act.[44]

The former English rural parishes continue to exist as parishes.[45] Urban parishes had not been local government authorities since 1933, but the Secretary of State for the Environment now has power to constitute parishes out of former urban districts or boroughs.[46] Wales, by contrast, has a new system of 'communities' covering the whole country, one for each of the former boroughs, urban districts, and rural parishes.[47]

In all the above areas the legal authority is the council,[48] which is a body corporate,[49] except in such parishes as have no council. Every parish must have a parish meeting, consisting of the local government electors and to be held at least once a year.[50] In addition, if the electors number not more than 150 and the parish meeting so resolves, the district council may establish a parish council; if the number exceeds 150 they must do so upon such a resolution; and if it exceeds 200 they must do so in any case.[51] A district council may also make orders grouping parishes under a common parish council, with the consent of the parish meetings.[52] Where the electors number 150 or less, the district council may dissolve the parish council on the application of the parish meeting.[53] In Wales a district council must establish a community council on application by the community meeting, and must dissolve one similarly, irrespective of numbers,[54] and grouping orders may be made as in England.[55] In parishes which have no parish council there are 'parish trustees' who are incorporated, can deal with parish property, and must obey the directions of the parish meeting.[56]

Once again Local Government Boundary Commissions have been created, one for England and one for Wales.[57] They may propose alterations or abolition of local government areas and the constitution of

[42] 1st sched., Pt. II (England); 4th sched., Pt. I (Wales).
[43] SI 1972 No. 2039.
[44] Act of 1972, 4th sched., Pt. II.
[45] Act of 1972, s. 1(6).
[46] Act of 1972, 1st sched., Pt. V.
[47] Act of 1972, s. 20(4).
[48] Act of 1972, ss. 2, 21.
[49] ss. 2(3), 14(2).
[50] ss. 9(1), 13.
[51] s. 9(2), (3).
[52] s. 11.
[53] s. 10.
[54] s. 28.
[55] s. 29.
[56] s. 13.
[57] Act of 1972, ss. 46, 53. See *Enfield LBC* v. *Boundary Commission* [1979] 3 All ER 747, where the House of Lords explained the Commission's duties.

new areas, including metropolitan areas, and the powers of the English
commission extend to the London boroughs.[58] The Secretary of State may
direct a review of any area and he can control the operations of the
commissions generally.[59] Subject to this control, they may review any area
at any time. The English Commission is to review all areas at intervals of
from ten to fifteen years.[60] Its first task was to propose the areas of the
districts in the English non-metropolitan counties, which the Secretary of
State then designated by order.[61] Any local authority may apply to the
appropriate commission for a review, but it may no longer seek to alter its
area, status, or electoral arrangements by promoting a Bill in Parliament.[62]

London government

The overhaul of local government in London took place a decade earlier
than in the rest of the country, under the London Government Act 1963,
also preceded by the report of a Royal Commission.[63] The Act replaced the
London County Council, created in 1888,[64] and the metropolitan borough
councils, created in 1899,[65] by the Greater London Council and thirty-two
London borough councils,[66] taking in a much larger area. The City of
London, with its ancient constitution intact, forms in effect an additional
London borough. The Inner Temple and the Middle Temple also retain
their ancient status as local authorities,[67] but they have little to do except for
paving and lighting and the collection of rates on behalf of the City, of
which they count as part.

   London therefore continued under a two-tier system, the London
boroughs corresponding generally to the metropolitan districts elsewhere,
until the abolition of the Greater London Council in 1986. The distribution
of functions between the Greater London Council and the London
boroughs was broadly similar to that in the metropolitan counties, except
that education, health, and welfare services belonged to the boroughs.
Passenger transport was provided by the London Transport Executive, of
which the Greater London Council had effective control. In the area of
Inner London (the old London County Council area), however, education

[58] ss. 47, 54.
[59] ss. 49, 56.
[60] s. 48.
[61] s. 1(4) and 3rd sched., para. 1; SI 1972 No. 2039.
[62] s. 70.
[63] Cmnd. 1164 (1960).
[64] Local Government Act 1888.
[65] London Government Act 1899.
[66] The GLC was incorporated but the London borough councils are not: the corporation
was the whole body of burgesses, i.e. electors: London Government Act 1963, s.1(2), (3).
[67] London Government Act 1963, s. 82.

belonged to the Greater London Council but was administered through the Inner London Education Authority, on which the Inner London boroughs were represented.[68] The metropolitan police were separately organised under the Home Secretary, as they still are.

London was reduced to a one-tier system by the Local Government Act 1985. The Inner London Education Authority was reconstituted as a directly elected authority and made subject to guidance from the Secretary of State. The London Fire and Civil Defence Authority was established as a joint authority of the London Boroughs. Control of passenger transport had already passed into the hands of the central government under the London Regional Transport Act 1984, by which the London Transport Executive was renamed London Regional Transport. Conservation functions were transferred to the Historic Buildings and Monuments Commission and a newly-created 'residuary body' took over various other tasks, as in the case of the metropolitan counties.

The Local Government Act 1972 had revised the constitutions of the Greater London Council and the London boroughs, abolishing the office of alderman, except in the City of London.[69] The constitution of the City consists of the Court of Common Hall, Court of Aldermen, and the Court of Common Council, the last being the important body for governmental purposes. The City still administers its own police force.

Allocation of functions

The principal functions of local government are parcelled out among the main authorities by a long series of provisions of the Act of 1972, which where necessary adapt the empowering enactments (such as the Education Act 1944, the Housing Act 1957 (now 1985) and the Town and Country Planning Act 1971) to the new hierarchy of authorities.[70] Only in the case of the former rural parishes was no reallocation required; their functions are inherited directly by the successor parishes in England and by the newly created communities in Wales.[71]

Subject to a certain amount of overlap, and subject also to special arrangements flowing from the extensive powers of co-operation and delegation given by the Act, the allocation of the most important functions in non-metropolitan areas is as shown in the table.[72]

[68] London Government Act 1963, s. 30.
[69] s. 8 and 2nd sched.
[70] Pt. IX.
[71] See s. 179(4).
[72] For a fuller catalogue see Department of Environment circular 121/72, annexe A (printed in (1972) 70(2) LGR 1348). Many local authorities have additional powers under local Acts of Parliament.

County council	District council	Parish or community council or meeting
Education	Housing	Footpaths
Town and country planning and development (S)	Town and country planning and development (S)	Allotments
Social services (S)	Public health and sanitary services	Bus shelters
Food and drugs (S)	Food and drugs (S)	Recreation grounds
Roads (mostly)	Minor urban roads	Village greens
Refuse disposal	Refuse collection	Burial grounds
Libraries	Entertainments	Parking places for motor cycles and bicycles
Highways	Recreation (S)	
Traffic	Rating	
Public transport	Coast protection	
Recreation (S)	Local licensing	
Police (A)		
Fire service (A)		

S = shared or divided service
A = subject to amalgamation schemes covering wider areas.

'Town and country planning and development' (outlined elsewhere[73]) includes the making of plans, the control of development and other functions under the Town and Country Planning Act 1971. 'Housing' includes slum clearance.[74] 'Social services' includes old people's and children's homes, welfare services for children, old people, the blind, the physically handicapped, and the chronically sick and disabled, and supplying temporary accommodation for those in urgent need.[75] An important power of county and district councils is that of compulsory purchase of land (also outlined elsewhere[76]), which is available, subject to ministerial approval, in conjunction with their other functions such as town development, slum clearance, housing, public buildings and works, coast protection schemes:[77] there are scores of statutes conferring this power.

---

[73] Below, p. 180.
[74] Below, p. 201.
[75] See Local Authority Social Services Act 1970, 1st sched., listing the numerous local authority social services. These range from the provision of homes to the supply of 'meals on wheels' and laundry facilities. Those listed under the National Health Service Act 1946 have since been transferred to the Secretary of State: see below, p. 214.
[76] Below, p. 172.
[77] Made under the Coast Protection Act 1949; see *Webb* v. *Minister of Housing and Local Government* [1965] 1 WLR 755 (below, p. 437).

Licensing powers are numerous and miscellaneous.[78] Among many other matters district councils license theatres, cinemas, pawnbrokers, moneylenders, riding establishments, dogs, and dealers in game. There is also a mass of local legislation which in particular places may apply to food vendors, hairdressers, pet shops, market porters, and other occupations. In some cases the Act will require a licence, in others it will require registration; but since either may be refused, the effect is the same. In some cases fire certificates must be obtained from the local authority. Formerly county councils were in charge of vehicle licensing, but this has been transferred to the Secretary of State, who nevertheless uses local authorities as his agents.[79]

Metropolitan areas

While they still existed the six metropolitan county councils had the usual county council functions, except that the district councils were in charge of education, social services, and libraries. After the 'abolition date' (1 April 1986) the district councils inherited planning, roads, waste disposal, land drainage, the administration of justice, and miscellaneous functions including licensing. Three joint authorities, consisting of members of the district councils, were constituted in each metropolitan county to administer the police, the fire service and civil defence, and passenger transport. Various other functions were transferred to statutory 'residuary bodies' appointed by the Secretary of State and intended to wind up the remaining affairs of the abolished authorities, in particular their debts, over a period of five years.

Constitution and election of councils

County and district councils have generally similar constitutions except in one respect. There are two quite different timetables for the election of councillors: either they may all be elected together and retire together every four years; or else a third of them may be elected in each of three years of the four-year cycle, retiring after four years' service. The Act of 1972 employs both of these systems, the former for the counties and the non-metropolitan districts and the latter for the metropolitan districts. But the non-metropolitan districts are given the option of adopting the system of election by thirds. Parliament has once again displayed indecision about

---

[78] On licensing see Hart, *Local Government*, 9th edn, ch. 28; Street, *Justice in the Welfare State*, ch. 4. The Local Government (Miscellaneous Provisions) Act 1982 gave new powers over public entertainments, sex establishments, street trading, take-away food shops, acupuncture, tattooing, and other things.

[79] Vehicle and Driving Licences Act 1969; Vehicles (Excise) Act 1971.

the pros and cons of the two systems.[80] Simultaneous election has the advantage of stimulating the electorate and counteracting apathy in local government. Election by thirds has the advantage of ensuring continuity of experience on the council.

The Act of 1972 provided for the simultaneous election of county councillors to take place in 1973 and every fourth year thereafter,[81] and for the simultaneous election of non-metropolitan district councillors to take place in 1973, 1976, 1979, and every fourth year thereafter,[82] thus ultimately spacing the district elections half way between the county elections. In metropolitan districts, and in other districts which have adopted election by thirds, the elections take place in every year when there is not a county election, one-third of the councillors being elected in such a year.[83] A non-metropolitan district council which wishes to adopt election by thirds, or having done so to revert to simultaneous election, must request the Secretary of State to make the necessary order by a two-thirds majority vote; but no request may be made within ten years of a previous one.[84] Simultaneous county elections are for single-member divisions.[85] Simultaneous district elections are for areas and members prescribed by the Secretary of State.[86] Elections by thirds are for multi-member wards, the number in each ward being divisible by three,[87] but a non-metropolitan district council wishing to adopt election by thirds may request single-member wards for part or all of its area.[88] Parish councillors are elected simultaneously, for three years in 1976 and for four years in 1979 and thereafter; their number (at least five) is fixed by the district council, which may divide the parish into electoral wards.[89] The franchise is virtually the same as the Parliamentary franchise, except that peers may vote.

In Greater London only simultaneous election is used and the period of office is three years. Elections for the Greater London Council and the metropolitan county councils were required in 1973 and every third year thereafter, but since they were due for abolition in 1986, the 1985 elections were cancelled and the members' tenure was prolonged.[90] For the London borough councils elections were required in 1974 and every third year

---

[80] There were similar differences under the Local Government Act 1933.
[81] s. 7(1).
[82] s. 7(8).
[83] s. 7(2), (8).
[84] s. 7(4)–(7).
[85] s. 6(2).
[86] s. 6(2).
[87] s. 6(2).
[88] s. 7(4).
[89] s. 16.
[90] Local Government (Interim Provisions) Act 1984.

thereafter. For the Greater London Council elections were by single-member districts, while for the London borough councils elections are by wards, the number of members for each being according to the borough charter, subject to any modification by the London Government Act 1963.[91]

Each county and district council must elect one of their number as chairman, as their first business at their annual meeting. They must also appoint a councillor as vice-chairman. The chairman and vice-chairman hold office for a year, and are eligible for re-election if still councillors. In cities and towns the chairman and vice-chairman will frequently bear the titles of mayor and deputy mayor, under the arrangement for preserving dignities already mentioned. But a dignitary who is disappearing from the scene is the alderman. Aldermen used to be elected by the councils of counties, county boroughs, and boroughs to serve for six years, and likewise in Greater London. But the Act of 1972 took steps to abolish them,[92] except only in the City of London.

A councillor must have attained twenty-one and be either a local government elector for the area or have resided, worked or occupied land there during the previous twelve months.[93] There are a number of disqualifications such as bankruptcy and a sentence of imprisonment;[94] the most important disqualification is the holding of any paid office or employment which in any way comes under the council, which disqualifies teachers in the council's maintained schools as well as others.[95] Disputed elections are determined on petition to the High Court under the Representation of the People Acts 1949 and 1969.

In addition to out-of-pocket expenses, councillors may claim attendance allowances, or alternatively 'financial loss allowances', for time spent on council business.[96] In principle these represent the loss which they suffer by giving their working time. They may also now be awarded 'special responsibility allowances'.[97] But they are entitled to no other remuneration: local government work is traditionally voluntary.

Operations and proceedings

Despite its power to make byelaws, mentioned below, a council is an executive rather than a legislative body. It exercises its powers directly in its

---

[91] 2nd sched., paras. 6, 7.
[92] 2nd sched., Pt. II, providing for a temporary reprieve in Greater London.
[93] Act of 1972, s. 79.
[94] s. 80.
[95] s. 80(3).
[96] s. 173; Local Government, Planning and Land Act 1980, s. 24.
[97] Act of 1980, s. 26.

own name, taking decisions by majority vote of those present at a meeting of the council.[98] But among these powers is a very extensive power of delegation, so that the council need not decide everything itself. Under the Act of 1972 a local authority may 'arrange for the discharge of any of their functions' by a committee, a sub-committee or an officer of the authority, or by any other local authority.[99] This is a wider power than had been given by the Local Government Act 1933, which permitted delegation to committees only,[1] and thus enforced a rigid 'committee system'. The policy of the Act of 1972 is to give councils greater freedom to organise their business in the most efficient way,[2] though naturally committees[3] are still used a great deal. The Act also reduced the number of cases where the council was required to act through specified committees, and where therefore it was not free to delegate otherwise. The most notable of the surviving exceptions are education committees and social services committees;[4] and only the authority itself may levy a rate or borrow money.[5] There are also wide powers for authorities to collaborate and to set up joint committees.[6] The legal aspects of delegation of power are discussed elsewhere.[7]

A detailed code of procedure for meetings of councils and committees and for parish and community meetings is contained in the Act.[8] Three days' notice must be given of county and district council meetings and of the business to be transacted.[9] The person presiding at a local authority or committee meeting has a casting vote.[10] Non-members of the authority may be appointed to a committee (unless disqualified[11]), except to a finance committee; but if it is to exercise any of the authority's powers they may not exceed one-third of the committee's membership.[12] Committees and

---

[98] Act of 1972, 12th sched., para. 39.

[99] s. 101.

[1] s. 85.

[2] As recommended by the Committee on the Management of Local Government, 1967, HMSO (chairman, Sir John Maud), and in The New Local Authorities: Management and Structure, 1972, HMSO (chairman: M. A. Bains).

[3] 'Committee' in this context means a body of more than one person: R v. Secretary of State for the Environment ex p. Hillingdon LBC [1986] 1 WLR 192, affirmed [1986] 1 WLR 807.

[4] s. 101(8), (9), (7).

[5] s. 101(6).

[6] s. 101(5).

[7] Below, p. 357.

[8] 12th sched.

[9] 12th sched., para. 4.

[10] 12th sched., para. 39.

[11] s. 104 disqualifies persons not qualified for membership of the authority, with certain exceptions for teachers.

[12] s. 102(3), (4).

sub-committees must be appointed by the authority or committee concerned: there is no power to co-opt.[13] Standing orders may be made for matters not governed by statute.[14] A councillor is entitled to attend meetings and see documents where he can show good reason, but in the case of a committee of which he is not a member he must show that it is necessary for the proper discharge of his duties, if the business is confidential.[15]

The public, including the press, have a right to attend meetings of local authorities and also meetings of their committees and sub-committees. In addition they are entitled to inspect agenda, minutes, reports, background papers, and other documents.[16] These rights are restricted where the business involves confidential information of certain kinds, such as information made confidential by government departments or by law, and personal information about employees, tenants, and children in care; negotiations about contracts, labour relations, and legal proceedings are also protected, among other matters. The authorities concerned include the Inner London Education Authority, combined police and fire authorities, and various other joint boards and committees. The campaign for a Freedom of Information Act has therefore made progress in local, if not in central, government.

There are criminal penalties for members of local authorities who take part in business in which they have a pecuniary interest. A member who 'has any pecuniary interest, direct or indirect, in any contract, proposed contract or other matter' which is under consideration when he is present must disclose the fact and may not speak or vote; and he may be excluded under standing orders.[17] The same rules apply to committee and sub-committee meetings.[18] 'Pecuniary interest' includes membership of a company, e.g. as shareholder, and partnership with anyone directly interested.[19] 'Any other matter' may include general policy, so that a director of a building company may not take part in a discussion of

---

[13] s. 102.

[14] 12th sched., para. 42; and see s. 106.

[15] R v. Birmingham City DC ex p. O. [1983] 1 AC 578; R v. Hackney LBC ex p. Gamper [1985] 1 WLR 1229.

[16] Public Bodies (Admission to Meetings) Act 1960, as extended by Local Government Act 1972, s. 100 and the Local Government (Access to Information) Act 1985. This is elaborate legislation. See also Health Service Joint Consultative Committees (Access to Information) Act 1986.

[17] Act of 1972, s. 94.

[18] s. 105. A local authority may require applicants for Committee membership to declare their own and their spouses' pecuniary and personal interests in a public register: R v. Newham LBC ex p. Haggerty (1986) 85 LGR 48.

[19] s. 95; but if a shareholding does not exceed the limits specified in s. 97(6) the member may speak and vote, but must still declare his interest.

contracting policy for building.[20] Nor need a pecuniary interest be immediately operative. Thus a tenant of a council house was held to be disqualified from debating the council's charges to its tenants.[21] But the Secretary of State has a dispensing power where the number of members disqualified is inconveniently large or dispensation is in the interests of the inhabitants,[22] and he has allowed council house tenants to speak and vote on matters of general housing policy.[23] The effect of interest or bias on the validity of an authority's decision is explained in chapter 14.

Many recommendations about operations and proceedings have been made by the Committee on the Conduct of Local Authority Business.[24]

Officers and employees

The policy of allowing greater freedom to local authorities in the management of their business was also applied by the Act of 1972 to their cadre of officials. Formerly it was mandatory for them to appoint many specified officers, such as a clerk (or town clerk), treasurer, surveyor, chief education officer, and so on.[25] Most of these requirements have now been repealed, leaving only a short list of obligatory appointments, which includes chief education officers, directors of social services and fire brigade officers; and the Greater London Council must still appoint surveyors.[26] A notable omission from this list is that of the clerk. Under the previous system the clerk was the head of the authority's staff and was normally a qualified solicitor. Consequently the administrative work pivoted round the legal department, contrasting with the central government and the civil service, in which lawyers in administrative positions are conspicuous by their absence.[27] Local authorities are now free to depart from their traditional organisation, and in fact many of them have appointed a 'chief executive' rather than a clerk of the old-fashioned type, thus emphasising policy and administration as opposed to legal guidance.

The main provisions of the Act of 1972 are that a local authority 'shall

---

[20] *Rands* v. *Oldroyd* [1959] 1 QB 204.

[21] *Brown* v. *Director of Public Prosecutions* [1956] 2 QB 369.

[22] s. 97. As regards parish and community councils this power belongs to the district council.

[23] Ministry of Housing and Local Government circular 5/67.

[24] 1986, Cmnd. 9797 (the Widdicombe Committee).

[25] Local Government Act 1933, ss. 98–104; Education Act 1944, s. 88; Local Authority Social Services Act 1970, s. 6.

[26] Act of 1972, s. 112(3), (4). Under 29th sched., para. 4 and s. 270(3), references in earlier Acts to specified officers are now to such officers as the authority may appoint for the purpose.

[27] See above, p. 59.

appoint such officers as they think necessary', who 'shall hold office on such reasonable terms and conditions, including conditions as to remuneration, as the authority . . . think fit'.[28] This freedom is restricted in a number of cases, as noted below, by the need to obtain ministerial approval or to conform to conditions laid down from Whitehall. Nevertheless local authorities have now been given a large measure of managerial autonomy.

In relation to the employing authority, its officers and employees serve under contracts of employment which are governed by the ordinary law. They have the benefit of statutory employment law, so that they can claim compensation for unfair dismissal or for being made redundant.[29] There are special provisions for pensions under the Superannuation Acts.

The liability of public authorities for wrongs done by their servants or agents is explained in a later chapter. Local authority officials and employees also bear the normal personal liability; in other words, the orders of their employer are no defence. But where the employee has acted in the council's business and has done some wrong for which, for some special reason, the council is not liable, the established practice is that the council should stand behind him and accept liability.[30] Treaurers responsible for the council's funds have a fiduciary duty to the electors to handle them properly.[31] Officers who have any direct or indirect pecuniary interest in any contract between their employing authority and other persons must give written notice of their interest, subject to prosecution and fine.[32]

Finance: revenue

The problems of the finance of local government are intensely political as well as economic. The political problems are centred round the fact that the revenue which local authorities can provide for themselves is quite unequal to their vastly extended functions. Consequently they depend upon central government grants, and inevitably the grants are subject to conditions. Local independence is therefore undermined by central control, to the point where some local authority services might rather be regarded as agency services for the central government, and confusion arises over

[28] s. 112. This does not allow gifts or retrospective payments: *Re Magrath (Decision of)* [1934] 2 KB 415; but it may include children's allowances: *Re Walker (Decision of)* [1944] KB 644. No other fee or reward may be accepted, under penalty of fine: s. 117.
[29] Employment Protection (Consolidation) Act 1978, Pts. V, VI.
[30] See *Ministry of Housing and Local Government* v. *Sharp* [1970] 2 QB 223 at 269, 275; below, p. 761.
[31] *A.-G.* v. *De Winton* [1906] 2 Ch. 106.
[32] Act of 1972, s. 117.

where responsibility and initiative really reside. As the scale and expense of local services has increased, the tendency has been for the central government to assert more and more control. Political tension is all the greater when the central government and local authorities are controlled by opposed political parties.

The revenue which local authorities raise for themselves consists partly of miscellaneous receipts such as rents, fees, and charges for services. But the primary source of their own revenue is rates. Rates are a local tax levied on the occupation of land according to the assessed annual value of the 'hereditament', i.e. the land and buildings occupied, and determined each year by declaring a rate of so many pence per pound of annual value. The law of rating can be traced from the Poor Relief Act of 1601 which instituted the parochial poor rate, and from church rates levied still earlier by vestries. Subject to numerous developments the parochial basis of collection lasted until the Rating and Valuation Act 1925 reorganised the system. The current statute is the General Rate Act 1967, which will be repealed when the new law of rates and charges takes effect in 1990, as mentioned below.

Rates are levied and collected by district councils, but they must at the same time collect the rates levied by county and parish councils and by various other authorities,[33] as notified to the district councils by precept.[34] There are many qualifications, reliefs, and exemptions: for example, agricultural land is wholly exempt and so is Crown land, but the Crown pays ex gratia; land occupied by charities is assessed at half rate; dwelling-houses qualify for a marginal relief specified by order, and rebates are given on grounds of personal need in the form of housing benefit.[35] The rating and de-rating of public utilities is the subject of particularly complex rules. Valuation is in the hands of the Inland Revenue and is thus not a local function; appeal lies to a local valuation court and thence to the Lands Tribunal.

The unsatisfactory features of rating are that it yields only about a third of the revenue needed by local authorities, bears unduly hardly on business and on householders, particularly those with large families and large houses, and fails to instil a sense of responsibility to the electorate. In some areas full rates are actually paid by less than a quarter of the electorate, and the national average is only about a third, so that the majority have little

---

[33] Including water authorities, joint metropolitan authorities, and the Inner London Education Authority.

[34] Act of 1972, ss. 149, 150. After a number of councils failed to set rates in an attempt to force the government to increase their grants an obligation to make a rate annually before April was imposed by the Local Government Act 1986, s. 1. Councillors were also liable to surcharge for the loss involved: *Smith* v. *Skinner* [1986] The Times, 6 March.

[35] Social Security Act 1986, s. 28, replacing earlier rate rebate schemes.

incentive to vote for economical policies. To fill this responsibility vacuum the central government has imposed 'rate-capping', i.e. a limit on the level of rates and precepts, on a number of high-spending local authorities.[36] Still more drastically, legislation now provides for the abolition of domestic rates and for their replacement by a 'community charge' payable by every citizen personally instead of by occupiers of land only. This revolutionary change is first being introduced in Scotland,[37] and is to follow in England and Wales with effect from April 1990, under an Act yet to be passed.[38]

For England and Wales the Bill provides for three varieties of community charge to be levied by district and London borough councils. The personal charge is payable by adults who have their sole or main residence in the local authority's area. The standard charge is payable by owners or tenants of dwelling-houses which are not the sole or main residences of individuals. The collective charge is payable by owners or tenants of domestic property designated as used wholly or mainly for short-term residence. Each authority's registration officer must maintain a register of persons chargeable by the authority and showing to which of the three varieties of charge they are subject. The charges are apportionable from day to day and a person liable to the collective charge may claim proportionate contributions from the other residents. Enforcement machinery is to be provided by regulations. Against entries in the register appeal lies to a 'valuation and community charge tribunal,' but the calculation and setting of charges and precepts may be challenged only by judicial review. There are various exceptions, reliefs, and rebates, for example for students, mental patients, and prisoners. Non-domestic rating is also to be reorganised, but it will remain based on the occupation of land and buildings. A novel feature is that the Secretary of State may impose central rating on prescribed classes of businesses through central non-domestic rating lists, collecting the rates himself.

Finance: grants and loans

During the nineteenth century local government came more and more to depend upon grants from the central government. These were normally earmarked grants in aid of specific services, usually calculated on a straight percentage basis and subject to the expenditure being approved. The faults of the system of grants in aid revealed themselves in due course: they encouraged extravagance, produced a bias towards grant-aided activities,

---

[36] Rates Act 1984, conferring power both to rate-cap designated authorities and also to impose a comprehensive scheme. The number rate-capped in 1987–8 was 17.

[37] Abolition of Domestic Rates, Etc. (Scotland) Act 1987.

[38] Local Government Finance Bill 1988. For the policy see Cmnd. 9714 (green paper).

and yet led to excessive central government interference. The Local
Government Act 1929 accordingly introduced a new system of 'block
grants', in aid of expenditure generally, and abolished the former
earmarked grants except in special matters such as police, housing, and
education. The amount of grant was adjusted by various systems of
weighting according to the population and rateable resources of each area:
the general rate grant was supplemented by what were called successively
exchequer equalisation grants[39] and rate deficiency grants;[40] and finally
both types of grant were merged in a single rate support grant under the
Local Government Act 1966, later replaced by the Local Government Act
1974.[41] The proportion of local government expenditure to be covered by
rate support grant in 1987–8 was 46 per cent.

Under the Act of 1974 the Secretary of State was required to divide the
grant into three 'elements', the needs element, the domestic element, and
the resources element. The needs element was designed to reflect
population factors such as the proportion of school children and old people;
but the Secretary of State had complete freedom to prescribe the relevant
factors. The domestic element reflected the loss of revenue by the partial
de-rating of dwelling-houses, which was to be made good by grant, again
as prescribed by the Secretary of State. The resources element reflected
rateable value per head of population. The needs element was not payable
to non-metropolitan district councils, unless regulations so provided, and
the domestic and resources elements were not payable to county councils.[42]

This system proved defective because the needs element was computed
with reference to expenditure and the resources element likewise tended to
favour high-spending authorities. A new system, designed to encourage
economy, was substituted by the Local Government, Planning and Land
Act 1980.[43] The needs and resources elements are now replaced by a block
grant based upon 'grant related expenditures' and calculated so as to give an
incentive to economy by setting a 'national threshold' of expenditure per
head of population above which rate support will fall away. In the
transitional period before the new system could take effect the Secretary of
State was given power to reduce rate support grants to local authorities
which set rates higher than a 'notional uniform rate', and by this means he
enforced economies on selected authorities.[44] The new system—so
complicated that the Secretary of State has himself misunderstood

[39] Local Government Act 1948.

[40] Local Government Act 1958.

[41] Pt. I. Under the Local Government Finance Bill 1988 the title will become 'revenue
support grant'.

[42] s. 2(3), (5).

[43] Pt. VI.

[44] But invalidly in some cases: *R* v. *Secretary of State for the Environment ex p. Brent LBC*
[1982] QB 593, fully expounding the complicated system.

it[45]—requires the Secretary of State to determine each year the aggregate amount of money available for rate support grants and, after consulting local authority associations, to lay a 'rate support grant report' before the House of Commons, which if approved by resolution then allows him to make payments accordingly. The Local Government Finance Act 1982 introduced yet further restrictions in the form of 'grant holdback', i.e. a reduction of grant to local authorities which exceeded their current expenditure targets as set by the Secretary of State.

Outside this complicated scheme there are still a number of earmarked grants, the most important being for police, housing, development schemes and relocation of population, and roads.

Most of the capital expenditure of local authorities is financed by borrowing, often by issuing loan stock or by borrowing from the Public Works Loan Board.[46] Although the Act of 1972 gives a very wide power to borrow money for any local government purpose,[47] this is severely restricted by its provision that borrowing requires the approval of the Secretary of State and compliance with any condition which he may impose.[48] The necessity for loan sanction enables the central government to control local authority borrowing in accordance with national policy on capital expenditure.

Finance: expenditure

Local councils are now statutory authorities, with the sole exception of the City of London, and they therefore have power to spend money only for such purposes as are authorised by Parliament.[49] But these purposes include what is reasonably incidental,[50] and the Act of 1972 expresses this principle in generous terms: it covers anything 'which is calculated to facilitate, or is conducive or incidental to, the discharge of any of their functions'.[51]

The Royal Commission in 1969 recommended that local authorities should be freed from the ultra vires doctrine and allowed to spend money for purposes of their own, so as to give them more scope for enterprise and

---

[45] Invalid calculations by the Secretary of State were legitimated retrospectively and for the future by Rate Support Grants Act 1986.

[46] For the methods permitted see Act of 1972, 13th sched., para. 2.

[47] s. 111.

[48] 13th sched., para. 1. Under para. 10 sanction is not required for loans to cover expenses pending receipt of revenue; an overdraft on current account is therefore permitted.

[49] Formerly boroughs founded by charter could claim the wider powers of chartered bodies: see below, p. 243. Under the Act of 1972 all local authorities are statutory: see ss. 1(10), 20(6).

[50] Below, p. 239.

[51] s. 111.

experiment.[52] A power of this kind is conferred by the Act of 1972, but subject to a strict financial limit. A local authority may incur expenditure not authorised by any other Act if in their opinion it is in the interests of their area or its inhabitants, and they may contribute to domestic charities and good causes; but they may not spend for these purposes in any year more than the product of a twopenny rate.[53]

Until 1980 the only central control over local capital expenditure was by means of loan sanction. But the Secretary of State then took power to control the aggregate amount of such expenditure under the Local Government, Planning and Land Act 1980.[54] Within the aggregate the local authority remained free to allot its expenditure as it wished, except that ministerial directions might be given to earmark specific amounts for projects of national or regional importance. Current expenditure came under direct central government control when 'rate-capping' was introduced by the Rates Act 1984, as already mentioned, the permitted rate being fixed by reference to approved expenditure.

The Act of 1980 imposed restrictions, mainly financial, on the works departments ('direct labour organisations') maintained by most councils for the upkeep of housing, roads, etc.[55] Separate accounts must now be kept so as to give a correct picture of the financial performance of these departments; they must show a proper return on capital employed; outside contractors must be allowed to compete with them in the classes of works specified in the Secretary of State's regulations; and a detailed annual report must be published in accordance with statutory rules.

The principles which require local authorities, like other public bodies, to spend money reasonably and with due regard to the interests of their ratepayers are explained later, in the context of the ultra vires doctrine generally.[56] Many examples of the restraints imposed upon them by administrative law will be found throughout this book. The courts have invalidated excessive wages,[57] excessive rent subsidies,[58] and free travel schemes.[59] But some of the decisions were given when the authorities' statutory powers were narrower than they are now.

---

[52] Cmnd. 4040 (1969), para. 323.

[53] s. 137, replacing Local Government (Financial Provisions) Act 1963.

[54] Pt. VIII.

[55] Pt. III.

[56] Below, p. 426.

[57] See below, p. 424. This is the case of *Roberts* v. *Hopwood* [1925] AC 578, a classic example of the working of the former district audit system. See also *Asher* v. *Secretary of State for the Environment* [1974] Ch. 208; *Lloyd* v. *McMahon* [1987] 2 WLR 821. Contrast *Pickwell* v. *Camden LBC* [1983] QB 962.

[58] *Taylor* v. *Munrow* [1960] 1 WLR 151; below, p. 417.

[59] *Prescott* v. *Birmingham Cpn.* [1955] Ch. 210; below, p. 426.

The audit system

Audit of accounts has a special importance in the system of local government—and also in administrative law, since it is one of the mechanisms of judicial review. The audit system is the means whereby improper expenditure can not only be brought to light but also charged personally to the councillors or others responsible. The certainty that irregularities will be exposed and charged in the audit and brought home to their authors is often a more effective deterrent than the vague and imperfect responsibility of councillors to their ratepayers. Every councillor and official is thus made conscious of his personal liability.

From 1844 to 1982 the central figure in this system was the district auditor, an official of the Department of the Environment who was thus, in effect, a central government inspector.[60] In 1982 the corps of auditors was detached from the Department and put under the Audit Commission, a new statutory body appointed by the Secretary of State and substantially controlled by him since he may give it binding directions.[61] The Commission's chief officer is the Controller of Audit, and auditors may be either officers of the Commission or independent accountants. The Commission must maintain a code of practice which must be approved by each House of Parliament.

All accounts of a local authority and its committees, a parish meeting, a combined police or fire authority, and certain other bodies must be audited annually in accordance with the Act of 1982.[62] The commission, and likewise the Secretary of State, may also direct an extraordinary audit at the request of an elector or at their own motion.[63]

The accounts are open to inspection and any local government elector for the area (or his representative) may appear before the auditor and object to any item.[64] If it appears to the auditor 'that any item of account is contrary to law he may apply to the court for a declaration that the item is contrary to law except where it is sanctioned by the Secretary of State'.[65] If the court so declares, it may also order that any person responsible for incurring or authorising any expenditure shall repay it in whole or in part; and if the expenditure exceeds £2,000, the court may order that a member of a local authority be disqualified from membership for a specified period. Councillors who vote for improper expenditure can therefore be ordered

---

[60] Local Government Act 1972, s. 156, allowing alternatively choice of an auditor approved by the Secretary of State.
[61] Local Government Finance Act 1982, Pt. III.
[62] s. 12.
[63] s. 22.
[64] s. 17. Written notice must first be given.
[65] s. 19.

to repay it personally. But the court is not to make any order if satisfied that the person responsible 'acted reasonably or in the belief that the expenditure was authorised by law'; and in any case it must have regard to all the circumstances, including personal means and ability to repay.[66] Both the auditor and the court are thus given discretionary powers which they may find it difficult to know how to exercise. This is in contrast to the pre-1972 system, under which the auditor had a mandatory duty to disallow unlawful expenditure and to surcharge it upon those responsible, subject to appeal to the court or the Secretary of State,[67] either of whom might remit a surcharge if satisfied that the person responsible ought fairly to be excused.[68]

If the auditor finds a failure to bring in any sum (unless sanctioned by the Secretary of State) or any loss or deficiency caused by wilful misconduct, he must certify that recompense is due from the person responsible.[69] Appeal lies to the court both in this case and where the auditor declines to apply to the court under the preceding paragraph; in the latter case the appellant is the objecting elector.[70] The auditor may be required to state his reasons in writing.[71] He has also a general duty to consider whether to make a report for the information of the council or of the public.[72]

The Secretary of State's power to 'sanction' irregularities can protect their authors personally from the penalties of the audit system. But the Secretary of State has no general power to make unlawful expenditure lawful, or to legalise misconduct, and it remains open to ratepayers and others concerned to resort to the ordinary legal remedies, e.g. to challenge expenditure by applying to the High Court for an injunction or declaration against it. The availability of these remedies is explained elsewhere.[73]

The audit and its consequences provide a kind of judicial procedure for testing the legality of expenditure. The auditor is not concerned with questions of policy. He must carry out his statutory duties in a judicial and independent spirit much in the manner of a statutory tribunal; and the Secretary of State has no power to interfere, except by granting his 'sanction'. The audit has at various times provided a battleground for acute political strife, when councillors have deliberately disobeyed the law and

[66] s. 19(3).
[67] Appeal lay only to the court if the amount related to a surcharge exceeding £500.
[68] Local Government Act 1933, s. 229. For an unsuccessful ministerial intervention see *R v. Minister of Health* [1927] 1 KB 765.
[69] s. 20.
[70] s. 20(3).
[71] s. 20(2).
[72] s. 15(3).
[73] Below, p. 603.

have been surcharged with the financial consequences of their misdeeds. On two occasions Parliament has intervened by legislation to relieve them of personal liability for surcharges, once in 1927 when the borough councillors of Poplar were unable, or at least unwilling, to repay the cost of excessive rates of wages,[74] and once in 1975 when some twenty or more councils had refused to apply the 'fair rent' system to their council houses as required by the Housing Finance Act 1972.[75] These were occasions when the regular application of the legal machinery proved to be politically unacceptable—in other words, when political rebellion succeeded. It is therefore not surprising that the Act of 1972 made the legal machinery more discretionary. Since then what may in some cases be essentially political questions have been put into the sole hands of the courts, the Secretary of State (except for his power to sanction) having no longer a part in the drama.

Political publicity

As a result of complaints about what was called 'overt political campaigning at public expense' by some local authorities the Local Government Act 1986 prohibited the publication by a local authority of any material which appeared to be designed to affect public support for a political party.[76] The Act also restricted the range of information which a local authority had power to publish, confining it to information about services and functions in its area. Prior to this legislation the courts had held that it was unlawful for local authorities to engage advertising agencies for the purpose of campaigning against government policy and legislation passing through Parliament, since their statutory power to publish information did not extend to attempts to persuade the public to agree with their politics.[77]

Byelaws

The Act of 1972 confers a wide power upon district and London borough councils 'to make byelaws[78] for the good rule and government of the whole or any part of the district or borough, as the case may be, and for the

---

[74] Audit (Local Authorities) Act 1927, s. 2(6).
[75] Housing Finance (Special Provisions] Act 1975.
[76] s. 2, prohibiting also financial support for such publication.
[77] *R v. Inner London Education Authority ex p Westminster City Council* [1986] 1 WLR 28; *R v. Greater London Council ex p Westminster City Council* [1985] The Times, 22 January.
[78] This is the statutory spelling, but 'by-law' is common, as in by-election, by-product, etc., 'by' meaning secondary. The original derivation may be from 'byr', meaning village or town, or from 'by', meaning town.

prevention and suppression of nuisances therein'.[79] This general power is not enjoyed by other authorities, but many statutes have conferred byelaw-making powers for particular purposes such as public health, housing and highways.[80] Furthermore, the general power given by the Act of 1972 may not be invoked where there is byelaw-making power under some other enactment.[81] It is therefore a residuary power merely.

Byelaws made under the Act of 1972 require confirmation by the Secretary of State,[82] and byelaws made under other Acts normally require ministerial confirmation.[83] They are therefore under firm central control. Confirming ministers issue model byelaws which local authorities will be expected to follow. Whether made under the Act of 1972 or otherwise, byelaws must be made under the authority's common seal and must be advertised and open to inspection for a month before the application for confirmation.[84] Unless some other Act authorises larger fines, the maximum penalty for infringement is a fine of £20 plus £5 per day for continuing offences.[85]

The law as to the validity of byelaws under the ultra vires doctrine is explained in the chapter on delegated legislation.

Central influence and control

After what has been said it is needless to emphasise that local government is subjected to central government in numerous and important ways. The Act of 1972 and other Acts conferring powers are shot through with restrictive provisions giving powers of yea or nay to the Secretary of State and ministers. After a review of the system in 1979[86] the Local Government, Planning and Land Act 1980 inaugurated a 'relaxation of controls',[87] repealing miscellaneous provisions requiring ministerial consent or allowing appeals to a minister and mitigating controls in various areas such as pollution, amenity, allotments and highways. But since at the same time the Act provided for sharply reduced rate support grants, and imposed new restrictions upon capital expenditure, its overall effect was to intensify central control. Since then the Local Government Finance Act

---

[79] s. 235.
[80] Public Health Act 1936 (e.g. ss. 61, 81, 104); Housing Act 1985, s. 23; Highways Act 1980, s. 186.
[81] s. 235(3).
[82] ss. 235(2), 236(7).
[83] See Act of 1972, s. 236(1), (7).
[84] s. 236(4), (5).
[85] s. 237.
[86] Cmnd. 7634 (1979) (White Paper).
[87] Pt. I; and see ss. 183, 188.

1982 and the Rates Act 1984 have given the central government a stranglehold on local authority revenue and expenditure.

Despite the lip-service paid to the need for financial independence, and the policy of reducing the number of earmarked grants, it is through financial administration that the central government's control makes itself most felt. The 'appropriate minister' may make regulations for prescribing standards and general requirements in relation to any function of a local authority,[88] and if he is satisfied that a local authority has fallen short of a reasonable standard, regard being had to any such regulations, he may, after hearing their representations, reduce their grant—though subject to the approval of the House of Commons.[89] With these powers in the background the central government is in a strong position to make its wishes felt in innumerable ways. It can restrict the authority's income by rate-capping. It can exercise tight control over capital expenditure, both through the power to withhold loan sanction and by restricting aggregate expenditure. It has control over the remaining earmarked grants.[90] It may make regulations as to all the details of accounts and audit.[91] In both great matters and small it maintains a powerful financial grip.

There is an abundance of other means of control also. In many matters ministers may give mandatory directions.[92] Departmental inspectors can keep a close watch on the schools, the fire service, and the police. Compulsory purchase of land is subject to ministerial approval.[93] So is the making of byelaws. So is the appointment of certain officers such as senior police officers.[94] So is the making of administrative schemes for certain services, such as school development plans.[95] So are a number of transactions in land.[96] These are only a few examples out of many. Ministers can also bring pressure to bear through their general powers to hold inquiries[97] and by giving advice and instructions in departmental circulars, which issue frequently to local authorities and are in many cases published.

Behind this powerful battery of weapons lies the ultimate sanction, the default power. This enables the minister, if he considers that the local

---

[88] Local Government Act 1974, s. 5(2).
[89] s. 5(1).
[90] e.g. housing grants may be made subject to any conditions: Housing Act 1985, 15th sched., Pt. II. Act 1958, s. 28.
[91] Act of 1972, s. 166.
[92] See also the wide supplementary power to make orders under Local Government Act 1972, s. 254.
[93] Below, p. 172.
[94] Below, p. 143.
[95] Education Act 1944, s. 11.
[96] e.g. Local Government Act 1972, ss. 122(3), 123(4).
[97] e.g. Act of 1972, s. 250. See below, p. 988.

authority is failing to perform some function as it should, to make a legally enforceable order directing it what to do, or to take over its administration himself, or to put it into the hands of another authority such as a county council, charging the cost to the defaulting authority. There is no overall default power to be found in the Act of 1972. But such powers have long been a feature of particular Acts, and may be seen for example in the Public Health Act 1936,[98] the Education Act 1944[99] and the Housing Act 1985[1] in a variety of forms but all with the same general effect. The Housing Finance Act 1972 contained a special default power, now repealed, enabling the Secretary of State to appoint a Housing Commissioner to perform any specified functions of the local authority in default[2]—a power which he had to exercise within a short time against councils which refused to obey the Act.[3] This was an exceptional occasion when default powers were called into play, but it showed that they do not always remain in the background.

Default powers are of importance in administrative law because the courts sometimes regard them as a substitute for other remedies, as will be explained in due course.[4]

Joint boards for special purposes

Where there are special reasons for one authority to administer a larger area than a normal local government area, a statutory joint board may be established by ministerial order. Powers of this kind are given by the Public Health Act 1936,[5] the Education Act 1944,[6] the Police Act 1964,[7] the Transport Act 1968,[8] the Town and Country Planning Act 1971,[9] and other Acts. Unlike joint committees of local authorities, these joint boards have their own corporate existence and their own powers, including the power to issue precepts for raising revenue through the rates. Normally, as under the Education Act and the Town and Country Planning Act, joint boards are composed of members of the local authorities in the area, nominated by those authorities themselves. But sometimes, as under the

---

[98] ss. 171–7.
[99] s. 99.
[1] s. 164 (the 'right to buy'). See *R* v. *Secretary of State for the Environment ex p. Norwich CC* [1982] QB 808.
[2] s. 95.
[3] See below, p. 748.
[4] See below, p. 747.
[5] s. 6 (united port health districts).
[6] s. 6 and 1st sched. (joint education boards).
[7] s. 3 (combined police authorities).
[8] s. 9 and 5th sched. (passenger transport authorities).
[9] s. 1 and 1st sched. (joint planning boards); see below, p. 184.

Transport Act, the minister may appoint some of the members; and under the Police Act, in accordance with the long-standing system, a third of the members of a combined police authority must be magistrates.

Water authorities

A new and independent system of water authorities, organised more like a nationalised industry than local authorities, was introduced by the Water Act 1973, which took effect in 1974 simultaneously with the Local Government Act 1972. The Act established ten regional water authorities for England and Wales, with the object of making them responsible for every part of the 'water cycle', including not only water supply but also water conservation, prevention of river pollution, sewerage and water disposal, land drainage, fisheries, and the use of inland waters for navigation and recreation. This has involved the take-over from local authorities of water supply, sewerage, and sewage disposal services, though the Act provides for sewage services to be supplied by district councils on the water authorities' behalf.[10]

Ministerial responsibility is divided between the Secretary of State for the Environment and the Minister of Agriculture, Fisheries and Food.[11] Between them they appoint the chairman and a number of the members of the water authorities, the relevant local authorities themselves appointing the other members, who need not be councillors.[12] The constitution of the water authorities is therefore much less democratic than that of local authorities. The two ministers may give them directions of a general character within their respective spheres.[13] They obtain their revenue through the rates by precepting upon district councils,[14] and have powers to make byelaws with ministerial approval. There is also a National Water Council with advisory and supervisory functions.[15]

COMPLAINTS AGAINST LOCAL GOVERNMENT

The ombudsman system extended

In 1974 the ombudsman system, which had been in operation since 1967 for the central government,[16] was extended to complaints against local authorities. There had been criticism of the fact that the Parliamentary

[10] s. 15.
[11] s. 1. The latter minister is responsible for land drainage and fisheries.
[12] s. 3.
[13] s. 5.
[14] See *Daymond* v. *Plymouth City Council* [1976] AC 609.
[15] s. 4.
[16] See above, p. 80.

Commissioner Act 1967 excluded all local authorities from its scope. This omission was made good by the Local Government Act 1974,[17] which took effect on 1 April 1974 along with the reorganisation of local government and the national health service. The legislation of 1974 is in many respects similar to that of 1967, so that this account of it need do little more than point out the main differences.

The Act of 1974 established two Commissions for Local Administration, one for England and one for Wales. The Parliamentary Commissioner for Administration is a member of both Commissions, but otherwise they consist of Local Commissioners appointed by the Crown, either full-time or part-time, and holding office, like the Parliamentary Commissioner, during good behaviour until retiring age.[18] For Scotland there is a single Commissioner for Local Administration, under separate legislation.[19] The English Commission at present consists of three Local Commissioners, each of whom covers one area of the country: one for London, the South-East and East Anglia; one for the North and North Midlands; and one for the rest of England.[20]

These Local Commissioners can deal with complaints against any local authority (including its committees, members, and officers), except a parish council.[21] Their jurisdiction also extends to any joint board composed exclusively of local authorities; to water authorities; and to police authorities (other than the Home Secretary, who falls under the Act of 1967),[22] and to certain others.[23] But they are not 'Parliamentary' commissioners, except in the sense that their work is of concern to the House of Commons' Select Committee on the Parliamentary Commissioner for Administration, who have several times taken evidence from them and given them support.[24]

Complaints, investigations and reports

As under the Act of 1967, the complainant must be a member of the public[25] who claims to have sustained injustice in consequence of

[17] Pt. III, subject to miscellaneous amendments made by Local Government Act 1988, 3rd sched.
[18] s. 23. The Crown may remove a Local Commissioner for incapacity or misbehaviour.
[19] Local Government (Scotland) Act 1975, Pt. II
[20] See *The Local Ombudsman* (the annual report of the English Commission).
[21] Local Government Act 1974, ss. 25, 34(1), as extended by Act of 1988, 3rd sched., para. 4. A parish council is included if acting for a county or district council: s. 25(4).
[22] s. 25.
[23] New town and urban development bodies, and the development board for rural Wales, were added by Local Government Act 1988, 3rd sched.
[24] See HC 254 (1979–80).
[25] Including a company or body of persons but excluding a local authority or government department: s. 27(1).

maladministration done in the exercise of the authority's administrative functions.[26] The complaint must be made in writing either to a Local Commissioner direct (as now allowed by the Act of 1988) or else to a member of the authority 'specifying the action alleged to constitute maladministration'.[27] In order to make sense of that expression the Court of Appeal has held that the complaint need only specify the action in connection with which the maladministration is alleged.[28] And, in any case, the Commissioner has power to determine conclusively whether a complaint is duly made.[29]

A member of a local authority receiving a complaint must refer it to a Local Commissioner, so that, unlike an MP under the Act of 1967, the member has no function as a 'filter' to eliminate ineligible complaints. If the Commissioner is satisfied that any such member has refused to refer it, he may if he thinks fit accept it direct from the complainant.[30] By contrast with the Act of 1967, therefore, there were discretionary arrangements for direct access to the local ombudsman under the Act of 1974. In 1984 a new practice was introduced whereby a complaint made direct, without prior reference to a member, was sent by the Commissioner to the civic head of the local authority with a request to refer it back to the Commissioner if it could not be settled by agreement.[31] Another difference is that the complainant must first have given the local authority a reasonable opportunity to investigate and reply to the complaint.[32]

There are provisions similar to those of the Act of 1967 for excluding cases where there is a remedy before a court of law or statutory tribunal, but they extend also to cases where there is a right of appeal to a minister, for example on a refusal of planning permission; and there is the same discretionary exception for cases where the Commissioner is satisfied that it is not reasonable to expect recourse to the legal remedy.[33] A Local Commissioner likewise has full discretion to decide whether to pursue a

[26] s. 26(1). A suitable representative may act on behalf of a complainant who has died or cannot act for himself: s. 27(2).

[27] s. 26(2) as amended by Act of 1988, 3rd sched., para. 5, which retains the expression quoted.

[28] R v. Local Commissioner for Administration ex p. Bradford MCC [1979] QB 287, refusing an application by the local authority to prohibit the Commissioner from investigating complaints by a mother who had unsuccessfully attempted to recover her children taken into care by the authority. In R v. Local Commissioner ex p. Eastleigh BC [1988] The Times, 15 March, the Court of Appeal declared that a Commissioner had exceeded his powers.

[29] s. 26(10).

[30] s. 26(2), (3). This happened in the Bradford case, above.

[31] Annual Report, 1985, p. 30.

[32] s. 26(5).

[33] s. 26(6). Like the Parliamentary Commissioner, the Local Commissioners appear to accept many cases where there would be legal remedies, e.g. where councillors with personal interests deal with planning applications: see Annual Report, 1981, p. 9.

complaint.[34] But he may not do so if it appears to affect all or most of the
inhabitants of the authority's area;[35] as for instance does the fixing of the
level of rates. There is the same prohibition as in the Act of 1967 against
questioning the merits of a discretionary decision taken without
maladministration.[36]

The rules as to investigations, and the powers given to Local
Commissioners for this purpose, are similar to those of the Act of 1967. The
report of an investigation must be sent to the complainant, the local
authority and the member who referred it originally; but it may not
identify, or contain particulars likely to identify, any person, unless the
Commissioner considers that necessary.[37] There are special arrangements
for publicising the report: the local authority must advertise it and then
make it available for public inspection (including copying) for three
weeks.[38] Information obtained in an investigation must not otherwise be
disclosed.[39] Either a minister of the Crown or a local authority may by
written notice prevent any disclosure of information or documents
(whether specific or a class) by the Commissioner or his staff on the ground
that this would be contrary to the public interest, but a local authority's
notice may be discharged by the Secretary of State.[40] The Commissioner
must give a month's notice to any government department which has
supplied information before using that information in a report,[41] so that the
department may consider whether to prevent its disclosure. Where an
investigation may overlap the jurisdiction of the Parliamentary Commissioner or the Health Service Commissioner, the Commissioners may
consult together.[42] In 1978 local authorities were empowered to pay
compensation for injustice caused by maladministration without having to
seek ministerial sanction on each occasion.[43]

Each Local Commissioner must make a general report annually to his
Commission.[44] Each Commission must similarly make an annual report to
a representative body of local authorities designated by the Secretary of

[34] s. 26(10).
[35] s. 26(7).
[36] s. 34(3).
[37] s. 30(1), (3).
[38] s. 30(4), (5).
[39] s. 32(2).
[40] s. 32(3), as amended by Local Government, Planning and Land Act 1980, s. 184.
Previously such a notice prevented disclosure to the Commissioner (*Re Liverpool City
Council* [1977] 1 WLR 995), but now he is put into the same position as the Parliamentary
Commissioner and there can be no restriction on disclosure to him.
[41] s. 32(5).
[42] s. 33.
[43] Local Government Act 1978.
[44] s. 23(11).

State, which must then publish it, with or without comments.[45] Each Commission must annually review the working of the system, and make its views known to local authorities through the representative body.[46] The Commission in England publishes these various reports and comments in its annual reports under the title *The Local Ombudsman*.

The Local Commissioners have on the whole had good success in obtaining satisfaction for the many injustices that they have found. But they have had more cause than the Parliamentary Commissioner to complain about recalcitrance in making amends. The Commission have recommended that there should be a remedy enforceable by a court of law, as in Northern Ireland,[47] and the House of Commons' Select Committee has suggested that the Committee itself should call refractory local authorities to account.[48] The Commissioners have also recommended, inter alia, that they should have jurisdiction over certain contractual, commercial, and personnel matters, that they should be able to act on their own initiative, and that complainants should be allowed direct access to them.[49] But none of these reforms has found favour with the government.[50]

Subjects excluded

There is a list of subjects which a Local Commissioner may not investigate,[51] which comprises:

legal proceedings;
investigation or prevention of crime;
contractual or commercial transactions, including passenger transport, docks and harbours, entertainments, industrial establishments and markets; but excluding the acquisition or disposal of land and certain statutory functions other than the procurement of goods and services;
personnel matters, including appointments, removals, pay, discipline, and superannuation;
educational matters, whether in maintained schools, colleges, or establishments for further education, including matters of conduct, curriculum, management, or discipline.

The Commission is dissatisfied with several of these exclusions, as already mentioned.

[45] s. 24.
[46] s. 23(12).
[47] Annual Report, 1987, p. 31.
[48] HC 448 (1985–6), para. 31. For a list of recalcitrant authorities see 122 HC Deb 679 (20 November 1987).
[49] Annual Report, 1985, p. 46. For supporting recommendations see Report on the Conduct of Local Authority Business (the Widdicombe Committee), Cmnd. 9797 (1986).
[50] Annual Report, 1986, p. 50.
[51] Act of 1974, s. 26(8) and 5th sched.

Results

Results for the last five years of the work of the Commission in England are shown in the table.

	1983	1984	1985	1986	1987
1. Complaints duly referred	2753	3034	3389	3502	4059
2. Investigations completed	2763	3019	3284	3134	3866
3. Maladministration with injustice found	1224	1426	1619	1097	1141
4. Satisfactory settlement obtained	1075	1244	1442	954	961
5. 3 as percentage of 2	44	47	49	35	30
6. 4 as percentage of 3	88	86	89	87	84

The great majority of complaints to the Commission concern planning and housing.

5

THE POLICE

Local police forces

The outstanding fact about the British police is that, except in London, they are not under the direct control of the central government: they are organised in local forces maintained by local authorities. The central government has effective regulatory power, reinforced by financial control, which ensures that, for example, the pay, dress, allowances, and other conditions of service in the police force are uniform throughout the country. But it has no power to give orders directly to local forces, and local chief constables have a high degree of independence from any kind of political control. This is an important facet of the constitution, and a prime safeguard against the evils of the police state. The Royal Commission of 1962, in a wide-ranging report, discounted the idea that a centralised police force would endanger liberty, and stressed rather the value of the association between local forces and local communities as its reason for recommending no change.[1] Nevertheless the aversion to a single state force in this country is deep-seated.

The reason for this independence is that the modern police system, replacing the inefficient system of constables inherited from the middle ages, was devised in the golden age of political liberty in the nineteenth century. In London the Metropolitan Police were established in 1829 and were put under the Home Secretary's control—where they remain to this day. The next step was to establish borough police forces as part of the general reform of the boroughs, but so lively was the fear of creating a government-controlled gendarmerie that each borough was made responsible for its own force by the Municipal Corporations Act 1835. The City of London, untouched by that Act, obtained its police in 1839 and kept control of them itself within its small enclave in the metropolitan area. The county justices were empowered to form county police forces in 1839, and were obliged to do so in 1856.

The weakness of this scheme of things lay in the numerous small borough forces. The solution was to merge them into the county forces,

---

[1] Royal Commission on the Police, Final Report, Cmnd. 1728 (1962), paras. 147–9. This Report is a mine of information on the evolution and administration of the police. For powerful advocacy of a single unified force see the memorandum of dissent by Professor A. L. Goodhart QC.

and this process was virtually completed by the Police Act 1946. Under the Police Act 1964, which followed the Report of the Royal Commission, police forces outside London were based on counties and county boroughs; but since some of those authorities were themselves too small to sustain efficient forces, the Act provided for both voluntary and compulsory amalgamation schemes, subject to the control of the Home Secretary. Under these powers large composite forces were formed and many of the smaller forces were exterminated. Finally the police had to be integrated with the enlarged local government areas which came into operation in 1974 under the Local Government Act 1972. This reform made it possible to transfer many of the amalgamated forces to the new and enlarged counties and metropolitan counties. The total number of forces in England and Wales is now reduced to forty-one, having been 123 at the time of the Royal Commission in 1961. Within this total the number of amalgamated forces (such as Thames Valley and West Mercia) fell from thirty-five to seven. Even so, it cannot yet be said that there is any prospect of a single state police force.

Administration and appointments

Local councils do not themselves administer their police forces directly, but must act through statutory police authorities, known as police committees. These committees are composed as to two-thirds of councillors, appointed by their councils, and as to one-third of magistrates, appointed by quarter sessions.[2] It was only under the Police Act 1964 that magistrates were admitted to the police authorities of boroughs, traditionally known as watch committees, all of which have now disappeared. But magistrates had always played an important part in the government of the county police. Originally the county justices were the sole county police authorities under the Act of 1839. But when most of their administrative work was transferred to the new county councils in 1888, they continued to provide half the members of the county police committee, then known as the standing joint committee. In Scotland magisterial participation has been abolished since 1929.[3] But England has preserved the link with the justices and has now extended it to all police authorities, with a uniform share of membership of one-third. The one exceptional case is London, where the Home Secretary himself is the police authority for the Metropolitan Police.

Chief constables and deputy[4] and assistant chief constables are appointed

---

[2] Police Act 1964, s. 2.
[3] See now Police (Scotland) Act 1956, s. 2.
[4] The office of deputy chief constable was abolished by the Police and Criminal Evidence Act 1984, s. 108, but every force must have an officer of the rank of deputy chief constable.

by the police authority, subject to the Home Secretary's approval. Lower ranks are appointed by the chief constable, subject to the Home Secretary's regulations.[5] With the Home Secretary's approval the police authority may require a chief constable or deputy or assistant chief constable to retire in the interests of efficiency.[6]

Central control

Along with much local autonomy there is much central control. Under the Police Act 1964[7] the Home Secretary has a general duty to promote the efficiency of the police; and he may make regulations 'as to the government, administration and conditions of service of police forces', covering (inter alia) qualifications, discipline, hours of duty, leave, pay and clothing. Parliament has thus conferred very wide regulatory power, which has been freely used. Regulations on such matters as hours of duty, pay, and clothing must be submitted in draft to the Police Council, a statutory body representing the interests both of members of the police forces and the police authorities, and their representations must be considered.[8] Regulations on certain other matters must similarly be submitted to a Police Advisory Board.[9] Regulations have imposed a uniform code for the administration of the numerous forces, and have made great inroads on local independence.[10] The Home Secretary is armed with other important powers, such as to require the police authority to retire a chief constable or a deputy or assistant chief constable in the interests of efficiency.[11] He can also fall back on the royal prerogative to provide for the peace of the realm, which has been held to entitle him to supply a police force with special riot equipment which the local police authority do not wish them to have.[12]

Controversy sometimes arises when the Home Secretary refuses consent to the appointment of a chief constable from within the same force. The Home Secretary's policy is to prevent 'inbreeding' by insisting that every chief constable should have had experience in a senior post in another force,[13] whereas the local police authority will often wish to appoint an

---

[5] ss. 7, 33.
[6] Police Act 1964, ss. 5(4), 33(3). The officer has a right to be heard both by the police authority and by the Home Secretary: ss. 5(5), 29(2).
[7] s. 33.
[8] s. 45(4).
[9] s. 46(3).
[10] See SI 1987 No. 851 (general) and SI 1985 Nos. 518, 519 (discipline).
[11] s. 29, giving the officer a right to a hearing.
[12] *R. v. Home Secretary ex p. Northumbria Police Authority* [1987] 2 WLR 998.
[13] Regulations require at least two years' service in another force in the rank of inspector or above.

officer who has had long service under them. In practice the police
authority will submit their short list of applicants to the Home Office and
will be informed in advance if they are unacceptable. It has been known for
the Home Office to threaten to withhold the grant (see below) in cases
where the police authority has resisted the Home Secretary's policy of
interchange.[14]

Finance supplies another instrument of central control, perhaps the most
efficient of all. The central government has for over a century made a grant
in aid of the cost of police services, which since 1918 has been 50 per cent.
No local authority can afford to dispense with this assistance. But, as the
price of it, its force must be certified as efficient by an inspector of
constabulary, who is an officer of the Crown; and the government may
withhold the grant wholly or partially unless satisfied that the force is
efficient and that the regulations are being duly observed. These
arrangements apply equally to the City of London Police. The
Metropolitan Police in London, though partly financed out of local rates,
are directly under the Home Secretary as police authority. The central
government can thus keep all police forces under close inspection and
control. In particular, the size of each local force is effectively decided in
Whitehall.

Nevertheless, a clear distinction is made between general regulation of
conditions of service and interference with the daily duties of the police in
enforcing the law. Ministers expressly recognise the principle that the
police are independent in their task of preserving law and order. No
ministerial responsibility is acknowledged for specific things that the police
do. The position is not quite the same in London, since the Home Secretary
in practice accepts a responsibility for the Metropolitan Police which may
be wider than his legal responsibilities strictly require,[15] or it may be that
this is attributable to the terms of the original Metropolitan Police Act
1829. As regards the rest of the country, the absence of ministerial
responsibility puts obstacles in the way of members of Parliament wishing
to criticise or discuss police administration and conduct. The Royal
Commission of 1962 recommended that ministers should be given
statutory responsibility for the efficiency of the police, though not for their
day-to-day actions.[16] This was why the Act of 1964 required the Home
Secretary to exercise his powers so as 'to promote the efficiency of the
police',[17] but this hardly alters the previous state of affairs.

---

[14] See Report of the Royal Commission, Cmnd 1728 (1962), para. 168. For an
unsuccessful challenge to the Home Secretary's policy see *Kilmarnock Magistrates* v. *Secretary
of State for Scotland* 1961 SC 350.

[15] Royal Commission's Report, Cmnd. 1728, para. 91.

[16] Para. 230.

[17] s. 28.

Legal status and responsibility of police officers

In their ordinary daily acts and decisions the police are as independent of the local police authority as they are of the central government. It is a mistake to suppose that because they do not take orders from the central government, therefore they must take orders from the police authority. The truth is that a police officer holds a public position, that of peace officer, in which he owes obedience to no executive power outside the police force. The chain of command therefore terminates at the chief constable, who is in effect an independent authority,[18] and must act free from all political influence, whether national or local. Despite all the regulatory powers which the central and local authorities share between them, the responsibility for deciding whether (for example) the police shall arrest or prosecute some particular person cannot rest upon any one but the police themselves. As it was put in an Australian case:[19]

The powers of a constable qua peace officer, whether conferred by common or statute law, are exercised by him by virtue of his office and cannot be exercised on the responsibility of any person but himself.

In the leading English case, where the police had by mistake arrested the wrong man on a criminal charge, an action for damages against the local police authority met with no success because the police, in making such an arrest, were acting on their own responsibility and not as servants of the local authority.[20] The legal link which could make the local authority liable was therefore missing. The position of a police officer was thus described by McCardie J:

He is a servant of the State, a ministerial officer of the central power, though subject, in some respects, to local supervision and local regulation.

And again:

The police, in effecting that arrest and detention, were not acting as the servants or agents of the defendants. They were fulfilling their duties as public servants and officers of the Crown sworn to 'preserve the peace by day and by night, to prevent robberies and other felonies and misdemeanours and to apprehend offenders against the peace'.

To show the position still more graphically, the learned judge said:

[18] See the Royal Commission's Report, Cmnd. 1728, para. 106. Both local and central authorities may call for reports under the Police Act 1964, ss. 12, 30.

[19] Griffith CJ in *Enever* v. *The King* (1906) 3 CLR 969, an Australian case cited in *Fisher* v. *Oldham Cpn.* (below).

[20] *Fisher* v. *Oldham Cpn.* [1930] 2 KB 364.

Suppose that a police officer arrested a man for a serious felony. Suppose, too, that the watch committee of the borough at once passed a resolution directing that the felon should be released. Of what value would such a resolution be? Not only would it be the plain duty of the police officer to disregard the resolution, but it would also be the duty of the chief constable to consider whether an information should not at once be laid against the members of the watch committee for a conspiracy to obstruct the course of criminal justice.

The Privy Council approved these passages in an Australian case,[21] and added:

To-day, as in the past, he (the police officer) is in common parlance described in terms which aptly define his legal position as 'a police officer', 'an officer of justice', 'an officer of the peace'. If ever he is called a servant, it is in the same sense in which any holder of a public office may be called a servant of the Crown or of the State.

The State of New South Wales here attempted unsuccessfully to show that a police officer was their servant, but the Privy Council made it clear that their contention was just as fallacious as the contention that the police are servants of local authorities. They do indeed hold office under the Crown: when appointed they swear that they will well and truly serve the sovereign in the office of constable. And a policeman has been held to be 'a person holding office under His Majesty' so as to make information obtained from him subject to the Official Secrets Acts.[22] But the oath no more makes him a servant of the Crown, in the sense of the relationship of master and servant, than does the oath taken by a judge.[23] For purposes of legal liability the constable in his functions as an officer of the peace is the servant of no one, neither of the Crown nor of the local authority nor of the chief constable.

Although the police have many statutory powers, their primary powers and duties as peace officers have long been based upon common law. Their general powers of arrest without warrant were however made statutory by the Criminal Law Act 1967,[24] and it has been held that their ordinary functions are 'statutory powers or duties' because the Police Regulations 1971 require them to perform all duties and attend to all matters within the scope of their office.[25]

---

[21] A.-G. for New South Wales v. Perpetual Trustee Co. Lt. [1955] AC 457 at 480; Griffiths v. Haines [1984] 3 NSWLR 653; cf. Wilts Police Authority v. Wynn [1981] QB 95 (police cadet not 'employee').

[22] Lewis v. Cattle [1938] 2 KB 454. See also Loat v. Andrews [1986] ICR 679, extending the definition to a local government employee working with the police.

[23] See above, p. 75.

[24] s. 2.

[25] George v. Garland [1980] RTR 77.

Independence of chief constables

The authorities just quoted apply with special force to a chief constable, since he has command over his force but no one has command over him. Lord Denning MR cited them with approval in describing the position of the Commissioner of the Metropolitan Police:[26]

The office of Commissioner of Police within the Metropolis dates back to 1829 when Sir Robert Peel introduced his disciplined force. The commissioner was a justice of the peace specially appointed to administer the police force in the metropolis. His constitutional status has never been defined either by statute or by the courts. It was considered by the Royal Commission on the Police in their Report in 1962 (Cmnd. 1728). But I have no hesitation in holding that, like every constable in the land, he should be, and is, independent of the executive. He is not subject to the orders of the Secretary of State, save that under the Police Act, 1964, the Secretary of State can call upon him to give a report, or to retire in the interests of efficiency. I hold it to be the duty of the Commissioner of Police of the Metropolis, as it is of every chief constable, to enforce the law of the land. He must take steps so to post his men that crimes may be detected; and that honest citizens may go about their affairs in peace. He must decide whether or no suspected persons are to be prosecuted; and, if need be, bring the prosecution or see that it is brought. But in all these things he is not the servant of anyone, save of the law itself. No Minister of the Crown can tell him that he must, or must not, keep observation on this place or that; or that he must, or must not, prosecute this man or that one. Nor can any police authority tell him so. The responsibility for law enforcement lies on him. He is answerable to the law and to the law alone.

Lord Denning went on to consider how far the law would interfere with a chief constable's exercise of his discretionary powers, saying:

For instance, it is for the Commissioner of Police of the Metropolis, or the chief constable, as the case may be, to decide in any particular case whether inquiries should be pursued, or whether an arrest should be made, or a prosecution brought. It must be for him to decide on the disposition of his force and the concentration of his resources on any particular crime or area. No court can or should give him direction on such a matter. He can also make policy decisions and give effect to them, as, for instance, was often done when prosecutions were not brought for attempted suicide. But there are some policy decisions with which, I think, the courts in a case can, if necessary, interfere. Suppose a chief constable were to issue a directive to his men that no person should be prosecuted for stealing any goods less than £100 in value. I should have thought that the court could countermand it. He would be failing in his duty to enforce the law.

This question of judicial control of the powers and duties of chief

[26] R. v. *Metropolitan Police Commissioner ex p. Blackburn* [1968] 2 QB 118 at 135. See also R. v. *Devon and Cornwall Chief Constable ex p. CEGB* [1982] QB 458.

constables will recur later, in connection with discretionary powers generally.[27]

Financial responsibility

Since police officers are nobody's servants in the exercise of their peace-keeping functions, it follows that no one is liable at common law for their misdeeds in the capacity of their employer. But if there were no way of charging to public funds the liability for wrongs committed by individual police officers, serious injury might be done and there might be no defendant worth suing. It was therefore the practice for the police authority to stand behind its police officers and pay the damages, much as the Crown used to do for its servants in the days before the Crown Proceedings Act 1947.[28] The Royal Commission recommended that, by analogy with that Act, the police authority should be given legal liability.[29] The Police Act 1964 in effect so provides in the case of subordinate police officers, by making them notional servants of the chief constable for purposes of liability and by requiring any damages or costs so awarded against the chief constable to be paid out of the police fund.[30] But this does not impose liability on any one else for the misdeeds of the chief constable himself. There is merely a general provision that the police authority 'may' pay damages or costs awarded against a member of their force, charging them to the police fund.[31] A chief constable, therefore, has no legal assurance that his police authority will stand behind him, though the Act now provides a legal basis for the practice of doing so.

It should be remembered that the legal independence of a police officer at common law is due to the special nature of his duties as a peace officer. It is possible that constables performing other duties might be held to be acting on behalf of other persons. Cases of that kind have occurred in South Africa, where the government have been held liable for careless driving by a constable ordered to take charge of a vehicle, and for negligent custody by a constable of an arrested person's motor-car.[32]

Relations with the public

It is impossible to examine the cases on the status of the police without marvelling at how few they are, and in how many respects their position

[27] Below, p. 403.
[28] The practice is described by the Royal Commission, Cmnd. 1728 (1962), para. 196. As to the Crown, see below, p. 812.
[29] Report (as above), para. 201.
[30] s. 48.
[31] s. 48(4).
[32] *Union Government* v. *Thorne* (1930) AD 47; *Lawrie* v. *Union Government* (1930) TPD 402.

and powers are still not clearly defined. The police have had remarkable success in avoiding challenge in the courts of law, even though they often stretch their powers and risk actions for trespass.[33] Yet the law does not give them wide discretionary powers: they must, for example, depose as to facts on oath before they can obtain a warrant for arrest; and in the cases where they may arrest a man without a warrant, they must be prepared to prove at least reasonable grounds for suspicion.[34] If they seize documents without legal warrant, the court will order them to be restored.[35] Like all other governmental agencies, they must show legal authority for what they do. Their independent position has no doubt contributed to their ability to avoid legal involvement.

In the last thirty years the standing of the police in the public eye has deteriorated in three ways. First, a series of cases in the 1950s brought to light malpractice and corruption. This led to the appointment of the Royal Commission which reported in 1962, but the problem persisted for some time thereafter. Secondly, in the 1970s bad relations developed between the police and immigrant communities in London and other big cities where there was much street crime, reaching a climax with the riots of 1981. Thirdly, there has been general dissatisfaction with the handling of complaints against the police (see next section). Lord Scarman's report on the Brixton riots[36] made a number of recommendations about training, discipline, and policing methods, and also about police–community relations, which the government accepted. Police authorities now have a statutory duty to make arrangements for obtaining the views of people in their area about policing and for obtaining their co-operation with the police in preventing crime.[37]

Complaints and discipline

The police are a disciplined force and have always been in charge of their own discipline, including the investigation of complaints, which is the responsibility of the chief constable.[38] But this makes them judges in their own cause, with the result that many complainants are left dissatisfied.[39]

---

[33] See *Ghani* v. *Jones* [1970] 1 QB 693 at 705.
[34] Police and Criminal Evidence Act 1984, ss. 24, 25.
[35] *Ghani* v. *Jones* (above).
[36] *The Brixton Disorders, 10–12 April 1981*, Cmnd. 8427.
[37] Police and Criminal Evidence Act 1984, s. 106.
[38] In the Metropolitan Police disciplinary cases are heard by senior officers, with a right of appeal to the Commissioner: 90 HC Deb. col. 2084 (5 December 1975).
[39] The problem is graphically illustrated by the Mars-Jones Report, Cmnd. 2526 (1964): see pp. 4, 122, 125. Senior police officers wishing to criticise the complaints procedure in evidence to the Royal Commission were deterred by the risk of endangering their careers and pensions: Cmnd. 2526, p. 55.

The institution of the Parliamentary Commissioner for Administration (ombudsman) has naturally led to a demand for some equally impartial system in the case of the police. A minority of the Royal Commission wished to see complaints handled by an independent ombudsman-type authority.[40] Occasionally an exceptional case may be made the subject of an independent inquiry[41] or even of a statutory tribunal of inquiry,[42] but these procedures are quite unsuitable for regular use.

There is little difficulty over the disciplinary procedure for chief constables (meaning all above the rank of chief superintendent), since proceedings must be held before an independent tribunal consisting of a person chosen by the police authority from a panel nominated by the Lord Chancellor, assisted by one or more assessors.[43] The tribunal sits in private, but if there is a complainant he may attend and put questions to the accused, at the tribunal's discretion. The tribunal makes a report to the police authority, who decide whether the accused should be dismissed, required to resign, or reprimanded. He has a right of appeal to the Home Secretary.[44] But this procedure operates only after disciplinary charges have been brought. It does not provide for the investigation of complaints. In the case of lower ranks the disciplinary and complaints procedures pose additional problems, since there is a conflict between the chief constable's disciplinary authority over his force and the public's demand for independent adjudication of complaints.

The Police Act 1964 provided only that the chief constable must arrange for the investigation of every complaint; that he might (and should if so directed by the Home Secretary) request the chief constable of another police area to provide an officer to hold the investigation; and that, unless satisfied that there had been no criminal offence, he should send the report of every investigation to the Director of Public Prosecutions. These arrangements did not meet the criticism that complaints against the police were investigated only by the police themselves, without any independent element. The police themselves came to realise that some such element was necessary, if only to retain public confidence. But there was serious anxiety about its effect on morale, discipline, and the maintenance of standards.

After lengthy public controversy the Police Act 1976 was passed. It established a central Police Complaints Board to which every chief constable was required to send the reports of investigations. The Board had power to recommend, and in the last resort to direct, the bringing of

[40] Cmnd. 1728 (1962), Appendix V.
[41] e.g. the Mars-Jones Report (above).
[42] e.g. Cmnd. 718 (1959). For this procedure see below, p. 1000.
[43] Police (Discipline) (Senior Officers) Regulations 1985, SI No. 519.
[44] Police Act 1964, s. 37, as amended by Police and Criminal Evidence Act 1984, s. 103; SI 1985 No. 576.

disciplinary charges, to be heard in serious cases by a tribunal consisting of the chief constable and two members of the Board in accordance with procedural regulations, with a right of appeal to the Home Secretary. But the new procedure failed to allay complaints that it was biased in favour of the police. Its defects were thought to have strained relations between the police and immigrant communities and to have contributed to the causes of the riots of 1981, and it once again became clear that an improved system would have to be devised. The outcome was Part IX of the Police and Criminal Evidence Act 1984.

This Act abolished the Police Complaints Board and in its place created the Police Complaints Authority, with a chairman appointed by the Crown and members appointed by the Home Secretary. No constable or former constable may be a member. Complaints against senior officers (above the rank of chief superintendent) are handled in the first instance by the local police authority (in London the Metropolitan Commissioner) and complaints against lower ranks by the chief constable. Failing settlement by conciliation, the authority or the chief constable must appoint one of their officers, or an officer from another force, to hold an investigation. The Police Complaints Authority is required to supervise the investigation of serious complaints, namely those involving death or serious injury, those specified in regulations,[45] and those referred to it by police authorities, chief constables, or the Commissioner.[46] They may also supervise other investigations where they think it desirable in the public interest. Their supervisory powers allow them to control the appointment of the police officer who is to conduct the investigation and to impose special requirements, and they must make a report on the conduct of the investigation to the referring authority after the investigating officer has himself made a report on it to them. The investigating officer's report on the complaint is made to the referring authority who must send a copy of it to the Director of Public Prosecutions unless satisfied that no criminal offence has been committed; but in the case of lower ranks the chief constable must decide whether the officer should be charged, and only if he so decides need he they report to the Director. In any event, in the case of lower ranks, the chief constable must inform the Authority whether he will bring disciplinary charges and if not, why not;[47] and the Authority may either refer the report on the complaint to the Director, or else direct the chief constable to prefer disciplinary charges.[48] Such charges are heard by a

[45] SI 1985 No. 673, specifying actual bodily harm, corruption, and a 'serious arrestable offence'.
[46] s. 89.
[47] s. 90.
[48] s. 93.

tribunal consisting of the chief constable and two members of the Authority who have not been concerned with the case.[49]

The Act makes many detailed provisions about procedures, about the receiving and recording of complaints, about their informal resolution where they are not serious enough for a prosecution or disciplinary charge, and about numerous matters to be prescribed by regulations.[50] The important facts about the new system are that the investigation of complaints is still carried out by the police themselves, but that the independent element, the new Authority, plays a larger part than before. The Authority can now monitor the whole procedure of formal investigations, though it remains to be seen whether their supervision will reassure public opinion sufficiently on the vital question of impartiality.

[49] s. 94.
[50] SI 1985 No. 518 (Police Discipline); No. 519 (Senior Officers—Discipline); No. 520 (Complaints—General); No. 671 (Complaints—Informal Resolution); No. 672 (Anonymous, Repetitious, etc., Complaints).

6

PUBLIC CORPORATIONS

GOVERNMENTAL CORPORATIONS

Use of corporate personality

As a legal organism the public corporation has many uses—so many, in fact, that it abounds at all levels of the governmental system.[1] It therefore has no regular form and no specialised function. It is employed wherever it is convenient to confer corporate personality. This may be done as much in the case of a government department as in that of a nationalised industry. Newly created government departments such as the Department of the Environment and the Department of Industry may be incorporated by making the Secretary of State a corporation sole, i.e. a corporation composed of a single person and his successors in office.[2] Local authorities are corporations aggregate, i.e. corporations composed of more than one person.[3] Many corporate bodies are cogs in the central government machine, such as the National Enterprise Board,[4] Regional Health Authorities,[5] the Housing Corporation,[6] and New Town Development Corporations.[7] There are other governmental or quasi-governmental corporations which are regulatory agencies, such as the Civil Aviation Authority,[8] the Independent Broadcasting Authority,[9] the Cable Authority,[10] and the National Dock Labour Board.[11] They shade off by degrees into many kinds of independent and more or less commercial bodies such as London Regional Transport,[12] Cable & Wireless Ltd. and British Petroleum Ltd. There is no stereotype.

Nevertheless the most conspicuous use of public corporations is as vehicles for the government's involvement in industry—an involvement

---

[1] For a synoptic (and selective) table see Garner, *Administrative Law*, 5th edn., 369.
[2] Above, p. 54.
[3] Above, p. 113.
[4] Industry Act 1975, s. 1. This Board is now inactive, as explained below.
[5] National Health Service Act 1977, 5th sched., para. 8.
[6] Housing Associations Act 1985, 1st sched.
[7] New Towns Act 1981, s. 3.
[8] Civil Aviation Act 1971.
[9] Independent Broadcasting Authority Act 1973.
[10] Cable and Broadcasting Act 1984.
[11] National Dock Work Regulation Act 1976.
[12] London Regional Transport Act 1984.

much reduced since 1979. Here too there is a wide spectrum, though with a common purpose. The corporations created for the nationalisation of industries such as the railways, coal, and electricity form one clearly recognisable class. Another class is composed of ordinary commercial companies in which the government has or had a shareholding, controlling or otherwise, such as Cable & Wireless Ltd. (wholly government owned until 1981), British Petroleum Ltd. (49 per cent shareholding until 1979, two government directors with powers of veto), and Short Bros. & Harland Ltd. (70 per cent shareholding). But in this class there are so many different degrees of participation and control that the denomination 'public corporation' is questionable. Until 1979 the government exercised powers of acquisition of and participation in industrial undertakings which were very extensive and flexible. It might acquire part or parts of some major undertaking which was in difficulties, as in the case of Rolls-Royce Ltd.[13] It might acquire shares, premises, plant and machinery, and might provide loans or services, in any industrial business under the Industry Act 1975, which gave extremely wide powers for the purposes (among others) of developing the national economy, promoting industrial efficiency and maintaining employment.

As its primary instrument for carrying out these purposes the Act of 1975 constituted a statutory corporation, the National Enterprise Board, which was not in law a Crown agency though obliged to obey any directions from the Secretary of State. Its powers for establishing and assisting any industry included 'extending public ownership into profitable areas of manufacturing industry'.[14] The Board might hold shares directly, as in the case of British Leyland. It made large investments in the motor vehicle, aerospace, machine tool and computer industries, amongst others. But in 1979 there was a reversal of policy: the Industry Act 1980 stripped the Board of its function of extending public ownership and substituted that of promoting private ownership by disposing of its assets.

Similarly under the Petroleum and Submarine Pipelines Act 1975 the British National Oil Corporation, created by the Act and subject to the directions of the Secretary of State for Energy, had powers of the widest kind for searching for, producing, and dealing with petroleum and for carrying out participation agreements, the policy of the legislation being both to make the state an oil producer and to secure for it a majority holding in commercial submarine oilfields. Here too the original policy was put into reverse so as to run down the state's participation in the industry.

---

[13] Rolls-Royce (Purchase) Act 1971. These assets were transferred from the National Enterprise Board to the Department of Industry in 1980 and sold to the public in 1987.
[14] s. 2(2).

Relevance in administrative law

Judged by the small number of cases which come before the courts, public corporations as such generate little friction in administrative law. The nationalised industries, as experience has shown, are in no position to resist their controlling ministries. As against the public, moreover, they have very few powers of a governmental character, apart from a few matters such as compulsory purchase of land (subject, as usual, to ministerial approval)[15] and railway byelaws. The problems of these corporations lie largely in fitting them into the established constitutional framework and in finding the right balance of power between them, the government, and Parliament. These are questions of constitutional rather than of administrative law. Nevertheless there are certain legal issues; and public corporations are so important an administrative mechanism that some information about them may be provided here.

It could indeed be said that the public corporation is sometimes used as a device for taking some administrative activity outside the range of administrative law. An illustration is the regulation of commercial television and sound broadcasting. The Independent Broadcasting Authority is in substance a licensing authority, controlling the transmission of programmes by commercial programme companies. But it operates this control by way of ordinary contracts, made simply as business transactions with the companies, so that what are in effect statutory licensing powers, which should be subject to the rules of administrative law, are disguised as private business. In 1968 the Authority abruptly and without public explanation switched valuable programme contracts from one company to another and it was estimated that some £11m. in share values changed hands overnight; and in 1980, when new contracts were being awarded, the IBA refused to renew them with two companies, and also insisted upon company reorganisations, under a procedure which was basically a private negotiation, without statutory rules or public hearings or published reasons or right of appeal.[16] Naturally there have been complaints that this was arbitrary government patronage instead of fair and public procedure with ministerial responsibility to Parliament.[17] In the United States, by contrast, the allocation of radio and television channels is controlled by a government licensing agency which holds elaborate public hearings in

[15] e.g. Electricity Act 1947, s. 7; Post Office Act 1969, s. 55; Civil Aviation Act 1971, s. 14.

[16] For the procedure see Report of the Select Committee on Nationalised Industry on the Independent Broadcasting Authority, HC 637 (1977–8), para. 96. Applications were to be published in part and comments in writing invited, but interviews were to be private. See also Briggs and Spicer, *The Franchise Affair* (1986).

[17] See HC 465, 1971–2, paras. 16, 33, 34; Schwartz and Wade, *Legal Control of Government*, 38.

accordance with published rules and subject to the Administrative Procedure Act of 1946 and judicial review.[18] The British technique saves much formality and expense, but it remains to be seen whether it will continue to be acceptable.

For present purposes there is no need to catalogue the numerous different types of public corporation, many of which have too little in common to illustrate any legal principle. It suffices to say that the public corporation is at present more in vogue than ever before, and more multifarious in its applications. Whenever Parliament is willing to grant a measure of autonomy, the public corporation is commonly employed. It has a legal existence of its own, and can be given statutory functions which can operate outside the normal organisation of the service of the Crown. It offers scope for many kinds of governmental experiment, under which central control, local control, and independence can be blended in any desired proportions.

Although corporations, notably ancient boroughs, had played a part in the system of government for many centuries, it was in the nineteenth century that they began to be used for new administrative purposes. An early example was that of the Poor Law Commissioners, established with corporate personality in 1834. It was employed for mixed bodies such as the Mersey Docks and Harbour Board, constituted in 1857 with a majority of elected members and some central government nominees, and the Port of London Authority, set up in 1908 with a generally similar constitution except that the nominated members represented local authorities as well as central government departments. Other examples were the Forestry Commission (1919), the British Broadcasting Corporation (1926), the London Passenger Transport Board (1933), and the British Overseas Airways Corporation (1939). Except in the case of the London Passenger Transport Board, whose members were appointed by independent trustees, membership of these corporations was controlled by the government.

A new era opened after the second world war, when the nationalisation of industry began, and it is the group of corporations established by the nationalising statutes which can best be discussed as a single class.

NATIONALISED INDUSTRY

Methods of nationalisation

The programme of nationalisation of industry carried out from 1945 onwards was designed to bring important industries into public ownership

---

[18] Schwartz and Wade (as above), 29, 107. The agency is the Federal Communications Commission.

so that they might be operated for the benefit of the public rather than for the benefit of shareholders. At the same time it was necessary to free them from the constant parliamentary investigation and criticism to which they would be subject if they were merely government departments, as the Post Office had been for three centuries prior to 1969. Nor can an industry be successfully run on civil service lines. It needs to be master in its own house and it must be given enough independence to encourage bold and far-sighted decisions and consistent long-term policies. The solution, it was supposed, was to put the nationalised industries into the hands of statutory corporations, intended to enjoy managerial liberty subject only to ministerial control in case the corporations' policy should conflict with the public interest. There was to be a distinction between broad policy and day-by-day administration the former being the sphere in which the government might intervene and the latter being the sphere of independent self-management. The interests of the public as customers were to be represented by statutory consumer councils or users' councils, entitled to be consulted and to make their wishes known to the corporations.[19] The hopes of the architects of this system not having been fulfilled in various respects, there has been since 1979 a large measure of denationalisation, effected by transferring the more profitable industries back to the private sector and vesting their assets in companies of the ordinary kind.

Two different techniques of nationalisation were followed in the period 1945–9. One was to set up a corporate body, such as the National Coal Board, and to transfer to it, by force of statute, all the assets belonging to the industry, with compensation for their owners. This was the method followed for the nationalisation of coal-mining, electricity, gas, railways, airlines, and road transport. The statute then gave special powers of control to the appropriate minister, empowering him to give general directions which the corporation was required to obey. The other technique was the compulsory acquisition of shares. The shares might then either be vested by the statute in a public corporation, as the shares in iron and steel companies were vested in the Iron and Steel Corporation, or else they might simply be held by the government, as was the case with nationalisation of the Bank of England; in either event, the control of the undertaking was then secured through the operation of the ordinary rules of company law as well as by giving the minister special powers.

---

[19] e.g. Electricity Act 1947, s. 7; Post Office Act 1969, s. 14; Gas Act 1972, s. 9. All, or nearly all, the members of these bodies are appointed by ministers. They have not in general proved very effective. A Broadcasting Complaints Commission was established by the Broadcasting Act 1980, replaced by Broadcasting Act 1981, s. 54.

The corporations

The chronological list of the nationalising statutes, and the corporations created or continued by them, with subsequent changes while they remained in public ownership, is as follows.

Bank of England Act 1946. No new corporation. The Bank of England was incorporated by royal charter in 1694.[20]

Coal Industry Nationalisation Act 1946. The National Coal Board.

Civil Aviation Act 1946. British Overseas Airways Corporation, which had existed since 1939[21]; British European Airways Corporation; British South American Airways Corporation (merged in BOAC in 1949 and later dissolved). The British Airways Board was created by the Civil Aviation Act 1971 and given control of BOAC and BEA. In 1973 BOAC and BEA were dissolved and their undertakings were transferred to the British Airways Board.[22] The management of the four major airports[23] was transferred to the British Airports Authority by the Airports Authority Act 1965.

Transport Act 1947. The British Transport Commission (in which all assets were vested). Various corporate Executives were also created, including the Railway Executive and the Road Transport Executive. All these bodies were replaced by the British Railways Board and three other Boards (London Transport Board, British Transport Docks Board, and British Waterways Board) under the Transport Act 1962. The Transport Act 1968 established the National Freight Corporation, the National Bus Company and other bodies. The London Transport Board was succeeded by the London Transport Executive in 1969[24] and by London Regional Transport in 1984.[25]

Electricity Act 1947. The Central Electricity Authority; Area Electricity Boards. The CEA was replaced under the Electricity Act 1957 by the Central Electricity Generating Board and the Electricity Council.

Gas Act 1948. Area Gas Boards; the Gas Council. The Area Boards were dissolved by the Gas Act 1972, which renamed the Gas Council as the British Gas Corporation.

Iron and Steel Act 1949. The Iron and Steel Corporation. This was replaced by the Iron and Steel Board on the denationalisation of the industry under the Iron and Steel Act 1953, by the National Steel Corporation on renationalisation under the Iron and Steel Act 1967, and finally by the British Steel Corporation in 1969. The principal Act is now the Iron and Steel Act 1975.

Aircraft and Shipbuilding Industries Act 1977. British Aerospace. British Shipbuilders.

This list could be extended by including corporations created for new

---

[20] The charter was authorised by statute: 5 & 6 W. & M. c. 20, s. 20.
[21] British Overseas Airways Act 1939.
[22] For the Board see British Airways Board Act 1977.
[23] Heathrow, Gatwick, Stansted, Prestwick.
[24] Transport (London) Act 1969.
[25] London Regional Transport Act 1984.

purposes, such as the Atomic Energy Authority (Atomic Energy Authority Act 1954) and the Independent Television Authority, now the Independent Broadcasting Authority (Television Act 1954, Broadcasting Act 1981). It might also include what could be called partially nationalising statutes such as the Rolls-Royce (Purchase) Act 1971, the Industry Act 1975 and the Petroleum and Submarine Pipe-lines Act 1975, already mentioned, under which state corporations can take shares in numerous industries, usually with a view to obtaining control. But this kind of participation is distinguishable only in degree from numerous other situations where the government or its agencies have acquired shares or interests in commercial or industrial undertakings.

Ministerial control

The nationalising statutes listed above contain many differences, but a common pattern can be seen throughout. The key provisions are that the power of appointment and removal of members of the corporation is vested in the Crown or in a minister, and that the minister may give to the corporation 'directions of a general character'. This formula, vague though it may be, is intended to express the distinction between the control over general policy in the public interest, for which some minister is responsible to Parliament, and the ordinary business management of the industry, in which the corporation is supposed to be free from interference. Some of the later statutes require ministerial directions to be laid before Parliament when given,[26] or even beforehand.[27] Any directions given under this power must be published in the corporation's annual report, which has to be laid before Parliament; but the minister is also given power to suppress publication if in his opinion it is contrary to the national interest.

These powers are enough to put the minister in a commanding position; but he also has important financial powers which by themselves give him a stranglehold. Programmes of reorganisation or development, if they involve substantial capital expenditure, are subject to his approval. He may have power to direct the corporation to discontinue any activity and dispose of any part of its undertaking or assets.[28] He may give directions,

[26] Under the Industry Act 1975, s. 7, the Secretary of State may give 'directions of a general or specific character', which must be laid before Parliament. Under the Petroleum and Submarine Pipe-lines Act 1975, ss. 4, 15, he may give 'general or specific directions' which the Corporation must publish in its annual report. Under the Aircraft and Shipbuilding Industries Act 1977, s. 4, he may give 'directions of a general character', which must be laid before Parliament.
[27] Certain directions under the British Airways Board Act 1977, s. 4, must be laid in draft.
[28] See below, p. 163.

particular as well as general, as to the use of surplus revenues, and often also as to other matters. He has control of the corporation's borrowing powers. For commercial purposes these are powers of life and death. But the minister need not, of course, use them. In fact the statutory power to give general directions has so far been used with marked restraint, and few directions of importance are to be found in the corporations' annual reports.

To judge by the small number of formal directions, however, would be highly misleading. In reality ministerial interference is frequent and pervasive. The important financial powers can be exercised informally; and in the background are the more general powers, which cast a deep shadow over the corporations' precarious independence. The minister has a powerful lever in his control over the appointment and tenure of the chairman and members. A chairman who is appointed for short term, perhaps three years, and who hopes for renewal of his appointment, is in no position to resist pressure from the minister, however informally applied. The supervising ministries are in constant touch with the corporations and they exercise much influence merely by holding the trump cards, without having to play them. Chairmen feel unable to act as public spokesmen for their industries, in case they may offend the minister. The Governor of the Bank of England is no longer the public mouthpiece of the City of London. Chairmen complain (usually after retirement) that the corporations have no genuine commercial independence and no freedom to follow long-term policies, since they are under constant political pressure and ministers do not look beyond the immediate crisis of the moment. The commercial independence that the corporations were intended to enjoy has therefore failed to materialise. They have fallen prey to political and bureaucratic influence. This is objectionable constitutionally as well as managerially, since ministers have exercised a great deal of power without accounting for it publicly and without giving Parliament the opportunity to comment.

This state of affairs was many times criticised by the House of Commons' Select Committee on Nationalised Industries while it still existed.[29] The Committee reported, for instance, that the Air Corporations were subject to 'a degree of control far in excess of that envisaged by the statutes'.[30] Thus BOAC, against their commercial judgment ordered too many Super VC-10 aircraft.[31] Similarly ministerial control was established over gas prices, although Area Boards were by statute responsible for fixing their own prices and were advised that the minister had no legal power to control

---

[29] The Committee ceased to exist when the new system of Select Committees was set up in 1979.

[30] Report from Select Committee on Nationalised Industries, 14 May 1959, pp. li, lii.

[31] Report of 9 June 1964, p. 22.

them.[32] In 1968 the Select Committee made a long report on ministerial control, condemning confusion and uncertainty of purpose, and saying that, despite the good intentions proclaimed in the government's white papers of 1961 and 1967,[33] the position was almost the exact opposite of what Parliament intended: instead of laying down broad policies and leaving management to the industries, the government had constantly interfered with management and given little clear guidance on policies.[34] The same theme recurred in later reports: ministerial interference with British Steel was of dubious benefit to the national interest but did patent damage to the Corporation;[35] and in controlling capital investment the attempts to observe the policy of the white papers were far from successful.[36] A minister himself told the Select Committee that there was 'an appalling record of private arm-twisting' in the relations between ministers and corporation chairmen.[37]

With a view to bringing the situation into the open the government in 1978 proposed that ministers should be given power to issue specific as well as general directions to the corporations, but that the directions should be laid before Parliament at the time and, in suitable cases, made subject to affirmative resolutions; and that where directions led to financial loss, the corporations should be compensated.[38] The Select Committee welcomed these proposals,[39] but before action was taken on them there was a change of government and the emphasis shifted to denationalisation.

Paradoxically, the ministerial power to give general directions, though little used for its true purpose, has been invoked as a means of escaping responsibility. In 1961 the government were attempting to enforce a 'pay pause' to prevent the constant rise of wages. A large wage claim was then pending before the Electricity Council. But the government declined to intervene, apparently because a particular wage claim could not be the subject of a 'general' direction.[40] Thus, while constantly exerting control behind the scenes, the government can shelter behind a narrow

[32] Report of 31 July 1961, pp. 18–20. Excessive ministerial interference with the London Transport Board is criticised in the Report of 3 August 1965, p. 27.

[33] Cmnd. 1337 and 3437 (financial and economic policy for nationalised industries).

[34] Report of 24 July 1968, p. 190. And see Reports of 14 May 1959, pp. li, lii; 9 June 1964, p. 91; 3 August 1965, p. 27.

[35] Report of 13 February 1973, p. xxvi.

[36] Report of 12 December 1973, para. 108.

[37] HC 636 (1977–8), Q 223 (Mr Tony Benn).

[38] Cmnd. 7131 (White Paper).

[39] HC 636 (1977–8), para. 59.

[40] See 649 HC Deb. cols. 1146–7; 650 HC Deb. cols. 238–9; (1965) 81 LQR at p. 363. Contrast the influence of the Ministry of Transport on wages paid by the London Transport Board: Report of 3 August 1965, p. 23.

interpretation of their formal powers when they do not wish to embroil
themselves.

DENATIONALISATION

Reversals of policy

The effects of excessive ministerial interference were especially obvious in
industries which were exposed, or ought to have been exposed, to
competition and market forces, such as air and road transport and
telecommunications. Measures have been enacted from 1980 onwards to
put the nationalising policy into reverse in a number of such cases, in
addition to the reversal of the National Enterprise Board's objectives as
already mentioned.[41]

The statutory pattern was to provide that on an appointed day the assets
of the public corporation should vest in a successor company nominated by
the Secretary of State. This company was to take the form of a normal
commercial company limited by shares. In the first instance the shares
would all be held by the government, but they would proceed to sell part
or all of them to private investors. The government might or might not
then retain a majority shareholding and might or might not take special
power to appoint directors. But it would have no power to give directions,
control capital investment, etc., otherwise than as shareholder under
normal company law. The model of British Petroleum Ltd., where
government and the public both held shares in an ordinary independent
company, was adopted as the prototype. Where the concern to be
denationalised was already an ordinary company, as in the case of Cable &
Wireless Ltd., all that was necessary was to authorise the government to put
a proportion of its shareholding on the market, as it did in 1981 and again in
1983 and 1985.[42] Some of its shares in British Petroleum Ltd. had already
been sold off in 1977, and the remainder were sold by instalments in 1979,
1983, and 1987. Shares in Jaguar motors were similarly sold in 1984 and in
Rolls-Royce in 1987.

In execution of this policy the British Aerospace Act 1980 provided for
the dissolution of British Aerospace and the transfer of its assets to a
company the shares of which were held by the Crown but put on sale in
1981 and 1985. The Transport Act 1980 provided for the transfer to the
private sector of the National Freight Corporation and for the relaxation of

---

[41] Above, p. 154. See [1987] MLR 16 (C. Graham and T. Prosser).
[42] Authorised by British Telecommunications Act 1981, s. 79.

the passenger vehicle licensing system so as to bring private bus operators into the industry. The Transport Act 1985 made provision for dismantling the National Bus Company under the Secretary of State's control. The Transport Act 1981 dealt with the docks, reconstituting the British Transport Docks Board under the name of Associated British Ports as a wholly owned subsidiary of a holding company limited by shares and subject to the Companies Act. The Civil Aviation Act 1980 applied the same policy to British Airways, the government's decision being to retain a majority shareholding in the new company but not to appoint directors. The Secretary of State pointed out how this would free the company from government control of its purchases of aircraft and of its borrowing powers, so conferring an entirely new measure of commercial liberty. The shares were sold in 1986. Other privatisation measures have resulted in the creation as independent companies of Britoil and Enterprise Oil,[43] British Telecom,[44] British Gas,[45] the Trustees Savings Bank,[46] and the British Airports Authority.[47] More major and minor measures are in prospect as the government liquidates its multifarious commercial involvements.

One form of denationalisation is to provide simply that the Secretary of State may order the corporation to discontinue any activity and to dispose of any part of its undertaking or assets as directed by him. A power of this kind over the British Steel Corporation is conferred by the Iron and Steel Act 1981, with a view to returning suitable parts of the industry to private business. Similar powers exist under the Transport Act 1981 in respect of British Railways, and were exercised under the Oil and Gas (Enterprise) Act 1982 for disposing of the British Oil Corporation's assets to the new companies Britoil and Enterprise Oil, whose shares were sold to the public in 1982–5.

In the background, however, there is an ultimate measure of government control. The constitutions of the new companies provide that the government retains a special share (commonly known as the 'golden share') which gives it paramount rights, e.g. to appoint directors and outvote all other shareholders, either at any time or for a certain term of years. The purpose is to protect the independence of the company so that it may not, for example, come under foreign control. In most cases there is a limit on the number of shares that any one shareholder, or overseas shareholder, may own, and sometimes the disposal of assets will require the consent of the holder of the special share, i.e. the government.

---

[43] Oil and Gas (Enterprise) Act 1982.
[44] Telecommunications Act 1984.
[45] Gas Act 1986.
[46] Trustee Savings Banks Act 1985.
[47] Airports Act 1986.

OTHER FEATURES

Degrees of control

Corporations which form part of the administrative structure of social services are usually more closely controlled by their ministers than are corporations whose primary business is industry or commerce. Regional and District Health Authorities under the National Health Service Act 1977, like Regional Hospital Boards under the National Health Service Act 1946, are subject to ministerial directions in all respects. So are New Town Development Corporations under the New Towns Act 1981 (dating from 1946). Even in the commercial sphere there is complete control over some corporations, for example the National Enterprise Board[48] and the Bank of England.[49]

At the other extreme there are statutory corporations which enjoy a very substantial degree of autonomy. The British Broadcasting Corporation, first constituted by royal charter in 1926 and at present chartered until 1996, operates under a statutory licence granted by the Home Secretary under the Wireless Telegraphy Act 1949.[50] The licence contains numerous restrictive conditions, both technical and political. In particular, the Corporation's members are appointed by the Crown; it may be required to transmit government announcements; and it may be required by the Home Secretary to refrain from transmitting any specified matter or class of matter—for example, the 'fourteen day rule' (imposed in 1955 and revoked in 1956) put a ban on broadcasts about matters to be debated in Parliament within the next fortnight. In this case the BBC showed how much stronger is its position than that of a nationalised industry: the government, as usual, wished to enforce the rule by informal pressure, but the BBC insisted on a formal directive which showed where the responsibility lay.

The accepted policy is that the BBC enjoys almost complete independence, subject only to standing directions forbidding it to give its own comments on current affairs and restricting party political broadcasts. Despite his extensive powers, the Home Secretary normally accepts responsibility only for the general framework within which the Corporation works. Similarly the Independent Broadcasting Authority, which in 1973 replaced the Independent Television Authority established by the Television Act 1954, may be required by the Home Secretary to transmit or refrain from transmitting particular items, and is subject to directions as

---

[48] Industry Act 1975, s. 7.
[49] Bank of England Act 1946, s. 4.
[50] Charter, 1981, Cmnd. 8313; Licence and Agreement, 1981, Cmnd. 8233.

to various matters including the hours of its programmes[51] (the ITA was also directed to obey the 'fourteen day rule' of 1955–6); but otherwise it is independent.

There are other public corporations of a more local character which likewise operate independently, such as the Port of London Authority (created in 1908) and the Mersey Docks and Harbour Board (created in 1857). There are government members of these boards, but they are in a minority among the other representatives elected by local interests. These mixed corporations have many of the traits of elected local authorities. The public corporation is a flexible device for the diffusion of responsibility, and it is often resorted to when the stereotyped organs of central or local government are for some reason unsuitable.

The Post Office

The Post Office has a special position, having been a government department in the full sense until turned into a public corporation by the Post Office Act 1969. Here therefore the device of the public corporation has been employed to increase rather than reduce the independence of a major industry.

The Secretary of State for Industry has the usual powers to give directions of a general character in the national interest and particular directions when required by national security or international relations. He appoints the chairman and members, and also has a number of special powers, including power to direct the corporation to dispose of any part of its undertaking or assets.[52] The Post Office's commercial independence therefore depends upon ministerial restraint, as in the case of the nationalised industries.

The Post Office has a statutory monopoly of the right to convey letters, subject to a catalogue of exceptions such as conveyance by the sender, 'personal friend', messenger, etc. This 'exclusive privilege' is now enshrined in the British Telecommunications Act 1981, which contains much about the Post Office as well as about telecommunications. But at the same time the Act gives the Secretary of State a wide licensing power under which he can authorise any person to compete with the Post Office. Licences have in fact been granted to a number of private firms operating special services, but on condition that they make a high minimum charge for each letter. The Secretary of State also has power to suspend the Post

---

[51] Broadcasting Act 1981, ss. 28, 29. The IBA's powers were extended by the Broadcasting Act 1980, which also established the Broadcasting Complaints Commission to deal with complaints against the BBC and the IBA (see now Broadcasting Act 1981, s. 54 and *R v. Broadcasting Complaints Commission ex p Owen* [1985] QB 1153).

[52] The powers are now specified by ss. 62–4 of British Telecommunications Act 1981.

Office monopoly wholly or partially by statutory instrument, subject to negative Parliamentary resolution.

It is expressly provided by the Act of 1969 that the corporation is not to be regarded as the servant or agent of the Crown or as entitled to any Crown status or to any general immunity from taxation.[53] But the Act preserved, and indeed extended, a wide statutory immunity from liability for wrongful acts, which government departments themselves do not enjoy. It is provided that neither the Post Office *nor any of its officers, servants, agents or sub-contractors* shall be liable in tort for what happens to anything in its post.[54] This is a breach of the principle that a public official is personally liable for wrongful injury.[55] A person who delivers a parcel to the Post Office and sees it damaged or destroyed before his eyes has, it seems, no civil remedy—though criminal proceedings will lie, and even carelessness is a statutory offence in such a case.[56] When a packet of travellers' cheques was stolen in the post by an airport employee, the airport authority successfully claimed immunity as a sub-contractor.[57] The Act did provide for a limited liability for registered packets,[58] but even this was hedged about with illogical limitations. It extended only to inland packets, so that a packet addressed to a foreign country was not covered, even though lost or damaged in this county.[59] The amount recoverable was limited by the fee paid, so that it was a form of statutory insurance rather than ordinary liability in tort.[60] The action had also to be brought within twelve months, instead of the usual six years.

Some mitigation of these immunities has now been made under the British Telecommunications Act 1981. The Act provides that the Post Office may make a statutory scheme in respect of inland packets for which it accepts liability.[61] It is therefore left to the Post Office to decide for itself in what cases it will pay compensation. The wide immunity of its employees etc. is not affected, and it is surprising that it is still tolerated.

---

[53] s. 6(5).

[54] s. 29, replacing Crown Proceedings Act 1947, s. 9. See *Stephen (Harold) & Co. Ltd.* v. *Post Office* [1977] The Times, 19 July.

[55] Below, p. 812.

[56] Post Office Act 1953, s. 59. See also s. 58 and *Gouriet* v. *Union of Post Office Workers* [1978] AC 435 (offence of detaining or delaying postal packet).

[57] *American Express Co.* v. *British Airways Board* [1983] 1 WLR 701, holding that breach of bailment is covered by the immunity, even though not tort.

[58] s. 30 (also dating from 1947).

[59] *Triefus & Co. Ltd.* v. *Post Office* [1957] QB 353, holding also that there is no liability in contract.

[60] See *Building and Civil Engineering Holidays Scheme Management* v. *Post Office* [1966] 1 QB 247.

[61] s. 70. The Post Office Scheme 1979 was amended for this purpose in 1982. But the limit of liability for an ordinary letter or parcel in 1987 was £20.

The law about interception of postal communications is explained below in connection with telephone tapping.

Telecommunications

Until 1981 the telephone, telegraph, and telecommunications services were a part of the Post Office, latterly known as British Telecom. They were detached by the British Telecommunications Act 1981 and assigned to a new corporation, British Telecommunications, on the ground that this high-technology industry required different management from the postal service, which is labour-intensive. This was a typical state corporation to which the Secretary of State could give directions of a general character. Three years later British Telecommunications was privatised, a new company being created under the Telecommunications Act 1984, which at the same time abolished the former corporation's monopoly and set up a licensing system, through which competitors could enter the field, under the control of the Secretary of State and the Director General of Telecommunications. One of the Director General's duties is the investigation of complaints.[62]

The Act of 1981 gave legal immunity from the law of tort both to the corporation and to its employees in respect of faults, failures, interruptions, delays, etc. in their services or errors or omissions in directories.[63] This continued the immunity which the Post Office had enjoyed formerly without evident good reason. The Act of 1984 repealed the exemption, which might well be done also in the case of the postal service.

Telephone tapping, a subject of long-standing controversy, is now regulated by the Interception of Communications Act 1985, which covers postal as well as telephonic messages. The Act was prompted by litigation which established that telephone tapping was not a tort at common law[64] but was a violation of the European Convention on Human Rights unless legally restricted by clear and precise rules.[65] The Act of 1984, which made telephone tapping an offence but gave the Home Secretary unlimited power to authorise it by warrant, failed to pass this test. The Act of 1985 has

---

[62] s. 49.

[63] s. 23.

[64] *Malone v. Metropolitan Police Commissioner* [1979] Ch. 344. It seems that there is no remedy for breach of contract since the telephone service is not contractual: see at 375. See also at 370 for the cryptic provision of the Post Office Act 1969, s. 80, which seems to have given legal recognition to the practice of authorising police interceptions by Home Secretary's warrant, established since 1937. See also Cmnd. 283 (1957) (Report of Committee of Privy Councillors).

[65] *Malone* case, European Court of Human Rights, Series A, No. 82 (2 August 1984), finding violation of Article 8 (respect for private life and correspondence).

now restricted the Home Secretary's power to cases where he considers that interception is necessary in the interests of national security, for the prevention or detection of serious crime, or for safeguarding the country's economic well-being against the acts or intentions of persons outside the British Islands; and there are a number of detailed restrictions and safeguards. A tribunal is constituted to investigate complaints. If it finds a contravention of the Act, the tribunal must report to the Prime Minister and it may quash the Home Secretary's warrant, order the destruction of intercepts, and direct the Home Secretary to pay specified compensation to the complaint. In addition there is a Commissioner who is charged with reviewing the working of the Act and with giving the tribunal whatever assistance it requires. But no evidence relating to offences or warrants may be given in any court or tribunal (save in the new tribunal itself) except in the case of certain criminal offences connected with confidentiality of communications. For most purposes, therefore, the tribunal offers the only remedy.

Responsibility to Parliament

Public corporations as such have no direct responsibility to Parliament. Ministers who have powers of control over them are responsible to Parliament in the normal way in so far as they have exercised, or failed to exercise, their statutory powers. In the case of the nationalised industries it was thought important to protect them from parliamentary interference. But, as has been seen, it is ministerial interference which has proved to be the danger. Much of this interference is not accounted for in Parliament. Parliamentary questions are accepted only on matters within the minister's statutory responsibilities, such as appointments and salaries of board members, capital expenditure and borrowing, and development programmes, subject to an indefinite exception for 'matters of sufficient public importance'.[66] Members of Parliament, knowing how much control is exercised by ministers informally, naturally feel frustrated by this rule. Less restricted opportunities occur in debates on the adjournment, on Supply days, and on the annual reports of the corporations and the periodical reports of the Select Committees. It has often been suggested that there ought to be some sort of ombudsman system for complaints about nationalised industries, in view of the limitations of the statutory consumer councils and users' councils, but nothing of the kind has been instituted.

For many years Parliament's most effective way of informing itself about the nationalised industries was the Select Committee on Nationalised Industries. At first, in 1955, there were difficulties over terms of reference:

---

[66] See 451 HC Deb. col. 1636 (7 June 1948).

the Committee was debarred from considering (inter alia) matters which were clearly the responsibility of ministers and also matters of day-to-day administration. Since hardly anything fell between these two stools, the Committee had to report that it was powerless. So in 1956 a new Select Committee was empowered simply 'to examine the Reports and Accounts of the Nationalised Industries', and in due course a comprehensive series of investigations was undertaken. But when the extended system of Select Committees, each dealing with a particular department, was established in 1979, the Committee was abolished. Since then the Committees have concerned themselves with public bodies associated with their departments and there have been reports on nationalised industries from the Industry and Trade Committee, the Transport Committee and the Treasury and Civil Service Committee, among others. As the industries have become adjusted to the balance of forces in the constitution, it has become plain that the original theories of nationalisation were unrealistic, and that Parliament has an important part to play.

Legal status and liability

Public corporations are as subject to the ordinary law, e.g. as to corporate powers,[67] taxation, and liability in tort, as are other corporate bodies, unless they enjoy some statutory exemption.[68] But it is important to ascertain which of them are in law servants of the Crown and thus able to claim the privileges of the Crown, such as the privilege of not being bound by certain statutes.[69]

Where the corporation has a sufficient degree of independence, neither the corporation nor its employees are legally servants of the Crown. The corporation is then itself vicariously liable for the torts (e.g. trespass or negligence) of its servants or agents in the same way as any other employer. The corporation's independence in law, precarious though it may be in fact, breaks the chain of command leading down from the Crown. The legal relationship of master and servant demands that the master shall have complete control of what the servant does. This test is not satisfied, in the case of a public corporation, merely because the minister may appoint and dismiss the members, or give directions 'of a general character', or

---

[67] e.g. *Smith* v. *London Transport Executive* [1949] 2 All ER 295 (bus service held authorised); *Roberts (Charles) & Co. Ltd.* v. *British Railways Board* [1965] 1 WLR 396 (Board's purposes held to extend to manufacture and sale of tank wagons but only for use in its own system).

[68] Constituent statutes often provide that public corporations shall have no authority to disregard any law and no exemption from taxes, rates, etc.; but this provision is declaratory of the ordinary law.

[69] For this see below, p. 827.

(probably) because he can give any kind of directions. In one case the British Transport Commission claimed to be able to eject a tenant from a house on the ground that the legislation protecting tenants did not apply to the Crown. But the Court of Appeal rejected the Commission's claim to Crown immunity.[70] Denning LJ considered the minister's various powers and said:

These are great powers but still we cannot regard the corporation as being his agent, any more than a company is the agent of the shareholders, or even of a sole shareholder. In the eye of the law, the corporation is its own master and is answerable as fully as any other person or corporation. It is not the Crown and has none of the immunities of privileges of the Crown. Its servants are not civil servants, and its property is not Crown property.

The Transport Act 1962 confirmed this decision by enacting that the corporations dealing with transport should not be regarded as servants or agents of the Crown or as entitled to any Crown immunity or privilege or as exempt from any tax or charge or as owners of Crown property.[71] Similar provisions have often been incorporated where an Act created a public corporation which was not intended to be a government department,[72] even where, like the British National Oil Corporation, it was subject to specific as well as general directions from a minister.[73]

It has also been held that the British Broadcasting Corporation is not an agency of the Crown and is therefore not entitled to the Crown's immunity from taxation.[74] The National Health Service, on the other hand, has been held to be in law part of 'the services of the Crown' for the purposes of the Crown's right to use patents[75] and to fall within 'the service of the Crown' for the purposes of the provisions of the Public Health Act 1936 about nuisances on Crown land.[76] The statutory health authorities which administer the health service, and which act on behalf of and subject to the instructions of the Secretary of State, are nevertheless, by a special provision, given the same legal rights and liabilities as if they were acting as principals.[77] The legal links between them and the Secretary of State are thus notionally severed for these purposes. The North Thames Gas Board was however held to be 'a public body' within a statutory definition

---

[70] *Tamlin* v. *Hannaford* [1950] 1 KB 18.

[71] s. 30.

[72] e.g. Electricity Act 1957, s. 38; Civil Aviation Act 1971, s. 1(4); Independent Broadcasting Authority Act 1973, s. 2(4).

[73] Petroleum and Submarine Pipe-lines Act 1975, s. 1(5).

[74] *British Broadcasting Corporation* v. *Johns* [1965] Ch. 32.

[75] *Pfizer Corporation* v. *Ministry of Health* [1965] AC 512.

[76] *Nottingham Hospital Management Committee* v. *Owen* [1958] 1 QB 50.

[77] National Health Service Act 1977, 5th sched., para. 15. In Scotland they are held not be be entitled to the Crown's immunity from interdict; *British Medical Association* v *Greater Glasgow Health Board* [1988] The Times, 20 May.

extending to 'local and public authorities of all descriptions'.[78] Similarly, also, the British Overseas Airways Corporation was held to be a public authority for the purposes of the provision (now repealed[79]) which set a one-year period of limitation in respect of acts done under 'any public duty or authority', despite the fact that the act in question was merely part of its commercial activities;[80] and the British Railways Board and the other transport boards were described in their constituent Act as 'public authorities'.[81]

[78] *R v. Manners* [1978] AC 43 (prosecution under Prevention of Corruption Acts 1889–1916).
[79] See below, p. 786.
[80] *Littlewood* v. *George Wimpey & Co. Ltd.* [1953] 1 WLR 426.
[81] Transport Act 1962, s. 1.

7

SOME GOVERNMENT FUNCTIONS

COMPULSORY PURCHASE OF LAND

Evolution of procedures

Powers of compulsory purchase of land under general statutory authority[1] are possessed by numerous government departments, local authorities, statutory corporations, and even by some commercial companies.[2] All these powers, however, are firmly under central government control, since every such purchase must be authorised by a minister, usually under the Acquisition of Land Act 1981, a consolidating Act which has replaced the Acquisition of Land (Authorisation Procedure) Act 1946.

It was first the canals, and then the railways, for which these powers were originally required on a large scale. The pioneers of compulsory purchase were therefore commercial companies. But every case required its own Act of Parliament. In the early period the procedure and provisions as to compensation were set out in full in each Act. But the mass of railway legislation, effected by private Bills, required a standardised system, and this was introduced by the Lands Clauses Consolidation Act 1845. From then on the common form clauses of that Act could be incorporated by reference; but a specific Act of Parliament still had to be obtained in every case. Meanwhile, however, something more like the modern system, which does not normally require Parliamentary sanction, had been introduced by the Defence Act 1842, which empowered the service departments to purchase land compulsorily for defence purposes if authorised by the Treasury and the Lord Lieutenant of the county; and this Act, as amended, still operates for those purposes.[3]

Later in the nineteenth century compulsory powers were needed for the new local government authorities, and were supplied in a new form of which the archetype is the Public Health Act 1875. That Act introduced the 'provisional order' procedure, under which a local authority, after

---

[1] There is today probably no such prerogative power: see below, p. 795.

[2] e.g. oil companies under the Pipe-lines Act 1962; but these require special Parliamentary procedure (see below).

[3] See Requisitioned Land and War Works Acts 1945 (Pt. VII) and 1948; Land Powers (Defence) Act 1958; *University College Oxford* v. *Secretary of State for Air* [1938] 1 KB 648. As to authorisation by the Lord Lieutenant (now no longer required) see *Hutton* v. *A.-G.* [1927] 1 Ch. 427; below, p. 556.

advertisement and notification to owners, might petition the Local Government Board for a provisional order incorporating the powers of the Act of 1845; but this order was inoperative unless confirmed by Act of Parliament, in the passage of which it could be opposed as if it were a private Bill. This hybrid administrative-and-legislative procedure, combining the worst of both worlds, was excessively cumbersome. Ultimately twentieth-century legislation brought into being the modern type of compulsory purchase order, exemplified by the Housing, Town Planning, etc. Act 1909: under this procedure the order took effect when confirmed by a minister, without reference to Parliament. For some time there were variations in various different Acts. But after 1946 a high degree of uniformity was achieved under the Acquisition of Land (Authorisation Procedure) Act 1946, which enacted what is now the standard procedure. That Act applied originally only to local authorities and the Minister of Transport. But subsequently it became the practice to adopt its machinery in most legislation,[4] in the case both of other ministers and of other bodies such as nationalised industries. In a few special cases, where additional safeguards are thought necessary, the order is also subject to 'special parliamentary procedure' under the Statutory Orders (Special Procedure) Act 1945, as mentioned below.

The legislation does not supply a very happy nomenclature. The first step is for the order to be 'made' by the minister, local authority or other body seeking it, but at this stage it has no legal effect as against the owner of the land.[5] It takes effect only when finally confirmed, and the hearing and determination of objections takes place between the 'making' and the confirmation. If the order is confirmed, the acquiring authority must within three years serve a 'notice to treat', which sets in motion the machinery for assessing compensation. At the same time the owner will prove his title and convey the land to the acquiring authority, or if necessary the authority may make a vesting order in its own favour.[6]

There are therefore two distinct stages in every compulsory purchase: first, the stage of authorisation, leading up to the confirmation of the order, when the policy of the matter is in question; and secondly, the stage of

---

[4] For lists of statutes which do and do not fall under the Act of 1981 see *Encyclopedia of Compulsory Purchase*, Pt. I, Appendices. Statutes which contain their own procedure include, in addition to the Defence Acts, the Housing Act 1985 (clearance areas), the Pipelines Act 1962, the New Towns Act 1981, and the Forestry Act 1967 (the last providing for special parliamentary procedure).

[5] Persons affected therefore have no right to be heard before the order is 'made': see below, p. 174. For the meaning of 'made' see *Iveagh (Earl)* v. *Minister of Housing and Local Government* [1964] 1 QB 395, holding that in some contexts 'made' means 'effectively made' i.e. confirmed.

[6] Compulsory Purchase (Vesting Declarations) Act 1981.

completion, when the compensation is assessed and the transfer of the land is effected. Compensation is dealt with in a later part of this book. The remainder of the operation is in most cases governed by the Acquisition of Land Act 1981 as regards the first stage, and by the Compulsory Purchase Act 1965 as regards the second stage.

County and district councils may be authorised to purchase land compulsorily for any of their statutory purposes, and whether inside or outside their area;[7] and district councils may be authorised to do so on behalf of parish councils if the district council finds after a local inquiry that suitable land cannot be acquired on reasonable terms by agreement.[8] Local authorities have very wide powers of acquisition for purposes of planning and development.[9] The Secretary of State for the Environment may acquire any land necessary for the public service.[10]

Authorisation procedure

The Act of 1981 requires a compulsory purchase order made by a local authority (which may be taken as a typical case) to be in the form prescribed by regulations and to describe the land by reference to a map.[11] It must then be advertised in local newspapers with particulars of its purpose and of the manner in which objections may be made, allowing for this purpose at least twenty-one days. Notice of a similar kind must be served on every owner, lessee, and occupier, except only tenants for a month or less. If none of these persons lodges an objection, the minister may confirm the order, with or without modification, provided that no additional land is included. If any of them duly object, the minister must arrange for a hearing for them and for the acquiring authority, or else hold a public local inquiry at which all interested persons may be heard.[12] He need not however do this if satisfied that the objections relate only to matters that can be dealt with by the tribunal which assesses compensation. Before deciding whether to confirm the order the minister must consider the objections and the report of any hearing or inquiry. Notice of confirmation of the order must again be published in the local press and served on the same persons as before.

Where the minister is himself the acquiring as well as the confirming authority, the Act of 1981 prescribes the same procedure, mutatis

---

[7] Local Government Act 1972, s. 121.

[8] Same, s. 125.

[9] Below, pp. 194, 197.

[10] Town and Country Planning Act 1971, s. 113.

[11] See Act of 1981, Pt. II for all the particulars in this paragraph.

[12] See below, p. 955, for such inquiries and for the statutory rules of procedure.

mutandis, except that the form of the initial order is not governed by regulations but is as the minister may determine.[13]

In statutes which do not incorporate the Act of 1981 the procedure for authorisation is usually closely similar, as it is for example in the provisions of the Housing Act 1985 dealing with compulsory acquisition for slum clearance,[14] the Pipe-lines Act 1962[15] and the Water Resources Act 1963.[16] The Town and Country Planning Act 1971 adopted the Act of 1946 (now 1981) for compulsory acquisition of land by local authorities for development, redevelopment, or improvement, and by the Secretary of State for use for the public service;[17] but in those cases the Secretary of State may disregard any objection which in his opinion is in substance an objection to the use proposed for the land in the development plan.[18] Under the New Towns Act 1981, which does not adopt the Acquisition of Land Act 1981 but provides a basically similar procedure, the Secretary of State is likewise empowered to disregard any objection to a compulsory purchase order which can be dealt with in the assessment of compensation or merely contends that the acquisition of land within the area of the new town is unnecessary or inexpedient.[19]

Special safeguards

Special protection is given by the Act of 1981 to land which has been acquired for the purposes of their undertaking by 'statutory undertakers', i.e. bodies supplying services such as gas, electricity, water, or transport under statutory authority. No such land may be taken by compulsory purchase unless the minister responsible for the undertaking in question certifies that the land can be spared or else replaced without serious detriment to the undertaking.[20]

Certain cases are subject to 'special parliamentary procedure' under the Statutory Orders (Special Procedure) Act 1945, which requires the order to be laid before Parliament by the minister with opportunity for objection by petition and subject to annulment by either House. The cases in question are the following.[21]

(a) Land owned by a local authority or acquired by a statutory undertaker for

[13] Act of 1981, 1st sched.
[14] s. 290 and 22nd sched.
[15] ss. 11, 12, and 2nd sched.
[16] s. 67 and 8th sched.
[17] ss. 112(4), 113(3).
[18] s. 132.
[19] 4th sched., para. 4(3).
[20] s. 16, subject to exceptions in s. 31.
[21] Act of 1981, ss. 17–20.

its undertaking, or held inalienably by the National Trust, if the body
concerned duly makes objection.

(b) Land forming part of a common or open space, or of an allotment under an
inclosure Act, unless the relevant minister certifies that suitable land will be
given in exchange or that (in the case of road-widening only) no
replacement is necessary.

(c) Land which is the site of an ancient monument or archaeological feature,
unless the relevant minister certifies that the acquiring authority has given a
satisfactory undertaking to preserve it.

But this restriction does not apply to acquisition of an interest in land if
made by a minister, a local authority or certain specified bodies.

Judicial review

The validity of a compulsory purchase order, made under the Act of 1981
or otherwise, is subject to limited judicial review, which must be sought
within six weeks of the date on which notice of confirmation of the order is
first published, on the ground that the order is not empowered to be
granted under the Act or that some statutory requirement has not been
complied with; and the court may then temporarily suspend the operation
of the order and, if the specified grounds are made out, may quash it.
Otherwise it may not be questioned in any legal proceedings whatsoever.[22]
The object of this drastic restriction of legal remedies is to enable the
acquiring authority to obtain a safe title to the land, so that it may proceed
to build houses, roads, etc., without risking large sums of public money.
This common statutory formula raises serious problems which are
discussed in the context of remedies generally.[23]

Procedure for completion

Once a compulsory purchase order has been confirmed and duly notified,
the stages for completing the transaction are normally as prescribed by the
Compulsory Purchase Act 1965, which replaced the Lands Clauses Acts but
preserved some of their oddities.[24] There is an overall time limit of three
years from the date on which the order becomes operative, after which the
powers of the acquiring authority lapse.[25] But, as explained elsewhere, the
court in any case requires the purchasing authority to proceed without
undue delay, and may hold that it has abandoned its powers if it delays

[22] Act of 1981, ss. 23–5.
[23] Below, p. 734.
[24] See e.g. s. 10(2).
[25] Compulsory Purchase Act 1965, s. 4, replacing Lands Clauses Consolidation Act 1845,
s. 123.

unreasonably or if its action indicates such an intention;[26] or, alternatively, the owner may compel it to proceed with the purchase,[27] and, if he has meanwhile suffered loss, he may sue for damages.[28] Naturally the authority may not depart from the authorised purpose.[29]

The first step is the 'notice to treat', which the acquiring authority must serve on all persons whom they can discover to be interested in the land.[30] If an owner is abroad or cannot be traced, they may have the land independently valued and pay the compensation money into court.[31] The notice to treat must demand particulars of each recipient's interest and claim. It may be withdrawn within six weeks of delivery of the claim, or where no claim is delivered within six weeks of the Lands Tribunal's final assessment.[32] This gives the acquiring authority a way of retreat if the land turns out to be much more valuable than expected. The transaction may also be frustrated if the owner exercises his right to resist the compulsory purchase of a part rather than the whole of a 'house, building or manufactory, or of a park or garden belonging to a house', though this right can be negated by the Lands Tribunal if it finds that there will be no serious detriment.[33] Service of a notice to treat does not make the acquiring authority the owner in equity (and so subject to risk) as does an ordinary contract of sale: that occurs only when compensation is agreed or assessed (there being then the equivalent of a sale price) or when the acquiring authority takes possession, if that is earlier.[34]

Once compensation is agreed or assessed, either party may sue for specific performance as if there were an ordinary contract of sale.[35] If the owner refuses or neglects to make out his title or to convey the land, the acquiring authority may pay the compensation money into court and execute a deed poll recording the circumstances, whereupon the legal

[26] Below, p. 268.
[27] Below, p. 260. The remedy is either mandamus or an action for specific performance. Mandamus is available before compensation is assessed, specific performance afterwards.
[28] *Bremer* v. *Haringey LBC* [1983] The Times, 12 May, where the council was held to have acted in bad faith.
[29] Below, p. 435.
[30] Compulsory Purchase Act 1965, s. 5.
[31] 2nd sched.
[32] Land Compensation Act 1961, s. 31.
[33] Compulsory Purchase Act 1965, s. 8. The language derives from the Lands Clauses Acts.
[34] *West Midland Baptist Association* v. *Birmingham Cpn.* [1970] AC 874 at 899, 911, overruling *Phoenix Assurance Co.* v. *Spooner* [1905] 2 KB 753; *Chilton* v. *Telford Development Cpn.* [1987] 1 WLR 872.
[35] Except as modified by statute, the ordinary law of vendor and purchaser then applies: *Harding* v. *Metropolitan Railway Co.* (1872) LR 7 Ch. App. 154; *Re Cary-Elwes' Contract* [1906] 2 Ch. 143.

ownership will vest in the authority absolutely.[36] In cases of urgency the acquiring authority may take over the land, before the compensation has been assessed, by executing a 'general vesting declaration' at least two months after publishing the notice of confirmation of the order, in which they must include prescribed particulars. Notices then have to be served upon owners and occupiers, after which at least a further twenty-eight days must be allowed. The land then vests in the acquiring authority on the vesting date specified in the declaration, and they can take possession of it at once.[37]

TOWN AND COUNTRY PLANNING

Planning control

Of all the administrative controls and services which multiply in the modern state, the one which generates most litigation in the courts is town and country planning. This book is replete with illustrations drawn from planning cases, and the following short account of the system will supply some background. Planning control aims to prevent the anti-social use of land, and to some extent also to promote the social use of it through 'positive planning' by local authorities. Primarily it is a comprehensive and drastic licensing system, under which every kind of 'development' of land requires permission, and the power to refuse permission is unrestricted. As a general rule, no compensation is paid for refusal of permission, so that the legislative scheme contains a large element of expropriation without compensation, a sacrifice which is imposed upon landowners for the general good, but which naturally provokes litigation. For the sake of equality of sacrifice and for raising public revenue Parliament has made a series of attempts to expropriate the development value of land altogether, so as to eliminate profit even where permission is granted. The latest of these measures was the Community Land Act 1975, now repealed.

The account given here is concerned mostly with the system of control. The general rules as to compensation will be found in the chapter on Liability of Public Authorities.

Planning before the Act of 1947

Planning is a twentieth-century governmental activity, though it has its roots in housing, just as housing has its roots in public health. The first step

[36] Compulsory Purchase Act 1965, s. 9.
[37] Compulsory Purchase (Vesting Declarations) Act 1981.

was taken by the Housing, Town Planning, etc. Act 1909, which empowered urban local authorities to make planning schemes; this was followed by an Act of 1919 which required the larger authorities to do so. The next major step was when the Town and Country Planning Act 1932 extended planning powers to rural authorities also, thus providing for the whole country. This Act introduced 'interim development control' to prevent development being blighted during the period, generally a long one,[38] between the local authority's resolution to prepare a scheme and the final confirmation of the scheme by the Minister of Health. If interim permission was given, the owner would be compensated if his development later turned out to conflict with the plan as confirmed. If permission was refused, the development could still be carried out, but at the owner's risk: if it conflicted with the final plan, he would receive no compensation if his building had to be demolished. There was a right of appeal to the minister against a refusal of permission or restrictive conditions. Buildings of special architectural or historic interest could be made the subject of preservation orders. This Act continued the earlier scheme of 'compensation and betterment', the theory being that the compensation paid for loss caused by restrictions would be balanced by charges collected for betterment, i.e. the profit brought by the plan to other owners.[39] But betterment proved difficult to collect and the liability for compensation proved a serious disincentive to local authorities.[40] This was the first of the series of unsuccessful financial schemes which have been a recurrent feature of planning control.

Progress having come to a halt during the war, the Town and Country Planning (Interim Development) Act 1943 imposed interim control in all areas, whether or not there had been a resolution to prepare a scheme. But powers of a wholly new character were conferred by the Town and Country Planning Act 1944, under which local planning authorities could acquire and develop land themselves, though subject, as in the case of all compulsory acquisition, to the consent of the minister. These powers covered not only areas devastated by bombing, which were the immediate cause of the Act, but also areas of 'bad lay-out and obsolete development' which needed comprehensive redevelopment. Local authorities thus acquired a new role of a creative character in addition to their role as arbiters of development carried out by private enterprise.

[38] By 1943 only some 4 per cent of the area of England and Wales was subject to confirmed schemes, but 70 per cent was subject to interim control.

[39] The local authority could recover 50 per cent of betterment under the Act of 1909 and 75 per cent under the Act of 1932.

[40] As explained in the Report of the Committee on Compensation and Betterment (1942) Cmnd. 6386 (the Uthwatt Report), which laid the foundations of the financial scheme of the Act of 1947.

The Planning Acts, 1947 and after

The modern system of planning law was inaugurated by the Town and Country Planning Act 1947. This was the first of a long series of Acts, underpinned by a mass of detailed regulations, which have several times been consolidated. The primary statute is now the Town and Country Planning Act 1971, but there are several other important Acts which must be described. It is legislation of formidable complexity.

The outstanding features of the Act of 1947 were that each local planning authority was required at once to prepare a detailed development plan for its area; that all development required permission and was exposed at once to enforcement proceedings if permission was not obtained, whether or not an overall plan for the area had been brought into effect; that no compensation was payable for refusal of permission; that on the grant of permission a 'development charge' was payable equal to the excess of the value of the land (with the permission) over its 'existing use value'; and that development rights then existing, which the Act in effect cancelled, should be indemnified by payment of compensation, for which a fund of £300m. was earmarked. As a corollary, compensation on the compulsory acquisition of land was limited to existing use value. The effect of these drastic provisions was that development rights in land were expropriated subject to a once-for-all payment from the central government. It was supposed that the price of land in the open market would likewise be limited to existing use value, but this proved to be a major miscalculation: the demand for land drove up prices to a much higher level, so that there was an inequitable difference between voluntary sale at full value and compulsory sale at existing use value. On the financial side the whole scheme of the Act was a sharp move away from the old system of compensation and betterment and towards the socialisation of land. The tight control imposed on development was a move in the same direction. Local authorities no longer needed to worry about their potential liability for compensation, and they could acquire land compulsorily much more cheaply.

Planning law falls into three separate compartments: the preparation of overall plans; the control of development; and the system of compensation. The system of compensation is explained in the chapter on the liability of public authorities,[41] and will be mentioned here only incidentally.

Overall plans

The local planning authorities designated by the Act of 1947 were the county and county borough councils. Each authority was required to

---

[41] Below, p. 795.

survey its area and within three years to put forward its development plan for the approval of the minister. These plans were to be subject to quinquennial review. The minister was obliged to hold an inquiry or hearing into objections, normally a public local inquiry. A new element was that the plan, even when approved, had no effect on the need to obtain planning permission for any particular development: it merely gave an indication of the probabilities of obtaining permission in any area, and it did not oblige the local planning authority to adhere to it. It would indicate the areas intended for industrial development, residential development, and so forth; it would include the road system; and it could designate areas as subject to compulsory acquisition for comprehensive redevelopment either by public or private enterprise. The plan itself would consist of written statements supplemented by detailed maps and diagrams, showing both the uses intended for each area and the stages in which development was to be carried out.

The simultaneous preparation of plans covering the whole country, and the lengthy public inquiries to which they gave rise, caused severe administrative indigestion, intensified by the requirement of quinquennial revision. As circumstances changed during this excessively slow and cumbersome process, long-term plans became unrealistic and impeded effective action. There were conflicting demands for more public consultation and at the same time for less administrative delay. The Town and Country Planning Act 1968 attempted to meet these complaints by unloading much of the detailed work from Whitehall and leaving it with local authorities. This was done by replacing the former monolithic development plan by a new two-tier system of structure plans and local plans.[42] In future only structure plans were to be the direct concern of the minister, and they would indicate broad planning policy only. Local plans would deal in detail with particular areas within the boundaries of a structure plan and would normally be approved by planning authorities themselves without ministerial intervention. At first this two-tier system did not correspond to the two-tier system of local government: only county councils were local planning authorities for both purposes. But under the Local Government Act 1972[43] county councils and district councils were made local planning authorities for their respective areas, and district councils became responsible for local plans. District councils have since been given increased powers, at the expense of county councils.[44] In the metropolitan counties and in Greater London district councils are now

[42] See Town and Country Planning Act 1971, Pt. II, as amended by Town and Country Planning (Amendment) Act 1972.
[43] s. 182.
[44] Local Government, Planning and Land Act 1980, s. 86.

in charge of both structural and local planning and make 'unitary development plans', as explained below. Both structure and local plans are subject to elaborate ministerial regulations as to their general form and content and the procedure for their adoption.[45]

Making of structure and local plans

The county council must prepare its structure plan after making a survey and after consultation with the district councils in its area.[46] The structure plan is to be a written statement, supplemented with diagrams and illustrations but not based on a map, formulating planning policy and general proposals and relating them to neighbouring areas. The plan must be publicised and potential objectors alerted in accordance with regulations governing public participation. It is then submitted to the Secretary of State for the Environment (now the minister responsible for planning) for his approval. Formerly the Secretary of State was required to hold a hearing (normally a public inquiry) for all objections. He must still consider objections duly lodged,[47] but under the Town and Country Planning (Amendment) Act 1972 he need no longer afford all objectors a hearing. He need now hold only an 'examination in public', at which he may select both the matters to be examined and the bodies and persons entitled to take part, subject to the discretion of the presiding officer to invite others to participate.[48] This is a further attempt to reduce the delays in which overall plans may get bogged down. Nevertheless it has been found necessary to empower the Secretary of State to direct a local planning authority to proceed with a local plan in advance of his approval of the structure plan, even though the two plans may not in the end be consistent.[49]

The examination in public is not at present subject to statutory procedural rules (though there is power to make them), but the Secretary of State publishes a code of practice describing how the subjects and participants will be selected and how the examination will be conducted.[50] Finally the Secretary of State may approve the plan with or without modifications, or may reject it in toto. The whole procedure of the

[45] SI 1982 No. 555.

[46] For details see Act of 1971, ss. 6–10 as amended by Act of 1972 and SI 1982 No. 555. s. 7(5) of the Act of 1971 requiring the indication of action areas was repealed by Local Government, Planning and Land Act 1980, 14th sched., para. 2.

[47] Unless they relate only to things to be done under certain highway orders or new town designation orders: Act of 1971, s. 16.

[48] Town and Country Planning (Amendment) Act 1972, s. 3.

[49] Local Government, Planning and Land Act 1980, s. 88. The local plan must 'conform generally to the structure plan as it stands for the time being'.

[50] Booklet *Structure Plans. The Examination in Public.* See Department of Environment circulars 36/73, 39/78, 23/81.

examination in public and the Secretary of State's part in it are subject to the supervision of the Council on Tribunals.[51] But the Secretary of State is required to make only 'such statement as he considers appropriate' of the reasons for his decision.[52]

Before local plans can be made the county council must make a 'local plan scheme' designating the parts of the county which are to be the subject of local plans and the authorities which are to prepare them.[53] These authorities (normally district councils) may then proceed to survey their areas and to make their detailed plans, with publicity and informal public participation much as in the case of structure plans. This is mandatory in the case of action areas (areas selected for comprehensive improvement or redevelopment in the near future) where the relevant structure plan has been approved. A local plan must consist of a map and written statement, but it does not have to be stereotyped as regards detail. It may be highly detailed about a redevelopment scheme to be carried out by the local authority, but much less detailed about one to be carried out by private developers. It must be certified by the county planning authority to be in general conformity with the structure plan; any difference of opinion over this is settled by the Secretary of State who may direct that the plan be revised.[54] If nevertheless a local plan is in conflict with the structure plan, the local plan prevails.[55]

The Secretary of State is not directly concerned with a local plan, though a copy of it must be sent to him and he has the power to call it in for his approval.[56] But objections duly made must be heard at a local inquiry or hearing before a Secretary of State's inspector, or where regulations permit before a person appointed by the local authority itself.[57] That authority must then consider the inspector's report, but is free to adopt its own plan, with or without modifications, or to reject it. Thus it has in the end to pass judgment on its own proposals. But before adopting its plan it must give notice both to the objectors and to the Secretary of State, and the Secretary of State may take time to consider whether to call in the plan at this final stage.[58] The local authority must if requested give reasons for its decision and its procedure is subject to the Tribunals and Inquiries Act 1971 and to the supervision of the Council on Tribunals.[59] Virtually the whole

[51] Act of 1971, s. 9(6), added by Act of 1972, s. 3.
[52] Act of 1971, s. 9(8), added by Act of 1972, s. 3. See below, p. 980.
[53] Act of 1971, s. 11A, added by Housing and Planning Act 1986, 10th sched.
[54] Act of 1971, s. 14(5), added by Local Government Act 1972, 16th sched., para. 3.
[55] Housing and Planning Act 1986, 10th sched., s. 15B.
[56] s. 14(3). He may reject it without leaving the local authority: *R v. Secretary of State for the Environment ex p. Southwark LBC* [1987] JPL 587.
[57] s. 13. This is subject to the above-mentioned exception under s. 16.
[58] SI 1982 No. 555, reg. 32.
[59] s. 13(1).

procedure is subject to the Secretary of State's control, by regulations or otherwise, and he has been given powers to direct the making, alteration, repeal, or replacement of any local plan.[60]

The legal validity of a structure plan or of a local plan, or of any alteration of it, may be questioned only within six weeks of the publication of the first notice of its approval or adoption,[61] under a form of provision which is discussed later.[62] Joint boards representing two or more county or district councils may be constituted by the Secretary of State as composite planning authorities for larger areas, or for special areas such as national parks.[63] In the case of national parks all planning powers of all kinds are exercised at county level only.[64]

The structure and local plans together form the 'development plan'. But despite all the statutory machinery, the plan has remarkably little direct effect. The legal problems of planning lie mostly in the day-to-day handling of applications for planning permission and enforcement, where the real teeth of the legislation are to be found.

Unitary development plans

When the Greater London Council and the Metropolitan county councils were abolished by the Local Government Act 1985 the London borough councils and the metropolitan district councils necessarily took over the task of making structure as well as local plans for their areas. The Act required them to incorporate both plans in a 'unitary development plan' in accordance with Secretary of State's regulations.[65] The plan must be divided into two parts, part 1 consisting of a general statement of policies similar to a structure plan, and part 2 containing detailed material corresponding to a local plan. The council has to publicise the plan, hold a local inquiry or hearing, and consider comments and objections. Before adopting it they must send a copy to the Secretary of State who has power to call it in in whole or in part for his approval, holding a local inquiry or hearing if the council have not already held one. Where only part 1 of the plan is called in the inquiry takes the form of an examination in public, subject to the Tribunals and Inquiries Act 1971 to the same extent as a structure plan. Two or more councils may join forces in a joint unitary

[60] Housing and Planning Act 1986, 10th sched.
[61] Act of 1971, ss. 242, 244.
[62] Below, p. 733.
[63] See SI 1973 No. 2061 (Peak District) and 1973 No. 2001 (Lake District), replacing earlier orders.
[64] Local Government Act 1972, s. 182(4).
[65] 1st sched.

plan. For Greater London there is a joint planning committee, with consultative functions, established by the boroughs.[66]

'Development'

The basic rule of planning law is that permission is required for development. 'Development' is very widely defined under two heads, as 'the carrying out of building, engineering, mining or other operations in, on, over or under land', or 'the making of any material change in the use of any buildings or other land'.[67] The second limb is expressly declared to include the use of a single dwelling-house as two or more dwelling-houses. On the other hand there are some important qualifications. A variety of things do not count as development, such as improvements or alterations to buildings, which do not materially affect external appearance, highway works, the use of buildings or land 'within the curtilage of a dwellinghouse'[68] for any purpose incidental to its enjoyment as such, use for agriculture or forestry, and change of use within the permitted 'use classes'.[69] 'Use classes' are groups of uses prescribed by order[70] which are freely interchangeable within each group; thus the use of an office may be changed for any purpose except financial or professional services, the use of a shop may be changed for most purposes (but not for the sale of hot food), a cinema may be changed to a bingo hall and a rag and bone dealer may change to a maggot breeder or gut scraper. Certain other things, though they count as development, are exempted from the requirement of permission by the General Development Order.[71] Examples are enlargements or alterations to a dwelling-house (including the building of a garage) not exceeding 15 per cent of its external cubic content or 70 cubic metres, whichever is the greater but with a maximum of 115 cubic metres; the erection of gates, walls, and fences within certain limits; painting (even this is assumed to be development); most agricultural and forestry buildings and works; and various ancillary industrial operations. The Secretary of State therefore has wide powers of adjusting the meaning and effect of development for the purposes of the Act. The courts have also

---

[66] s. 5.
[67] Town and Country Planning Act 1971, s. 22 (this is the original definition from the Act of 1947).
[68] This means the garden or land adjacent and used for household purposes: see *Pilbrow* v. *Vestry of St. Leonard, Shoreditch* [1895] 1 QB 433; *Re St. George's, Oakdale* [1976] Fam. 210.
[69] s. 22(2).
[70] Town and Country Planning (Use Classes) Order 1987, SI No. 764.
[71] Town and Country Planning General Development Order 1977, SI No. 289; 1980, No. 1946; 1981, No. 245; 1987, No. 765.) The order may (and does) allow the Secretary of State to withdraw the permission in any particular case or area: Act of 1971, s. 24(5).

been concerned with its meaning in many cases.[72] Whether there has been a 'material change in the use' is held to be 'a question of fact and degree', as explained elsewhere.[73]

Planning permission

Permission must be sought from the local planning authority (the district council). If it is granted, it may be (and normally is) made subject to conditions, but the conditions must be reasonable and within the true purposes of the Act.[74] The planning authority must have regard to the development plan but is at liberty to depart from it, provided that any substantial departure must first be advertised, allowing time for objections, and notified with particulars to the Secretary of State.[75] The Secretary of State may call in any application for his own determination after inquiry or hearing,[76] and this is often done where there is strong local opposition. Applications for certain uses, such as cinemas, bingo halls, slaughterhouses, or cemeteries, must be advertised by notices both in the local press and on the site.[77] Applications by non–owners must be notified to the owners and others interested in the land.[78] A public register of all applications must be maintained by the planning authority,[79] so that with sufficient vigilance it is possible for neighbours and others to keep themselves informed. If there is no decision on an application within eight weeks, it is deemed to have been refused, so that an appeal can then be made.[80] Until 1981 planning applications were free of charge, but a scale of fees has since been imposed.[81]

Planning authorities do not formally hold hearings before refusing permission,[82] but if they propose to refuse or if opposition has been

---

[72] e.g. *East Barnet Urban District Council* v. *British Transport Commission* [1962] 2 QB 484; *Birmingham Cpn.* v. *Habib Ullah* [1964] 1 QB 178; *James* v. *Minister of Housing and Local Government* [1968] AC 409; *Webber* v. *Ministry of Housing and Local Government* [1968] 1 WLR 29; *Coleshill & District Investment Ltd.* v. *Minister of Housing and Local Government* [1969] 1 WLR 746; *Burdle* v. *Secretary of State for the Environment* [1972] 1 WLR 1207.

[73] Below, p. 941.

[74] See below, p. 431.

[75] SI 1977 No. 289, art. 14; direction in Ministry of Housing and Local Government circular no. 96/75. See *Gregory* v. *Camden London Borough Council* [1966] 1 WLR 899; below, p. 692.

[76] Act of 1971, s. 35.

[77] Act of 1971, s. 26; SI 1977 No. 289, para. 8.

[78] Act of 1971, s. 27.

[79] Act of 1971, s. 34.

[80] Act of 1971, s. 37; SI 1977 No. 289, art. 7(6). Alternatively a decision may be demanded: *Bovis Homes (Scotland) Ltd.* v. *Inverclyde DC* 1982 SLT 473.

[81] Local Government, Planning and Land Act 1980, s. 87; SI 1983 No. 1674. The fee for a dwelling-house is £66.

[82] See below, p. 551.

expressed they will often adjourn the case in order to receive representations in writing. They have wide powers to delegate the decision of planning applications and similar matters to their officers.[83] They can give rulings, on the application of would-be developers, to determine whether planning permission is required.[84]

Planning permission enures for the benefit of the land and all persons interested in it, so that it is not lost by inactivity or abandonment.[85] It may be revoked or modified by the local planning authority in respect of building operations not yet completed and changes of use not yet carried out. But then there is a right to compensation for abortive expenditure or other loss incurred.[86] Revocation or modification requires the consent of the Secretary of State unless it is unopposed and unlikely to involve compensation; and in any case any party affected has a right to be heard by a Secretary of State's inspector.[87] As a final reserve power the local planning authority may order the discontinuance of any use or the alteration or removal of any buildings or works, even though authorised; but this may be done only with the consent of the Secretary of State, and compensation is payable not only for depreciation of the land but also for the expenses of compliance.[88]

The Secretary of State may himself grant planning permission by means of a development order, either for general classes of development (as already illustrated) or for any specific case.[89] But persons thereby affected have no procedural rights, so that neighbours were not entitled to be heard when a development order authorised the extension of an airport.[90]

Local authorities and public corporations are not exempted from the need to obtain planning permission for development which they wish to carry out on their own land. Their position is however eased in three respects. First, they may, in effect, grant permission to themselves by following the procedure prescribed by regulations, registering their project in the register of planning applications, giving notice to owners and others concerned, and advertising where the class of development so requires.[91] If the Secretary of State does not call in the case, a resolution may be passed which operates as deemed permission from him. Secondly, many of their

---

[83] Local Government Act 1972, s. 101.
[84] Act of 1971, s. 53.
[85] *Pioneer Aggregates Ltd* v. *Secretary of State for the Environment* [1985] AC 132.
[86] Act of 1971, ss. 45, 164. See below, p. 805.
[87] ss. 45, 46.
[88] ss. 51, 170.
[89] s. 24.
[90] *Essex County Council* v. *Ministry of Housing and Local Government* (1967) 18 P & CR. 531 (Stansted Airport); below, p. 573.
[91] Act of 1971, s. 270; SI 1976 No. 1419, para. 4.

normal operations are permitted under the General Development Order;[92] and thirdly, planning permission is deemed to have been granted for any development which has been given ministerial authorisation, either expressly or by confirmation of a compulsory purchase order, grant, or loan sanction.[93]

The legislation does not bind the Crown, so that government departments can develop their land without legal restriction.[94]

Enterprise zones and simplified planning zones

Enterprise zones and simplified planning zones are two devices aiming to encourage enterprise and development by reducing bureaucratic controls.

Enterprise zones were introduced by the Local Government, Planning and Land Act 1980 in order to assist redevelopment in the inner cities.[95] Since they confer valuable financial privileges including exemption from taxes and rates, they may be established only on the initiative of the Secretary of State and subject to the consent of the Treasury and annulment by either House of Parliament. If the Secretary of State invites a local authority to prepare a scheme, they may proceed to adopt one after giving it adequate publicity and considering representations. If the validity of the scheme is not challenged within six weeks, the Secretary of State may designate the area as an enterprise zone for a fixed period (in practice ten years). The planning consequences are that planning permission is thereby granted automatically for any development or class of development specified in the scheme, but subject to whatever conditions the scheme contains. The scheme may, for example, confer outline permission only.

Simplified planning zones have been devised to operate on a wider basis under the Housing and Planning Act 1986.[96] Here the initiative rests with the local authority and there are no fiscal privileges. Every planning authority must consider whether it should make one or more schemes for such zones. Every scheme, after preliminary publicity and consideration of representations, must be opened to public inspection and subjected to public inquiry in the usual way. The Secretary of State must be informed throughout and all the steps must be in accordance with regulations, with default powers in the background. Furthermore, any one may request the planning authority to make a scheme and if they refuse he may require them to refer the request to the Secretary of State, who may direct the

---

[92] Above, p. 185.
[93] Act of 1971, s. 40.
[94] *Ministry of Agriculture* v. *Jenkins* [1963] 2 QB 317; below, p. 827.
[95] s. 179 and 32nd sched.
[96] s. 25 and 6th sched.

making of a scheme. Approval of a scheme by the Secretary of State means that planning permission is automatically granted for any development or class of development specified in the scheme, and conforming to any conditions contained in it, for a period of ten years.[97] The scheme thus operates like a local general development order.

Appeals and judicial review

No one has any right of appeal against the grant of planning permission. The theory of planning control is that the only parties concerned are the applicant and the planning authority, and that permission merely legitimates what the owner was previously at liberty to do on his land in any case.[98] The permission in no way entitles him to infringe the legal rights of others, e.g. by building so as to obstruct their light or operating an industry which is a nuisance.

Against refusal of permission, and against any condition attached to permission, there is a right of appeal to the Secretary of State, who must afford an oral hearing.[99] This will generally involve a public inquiry before a departmental inspector, in which all members of the public will be allowed to take part, unless the appellant opts (as the great majority of appellants in fact do) for one of the alternative procedures of informal hearing or appeal on written representations only.[1] Formerly much delay was caused by the over-centralisation of thousands of appeals in the department. But most appeals may now be determined by the inspector himself under delegated powers, which have been extended by stages until now they apply to all appeals against refusal of planning permission, against conditions, and against enforcement notices except appeals by statutory undertakers (such as nationalised industries) which concern some other minister as well as the Secretary of State.[2] On an appeal the case may be dealt with as if at first instance,[3] so that an appeal against conditions may result in a refusal. This right of appeal is basically for purposes of planning policy. But in two cases there is a further appeal from the Secretary of State's decision to the High Court on a point of law: where a ruling is given on the question whether planning permission is required, as mentioned

[97] Development begun within the ten years remains permitted.
[98] See *Buxton* v. *Minister of Housing and Local Government* [1961] 1 QB 278, discussed below, p. 744. Judicial review is another matter: see below.
[99] Act of 1971, s. 36.
[1] See below, p. 990, for these procedures.
[2] Act of 1971, 9th sched.; SI 1981 No. 804.
[3] s. 36(3). See *Stringer* v. *Minister of Housing and Local Government* [1970] 1 WLR 1281 (below, p. 373).

above; and where the appeal is against an enforcement notice, as mentioned below.[4]

The right to challenge the validity of planning decisions and orders in the High Court—that is to say, the right to invoke judicial review—is subject to complex provisions which in specified cases allow challenge to be made only within six weeks and only on the grounds that the decision or order is not within the powers of the legislation or that substantial prejudice has been suffered by failure to comply with some requirement. The planning authority may use this procedure to challenge a grant of planning permission by the Secretary of State on appeal.[5] The effect of this statutory version of judicial review, which in an important group of Acts of Parliament has displaced the ordinary review under common law, is investigated elsewhere.[6] The court may also grant ordinary remedies, such as certiorari, where they are not excluded by the Act, e.g. to quash a planning permission containing conditions which are ultra vires, or granted in breach of the principles of natural justice.[7]

Enforcement

The sanction against a breach of planning control is the enforcement notice. This is served by the local planning authority on the owner and the occupier and any one else materially affected, and it must specify the date (at least twenty-eight days after service) when it is to take effect, the time allowed thereafter for compliance, and the steps required to be taken,[8] e.g. the demolition of a building erected without permission, or the discontinuance of some new unauthorised use. In the case of a change of use the notice may be served after any interval of time, except where the change is to use as a single dwelling-house. In other cases, including cases of breach of conditions attached to a planning permission for building or other operations, there is a time limit of four years from the breach.[9] Failure to comply with an enforcement notice is punishable by fine, with additional daily fines for continuing disobedience after conviction.[10] In the case of offending buildings etc. the local planning authority may enter the land and remove them at the cost of the owner.[11] In urgent cases it may also

[4] Act of 1971, ss. 246, 247.
[5] Act of 1971, s. 245(2).
[6] Below, p. 734.
[7] See below, pp. 431, 476.
[8] Act of 1971, s. 87.
[9] s. 87(3).
[10] s. 89.
[11] s. 91.

serve a stop notice so as to prevent offending operations from continuing during the period before the enforcement notice takes effect, and subject to similar penalties,[12] but there is a right to compensation if the proceedings turn out to be unjustified.[13]

Against an enforcement notice there is a right of appeal to the Secretary of State, with a further appeal to the High Court on a question of law; and meanwhile the notice does not take effect.[14] The Secretary of State has very wide powers, not only as to the details of the breach and the enforcement notice, but also as to the planning merits, and he may if he thinks fit grant planning permission; he may also amend or vary the enforcement notice. On certain of the grounds on which an enforcement notice may be disputed this appeal is the only available remedy, recourse to the courts being excluded by the Act.[15] But there has been much litigation over the formalities of enforcement notices, which the courts require to indicate fairly the contravention and the steps to be taken to remedy it, without undue emphasis on mere technicalities.[16]

This system of enforcement proved inadequate for the control of caravan sites. Unauthorised development was not in itself an offence, and an enforcement notice might not take effect for a long time if there was first an appeal to the Secretary of State and then perhaps an appeal on a point of law which might be carried to the House of Lords. When finally the notice was upheld, the offender had only to move the caravans to an adjacent field and begin again.[17] This abuse was first countered by obtaining injunctions with the assistance of the Attorney-General.[18] The Caravan Sites and Control of Development Act 1960 then imposed special statutory penalties, making it an offence to use a caravan site, whether or not previously authorised, without a site licence from the local authority, normally the district council.[19] No site licence could be granted unless planning permission had first been obtained; once planning permission was obtained, however, a site licence had to be granted, but might be (and normally was) subject to conditions for controlling the numbers and types

---

[12] s. 90, as amended by Town and Country Planning (Amendment) Act 1977.

[13] s. 177.

[14] s. 88.

[15] s. 243, including the grounds that the matters alleged are not a breach, that the four-year limit has expired, and that the notice was not duly served.

[16] *Munnich* v. *Godstone Rural District Council* [1966] 1 WLR 427. See e.g. *East Riding County Council* v. *Park Estate (Bridlington) Ltd.* [1957] AC 233; *Dudley Bowers Amusements Enterprises Ltd.* v. *Secretary of State for the Environment* (1986) 52 P & CR 365.

[17] For full explanation see *Mixnam's Properties Ltd.* v. *Chertsey Urban District Council* [1964] 1 QB 214 at 235 (Diplock LJ), affirmed [1965] AC 735.

[18] See below, p. 610.

[19] Pt. I. This is still in force, independently of the Act of 1971.

of caravans, for preserving amenity, ensuring proper fire precautions and sanitary arrangements, and so forth.[20] Caravan sites were thus subjected to a regime which went beyond normal planning control and which had effective sanctions. The Act gave a right of appeal to a magistrates' court against any site licence condition which was unduly burdensome.[21] It also exempted various minor and temporary uses of caravans.[22] Local authorities have power to provide caravan sites and facilities for them[23] and are officially encouraged to do so for some purposes, e.g. for the use of gipsies.

Other features of planning law

In addition to the regular system of control of development, planning law has or had a number of branches which may be mentioned briefly.

Industrial development and office development were both formerly subject to special licensing arrangements which required a preliminary authorisation from the Secretary of State before a planning application could be made, except that an industrial development certificate was not required in a 'development area', i.e. an area where it is the policy to attract industry.[24] But both these controls have been abolished.[25] A remarkable feature of both of them was that the elaborate statutory rules made no provision for any procedure, any right to be heard, or any appeal.[26]

Buildings of special architectural or historic interest are protected by the 'listed building' system. Lists are compiled or approved by the Secretary of State, and it is an offence to demolish, alter, or injure a listed building without a 'listed building consent' from the local planning authority or the Secretary of State.[27] An unlisted building may also be protected temporarily by the local planning authority by means of a building preservation notice, which operates for six months.[28] There is no provision

[20] Act of 1960, s. 5, requiring the local authority to have regard to the Secretary of State's 'model standards for caravan sites'.

[21] s. 7.

[22] 1st sched.

[23] Act of 1960, s. 24.

[24] Act of 1971, ss. 66–86.

[25] Industrial development control was suspended by SI 1981 No. 1826 and office development control was terminated by SI 1979 No. 908. ss. 66–86 of the Act of 1971 are now repealed: Housing and Planning Act 1986, 12th sched.

[26] See below, p. 561.

[27] Act of 1971, ss. 54, 55 as amended by Local Government, Planning and Land Act 1980, s. 90 and by Housing and Planning Act 1986, s. 49 and sched. 9.

[28] s. 58.

for the owner to be heard, or even notified, before his building is listed,[29] but there is a statutory procedure for applications for listed building consent, including a right of appeal to the Secretary of State against refusal of consent by the local planning authority.[30] Refusal or revocation of consent may entitle the owner to compensation, provided that he has exercised his right of appeal.[31] A listed building may also be acquired compulsorily for the purpose of preserving it.[32]

'Conservation areas' are required to be designated by local planning authorities, where they determine that it is desirable to preserve or enhance some area of special architectural or historic interest; and the Secretary of State may do likewise. Only other local authorities need be consulted. All buildings in the area are then protected as if they were listed buildings, subject to specified exceptions, and trees are protected as if they were subject to tree preservation orders.[33]

Tree preservation orders may be made by local planning authorities in the interests of amenity.[34] Unless unopposed, a tree preservation order requires the confirmation of the Secretary of State, who must consider objections and representations. It may prohibit the felling of trees without the authority's consent and it may require felled areas to be suitably replanted, subject to compensation in some cases[35] and subject to fines for disobedience.[36] A provisional order may also be made without confirmation, so as to preserve the status quo for a maximum period of six months.[37]

The local planning authority's ultimate power to order the cessation of any use or the removal of buildings has already been noted.

Eyesores and derelict land may be dealt with under a provision empowering the local planning authority to serve a notice requiring the abatement of injury to amenity caused by the condition of any land in or adjoining their area.[38] The authority may take the necessary action itself and recover the cost from the owner. Non-compliance is punishable by

[29] s. 54(3) merely requires the Secretary of State to consult persons or bodies interested in such buildings generally. Officials compiling lists are instructed not to notify owners: see *Amalgamated Investment Co. Ltd.* v. *Walker Ltd.* [1977] 1 WLR 164, where this practice caused heavy loss.
[30] 11th sched., Pt. I.
[31] ss. 171, 172; also 173 (building preservation notices).
[32] ss. 114–17.
[33] Act of 1971, s. 277 as amended by Town and Country Amenities Act 1974, ss. 1, 8.
[34] Act of 1971, s. 60.
[35] ss. 174, 175.
[36] s. 102.
[37] s. 61.
[38] Act of 1971, s. 65 as amended by Housing and Planning Act 1986, s. 46. See *Stephens* v. *Cuckfield Rural District council* [1960] 2 QB 373.

fine, but there is a right of appeal against the notice to a magistrates' court and thence to the Crown Court.[39]

Advertisements are subject to detailed control under a lengthy code of regulations which the Secretary of State is empowered to make in the interests of amenity or public safety.[40] Where they comply with these regulations they do not require planning permission, even though they may constitute development.[41] Infringement is punishable by fine.[42] 'Areas of special control' may be established, e.g. for open countryside, where in general no advertisements are to be permitted, subject to narrow exceptions. In other areas advertisements require the consent of the local planning authority or of the Secretary of State, subject to a catalogue of exceptions such as traffic signs, business and directional signboards, and temporary advertisements, e.g. 'for sale'.

Public access to open country may be secured by an access order made by a local planning authority under the National Parks and Access to the Countryside Act 1949.[43] An access order must be confirmed by the Secretary of State who must, if objections or representations are lodged, first hold a public inquiry or hearing in the same general manner as on a planning appeal.[44] The effect of an access order is that persons on the land solely for purposes of recreation are not to be treated as trespassers provided that they observe the prescribed conditions, which broadly speaking require good behaviour and the avoidance of agricultural land and places such as gardens and quarries.[45]

In addition to all these powers and controls, the Act of 1971 allows the Secretary of State to authorise the compulsory acquisition of land by local authorities for development, redevelopment, or improvement or for any purpose necessary for proper planning, including the relocation of population or industry.[46] The standard compulsory purchase procedure applies. The Secretary of State also has power, subject to advertisement and consideration of objections, to order the stopping up or diversion of highways where this appears necessary to enable permitted developments to be carried out.[47]

A system of control, analogous to planning control, over hazardous substances was imposed by the Housing and Planning Act 1986.[48]

[39] ss. 104–7.
[40] Act of 1971, s. 63; SI 1969 No. 1532; 1975 No. 898.
[41] Act of 1971, s. 64.
[42] s. 109.
[43] ss. 59–83, as amended by the Countryside Act 1968.
[44] s. 65 and 1st sched.
[45] s. 60.
[46] s. 112 as extended by Local Government, Planning and Land Act 1980, s. 91.
[47] ss. 209–14.
[48] s. 30.

NEW TOWNS, TOWN DEVELOPMENT AND URBAN DEVELOPMENT

New towns

A particularly creative planning function, though one committed to special statutory authorities, is the improvement of the distribution of population by the creation of new towns. Statutory machinery for this was first provided by the New Towns Act 1946, replaced first by the New Towns Act 1965 and secondly by the New Towns Act 1981.

It is for the Secretary of State for the Environment to designate the area of a new town, which may if desired include an existing town. He must first publish a draft order and if objections are duly lodged he must hold a public inquiry 'with respect to the objection'; then he must consider the inspector's report and determine whether or not to make the order.[49] Since he is both the initiating and confirming authority, he cannot be expected to be an impartial arbiter. The order for the first of the new towns (Stevenage) was unsuccessfully challenged, as related elsewhere, on the ground that the minister had displayed bias in advance.[50] The validity of the order may be questioned only within six weeks.[51]

The next step is for the Secretary of State to establish a development corporation for the new town, which has full powers to carry out development, building, provision of services, commercial transactions, and so forth.[52] Plans must be submitted from time to time to the Secretary of State who may approve or vary them by development order, and who may give directions to the development corporation.[53] Planning control is accordingly taken out of the hands of the local planning authorities during the initial development. The development corporation has powers of compulsory purchase, with expedited completion if so directed by the Secretary of State.[54] The new town may be made a united district for the purpose of the Public Health Act 1936, and the development corporation may be authorised to provide services such as transport and sewerage.[55] But otherwise the new town does not alter the ordinary responsibilities of the local authorities and it has no effect on local government areas. With the Secretary of State's approval the development corporation may transfer to a suitable local authority any part of their undertaking or property.[56]

[49] Act of 1981, s. 1 and 1st sched.
[50] Below, p. 491.
[51] 1st sched., paras. 6, 7.
[52] Act of 1965, ss. 3–6.
[53] s. 5.
[54] ss. 10–16.
[55] ss. 33–4.
[56] s. 39.

When the development corporation has substantially finished its work it will be dissolved by the Secretary of State and its remaining property will be transferred to the Commission for the New Towns.[57] This Commission is a permanent body which holds and manages the property of the dissolved development corporations, and has power to use their assets on a commercial basis for the benefit of the towns from which they derive.[58] In law the Commission is not a servant or agent of the Crown, but it is subject to directions from the Secretary of State;[59] it is thus a typical public corporation.

The Commission and the development corporations have power to dispose of their land to private purchasers, but the sale of freeholds or leases longer than ninety-nine years requires authority from the Secretary of State, who may in any case control the use of the power. He may put pressure on them to make sales by calling for repayment of capital advanced to them, and also by excluding from their area any specified land, which must then be sold.[60]

Town development

A less radical alternative to creating new towns is to encourage the expansion of the smaller existing towns and the reception by them of 'overspill' population from the great cities or other overcrowded areas. Powers for this purpose were conferred upon local authorities by the Town Development Act 1952.[61] In this case there are no new statutory bodies: the existing local authorities undertake the operations themselves, though the Secretary of State may constitute them into joint bodies if occasion requires.[62]

The Act authorises local authorities, with the consent of the Secretary of State, to exercise any of their powers, e.g. to provide housing, for the benefit of areas other than their own, if this will relieve congestion or over-population elsewhere.[63] There are provisions for grants both from the central government and from the local authorities exporting surplus population. Wide powers are given for local authorities to collaborate, either through agency or otherwise, under agreements approved by the Secretary of State or under orders made by him. The authority which is

[57] s. 41.
[58] ss. 35–7.
[59] ss. 35(2), 37(2).
[60] ss. 2, 17, 63–4.
[61] As amended by the Local Government Act 1972, s. 185 and 18th sched., and Local Government, Planning and Land Act 1980, s. 124.
[62] Act of 1952, s. 12.
[63] ss. 1, 5.

exporting population may be authorised to acquire land and to carry out development in the importing authority's area. There is no dispensation from normal planning control.[64] This machinery has been put to use in a series of arrangements for relieving the congestion of London.

Urban development

In order to 'secure the regeneration' of decayed urban areas such as the London and Liverpool docklands, new machinery for 'urban development' is provided by the Local Government, Planning and Land Act 1980.[65] An urban development corporation, modelled in general on a new town development corporation, may be constituted by the Secretary of State after he has designated an urban development area.[66] The corporation then has extensive powers to acquire land, carry out building, development and other operations, and generally to do anything required for the purpose of 'encouraging the development of existing and new industry and commerce, creating an attractive environment and ensuring that housing and social facilities are available to encourage people to live and work in the area'.[67] The intention is that the corporation should be a relatively short-term phenomenon, operating in conjunction with private enterprise and handing its area back to the ordinary local authorities when development has been stimulated sufficiently.

An urban development corporation is not in law a Crown agency, but it is under close control by the Secretary of State. He appoints all its members and he may give directions restricting its functions or requiring it to exercise them in any specified way. He may approve its development plans by special development order and he may make it the planning, housing, and (in some respects) public health authority for its area. Finally, when its task is done and its property duly disposed of, he may dissolve it.

COMMUNITY LAND ACT 1975–1980

Nationalisation of development

The planning system outlined in the preceding pages was radically affected by the scheme for community land contained in the Community Land Act

[64] s. 21.
[65] Pt. XVI.
[66] s. 136. The former restriction to metropolitan areas no longer applies: Housing and Planning Act 1986, s. 47.
[67] See Merseyside Development Corporation (Area and Constitution) Order, SI 1981 No. 481.

1975. But the Act was repealed in 1980, after a change of government and before it could be brought fully into effect.[68] This abbreviated account of it is primarily of historical interest. Although certain parts of the Act have survived, its policy and main structure are abolished. Its principal surviving remnant is the Land Authority for Wales, which was constituted to deal with developable land in Wales instead of the local authorities, which in Wales are sometimes inconveniently small.[69] The Act of 1975 was exceptional even by modern standards in being a piece of skeleton legislation conferring very wide powers, the true nature of which would be revealed by regulations and directions issued by the Secretary of State, whose control over the whole operation was virtually unlimited. The effective agents, however, were to be local authorities.

A primary objective was to make yet another attempt to expropriate the development value of land for the benefit of the community as a whole. This aspect is to be explained later as part of the section on compensation. Here it will suffice to describe briefly the general scheme of the legal machinery, which never passed beyond a transitional stage.

Broadly stated, the aim was to nationalise most commercial development. Instead of confining itself to permitting or not permitting development by private enterprise, a local authority was to involve itself positively in development by acquiring the land in question. Having acquired the land, it might then develop it itself or dispose of it to a private developer, buying at current use value and selling or letting at full market value, and so taking the development value for public funds. The principle was that land required for 'relevant development' should pass either into or through public ownership.

'Relevant development' meant development as defined by the planning legislation, with exceptions which included the building of a single dwelling-house and development of any class prescribed by regulations.[70]

Introduction by stages

The Act was to be brought into force by stages, marked by 'appointed days' and 'relevant dates'. 'Land acquisition and management schemes' had to be prepared for each county by the various local authorities acting jointly and subject to the control of the Secretary of State, allotting functions between them according to their respective responsibilities for planning, housing, local government, and so forth. There followed the

---

[68] Local Government, Planning and Land Act 1980, s. 101.

[69] Act of 1975, s. 8; Act of 1980, Pt. XII. The Authority is subject to detailed directions by the Secretary of State but it is not a Crown agency.

[70] s. 3(2); SI 1976 No. 331.

'first appointed day' on 6 April 1976,[71] when the new powers of acquisition became exercisable. The principal power was simply to acquire by agreement or compulsorily 'any land which, in their opinion, is suitable for development'.[72] This was hardly wider than the powers already conferred by the planning legislation,[73] but its bald form signalised the new policy of development through the agency of public authorities. Under each land acquisition and management scheme the various local authorities were to use their power of acquisition with a view to developing the land themselves and then disposing of it, or else making it available for development by others.[74] For this purpose they had to have regard to 'the desirability of bringing development land into public ownership', to the development plan for their area, and to planning policy generally.

The next stage was to be the 'relevant date'. This meant the date of the entry into force of an order made by the Secretary of State designating classes of relevant development for some particular area. Upon this date the power of acquisition became a duty: the local authorities had to arrange for one or other of them to acquire all land which was needed for development designated in the order, so passing all such land through public ownership. But this applied only to land which would be needed within ten years at any given time. The object of the 'relevant date' machinery was to allow the compulsory stage to be introduced piecemeal, for administrative reasons. For these and related purposes nearly 200 orders, circulars, etc., were issued under the Act. But no 'relevant date' had arrived before it was repealed.

Finally, when all relevant development had been designated by orders covering all areas of Great Britain, the 'second appointed day' was to be declared. This was to be the date for the adoption of current use value as the basis of compensation on compulsory purchase, as explained later.[75]

But that great day never arrived. When the Act was repealed such land as had in fact been acquired after the first appointed day was treated as acquired for planning purposes.[76]

Effect on planning permissions

The Community Land Act 1975 demanded important modifications in the system of planning permissions under the Town and Country Planning

---

[71] s. 7 and SI 1976 No. 330 (for Scotland, No. 662, appointing 1 September 1976).

[72] s. 15. The standard procedure for compulsory acquisition applied as modified by the complex provisions of the 4th sched.: see above, p. 174.

[73] Above, p. 194.

[74] 5th sched., para. 2.

[75] Below, p. 799.

[76] Act of 1980, 17th sched., para. 11.

Act 1971. The principle of these modifications was that planning permission for relevant development was to be automatically suspended until the land had been taken into public ownership for development. But the principle was to operate in this simple form only when the public ownership was compulsory, i.e. when planning permission was granted after the 'relevant date'. For the earlier transitional stages there were more complicated rules. If the permission was granted before the relevant date, it was suspended only if the local authority served a notice within two months declaring that they wished to acquire the land. If they did not do so, they lost their power to acquire the land within the next five years. If they did so, notice of any compulsory purchase order had to be published within twelve months and there was a restricted timetable for the remaining stages of the purchase. But if the application for planning permission was made before the first appointed day, the option was first given to the applicant: planning permission granted before the relevant date was then suspended only if the applicant served a notice of election calling upon the local authority to decide whether they wished to acquire the land, subject to the same rules as above. None of these rules is any longer enforceable.[77]

HOUSING

Provision of housing

One of the most important and expensive activities of the welfare state is the provision of housing, now undertaken on a vast scale by local authorities under the usual central government supervision and with the usual central government subsidies.[78] Approximately a third of all the rented accommodation in the country is supplied by district councils, who are the local housing authorities and who are thus the country's greatest landlords. This is an area in which they enjoy a large measure of liberty for enterprise and experiment in planning and executing their housing projects, despite the ministerial control which is always in the background and which, in particular, dictates financial policy. In the development of a housing project ministerial control will usually operate at three different stages: first, when the compulsory purchase order for acquiring the land requires confirmation; secondly, when loan sanction is required for raising the capital; and thirdly, when subsidies are needed for letting the houses at uneconomic rents. Once the houses are built and let, however, the local authority's managerial freedom is no longer as great as it used to be. For in

---

[77] Act of 1980, 17th sched., paras. 8, 13.
[78] The primary power to provide housing is in the Housing Act 1985, s. 9.

1980 council house tenants were for the first time given two valuable rights: the right to security of tenure; and the right to buy their houses or, in the case of flats, to take long leases.

The Labouring Classes Lodging Houses Act 1851, characteristically entitled in its time, was the first statute which empowered local authorities to build and let houses. Later milestones in housing legislation were the Public Health Act 1875 and the Housing of the Working Classes Act 1890, which were concerned not only with the supply of better housing but with the abolition of intolerably bad housing by means of closing and demolition orders. Additional powers were given in a long succession of Acts, which provided also for central government subsidies. The housing shortages produced by the two world wars supplied additional stimulus. Slum clearance was the dominant theme of the Housing Acts of 1930 and 1935. But the restriction to the 'working classes' lasted until removed by the Housing Act 1949. All the surviving enactments were ultimately consolidated in the Housing Act 1957, which with much amendment, especially by the Housing Act 1980, survived until it was replaced by the Housing Act 1985, now the primary statute. Between these various milestones there has been much legislation concerned with the complex system of grants and subsidies, as to which there have been sharp changes of policy.[79] The Housing Finance Act 1972 was designed to reduce rent subsidies by putting council houses onto the same 'fair rent' basis as other rent-controlled houses; but this was repealed by the Housing Rents and Subsidies Act 1975. The steps taken against some councils which refused to obey the Act of 1972 are noted elsewhere.[80] The Act of 1975 was in its turn superseded by the Act of 1980, which is now mostly incorporated in the Act of 1985.[81]

Council houses are subject to a legal regime of their own, now to be found in the Act of 1985.

Slum clearance

The most sweeping of all housing powers is that of slum clearance, and the litigation which it has provoked has made major contributions to administrative law.[82] The same basic procedure is used as for compulsory purchase, orders being first made by local authorities and then submitted to the Secretary of State for confirmation, with the usual procedure for a

---

[79] Subsidies in aid of a local authority's housing revenue account are payable under the Housing Act 1985, s. 421.

[80] Below, p. 748.

[81] Repeals of the Acts consolidated in the Act of 1985 are set out in Housing (Consequential Provisions) Act 1985, 1st sched.

[82] For examples see below, pp. 323, 508.

public inquiry or a hearing of objections prior to confirmation. The governing enactment is now the Housing Act 1985, Part IX.

The local authority must first be satisfied from an official representation or other information in their possession that the houses in the area are unfit for human habitation (as defined by the Act[83]) or dangerous or injurious to health and that the other buildings are similarly defective; and that the most satisfactory course is total demolition. A map must then be made excluding any sound buildings, and a resolution must be passed declaring a clearance area. But there are two conditions: suitable accommodation must be made available for the displaced inhabitants; and the local authority must have sufficient financial resources. At this stage the local authority need not consult the owners: the only person who need be informed of the resolution is the Secretary of State.[84]

Once the land has been declared to be a clearance area, two alternative procedures are possible. The local authority's immediate obligation is to purchase the land either by agreement or compulsorily and to arrange for the demolition of the buildings on it.[85] It will then become owner of the land which it can clear and, if it wishes, redevelop, bearing the cost itself.[86] Even if a compulsory purchase order has already been submitted to the Secretary of State, he may authorise the parties to proceed instead by agreement.[87] To proceed by agreement is often no hardship to the owner, since he will probably be relieved of unremunerative rent-controlled tenants who will be rehoused at public expense, and the cleared site may be worth much more than the slum. By making a compulsory purchase order, subject to limited compensation as explained elsewhere, the local authority can itself reap the profit of redeveloping the site. It has a free choice, and is not obliged to proceed by agreement rather than by compulsory purchase merely because it knows that the owner is willing and able to comply.[88] A compulsory purchase order also has the advantage that it may include any land surrounded by the clearance area which is reasonably necessary in order to secure a convenient clearance area and also any adjoining land which is reasonably necessary for the development or use of the cleared area;[89] and it may include areas where the only defect is the bad arrangement of buildings or narrow streets.

---

[83] s. 604.

[84] s. 289.

[85] The former alternative of a clearance order, requiring the owner to demolish the buildings himself, was abolished by Housing Act 1974, s. 108.

[86] s. 290.

[87] s. 292.

[88] *Robins (E.) Ltd.* v. *Minister of Health* [1939] 1 KB 520.

[89] Housing Act 1985, s. 290(3). See *Coleen Properties Ltd.* v. *Minister of Housing and Local Government* [1971] 1 WLR 433 (below, p. 325).

Compulsory purchase in a clearance area is governed by a procedure of its own and not by the Acquisition of Land Act 1981.[90] The order must be advertised and notices must be served on owners and occupiers much as in the case of other compulsory purchase orders, and it must then be submitted to the Secretary of State. The Secretary of State must hold the usual public local inquiry or hearing if there are objections, and must consider the objections and the report of the hearing before confirming or rejecting the order. If the ground of objection is that some building is not unfit for human habitation, the local authority must give the objector particulars of the alleged unfitness and the hearing must be at least fourteen days later; the objector also has a right to a statement of reasons from the Secretary of State.[91] The order may be confirmed with modifications, but not so as to bring in any additional land. The Secretary of State may however exclude any land from the clearance area but nevertheless authorise its compulsory purchase;[92] this will give the owner a more favourable basis of compensation.[93] There is power to postpone the operation of the order in the case of houses which are considered to be tolerable for the time being.[94]

Like other compulsory purchase orders and many orders affecting land, these orders must be challenged within six weeks if their legal validity is to be disputed.[95] Within that time the standard form of statutory remedy may be sought; the scope of this is fully discussed elsewhere.[96]

Redevelopment and improvement

The Housing Acts of 1935 and 1957 contained powers for schemes of redevelopment, to be made by local authorities with ministerial approval, in areas containing fifty or more working-class houses at least a third of which were overcrowded or unfit for habitation.[97] These were wider in some respects than the powers of slum clearance, but before any substantial use had been made of them they were in practice superseded by the wider powers conferred by the planning legislation. The Housing Act 1969 supplied still more extensive powers for the designation of 'general improvement areas', in order to encourage, without class distinction, the

[90] The procedure is set out in Housing Act 1985, 22nd sched.
[91] SI 1976 No. 74, rule 10.
[92] 22nd sched., para. 5(3).
[93] See *Ashbridge Investments Ltd.* v. *Minister of Housing and Local Government* [1965] 1 WLR 1320; and below, p. 690.
[94] Housing Act 1985, s. 301.
[95] 22nd sched., para. 7.
[96] Below, p. 734.
[97] Housing Act 1957, s. 55.

rehabilitation of run-down residential areas where better housing and amenities are needed.[98] These powers are now contained in the Housing Act 1985.[99]

A general improvement area need merely be 'a predominantly residential area' in which the local authority consider that living conditions ought to be improved. The resolution designating it must be advertised and brought to the attention of owners and residents and copied to the Secretary of State; but the Secretary of State need not confirm it, though he needs to confirm any compulsory purchase made under the powers. These powers are to carry out works, or acquire land either by agreement or compulsorily, and to let or otherwise dispose of land.

Additional categories of a similar kind were added by the Housing Act 1974, which authorised the designation of 'housing action areas' and 'priority neighbourhoods'. A housing action area[1] is an area where the local authority find that the living conditions are unsatisfactory and can most effectively be dealt with within a period of five years. It may include land which was formerly in a general improvement area or a priority neighbourhood. Its designation does not require the prior approval of the Secretary of State, but he has powers of partial or total veto. Subject to this, the Act confers very wide powers of compulsory purchase (if duly authorised) and of providing housing, whether by building, conversion, or improvement, of carrying out repairs, of management, of providing furniture, fittings, or services, and of making grants or otherwise assisting owners or tenants to carry out 'environmental works' for improving housing or amenities. Financial contributions may be made by the Secretary of State. A priority neighbourhood[2] is an area surrounding or adjoining a housing action area or a general improvement area where living conditions are unsatisfactory but it is not practicable to invoke the powers relating to housing action areas or general improvement areas. The procedure and powers conferred are generally similar to those which apply to housing action areas. But the Housing Act 1980 put an end to the creation of priority neighbourhoods, without prejudice to those already existing.[3]

Individual houses

Long before local authorities were given comprehensive powers of slum clearance they were empowered to take action against individual houses

---

[98] s. 253.
[99] Pt. VIII.
[1] Housing Act 1985, s. 239.
[2] Housing Act 1974, Pt. VI.
[3] s. 109.

which were unfit for human habitation. The standard of fitness is now prescribed by the Housing Act 1985 in terms of nine matters: repair, stability, freedom from damp, internal arrangement, natural lighting, ventilation, water supply, drainage and sanitary conveniences, and facilities for storage, preparation, and cooking of food and for the disposal of waste water. A house is unfit for human habitation if so defective in one or more of these matters that it is not 'reasonably suitable for occupation'.[4]

Every local authority has the duty to inspect houses in its area and to keep records. Before it may take action against an unfit house it is no longer necessary first to have an unfavourable report from its medical officer of health: it may act on any information in its possession.[5] If the house is capable of being rendered fit at reasonable expense, the local authority must serve a repair notice upon 'the person having control of the house' requiring him to carry out specified repairs, subject to appeal to the county court;[6] and in case of default it may do the repairs itself and charge the cost to the defaulter. If the house cannot be so rendered fit, the local authority must serve upon the person in control of it a notice saying that they will consider the position and any offer as to reconstruction or user which he may make. If no satisfactory undertaking is forthcoming, or if an undertaking is broken, the local authority must make a demolition order requiring the house to be pulled down;[7] but if part only is unfit, or if demolition would be injurious to neighbouring buildings, they must instead make a closing order prohibiting the use of the house, or the unfit part of it, for any purpose not approved by the local authority.[8] There are the same rights of appeal, and the same default powers, as in the case of repair notices. There is no power to postpone the making of these various orders as there is in the case of clearance orders. There are also no restrictions on challenging their validity in the ordinary way.

Housing the homeless

A duty to find accommodation for the homeless was put upon local authorities by the Housing (Homeless Persons) Act 1977, since replaced by the Housing Act 1985, Part III. The duty arises where the homeless person has a priority need, provided that he has not become homeless intentionally. For this purpose a person is homeless if he has no accommodation which he is entitled to occupy or if he is prevented from

---

[4] s. 604.
[5] ss. 189, 264.
[6] s. 189.
[7] s. 265. As to compensation, see below, p. 800.
[8] ss. 265, 277.

entering his home or threatened with violence. He has a priority need if he has children living with him, or is the victim of flood, fire, or other disaster, or is vulnerable for any special reason such as old age, mental handicap, or physical disability. But he is treated as homeless intentionally if he deliberately does anything causing loss of available accommodation, knowing the facts of the situation. The Act applies also to persons threatened with homelessness, if it is likely to occur within 28 days.

The homeless person must make application to the authority, whose first duty is to inquire into the facts of the case. If then they are satisfied that he fulfils the conditions, they must 'secure that accommodation becomes available for his occupation'. A decision of the House of Lords, holding that the bare word 'accommodation' did not mean 'appropriate' or 'reasonable' accommodation,[9] was reversed by the Housing and Planning Act 1986, providing that a person shall not be treated as having accommodation unless it is accommodation which it would be reasonable for him to continue to occupy.[10]

If not satisfied that the homeless person has a priority need the authority need only give 'advice and appropriate assistance'. If satisfied that he became homeless intentionally, they must secure accommodation for him for long enough to give him a reasonable opportunity of finding it for himself. But if he has a local connection with another authority's area, and none with the area where he applies, he may be referred to the other authority. In administering the Act authorities must have regard to guidance given by the Secretary of State, who has published a code for the purpose.

It has been held that a person may be treated as intentionally homeless if he acquiesces in accommodation being given up by a person with whom he lives,[11] and also if he gives up accommodation abroad to come to this country, even though meanwhile he has stayed with relatives here.[12] On the other hand the benefit of the Act may be claimed by any one lawfully in this country, including immigrants.[13] If the local authority wrongly rejects a claim it is subject to the usual remedies of judicial review,[14] and may also be liable in damages for breach of statutory duty.[15]

---

[9] R. v. Hillingdon LBC ex p. Puhlhofer [1986] AC 484.

[10] s. 14, allowing regard to be had to local conditions. In R. v. South Herefordshire DC ex p. Miles (1983) 17 HLR 82 it was held unreasonable for a couple with three children to continue to occupy a small rat-infested hut with no main services.

[11] R. v. North Devon DC ex p. Lewis [1981] 1 WLR 328.

[12] De Falco v. Crawley BC [1980] QB 460; and see Dyson v. Kerrier DC [1980] 1 WLR 1205.

[13] R. v. Hillingdon LBC ex p. Streeting [1980] 1 WLR 1425; same ex p. Islam [1981].

[14] As preceding note.

[15] Thornton v. Kirklees MBC [1979] QB 626.

The Act has produced much litigation, most of it by way of judicial review, accompanied by misgiving whether it 'is as well considered as it is undoubtedly well intentioned'.[16]

Tenure and enfranchisement in the public sector

Until 1980 lettings by public authorities were outside any system of rent control and protection of tenure like that which operated in the private sector, except for the period 1972–5 when council houses were brought within the 'fair rent' provisions of the Rent Acts. Local authorities could therefore eject their tenants or increase their rents with no restraint other than the terms of their leases or agreements and their legal duty to exercise their powers reasonably.[17] In fact council house rents were in general well below rents in the private sector, being heavily subsidised. But there was no legal security of tenure.

The Housing Act 1980 introduced 'secure tenancies'.[18] The protection applies to tenancies of dwelling-houses let by local authorities (and certain other bodies such as housing associations and new town development corporations) where the house is the tenant's only or principal home.[19] A fixed-term tenancy on its expiry continues automatically as a periodic tenancy. No protected tenancy can be brought to an end without an order of the court, and the court may make an order for possession only on one of the numerous grounds set out in the Act, such as non-payment of rent or unneighbourly conduct or neglect of the building. Occupants who are in law licensees rather than tenants are equally protected, unless they were squatters originally. A secure tenant may not sublet or part with possession without the landlord's consent (not to be unreasonably withheld), but he cannot be prevented from taking lodgers. Subletting or assignment puts an end to the security of tenure, except in a few special cases. On the tenant's death the tenancy vests automatically in the widow or widower or, if none, in a member of the tenant's family who has lived with him for the previous twelve months (if the family cannot agree, the landlord may choose the successor); but only one such succession is allowed. The rent under a secure tenancy is governed by the terms of the lease and the policy of the local authority, but the tenant (or a successor spouse) cannot be charged additional rent for improvements made at his own expense.

[16] *R. v. Hillingdon LBC ex p. Islam* (above) (Lord Wilberforce).
[17] See below, p. 400. Rents must be reasonable: Housing Act 1985, s. 24; and may be differential: below, p. 427.
[18] s. 28, replaced by Housing Act 1985, s. 79.
[19] There are various exceptions, including employees' tied houses, lettings to students, and lettings to homeless persons during the first year: Act of 1985, 1st sched.; and see *Harrison* v. *Hammersmith LBC* [1981] 1 WLR 650.

Secure tenants of two years' standing were at the same time granted rights of enfranchisement on indulgent terms.[20] In the case of a house the tenant is entitled to buy the freehold; and in the case of a flat he is entitled to buy a long lease of 125 years at a rent of £10 per annum; and in either case he has the right to a mortgage covering the whole or part of the purchase money plus costs, subject to a ceiling fixed by the Secretary of State by reference to the tenant's income. The price in the case of a house is the open market value minus a statutory discount of 32 per cent for a tenant of less than two years' standing, increasing by 1 per cent per year of tenancy to a maximum of 60 per cent; in the case of a flat the figures are 44, 2, and 70 respectively.[21] The terms of the mortgage, if claimed and if not agreed, can be settled by the county court. The period for repayment of the capital by instalments is 25 years, unless otherwise agreed; the Secretary of State has power to vary it but not retrospectively. These valuable privileges are subject to a list of exceptions for special cases,[22] and also to provisions requiring repayment of the discount, or a proportionate part of it, if the new owner sells within five years.[23] The Secretary of State has default powers for coercing resistant local authorities.[24]

Rent restriction and tenure in the private sector

Housing law is not exclusively concerned with public authorities and their powers. In the private sphere the relationship of landlord and tenant is drastically controlled by the Rent Act 1977, in which is consolidated the mass of highly complex legislation going back to 1915. It is designed to protect tenants by keeping down their rents and by preventing their eviction. Most of it is outside the domain of administrative law, being part of the law of property in land.[25] But many questions of jurisdiction and judicial control have arisen in connection with rent tribunals and rent assessment committees, whose decisions have often been quashed by the courts on various grounds of ultra vires. A little may therefore be said about the scheme of the Act, with the warning that such a brief description must neglect much detail.

The Rent Act does not apply to lettings by public authorities; it does not

[20]   See now Housing Act 1985, s. 118, incorporating amendments made by Housing and Building Control Act 1984.
[21]   Housing Act 1985, s. 129 as amended by Housing and Planning Act 1986, s 2.
[22]   Housing Act 1985, 5th sched., as amended by Housing and Planning Act 1986, s. 1.
[23]   Act of 1985, s. 155, tapering the sum at 20 per cent p.a.
[24]   Act of 1985, s. 164. See R. v. Secretary of State for the Environment ex p. Norwich City Council [1982] QB 808.
[25]   For full details see Megarry, The Rent Acts, 10th edn.; for a concise account, Megarry and Wade, Real Property, 5th edn. 1085. Litigation has been immense.

bind the Crown or government departments,[26] nor does it apply to local authorities or to new town development corporations. With these and a few other exceptions, it applies to every dwelling-house within certain limits of rateable value which is let at a rent not less than two-thirds of its rateable annual value in (or if necessary, after) 1965. The limits of rateable value have been altered many times, notably when the Rent Act 1957 reduced them to £40 in London and £30 elsewhere (at 1956 values) thereby decontrolling large numbers of houses and when the Rent Act 1965 raised them to £400 in London and £200 elsewhere (at 1965 values), thereby reversing the policy of working towards a free market. The present limits are £1,500 in London and £750 elsewhere (at 1973 values), representing a considerable extension of control despite the rating revaluation which had taken place in the meantime.[27]

A normal tenancy which falls within the Rent Acts is a 'protected tenancy'. When it expires or is determined by due notice, the tenant may remain in possession under a 'statutory tenancy', which the landlord may determine only if he obtains an order of the county court on certain specified grounds, e.g. that the tenant has broken his covenants or that the landlord reasonably requires the house for himself or his family.[28] If the statutory tenancy is also a 'regulated tenancy', as the majority of statutory tenancies now are, the landlord may nevertheless recover the house for certain purposes, such as for his own use (where he lived in it before) or as a retirement home (even where he did not); or in certain cases of short lettings to students or as holiday homes; or where the letting is, or was originally, a 'shorthold tenancy' of from one to five years under the Housing Act 1980.[29] But this right is in most cases dependent on notice of it being given at the beginning of the tenancy.[30]

All regulated tenancies are subject to the 'fair rent' system, introduced by the Rent Act 1965.[31] This enables the landlord, the tenant, or the local authority to apply to the local rent officer for the registration, in accordance with the Act, of a fair rent, which is assessed by the rent officer after hearing the parties. A fair rent is basically an open market rent, disregarding any local scarcity of housing and anything done voluntarily by the tenant or his predecessors to the benefit or detriment of the property; and it may be

[26] Housing Act 1980, s. 73, providing however that tenants of the Crown Estate Commissioners and of the Duchies of Cornwall and Lancaster are protected.
[27] Rent Act 1977, s. 4.
[28] Rent Act 1977, ss. 2, 98.
[29] ss. 51–5. Another new form of tenancy created by this Act (s. 56) is an 'assured tenancy' of a newly constructed building granted by a body approved by the Secretary of State.
[30] Rent Act 1977, s. 98(2).
[31] Rent Act 1977, Pts. III, IV, as amended by Housing Act 1980 ss. 59–63. But 'shorthold tenancies' outside London are now exempt: SI 1981 No. 1578.

either higher or lower than the previous rent. Either party can dispute the rent officer's decision before a rent assessment committee, which is a statutory tribunal. A registered rent holds good for three years. As well as regulated tenancies there used to be 'controlled tenancies',[32] a diminishing class of the poorer houses which had been controlled under the pre-1965 system, the rent being restricted to the rateable value multiplied by a factor varying with the tenant's liability for repair and adjusted according to the incidence of rates and various other expenses. But those tenancies were abolished when the Housing Act 1980 converted them into regulated tenancies, so as to bring them within the more flexible fair rent system.[33]

The system of rent rebates and allowances to needy tenants established by the Housing Finance Act 1972 was replaced by a system of 'housing benefits', also administered by local authorities, under the Social Security and Housing Benefits Act 1982 and the Social Security Act 1986.[34]

Furnished tenancies

Furnished lettings were outside the Rent Acts altogether until the Furnished Houses (Rent Control) Act 1946 set up rent tribunals with power to reduce (but not increase) any furnished rent to a reasonable figure. Under the Rent Act 1957, however, control was limited to houses within the Rent Act limits of value, and the tribunal might increase the rent. There were provisions, over which the tribunal had discretionary control, for preventing landlords from evicting tenants because the case had been referred to the tribunal,[35] and the tribunal could grant successive extensions of tenure for a period of up to six months on each occasion. An owner-occupier could guard against this by giving a statutory notice to the tenant when letting the house; this enabled him to recover it for occupation by himself or a member of his family who was then living with him in it. But these rules ceased to apply to furnished tenancies when the Rent Act 1974 turned them into regulated tenancies, thus bringing them within the fair rent system, with the normal Rent Act protection of tenure. The former rules now operate only in certain excepted cases, as where a substantial part of the rent is paid for services or where the landlord resides on the premises or shares part of them with the tenant, whether or not the tenancy is furnished.[36] The 1946-style rent tribunals were therefore left with little to do, and in 1980 their functions were taken over by rent assessment

---

[32] Rent Act 1977, s. 17.
[33] s. 19; SI 1980 No. 1555.
[34] s. 28 in both cases.
[35] The reference might also be made by the local authority.
[36] Rent Act 1977, ss. 21, 22.

committees.[37] Unlawful eviction and harassment of residential tenants are criminal offences; and even where the tenancy is not protected by the Rent Act and the lease has expired, the owner may not eject the ex-tenant without a court order.[38]

Agricultural, business and long-term tenancies

Agricultural tenants have the benefit of the Agricultural Holdings Act 1948, as amended, which in effect gives them security of tenure for life provided they are not guilty of bad husbandry or breach of covenant, and which makes the rent reviewable by arbitration every three years. Members of their families, if properly qualified, have rights of succession under the Agriculture (Miscellaneous Provisions) Act 1976. Both the agricultural land tribunals, which decide disputes as to tenure, and the agricultural arbitrators, who assess rents, are statutory tribunals.[39]

Bare mention will suffice for two further systems of protection, since they are the concern of the ordinary courts and not of administrative law.[40] These are the systems introduced by the Landlord and Tenant Act 1954, for the protection of business tenancies; and by the same Act and the Leasehold Reform Act 1967, for the protection of tenants under expiring long leases of houses held at ground rents (e.g. for 99 years), who under the latter Act are allowed in many cases to buy or rent the property compulsorily on terms which represent the value of the site only, thus expropriating the landlord's interest in the house.[41] This is the only case in the private sector in which a right of enfranchisement has been granted by Parliament as a solution to the problems of the leasehold system.[42]

No contracting out

The legislation which protects residential and agricultural tenants is mandatory in its terms and overriding in its effect. Tenants cannot contract out of the statutory protection by agreeing not to exercise their rights, nor can they waive them in any way which will be legally binding.[43] The

[37] Housing Act 1980, s. 72; below, p. 921.
[38] Protection from Eviction Act 1977.
[39] For a short account see Megarry and Wade, *Real Property*, 5th edn., 1094.
[40] See Megarry and Wade (as above), 1086, 1125.
[41] See below, p. 796.
[42] Another instance is the right granted by the Law of Property Act 1925, s. 153; but this is for technical and not social reasons.
[43] *Artizans etc. Co. Ltd.* v. *Whitaker* [1919] 2 KB 301; *Johnson* v. *Moreton* [1980] AC 37 (where the House of Lords discussed the policy of such legislation in the agricultural context). But the landlord can waive his statutory rights: *Elsden* v. *Pick* (1980) 40 P & CR 550.

statutes in fact contain no provision to this effect, but from the beginning the courts have had no difficulty in holding that this was their intention.

THE NATIONAL HEALTH SERVICE

The scheme of 1946

The health service, and the connected welfare services, provided both on a national and a local basis, are a vital area of public administration which however produce little material for administrative law outside the sphere of tribunals, which are discussed later. A summary account of the administrative arrangements will therefore be adequate for present purposes.

The national health service was organised under two primary statutes, the National Health Service Act 1946 and the National Health Service Reorganisation Act 1973, which were consolidated along with connected legislation in the National Health Service Act 1977. The Act of 1946, which first created the service, made it the general duty of the Minister of Health to see that the service was provided, and to finance it from central government funds. But administratively the Act distinguished sharply between hospitals[44] and specialist services, which were directly provided by the minister, and general practitioner services (and also dental, pharmaceutical, and ophthalmic services), which were provided separately in each county by executive councils made up of county councillors, ministerial appointees, and local doctors, dentists, and pharmacists. Each county (or county borough) council was made the local health authority, with responsibility for certain things such as health centres, maternity and midwifery services, and ambulances. But the main responsibility, outside the hospitals, rested upon the executive councils, which had a considerable degree of independence as local authorities, subject only to the minister's default powers.[45] These councils worked in collaboration with local medical (and dental, etc.) committees, made up of local practitioners; and there were medical practices committees concerned with the distribution of practices. Complaints that a practitioner had failed to fulfil his obligations under his terms of service, such as complaints by patients against their doctors, were heard by service committees appointed by the executive councils under ministerial regulations[46] and made up partly of members of the councils and partly of representative practitioners; they reported to the executive council, which could withhold part of the

---

[44] Including mental hospitals where patients are detained: Mental Health Act 1959, ss. 97, 98.

[45] Act of 1946, s. 43.

[46] SI 1956 No. 1077.

practitioner's remuneration, or limit the number of his patients, or represent to the National Health Service Tribunal that he should be removed from the service. The appeal system, including the ultimate right of appeal to the minister, is explained in the chapter on tribunals.[47]

The reorganisation of 1973

The Act of 1973 reorganised the main administrative framework so as to constitute a unified hierarchy of authorities under the Secretary of State for Social Services, dealing alike with hospitals, consultants, and family practitioners. The principal authorities are corporate bodies, and though they are subject in almost all respects to directions by the Secretary of State, they and their employees (numbering over 900,000) are treated as a separate service, outside the civil service. In law, however, they are servants of the Crown.[48] Complaints about hospitals being exempt from the food and health and safety legislation, on account of Crown immunity,[49] were met by the National Health Service (Amendment) Act 1986, which applied this legislation to them.

For England there was a two-tier structure consisting of regional health authorities and area health authorities. There were fourteen regions containing between them ninety areas, which were conterminous with local government areas.[50] For Wales there was a system of eight areas only. The areas have however since been reorganised into a system of districts.[51] Each district authority has to establish a family practitioner committee, which corresponds generally to the former executive council, and which is required by regulations to establish service committees for dealing with complaints, much as before.[52] The functions of these authorities are not allotted by the Act, which provides merely an extremely flexible system of delegation, by which the Secretary of State can give directions as to the functions of regional and district health authorities and, subject to his overriding powers, regional authorities may delegate to district authorities.[53] Some of these directions are required to be embodied in regulations, but many need not be.[54]

[47] Below, p. 906.
[48] See above, p. 67.
[49] See below, p. 827.
[50] The areas corresponded with counties, metropolitan districts, and London boroughs, some of the latter being grouped.
[51] See SI 1981 Nos. 1837, 1838, and later amendments.
[52] Act of 1977, s. 10; Health and Social Security Act 1984, s. 5; National Health Service (Service Committees and Tribunal) Regulations 1974, SI Nos. 455, 907.
[53] Act of 1977, ss. 13, 14. For details see National Health Service Functions (Directions to Authorities) Regulations 1982, SI No. 287; 1984, No. 1577.
[54] Act of 1977, s. 18.

The former local health authorities have disappeared, and their duties now belong to the Secretary of State;[55] but a community health council is established for each district, and the health authorities have the duty of co-operating with the local authorities for purposes of health and welfare, with the assistance of joint consultative committees.[56] In the regions there are local advisory committees representative of the various classes of practitioners.[57] The reorganisation took effect in 1974 simultaneously with the reorganisation of local government.

The short-lived Health Services Board, constituted by the Health Services Act 1976 for the purpose of phasing out facilities for private patients in NHS hospitals, was abolished by the Health Services Act 1980, when the policy was reversed.

WELFARE AND SOCIAL SECURITY

The welfare state

The operations of the welfare state are naturally much to the fore in administrative law, since benefits are distributed to very large numbers of people under elaborate statutory machinery. But as in the case of the national health service, which itself is a major part of the welfare system, the legal problems are mainly concentrated in the field of tribunals, and are given full treatment elsewhere.[58] All the statutory schemes of welfare and social security make extensive use of statutory tribunals for deciding disputes about entitlement to benefits and various other matters. Each of these schemes has its own built-in adjudicatory system. These tribunals are a major topic of administrative law, both with regard to their organisation and working and with regard to the control over them which the ordinary courts exercise. The smooth running of the welfare state demands speedy, simple, and informal procedures for disposing of innumerable disputed claims, and a whole new system of judicature has been created by Parliament for this purpose. It also demands a great deal of delegated legislation. The mass of enacted law is supplemented by an even greater mass of regulations, resulting in a body of law of formidable size and repellent complexity, which is incessantly changing. Within the bounds of this book it is only possible to say a little about the administrative structure generally.

Welfare and social security services fall into two distinct classes: those

[55] s. 3.
[56] ss. 20–2.
[57] s. 19.
[58] Below, p. 894.

where the benefit is provided in kind, and those where it is paid in cash. Into the former class fall the national health service, which provides the services of doctors, dentists, etc., at public expense, and the personal social services, as they are called, administered by local authorities under the Local Authority Social Services Act 1970 and other Acts, as mentioned earlier.[59] Into the latter class fall the various benefits provided by the national insurance system (as it was known until 1973), together with child benefit and supplementary benefit (as it was known until 1988), this last being the lineal descendant of the old poor law, of which something has been said already.[60] These cash benefits can themselves be divided into two classes: those financed at least partially out of contributions by the beneficiaries, as are unemployment, sickness and industrial injury benefits; and those which are non-contributory, as are some retirement pensions, child benefit and supplementary benefit. The non-contributory class can be further subdivided: supplementary benefit is subject to means test, but retirement pensions and child benefit are not. Except where otherwise indicated, all these benefits are administered by the Department of Health and Social Security.

The origins of the welfare state lie in the Workmen's Compensation Act 1897, the Old Age Pensions Act 1908, and the National Insurance Act 1911. The Act of 1908 introduced old-age pensions for those over 70 which were non-contributory but subject to means test. The Acts of 1897 and 1911 introduced compulsory insurance for employees against accidents at work, ill health and unemployment, financed mainly by contributions from employers and employees. The workmen's compensation scheme was operated through insurance companies and led to an excessive amount of litigation in the courts (mostly about whether an accident was in the course of employment) until it was replaced by a state-administered scheme under the National Insurance (Industrial Injuries) Act 1946, which set up statutory tribunals. The Act of 1911, on the other hand, employed tribunals from the start, and its basic administrative and adjudicatory structure may still be seen in the much wider social security system of today. That system was inaugurated by the National Insurance Act 1946,[61] which has since been extended and replaced by a long succession of later Acts. Many of them were consolidated in the Social Security Act 1975, which is now the principal Act, though by no means the last.[62] The nomenclature of

[59] Above, p. 116.
[60] Above, p. 105.
[61] Preceded by the Beveridge Report (*Social Insurance and Allied Services*), 1942, Cmd. 6404.
[62] Seven social security statutes were enacted in 1974 and 1975 alone. Since then the average is one a year. The latest is the Social Security Act 1988.

'insurance' had already mostly been eliminated by the Social Security Act 1973 in favour of a 'scheme of social security contributions and benefits'. The Act of 1975 included the industrial injuries legislation as an integral part of this scheme.[63] But there was separate legislation for child benefit,[64] supplementary benefit,[65] and family income supplement,[66] much of which has now been replaced by the Social Security Act 1986, substituting 'income support' for supplementary benefit and 'family credit' for family income supplement.[67] Housing benefit, administered by local authorities, was introduced in 1982 in substitution for the rent and rate rebates formerly allowed.[68] It is now governed by the Act of 1986.[69] About a third of all households receive this benefit.

The Secretary of State is advised by the Social Security Advisory Committee, a statutory body established originally by the National Insurance Act 1946.[70] The committee must be consulted about proposed regulations[71] and its report must be laid before Parliament along with the regulations themselves. It deals with the whole area of social security, including child benefit and income support, with the exception of industrial injuries, for which the corresponding body is the Industrial Injuries Advisory Council.[72]

Social security benefits[73]

The contributory benefits provided under the Social Security Act 1975 were set out in the Act as follows:[74]

  (a) unemployment benefit (with earnings-related supplement[75] and increase for adult and child dependants);

---

[63] s. 50.

[64] Child Benefit Act 1975.

[65] Supplementary Benefits Act 1976.

[66] Family Income Supplements Act 1970.

[67] s. 20.

[68] Social Security and Housing Benefits Act 1982.

[69] ss. 20(7), 28. The prescribed scheme is SI 1987 No. 1971.

[70] Social Security Act 1980, ss. 9, 10. The former National Insurance Advisory Committee was restricted to the area of national insurance.

[71] With the exceptions specified in 3rd sched., Pt. II.

[72] Social Security Act 1975, s. 141.

[73] For details and comment on these and other services (including supplementary benefit) see Ogus and Barendt, *The Law of Social Security* (2nd edn., with supplements); Pearl and Gray, *Social Welfare Law*; Calvert, *Social Security Law* (2nd edn.); Smith and Hoath, *Law and the Underprivileged*. For the system of adjudication see Sir R. Micklethwait, *The National Insurance Commissioners*. Informative booklets are published by the Department of Health and Social Security.

[74] s. 12.

[75] This supplement was abolished by Social Security (No. 2) Act 1980, s. 4.

(b) sickness benefit (with earnings-related supplement,[75] and increase for adult and child dependants);

(c) invalidity benefit, comprising:
   (i) invalidity pension (with increase for adult and child dependents),
   (ii) invalidity allowance;

(d) maternity benefit, comprising:
   (i) maternity grant,
   (ii) maternity allowance (with earnings-related supplement,[75] and increase for adult and child dependants);

(e) widow's benefit, comprising
   (i) widow's allowance (with earnings-related addition,[76] and increase for child dependants),
   (ii) widowed mother's allowance (with increase for child dependants),
   (iii) widow's pension;

(f) retirement pensions of the following categories:[77]
   Category A, payable to a person by virtue of his own contributions (with increase for adult and child dependants), and
   Category B, payable to a woman by virtue of her husband's contributions (with increase for child dependants);

(g) child's special allowance;

(h) death grant.

The Act of 1986 abolished death grant.[78] For widow's allowance it substituted a fixed tax-free 'widow's payment'[79] and for maternity grant it substituted a payment from the Social Fund,[80] for which see below.

The rates of benefit may vary according to a number of circumstances, such as the contributions paid and responsibility for children and dependants.[81] Unemployment benefit is available for a maximum of 312 days to employees for whom contributions have been paid both by themselves and their employers; it is not available to the self-employed.[82] Nor is it available to any one thrown out of work by a strike, if he is 'participating in or financing or directly interested in the trade dispute' or belongs to a grade or class of workers who are doing so,[83] unless the

[76] As previous note.
[77] The scheme for these pensions was radically altered by the Social Security Pensions Act 1975.
[78] s. 41.
[79] s. 36.
[80] ss. 32, 38. Women in employment were by s. 46 given the right to maternity pay from their employers.
[81] Act of 1975, Pt. II, ch. III.
[82] ss. 13(1), 18.
[83] s. 19. See e.g. Punton v. Ministry of Pensions and National Insurance (No. 2) [1963] 1 WLR 1176 (below, p. 601) (refusal of benefit on the ground that the insured was directly interested in the strike).

unemployment is due to redundancy.[84] The 'voluntary unemployed', i.e. those dismissed for misconduct or refusing suitable employment, are disqualified for the first 13 weeks.[85] There is a great deal of elaborate law about this benefit.

All contributory benefits are subject to the statutory contribution conditions being satisfied.[86] The conditions are complicated, but roughly speaking they require a full year's contributions to have been paid. Contributions, which formerly were mostly flat-rate, are now wholly earnings-related. The government subsidises the system by an annual contribution from the exchequer amounting to about a fifth of the net total of contributions.[87]

The non-contributory benefits are the following.[88]

(a) attendance allowance (this is for the severely disabled who require constant attendance);

(b) non-contributory invalidity pension (with increase for adult and child dependants);

(c) invalid care allowance (with similar increase);

(d) guardian's allowance (this is for a child of which the insured is guardian);

(e) retirement pensions of categories C and D (these are mainly for persons over eighty);

(f) age addition to retirement pension of a person over eighty.

Along with these benefits may be mentioned child benefit, since although it is provided under separate legislation, it is likewise non-contributory and likewise not subject to means test. This benefit was first introduced by the Family Allowances Act 1945, when it was not payable in respect of the first child and was subject to income tax. Both these restrictions were removed by the Child Benefit Act 1975, under which a flat-rate tax-free weekly allowance is paid for each child while under the school-leaving age (approximately fifteen) or up to the age of nineteen if under full-time education or apprenticeship. In a normal two-parent family the allowance is due to the wife,[89] but this may be varied by a magistrates' order.

The rates of benefit are laid down in the Social Security Act 1975,[90] but are subject to annual review by the Secretary of State,[91] who must increase

---

[84] Social Security Act 1986, s. 44.

[85] Act of 1975, s. 20, Act of 1986, s. 43 (extending the former period of 6 weeks).

[86] Act of 1975, 3rd sched.

[87] s. 1(5).

[88] Pt. II, ch. II.

[89] Child Benefit Act 1975, 2nd sched., para. 3. Income tax allowances for children were simultaneously withdrawn.

[90] 4th sched.

[91] For the 1988 rates see 121 HC Deb. 195 (27 October 1987).

them (by an order approved in draft by both Houses of Parliament) if he concludes that they have not retained their value in relation to prices;[92] but since 1980 he may reduce this up-rating by up to 5 per cent of the benefit.[93] The rates of child benefit are prescribed by regulations subject likewise to Parliament's approval.[94] The Secretary of State must review them annually but is not obliged to increase them.

A claim to social security benefit or child benefit is adjudicated in the first instance locally by an 'adjudication officer', who is an employee of the Department of Health and Social Security.[95] Appeal lies to a social security appeal tribunal, which is independent; there is a further appeal (on both fact and law) to a Social Security Commissioner, who is a barrister or solicitor of at least ten years' standing and is comparable to a circuit judge;[96] and appeal on a point of law (only) then lies to the Court of Appeal.[97] But if the local tribunal was unanimous appeal to a commissioner requires leave from the chairman of the tribunal or the commissioner; and appeal from a commissioner requires leave from him or from the court.[98] A trade union or welfare association may appeal to a commissioner on behalf of one of its members. But certain important questions, such as whether a person is an employee or self-employed and whether contribution conditions are satisfied, are reserved for adjudication by the Secretary of State, i.e. by one of his officials, subject to a right of appeal to the High Court on a question of law.[99] Entitlement to attendance allowance, also, is determined by the Attendance Allowance Board, subject to appeal (with leave) to a Social Security Commissioner on a question of law.[1] On all these matters there are powers to review decisions which are shown by fresh evidence to have been wrong or where circumstances have changed, with similar rights of appeal.[2] Except where appealable, decisions are 'final'.[3]

---

[92] s. 125, subject to certain exceptions and as amended by Social Security Act 1980, s. 1. There is a wide power to increase benefits under the Social Security Act 1975, s. 124.

[93] Social Security (No. 2) Act 1980, s. 1.

[94] Child Benefit Act 1975, ss. 5, 22.

[95] Social Security Act 1975, ss. 97-9; Child Benefit Act 1975, s. 7; Health and Social Services and Social Security Adjudications Act 1983, 8th sched., renaming the former national insurance officer and national insurance local tribunals.

[96] Social Security Act 1975, ss. 97, 101; Social Security Act 1979, s. 9; Social Security Act 1986, s. 52(2).

[97] Social Security Act 1980, s. 14.

[98] Act of 1980, ss. 14, 15.

[99] Act of 1975, ss. 93, 95. See below, p. 902.

[1] ss. 105, 106.

[2] ss. 96, 104, 106.

[3] s. 117. See below, p. 720.

Industrial injuries

The industrial injuries insurance scheme, replacing the Workmen's Compensation Acts, was established by the National Insurance (Industrial Injuries) Act 1946, at the same time as the modern system of national insurance. The two systems were governed by separate legislation until they were brought together in the Social Security Act 1975.[4]

Industrial injuries benefits are payable in respect of injuries suffered by employees in the course of their employment. Contributions are paid by employers and employees as part of their national insurance contributions, and there are no contribution conditions to be satisfied before benefits can be paid. The benefits are injury benefit, disablement benefit, and industrial death benefit.[5] Injury benefit is payable at a flat rate, plus additions for family responsibilities, for not more than twenty-six weeks when the claimant is incapable of work as a result of the injury.[6] Thereafter, if suffering from loss of physical or mental faculty, as assessed in accordance with the Act on a percentage scale, he may claim disablement benefit in the form of disablement gratuity (sometimes payable by instalments) if the assessed loss of faculty is less than 20 per cent, and of disablement pension if it is greater.[7] A disablement pension is related to the degree of disablement but not to earnings. It is increased for family responsibilities and for unemployability caused by the loss of faculty and in cases of special hardship or special needs.[8] It is payable whether or not the claimant is in employment. In addition, other social security benefits can in some cases be drawn. Death benefit takes the form of pensions payable to widows and other relatives maintained by the deceased employee.[9] The statutory rates of benefit may be increased by an order of the Secretary of State approved in draft by both Houses of Parliament.[10]

Claims to injury benefit are adjudicated by an adjudication officer with the same rights of appeal as in other social security claims.[11] Questions as to disablement are referred to one (normally) or more 'adjudicating medical practitioners,'[12] from whom appeal lies to a medical appeal tribunal and

---

[4] See Pt. II, ch. IV.

[5] s. 50. For the 1988 rates see 121 HC Deb 195 (27 October 1987).

[6] s. 56.

[7] s. 57. For the problems of assessment under the 'paired organs' regulations see below, p. 313.

[8] ss. 58–66.

[9] ss. 67–75.

[10] ss. 124, 125 (requiring annual review).

[11] ss. 97–101. Before the National Insurance Act 1966 the National Insurance Commissioners adjudicated these appeals in the separate capacity of Industrial Injuries Commissioners.

[12] Substituted for the former medical boards by Health and Social Services and Social Security Adjudications Act 1983, 8th sched., para. 21.

thence (with leave of the tribunal or commissioner) to a Social Security Commissioner on a point of law.[13] Subject only to these rights of appeal, decisions are 'final'.[14] Formerly there was great uncertainty whether this provision prevented a medical board (as it then was) from finding that a disability, e.g. a bad heart, had not been caused by the accident when the local tribunal had awarded injury benefit on the footing that it had been so caused; but it is now enacted that no finding of fact shall be conclusive for the purpose of any further decision, so that the medical board may act on its own opinion.[15] There is a wide power to review decisions, e.g. where there is fresh evidence or unforeseen aggravation of the injury.[16]

Income support and family credit

The ultimate safety-net of the welfare state is 'income support', known before 1988 as supplementary benefit, before 1966 as national assistance, and before 1948, in plainer English, as the poor law. The object of these verbal changes has been to break away from the patronising vocabulary of pauperism and state charity, and to represent the relief of poverty as an extension of state-provided social security benefits, to which the claimant has a legal right. When the penultimate change was made in 1966 emphasis was put on the 'legal right' basis and at the same time the administration was amalgamated so far as possible with that of national insurance. Formerly it had been in the hands of a separate and legally independent body, the National Assistance Board. After 1966 it was under the Supplementary Benefits Commission, a corporate body which was part of the Department of Health and Social Security.[17] In 1980 the Commission was abolished, its executive functions remaining in the Department and its advisory functions passing to the Social Security Advisory Committee.[18] The principal Act is now the Social Security Act 1986, effective from April 1988, under which supplementary benefit is replaced by income support.[19] This is skeleton legislation, however, and most of the details are to be found in the regulations made under the Act.

---

[13] ss. 108–12. The ban on appeals in the first two years was removed by the Act of 1983, 8th sched., para. 22.

[14] s. 117, containing qualifications as to industrial accidents.

[15] In *R. v. National Insurance Commissioner ex p. Hudson* [1972] AC 944 a special House of Lords of seven decided by four to three that the medical board was bound by the earlier decision. This decision was promptly reversed by the National Insurance Act 1972, s. 5, now incorporated in the Act of 1975, s. 117.

[16] s. 110.

[17] Supplementary Benefit Act 1966 (originally entitled Ministry of Social Security Act 1966 but renamed by Social Security Act 1973, s. 99(18)).

[18] Social Security Act 1980, s. 6.

[19] s. 20.

The principle of the legislation is that every member of the population over sixteen years of age is entitled to a certain minimum level of cash income.[20] The other benefits by no means necessarily provide this minimum level, so that supplementary benefit has to play a large part, for example, in the maintenance of unemployed workers and their families, and of old-age pensioners. It is therefore a most necessary and expensive service. The rate of benefit is computed according to the difference between the recipient's resources and his requirements, in accordance with the prescribed scheme.[21] This calculation depends on many variables, such as family obligations, rent and rates; and it necessarily involves a means test. Despite the emphasis on legal rights, there are important discretionary elements in the system, e.g. in the power to make special payments to meet exceptional expenses, including maternity and funeral expenses.[22] Under the Act of 1986 these payments are made from the Social Fund, administered by social fund officers appointed by the Secretary of State and monitored by the Social Fund Commissioner and a corps of inspectors. Social fund officers' awards are reviewable by the awarding officer or another social fund officer, or by a social fund inspector; but there is no other right of appeal.[23] These arrangements emphasise the difference between the regular and discretionary relief which may be given. One of the regular rules is the controversial cohabitation rule, under which a man and a woman cohabiting as man and wife are treated like a husband and a wife, whose resources must be aggregated.[24] The 'wage-stop', which formerly prevented supplementary benefit from exceeding the claimant's normal earnings, was abolished in 1975.

There are restrictions on the award of benefit to strikers and their families. A claimant 'participating in or directly interested in' a trade dispute at his place of employment is disqualified.[25] He may however receive benefit from the Social Fund and he may claim benefit for the other members of his family. In 1980 the restrictions were tightened and a fixed sum was made deductible from any benefit claimable.[26] The object was to make trade unions bear a larger share of the cost of strikes, but the new restrictions were not confined to their members.

[20] Act of 1986, s. 20(3).

[21] SI 1987 No. 1967.

[22] Act of 1986, s. 32, as amended by Social Fund (Maternity and Funeral Expenses) Act 1987 and by Social Security Act 1988, 3rd sched.

[23] Except as to funeral and maternity payments where appeal lies to a social security appeal tribunal. The abolition of the former general right of appeal was criticised by the Council on Tribunals in a special report, Cmnd. 9722 (1986). The regulations are SI 1988 Nos. 34, 35, 36.

[24] Child Benefit Act 1975, s. 19.

[25] Act of 1986, s. 23, replacing Act of 1976, s. 8.

[26] Social Security (No. 2) Act 1980.

Claims to income support are made to an adjudication officer with a right of appeal to a social security appeal tribunal as in the case of claims to other benefits. Claims to social fund payments are made to social fund officers as already described. From the appeal tribunal there is the same further appeal to the Commissioner and to the courts as in other cases.[27] The tribunal's decisions are also subject to judicial review on any of the normal grounds.

An additional benefit, family income supplement, was introduced in 1970. It is now paid under the Social Security Act 1986 and renamed 'family credit'.[28] It provides a fixed weekly allowance for families with low income and one or more dependent children, where one parent is in remunerative work and the total family income is below the prescribed level. Accordingly it involves a means test. Once granted, benefit continues for twenty-six weeks regardless of change of circumstances. Administration is as for income support, with the same rights of appeal.

Disappointed applicants for housing benefit may appeal to a Housing Benefit Review Board.[29]

IMMIGRATION, DEPORTATION AND EXTRADITION

Control of immigration

At common law the Crown has the prerogative power to refuse an alien admission to the realm.[30] In all other respects aliens in Britain enjoy normal civil rights and have the benefit of the ordinary law.[31] But they are subject to controls and restrictions under statutes which confer wide discretionary powers upon the Home Secretary, backed up by powers of detention and deportation; and the consequences for individuals may be extremely severe. Immigration cases are now a prominent feature of administrative law, and in particular they are the part of the subject where the remedy of habeas corpus plays its most conspicuous part.

The Aliens Act 1905 established immigration officers at the main ports with powers to refuse admission to 'undesirable aliens', such as those with no means of support or serious criminal convictions; but there was a right

[27] Above, p. 219. Two appeals reached the House of Lords in *Supplementary Benefits Commission* v. *Jull* [1981] AC 1025.

[28] s. 20(5). The regulations are SI 1987 No. 1973.

[29] Constituted by the local authority under SI 1982 No. 1124.

[30] *Musgrave* v. *Chun Teeong Toy* [1891] AC 472; *R.* v. *Home Secretary ex p. Thakrar* [1974] QB 684. The prerogative power is preserved by Immigration Act 1971, s. 35(5). Probably there was no such power to expel aliens otherwise in peacetime: see Dicey, *The Law of the Constitution*, 225; (1963) 12 ICLQ 414 (C. Thornberry).

[31] Below, p. 830.

of appeal to a local appeal board. The Aliens Restriction Act 1914, passed
on the outbreak of war, gave the Crown virtually unlimited powers to
control, detain, restrict and deport aliens in times of war or great
emergency, with no procedural safeguards. Those powers were continued
into peacetime by the Aliens Restriction (Amendment) Act 1919, and
though the Act had to be renewed annually, its only safeguard was that
Orders in Council had to be laid before Parliament and could be
disapproved.[32] Emergency legislation was carried forward in this makeshift
way until it was replaced by the Immigration Act 1971, though a system of
appeals was introduced by the Immigration Appeals Act 1969.

The acute problems of immigration law are concerned not with aliens
but with citizens of the British Commonwealth.[33] Originally every one
within the allegiance of the Crown was a British subject and free to enter
Britain. When the independent countries of the Commonwealth came to
define their own citizenship for themselves, the comprehensive British
nationality gave way to a group of citizenships within the Commonwealth. The British Nationality Act 1948 defined 'citizens of the United
Kingdom and Colonies' as a single group. Freedom of entry, however,
continued as before, since no Commonwealth citizen was an alien. It was
only when unprecedented numbers began to arrive from the West Indies,
India and Pakistan that controls were imposed as a 'temporary provision'
by the Commonwealth Immigrants Act 1962.

The Act imposed restrictions on Commonwealth citizens unless they
were born in the United Kingdom or held passports issued by the United
Kingdom government. Natives of the colonies thus lost the right of
immigration, despite their common citizenship with the United Kingdom.
But even tighter restrictions were imposed by the Commonwealth
Immigrants Act 1968 in order to prevent immigration by large numbers of
Kenyans of Asian origin who held passports issued by the government of
the United Kingdom under the arrangements made when Kenya became
independent in 1963. The right of entry was confined by the Act of 1968 to
Commonwealth citizens who were born, naturalised, adopted or registered in the United Kingdom, or who had a parent or grandparent so
qualified. This was acutely controversial legislation, which arguably
violated both the European Convention on Human Rights[34] and the

---

[32] The Aliens Order 1953, SI No. 1671, replaced many earlier orders.

[33] See J. M. Evans, *Immigration Law* (2nd edn.); T. E. Smith, *Commonwealth Migration*.

[34] The Commission declared a group of complaints well founded (Yearbook, 1970,
p. 928), but they were not referred to the Court of Human Rights and were not taken
further by the Committee of Ministers. For this case see HC 434 (1979–80). Many Kenyan
Asians had meanwhile been allowed to enter the UK. The UK has been unable to ratify the
Fourth Protocol of the European Convention on Human Rights since it protects the right to
enter the country of which one is a national (art. 3).

assurances given to the Kenyan Asians. In its terms it did not discriminate according to race or colour, but its design was to check immigration by the coloured peoples of the Commonwealth. In fact many such immigrants continued to be admitted,[35] but the grant or refusal of permission was entirely within the Home Secretary's discretion and his policy was explained in statements to Parliament.

The Acts of 1971 and 1981

The supposedly temporary Acts of 1919, 1962 and 1968 were ultimately replaced by the Immigration Act 1971, which at the same time replaced the Immigration Appeals Act 1969. It has been amended by the British Nationality Act 1981, as explained below. It applies to Commonwealth citizens and to aliens alike. The definitions in the Acts of 1971 and 1981 are complicated and they can only be imprecisely summarised here.

The Act of 1971 defined the 'right of abode', meaning the right to live in the United Kingdom and to come and go freely.[36] In order to enjoy that right a person had to be (a) a citizen of the United Kingdom and Colonies who was such by birth, adoption, naturalisation or registration in the United Kingdom or who had a parent or grandparent (natural or adoptive) similarly qualified, or who had been settled and ordinarily resident in the United Kingdom for the last five years; (b) a Commonwealth citizen born to or adopted by a citizen of the United Kingdom and Colonies by birth; or (c) the wife or former wife of someone qualified under (a) or (b). All other immigrants were subject to the discretionary control of the Home Secretary, with the exception of those coming from within the British Isles (thus exempting those coming from the Irish Republic), certain others such as seamen and diplomats, and nationals of EEC countries who had overriding rights under the Treaty of Rome and the European Communities Act 1972.[37] Immigration officers might refuse admission or grant it permanently or temporarily or subject to any conditions; and the Home Secretary might grant, refuse or vary leave to remain.

The Home Secretary is required to make rules of practice for his administration of the Act and to lay them before Parliament, and to make such changes as appear to be required if they are disapproved—as in fact the first rules were.[38] The Immigration Rules[39] are an elaborate code, covering leave to remain as well as leave to enter. They provide for example for

[35] Notably many thousands of Asians expelled from Uganda in 1972.

[36] ss. 1, 2. The Act conferred the title 'patrial' on those entitled to the right, but that was eliminated by British Nationality Act 1981, s. 39.

[37] See *Van Duyn* v. *Home Office* [1975] Ch. 358.

[38] 846 HC Deb 1343 (22 November 1972). The present rules were at first disapproved: 34 HC Deb 355, 435 (15 December 1982).

[39] The present rules are set out in HC 169 (February 1983), subject to later amendments.

temporary visitors, students and au pair girls; for those seeking employment, who must first have obtained a work permit unless nationals of EEC countries or otherwise dispensed; for those coming for settlement, who must usually have obtained an entry clearance or voucher before leaving their country of origin; and for those seeking asylum, who must show 'well-founded fear of being persecuted for reasons of race, religion, nationality, membership of a particular social group or political opinion',[40] though admission is always at the Home Secretary's discretion.[41] The rules provide also for variation of leave to enter or remain and for deportation.

Basically the immigration rules are administrative instructions from the Home Secretary to immigration officers and statements of policy and practice. But they have acquired something of the status of rules of law, since in the long series of immigration cases the courts have given them a measure of legal effect, and the Act requires them to be followed by the adjudicators and tribunal who determine appeals.[42]

The British Nationality Act 1981, which came into force in 1983, narrowed the definition of British citizenship so as to make it conform with the restricted right of abode under the Act of 1971 as amended. Any one entitled to this right was a 'British citizen'. The right of abode was confined to British citizens and those Commonwealth citizens who at the commencement of the Act of 1981 had the right of abode by virtue of parentage or (in the case of a woman) marriage.[43] Colonial citizens were excluded from British citizenship and became 'citizens of British Dependent Territories'. A third class of 'British overseas citizens' was created for former citizens of the United Kingdom and Colonies who at the commencement of the Act did not qualify as either British citizens or citizens of British Dependent Territories. Commonwealth citizenship was retained, comprising the three classes of British citizens and citizens of the countries listed in a schedule, but it will have little legal significance in future.

Deportation

Under the Aliens Restriction Acts the Home Secretary was given full power to make orders for the deportation of aliens, and under the Aliens Order 1953 these were crystallised into two cases: where a court so recommended after convicting the alien of serious crime; and where the

---

[40] Rule 73. See *R.* v. *Home Secretary ex p. Awuku* [1987] The Times, 3 October; *R.* v. *Home Secretary ex p. Sivakumaran* [1988] 2 WLR 92.

[41] See *Re Vilvarajah* [1987] The Times, 31 October (fear of persecution well founded but admission refused on account of deception).

[42] See below, p. 858, for the legal status of the rules.

[43] s. 39, amending the Act of 1971.

Home Secretary deemed deportation to be 'conducive to the public good'.[44] No British subject or Commonwealth citizen was liable to deportation until the Commonwealth Immigrants Act 1962 made it a necessary accompaniment of the restrictions then imposed. That Act made Commonwealth citizens deportable on a court's recommendation after conviction for an offence punishable with imprisonment (which included illegal entry and overstaying) but not on the ground of 'the public good'. In addition they could be removed without a deportation order on the directions of an immigration officer if refused entry, and the captain or owner of a ship or aircraft could be directed to return them to their own countries at public expense.

The Immigration Act 1971 treats aliens and Commonwealth citizens alike, making them all, if not entitled to the right of abode, liable to deportation on the 'public good' ground as well as for overstaying, breach of condition (such as a condition against taking employment), membership of a deportee's family, and recommendation by a court after conviction. Illegal entrants, i.e. those who enter or seek to enter in breach of the law,[45] can be dealt with by immigration officers without deportation orders (though also liable to fine and imprisonment), and may be detained pending a decision and then removed as under the Act of 1962. Carriers who bring would-be immigrants without proper documents may be made to bear the expense of their return.[46]

Rights of appeal

Apart from the short-lived right of appeal under the Aliens Act 1905, the law gave no right of appeal whatever against deportation orders or immigration restrictions, even after these were applied to Commonwealth citizens, until 1969. The system was so deficient in justice that the Home Secretary had to arrange for administrative hearings in many deportation cases in order to comply with the European Convention on Establishment of 1956.[47] At long last the Immigration Appeals Act 1969 set up tribunals consisting of adjudicators (appointed by the Home Secretary) to whom appeal could be made on the spot at seaports and airports and the Immigration Appeal Tribunal (appointed by the Lord Chancellor) to which further appeal would lie. The provisions of 1969 were reproduced with some amendment in the Immigration Act 1971.[48]

[44] This expression appears to derive from the Aliens Order 1920 SR & O No. 448, art. 12(6).
[45] See below, p. 460.
[46] Immigration (Carriers' Liability) Act 1987.
[47] See below, p. 576.
[48] Pt. II.

Under the Act of 1971 appeal lies to an adjudicator, with further appeal to the tribunal, against a deportation order based upon overstaying or breach of condition.[49] Where the basis is membership of a deportee's family, appeal lies direct to the tribunal, together with any appeal by the deportee himself. Where a court has recommended deportation after conviction, the recommendation is appealable to a higher criminal court, but there is no appeal against the Home Secretary's decision. Where the basis is that deportation is 'conducive to the public good', appeal lies to the tribunal except where the reasons concern national security or international relations or 'other reasons of a political nature', in which case there may be a non-statutory hearing before a panel of three persons who will advise the Home Secretary but who have no legal obligation to particularise the charge, give reasons for their conclusions or disclose their report. In all cases, however, a person ordered to be deported or removed may appeal to an adjudicator, and thence to the tribunal, against the intended destination.

Immigration restrictions are also in most cases appealable, but there are important qualifications. There is no appeal in most cases where a claim to the right of abode is based upon residence or parentage. A person refused leave to enter the country may not appeal while he is still in it, and must therefore make his appeal in writing from abroad, unless he holds an entry clearance or a work permit. If the ground for refusal is a decision by the Home Secretary personally that 'his exclusion is conducive to the public good', he may appeal only against the intended destination.[50] Subject to that, he may appeal to an adjudicator against refusal of leave to enter, refusal of a certificate of entitlement to entry or entry clearance, and against directions for his removal.[51] If admitted, he may appeal against conditions imposed upon him, except where it is a 'public good' case involving national security etc. (as above), or where the conditions are imposed generally by statutory instrument.[52] There is no appeal against refusal of a work permit.

An adjudicator must allow the appeal if he finds that the decision was not in accordance with law or with the immigration rules, or if he considers that discretion should have been exercised differently, and he may review any finding of fact.[53] The tribunal may make any determination that could have been made by the adjudicator.[54]

Procedural rules for these appeals are made by the Home Secretary.[55]

[49] Act of 1971, s. 15. The Immigration Bill 1988 proposes to restrict this right except where the deportation order is not justified by the reasons stated in it or where leave to enter was given more than seven years previously.

[50] ss. 15(4), 17.

[51] ss. 13, 17.

[52] s. 14.

[53] s. 19.

[54] s. 20.

[55] SI 1984 No. 2041.

Appeals from an adjudicator to the tribunal require leave from one or other of them in almost all cases. Both are subject to the general law of statutory tribunals and are under the supervision of the Council on Tribunals.

No appeal lies from the tribunal to the courts of law. The numerous immigration and deportation cases which come before the courts are therefore cases of judicial review, where an immigrant seeks habeas corpus or some other prerogative remedy on the ground that the action taken against him was unlawful. Many instances will be found in this book of the quashing of decisions of immigration officers, the Home Secretary, adjudicators and the tribunal, for example for violation of natural justice, or for failure to take the right matters into account. Even a decision of the Home Secretary that a person's exclusion is conducive to the public good may be quashed if based on insufficient grounds.[56] In the past the courts have been unduly hesitant in extending some of their principles into this area, despite the obvious need for the full protection of administrative law against drastic discretionary decisions which may cause great personal hardship.[57] But since the revival of judicial review immigrants have had many successes in the courts.

Extradition of fugitive offenders

Extradition is the surrender by one country to another of some person charged with or convicted of serious crime. The law provides for it in three different ways. In the case of many foreign countries there is an extradition treaty specifying the extradition offences, which is made effective by an Order in Council under the Extradition Acts 1870–1935. In the case of Commonwealth countries and dependencies of the United Kingdom extradition is effected under the Fugitive Offenders Act 1967, which defines the offences and empowers the Crown to designate the countries concerned by Order in Council. In the case of the Republic of Ireland there is summary machinery under the Backing of Warrants (Republic of Ireland) Act 1965, whereby Irish warrants for arrest are indorsed by a magistrate in the United Kingdom and the fugitive is then arrested and surrendered. The Extradition Acts have now been replaced by the Criminal Justice Act 1988[58] which is designed to facilitate extradition to countries with legal systems like Britain's and to enable Britain to ratify the European Convention on Extradition of 1957.

---

[56] R. v. Immigration Appeal Tribunal ex p. Patel [1986] The Independent, 10 December (quashing the decision of the tribunal); reversed [1988] 2 WLR 1165 (HL).

[57] See below, p. 460.

[58] Pt. I, repealing the Extradition Acts, but without affecting the operation of arrangements made under them.

Extradition is less prominent in administrative law than are immigration and deportation, since the legislation and the case-law are concerned more with courts of law than with administrative authorities. Nevertheless some of the decisions are relevant to general principles of judicial review, and most of them illustrate the remedy of habeas corpus.

Under the Extradition Acts the criminal conduct alleged by the foreign country must also be a crime in British law,[59] as well as being specified in the treaty and the schedule of the Act of 1870, as amended; and the evidence must be such as would justify committal for trial in England. The Act of 1988 has eliminated this last requirement where there are general extradition arrangements such as those of the European Convention.[60] In no case may a fugitive be surrendered if his offence is 'of a political character' or if there is an ulterior motive to punish him for such an offence. To this extent the law recognises the right of political asylum, which is recognised also in the immigration rules, as already mentioned. There is no statutory definition of 'political character' and the House of Lords has held that a judicial definition would not be desirable.[61] A political offence need not necessarily be an attempt to overthrow a government or to change the constitution of a state. The underlying idea is, in Lord Radcliffe's words, 'that the fugitive is at odds with the state that applies for his extradition on some issue connected with the political control or government of the country'.[62] Mutiny at sea for the purpose of escaping from a communist country has been held to be a political offence,[63] but not a bomb outrage by an anarchist.[64] For similar reasons treason and sedition are not extraditable crimes. But some modern forms of criminality have had to be outlawed by statute. Genocide is not to be treated as a political offence.[65] Nor are a long list of crimes, including murder, kidnapping, wounding, hijacking, and offences involving explosives, firearms, or nuclear material[66] *vis-à-vis* countries which are parties to the European Convention on the Suppression of Terrorism or to which the legislation is extended by order of the Home Secretary.[67] In exchange, however, there is the safeguard, adopted from the Fugitive Offenders Act 1967, that extradition is to be refused if the fugitive is likely to be penalised on account of his race,

---

[59] *Re Nielsen* [1984] AC 606; *Government of the United States of America* v. *McCaffery* [1984] 1 WLR 867.

[60] s. 6(4).

[61] *R.* v. *Brixton Prison Governor ex p. Schtraks* [1964] AC 556.

[62] [1964] AC at 591.

[63] *R.* v. *Brixton Prison Governor ex p. Kolczynski* [1955] 1 QB 540.

[64] *Re Meunier* [1894] 2 QB 415.

[65] Genocide Act 1969, s. 2.

[66] Added by Criminal Justice Act 1988.

[67] Suppression of Terrorism Act 1978.

religion, nationality or political opinions.[68] Large inroads have therefore been made into the traditional right of political asylum, though there is now better provision against racial and political persecution.

The Fugitive Offenders Act 1967[69] operates in a generally similar manner vis-à-vis Commonwealth and colonial countries, though without the need for treaties. The alleged offence must be punishable with at least twelve months' imprisonment under both British and the relevant foreign law. Evidence must be produced which would justify trial in this country. The court may free the fugitive on habeas corpus if of opinion that it would be unjust or oppressive to return him because his offence was trivial or too much time has since elapsed or the charge is not made in good faith.[70] He is not to be returned if his offence was of a political character or if he is likely to be penalised on account of his race, religion, nationality or political opinions.

The procedure under the Extradition Acts, the Fugitive Offenders Act and the Criminal Justice Act is that the Home Secretary, on receiving a request, authorises a metropolitan magistrate to issue a warrant for the fugitive's arrest, upon which he is brought before the magistrate and the evidence is investigated. If the evidence satisfies the statutory requirements,[71] the fugitive is committed to prison and in due course returned, though he must be allowed fifteen days in which to apply for habeas corpus. If either the Home Secretary or any of the courts considers that he is entitled to the benefit of the rules about political offences, racial (etc.) persecution or triviality of offence (etc.) they may direct his release at any stage of the proceedings; and he may secure his release on judicial review if the proceedings are legally defective. The Home Secretary has general control throughout.

PRISON ADMINISTRATION AND DISCIPLINE

Statutory framework

In the last few years prisoners have become a conspicuous class of litigants and have won a number of successes both in English courts and in the European Court of Human Rights. Some brief details about the administration of prisons, and in particular about disciplinary charges and adjudications, may therefore be given here.

Prisons are the responsibility of the Home Secretary under the Prison

[68] See now Criminal Justice Act 1988.
[69] Replacing Fugitive Offenders Act 1881 and as amended by the Act of 1987.
[70] The Act of 1987 also contains this safeguard.
[71] See R. v. Governor of Ashford Remand Centre ex p. Postlethwaite [1987] 3 WLR 365.

Act 1952. Under that Act, as amended, he makes the Prison Rules,[72] which are supplemented by standing orders. After stating that 'the purpose of the training and treatment of convicted prisoners shall be to encourage and assist them to lead a good and useful life' the rules provide for privileges, remission of sentence (with a maximum of one third[73]), religion, medical attention, work, education, correspondence, discpline,[74] and many other matters. There is a catalogue of offences against discipline followed by detailed provisions about charges, adjudication and punishment.

The Act and the rules provide also that for every prison there shall be a board of visitors which shall include at least two justices of the peace.[75] Members of these boards are appointed by the Home Secretary, usually on the advice of the chairman or members of the board in question, and a member will normally serve for many years. Boards of visitors have both pastoral and disciplinary functions, which they perform as a voluntary social service. In the former guise they have to satisfy themselves (inter alia) as to the condition and management of the prison and the treatment of prisoners, to hear prisoners' complaints, to inspect their food and to report deficiencies to the governor; and they may visit any prisoner at any time and converse with him in private. Their disciplinary functions are explained below.

The statutory boards of visitors must be distinguished from the informally organised prison visitors who undertake to visit and befriend prisoners in many prisons, the arrangements being voluntary on both sides. These visitors need the approval of the Home Office, but they play no part in prison administration and have no prescribed duties or powers.

Discipline and adjudication

A prisoner remains entitled to all his civil rights except in so far as they are taken away by legislation.[76] He has the right of access to the courts, which includes the right to consult a solicitor,[77] and any attempt by the prison authorities to impede it may be treated as contempt of court.[78] Through a Member of Parliament he may complain to the Parliamentary Commis-

---

[72] SI 1964 No. 388 as amended up to 1987 No. 2176.

[73] One half in the case of a sentence not exceeding 12 months: SI 1987 No. 1256.

[74] See [1981] PL 228 (G. Zellick).

[75] s. 6 and rule 92. Detailed information about boards of visitors may be found in *Campbell and Fell* v. *UK*, cited at the end of this section.

[76] *Raymond* v. *Honey* [1983] 1 AC 1 at 10. Prisoners may not vote for or be elected to Parliament under the Representation of the People Acts 1981 and 1983 respectively.

[77] *R.* v. *Home Secretary ex p. Anderson* [1984] QB 778.

[78] *Raymond* v. *Honey* (above) (governor's temporary stopping of application to court held contempt but no penalty imposed).

sioner for Administration. Any disciplinary penalty imposed on him must be authorised by the Prison Act or by the Rules.

The rules provide that minor disciplinary offences are dealt with by the prison governor, who can impose a variety of punishments (known as 'awards'), such as cellular confinement for up to 3 days, stoppage of privileges or earnings for up to 28 days, and forfeiture of remission of sentence for up to 28 days.[79] More serious charges, such as attempted escape or assault on a prison officer, are adjudicated by the board of visitors, who may impose similar penalties for longer periods and may order forfeiture of remission for up to 180 days, or longer in the case of the gravest offences such as mutiny.[80]

The prison rules provide that a prisoner charged with an offence against discipline shall be informed of the charge as soon as possible and shall be given a full opportunity of hearing what is alleged against him and of presenting his own case.[81] The courts apply the principles of natural justice to proceedings before boards of visitors, so that the prisoner may be entitled to call an important witness, including a prisoner from another prison.[82] In the past he was not allowed representation, legal or otherwise, but the courts have held that a board of visitors have power to allow representation and ought normally to do so where there is a serious charge, such as mutiny, and fairness so demands.[83] In principle the awards of boards of visitors are open to challenge on any of the various grounds on which judicial review is available.

Governors' adjudications, on the other hand, were until recently held to be beyond the reach of judicial review altogether, so that a prisoner had no legal remedy against unfair procedure or other injustice in a governor's case. The courts did not explain satisfactorily why they made this distinction, admitting that it was pragmatic rather than logical. The House of Lords, however, have now swept it away, holding that judicial review is as necessary in these cases as in others.[84]

There is no provision for appeal against the awards of either prison governors or prison visitors.

Proposals for reform

After a series of cases in the courts had revealed deficiencies in prison adjudications the government set up a committee to review the disciplinary

[79] Rule 50, as amended by SI 1974 No. 713. Some 95 per cent of offences are dealt with by governors.
[80] Rules 51, 52, amended as above. Visitors' adjudications are about 3,000 annually.
[81] Rule 49.
[82] Below, p. 575.
[83] Below, p. 546.
[84] Below, p. 575.

offences applying to prisoners and the arrangements for their investigation, adjudication and punishment, having regard in particular to (inter alia) the need for 'a disciplinary system which is swift, fair and conclusive'. The committee's principal recommendation was that boards of visitors should lose their disciplinary and judicial functions and that these should be transferred to an independent body, the Prison Disciplinary Tribunal.[85] Their overriding concern was that 'justice must be seen to be done' and that the adjudicating body should be 'clearly seen to be wholly independent of the prison system' and its administration. In the light of legal developments they found it 'inconceivable to us that the present system can continue without structural reform'.[86]

It was recommended that the new tribunal should have a circuit judge as president and should sit in a number of panels, each with a legally qualified chairman (appointed by the Lord Chancellor) and two lay members. The tribunal should be able to order loss of remission up to 120 days, or 180 days for multiple offences. Legal representation should be allowable in discretion before the tribunal but not in governors' hearings. There should be rights of appeal from the governor, if he orders more than seven days' loss of remission, to the tribunal and from the tribunal in all cases to an appeal tribunal, with leave of the latter. There were many other recommendations about offences, punishments and disciplinary procedures.

The government's first reaction, published in a white paper,[87] was to accept the great majority of these proposals, including the new tribunal, but to reject several that were important. It was not agreed that the new tribunal should have legally qualified chairmen, or a president, or that there should be an appeal tribunal; but it was agreed that the tribunal should have access where necessary to legal and procedural advice. A year later, however, the government announced that it had changed its mind, being able to find no consensus in favour of the committee's plan.[88] Boards of visitors were to retain their disciplinary functions and there was to be no new tribunal; but the boards would be given access to expert and legal advice and there would be arrangements for training. Miscellaneous recommendations of the commitee, as approved by the government, would take effect by amendment of the prison rules and standing orders. But the structural reform, which the committee considered to be inevitable, is not to take place.

---

[85] Report of the Prior Committee, Cmnd. 9641 (1985).
[86] Paras. 5.31, 5.50, 5.53.
[87] Cmnd. 9920 (1986).
[88] 489 HL Deb 654 (29 October 1987). The opposition of many boards of visitors seems to have been significant.

European human rights

In a number of cases prisoners have been able to claim the protection of the European Convention on Human Rights and Fundamental Freedoms. Unlike most of the other member states, Britain has failed to incorporate the Convention into the law of the land and it therefore confers no rights which the courts can enforce; but Britain recognises the right of individual petition to the European Commission of Human Rights at Strasbourg, and the Commission can bring the complaints of individuals, including prisoners, before the European Court of Human Rights. The government has an international obligation to give effect to the decisions of the Court.

The strict censorship formerly imposed on prisoners' correspondence was successfully challenged by prisoners in two cases which led to drastic changes in standing orders and much greater freedom for prisoners to consult legal advisers, Members of Parliament and others.[89] The Republic of Ireland obtained a judgment against the United Kingdom for 'inhuman or degrading treatment' of detainees in Northern Ireland.[90] Under the requirement that 'in the determination of his civil rights and obligations or of any criminal charge against him, everyone is entitled to a fair and public hearing within a reasonable time by an independent and impartial tribunal established by law' and that 'judgment shall be pronounced publicly', the court upheld complaints by two prisoners that they were not allowed legal assistance or representation and that the board of visitors' decision was not made public; but it was accepted that the visitors were 'an independent and impartial tribunal' and that the hearing in private fell within the exceptions allowed.[91] In a case where a prisoner serving a life sentence was released on licence (parole) and then recalled to prison, the court accepted that the Parole Board was independent and impartial; but it held that, since the Board was advisory only, and did not disclose material adverse to the prisoner, it violated the right of everyone deprived of his liberty to have the lawfulness of his detention decided by a court—a right which implies a full and fair judicial procedure and is not satisfied by the limited possibilities of judicial review.[92] This decision means that a proper judicial procedure for the recall of paroled prisoners will have to be devised.

The European Court of Human Rights has brought about these notable improvements in prison administration and discipline in fulfilment of its maxim that 'justice cannot stop at the prison gate'.[93]

[89] *Golder* v. *UK* (1975) Series A, No. 18; *Silver* v. *UK* (1983) Series A, No. 61. See [1981] *PL* 435 (G. J. Zellick).
[90] *Ireland* v. *UK* (1978) Series A, No. 25.
[91] *Campbell and Fell* v. *UK* (1984) Series A, No. 80.
[92] *Weeks* v. *UK* (1987) Series A, No. 114.
[93] See *Campbell and Fell* (above) at 35.

PART III
POWERS AND JURISDICTION

8

LEGAL NATURE OF POWERS

Statutory powers and duties

Public administration is carried out to a large extent under statutory powers, conferred upon public authorities by innumerable Acts of Parliament. Statutory duties, imposed similarly, also play their part, but it is a minor one in comparison with powers. This is because powers confer discretion whether to act or not to act, and also, in many cases, what action to take, whereas duties are obligatory and allow no option. It is the element of discretion which raises the most numerous and most difficult problems in the law.

When the question arises whether a public authority is acting lawfully or unlawfully, the nature and extent of its power or duty has to be found by seeking the intention of Parliament as expressed or implied in the relevant Act. The principles of administrative law are generalised rules of statutory interpretation. They do not derive from a written constitution which safeguards them against amendment by everyday legislation: an Act of Parliament is sovereign, and all legal rights are at its mercy. Despite this insecure foundation, the courts have developed and refined a great many effective rules for the control of statutory power. Since so much of this book is concerned with them, an abundance of examples will soon be found. The dominating source of power is Parliament, but there are certain other sources, to be mentioned below, which do not have a statutory basis. These are the royal prerogative; corporate and contractual powers; and non-legal powers.

Acts reasonably incidental

A statutory power will be construed as impliedly authorising everything which can fairly be regarded as incidental or consequential to the power itself; and this doctrine is not applied narrowly.[1] For example, a local authority may do its own printing and bookbinding.[2] Buses may be run a short distance beyond the end of the authorised route if there is no other

---

[1] *A.-G.* v. *Great Eastern Railway* (1880) 5 App. Cas. 473; *A.-G.* v. *Smethwick Cpn.* [1932] 1 Ch 563.

[2] *A.-G.* v. *Smethwick Cpn.* (above)

practicable way of turning them round.[3] Housing authorities may charge differential rents according to their tenants' means,[4] may subsidise their tenants,[5] and may insure their effects.[6] A Board charged with the organisation of the totalisator may make contracts with firms for the collection of off-the-course bets, but may not subsidise one of the firms.[7] The Home Secretary may make charges to prisoners for privileges allowed to them.[8] Statutory powers therefore have considerable latitude, and by reasonable construction the courts can soften the rigour of the ultra vires principle. Although this book contains so many instances of that principle being infringed, it must be remembered that the courts intervene only where the thing done goes beyond what can fairly be treated as incidental or consequential.[9]

Local authorities enjoy a wide 'incidental' power under the Local Government Act 1972: they may do anything 'which is calculated to facilitate, or is conducive or incidental to, the discharge of any of their functions'.[10]

The royal prerogative

In earlier times the Crown wielded extensive powers over its subjects under the royal prerogative, which was part of the common law. In the seventeenth century the Crown had power to imprison people[11] and to impose taxation[12] in its own discretion. But in the course of constitutional history the Crown's oppressive powers have been stripped away, and for administrative purposes the prerogative is now a much-attenuated remnant. Numerous statutes have expressly restricted it, and even where statute merely overlaps it the doctrine is that the prerogative goes into abeyance.[13] It is, in any case, defined by law, that is to say by judicial

[3] *A.-G. v. Leeds Cpn.* [1929] 2 Ch 291.

[4] *Smith v. Cardiff Cpn.* (No. 2) [1955] Ch 159.

[5] *Evans v. Collins* [1965] 1 QB 580; and see *Luby v. Newcastle-under-Lyme Cpn.* [1965] 1 QB 214.

[6] *A.-G. v. Crayford Urban District Council* [1962] Ch 575.

[7] *A.-G. v. Racecourse Betting Control Board* [1935] Ch 34.

[8] *Becker v. Home Office* [1932] 2 QB 407.

[9] See *Ski Enterprises v. Tongariro National Park Board* [1964] NZLR 884 (exclusive concessions for long terms beyond powers of Board); *Felixstowe Dock & Rly Co. v. British Transport Docks Board* [1976] 2 Ll R 656 (Board empowered to make agreements incidental to promotion of Bills in Parliament).

[10] s. 111; above, p. 127.

[11] *Darnel's Case* (1627) 3 St Tr 1.

[12] *Bate's Case* (1606) 2 St Tr 371.

[13] *A.-G. v. De Keyser's Royal Hotel* [1920] AC 508; *R. v. Home Secretary ex p. Northumbria Police Authority* (below).

decisions.[14] Prerogative powers may also, it seems, be atrophied by mere disuse. Thus the Crown used to employ the prerogative writ ne exeat regno to prevent a person leaving the country; but the courts have now held for many years that this remedy is granted only to a creditor for the restraint of an absconding debtor.[15] Although the Crown has been deprived of its former powers of invading the rights and liberties of subjects, there are still a few prerogative powers which can have unwelcome legal effects on individuals. By declaring war the Crown can prevent trade with the enemy and can intern enemy aliens—though in wartime these matters are normally covered by legislation.[16] The Crown has special powers in foreign affairs, e.g. under the doctrine of act of state, which is discussed later.[17] But there is no prerogative power to enforce treaties.[18] The prerogative, in fact, has ceased to be a significant source of administrative power as against the citizen. It still comprises power to take action to preserve the peace,[19] to grant legal favours such as corporate personality or peerage, and it comprises many constitutional powers, such as the power to summon and dissolve Parliament and to assent to bills.

'Prerogative' power is, properly speaking, legal power which appertains to the Crown but not to its subjects. Blackstone explained the correct use of the term.[20]

It signifies, in it's etymology (from prae and rogo) something that is required or demanded before, or in preference to, all others. And hence it follows, that it must be in it's nature singular and eccentrical; that it can only be applied to those rights and capacities which the king enjoys alone, in contradistinction to others, and not to those which he enjoys in common with any of his subjects; for if once any one prerogative of the crown could be held in common with the subject, it would cease to be prerogative any longer.

Although the courts may use the term 'prerogative' in this sense, they have fallen into the habit of describing as 'prerogative' every power of the

[14] *Case of Proclamations* (1611) 12 Co Rep 74; *A.-G.* v. *De Keyser's Royal Hotel* (above); *Burmah Oil Co.* v. *Lord Advocate* [1965] AC 75. See [1973] CLJ 287 (B. S. Markesinis).

[15] See below, p. 617.

[16] Much wider powers than those of the prerogative are in fact conferred, as by the Emergency Powers (Defence) Act 1939.

[17] Below, p. 829.

[18] *Walker* v. *Baird* [1892] AC 491; below, p. 830.

[19] *R.* v *Home Secretary ex p. Northumbria Police Authority* [1988] 2 WLR 590 (special riot equipment issued to police against wishes of police authority).

[20] Bl Comm 1.239. In *Re Ferdinand, Ex-Tsar of Bulgaria* [1921] 1 Ch. 107 at 139 Warrington LJ said that 'prerogative properly describes the power and authority of the king in relation to his own subjects' as opposed to 'persons owing no allegiance to him,' and he doubted whether the Crown's power to seize the property of enemy aliens within the realm was a prerogative power. Since aliens within the jurisdiction in time of peace enjoy the same civil rights as subjects, the proposition is questionable.

Crown which is not statutory.[21] For example, the Court of Appeal has described the administrative scheme for compensating victims of violent crime as established 'under the prerogative'.[22] The scheme was set up by executive action without statutory authority, and the compensation distributed by the Criminal Injuries Compensation Board (out of moneys voted by Parliament) consists technically of ex gratia payments. But anyone may set up a trust or other organisation to distribute money, and for the government to do so involves no 'prerogative' power. Similarly the House of Lords has held that the Crown's powers of control over the civil service are part of the royal prerogative,[23] although in their essence they are merely the powers which any employer has over his employees. A true prerogative power, such as the power to declare war or to create a peer, involves something which no subject may do. Similarly the issue or denial of passports is sometimes said to be a prerogative power, but more probably it involves no legal power at all.[24] The Crown's power to make international treaties is also often called a prerogative power,[25] but since it cannot affect the law administered by the courts it is not, in the domestic sense, a true legal power either.

Corporate powers

One lingering effect of the royal prerogative, at least in theory, is on the powers of corporations. The Crown has the prerogative power of incorporation and can thus incorporate bodies by royal charter, for example boroughs, universities and colleges, professional societies, and the British Broadcasting Corporation.[26] But the great majority of corporations, including most trading companies, and many governmental corporations such as county councils, are incorporated by statute. This leads to a difference in the scope of their powers which was thus expressed in a case about Leeds Corporation:[27]

---

[21]   This loose usage may derive from Dicey, *The Law of the Constitution*, 10th edn, 425: see Wade, *Constitutional Fundamentals*, 49. For further comment see (1985) 101 LQR 180 at 190, cited in *R. v. Panel on Take-overs and Mergers ex p. Datafin Plc* [1987] QB 815 where Lloyd LJ accepts the distinction made in the text, and the Court of Appeal plays down the supposed prerogative element in *ex p. Lain* (below).

[22]   *R. v. Criminal Injuries Compensation Board ex p. Lain* [1967] 2 QB 864 at 881, 883.

[23]   *Council of Civil Service Unions v. Minister for the Civil Service* [1985] AC 374. For these powers see above, p. 56.

[24]   See below, p. 392.

[25]   As in *Laker Airways Ltd. v. Dept. of Trade* [1977] QB 643.

[26]   The Crown could also make an individual office-holder and his successors a corporation sole. One of the few examples is the Master of Pembroke College, Oxford: Halsbury's *Laws of England*, 4th edn., vol. ix, para. 1233.

[27]   *A.-G. v. Leeds Cpn.* [1929] 2 Ch 291.

The corporation was incorporated by royal charter in the year 1627 in the reign of King Charles I. The fact that it is incorporated by royal charter is of importance, because a corporation so constituted stands on a different footing from a statutory corporation, the difference being that the latter species of corporation can only do such acts as are authorised directly or indirectly by the statute creating it; whereas the former can, speaking generally, do anything that an ordinary individual can do.

In other words, the law allows the Crown to create only corporations with complete legal personality and with full power to hold property, make contracts, and so forth. Such corporations may be empowered by their charters to make byelaws, enforceable by fines, provided that they are reasonable.[28] There are remedies against violation of the charter: it is liable to be revoked in scire facias proceedings,[29] members of the corporation can apply for an injunction,[30] and so can the Attorney-General.[31] But the terms of the charter are regarded as a kind of bargain between the corporation and the Crown,[32] and unauthorised transactions are not void as against the rest of the world.[33]

A statutory corporation is entirely different. Its objects and powers are solely those which Parliament has laid down expressly or impliedly in the constituent Act:[34] beyond these it is legally incapable of doing anything, so that any act which is ultra vires is wholly void in law. If therefore it borrows money in excess of a statutory limit, it is not liable to repay because it cannot contract such a debt.[35] If it covenants that it will not exercise a power of compulsory purchase, the covenant is entirely void.[36] This rigid doctrine has been radically modified in favour of persons dealing in good faith with a company;[37] but that applies only as regards companies incorporated under the Companies Acts and not to public authorities incorporated otherwise.

[28] See the *Ipswich Tailors' case* (1614) 11 Co Rep 53; *Slattery* v. *Naylor* (1888) 13 App Cas 446 at 452. Subject to a few exceptions based on ancient custom or prescription, such byelaws could not bind non-members of the corporation unless empowered by statute: *Halsbury's Laws of England*, 4th edn., ix. 756.

[29] Halsbury (as above), paras. 1332, 1396. An affected person may sue with the Attorney-General's fiat.

[30] *Jenkin* v. *Pharmaceutical Society* [1921] 1 Ch 392.

[31] Either on his own motion or on behalf of an affected person: Halsbury (as above), para. 1342.

[32] *Baroness Wenlock* v. *River Dee Co.* (1885) 36 Ch D 674 at 685 n. (Bowen LJ).

[33] *A.-G.* v. *Leicester Cpn.* [1943] Ch. 86.

[34] See e.g. *Re Westminster CC* [1986] AC 668 (unlawful payments by Greater London Council).

[35] *Baroness Wenlock* v. *River Dee Co.* (1885) 10 App Cas 354.

[36] *Triggs* v. *Staines UDC* [1969] 1 Ch 10; below, p. 377.

[37] European Communities Act 1972, s. 9.

Most governmental corporations are statutory, for example incorporated government departments, county councils, district councils and parish
councils. But formerly there were boroughs created by royal charter, and
these could sometimes successfully invoke the wider powers of chartered
corporations. Thus the Corporation of Leicester, which had statutory
power to run bus services within the city, was able to make a valid contract
for the purpose of a bus undertaking operating outside the city; and
although it could not pay the purchase money out of its bus service reserve
fund, since that was restricted by statute, it could pay from its rate fund
which was not (as it was held) so restricted.[38] This distinction is now of
historical interest only as regards local authorities, all of which became
statutory in 1974.[39] In any case it conferred little real liberty on borough
corporations, since their powers were restricted by statute in many respects,
and they are subject to a fiduciary duty to apply their funds for proper
purposes only.[40] It is of more significance that a small margin of freedom to
spend funds for purposes of their own has been given to local authorities
generally by the Local Government Act 1972.[41]

Since a statutory authority's powers are confined by the terms of the
statute, any wider powers which a private owner could exercise are not
available to them. A dock company in which the docks are vested,
accordingly, cannot prevent people from using the docks by relying on an
owner's power to exclude whom he wills, if its statutory powers provide
only for it to regulate the use of the docks by all comers.[42] A public
authority's statutory powers must, moreover, be exercised reasonably and
in accordance with natural justice, so that it cannot arbitrarily evict a tenant
or deny the use of a football ground in a way that might be lawful for a
private landlord.[43]

Contractual powers

Public authorities, like other people, frequently acquire powers by
contract, for example where a local authority lets houses on lease and under
the terms of the lease has power to increase the rent. Contractual powers are
important in some administrative areas, but they do not demand much
attention in administrative law since the ordinary law of contract provides

[38] *A.-G.* v. *Leicester Cpn.* [1943] Ch 86. See Hart, *Local Government and Administration,* 9th
edn., 309.
[39] See above, p. 113.
[40] Below, p. 426.
[41] Above, p. 128.
[42] *London Association of Shipowners* v. *London & India Docks Joint Committee* [1892] 3 Ch.
242; *British Trawlers Federation Ltd.* v. *L. & N. E. Rly Co.* [1933] 2 KB 14.
[43] See below, pp. 400 (reasonableness), 559 (natural justice).

adequate machinery for their enforcement and control. Consequently they are not within the scope of the remedies discussed in this book and the system of judicial review. Something will however be said later about the use of contracts in the mechanism of government.[44]

Non-legal powers

For the sake of completeness it must be added that the courts have in several cases treated non-statutory bodies as subject to the restraints of administrative law as if they were statutory. These bodies are the Criminal Injuries Compensation Board, the Civil Service Appeal Board and the Panel on Take-overs and Mergers, and their cases are best explained later in the context of the remedies which the courts can award.[45] None of them were created or given powers by Parliament, so in theory none of them could do any legal act with which administrative law should be concerned. But the courts treated them as de facto public authorities and held that their actions were subject to judicial review and to legal remedies. At present these cases are sporadic and appear to be anomalous. But it is probable that they will multiply and so open new vistas of judicial review, enabling the courts to penetrate into many areas which were previously beyond their reach.

Another abnormal case is that of the police, who have certain powers and duties at common law in their capacity as officers of the peace, in addition to the many powers and duties conferred upon them by statute. Consequently the court may be able to order the police to carry out their duties even where these are not statutory, as several decisions indicate.[46]

There may even be cases where the principles of judicial review will be applied so as to restrict the powers of a private landowner without any element of contract, for example so as to prevent him from ejecting a race-goer from a racecourse.[47] But such cases, if they exist, lie outside the field of administrative law.

EXPRESS REQUIREMENTS AND CONDITIONS

Mandatory or directory conditions

Acts of Parliament conferring power on public authorities very commonly impose conditions about procedure, for example by requiring that a notice shall be served or that action shall be taken within a specified time or that the decision shall state reasons. If the authority fails to observe such a

[44] Below, pp. 788, 831.
[45] Below, p. 640.
[46] Below, p. 403.
[47] See *Forbes* v. *New South Wales Trotting Club* (1979) 25 ALR1 (below, p. 471).

condition, is its action ultra vires? The answer depends upon whether the condition is held to be mandatory or directory. Non-observance of a mandatory condition is fatal to the validity of the action. But if the condition is held to be merely directory, its non-observance will not matter for this purpose. In other words, it is not every omission or defect which entails the drastic penalty of invalidity.

The distinction is not quite so clear-cut as this suggests, since the same condition may be both mandatory and directory: mandatory as to substantial compliance, but directory as to precise compliance. Where, for example, a local authority were empowered to assess coast protection charges on landowners within six months but did so after 23 months, the delay was so excessive that there was total non-compliance with the condition, and the assessments were void; but had the excess been a few days only, they would probably have been valid.[48] The court may readily find reasons for overlooking trivial or unimportant irregularities.[49]

Sometimes the legislation makes it plain what the effect of non-observance is to be. But more often it does not, and then the court must determine the question. This the court does by weighing the inconvenience of holding the condition ineffective against the inconvenience of insisting upon it rigidly.[50] It is a question of construction, to be settled by looking at the whole scheme and purpose of the Act and by weighing the importance of the condition, the prejudice to private rights, and the claims of the public interest.[51] Little reliable guidance can be drawn from rules which have been suggested in some cases, for example that conditions governing rights are to be applied more strictly than conditions governing duties—though this distinction helps to explain some of the decisions.[52] The construction of the Act should not be affected by the facts of the particular case,[53] but those facts may induce the court to withhold a discretionary remedy.[54] In any case, judges faced with these questions of construction may regard categories such as mandatory and directory as presenting 'not so much a stark choice of alternatives but a spectrum of possibilities in which one compartment or description fades gradually into another'.[55]

---

[48] *Cullimore* v. *Lyme Regis Cpn.* [1962] 1 QB 718. Compare *James* v. *Minister of Housing and Local Government* (below).

[49] e.g. *Re Bowman* [1932] 2 KB 621; *R.* v. *Dacorum Gaming Licensing Committee* [1971] 3 All ER 666; *Sheffield CC* v. *Graingers Wines Ltd.* [1977] 1 WLR 1119.

[50] *R.* v. *Rochester (Mayor)* (1857) 7 E & B 910.

[51] *Howard* v. *Bodington* (1877) 2 PD 203; *Coney* v. *Choyce* [1975] 1 WLR 422.

[52] See *Caldow* v. *Pixell* (1877) 2 CPD 562; *Montreal Street Railway Co.* v. *Normandin* [1917] AC 170; *Clayton* v. *Heffron* (1960) 105 CLR 214 at 247.

[53] *Cullimore* v. *Lyme Regis Cpn.* (above).

[54] *Coney* v. *Choyce* (above).

[55] *London & Clydeside Estates Ltd.* v. *Aberdeen DC* [1980] 1 WLR 182 (Lord Hailsham LC).

The courts also sometimes vary their terminology, as by contrasting 'imperative' with 'mandatory' (meaning mandatory and directory respectively).[56] In one case the Court of Appeal held that a planning authority could validly give a decision without stating reasons as required by the Act, but called the condition mandatory in the sense that the duty to state reasons could be enforced by mandamus.[57] But the availability of that remedy has nothing to do with the question whether the decision itself is valid, and the normal conclusion, applying the test laid down in a great number of cases, would have been to hold the condition to be directory.

It is possible for whole areas of statutory law to be treated as merely directory. This has been held in respect of certain provisions of the Prison Act 1952 and the whole of the prison rules[58] made under it, so that a prisoner not treated in accordance with the Act or the rules has no legal remedy.[59] Yet the same rules have been treated as enforceable in determining a prisoner's right to correspond with his solicitor and to make an application to the court[60] and to receive prompt notice of a disciplinary charge.[61]

Procedural and formal requirements

Procedural safeguards, which are so often imposed for the benefit of persons affected by the exercise of administrative powers, are normally regarded as mandatory, so that it is fatal to disregard them. Where there is a statutory duty to consult persons affected, this must genuinely be done,[62] and reasonable opportunity for comment must be given.[63] Where a proposal or scheme is required to be published it must be accurately

---

[56] As in *Howard* v. *Bodington* (above). See also below, p. 250, n. 84.

[57] *Brayhead (Ascot) Ltd.* v. *Berks CC* [1964] 2 QB 303.

[58] SI 1964 No. 388 as amended.

[59] *Arbon* v. *Anderson* [1943] KB 252; *Becker* v. *Home Office* [1972] 2 QB 407; *R.* v. *Hull Prison Visitors ex p. St. Germain* [1979] QB 425; *Williams* v. *Home Office* (No. 2) [1981] 1 All ER 1211. For an exception see *R.* v. *Home Secretary ex p. Herbage* (No. 2) [1987] QB 1077 (below, p. 575).

[60] *Raymond* v. *Honey* [1983] 1 AC 1. See also *Guilfoyle* v. *Home Office* [1981] QB 309 (rules strictly construed by Court of Appeal in rejecting right to correspond with solicitor concerning petition to European Commission of Human Rights).

[61] *R.* v. *Board of Visitors of Dartmoor Prison ex p. Smith* [1987] QB 106;below, p. 250. See also *R.* v. *Home Secretary ex p. Anderson* [1984] QB 778 (prison rule restricting access to legal advisers held ultra vires).

[62] *Grunwick Processing Laboratories Ltd.* v. *ACAS* [1978] AC 277; *Agricultural* (etc.) *Training Board* v. *Aylesbury Mushrooms Ltd.* [1972] 1 WLR 190 (below, p. 339).

[63] *Re Union of Benefices of Whippingham and East Cowes, St James'* [1954] AC 245; *Port Louis Cpn.* v. *A.-G. of Mauritius* [1965] AC 1111; and see below, p. 885 (delegated legislation).

described[64] and any one entitled to object must be allowed adequate time. Four days' notice of a local authority's scheme for setting up comprehensive schools was held wholly unreasonable and inadequate, so that the scheme was void.[65] An identical scheme had previously been held void and prohibited by injunction, because public notice of it had not been given as required by the Education Act 1944.[66] The object of requiring notice was to give an opportunity for objections to be made to the Minister before he decided whether to confirm the scheme. But this procedure was required only where the scheme involved setting up new schools or ceasing to maintain old ones. The local authority had wrongly supposed that they were not ceasing to maintain their former schools. It was held to be clearly implicit in the design of the Act that the Minister could not approve the scheme until the statutory procedure had been observed, and it was said[67]

. . . it is imperative that the procedure laid down in the relevant statutes should be properly observed. The provisions of the statutes in this respect are supposed to provide safeguards for Her Majesty's subjects. Public Bodies and Ministers must be compelled to observe the law; and it is essential that bureaucracy should be kept in its place.

The same case contains a contrasting example of directory requirements. Objections had been duly invited in respect of other schools covered by the scheme, but the Act also required that their specifications should be approved by the Minister. The local authority was proceeding with its scheme without submitting specifications for approval, but it was held that the court would not intervene, in the absence of objection by the Minister, even though the local authority was 'flying in the face of the intention which Parliament manifested'.[68]

Contrasting examples also appeared in another comprehensive school case, where the regulations requiring public notice of the scheme were held to be mandatory as regards substantial compliance, but merely regulatory as to some minor details.[69] Substantial compliance also sufficed where a local authority, in arranging for the adoption of a child, failed to notify the mother in writing but in fact made the position clear to her.[70] In a planning

---

[64] *Wilson* v. *Secretary of State for the Environment* [1973] 1 WLR 1083 (notice describing land wrongly). See also *Legg* v. *Inner London Education Authority* [1972] 1 WLR 1245; *Coney* v. *Choyce* (above).

[65] *Lee* v. *Dept. of Education and Science* (1967) 66 LGR 211. See similarly *R.* v. *Brent LBC ex p. Gunning* (1985) 84 LGR 168.

[66] *Bradbury* v. *Enfield LBC* [1967] 1 WLR 1311.

[67] At 1325 (Danckwerts LJ).

[68] At 1335 (Diplock LJ).

[69] *Coney* v. *Choyce* [1975] 1 WLR 422. Contrast *Mukta Ben* v. *Suva CC* [1980] 1 WLR 767 (non-publication of notice of compulsory purchase order not fatal: directory only).

[70] *Re T* [1986] Fam. 160.

case the requirement that a notice of appeal against an enforcement notice should state the grounds of appeal was held to be merely directory, but the time limit for appeal was held to be mandatory.[71] The requirement that a planning application involving a departure from the development plan should be advertised as such has been held to be merely directory;[72] but the omission from a planning authority's statutory advertisement of details about the lodging of objections resulted in the invalidity of a planning permission.[73]

In notices affecting private rights, particularly where the effect is penal, scrupulous observance of statutory conditions is normally required. A demand for industrial training levy[74] and a certificate of 'alternative development'[75] have both been held void for failure to indicate, as required by statute, that there was a right of appeal. An enforcement notice is void if it fails to state, as it should, the time allowed for compliance.[76] A demand for a payment is void if it is signed by the borough treasurer instead of by the town clerk.[77] Where an Act requires consent in writing from the local authority carrying on an 'offensive trade', the requirement of writing is mandatory.[78]

Requirements which are less substantial, and more like matters of mere formality, may fall on either side of the line. Some of the cases concern delegated legislation, and are discussed elsewhere.[79] The omission from a clearance order of a note giving directions for the filling up of the form of order was held to be immaterial.[80] The provision of the Rent Act 1965 that a rent officer should consider 'the rent specified in the application' was held to contain a mandatory condition, so that an application which did not specify the desired rent was a nullity and the defect could not be waived.[81] The court distinguished an earlier case in which the application to a rent tribunal had failed to give the name of the landlord as required by regulations made under the relevant Act. The regulations were held to be merely directory in this respect, since the Act itself contained no such

---

[71] *Howard v. Secretary of State for the Environment* [1975] QB 235.
[72] *R. v. St Edmundsbury BC ex p. Investors in Industry Commercial Properties Ltd.* [1985] 1 WLR 1168; and see *Co-operative Retail Services Ltd.* v. *Taff-Ely BC* (1979) 39 P & CR 223.
[73] *R. v. Lambeth LBC ex p. Sharp* (1984) 50 P & CR 284.
[74] *Agricultural (etc.) Industry Training Board* v. *Kent* [1970] 2 QB 19. See similarly *Rayner* v. *Stepney Corporation* [1911] 2 Ch. 312 (closing order void).
[75] *London & Clydeside Estates Ltd.* v. *Aberdeen DC* [1980] 1 WLR 182.
[76] *Burges v. Jarvis* [1952] 2 QB 41.
[77] *Graddage v. Haringey London Borough Council* [1975] 1 WLR 241.
[78] *Epping Forest DC v. Essex Rendering Ltd.* [1983] 1 WLR 158 HL.
[79] Below, p. 873.
[80] *Re Bowman* [1932] 2 KB 621.
[81] *Chapman v. Earl* [1968] 1 WLR 1315.

requirement.[82] But many cases show that even where the requirement is in the Act itself, it is possible for it to be held directory only.[83] 'No universal rule can be laid down for the construction of statutes, as to whether mandatory enactments shall be considered directory only or obligatory, with an implied nullification for disobedience'.[84]

A requirement of the prison rules that a charge against a prisoner should be laid 'as soon as possible' was held by the Court of Appeal to be mandatory, thus invalidating a charge laid in May for an offence committed in February.[85]

The possibility that a public authority may have power to waive an otherwise mandatory procedural requirement is mentioned below.[86]

Time limits

It has often been held that an act may be validly done after the expiry of a statutory time limit. Thus a rating list was upheld even though made and transmitted after the required dates.[87] A local planning authority, which is required by regulations to give notice of its decision within two months, was held able to give a valid decision after three months.[88] An earlier case[89] holding that a delay of over two years would invalidate the decision has been disapproved, but it is not entirely clear that so long a delay may not still be fatal.[90]

Time limits may be held to be mandatory where the rights of other persons depend on them or they are of special importance. In an oft-cited case a bishop received a complaint against a clergyman but failed to send a copy of it to the clergyman within the statutory twenty-one days. All subsequent proceedings in the case were void.[91] So was a planning appeal lodged out of time, as mentioned above.[92] So was a scheme of charges for

---

[82] *Jackson (Francis) Developments Ltd.* v. *Hall* [1951] 2 KB 488; and see *R.* v. *Lincolnshire Appeal Tribunal ex p. Stubbins* [1917] 1 KB 1; *R.* v. *Devon and Cornwall Rent Tribunal ex p. West* (1974) 29 P & CR 316.

[83] e.g. *Margate Pier Co.* v. *Hannam* (1819) 3 B & Ald 266; *Caldow* v. *Pixell* (above); *Montreal Street Railway Co.* v. *Normandin* (above).

[84] *Liverpool Borough Bank* v. *Turner* (1861) 2 De GF & J 507 (Lord Campbell).

[85] *R.* v. *Board of Visitors of Dartmoor Prison ex p. Smith* [1987] QB 106.

[86] Below, p. 267.

[87] *R.* v. *Ingall* (1876) 2 QBD 199.

[88] *James* v. *Minister of Housing and Local Government* [1966] 1 WLR 135, approved on this point [1967] 1 WLR 171 (HL); and see *Chelmsford Rural District Council* v. *Powell* [1963] 1 WLR 123 (additional ground of appeal allowed out of time); *R.* v. *Inspector of Taxes ex p. Clarke* [1971] 2 QB 640.

[89] *Edwick* v. *Sunbury-on-Thames UDC* [1962] 1 QB 229.

[90] See [1966] 1 WLR at 142 (Lord Denning MR).

[91] *Howard* v. *Bodington* (1877) 2 PD 203.

[92] *Howard* v. *Secretary of State for the Environment* (above).

coast protection works which was made long after the appointed time.[93] So was an election petition which was presented after the prescribed time had expired.[94] But time limits governing electoral procedure may sometimes be exceeded with impunity, as where a list of voters was revised after the time appointed by the Act.[95] In New Zealand the court understandably refused to invalidate a general election, even though the Governor-General's warrant was issued unduly late.[96] These are cases where public policy clearly requires some latitude.

Failure to state reasons

The great majority of statutory tribunals are required by the Tribunals and Inquiries Act 1971 to give reasons for their decisions on request. The qualified duty imposed by the Act is often supplemented by an unqualified duty imposed by procedural regulations. The Act likewise applies to decisions of Ministers taken after public inquiries. And other statutes and regulations sometimes impose a like duty. This duty may be broken either because no reasons are given or because the reasons given are inadequate. The general nature of this duty is discussed elsewhere.[97] Here we are concerned with the effect of a breach of it.

In the case already mentioned the Court of Appeal held that a condition attached to a grant of planning permission was not invalidated by the planning authority's omission to state reasons in writing as required by the General Development Order.[98] Though described as mandatory, the requirement was in effect held to be directory. This decision seems reasonable in the circumstances. Planning authorities impose common-form conditions in many cases, and it would be a serious inconvenience to invalidate any condition for which separate reasons were not given. On the other hand, where it is a case of failure to explain the authority's main decision, the court will intervene not merely if no reasons were given but also if they are unsatisfactory. In one such case, where the reasons given by an agricultural arbitrator did not explain what breaches of covenant had been committed by the tenant, this was held to be error on the face of the

---

[93] *Cullimore* v. *Lyme Regis Corporation* [1962] 1 QB 718.
[94] *Devan Nair* v. *Yong Kuan Teik* [1967] 2 AC 31.
[95] *R.* v. *Rochester (Mayor)* (1857) 7 E & B 910.
[96] *Simpson* v. *A.-G.* [1955] NZLR 271.
[97] Below, p. 934.
[98] *Brayhead (Ascot) Ltd.* v. *Berks CC* [1964] 2 QB 303; above, p. 247. See likewise *R.* v. *Liverpool CC ex p. Liverpool Taxi Fleet Operators' Association* [1975] 1 WLR 701, where however it is suggested that the court might intervene if the irregularity caused 'significant injury'. In *Greene* v. *Home Secretary* [1942] AC 284 failure to state reasons correctly did not invalidate a detention order.

award and it was set aside.[99] And in a planning case, where the Minister's decision of an appeal was accompanied by obscure and unsatisfactory reasons, the decision was quashed for non-compliance with the procedural rules which govern these appeals and require decisions to be reasoned.[1]

Later decisions have clearly held that a statutory duty to give reasons is normally mandatory, so that in default of adequate reasons the decision is a nullity and will be quashed. Decisions of immigration appeal tribunals,[2] industrial relations tribunals[3] and mental health review tribunals[4] have been invalidated accordingly. So have the decisions of ministers taken after statutory inquiries.[5] The whole tenor of the case-law is that the duty to give satisfactory reasons is a duty of decisive importance which cannot lawfully be disregarded. They are supported by an earlier decision that where licensing justices were required by statute to specify the grounds of their decision, failure to do so made their proceedings wholly defective, so that they could be required by mandamus to rehear the application de novo.[6] The justices were empowered to refuse an application on one of four specified grounds, and it was held that this implied a duty to state the ground of refusal.[7]

Provisions as to irregularity

Statutes occasionally make specific provision for the effect of non-observance of their requirements. Thus the Licensing Act 1964, after setting out a list of disqualifying circumstances for justices sitting to grant liquor licences, provides: 'No objection shall be allowed to any justices' licence on the ground that it was granted by justices not qualified to grant it.'[8] The Agriculture Act 1947, after prescribing the mode of appointment of members of agricultural land tribunals, provides that the tribunal's acts shall be valid notwithstanding that it is afterwards discovered that there was a defect in the appointment of a member.[9] The latter provision has been

---

[99] *Re Poyser and Mills' Arbitration* [1964] 2 QB 247; below, p. 936.

[1] *Givaudan & Co. Ltd.* v. *Minister of Housing and Local Government* [1967] 1 WLR 250.

[2] *R.* v. *Immigration Appeal Tribunal ex p. Khan (Mahmud)* [1983] QB 790.

[3] *Norton Tool Co. Ltd.* v. *Tewson* [1973] 1 WLR 45; *Alexander Machinery (Dudley) Ltd.* v. *Crabtree* [1974] ICR 120; *Guest* v. *Alpine Soft Drinks Ltd.* [1982] ICR 110; and other cases cited below, p. 936.

[4] *R.* v. *Mental Health Review Tribunal ex p. Clatworthy* [1985] 3 All ER 699; *R.* v. *Mental Health Review Tribunal ex p. Pickering* [1986] 1 All ER 99.

[5] Below, p. 974.

[6] *R.* v. *Thomas* [1892] 1 QB 426. See also *R.* v. *Sykes* (1875) 1 QBD 52; *ex p. Gorman* [1894] AC 23.

[7] The Licensing Act 1964, s. 12(6) now requires grounds of refusal to be specified.

[8] s. 193(8). For the restrictive interpretation given to this section see below, p. 482.

[9] Sched.

successfully invoked where an appointment appeared to be defective.[10] Procedural regulations sometimes contain similar clauses to the effect that failure to comply with them shall not invalidate the proceedings.[11] It is open to doubt whether such clauses would protect serious procedural errors, and it is unlikely that they would validate any procedure which violated the principles of natural justice.[12]

Irregularities may also be cured under statutory powers of modification. Clearance orders under the Housing Acts, for example, may be confirmed by the Minister with or without modification, and he has power to modify an invalid order so as to make it a valid one. Thus where the local authority's order provided that the land acquired might be disposed of in ways not permitted by the Act, the Minister modified the order so as to confine the future use of the land to rehousing and thus saved it from invalidity.[13] Similarly an order has been validated by extending an excessively short time limit.[14] Under the Town and Country Planning Act 1971[15] the Secretary of State may correct an error in an enforcement notice in deciding an appeal against it, if satisfied that the error is not material.

The common form of enactment which allows the validity of housing, planning and other orders to be challenged only within six weeks gives the court power to quash the order if it is not within the powers of the Act or if failure to comply with requirements of the Act has caused the interests of the applicant to be substantially prejudiced. This formula is discussed in a later chapter, where it is suggested that its two limbs ('not within the powers' and 'failure to comply with requirements') should be interpreted as distinguishing between mandatory and directory conditions.[16]

CONCLUSIVENESS, MISTAKE AND FRAUD

Revocable and irrevocable action

It may be necessary to determine whether there is power to revoke or modify the decisions or orders of an administrative authority or tribunal.[17] The question here is whether the authority itself has power to do this. This is different from the question whether some other authority has power to

---

[10] *Woollett* v. *Minister of Agriculture and Fisheries* [1955] 1 QB 103.
[11] e.g. Plant Variety Rights Tribunal Rules 1965 (SI 1965 No. 1623), rule 21.
[12] See below, p. 482.
[13] *R.* v. *Minister of Health ex p. Yaffe* [1931] AC 494.
[14] *Re Bowman* [1932] 2 KB 621.
[15] s. 88(4). See *Miller-Mead* v. *Minister of Housing and Local Government* [1963] 2 QB 196.
[16] Below, p. 741.
[17] On this subject see [1982] PL 613 (M. Akehurst).

do so, which may be affected by a statutory provision that the decision 'shall be final', as explained elsewhere.[18]

In the interpretation of statutory powers and duties there is a rule that, unless the contrary intention appears, 'the power may be exercised and the duty shall be performed from time to time as occasion requires'.[19] But this gives a highly misleading view of the law where the power is a power to decide questions affecting legal rights. In those cases the courts are strongly inclined to hold that the decision, once validly made, is an irrevocable legal act and cannot be recalled or revised. The same arguments which require finality for the decisions of courts of law apply to the decisions of statutory tribunals, ministers and other authorities.

For this purpose a distinction has to be drawn between powers of a continuing character and powers which, once exercised, are finally expended so far as concerns the particular case. An authority which has a duty to maintain highways or a power to take land by compulsory purchase may clearly act 'from time to time as occasion requires'. But if in a particular case it has to determine the amount of compensation or to fix the pension of an employee, there are equally clear reasons for imposing finality. Citizens whose legal rights are determined administratively are entitled to know where they stand.

There is a third class of cases where there is power to decide questions affecting private rights but where there is also an inherent power to vary an order[20] or power to entertain fresh proceedings and make a different decision. Decisions on licensing applications and other decisions of policy will usually fall into this class, since policy is essentially variable. Thus, as mentioned earlier,[21] decisions on planning applications may be varied at any time if a fresh application is submitted.

There are also cases where a power of review is expressly given by statute. The social security authorities, for example, have extensive powers to review their decisions on grounds of fresh evidence, change of circumstances, or mere mistakes.[22] Powers of much the same kind have been conferred on industrial tribunals.[23] But if it proposes to vary its decision under such a power the tribunal should first hear any party prejudiced.[24] Even where such powers are not conferred, it is possible that

[18] Below, p. 720.
[19] Interpretation Act 1978, s. 12. For the power to modify legislative orders see below, p. 852.
[20] As in *Re Wilson* [1985] AC 750 (justices' order as to payment of fines; Interpretation Act 1978 invoked).
[21] Above, p. 187.
[22] Below, p. 933.
[23] Below, p. 934.
[24] *Times Newspapers Ltd.* v. *Fitt* [1981] ICR 637.

statutory tribunals would have power, as has the High Court, to correct accidental mistakes; to set aside judgments obtained by fraud; and to review a decision where facts subsequently discovered have revealed a miscarriage of justice.[25] In the absence of such special circumstances the tribunal's decision is irrevocable as soon as it has been communicated to the parties, even though orally[26] and even though the reasons for it remain to be given later.[27]

A mistake may lead to action being taken upon a wholly wrong basis so that some different action needs to be substituted. This happened where a local education authority agreed to pay the cost of school transport for a girl, supposing that she lived more than three miles from the school and that they therefore had a statutory duty to pay. When it was found that the distance was less than three miles, so that they had a power to pay but no duty, they refused to do so. The Court of Appeal rejected the plea that the original decision was irrevocable, since it was not taken in the exercise of any power to determine a question of legal right and could not affect the duty to exercise discretion when the true facts appeared.[28]

Cases of irrevocability

The following cases illustrate situations in which the court will hold administrative decisions to be irrevocable. A local authority, proposing to make up a street and apportion the expense among the frontagers, gave notice that it would follow one of the two alternative statutory procedures. It was held unable to revoke this decision when it later wished to follow the other procedure.[29] Although the court said that the authority's notice would estop it, the true ground of decision was probably that the election, once formally made, was a legal act which there was no power to undo. That was certainly the operative ground where the Westminster Council was held unable to vary an excessive award of compensation to a redundant employee.[30] The district auditor had disallowed the excess as unlawful

---

[25] See RSC 1965, O 20 r 11 (though the jurisdiction is inherent); *Hip Foong Hong* v. *H. Neotia & Co.* [1918] AC 888 (PC). For the position of tribunals see further below, p. 933.

[26] *Lamont* v. *Fry's Metals Ltd.* [1985] ICR 566.

[27] *Jowett* v. *Bradford (Earl)* [1977] ICR 342; *R.* v. *Cripps ex p. Muldoon* [1984] QB 686; R. v. *Oxford Regional Mental Health Review Tribunal ex p. Home Secretary* [1988] AC 120. Contrast *Hanks* v. *Ace High Products* [1978] ICR 1155; *R.* v. *Greater Manchester Valuation Panel ex p. Shell Chemicals Ltd.* [1982] QB 255.

[28] *Rootkin* v. *Kent CC* [1981] 1 WLR 1186.

[29] *Gould* v. *Bacup Local Board* (1881) 50 LJMC 44.

[30] *Livingstone* v. *Westminster Cpn.* [1904] 2 KB 109. And see *Battelley* v. *Finsbury Borough Council* (1958) 56 LGR 165 (no power to revoke engagement of employee). Scots examples are *Campbell* v. *Glasgow Police Cmrs.* (1895) 22 R. 621; *Blackley* v. *Ayr CC* 1934 SLT 398.

expenditure and surcharged the councillors; but the High Court discharged them for the reason that it was for them to find the facts, and even if they had done so wrongly they had acted within their jurisdiction and made a valid determination which they had no power to reconsider or reduce. Similarly where the War Damage Commission had written to the owner of damaged property saying that it had been classified as 'not total loss', so that the statutory compensation would be on a 'cost of works' basis, the Commission were held unable to alter the classification to 'total loss', which they later decided was right.[31] These might be represented as cases of estoppel, but in truth they depend on the principle that a statutory power to decide is often a power to decide once and once only. In the case last mentioned Vaisey J accepted the principle in these words:[32]

> . . . where Parliament confers on a body such as the War Damage Commission the duty of deciding or determining any question, the deciding or determining of which affects the rights of the subject, such decision or determination made and communicated in terms which are not expressly preliminary or provisional is final and conclusive, and cannot, in the absence of express statutory power or the consent of the person or persons affected, be altered or withdrawn by that body.

The suggestion that a conclusive decision can be altered with the consent of the person affected needs qualification, since consent by itself cannot confer power which does not exist.[33] If a public authority makes a grant or gives a licence, it will not normally be able to revoke or alter its decision. But if it refuses a grant or a licence, it may be able to allow a renewed application, not because its first decision was not conclusive, but because it has a continuing power, and perhaps duty, to allow applications at any time.[34]

In the War Damage Commission case it was held that the Commission's decision was none the less binding because it was conveyed by an informal letter.[35] Where formalities are not prescribed by the Act in such a way as to make them mandatory, there is no reason why informal notification of the decision should not be fully conclusive.

Similarly where an immigration officer gives an immigrant leave to enter and remain in the country, this is conclusive of his right to do so even

---

[31] *Re 56 Denton Road, Twickenham* [1953] Ch. 51. See similarly *Employment and Immigration Commission v. Macdonald Tobacco Inc.* (1981) 121 DLR (3d) 546.

[32] At 802.

[33] Below, p. 264.

[34] See *R. v. Hertfordshire CC ex p. Cheung* [1986] The Times, 4 April (student grants, previously refused, allowed after *R. v. Barnet LBC ex p. Shah* [1982] 2 AC 309 showed that refusals were wrong in law).

[35] As also in *A.-G. v. Hughes* (1889) 81 LT 679; *Robertson v. Minister of Pensions* [1949] 1 KB 227.

if the immigration officer acts under a mistake.[36] It is otherwise, of course, if he has no legal authority to grant leave in the circumstances,[37] or if he grants it because of misrepresentation by the immigrant, as explained below.

Fraud and misrepresentation

An order or determination will not be conclusive if it has been obtained by fraud or misrepresentation. Denning LJ once said:[38]

No judgment of a court, no order of a Minister, can be allowed to stand if it has been obtained by fraud. Fraud unravels everything.

In administrative law, which was not the context of this statement, there is only scanty material to illustrate it, although in principle it ought to be correct. The only field in which there are examples is immigration law, where it is held that leave to enter given by an immigration office is vitiated if it has been obtained by any kind of fraud, deception, or misrepresentation on the part of the immigrant.[39] The House of Lords once went so far as to hold, in an exceptional decision, that an immigrant had a positive duty to disclose all material facts, even if he was not asked about them, and that if he failed to volunteer relevant information he was guilty of deception.[40] But in a later decision the House retracted this severe ruling.[41]

A decision of an inferior tribunal obtained by fraud, for example by perjured evidence, may be quashed by the High Court on certiorari.[42]

Misrepresentation by a public authority may bring into play the doctrine of estoppel[43] and it may amount to an abuse of power which the court will control.[44] It may also be a tort for which the court will award damages.[45]

---

[36] *R. v. Home Secretary ex p. Ram* [1979] 1 WLR 148.
[37] *R. v. Home Secretary ex p. Choudhary* [1978] 1 WLR 1177.
[38] *Lazarus Estates Ltd.* v. *Beasley* [1956] 1 QB 702 and 712. cf. *R. v. Wolverhampton Crown Court ex p. Crofts* [1983] 1 WLR 204.
[39] *R. v. Home Secretary ex p. Hussain* [1978] 1 WLR 700; *Same ex p. Choudhary* (above); *Same ex p. Zamir* [1980] AC 930.
[40] *R. v. Home Secretary ex p. Zamir* (above). See below, p. 460. Contrast *R. v. Home Secretary ex p. Mangoo Khan* [1980] 1 WLR 569; *Same ex p. Jayakody* [1982] 1 WLR 405.
[41] *R. v. Home Secretary ex p. Khawaja* [1984] AC 74.
[42] *R. v. Gillyard* (1848) 12 QB 527; *R. v. Fulham &c Rent Tribunal ex p. Gormly* [1951] 2 All ER 1030.
[43] Below, p. 261.
[44] Below, p. 423.
[45] As in *Bennett (Potatoes) Ltd.* v. *Secretary of State for Scotland* 1986 SLT 665 (government inspector without reasonable basis falsely certified potatoes as pest-free: damages awarded for fraudulent misrepresentation though without intent to deceive).

POWER OR DUTY—WORDS PERMISSIVE OR OBLIGATORY

When 'may' means 'must'

The hallmark of discretionary power is permissive language using words
such as 'may' or 'it shall be lawful', as opposed to obligatory language such
as 'shall'. But this simple distinction is not always a sure guide, for there
have been many decisions in which permissive language has been construed
as obligatory. This is not so much because one form of words is interpreted
to mean its opposite, as because the power conferred is, in the circumstances
prescribed by the Act, coupled with a duty to exercise it in a proper case.
Cotton LJ once said:[46]

I think that great misconception is caused by saying that in some cases 'may' means
'must'. It never can mean 'must', so long as the English language retains its
meaning; but it gives a power, and then it may be a question in what cases, where a
Judge has a power given him by the word 'may', it becomes his duty to exercise it.

This view of the matter was adopted in a case where the Act provided that
the county court 'may' make an order for possession in proceedings by a
landlord against a tenant: it was held that, on proof of the relevant facts, the
court was bound to make the order.[47] There have been many similar
decisions concerning the powers of courts of law, since they have a general
duty to enforce legal rights.[48] Public authorities have a duty, likewise, to
exercise their powers as the public interest requires. Coleridge J said in a
case concerning the Tithe Commissioners:

The words undoubtedly are only empowering; but it has been so often decided as
to become an axiom that in public statutes words only directory, permissory, or
enabling, may have a compulsory force where the thing to be done is for the public
benefit or in advancement of public justice.[49]

The application of this doctrine to action of an administrative character is
shown by two contrasting decisions of the House of Lords. In *Julius v. Lord
Bishop of Oxford*[50] the statute said that 'it shall be lawful' for a bishop to issue
a commission of inquiry in case of alleged misconduct by a clergyman,
either on the application of a complainant or of his own motion; and the

[46] *Re Baker* (1890) 44 Ch D 262 at 270, following *Julius v. Lord Bishop of Oxford* (below).
[47] *Sheffield Cpn. v. Luxford* [1929] 2 KB 180.
[48] See cases catalogued under 'May' in Stroud's *Judicial Dictionary*. Examples are *Shelley
v. London County Council* [1949] AC 56; *Peterborough Corporation v. Holdich* [1956] 1 QB 124;
Re Shuter [1960] 1 QB 124.
[49] *R. v. Tithe Commissioners* (1849) 14 QB 459 at 474.
[50] (1880) LR 5 App Cas 214, reviewing cases going back to *Blackwell's Case* (1683) 1 Vern
152, in which permissive words were held mandatory. See also *Lawrence Building Co. v.
Lanarkshire CC* 1977 SLT 110.

question was whether, complaint having been made by a parishioner, the bishop was entitled to refuse to act. The House of Lords held that the permissive wording gave the bishop discretion, and that he had no mandatory duty except, perhaps, to hear and consider the application—as he had done. For it was evident from the form and policy of the Act that the power was given to the bishop in order that he might exercise his judgment and disallow applications which were unsubstantial or unmeritorious. Otherwise clergymen might be harried with innumerable vexatious inquiries. In the contrasting case, *Padfield* v. *Minister of Agriculture, Fisheries and Food*,[51] the question was also whether action need be taken on a complaint. The Agricultural Marketing Act 1958 provided for the reference of certain complaints to a committee of investigation 'if the Minister in any case so directs'. The Minister refused to act on a complaint by a group of milk producers against the Milk Marketing Board. But his reasons were held to be inconsistent with the policy of the Act, which was that relevant and substantial complaints should go to the committee in the absence of good reasons to the contrary. The permissive words gave the minister discretion, but he was not entitled to use his discretion in such a way as to thwart the policy of the Act. Primarily, therefore, this is a leading example of the abuse of discretion, and it is in that context that it is considered later.[52]

Statutory construction

Whether a power, expressed in merely permissive language, is accompanied by a duty to exercise it in certain circumstances requires consideration of the whole statutory context in which the power is given. A power to levy rates, for example, is often given in the form that the local authority 'may' levy them for particular purposes or in particular cases, yet the court will readily conclude that where the prescribed conditions exist, there is a duty to impose the rate.[53] Where a licensing authority 'may' grant a licence to an applicant with certain qualifications, the policy of the Act may be that licences are not to be withheld from qualified applicants unless there is some valid objection. Thus where the Home Secretary was given power to license cabs on such conditions as he might by order prescribe, the Court of Appeal doubted whether he was intended to have absolute discretion to put many thousands of cab-drivers out of business even where they fulfilled the

---

[51] [1968] AC 997. See similarly *Car Owners' Mutual Insurance Co. Ltd.* v. *Treasurer of the Commonwealth of Australia* [1970] AC 527, where the Privy Council held that the Treasurer was obliged to certify that the company had satisfied the requirements for recovery of its deposited funds, despite the statutory condition 'if the Treasurer so certifies'.

[52] Below, p. 401.

[53] *R.* v. *Barlow* (1693) 2 Salk. 609; *R.* v. *Barclay* (1882) 8 QBD 486.

conditions.[54] In fact the Home Secretary had validly delegated his power to the commissioner of police subject to two specific reservations, and it was held that the commissioner was not therefore empowered to refuse licences on other grounds. So likewise, where the Acts says that a licence 'may be issued' and 'may be revoked' without saying in what circumstances, there may be a duty to issue it and a duty not to revoke it except for a good legal reason: an arbitrary revocation of a television licence by the Home Secretary was accordingly declared unlawful by the Court of Appeal.[55]

Where a local authority 'may grant permission' for land to be used as a caravan site, this must in some circumstances mean 'shall grant permission', where the context so implies.[56] And where a regulatory power is given for the purpose of policing the fulfilment of prescribed conditions, it is natural to infer a mandatory duty in other cases.[57] These exercises in statutory interpretation are only another facet of the principle that discretion must be exercised on proper legal grounds and in accord with the policy of the Act.[58] In this way the court may counteract the tendency of legislation to enlarge executive discretion by loosely using the language of power instead of that of duty, in the manner to which government draftsmen are addicted.

The interpretation of permissive language as mandatory in certain circumstances may be assisted by qualifying words in the context, such as 'unless sufficient cause is shown to the contrary'[59] or 'if satisfied that there is proper ground for doing so'.[60] It may also be assisted by the hardship that might otherwise be caused by indefinite delay and uncertainty. It was for this reason that a public authority's power to proceed with a compulsory purchase of land, once the compulsory purchase order was authorised, could be enforced as a duty by the person from whom the land was to be taken, and who might otherwise have been left with unmarketable land on his hands for an indefinite period.[61]

---

[54] *R.* v. *Metropolitan Police Commissioner ex p. Holloway* [1911] 2 KB 1131. See also *R.* v. *Tynemouth Rural District Council* [1896] 2 QB 451 (building plans disapproved for improper reasons: approval ordered). Contrast *Patmor Ltd* v. *City of Edinburgh District Licensing Board* 1987 SLT 492.

[55] *Congreve* v. *Home Office* [1976] QB 629; for this case see below, p. 406.

[56] *Hartnell* v. *Minister of Housing and Local Government* [1965] AC 1134 at 1158 (Lord Reid). See similarly *A.-G.* v. *Antigua Times Ltd.* [1976] AC 16.

[57] As in *R.* v. *Newcastle on Tyne Corporation ex p. Veitch* (1889) 60 LT 963 (no discretion to withhold approval of plans conforming to building byelaws).

[57] See   [58] Below, p. 416. For the recent *Tower Hamlets* case see below, p. 419.

[59] As in *Re Shuter* [1960] 1 QB 142.

[60] As in *Annison* v. *District Auditor for St. Pancras* [1962] 1 QB 489 at 497.

[61] *Birch* v. *St. Marylebone Vestry* (1869) 20 LT 697. The Compulsory Purchase Act 1965, s. 4, limits the powers of the acquiring authority to a period of three years from the operative date of the compulsory purchase order: see above, p. 176.

ESTOPPEL

Estoppel and public authorities

The basic principle of estoppel is that a person who by some statement or representation of fact causes another to act to his detriment in reliance on the truth of it is not allowed to deny it later, even though it is wrong. Justice here prevails over truth. Estoppel is often described as a rule of evidence, but more correctly it is a principle of law.[62] As a principle of common law it applies only to representations about past or present facts. But there is also an equitable principle of 'promissory estoppel' which can apply to public authorities.[63] In a class by itself is estoppel by judgment, res judicata, which is treated separately.[64] This last is also known as issue estoppel, since it is a rule against the relitigation of the same issue between the same parties.

Legal rules about estoppel and waiver are applicable to public authorities as well as to other persons. A city corporation may be estopped from denying that payments made to it in satisfaction of a liability for rates are 'rates actually levied',[65] and a county council may, by giving an employee a certain status for superannuation, estop itself from denying that status later.[66] Similarly a public authority which lets land on lease is bound by the usual rule that acceptance of rent with knowledge of a breach of covenant by the tenant amounts to waiver of the lessor's right of forfeiture for the breach.[67] A local authority which agrees that a landowner may have access to a road from a particular plot may not, after the owner has fenced the plot and agreed to sell it, revoke the permission given.[68] If they negotiate the purchase of land for road widening and encourage the owner to incur expenditure on an alternative site, they may not then discontinue the

---

[62] *Canada & Dominion Sugar Co. Ltd.* v. *Canadian National (West Indies) Steamships Ltd.* [1947] AC 46 at 56.

[63] *Robertson* v. *Minister of Pensions* [1949] 1 KB 227 (but see below, p. 382); *Roberts & Co. Ltd.* v. *Leicestershire CC* [1961] Ch 555 (council estopped from denying terms of contract); the *Crabb* and *Salvation Army* cases (below). When affecting land, as in those cases, it may be called 'proprietary estoppel'.

[64] Below, p. 268.

[65] *North Western Gas Board* v. *Manchester Corporation* [1964] 1 WLR 64. Cf. *Gould* v. *Bacup Local Board* (1881) 50 LJMC 44 (election to follow one of the alternative statutory procedures held binding); *Roberts & Co. Ltd.* v. *Leicestershire CC* [1961] Ch. 555 (council estopped from denying terms of contract).

[66] *Algar* v. *Middlesex County Council* [1945] 2 All ER 243. But cases of this kind may be better explained by the rule that such determinations are inherently irrevocable: see above, p. 255.

[67] *Davenport* v. *R.* (1887) 3 App. Cas. 115; *R.* v. *Paulson* [1921] 1 AC 271. See also *Plimmer* v. *Wellington Cpn.* (1884) 9 App. Cas. 699; *Orient Steam Navigation Co.* v. *The Crown* (1925) 21 Ll LR 301 (below, p. 824); *Canadian Pacific Railway Co.* v. *R.* [1931] AC 414.

[68] *Crabb* v. *Arun DC* [1976] Ch. 179.

purchase.[69] As several of these cases show, the principle of estoppel applies equally to the Crown.[70]

But, just as with contracts, the ordinary rules must give way where their application becomes incompatible with the free and proper exercise of an authority's powers or the due performance of its duties in the public interest. Where the normal principles of justice are forced to give way, hard cases naturally result. It is possible for a citizen to be seriously misled by a public authority in a manner which ought, under the normal rules, to give rise to an estoppel which would compel the authority to stand by its representations; but nevertheless there may be no legal remedy. These cases, where the rules of public and private law are irreconcilable, will be found in a later section on discretionary power.[71] Some of them concern the Crown.

An essential element in estoppel is that the aggrieved party should have been induced to act to his detriment. In one case, where a planning application had been refused by a planning authority, but by mistake their planning officer notified the applicant that it had been granted, no estoppel was possible because the mistake was discovered and corrected before the applicant had acted to his detriment in any way.[72]

Estoppel and ultra vires

In public law the most obvious limitation on the doctrine of estoppel is that it cannot be invoked so as to give an authority powers which it does not in law possess. In other words, no estoppel can legitimate action which is ultra vires. Thus where an electricity authority, by misreading a meter, undercharged its customer for two years, it was held that the accounts it delivered did not estop it from demanding payment in full;[73] for the authority had a statutory duty to collect the full amount, and had no power to release the customer, expressly or otherwise. Where a local planning authority served an invalid discontinuance notice, the landowner's acquiescence could not estop him from later denying its validity.[74] Nor could a parish council, which had no power to undertake to allow a neighbouring district to make use of its sewers, be estopped by its long

---

[69] *Salvation Army Trustee Co.* v. *West Yorkshire CC* (1980) 41 P & CR 179, explained in *A.-G. of Hong Kong* v. *Humphreys Estate (Queen's Gardens) Ltd* [1987] AC 114.

[70] See n. 67.

[71] Below, p. 381.

[72] *Norfolk CC* v. *Secretary of State for the Environment* [1973] 1 WLR 1400.

[73] *Maritime Electric Company* v. *General Dairies Ltd.* [1937] AC 610. See likewise *R.* v. *Blenkinsop* [1892] 1 QB 43 (rate demand too low: no estoppel); *Norfolk County Council* v. *Secretary of State for the Environment* (above).

[74] *Swallow and Pearson* v. *Middlesex County Council* [1953] 1 WLR 422.

acquiescence from terminating such an arrangement.[75] Where a minister took possession of land under statutory powers of occupation which did not extend to the grant of leases, he was not estopped from denying that he had granted a lease, even though he had expressly purported to 'let' the land to a 'tenant'.[76] The result was the same where the supposed landlord was a local authority which had failed to obtain the requisite consent from the minister, so that the lease was void. Accordingly the local authority were at liberty to deny the validity of their own 'lease', contrary to the rules which govern private lettings.[77] No arrangement between the parties could prevent either of them from asserting the fact that the lease was ultra vires and void. Nor can any kind of estoppel give a tribunal wider jurisdiction than it possesses.[78]

Another limitation is that the principle of estoppel does not operate at the level of government policy. A government department which encourages an airline to invest in aircraft on the understanding that its licence will be continued is not estopped, if there is a change of government and a reversal of policy, from withdrawing the licence.[79] Many people may be victims of political vicissitudes, and 'estoppel cannot be allowed to hinder the formation of government policy'.

Estoppels have, however, been allowed to operate against public authorities in minor matters of formality, where no question of ultra vires arises. In one case Lord Denning MR said:[80]

Now I know that a public authority cannot be estopped from doing its public duty, but I do think it can be estopped from relying on technicalities . . .

He then held that the court could ignore the fact that the proper statutory application had not been made before a planning authority's determination, since the authority itself had led the landowner to suppose that it was not required; and the authority was therefore estopped from taking the objection. The same doctrine was applied in a case where a mother was out of time in lodging a statutory notice of objection to a local authority's order assuming parental rights over her child; the authority was estopped from

[75] *Islington Vestry* v. *Hornsey Urban Council* [1900] 1 Ch. 695.
[76] *Minister of Agriculture and Fisheries* v. *Matthews* [1950] 1 KB 148, citing an unreported decision of the Court of Appeal; *R.* v. *Rushbrooke* [1958] NZLR 877.
[77] *Rhyl UDC* v. *Rhyl Amusements Ltd.* [1959] 1 WLR 465.
[78] *Secretary of State for Employment* v. *Globe Elastic Thread Co. Ltd.* [1980] AC 506.
[79] *Laker Airways Ltd.* v. *Department of Trade* [1977] QB 643. The quotation is from Lawton LJ.
[80] *Wells* v. *Minister of Housing and Local Government* [1967] 1 WLR 1000 at 1007, approved in *Western Fish Products Ltd.* v. *Penwith DC* (1978) 38 P & CR 7 (see below, p. 384).

insisting on the time limit because its officers had misled the mother into supposing that a previous notice of objection was still effective.[81]

A public authority, furthermore, has a duty to act fairly and consistently. If it acts in a contradictory and misleading manner, this may amount to an abuse of discretion which the court can condemn. The immigration authorities acted in a 'Machiavellian and unconscionable' way when they abandoned deportation proceedings against an immigrant but three years later refused him readmission on the same grounds.[82] In this case the judge accepted a plea of estoppel, but plainly it was a case of abuse of power, to be classed with others explained later.[83] Where there is such unreasonable or unfair conduct there is no need to resort to the doctrine of estoppel.

WAIVER AND CONSENT

Primary rules

Waiver and consent are in their effects closely akin to estoppel, and not always clearly distinguishable from it. But no rigid distinction need be made, since for present purposes the law is similar. The primary rule is that no waiver of rights and no consent or private bargain can give a public authority more power than it legitimately possesses. Once again, the principle of ultra vires must prevail when it comes into conflict with the ordinary rules of law. A contrasting rule is that a public authority which has made some order or regulation is not normally at liberty to waive the observance of it by exercising a dispensing power. The principle here is that law which exists for the general public benefit may not be waived with the same freedom as the rights of a private person. In other cases, where neither of these rules is infringed, waiver and consent may operate in a normal way so as to modify rights and duties.

It has often been laid down that no amount of waiver or consent can extend a public authority's powers or validate action which is ultra vires. In one case a tenant had applied to a rent tribunal and obtained an order substantially reducing his rent, but later discovered that the house had been let at a date which put it outside the tribunal's jurisdiction. He then applied to the county court, which in that case would have had jurisdiction. The High Court granted mandamus to compel the county court to decide the case, despite the fact that both parties had previously acquiesced in the rent

---

[81] *Re L (AC) (an infant)* [1971] 3 All ER 743.
[82] *R. v. Immigration Appeal Tribunal ex p. Patel* [1986] The Independent, 10 December; reversed [1988] 2 WLR 1165 (HL).
[83] Below, p. 423.

tribunal's order.[84] The issue was one of jurisdictional fact and the court before which it was raised was obliged to determine it. For the same reasons an agreement with the landlord that the tenancy is furnished, when in fact it is not, cannot estop the tenant from later claiming an unfurnished tenancy.[85] In a planning case concerning a caravan site, the Court of Appeal held that the site-owner could apply for a declaration that the planning authority's enforcement notice was bad in law, even though he had pleaded guilty to contravention of the notice in previous criminal proceedings.[86] If the notice was in reality bad, no previous acquiescence could preclude him from contesting it. Exactly the same point determined an earlier enforcement notice case in which the landowners on whom the notice had been served applied for planning permission on the footing that the notice was valid. They were held entitled, nevertheless, to dispute its validity subsequently.[87] Parker J said: 'I do not think that any amount of so-called waiver or approbation can make a document like this, which is patently and wholly invalid, into a valid document.' The House of Lords confirmed this principle in a case where a party had acquiesced in proceedings before the Lands Tribunal which were later held to be outside that tribunal's jurisdiction. Lord Reid said: '. . . in my judgment, it is a fundamental principle that no consent can confer on a court or tribunal with limited statutory jurisdiction any power to act beyond that jurisdiction, or can estop the consenting party from subsequently maintaining that such court or tribunal has acted without jurisdiction.'[88]

Procedure and jurisdiction

The primary rule is subject to various qualifications. One of these concerns conditions which are merely procedural, but which may nevertheless be mandatory and so affect jurisdiction. Thus where a county court, which for this purpose is analogous to a statutory tribunal, could entertain proceedings against persons residing outside its area only on condition that leave was obtained, it was held that such a person who appeared on the first day as defendant without raising objection could not challenge the court's jurisdiction on a later day.[89] Although the court held that the question

---

[84] *R.* v. *Judge Pugh ex p. Graham* [1951] 2 KB 623. See similarly *Farquharson* v. *Morgan* [1894] 1 QB 552; *Wilkinson* v. *Barking Corporation* [1948] 1 KB 721.

[85] *Welch* v. *Nagy* [1950] 1 KB 455; likewise *Chapman* v. *Earl* [1968] 1 WLR 1315 (invalid application by tenant to rent officer: landlord's participation in proceedings not waiver).

[86] *Munnich* v. *Godstone Rural District Council* [1966] 1 WLR 427.

[87] *Swallow & Pearson* v. *Middlesex County Council* [1953] 1 WLR 422.

[88] *Essex Incorporated Congregational Church Union* v. *Essex County Council* [1963] AC 808. See also *London Cpn.* v. *Cox* (1867) LR 2 HL 239 at 283; *Bradford City MC* v. *Secretary of State for the Environment* (1986) 53 P & CR 55 (below, p. 790).

[89] *Moore* v. *Gamgee* (1890) 25 QBD 244.

'would come under the head of procedure rather than under the head of jurisdiction', the condition was probably jurisdictional. In an earlier case[90] of a similar kind Erle J had said: 'But jurisdiction is sometimes contingent; in such a case, if the defendant does not, by objecting at the proper time, exercise his right of destroying the jurisdiction, he cannot do so afterwards.' This probably reveals the correct principle, that there are some conditions which are jurisdictional only if pleaded at the right time. This conforms, in particular, to the decisions on the rules of natural justice. If a person disqualified by interest or bias takes part in an adjudication, that goes to jurisdiction and renders the decision void. But if the party affected knows the facts and raises no objection at the outset, he is taken to have waived it and cannot raise it later. As explained elsewhere,[91] there is nothing illogical in this. The correct rule, it must be assumed, is that jurisdiction is lost if the objection is raised at the proper time, but not otherwise. Erle J's remark explains why it is fallacious to suppose that a condition cannot be jurisidictional merely because it can be waived.

In the House of Lords, in the case already cited,[92] Lord Hodson said: 'Had the question been procedural only no difficulty would have arisen, for the parties had consented to the course taken before the Lands Tribunal,' but he then held that the statutory condition was absolute so that the parties had no power to confer jurisdication where none existed. Lord Devlin, on the other hand, appeared to enunciate a theory of judicial control under which, if there was jurisdiction to enter on the inquiry, no error in the course of the inquiry could go to jurisdiction, so that any such error could be waived. Theories of this kind have from time to time found favour with judges, but they have been firmly rejected by the House of Lords in other cases where the question has been more fully considered.[93] As explained elsewhere,[94] they are inconsistent with the fundamental theory of jurisdiction which English law has developed, which holds that many kinds of fundamental error in the course of an inquiry may carry the inquiring authority outside its jurisdiction.

[90] *Jones* v. *James* (1850) 19 LJQB 257.

[91] Below, p. 494.

[92] *Essex Incorporated Congregational Church Union* v. *Essex County Council* [1963] AC 808 (above).

[93] Lord Devlin's theory corresponds to his opinion in *Ridge* v. *Baldwin* [1964] AC 40, that error in the course of the inquiry rendered the decision voidable, not void; but the majority of the House of Lords rejected this decisively: below, p. 526. Likewise in *Anisminic Ltd.* v. *Foreign Compensation Commission* [1969] 2 AC 147 the House rejected the notion that a mere mistake in the course of the inquiry could not go to jurisdiction. Lord Reid there (at 234) corrected his remarks in *R.* v. *Governor of Brixton Prison ex p. Armah* [1968] AC 192, which appeared to adopt a theory of jurisdiction similar to Lord Devlin's.

[94] Below, p. 294.

Non-jurisdictional waiver

Where problems of jurisdiction do not arise, a person entitled to the benefit of some statutory rule or condition may be able to waive the benefit of it. Thus one party to an action in the county court may waive the statutory time limit on his opponent's right of appeal.[95] But this doctrine does not apply to planning permission, which under the planning legislation enures for the benefit of the land and its successive owners, so that termination of the permitted operations by one owner does not amount to waiver or abandonment of the permission.[96]

Personal benefit and public policy

It may be difficult to decide whether a statutory condition exists solely for a person's benefit so that he may waive it on the principle *quilibet potest renuntiare juri pro se introducto*. It may, on the contrary, embody some public policy which an individual has no power to modify. On this latter ground the Court of Appeal of New Zealand held that the Commissioner of Inland Revenue had no power to waive the thirty-day time limit on appeals from the Taxation Board of Review to the High Court, even though he was willing to do so in a case where the taxpayer's solicitor had been ill.[97] As Turner J put it, 'the due and impartial administration of a revenue statute' is 'a matter in which every citizen has an interest'. In this decision a sound principle may have been carried too far, since it must surely be even more in the public interest that accidents should not prevent tax liability from being correctly adjudicated. More recently the Court of Appeal in England has shown itself favourable to the contention that a planning authority may waive the prescribed formalities for applications in planning matters.[98] Lord Denning MR said:[99]

I take the law to be that a defect in procedure can be cured, and an irregularity can be waived, even by a public authority, so as to render valid that which would otherwise be invalid.

But these decisions were strongly motivated by the court's desire to contrive some binding legal basis for the informal advice often given to enquirers by planning authorities and their officers; but to this, as will be

---

[95] *Park Gate Iron Co. Ltd.* v. *Coates* (1870) LR 5 CP 634.

[96] *Pioneer Aggregates (UK) Ltd.* v. *Secretary of State for the Environment* [1985] AC 132.

[97] *Reckitt & Colman (New Zealand) Ltd.* v. *Taxation Board of Review* [1966] NZLR 1032, following earlier New Zealand and Canadian cases.

[98] *Wells* v. *Minister of Housing and Local Government* [1967] 1 WLR 1000; *Lever Finance Ltd.* v. *Westminster London Borough Council* [1971] 1 QB 222.

[99] In the *Wells* case at 1007.

shown, there are serious legal objections.[1] There is force in the dissenting view of Russell LJ that a planning authority, as 'the guardian of the planning system', is 'not a free agent to waive statutory requirements', and that the law should not be made to conform to 'a thoroughly bad administrative practice'.[2]

No power to dispense

Where something more than mere procedure or formality is in question, a public authority cannot exercise a dispensing power by waiving compliance with the law. For this would amount to an unauthorised power of legislation. There is therefore no power for a local authority to waive compliance with its binding byelaws;[3] nor is any such power possessed by the minister with whose consent the byelaws are made.[4] Still less is there any power to grant dispensations from the ordinary law, e.g. as to obstruction of the highway.[5]

Abandonment

A public authority which fails to proceed with a compulsory purchase order may be held to have abandoned it and so to have lost the power to enforce it.[6]

RES JUDICATA

Principles and distinctions

One special variety of estoppel is res judicata. This results from the rule which prevents the parties to a judicial determination from litigating the same question over again, even though the determination is demonstrably wrong. Except in proceedings by way of appeal, the parties bound by the judgment are estopped from questioning it. As between one another, they

---

[1]   Below, p. 382.

[2]   In the *Wells* case (above) at 1015.

[3]   *Yabbicom* v. *King* [1899] 1 QB 444; *Bean (William) & Sons* v. *Flaxton Rural District Council* [1929] 1 KB 450; below, p. 862.

[4]   *Bean (William) & Sons* v. *Flaxton Rural District Council* (above).

[5]   *Redbridge London Borough Council* v. *Jacques* [1970] 1 WLR 1604; *Cambridgeshire County Council* v. *Rust* [1972] 2 QB 426.

[6]   *Tiverton and North Devon Railway Co.* v. *Loosemore* (1884) 9 App Cas 480; *Grice* v. *Dudley Corporation* [1958] Ch. 329; *Simpsons Motor Sales Ltd.* v. *Hendon Cpn.* [1964] AC 1088.

may neither pursue the same cause of action again, nor may they again litigate any issue which was an essential element in the decision. These two aspects are sometimes distinguished as 'cause of action estoppel' and 'issue estoppel'. It is the latter which presents most difficulty, since an issue 'directly upon the point' has to be distinguished from one which 'came collaterally in question' or was 'incidentally cognisable'.[7] In any case, 'there must a lis or issue and there must be a decision'.[8]

Like other forms of estoppel already discussed, res judicata plays a restricted role in administrative law, since it must yield to two fundamental principles of public law: that jurisdiction cannot be exceeded; and that statutory powers and duties cannot be fettered.[9] Within those limits, however, it can extend to a wide variety of statutory tribunals and authorities which have power to give binding decisions.[10] It is by no means confined to courts of law in the strict sense.

Res judicata is sometimes confused with the principle of finality of statutory decisions and acts, and thus with the general theory of judicial control. If a public authority has statutory power to determine some question, for example the compensation payable to an employee for loss of office,[11] its decision once made is normally final and irrevocable. This is not because the authority and the employee are estopped from disputing it, but because, as explained elsewhere,[12] the authority has power to decide only once and thereafter is without jurisdiction in the case. Conversely, where a statutory authority determines some matter within its jurisdiction, its determination is binding not because of any estoppel but because it is a valid exercise of statutory power. The numerous cases which hold that a decision within jurisdiction is unchallengeable[13] have therefore no necessary connection with res judicata. Res judicata does nothing to make the initial decision binding: it is only because the decision is for some other reason binding that it may operate as res judicata in later proceedings raising the same issue between the same parties.

How easily these questions may appear to overlap may be seen in a case

[7] These phrases were used in *The Duchess of Kingston's Case* (1776) 20 St Tr 355, 538 n., in which the rules were laid down. See Spencer Bower and Turner, *Res Judicata*.

[8] *Vernon v. Inland Revenue Commissioners* [1956] 1 WLR 1169 at 1178, holding that the Attorney-General was not estopped from disputing the purposes of a charity by having been party to an order of the court which did not put that question in issue.

[9] Above, p. 262.

[10] For a wide statement of the principle see *Administration of Papua and New Guinea v. Daera Guba* (1973) 130 CLR 353. For an example see *McLoughlin v. Gordons (Stockport) Ltd.* [1978] ICR 561 (industrial tribunal).

[11] As in *Livingstone v. Westminster Corporation* [1904] 2 KB 109.

[12] Above, p. 255.

[13] See above, p. 42.

where a schoolteacher, who had enlisted for war service, claimed additional
pay from the local authority which had undertaken to make up his service
pay to the level of his teacher's pay. The dispute was referred to the
National Arbitration Tribunal, which ruled against him, and he then
brought proceedings in the High Court. The questions were whether there
was a 'trade dispute' within the Tribunal's statutory jurisdiction, and
whether it had jurisdiction over private (as opposed to national) service
agreements. These being answered in the affirmative, the Tribunal's award
was held conclusive[14]—from which it followed, the judge said, that it was
res judicata.[15] But in fact the case seems to belong to the common class
where a specific matter is allotted by statute to a specific tribunal so that the
tribunal's award, within its jurisdiction, is conclusive.[16] Where the question
in issue is one of jurisdiction, no estoppel can prevent the court from
determining it.[17] Once it is determined in favour of the tribunal, no
estoppel is needed to bind the parties conclusively. If in the case of the
teacher there had been an 'issue estoppel'—if, for example, the tribunal had
determined that he belonged to a particular category, and he disputed this
in later proceedings against the local authority—a true res judicata might
have been pleaded. So where an industrial tribunal found that an employee
had been fairly dismissed, he was not allowed to litigate substantially the
same issue in a High Court action for breach of contract.[18]

Administrative cases

Res judicata in an administrative context is illustrated by a decision of the
House of Lords about the making up of Sludge Lane, Wakefield.
Adjoining landowners disputed their liability to contribute to the costs
incurred by the Corporation on the ground that Sludge Lane was a public
rather than a private road, and so chargeable to the ratepayers generally
rather than to the frontagers. A local Act empowered two justices to
determine the objection, and they determined it in favour of the frontagers.
Three years later the Corporation undertook further works and again
attempted to charge the frontagers, who were mostly the same persons as
before. The justices refused to reconsider the matter, holding it to be res
judicata; and after being reversed in the King's Bench Division and upheld

---

[14] *Re Birkenhead Cpn.* [1952] Ch. 359.
[15] At 379.
[16] e.g. *IRC* v. *Pearlberg* [1953] 1 WLR 331; *Healey* v. *Minister of Health* [1955] 1 QB 221;
R. v. *Paddington &c Rent Tribunal ex p. Perry* [1956] 1 QB 229; *Davies* v. *Price* [1958] 1 WLR
434.
[17] See above, p. 262.
[18] *Green* v. *Hampshire CC* [1979] ICR 861.

in the Court of Appeal, their decision was upheld in the House of Lords.[19] The House of Lords was prepared to treat the original decision as a judgment in rem,[20] binding on everyone. Lord Davey said that, alternatively, it would bind all who were given notice and an opportunity to object. Such an estoppel would, on ordinary principles, bind their successors in title also.[21]

The House of Lords distinguished *R* v. *Hutchings*,[22] a superficially similar case where the justices had held that the disputed road was a public highway and had dismissed the local board's application for the enforcement of its levy on the frontager. Five years later the same board made another levy on the same frontager which a magistrate upheld. The Court of Appeal held that this was correct and that there was no res judicata. The reason was that the Public Health Act 1875, unlike the local Act in Wakefield, gave the justices no power to determine finally whether the street was public or private. Their only power was to decide whether the levy was properly assessed or not. If its validity was disputed on the ground that it was ultra vires, the magistrate had indeed to determine that issue before proceeding further; but it was only a matter 'incidentally cognisable' which created no estoppel. That is to say, it lay outside the limited area within which justices could give an unchallengeable decision.[23] Otherwise, said Lord Selborne LC, there might be two laws operating simultaneously in opposite directions as against different persons in exactly the same circumstances.[24]

The reasoning of the last-mentioned case has played an important part in a series of later decisions about assessments for rates and taxes. In these it has been repeatedly held that matters decided for the purposes of one year's assessment or of one rating list do not amount to res judicata for the purposes of later assessments or lists. A medical society successfully established before the Lands Tribunal in 1951 that it was entitled to exemption from rates under the Scientific Societies Act 1843. In 1956 a new valuation list had to be made and the valuation officer again attempted to assess the society, and on his appeal to the Lands Tribunal the society

[19] *Wakefield Cpn.* v. *Cooke* [1904] AC 31. See similarly *Armstrong* v. *Whitfield* (1973) 71 LGR 282 (determination as to public right of way conclusive in later proceedings).

[20] For this see also *A.-G.* v. *Honeywill* (1972) 71 LGR 81; *Armstrong* v. *Whitfield* (above); *Emms* v. *R.* [1979] 2 SCR 1148 (judgment invalidating regulation held binding upon all affected by it).

[21] See *Halsbury's Laws of England,* 4th edn., xvi. 1041.

[22] (1881) 6 QBD 300.

[23] See at 305.

[24] But this possibility is always inherent in the law of res judicata, e.g. where parties are bound by a judgment which is later overruled in proceedings between other parties. Lord Selborne perhaps meant that it was particularly inappropriate in public law.

pleaded res judicata. Although it was admitted that there had been no relevant change of circumstances, the House of Lords disallowed this plea and ruled that the question must again be decided on its merits.[25] It was held that decisions relating to a different list were irrelevant, since the local valuation court had jurisdiction to determine cases for the purpose of one list only at any one time. The same point has been settled, after some difference of opinion, in a line of income tax cases. Thus where a trust in Ceylon had been held to be a charity, and so exempt from income tax, by the statutory board of review, this was held to be conclusive only in the relevant year of assessment, and to be open to challenge by the Commissioner of Income Tax in any subsequent year.[26] The Privy Council emphasised that the important consideration was the limited nature of the question that was within the tribunal's jurisdiction: each year's assessment was a different operation and there was no 'eadem quaestio' of the kind required for res judicata.

The search for a principle

The above-mentioned decisions on rates and taxes have carried the doctrine of *R* v. *Hutchings*,[27] which they profess to follow, far beyond its apparent boundaries. That case merely illustrates the familiar principle that where jurisdictional questions are raised before a tribunal of limited jurisdiction, the tribunal must necessarily determine them for its own purposes but its determination may be reviewed in the High Court.[28] It follows that the tribunal's determination cannot be conclusive, whether as res judicata or otherwise. But it is plain that the question whether a taxpayer or ratepayer is entitled to exemption, if raised before a revenue tribunal, is not 'collateral' or' incidental' in any such sense: it falls squarely within the range of questions which it is the tribunal's business to decide conclusively. The tax and rate cases observe no such distinction, and the Privy Council admit that they may form 'a somewhat anomalous branch' of res judicata.[29] It should likewise be admitted that no help is to be derived from trying to distinguish judicial from administrative functions[30] (that favourite

---

[25] *Society of Medical Officers of Health* v. *Hope* [1960] AC 551.
[26] *Caffoor* v. *Commissioner of Income Tax* [1961] AC 584, following *Broken Hill Proprietary Company Ltd.* v. *Broken Hill Municipal Council* [1926] AC 94 and *Inland Revenue Commissioners* v. *Sneath* [1932] 2 KB 362; not following *Hoystead* v. *Commissioner of Taxation* [1926] AC 155.
[27] Above.
[28] Below, p. 283.
[29] *Caffoor* (as above) at 599.
[30] *Caffoor* (as above); and see [1965] PL 237 at 241 (G. Ganz).

fallacy[31]): all that res judicata requires is some power to adjudicate. Nor does there appear to be merit in the argument that there is no *lis* because the taxing or rating officer is a neutral party rather than an opponent.[32] Law based on such sophistries must lack a firm foundation.

Yet a firm foundation exists, and can be traced through a series of judicial opinions. The principle is simply that an assessing officer has a statutory public duty to make a correct assessment on the taxpayer or ratepayer on each occasion, and that no estoppel can avail to prevent him doing so. Just as an electricity company cannot be estopped from charging the full price of electricity, if it has a statutory duty,[33] so an assessing officer 'cannot be estopped from carrying out his duties under the statute.'[34] A county court, similarly, must determine a statutory standard rent on the correct facts, and no estoppel or res judicata from earlier proceedings can discharge the court from this duty.[35] This doctrine fits easily into the framework of public law. It carries altogether more conviction that the formalistic distinctions discussed above, which fail to take account of the special character of public power and duty. Its force is all the more obvious if it is remembered that res judicata, like other forms of estoppel, is essentially a rule requiring a party to accept some determination of fact or law which is wrong.[36] For if the determination is right, no substantive question arises. There are self-evident objections to requiring public authorities to act on wrong assumptions. Public powers and duties, as has been seen elsewhere,[37] cannot be fettered in such ways. There is no inconsistency in giving conclusive force to a tax tribunal's decision on an assessment for the year in question, since that is given the force of law by statute, not by mere estoppel.

The same principle ought to apply in all situations where powers have to be exercised in the public interest. Suppose that certain disciplinary charges are made against a schoolteacher whose removal can be required by the education authority only on educational grounds, that no educational

---

[31] See below, pp. 518, 634

[32] The House of Lords lent countenance to this in *Society of Medical Officers of Health* v. *Hope* [1960] AC 551. Cf. *Inland Revenue Commissioners* v. *Sneath* [1932] 2 KB 362.

[33] See *Maritime Electric Company* v. *General Dairies Ltd.* [1937] AC 610; above, p. 262.

[34] *Society of Medical Officers of Health* v. *Hope* [1960] AC 551 at 568 (Lord Keith), citing the *Maritime Electric Company* case (above) and the opinion of Lord Parker of Waddington in *Inland Revenue Commissioners* v. *Brooke* [1915] AC 478 at 491. See also *Bradshaw* v. *M'Mullen* [1920] 2 IR (HL) 412 at 425; *Inland Revenue Commissioners* v. *Sneath* [1932] 2 KB 362 at 382 (Lord Hanworth MR). For a similar principle of public policy in matrimonial law see *Hudson* v. *Hudson* [1948] P 292.

[35] *Griffiths* v. *Davies* [1943] KB 618; *R.* v. *Pugh* [1951] 2 KB 623; above, p. 265.

[36] This was the reason for the old saying 'estoppels are odious': e.g. *Baxendale* v. *Bennett* (1878) 3 QBD 525 at 529. An instance is *Priestman* v. *Thomas* (1884) LR 9 PD 210, where the estoppel obliged the parties to accept a forged will.

[37] Above, p. 262.

grounds are shown before the authority's disciplinary committee, and that the complaint is dismissed. What is the position if it is later discovered that there were in fact good educational grounds on which the teacher ought to have been removed? The answer should be that the education authority always has the power to require removal when such grounds in fact exist; that this is a power which it must exercise in the public interest; that its powers cannot be fettered by any estoppel, by res judicata or otherwise; and that it is therefore free to act on the fresh evidence. The additional dimension of the public interest is what makes the difference.

Where, on the other hand, an immigrant's right to an entry certificate was established in his favour by an adjudicator, but the Home Office later discovered evidence suggesting that he might be an illegal entrant, the court refused to admit that evidence in later proceedings and held that the adjudicator's decision came very close to rendering the immigrant's status res judicata.[38] Thus they treated his status as a matter more of private right than of public interest. Where an inspector had ruled that certain properties were hotels for planning purposes, another inspector three years later could not rule that they were hostels.[39]

Jurisdictional questions

No question of res judicata can derogate from the rule that a determination which is ultra vires may always be challenged in the High Court. This is no more than a corollary of the main principle of jurisdictional control, which ordains that no tribunal can give itself jurisdiction which it does not possess.[40] It is also a corollary of the proposition that a litigant who relies on the decision of an inferior tribunal must be prepared, if challenged, to prove that the tribunal had jurisdiction.[41] No res judicata can therefore prejudice that issue. Since such a wide range of questions are held to go to jurisdiction, the scope of res judicata in administrative law is limited.

---

[38] R. v. Home Secretary ex p. Momin Ali [1984] 1 WLR 663, no doubt assisted by the fact that the fresh evidence was weak.

[39] Thrasyvoulou v. Secretary of State for the Environment [1988] 3 WLR 1.

[40] See below, p. 281. In American law, where the jurisdictional principle is less sacrosanct, a decision which is ultra vires may sometimes produce estoppel by res judicata. See Davis, Administrative Law Treatise, 18.07: 'To say that a tribunal cannot confer power upon itself by making a finding that it has jurisdiction is entirely logical. But equally logical is the proposition that every tribunal has jurisdiction to determine its own jurisdiction and that if the parties have litigated the question once, the policies against relitigation are fully applicable.' The second proposition is not logical in English law, since the first litigation, unlike the second, is before a tribunal which has no power to decide the question conclusively. The proposition is logical only where the tribunal has the same power in both cases.

[41] See above, p. 262.

This is illustrated by the case already cited, where a tenant had applied to a rent tribunal and obtained an order substantially reducing his rent, but later discovered that the house had been let at a date which put it outside the jurisdiction of the tribunal but within the jurisdiction of the county court, and the High Court granted mandamus to compel the county court to decide the case.[42] The rent tribunal's assumption of jurisdiction could not be conclusive, for otherwise it would have power to give itself jurisdiction which did not belong to it. Consequently neither the order of the tribunal nor the acquiescence of the parties could make the question res judicata or create any estoppel. In an analogous New Zealand case, where an order had been made under the Fair Rents Act without considering whether the house was let between the dates required for the Act to apply, it was held that this jurisdictional question must be tried on the evidence by the reviewing court, and a plea of res judicata was expressly rejected.[43] Likewise a county court's order in favour of a landlord under the Small Tenements Recovery Act 1838 is contingent upon the landlord being truly the owner, so that the question of title to the land may be litigated subsequently between the same parties.[44] In the same class may be included the road-making case previously explained, where the decision of the justices did not produce res judicata as to the validity of the local authority's levy, since they had only incidental jurisdiction over that question.[45]

These decisions reveal an important limit to the plea of res judicata when based on the decision of an inferior tribunal. The plea is of no avail in two quite different situations: first, where the tribunal has no jurisdiction over the matter at all; and secondly, where it has the power and duty to decide, but no power to decide conclusively. The first category is self-explanatory. The second category is the same as that of questions of jurisdictional fact and jurisdictional law. Those are questions affecting the tribunal's own jurisdiction which the tribunal is obliged to decide, in order that it may know whether it ought to proceed further, but which for fundamental reasons (discussed elsewhere) cannot be determined by the tribunal conclusively but remain open to challenge in the High Court. To allow res judicata to be pleaded to protect such determinations would be to cut off access to the High Court in exactly the situations where it is most necessary for the purposes of jurisdictional control. The need to preserve this indispensable control over public authorities of all kinds must take priority over the rule of res judicata which in other cases forbids the relitigation of a question necessarily determined between given parties by a given tribunal.

---

[42] *R. v. Pugh (Judge) ex p. Graham* [1951] 2 KB 623.
[43] *Bethune v. Bydder* [1938] NZLR 1.
[44] *Hodson v. Walker* (1872) LR 7 Ex. 55.
[45] *R. v. Hutchings* (1881) 6 QBD 300; above, p. 271.

Error on the face. Prerogative remedies

There being no such thing as jurisdiction by estoppel, there can be no effective plea of res judicata in the multitudinous disputes over jurisdiction which make up so much of administrative law. Indeed, both branches of the law of judicial control are exempt from this plea: jurisdictional cases are exempt for the reasons just given; and cases of mere error on the face of the record[46] are exempt because, since the remedy is by certiorari against the deciding body, the proceedings will never be between the same parties as the previous proceedings. The requirement of identity of parties will seldom be satisfied where prerogative remedies are employed. In a wartime case a detainee obtained release on habeas corpus on grounds which the House of Lords in another case held to be insufficient. In an action against the Home Secretary for false imprisonment he claimed that the illegality of his detention was res judicata. The judge held that this plea failed, 'if only because the parties are different'.[47]

It is also probable that the doctrine of res judicata is inherently inapplicable to proceedings for habeas corpus,[48] certiorari, and the other prerogative remedies. Formerly there were grounds for holding that the court's rulings in such cases were not technically judgments capable of producing res judicata.[49] A more persuasive reason is that in these procedures the court 'is not finally determining the validity of the tribunal's order as between the parties themselves' but 'is merely deciding whether there has been a plain excess of jurisdiction or not'.[50] They are a special class of remedies designed to maintain due order in the legal system, nominally at the suit of the Crown,[51] and they may well fall outside the ambit of the ordinary doctrine of res judicata. But the court may refuse to entertain questions which were or could have been litigated in earlier proceedings, when this would be an abuse of legal process;[52] and in the case of habeas corpus there is a statutory bar against repeated applications made on the same grounds.[53]

This reasoning was approved by a Divisional Court and by the Court of Appeal in a case where a London borough, after securing the quashing of

---

[46] For this see below, p. 303.
[47] *Budd* v. *Anderson* [1943] KB 642. The report does not say who were the parties to the habeas corpus proceedings. Cf. *R.* v. *Brixton Prison Governor ex p. Savarkar* [1910] 2 KB 1056 (different issue).
[48] *Re Hastings (No. 2)* [1959] 1 QB 358 at 371; *R.* v. *Pentonville Prison Governor ex p. Tarling* [1979] 1 WLR 1417 at 1422.
[49] See Lord Goddard CJ, 'A Note on Habeas Corpus', (1949) 65 LQR 30 at 35.
[50] *R.* v. *Fulham &c. Rent Tribunal ex p. Zerek* [1951] 2 KB 1 (Devlin J).
[51] See below, p. 616.
[52] See the *Tarling* case (above and the *Momin Ali* case (below).
[53] Below, p. 618.

the Secretary of State's order to reduce their rate support grant, failed in a further claim that their success in the first proceedings precluded the Secretary of State from later making a similar reduction order. Both courts were of the opinion that the doctrine of issue estoppel was not to be relied upon in proceedings for judicial review.[54]

The proper sphere of res judicata

The foregoing discussion has revealed a variety of reasons for rejecting arguments founded on res judicata in cases involving public powers and duties or raising issues of jurisdiction. Is there then any positive role which this plea ought to play in administrative law? The answer to this question must be largely conjectural, since judicial decisions are lacking. The following suggestions can only be put forward tentatively.

Where there are no special reasons for rejecting the plea, it is just as necessary in public law as elsewhere. Parties ought not to be allowed to litigate the same issues repeatedly. It seems certain that the High Court would reject any attempt to relitigate the legality of an administrative decision or order where it had itself refused relief in earlier proceedings. There may be a technical doubt in the case of the prerogative remedies since, as mentioned above, it used to be considered that there was no judgment; and this technicality was thought to underlie the supposed rule, now rejected, that an applicant for habeas corpus could make the same application successively to one judge after another and demand a decision on the merits.[55] But in reality it is plain that the court gives a decision, and there is no reason why the ordinary objections to relitigation should not apply.

Where the initial proceedings are brought before an inferior tribunal and the later proceedings are brought in the High Court, the question is likely to be more difficult. If for example a tenant applies to a rent tribunal for a reduction of rent and the rent payable is disputed between landlord and tenant, the tribunal must determine it. If the tribunal dismisses the reference, so that no rent is registered, can the landlord assert his claim to a higher rent in the High Court or the county court? Similarly if in an employee's claim to a redundancy payment an industrial tribunal determines the amount of his weekly wages, can he or his employer assert in other proceedings that this determination was wrong? These questions

---

[54] R. v. Secretary of State for the Environment ex p. Hackney LBC [1983] 1 WLR 524, [1984] 1 WLR 592, approving the last ten lines of the preceding paragraph, and confirmed in R. v. Home Secretary ex p. Momin Ali [1984] 1 WLR 663.

[55] For its rejection see Re Hastings (No. 2) [1959] 1 QB 358, (No. 3) [1959] Ch 368; below, p. 618.

are not likely to affect jurisdiction, and there is no general reason why the decision of an inferior statutory tribunal cannot create an issue estoppel.[56] But there is no telling when the court might not invoke the concept of limited jurisdiction as it was applied to non-jurisdictional questions in the tax and rate cases,[57] and hold that, since the tribunal's jurisdiction was merely to decide whether the rent should be altered or a redundancy payment awarded, all other questions were 'collateral' or 'incidental'. The authorities establish two contradictory possibilities.

Relatively few decisions of administrative authorities or tribunals determine questions between parties of the kind just instanced. More commonly they decide applications for benefits, permissions, or licences, and if there is any 'other party' at all, it will be a public authority. A national insurance tribunal may decide that A and B are man and wife, or an immigration appeal tribunal may decide that a would-be immigrant has a criminal record. Even if the administrative authorities are regarded as genuine parties,[58] it is unlikely that the same question could arise between the same parties before a court of law.

A large class of administrative cases must also be ruled out because they involve public policy. In licensing cases of all kinds it is usually inherent in the system of control that applications may be made at any time and may be renewed. Thus planning permission may be sought repeatedly over many years and each application must be considered on its merits.[59] As will be seen, the discretionary power of a public authority cannot normally be fettered, even by its own decisions.[60] Res judicata rests on the theory of an unchanging law, whereas policy must be free to change at any moment, as the public interest may require.

[56] *Marginson* v. *Blackburn Borough Council* [1939] 2 KB 426 (county court).

[57] See above, p. 271.

[58] See *Society of Medical Officers of Health* v. *Hope* [1960] AC 551; *Inland Revenue Commissioners* v. *Sneath* [1932] 2 KB 362; above, p. 272.

[59] As in *Westminster Bank Ltd.* v. *Beverley Borough Council* [1971] AC 508; and see *Thrasyvoulou* v. *Secretary of State for the Environment* [1988] 3 WLR 1 (above, p. 274)..

[60] Below, p. 371.

9

JURISDICTION OVER FACT AND LAW

ERROR OUTSIDE JURISDICTION

Objective boundaries of subjective powers

The courts of law have inherent jurisdiction, as a matter of common law, to prevent administrative authorities from exceeding their powers or neglecting their duties. At this point we are concerned with powers, and primarily with the application of the principle of ultra vires in conjunction with the principle of objectivity. In the case, for example, of the Home Secretary's power to deport an alien, the principle of objectivity ordains that the question whether some person is truly an alien should, if disputed, be determined by the court. If the Act had said 'any person who in the opinion of the Home Secretary is an alien' the decision would be for the Home Secretary, though subject to judicial review on various grounds. Subjective expressions of that kind extend the area of discretion.

Wide discretionary powers are very commonly conferred upon ministers, tribunals and other public bodies, and the courts' powers of review over them are explained in later chapters. Here we must investigate the objective boundaries of these powers and the way in which the courts police them.[1] All discretionary powers have objective limits of some kind, but the problem lies in identifying them. It is easy to see that the question whether an alien ought to be deported is for decision by the Home Secretary but that the question whether a person is really an alien must be determined by the court.[2] Other cases, unfortunately, are often less clear.

The same distinction is sometimes expressed in terms of the liberty to err. It is inherent in all discretionary power that it includes the power to make mistakes, that is to say, to decide freely, without liability to correction, within the area of discretion allowed by the law. The principle was clearly expressed long ago by Holt CJ,[3] who spoke of

this diversity, (viz.) that if the commissioners had intermeddled with a thing which was not within their jurisdiction, then all is coram non judice,[4] and that may be given in evidence upon this action; but 'tis otherwise if they are only mistaken in

---

[1] We are not here concerned with appeals, which are always statutory. See above, p. 36.

[2] As explained in *R. v. Home Secretary ex p. Khawaja* [1984] AC 74 in terms of the power to deport an illegal entrant (below, p. 460).

[3] *Fuller* v. *Fotch* (1695) Carthew 346.

[4] i.e. null and void.

their judgment in a matter within their conusance, for that is not inquirable, otherwise than upon an appeal.

Lord Reid echoed this in a modern case by saying of a magistrate or tribunal: 'if he has jurisdiction to go right he has jurisdiction to go wrong'.[5] Even though so many kinds of 'going wrong' have now been brought within the scope of judicial review, it always remains true that there is some area of discretion within which the administrator has a free hand.[6]

The principle of objectivity authorises the courts to define that area of freedom. It is only one of the many weapons in their armoury, but it is of primary importance. Without it they would be powerless to prevent serious usurpations. A public authority might then, by making some mistake as to the extent of its powers, do something which the statute never intended to permit. The object of the courts is to prevent this at all costs by standing guard over the frontiers of free discretion. In other words, the minister or other body must not be allowed to be the judge of the extent of his own powers.

In this area 'jurisdiction' is a hard-worked word. Commonly it is used in its broadest sense, meaning simply 'power'. In some contexts it will bear the narrower sense of 'power to decide' or 'power to determine', but there will be no technical difference. In fact, except in the special case of error on the face of the record, the principle here at work is basically that of ultra vires, which is synonymous with 'outside jurisdiction' or 'in excess of power'.[7]

With these preliminaries in mind we must now inquire how far administrative authorities are at liberty to decide questions of fact and questions of law, and how far their decisions may be final and conclusive.[8] The foundations of the law are long-established rules of some complexity which are in the process of being replaced by simpler and broader rules giving the courts a general jurisdication to intervene whenever mistakes of law or fact are the cause of injustice. An overall view of the position will be found in the summary at the end of this chapter.

Jurisdictional and non-jurisdictional fact

Certain mistakes of fact can carry an administrative authority or tribunal outside its jurisdiction.[9] A rent tribunal, for example, may have power to

---

[5] R. v. *Governor of Brixton Prison ex p. Armah* [1968] AC 192 at 234. As to this see below, p. 294.

[6] See e.g. *Anisminic Ltd.* v. *Foreign Compensation Commission* [1969] 2 AC 147 at 207 (Lord Wilberforce).

[7] See above, p. 39.

[8] See [1984] OJLS 22 (J. Beatson); [1987] LQR 66 (G. L. Peiris).

[9] On this subject see de Smith, *Judicial Review of Administrative Action*, 4th edn., 110; Jaffe, *Judicial Control of Administrative Action*, chs. 14, 15; Rubinstein, *Jurisdiction and Illegality*, 212.

reduce the rent of a dwelling-house. If it mistakenly finds that the property is a dwelling-house when in fact it is let for business purposes,[10] and then purports to reduce the rent, its order will be ultra vires and void. For its jurisdiction depends upon facts which must exist objectively before the tribunal has power to act. As to these 'jurisdictional facts' the tribunal's decision cannot be conclusive, for otherwise it could by its own error give itself powers which were never conferred upon it by Parliament. The fact that the tribunal's order appears good on its face can avail nothing. It will be quashed on certiorari if the applicant can show that the true facts do not justify it. For this purpose, accordingly, any available evidence may be put before the court.[11]

Although 'jurisdictional fact' has long been part of the currency of administrative law,[12] English judges have previously preferred to speak of 'collateral questions'.[13] A classic statement comes from a case of 1853[14] in which Coleridge J said:

Now it is a general rule, that no Court of limited jurisdiction can give itself jurisdiction by a wrong decision on a point collateral to the merits of the case upon which the limit to its jurisdiction depends; and however its decision may be final on all particulars, making up together that subject-matter which, if true is within its jurisdiction, and, however necessary in many cases it may be for it to make a preliminary inquiry, whether some collateral matter be or be not within the limits, yet, upon this preliminary question, its decision must always be open to inquiry in the superior Court.

This is merely to say that it is always for the court to enforce the statutory conditions limiting the extent of a power, i.e. to enforce the principle of ultra vires.

---

[10] As in *R.* v. *Hackney* (etc.) *Rent Tribunal ex p. Keats* [1951] 2 KB 15. See below, p. 291.

[11] See below, p. 286. Formerly the order had to show jurisdiction: below, p. 456.

[12] The earliest recognisable case appears to be *Terry* v. *Huntington* (1668) Hardr. 480 (successful action against commissioners of excise for levying duty on 'low wines' when they had powers only as to 'strong wines'). Hale CB called this 'a stinted, limited jurisdiction' and said: 'though the information before them supposes the matter to be within their power and jurisdiction; yet the party is not thereby concluded, but that he may aver the contrary.' See likewise *Fuller* v. *Fotch* (1695) Carth. 346. In (1929) 45 LQR 479 (D. M. Gordon) *St. John's Case* (1601) 5 Co. Rep. 61b is cited as an early example of collateral fact, but the report is inadequate for this purpose; so is the report of the same case as *Gardener's Case* (1600) Cro. Eliz. 821: see Rubinstein, *Jurisdiction and Illegality*, 62.

[13] Probably the first appearance of 'jurisdictional fact' in an English law report was in *Anisminic Ltd.* v. *Foreign Compensation Commission* [1969] 2 AC 147 at 208, 242 (Lord Wilberforce and Browne J). See also *R.* v. *Home Secretary ex p. Khawaja* [1984] AC 74 at 101 (Lord Wilberforce); 'precedent fact' also occurs in several speeches.

[14] *Bunbury* v. *Fuller* (1853) 9 Ex. 111 (assistant tithe commissioner's jurisdiction dependent on fact that land was not previously discharged from tithe; this fact held collateral). Contrast *Tithe Redemption Commission* v. *Wynne* [1943] KB 756, where the Tithe Act 1936 gave the Commission conclusive jurisdiction over a similar question.

Many facts on the other hand will not be jurisdictional, since they will have no bearing on the limits of the power. A rent tribunal's findings as to the state of repair of the property, the terms of the tenancy, and the defaults of landlord or tenant will probably not affect its jurisdiction in any way and will therefore be immune from jurisdictional challenge.[15]

The distinction which has to be made in these cases is that between the primary or central question which the tribunal has power to decide conclusively itself, and other questions which circumscribe the scope of that power. This is what is meant by the contrast made in the above quotation between 'the merits of the case' and a point which is 'collateral', and by the contrasts made by Lord Goddard CJ, as quoted below,[16] between 'the main question which the tribunal have to decide' and other questions on which 'the existence of jurisdiction depends'. In the above examples the central question for the rent tribunal's decision is whether the rent ought to be reduced. No court of law can review their decision on this question if it is validly made within their jurisdiction. The collateral questions, such as whether the letting is furnished or unfurnished, or whether it is for residential or business purposes, or whether a premium has been paid, are questions which determine whether a situation has arisen in which the tribunal may proceed to exercise its primary power. These are therefore questions which a court of law may review in order to keep the tribunal within its proper sphere. Difficult as this distinction may be to apply in some cases, it is clear in principle and fundamental in importance.

Jurisdictional law

In the past the same distinction was applied to questions of law. For example, a rent tribunal had power to reduce a rent where it appeared that a premium had been paid; but where the payment had in fact been made in respect of work done by the landlord and not in respect of the grant of the lease, it was not in law a premium. By treating it as such the tribunal made a mistake of law and acted in excess of its powers, and its order was quashed.[17] If the payment had truly been a premium, but the tribunal had mistakenly held that it was not one in law and had made no order, their error would have amounted to refusal of jurisdiction and the court could have ordered them to hear and decide the case.

---

[15] Thus in *Terry* v. *Huntington* (above) Hale CB said: 'But if they should commit a mistake in a thing that were within their power, that would not be examinable here.' For further examples see below, p. 288.

[16] p. 284.

[17] *R.* v. *Fulham (etc.) Rent Tribunal ex p. Philippe* [1950] 2 All ER 211. Another example is *R.* v. *Tottenham District Rent Tribunal ex p. Fryer Ltd.* [1971] 2 QB 681 (question whether reference to tribunal validly withdrawn).

Now, however, the courts appear to be taking a new position, holding that every error of law by a tribunal must necessarily be jurisdictional. This is a deduction from the decision of the House of Lords in the *Anisminic* case, which stretched the concept of jurisdictional error of law to such a point that the concept of non-jurisdictional error may disappear. This complication, which could have important repercussions in several areas, must be explained later.[18] For present purposes it means that any error of law made by a tribunal, if material to its decision, may render the decision ultra vires. In future, therefore, the distinction between errors which do and do not affect jurisdiction may apply only to errors of fact. 'Jurisdictional fact' will then continue to present problems, while 'jurisdictional law' will not. Moreover, it will become necessary to distinguish questions of law from questions of fact—a matter upon which judicial opinions are habitually inconsistent.[19]

Power to determine jurisdictional questions

Where a jurisdictional question is disputed before a tribunal, the tribunal must necessarily decide it.[20] If it refuses to do so, it is wrongfully declining jurisdiction and the court will order it to act properly.[21] Otherwise the tribunal or other authority 'would be able to wield an absolutely despotic power, which the legislature never intended that it should exercise'.[22] It follows that the question is within the tribunal's own jurisdiction, but with this difference, that the tribunal's decision about it cannot be conclusive. This also was explained in the classic case:[23]

Suppose a judge with jurisdiction limited to a particular hundred, and the matter is brought before him as having arisen within it, but the party charged contends that it arose in another hundred, this is clearly a collateral matter independent of the merits; on its being presented, the judge must not immediately forbear to proceed, but must inquire into its truth or falsehood, and for the time decide it, and either proceed or not with the principal subject-matter according as he finds on that point; but this decision must be open to question, and if he has improperly either forborne or proceeded on the main matter in consequence of an error, on this the

[18] Below, p. 299.

[19] See below, p. 938.

[20] Unless, perhaps, trial by a court is more suitable: see the *Zerek* case (below) at 13 (Devlin J); or unless statute provides otherwise: *R. v. Kensington Rent Officer ex p. Noel* [1978] QB 1.

[21] *R. v. Marsham* [1892] 1 QB 371; *R. v. Pugh (Judge) ex p. Graham* [1951] 2 KB 623; *R. v. Camden LB Rent Officer ex p. Ebiri* [1981] 1 WLR 881.

[22] *R. v. Marsham* (above) at 379.

[23] *Bunbury v. Fuller* (1835) 9 Ex. 111 (above). See also *R. v. Special Commissioners of Income Tax* (1888) 21 QBD 313 at 319, quoted below, p. 287.

Court of Queen's Bench will issue its mandamus or prohibition to correct his mistake.[24]

Similarly Lord Goddard CJ explained that[25]

if a certain state of facts has to exist before an inferior tribunal have jurisdiction, they can inquire into the facts in order to decide whether or not they have jurisdiction, but cannot give themselves jurisdiction by a wrong decision upon them; and this court may, by means of proceedings for certiorari, inquire into the correctness of the decision. The decision as to these facts is regarded as collateral because, though the existence of jurisdiction depends on it, it is not the main question which the tribunal have to decide.

A collateral question is thus to be contrasted with 'the main question', or 'the actual matter committed to its decision',[26] upon which the tribunal's own decision is conclusive.

All this doctrine applies just as much to ordinary administrative action as it does to the decisions of courts and tribunals. Jurisdictional questions are less likely to be raised in the former case, since normally no power to determine questions of fact or law will have been given. Nevertheless such powers are occasionally claimed. One instance was where a local authority had power to take land compulsorily for housing provided that it was not 'part of any park, garden or pleasure ground'.[27] An order made by the authority and confirmed by the minister was quashed on the ground that the land was in fact parkland. This on its face was a simple case of ultra vires. But the minister contended that it was for the acquiring authority and himself to determine the facts, and that their findings of fact were conclusive. The Court of Appeal rejected this argument, holding that the fact in question was collateral and applying the classic rule that collateral facts must be determinable ultimately by the court. Luxmoore LJ said:

In such a case it seems almost self-evident that the court which has to consider

---

[24] On territorial error see *Vevers* v. *Mains* (1888) 4 TLR 724; contrast *Re Smith* (1858) 3 H & N 227 and see (1929) 45 LQR at p. 486, (1966) 82 LQR at p. 518 (D. M. Gordon).

[25] *R.* v. *Fulham (etc.) Rent Tribunal ex p. Zerek* [1951] 2 KB 1 at 6 (Devlin J at 10 is equally clear). See similarly *R.* v. *Lincolnshire Justices ex p. Brett* [1926] 2 KB 192 at 202; *R.* v. *Pugh (Judge) ex p. Graham* [1951] 2 KB 623; *Re Purkiss' Application* [1962] 1 WLR 902 at 914 (Diplock LJ); *Anisminic Ltd.* v. *Foreign Compensation Commission* [1969] 2 AC 147 at 174 (Lord Reid); *R.* v. *Croydon &c. Rent Tribunal ex p. Ryzewska* [1977] QB 876; *R.* v. *Camden LB Rent Officer ex p. Ebiri* [1981] 1 WLR 881.

[26] *R.* v. *Lincolnshire Justices* (above) at 202 (Atkin LJ).

[27] *White and Collins* v. *Minister of Health* [1939] 2 KB 383. Another such case is *R.* v. *Bradford* [1908] 1 KB 365 (power to license surveyor of highways to excavate from enclosed lands 'not being a . . . park'. Held: land was a park, so licence was quashed). See the statement of principle by Channell J at 372. See similarly *R.* v. *Armagh JJ* [1924] 2 IR 55; *Re Newhill Compulsory Purchase Order* [1938] 2 All ER 163; *R.* v. *Blakely ex p. Association of Architects of Australia* (1950) 82 CLR 54; *State* v. *Durcan* [1964] IR 279.

whether there is jurisdiction to make or confirm the order must be entitled to review the vital findings on which the existence of the jurisdiction relied upon depends.

It is obvious that, if this were not so, the statutory exemption in favour of parkland would, legally speaking, be illusory.

The Home Secretary's statutory power to deport aliens is similarly limited by the word 'alien'. Whether a person is, in fact or in law, an alien or a British subject is a question which the court must determine in the case of dispute.[28] Alien nationality is the preliminary or collateral condition on which the Home Secretary's power depends. If he could determine this himself conclusively, a British subject mistakenly taken for an alien would have no legal protection, and plainly this would be intolerable. The Home Secretary's power to deport an 'illegal entrant' is limited in the same way, so that it is for the court to decide objectively on the evidence whether a person has or has not entered the country illegally. The House of Lords made a grave error, fortunately since corrected, when they held that this decision was for the Home Secretary, provided only that he was not acting on no evidence and not acting unreasonably.[29] If the court fails to stand guard over facts and requirements expressed objectively in the Act, it surrenders the rule of law to the rule of executive discretion. It is essential, therefore, that 'where the exercise of executive power depends upon the precedent establishment of an objective fact, the courts will decide whether the requirement has been satisfied'.[30]

There is a vital distinction, therefore, between expressions which are objective, such as 'an alien' or 'an illegal entrant', and those which are subjective, such as 'a person who the Home Secretary is satisfied' is an alien or an illegal entrant. In the latter case the decision is for the Home Secretary, subject to judicial review if he should act on no evidence, unreasonably, under a mistake of jurisdictional law, etc. The doctrine of

---

[28] R. v. Home Secretary ex p. Duke of Chateau Thierry [1917] 1 KB 922 at 930; Eshugbayi Eleko v. Officer Administering Government of Nigeria [1931] AC 662 at 670; R. v. Home Secretary ex p. Budd [1942] 2 KB 14 at 22. In Khawaja's case (below) Lord Wilberforce said: 'The best known example of this is Eshugbayi Eleko v. Government of Nigeria [1931] AC 662, where the discretionary power was exercisable only if the person affected was a native chief, so that whether he was such a chief or not was what is sometimes called a jurisdictional or collateral fact.'

[29] R. v. Home Secretary ex p. Zamir [1980] AC 930, corrected in R. v. Home Secretary ex p. Khawaja [1984] AC 74; see below, p. 460.

[30] Khawaja's case (above) at 110 (Lord Scarman). In R. v. Hillingdon LBC ex p. Puhlhofer [1986] AC 484 the House of Lords treated 'accommodation' under the Housing (Homeless Persons Act) 1977 subjectively, but the report fails to make it clear that this was in accordance with the Act, which gives discretion to the housing authority 'if they are satisfied'.

jurisdictional fact and law is thus a corollary of the principle of objectivity which is the sheet anchor of the rule of law.

There are many other possible examples.[31] Any ultra vires case can raise questions of jurisdictional fact or law if the public authority claims power to decide any question which defines the scope and limits of its power. Where a minister must have 'reasonable cause to believe' something, he may claim that it is for him to decide the question of reasonableness, whereas it is a jurisdictional matter to be decided by the court.[32] It must be remembered that the courts often show themselves unwilling to resign their control of such questions merely because the power is conferred in subjective terms. In the rent tribunal case already cited the words were 'where it appears to the tribunal that a premium has been paid', but the court quashed the tribunal's order nevertheless when it was shown that the payment made was not in law a premium, so that the tribunal had misdirected itself in law.[33] Decisions of this kind have become more frequent as the developing law of judicial review has brought discretionary powers under stricter control, as will appear when subjective language is more fully discussed later.[34]

Borderline cases

As a general rule, limiting conditions stated in objective terms will be treated as jurisdictional, so that the court will consider any admissible evidence of their non-fulfilment.[35] In the majority of cases these 'limiting conditions' are easy to identify. But there are borderline cases where the question may, on a true view, be part of the matter which the administrative authority is empowered to decide conclusively, so that it is squarely within its jurisdiction. One such was where a taxpayer was entitled to a repayment if 'within or at the end of the year' he could show to

---

[31] Numerous examples of questions held to be collateral or not are collected in (1929) 45 LQR at pp. 479–82 and in (1960) 1 UBCLR 185 (D. M. Gordon).

[32] See the *Liversidge* and *Rossminster* cases, below, pp. 457, 459. *Liversidge* was the most notorious of the lapses from objectivity.

[33] R. v. *Fulham (etc.) Rent Tribunal ex p. Philippe* [1950] 2 All ER 211; above, p. 282. See also *Relton & Sons (Contracts) Ltd.* v. *Whitstable Urban District Council* (1967) 201 EG 955 ('where it appears to the appropriate authority that an existing highway should be converted into a new street . . .': no power to decide conclusively that highway was not already a new street, since this was a 'fundamental matter'.)

[34] Below, p. 445.

[35] The cases usually refer to affidavit evidence since prerogative remedies are in question: e.g. R. v. *Bolton* (1841) 1 QB 66; *Re Baker* (1857) 2 H & N 219; R. v. *Bradley* (1894) 70 LT 379; R. v. *Radcliffe (Judge) ex p. Oxfordshire County Council* [1915] 3 KB 418; R. v. *Board of Control ex p. Rutty* [1956] 2 QB 109: R. v. *Northumberland Compensation Appeal Tribunal ex p. Shaw* [1952] 1 KB 338 at 352, 353.

the assessing commissioners that he had overpaid. The claims were made two years and more after the relevant year, but passed by the assessing commissioners. The Special Commissioners then refused to pay, holding that the assessing commissioners had no power to accept the claims in the circumstances. But Lord Esher MR held that it was for the assessing commissioners to determine conclusively whether the conditions of claim were satisfied, and that the Special Commissioners were therefore obliged to make the repayment.[36] He distinguished in abstract terms the two situations which the legislature might create:[37]

It may in effect say that, if a certain state of facts exists and is shown to such tribunal or body before it proceeds to do certain things, it shall have jurisdiction to do such things, but not otherwise. There it is not for them conclusively to decide whether that state of facts exists, and, if they exercise the jurisdiction without its existence, what they do may be questioned, and it will be held that they have acted without jurisdiction. But there is another state of things which may exist. The legislature may intrust the tribunal or body with a jurisdiction, which includes the jurisdiction to determine whether the preliminary state of facts exists as well as the jurisdiction, on finding that it does exist, to proceed further or do something more.

A case which naturally falls into the latter category is where a magistrate has jurisdiction to convict on certain facts being proved before him. This is the explanation of the famous 'bum–boat case',[38] in which the magistrates had power to order the forfeiture of any boat suspected of carrying stolen cargo. They were sued in trespass by the owner of a boat so condemned, who wished to show that his vessel was too large to be a boat within the meaning of the Act. The court refused to hear this evidence, holding that the question was within the jurisdiction of the magistrates and that their order, being good on its face, was therefore conclusive. Whether the boat was within the Act was no more jurisdictional than any other ingredient in the situation which the magistrates had to adjudge. In other words, it was within the central area of their jurisdiction and not in any way collateral. Similarly where justices had power to make a bastardy order 'if the evidence of the mother be corroborated in some material particular by other evidence to the satisfaction of the said justices' it was held that it was for the justices to determine finally whether the other evidence was really corroborative or not, and that even if it was not, the court could not

---

[36] R. v. Special Commissioners of Income Tax (1888) 21 QBD 313. Lindley LJ was doubtful on this question.

[37] At 319. This passage was approved by the House of Lords in Anisminic Ltd. v. Foreign Compensation Commission [1969] 2 AC 147.

[38] Brittain v. Kinnaird (1819) 1 Br & B 432. See likewise Cave v. Mountain (1840) 1 M & G 257; Allen v. Sharp (1848) 2 Ex. 352; R. v. Dayman (1857) 7 E & B 672 ('new street'); Ex p. Vaughan (1866) LR 2 QB 114; R. v. Bradley (1894) 70 LT 379 (justices empowered to determine conclusively what is 'highway').

intervene.[39] This decision proceeded not on the subjective language ('to the satisfaction of the said justices') but on the distinction between 'a collateral issue independent of the merits' and 'one of the points involved in the actual matter committed to' the justices' decision. In cases of this class, therefore, jurisdictional objections less commonly succeed. It is natural to regard questions of fact determining guilt or innocence in courts of law as the primary and central questions for decision by these courts and not as preliminary conditions to the power to decide the punishment.[40] In Lord Goddard CJ's terms,[41] they are within 'the main question which the tribunal have to decide', as opposed to being collateral.

Administrative cases

In administrative cases the prescribed statutory ingredients will more readily be found to be collateral. This is probably because, in contrast to the judicial cases just discussed, the central question committed to the administrative authority will commonly be whether to exercise some discretionary power, and the prescribed statutory ingredients will more naturally be regarded as preliminary or collateral conditions. For example, where licensing justices are empowered to grant extensions of hours on 'special occasions', the court will review the question whether there really was a special occasion within the meaning of the Act, which it treats as a jurisdictional condition.[42] As usual with administrative powers, the court is determined to enforce their legal limits and to prevent their abuse. But however strict the court may be, there will always be a residuum of jurisdiction within which the power of determination is conclusive. Perhaps the most frequently cited such case was where justices made an order for the removal of a pauper, who had been in prison for smuggling, from a house belonging to the parish. It was contended that the occupant was not a pauper and that the decision was wrong on the evidence. The court refused to investigate the evidence, holding that the whole matter was within the jurisdiction of the justices and distinguishing cases where their jurisdiction depended upon some objective fact.[43] The statute was not

---

[39] R. v. *Lincolnshire Justices ex p. Brett* [1926] 2 KB 192.

[40] See *Canadian Union of Public Employees* v. *New Brunswick Liquor Cpn.* (1979) 97 DLR (3d) 417, citing this comment.

[41] As quoted above, p. 284.

[42] R. v. *Sussex JJ* [1933] 2 KB 707 (period of summer time: 'clearly . . . excess of jurisdiction'); R. v. *Metropolitan Police Commissioner ex p. Ruxton* [1972] 1 WLR 232. Similarly as to 'special reasons'; R. v. *Liverpool City Council ex p. Liverpool Taxi Fleet Operators' Association* [1975] 1 WLR 701; and as to 'special circumstances': R. v. *Home Secretary ex p. Mehta* [1975] 1 WLR 1087.

[43] R. v. *Bolton* (1841) 1 QB 66 (Lord Denman CJ). See similarly *Ex. p. Vaughan* (1866) LR 2 QB 114. Cf. *Allen* v. *Sharp* (1848) 2 Ex. 352; R. v. *Young* (1883) 52 LJMC 55.

even recited, and no collateral or jurisdictional question was raised—even though it would seem that there might have been room for such questions. The case is one of the long series which fall into the second category distinguished by Lord Esher MR and which establish that where the whole matter is considered to be within the jurisdiction of the adjudicating body, its order cannot be quashed by the court merely on the ground that it is mistaken.[44] This elementary rule was often stated in the form that where the subject–matter was within the jurisdiction, an order valid on its face was conclusive.[45]

In fact there are relatively few other examples of questions which might have been considered to be collateral being held to be conclusively determinable by an administrative authority.[46] Where 'every officer' of an authority was entitled to apply to a district board for compensation for loss of office, the question whether an applicant was truly an officer was held to be a matter entirely for the board, being the very point they were to inquire into;[47] and similarly where the question was as to his rate of pay.[48] Where licensing justices were empowered to sit 'for the purpose of granting licences to persons keeping or being about to keep inns, alehouses and victualling houses' the majority of the Court of Appeal concluded that it was for the justices to decide conclusively whether any particular applicant fell within this description, and that a mere mistake did not affect their jurisdiction.[49] Where the Price Commission had to calculate the net profits of a business 'in accordance with generally accepted accounting principles' the Court of Appeal declined to review the Commission's findings of fact as to what these principles were and as to what items were consequently allowable, holding that the legislation clearly implied that these were matters for the Commission and not for the courts; for the statutory

---

[44] The case is put into correct perspective, and contrasted with cases where jurisdiction is in issue, by Lord Denman CJ himself in *R.* v. *Justices of Buckinghamshire* (1843) 3 QB 800; by all the judges in *Ex. p. Vaughan* (1866) LR 2 QB 114; by Sir J. Colville in *Colonial Bank of Australasia* v. *Willan* (1874) LR 5 PC 417 at 443; by Gibson J in *R.* v. *Mahony* [1910] 2 IR 695 at 739; by Lord Sumner in *R.* v. *Nat Bell Liquors Ltd.* [1922] 2 AC 128 at 154; and by Browne J in *Anisminic Ltd* v. *Foreign Compensation Commission* [1969] 2 AC 147 at 242. None of these decisions conflicts in any way with the principle of *Bunbury* v. *Fuller*, above, p. 281. This is explained particularly clearly in *Colonial Bank of Australasia* v. *Willan* (above).

[45] As in *Brittain* v. *Kinnaird* (above; *R.* v. *Bolton* (above); *Colonial Bank of Australasia* v. *Willan* (above).

[46] Examples are *R.* v. *Dayman, Ex p. Vaughan*, and *R.* v. *Bradley*, cited above, p. 287 n. 38. But *Liversidge* v. *Anderson* [1942] AC 206 and *R.* v. *Home Secretary ex p. Zamir* [1980] AC 930 might be added. For these cases see below, pp. 457, 460.

[47] *R.* v. *St. Olave's District Board* (1857) 8 E & B 529.

[48] *Livingstone* v. *Westminster Cpn.* [1940] 2 KB 109.

[49] *R* v. *Woodhouse* [1906] 2 KB 501 (upheld on this point but reversed on other grounds: [1907] AC 420). cf. *State* v. *Durcan (Judge)* [1964] IR 279.

scheme of price control required expert, quick, and final decisions.[50] But the same court granted a declaration that a method of calculating depreciation, though used only by few companies, would qualify, as a matter of law, as falling within 'generally accepted accounting principles'.[51] The fine distinction between these cases is perhaps that the second, but not the first, raised a question of law on the interpretation of the price code, which the court treated as a reviewable question of law; but this would seem to be a matter of presentation rather than of substance.

Whether the meaning of 'houses' was a collateral question for the purposes of clearance orders (now abolished[52]) was a matter of some doubt under decisions of the Court of Appeal. A local authority might make a clearance order where they were satisfied 'that the houses in that area are unfit for human habitation', and the order required confirmation by the minister. In one case the court treated the meaning of 'house' as a matter entirely for the court, i.e. as a jurisdictional condition, and it seems to have been assumed without argument that this was correct.[53] In a later case the court held that the question 'house or not a house', just like the question 'fit or unfit', was a question for the minister to determine finally, provided that he did not commit other errors of the kind that the court can control on other grounds.[54] But this was in the context of the minister's power to modify a clearance order 'if the minister is of opinion' that any land ought not to have been included in it, and this subjective language naturally influenced the court. The implication of the decision was that confirmation by the minister is in any case conclusive that the buildings in the clearance area are 'houses'.

Excess or abuse of power

The doctrine of collateral fact and law is always liable to be brought into play if the court suspects an excess or abuse of power. This is especially true where personal liberty is at stake, so that some habeas corpus cases show an

---

[50] *General Electric Co. Ltd.* v. *Price Commission* [1975] ICR 1.

[51] *Associated Portland Cement Manufacturers Ltd.* v. *Price Commission* [1975] ICR 27, decided within a month of the previous case but not referring to it. In principle the decisions appear contradictory, since in the second the commission should have been able to find as a fact that generally accepted accounting principles did not admit the method in question. But this does not seem to have been pleaded.

[52] Above, p. 202.

[53] *Re Butler* [1939] 1 KB 570. See likewise *Quiltotex Co. Ltd.* v. *Minister of Housing and Local Government* [1966] 1 QB 704; and compare *Lake* v. *Bennett* [1970] 1 QB 663.

[54] *Ashbridge Investments Ltd.* v. *Minister of Housing and Local Government* [1965] 1 WLR 1320 (unreserved judgments, reversing the High Court's decision that 'house' was jurisdictional); for this case see below, p. 324.

exceptional willingness to treat incidental facts as collateral.[55] A relatively clear case was where a board of control was empowered to place a mental defective in an institution if 'found neglected', but the evidence showed that this condition was not satisfied.[56]

Another fruitful field for this doctrine is that of preventing statutory tribunals from dealing with matters which do not belong to them. Good illustrations are the decisions on the jurisdiction of rent tribunals, which had separate jurisdictions over furnished and unfurnished dwelling-houses. The court would review the questions whether a tenancy truly existed or had been already determined;[57] whether there was a reference before the tribunal;[58] whether letting was for residential or for business purposes';[59] whether the property was furnished or unfurnished;[60] and whether a payment was in law a premium.[61] Quashing a decision where the tribunal had found that a business letting was a mere sham to disguise the letting of a dwelling-house, but the evidence before the court showed that finding to be unjustified, Lord Goddard CJ said: 'A more dangerous usurpation of power by one of these tribunals it is impossible to imagine.'[62]

In numerous cases Australian and Canadian courts have found collateral error invalidating the decisions of tribunals concerned with labour relations;[63] and in controlling administrative jurisdiction generally they observe the same fundamental distinction as does English law.[64]

Disputed questions of fact

Although the contrast between questions which do and do not go to jurisdiction was in principle clear-cut, it was softened by the court's

[55] See cases cited by Hilbery J in R. v. Board of Control ex p. Rutty [1956] 2 QB 109: Re Bailey (1854) 3 E & B 607; Re Baker (1857) 2 H & N 219; Re Authers (1889) 22 QBD 345; R. v. Radcliffe (Judge) ex p. Oxfordshire County Council [1915] 3 KB 418.

[56] R. v. Board of Control ex p. Rutty (above) (Hilbery and Devlin JJ). For the scope of habeas corpus in such cases see below, p. 620.

[57] R. v. London (etc.) Rent Tribunal ex p. Honig [1951] 1 KB 641.

[58] R. v. Tottenham Districts Rent Tribunal ex p. Fryer Ltd. [1971] 2 QB 681.

[59] R. v. Hackney (etc.) Rent Tribunal ex p. Keats [1951] 2 KB 15.

[60] R. v. Blackpool Rent Tribunal ex p. Ashton [1948] 2 KB 277; R. v. Fulham (etc.) Rent Tribunal ex p. Zerek [1951] 2 KB 1.

[61] R. v. Fulham (etc.) Rent Tribunal ex p. Philippe [1950] 2 All ER 211.

[62] In the Keats case (above) at 15. But it is not right that the tribunal may not enter into the question: see the correction in the Zerek case (above) at 7.

[63] e.g. R. v. Hickman (1945) 70 CLR 598; Mutual Life and Citizens' Assurance Co. Ltd. v. A.-G. for Queensland (1961) 106 CLR 48; Metropolitan Life Insurance Co. v. International Union of Operating Engineers (1970) 11 DLR (3d) 336.

[64] e.g. R. v. Commonwealth Rent Controller (1947) 75 CLR 361; Bell v. Ontario Human Rights Commission (1971) 18 DLR (3d) 1; Parkhill Bedding and Furniture Ltd v. International Molders Union (1961) 26 DLR (2d) 589, classifying earlier cases.

unwillingness to enter upon disputed questions of fact in proceedings for judicial review.[65] Evidence of facts is normally given on affidavit; and although the rules of court made provision for cross-examination, interrogatories, and discovery of documents, and for the trial of issues of fact,[66] the court did not often order them.[67] The procedure was thus not well adapted for trying disputed facts. If the inferior tribunal had itself tried them, 'the court will not interfere except upon very strong grounds'.[68] There had to be 'a clear excess of jurisdiction' without the trial of disputed facts de novo.[69] Questions of law and questions of fact were therefore to be distinguished, as was explained by Devlin J:[70]

Where the question of jurisdiction turns solely on a disputed point of law, it is obviously convenient that the court should determine it then and there. But where the dispute turns on a question of fact, about which there is a conflict of evidence, the court will generally decline to interfere.

Lord Wilberforce similarly described the position of the court which hears applications for judicial review:[71]

It considers the case on affidavit evidence, as to which cross-examination, though allowable, does not take place in practice. It is, as this case well exemplifies, not in a position to find out the truth between conflicting statements.

In cases of conflict of evidence, therefore, the court was disinclined to do more than ascertain that there was evidence before the tribunal which would justify a reasonable tribunal reaching the same conclusion.[72] It appears also that the same doctrine was applied to statutory applications to quash, since these are in principle similar to applications for judicial review.[73]

A system of judicial review which cannot cope with crucial questions of

---

[65] For the procedure see below, p. 672.

[66] Under RSC 1965, O. 33 r. 3;; O. 53 r. 8.

[67] A rare instance is *R. v. Stokesley, Yorkshire, Justices ex p. Bartram* [1956] 1 WLR 254.

[68] *Elston v. Rose* (1868) LR 4 QB 4 at 7.

[69] *R. v. Fulham (etc.) Rent Tribunal ex p. Zerek* [1951] 2 KB 1 at 11, reviewing the authorities. See also *Colonial Bank of Australasia v. Willan* (1874) LR 5 PC 417 at 442 ('a manifest defect of jurisdiction').

[70] In the *Zerek* case (above). See likewise *Elston v. Rose* (above).

[71] *R. v. Home Secretary ex p. Zamir* [1980] AC 930 at 949. See also below, p. 460.

[72] *Brown v. Cocking* (1868) LR 3 QB 672 at 675 (stating the rule somewhat strictly); *R. v. Hackney (etc.) Rent Tribunal ex p. Keats* as explained in *R. v. Fulham (etc.) Rent Tribunal ex p. Zerek* [1951] 2 KB 1 at 7.

[73] *Re Bowman* [1932] 2 KB 621 at 634; *Re Newhill Compulsory Purchase Order 1937* [1938] 2 All ER 163; *Ashbridge Investments Ltd. v. Minister of Housing and Local Government* [1965] 1 WLR 1320; *Coleen Properties Ltd. v. Minister of Housing and Local Government* [1971] 1 WLR 433. For these cases see below, p. 324.

fact (as jurisdictional facts necessarily are) is seriously defective. One purpose of the procedural reforms made in 1977, and described later,[74] was to remove exactly this defect by providing for cross-examination, etc., so that disputed facts could be tried. Lord Wilberforce's above-quoted statement comes from an unfortunate and discredited decision of the House of Lords.[75] The correct rule, it is submitted, is that stated by Lord Diplock in a later case, that cross-examination should now be allowed whenever the justice of the case so requires, and on the same basis as in ordinary proceedings.[76]

The 'original jurisdiction' fallacy

Collateral or jurisdictional questions of the class discussed above are essentially objective so far as the inferior tribunal is concerned.[77] The facts and legal consequences which will give the tribunal jurisdiction either exist or they do not. All such questions are necessarily external to and independent of the tribunal's own proceedings, in the sense that their final determination, in case of dispute, cannot be affected by any act or decision of the tribunal itself. If the land is a park, and so exempt from compulsory purchase, or if the house is let for business purposes, and so exempt from the rent tribunal's power to reduce the rent, these facts must have been so at the outset, so that on a true objective view the tribunal was never entitled to entertain the case at all.

Many judges have therefore made a contrast between jurisdictional questions determinable at the outset and mere error made within jurisdiction during the course of the inquiry. A favourite quotation has been from Lord Denman CJ:[78]

The question of jurisdiction does not depend on the truth or falsehood of the charge, but upon its nature; it is determinable on the commencement, not at the conclusion, of the inquiry; and affidavits, to be receivable, must be directed to what appears at the former stage, and not to the facts disclosed in the progress of the inquiry.

Similarly Lord Sumner said of a magistrate:[79]

---

[74] Below, p. 671.

[75] See below, p. 460.

[76] *O'Reilly* v. *Mackman* [1983] 2 AC 237 at 282; below, p. 678.

[77] They are subjective in that their existence depends upon the findings of the reviewing court, but those findings are objective *vis-à-vis* the tribunal.

[78] *R.* v. *Bolton* (1841) 1 QB 66 at 74, described by Lord Denning MR as the start of 'a black-out against any development of administrative law': *O'Reilly* v. *Mackman* [1983] 2 AC 237 at 253.

[79] *R.* v. *Nat Bell Liquors Ltd.* [1922] 2 AC 128 at 151.

... if his jurisdiction to entertain the charge is not open to impeachment, his subsequent error, however grave, is a wrong exercise of a jurisdiction which he has, and not a usurpation of a jurisdiction which he has not ...

And Lord Reid also once said:[80]

If a magistrate or any other tribunal has jurisdiction to enter on the inquiry and to decide a particular issue, and there is no irregularity in the procedure, he does not destroy his jurisdiction by reaching a wrong decision. If he has jurisdiction to go right he has jurisdiction to go wrong. Neither an error in fact nor an error in law will destroy his jurisdiction.

In their own time and context[81] these statements were unexceptionable: they expressed the traditional doctrine that so long as jurisdiction existed, mere error as such would not destroy it. But it does not in the least follow that no sort of error made in the course of the proceedings can affect jurisdiction. Some question may arise which the tribunal is incompetent to determine;[82] or some point may be decided in bad faith or in breach of natural justice or on irrelevant grounds or unreasonably, all of which faults go to jurisdiction and render the proceedings a nullity.[83]

Lord Reid guarded himself with this necessary qualification in a later case,[84] pointing out that 'the word "jurisdiction" has been used in a very wide sense' and would be better confined to 'the narrow and original sense of the tribunal being entitled to enter on the inquiry in question'. In fact 'jurisdiction' has traditionally borne the wide sense, synonymous with 'power'; for plainly a tribunal must not only have jurisdiction at the outset but must retain it unimpaired until it has discharged its task. Lord Pearce explained this with impeccable logic in the same case, in words already quoted, pointing out that if a tribunal in the course of its inquiry addressed

---

[80] R. v. Governor of Brixton Prison ex p. Armah [1968] AC 192 at 234. Contrast Lord Upjohn's remarks at 257. See also Lord Devlin's opinion in Essex Incorporated Congregational Church Union v. Essex County Council [1963] AC 808, cited above, p. 265.

[81] And under the law as it stood before the Anisminic case (below).

[82] See Colonial Bank of Australasia v. Willan (1874) LR 5 PC 417 at 444: 'There is a third class of cases, in which the Judge of the inferior court, having legitimately commenced the inquiry, is met by some fact which, if established, would oust his jurisdiction and place the subject-matter of the inquiry beyond it.' Examples are then given of question of title to land arising before the tribunal incompetent to try them.

[83] Above, p. 42; below, p. 351.

[84] Anisminic Ltd. v. Foreign Compensation Commission [1969] 2 AC 147 at 171. Lord Reid also said: 'I understand that some confusion has been caused by my having said . . . that if a tribunal has jurisdiction to go right it has jurisdiction to go wrong.' But more probably confusion would be caused by 'Neither an error in fact nor an error in law will destroy his jurisdiction', a statement inconsistent with Lord Reid's own decision in the Anisminic case, unless limited to its proper context.

itself to the wrong question or violated the rules of natural justice, it thereby stepped outside its jurisdiction.[85] If the tribunal's determination is in the end a nullity, it must at some point have exceeded its powers. In the same case Lord Justice Diplock said:[86]

'Jurisdiction' is an expression which is used in a variety of senses and takes its colour from its context.

But any attempt to confine 'jurisdiction' to one sort of power rather than another is certain to produce confusion.

Theory versus reality. The 'theory of jurisdiction'

The distinction between jurisdictional (or collateral) and other questions, emphasised so strongly in the foregoing discussion, has been made the object of a frontal attack. It has been contended[87] that the whole distinction is logically baseless and ought to be repudiated. A tribunal's findings, it is argued, ought to be equally conclusive on every matter which it must investigate in order to discharge its task; and none of them can be classed apart as collateral or preliminary or jurisdictional, so as to be automatically reviewable in the High Court when no appeal is given. No English court has ever adopted this theory, or even discussed it.[88] But so forcefully and learnedly has it been advocated that one distinguished author dignified it with the name of the 'pure' theory of jurisdiction,[89] and expounded it as 'a coherent theory of the concept of jurisdiction' which was coming into favour in the first half of the nineteenth century, though emphatically repudiated later.[90] Yet the courts, in reality, seem never to have been conscious of it at any time, so that they never had occasion to repudiate it. The theory is not so much pure as simple: it merely ignores the distinction upon which judicial review is founded. So far from being coherent, it is

---

[85] At 195, quoted above, p. 43.

[86] In the *Anisminic* case in the Court of Appeal, [1968] 2 QB 862 at 889.

[87] By Mr D. M. Gordon QC in a series of articles: 'The Relation of Facts to Jurisdiction' (1929) 45 LQR 459; 'Observance of Law as a Condition of Jurisdiction' (1931) 47 LQR 386, 557; *Tithe Commutation Commission* v. *Gwynne* (1944) 60 LQR 250; 'Conditional or Contingent Jurisdiction of Tribunals' (1960) 1 UBCLR 185; 'Jurisdictional Fact: An Answer' (1966) 82 LQR 515; and see (1960) 76 LQR 306; (1966) 82 LQR 263. Mr Gordon's thesis is supported in (1971) 9 Osgoode Hall LJ 203 at 210 (P. W. Hogg); but it seems to lack followers outside Canada.

[88] Many cases hold that a tribunal is at liberty to go wrong within its jurisdiction (see above, pp. 279, 288); but none of them holds that it may conclusively determine the boundaries of its jurisdiction.

[89] De Smith, *Judicial Review of Administrative Action,* 4th edn., 112.

[90] De Smith (as above), 110, 120.

irreconcilable with the fundamental rules of subordination without which the legal system itself cannot be coherent. This controversy, though wholly academic, is worth a digression since it throws light on the highly important reasons underlying the policy which the courts themselves have steadily pursued.

According to the 'theory of jurisdiction', a rent tribunal which has power to fix the rents of furnished but not unfurnished houses ought to have just the same jurisdiction over the question 'furnished or unfurnished' as it has over the question 'reasonable or unreasonable rent'. Similarly magistrates who have jurisdiction in county A but not in county B, if they find that an offence was committed in county A, ought not to be liable to have their decision quashed if it can be shown that the offence was in fact committed in county B.[91] It is conceded that these facts, if disputed, must initially be determined by the tribunal, which therefore has this jurisdiction over them. Since it is irrational to say that jurisdiction gives only power to decide correctly and not power to decide incorrectly,[92] that jurisdiction must extend to determining them incorrectly. Since it is also conceded that magistrates, acting within their jurisdiction, have conclusive power to find an innocent man guilty, and that the High Court has no power to review the conviction (except where appeal is provided), why should the magistrates be denied exclusive power to find where the offence was committed? Any attempt to differentiate these findings can lead only to logical absurdity, as is shown also by the fact that no clear guidelines for differentiating them can be formulated.

The insuperable objection to this theory is based both on legal logic and on practical policy. It would destroy the whole conception of 'stinted, limited jurisdiction', as Hale CB called it,[93] since it would make inferior tribunals the final judges of the limits of their own powers. A rent tribunal might determine that a large mansion was a furnished flat, the Home Secretary might deport a British subject by finding that he was an alien,[94] and a minister might take parkland, contrary to the Act, under a compulsory purchase order. If the High Court could not control such excesses, there would be no means of enforcing the doctrine of ultra vires. That doctrine is the sheet anchor of the rule of law, and the doctrine of collateral or jurisdictional questions is its indispensable corollary. To attack

---

[91] Such territorial questions are normally jurisdictional: see *R. v. Sandbach JJ ex P. Smith* [1951] 1 KB 62.

[92] But this is the fallacy: see below.

[93] Above, p. 281.

[94] In 82 LQR at p. 269 Mr Gordon contends that this is a different class of case from that of a tribunal. But in both cases alike there is statutory power conditional on certain questions, and no relevant difference is to be found. See above, p. 288.

the latter doctrine is to attack an essential part of the system of judicial control, of which the courts have made fruitful use. This, therefore, is its true logical basis, and it is mistaken to suppose that it is a weaker logical basis than any other—indeed, it is the most logical basis possible, since it follows necessarily from constitutional fundamentals.

The essential legal policy

As in so many legal situations, several different approaches are possible logically. The choice of the courts is determined by their evaluation of the underlying legal policy. In this case they could not have chosen otherwise without opening the door to arbitrary power and abandoning their task of protecting the citizen against illegal acts of government. Their reasons for clinging so faithfully to their principles have never been given better expression from the bench than in a judgment of Farwell LJ:[95]

No tribunal of inferior jurisdiction can by its own decision finally decide on the question of the existence or extent of such jurisdiction: such question is always subject to review by the High Court, which does not permit the inferior tribunal either to usurp a jurisdiction which it does not possess . . . or to refuse to exercise a jurisdiction which it has . . . Subjection in this respect to the High Court is a necessary and inseparable incident to all tribunals of limited jurisdiction; for it is a contradiction in terms to create a tribunal with limited jurisdiction and unlimited power to determine such limit at its own will and pleasure—such a tribunal would be autocratic, not limited—and it is immaterial whether the decision of the inferior tribunal on the question of the existence or non-existence of its own jurisdiction is founded on law or fact . . .

If administrative tribunals and authorities could trespass uncontrollably outside their proper fields, there would no longer be order in the legal system. Order can be preserved only if jurisdictional demarcation disputes can always be carried to the regular courts of law, and so brought within a unified hierarchy of authority.

To emphasise this vital legal policy is not to concede that there is any logical weakness in the distinctions on which jurisdictional control is founded. The classical doctrine of collateral or jurisdictional questions rests on the clear distinction between questions which fall within the tribunal's limited power only if answered one way, and questions which fall within it whether answered either way. There is no logical reason why all such

---

[95] R. v. Shoreditch Assessment Committee ex p. Morgan [1910] 2 KB 859 at 880; approved in Anisminic Ltd. v. Foreign Compensation Commission [1969] 2 AC 147 at 197, 209 and 233 by Lords Pearce and Wilberforce and by Browne J, who cited it with reference to (1966) 82 LQR 226 (Wade).

questions should be classed together indiscriminately, and the so-called 'theory of jurisdiction' is fallacious in asserting the contrary.[96] Many of the examples used to support it are cases of convictions by magistrates, in which as already pointed out[97] it is natural to treat all the ingredients of the offence as equally within the magistrates' determinative powers. But this is merely to say that these cases are in the 'jurisdiction either way' category; it is not to say that the other category ought not to exist. And the decisions holding that a conviction by magistrates, if good on its face, is conclusive are cases where no jurisdictional fact was in issue[98]—or, putting it another way, they were cases where it was attempted to make a jurisdictional fact out of what was clearly not one.

Admittedly the question 'jurisdictional or not jurisdictional' will sometimes be a difficult question of construction when the terms of the Act are inconclusive. But administrative law, and indeed all law, is riddled with difficulties of that kind, and their mere existence proves or disproves nothing. The distinction between mandatory and directory conditions,[99] for example, presents exactly analogous difficulties, but is none the less genuine on that account. It is by no means a bad thing that the courts have flexible instruments at their disposal, and are not confined by rigid theories. If occasionally they push them to extremes, as in the *Anisminic* case,[1] they are thus able to demonstrate that, when faced with exceptionally drastic legislation, they can stretch their powers to meet the challenge.

Although in the remainder of this chapter we will see signs that the courts may feel strong enough to dispense with jurisdictional arguments, the ultra vires principle is bound to remain the foundation of their power. It played a prominent part in the series of cases which began with *Anisminic*, leading into problems not yet resolved. At a time when the courts are mobilising all their resources for controlling governmental power it is unlikely that they will discard the principles which have served them well for centuries. Their addiction to the technicalities of jurisdictional review is not a mere aberration. It is the consequence of their constitutional position *vis-à-vis* a sovereign legislature: only by showing that they are obeying its commands can they justify their interventions.[2] By one means or another, therefore, the doctrine of ultra vires must be stretched to cover the case. The courts of the United States, with their entrenched constitutional status,

---

[96] The fallacy is observed by Lord Wilberforce in the *Anisminic* case (above) at 209. The classical doctrine of English law is 'rooted in first principles and common sense': *State* v. *Durcan (Judge)* [1964] IR 279 at 283.

[97] Above, p. 287.

[98] Above, p. 287.

[99] Above, p. 245.

[1] Above, p. 283; below, p. 725.

[2] See above, p. 41.

can afford to dispense with these subtleties. The position of British judges is fundamentally different.

All error of law to be reviewable?

The *Anisminic* case[3] is now the leading example of jurisdictional error by a tribunal in the course of its proceedings. It is also an extreme example of an error of law, which might have been considered an error within jurisdiction, being held to be jurisdictional. The Foreign Compensation Commission had rejected a claim for compensation for a property already sold to a foreign buyer on the erroneous ground that the statutory Order in Council required that the successor in title should have been of British nationality at a certain date. The majority of the House of Lords held that this error destroyed the Commission's jurisdiction and rendered their decision a nullity, since on a true view of the law they had no jurisdiction to take the successor in title's nationality into account. Plainly the Commission had jurisdiction in Lord Reid's narrow sense, for they had power to entertain and determine the claim. But by asking themselves the wrong question, and by imposing a requirement which they had no authority to impose, they were held to have overstepped their powers. By stretching the concept of jurisdictional error the House of Lords were able to justify their power to intervene and to declare the Commission's decision to be ultra vires and a nullity.

But it was soon seen that the concept had been stretched to breaking-point. For it requires only a simple verbal manipulation to represent any error of law as the result of the tribunal asking itself a wrong question or imposing some wrong requirement. By such logic (if logic it be) any and every error of law could be shown to involve excess of jurisdiction. Thus the House of Lords, while purporting to uphold the distinction between errors of law which went to jurisdiction and errors of law which did not, in fact undermined it. A tribunal had now, in effect, no power to decide any question of law incorrectly: any error of law would render its decision liable to be quashed as ultra vires.[4]

This radical conclusion was first drawn by Lord Diplock in a published lecture, saying that the *Anisminic* case 'renders obsolete the technical distinction between errors of law which go to "jurisdiction" and errors of law which do not'.[5] Then it was adopted by Lord Denning MR (supported

---

[3] Above. The case is discussed in (1969) 85 LQR 198 (Wade); [1970] PL 358 (B. C. Gould); (1971) 34 MLR 1 (D. M. Gordon).

[4] For discussion see (1984) 4 OJLS 22 (J. Beatson).

[5] [1974] CLJ 233 at 243 (the de Smith memorial lecture). For a similar comment see (1969) 85 LQR at 211.

by Eveleigh LJ but opposed by Geoffrey Lane LJ) in the *Pearlman* case, holding that the decision of a county court could be quashed for error of law, the normal right of appeal having been cut off by statute.[6] Observing that the House of Lords had reduced the former distinction to a mere matter of words, Lord Denning said:

I would suggest that this distinction should now be discarded. . . . The way to get things right is to hold thus: no court or tribunal has any jurisdiction to make an error of law on which the decision of the case depends. If it makes such an error, it goes outside its jurisdiction and certiorari will lie to correct it.

Geoffrey Lane LJ, dissenting, pointed out that (as is undoubtedly true) the House of Lords in the *Anisminic* case intended to maintain the established distinction between error of law within jurisdiction and error of law outside jurisdiction; and he held that the county court's error was within jurisdiction, and not therefore subject to judicial review. His opinion has been followed, in preference to that of Lord Denning, by the Privy Council in a case from Malaysia, in which they reached the same conclusion as regards the error (if any) in an award of an industrial court.[7] The High Court of Australia has followed the Privy Council.[8]

Lord Denning's opinion has however been upheld in an important speech by Lord Diplock in the *Racal* case in the House of Lords.[9] That case was concerned with a decision of a High Court judge which statute had made unappealable. A decision of the High Court is not subject to judicial review, so the case did not raise any question of error by an inferior

---

[6] *Pearlman* v. *Harrow School Governors* [1979] QB 56 (the county court had determined that the installation of central heating was not a 'structural alteration or addition' by a tenant). Lord Denning repeated his proposition, aligning it with Lord Diplock's in the *Racal* case (below), in *R.* v. *Chief Immigration Officer, Gatwick Airport ex p. Kharrazi* [1980] 1 WLR 1396. See also *Watt* v. *Lord Advocate* 1979 SLT 137.

[7] *South East Asia Fire Bricks Sdn Bhd.* v. *Non-Metallic Mineral Products Manufacturing Employees Union* [1981] AC 363, decided ten days before the House of Lords gave judgment in the *Racal* case, below.

[8] *Houssein* v. *Under Secretary, Department of Industrial Relations* (1982) 38 ALR 577; *Hockey* v. *Yelland* (1984) 56 ALR 215. See also *Glenvill Homes Pty Ltd.* v. *Builders Licensing Board* [1981] 2 NSWLR 608; *New Zealand Engineering (etc.) Union* v. *Court of Arbitration* [1976] 2 NZLR 283; *Eastern (Auckland) Rugby Football Club Inc.* v. *Licensing Control Commission* [1979] 1 NZLR 367, where Speight J follows Geoffrey Lane LJ's dissent as preferable 'for conservatively-minded people'.

[9] *Re Racal Communications Ltd.*, reported as *Re A Company* [1981] AC 374 (challenge to order of High Court judge authorising compulsory inspection of company's books). Lord Keith concurred with Lord Diplock in general terms. Lord Edmund-Davies supported the Privy Council (in which he had sat) and Geoffrey Lane LJ, and therefore disagreed with Lord Diplock as to the effect of *Anisminic*. Lords Salmon and Scarman merely held (with respect, correctly) that *Anisminic* had nothing to do with the case. *Anisminic* was concerned with judicial review of an inferior tribunal. *Racal* was concerned with appeal from a High Court judge.

tribunal. But Lord Diplock, taking the opportunity to corroborate the view expressed in his lecture, said:

The break-through made by *Anisminic* was that, as respects administrative tribunals and authorities, the old distinction between errors of law that went to jurisdiction and errors of law that did not, was for practical purposes abolished. Any error of law that could be shown to have been made by them in the course of reaching their decision on matters of fact or of administrative policy would result in their having asked themselves the wrong question with the result that the decision they reached would be a nullity.

He then held that inferior courts (such as the county court) might still be held to have authority to make errors of law within their jurisdiction, so that as regards such courts (as opposed to tribunals) the old distinction between jurisdictional and non-jurisdictional error would survive.[10] In a subsequent speech, however, in which he again expounded his interpretation of 'the landmark decision' in *Anisminic*, Lord Diplock included inferior courts along with tribunals as bodies to which the old distinction would no longer apply;[11] and a strong divisional court has followed this later analysis in holding that the Court could review the finding of a coroner's inquest on the basis that any significant mistake of law would destroy jurisdiction.[12]

Anisminic: two views and three possibilities

Sharply conflicting views about the *Anisminic* case and its effects thus prevail in the House of Lords and in the Privy Council.[13] The inherent contradiction in that 'legal landmark', as Lord Diplock called it, lies in the inconsistency between the reasoning and the result. If regard is had primarily to the reasoning, the old distinction between errors within and without jurisdiction ought still to be in force as (in Lord Wilberforce's words) 'a crucial distinction which the court has to make'.[14] On this view,

[10] In *Bulk Gas Users Group* v. *Attorney-General* [1983] NZLR 129 Cooke J suggests that the rival *Pearlman/Racal* and *South East Asia Fire Bricks* propositions can thus be reconciled by regarding the tribunal in the latter case as akin to a court.

[11] *O'Reilly* v. *Mackman* [1983] 2 AC 237 at 278, the whole House concurring in general terms.

[12] *R.* v. *Greater Manchester Coroner ex p. Tal* [1985] QB 67, where the application failed since no mistake was shown. A coroner's inquest was held to be a court in *R.* v. *Surrey Coroner ex p. Campbell* [1982] QB 661.

[13] In addition to the primary conflict there are contradictory cross-currents. Lord Diplock approves Geoffrey Lane LJ's dissent in *Pearlman*, but that dissent was based upon the interpretation of *Anisminic* which Lord Diplock rejects. Lord Keith was an assenting member of the Privy Council in *South East Asia Fire Bricks* but in *Racal* he expresses agreement with Lord Diplock's opinion.

[14] [1969] 2 AC at 210.

which is that of the Privy Council and of Geoffrey Lane LJ, *Anisminic* upheld the established distinction but applied it to the facts in a manner which is difficult to explain. If regard is had primarily to the result, on the other hand, one is driven to conclude that the old distinction has been manipulated out of existence. This is the view taken by Lord Denning and Lord Diplock. It results in a notable extension of judicial review, since every error of law made by an administrative tribunal or authority, if decisive of the case, will now render its decision liable to be quashed. This is yet a further step in the direction of making the courts the conclusive arbiters on all questions of law. Australian and Canadian legislation has moved in the same direction.[15]

If the law is now to be as laid down by Lord Denning and Lord Diplock, there will be important repercussions in other areas. The law as to error of law on the face of the record will become redundant.[16] On the other hand, the situations in which the court may disregard statutes which take away legal remedies will be extended. It is in the context of such statutes, which were in issue throughout this series of cases, that the problem takes on a special importance. That aspect of it must be explained later in conjunction with the law of remedies.[17] All that can be said with certainty at the present stage is that there is a medley of contradictory opinions in the appellate courts and the conflict between the rival interpretations of *Anisminic* is unresolved.

What can perhaps be said, nevertheless, is that the main current of judicial opinion is running in favour of holding all error of law to be reviewable. This may be achieved either by adopting the Denning–Diplock analysis, as in the above-mentioned decision of the Divisional Court, or else by simply ignoring all the esoteric argument about jurisdiction and holding that error of law is inherently something that it is the business of the court to remedy. Lord Denning himself had spoken in the latter sense even in pre-*Anisminic* times, saying that a minister's decision could be quashed 'if he has given a wrong interpretation to the words of a statute . . . or has otherwise gone wrong in law';[18] and his later remark that the court would quash if a minister 'plainly misdirects himself in fact or in law' was approved in the House of Lords.[19] Lord Diplock, without referring to his *Anisminic* thesis, has said that 'the decision-maker must understand correctly the law that regulates his decision-making power and must give effect to it', otherwise the court will review for 'illegality'.[20] And

---

[15] See below, p. 309.
[16] Below, p. 308.
[17] Below, p. 725.
[18] In the *Ashbridge Investments* case, quoted below, p. 324.
[19] See below, p. 328.
[20] *Council of Civil Service Unions* v. *Minister for the Civil Service* [1985] AC 374 at 410.

Lord Templeman has said that judicial review is available 'where a decision-making authority ... commits an error of law'.[21] These were *obiter dicta*, but are none the less significant and authoritative. In a series of immigration cases, furthermore, the courts have quashed decisions on account of misconstruction or misapplication of the immigration rules, treating such errors as automatically reviewable, without further explanation.[22]

With these decisions and opinions the courts seem to have prepared the ground for holding any error of law to be reviewable. If this is now to be the acknowledged rule, large parts of this chapter, including all the foregoing discussion of jurisdictional law and all the following account of error on the face of the record, will pass into history. Presumably the courts will allow the same margin of error as they have done under the latter head, so as not to interfere with minor errors of interpretation;[23] but otherwise their dominion over all questions of law will be absolute. In the words of Sir Robin Cooke,[24] speaking extra-judicially,

Whatever different shades of opinion there may be about refinements, we are on the brink of open recognition of a fundamental rule of our mainly unwritten constitution: namely that determination of questions of law is always the ultimate responsibility of the courts of general jurisdiction.

ERROR ON THE FACE OF THE RECORD

Error within jurisdiction

It is now necessary to explain a unique legal doctrine, deriving from early times, by which the courts can quash proceedings which display mistake of law on their face. The reader must be warned, however, that for the reasons explained in the foregoing paragraphs this doctrine seems likely to have outlived its utility and may prove to be of historical interest only.

A mistake of law which appears 'on the face of the record' of the proceedings is, so to speak, an affront to the law which cannot be overlooked. This doctrine was developed quite independently of any question of jurisdiction. A tribunal might have misinterpreted a statute or regulation while keeping fully within its jurisdiction, and provided that

---

[21] *R. v. Inland Revenue Commissioners ex p. Preston* [1985] AC 835 at 862.

[22] See below, p. 858. In the *Kharrazi* case, there cited, Lord Denning MR adopted the jurisdictional argument while Waller and Dunn L JJ ignored it, holding simply that the decision could be quashed if there was error of law.

[23] Below, p. 317.

[24] *Judicial Review of Administrative Action in the 1980s*, p. 10.

this was not self-evident on its record, its adjudication could not be quashed. But where it was self-evident, the urge to intervene was more than judicial flesh and blood could resist.

This is the one region in which the doctrine of ultra vires is not dominant—the one region, in other words, where the courts are able to interfere with statutory determinations even though they are within jurisdiction. The standard jurisdictional test, which is usually the mainstay of the court's power, is replaced simply by the test of correctness. For once it is a question of 'right or wrong' instead of a question of 'lawful or unlawful'. Nevertheless the proceeding is not an appeal. It is a distinct branch of the High Court's inherent jurisdiction over inferior tribunals.

Judged by the usual principle of ultra vires, which elsewhere reigns supreme, this jurisdiction in the High Court is anomalous, since in principle a tribunal which keeps within its jurisdiction ought to be immune from judicial molestation. But the doctrine's justification is supplied by its history. When in the seventeenth century the remedy of certiorari was first used to control statutory powers, its primary object was to call up the record of the proceedings into the Court of King's Bench; and if the record displayed error, the decision was quashed. What is now an exception was then a primary rule, and it was not founded on any idea of jurisdiction or ultra vires. But if the applicant wanted to go outside the record, and bring other evidence to show some abuse of the power, the court would quash only where an excess of jurisdiction could be shown.[25] If the record itself showed an excess of jurisdiction, the court could as well quash for that as for any other defect.[26] If the record did not show it, additional evidence had to be given, and in proceedings for certiorari that had to be done by affidavit. Hence came the rule that affidavits were admitted only to show want of jurisdiction.[27] But that rule emerged only gradually in the eighteenth century.[28] Although it provided the opening through which the wide ultra

---

[25] Parts of this passage were adopted by Lawton LJ in *R. v. West Sussex Quarter Sessions ex p. Johnson Trust Ltd.* [1974] 1 QB 24 at 40.

[26] In *R. v. Glamorganshire (Inhabitants)* (the Cardiff Bridge case) (1700) 1 Ld. Raym. 580 Holt CJ rejected the decision in *Ball v. Pattridge* (1666) 1 Sid. 296 that excess of jurisdiction (by the Commissioners of Fens) could be tried only in an action for damages and not on certiorari, saying: 'For this Court will examine the proceedings of all jurisdictions erected by Act of Parliament. And if they, under pretence of such Act, proceed to encroach jurisdiction to themselves greater than the Act warrants, this Court will send a certiorari to them to have their proceedings returned here.' In *R. v. Burnaby* (1703) 2 Ld. Raym. 900 Holt CJ's view was rejected by the other judges (who quashed for defects of form). But from then on it prevailed. See also *Groenvelt v. Burwell* (1700) 1 Ld. Raym. 454 at 496.

[27] *R. v. Bolton* (1841) 1 QB 66; *R. v. Nat Bell Liquors Ltd.* [1922] 2 AC 128 at 155–6, 160; *R. v. Northumberland Compensation Appeal Tribunal ex p. Shaw* [1951] 1 KB 711 at 719;

[28] Rubinstein, *Jurisdiction and Illegality*, 70. At p. 69 it is said that *R. v. Oulton Inhabitants* (1735) Cas. t. Hard. 169 shows that affidavits were still then refused; but the case does not seem to concern jurisdictional error.

vires doctrine made its way into the law, this was a development which came later than the jurisdiction to review the record for error of any description, a jurisdiction firmly established in the time of Lord Holt CJ, about the year 1700.[29] Review of the record was therefore the original system of judicial control, adopted when the Court of King's Bench took over the work of supervising inferior tribunals and administrative bodies, such as Justices of the Peace and the Commissioners of Sewers, after the Star Chamber and the conciliar courts had been abolished.[30]

Decline of non-jurisdictional review

The development of this early system was blighted by parliamentary interference, prompted by judicial pedantry. Review of the record became excessively formal, and many orders were quashed on what one judge described as 'lamentable and disgraceful technicalities'.[31] As Denning LJ explained,[32]

Ever since the days of Holt CJ the Court of King's Bench has been extremely strict to see that all was in order. Everything necessary to support the conviction had to appear on the face of the record. . . . If there was any defect in point of form, or any error in point of law, appearing on the face of the record, the conviction would be removed into the King's Bench and quashed. Nothing could be supplied by argument or intendment.

Although in those days little distinction was made in general between the criminal jurisdiction and the administrative functions of justices of the peace (e.g. maintaining roads and administering the poor law), there was one significant difference in that for their administrative acts a much simpler record was acceptable to the King's Bench.[33] Primarily therefore it was the quashing of convictions for trivial defects that caused complaint. Parliament remedied this abuse in two different ways: first by inserting 'no-certiorari clauses' in many statutes from the seventeenth century onwards;[34] and secondly by enacting in the nineteenth century that criminal convictions need be supported only by a very short record,

[29] See n. 26, above.
[30] Holdsworth, *History of English Law*, vi. 56, 112, 263; x. 155. The Court of Session has deplored the lack of any corresponding jurisdiction in Scotland: *Watt* v. *Lord Advocate* 1979 SLT 137.
[31] *R.* v. *Ruyton (Inhabitants)* (1861) 1 B & S 534 at 545.
[32] *R.* v. *Northumberland Compensation Appeal Tribunal ex p. Shaw* [1952] 1 KB 338 at 348.
[33] As above, at 349.
[34] For these see below, p. 722. Another remedy was to empower the court to correct defects in the record that were not material, as was done by the Quarter Sessions Act 1849 (12 & 13 Vict., c. 45), s. 7.

omitting the charge and the evidence and the reasoning which were required to be set out previously.[35] No-certiorari clauses simply forbade the court to grant this remedy in many particular cases. The short form of conviction, on the other hand (to quote a celebrated judgment of Lord Summer)[36]

did not stint the jurisdiction of the Queen's Bench, or alter the actual law of certiorari. What it did was to disarm its exercise. The effect was not to make that which had been error, error no longer, but to remove nearly all opportunity for its detection. The fact of the record 'spoke' no longer: it was the inscrutable face of a sphinx.

The combined effect of these events was to divert the energies of the courts away from control of the record and towards the development of the ultra vires doctrine. That was not restricted in any way by what appeared on the record, and evidence to show an excess of jurisdiction was always admissible.[37] Furthermore, the courts circumvented the no-certiorari clauses by holding that they were intended only to prevent quashing for trivial errors on the record within jurisdiction, and not to protect excesses of jurisdiction at all. It was for these reasons that the courts were led to concentrate on jurisdictional control, which had a firm constitutional basis,[38] rather than on review of the record, which was often merely formalistic. This also explains why the jurisdictional principle was extended to lengths which made it, in its turn, seem artificial: for, being the most defensible and flexible doctrine, it was pressed into service for nearly all purposes.[39]

The doctrine revived

The result of this process of evolution was that the power of review for mere error on the face of the record was almost wholly forgotten after 1848, until it was dramatically revived in 1950. So complete was the lapse of memory that in 1944, when administrative law was at its nadir, the Court of Appeal held that there was no such jurisdiction and no sign that it had ever existed, so that an alleged mistake of law in the award of a

---

[35] Summary Jurisdiction Act 1848. The Summary Jurisdiction Act 1857 provided for an appeal by case stated on a point of law; this rendered certiorari unnecessary in many cases (see s. 10), as explained below, p. 315.

[36] R. v. *Nat Bell Liquors Ltd.* [1922] 2 AC 128 at 159. See also the account given by Cave J in R. v. *Bradley* (1894) 70 LT 379.

[37] Above, p. 281.

[38] Above, p. 42.

[39] Above, p. 42.

statutory claims tribunal could not be challenged.[40] Fortunately this could be shown to be contrary to a decision of the House of Lords, one of the few cases that had occurred during the century of amnesia.[41] When the issue again came before the courts in 1950, therefore, the outcome was entirely different. Error of law on the face of the record was re-established as a ground of review and rapidly rose to great popularity. For it was particularly well suited to the needs of the time. Statutory tribunals had greatly increased both in number and power; Parliament, averse to judicial interference, had given few rights of appeal; and there was public complaint.[42] Here, therefore, was an opportunity for the courts to undertake to correct errors by tribunals which patently misapplied the law. The time was ripe for the *Northumberland* case,[43] in which by reviving the old jurisdiction over the record the courts recovered much lost control, as they were increasingly to do in other ways during the next twenty years.

This case turned upon the amount of compensation payable to the clerk to a hospital board in Northumberland who had lost his post in 1949 after the National Health Service was introduced. He claimed that not only his service with the hospital board, but also his earlier service with the local authority ought to be included in calculating his statutory compensation. The Compensation Appeal Tribunal were required to apply the regulations made under the Act, which as a matter of law required both periods of service to be taken into account. In their decision dismissing the appeal the tribunal stated that there had been these two periods of service, but that in their judgment it was only the second period which should count. The order therefore contained a manifest error of law, and on this ground it was quashed. Denning LJ said:

We have here a simple case of error of law by a tribunal, an error which they frankly acknowledge. It is an error which deprives Mr. Shaw of the compensation to which he is by law entitled. So long as the erroneous decision stands, the

[40] *Racecourse Betting Control Board* v. *Secretary for Air* [1944] Ch. 114. This was on a motion to set aside the award, but Lord Greene MR and Goddard LJ expressly denied that certiorari would lie. Lord Goddard CJ changed his mind in the *Northumberland* case, below. The Canadian courts did not fall into this error: *R.* v. *Logan ex p. McAllister* [1974] 4 DLR 676; *John East Ironworks* v. *Labour Relations Board of Saskatchewan* [1949] 3 DLR 51.

[41] *Walsall Overseers* v. *L. & N.W. Rly* (1878) 4 App. Cas. 30, giving an account of earlier practice. Lord Cairns LC said (at 39): '. . . The Court of Queen's Bench might be asked to have the order brought into it, and to look at the order, and view it upon the face of it, and if the Court found error upon the face of it, to put an end to its existence by quashing it; not to substitute another order in its place, but to remove that order out of the way, as one which should not be used to the detriment of any of the subjects of Her Majesty.'

[42] See below, p. 911.

[43] *R.* v. *Northumberland Compensation Appeal Tribunal ex p. Shaw* [1952] 1 KB 338. See Sawer, (1956) U of WALR 24; Abel, (1963) 15 U of Tor LJ 102.

compensating authority dare not pay Mr. Shaw the money to which he is entitled
lest the auditor should surcharge them. It would be quite intolerable if in such a case
there were no means of correcting the error.

The Court thus upheld the decision of the King's Bench Division,[44] where
Lord Goddard CJ had been the first to see that the decision of 1944 was
wrong, although he had been party to it, and that the court ought to follow
the old authorities. He also said:[45]

I think it is beneficial in this case that we should do so, not merely having regard to
the facts of this case, but because so many tribunals have now been set up, all of
whom, I am certain, desire to do their duty in the best way, and are often given
very difficult sets of regulations and statutes to construe.

How true this was was soon shown by the number of applications for
certiorari which came before the courts on this ground in the ensuing years.
These cases left a particularly deep mark on the national insurance and
industrial injuries system, as mentioned elsewhere.[46]

Jurisdiction—relevant or irrelevant?

In the *Northumberland* case both courts were careful to point out that there
had been no excess of jurisdiction: the tribunal had complete power over
the case in question, but had simply gone wrong in law. The High Court's
power to intervene on this ground, though not respectable historically,
thus appears anomalous in modern administrative law since it is the only
branch of judicial review which is not anchored to concepts of jurisdiction
and ultra vires.[47] Of course, if the error happens to be jurisdictional as well
as apparent on the face of the record, the court can quash for either or both
reasons.[48]

But now, as has been explained earlier, a powerful school of thought
maintains that by its decision in the *Anisminic* case the House of Lords has
destroyed the possibility that a tribunal may make an error of law and yet
remain within its jurisdiction.[49] Although there are acute differences of
opinion in the highest courts, a proposition supported by Lord Denning

[44] [1951] 1 KB 711, an unreserved judgment of notable quality.
[45] At p. 724. See also the comments of Griffiths LJ in R. v. *Knightsbridge Crown Court ex p. International Sporting Club Ltd.* [1982] QB 304.
[46] Below, p. 319.
[47] This inconsistency has sometimes led judges to hold that error on the face must be a species of jurisdictional error. Lord Sumner appears to have so held in R. v. *Nat Bell Liquors Ltd.* [1922] 2 AC 128 at 155 (lines 1–2), 157 (lines 8–13); and in R. v. *Mahony* [1910] 2 IR 695 at 722 Palles CB (dissenting) so held in 'an unmistakably Irish syllogism': Rubinstein, *Jurisdiction and Illegality*, 93.
[48] An example is R. v. *Chichester RDC* [1960] 1 WLR 197.
[49] Above, p. 299.

and Lord Diplock must be of great authority. If their interpretation prevails, all the law about error on the face of the record will become redundant, since every error of law will be an excess of jurisdiction and court can then quash the tribunal's decision as ultra vires independently of the record—a result since accepted as correct in a case where the court said:[50]

Since *Anisminic* the requirement that an error of law within the jurisdiction must appear on the face of the record is now obsolete.

Lord Diplock had made the same point in his lecture already quoted;[51] saying that the *Anisminic* case

renders obsolete the technical distinction between errors of law which go to 'jurisdiction' and errors of law which do not. In doing so it enlarges the material that can be made available to the court on certiorari to found an inference that those responsible for an administrative decision have erred in law. So technicalities as to what constitutes the 'record' for the purposes of review no longer matter.

Whether the decision really effected fundamental changes of this kind, without any apparent intention on the part of the House of Lords, is an unresolved controversy, as already pointed out. If it has, the law of judicial review will in some ways be simplified and improved. For there is no real merit in the distinction between errors which appear on the face of the record and those which do not. It is a legacy from an older and more formalistic era of legal history which might well be eliminated—as has indeed been done in several Commonwealth jurisdictions.[52] It is a pity that this simple reform has not been effected directly, instead of in terms of 'esoteric distinctions'[53] between intra-jurisdictional and extra-jurisdictional errors of law, a fertile source of doubt and difficulty.

Since it is not yet certain that the views of Lord Denning and Lord Diplock will prevail, it may be premature to consign the law about review of the record to the limbo from which it was rescued in 1950. It has played an important part in the extension of judicial review since that date and it

---

[50] *R. v. Greater Manchester Coroner ex p. Tal* [1985] QB 67 at 82 (above, p. 301). The words 'within the jurisdiction' may be inadvertent, since ex hypothesi the error is outside jurisdiction. The principal error alleged, but not proved, was the admission of hearsay evidence. See similarly *R. v. Knightsbridge Crown Court ex p. The Aspinall Curzon Ltd.* [1982] The Times, 16 December, holding that the facilities for discovery etc. now available under RSC Order 53 (below, p. 672) have deprived the record of its importance.

[51] (1974) 33 CLJ 233 at 243; above, p. 299.

[52] e.g. Canada (Federal Court Act 1970, s. 28); Australia (Administrative Decisions (Judicial Review) Act 1977, s. 5). These Acts empower the court to quash for error of law whether or not it appears on the record.

[53] Lord Diplock in *O'Reilly* v. *Mackman* [1983] 2 AC 237 at 278.

may possibly do so in the future. Its main rules are described in the following pages.

Certiorari usually the only remedy

One symptom of the anomalous character of 'face of the record' review is that certiorari is usually the only available remedy. Action which is ultra vires can be rectified in many ways: by actions for damages, or injunctions, or declaratory judgments, as well as by habeas corpus, prohibition, or certiorari.[54] Mere error on the record, on the other hand, has no general invalidating effect; it merely renders the erroneous order liable to be quashed on certiorari. An act which is ultra vires is null and void and of no legal effect. An order which merely displays error on its face is void when quashed by certiorari, but until then, not being vitiated by excess of jurisdiction, it is legal and valid. It may accordingly be described as voidable.[55] It is of no avail, therefore, in proceedings for a declaratory judgment to attack an order for mere error of law on its face.[56] All that the court can declare is that the order, though it may contain a mistake, is valid. Even if the court were to declare that the order displayed error on its face, this would not render the order ineffective if it was itself intra vires. Nor has this position been changed by the new rules of court which have introduced a single procedure for certiorari and declaration alike; for the rules deal with the procedure for applying for these remedies and do not alter their effect when awarded.[57]

To the rule that certiorari is the only remedy there appear to be two exceptions. First, the remedy of prohibition, which often goes hand in hand with certiorari,[58] may be available to prohibit the execution of an order showing error on its face in cases where certiorari will not lie, as in the case of an ecclesiastical court.[59] The same ought to be true of cases where mandamus is used, conventionally though unnecessarily, as a substitute for certiorari, as in liquor licensing cases.[60] Secondly, it is never safe to rule out the remedy of habeas corpus, since courts may stretch their powers when personal liberty is at stake. In principle habeas corpus is not available to review the merits of a decision (as opposed to the jurisdiction), for the rule

---

[54] See chs. 16, 17.

[55] See below, p. 349.

[56] *Punton* v. *Ministry of Pensions and National Insurance (No. 2)* [1964] 1 WLR 226; below, p. 601.

[57] See below, p. 671.

[58] See below, p. 626.

[59] See below, p. 646.

[60] See below, p. 658.

is that it may not be used as an indirect appeal.[61] But where detention is under an administrative order vitiated by error on its face, the court will naturally wish to release the detainee; and at least two decisions of the House of Lords support this possibility.[62] Strictly speaking there should be a certiorari to remove the cause as well as a habeas corpus to remove the body, but this formality is unlikely to be insisted upon where the order of detention or the matter accompanying it is bad on its face.[63]

It is clear at least that error on the face is not remediable by non-prerogative remedies such as damages, injunction or declaration. Apart from this difference, quashing for error on the face is generally similar to quashing for excess of jurisdiction. Certiorari is available against administrative authorities generally on a very wide basis.[64] It is never a mode of appeal, for the reviewing court cannot substitute its own judgment: the court can only remove the offending order out of the way, as Lord Cairns LC put it.[65] But in doing so the court will naturally indicate where the error lies. The tribunal or other deciding authority will then have to dispose of the case, since its previous order is annulled, and will know how to do so correctly.[66]

Another similarity with jurisdictional review is that the court's power to quash is unaffected by a statutory provision that the tribunal's decision shall be final.[67] But a provision that the decision shall not be questioned in legal proceedings, or shall not be subject to certiorari, brings out the difference: it prevents review for mere error on the face, but not for excess of jurisdiction. This is explained in a later chapter.[68]

What is 'the record'?

It is essential[69] that the error should appear 'on the face of the record'. This requirement dates back to a period of formalism, and to modern judges, who are inclined to find a remedy for any serious misapplication of law, it

[61] R. v. *Board of Control ex p. Rutty* [1956] 2 QB 109, discussed below, p. 620.
[62] R. v. *Governor of Brixton Prison ex p. Armah* [1968] AC 192 at 235 (Lord Reid) and 257 (Lord Upjohn); Lord Pearce (at 254) however speaks in terms of jurisdiction, although for that purpose any evidence could be given in any case. See also R. v. *Governor of Pentonville Prison ex p. Sotiriadis* [1975] AC 1 at 30 (Lord Diplock), where the exception should perhaps apply to all habeas corpus cases and not extradition cases only. For these decisions see below, p. 622.
[63] See the *Armah* case (above) at 234–5, 254.
[64] Below, p. 628.
[65] See above, p. 307, n. 41.
[66] See R. v. *Northumberland Compensation Appeal Tribunal ex p. Shaw* [1952] 1 KB 338 at 347, 354 (Denning LJ).
[67] R. v. *Medical Appeal Tribunal ex p. Gilmore* [1957] 1 QB 574: below, p. 720.
[68] Below, p. 724.
[69] But see Lord Diplock's comment, above, p. 309.

appears artificial. They therefore allow considerable latitude. In the
Northumberland case itself the tribunal's mistake could not be deduced from
its recorded decision, which did not mention the correct argument which it
had wrongly rejected. But this would have appeared if the claim and the
notice of appeal had also been submitted, which the court held should have
formed part of the record; and since the mistake had been admitted in open
court, this was held to conclude the matter.[70]

In the same case Denning LJ summed up the requirements of a proper
record, distinguishing between civil and criminal cases as mentioned
earlier. The authorities for civil cases showed, he said,[71] that

the record must contain at least the document which initiates the proceedings; the
pleadings, if any; and the adjudication; but not the evidence, nor the reasons, unless
the tribunal chooses to incorporate them. If the tribunal does state its reasons, and
those reasons are wrong in law, certiorari lies to quash the decision.

The authorities likewise showed that if the necessary materials were not
submitted, the court could order the tribunal to supply them, on pain of
having its decision quashed.[72] This does not mean that the court can call for
material to supplement the record, e.g. statements of reasons where those
are not required by law. It means merely that the essential items which
make up a legal record can be called for. A tribunal cannot be allowed to
frustrate judicial review by withholding documents which are part of the
record of the proceedings before it. It can also be ordered to supply
particulars which it has a legal duty to incorporate in its decision (as where
procedural regulations require a statement of reasons), thus saving a
separate application for mandamus.[73] If it voluntarily supplies particulars,
as by filing an affidavit in certiorari proceedings, that too is part of the
record.[74] So is a letter explaining the reasons for an administrative decision,
even if sent some time later and not to the party himself.[75]

The House of Lords has been willing to assume, without deciding, that

[70] [1952] 1 KB at 344, 354, 355.
[71] At p. 352. But see Lord Tucker's reservations in *Baldwin & Francis Ltd.* v. *Patents Appeal Tribunal* [1959] AC 663 at 687, questioning whether the record means anything more than the order or decision as recorded. This has not deterred the Court of Appeal from going beyond the order: see *R.* v. *Patents Appeal Tribunal ex p. Swift & Co.* [1962] 2 QB 647 (application and specification admitted in patent case). A narrow view of 'the record' appears in *R.* v. *District Court, Queensland ex p. Thompson* [1968] ALR 509 (reasons stated in writing not part of record since not part of formal order).
[72] At p. 352.
[73] *R.* v. *Medical Appeal Tribunal ex p. Gilmore* [1957] 1 QB 574 at 582 (finding of fact and reasons required by regulations).
[74] *R.* v. *Southampton Justices ex p. Green* [1976] QB 11 at 22.
[75] *R.* v. *Supplementary Benefits Commission ex p. Singer* [1973] 1 WLR 713 (Commission's decision quashed for error appearing in letter from Department of Health and Social Security).

the record of a decision of the Patents Appeal Tribunal includes the rival patent specifications and the decision of the superintending examiner.[76] But even on that assumption the alleged error was held to be not apparent on the record, so that certiorari was refused. This case is the leading example of error (if any) not shown by the record and therefore not remediable. It does however indicate that the House of Lords approves of the jurisdiction which the *Northumberland* case brought back to life. The Court of Appeal has also held that the record in a patent case includes the application and specification.[77]

In habeas corpus cases, where the court is naturally inclined to be generous, the record appears to include depositions of evidence which were before the tribunal which ordered the detention of the prisoner.[78]

The record extends to include any document referred to in the primary documents. This was established in a case where a colliery pick-sharpener, who already had one injured eye, suffered an injury to the other eye and claimed disablement benefit. The tribunal assessed him at a low rate of benefit, failing to take due account of the regulations governing injury to 'paired organs'[79] which entitled him to a higher assessment due to the previous injury. This mistake did not appear on the face of the award, which said nothing about the other eye; but it quoted a specialist's report which, when produced in full, gave the complete facts and made it apparent that the regulations had been ignored or misconstrued. The inadequate award was therefore quashed.[80]

It seems clear that mere evidence is not part of the record, unless the tribunal chooses to make it so.[81] Quashing for want of evidence is discussed in the next section.

It is now settled that mere spoken words can be part of the record, contradictory though this might seem. In one case[82] the court quashed an oral decision of magistrates who had imposed a fine for a continuing

---

[76] *Baldwin & Francis Ltd.* v. *Patents Appeal Tribunal* [1959] AC 663. Lord Denning held that the error did appear on the record but that certiorari should be withheld in discretion because other remedies were more suitable. Contrast *R.* v. *Patents Appeal Tribunal ex p. Geigy SA* [1963] 2 QB 728.

[77] *R.* v. *Patents Appeal Tribunal ex p. Swift & Co.* (above).

[78] See below, p. 621.

[79] The obscurity of these regulations has baffled the courts as well as tribunals: see *R.* v. *Industrial Injuries Commissioner ex p. Cable* [1968] 1 QB 729.

[80] *R.* v. *Medical Appeal Tribunal ex p. Gilmore* [1957] 1 QB 574. Contrast the stricter rule in arbitration proceedings, where a mere reference does not suffice: *Giacomo Costa Fu Andrea* v. *British Italian Trading Co. Ltd.* [1963] 1 QB 201.

[81] *Re Allen & Matthews' Arbitration* [1971] 2 QB 518.

[82] *R.* v. *Chertsey Justices, ex p. Franks* [1961] 2 QB 152, criticised in (1961) 77 LQR 157 (R. E. Megarry), 322 (D. M. Gordon). Contrast *R.* v. *Newington Licensing Justices* [1948] 1 KB 681 at 686: 'certiorari does not lie to quash an oral statement'.

offence at a flat rate per day for a period of over fourteen months, their jurisdiction being limited to offences committed within the last six months. Since the magistrates plainly exceeded their jurisdiction, the case looked like a straightforward example of ultra vires. But it has since been treated as a case of error on the face and several other decisions have shown that the court's practice is to quash for mistakes of law appearing in oral judgments of statements of reasons.[83] A transcript of an oral statement is thus acceptable as part of the record. This development, admittedly a departure from earlier decisions, is designed to amplify the system of judicial review and to avoid formalism. The policy of the judges also accords with that of Parliament. Since 1958 statutory tribunals have been compellable to give reasons for their decisions upon request; the reasons may be written or oral, and in either case they are to be taken 'to be incorporated in the record'.[84] The obvious intention of this provision is that mistakes of law in oral reasons should be reviewable in the case of tribunals, and it would make no sense for the courts to hold otherwise in other cases.

Reasons and speaking orders

At common law there was no need for the record in a civil case to set out the tribunal's reasoning. The reasoning was the part of the proceedings which was most likely to contain substantial error, but originally the law was concerned more with form than with substance. Yet a tribunal was always at liberty to incorporate its reasoning in its record, and if it did so the court would review it. There would then be a 'speaking order', carrying its reasons on its face.[85] The tribunal could not be compelled to 'speak' in this way, so that an unspeaking order, if within jurisdiction, could not be quashed.[86] But during the eighteenth century it became the practice that magistrates would state a case for the opinion of the Court of King's Bench on any question which they thought to be of difficulty.[87] The mechanism for removing the matter to the King's Bench was certiorari; and provided that that remedy had not been taken away by statute, the practice enabled

---

[83] See *R. v. Knightsbridge Crown Court ex p. International Sporting Club Ltd.* [1982] QB 304, citing and explaining other cases concerned with courts of law and the Divisional Court's practice.

[84] Tribunals and Inquiries Act 1971, s. 12(5), replacing the Act of 1958, s. 12(3).

[85] *Walsall Overseers* v. *L. & N.W. Rly Co.* (1878) 4 App. Cas. 30 at 40; *R. v. Nat Bell Liquors Ltd.* [1922] 2 AC at 155; *R. v. Northumberland Compensation Appeal Tribunal ex p. Shaw* [1952] 1 KB 338.

[86] *R. v. Oulton (Inhabitants)* (1735) Cas. t. Hard. 169; *R. v. Preston-on-the-Hill (Inhabitants)* (1736) Burr. Set. Cas. 77; the *Walsall* and *Nat Bell* cases (preceding note).

[87] *R. v. Chantrell* (1875) LR 10 QB 587 at 589. This replaced the older practice of reserving questions for the opinion of the judge of assize: *R. v. Chantrell*; the *Walsall* case (above).

the courts to exercise a wide reviewing power over the inferior tribunal's reasoning. After the Summary Jurisdiction Act 1857 introduced a statutory appeal by way of case stated from magistrates, this use of certiorari naturally declined. There was also a practice whereby the parties could by agreement refer a question to the court for consideration on certiorari.[88]

When quashing for error on the face was reintroduced in 1951, it found a ready application in the wide field of modern statutory tribunals from which Parliament had provided no appeal. Some of them gave reasons for their decisions, but many did not. Not only was there no legal means of procuring speaking orders:[89] there was some fear that the High Court's revived powers might induce tribunals to be more reticent than before. The defect was remedied by the Tribunals and Inquiries Act 1958 which, as explained elsewhere,[90] introduced a legal right to reasoned decisions, so that speaking orders could be obtained on demand. It was significant that, as mentioned already, it provided that reasons given under the Act should be treated as incorporated in the record. This made it clear that Parliament approved the reassertion of the High Court's powers. The Act and the traditional jurisdiction over the record then combined to bring tribunals' reasons within the scope of judicial review. This was a development of great importance. But the court still has no general power to compel the statement of reasons in cases where the Act does not apply.

Where it can be seen from the record that the reasons given are insufficient to satisfy the requirements of the Act, this in itself is error on the face of the record for which the court can quash.[91] The tribunal will then have to give a further decision embodying adequate reasons.

A tribunal whose decision is under attack may itself supply further explanation of it by affidavit in defending certiorari proceedings. Its affidavit can then be treated as part of the record, and if it discloses error the decision will be quashed.[92]

What errors are controllable

In the *Northumberland* case and all the later cases where orders have been quashed for mere error on the face, the error has been one of law. And it has

[88] R. v. *Northumberland Compensation Appeal Tribunal ex p. Shaw* [1952] 1 KB 338 at 353 (Denning LJ). But the modern instances cited do not show the survival of this practice, being either cases of refusal of jurisdiction (by refusing to hear evidence) or of excess of jurisdiction (by a breach of natural justice). A no-certiorari clause would bar such proceedings: R. v. *Chantrell* (above).

[89] Except where an Act or regulations so required: see R. v. *Medical Appeal Tribunal ex p. Gilmore*, above, p. 313.

[90] Below, p. 934.

[91] Re *Poyser & Mills Arbitration* [1964] 2 QB 467.

[92] R. v. *Southampton Justices ex p. Green* [1976] QB 11 at 22 (Browne LJ).

several times been laid down that only error in law is so controllable.[93] But the ambit of error of law is wide. It includes, for example, procedural mistakes, as where a tribunal wrongly refused an adjournment which was necessary in order to allow the applicant to produce relevant evidence.[94] It may be presumed that 'law' here carries the same wide meaning as it does for the purpose of defining the right of appeal on the point of law, explained elsewhere.[95] Accordingly it will include wrong inferences drawn from the facts of the case for the purpose of statutory definitions as well as any form of statutory misinterpretation. Even misinterpretation of non-statutory rules may be treated as error of 'law'. This anomaly is discussed later.[96]

The error of law must be fundamental to the decision and a cause of injustice. If the decision would have been the same without it, it will not be quashed.[97]

Errors of fact can be reached to this extent, that the court will quash where the finding of fact is manifestly based on no evidence, i.e. no evidence on which a reasonable tribunal could act.[98] This is an application of the settled rule that to find facts unsupported by evidence is to err in law.[99] But it offers little scope for the court, since evidence is not part of the record unless so incorporated by the tribunal of its own volition. A different basis for 'no evidence' cases has therefore been sought elsewhere.[1] In habeas corpus cases, it must be remembered, the court may assume a wider power to treat evidence as part of the record.[2]

Perhaps also the door should be left open for purely factual error which may appear in an order, either because it contradicts itself on some finding of fact or because it finds some fact contrary to common knowledge of which judicial notice can be taken. A decision which on its face was obviously unsatisfactory for some such reason might well be quashed, since it is no less objectionable on its face than if vitiated by error of law. The true

[93] *Anisminic Ltd.* v. *Foreign Compensation Commission* [1968] 2 QB 862 at 892 (Diplock LJ): *R.* v. *Criminal Injuries Compensation Board ex p. Staten* [1972] 1 WLR 569 (error of fact: certiorari refused); *Gould* v. *Wily* [1960] NZLR 960.

[94] *R.* v. *Medical Appeal Tribunal ex p. Carrarini* (1966) 1 WLR 883.

[95] Below, p. 938.

[96] Below, p. 640.

[97] *R.* v. *Knightsbridge Crown Court ex p. Marcrest Properties Ltd.* [1983] 1 WLR 300, holding that if, which was not decided, any error of law renders the decision ultra vires, the court would refuse certiorari in its discretion; *R.* v. *Chief Registrar of Friendly Societies ex p. New Cross Building Society* [1984] QB 227 at 260.

[98] *R.* v. *Roberts* [1908] 1 KB 407 at 423 (the decision that the court could in any case quash for error of fact depended on an exceptional statutory jurisdiction).

[99] See below, p. 320.

[1] Below, p. 320.

[2] Above, p. 310.

principle may be that the court can quash any decision which is clearly bad on its face, and that errors of fact are normally unreviewable because they do not so appear.

Allowable margin of error

Where the error is not really clear or is insignificant the court may give the tribunal the benefit of the doubt: as Lord Tucker once said, 'the inscrutable face of the sphinx' and 'the ambiguous voice of the oracle' may be much the same for this purpose.[3] In any case, certiorari is always a discretionary remedy. Lord Denning MR has declined to intervene in the absence of 'a real error of law', meaning something more than a borderline question.[4] The Industrial Injuries Commissioner had disallowed a claim to injury benefit by a workman who suffered an accident in a factory while waiting to use a smoking booth five minutes after the end of the ten-minute break allowed for that purpose; and the question was whether he was then 'in the course of his employment'. Lord Denning said:

This is one of those questions which, as it seems to me, the legislature had decided should not be brought up to the courts of law for decision, but should be entrusted to the specialised statutory authorities for determination. It may occasionally be of use, if there is a real error of law, for a case to be brought before this court, but not in such a case as this. No error of law is shown here.

This suggests that the court may show restraint where the question is one particularly within the province of the tribunal. Parliament had undoubtedly intended originally that these insurance questions should not come before the courts of law at all. The same was true of supplementary benefit appeal tribunals, the decisions of which were to be 'conclusive for all purposes'.[5] The Court of Appeal has in their case refused to grant certiorari even where an error of law was shown, since the tribunal's decision represented the better way of administering the Act.[6] Lord Denning MR said:

It is plain that Parliament intended that the Supplementary Benefit Act 1966

---

[3] *Baldwin & Francis Ltd.* v. *Patents Appeal Tribunal* [1959] AC 663 at 687.

[4] *R.* v. *Industrial Injuries Commissioner ex p. Amalgamated Engineering Union (No. 2)* [1966] 2 QB 31. Contrast *R.* v. *National Insurance Commissioner ex p. Michael* [1977] 1 WLR 109. But the court will be slow to interfere with decisions of national insurance commissioners, particularly if long accepted and acted upon: *R.* v. *National Insurance Commissioner ex p. Stratton* [1979] QB 361.

[5] As to this see below, p. 720.

[6] *R.* v. *Preston Supplementary Benefits Appeal Tribunal ex p. Moore* [1975] 1 WLR 624 (refusal of benefit to four students living together and claiming to be householders, perhaps correctly in law). See also *R.* v. *Barnsley Supplementary Benefits Appeal Tribunal ex p. Atkinson* [1976] 1 WLR 1047.

should be administered with as little technicality as possible. It should not become a happy hunting ground for lawyers. The courts should hesitate long before interfering by certiorari with the decisions of the appeal tribunals. . . . The courts should not enter into a meticulous discussion of the meaning of this or that word in the Act. They should leave the tribunals to interpret the Act in a broad reasonable way, according to the spirit and not to the letter.

He added that the courts should interfere only when the decision of the tribunal is unreasonable, in the sense that no tribunal acquainted with the ordinary use of language could reasonably reach that decision. The court should be ready to lay down broad guidelines, to promote uniformity of decision, but should refuse to be used as a court of appeal.

This tolerant policy in reviewing for an error on the face of the record may suitably be applied to many tribunals, allowing them reasonable latitude of interpretation in areas where they themselves are the specialists. A similar criterion is used for judicial review in the United States.[7]

Review of the record in wider context

In the light of later events, the rediscovery of the power of review for error on the face of the record can be seen as the first stage of the movement towards bringing decisions on questions of law back within the superintendence of the ordinary courts. In the social legislation of the late 1940s statutory tribunals were given an excessive degree of independence, and the lack of rights of appeal was strongly felt.[8] Eventually the Tribunals and Inquiries Act 1958 gave many new rights of appeal on questions of law,[9] thus reducing the need for applications to quash by certiorari—though the existence of a right of appeal does not mean that certiorari may not be granted if preferred.[10] The Act of 1958 also safeguarded the remedy by certiorari against earlier Acts which had taken it away.[11] And, as already noticed, it confirmed and extended the use of that remedy by granting a right to reasoned decisions which automatically became part of the record. This machinery enables virtually any error of law to be dragged forth into the light for judicial inspection and correction; and the notion that statutory tribunals can be final arbiters on matters of law has fallen far back from the high-water mark which it had previously attained.

---

[7] Schwartz and Wade, *Legal Control of Government*, 232.

[8] See e.g. *R. v. Northumberland Compensation Appeal Tribunal ex p. Shaw* [1952] 1 KB 338 at 346 (Singleton LJ); *R. v. Medical Appeal Tribunal ex p. Gilmore* [1957] 1 QB 574 at 587 (Romer LJ).

[9] Below, p. 917.

[10] Below, p. 712.

[11] Below, p. 729.

The continuing utility of 'face of the record' review is well shown by the succession of cases on national insurance and industrial injuries (later merged into the scheme of social security). In these matters the Act of 1958 provided no appeal to the courts,[12] since the system contained its own appeal tribunals and they were of high quality. The scheme of the original legislation of 1946–8 was undoubtedly that disputes over claims to benefit should be altogether banished from the ordinary courts. Since the courts were then believed to have no jurisdiction over mere error, no special legislative provision seemed necessary. But the whole situation was changed by the *Northumberland* decision, just at the time when it was felt that the courts had been too rigorously excluded. The tribunals themselves welcomed this development, which gave them the guidance of the courts of law on some of the difficult legal questions with which the legislation abounded. Even though those questions occasionally prove almost too difficult for the House of Lords,[13] there can be little doubt that this limited measure of judicial supervision is beneficial. The courts have intervened in a stream of cases, and their arm has proved long enough to reach even bodies constituted administratively and devoid of statutory power.[14]

FINDINGS, EVIDENCE AND JURISDICTION

Findings of fact. 'No evidence'

Findings of fact are the domain where a deciding authority or tribunal can fairly expect to be master in its own house. Provided only that the facts are not collateral or jurisdictional, the findings will in general be exempt from review by the courts, which will in any case respect the decision of the body that saw and heard the witnesses or took evidence directly. Just as the courts look jealously on decisions by other bodies on matters of law, so they look indulgently on their decisions on matters of fact.

But the limit of this indulgence is reached where findings are based on no satisfactory evidence at all. It is one thing to weigh conflicting evidence which might justify a conclusion either way. It is another thing altogether to make insupportable findings. This is an abuse of power and may cause grave injustice. At this point, therefore, the court is disposed to intervene. Lately there have been clear indications that the court was seeking a basis for such a jurisdiction, and it has been possible to predict that this would be the next important development.

---

[12] A right of appeal has since been given: below, p. 908.
[13] See *R. v. National Insurance Commissioner ex p. Hudson* [1972] AC 944, above, p. 221.
[14] See below, p. 640.

'No evidence' does not mean only a total dearth of evidence. It extends to any case where the evidence, taken as a whole, is not reasonably capable of supporting the finding;[15] or where, in other words, no tribunal could reasonably reach that conclusion on that evidence.[16] This 'no evidence' principle clearly has something in common with the principle that perverse or unreasonable action is unauthorised and ultra vires.[17] It also has some affinity with the substantial evidence rule of American law, which requires that findings be supported by substantial evidence on the record as a whole.[18] In the United States this rule has virtually eliminated the need to inquire whether facts are jurisdictional, since the same test is applied whether they are so or not. English law allows them to be inquired into fully if jurisdictional, but not at all if not—or so at least the law was previously. If English law, as now seems likely, develops a general 'no evidence' rule for judicial review, alongside the rule already existing for appeal, this will only be following the American lead.[19]

The basis of review for 'no evidence'

Desirable as it may be to invalidate decisions based upon insupportable findings, there has been difficulty in fitting such a jurisdiction into the regular categories of judicial review. There is, indeed, the well established rule that to find facts on no evidence is to err in law. This rule is constantly applied in cases of appeal, where statute gives a right of appeal on a point of law only, so that this limited right of appeal is made to extend to unjustifiable findings of fact.[20] Judges are so familiar with it in that context that they may instinctively resort to it in cases of review. But review must be based either on jurisdictional error or error on the face of the record. The latter doctrine will clearly be of little use, since it will be only rarely that the record will show on what evidence the findings of fact are based. This was not so formerly in the case of the magistrates' decisions before the Summary Jurisdiction Act 1848, as has been seen; but modern procedure has largely eliminated the possibility.[21]

---

[15] *Allinson* v. *General Medical Council* [1894] 1 QB 750 at 760, 763; *Lee* v. *Showmen's Guild of Great Britain* [1952] 2 QB 329 at 345.

[16] *R.* v. *Roberts* [1908] 1 KB 407 at 423.

[17] Below, p. 407.

[18] Administrative Procedure Act (USA, 1946), s. 10(*e*); *Universal Camera Corporation* v. *National Labor Relations Board*, 340 US 474 (1951); Schwartz and Wade, *Legal Control of Government*, 228. American administrative procedure facilitates this control by providing a full record of evidence.

[19] For the position in Canada see (1972) 37 Sask LR 48 (D. W. Elliott).

[20] See e.g. *Hemns* v. *Wheeler* [1948] 2 KB 61 at 65; below, p. 938.

[21] Above, p. 305.

The question then must be whether a 'no evidence' rule can be forced into the mould of ultra vires. To do this would hardly be to strain it beyond the limits of the doctrine of reasonableness, as applied in so many cases. But judges of high authority have long held that this was the point where intervention must cease. The locus classicus is the celebrated opinion given by Lord Sumner in a Privy Council case from Canada, where a firm had been convicted before a magistrate for selling liquor contrary to the local Liquor Act. The only evidence of the fact of sale was that of an *agent provocateur* of the police, which was the subject of a number of objections. Could the inferior court's decision be quashed as ultra vires (as opposed to being challenged on appeal) because they had no proper evidence before them? In rejecting the contention that 'want of evidence on which to convict is the same as want of jurisdiction to take evidence at all', Lord Sumner said:[22]

This, clearly, is erroneous. A justice who convicts without evidence is doing something which he ought not to do, but he is doing it as a judge, and if his jurisdiction to entertain the charge is not open to impeachment, his subsequent error, however grave, is a wrong exercise of a jurisdiction which he has, and not a usurpation of a jurisdiction which he has not. . . . To say that there is no jurisdiction to convict without evidence is the same thing as saying that there is jurisdiction if the decision is right, and none if it is wrong. . . .

The principle was the same for administrative authorities and tribunals and was often stated by Lord Goddard CJ, both in approving a favourite quotation[23] about error within jurisdiction and also when he said:[24]

If it is acting within its jurisdiction, it is now settled law that absence of evidence does not affect the jurisdiction of the tribunal to try the case, nor does a misdirection by the tribunal to itself in considering the evidence nor what might be held on appeal to be a wrong decision in point of law.

To these authorities can be added statements by Lord Reid and Lord Diplock that lack of evidence raises no question of jurisdiction.[25] And there is no dearth of similar judicial rulings.[26]

But there is a current of opinions to the contrary which has recently been

---

[22] *R.* v. *Nat Bell Liquors Ltd.* [1922] AC 128 at 151, described by Lord Denning MR as the darkest moment of the 'black-out of any development of administrative law': *O'Reilly* v. *Mackman* [1983] 2 AC 237 at 253.

[23] From Halsbury's Laws of England, 3rd ed., vol. 11, p. 62.

[24] *R.* v. *Ludlow* [1947] KB 634.

[25] *R.* v. *Governor of Brixton Prison ex p. Armah* [1968] AC 192 at 234; *R.* v. *Governor of Pentonville Prison ex p. Sotiriadis* [1975] AC 1 at 30.

[26] A notable instance is *R.* v. *Mahony* [1910] 2 IR 695, where the older law is very fully discussed by Gibson J.

gathering force. Lord Atkinson said in one case that 'an order made without any evidence to support it is in truth, in my view, made without jurisdiction'.[27]

Even Lord Sumner's classic judgment appears to proceed partly on the footing that to make any error of law is to exceed jurisdiction,[28] inconsistent as this is with the extract quoted above. In criminal cases prior to the Summary Jurisdiction Act 1848 the courts were fully accustomed to quashing magistrates' convictions on account of 'no evidence', since in those days the evidence was incorporated in the record and consequently appeared on its face.[29] When this control went into abeyance after the Act, in the manner explained by Lord Sumner,[30] judges would naturally turn to the ultra vires doctrine as a substitute.[31] This has been done in Canada, where it has been held that 'the legislative grant of power is upon the condition that the statutory tribunal will only proceed where it has evidence to go on', the statutory condition being implied in just the same way as in the case of natural justice, reasonableness and other familiar conditions.[32] Furthermore, a 'no evidence' doctrine has become established in habeas corpus cases, where in principle the court should intervene on grounds of jurisdiction only.[33] Sometimes judges would generalise as if the doctrine was of universal application.[34] Or they might hold that decisions unsupported by evidence were capricious or unreasonable,[35] or given upon

[27] *Folkestone Cpn.* v. *Brockman* [1914] AC 338 at 367.
[28] See above, p. 308, n. 47.
[29] See *R.* v. *Mahony*, above, at pp. 703, 710, 716 (Palles CB dissenting at pp. 721–2).
[30] Above, p. 306.
[31] See *Bailey's Case* (1854) 3 E & B 607; *Allinson* v. *General Medical Council* [1894] 1 QB 750 at 760; *R.* v. *Mahony* [1910] 2 IR 695 at 722 (Palles CB, dissenting); *Lee* v. *Showmen's Guild* [1952] 2 QB 329 at 340, 345 (but there the power was contractual, not statutory).
[32] *Westburne Industrial Enterprises Ltd.* v. *Labour Relations Board* [1973] 6 WWR 451 affirmed [1974] 1 WWR 572. The judgment of Berger J is particularly clear. For other Canadian authorities see Reid, *Administrative Law and Practice*, 337; (1972) 37 Sask. LR 48 (D. W. Elliott).
[33] For these see below, p. 622.
[34] As in *R.* v. *Board of Control ex p. Rutty* [1956] 2 QB 109 at 124; *R.* v. *Birmingham Compensation Appeal Tribunal* [1952] 2 All ER. 100 (error of statutory interpretation represented as 'no evidence'); *Ashbridge Investments Ltd.* v. *Minister of Housing and Local Government* [1965] 1 WLR 1320 at 1327–8 (representing the case of *White and Collins v. Minister of Health*, discussed above, p. 284, as one of 'no evidence', whereas it was expressly decided on the ground of excess of jurisdiction); *R.* v. *Governor of Brixton Prison ex p. Armah* [1968] AC 192 at 257 (wide statement by Lord Upjohn); *R.* v. *Governor of Brixton Prison ex p. Ahsan* [1969] 2 QB 222.
[35] As suggested in *Osgood* v. *Nelson* (1872) LR 5 HL 636; and see *Folkestone Cpn.* v. *Brockman* [1914] AC 338 at 355; *Minister of National Revenue* v. *Wrights' Canadian Ropes Ltd.* [1947] AC 109; *Argosy Co Ltd.* v. *IRC* [1971] 1 WLR 514.

wrong legal grounds,[36] and so ultra vires for other reasons. The House of Lords has held that an immigration officer, who has power to refuse leave to enter the country if satisfied of certain facts, is on 'normal principles' not at liberty to refuse it if there is no evidence to support his decision.[37] The House has similarly quashed a local authority's determination that an immigrant from Bangladesh was 'intentionally homeless' when there was no evidence that the home which he was supposed to have left was ever available to him.[38] The Court of Appeal has quashed a decision of the Secretary of State for Transport when his decision letter stated that he was not satisfied on a number of matters without showing any basis of evidence for his conclusions.[39] In none of these cases was the legal basis of a 'no evidence' rule discussed: it was simply assumed to exist.

The principles of natural justice may also supply the basis of this rule, according to a series of opinions of Lord Diplock. In the first of these he indicated that the principles of natural justice require that a tribunal's decisions be based on some evidence of probative value.[40] Speaking in two cases for the Privy Council he held that a minister dealing with an application for registration of citizenship must act on 'evidential material of probative value' if his decision is to be valid,[41] and that the same rule applied, as a matter of natural justice, to a judge acting as a statutory royal commissioner.[42] The attraction of this theory is that it finds a suitable home for the rule in the expanding field of natural justice.[43]

The Housing Act cases

Clear indications that the courts are disposed to adopt a 'no evidence' rule are in a series of decisions under the Housing Acts. These may be subject to reservations, partly because they concern statutory rather than common law powers of review and partly because none of them mentions the weighty adverse authority of Lord Sumner, Lord Goddard, and Lord Reid. Nevertheless they probably mark a turning point. All were decided

---

[36] Examples are R. v. Flintshire CC Licensing Committee [1957] 1 QB 350; R. v. Australian Stevedoring Industry Board ex p. Melbourne Stevedoring Co. (1953) 88 CLR 100 at 119–20.

[37] R. v. Home Secretary ex p. Zamir [1980] AC 930.

[38] R. v. Hillingdon LBC ex p. Islam [1983] 1 AC 688.

[39] R. v. Secretary of State for Transport ex p. Cumbria CC [1983] RTR 129.

[40] R. v. Deputy Industrial Injuries Commissioner ex p. Moore [1965] 1 QB 456. See also Burwoods (Caterers) Ltd. v. SS for Environment [1972] Est. Gaz. Dig. 1007.

[41] A.-G. v. Ryan [1980] AC 718. See also Ong Ah Chuan v. Public Prosecutor [1981] AC 648 at 671.

[42] Mahon v. Air New Zealand Ltd. [1984] AC 808, where this was a principal ground of decision.

[43] See below, p. 546.

under the provision of the Housing Act which prohibits judicial review except on the ground that the order 'is not within the powers of this Act or that any requirement of this Act has not been complied with'. For the purposes of the present argument it must be assumed that this formula has the same meaning as the doctrine of ultra vires. Whether that assumption is right is discussed elsewhere in this work.[44]

In the first case, where the local authority had power to make a clearance order if they were satisfied that the houses were unfit for human habitation, the judge reserved the question whether the order would be quashed if there was before the local authority no material upon which they could, as reasonable people, be satisfied.[45] Next, in a case where the power was to purchase land adjoining a clearance area where that was reasonably necessary for the scheme, the same judge held that if the court found that there was no material on which the minister could have found that it was reasonably necessary, the court would not hesitate to quash the minister's order.[46] In 1965 the Court of Appeal made an important pronouncement in a case where the minister was empowered to modify the order if he was of opinion that any land ought not to have been included. Lord Denning MR said:[47]

Under this section it seems to me that the court can interfere with the Minister's decision if he has acted on no evidence; or if he has come to a decision to which on the evidence he could not reasonably come; or if he has given a wrong interpretation to the words of the statute; or if he has taken into consideration matters which he ought not to have taken into account, or vice versa; or has otherwise gone wrong in law. It is identical with the position when the court has power to interfere with the decision of a lower tribunal which has erred in point of law.

No mention was made of the authorities adverse to a 'no evidence' rule, or

---

[44] Below, p. 739.
[45] *Re Bowman* [1932] 2 KB 621. But the same judge (Swift J) expressly held that the minister's confirmation order could not be attacked on this ground: *Re Falmouth Clearance Order* [1937] 3 All ER 308. See also *Re London County Council (Riley Street, Chelsea) Order* [1938] 2 All ER 484; *Goddard* v. *Minister of Housing and Local Government* [1958] 1 WLR 1151.
[46] *Sheffield Burgesses* v. *Minister of Health* (1935) 52 TLR 171, [1935] All ER Rep. 703.
[47] *Ashbridge Investments Ltd.* v. *Minister of Housing and Local Government* [1965] 1 WLR. 1320 at 1326 (unreserved judgment). See also *Gordondale Investments Ltd.* v. *Secretary of State for the Environment* (1971) 70 LGR 158; *British Dredging (Services) Ltd.* v. *Secretary of State for Wales* [1975] 1 WLR 687; *R.* v. *Secretary of State for the Environment ex p. Ostler* [1977] QB 122 at 123; and also *Howard* v. *Minister of Housing and Local Government* (1967) 65 LGR 257 at 262; *Re Watch House, Boswinger* (1976) 66 LGR 6 at 17; *A. B. Motor Co. of Hull Ltd.* v. *Minister of Housing and Local Government* (1969) 67 LGR 689; *General Electric Co Ltd.* v. *Price Commission* [1975] ICR 1, where Lord Denning also summarises principles of judicial review.

of the rule that error of law must, if not jurisdictional, appear on the face of the record. The statement has, however, been frequently applied since,[48] as if it were an epitome of the principles of judicial review generally. In particular the Court of Appeal applied it in the first case in which an order of the minister was quashed for 'no evidence'. In all the previous cases it had been found that sufficient evidence had existed. In the *Coleen Properties* case[49] it was found that no evidence existed. Here again the power was that of purchasing land adjoining a clearance area where that was reasonably necessary for the scheme. At a public inquiry no evidence had been called that the acquisition was reasonably necessary, and the inspector had recommended against it; but the minister rejected the inspector's advice, on no additional evidence of any kind, and included the property, which was in first-class condition, in the compulsory purchase order. Consequently this part of it was quashed.

These decisions are difficult to assess since, as has happened so often in administrative law, the courts referred only to cases decided under the Act in question and not to the general principles previously established under other Acts. One possible view of them is that they are merely cases of ordinary ultra vires. Where there is power to take adjacent land only if this is reasonably necessary, this is a condition of the validity of the order: if the necessity does not, on the evidence, appear to the court, the order is ultra vires. This is the ordinary doctrine of jurisdictional fact, and it seems clearly to have operated in the *Coleen Properties* case.[50] The court's position may be merely this: that where the matter is peculiarly within the province of the minister, as is the question whether a clearance scheme is practicable without acquiring adjacent land, the minister's decision will not be questioned, provided only that it is based on some relevant evidence. No difference is taken on the ground of subjective wording, so that the position is apparently the same whether the requirement of the Act is subjective ('if the local authority is satisfied', 'if the Minister is of opinion') or objective ('land the acquisition of which is reasonably necessary').[51] The attraction of

[48] See preceding note.
[49] *Coleen Properties Ltd.* v. *Minister of Housing and Local Government* [1971] 1 WLR 433. See also *Sabey (H.) & Co. Ltd.* v. *Secretary of State for the Environment* [1978] 1 All ER 586. In *R.* v. *Secretary of State for the Environment ex p. Powis* [1981] 1 WLR 584 the Court of Appeal held that the principle of the *Coleen* case did not apply to a finding of the Secretary of State in a planning case where the Act allowed written representations only and not a public hearing, since he 'must assess the submissions and reach his conclusion as best he can on the material put before him.' Yet unsupported findings would seem to be no less objectionable in that situation. The report also indicates (at 595A, B) that there was in fact evidence.
[50] See at pp. 439C (Sachs LJ), 442B (Buckley LJ).
[51] In the latter case the interpretation could be criticised as a departure from the principle of objectivity. There is a clear parallel with the doctrine adopted in immigration cases, in which the requirement of evidence is also stressed: see below, p. 460.

this explanation is that it avoids any conflict between the Housing Act cases and the classic authorities.

Is the 'no evidence' rule now established?

Despite reservations about the *Coleen Properties* case, and despite the lack of any decision reviewing the authorities for and against a 'no evidence' rule, it seems clear that this ground of judicial review ought now to be regarded as established on a general basis. There have been so many sporadic references to it on this assumption, and it conforms so well to other developments in administrative law, that one can only assume that the older authorities to the contrary, impressive though they are, may now be consigned to the limbo of history. 'No evidence' seems destined to take its place as yet a further branch of the principle of ultra vires, so that Acts giving powers of determination will be taken to imply that the determination must be based upon some acceptable evidence. If it is not, it will be treated as 'arbitrary, capricious and obviously unauthorised'.[52]

The time is ripe for this development as part of the active judicial policy of preventing abuse of discretionary power. To find facts without evidence is itself an abuse of power and a source of injustice, and it ought to be within the scope of judicial review. This is recognised in other jurisdictions where the grounds of review have been codified by statute. In Australia the Administrative Decisions (Judicial Review) Act 1977 expressly authorises review on the ground that there was 'no evidence or other material' to justify the decision where some particular matter has to be established,[53] and a somewhat analogous provision has been enacted in Canada.[54]

Wrongful rejection of evidence

If a tribunal wrongly refuses to receive evidence on the ground that it is irrelevant or inadmissible, this error does not go to jurisdiction and the court cannot intervene unless the error appears on the face of the record.[55] But there will be a jurisdictional error if the reason for rejecting the evidence is a mistaken belief by the tribunal that it has no business to

---

[52] So described in the USA by the Attorney General's Committee on Administrative Procedure, Report p. 88 (1941).

[53] ss. 5, 6. See similarly the Administrative Justice Act 1980 of Barbados, s. 4.

[54] Federal Court Act 1971, s. 28(1). See also Law Reform Commission of Canada, Report No. 14 (1980), recommendation 4. 3.

[55] Subject to the possible effect of the *Racal* case (above, p. 300) and to the possibility that self-misdirection as to law may be equivalent to declining jurisdiction: *R. v. Wells Street Magistrate ex p. Westminster CC* [1986] 1 WLR 1046.

investigate the question at all. This was the case where a magistrate refused to hear evidence, in defence to a charge of failing to pay the apportioned cost of paving a street, to the effect that the apportionment by the board of works included improper items.[56] He was thus improperly refusing to allow jurisdictional facts to be disputed. Going somewhat further, the court quashed the refusal of an inspector, conducting an inquiry into a compulsory purchase order, to hear relevant evidence relating to the owner's conduct as landlord;[57] the court emphasised that the inspector's error was fundamental to the conduct and utility of the inquiry as distinct from a mere error of judgment. In Ontario a labour board's order was quashed where it had refused to receive evidence about resignations from a trade union where the question was whether a majority of employees were members in good standing.[58] In such cases the tribunal can be ordered to determine the question properly.[59]

As can be seen, the distinction between declining jurisdiction and merely refusing to admit certain evidence is 'sometimes rather nice'.[60] But in principle it is a clear-cut matter. It has nothing to do with the legal rules as to admissibility of evidence, which in general do not apply to statutory tribunals.[61] The question is simply whether the tribunal has failed in its duty to inquire fully into the case before it.

Discovery of fresh evidence

Where some tribunal or authority has power to decide questions of fact, and no power to reopen its own decisions,[62] its decision cannot be reviewed by the High Court merely on the ground that fresh evidence, which might alter the decision, has since been discovered. This is because the decision is within jurisdiction and there is no basis on which the court can intervene. The remedy of certiorari will therefore not lie in such a case.[63] But, for the same reason, there is an important exception: if the fresh evidence relates to a fact which goes to jurisdiction, so that it may be possible to show subsequently that the decision was without jurisdiction and void, this evidence may be used in later proceedings to invalidate the decision, as

[56] R. v. Marsham [1891] 1 QB 371.
[57] R. v. Secretary of State for the Environment ex p. Kensington and Chelsea RBC [1987] The Times, 30 January.
[58] Toronto Newspaper Guild v. Globe Printing Co. [1953] 3 DLR 561.
[59] As in R. v. Marsham (above) (mandamus).
[60] R v. Marsham (above) at p. 378 (Lord Esher MR).
[61] See below, p. 925.
[62] See above, p. 254.
[63] R. v. West Sussex Quarter Sessions ex p. Johnson Trust Ltd. [1974] QB 24 (Lord Denning MR dissenting); and see R. v. Home Secretary ex p. Momin Ali [1984] 1 WLR 663 (above, p. 274).

explained in the context of res judicata.[64] This is a necessary consequence of the doctrine of jurisdictional fact.[65]

Where it is later discovered that an order was outside jurisdiction, the court has inherent power to quash consequential orders made on the footing that the original order was valid, even though the later orders, taken by themselves, were within jurisdiction.[66]

Error of material fact

Recent cases contain suggestions of a further ground of judicial review, 'misunderstanding or ignorance of an established and relevant fact',[67] or acting 'upon an incorrect basis of fact'.[68] In a case where the Secretary of State had power to give directions if he was satisfied that the local education authority were acting unreasonably, Lord Wilberforce, in explaining that such powers were to some extent subject to judicial review, said:[69]

If a judgment requires, before it can be made, the existence of some facts, then, although the evaluation of those facts is for the Secretary of State alone, the court must inquire whether those facts exist, and have been taken into account, whether the judgment has been upon a proper self-direction as to those facts, whether the judgment has not been made upon other facts which ought not to have been taken into account. If those requirements are not met, then the exercise of judgment, however bona fide it may be, becomes capable of challenge.

and he approved a remark by Lord Denning MR in another case that the court could intervene if a minister 'plainly misdirects himself in fact or in law'.[70] Effect was given to these ideas when the court quashed a Secretary of State's decision owing to a mistake of fact in his inspector's report which said that a site had never been proposed as green belt when in fact it had been;[71] and when the Court of Appeal held that it could quash a local

[64] See above, p. 274, and *R. v. Pugh (Judge)* [1951] 2 KB 623; *R. v. Secretary of State for the Environment ex p. Powis* [1981] 1 WLR 584. Fraud or perjury by a party may also be proved by fresh evidence; ibid.

[65] See above, p. 280.

[66] *R. v. Middleton, Bromley and Bexley Justices ex p. Collins* [1970] 1 QB 216 (pleas of guilty on mistaken assumption that earlier conviction was valid: later convictions quashed).

[67] *Secretary of State for Education and Science v. Tameside MBC* [1977] AC 1014 at 1030 (Scarman LJ, giving examples).

[68] At 1047 (Lord Wilberforce). See similarly *Laker Airways Ltd. v. Department of Trade* [1977] QB 643 at 706 (Lord Denning MR).

[69] The *Tameside* case (above) at 1047.

[70] *Secretary of State for Employment v. ASLEF (No. 2)* [1972] 2 QB 455 at 493, repeated in *Smith v. Inner London Education Authority* [1978] 1 All ER 411.

[71] *Hollis v. Secretary of State for the Environment* (1982) 47 P & CR 351. The suggestion (at 360) that the Secretary of State must have been in possession of the true facts does not seem to be relevant. For a restrictive interpretation of Lord Wilberforce's words see *R. v. London Residuary Body ex p. Inner London Education Authority* [1987] The Times, 24 July.

authority's decision which was 'flawed by an error of fact' as to the content of a judgment of the House of Lords.[72] Similarly in New Zealand it was held that a minister's decision was invalid for failure to take into account the true facts, a medical referee having misled him by an inadequate report.[73]

This ground of review has long been familiar in French law[74] and it has been adopted by statute in Australia.[75] It is no less needed in this country, since decisions based upon wrong facts are a cause of injustice which the courts should be able to remedy. If a 'wrong factual basis' doctrine should become established, it would apparently be a new branch of the ultra vires doctrine, analogous to finding facts based upon no evidence or acting upon a misapprehension of law.[76] A minister, for example, would have to show not only that he decided reasonably on the material before him, but that he had the relevant material before him in correct form. This would tighten still further the court's control over administrative findings of fact and would consign much of the old law about jurisdictional fact, etc., to well-deserved oblivion. It would make judicial review into a comprehensive system, about to correct serious errors of all kinds.

SUMMARY OF RULES

Jurisdiction over fact and law: summary

At the end of a chapter which is top-heavy with obsolescent material it may be useful to summarise the position as shortly as possible. The overall picture is of an expanding system struggling to free itself from the trammels of the classical doctrines laid down in the past. In this transitional period it is not yet safe to say that the classical doctrines are obsolete and that the broad and simple principles of review, which clearly now commend themselves to the judiciary, will entirely supplant them. There are many pointers, but not enough categorical decisions of overriding authority. A summary can

[72] R. v. *Hertfordshire CC ex p. Cheung* [1986] The Times, 4 April and Lexis (refusal to reconsider students' grant applications quashed). See similarly R. v. *Home Secretary ex p. Awuku* [1987] The Times, 3 October (immigration officer's decision quashed for 'material errors of fact' and breach of natural justice).

[73] *Daganayasi* v. *Minister of Immigration* [1980] 2 NZLR 130 (Cooke J., Richardson J preferring to express no opinion).

[74] CE 20 janv. 1922, *Trépont*, established 'fait matériellement inexact' as a ground of review.

[75] Administrative Decisions (Judicial Review) Act 1977 (Cth) s. 5(3)(b), allowing judicial review where 'the person who made the decision based the decision on the existence of a particular fact, and that fact did not exist'; similarly s. 6(3)(b).

[76] See above, p. 326.

therefore only state the long-established rules together with the simpler and broader rules which are now emerging and which seem likely to supersede them, much for the benefit of the law. Together they are as follows.

Errors of fact

Established rule: The court will quash only if the error is jurisdictional.[77]

Emergent rule: The court will quash if a decisive fact was
(a) found on the basis of no evidence;[78] or
(b) wrong, misunderstood or ignored.[79]

Errors of law

Established rule: The court will quash only if the error is
(a) jurisdictional;[80] or
(b) on the face of the record.[81]

Emergent rule: The court will quash for any decisive error because
(a) all errors are now jurisdictional;[82] or
(b) all errors are reviewable anyway.[83]

[77] Above, p. 280.
[78] Above, p. 326.
[79] Above, p. 328.
[80] Above, p. 282.
[81] Above, p. 303.
[82] Above, p. 299.
[83] Above, p. 302.

10

PROBLEMS OF INVALIDITY

COLLATERAL PROCEEDINGS

Collateral challenges allowed

As will be stressed later in this chapter, the court will treat an administrative act or order as invalid only if the right remedy is sought by the right person in the right proceedings. The question now is what are the right proceedings in which the validity of the act or order can be challenged. It may be challenged directly, as in proceedings for certiorari to quash it or for a declaration that it is unlawful. But it may also be challenged collaterally, as for example by way of defence to a criminal charge, or by way of defence to a demand for some payment.[1]

There is some difficulty over terminology, since the House of Lords has held, in a case of the last-mentioned kind,[2] that an issue is not truly collateral if it is the central issue which has to be decided. But, as the examples in this section illustrate, it is not the central character of the issue which matters (for any decisive issue is necessarily central) but the nature of the proceedings in which the issue is raised. In the following discussion 'collateral' will be used in its customary sense, as applying to proceedings which are not themselves designed to impeach the validity of some administrative act or order.

As a general rule, the court will allow the issue of invalidity to be raised in any proceedings where it is relevant. Where some act or order is invalid or void, the consequences are followed out logically: consequential acts are also invalid. An illustration is the House of Lords' decision in the case, mentioned later, where a man prosecuted for carnal knowledge of a detained mental defective was able to plead that the detention order under which the defective was held had not been validly made: the detention order was a nullity and an essential element of the offence was therefore lacking.[3] Many comparable examples are to be found throughout the field of judicial review. A firm may resist a demand for purchase tax by showing

---

[1] On collateral challenge see Rubinstein, *Jurisdiction and Illegality*, ch. 3.

[2] The *Wandsworth* case (below).

[3] *Director of Public Prosecutions* v. *Head* [1959] AC 83 (below, p. 349); cf. *Dillon* v. *R.* [1982] AC 484.

that the assessment is made under an invalid regulation,[4] and a ratepayer may similarly resist a rate demand.[5] A local authority's tenant, sued for increased rent, may contend in his defence that the increase was ultra vires and void.[6] Gipsies occupying a local authority's land may resist proceedings for their ejection on the ground that the decision to eject them was unreasonable.[7] The validity of regulations about the registration of land charges may be disputed in proceedings for the recovery of compensation paid by a government department.[8] A local authority may plead the invalidity of its own repairs notices in resisting tenants' applications for grants to meet the cost of compliance.[9] The invalidity of a local planning authority's enforcement notice may be pleaded in defence to a criminal charge of disobedience to it,[10] and so may the invalidity of a byelaw, in whatever court the plea is made.[11] An appeal against convictions for bribery before a statutory tribunal may succeed on the ground that the members of the tribunal were invalidly appointed, so that the tribunal was without jurisdiction.[12] In particular, any questions affecting the jurisdiction of a tribunal can normally be raised in collateral proceedings, for the reasons already explained.[13] The writ of habeas corpus allows a prisoner to raise all questions capable of affecting the validity of his detention, and in most of its applications can be considered a means of collateral attack.[14]

The doctrine cannot be carried to the point of dispensing altogether with

---

[4] *Commissioners of Customs & Excise* v. *Cure and Deeley Ltd.* [1962] 1 QB 340; below, p. 449. See likewise *R.* v. *Commissioners of Customs and Excise ex p. Hedges and Butler Ltd.* [1986] 2 All ER 164.

[5] *Daymond* v. *Plymouth City Council* [1976] AC 609.

[6] *Wandsworth LBC* v. *Winder* [1985] AC 461, where the House of Lords rejected an argument based on *O'Reilly* v. *Mackman* [1983] 2 AC 237 to the effect that judicial review was the only available remedy (see p. 686, below); and see similarly *R.* v. *Jenner* [1983] 1 WLR 873.

[7] *West Glamorgan CC* v. *Rafferty* [1987] 1 WLR 457. Contrast *Waverley BC* v. *Hilden* [1987] The Times, 9 June.

[8] *Ministry of Housing and Local Government* v. *Sharp* [1970] 2 QB 223; below, p. 761.

[9] *R.* v. *Lambeth BC ex p. Clayhope Properties Ltd.* [1987] The Times, 17 June.

[10] *Scarborough BC* v. *Adams* (1983) 47 P & CR 133; *R.* v. *Reading Crown Court ex p. Hutchinson* [1987] 3 WLR 1062, criticising and not following *Quietlynn Ltd.* v. *Plymouth CC* [1987] 3 WLR 189 where it was held that such defences were no longer allowable in criminal courts.

[11] *R.* v. *Reading Crown Court ex p. Hutchinson* (above); *Staden* v. *Tarjanyi* (1980) 78 LGR 614.

[12] *Bribery Commissioner* v. *Ranasinghe* [1965] AC 172; compare *Ranaweera* v. *Ramachandran* [1970] AC 962 (Lord Diplock, dissenting). But no mention was made of the doctrine of officers and judges de facto: see below, p. 336.

[13] Above, p. 274.

[14] As in *R.* v. *Board of Control ex p. Rutty* [1956] 2 QB 109; *R.* v. *Brixton Prison Governor ex p. Ahsan* [1969] 2 QB 22. For these cases see below, p. 620. Rubinstein, *Jurisdiction and Illegality*, 107.

some legal requirement such as a licence. If the licensing authority refuses a licence invalidly, for example unreasonably or in breach of natural justice, this cannot be pleaded in defence to a charge of acting without a licence.[15] Even where there is a duty, as opposed to discretionary power, to grant the licence, the position must be the same, since no collateral plea can supply a licence which does not exist.

Conversely, but less reasonably, a person may be convicted for selling liquor where his licence is void because of some legal defect.[16] This again illustrates the error of regarding nullity as an absolute rather than a relative concept.[17] The correct attitude would probably be to treat the defective licence, at least if regular on its face, as a licence de facto, on the same principle as with officers de facto, mentioned below. In some situations the courts have sensibly adopted this type of solution, refraining from pushing the doctrine of nullity to extremes. A case in point is that of officers executing warrants and other orders, who are in general protected if there is no evident invalidity on the face of the warrant or order.[18]

A comparable distinction was made where actions for damages were brought against magistrates and judges of inferior courts on account of orders made by them outside their jurisdiction.[19] If the order was bad on its face the court would treat it as invalid. But if the jurisdictional defect was not visible on the face, the court would require the order first to be quashed in separate proceedings before the action for damages could be entertained.[20] Collateral attack was thus allowed in the first case but not in the second.

Collateral challenges not allowed

There are a number of situations in which the court will not permit an order to be challenged in collateral proceedings. These flow partly from the familiar distinctions based on jurisdiction, but partly also they are

---

[15] *Quietlynn Ltd.* v. *Plymouth CC* (above), which involved such a situation (operation of sex shops without licence), might more suitably have been decided on this ground. In fact no invalidity was found.

[16] *R.* v. *Downes* (1790) 3 TR 560 (licence granted in private instead of public session); *Pearson* v. *Broadbent* (1870) 36 JP 485 (licence granted under repealed section of Act). See Rubinstein (as above), 43.

[17] See below, p. 353.

[18] *Shergold* v. *Holloway* (1735) 2 Str. 1002; *Andrews* v. *Marris* (1841) 1 QB 3; *Demer* v. *Cook* (1903) 88 LT 629. See also Constables Protection Act 1750; *Horsfield* v. *Brown* [1932] 1 KB 355; *Sirros* v. *Moore* [1975] QB 118; *Maharaj* v. *A.-G. of Trinidad and Tobago* (No. 2) [1979] AC 385 at 397.

[19] For their liability see below, p. 784.

[20] *O'Connor* v. *Isaacs* [1956] 2 QB 288 at 304 and cases there cited by Diplock J.

exceptions to the general rule stated above, made for reasons of convenience.

The first class of cases is one which used to be prominent but which, as a result of the *Anisminic* case, may now be non-existent.[21] It comprised cases where an order was made within jurisdiction but was vitiated by mere error on its face. This was the anomalous case where the court had power to quash what was ex hypothesi a valid act. In these cases certiorari was the only remedy and the order could not be treated as invalid in any other proceedings. The operation of this doctrine and the historical reasons underlying it have been explained already.[22] The distinction between cases of this kind and cases of ultra vires is again illustrated by the case of the acquittal on the charge of carnal knowledge of a detained mental defective: the majority of the House of Lords held that the detention order was ultra vires and void, and so they acquitted: the minority view was that the order was only voidable for error on its face, so that in consequential criminal proceedings it should be treated as valid, not having been quashed by certiorari, and the accused should be convicted.[23]

Next come cases where it is held that some statutory remedy, such as a right of appeal, is the only remedy available. These are similar in principle to the cases last instanced, the only difference being that an exclusive remedy is prescribed by statute rather than by common law. No challenge to the validity of the order can therefore be made in collateral proceedings, or even in direct proceedings other than those prescribed. This class of cases is discussed in connection with remedies.[24] An example was where a vestry served a notice requiring a householder to provide a water closet with proper doors and coverings under an Act which gave a right of appeal to the County Council: on the words of the Act it was held that the statutory appeal was the only remedy and that in enforcement proceedings before a magistrate the householder could not contest the validity of the notice.[25]

There may also be cases where, although there is no special statutory remedy, it would be contrary to the scheme of the Act to allow the validity of an order to be disputed collaterally in enforcement proceedings. Such a case was where the mother of a child with scarlet fever refused to obey a magistrate's order for the removal of the child to hospital: when prosecuted for obstructing execution of the order the mother was not allowed to contest its validity, since the intention of the Act was that there should be summary powers for dealing urgently with infectious diseases, without the

---

[21] As explained above, p. 302.

[22] Above, p. 303.

[23] *Director of Public Prosecutions* v. *Head* (above). The minority view was that of Lord Denning.

[24] Below, p. 716.

[25] *Vestry of St. James and St. John, Clerkenwell* v. *Feary* (1890) 24 QBD 703.

usual right to notice and hearing: the removal order was therefore to be obeyed, whether right or wrong.[26] The court indicated, however, that its validity might have been challenged directly by certiorari or habeas corpus after the removal.

It seems possible that there may be good grounds for disallowing collateral challenge in cases of breach of the principles of natural justice. If some order is made against a person without giving him a fair hearing as required by the principles of natural justice, he can have the order set aside as void. But it does not necessarily follow that he can dispute its validity if prosecuted for disobedience. No English court appears yet to have faced this question. But it has been held in Australia that criminal proceedings for enforcement of the order are not suitable proceedings for questioning its validity on the ground that a fair hearing was not given. The accused's lorry had been rated by the registrar of motor vehicles as having a load capacity of over eight tons, which brought it under regulations requiring certain records and payments. On a prosecution for failure to provide these, the courts refused to enter into the accused's defence that the rating of his vehicle was void because the registrar had not heard his objections.[27] One obvious difficulty was that the registrar was not a party to the proceedings; but this may not be conclusive, since the same difficulty may arise in many cases of collateral challenge, and it may also be possible to bring in the necessary party. The court reached its conclusion by holding that the rating would be at most voidable rather than void, following as best they could the paradoxical decision of the Privy Council which is criticised elsewhere as an unsound authority.[28] It may be that the right to complain of a breach of natural justice is not only strictly personal to the individual concerned[29] but is also confined to direct proceedings against the authority or tribunal, as in an application for certiorari, an action for a declaration, or an action for damages based on the nullity of the order. But in the absence of English authority this is little more than conjecture.

The correct conclusion is probably that there can be no hard and fast rules for determining when the court may or may not allow collateral challenge. In some situations it will be suitable and in others it will be unsuitable, and no classification of the cases is likely to prove exhaustive.

[26] R. v. Davey [1899] 2 QB 301. See below, p. 530. Compare Children's Aid Society of Metropolitan Toronto v. Lyttle (1973) 34 DLR (3d) 127 (collateral challenge to wardship order by way of adoption proceedings not allowed).
[27] Hinton Demolition Pty. Ltd. v. Lower (No. 2) [1971] 1 SASR 512 (Supreme Court of South Australia). That such cases are not solved by any doctrine of 'void or voidable' but rather depend always upon the court's willingness to grant remedies is explained below, p. 353.
[28] Durayappah v. Fernando [1967] 2 AC 337, for which see below, pp. 527, 537.
[29] Below, p. 537.

Officers and judges de facto

In one class of cases there is a long-standing doctrine that collateral challenge is not to be allowed: where there is some unknown flaw in the appointment or authority of some officer or judge. The acts of the officer or judge may be held to be valid in law even though his own appointment is invalid and in truth he has no legal power at all.[30] The logic of annulling all his acts has to yield to the desirability of upholding them where he has acted in the office under a general supposition of his competence to do so. In such a case he is called an officer or judge de facto, as opposed to an officer or judge de jure.

The House of Lords applied this principle to an administrative authority so as to uphold a rate levied by a vestry although a number of the vestrymen had not been duly elected. Lord Truro LC described them as vestrymen de facto and said:[31]

You will at once see to what it would lead if the validity of their acts, when in office, depended upon the propriety of their election. It might tend, if doubts were cast upon them, to consequences of the most destructive kind. It would create uncertainty with respect to the obedience to public officers, and it might lead also to persons, instead of resorting to ordinary legal remedies to set right anything done by the officers, taking the law into their own hands.

In another administrative case the court upheld a distress levied by a collector of land tax who did not have the residential qualification required for his appointment.[32] The same doctrine has been applied to invalidly appointed judges and magistrates: a distress warrant was held valid although granted by a magistrate who had not taken the necessary oath;[33] and when the appointment of a judge of the Supreme Court of New Zealand was found to be void,[34] a prisoner whom he had sentenced at the time when he was supposed to be a judge failed to secure release.[35] Similarly, in the days when judges' appointments were automatically

[30] For discussion see Rubinstein, *Jurisdiction and Illegality*, 205; Owen Dixon (later Sir O. Dixon CJ), *Res Judicatae* (Melbourne, 1938), i. 285; (1955) 71 LQR 100 at 106 (R. B. Cooke); [1978] PL 42 (P. Mirfield). There are many American decisions, notably *State* v. *Carroll* (1871) 38 Conn. 449, 9 Am 409, where early authorities are reviewed. For an example from Roman law see [1967] *Irish Jurist* 269 (A. M. Honoré), citing a case where a slave was elected praetor.
[31] *Scadding* v. *Lorant* (1851) 3 HLC 418 at 447.
[32] *Waterloo Bridge Co.* v. *Cull* (1859) 1 E. & E. 245.
[33] *Margate Pier Co.* v. *Hannam* (1819) 3 B & Ald 266.
[34] See *Buckley* v. *Edwards* [1892] AC 387 (appointment invalid since no salary appropriated).
[35] *Re Aldridge* (1893) 15 NZLR 361. This case contains a learned review of the law, except that it makes no mention of *Scadding* v. *Lorant* (above).

determined by the demise of the Crown, their judgments and acts remained valid until news of the monarch's death in fact arrived.[36]

The decisions indicate that the doctrine will apply only where the office-holder has 'colourable authority' or some colour of title to the appointment. Where the registrar of the Bedford Level company employed a deputy to register land titles within the Level, it was held that registrations effected by the deputy after the death of the registrar was known were invalid: the deputy's authority expired on the death of his principal, and once the death was generally known the deputy could not be taken to have any colour of authority to act. Lord Ellenborough CJ said:[37]

An officer de facto is one who has the reputation of being the officer he assumes to be, and yet is not a good officer in point of law.

So a divorce granted in 1970 by a Rhodesian judge, appointed under the unconstitutional Rhodesian regime established in 1965, was held to be invalid in England, since it was notorious in both countries that the Rhodesian regime had been declared unlawful by Act of Parliament and Order in Council;[38] accordingly the judge had no colour of title to his office in the eyes of English law. The basis of the de facto principle is that the public must be able to rely on the acts of judges and officers so long as there is no reason to suppose that they are not validly appointed.

The de facto doctrine has a long history and has been applied to a wide variety of officers. It was even said to have applied to the monarchy, so that it might validate acts done in the names of kings whose title to the throne was considered illegitimate and who were kings 'in fact and not in law'.[39] At the other end of the scale the doctrine was invoked from an early date to uphold copyhold titles enrolled by stewards of manors who were not properly appointed.[40] Offices were long considered to be a form of property,[41] and wrongful possession of an office may be compared with wrongful possession of land: just as a wrongful occupier of land may validly exercise an owner's powers (to convey, sue for trespass, etc.) against

---

[36] *Crew* v. *Vernon* (1627) Cro. Car. 97.

[37] *R.* v. *Bedford Level Corporation* (1805) 6 East 356 at 368.

[38] *Adams* v. *Adams* [1971] P. 188. For criticism see Lord Denning MR (dissenting) in *Re James* [1977] Ch. 41 at 65. The law was changed by SI 1972 No. 1718.

[39] These words ('en fait et nient en droit') are from the Act of 1461 (1 Edw. IV, cap. I) which on the accession of Edward IV removed doubts as to the judgments given in the reigns of Henry IV, Henry V and Henry VI, then considered usurpers. This Act was said to be declaratory of the common law: see *Re Aldridge* (above) at 369; but this was doubted in *Adams* v. *Adams* (above) at 213. See [1967] CLJ 214 (A. M. Honoré); [1972B] CLJ at 150 (D. E. C. Yale).

[40] See *Knowles* v. *Luce* (1580) Moore (KB) 109 at 112; *Parker* v. *Kett* (1701) 1 Ld. Raym. 658.

[41] See (1945) 61 LQR 240 at 249 (D. W. Logan).

all but the true owner, merely on the strength of the fact of possession,[42] so the wrongful occupier of an office may validly exercise its powers as against members of the public merely on the strength of his authority de facto. Both titles to land and unlawful administrative acts are subject to a similar principle of relativity.[43] In many legal situations it is a mistake to suppose that the consequences of invalidity should be worked out with rigid logic and without regard to facts.

In a number of reported cases the possibility of authority de facto does not seem to have been argued, for example where the Privy Council set aside penalties for bribery imposed by the Bribery Commission in Ceylon because the commissioners had not been appointed by the proper body,[44] and where the High Court declared a trial void because the deputy recorded was a solicitor and not a barrister as required by statute.[45]

PARTIAL INVALIDITY

Severance of good from bad

An administrative act may be partially good and partially bad. It often happens that a tribunal or authority makes a proper order but adds some direction or condition which is beyond its powers. If the bad can be cleanly severed from the good, the court will quash the bad part only and leave the good standing. One example was where a licensing authority allowed an applicant's appeal but wrongly ordered him to pay costs, which it had no power to do; the court quashed only the order as to costs.[46] Another was where a disciplinary board validly acquitted a public servant on some charges but invalidly convicted him on others.[47] The same principle applies to orders of courts of law, as where an unauthorised order for disqualification or forfeiture is added to a valid conviction.[48] It also seems possible that a single order may be good against some persons and bad against others. In one case, where a training board was under a mandatory duty to consult certain trade organisations and trade unions, the order was

---

[42] Megarry and Wade, *Real Property*, 5th edn., 103. The analogy was observed by Manwood CB in *Knowles* v. *Luce* (above) and *Leak* v. *Hall* (1597) Cro. Eliz. 533 (customs officer de facto), and by Owen Dixon in *Res Judicatae* (1938) at 288.

[43] See below, p. 351; as to title to land, Megarry and Wade (as above).

[44] *Bribery Commissioner* v. *Ranasinghe* [1965] AC 172; above, p. 332.

[45] *R.* v. *Cronin* (1940) 27 Cr. App. R. 179. But here there may have been no 'colourable authority'. Contrast *Re James* [1977] Ch. 41 at 66; *Campbell* v. *Wallsend Engineering Co.* [1978] ICR 1015; and see Cross, *Evidence*, 5th edn., 46.

[46] *R.* v. *Bournemouth Licensing Justices ex p. Maggs* [1963] 1 WLR 320.

[47] *Bowman* v. *State and State Services Commission* [1972] NZLR 78.

[48] e.g. *R.* v. *Llandrindod Wells Justice ex p. Gibson* [1968] 1 WLR 598.

held to be good as against those that had been consulted and bad against those that had not been.[49] In this case the remedy was necessarily a declaratory judgment.

Where an order is not divisible into component parts but is a single whole the court may decline to sever the bad from the good, as it did where the Secretary of State for Transport miscalculated the sum which he ordered the Greater London Council to pay to London Regional Transport and unlawfully overcharged them by some £10 million.[50] But there is no 'blue pencil rule' requiring the bad part of the order to be identifiable in the order itself. Thus a local authority's order which appropriated land for planning purposes, but which included a small plot which was outside its powers, was held to be severable and valid as regards the remainder, even though it treated all the land as a single area.[51] These cases depend not upon rigid rules but upon the balance of advantage as perceived by the court.

It may be no easier to draw the line where the authority is empowered to demand information and demands more than is permitted. In the well-known case of *Dyson* v. *Attorney-General*,[52] where the Act required the taxpayer to make a return under penalty, it was held that the tax commissioners' demand was wholly invalid where they included an unauthorised question in the form of return which they required. This was because the penalties of the Act applied to a return which was one and indivisible and which could not be split into good and bad parts.[53] But where the power is to demand such information as is thought necessary or as may be required for some purpose, a demand which is partly within the power and partly in excess of it may be severed, so that it is valid to the extent that it falls within the Act and no further.[54] The mere inclusion of an unauthorised item will not therefore exonerate the recipient. But 'it may well be that if the excess is so entwined with the valid as to be separable from it only with difficulty, then the whole of the requirement will be bad: the subject ought not to be required to perform delicate feats of surgery upon what is in substance a single requirement.'[55]

The court may be particularly disinclined to perform feats of surgery

---

[49] *Agricultural Horticultural and Forestry Industry Training Board* v. *Aylesbury Mushrooms Ltd* [1972] 1 WLR 190. See also below, p. 875.

[50] *R.* v. *Secretary of State for Transport ex p. Greater London Council* [1986] QB 556, containing an extensive review of authorities by McNeill J, who quashed the whole order.

[51] *Thames Water Authority* v. *Elmbridge BC* [1983] QB 570.

[52] [1912] 1 Ch. 158; below, p. 595.

[53] See Farwell LJ at p. 171.

[54] *Potato Marketing Board* v. *Merricks* [1958] 2 QB 316; *Royal Bank of Canada* v. *IRC* [1972] Ch. 665.

[55] Megarry J in the *Royal Bank of Canada* case, above.

where an invalid condition is one of the terms on which a discretionary power is exercised. If an invalid condition is attached to a licence or to planning permission, the permission without the condition may be such as the licensing authority would not have been willing to grant on grounds of public interest. The right course for the court is then to quash the whole permission, so that a fresh application may be made. An example is where a local authority, in granting a licence for open-air rock concerts, attached an invalid condition requiring the promoter to reimburse the cost of policing them. Since the court regarded the condition as an essential part of the permission, it quashed the whole licence.[56] The same was done in two planning cases, described elsewhere, where the permission was made subject to conditions which went beyond the proper scope of planning law.[57] The House of Lords approved this practice in a later case in which they held, though by a narrow majority, that they could not sever a planning condition requiring that the permission should lapse after three years unless in the meantime detailed plans were approved by the planning authority.[58] Lord Morris then said:[59]

There might be cases where permission is granted and where some conditions, perhaps unimportant or perhaps incidental, are merely superimposed. In such cases if the conditions are held to be void the permission might be held to endure, just as a tree might survive with one or two of its branches pruned or lopped off. It will be otherwise if some condition is seen to be a part, so to speak, of the structure of the permission so that if the condition is hewn away the permission falls away with it.

Planning conditions do not all necessarily fall into the latter class. Conditions improperly restricting the 'existing use rights' of owners have been treated as severable;[60] so have conditions which imposed rent control and other excessive restrictions on a caravan site;[61] so has a condition requiring a developer to provide small shops in addition to a supermarket;[62]

---

[56] R. v. North Hertfordshire DC ex p. Cobbold [1985] 3 All ER 486.

[57] Hall & Co. Ltd. v. Shoreham-by-Sea UDC [1964] 1 WLR 240 (below, p. 433); R. v. Hillingdon LBC ex p. Royco Homes Ltd. [1974] QB 720 (below, p. 432). See similarly British Airports Authority v. Secretary of State for Scotland 1979 SLT 197.

[58] Kingsway Investments (Kent) Ltd. v. Kent CC [1971] AC 72 (the condition was in fact held valid). See similarly Newbury District Council v. Secretary of State for the Environment [1981] AC 578.

[59] At p. 102.

[60] Hartnell v. Minister of Housing and Local Government [1965] AC 1134 (severability assumed without discussion); Allnat London Properties Ltd. v. Middlesex CC (1964) 62 LGR 304.

[61] Mixnam's Properties Ltd. v. Chertsey UDC [1965] AC 735; below, p. 431. Here also severability was assumed without discussion.

[62] R. v. St Edmundsbury BC ex p. Investors in Industry Commercial Properties Ltd [1985] 1 WLR 1168.

and so has a condition requiring any dispute about the observance of conditions to be referred to a consultant for conclusive determination.[63] A compulsory purchase order was severed where it wrongly included property which was in good condition and which was not reasonably necessary for the development of the adjacent clearance area.[64] Severance has also been allowed where the order was of a legislative character, as explained elsewhere.[65]

STANDARD AND BURDEN OF PROOF

The standard of proof

Nearly all the cases which concern administrative law are civil, as opposed to criminal, proceedings. The standard of proof of facts, accordingly, is the civil standard, based on the balance of probabilities, as contrasted with the criminal standard which requires proof beyond reasonable doubt. Even where, as sometimes in disciplinary proceedings, the language of the Act or regulations has a criminal flavour, speaking of 'offences' 'charges', and 'punishments', the standard of proof remains the civil standard.[66]

But the civil standard is flexible, so that the degree of probability required is proportionate to the nature and gravity of the issue. Where personal liberty is at stake, for example, the court will require a high degree of probability before it will be satisfied as to the facts justifying detention;[67] and the requirement will not be much lower in matters affecting livelihood and professional reputation, or where there is a charge of fraud or moral turpitude.[68] Lord Scarman has indeed said that the choice between the two standards is largely a matter of words, asking how, if a court has to be satisfied of some crucial fact, it can entertain a reasonable doubt.[69]

Disciplinary offences in prisons are evidently treated as criminal, so that the criminal standard applies.[70]

---

[63] *Turner* v. *Allison* [1971] NZLR 833.

[64] *Coleen Properties Ltd.* v. *Minister of Housing and Local Government* [1971] 1 WLR 433.

[65] Below, p. 874.

[66] *R.* v. *Hampshire CC ex p. Ellerton* [1985] 1 WLR 749 (disciplinary proceedings against fire officer).

[67] *R.* v. *Home Secretary ex p. Khawaja* [1984] AC 74; and see *Eshugbayi Eleko* v. *Government of Nigeria* [1931] AC 662.

[68] *Bhandari* v. *Advocates Committee* [1956] 1 WLR 1442; *R.* v. *Milk Marketing Board ex p. Austin* [1983] The Times, 21 March; and see *R.* v. *South Glamorgan Health Authority ex p. Phillips* [1986] The Times, 21 November (tribunal's rules specified criminal standard).

[69] [1984] AC at 112, 113.

[70] *R.* v. *Home Secretary ex p. Tarrant* [1985] QB 251 at 285.

The burden of proof

Where the validity of an administrative act or order is attacked, the incidence of the burden of proof may vary with the circumstances. The burden of proof naturally lies in the first instance upon the plaintiff or complainant. Whether he can transfer it to the defendant public authority depends upon the nature of the act.

If the act is one which in the absence of statutory power would be a trespass or other wrongful injury, the plaintiff has only to prove the facts which would constitute the wrong and the burden of proof then passes to the public authority, which has to show justification. Thus a government official seizing a man's goods bears the onus of proof that he had power to do so.[71] A highway authority which removes a supposed obstruction can be put to proof of its power, and if it cannot show this it will be liable in damages for trespass.[72] A local authority empowered to eject a tenant for housing purposes must give some evidence that it is acting for those purposes.[73] An immigrant detained on the ground that he landed unlawfully within the previous twenty-four hours is entitled to release by habeas corpus if there is no proof either way of the time at which he landed.[74] Lord Atkin once said:[75]

In accordance with British jurisprudence no member of the executive can interfere with the liberty or property of a British subject except on the condition that he can support the legality of his action before a court of justice. And it is the tradition of British justice that judges should not shrink from deciding such issues in the face of the executive.

This was in a case where a Nigerian native chief had been deported to another area but the power to do so depended on a number of conditions. The Privy Council held that it was for the executive to show that these conditions existed and they remitted the case to the court in Nigeria.

Where, on the other hand, the administrative act is some decision or order which in itself inflicts no legal wrong, the complainant's task will be to raise a prima facie case of irregularity, and the burden of proof lies upon him. This is equally so where there is an invasion of his liberty or property but he alleges not that the statutory conditions are not satisfied but that

[71] *R. v. Inland Revenue Cmrs ex p. Rossminster Ltd.* [1980] AC 952 at 1011. Likewise with compulsory purchase: *Prest v. Secretary of State for Wales* (1983) 81 LGR 193.
[72] *Murray v. Epsom Local Board* [1897] 1 Ch. 35 at 40.
[73] *St. Pancras Borough Council v. Frey* [1963] 2 QB 586; *Harpin v. St. Albans Cpn.* (1969) 67 LGR 479. For doubt on these decisions see *Bristol District Council v. Clark* [1975] 1 WLR 1443 at 1448 (CA).
[74] *R. v. Governor of Brixton Prison ex p. Ahsan* [1969] 2 QB 222.
[75] *Eshugbayi Eleko v. Government of Nigeria* [1931] AC 662 at 670. See to the same effect *R. v. Home Secretary ex p. Khawaja* [1984] AC 74 (below, p. 460).

there is some ulterior defect, for example bad faith.[76] It has often been laid down that the onus of proof rests upon the party alleging invalidity.[77] In other words, there is a presumption that the decision or order is properly and validly made, a presumption sometimes expressed in the maxim *omnia praesumuntur rite esse acta*. In a war-time case where it was unsuccessfully contended that the minister had no adequate grounds connected with national defence for making an order taking control of a colliery business, Lord Greene MR said:[78]

It is a settled principle, in dealing with documents of this kind, that the rule of *omnia rite esse acta* is to be applied and, therefore, when it is stated by the Ministry in the proper way that it appears to the Minister of Fuel and Power that certain things are so, it is to be taken that that is an accurate statement unless and until the contrary is proved.

A judge has also spoken of 'the clearly established presumption that statutory duties are duly and properly performed'.[79] An administrative authority cannot therefore be put to proof of the facts or conditions on which the validity of its order must depend, unless the party attacking it can first produce evidence which will shift the burden of proof off his own shoulders. How much evidence is required for this purpose will always depend upon the nature of the case. If an order has an apparent fault on its face, the burden is easily transferred. But if the grounds of attack are bad faith or unreasonableness,[80] the plaintiff's task is heavier. So it is also where the authority must be satisfied of something or form some opinion.[81] If no evidence to the contrary is offered, it will be presumed in favour of the authority that it was duly satisfied or of opinion accordingly.[82] Likewise where tax commissioners were empowered to require 'such particulars as they think necessary', but gave no supporting evidence beyond affirming that they did so think, their order was upheld in the absence of positive evidence from the taxpayer that their wide powers had been in any way abused.[83]

---

[76] *Greene v. Home Secretary* [1942] AC 284 as explained in *Ahsan's* case, above.

[77] *Minister of National Revenue v. Wright's Canadian Ropes Ltd.* [1947] AC 109 at 122; *Associated Provincial Picture Houses Ltd. v. Wednesbury Cpn.* [1948] 1 KB 223 at 228; *Fawcett Properties Ltd. v. Buckingham County Council* [1959] Ch. 543 at 575, affirmed [1961] AC 636.

[78] *Point of Ayr Collieries Ltd. v. Lloyd-George* [1943] 2 All ER 546.

[79] *Wilover Nominees Ltd. v. Inland Revenue Commissioners* [1973] 1 WLR 1393 at 1399 (Goulding J), affirmed [1974] 1 WLR 1342.

[80] See *Potato Marketing Board v. Merricks* [1958] 2 QB 316 at 331; *Cannock Chase DC v. Kelly* [1978] 1 WLR 1 (no obligation on council to justify reasonableness of eviction of tenant).

[81] See the *Point of Ayr Collieries* case, above.

[82] *Stoke-on-Trent CC v. B & Q (Retail) Ltd.* [1984] Ch. 1, affirmed [1984] AC 754.

[83] *Wilover Nominees Ltd. v. Inland Revenue Commissioners* [1974] 1 WLR 1342.

A situation in which the presumption of regularity does not apply is where the jurisdiction of an inferior tribunal is challenged in collateral proceedings.[84] This rule, however, is concerned not so much with the initial burden of proof as with the matters that may be put in issue. Willes J expressed it as follows:[85]

Another distinction is, that whereas the judgment of a superior Court unreversed is conclusive as to all relevant matters thereby decided, the judgment of an inferior Court, involving a question of jurisdiction, is not final.

And he added, quoting from another case,[86] that 'the rule, that in inferior Courts and proceedings by magistrates the maxim *omnia praesumuntur rite esse acta* does not apply to give jurisdiction, never has been questioned'. Accordingly if a weekly rent is reduced by order of a rent tribunal from £5 to £3, the landlord can still sue for £5 and, when met with the defence that the tribunal has ordered a reduction, he may show if he can that the tribunal had no jurisdiction.[87] This is a corollary of the rule, discussed earlier,[88] that a tribunal cannot give itself additional jurisdiction by its own mistaken decision.

Personal liberty

In cases of habeas corpus there is a principle which 'is one of the pillars of liberty',

that in English law every imprisonment is prima facie unlawful and that it is for a person directing imprisonment to justify his act.[89]

Accordingly the detaining authority must be able to give positive evidence that it has fulfilled every legal condition expressly required by statute, even in the absence of contrary evidence from the prisoner. This was held in a case where clandestine immigrants had been arrested but where there was power to detain them only if they had landed within the previous twenty-

---

[84] There seems even to have been a presumption of irregularity, in that the order was presumed void unless it showed jurisdiction upon its face: *Taylor* v. *Clemson* (1842) 2 QB 978 at 1031.

[85] *City of London* v. *Cox* (1866) LR 2 HL 230 at 262.

[86] *R.* v. *All Saints, Southampton* (1828) 7 B. & C. 785 (Holroyd J). See likewise *Briscoe* v. *Stephens* (1824) 2 Bing. 213.

[87] *R.* v. *Fulham & c. Rent Tribunal ex p. Zerek* [1951] 2 KB 1 at 10. And see *R.* v. *Judge Pugh ex p. Graham* [1951] 2 KB 623.

[88] Above, p. 281.

[89] *Liversidge* v. *Anderson* [1942] AC 206 at 245 (Lord Atkin), confirmed in the *Khawaja* case (below) at 110 (Lord Scarman). And see *R.* v. *Home Secretary ex p. Ram* [1979] 1 WLR 148.

four hours. The immigrants failed to show that they had landed before that time and the authorities failed to show that they had landed within it. In this situation it was held that they must be released.[90] Accordingly it is not enough for the custodian to make a return which is valid on its face, unless there is no challenge to the conditions which must be satisfied.[91] If there is such a challenge, the custodian must accept the burden of proof of their existence. This rule is indeed an example of the principle stated at the outset, since unjustified detention is trespass to the person. It is particularly important that the principle should be preserved where personal liberty is at stake. It has recently been corroborated in a decision of the House of Lords which, though not primarily concerned with habeas corpus, explains the burden of proof which lies upon those who have power to detain and remove immigrants, and for this purpose equates habeas corpus with the other remedies of judicial review.[92]

In the past, unfortunately, the protection of liberty has been weakened by judges who have held that a return from the custodian which is valid on its face puts the burden of disproving it upon the prisoner.[93] For the return is merely a statement of the facts which are alleged to justify the detention, and does not in itself provide any evidence of their existence. Administrative detention is a different matter from detention by order of a court of competent jurisdiction, where the return is conclusive.[94] To throw the burden of proof onto administrative prisoners contradicts the principle stated by Lord Atkin[95] and puts the individual in danger of being detained upon allegations which he may have no means of disproving. It was in order to require proper proof of the facts stated in returns by gaolers that

[90] *Ahsan's* case, above. See also *R. v. Home Secretary ex p. Badaike* [1977] The Times, 3 May (habeas corpus granted).

[91] See Lord Parker CJ in *Ahsan's* case, above, at 231.

[92] *R. v. Home Secretary ex p. Khawaja* [1984] AC 74, especially at 105 (Lord Wilberforce) and 110 (Lord Scarman). Lord Scarman's later statement that a prisoner carries the initial burden of proof is difficult to understand, since the fact of imprisonment makes a prima facie case, as Lord Scarman acknowledges.

[93] *R. v. Home Secretary ex p. Greene* [1942] 1 KB 87 at 116; *Greene v. Home Secretary* [1942] AC 284 at 295; *R. v. Risley Remand Centre Governor ex p. Hassan* [1976] 1 WLR 971 (rejecting *Ahsan's* case, above, on an unjustifiable distinction between British subjects and aliens and adopting the opinion of the dissenting judge). In *R. v. Home Secretary ex p. Zamir* [1980] 3 WLR at 253 Lord Wilberforce is reported as saying that it was for the detainee to show that his detention was unlawful; but in [1980] AC at 947 these words are omitted. See also Sharpe, *Habeas Corpus*, 82.

[94] See *Liversidge v. Anderson* [1942] AC 206 at 245 (Lord Atkin); *Greene v. Home Secretary* (above) at 294 (Lord Maugham, erroneously extending the rule to administrative detention also); and see below, p. 624.

[95] Quoted above, p. 342. In *Liversidge* v. *Anderson* (above) at 247 Lord Atkin said: 'A minister given only a limited authority cannot make for himself a valid return by merely saying I acted as though I had authority. His ipse dixit avails nothing.'

the Habeas Corpus Act 1816 empowered the court 'to examine into the truth of the facts set forth in such return' in non-criminal cases.[96] But this protection becomes nugatory if the initial burden of proof is put upon the prisoner. Despite the obvious confusion between allegation and evidence, judges have too readily committed themselves to this dangerous proposition, instead of requiring the custodian to produce at least enough evidence of legality to call for rebuttal. The burden should revert to the prisoner only where his case is based on an allegation of bad faith or breach of natural justice or some such vitiating element, in accordance with the normal rules.[97] If, on the other hand, an allegation of fraud is made against him, the burden of proof is of course upon the party making it.[98]

INTERIM EFFECT OF DISPUTED ORDERS

Effectiveness pending determination

The House of Lords has held that there is a presumption of validity in favour of a disputed order during the time that must elapse before the court can decide the question; and even where temporary obedience to the disputed order caused the irreparable loss of a large sum of money, the House refused to impose terms which would protect the person affected.[99] This was in a case where a supplier of drugs (used in large quantities in the national health service) claimed that a price-fixing order was invalid because of improper procedure by the Monopolies Commission. The cost to the supplier of obeying the order pending final determination of its validity in about two years' time was estimated at £8m. When the Crown sought to enforce the disputed order immediately by interim injunction, the supplier asked for the usual undertaking in damages to protect him in case the order should prove to have been invalid. The House of Lords refused this protection, holding that a sufficiently strong prima facie case had not been shown. They held, further, that the order must meanwhile be presumed to be valid and must be obeyed. The problems arising in this situation will recur later, partly in the section on 'void or voidable'[1] and

---

[96] See the *Khawaja* case (above) at 110 (Lord Scarman).

[97] As in *R. v. Brixton Prison Governor ex p. Soblen* [1963] 2 QB 243 at 281 (deportation order alleged to be a sham).

[98] *R. v. Home Secretary ex p. Momin Ali* [1984] 1 WLR 663.

[99] *Hoffman–La Roche & Co. v. Secretary of State for Trade and Industry* [1975] AC 295. The logic is criticised by Lord Wilberforce in his dissenting speech. The European Court has decided similarly: *Granaria BV v. Hoofproduktschap voor Akkerbouwprodukten* (case 101/78) [1979] 3 CMLR 124. Compare *A.-G. v. Wright* [1988] 1 WLR 164.

[1] Below, p. 351.

partly in the context of liability for loss caused by the making of invalid orders.[2]

Inconsistently with this presumption of validity, judges sometimes resort to the unrealistic argument that if the order is void no one need obey it or suffer loss, all persons being presumed to know the law.[3] In a case where an Australian local authority had imposed building restrictions which were ultra vires and void the Privy Council rejected the landowner's claim for loss of development value during the period before the invalidity of the restrictions was established in litigation.[4] The local authority had failed to comply with certain requirements, including a requirement of notice and hearing, and the Privy Council said:

The effect of the failure is to render the exercise of the power void and the person complaining of the failure is in as good a position as the public authority to know that that is so. He can ignore the purported exercise of the power. It is incapable of affecting his legal rights.

The Court of Appeal has similarly held that maintenance payments made by a husband under a justices' order could not be recovered in an action against the justices when the order was later found to have been made without jurisdiction, since there was no obligation to obey the void order.[5]

But the argument that void orders need not be obeyed 'bears no relation to the facts', as Denning LJ once aptly said in a case where a member of a trade union had been wrongfully expelled.[6] He continued:

The exclusion may have been a nullity in law but it was far from being a nullity in fact. . . . It deprived him of his livelihood and caused him great damage.

Similarly in a notable Canadian case, where damages were recovered for the wrongful (and void) revocation of a liquor licence, Rand J said:[7]

The revocation was de facto, it was intended to end the privilege and to bring about the consequences that followed. As against the respondent, the appellant was entitled to treat the breach of duty as effecting a revocation and to elect for damages.

[2] Below, p. 776.
[3] As in *Wood* v. *Wood* (1874) LR 9 Ex 190 (no damages for wrongful expulsion from business association since expulsion was void and plaintiff therefore remained a member); and see *Stott* v. *Gamble* [1916] 2 KB 504 at 508; *Thompson* v. *British Medical Association* [1924] AC 764 at 775.
[4] *Dunlop* v. *Woollahra Municipal Council* [1982] AC 158. For the possibility of an action for negligence in such a case see below, p. 779.
[5] *O'Connor* v. *Isaacs* [1956] 2 QB 288.
[6] *Bonsor* v. *Musicians' Union* [1954] 1 Ch. 479 at 513. Since trade union membership is a matter of contract, the exclusion would have been a breach of contract rather than a nullity.
[7] *Roncarelli* v. *Duplessis* (1959) 16 DLR (2d) 689 at 708; below, p. 405. Similarly in *Ridge* v. *Baldwin* [1964] AC 40 the chief constable was dismissed de facto in the period before it was established that his dismissal was void; see below, p. 517.

By treating void acts as operative de facto the courts can escape from the more inconvenient consequences of carrying their doctrine of nullity to its logical conclusions. Further examples will be found elsewhere.[8] As is explained below,[9] 'void' is a relative concept, and there is no absurdity in treating an order as void for some purposes but valid for others. The judgments which hold that no one need obey a void order or suffer damage from it are therefore tainted by faulty reasoning, and would be better based upon the non-liability of public authorities for action taken in good faith and without malice or negligence.[10]

Recovery of money paid

Another question which can arise in connection with an invalid order is whether it is possible to recover some payment made in the interim before its invalidity was established. But that question belongs to a later chapter.[11]

Orders of superior courts

From what has been said above it follows *a fortiori* that the order of a superior court, such as the High Court, must always be obeyed, no matter what flaws it may be thought to contain. Thus a party who disobeys a High Court injunction is punishable for contempt of court even though it was granted in proceedings deemed to have been irrevocably abandoned owing to the expiry of a time limit.[12] More about the orders of superior courts will be found at the end of the following section on void or voidable.

VOID OR VOIDABLE?

Proper basis of the distinction

A source of complication introduced in certain decisions of recent years is the question whether unlawful administrative acts are void or voidable.[13] Up to a point there is a sound basis for this distinction. But attempts have been made to carry it beyond that point and to use it as a means of turning firm rules of law into matters of discretion. Although it is now reasonably clear that these attempts have failed, a good deal of confusing reasoning has accumulated and requires to be sorted out.

[8] Above, p. 336 (officers and judges de facto).
[9] p. 352.
[10] This was indeed the primary basis of the *Dunlop* case, above; see below, p. 780.
[11] Below, p. 790.
[12] *Isaacs* v. *Robertson* [1985] AC 97.
[13] For discussion see (1967) 83 LQR 499, (1968) 84 LQR 95 (Wade); 31 MLR 2, 138 (M. B. Akehurst); [1977] NZLJ 284 (J. F. Northey); [1981] CLP 43 (D. Oliver).

'Void or voidable' is a distinction which applies naturally and without difficulty to the basic distinction between action which is ultra vires and action which is liable to be quashed for error on the face of the record. Action which is ultra vires is unauthorised by law, outside jurisdiction, null and void, and of no legal effect.[14] But an order vitiated merely by error on its face is, as has been seen, intra vires and within jurisdiction, but liable to be quashed because of the exceptional powers of control which the courts established three centuries ago and which they recently revived.[15] Such an order is voidable, being intra vires and valid and effective, unless and until the court quashes it. An order which is ultra vires within any of the ramifications of that doctrine, e.g. because of unreasonableness or wrong grounds or violation of statutory requirements, can only be void: once the court condemns it as being void, it is seen to have been destitute of all legal effect from the outset. An order which is merely voidable, on the other hand, has legal effect up to the time when it is quashed, and in respect of that period it remains a valid order even after being quashed. An additional example of a voidable order is the order of a court or tribunal which is not liable to be quashed as ultra vires but which is subject to appeal on its merits: unless and until reversed on appeal, it is a valid order.[16]

The difference which this distinction may make is shown by the case of a man convicted of carnal knowledge of a detained mental defective, who appealed successfully on the ground that the defective was not legally detained since the Home Secretary's detention order was invalid, not being supported by the medical certificates required by statute.[17] The House of Lords held that the detention order was ultra vires and void and the conviction therefore wrong. But Lord Denning, dissenting on this point, held that it was a case of mere error on the face of the record and within jurisdiction, so that the detention order was voidable only and was valid and effective at the time of the offence, so justifying the conviction.[18] This is a rare example of a decision turning upon an intelligible distinction between void and voidable.

Deviations and complications

The point at which intelligibility ceased was when judges began to suggest that even ultra vires action might be merely voidable. This paradoxical

[14] But see below, p. 352, for necessary qualifications.

[15] Above, p. 303.

[16] As in *Re F. (Infants) (Adoption Order: Validity)* [1977] Fam. 165 (adoption order held voidable because liable to be set aside on appeal).

[17] *Director of Public Prosecutions* v. *Head* [1959] AC 83.

[18] Yet it would seem that the order in question was necessarily ultra vires, whether or not the defect appeared on its face.

opinion was first advanced by the dissenting judges in *Ridge* v. *Baldwin*,[19] a case of denial of natural justice which in no way appeared on the record and which the court therefore could only condemn on the footing that the action was ultra vires and void—as the majority judges duly held. This and other cases on natural justice are discussed in that context separately.[20] They offer particularly strong proof that administrative action which is ultra vires is void and not voidable, and that judicial attempts to maintain the contrary conflict not only with the strong current of authority but also with the basic logic of administrative law. Yet for some time after *Ridge* v. *Baldwin* Lord Denning MR expressed opinions to the effect that irregular administrative acts might be voidable only. Prominent among these was his judgment in a rating case, where a ratepayer challenged the whole valuation list on the ground that it was compiled on an entirely wrong basis, contrary to the directions in the statute. This claim failed on the facts, but on the hypothesis that it was justified Lord Denning said that the valuation officer was acting within his jurisdiction but erroneously, so that the list was merely voidable and good until set aside.[21] But if the valuation officer was indeed acting intra vires, the court should have had no power to intervene at all, there being no error on the face of any record.

More recently, however, Lord Denning has retracted these opinions. In a case where a court registrar's order was made under a fundamental mistake and contrary to natural justice Lord Denning said that 'on being set aside, it is shown to have been a nullity from the beginning and void', and that he would adopt the meanings of 'void' and 'voidable' given in this book.[22] In one of his own books, also, he confesses that some of his earlier statements were unguarded and that a decision reached in violation of natural justice or made in bad faith is void, in accordance with the *Anisminic* case.[23]

Both in *Ridge* v. *Baldwin* and the *Anisminic* case[24] the House of Lords has

---

[19] [1964] AC 40.

[20] Below, p. 526.

[21] *R.* v. *Paddington Valuation Officer ex p. Peachey Property Corporation Ltd.* [1966] 1 QB 380 at 402. Compare his similar remarks in *Director of Public Prosecutions* v. *Head* (above) at 111 and in *MacFoy* v. *United Africa Co. Ltd.* [1962] AC 152 at 160. In *James* v. *Minister of Housing and Local Government* [1966] 1 WLR 135 (reversed on other grounds, [1967] 1 WLR 171) Lord Denning suggested that a planning authority's decision, given after the permitted two months, was 'not void but at most voidable'; but since the time limit was directory only, the question did not appear to arise. In *R.* v. *Secretary of State for the Environment ex p. Ostler* [1977] QB 122 he said that bad faith or breach of natural justice would make an order voidable only and not a nullity.

[22] *Firman* v. *Ellis* [1978] QB 886, generously confirmed in *The Discipline of Law*, 77 ('I confess that at one time I used to say that such a decision was not void but only voidable. But I have seen the error of my ways').

[23] *The Discipline of Law*, 108, withdrawing his remarks in the *Ostler* case, above.

[24] *Anisminic Ltd.* v. *Foreign Compensation Commission* [1969] 2 AC 147 at 170 (Lord Reid).

made it clear that 'there are no degrees of nullity' and that errors such as bad faith, wrong grounds and breach of natural justice all necessarily involve excess of jurisdiction and therefore nullity.[25] This was merely to restate what has always been a fundamental rule.[26] Lord Diplock has made it clear that 'void' is the correct term in any such context, saying:[27]

It would, however, be inconsistent with the doctrine of ultra vires as it has been developed in English law as a means of controlling abuse of power by the executive arm of government if the judgment of a court in proceedings properly constituted that a statutory instrument was ultra vires were to have any less consequence in law than to render the instrument incapable of ever having had any legal effect . . .

Self-evident though this proposition is, it should help judges who have to cut a way through the verbal entanglement that some of the decisions have created.

Remedies and relativity

In the rating case cited above Lord Denning MR said that if a rating list is so defective that it is a nullity 'there is no need for an order to quash it. It is automatically null and void without more ado.'[28] Here also there is a logical difficulty, since unless an order of the court is obtained, there is no means of establishing the nullity of the list. It enjoys a presumption of validity,[29] and will have to be obeyed unless a court invalidates it. In this sense every unlawful administrative act, however invalid, is merely voidable. But this is no more than the truism that in most situations the only way to resist unlawful action is by recourse to the law. In a well-known passage Lord Radcliffe said:[30]

An order, even if not made in good faith, is still an act capable of legal consequences. It bears no brand of invalidity upon its forehead. Unless the necessary proceedings are taken at law to establish the cause of invalidity and to get it quashed or otherwise upset, it will remain as effective for its ostensible purpose as the most impeccable of orders.

[25] Above, p. 42.
[26] [1969] 2 AC at 171, 195, 207.
[27] In the *Hoffman–La Roche* case (below) at 365.
[28] *R. v. Paddington Valuation Officer ex p. Peachey Property Corporation Ltd.* (above). The person concerned may of course choose to ignore a patently illegal order and merely plead it as a defence if necessary, as pointed out by Lord Hailsham LC in *London & Clydeside Estates Ltd.* v. *Aberdeen District Council* [1980] 1 WLR 182 at 189. See also below p. 643 (certiorari to quash nullities).
[29] *Hoffman–La Roche* v. *Secretary of State for Trade and Industry* [1975] AC 295. See above, p. 346.
[30] *Smith* v. *East Elloe Rural District Council* [1956] AC 736 at 769.

This must be equally true even where the 'brand of invalidity' is plainly visible: for there also the order can effectively be resisted in law only by obtaining the decision of the court. The necessity of recourse to the court has been pointed out repeatedly in the House of Lords and Privy Council, without distinction between patent and latent defects.[31] Lord Diplock has spoken still more clearly,[32] saying that

it leads to confusion to use such terms as 'voidable', 'voidable ab initio', 'void' or 'a nullity' as descriptive of the status of subordinate legislation alleged to be ultra vires for patent or for latent defects, before its validity has been pronounced on by a court of competent jurisdiction.

The words 'patent or latent' show that it makes no difference for this purpose[33] whether the order bears a 'brand of invalidity upon its forehead'. Lord Diplock pointed out that the order would be presumed to be valid unless the presumption was rebutted in competent legal proceedings by a party entitled to sue. He added that there might be no one entitled to sue, for example if a statutory time limit had expired. In that case the order would have to stand. Cooke J expressed the same idea in a New Zealand case:[34] 'Except perhaps in comparatively rare cases of flagrant invalidity, the decision in question is recognised as operative unless set aside.'

The truth of the matter is that the court will invalidate an order only if the right remedy is sought by the right person in the right proceedings and circumstances. The order may be hypothetically a nullity, but the court may refuse to quash it because of the plaintiff's lack of standing,[35] because he does not deserve a discretionary remedy,[36] because he has waived his rights,[37] or for some other legal reason. In any such case the 'void' order remains effective and is, in reality, valid. It follows that an order may be

---

[31] As by Lord Morris in *Ridge* v. *Baldwin* [1964] AC 40 at 125; by the Privy Council (Lord Wilberforce) in *Calvin* v. *Carr* [1980] AC 574 at 589–90; by Lord Hailsham LC in *London & Clydeside Estates Ltd.* v. *Aberdeen DC* [1980] 1 WLR 182 at 189. Lord Morris's remarks were misunderstood by the Privy Council in *Durayappah* v. *Fernando* [1967] 2 AC 337, for which see below, p. 527.

[32] In the *Hoffman–La Roche* case (above) at 366.

[33] It may make a difference for other purposes such as collateral challenge (above, p. 334).

[34] *A. J. Burr Ltd.* v. *Blenheim Borough* [1980] 2 NZLR 1 at 4.

[35] As in *Gregory* v. *Camden London Borough Council* [1966] 1 WLR 899; below, p. 692.

[36] As in *Lovelock* v. *Minister of Transport* (1980) 40 P & CR (compulsory purchase order for green belt land needed for motorway held perhaps void for failure to take account of relevant considerations but remedy sought too late). Lord Denning MR there said 'I have got tired of all the discussion about "void" and "voidable". It seems to me to be a matter of words—of semantics—and that is all. The plain fact is that, even if such a decision as this is "void" or a "nullity", it remains in being unless and until some steps are taken before the courts to have it declared void.' Sir John Donaldson MR made a similar statement in *R.* v. *Panel on Take-overs and Mergers ex p. Datafin Plc* [1987] QB 815, quoted below, p. 641.

[37] As to waiver see above, p. 264, and below, pp. 482, 537.

void for one purpose and valid for another;[38] and that it may be void against one person but valid against another.[39] A common case where an order, however void, becomes valid is where a statutory time limit expires after which its validity cannot be questioned.[40] The statute does not say that the void order shall be valid; but by cutting off legal remedies it produces that result.[41]

Similarly with remedies withheld in discretion: the court may hold that an attack on the validity of some act or order succeeds, but that no remedy should be granted. The court then says, in effect, that the act is void but must be accepted as valid. An example was where in making social security regulations the Secretary of State neglected his mandatory duty to consult organisations concerned: the court granted a declaration to this effect, but declined in its discretion to quash the regulations.[42] The net result of this contradictory course was that the regulations stood, and were therefore valid.

'Void' is therefore meaningless in any absolute sense. Its meaning is relative, depending upon the court's willingness to grant relief in any particular situation. If this principle of legal relativity is borne in mind, confusion over 'void or voidable' can be avoided.[43] A case could be made for using either term in relation to invalid acts. But so long as the ultra vires doctrine remains the basis of administrative law, the correct epithet must be 'void'.

Judicial discretion

One motive for holding administrative acts to be voidable, when according to principle they are void, may be a desire to extend the

[38] It may be valid for the purpose of being appealed against but for no other purpose: see below, p. 946.

[39] If in *Ridge* v. *Baldwin* (above) the chief constable had accepted his dismissal, its voidness could not have been asserted by other people; it would have been void against the chief constable, but valid against others: see *Durayappah* v. *Fernando* (above) at 352–3. See also *Agricultural & Training Board* v. *Aylesbury Mushrooms Ltd.* [1972] 1 WLR 190 (industrial training order valid against organisations duly consulted but void against those not consulted).

[40] As in *Smith* v. *East Elloe RDC* [1956] AC 736; *R.* v. *Secretary of State for the Environment ex p. Ostler* [1977] QB 122; below, pp. 741, 738.

[41] Lord Diplock makes a statement to the same effect in *O'Reilly* v. *Mackman* [1983] 2 AC 237 at 283F.

[42] *R.* v. *Secretary of State for Social Services ex p. Association of Metropolitan Authorities* [1986] 1 WLR 1. For this and other such cases see below, p. 711.

[43] See in particular the remarks of Lord Hailsham LC in the *London & Clydeside Estates* case (above) and of Cooke J in *A. J. Burr Ltd.* v. *Blenheim Borough* (above). For an analogy with the relativity of titles to land see above, p. 337. For further discussion see M. Taggart in *Judicial Review of Administrative Action in the 1980s* (Oxford University Press), 70.

discretionary power of the court. This policy, and the dangers of it, are to be seen particularly clearly in the cases on the right to a fair hearing, which are considered separately later.[44] There are grave objections to giving the courts discretion to decide whether governmental action is lawful or unlawful: the citizen is entitled to resist unlawful action as a matter of right, and to live under the rule of law, not the rule of discretion. 'To remit the maintenance of constitutional right to the region of judicial discretion is to shift the foundations of freedom from the rock to the sand.'[45] The true scope for discretion is in the law of remedies, where it operates within narrow and recognised limits and is far less objectionable. If the courts were to undermine the principle of ultra vires by making it discretionary, no victim of an excess or abuse of power could be sure that the law would protect him.

Another serious consequence would be that the declaratory judgment, a very valuable remedy, would as the law now stands lose much of its efficacy, since it is of use only against action which can be declared to be ultra vires, i.e. void from the outset.[46]

The superior courts

As Lord Diplock explained in a Privy Council case, speaking of superior courts such as the High Court,[47]

The contrasting legal concepts of voidness and voidability form part of the English law of contract. They are inapplicable to orders made by a court of unlimited jurisdiction in the course of contentious litigation. Such an order is either irregular or regular. If it is irregular it can be set aside by the court that made it upon application to that court; if it is regular it can only be set aside by an appellate court upon appeal if there is one to which an appeal lies.

Lord Diplock also said that where there was a defect such as breach of the rules of natural justice a party might have the order set aside ex debito justitiae (meaning as of right) without recourse to the rules about irregularity which give the judge discretion.

An example of a superior court's order being held to be void was where the Court of Appeal allowed an appeal in a case where appeal was expressly prohibited by statute and on further appeal its decision was held by the House of Lords to be without jurisdiction and a nullity.[48] But, as already explained,[49] such an order must always be obeyed, whatever its legal defects, unless and until it is set aside.

[44] Below, p. 535.
[45] *Scott* v. *Scott* [1913] AC 417 at 477 (Lord Shaw).
[46] Below, p. 601, subject to the new doctrine there mentioned.
[47] *Isaacs* v. *Robertson* [1985] AC 97 at 103.
[48] *Re Racal Communications Ltd.*, reported as *Re a Company* [1981] AC 374; above, p. 300.
[49] Above, p. 346.

PART IV
DISCRETIONARY POWER

11

RETENTION OF DISCRETION

DISCRETIONARY POWER

In this and the next following chapter the rules which govern discretionary power must be examined in detail. All legal power, as opposed to duty, is inevitably discretionary to a greater or lesser extent, but now the emphasis falls upon the nature of discretion itself and the standards upon which the courts insist in order that it may be exercised in a proper and lawful way in accordance with the presumed intentions of the legislature that conferred it. First, in this chapter, come the rules which ensure that discretionary power should be wielded only by those to whom it is given and that they should retain it unhampered by improper constraints or restrictions. Next, in chapter 12, comes the sovereign principle that powers must be exercised reasonably and in good faith and on proper grounds—in other words, that they must not be abused. This is one of the twin pillars that uphold the structure of administrative law. The other is natural justice, the subject of Part V. The law can thus control, to a limited but important extent, both the substance of discretionary decisions and the procedure under which they are made.

DELEGATION

Inalienable discretionary power

An element which is essential to the lawful exercise of power is that it should be exercised by the authority upon whom it is conferred, and by no one else. The principle is strictly applied, even where it causes administrative inconvenience, except in cases where it may reasonably be inferred that the power was intended to be delegable. Normally the courts are rigorous in requiring the power to be exercised by the precise person or body stated in the statute, and in condemning as ultra vires action taken by agents, sub-committees, or delegates, however expressly authorised by the authority endowed with the power.

One aspect of this principle is the rule that the participation of non-members in the deliberations or decisions of a collective body may invalidate its acts. The decision of a disciplinary committee, for example, is likely to be invalid if any non-member of the committee has taken part in its proceedings.[1] It is not clear that the mere presence of a non-member will be fatal,[2] although in one case Lord Wright MR said:

> It would be most improper on general principles of law that extraneous persons, who may or may not have independent interests of their own, should be present at the formulation of that judicial decision.[3]

A recognised exception is the right of magistrates to have the assistance of their clerk on questions of law.[4]

The maxim *delegatus non potest delegare* is sometimes invoked as if it embodied some general principle that made it legally impossible for statutory authority to be delegated. In reality there is no such principle; and the maxim plays no real part in the decision of cases, though it is sometimes used as a convenient label. Its proper home is in the law of agency, where it expresses the point that a principal who must accept liability for the acts of his agent need not accept it for the acts of his agent's agent; but even here there are wide exceptions. In the case of statutory powers the important question is whether, on a true construction of the Act, it is intended that a power conferred upon A may be exercised on A's authority by B. The maxim merely indicates that this is not normally allowable.[5] For this purpose no distinction need be drawn between delegation and agency. Whichever term is employed, the question of the true intent of the Act remains. It is true that the court will more readily approve the employment of another person to act as a mere agent than the wholesale delegation of the power itself. But this is due not to any technical difference between agency and delegation but to the different degress of devolution which either term can cover. The vital question in most cases is whether the statutory discretion remains in the hands of the proper authority, or whether some other person purports to exercise it. Thus where the Act said that an inspector of nuisances 'may procure any sample' of goods for analysis, it was held that the inspector might validly send his assistant to buy a sample of coffee.[6] This might be described as mere agency as opposed to delegation. But that would obscure the true ground, which was that the inspector had in no way authorised his assistant to exercise the discretion

---

[1] *Lane* v. *Norman* (1891) 66 LT 83; *Leary* v. *National Union of Vehicle Builders* [1971] Ch. 34; *Ward* v. *Bradford Corporation* (1971) 70 LGR 27. But see *Wislang* v. *Medical Practitioners Disciplinary Committee* [1974] 1 NZLR 29.

[2] See *Leary's* case, above, at 53.

[3] *Middlesex County Valuation Committee* v. *West Middlesex Assessment Area Committee* [1937] Ch. 361.

[4] See *Ward's* case, above, at 33.

[5] For discussion see *Re S.* (A Barrister) [1970] 1 QB 160; (1943) 21 Can BR 257 (J. Willis); (1972) 2 Auck ULJ 85 (P. H. Thorp).

[6] *Horder* v. *Scott* (1880) 5 QBD 552.

legally reposed in himself. For similar reasons there can be no objection to the Commission for Racial Equality using its officers to collect information in its investigations.[7]

Examples of delegation

The following are characteristic cases where action was held ultra vires because the effective decision was taken by a person or body to whom the power did not properly belong.

(a) Under wartime legislation local committees were empowered to direct farmers to grow specified crops on specified fields. A committee decided to order eight acres of sugar beet to be grown by a farmer, but left it to their executive officer to decide on which field it should be grown. The farmer, prosecuted for disobedience, successfully pleaded that the direction was void, since the executive officer had no power to decide as to the field.[8] The right procedure would have been for the committee to have obtained the officer's recommendation and to have decided the whole matter itself.

(b) Registered dock workers were suspended from their employment after a strike. The power to suspend dockers under the statutory dock labour scheme was vested in the local Dock Labour Board. The suspensions were made by the port manager, to whom the Board had purported to delegate its disciplinary powers. The dockers obtained declarations that their suspension was invalid since the Board had no power to delegate its functions and should have made the decision itself.[9]

(c) In a similar case where a registered dock worker was dismissed the House of Lords granted a declaration that the dismissal was invalid because the Board, instead of deciding itself, had entrusted the whole matter to a disciplinary committee.[10]

(d) A local board had power to give permission for the laying of drains. They empowered their surveyor to approve straightforward applications, merely reporting the number of such cases to the Board. It was held that the Board itself must decide each application, and that delegation to the surveyor was unlawful.[11] The result was the same

---

[7] R. v. *Commission for Racial Equality ex p. Cottrell & Rothon* [1980] 1 WLR 1580.

[8] *Allingham* v. *Minister of Agriculture and Fisheries* [1948] 1 All ER 780.

[9] *Barnard* v. *National Dock Labour Board* [1953] 2 QB 18.

[10] *Vine* v. *National Dock Labour Board* [1957] AC 488; see similarly *Young* v. *Fife Regional Council* 1986 SLT 331 (committee wrongly delegated to sub-committee).

[11] *High* v. *Billings* (1903) 89 LT 550. Similarly *Vic Restaurant Inc.* v. *City of Montreal* (1958) 17 DLR (2d) 81 (licensing power delegated to police).

where a local education committee left it to its chairman to fix the date of closure of a school[12] and where the Monopolies Commission allowed its chairman to decide that a company's take-over proposal had been abandoned.[13]

From these typical cases it might be supposed that the question was primarily one of form. Convenience and necessity often demand that a public authority should work through committees, executive officers, and other such agencies.[14] The law makes little difficulty over this provided that the subordinate agencies merely recommend, leaving the legal act of decision to the body specifically empowered.[15] It is obvious that in many such situations the real discretion will be exercised by the agency that recommends, and that in substance the law allows this function to be delegated. Nevertheless it is more than a matter of observing legal forms. The valid exercise of a discretion requires a genuine application of the mind and a conscious choice by the correct authority.

A public body which blindly rubber-stamps its officers' recommendations will therefore be acting unlawfully, as already seen in the case of the local board which had power to approve drains but allowed its surveyor to approve straightforward applications, merely reporting the numbers of such cases to the board.[16] Similarly a labour relations board, which had power to determine whether a trade union was supported by a majority of employees, could not validly commission one of its officers to determine this question and then merely adopt his decision.[17] In both these cases the decision would have been valid had it been taken on a report and recommendation from the officer which the board genuinely considered before determining the question itself. The same distinction was applied in Ceylon to a board which had power to appoint trustees of a mosque. They consulted a Member of Parliament who supplied a list of names including his own, all of whom the board appointed. It was held that the board had merely adopted a ready-made decision by an outsider and that such appointments were void.[18] There can be no legal objection to a public body obtaining advice and consulting suitable persons, but it is vital that it should genuinely keep the decision in its own hands.

[12] R. v. Secretary of State for Education and Science ex p. Birmingham CC (1984) 83 LGR 79 (Secretary of State's approval quashed).
[13] R. v. Monopolies and Mergers Commission ex p. Argyll Group Plc [1986] 1 WLR 763 (Secretary of State's consent not quashed: see below, p. 710).
[14] See below, p. 364.
[15] Hall v. Manchester Cpn. (1915) 79 JP 385 (HL); distinguished in Cohen v. West Ham Cpn. [1933] Ch. 814.
[16] High v. Billings (1903) 89 LT 550.
[17] Labour Relations Board of Saskatoon v. Spears [1948] 1 DLR 340.
[18] Cader v. Commissioners for Mosques (1963) 66 NLR 16.

Unauthorised discretion or consent

Sometimes the judicial aversion to delegation is carried to lengths which make administration difficult, a tendency which is particularly marked in the Canadian cases. In one of these the Governor in Council was empowered to make regulations for the control of immigration with reference to specified criteria such as the immigrant's unsuitability. The court condemned a regulation which denied admission to persons who were unsuitable in the opinion of a special inquiry officer[19]—though it is hard to see how the criterion could have been applied without some such delegation. A clearer case was where an immigration adjudicator, hearing an appeal, found facts which gave a discretion to the Secretary of State but wrongly exercised it himself.[20] In a case from Ceylon the Governor-General had power to appoint a commission of inquiry into any matter in which in his opinion it would be in the interests of the public safety or welfare. He appointed a commissioner to inquire into all such government contracts as the commissioner in his absolute discretion might think of sufficient importance to the public welfare to warrant inquiry. The Privy Council held this to be unlawful delegation, since the subject of inquiry should have been chosen according to the Governor-General's opinion, not the Commissioner's.[21] But the House of Lords upheld notices issued by a rating authority's subordinate officer where the Act said: 'Where the rating authority are of opinion . . .', and the only opinion formed was that of the subordinate.[22] It was said that the Act plainly contemplated rate-collection by subordinates and this construction was assisted by the very wide powers conferred upon local authorities.[23]

Another legal pitfall is the requirement of some extraneous person's consent, which may be held to put the decision effectively into that person's hands. A county council erred in this respect when it licensed a cinema on condition that no film should be shown which had not been certified by the British Board of Film Censors, an unofficial body established by the film industry.[24] The council were empowered to impose such conditions as they might determine, but this condition was held unreasonable and ultra vires as 'putting the matter into the hands of a third person or body not possessed of statutory or constitutional authority'. But this case was only just on the wrong side of the line. A similar condition imposed by another council

---

[19] *A-G of Canada* v. *Brent* [1956] SCR 318.
[20] *R.* v. *Home Secretary ex p. Malik* [1981] The Times, 18 November.
[21] *Ratnagopal* v. *A-G* [1970] AC 974.
[22] *Provident Mutual Life Assurance Association* v. *Derby CC* [1981] 1 WLR 173 (Lord Bridge dissenting).
[23] See below, p. 364.
[24] *Ellis* v. *Dubowski* [1921] 3 KB 621.

survived challenge since it contained the words 'without the consent of the council' and so preserved the council's own power to decide in the last resort.[25] Thus the court was able to validate an eminently reasonable administrative policy. Similarly in New Zealand, where the Govenor-General had power to make regulations for the control of civil aviation, the court upheld a regulation prohibiting the towing of aircraft except with the permission of the Director of Civil Aviation.[26] If the courts make it impossible for conditions of this kind to be imposed, good administration may be hampered for doctrinaire reasons.[27] It is obvious that some dispensing or licensing power will often need to be given to subordinate officials, and that general powers of regulation should be construed so as to permit this in suitable cases.

Agency and administration

Unlawful delegation must be distinguished from lawful agency. A public authority is naturally at liberty to employ agents in the execution of its powers, as for example by employing solicitors in litigation, surveyors in land transactions, and contractors in road-building. The essential thing is that it should take its decisions of policy itself, and observe any statutory requirements scrupulously.[28] It may be allowed to ratify the acts of its agents retrospectively, both under the ordinary rules of agency and under liberal interpretation of statute.[29] Occasionally the court may even invoke the rules of agency to justify a questionable delegation. This happened where the Westminster City Council's public health committee had authorised their chairman to deal with urgent matters in the vacation, and the chairman instituted proceedings for nuisance which the committee ratified at their next meeting.[30] This was an indulgent decision and it was not unanimous. Normally a stricter rule prevails, so that where the Act allows proceedings to be instituted by an officer authorised by resolution, a

---

[25] *Mills* v. *London County Council* [1925] 1 KB 213. See *R.* v. *Greater London Council ex p. Blackburn* [1976] 1 WLR 550.

[26] *Hookings* v. *Director of Civil Aviation* [1957] NZLR 929, reviewing earlier cases.

[27] An extreme case is *Re Davies & Village of Forest Hills* (1964) 47 DLR (2d) 392.

[28] Thus local authorities taking legal proceedings through their officers must expressly authorise them under Local Government Act 1972, s. 223; a mere resolution to take proceedings is inadequate: *Bob Keats Ltd.* v. *Farrant* [1951] 1 All ER 899. cf *Becker* v. *Crosby Cpn.* [1952] 2 All ER 1350 (notice to quit signed by wrong officer).

[29] As in *Warwick RDC* v. *Miller-Mead* [1962] Ch. 441 (council empowered to sue for nuisance resolved to sue three days after writ issued by their solicitors; held, valid).

[30] *R.* v. *Chapman ex p. Arlidge* [1918] 2 QB 298. In *Firth* v. *Staines* [1897] 2 QB 70, there relied upon, the Act expressly authorised subsequent approval.

later resolution cannot validly ratify action already taken.[31] It must be emphasised that all these cases turn on the implications of various statutory provisions: there is no rigid rule. But in general the court is likely to be more strict where the issue is one of substance as opposed to formality. The Court of Appeal summarily dismissed the National Dock Labour Board's claim to have ratified the suspension of dock workers who had been invalidly suspended by the port manager, since this was serious disciplinary action which only the Board itself was competent to take.[32] It dismissed no less firmly a minister's claim to have ratified the irregular requisitioning of a house by a local authority under powers validly delegated by the minister.[33] It refused, likewise, to allow a planning authority to ratify a planning permission issued by its clerk without any authority.[34]

In one doubtful decision it was held in effect that delegation of its powers by a local planning authority was justified by a general practice, though the practice had no legal basis.[35] In another case Denning LJ said: 'While an administrative function can often be delegated, a judicial function rarely can be. No judicial tribunal can delegate its functions unless it is enabled to do so expressly or by necessary implication.'[36] The decisions in fact show that the courts do not normally allow the delegation even of administrative functions if they involve the exercise of discretion. There is no general principle that administrative functions are delegable. The principle is rather that, where any sort of decision has to be made, it must be made by the authority designated by Parliament and by no one else. Occasionally the court will allow some degree of delegation on the ground that the matter is merely administrative,[37] particularly in the case of a body which has to make investigations, such as the Race Relations Board.[38] It is doubtless correct that the general objections to delegation apply with special force to judicial functions, particularly if they affect personal liberty or are disciplinary.[39] The extent to which the courts will allow the delegation of

---

[31] *Bowyer Philpott & Payne Ltd.* v. *Mather* [1919] 1 KB 419 (legal proceedings).

[32] *Barnard* v. *National Dock Labour Board* [1953] 2 QB 18. See similarly *Vine* v. *National Dock Labour Board* [1957] AC 488. In both cases the judicial or quasi-judicial nature of the function was emphasised.

[33] *Blackpool Cpn.* v. *Locker* [1948] 1 KB 349.

[34] *A.-G. ex rel. Co-operative Retail Services Ltd.* v. *Taff-Ely BC* (1979) 39 P & CR 233, affirmed (1981) 42 P & CR 1.

[35] *Lever Finance Ltd.* v. *Westminster London Borough Council* [1971] 1 QB 222.

[36] *Barnard* v. *National Dock Labour Board* (above) at 40.

[37] e.g. *Bridge* v. *R.* [1953] 1 DLR 305; *Hookings* v. *Director of Civil Aviation* [1957] NZLR 929. See also the *Provident Mutual Life Assurance* case (above, p. 361).

[38] *R.* v. *Race Relations Board ex p. Selvarajan* [1957] 1 WLR 1686.

[39] See *R.* v. *Chiswick Police Station Superintendent ex p. Sacksteder* [1918] 1 KB 578 at 591; *General Medical Council* v. *UK Dental Board* (below).

fair hearings required by the principles of natural justice is explained elsewhere.[40]

Statutory power to delegate

Since in practice government demands a great deal of delegation, this has to be authorised by statute, either expressly or impliedly. The whole of the committee system, as operated by local authorities, is dependent upon the powers of delegation conferred by statute, currently by the Local Government Act 1972. This empowers local authorities to arrange for the discharge of any of their functions by committees, sub-committees, or officers of the authority or by any other local authority, or by acting jointly with other local authorities through joint committees, etc.[41] Certain functions are excepted, notably the levying of rates and the borrowing of money.[42] Local planning authorities are given similar powers,[43] and may also delegate to their officers the decision of certain classes of planning applications.[44] Statutory powers of delegation are necessarily very numerous. They will be construed in the same way as other powers, and will not therefore extend to subdelegation in the absence of some express or implied provision to that effect.[45] The delegate must also keep within the bounds of the power actually delegated, which may be narrower than that possessed by the delegating authority; it will be no defence that that authority could, had it wished, have delegated wider power.[46]

A statutory power to delegate functions, even if expressed in wide general terms, will not necessarily extend to everything. Thus it has been held that the General Medical Council must itself exercise its disciplinary powers over dentists and cannot delegate them to its executive committee, even though it has express statutory powers to act through such a committee for the purpose of its functions under the Dentists Acts.[47] In the case of important judicial and disciplinary functions the court may be disposed to construe general powers of delegation restrictively.

---

[40] Below, p. 552.
[41] ss. 101, 102. The Local Government Act 1933, s. 85, gave power to 'delegate' functions to committees, but not to sub-committees. The Act of 1972 avoids using that word.
[42] s. 101(6).
[43] Town and Country Planning Act 1971, sched. 2 (dating from 1968).
[44] Same Act, s. 4, (dating from 1968). In *Lever Finance Ltd.* v. *Westminster London Borough Council* [1971] 1 QB 222 Sachs. LJ held that delegation might be implied and that the requirement of notification in writing (s. 4(5)) might be disregarded.
[45] For an example of authorised subdelegation see n. 41 above.
[46] *Cook* v. *Ward* (1877) 2 CPD 255; *Blackpool Cpn.* v. *Locker* [1948] 1 KB 349.
[47] *General Medical Council* v. *UK Dental Board* [1936] Ch. 41.

A statutory power to delegate will normally include a power to revoke the delegation when desired.[48] While the delegation subsists it may be arguable whether the delegating authority is denuded of its power or is able to exercise it concurrently with the delegate. This question arose where under statutory authority the executive committee of a county council delegated to a sub-committee its powers to make regulations for the control of rabies; but before the sub-committee had done anything the executive committee, without revoking the delegation, itself issued regulations for the muzzling of dogs. These regulations were upheld, but on inconsistent grounds, one judge holding that the executive committee had resumed its powers and the other that it had never parted with them, and that 'the word "delegate" means little more than an agent'.[49] In a later case the latter view prevailed, on the ground that 'one cannot divest oneself of one's statutory duties'.[50] But the contrary was held by the Court of Appeal where a minister had formally delegated to local authorities his power to requisition houses. By doing this he had for the time being divested himself of his powers, so that an invalid requisition by the local authority could not be cured by their acting in his name; and the court rejected the contention that delegation was a form of agency.[51] The Local Government Act 1972 expressly preserves the powers of a local authority concurrently with those delegated to its committees, etc.[52]

Implied power to delegate is not commonly found in peacetime legislation. Under wartime powers, which are necessarily very wide and which necessarily demand much delegation and subdelegation, the implication is almost irresistible. The Defence of the Realm legislation in the first world war contained no express power to delegate, but there was no ligation attempting to challenge any of the government's acts on this ground. Under similar legislation in Canada in the second world war the Supreme Court held that the power to make regulations must necessarily be delegable, so that it could be delegated by the Governor-General to the Controller of Chemicals.[53] The corresponding legislation in the United Kingdom permitted delegation and subdelegation expressly.[54] Under an Act obliging the owners of cars to identify their drivers if so required 'by or

---

[48] But not retrospectively: *Battelley* v. *Finsbury Borough Council* (1958) 56 LGR 165 (council unable to repudiate appointment of employee made by committee under delegated power). For revocability see above, p. 253 and *Manton* v. *Brighton Cpn.* [1951] 2 KB 393.

[49] *Huth* v. *Clark* (1890) 25 QBD 391 (Lord Coleridge CJ and Wills J).

[50] *Manton* v. *Brighton Cpn.* (above). See similarly *Gordon, Dadds & Co.* v. *Morris* [1945] 2 All ER 618.

[51] *Blackpool Cpn.* v. *Locker* [1948] 1 KB 349.

[52] s. 101(4).

[53] *Re Chemicals Regulations* [1943] SCR 1.

[54] Emergency Powers (Defence) Act 1939, s. 1(3); below, p. 854.

on behalf of' a chief constable, it was held that police officers who normally handled traffic cases had implied delegated authority to sign notices on behalf of the chief constable by reason of their position, without any express authorisation.[55] But the court emphasised that express authority was highly desirable, and the case must be regarded as on the borderline. It was made clear that the police cannot claim the benefit of the doctrine which applies to ministers and officials in government departments.

Government departments

Departments of the central government have the benefit of a special rule whereby officials may act in their ministers' names without any formal delegation of authority. When powers are conferred upon ministers who have charge of large departments, it is obvious that they will often not be exercised by the minister in person. Parliament is well aware of this, and ministerial powers are therefore taken to be exercisable by officials of the minister's department acting in his name in the customary way. In the leading case the owner of a factory challenged a wartime requisitioning order made on behalf of the Commissioners of Works (as the ministry was then called). The Commissioners had power to requisition land 'if it appears to that authority to be necessary or expedient to do so'. But they themselves never met or transacted business as a body: their powers were exercised entirely by their officials. The requisitioning order was signed by an assistant secretary, who was solely in charge of the case, and it was never considered by any of the Commissioners. The Court of Appeal held that this procedure was open to no legal objection.[56] Lord Greene MR said:[57]

It cannot be supposed that this regulation meant that, in each case, the minister in person should direct his mind to the matter. The duties imposed upon ministers and the powers given to ministers are normally exercised under the authority of the ministers by responsible officials of the department. Public business could not be carried on if that were not the case. Constitutionally, the decision of such an official is, of course, the decision of the minister. The minister is responsible. It is he who must answer before Parliament for anything that his officials have done under his authority. . . .

Consequently many ministerial powers are exercised by officials who recite 'I am directed by the Minister', 'the Minister is of the opinion', and so forth, when in reality they are acting on their own initiative. If the proper official

---

[55] *Nelms* v. *Roe* [1970] 1 WLR 4.

[56] *Carltona Ltd.* v. *Commissioners of Works* [1943] 2 All ER 560. See similarly *Point of Ayr Collieries Ltd.* v. *Lloyd-George* [1943] 2 All ER 546; *Re Golden Chemical Products Ltd.* [1976] Ch. 300.

[57] In the *Carltona* case at 563.

is acting in his capacity as such, his assumption of ministerial authority is lawful.[58] This doctrine is assumed to extend equally to legislative powers, since it is common practice for officials to issue statutory regulations under powers vested in their ministers.[59]

Strictly speaking there is not even delegation in these cases. Delegation requires a distinct act by which the power is conferred upon some person not previously competent to exercise it. But the authority of officials to act in their ministers' names derives from a general rule of law and not from any particular act of delegation.[60] Legally and constitutionally the act of the official is the act of the minister, without any need for specific authorisation in advance or ratification afterwards. Even where there are express statutory powers of delegation they are not in fact employed as between the minister and his own officials.[61] Such legal formalities would be out of place within the walls of a government department, as is recognised by Parliament's practice of conferring powers upon ministers in their own names. The case is of course different where the official is to be empowered to act in his own name rather than the minister's. Thus the power for inspectors to decide certain kinds of planning appeals must be delegated by the minister by statutory instrument, as required by the Act.[62]

The limits of this doctrine must be noticed. It applies only to the departments of the central government, and not therefore to local government authorities and other statutory bodies, as is plain from the examples already given.[63] It does not apply to the police.[64] Even within the central government the powers conferred upon a specified minister may not be exercised in his name by another minister[65] or the latter's officials, whether or not the minister has purported to authorise this expressly.[66] For

[58] See also *Lewisham BC* v. *Roberts* [1949] 2 KB 608; *Woollett* v. *Minister of Agriculture and Fisheries* [1955] 1 QB 103; *R.* v. *Skinner* [1968] 2 QB 700. For the position when the official is not authorised see below, p. 382.

[59] This is the practice, for certain classes of orders, in the Department of the Environment, the Department of Trade, and the Ministry of Agriculture, Fisheries and Food.

[60] *Lewisham BC* v. *Roberts* (above); *R.* v. *Skinner* (above).

[61] See *Carltona Ltd.* v. *Commissioners of Works* (above); *Lewisham BC* v. *Roberts* (above).

[62] Town and Country Planning Act 1971, sched. 9.

[63] Above, p. 359.

[64] *Nelms* v. *Roe* (above).

[65] But powers conferred upon 'the Secretary of State' are exercisable by any Secretary of State: above, p. 52.

[66] *Jackson Stansfield & Sons* v. *Butterworth* [1948] 2 All ER 558. But there the Minister of Works had purported to authorise the clerks of local authorities to issue building licences in his name, under the direction of local authorities, and used the Minister of Health as means of communication only. In fact the licence was held void since it was given by word of mouth only. The case revealed much legal and administrative confusion. Clearer guidance is given by *Lavender & Sons Ltd.* v. *Minister of Housing and Local Government* [1970] 1 WLR 1231, holding that one minister may not share his powers with another: see below, p. 368.

Parliament must have intended that only the designated minister should act. There may be cases where the power is of such a special kind that the minister must exercise it personally and not through officials. A wartime detention order has been assumed to be one such matter;[67] an order for the deportation of an alien has been held to be another;[68] and the same may well be true of an order for the return of a fugitive offender.[69]

SURRENDER, ABDICATION, DICTATION

Power in the wrong hands

Closely akin to delegation, and scarcely distinguishable from it in some cases, is any arrangement by which a power conferred upon one authority is in substance exercised by another. The proper authority may share its power with some one else, or may allow some one else to dictate to it by declining to act without their consent or by submitting to their wishes or instructions. The effect then is that the discretion conferred by Parliament is exercised, at least in part, by the wrong authority, and the resulting decision is ultra vires and void. So strict are the courts in applying this principle that they condemn some administrative arrangements which must seem quite natural and proper to those who make them. In this class might be included the case of the cinema licensing authority which, by requiring films to be approved by the British Board of Film Censors, was held to have surrendered its power of control[70] and also the case of the Police Complaints Board, which acted as if it were bound by a decision of the Director of Public Prosecutions when only required to 'have regard' to it.[71] This doctrine has even been applied to voting by local councillors.[71a]

Ministers and their departments have several times fallen foul of the same rule, no doubt equally to their surprise. The Minister of Housing and Local Government made it a rule to refuse planning permission for gravel-working on top-class agricultural land whenever the application was opposed by the Minister of Agriculture. The court held that this was to put the decisive power into the hands of the wrong minister and that a decision so taken must be quashed.[72] Similarly the court invalidated a reinstatement

[67] *Liversidge* v. *Anderson* [1942] AC 206 (see Lord Maugham at p. 224). But see *Re Golden Chemical Products Ltd.* [1976] Ch. 300 at 310.

[68] *R.* v. *Chiswick Police Station Superintendent ex p. Sacksteder* [1918] 1 KB 578 at 585, 591.

[69] See *R.* v. *Brixton Prison Governor ex p. Enahoro* [1963] 2 QB 455 (point assumed but not decided). See also *Minister for Aboriginal Affairs* v. *Peko-Wallsend Ltd.* (1986) 60 ALJR 560.

[70] *Ellis* v. *Dubowski*, above, p. 361.

[71] *R.* v. *Police Complaints Board ex p. Madden* [1983] 1 WLR 447.

[71a] *R.* v. *Walton Forest LBC ex p. Baxter* [1988] 2 WLR 257 (CA), upholding votes based on party policy.

[72] *Lavender & Sons Ltd.* v. *Minister of Housing and Local Government* [1970] 1 WLR 1231.

order made under wartime labour regulations by a national service officer, who was empowered to direct reinstatement of workers dismissed for misconduct.[73] For the officer was acting under directions from the minister, whereas he was a statutory authority in his own right and should have exercised his personal discretion. The minister's directions were merely that there should be reinstatement wherever the appeal board was unanimous. But in fact the minister had no power to lay down any such rule, however reasonable. Even where there is a right of appeal to the minister, and it may seem sensible to take account of his practice, it has been held that this must not be adopted uncritically; but this was a case where the Act specifically required a local authority to follow certain rules, which did not extend to the departmental practice which they followed wrongly.[74]

Clear-cut cases of unlawful dictation have occurred in other jurisdictions where ministers have attempted to interfere for political reasons. In one, the Prime Minister of Quebec gave instructions for the cancellation of a liquor licence where the licensee was supporting an unpopular section of the community;[75] in another, an Indian minister was alleged to have procured the taking-over by the state of businesses belonging to his political opponents.[76] If the minister's intervention is in fact the effective cause, and if the power to act belongs to a body which ought to act independently, the action taken is invalid on the ground of external dictation as well as on the obvious grounds of bad faith or abuse of power.[77]

Permissible guidance

Clearly these rules ought not to be carried to the length of preventing one government department from consulting another, or of preventing government agencies from acting in accordance with government policy. There must always be a difference between seeking advice and then genuinely exercising one's own discretion, on the one hand, and, on the other hand, acting obediently or automatically under some one else's advice or directions. A licensing authority, for instance, may quite properly take account of government policy in its decisions, provided that it genuinely decides each case itself. A borderline case divided opinions in the High Court of Australia where the majority held that the Director-General of Civil Aviation might refuse import licences for aircraft following the

[73] *Simms Motor Units Ltd.* v. *Minister of Labour* [1946] 2 All ER 201.
[74] *R.* v. *Stepney Cpn.* [1902] 1 KB 317.
[75] *Roncarelli* v. *Duplessis* (1959) 16 DLR (2d) 689 (licensee repeatedly provided bail for Jehovah's Witnesses).
[76] *Rowjee* v. *Andhra Pradesh* AIR [1964] SC 962.
[77] See below, p. 405.

Government's policy of not allowing new operators to enter the interstate air freight business.[78]

OVER-RIGID POLICIES

Policy and precedent

An authority can fail to give its mind to a case, and thus fail to exercise its discretion lawfully, by blindly following a policy laid down in advance.[79] It is a fundamental rule for the exercise of discretionary power that discretion must be brought to bear on every case: each one must be considered on its own merits and decided as the public interest requires at the time. The Greater London Council was criticised for disregard of this principle when it proceeded to make a large subsidy to the London bus and underground services as a matter of course because the ruling party had promised to do so in their election campaign.[80] They regarded themselves as irrevocably committed in advance, whereas their duty was to use their discretion. Nor may a local authority lawfully refuse all applications for housing for children of families considered to be 'intentionally homeless',[81] since the power to provide housing implies a duty to consider the different circumstances of each child.[82] Nor, for the same reason, may they automatically proceed to recondition substandard houses as soon as the owner has failed to comply with an improvement notice.[83] Nor may they refuse to repay rates overpaid if their policy is based upon advice which interprets their statutory discretionary power too narrowly.[84] Where the Secretary of State's policy was to disallow all merely local objections to the allocation of land for gipsies, the court held it unlawful for undue rigidity.[85] Where he made a rule that he would refuse grants to all projects already started before the grant application he fettered his discretion unlawfully.[86]

---

[78] R. v. Anderson ex p. Ipec-Air Pty. Ltd. (1965) 113 CLR 177.

[79] For discussion see (1972) 18 McGill LJ 310 (H. L. Molot); [1976] PL 332 (D. J. Galligan).

[80] Bromley LBC v. Greater London Council [1983] 1 AC 768 (Lords Diplock and Brandon).

[81] See above, p. 205.

[82] A-G ex rel. Tilley v. Wandsworth LBC [1981] 1 WLR 854 (declaration that resolution was unlawful).

[83] Elliott v. Brighton BC (1980) 79 LGR 506.

[84] R. v. Rochdale MBC ex p. Cromer Ring Mill Ltd. [1982] 3 All ER 761.

[85] R. v. Secretary of State for the Environment ex p. Hatton BC (1983) 82 LGR 662; and see R. v. Home Secretary ex p. Bennett [1986] The Times, 18 August (Home Office circular set unduly rigid criteria for approval of police rent allowance applications).

[86] R. v. Secretary of State for Transport ex p. Sherriff & Sons Ltd. [1986] The Times, 18 December.

The Court of Appeal has held that a local council's resolution might be quashed if councillors who voted for it did so under the orders of their political party instead of exercising their own judgment as their duty required.[87]

In enforcing this rule the courts are underlining the difference between judicial and administrative processes. The legal rights of litigants are decided according to legal rules and precedents which are sometimes held to prevail over the court's own opinion. But if an administrative authority acts in this way its decision is ultra vires and void. It is not allowed to 'pursue consistency at the expense of the merits of individual cases'.[88] This doctrine is applied even to statutory tribunals, despite their resemblance to courts of law.[89] Indeed, the quotation comes from a case in which it was held that the Transport Tribunal ought not to hold itself bound by its own precedents. But that tribunal, as explained elsewhere,[90] is in effect a licensing authority which takes decisions based on administrative policy, and it is the nature of the decision that counts rather than the outward appearance of the deciding body.

Just how far they may enforce a fixed policy is often a difficult question for authorities granting licences or permits. A clear instance was where an applicant for permission to sell pamphlets in public parks for the benefit of the blind was told that the Council had decided to grant no such permits, and could make no exception even in the most deserving case. The court regarded that 'not as the adoption of a policy in the exercise of a discretion but as a refusal to exercise any discretion',[91] and granted mandamus to compel the Council to consider the application.[92] It did not follow that they must give permission, or that they might not follow a policy: their duty was merely to exercise their discretion in each case, and not to shut the door indiscriminately either on all applicants or on applicants who did not conform to some particular requirement. This duty may well have some connection with the duty to give a fair hearing before refusing a licence.

[87] R. v. Waltham Forest LBC ex p. Waltham Forest Ratepayers Action Group [1987] The Times, 2 October (no unlawful fettering of discretion found).

[88] Merchandise Transport Ltd. v. British Transport Commission [1962] 2 QB 173 at 193.

[89] See R. v. Greater Birmingham Appeal Tribunal ex p. Simper [1974] QB 543 (tribunal applied rule of thumb instead of exercising discretion: decision quashed); R. v. Criminal Injuries Compensation Board ex p. RJC [1978] The Times, 21 January (discretion fettered by policy statement).

[90] Below, p. 901.

[91] Bankes LJ in R. v. Port of London Authority ex p. Kynoch Ltd. [1919] 1 KB 176 at 185.

[92] R. v. London County Council ex p. Corrie [1918] 1 KB 68. cf. Sagnata Investments Ltd. v. Norwich Cpn. [1971] 1 QB 614 (rigid policy against amusement arcades: no exercise of discretion. This was decided on appeal, not on judicial review). For a case of statutory permission to adopt a rigid policy of refusal see R. v. Herrod ex p. Leeds City District Council [1976] QB 540.

One member of the court said: that the 'prima facie right to be heard' was 'one of those public safeguards which we should always struggle to preserve'.[93]

Consequently a local education authority may follow its own rules in allotting pupils to schools, provided that its motives are not unreasonable, capricious or irrelevant, and provided that it is ready to consider exceptional cases.[94] Where it is at liberty to make a choice between conflicting policies, it may decide to make no exceptions, as where it adopts a policy of making all schools in its area into comprehensive schools and abolishing all grammar schools.[95] But even then it is in a stronger position if it has listened fairly to the objections of parents and others concerned.

Licensing authorities

The rule has often been canvassed in liquor licensing cases where the licensing justices have adopted some restrictive policy, for example for reducing the number of licences in their area.[96] If the justices refuse renewal of a licence under some new policy without considering the application on its merits, their decision will be quashed.[97] But there can be no objection to a declared policy provided that the application is properly heard and considered in each case. Thus where the justices announced publicly that they would renew restricted licences only subject to the same restrictions, save in very exceptional cases, and subsequently decided a case saying: 'The bench carefully considered the application but is not prepared to alter the policy', the court upheld its decision.[98] The court is careful not to inhibit public authorities from laying down policies, since consistent administrative policies are not only permissible but highly desirable. And it is no less desirable that policies should be made public, so that applicants may know what to expect. But the policies must naturally be based on proper and relevant grounds. The justices erred, therefore, in refusing an occasional licence under a policy of never allowing more than two such licences a year to any one applicant.[99] Even though they considered the case and were

---

[93] Sankey J (at 75).

[94] *Cumings* v. *Birkenhead Cpn.* [1972] Ch. 12, where Lord Denning MR expounds the rules as to policy.

[95] *Smith* v. *Inner London Education Authority* [1978] 1 All ER 411.

[96] *Boyle* v. *Wilson* [1907] AC 45.

[97] *R.* v. *Windsor Licensing Justices ex p. Hodes* [1983] 1 WLR 685.

[98] *R.* v. *Torquay Licensing Justices ex p. Brockman* [1951] 2 KB 784, distinguishing *R.* v. *Walsall Justices* (1854) 18 JP 757 (refusal to hear any application for new licences) and following *R.* v. *Holborn Licensing Justices* (1926) 42 TLR 778 (fixed policy but case duly considered).

[99] *R.* v. *Rotherham Licensing Justices ex p. Chapman* (1939) 55 TLR 718 (explained in the *Torquay* case, above). See also *Perilly* v. *Tower Hamlets London Borough Council* [1973] QB 9 (mistaken rule of 'first come first served').

prepared to make exceptions, they acted on a policy different from that which the Act imposed upon them, which was public convenience. Similarly where the justices had refused a licence to sell liquor to one theatre, and for the sake of consistency felt obliged to refuse one to another theatre which had enjoyed it for fifty years previously, the decision was set aside since the statutory purpose was 'for ensuring order and decency' and the justices' motive was primarily to enforce consistency.[1] These decisions are merely examples of the abuse of discretionary power, discussed elsewhere.[2] None of them is in any way hostile to the adoption of a policy as such.

Bankes LJ stated the basic distinction in a frequently cited judgment. He contrasted two classes of cases: 'cases where a tribunal in the honest exercise of its discretion has adopted a policy, and, without refusing to hear an applicant, intimates to him what its policy is, and that after hearing him it will in accordance with its policy decide against him, unless there is something exceptional in his case'; and 'cases where a tribunal has passed a rule, or come to a determination, not to hear any application of a particular character by whomsoever made'.[3] Accordingly the Port of London Authority, which was empowered to grant or withhold permission for the construction of docks, was allowed to enforce its policy of refusing permission, after due consideration, in cases where the new dock would come into competition with its own docks.

Ministers and national policy

Ministerial policies are subject to the same principles as the policies of other authorities. Accordingly it was unobjectionable for the Minister of Housing and Local Government, in deciding planning appeals, to follow a policy of discouraging development likely to interfere with the Jodrell Bank radio telescope, provided that he judged each individual case fairly.[4] The Home Secretary is likewise entitled to pursue a policy of discrimination against foreign students of 'scientology' by refusing to renew their residence premits, subject to the same qualification;[5] and he may change his policy so as to refuse release on licence ('parole') to certain classes of prisoners in all but the most exceptional cases, so long as each case is examined individually.[6] The law as stated by Bankes LJ applied in these

---

[1] R. v. *Flintshire CC Licensing Committee ex parte Barrett* [1957] 1 QB 350.
[2] See particularly R. v. *Birmingham Planning Committee ex p. Kennedy* [1972] 2 QB 140 (unlawful requirement that licences be purchased), below, p. 421.
[3] R. v. *Port of London Authority ex p. Kynoch Ltd.* [1919] 1 KB 176 at 182.
[4] *Stringer* v. *Ministry of Housing and Local Government* [1970] 1 WLR 1281.
[5] *Schmidt* v. *Home Secretary* [1969] 2 Ch. 149.
[6] *Re Findlay* [1985] AC 318. Opinions in the Divisional Court and the Court of Appeal were divided.

cases. It was reviewed by the House of Lords in another case where the Board of Trade had made it a rule to refuse all applications for investment grants for items costing less than £25.[7] The claimants had invested over £4m. in oxygen cylinders, but since each cylinder cost only about £20 the Board refused a grant, after giving full consideration to the case. The Act said merely that the Board 'may make' a grant. The House of Lords upheld the Board's action. Lord Reid said: '. . . if the Minister thinks that policy or good administration requires the operation of some limiting rule, I find nothing to stop him'. He added the familiar proviso: 'provided that the authority is always willing to listen to anyone with something new to say—of course I do not mean to say that there need be an oral hearing'. But he sounded a caveat against taking Bankes LJ's formula literally in every case; and Lord Dilhorne carried this further, saying: 'it seems somewhat pointless and a waste of time that the Board should have to consider applications which are bound as a result of its policy decision to fail'. There may thus be room for some relaxation of the requirement of consideration of every application on its merits, at any rate in cases involving a national policy where applications are multitudinous. And there is no real difference in this context between a 'policy' and a 'rule'.

In a strongly contrasting case a minister resolved to turn a deaf ear to all pleas for a change of policy and his decision was quashed.[8] He had consulted local authorities generally before obtaining statutory power to reduce the central government's rate support grant to those whose expenditure was in his view excessive. After the Act was passed he refused to receive further representations and decided on reductions in the case of several authorities. He was held to have fettered his discretion unlawfully by settling and announcing his policy before he obtained his powers and then refusing to consider any appeals for exceptions. He had disregarded his duty 'to listen to any objector who shows that he may have something new to say'. He had also disregarded the principles of natural justice.[9]

Sometimes a minister will have power to make regulations covering the same ground as some policy which he has adopted, and it may then be argued that he should enforce his policy openly by making regulations, which may be subject to Parliamentary scrutiny, rather than covertly by exercising discretion in each case. This argument was rejected by the Court of Session in a case where the Secretary of State had refused to approve the appointment of a chief constable on the ground that he came from within

---

[7] *British Oxygen Co. Ltd.* v. *Board of Trade* [1971] AC 610 cf. *Kilmarnock Magistrates* v. *Secretary of State for Scotland* (below).

[8] *R.* v. *Secretary of State for the Environment ex p. Brent LBC* [1982] QB 593 (Divisional Court).

[9] See below, p. 556.

the local force.[10] The Secretary of State had both a discretionary power to withhold consent and also power to prescribe the qualifications of chief constables by regulation but he had made no regulation embodying his policy for rejecting internal appointments. There might perhaps be cases where a regulation-making power could be held to exclude administrative discretion; but where both powers are conferred by the same statute it is reasonable to allow the minister to choose between them; and it is, indeed, his duty to decide every case as he believes the public interest requires at the time.

Indiscriminate action

It undoubtedly remains true that the court will not accept the indiscriminate use of a power where cases ought to be considered on their own merits. If a local authority has power to refer furnished lettings to a rent tribunal, in order to obtain adjudication of the rent, it may not adopt a rule of referring all tenancies in any block of flats where two or more reductions of rent have previously been ordered, whether or not the tenants have complained.[11] For it is inherent in the power to refer that there should be some reasonable and specified ground for doing so in each particular case. If the authority has power to require owners of unfit houses to repair them, or else to repair them itself at the owner's expense, it may not give standing orders that the latter course shall always be taken without regard to individual circumstances.[12] There can be no substitute for the genuine exercise of discretion on every occasion.

RESTRICTION BY CONTRACT OR GRANT

Contractual fetters on discretion

Just as public authorities must have policies, so they must make contracts. Like policies, contracts may be inconsistent with the authorities' proper exercise of their powers. But, unlike policies, contracts are legally binding commitments, and therefore they present more difficult problems. The general principle is the same: an authority may not by contract fetter itself

---

[10] *Kilmarnock Magistrates* v. *Secretary of State for Scotland* 1961 SC 350 (Secretary of State's decision upheld). This question has been much litigated in the United States: see Schwartz and Wade, *Legal Control of Government*, 93.

[11] *R.* v. *Paddington and St. Marylebone Rent Tribunal ex p. Bell London & Provincial Properties Ltd.* [1941] 1 KB 666 (below, p. 422). cf. *Wood* v. *Widnes Cpn.* [1898] 1 QB 463 (over-rigid policy of requiring installation of water-closets).

[12] *Elliott* v. *Brighton BC* (1980) 79 LGR 506.

so as to disable itself from exercising its discretion as required by law. Its paramount duty is to preserve its own freedom to decide in every case as the public interest requires at the time.[13] But at the same time its powers may include the making of binding contracts, and it may be most important that it should make them. Since most contracts fetter freedom of action in some way, there may be difficult questions of degree in determining how far the authority may legally commit itself for the future.[14]

Two leading decisions of the House of Lords may be contrasted. In the *Ayr Harbour* case the harbour trustees had been incorporated by a local Act of Parliament with power to acquire compulsorily certain specified land for the purpose of carrying out certain specified works. On the acquisition of one part of the land they wished to give an undertaking to the former owner that he should have unobstructed access from his adjoining land to the harbour, thus reducing the compensation payable for injurious affection of that land. The House of Lords held that any such undertaking would be incompetent.[15] The trustees had specific statutory power to build, etc., on the land in question, and they could not strip themselves of this power by making a bargain. Lord Blackburn emphasised that the powers were entrusted to them by the legislature of the public good, and that a contract purporting to bind them and their successors not to exercise the powers was therefore void.

In the *Birkdale Electricity* case the House of Lords refused to apply this doctrine to an agreement by a statutory electricity company not to raise its charges above those of the adjoining electricity authority, the Corporation of Southport.[16] The company had statutory power to charge what it wished, subject to certain limits, and it was contended that any contract which fettered its exercise of this power could not be binding. But the House of Lords refused to accept an argument which would invalidate many ordinary trading contracts made by statutory authorities in the due management of their businesses. The *Ayr Harbour* case was distinguished as one where the trustees 'renounced a part of their statutory birthright' by offering 'to sterilize part of their acquisition, so far as the statutory purpose of their undertaking was concerned.'[17] In other words, there was a clear incompatability between their specific statutory purposes and the contract which they wished to make. The electricity company, on the other hand, should have commercial liberty as part of its statutory birthright of selling

---

[13] See *Denman Ltd.* v. *Westminster Cpn.* [1906] 1 Ch. 464 at 476.

[14] See [1971] PL 288 (P. Rogerson).

[15] *Ayr Harbour Trustees* v. *Oswald* (1883) 8 App. Cas. 623.

[16] *Birkdale District Electric Supply Company* v. *Southport Cpn.* [1926] AC 355, criticising *York Cpn.* v. *Henry Leetham & Sons Ltd.* [1924] 1 Ch. 557 (contract assuring fixed river tolls for twenty years held inconsistent with power to increase tolls as required).

[17] *Birkdale* (as above) at pp. 371–2 (Lord Sumner).

electricty, and that liberty should include power to make binding contracts. It would be absurd if the existence of statutory powers invalidated 'mere contracts restricting the undertakers' future freedom of action in respect of the business management of their undertaking'.[18]

Compatibility of powers

The important question is whether there is incompatibility between the purposes of the statutory powers and the purposes for which the contract is made. In cases where there is no commercial element the court is normally ready to condemn any restriction on a public authority's freedom to act in the public interest. Thus a planning authority cannot bind itself by contract either to grant[19] or to refuse[20] planning permission in the future. In one case a local authority designated a sports ground as a proposed public open space, but made a formal agreement with the owner that this designation should cease to operate if the authority had not purchased the land by a certain time, that it would not purchase the land either voluntarily or compulsorily during a certain period, and that it would not make any claim for betterment. All these undertakings were void as clearly incompatible with the authority's duty to preserve its powers intact.[21] On the other hand it has been held to be compatible with the powers of a city council to give a public assurance that it would not increase the number of licensed taxicabs until a local Act of Parliament had been obtained.[22] This was not, apparently, a contractually binding undertaking,[23] but it influenced the Court of Appeal to hold that the council failed to act fairly and could not lawfully proceed without hearing those affected and paying due regard to its own assurance.

It follows *a fortiori* that a contract can contain no implied term which conflicts with the freedom to exercise a governmental power. This

---

[18] As above.

[19] *Ransom & Luck Ltd.* v. *Surbiton Borough Council* [1949] Ch. 180 (contract not to revoke permission). But see *Windsor and Maidenhead RBC* v. *Brandrose Investments Ltd.* [1983] 1 WLR 509 (relief refused in discretion).

[20] *Stringer* v. *Minister of Housing and Local Government* [1970] 1 WLR 1281 (formal agreement with Manchester University to discourage development in the area of the Jodrell Bank radio telescope).

[21] *Triggs* v. *Staines Urban District Council* [1969] 1 Ch. 10.

[22] *R.* v. *Liverpool Corporation ex parte Liverpool Taxi Fleet Operators' Association* [1972] 2 QB 299. For its 'acting fairly' context see below, p. 521.

[23] Lord Denning MR said: 'So long as the performance of the undertaking is compatible with their public duty, they must honour it.' He also said that 'it certainly was binding unless overridden by some imperative public interest'. No such obligation was mentioned by the other members of the court, but unilateral undertakings have since been held binding in other cases: see below, p. 423.

consideration determined a case where the London Corporation had contracted with a firm of barge-owners for the removal by water of large quantities of refuse, on terms fixed in 1936 which later proved unprofitable to the firm. The Corporation was also the port health authority and responsible for making byelaws. During the period of the contract they made new byelaws imposing more stringent requirements on barges, which would have added to the firm's losses. The firm claimed that the contract for refuse-collecting necessarily implied an undertaking by the Corporation to refrain from altering its byelaws to the firm's disadvantage, and that for breach of this undertaking they were entitled to rescind. The Court of Appeal held that there could be no question of implying a term which, even if express, could not be legally binding, since the Corporation could not contract out of its statutory duties as port health authority.[24] There would seem to be no objection to a term, express or implied, under which the Corporation would undertake, if it should change the byelaws, to compensate the contractor. This is the result achieved in French law by the doctrine of *fait du prince*, under which a government contractor can claim an equitable adjustment if the government, by use of its paramount powers, upsets the calculations on which the contract was made.[25]

The principles which forbid the fettering of public authorities' powers by contract apply equally to covenants and grants in property transactions. If the Crown grants a lease, this cannot prevent the Crown from requisitioning the property under wartime statutory powers.[26] In this case the Crown cannot be said to have 'evicted' the tenant, and thus released him from liability for the rent, since the taking of the premises by requisition was a lawful act. Nor can the usual implied covenant for quiet enjoyment include any implication that the power of requisition will not be exercised, since clearly that power must in the public interest be paramount.[27] Similarly if the government acquires land for national defence, they have overriding power to use the land as an airfield even though it is subject to a restrictive covenant limiting its use to

---

[24] *Cory (William) & Son Ltd.* v. *London Corporation* [1951] 2 KB 476. It was conceded that the new byelaws would frustrate the contract, but the firm was claiming immediate rescission as for breach.

[25] See Mitchell, *The Contracts of Public Authorities*, 193. For criticism see P. Rogerson, [1971] PL at p. 300, suggesting that an automatic right to compensation unduly favours those who contract with public authorities as compared with other contractors who may suffer equal loss from acts of government. In principle all contractors should cover themselves against this risk, but there are special reasons for implying an indemnity when it is within the power of one contracting party to alter the situation to the disadvantage of the other.

[26] *Commissioners of Crown Lands* v. *Page* [1960] 2 QB 274 (CA).

[27] There is no implied term that the powers shall be exercisable; no covenant can prevent them from being exercisable.

agriculture[28]—and it can make no difference whether the covenant was made by the government itself or by some predecessor in title.

Valid commitments

It would be quite wrong to conclude that a public authority can 'escape from any contract which it finds disadvantageous by saying that it never promised to act otherwise than for the public good'.[29] There will often be situations where a public authority must be at liberty to bind itself for the very purpose of exercising its powers effectively. The Bournemouth Corporation, on acquiring land for a public park, entered into a restrictive covenant with the vendor that the land should be used as a pleasure ground free from building or erections. The Corporation wished to erect public lavatories, having specific statutory power to do so in any public park. The Court of Appeal held that they were bound by their covenant, and refused to accept that there was any analogy with the *Ayr* case.[30] The land had been acquired for an express purpose and there was nothing contrary to that purpose in the observance of the covenant. Similarly a local authority, on acquiring land for allotments, could validly covenant that it would be used only for that purpose.[31] If it were otherwise, local authorities would often find it very difficult to acquire land by agreement. This is another case where the 'statutory birthright' must include power to make binding promises. And, of course, such a power may be conferred by statute.[32]

The truth is that multi-purpose authorities, such as local councils, are equipped with a great many different powers for different purposes, and that some of these may necessarily be inconsistent with others. It cannot be right to restrict the exercise of power which the authority wishes to use in some particular situation, because some other power, which the authority does not then wish to use, would then become unusable. A local authority which has power to maintain public parks may thus quite properly dedicate a part to public use, even though this makes it impossible for the future for it to exercise its general powers of letting the land in question.[33]

The Court of Appeal has indicated that in the case of overlapping and conflicting powers the first thing to ascertain is the object for which the

---

[28] *Marten* v. *Flight Refuelling Ltd.* [1962] Ch. 115 (covenant by predecessor in title).

[29] *Commissioners of Crown Lands* v. *Page* (above) at 293 (Devlin LJ).

[30] *Stourcliffe Estates Co. Ltd.* v. *Bournemouth Cpn.* [1910] 2 Ch. 12. See similarly *R.* v. *Hammersmith and Fulham LBC ex p. Beddowes* [1987] QB 1050.

[31] *Leicester (Earl)* v. *Wells-next-the-Sea Urban District Council* [1973] Ch. 110.

[32] *Windsor BC* v. *Brandcote Investments Ltd.* [1981] 1 WLR 1083 (statutory agreement with planning authority).

[33] *Blake* v. *Hendon Cpn.* [1962] 1 QB 283.

land is held. All other powers are subordinate to the main power to carry out the statutory object and can be used only to the extent that their exercise is compatible with that object.[34] This principle was applied, though without being cited, in a case where the Wolverhampton Corporation had granted to a company the right to use the municipal airport for ninety-nine years. After thirty-five years the Corporation decided to discontinue the airport and use the land as a housing estate. But the Vice-Chancellor held that it had no right to do so in breach of its commitment to the company, which had been validly made.[35] He said:

Obviously, where a power is exercised in such a manner as to create a right extending over a term of years, the existence of that right pro tanto excludes the exercise of other statutory powers in respect of the same subject matter, but there is no authority and I can see no principle upon which that sort of exercise could be held to be invalid as a fetter upon the future exercise of powers.

In this case as in many others the court was pressed with the *Ayr* case. But it is quite evident that the doctrine of that case will not be extended to the point where it can be invoked by a public authority as a pretext for escaping from obligations which it has deliberately and properly contracted.

Non-contractual cases

It has several times been held that a non–contractual undertaking may bind a public body. One case was where a taxicab licensing authority gave a public undertaking not to increase the number of licences for a certain time. Although this was a mere statement of future policy, which in general cannot be restricted by agreement, it was said that the undertaking 'certainly was binding unless overridden by some imperative public interest.'[36] That such an undertaking could create a legal obligation was a novel proposition. But it has since fallen into place as part of the doctrine that breach of an undertaking may lead to inconsistent and unfair action amounting either to an abuse of power[37] or else to a breach of the principles of natural justice.[38]

The grant of an easement, such as a right of way, may or may not be compatible with a public body's statutory powers and duties. This question

[34] *Blake v. Hendon Cpn* (above) at pp. 301–2, following *British Transport Commission v. Westmorland County Council* (below).
[35] *Dowty Boulton Paul Ltd. v. Wolverhampton Cpn.* [1971] 1 WLR 204.
[36] *R. v. Liverpool Cpn. ex p. Liverpool Taxi Fleet Operators' Association* [1972] 2 QB 299 (Lord Denning MR). For this case see above, p. 377.
[37] See below, p. 423.
[38] See below, p. 521.

has often arisen,[39] but many of the cases concern railway companies and other non-governmental bodies, outside the field of administrative law. They were considered by the House of Lords in a case where a railway company had allowed the public to use a bridge over their railway for so long that dedication as a public highway was to be presumed. The question was whether the dedication of a highway was inconsistent with the company's statutory objects and powers, including their power to demolish the bridge in certain circumstances. This was answered in the negative,[40] and it was laid down that the test of consistency was not to be applied with undue rigour, as had occurred in some earlier cases.[41] It was to be based on 'consideration of reasonable probabilities'[42] and it was to be a 'pragmatic test', bearing in mind that it would be a grave impediment to public amenity if railways were legally incompetent to create public rights of way across their lines.[43]

ESTOPPEL—MISLEADING ADVICE

Estoppel and discretion

The doctrine of estoppel must be prevented not only from enlarging the powers of public authorities illegitimately, as already explained:[44] it must also be prevented from cramping the proper exercise of their discretion. The principle here is the same as in the case of contracts, already discussed, and it is equally capable of causing hardship.[45] The leading cases concern misleading official rulings.

The employees of public authorities may often be asked to advise or rule upon some question which only their employing authority can decide. Expense may reasonably be incurred in reliance on the advice given, but if

[39] See *R. v. Leake (Inhabitants)* (1833) 5 B & Ad 469 and later cases cited in *British Transport Commission v. Westmorland County Council* (below).

[40] *British Transport Commission v. Westmorland County Council* [1958] AC 126.

[41] *Mulliner v. Midland Railway* (1879) 11 Ch. D. 611; *Paterson v. Provost (&c.) of St. Andrews* (1881) 6 App. Cas. 833. Both these decisions are hostile to the creation of public rights of way by authorities with limited powers. The second concerned a road on the St Andrews golf links.

[42] *British Transport Commission v. Westmorland County Council* (above) at p. 144 (Lord Simonds).

[43] *British Transport Commission* (as above) at pp. 153, 156 (Lord Radcliffe).

[44] Above, p. 262. For discussion see [1981] CLP 1 (A. W. Bradley); (1977) 93 LQR 398 (P. P. Craig); [1972] PL 43 (M. A. Fazal); [1965] PL 237 (G. Ganz); (1953) 53 Col LR 374 (F. C. Newman).

[45] See the *Laker Airways* case, above, p. 263.

it turns out to be wrong there is usually no legal remedy. The authority's freedom to decide as it thinks the public interest requires must on no account be compromised, hard though the result may be. A notable illustration was a case where a company had bought land for use as a builder's yard, on the understanding that it had an existing use right for that purpose, so that no planning permission would be required.[46] In order to make sure of this before committing themselves to the purchase, the company consulted the borough surveyor, an employee of the planning authority, who confirmed that the right existed and that no planning permission was necessary. But this advice was wrong, and eventually the planning authority served an enforcement notice to stop the company from using the land as a builders' yard. It was held, though reluctantly, that this notice was enforceable, and that no advice or assurance from the borough engineer could hamper the planning authority's free and unhindered discretion, which they had a duty to exercise in the public interest. In the same way a local education authority's decision to pay the school transport costs of a pupil could not estop them from revoking it when it was found to have been taken under a mistake as to the facts.[47]

In endeavouring to protect the citizen against such hardships the courts have strained the law and given doubtful decisions. An irregular departmental decision was held binding on the Crown in a case where an army officer claimed a disablement pension on account of war injury. The War Office wrote to him that 'Your disability has been accepted as attributable to military service.' But for this injury the responsible department was the Ministry of Pensions, which the War Office had not consulted. The Ministry later decided that the disability was not attributable and the pension appeal tribunal upheld that decision. In reliance on the War Office letter the claimant had refrained from getting a medical opinion and assembling other evidence which might have strengthened his case against the Ministry. On appeal to the court, Denning J reversed the decisions of the Ministry and the tribunal, holding that the Crown was bound by the War Office letter.[48] He invoked two doctrines of his own creation: that assurances intended to be acted upon and in fact acted upon were binding; and that where a government department wrongfully assumes authority to perform some legal act, the citizen is entitled to assume that it has the authority. He also dismissed the contentions that

---

[46] *Southend-on-Sea Corporation* v. *Hodgson (Wickford) Ltd.* [1962] 1 QB 416. See also *Brooks and Burton Ltd.* v. *Secretary of State for the Environment* (1977) 75 LGR 285, reversed on other grounds [1977] 1 WLR 1294 but approved on this point in *Western Fish Products Ltd.* v. *Penwith DC* (1978) 38 P & CR 7.

[47] *Rootkin* v. *Kent CC* [1981] 1 WLR 1186 (above, p. 255).

[48] *Robertson* v. *Minister of Pensions* [1949] 1 KB 227. See also *Re L (AC) (an infant)* [1971] 3 All ER 743 (above, p. 263).

estoppels do not bind the Crown ('that doctrine has long been exploded') and that the Crown cannot fetter its future executive action.[49]

The proposition about wrongfully assumed authority was emphatically repudiated by the House of Lords in a later case in which Denning LJ had again put it forward. The question was whether ship repairs, which could be lawfully executed only under written licence, could in effect be validly authorised merely by oral permission from the licensing officer. Could the licensee rely on the licensing officer's purported authority to grant an oral licence? The House of Lords answered this firmly in the negative.[50] Although this was a somewhat stronger case, in that there would otherwise have been a violation of an express statutory prohibition, it would seem necessary to reject the whole notion of estoppel of a public authority by wrongful assumption of statutory authority.[51] For it clearly conflicts with the basic rule that no estoppel can give the authority power which it does not possess. Just as there was no power to license ship repairs orally, so there was no power for the War Office to award pensions which in law were available only from the Ministry of Pensions.

Nevertheless the Court of Appeal has held a local planning authority bound by wrong statements made by its own officers, in apparent defiance of the rules against both delegation and estoppel. After planning permission had duly been given for the building of a group of houses in London, the builder submitted a revised plan and asked for approval of the variations. The planning officer had lost the file with the original plan and, thinking that the variations were not material, told the builder that no further permission would be needed. In fact the variations brought the new houses much closer to existing houses, and when one of them was already nearly finished the planning authority refused permission and threatened enforcement. The Court of Appeal granted a declaration that there was already a valid planning permission for the house on the altered site.[52] But in fact the planning officer had no power to grant planning permission at all, and the planning authority itself had not done so in respect of the new site. Lord Denning MR held that the practice of allowing the planning officer to rule that variations were not material gave him 'ostensible

---

[49] See below, p. 831.

[50] *Howell* v. *Falmouth Boat Construction Co. Ltd.* [1951] AC 837. See also *A-G for Ceylon* v. *A. D. Silva* [1953] AC 461, quoted below, p. 385.

[51] In this context estoppel has a wider sense than estoppel by representations of fact, and includes representations of law. For ostensible agency in contract see below, p. 822.

[52] *Lever Finance Ltd.* v. *Westminster London Borough Council* [1971] 1 QB 222 (judgments not reserved). Sachs LJ held that on the facts the planning authority had delegated its power to the planning officer under Town and Country Planning Act 1968, s. 64; statutory formalities had not been observed, but perhaps they could have been treated as merely directory.

authority', since the planning authority might have delegated its powers to him and the builder was entitled to assume that the necessary resolution had been passed.[53] He also stated that a public authority may be bound by representations made by their officer within this ostensible authority if some other person acts on them.[54] These two propositions were virtually the same as those that had been rejected by the House of Lords in the ship-licensing case,[55] but this was not cited.

The unfortunate features of the Court of Appeal's decision were first that it sacrificed the interests of the neighbouring house-owners, who were forced to accept houses overlooking them much more closely than the planning authority would have permitted. Secondly, it sacrificed the public interest, since the court deprived the responsible public authority of the powers of control which the Act assigned to them and to them only. As has been amply illustrated, the court is normally careful to prevent any legal doctrines from impeding the free exercise of statutory discretion in the public interest by the proper body.

Wrestling with the problems so created, another Court of Appeal supplied a partial corrective in a case where a firm purchased a disused factory for the purpose of manufacturing fish products and incurred expenditure after being told orally on behalf of the local authority's chief planning officer that application for an 'established use' certificate would be 'purely a formality'.[56] The local authority eventually refused the certificate and refused planning permission. Dismissing the firm's claim, the court held that there were only two kinds of exception to the principle that a public authority could not be estopped from exercising its duties and powers. One exception was where it had statutory power to delegate functions to its officers and there were special circumstances to justify the applicant in thinking that the officer thus had power to bind the authority by an irrevocable decision. The earlier Court of Appeal case was brought within this exception because of the evidence of a widespread practice of allowing planning officers to authorise immaterial modifications of approved plans. But the mere holding of such an office was not enough, and the court rejected Lord Denning's proposition that any one dealing with a planning officer is entitled to assume that he is authorised to make

[53] The Town and Country Planning Act 1968, s. 64, was already in force. It was on this ground that the *Southend* case (above, p. 382) was distinguished.

[54] This must mean 'acts on them to his detriment': *Norfolk County Council* v. *Secretary of State for the Environment* [1973] 1 WLR 1400, where Lord Widgery CJ accepted Lord Denning's proposition with this addition. For this case see above, p. 262. See also *Rootkin* v. *Kent CC* [1981] 1 WLR 1186; *A-G* v. *Taff-Ely BC* [1981] 42 P & CR 1.

[55] *Howell* v. *Falmouth Boat Construction Co. Ltd.* (above).

[56] *Western Fish Products Ltd.* v. *Penwith DC* (1978) 38 P & CR 7 (later reported in [1981] 2 All ER 204) (unanimous judgment).

binding decisions. The court also stressed the injustice to third parties and to the public where a planning authority is held bound by an estoppel to allow development which flouts its planning policy.

The other exception is where the authority waives a procedural requirement relating to some application made to it, whereupon it may be estopped from relying on the lack of formality.[57] As already explained,[58] this is an established exception in cases where it does not hamper the authority in the discharge of its statutory functions.

Despite these restrictive rules, the Court of Appeal has since held the Crown estopped by a colonial governor's letter wrongly stating that an applicant's children already had British citizenship, so that he discontinued an application for their registration. Registration was discretionary, but it was conceded that it would have been granted. The House of Lords, however, found other reasons for rejecting the Crown's argument that it was now too late to rectify the mistake, while noting that the element of discretionary power might have made it difficult to establish an estoppel.[59]

The solution: compensation

The dilemma which misleading rulings can create is certainly painful. But it does not follow that the right solution is to disregard the public interest, together with the interest of those whom the law is intended to protect. If the force of law is given to a ruling from an official merely because it is wrong, the official who has no legal power is in effect substituted for the proper authority, which is forced to accept what it considers a bad decision.[60] To legitimate ultra vires acts in this way cannot be a sound policy, being a negation of the fundamental canons of administrative law. As the Privy Council said in an analogous case of a Crown officer who made an unauthorised contract:[61]

It may be said that it causes hardship to a purchaser . . . if the burden of ascertaining whether or not the Principal Collector has authority to enter into the sale is placed upon him. This undoubtedly is true. But . . . to hold otherwise would be to hold

---

[57] The court cites *Wells* v. *Minister of Housing and Local Government* [1967] 1 WLR 1000, where the waiver was by the authority itself. It seems that officers of the authority may also raise estoppels of this kind: *Re L (AC) (an infant)* [1971] 3 All ER 743 (above, p. 264).

[58] Above, p. 267.

[59] *Gowa* v. *Attorney-General* [1985] 1 WLR 1003. The Court of Appeal's decision is reported briefly in [1984] The Times, 27 December.

[60] In *Wells* v. *Minister of Housing and Local Government* (above) Russell LJ, dissenting, attributed that policy to the natural indignation that the practice should operate as a trap for the unwary, adding that 'the question is, I think one of a law not to be decided by a thoroughly bad administrative practice'.

[61] *A-G for Ceylon* v. *A. D. Silva* [1953] AC 461 at 480.

that public officers had dispensing powers because they then could by unauthorised acts nullify or extend the provisions of the Ordinance. Of the two evils this would be the greater one.

Nor should it make any difference that the decision forced upon the public authority is one which would have been within its powers, as opposed to one which would have been outside them.[62] For decisions which are against the public interest, in the view of the proper authority, are scarcely less objectionable if intra vires than if ultra vires. The Court of Appeal has now very properly recognised the dangers of giving rein to the doctrine of estoppel in public law and has said that its extension cannot be justified beyond the two exceptions explained above.[63]

The only acceptable solution, therefore, is to enforce the law but to compensate the person who suffered the loss by acting on a ruling from the ostensibly proper official. If the ruling leads to the erection of a house without planning permission, and the planning authority thinks it wrong to give permission, the house should be demolished and the builder should be compensated, in the same way as when a valid planning permission is revoked and compensation is paid for abortive expenditure.

The Parliamentary Commissioner for Administration has given a lead in the right direction by obtaining compensation in a number of such cases, for example for an importer who had to pay purchase tax on a car imported on the faith of a prior official assurance that it would be duty-free.[64] The giving of wrong rulings by officials is maladministration and this is the correct basis for redress. French law has found no difficulty in reaching this solution[65] and English law should equally well be able to reach it. It is on all accounts better than manipulating the law so as to uphold acts which are ultra vires or contrary to the public interest, in an attempt to make two wrongs into a right. It is true that many people have to rely on legal or other advice which may prove to be wrong, but there is a special claim to redress where loss is caused by a wrong ruling from a governmental authority on whose guidance the citizen is entitled to rely.

In a growing number of cases a solution has been found in the tort of negligent misstatement, now being developed by the courts.[66] Although

---

[62] De Smith, *Constitutional and Administrative Law*, 4th edn., 402 and M. A. Fazal, [1972] PL 43, suggest this distinction.

[63] In the *Western Fish Products* case (above); and see *Rootkin* v. *Kent CC* (above).

[64] See above, p. 91.

[65] The Conseil d'État treats misleading official advice as *faute de service*: see CE 10 juill. 1964, *Duffaut*, Rec. 399; CE 17 déc. 1965, *Jaquet*, Rec. 699. In both cases planning authorities misled purchasers of land by informing them that there were no restrictions on building, whereas the lands were reserved for an airfield and a university respectively; and when permission to build was later refused, the purchasers recovered compensation from the state.

[66] *Hedley Byrne & Co. Ltd.* v. *Heller & Partners Ltd.* [1964] AC 465 is the root case.

negligence is not always easy to prove, it is sometimes self-evident in cases of wrong official rulings. A local authority has been held liable for the failure by one of its clerks to search the local register of land charges with due care, thus causing pecuniary loss.[67] A government department has been held liable similarly for negligently advising an exporter that he would be insured against loss when in fact he was not.[68] And other examples are accumulating. Wrong advice or assurances given by officials of planning authorities might make them liable similarly, so as to compensate the misguided developer and avoid the legitimation of wrongful assumption of authority. This head of liability is further discussed below in the wider context of negligent government acts and decisions.[69]

Misleading official advice may, in addition, be a contributory factor to action by a public authority which is so unfair and inconsistent that it amounts to an abuse of power.[70] Where local authorities wrongly advised students that they were ineligible for grants, thus deterring them from making their applications in time, and then refused grants on the ground that the applications were late, the refusals were quashed as unfair and irrational and an abuse of discretion[71]—a form of maladministration amply illustrated in the following chapter.

Wrong official advice may also sometimes be a good defence to a criminal charge, but only where there would be no offence if the advice given were correct.[72]

---

[67] *Ministry of Housing and Local Government* v. *Sharp* [1970] 2 QB 223.
[68] *Culford Metal Industries Ltd.* v. *Export Credits Guarantee Department* [1981] The Times 25 March.
[69] Below, p. 762.
[70] See below, p. 423.
[71] *R.* v. *West Glamorgan CC ex p. Gheissary* [1985] The Times, 18 December.
[72] *Cambridgeshire County Council* v. *Rust* [1972] 2 QB 426.

12

ABUSE OF DISCRETION

RESTRICTION OF DISCRETION

Discretion limited by law

It used to be thought to be classical constitutional doctrine that wide discretionary power was incompatible with the rule of law.[1] But this dogma cannot be taken seriously today, and indeed it never contained much truth. What the rule of law demands is not that wide discretionary power should be eliminated, but that the law should be able to control its exercise. Modern government demands discretionary powers which are as wide as they are numerous. Parliamentary draftsmen strive to find new forms of words which will make discretion even wider, and Parliament all too readily enacts them. It is the attitude of the courts to such seemingly unbounded powers which is perhaps the most revealing feature of a system of administrative law.[2]

The first requirement is the recognition that all power has legal limits. The next requirement, no less vital, is that the courts should draw those limits in a way which strikes the most suitable balance between executive efficiency and legal protection of the citizen. Parliament constantly confers upon public authorities powers which on their face might seem absolute and arbitrary. But arbitrary power and unfettered discretion are what the courts refuse to countenance. They have woven a network of restrictive principles which require statutory powers to be exercised reasonably and in good faith, for proper purposes only, and in accordance with the spirit as well as the letter of the empowering Act. They have also, as explained elswhere, imposed stringent procedural requirements.[3] Here we are concerned with the substance of administrative discretion.

[1] Dicey, *Law of the Constitution*, 9th edn., 202.
[2] For discussion see Galligan, *Discretionary Power*. For the corresponding law in France see [1986] PL 99 (J. Bell); [1987] PL 287 (R. Errera). For the USA see Schwartz, *Administrative Law*, 2nd edn., 613; (1986) 54 *Geo. Wash L. Rev.* 469 (C. H. Koch); Schwartz and Wade, *Legal Control of Government*, 260, 262; (1966) 82 LQR 226 at 247 (Wade); Davis, *Discretionary Justice*, discusses problems of discretionary power in the United States but says little about the role of the courts. See also Davis, *Discretionary Justice in Europe and America*. For criticism see [1984] PL 570 (R. Baldwin and K. Hawkins). Note also Recommendation R(80)2 of the Committee of Ministers, Council of Europe (11 March 1980).
[3] Below, p. 465.

Discretion is an element in all power, as opposed to duty, so that 'abuse of discretion' could be made to include most of administrative law. But it is more convenient to confine this rubric to a central group of rules which are difficult to separate from one another, leaving aside what can readily be classified under other headings. This has the advantage of emphasising the policy of the courts in the area where they have to come closest to sitting in judgment on the merits, as such, of governmental acts and decisions. It is an area where wide choices are open to them. If they choose to shelter behind literal interpretation, and take the words of each Act at face value, they could absolve themselves from many difficult problems. By insisting, as they do, that the implications of an enactment are as significant as its express provisions, and that powers given for public purposes are as it were held upon trust, they embroil themselves with the policy, motives, and merits of administrative action. At the same time they must confine themselves to applying recognisable principles of law, since at all costs they must not expose themselves to the charge of usurping executive power.

Having pushed their doctrines to remarkable lengths in some cases, the courts have staked their claim to a kind of constitutional restraining power. While their paramount duty is loyal obedience to Parliament, it is for them to say what Parliament really means. Parliament—or, more realistically, the government which controls Parliament—is impatient of any restraint, and constantly confers what appear to be unfettered powers, or attempts to take away judicial remedies. The courts as constantly react by devising some means of preserving the legal principles of control. In so doing they preserve the rule of law, of which Parliament appears surprisingly heedless. If legislation were more restrained, the courts would not be called upon to perform such striking feats of interpretation. They are a kind of legal antidote to the unqualified sovereignty of Parliament, redressing the balance of forces in the constitution.

Although it has been laid down in the House of Lords, and repeated by other judges, that judicial review means 'review of the manner in which the decision was made,'[4] the context of this statement shows that it was not intended to affect the established grounds of review which, as the whole of this chapter illustrates, extend to the substance as well as the manner of the making of administrative decisions and acts.

Basis of judicial review

In requiring statutory powers to be exercised reasonably, in good faith, and on correct grounds, the courts are still working within the bounds of the

---

[4] *Chief Constable of North Wales Police* v. *Evans* [1982] 1 WLR 1155 at 1174 (Lord Brightman). Review for unreasonableness in the *Wednesbury* sense is expressly recognised.

familiar principle of ultra vires. The analysis involves no difficulty or mystique. Offending acts are condemned simply for the reason that they are unauthorised. The court assumes that Parliament cannot have intended to authorise unreasonable action, which is therefore ultra vires and void.[5] This is the express basis of the reasoning in many of the cases cited below.[6] Two particularly well-known statements may be instanced. One is from Lord Russell of Killowen CJ, who said that if a local authority's byelaws were manifestly unjust or oppressive

the Court might well say, 'Parliament never intended to give authority to make such rules; they are unreasonable and ultra vires.'[7]

The other is from Lord Greene MR, who in a judgment discussed later said that where an act was challenged as being unreasonable, the court's only task was

to see whether the local authority have contravened the law by acting in excess of the powers which Parliament has confided in them.[8]

It is, indeed, self-evident that the decisions rest on this elementary principle, since if the action in question is found to be intra vires the court has no power to interfere.[9] The same result is attained in some cases by saying that, where a decision is bad for unreasonableness, the authority has failed to exercise its discretion at all.[10]

A necessary corollary is that, as usual throughout administrative law, we

---

[5] Above, p. 42. No contrary conclusion is to be drawn from the conflicting statements in *Smith* v. *East Elloe Rural District Council* [1956] AC 736, which were concerned with a particular statutory formula and which, in any case, failed to take account of important principles: see below, p. 741.

[6] e.g. *Short* v. *Poole Corporation* [1926] Ch. 66; *Hall & Co. Ltd.* v. *Shoreham-by-Sea Urban District Council* [1964] 1 WLR 240; *Mixnam's Properties Ltd.* v. *Chertsey Urban District Council* [1965] AC 735 at 753 (Lord Radcliffe); *Hartnell* v. *Minister of Housing and Local Government* [1965] AC 1134 at 1173 (Lord Wilberforce); *Roncarelli* v. *Duplessis* (1959) 16 DLR (2d) 689, quoted below, p. 405.

[7] *Kruse* v. *Johnson* [1898] 2 QB 91 at 100.

[8] *Associated Provincial Picture Houses Ltd.* v. *Wednesbury Cpn.* [1948] 1 KB 223 at 234. On this Lord Reid said in *Westminster Bank Ltd.* v. *Beverley Borough Council* [1971] AC 508 at 530: 'The word "unreasonable" is not at all an apt description of action in excess of power, and it is not a very satisfactory description of action in abuse of power. So in the chapter of the law the word has come to acquire a rather artificial meaning.' But this dictum departs from long-settled usage.

[9] Except in the case, not here applicable, of error on the face of the record: above, p. 303.

[10] e.g. in *R.* v. *St. Pancras Vestry* (1890) 24 QBD 371 at 375; *R.* v. *Board of Education* [1910] 2 KB 165 at 175; *Williams* v. *Giddy* [1911] AC 381 at 386; *R.* v. *Port of London Authority ex p. Kynoch* [1919] 1 KB 176 at 183. In licensing cases this analysis may be due to the preference for mandamus as a remedy, based on the mistaken idea that certiorari will not lie: see below, p. 634.

are concerned with acts of legal power, i.e. acts which, if valid, themselves produce legal consequences.[11] Courts of law have nothing directly to do with mere decisions of policy, such as decisions by the government that Britain shall join the European Communities (even though a treaty is concluded)[12] or that grammar schools shall be replaced by comprehensive schools.[13] Such decisions have no legal impact until statutory powers are conferred or invoked. But as soon as Parliament confers some legal power it becomes the business of the courts to see that the power is not exceeded or abused.

This logic, fundamental though it should be, is not invariably respected. It has been held that two non-statutory bodies, the Criminal Injuries Compensation Board and the Panel on Take-overs and Mergers, are subject to judicial review on the same general basis as if they were statutory. In the latter case, moreover, the court asserted its jurisdiction in such wide terms that it may have opened the door to the control of other comparable bodies. These exceptional decisions, discussed later,[14] were prompted by the courts' determination to act 'in defence of the citizenry'[15] against abuse of power by important bodies of a governmental or quasi-governmental nature, and not to let them escape merely because of their non-statutory character. If these judicial forays prove successful, they are likely to open up an important new field for administrative law.

The royal prerogative

The prerogative powers of the Crown[16] have traditionally been said to confer discretion which no court can question;[17] and there was long a dearth of authority to the contrary. But it may be that this was because the decided cases involved discretions which are, as has been laid down in the House of Lords, inherently unsuitable for judicial review, 'such as those relating to the making of treaties, the defence of the realm, the prerogative of mercy, the grant of honours, the dissolution of Parliament and the appointment of ministers as well as others'.[18] But at the same time the

---

[11] Subject to the anomaly noted below, p. 638, as to 'decisions'.

[12] *Blackburn* v. *A.-G.* [1971] 1 WLR 1037.

[13] *Secretary of State for Education and Science* v. *Tameside Metropolitan Borough Council* [1977] AC 1014; below, p. 450.

[14] Below, p. 640.

[15] Sir John Donaldson MR in *R.* v. *Panel on Take-overs and Mergers ex p. Datafin Plc* [1987] 2 WLR at 715.

[16] See above, p. 240.

[17] Bl. Comm. 250, 252.

[18] *Council of Civil Service Unions* v. *Minister for the Civil Service* [1985] AC 374 at 418 (Lord Roskill). For this case see below, p. 574.

House of Lords held that the Crown's power to dismiss civil servants was reviewable, so that it was subject to the principles of natural justice; and this power, though it would seem to be no more than anyone's power to employ servants, was ascribed to the royal prerogative. In principle, it was held, administrative action is reviewable without distinction as to the origin of the power, whether it be statute or common law.[19] In a later case also a divisional court held that the dismissal of a civil servant involved 'a sufficient public law element' to be subject to judicial review.[20] So now it may be said that the royal prerogative does not *per se* confer unreviewable discretion, but that many of the powers contained in it will be of a kind with which the courts will not concern themselves.

These propositions are founded on the wide definition of prerogative which has been criticised earlier.[21] The making of treaties, for example, has no effect on the law of this country,[22] so that there is no exercise of power which can concern the courts. It might be called prerogative without power, while the employment of civil servants might be called power without prerogative. A case where there may be neither prerogative nor power is the grant and refusal of passports, which is claimed to be wholly within the prerogative and discretion of the Crown.[23] A passport is merely an administrative device, the grant or cancellation of which probably involves no direct legal consequences,[24] since there appears to be no justification for supposing that, in law as opposed to administrative practice, a citizen's right to leave or enter the country is dependent upon the possession of a passport.[25] If their loose definition of prerogative should enable the courts to bring this supposed power under legal control, as has

---

[19] So confirming a remark of Lord Devlin in *Chandler* v. *Director of Public Prosecutions* [1964] AC 763 at 809–10. Note the similar attitude of the Court of Appeal in *R.* v. *Panel on Take-overs and Mergers ex p. Datafin Plc* (above). See also [1973] CLJ 287 at 293 (B. S. Markesinis).

[20] *R.* v. *Civil Service Appeal Board ex p. Bruce* [1987] The Times, 22 June (relief refused since applicant was taking proceedings in an industrial tribunal). A naval officer's disqualification for promotion was held potentially reviewable in *Bradley* v. *Attorney-General* [1986] 1 NZLR 176.

[21] Above, p. 242.

[22] *The Parlement Belge* (1879) 4 PD 129; *Walker* v. *Baird* [1892] AC 491; *Blackburn* v. *A.-G.* [1971] 1 WLR 1037. But it is often called 'prerogative', as in the *Laker Airways* case, below.

[23] See 209 HL Deb col. 860 (16 June 1958); 764 HC Deb cols. 1041 ff. (14 May 1969). The government has refused to agree to a statutory right as advocated in *Going Abroad* (a JUSTICE booklet): 416 HL Deb col. 558 (22 January 1981).

[24] Under the Immigration Act 1971, 2nd sched., para 4(2)(*a*) an immigration officer may now require production of either a passport or some other document satisfactorily establishing identity and nationality.

[25] See Bl. Comm. (14th edn.,), i. 265; Halsbury (4th edn.), viii. 636. Passports and the Individual's Right to Travel, The Times, 7 August 1968; Wade, *Constitutional Fundamentals*, 50. For the more favourable law in France see [1986] PL 637, 1987 PL 464 (R. Errera).

been done in other countries,[26] it will have proved useful if not logical. A decision to this effect has, indeed, already been given.[27]

At least it is now judicially recognised that prerogative power is as capable of abuse as is any other power, and that the law can sometimes find means of controlling it. The prerogative has many times been restricted both by judicial decision and by statute.[28] It is for the court to determine the legal limits of the prerogative, and they may include the same requirement of reasonable and proper exercise as applies to statutory powers—though with this difference, that it cannot be based upon the presumed intention of Parliament. In one unusual case, where a Parliamentary basis could be found because action taken by a minister under a treaty was held to be impliedly prohibited by a statute,[29] Lord Denning MR discussed the nature of the prerogative and said:[30]

Seeing that the prerogative is a discretionary power to be exercised for the public good, it follows that its exercise can be examined by the courts just as any other discretionary power which is vested in the executive.

Then after citing cases of abuse of statutory power he concluded:

Likewise it seems to me that when discretionary powers are entrusted to the executive by the prerogative—in pursuance of the treaty-making power—the courts can examine the exercise of them so as to see that they are not used improperly or mistakenly.

But this last remark was said in the House of Lords to be 'far too wide';[31] and admittedly it is not easy to suggest examples where the court might intervene, except in the case of powers which are not, in fact, unique to the Crown such as the power to appoint and dismiss servants. Could the court go further and entertain a complaint that, for example, a royal pardon had been obtained by fraud or granted by mistake or for improper reasons?[32]

---

[26] *Kent* v. *Dulles* 375 (1958); *US* v. *Laub* 385 US 475 (1967); *Lund* v. *Rusk* 398 F. 2d 940 (1967); in the Irish Republic: *State (M.)* v. *A.-G.* [1978] IR 73; and in India: *Satwant Singh* v. *Ramarathnam* AIR 1967 SC 1836.

[27] *R.* v. *Secretary of State for Foreign and Commonwealth Affairs ex p. Everett* [1987] The Times, 10 December (refusal of passport quashed for rigid application of policy and failure to consider applicant's circumstances).

[28] As in *Entick* v. *Carrington* (1765)19 St. Tr. 1030; *A.-G.* v. *De Keyser's Royal Hotel* [1920] AC 508; *Burmah Oil Co* v. *Lord Advocate* [1965] AC 75.

[29] *Laker Airways Ltd.* v. *Department of Trade* [1977] QB 643; below, p. 418.

[30] Lord Denning claimed support from Blackstone but did not mention that he insists that the prerogative, within its limits, is uncontrollable by the courts.

[31] By Lord Roskill in the *Civil Service Unions* case (above) at 416.

[32] According to *Hanratty* v. *Butler* [1971] The Times, 12 May, the discretion is absolute. In 1948, when the death penalty for murder was suspended administratively by granting commutation, Lord Goddard CJ suggested that this was contrary to the prohibition of the suspending power in the Bill of Rights 1688: 156 HL Deb 117 (2 June 1948); but that would have been the familiar restriction by statute.

May it now be held that a passport should not be withheld or revoked except on grounds which pass the tests of reasonableness, fairness, etc., of administrative law?[33] It is in the sphere of the prerogative strictly so called, i.e. where it confers true legal power taking effect within the jurisdiction of the courts, that there would seem to be little scope for judicial review of the discretion exercised by the Crown and its officers.

Intentions imputed to Parliament

For more than three centuries it has been accepted that discretionary power conferred upon public authorities is not absolute, even within its apparent boundaries, but is subject to general legal limitations. These limitations are expressed in a variety of different ways, as by saying that discretion must be exercised reasonably and in good faith, that relevant considerations only must be taken into account, that there must be no malversation of any kind, or that the decision must not be arbitrary or capricious. They can all be comprised by saying that discretion must be exercised in the manner intended by the empowering Act. As Griffiths LJ has said:[34]

Now it goes without saying that Parliament can never be taken to have intended to give any statutory body a power to act in bad faith or a power to abuse its powers. When the court says it will intervene if the particular body acted in bad faith it is but another way of saying that the power was not being exercised within the scope of the statutory authority given by Parliament. Of course it is often a difficult matter to determine the precise extent of the power given by the statute particularly where it is a discretionary power and it is with this consideration that the courts have been much occupied in the many decisions that have developed our administrative law since the last war.

In attempting to discover the intention to be imputed to Parliament, the court must pick its way between conflicting presumptions. On the one hand, where Parliament confers power upon some minister or other authority to be used in discretion, it is obvious that the discretion ought to be that of the designated authority and not that of the court. Whether the discretion is exercised prudently or imprudently, the authority's word is to be law and the remedy is to be political only. On the other hand, Parliament cannot be supposed to have intended that the power should be open to serious abuse. It must have assumed that the designated authority would act properly and responsibly, with a view to doing what was best in the public interest and most consistent with the policy of the statute. It is from this presumption that the courts take their warrant to impose legal bounds on even the most extensive discretion. The apparent contradiction

---

[33] As in the *Everett* case, above.
[34] *R. v. Commission for Racial Equality ex p. Hillingdon LBC* [1982] QB 276.

of the propositions between which the courts have to steer is well brought out in two contrasting statements by Lord Halsbury. In one case he said:[35]

Where the legislature has confided the power to a particular body, with a discretion how it is to be used, it is beyond the power of any court to contest that discretion.

But in an earlier case he had already made the necessary qualification:[36]

... 'discretion' means when it is said that something is to be done within the discretion of the authorities that that something is to be done according to the rules of reason and justice, not according to private opinion: *Rooke's Case*; according to law and not humour. It is to be, not arbitrary, vague, and fanciful, but legal and regular. And it must be exercised within the limit, to which an honest man competent to the discharge of his office ought to confine himself.

This passage describes the administrative discretion of justices of the peace in deciding applications for liquor licences. The middle sentence is borrowed from Lord Mansfield, who used the same words in describing the discretion of a court of law in allowing bail to prisoners.[37]

THE PRINCIPLE OF REASONABLENESS

Early decisions

The characteristically legal conception of discretion just explained is firmly established and dates at least from the sixteenth century. *Rooke's* case,[38] referred to by Lord Halsbury, contains a well-known statement made in 1598 which has lost nothing of its accuracy in nearly 400 years. The Commissioners of Sewers had levied charges for repairing a river bank, but they had thrown the whole charge on one adjacent owner instead of apportioning it among all the owners benefited. In law they had power to levy charges in their discretion. But this charge was disallowed as inequitable and the report proceeds, in Coke's words:

... and notwithstanding the words of the commission give authority to the commissioners to do according to their discretions, yet their proceedings ought to be limited and bound with the rule of reason and law. For discretion is a science or understanding to discern between falsity and truth, between wrong and right, between shadows and substance, between equity and colourable glosses and pretences, and not to do according to their wills and private affections; for as one saith, *talis discretio discretionem confundit.*

[35] *Westminster Cpn.* v. *London & North Western Railway Co.* [1905] AC 426.
[36] *Sharp* v. *Wakefield* [1891] AC 173.
[37] *R.* v. *Wilkes* (1770) 4 Burr. 2527 at 2539.
[38] (1598) 5 Co. Rep. 99b.

In a very similar case of 1609 the same doctrine is repeated;[39] and it recurs elsewhere in Coke's works.[40] In 1647 it is laid down that

wheresoever a commissioner or other person hath power given to do a thing at his discretion, it is to be understood of sound discretion, and according to law, and that this court hath power to redress things otherwise done by them.[41]

To the same effect is a reporter's note of 1666, where the court had granted certiorari against the Commissioners of Fens merely on an allegation 'that they had proceeded unreasonably' for 'this court may judge whither they have pursued their powers'.[42]

An eighteenth-century illustration is the case of the paving commissioners for Wapping, who had power to make alterations in streets 'in such a manner as the commissioners shall think fit'. In order to give a regular incline to a certain street they raised part of it by six feet, thus obstructing the plaintiff's doors and windows. The court held that 'the commissioners had grossly exceeded their powers, which must have a reasonable construction. Their discretion is not arbitrary, but must be limited by reason and law.'[43] These words clearly echo the decisions of the previous century.

Some later authorities

That the general principle remains unchanged is shown by an abundance of later statements of high authority, such as Lord Halsbury's already cited. In a case about a local authority's power to erect public conveniences Lord Macnaghten said:

It is well settled that a public body invested with statutory powers such as those conferred upon the corporation must take care not to exceed or abuse its powers. It must keep within the limits of the authority committed to it. It must act in good faith. And it must act reasonably. The last proposition is involved in the second, if not in the first.[44]

Lord Macnaghten likewise said, in a case where the Public Service Board of New South Wales had awarded a retiring civil servant a derisory gratuity of one penny per year of service:

---

[39] *Keighley's Case* (1609) 10 Co. Rep. 139a.
[40] See Co. Litt. 227b: 'for as by the authority of Littleton, *discretio est discernere per legem, quid sit justum,* that is to discern by the right line of law, and not by the crooked cord of private opinion, which the vulgar call discretion.' See also *Hetley* v. *Boyer* (1614) Cro. Jac. 336 (Coke CJ). cf. 4 Co. Inst. 41.
[41] *Estwick* v. *City of London* (1647) Style 42.
[42] *R.* v. *Commissioners of Fens* (1666) 2 Keb. 43.
[43] *Leader* v. *Moxon* (1773) 2 W. Bl. 924 (successful action for damages).
[44] *Westminster Corporation* v. *L &NW Railway* [1905] AC 426 at 430.

Nobody, of course, can dispute that the Government or the Board had a discretion in the matter. But it was not an arbitrary discretion, as Pring J. seems to think. It was a discretion to be exercised reasonably, fairly, and justly.

Consequently the Privy Council held that the award was a mere sham and pretence, and tantamount to a refusal to exercise the statutory discretion.[45]

An extensive repertory of similar statements is to be found in the speeches of the Law Lords in *Roberts* v. *Hopwood*, a celebrated case where the whole issue revolved round reasonableness. The district auditor had disallowed as 'contrary to law' the over-generous wages paid by the Borough Council of Poplar to their employees under an Act empowering them to pay such wages as they 'may think fit'. What limit should the law set to this apparently unbounded discretion? In upholding the auditor the House of Lords decided unanimously that the Council were not at liberty to pay more than what was reasonable in the light of rates of wages generally.[46] Lord Sumner said that the words 'as they think fit' contained a necessary implication both of honesty and of reasonableness, and that the admitted implication as to bad faith was wide enough to include both.[47] This is precisely what Lord Macnaghten had said. Lord Sumner added:

There are many matters which the courts are indisposed to question. Though they are the ultimate judges of what is lawful and what is unlawful to borough councils, they often accept the decisions of the local authority simply because they are themselves ill equipped to weigh the merits of one solution of a practical question as against another. This, however, is not a recognition of the absolute character of the local authority's discretion, but of the limits within which it is practicable to question it.[48]

Lord Wrenbury, dealing with the argument that that Act did not say 'such reasonable wages' or 'as they reasonably think fit', said that to his mind there was no difference in the meaning, whether those words were in or out.[49] He laid down the law as follows:

A person in whom is vested a discretion must exercise his discretion upon reasonable grounds. A discretion does not empower a man to do what he likes merely because he is minded to do so—he must in the exercise of his discretion do not what he likes but what he ought. In other words, he must, by the use of his reason, ascertain and follow the course which reason directs. He must act reasonably.[50]

---

[45] *Williams* v. *Giddy* [1911] AC 381.
[46] *Roberts* v. *Hopwood* [1925] AC 578; below, p. 424.
[47] At p. 604.
[48] At p. 606.
[49] At p. 613.
[50] At p. 613.

Vitality of the principle today

The principle of reasonableness has become one of the most active and conspicuous among the doctrines which have vitalised administrative law in recent years. Although the principle itself is ancient, the cases in which it was invoked were few and far between until in 1968 the *Padfield* case[51] opened a new era. Today, on the other hand, it appears in reported cases almost every week, and in a substantial number of them it is invoked successfully. Its contribution to administrative law on the substantive side is equal to that of the principles of natural justice on the procedural side.

This doctrine is now so often in the mouths of judges and counsel that it has acquired a nickname, taken from a case decided twenty years before *Padfield*, the *Wednesbury* case.[52] The reports now are freely sprinkled with expressions like 'the *Wednesbury* principle', '*Wednesbury* unreasonableness', or 'on *Wednesbury* grounds.' As Lord Scarman has explained,[53]

'*Wednesbury* principles' is a convenient legal 'shorthand' used by lawyers to refer to the classical review by Lord Greene MR in the *Wednesbury* case of the circumstances in which the courts will intervene to quash as being illegal the exercise of administrative discretion.

One of the grounds of review, he added, is 'unreasonableness in the *Wednesbury* sense'. In the same case Lord Bridge referred to the exercise of power 'unreasonably in what, in current legal jargon, is called the "*Wednesbury*" sense'. '*Wednesbury*' is now a common and convenient label indicating the special standard of unreasonableness which has become the criterion for judicial review of administrative discretion. It is explained in that context below, where the key passage from the judgment of Lord Greene MR is set out in full.[54]

In an important ex cathedra statement of the grounds for judicial review Lord Diplock preferred the term 'irrationality', explaining it as 'what can by now be succinctly referred to as *Wednesbury* unreasonableness'.[55] But it is questionable whether 'irrationality' is a better word. Virtually all administrative decisions are rational in the sense that they are made for intelligible reasons, but the question then is whether they measure up to the legal standard of reasonableness. These are two different things, and for legal purposes they are best differentiated by the established terminology. For the sake of clarity as well as consistency it will be best to employ

---

[51] Below, p. 401.

[52] Below, p. 407.

[53] *R. v. Secretary of State for the Environment ex p. Nottinghamshire CC* [1986] AC 240 at 249.

[54] Below, p. 407. For a general account see [1987] CLJ 53 (G. L. Peiris).

[55] *Council of Civil Service Unions* v. *Minister for the Civil Service* [1985] AC 374 at 410.

'unreasonableness' as the key word, and it seems that the courts are in fact still doing so.[56]

The expression 'arbitrary and capricious' is sometimes used as a synonym for 'unreasonable';[57] and in one case this has been transmuted into 'frivolous or vexatious' and 'capricious and vexatious'.[58] But the meaning of all such expressions is necessarily the same, since the true question must always be whether the statutory power has been abused.

No unfettered discretion in public law

The common theme of all the authorities so far mentioned is that the notion of absolute or unfettered discretion is rejected. Statutory power conferred for public purposes is conferred as it were upon trust, not absolutely—that is to say, it can validly be used only in the right and proper way which Parliament when conferring it is presumed to have intended. Although the Crown's lawyers have argued in numerous cases that unrestricted permissive language confers unfettered discretion, the truth is that, in a system based on the rule of law, unfettered governmental discretion is a contradiction in terms.[59] The real question is whether the discretion is wide or narrow, and where the legal line is to be drawn. For this purpose everything depends upon the true intent and meaning of the empowering Act.

The powers of public authorities are therefore essentially different from those of private persons. A man making his will may, subject to any rights of his dependants, dispose of his property just as he may wish.[60] He may act out of malice or a spirit of revenge, but in law this does not affect his exercise of his power. In the same way a private person has an absolute power to allow whom he likes to use his land, to release a debtor, or, where the law permits, to evict a tenant, regardless of his motives.[61] This is unfettered discretion. But a public authority may do none of these things unless it acts reasonably and in good faith and upon lawful and relevant

---

[56] e.g. in the *Nottinghamshire* case, above. 'Irrational' may apply to mistakes of various kinds, as in *R. v. Secretary of State for Transport ex p. Greater London Council* [1986] QB 556, where the Secretary of State acted 'unlawfully, irrationally and procedurally improperly' in directing the GLC to make an excessive payment to London Regional Transport.

[57] e.g. in *Weinberger v. Inglis* [1919] AC 606; *Roncarelli v. Duplessis* (above). This is the established formula in the United States: see below, n. 65.

[58] *R. v. Barnet and Camden Rent Tribunal ex p. Frey Investments Ltd.* [1972] 2 QB 342.

[59] A particularly clear decision to this effect is that of Sachs J in *Commissioners of Customs and Excise v. Cure and Deeley Ltd.* [1962] 1 QB 340, especially at pp. 366–7.

[60] See *Re Brocklehurst* [1978] Ch. 14.

[61] As in *Chapman v. Honig* [1963] 2 QB 502 (tenant gave evidence against landlord, who then evicted him. Lord Denning MR dissented).

grounds of public interest. So a city council acted unlawfully when it refused unreasonably to let a local rugby football club use the city's sports ground,[62] though a private owner could of course have refused with impunity. Nor may a local authority arbitrarily release debtors,[63] and if it evicts tenants, it must act reasonably and 'within the limits of fair dealing'.[64] The whole conception of unfettered discretion is inappropriate to a public authority, which possesses powers solely in order that it may use them for the public good.

There is nothing paradoxical in the imposition of such legal limits. It would indeed be paradoxical if they were not imposed. Nor is this principle an oddity of British or American law:[65] it is equally prominent in French law.[66] Nor is it a special restriction which fetters only local authorities: it applies no less to ministers of the Crown.[67] Nor is it confined to the sphere of administration: it operates wherever discretion is given for some public purpose, for example where a judge has a discretion to order jury trial.[68] It is only where powers are given for the personal benefit of the person empowered that the discretion is absolute. Plainly this can have no application in public law.

For the same reasons there should in principle be no such thing as unreviewable administrative discretion, which should be just as much a contradiction in terms as unfettered discretion. The question which has to

---

[62] *Wheeler* v. *Leicester CC* [1985] AC 1054, explained below, p. 420.

[63] *A.-G.* v. *Tynemouth Union* [1930] 1 Ch. 616.

[64] *Bristol District Council* v. *Clark* [1975] 1 WLR 1443; *Cannock Chase DC* v. *Kelly* [1978] 1 WLR 1, holding that a local authority is under a stricter obligation than a private landlord but need not explain its reasons; *Sevenoaks DC* v. *Emmott* (1979) 39 P & CR 404 (from which the quotation comes). See also *Webster* v. *Auckland Harbour Board* [1983] NZLR 646; *West Glamorgan CC* v. *Rafferty* [1987] 1 WLR 457 (unlawful eviction of gipsies).

[65] In the United States s. 10(3) of the federal Administrative Procedure Act of 1946, in this respect restating the previous law, requires the court to set aside decisions which are arbitrary, capricious, an abuse of discretion, or otherwise not in accordance with law. See Schwartz and Wade, *Legal Control of Government*, 262, 337.

[66] It is well stated in Vedel and Delvolvé, *Droit administratif*, 9th edn., 803: 'En droit privé . . . un particulier peut agir par raison, par intérét, par générosité, par caprice; le contrôle du juge ne s'exercera qu'à l'encontre d'un but illicite ou immoral. Au contraire, il n'existe pas en droit administratif de principe d'autonomie de la volonté. La volonté de l'Administration n'est pas autonome; l'Administration ne doit se décider que pour des raisons de fait ou de droit ayant existence objective réelle et adéquates à l'acte fait.'

[67] e.g. *Commissioners of Customs and Excise* v. *Cure and Deeley Ltd.* [1962] 1 QB 340; *Padfield* v. *Minister of Agriculture, Fisheries and Food* (below); *Congreve* v. *Home Office*, below, p. 406; and see the *Tameside* case, below, p. 450.

[68] *Ward* v. *James* [1966] 1 QB 273. For rejection of 'absolute discretion' see at p. 292 (Lord Denning MR). Similar law governs the discretionary powers of professional bodies and trustees: see e.g. *R.* v. *Askew* (1768) 4 Burr. 2186 at 2189 (admission to College of Physicians); *Re Baden's Deed Trusts* [1971] AC 424 at 456.

be asked is what is the scope of judicial review, and in a few special cases the scope for the review of discretionary decisions may be minimal.[69] It remains axiomatic that all discretion is capable of abuse, and that legal limits to every power are to be found somewhere.[70]

Judicial rejection of unfettered discretion

In two strong and almost simultaneous decisions of 1968 the House of Lords and the Court of Appeal boldly applied the law as so often laid down. In one, the House of Lords asserted legal control over the allegedly absolute discretion of the Minister of Agriculture and held that he had acted unlawfully. In the other, related in the next section, the Court of Appeal decided that they had power to condemn discriminatory action by the police in enforcing the criminal law, a species of discretion which is particularly difficult to challenge.

In *Padfield* v. *Minister of Agriculture, Fisheries and Food*[71] the House of Lords had to consider a dispute under the milk marketing scheme established under the Agricultural Marketing Act 1958. The Act provided for a committee of investigation which was to consider and report on certain kinds of complaint 'if the Minister in any case so directs'. The milk producers of the region close to London complained that the differential element in the price fixed for their milk by the Milk Marketing Board was too low, since it ought to reflect the increased cost of transport from other regions but had not been revised since the second world war. But since that region was in a minority on the Board, and any increase would be at the expense of the other regions, the Board could not be persuaded to act. The minister had power, if the committee of investigation so recommended, to make an order overriding the Board. But he refused to direct the committee to act, saying that since the producers were represented on the board they should be content with 'the normal democratic machinery' of the marketing scheme. His officials also added, incautiously, that if the committee made a favourable report the minister might be expected to take action on it. The whole object of the minister's overriding power, however, was that he might correct the 'normal democratic machinery' where necessary; and the suggestion that he might be embarrassed by a favourable report was, as Lord Reid said, 'plainly a bad reason'. It was held that where there was a relevant and substantial complaint the minister had a duty as well as a power and that he could not use his discretion to frustrate

---

[69] As in the case of some prerogative powers (above, p. 391).

[70] Most of this section, as it stood in the previous edition, was approved by the House of Lords in *R*. v. *Tower Hamlets LBC ex p. Chetnik Developments Ltd* [1988] 2 WLR 654 at 660.

[71] [1968] AC 997.

the policy of the Act. Otherwise he would be rendering nugatory a safeguard provided by the Act and depriving the producers of a remedy which Parliament intended them to have. Mandamus was therefore granted to compel the minister to act as the law required.

Lord Reid expressly rejected 'the unreasonable proposition that it must be all or nothing—either no discretion at all or an unfettered discretion'. He said:

Parliament must have conferred the discretion with the intention that it should be used to promote the policy and objects of the Act; the policy and objects of the Act must be determined by construing the Act as a whole and construction is always a matter of law for the court. In a matter of this kind it is not possible to draw a hard and fast line, but if the Minister, by reason of his having misconstrued the Act or for any other reason, so uses his discretion as to thwart or run counter to the policy and objects of the Act, then our law would be very defective if persons aggrieved were not entitled to the protection of the court.

Lord Upjohn said that the minister's stated reasons showed a complete misapprehension of his duties, and were all bad in law. The scarcely veiled allusion to fear of parliamentary trouble was, in particular, a political reason which was quite extraneous and inadmissible. One of the fundamental matters confounding the minister's attitude was his claim to 'unfettered' discretion:

First, the adjective nowhere appears in section 19 and is an unauthorised gloss by the Minister. Secondly, even if the section did contain that adjective I doubt if it would make any difference in law to his powers, save to emphasise what he has already, namely that acting lawfully he has a power of decision which cannot be controlled by the courts; it is unfettered. But the use of that adjective, even in an Act of Parliament, can do nothing to unfetter the control which the judiciary have over the executive, namely that in exercising their powers the latter must act lawfully and that is a matter to be determined by looking at the Act and its scope and object in conferring a discretion upon the Minister rather than by the use of adjectives.

Having thus decisively rejected the notion of unfettered discretion, at the initial stage, the House of Lords went on to indicate that the minister might in the end decline to implement the committee's report, and that the assessment of the balance of public interest would be for him alone. Lord Reid said:

He may disagree with the view of the committee as to public interest, and, if he thinks that there are other public interests which outweigh the public interest that justice should be done to the complainers, he would be not only entitled but bound to refuse to take action. Whether he takes action or not, he may be criticised and held accountable to Parliament but the court cannot interfere.

In the end, perhaps predictably, the committee reported in favour of the complainants, but the minister refused to take action. No doubt even his ultimate discretion could be abused unlawfully if he could be shown to have acted on inadmissible grounds, e.g. from personal spite. But the distinction drawn by the House of Lords well shows how a statute which confers a variety of discretionary powers may confer wider or narrower discretion according to the context and the general scheme of the Act. Translated into terms of the traditional rule that powers must be exercised reasonably, this means that the standard of reasonableness varies with the situation. The pitfalls which must always be avoided are those of literal verbal interpretation and of rigid standards.

The importance of the House of Lords' decision was underlined by Lord Denning MR:[72]

The discretion of a statutory body is never unfettered. It is a discretion which is to be exercised according to law. That means at least this: the statutory body must be guided by relevant considerations and not by irrelevant. If its decision is influenced by extraneous considerations which it ought not to have taken into account, then the decision cannot stand. No matter that the statutory body may have acted in good faith; nevertheless the decision will be set aside. That is established by *Padfield* v. *Minister of Agriculture, Fisheries and Food* which is a landmark in modern administrative law.

Another potentially significant aspect of the case was that the House of Lords refused to accept that the court's control could be evaded by omitting to specify the grounds of decision.[73]

A particularly striking example of a minister's discretionary power being fettered by the policy of an Act of Parliament is the *Laker Airways* case, explained below.[74]

The Privy Council has held that the discretion of the Malaysian head of state to revoke a proclamation of emergency is not entirely unfettered, and that failure to revoke it after he no longer considers it to be necessary would be an abuse of his discretion.[75]

Discretionary police powers

The discretion possessed by the police in enforcing the criminal law was considered by the Court of Appeal in a case in which the applicant complained, merely as a citizen, that the police had adopted a policy of not

---

[72] *Breen* v. *Amalgamated Engineering Union* [1971] 2 QB 175 at 190; See similarly *Secretary of State for Employment* v. *ASLEF* (No. 2) [1972] 2 QB 455 at 493; *Secretary of State for Education and Science* v. *Tameside Metropolitan Borough Council* [1977] AC 1014.

[73] See below, p. 418.

[74] p. 418.

[75] *Teh Cheng Poh* v. *Public Prosecutor, Malaysia* [1980] AC 458, holding that the duty would be enforceable by mandamus to the responsible ministers.

prosecuting London gaming clubs for illegal forms of gaming.[76] The Commissioner's confidential instructions, when revealed to the court, substantially bore out the complaint, being based on the uncertainty of the law and the expense and manpower required to keep the clubs under observation. But while the case was pending the law was clarified, fresh instructions were issued, and the Commissioner undertook to withdraw the former instructions. The court therefore found no occasion to intervene. But they made it clear that the Commissioner was not an entirely free agent as his counsel contended. He had a legal duty to the public to enforce the law and the court could intervene by mandamus if, for example, he made it a rule not to prosecute housebreakers. On the other hand the court would not question his discretion when reasonably exercised, e.g. in not prosecuting offenders who for some special reason were not blameworthy in the way contemplated by the Act creating the offence. The court criticised the police policy of suspending observation of gaming clubs, as being clearly contrary to Parliament's intentions; and had it not been changed, they would have been disposed to intervene. But the police have a wide discretion in their operational decisions and their choice of methods, for instance if they call off the pursuit of robbers in a disturbed area because of concern for the safety of their officers.[77]

In 1972 the same public-spirited citizen brought similar proceedings, asking the court to order the police to take more effective action to enforce the law against the publication and sale of pornography. The Metropolitan Police were given instructions not to institute prosecutions or apply for destruction orders without the approval of the Director of Public Prosecutions; and it was shown that much pornographic literature was flagrantly offered for sale without interference by the police. The Court of Appeal found that the efforts of the police had been largely ineffective, but that the real cause of the trouble was the feebleness of the Obscene Publications Act 1959. Accordingly it could not be said that the police were failing in their duty, and an order of mandamus was refused.[78] It was again made clear that if the police were carrying out their duty to enforce the law, the court would not interfere with their discretion; but that the court would do so in the extreme case where it was shown that they were neglecting their duty. And the applicant was commended for having performed a public service by his proceedings.

[76] R. v. Metropolitan Police Commissioner ex p. Blackburn [1968] 2 QB 118. See also Adams v. Metropolitan Police Cmr. [1980] RTR 289.

[77] R. v. Oxford ex p. Levey [1986] The Times, 1 November.

[78] R. v. Metropolitan Police Commissioner ex p. Blackburn (No. 3) [1973] 1 QB 241. The applicant made another attempt in 1980 but with no better success: The Times, 7 March 1980 (reporting that the applicant referred to Lord Denning MR as 'the greatest living Englishman' and received the retort 'tell that to the House of Lords').

These cases are examples of the court's power to control the exercise of a non-statutory discretionary power, for the law governing prosecution by the police has never been enacted. They show that statutory implication is not the indispensable basis of the principle that the discretion of public authorities is never unfettered. Its real basis is that nothing else is compatible with a proper system of administrative law.

Police powers of arrest on suspicion are now statutory and are, as the House of Lords has held, reviewable on 'Wednesbury principles'.[79]

Abuse of licensing powers

The law was admirably stated by a Canadian judge in a celebrated case where a liquor licence had been unlawfully cancelled for extraneous political reasons, purportedly under an Act which said that the liquor commission 'may cancel any permit at its discretion'. Rand J. said:[80]

In public regulation of this sort there is no such thing as absolute and untrammelled 'discretion', that is that action can be taken on any ground or for any reason that can be suggested to the mind of the administrator; no legislative Act can, without express language, be taken to contemplate an unlimited arbitrary power, exercisable for any purpose, however, capricious or irrelevant, regardless of the nature or purpose of the statute. Fraud and corruption in the Commission may not be mentioned in such statutes but they are always implied as exceptions. 'Discretion' necessarily implies good faith in discharging public duty; there is always a perspective within which a statute is intended to operate; and any clear departure from its lines or objects is just as objectionable as fraud or corruption. Could an applicant be refused a permit because he had been born in another Province or because of the colour of his hair? The ordinary language of the Legislature cannot be so distorted.

In this case a restaurant proprietor's liquor licence had been cancelled by the Quebec Liquor Commission at the instigation of the Prime Minister of Quebec, for the reason that the proprietor habitually stood bail for members of the sect of Jehovah's Witnesses, who were a nuisance to the police. The Supreme Court of Canada awarded damages against the Prime Minister and stigmatised the cancellation as

a gross abuse of legal power expressly intended to punish him for an act wholly irrelevant to the statute, a punishment which inflicted on him, as it was intended to do, the destruction of his economic life as a restaurant keeper within the Province.

---

[79] *Mohammed-Holgate* v. *Duke* [1984] AC 437 (complaint of irrelevant considerations failed).

[80] *Roncarelli* v. *Duplessis* (1959) 16 DLR (2d) 689 at 705. The other quotations below are from the same judgment.

And in addition it was said:

To deny or revoke a permit because a citizen exercises an unchallengeable right
totally irrelevant to the sale of liquor in a restaurant is equally beyond the scope of
the discretion conferred.

As well as affording an outstandingly clear example of the abuse of
executive power, this case illustrates the personal liability of ministers[81] and
the possibility of a remedy in damages for maladministration.[82]

In a comparable English case the revocation of television licences by the
Home Office was condemned by the Court of Appeal.[83] The Home
Secretary had a statutory power to revoke or vary any licence under the
Wireless Telegraphy Act 1949, and he elected to use this power to cancel
the licences of persons who took them out during the currency of their
previous licences in order to avoid a sharp increase in the licence fee. The
increase took effect on a fixed date and it was in no way unlawful for a
licence-holder to obtain a new licence before that date at the lower fee. The
Home Office had no power to prevent this, but they tried to enforce a
policy of exacting the higher fee by resorting to their power to revoke
licences. This was held to be a clear abuse of the power and also an illegal
attempt to levy money for the use of the Crown contrary to the Bill of
Rights 1688. Lord Denning MR said:

But when the licensee has done nothing wrong at all, I do not think the Minister
can lawfully revoke the licence, at any rate, not without offering him his money
back, and not even then except for good cause. If he should revoke it without
giving reasons, or for no good reason, the courts can set aside his revocation and
restore the licence. It would be a misuse of the power conferred on him by
Parliament: and these courts have the authority—and, I would add, the duty—to
correct a misuse of power by a minister of his department, no matter how much he
may resent it or warn us of the consequences if we do.

In effect, the Home Office had tried to use their licensing powers to obtain
taxing powers which had not been conferred on them. Their handling of
the affair was also strongly criticised by the Parliamentary Commissioner
for Administration.[84]

Other examples of the legal limits to the discretion of licensing
authorities are given below.[85]

---

[81] Below, p. 812.
[82] Below, p. 777.
[83] *Congreve* v. *Home Office* [1976] QB 629. See (1976) 92 LQR 331. The Home Office had
issued many thousands of demands and had to undertake a big operation to repay money
unlawfully received.
[84] HC 680 (1974–5); above, p. 90.
[85] Below, p. 428.

The standard of reasonableness

The doctrine that powers must be exercised reasonably has to be reconciled with the no less important doctrine that the court must not usurp the discretion of the public authority which Parliament appointed to take the decision. Within the bounds of legal reasonableness is the area in which the deciding authority has genuinely free discretion. If it passes those bounds, it acts ultra vires. The court must therefore resist the temptation to draw the bounds too tightly, merely according to its own opinion. It must strive to apply an objective standard which leaves to the deciding authority the full range of choices which the legislature is presumed to have intended.[86] Decisions which are extravagant or capricious cannot be legitimate. But if the decision is within the confines of reasonableness, it is no part of the court's function to look further into its merits. 'With the question whether a particular policy is wise or foolish the court is not concerned; it can only interfere if to pursue it is beyond the powers of the authority.'[87] As Lord Hailsham LC has said, two reasonable persons can perfectly reasonably come to opposite conclusions on the same set of facts without forfeiting their title to be regarded as reasonable.[88]

This is not therefore the standard of 'the man on the Clapham omnibus'.[89] It is the standard indicated by a true construction of the Act which distinguishes between what the statutory authority may or may not be authorised to do. It distinguishes between proper use and improper abuse of power. It is often expressed by saying that the decision is unlawful if it is one to which no reasonable authority could have come. This is the essence of what is now commonly called 'Wednesbury unreasonableness', after the now famous case in which Lord Greene MR expounded it as follows.[90]

It is true that discretion must be exercised reasonably. Now what does that mean? Lawyers familiar with the phraseology used in relation to exercise of statutory discretions often use the word 'unreasonable' in a rather comprehensive sense. It has frequently been used and is frequently used as a general description of the things that must not be done. For instance, a person entrusted with a discretion must, so to speak, direct himself properly in law. He must call his own attention to the matters which he is bound to consider. He must exclude from his consideration matters

---

[86] This passage was approved by the Court of Appeal in R. v. Boundary Commission ex p. Foot [1983] QB 600 (unsuccessful challenge to Commission's decisions fixing boundaries of parliamentary constituencies).

[87] Short v. Poole Cpn. [1926] Ch. 66 and 91 (Warrington LJ).

[88] Re W. (An Infant) [1971] AC 682 at 700.

[89] [1933] 1 KB 205 at 224.

[90] Associated Provincial Picture Houses Ltd. v. Wednesbury Corporation [1948] 1 KB 223 at 229, for which see below, p. 430.

which are irrelevant to what he has to consider. If he does not obey those rules, he may truly be said, and often is said, to be acting 'unreasonably'. Similarly, there may be something so absurd that no sensible person could ever dream that it lay within the powers of the authority. Warrington LJ in *Short* v. *Poole Corporation*[91] gave the example of the red-haired teacher, dismissed because she had red hair. This is unreasonable in one sense. In another it is taking into consideration extraneous matters. It is so unreasonable that it might almost be described as being done in bad faith; and, in fact, all these things run into one another.

This has become the most frequently cited passage (though most commonly cited only by its nickname) in administrative law. It explains how 'unreasonableness', in its classic formulation, covers a multitude of sins. These various errors commonly result from paying too much attention to the mere words of the Act and too little to its general scheme and purpose, and from the fallacy that unrestricted language naturally confers unfettered discretion.

Unreasonableness has thus become a generalised rubric covering not only sheer absurdity or caprice, but merging into illegitimate motives and purposes, a wide category of errors commonly described as 'irrelevant considerations', and mistakes and misunderstandings which can be classed as self-misdirection,[92] or addressing oneself to the wrong question.[93] But the language used in the cases shows that, while the abuse of discretion has this variety of differing legal facets, in practice the courts often treat them as distinct. When several of them will fit the case, the court is often inclined to invoke them all. The one principle that unites them is that powers must be confined within the true scope and policy of the Act.

Taken by itself, the standard of unreasonableness is nominally pitched very high: 'so absurd that no sensible person could ever dream that it lay within the powers of the authority' (Lord Greene MR); 'so wrong that no reasonable person could sensibly take that view' (Lord Denning MR);[94] 'so outrageous in its defiance of logic or of accepted moral standards that no sensible person who had applied his mind to the question to be decided could have arrived at it' (Lord Diplock).[95] It might seem from such language that the deliberate decisions of ministers and other responsible public authorities could almost never be found

[91] [1926] Ch. 66.
[92] An example of self-misdirection was where the minister was given misleading advice, misunderstood his default powers, and gave invalid directions to a local health authority: *Lambeth LBC* v. *Secretary of State for Social Services* (1980) 79 LGR 61. The mistake was rectified by National Health Service (Invalid Direction) Act 1980.
[93] Examples are *Niarchos* v. *Secretary of State for the Environment* (1977) 76 LGR 480; *Anisminic Ltd.* v. *Foreign Compensation Commission* [1969] 2 AC 147 (above, p. 299).
[94] In the *Tameside* case [1977] AC at 1026.
[95] In *Council of Civil Service Unions* v. *Minister for the Civil Service* [1985] AC at 410.

wanting. But, as may be seen in the following pages, there are abundant instances of legally unreasonable decisions and actions at all levels. This is not because public authorities take leave of their senses,[96] but because the courts in deciding cases tend to lower the threshold of unreasonableness to fit their more exacting ideas of administrative good behaviour.[97]

There is ample room, within the legal boundaries, for radical differences of opinion in which neither side is unreasonable. A number of statements to this effect were made in the Court of Appeal and the House of Lords in the case of the Tameside schools, discussed below.[98] Lord Denning MR pointed out the error of confusing differences of opinion, however strong, with unreasonableness on the part of one side or the other. One party may call the other 'quite unreasonable' when he is well within the legal limits of reasonableness. This was the distinction which the Secretary of State failed to make, as the House of Lords emphatically confirmed. Lord Diplock said:[99]

The very concept of administrative discretion involves a right to choose between more than one possible course of action upon which there is room for reasonable people to hold differing opinions as to which is to be preferred.

In the same vein Lord Hailsham LC has said that 'not every reasonable exercise of judgment is right, and not every mistaken exercise of judgment is unreasonable'.[1]

Judges have sometimes given examples of what might be called pure unreasonableness. In a controversy which upheld a local authority's power to erect a urinal near Buckingham Palace, Turner LJ said that it would not be lawful to do so 'in front of any gentleman's house'.[2] Similarly the power to erect rails and fences in streets for the protection of pedestrians would not justify a high closeboarded fence which would interfere with light.[3] The authority 'is bound to have some regard to the interest of those who may suffer for the good of the community'.[4] As concrete instances of pure

---

[96] Lord Scarman used this phrase in *R. v. Secretary of State for the Environment ex p. Nottinghamshire CC* [1986] AC at 247.

[97] cf. [1987] PL 368 at 372 (J. Jowell and A. Lester).

[98] Below, p. 450.

[99] [1977] AC at 1064.

[1] *Re W. (An Infant)* [1971] AC 682 at 700. For a 'grave error of judgment' held not to be unreasonable see *R. v. Independent Broadcasting Authority ex p. Whitehouse* [1984] The Times, 14 April.

[2] *Biddulph v. Vestry of St. George, Hanover Square* (1863) 33 LJ Ch 411 at 417.

[3] *Dormer v. Newcastle upon Tyne Cpn.* [1940] 2 KB 204 at 217.

[4] *Westminster Cpn. v. London and North Western Railway* [1905] AC 426 at 433 (Lord Macnaghten).

unreasonableness may be cited the case of the penny-a-year gratuity;[5] a case where a minister allowed only four days for objections to be made to a scheme for a comprehensive school;[6] and a case where a local authority, having lodged homeless persons temporarily in a hotel, then served notices requiring the hotel to conform to the Housing Act standards applicable to private houses.[7] More numerous are the cases which can be classified under particular subheads such as improper motives or irrelevant considerations, which are grouped separately below.

Ministerial policy and parliamentary approval

Ministers' decisions on important matters of policy are not on that account sacrosanct against the unreasonableness doctrine, as is shown by a number of leading cases such as the *Padfield* and *Congreve* cases already discussed and the *Tameside* case discussed below. Further examples will be found in the context of delegated legislation, since the courts have several times held ministerial regulations to be void for unreasonableness.[8]

A three-judge divisional court provided another striking instance in granting declaratory relief to prisoners serving life sentences whose prospects of release on licence ('parole') were sharply reduced after a change of policy by the Home Secretary.[9] The new policy had first been challenged by other prisoners on the ground that the Parole Board had not been consulted and that the Home Secretary had fettered his discretion, but the House of Lords upheld it.[10] The Home Secretary then decided to make a practice of waiting for three or four years before asking the judge who had passed a life sentence for his opinion on the term of imprisonment which the convict ought to serve. This delay was held to be an unfair restriction on the implementation of the parole policy which in some cases would extend the term of imprisonment unjustly, contrary to what the judge would have advised if consulted at the time of conviction. It was held that a minister could not lawfully maintain a policy when the application of it was, in part at least, shown to give rise to injustice; and that the policy of delayed reference to the judge was unreasonable in the *Wednesbury* sense. The decision is all the more notable in that the unreasonable action was not itself the exercise of a statutory power, as it was in the cases mentioned above, but was merely preparatory to the exercise of the statutory function

---

[5]   *Williams* v. *Giddy* [1911] AC 381 (above, p. 396).
[6]   *Lee* v. *Department of Education and Science* (1967) 66 LGR 211.
[7]   *R.* v. *Hackney LBC ex p. Evenbray Ltd.* [1987] The Times, 15 September.
[8]   Below, p. 868.
[9]   *R.* v. *Home Secretary ex p. Handscomb* [1987] The Times, 4 March; The Independent, 3 March.
[10]   *Re Findlay* [1985] AC 318.

of referring cases to the Parole Board. The real misdeed, therefore, was the failure to consider whether to take the latter step at the proper time.

A decision of the House of Lords suggests that parliamentary approval may confer some degree of immunity, and that there may be different degrees of unreasonableness, with abuse of power at one end of the scale and mere misjudgment at the other. The House held that, where a minister's order has been laid before Parliament and approved, the court is not concerned with its reasonableness unless it also constitutes an abuse of power, or there is some misconduct or mistake of law.[11] Unreasonableness here merges into other grounds of review as the House of Lords emphasises that it is not for judges to trespass upon the area where decisions are matters of political judgment. It remains to be seen, however, whether this will lead to any change in the established judicial policy, which is that, in accordance with constitutional principle,[12] parliamentary approval does not affect the normal operation of judicial review, whether for unreasonableness or otherwise, unless embodied in an Act. Once again, the decisions on delegated legislation, which is normally approved by Parliament, provide clear illustrations.

Relevant and irrelevant considerations

There are many cases in which a public authority has been held to have acted from improper motives or upon irrelevant considerations, or to have failed to take account of relevant considerations, so that its action is ultra vires and void. It is impossible to separate these cleanly from other cases of unreasonableness and abuse of power, since the court may use a variety of interchangeable explanations, as was pointed out by Lord Greene.[13] Regarded collectively, these cases show the great importance of strictly correct motives and purposes. They show also how fallacious it is to suppose that powers conferred in unrestricted language confer unrestricted power.

Lord Esher MR stated the 'irrelevant considerations' doctrine in a case where a vestry had mistakenly fixed the pension of a retiring officer on the erroneous assumption that they had no discretion as to the amount:[14]

But they must fairly consider the application and not take into account any reason for their decision which is not a legal one. If people who have to exercise a public

---

[11] *R. v. Secretary of State for the Environment ex p. Nottinghamshire CC* [1986] AC 240 (unsuccessful complaint of unreasonably low 'expenditure target' set by Secretary of State). See similarly *City of Edinburgh DC* v. *Secretary of State for Scotland* 1985 SLT 551.

[12] See above, p. 29.

[13] Above, p. 407. See [1976] CLJ 272 (G. D. S. Taylor).

[14] *R. v. St Pancras Vestry* (1890) 24 QBD 371 at 375.

duty by exercising their discretion take into account matters which the courts consider not to be proper for the exercise of their discretion, then in the eye of the law they have not exercised their discretion.

The doctrine applies equally to failure to take account of some consideration which is necessarily relevant, such as the respective costs of rival proposals[15] or the availability of more suitable land.[16] Cooke J explained in a New Zealand case that 'the more general and the more obviously important the consideration, the readier the court must be to hold that Parliament must have meant it to be taken into account'.[17]

Under many statutes the discretion conferred is extensive, and it is no concern of the court to restrict it artificially by limiting the considerations that are relevant. A minister may be entitled to take account of every factor that may affect the public interest,[18] but it does not follow that he is obliged to do so. In another New Zealand case Cooke J pointed out 'the difference between obligatory considerations (i.e. those which the Act expressly or impliedly requires the Minister to take into account) and permissible considerations (i.e. those which can properly be taken into account but do not have to be)'.[19] Where there is overlap between different areas of policy, for example housing and planning, the court may decline to make a rigid dichotomy between them so as to confine a housing authority to 'housing' considerations only.[20] The court will intervene in two situations. The first is where the authority has acted on grounds which the statute never intended to allow, so that the statutory power is exceeded. The second is where the authority has failed to take proper account of something that the statute expressly or impliedly required it to consider,[21] even though it may not have been known at the time.[22] But under this second head the implied requirement may be wide. In deciding whether to deport an immigrant the Secretary of State 'on classic *Wednesbury* principles . . . is bound to take

---

[15] *Eckersley* v. *Secretary of State for the Environment* [1977] JPL 580; *Prest* v. *Secretary of State for Wales* (1982) 81 LGR 193; *R.* v. *Brent LBC ex p. Gunning* (1985) 84 LGR 168.

[16] *Brown* v. *Secretary of State for the Environment* (1978) 40 P & CR 285 (provision of land for gipsies). See also *City Cabs (Edinburgh) Ltd* v. *Edinburgh DC* 1988 SLT 184.

[17] *CREEDNZ* v. *Governor-General* [1981] 1 NZLR 172, applied in *R.* v. *Hillingdon Health Authority ex p. Goodwin* [1984] ICR 800 (decision to close hospital quashed for failure to take account of doctors' interests).

[18] See e.g. *Rother Valley Railway Co. Ltd.* v. *Ministry of Transport* [1971] 1 Ch. 515.

[19] *Ashby* v. *Minister of Immigration* [1981] 1 NZLR 222 at 224 (admission of South African rugby football team unsuccessfully challenged).

[20] *Hanks* v. *Minister of Housing and Local Government* [1963] 1 QB 999; see below, p. 436, for this and contrasting cases.

[21] *CREEDNZ* v. *Governor-General* (above); and see *Ashby* v. *Minister of Immigration* (above).

[22] *R.* v. *Immigration Appeal Tribunal ex p. Hassanin* [1987] 1 WLR 1448 (cases remitted to appeal tribunals to consider all the relevant circumstances).

account of all relevant considerations', so that an adjudicator misdirects himself in law if he refuses to take account of the immigrant's special value to his own community.[23] A threat by that community to instigate a strike, on the other hand, would be improper and therefore irrelevant.[24] The range and flexibility of this judicial technique are obvious, and equally obvious is the difficulty of reducing it to precise rules.

Examples of the doctrine

A clear case of abuse of power prompted by an irrelevant consideration was where some local authorities refused to provide certain newspapers in their public libraries. Their reason for the ban was that they were politically hostile to the newspapers' proprietors, who had dismissed many of their workers when they went on strike. The ulterior political object of the local authorities was irrelevant to their statutory duty to provide 'a comprehensive and efficient library service'.[25] Another example was where the Secretary of State had power to prescribe 'the appropriate contribution' of local authorities to a fund for financing further education, and prescribed a formula based on the rateable resources of each area, so that the richer local authorities were made to subsidise the poorer. It was held that relative resources were an irrelevant consideration, since a local authority's rate fund should be used for the benefit of its own area and there was nothing in the empowering Act to justify the redistribution of resources.[26]

A group of cases concern the dismissal of schoolteachers. Where education authorities had power to require the dismissal of teachers 'on educational grounds' they acted ultra vires in requiring dismissals in order to save expenditure[27] or because a teacher took an afternoon off in poignant circumstances.[28] But where they had an unrestricted power of dismissal themselves, they were held entitled to dismiss teachers who were married women on the grounds that housewives were less satisfactory and were less

---

[23] R. v. Immigration Appeal Tribunal ex p. Bakhtaur Singh [1986] 1 WLR 910 (Lord Bridge). See also R. v. Immigration Appeal Tribunal ex p. Bastiampillai [1983] 2 All ER 844 (failure to take account of immigrant's circumstances); R. v. Immigration Appeal Tribunal ex p. Kumar [1986] The Times, 13 August (disregard of husband's proved devotion in alleged marriage of convenience); R. v. Home Secretary ex p. Bugdaycay [1987] AC 514 (failure to consider danger to deportee).

[24] Bakhtaur Singh's case (above).

[25] R. v. Ealing LBC ex p. Times Newspapers Ltd. (1986) 85 LGR 316.

[26] R. v. Secretary of State for Education and Science ex p. Inner London Education Authority [1985] 84 LGR 454.

[27] Hanson v. Radcliffe Urban Council [1922] 2 Ch. 490; Sadler v. Sheffield Cpn. [1924] 1 Ch. 483; R. v. Liverpool CC ex p. Ferguson [1985] The Times, 20 November.

[28] Martin v. Eccles Cpn. [1919] 1 Ch. 387.

in need of employment than single women.[29] These grounds were not alien or irrelevant to the statutory purpose of maintaining efficient schools. But the dismissal of teachers was ultra vires where the sole ground for it was that the teachers refused to collect money for pupils' meals: for the Education Act 1944 expressly provided that the Minister could not impose this requirement, and it was not therefore a relevant and valid ground of dismissal.[30]

Incessant litigation over planning and compulsory purchase, illustrated more fully below,[31] has produced a meticulous style of review[32] in which the doctrine of relevant and irrelevant considerations is frequently employed. One case carried it to a new point in quashing a decision of the Secretary of State for paying too much regard to a relevant consideration and so misdirecting himself.[33] His error was to regard a long-expired planning permission as a 'vitally material consideration' requiring the granting of a new permission, when in fact that consideration was relevant but not dominant; and so he came to a perverse decision. With somewhat similar reasoning the Court of Appeal quashed a compulsory purchase order because the Secretary of State failed to take account of an offer by the landowner which would have made an alternative site less rather than more expensive.[34] It is in decisions such as these that the courts may be said to employ something like the American doctrine of 'hard look review'.[35]

Another way of expressing the irrelevant considerations doctrine is to say that a wrong test has been applied. In refusing an application for political asylum on the ground that he was not persuaded that the applicant would be singled out for persecution in his own country the Home Secretary failed to apply the right test, which was whether the applicant

---

[29] *Short v. Poole Cpn.* [1926] Ch. 66. cf. *Price v. Rhondda Urban Council* [1923] 2 Ch. 372.

[30] *Price v. Sunderland Cpn.* [1956] 1 WLR 1253.

[31] Below, pp. 431, 435.

[32] Summarised in *Seddon Properties Ltd.* v. *Secretary of State for the Environment* (1978) 42 P & CR 26.

[33] *South Oxfordshire DC* v. *Secretary of State for the Environment* [1981] 1 WLR 1092. cf. *Westminster Renslade Ltd.* v. *Secretary of State for the Environment* (1983) 48 P & CR 255; *Surrey Heath BC* v. *Secretary of State for the Environment* [1986] The Times, 3 November.

[34] *Prest v. Secretary of State for Wales* (1982) 81 LGR 193.

[35] The hard look doctrine was originally one of judicial restraint, restricting review of decisions of policy provided that the *agency* had taken a hard look at the whole matter, and decided rationally: *Greater Boston Television Corp.* v. *FCC* 444 F. 2d 841 (1970). But the same title has been given to an intensive technique of review where the *court* investigates relevance of motives, adequacy of evidence and preparatory studies, and other such factors, as in *Sierra Club* v. *Castle* 657 F. 2d 298 (1981) and *Motor Vehicle Manufacturers Association* v. *State Farm Mutual Automobile Insurance Co.* 463 US 29 (1983). In the latter case the Supreme Court set aside the revocation of a government order about car seatbelts for failure to consider the available options and lack of rational connection between the facts and the decision.

had a well-founded fear of being persecuted for the reasons specified in the international convention on the status of refugees.[36] In the same category, perhaps, was the Home Secretary's 'unreasonable and perverse' decision to refuse concessionary television licences to residents in old people's homes, which the court quashed because he imposed a requirement which was irrelevant to the statutory qualifications.[37]

Qualifications and extensions

There are some situations in which the presence of irrelevant motives will not necessarily be fatal. The most obvious are where they do not in fact affect the action taken or where they operate in the complainant's favour,[38] or where they are merely redundant. Thus where the Broadcasting Complaints Commission declined to entertain a complaint by a party leader that his party was given too little broadcasting time, giving a number of good reasons but including the irrelevant reason that the task would be burdensome, their decision was within their lawful discretion.[39] Irrelevant considerations may also be innocuous if the action taken is reasonable in itself. In fixing the level of pay of its employees, which is required by the court to be reasonable, a local authority may act on entirely wrong grounds and yet its payments, if not in themselves excessive, are not unlawful. Of this situation Lord Sumner said:[40]

If, having examined the expenditure and found clear proof of bad faith, which admittedly would open the account, the auditor found that the councillors' evil minds had missed their mark, and the expenditure itself was right, then the expenditure would not be 'contrary to law' and could not be disallowed.

This therefore appears to be a case where objective and not subjective consideration may prevail. The reasoning was invoked in a later case to justify the payment of children's allowances by way of additional salary.[41]

The European Convention on Human Rights and Fundamental Freedoms of 1950[42] is now treated by the courts as a factor to be taken into account, presumably by implication in statutes passed since that date. Lord Widgery CJ has said that regard ought to be had to the Convention when

[36] R. v. Home Secretary ex p. R. [1987] The Times, 8 June (Home Secretary's decision quashed).
[37] R. v. Home Secretary ex p. Kirklees BC [1987] The Times, 24 January (unjustified requirement of exclusive services of housing steward).
[38] Hanks v. MHLG (above) at 1020.
[39] R. v. Broadcasting Complaints Commission ex p. Owen [1985] QB 1153. See also R. v. Secretary of State for Social Services ex p. Wellcome Foundation Ltd. [1987] 1 WLR 1166.
[40] Roberts v. Hopwood [1925] AC 578 at 604; below, p. 424.
[41] Re Walker's Decision [1944] KB 644; below, p. 427.
[42] Cmd. 8969 (1953).

an issue in this country makes it relevant, and that the omission of a factor which ought to be taken into account makes a decision a nullity.[43] This is one aspect of the increasing desire of the judiciary to give some legal effect to the Convention, which Parliament has failed to incorporate into the law of the land.[44]

In 1975 the government, wishing to enforce a policy of wage control but not wishing to seek legislation, decided to refuse discretionary assistance of various kinds to firms which paid higher wages than they approved.[45] Grants under the Industry Act 1972 and the Export Credits Guarantees Act 1975 and also payments of 'temporary employment subsidy' were among those to be refused. The government compiled a 'blacklist' of offending firms and called upon local authorities, nationalised industries, and other bodies (including universities) not to place contracts with them. This policy provoked much political protest, but no litigation reached the courts before the policy collapsed in 1978. The question whether resort to these expedients was an abuse of discretion was therefore never tested. It seems unlikely that the courts could or should assert any control over the government's freedom to place its contracts as it wishes. But the use of statutory powers for ulterior purposes not contemplated by Parliament might well have provided further material for this chapter.

'Illegitimate motives', 'irrelevant considerations' and their associated doctrines have many ramifications. They embrace a large area of the ultra vires rule and the decisions are numerous. Many of the best examples can be grouped according to their subject-matter under the titles which follow. But these categories must not be regarded as rigid. The courts have many strings to their bow and many of their arguments are interchangeable.[46]

CATEGORIES OF UNREASONABLENESS

Opposition to the policy of Parliament

From time to time public authorities have set their faces against the policy of an Act, and either declined to implement it or else attempted to frustrate

[43] *R. v. Home Secretary ex p. Bhajan Singh* [1976] QB 198; see also the observations of the Court of Appeal, there reported. Contrast *Ashby* v. *Minister of Immigration* [1981] 1 NZLR 222, holding that in issuing entry permits to a South African football team the minister was not required to take account of an international convention on racial discrimination.

[44] For other aspects see below, p. 497.

[45] The policy was announced in White Papers of 1975–8, Cmnd. 6151, 6507, 6882, 7293. For the whole affair see [1978] PL 333 (G. Ganz).

[46] See e.g. *Wheeler* v. *Leicester City Council* [1985] AC 1054, where arguments based on unfairness, unreasonableness and abuse of power are intermingled. See also [1987] PL 368 (J. Jowell and A. Lester) for various facets of the *Wednesbury* doctrine.

it. Needless to say, this is an unlawful motive. In a case under the old poor law, where justices of the peace had discretion to enforce parochial contributions if they 'shall think fit', the justices refused to make an order against one parish because they thought it unfair that, having no paupers, it should be made to contribute, and the justices' order was condemned as arbitrary and illegal.[47] An analogous modern case arose from a London borough council's hostility to the policy of the Rent Act 1957. Certain classes of houses, formerly under requisition, remained in the occupation of tenants whose rents could not be increased 'except so far as the local authority may from time to time determine'; and the local authority had to compensate the owners by paying them the difference between the rent so determined and the rent which would otherwise be payable. The object of the Rent Act 1957 was to allow rents to rise to more realistic levels. Therefore the compensation payable to the owners would be greatly increased unless the local authority approved higher rents for the tenants. The St Pancras borough council refused to do this, being opposed to higher rents generally and wishing to 'protect the tenants from the Rent Act'. Lord Parker CJ held that this policy rendered the council's decision 'purely arbitrary' and disregarded the council's duty to their ratepayers, on whom the cost of the compensation would fall.[48] Their legal duty therefore was to review the rents, taking account of the relevant consideration that rents had been allowed to rise. The district auditor had accordingly been right in disallowing the additional compensation which the council had unlawfully paid. In later proceedings it was held that the councillors responsible had acted honestly but unreasonably, and ought not to be relieved from the auditor's surcharges.[49]

A simple and blatant device aimed at nullifying the effect of an Act of Parliament was where a housing authority, determined not to make a general increase of rents as required by the Act, charged the whole of the required increase onto a single vacant house, putting up its weekly rent from £7 to £18,000. The court had no difficulty in holding this an unlawful abuse.[50]

The *Padfield* case,[51] already discussed, shows the 'statutory policy' doctrine as applied to a minister of the Crown. The House of Lords held that in refusing to refer the milk producers' complaint to the statutory committee the minister had acted so as to frustrate the policy of the Act, despite the fact that its words were merely permissive; and that the political

[47] *R.* v. *Boteler* (1864) 4 B & S 959.
[48] *Taylor* v. *Munrow* [1960] 1 WLR 151.
[49] *Annison* v. *District Auditor for St. Pancras* [1962] 1 QB 489.
[50] *Backhouse* v. *Lambeth London Borough Council* [1972] The Times, 14 October.
[51] *Padfield* v. *Minister of Agriculture Fisheries and Food* [1968] AC 997; above, p. 401.

and other reasons given were irrelevant and indicative of unlawful motives. It is particularly important to notice how closely the House of Lords scrutinised the minister's reasons, as governing the validity of the action. One of the reasons given in a departmental letter was that the minister would have to consider whether, if he allowed the producers' complaint to be referred to the statutory committee and they upheld it, he would be expected to give effect to the committee's recommendations. Lord Upjohn said:

This fear of parliamentary trouble (for, in my opinion, this must be the scarcely veiled meaning of the letter) if an inquiry was ordered and its possible results is alone sufficient to vitiate the Minister's decision which, as I have stated earlier, can never validly turn on purely political considerations; he must be prepared to face the music in Parliament. . . .

There could scarcely be a better example of the principle that statutory powers, however, permissive, must be used with scrupulous attention to their true purposes and for reasons which are relevant and proper.

The House of Lords also rejected the Crown's argument that the minister need have given no reasons and that therefore such reasons as he volunteered to give could not be criticised. Going still further, the House declared that if in such a case he refused to give any reasons, the court might have to assume that he had no good reasons and was acting arbitrarily.[52] In other words, the minister may not be able to disarm the court by taking refuge in silence. In this way the court would have power to impose, in effect, an obligation to give reasons for discretionary decisions. But there is as yet no sign of this becoming the practice. Despite the general obligation to act reasonably, a local authority need not give reasons for evicting a tenant,[53] nor need a minister do so for making orders and giving directions for the protection of trading interests.[54]

A determined ministerial attempt to frustrate the policy of an Act was condemned by the Court of Appeal in the *Laker Airways* case.[55] The company had been granted a licence for a low-cost transatlantic air service by the Civil Aviation Authority, one of whose statutory duties was to secure that at least one independent British airline had opportunities to

---

[52] [1968] AC at 1032, 1053, 1061. See similarly *Secretary of State for Employment* v. *ASLEF* (No. 2) [1972] 2 QB 455 at 493 (Lord Denning MR) and *Minister of National Revenue* v. *Wright's Canadian Ropes Ltd.* [1947] AC 109 at 123 (below, p. 454); and compare *Fiordland Venison Ltd.* v. *Minister of Agriculture* [1978] 2 NZLR 341 (minister's reasons inferred from evidence and held improper; applicant held entitled to licence in the absence of good reasons for refusing it).
[53] *Cannock Chase DC* v. *Kelly* [1978] 1 WLR 1.
[54] *British Airways Board* v. *Laker Airways Ltd.* [1985] AC 58.
[55] *Laker Airways Ltd.* v. *Department of Trade* [1977] QB 643.

compete with British Airways. In 1975 the government announced a policy of preventing competition and the Secretary of State issued 'guidance' to the CAA, in terms approved by both Houses of Parliament, requiring them to revoke the company's licence. Under the Civil Aviation Act 1971 the Secretary of State had power to give the CAA guidance in the performance of their functions and the CAA had to obey. But the guidance given in this case clearly conflicted with their functions since one of them was to give opportunities to independent airlines. The guidance was therefore ultra vires and invalid.[56] The Secretary of State had also announced that he would withdraw the company's designation as an approved airline under the agreement with the United States, so that it would not obtain landing rights in America. This step was likewise declared to be unlawful. For its object, again, was to frustrate the express provision of the Act about allowing competition and to render licences properly granted by the CAA worthless. The Act, it was held, by necessary implication prohibited the Crown from pursuing this unlawful object, even though the Crown was acting, as it claimed, under the royal prerogative in the sphere of foreign affairs. Lord Denning MR held further that the Crown was abusing the prerogative, as explained earlier.[57] The use of the doctrine of implied prohibition to restrain action which would normally be beyond the court's control is a particularly striking feature of this decision.

Failure to take account of the policy of Parliament caused the quashing of a local council's refusal to refund rates overpaid. The council had discretionary power under the Act to make repayments, but had refused to exercise it for various bad reasons, without regard to the Act's policy that injustice should be remedied.[58]

Penalising the innocent

One element in the abuse of power condemned by the Court of Appeal in the television licences case, already encountered, was the penalising of licence-holders for doing something quite lawful, namely taking out new licences at any time they might wish.[59] The House of Lords emphasised the same point in a later case where a city council had refused, contrary to its

---

[56] For another mistake by a Secretary of State as to his powers of giving directions see *R. v. Secretary of State for Social Services ex p. Lewisham (etc.) LBC* [1980] The Times, 26 February (default powers misunderstood).

[57] See above, p. 393.

[58] *R. v. Tower Hamlets LBC ex p. Chetnik Developments Ltd.* [1988] 2 WLR 654. See also *R. v. Burnham Primary and Secondary Committee ex p. Professional Association of Teachers* [1985] The Times, 30 March (exclusion of teachers' association frustrated policy of Act).

[59] Above, p. 406. See likewise *Roncarelli v. Duplessis*, above, p. 405.

previous practice, to allow a local rugby football club to use the city's sports ground because three of its members had played in South Africa.[60] The House held that it was unreasonable thus to punish the club for not conforming to the council's political attitudes, and Lord Templeman said:

A private individual or a private organisation cannot be obliged to display zeal in the pursuit of an object sought by a public authority and cannot be obliged to publish views dictated by a public authority. . . . The council could not properly seek to use its statutory powers of management or any other statutory powers for the purposes of punishing the club when the club had done no wrong.

The council's decision was therefore quashed, with provision for declaratory or injunctive relief if necessary, thus in effect compelling the council to allow the club to use its sports ground. In a similar case a London borough adopted a policy of boycotting the products of an oil company because it did business in South Africa, and since this was not an unlawful activity the council's resolution was quashed and its enforcement restrained by injunction.[61]

Financial motives

A laudable desire to save public money has led many authorities into the error of using their powers for financial profit when that is not a legitimate purpose. This has already been illustrated by the case of the planning condition which wrongfully required the applicant to provide a strip of roadway at his own expense.[62] Similarly a local authority was not entitled, as a condition of approving building plans, to stipulate that the applicant should provide and pay for sewers outside his own property: this, said Lord Russell CJ, was 'utterly unreasonable'.[63] An education authority which has power to require the dismissal of teachers on 'educational grounds' may not do so merely to save money.[64]

The city of Sydney exceeded its powers of acquiring land for 'carrying out improvements in or remodelling any portion of the city' when it made a compulsory purchase order for land merely in order to obtain the rise in value which the extension of a street would bring about, without any intention of improving or remodelling.[65] In another Australian case a

---

[60] *Wheeler* v. *Leicester City Council* [1985] AC 1054.

[61] *R.* v. *Lewisham LBC ex p. Shell UK Ltd.* [1987] The Times, 23 December.

[62] *Hall & Co. Ltd.* v. *Shoreham-by-Sea Urban District Council* [1964] 1 WLR 240; below, p. 433.

[63] *R* v. *Tynemouth District Council* [1896] 2 QB 219.

[64] *Sadler* v. *Sheffield Cpn.* [1924] 1 Ch. 483; below, p. 442.

[65] *Sydney Municipal Council* v. *Campbell* [1925] AC 338. Compare *Denman & Co. Ltd.* v. *Westminster Cpn.* [1906] 1 Ch. 464 at 476.

statutory committee was given wide wartime powers to ensure adequate supplies of vegetable seeds, and was also empowered to trade in seeds. It was held that orders prohibiting merchants from dealing in certain seeds would be ultra vires if made primarily for the purpose of improving the profitability of the committee's trading operations rather than for ensuring supplies.[66]

Two liquor licensing cases firmly underline the same point. In one, the licensing justices required the applicant to pay £1,000, which they intended to use to reduce the rates or for some other public purpose. The court had no difficulty in holding that the justices had taken illegitimate factors into account in a wholly unjustifiable way.[67] In the other case an elaborate system had been set up by the statutory licensing planning committee in Birmingham to deal with the licences relating to the many public houses destroyed in the second world war. With Home Office approval and for some twenty years they had refused to approve applications unless the applicant purchased outstanding licences sufficient to cover his estimated sales. The main object of the policy was to relieve the city of the cost of compensating the holders of the outstanding licences. At the current market price of these licences the proprietors of a large new hotel would have had to pay over £14,000. At their instance the Court of Appeal condemned the whole system as unreasonable.[68] Lord Denning MR said:

I think it is unreasonable for a licensing planning committee to tell an applicant: 'We know that your hotel is needed in Birmingham and that it is well placed to have an on-licence, but we will not allow you to have a licence unless you buy out the brewers.' They are taking into account a payment to the brewers which is a thing they ought not to take into account.

The condition was therefore 'bad because it is unreasonable'.

In this class also is to be included the television licence case, already recounted, in which the Court of Appeal held that the Home Secretary could not lawfully exercise his power to revoke a licence for the purpose of compelling the licensee to pay an additional fee which had not been authorised by Parliament.[69] The revocation was invalid not only on general

---

[66] *Yates (Arthur) & Co. Pty. Ltd.* v. *Vegetable Seeds Committee* (1945) 72 CLR 37. cf. *Bailey* v. *Conole* (1931) 34 WALR 18 (regulations prescribing bus routes invalid since object was to protect state-owned trains from competition).

[67] *R.* v. *Bowman* [1898] 1 QB 663. See similarly *R.* v. *Sheffield Justices ex p. Rawson* (1927) 44 TLR 43 (offer to pay £1,250 to compensation fund). cf. *Marshal Shipping Co.* v. *R.* (1925) 41 TLR 285; *R.* v. *LCC* [1931] 2 KB 215 at 232. Contrast *Becker* v. *Home Office* [1972] 2 QB 407 (above, p. 240).

[68] *R.* v. *Birmingham Licensing Planning Committee ex p. Kennedy* [1972] 2 QB 140.

[69] *Congreve* v. *Home Office* [1976] QB 629; above, p. 406.

grounds of unreasonableness but also because it was an attempt to levy money for the use of the Crown without the authority of Parliament, contrary to the Bill of Rights 1688.

The Crown is not subject to this branch of the doctrine of unreasonableness when using its ordinary powers as an owner of land. Accordingly there can be no objection to the demand by an official in Hong Kong, acting as land agent for the Crown, for the payment of a high premium as the price of waiving restrictions in a lease of Crown land.[70]

Indiscriminate action

The indiscriminate or excessive use of power is illustrated by the case of a London borough council which made it a rule to refer to the rent tribunal all the tenancies in any block of flats where two or more reductions of rent had been awarded.[71] Although the Act contained no express restriction on the council's power to reduce the rent, it was held that it was an abuse to make a single block reference of over three hundred tenancies without any consideration of the individual cases and without any specific complaint against the landlord. The disputed reference in fact contained so many inaccuracies that it was not a genuine exercise of the power, and furthermore the council had taken account of the irrelevant consideration that the flats were allegedly below the highest building standards. This decision was distinguished in a later case where another London council had considered each case with care in a reference of twenty-two tenancies, and where the only complaint was that most of the tenants themselves did not wish the reference to be made.[72] The council here was plainly acting responsibly and intra vires, within the bounds of its discretion. But the Court of Appeal went out of their way to say that the doctrine of relevant and irrelevant considerations ought not to apply at all to a decision which does not itself infringe rights and merely causes something to be investigated. This novel proposition was probably not intended to make a breach in the long-settled rules of judicial review, since the court appears to have assumed that the 'relevant considerations' doctrine was violated whenever anything which might be thought relevant was not considered or any sort of mistake was made. In reality that doctrine applies only where the relevant considerations neglected or the irrelevant considerations adopted are so serious as to put the decision outside the powers of the statute.[73] The problem disappears if it is understood that the 'relevant

---

[70] *Hang Wah Chong Investment Co. Ltd. v. A.-G. of Hong Kong* [1981] 1 WLR 1141.

[71] *R. v. Paddington &c. Rent Tribunal ex parte Bell London and Provincial Properties Ltd.* [1949] 1 KB 666.

[72] *R. v. Barnet etc. Rent Tribunal ex parte Frey Investments Ltd.* [1972] 2 QB 342.

[73] See *R. v. St Pancras Vestry* (1890) 24 QBD 371 (above, p. 411).

considerations' doctrine is necessarily a species of the genus 'ultra vires', and cannot be used to impugn a proper and reasonable decision.

Inconsistency, unfairness and breach of undertakings

Inconsistency of policy may also amount to an abuse of discretion, particularly when undertakings or statements of intent are disregarded unfairly[74] or contrary to the citizen's legitimate expectation.[75] The Privy Council, in holding that the Government of Hong Kong must honour its published undertaking to treat each deportation case on its merits, has applied 'the principle that a public authority is bound by its undertakings as to the procedure it will follow, provided they do not conflict with its duty'.[76] The Court of Appeal made strong comments when quashing the refusal of the Home Office to allow a Pakistani, settled in England, to bring in his young nephew with a view to his adoption, since the Home Office had issued a circular specifying the conditions which need to be satisfied but had, by 'grossly unfair administration', refused admission on an altogether different ground. If the published policy was to be changed, the applicant should be given 'full and serious consideration whether there is some overriding public interest' justifying the new departure.[77] In another case the court condemned 'Machiavellian and unconscionable' conduct by the immigration authorities in treating an immigrant as an illegal entrant after they had abandoned this charge against him three years earlier.[78] In the same way the Court of Appeal held that a public authority has a duty to act with fairness and consistency in its dealings with the public, and that if it makes inconsistent decisions unfairly or unjustly it misuses its powers. Consequently the Price Commission was declared unable to issue a new ruling contradicting its previous statement that tax payments were a permissible item of costs for the purpose of calculating increases of price by television programme contractors.[79] One element of the unfairness was

---

[74] *R. v. Inland Revenue Commissioners ex p. Preston* [1985] AC 835 (complaint not made good).

[75] See the *Hong Kong* and *Ruddock* cases, below.

[76] *Attorney-General of Hong Kong* v. *Ng Yuen Shiu* [1983] 2 AC 629, approving *R. v. Liverpool Cpn. ex p. Liverpool Taxi Fleet Operators' Association* [1972] 2 QB 299. For these and other 'legitimate expectation' cases see below, p. 520.

[77] *R. v. Home Secretary ex p. Asif Mahmood Khan* [1984] 1 WLR 1337 (Parker LJ). The Home Secretary 'in effect made his own rules, and stated those matters which he regarded as relevant and would consider in reaching his decision' and 'misdirected himself according to his own criteria and acted unreasonably' (Dunn LJ).

[78] *R. v. Immigration Appeal Tribunal ex p. Patel* [1986] The Independent, 10 December; above, p. 264. But the House of Lords reversed: [1988] 2 WLR 1165.

[79] *HTV Ltd* v. *Price Commission* [1976] ICR 170, cited with approval in the *Preston* case (above).

that the contractors had been led to believe that they could safely act on the ruling given to them. In a case about telephone tapping it was held that the Home Secretary's published criteria for regulating this form of espionage created a legitimate expectation that they would be properly observed and that the court might grant relief if they were violated without any published change of policy.[80]

These are revealing decisions. They show that the courts now expect government departments to honour their published statements or else to treat the citizen with the fullest personal consideration. Unfairness in the form of unreasonableness here comes close to unfairness in the form of violation of natural justice,[81] and the doctrine of legitimate expectation can operate in both contexts. It is obvious, furthermore, that this principle of substantive, as opposed to procedural, fairness may undermine some of the established rules about estoppel and misleading advice, which tend to operate unfairly.[82] Lord Scarman has stated emphatically that unfairness in the purported exercise of a power can amount to an abuse or excess of power,[83] and this seems likely to develop into an important general doctrine.

Misplaced philanthropy

Statutory authorities have sometimes made use of their wide general powers in order to confer social or economic benefits on particular sections of the community. In several such cases they have gone beyond the true limits of their powers. The policy of the courts is in general hostile to the use of public funds, such as rates, for new social experiments. Local authorities are subject to a fiduciary duty to use their revenues with due restraint.

The leading case in this group is *Roberts* v. *Hopwood*.[84] A minimum weekly wage of £4 for men and women equally was established in 1920 by the Poplar Borough Council, representing themselves as 'model socialist employers'. This in itself was very substantially above the previous rates, and soon became relatively higher still due to a sharp fall in the cost of living and in wages. But the council insisted on continuing the £4 rate,

---

[80] *R.* v. *Home Secretary ex p. Ruddock* [1988] QB 000. The relief sought (declaration and damages for misfeasance) was refused since no violation was shown. The events took place before the Interception of Communications Act 1985 was in force.

[81] See below, p. 520.

[82] Above, pp. 261, 381. See in particular *R.* v. *West Glamorgan CC ex p. Gheissary* [1985] The Times, 18 December (above, p. 387). For discussion see [1981] CLP 1 (A. W. Bradley).

[83] In the *Preston* case (above) at 852.

[84] [1925] AC 578. Contrast *Pickwell* v. *Camden LBC* [1983] QB 962 (payment of wages above national level; auditor's challenge failed).

maintaining that this was within their power to pay their servants 'such salaries and wages as (they) may think fit'. In due course the district auditor disallowed the wage payments, in so far as they exceeded current market rates, as being 'contrary to law', and surcharged the councillors personally. A long struggle over the surcharges began, in the course of which the auditor's ruling was unanimously upheld by the House of Lords, and an order of the Minister of Health, purporting to free the councillors from liability, was held invalid by the High Court. Ultimately, when the surcharges had accumulated far beyond the councillors' personal means, they were remitted by Act of Parliament.[85]

The basis of the decision of the House of Lords, as already noted, was that the wages paid were excessive and unreasonable in such a degree that they were beyond the council's powers. The council's philanthropic purposes were not in law relevant considerations: their duty was not to give their ratepayers' money away in what were in substance gifts, but to take due account of the relevant factor of current market rates. They had misled themselves by 'eccentric principles of socialistic philanthropy'.[86]

Despite remarks such as the last, and despite criticisms from literal-minded people, there is no doubt that this decision was fully in accord with the settled policy of limiting discretionary powers. It was followed where councillors of another London borough were surcharged for failing to increase rents in an attempt to resist the policy of the Rent Act 1957, as already explained.[87] It was also accepted by the Court of Appeal as supporting their decision in the *Birmingham* case, discussed below. It had also been foreshadowed earlier when Farwell LJ had said:[88]

The auditor does not claim . . . to exercise any control over questions of policy; but he does claim the right to check and challenge all items of administration. It is not easy to draw the line between policy and administration, or to give a definition except by way of example, but in my opinion the establishment of a works committee would be a question of policy into which the auditor could not go, but the payment of abnormally high wages to the workmen employed by such committee would be a matter of administration.

Another restrictive decision comes from the general strike of 1926. After the strike, when the poor law guardians had been empowered to give relief to miners' families by way of loan, the Tynemouth guardians resolved to

---

[85] Audit (Local Authorities) Act 1927, s. 2(6). For a good account of the whole contest and its political background, including the imprisonment of thirty councillors for failing to levy rates, see B. Keith-Lucas [1962] *Public Law* 52; N. Branson, *Poplarism*.

[86] At 594 (Lord Atkinson).

[87] *Taylor* v. *Munrow* [1960] 1 WLR 151; above, p. 417.

[88] *R.* v. *Roberts* [1908] 1 KB 407 at 435 (unsuccessful appeal by the same auditor who played a leading part in *Roberts* v. *Hopwood*).

cancel the outstanding debts.[89] This was held to be ultra vires since the guardians, unlike a private creditor, had no power to remit debts,[90] and because, in any case, it was unreasonable to do so where there was no evidence of inability to repay. The idea that runs through these cases is that public money must be administered with responsibility and without extravagance. This appears to mean that it is not available for charity.

The generosity of local authorities, in particular, is restrained by the doctrine that they owe a fiduciary duty to their ratepayers analogous to that of trustees. This means that, in deciding upon their expenditure, they must hold a balance fairly between the recipients of the benefit and the ratepayers who have to bear the cost. The courts have given two notable illustrations of this doctrine. In the first, the Court of Appeal invalidated the Birmingham City Council's concession to old-age pensioners, by which if resident in the city they could travel free of charge on the corporation's buses and trams.[91] These services were operated under Acts of Parliament which empowered the corporation to impose 'such fares and charges as they may think fit'. They were already run at a loss, and the additional cost of the concession was some £90,000 a year. At the instance of a ratepayer the court granted a declaration that the concession was illegal. The corporation's fiduciary duty to its ratepayers meant that it was not free to saddle them with the cost of subsidising one particular class of the community. Philanthropy was no part of the management of a transport undertaking which the corporation ought to operate 'substantially on business lines'. This would not necessarily exclude free or cheap travel for children, which might well be commercially justifiable. But it did exclude concessions made merely 'on benevolent or philanthropic grounds'. Ultimately, however, local authorities were given power to allow free travel to certain specified classes of the community by the Travel Concessions Act 1964.[92]

The second illustration was the invalidation by the House of Lords of the supplementary rate levied by the Greater London Council for the purpose of financing a 25 per cent cut in the London bus and underground fares.[93] This cut was made in fulfilment of electoral promises. But it had to be paid for by all the ratepayers of Greater London, for whom it was exceptionally expensive since it involved a loss of government grant which approximately doubled the rate. In deciding to fulfil its election promises without

[89] *A.-G.* v. *Tynemouth Union* [1930] 1 Ch. 616, also following *Roberts* v. *Hopwood.*
[90] See above, p. 400.
[91] *Prescott* v. *Birmingham Cpn.* [1955] Ch. 210.
[92] Concessions already in operation had been legitimated by the Public Service Vehicles (Travel Concessions) Act 1955.
[93] *Bromley LBC* v. *Greater London Council* [1983] 1 AC 768.

regard to the exceptional burden thrown upon the ratepayers the GLC was held to have neglected its fiduciary duty to hold the balance fairly, as well as to have failed in its statutory duties.[94] It had power to subsidise the transport services, but it also had a duty to encourage their economic operation rather than to drive them into loss deliberately, leaving the ratepayers to foot the bill.

A paternal concern for human welfare motivated a caravan site licensing authority's requirements that there should be rent control, security of tenure, and no restrictions on the tenants' liberty to shop where they wanted or to form tenants' associations. We have already seen how the House of Lords invalidated these conditions as being unreasonably remote from the purposes of the Act controlling the use of land for caravan sites.[95]

Permissible philanthropy

One form of social assistance which the law has allowed is the charging of differential rents to tenants of local authorities.[96] This is held to be reasonably incidental to their managerial powers over their houses. They may therefore adjust rents according to the means of individual tenants, either by granting rebates or by adding surcharges to a low basic rent. This is clearly philanthropy, but it is philanthropy authorised by Parliament. For the underlying policy of the housing legislation, which empowers the authorities to make 'such reasonable charges . . . as they may determine', is to provide houses for those who cannot afford economic rents, but not to subsidise those who can afford them.[97] This policy was prayed in aid by one tenant of a council house who challenged the legality of a uniform increase of rents on the ground that the council was *not* operating a differential scheme, and did not consider the means of each of its tenants. The court had no difficulty in upholding the council.[98] Here is one field where a wide range of differing social policies is within the bounds of the discretion conferred, and where the court will not (as elsewhere it may[99]) seize upon the word 'reasonable' as importing a rigid legal standard.

Children's allowances have also been held to be a legitimate element in wages paid by local authorities.[1] Following the lead of *Roberts* v. *Hopwood*,

---

[94] For that aspect see below, p. 615.
[95] *Mixnam's Properties Ltd.* v. *Chertsey Urban District Council* [1965] AC 735; below, p. 431.
[96] *Leeds Cpn.* v. *Jenkinson* [1935] 1 KB 168; *Smith* v. *Cardiff Cpn. (No. 2)* [1955] Ch. 159; *Summerfield* v. *Hampstead Borough Council* [1957] 1 WLR 167.
[97] See *Smith* v. *Cardiff Cpn.* (above) at 170.
[98] *Luby* v. *Newcastle-under-Lyme Cpn.* [1964] 2 QB 64.
[99] See below, p. 456.
[1] *Re Walker's Decision* [1944] KB 644.

the district auditor for Birmingham disallowed the payments and surcharged the councillors, holding that the size of an employee's family was an irrelevant consideration in determining his salary. But the Court of Appeal quashed these orders, on the ground that children's allowances were a recognised benefit which many employers had reasonably paid, and which therefore were within the council's powers. The strength of the council's case was that, instead of increasing all salaries to the pre-war level in terms of real values, they were increasing them selectively in order to benefit the class which suffered most. Since all the salaries were therefore within the range of what the council might reasonably pay, the allowances for children were intra vires. In *Roberts* v. *Hopwood* Lord Sumner had said that even where the motive was improper the expenditure would be lawful if there was no excess over what was reasonable.[2] Here therefore the council's discretion was wide enough to allow some scope for philanthropy.

Improper licensing decisions

Miscellaneous licensing powers are very numerous, and are often conferred in widely permissive terms. The courts are vigilant to restrict the discretion of licensing authorities to the true purposes of the empowering Act, and to disallow arbitrary or oppressive refusals or revocations or improper conditions. In licensing there is naturally wide scope for the question of relevant and irrelevant considerations. A century ago, for example, a local authority might not withhold approval of building plans on the ground that the building was unsuitable for the neighbourhood.[3] Today this has become a highly relevant consideration for the refusal of planning permission, although in both cases alike the Acts merely give power to grant or withhold consent.

Among the many examples of the abuse of licensing powers pride of place is claimed by the three cases, one Canadian and two English, in which ministers have attempted to procure the cancellation of licences for improper reasons. These have already been related.[4] The Court of Appeal quashed the revocation of a market trader's licence on the ground that to deprive him of his livelihood was an excessive penalty in relation to his

---

[2] [1925] AC 578 at 604, quoted above, p. 415.

[3] *R.* v. *Newcastle on Tyne Cpn. ex p. Veitch* (1889) 60 LT 963. cf. *Marshall* v. *Blackpool Cpn.* [1935] AC 16 (power to approve plans for access across footpaths to street does not empower refusal of approval of proper plans because access might impede traffic; Act not intended to restrict owner's right of access); *Davies* v. *Bromley Cpn.* [1908] 1 KB 170 (plans allegedly rejected out of spite).

[4] Above, pp. 405, 406.

offence, which was indulgence in abusive language.[5] There is a similar 'principle of proportionality' in European law by which excessive penalties can be set aside.[6] Lord Diplock has spoken of the possible adoption of this principle in English law[7] but it would seem to be already available as inherent in the principle of reasonableness.

In the long history of liquor licensing the courts have quashed many decisions of licensing justices and examples have already been given.[8] It has been held irrelevant for the justices, when considering whether the applicant is a fit and proper person, to take account of the way he proposed to do business, the terms agreed between him and the brewery company, and the price of the beer to be supplied.[9] In considering an application for enlarging licensed premises it is an irrelevant ground of refusal that the licensee will obtain a valuable addition to his trade without paying the levy for monopoly value;[10] but this factor is relevant on an application for transfer of the licence to superior premises, since it is then reasonable to insist on a new application.[11] To require the surrender of some other licence as a condition of the grant of a licence is illegitimate.[12] And so is to require a payment.[13] Licensing justices must also pursue a consistent policy and may not refuse renewal of a licence unless their new policy is justified by a genuine change of circumstances.[14] Where a refreshment licence was refused to a theatre which had enjoyed it for over fifty years, on the ground that it should be treated equally with a new theatre where an application had been refused, and because there were other facilities nearby, the licensing committee were held to have given too little weight to the fifty years' enjoyment and too much to rigid consistency.[15] In this case the court was virtually acting as a court of appeal and reversing a decision with which

---

[5] *R.* v. *Barnsley Metropolitan Borough Council ex p. Hook* [1976] 1 WLR 1052; and see *R.* v. *Brent LBC ex p. Assegai* [1987] The Independent, 12 June (citizen banned from access to local authority premises: penalty disproportionate to offence).

[6] Examples are *R.* v. *Intervention Board for Agricultural Produce ex p. ED & F Man (Sugar) Ltd* [1986] 2 All ER 115; *Buitoni SA* v. *Fonds des Marchés Agricoles* [1979] 2 CMLR 665; *Commission of the European Communities* v. *U.K.* (case 261/85) [1988] The Times, 6 February (disproportionate ban on milk imports).

[7] *Council of Civil Service Unions* v. *Minister for the Civil Service* [1985] AC at 410.

[8] Above, p. 421.

[9] *R.* v. *Hyde Justices* [1912] 1 KB 645.

[10] *R.* v. *Wandsworth Licensing Justices ex p. Whitbread & Co. Ltd.* [1921] 3 KB 487 (this levy represents the difference in value between licensed and unlicensed premises and is payable to the exchequer).

[11] *R.* v. *Southampton County Confirming Committee ex p. Slade* [1929] 1 KB 645 (not citing the *Wandsworth* case, above).

[12] *R.* v. *Wandsworth Licensing Justices* (above).

[13] See above, p. 421.

[14] *R.* v. *Windsor Licensing Justices ex p. Hodes* [1983] 1 WLR 685.

[15] *R.* v. *Flintshire County Licensing Committee ex p. Barrett* [1957] 1 QB 350.

it disagreed. It could not be said that the committee had failed to take into account the rival considerations, each of which was relevant: they had assessed them carefully, but the court assessed them otherwise. Nor could it be said that the decision was so unreasonable as to be beyond the committee's powers.

In other cases the courts have allowed a considerable freedom of discretion to licensing justices, when satisfied that they were acting bona fide for the true purposes of the Licensing Acts.[16] But they abuse their discretion if they require a licensee to enter into a binding undertaking restricting his licence in a case where they are not themselves empowered to impose conditions.[17]

Complication has been caused by the introduction of licensing planning committees from whom a certificate of non-objection must be obtained before application for a justices' liquor licence may be made. The committees have to consider an area as a whole, with reference to the number, nature, and distribution of licensed premises and the accommodation and facilities provided in them.[18] It has been held that they may not legitimately insist on a bingo club requiring membership for twenty-four rather than forty-eight hours before supplying liquor,[19] nor may they object to mobile trolley bars being used in cinemas,[20] since these are matters of detail for the licensing justices and irrelevant for the committee's purposes.

Cinema licensing is a field where the courts are reluctant to interfere, since the disputed questions are usually well within the range of the local authority's discretion. Conditions barring children, even when accompanied by adults, from cinemas on Sundays[21] or barring Sunday opening altogether,[22] have been upheld as not unreasonable. The general principles stated by Lord Greene MR in the leading case have already been quoted.[23] He criticised an earlier decision in which the court had disallowed conditions restricting children from attending cinemas after certain hours, and had held that concern for the health and welfare of children generally was not a relevant factor.[24] The 'irrelevant considerations' argument was also rejected in an earlier wartime case where a licence was refused because

---

[16] e.g. *Sharp* v. *Wakefield* [1891] AC 173; *Leeds Corporation* v. *Ryder* [1907] AC 420.

[17] *R.* v. *Edmonton Licensing Justices ex p. Baker* [1983] 1 WLR 1000.

[18] Licensing Act 1964, s. 119, replacing earlier Acts.

[19] *Fletcher* v. *London (Metropolis) Licensing Planning Committee* [1976] AC 150.

[20] *R.* v. *London (Metropolis) Licensing Planning Committee ex p. Maynard* [1976] The Times, 11 May.

[21] *Harman* v. *Butt* [1944] KB 491; *Associated Provincial Picture Houses Ltd.* v. *Wednesbury Cpn.* [1948] 1 KB 223.

[22] *London County Council* v. *Bermondsey Bioscope Ltd.* [1911] 1 KB 445.

[23] Above, p. 407.

[24] *Theatre de Luxe (Halifax) Ltd.* v. *Gledhill* [1915] 2 KB 49.

the cinema company was controlled by enemy aliens.[25] But the Court of Appeal upheld a complaint that the Greater London Council was using an unduly permissive test of obscenity and licensing indecent films, thereby misusing their licensing power.[26]

A good example of irrelevant grounds in transport licensing was where the commissioner of police refused cab licences to all proprietors whose vehicles were on hire-purchase.[27] In New Zealand the court has condemned a refusal of foreign investment facilities when the motives of the authorities were outside the purposes of the Act.[28]

The planning cases discussed next might also be considered to illustrate illegitimate licensing decisions.

Unreasonable planning decisions

The importance of the statutory background and context is well illustrated by a group of planning cases. A local planning authority may grant permission 'subject to such conditions as they think fit',[29] and the court is disposed to construe such conditions benevolently.[30] But it has been repeatedly held that such conditions are invalid unless they 'fairly and reasonably relate to the permitted development'.[31] Many planning conditions have been condemned by the application of this test. The House of Lords similarly invalidated conditions imposed by a caravan site licensing authority, although it had power to grant licences 'subject to such conditions as the authority may think it necessary or desirable to impose'.[32] Among numerous conditions were: that site rents should be agreed with the authority, that there should be security of tenure comparable to that in rent-controlled houses, that no premium should be charged for a site, and that there should be no restrictions on commercial or political activity. These conditions, designed to benefit the tenants personally rather than to

[25] R. v. *London County Council ex parte London & Provincial Electric Theatres Ltd.* [1915] 1 KB 446.

[26] R. v. *Greater London Council ex p. Blackburn* v. [1976] 1 WLR 550.

[27] R. v. *Metropolitan Police Commissioner ex p. Randall* (1911) 27 TLR 505; cf. R. v. *Brighton Cpn. ex p. Thomas Tilling Ltd.* (1916) 85 LJKB 1552.

[28] *Rowling* v. *Takaro Properties Ltd.* [1975] 2 NZLR 62 (doubted by the Privy Council in the sequel case: [1988] 2 WLR 418 at 435).

[29] Town and Country Planning Act 1971, s. 29(1) (repeating earlier Acts).

[30] *Fawcett Properties Ltd.* v. *Buckingham County Council* [1961] AC 636 at 679; *Hall & Co. Ltd.* v. *Shoreham-by-Sea Urban District Council* [1964] 1 WLR 240. A condition is not invalid because it depends on events beyond the applicant's control: *Grampian Regional Council* v. *Aberdeen DC* (1983) 47 P & CR 633 (House of Lords upheld condition requiring that a public road should first be closed).

[31] *Pyx Granite Co Ltd.* v. *Ministry of Housing and Local Government* [1958] 1 QB 544 at 572 (Lord Denning), affirmed [1960] AC 260.

[32] *Mixnam's Properties Ltd.* v. *Chertsey Urban District Council* [1965] AC 735.

control the use made of the land, were held to be 'a gratuitous interference with the rights of the occupier' and 'wholly unnecessary for the good governance of the site', and therefore ultra vires. Lord Upjohn, who used these words, stressed the principle that conditions such as these must be reasonable.

Planning conditions are likewise unreasonable if, instead of relating to the permitted development, they attempt to restrict the owner's existing use rights in his land; for it is the policy of the legislation to preserve these rights and to give compensation for restriction of them. The House of Lords therefore held a planning condition to be ultra vires and void because it allowed only six caravans to be stationed on the site:[33] for although there had been only six previously, the existing use right included the right to increase the number up to the point where there would be a material change of use. But the principle of this case is confined, it seems, to situations where the owner is given nothing in exchange. If he is given permission for some new development over and above his existing use rights, there may be valid conditions restricting his existing use rights on other land or requiring him to remove buildings on other land. So where British Railways were given permission to rebuild a station subject to a condition that part of the land should always be used as a car park, this condition was valid although it restricted existing use rights in the land in question.[34] A condition requiring the removal of buildings, however, is likely to be void if attached to a permission for their use in some particular way.

Planning conditions sometimes require new buildings to be used for particular purposes.[35] A condition restricting the occupants of new cottages to persons employed in agriculture or forestry was upheld by the House of Lords as being within the policy of the Act.[36] But a Divisional Court held it unreasonable and ultra vires to require a builder to let his houses to persons on the local authority's housing waiting list, for then he was being asked to undertake part of their own duties as housing authority.[37]

---

[33] *Hartnell* v. *Minister of Housing and Local Government* [1965] AC 1134, holding the minister's confirming order to be 'unreasonable and ultra vires' (Lord Wilberforce at 1173). See similarly *Allnat London Properties Ltd.* v. *Middlesex County Council* [1964] 62 LGR 304 (factory site wrongly restricted); *British Airports Authority* v. *Secretary of State for Scotland* 1979 SLT 197 (unreasonable restrictions on flying).

[34] *Kingston-upon-Thames Royal London Borough Council* v. *Secretary of State for the Environment* [1973] 1 WLR 1549. See also the *British Airports Authority* case, above.

[35] *Newbury District Council* v. *Secretary of State for the Environment* [1981] AC 578 (condition requiring removal of warehouses after ten years void).

[36] *Fawcett Properties Ltd.* v. *Buckingham County Council* [1961] AC 636.

[37] *R.* v. *Hillingdon London Borough Council ex p. Royco Homes Ltd.* [1974] QB 720. See similarly *Lowe (David) & Sons Ltd.* v. *Musselburgh Cpn.* 1974 SLT 5; *Westminster Renslade Ltd.* v. *Secretary of State for the Environment* (1983) 48 P & CR 255.

A striking example of an invalid planning condition was one which required the landowners to construct a strip of roadway along their entire frontage and to give public right of passage over it.[38] The Court of Appeal invalidated this as an attempt to secure a widening of the adjacent road at the landowners' expense, so as to avoid using the powers of the Highways Act 1959 (now 1980), which would require compensation to be paid. The object, i.e. to widen the road, was held to be perfectly reasonable in itself, but the conditions which attempted to put the expense onto the landowner by the use of planning powers were 'so unreasonable that they must be held to be ultra vires'.[39] This decision has several times been approved,[40] though it must not be taken to establish a principle that, where there are two alternative procedures, the more expensive one must be followed.[41] It shows that on the question of reasonableness it is not enough to consider merely the context and purposes of the statute conferring the disputed power: there may be other statutes such as the Highways Act which lay down procedures or confer rights for specific purposes which merely general powers ought not to be capable of overriding, on the principle *generalia specialibus non derogant*. Interaction with other statutes thus imposes still further limits on the indefinite discretionary powers with which statutes are so freely strewn.

The Court may quash the Secretary of State's decision of a planning appeal if it is one which on the evidence he could not reasonably make, as where he refused permission for the continuance of office use in a residential area, when the only reasonable conclusion was that conversion of the premises for residential use was unjustifiably expensive.[42] And where his decision to reopen a planning inquiry can only be described as perverse, that will be quashed likewise.[43]

A way of escape from the strictness of judicial control in this area has been found by many local planning authorities in the device of planning agreements, which they have statutory power to make. An applicant for planning permission will often be willing to agree to give the local

[38] *Hall & Co. Ltd.* v. *Shoreham-by-Sea Urban District Council* [1964] 1 WLR 240.

[39] At 251 (Willmer LJ). See similarly *Bradford Metropolitan Council* v. *Secretary of State for the Environment* (1986) 53 P & CR 55 (Secretary of State rightly disallowed condition requiring road-widening as manifestly unreasonable).

[40] By Lord Wilberforce in *Hartnell's* case (above), where similar reasoning was used; by Lord Widgery CJ in the *Hillingdon* case (above); and see *Hoveringham Gravels Ltd.* v. *Secretary of State for the Environment* [1975] 1 QB 754 (Orr LJ).

[41] See below (overlapping powers).

[42] *Niarchos* v. *Secretary of State for the Environment* [1977] 76 LGR 480; and see *Forkhurst* v. *Secretary of State for the Environment* (1982) 46 P & CR 89 (inspector's decision quashed as unreasonable).

[43] *Niarchos (London) Ltd* v. *Secretary of State for the Environment* (1980) 79 LGR 264.

authority some benefit, such as land for street widening or office accommodation, if given to understand that he is unlikely to obtain permission otherwise. The legality of this evasive practice has however been questioned.[44]

Overlapping powers and compensation

Another feature of planning law is that the very wide powers of planning authorities may overlap more specific powers, and that the choice of power may affect the right to compensation. This problem arose where a borough council, as planning authority, persistently refused planning permission for building alongside a road, because, in its capacity of highway authority, it had nebulous plans for widening the road in the future. Meanwhile the land suffered prolonged 'planning blight'. As highway authority the council had power to prescribe an improvement line under the Highways Act 1959 (now 1980). But the council did not invoke that power, since the Highways Act required compensation to be paid for the blight inflicted, and the Ministry of Transport's policy was to refuse grants towards such compensation since the same result could be attained free of charge by the use of planning powers. Was it lawful for the council to use its general planning powers, which taken by themselves were sufficient, when Parliament had provided a different procedure for this specific purpose and had given a right to compensation? The House of Lords[45] found the solution in a provision that planning powers may be freely exercised despite any other legislation regulating development which was in force before the original planning Act of 1947,[46] which they interpreted so as to include provisions repealing and re-enacting such legislation (as did the Highways Act 1959 as regards improvement lines). But they also gave clear indications that there was no legal objection to the use of planning powers in preference to more specific powers requiring compensation.[47]

In a later case Lord Denning MR said broadly that the House of Lords had held that where there were two such alternative courses of action, a public authority might adopt the one which did not give rise to compensation.[48] It must be remembered that the planning legislation of 1947 introduced a new philosophy of uncompensated control, so that it may be logical to make this prevail over earlier legislation which paid more

[44] See below, p. 790.
[45] *Westminster Bank Ltd* v. *Beverley Borough Council* [1971] AC 508, upholding the refusal of planning permission by the local authority and the minister.
[46] Town and Country Planning Act 1962, s. 220, now replaced by s. 289 of the Act of 1971. This provision was not cited in the courts below, nor in *Hall & Co.'s* case (above).
[47] See especially at 530 (Lord Reid).
[48] *Hoveringham Gravels Ltd.* v. *Secretary of State for the Environment* [1975] QB 754 at 763. Orr and Scarman LJJ confined their remarks to the planning legislation.

respect to rights of property.[49] This reasoning may not necessarily conflict with that adopted by the Court of Appeal in the *Shoreham* case.[50] The basis of the latter may be that a condition requiring a developer to present the public with a free roadway is something quite extraneous to the permitted development and also an unjustifiable demand that he should give up his existing rights of ownership.[51]

Compulsory purchase of land

Wrong or irrelevant purposes have often vitiated compulsory purchase orders or schemes depending upon them, as has already been shown in other contexts.[52] In several cases the illegal element was some bargain with the owner or a third party for putting the land to some use outside the powers of the Act[53] or some plan for disposing of it when the Act required it to be redeveloped.[54] The motives behind a compulsory purchase order made by the Central Land Board were canvassed in a case where, although the House of Lords ultimately upheld the order, a forceful dissenting judgment made out a strong case against it.[55] Under the law then in force persons granted planning permission had to pay a 'development charge', representing the value of the permission, so that development rights were in effect expropriated. Compulsory purchase for public purposes was accordingly effected at 'existing use value' and it was intended that land should change hands at this value. In fact it did not, since the Act did not impose price control, and demand drove up prices. The Central Land Board, empowered to acquire land compulsorily for permitted develop-ment, made an order for the acquisition of land which the intending developer was unable to obtain except at a high price. It was suspected that the Board's object was to make an example and to use its powers *in terrorem* for a purpose not authorised by the Act, i.e. to enforce price control.[56] Denning LJ held this to be a usurpation of the legislative powers of Parliament, having a purpose for which Parliament had deliberately refrained from legislating. He said:[57]

But there is a principle at stake which is far more important than the stopping of

---

[49] See the *Westminster Bank* case (above) at 529, 535.

[50] *Hall & Co. Ltd.* v. *Shoreham-by-Sea Urban District Council* (above).

[51] This distinction is taken by Orr LJ in the *Hoveringham Gravels* case (above) at 765.

[52] Above, p. 420.

[53] *Denman & Co. Ltd.* v. *Westminster Cpn.* [1906] 1 Ch. 464; *London & Westcliff Properties Ltd.* v. *Minister of Housing and Local Government* [1961] 1 WLR 519.

[54] *R.* v. *Minister of Health ex parte Davis* [1929] 1 KB 619.

[55] *Fitzwilliam (Earl)'s Wentworth Estates Co.* v. *Minister of Town and Country Planning* [1952] AC 362.

[56] [1951] 2 KB 284 at 300.

[57] [1951] 2 KB at 311–13.

one particular piece of profiteering. The principle is that the legislative power in this country resides in Parliament and not in the government departments. [Powers] must not be used for an ulterior object which is not authorised by law, however desirable that object may seem to them to be in the public interest.

But the House of Lords held that the powers conferred were wide enough to cover the Board's objectives.

In another compulsory purchase case the court declined to make a sharp distinction between 'housing' and 'planning' considerations, holding that a housing authority might legitimately take account of factors which were also relevant for the planning authority.[58] In these fields it is obvious that many relevant factors will overlap. On the other hand, a local authority may not use its housing powers merely for the purpose of obtaining a highway;[59] and a caravan site licensing authority, which is concerned with the use of the particular site, cannot lawfully take account of 'pure planning' considerations, such as that the site is in the green belt.[60] There are however numerous aspects such as amenity, transport, schools and shopping facilities which are relevant both to planning and to site licensing, so that here again there is a wide area of common ground.[61]

A compulsory purchase order, when confirmed by the minister, authorises the purchase for the particular purpose then specified. If later the purpose changes, the authority no longer holds good. Where, accordingly, a local authority obtained an order for the purpose of road widening and building a market hall, they were unable to enforce it for other purposes after abandoning their earlier plans.[62] But a mere change of circumstances rendering the attainment of the objective more remote will not necessarily have this effect.[63]

Powers of compulsory purchase, like other powers, must be exercised reasonably, and all the more so because they expropriate an owner against his will. An order may be quashed as unreasonable if the authority making it already possesses, or can acquire by agreement, other land which is equally suitable for its purposes.[64]

---

[58] *Hanks* v. *Minister of Housing and Local Government* [1963] 1 QB 999.

[59] *Meravale Builders Ltd.* v. *Secretary of State for the Environment* (1978) 77 LGR 365.

[60] *Esdell Caravan Parks Ltd.* v. *Hemel Hempstead Rural District Council* [1966] 1 QB 895 (CA).

[61] Same case at 925 (Lord Denning MR).

[62] *Grice* v. *Dudley Cpn.* [1958] Ch. 329 (declarations that notice to treat and compulsory purchase order were no longer effective).

[63] *Simpsons Motor Sales Ltd.* v. *Hendon Cpn.* [1964] AC 1088 (Lord Evershed at pp. 1126–7 curiously refers to the court's jurisdiction as if it were a branch of equity in the technical sense. The only equitable aspect of the case was that part of the relief asked for was an injunction, but this was not material).

[64] *Brown* v. *Secretary of State for the Environment* (1978) 40 P & CR 285; *Prest* v. *Secretary of State for Wales* (1982) 81 LGR 193.

The acquiring authority is usually empowered to take as much land as it judges to be necessary for the statutory purpose. But where it takes more than could reasonably be considered necessary, it acts ultra vires. It cannot therefore take the whole of the site where it requires no more than a few feet for street widening.[65] The Court of Appeal quashed a compulsory purchase order made ostensibly for a sea-wall but including a large piece of land said to be required for coast protection purposes but in fact intended for a paved access way which was to be a sort of promenade and was not in fact needed for coast protection at all.[66]

Tax concessions

Judges have often criticised the practice of the Commissioners of Inland Revenue in making extra-statutory concessions to taxpayers, thereby discriminating between them in their free discretion but without any legal basis.[67] Some of these concessions are made regularly according to published rules;[68] for example, money paid to coalminers in lieu of their entitlement of free coal is, by concession, not assessed to tax. One concession, strongly criticised in the House of Lords, was made under a statute which had been held to make each of a number of joint beneficiaries under a family settlement severally liable for the whole of the tax on the whole income of the fund. Instead of taking steps to amend the law, the tax authorities tempered its application by concession, assessing each taxpayer with his own proportion only. Lord Wilberforce stigmatised this state of affairs as arbitrary, unjust and unconstitutional; for, as Walton J had said at first instance, 'one should be taxed by law, and not be untaxed by concession'. Since the House of Lords held that the oppressive interpretation of the taxing Act was wrong, it was unnecessary to decide whether taxation by administrative discretion was unlawful.[69] But Lord Wilberforce said that unless it was expressly authorised by Act of Parliament 'the courts, acting on constitutional principles, not only should not but cannot validate it.'

In another case, however, the House upheld concessions by which

---

[65] Gard v. Commissioners of Sewers of City of London (1885) 28 Ch. D. 486; Denman & Co. Ltd. v. Westminster Cpn. [1906] 1 Ch. 464; Bartrum v. Manurewa Borough [1962] NZLR 21 (acquisition for benefit of neighbouring owner rather than for public benefit).

[66] Webb v. Minister of Housing and Local Government [1965] 1 WLR 755.

[67] See the opinions of Lord Wilberforce, Lord Edmund-Davies and Walton J in the Vestey case (below).

[68] The Inland Revenue publish a booklet on them with annual supplements. This has been called 'administrative quasi-legislation': (1944) 60 LQR 125, 218 (R. E. Megarry). See also R. v. Customs & Excise Commissioners ex p. Cook [1970] 1 WLR 450; below, p. 698.

[69] Vestey v. Inland Revenue Commissioners [1980] AC 1148.

workers in the printing industry were exonerated from liability for arrears of tax on casual earnings, which had been evaded on a large scale for some years. The tax authorities made a concession to the workers under which the arrears would be discharged if proper tax returns were made for the future. Despite evidence that the concession might have been motivated by fear of a printers' strike, it was held to have been made under an arrangement which was within the managerial powers and discretion of the authorities.[70] At the same time it was said that improper concessions might be the subject of intervention by the court. That indeed occurred in a later case where the tax authorities accepted a valuation 'which no reasonable authority properly directing itself could reach', so that it was declared unlawful by the Court of Appeal.[71]

Unreasonable regulations

The principle of reasonableness applies just as much to the making of rules and regulations as it does to other administrative action. This is explained in the chapter on delegated legislation, where some striking examples will be found.

Miscellaneous cases; undue delay

No list of categories will cover all cases, since the possibilities of abuse are infinite.

The courts are always disposed to intervene where the action is arbitrary or oppressive. If the Commission for Racial Equality uses its formidable powers to make a roving investigation without having reasonable grounds for suspecting racial discrimination, its proceedings may be condemned as unreasonable and vexatious.[72]

A clear instance of 'collateral purpose' was where a chief constable had retired on pension because of infirmity and lived abroad to avoid his creditors. The police authority called him up for medical examination, and when he did not attend, cancelled his pension. It was proved that their object was not to obtain medical information but to bring him within reach of his creditors and he was granted mandamus to restore his pension.[73] An

---

[70] R. v. *Inland Revenue Commissioners ex p. National Federation of Self-Employed and Small Businesses Ltd.* [1982] AC 617. See also R. v. *Inspector of Taxes, Reading, ex p. Fulford-Dobson* [1987] 3 WLR 277.

[71] R. v. *Attorney-General ex p. Imperial Chemical Industries plc* [1986] The Times, 27 February, [1987] CMLR 72 (under-valuation of ethane gas).

[72] R. v. *Commission for Racial Equality ex p. Hillingdon LBC* [1982] QB 276.

[73] R. v. *Leigh (Lord)* [1897] 1 QB 132. Similarly a local authority may not use its power to acquire land, even by agreement, where its real object is to remove gipsies from it: *Costello v. Dacorum DC* (1980) 79 LGR 133.

alien may challenge the legality of his deportation on the ground that its real purpose is to comply with a request from his country of origin, so that it is extradition in disguise.[74]

Delay in performing a legal duty may also amount to an abuse which the law will remedy. Where a British 'patrial' was entitled by statute to enter the country 'without let or hindrance', but the Home Office refused her the necessary certificate of patriality except by an administrative procedure which would have made her wait for over a year,[75] the Court of Appeal held that the certificate could not be arbitrarily refused or delayed and ordered its issue, citing Magna Carta 1215: 'to no one will we delay right or justice'.[76] Where police officers were not given the formal notice of complaints made against them for over two years, this excessive delay invalidated the disciplinary proceedings.[77] Where the Advisory, Conciliation and Arbitration Service deferred proceeding with inquiries into a recognition issue at the instance of a trade union, the House of Lords held that excessive deferment, amounting to abdication of the Service's functions, would be unlawful; but the majority also held that the deferment was not excessive in the circumstances.[78] Likewise the House has held that delay by the tax authorities may, if unfair, amount to abuse of power; but again the complaint failed on the facts.[79]

It may be possible for total inactivity to amount to abuse of discretion. The Privy Council has suggested that this would be the case if the Malaysian head of state failed to revoke a proclamation of emergency once he no longer considered it necessary for its proper purpose.[80] That is another way of saying that in those circumstances he would become subject to a legal duty to proclaim the end of the emergency.

MIXED MOTIVES

Duality of purpose

Sometimes an act may serve two or more purposes, some authorised and some not, and it may be a question whether the public authority may kill

[74] *R. v. Brixton Prison Governor ex p. Soblen* [1963] 2 QB 243 at 302. For this case see below, p. 441.

[75] *R. v. Home Secretary ex p. Phansopkar* [1976] QB 606. See also *R. v. Durham Prison Governor ex p. Hardial Singh* [1984] 1 WLR 704 (delay in effecting deportation).

[76] Magna Carta 1215, c. 29.

[77] *R. v. Merseyside Chief Constable ex p. Calveley* [1986] QB 424.

[78] *Engineers' and Managers' Association* v. *ACAS* [1980] 1 WLR 302.

[79] *R. v. Inland Revenue Cmrs. ex p. Preston* [1985] AC 835.

[80] *Teh Cheng Poh* v. *Public Prosecutor, Malaysia* [1980] AC 458 (suggesting that mandamus might lie against members of the cabinet on whose advice he would act).

two birds with one stone. The general rule is that its action will be lawful provided that the permitted purpose is the true and dominant purpose behind the act, even though some secondary or incidental advantage may be gained for some purpose which is outside the authority's powers. There is a clear distinction between this situation and its opposite, where the permitted purpose is a mere pretext and a dominant purpose is ultra vires.

A leading example is the decision of the House of Lords upholding the legality of the subway crossing the foot of Whitehall in London.[81] The Westminster Corporation had no power to construct subways, but they had power to construct public conveniences. They located the conveniences under the street with access from both sides, so that a subway naturally resulted. The House of Lords had no doubt that the 'primary object of the council was the construction of the conveniences with the requisite and proper means of approach thereto and exit therefrom'.[82] Accordingly 'that the public may use it for a purpose beyond what the statute contemplated is nothing to the purpose'.[83] Distinguishing the opposite situation, Lord Halsbury said:

I quite agree that if the power to make one kind of building was fraudulently used for the purpose of making another kind of building, the power given by the Legislature for one purpose could not be used for another.

And Lord Macnaghten said:

In order to make out a case of bad faith it must be shown that the corporation constructed this subway as a means of crossing the street under colour and pretence of providing public conveniences which were not really wanted at that particular place.

The Court of Appeal closely followed these statements in upholding the power of a city corporation to make and improve a roadway even though their immediate motive was to attract speed trials of motor cars.[84] The speed trials indeed provided the occasion for the work being done at the particular time; but that was no reason why the corporation could not use its road-making powers for an improvement which was shown to be genuine and desirable in its own right, and which could not be said to be a merely pretended purpose for the sake of a different and unlawful objective. By contrast, the Inner London Education Authority acted unlawfully in launching an expensive publicity campaign in protest against cuts in its expenditure imposed by the government. The ILEA had power to publish information on local government affairs, but 'a, if not the, major

[81] *Westminster Cpn. v. London and North Western Railway* [1905] AC 426.
[82] At 433 (Lord Macnaghten).
[83] At 428 (Lord Halsbury).
[84] *R. v. Brighton Cpn. ex p. Shoosmith* (1907) 96 LT 762.

purpose' of their campaign was to persuade the public that they were being hardly treated, and this purpose was unauthorised.[85]

The same distinction was made by the Court of Appeal where an order for the deportation of an alien to the United States was challenged on the ground that the Home Secretary was in fact motivated by a request from the United States for the surrender of the alien. Since the offence with which the alien was charged was not a legal ground of extradition, it was argued that the Home Secretary's real object was unlawful extradition, and that the deportation order was a mere disguise. Lord Denning MR said that everything depended upon the purpose with which the act was done.[86]

If, therefore, the purpose of the Home Secretary in this case was to surrender the applicant as a fugitive criminal to the United States of America because they had asked for him, then it would be unlawful. But if the Home Secretary's purpose was to deport him to his own country because the Home Secretary considered his presence here to be not conducive to the public good, then the Home Secretary's action is lawful. It is open to these courts to inquire whether the purpose of the Home Secretary was a lawful or an unlawful purpose. Was there a misuse of the power or not? The courts can always go behind the face of the deportation order in order to see whether the powers entrusted by Parliament have been exercised lawfully or no.

On the facts the court found that there was every reason to suppose that the Home Secretary was acting from proper 'deportation' motives. His power to deport, and his power to prescribe the country of destination, was in no way diminished by the fact that he was at the same time assisting the United States government, and might indeed be glad to do so.

Overlapping motives

Cases where the dominant motive is improper are, of course, cases of ultra vires, and a number of them have been cited in the context of wrong purposes and irrelevant considerations. Examples are the case of the caravan site licensing authority which wrongly attempted to act as a planning authority in order to protect the green belt,[87] and the case of the town council which compulsorily acquired land ostensibly for coast protection

---

[85] *R. v. Inner London Education Authority ex p. Westminster CC* [1986] 1 WLR 28. See similarly *R. v. Greater London Council ex p. Westminster CC* [1984] The Times, 27 December; *R. v. Lewisham LBC ex p. Shell UK Ltd.* [1987] The Times, 23 December.

[86] *R. v. Brixton Prison Governor ex p. Soblen* [1963] 2 QB 302; and see *R. v. Bow Street Magistrates ex p. Mackeson* (1981) 75 Crim. App. R. 24, where the court quashed charges on account of 'disguised extradition' by way of deportation from Zimbabwe.

[87] *Esdell Caravan Parks Ltd. v. Hemel Hempstead Rural District Council* [1966] 1 QB 895; above, p. 436.

but in reality for public amenity.[88] Similarly the High Court of Australia invalidated a local authority's scheme for the resumption (acquisition) of land for road improvement, since a substantial part of the land was to be sold off and not therefore acquired for 'the improvement and embellishment of the area'.[89] The High Court said:[90]

> But the evidence establishes that one purpose at least of the Council in attempting to acquire the land now required to construct the new road is to appropriate the betterments arising from its construction. In *Municipal Council of Sydney* v. *Campbell*[91] this was the sole purpose. But in our opinion it is still an abuse of the Council's powers if such a purpose is a substantial purpose in the sense that no attempt would have been made to resume this land if it had not been desired to reduce the cost of the new road by the profit arising from its re-sale.

Where schoolteachers can be dismissed only on 'educational grounds' it has been said that this means educational grounds only, so that if the grounds are both educational and non-educational, the power is not well exercised.[92] But if in fact there were sufficient educational grounds, and these supplied the true motive, it seems unlikely that additional non-educational grounds would vitiate the dismissal. The whole question ought to be one of the substantial purpose, in the sense explained by the High Court of Australia. It is for the education authority to show that its purposes are proper, and if it fails to show that educational purposes predominate, its action will be void.

An alternative route to the same result may be found by invoking the doctrine of irrelevant considerations. If the decision has been materially influenced by an unauthorised purpose, it can be said that an irrelevant consideration has been taken into account, so that the decision cannot stand.[93]

GOOD FAITH

Bad faith not dishonesty

The judgments discussed in the last few pages are freely embellished with references to good and bad faith. These add very little to the true sense, and

---

[88] *Webb* v. *Minister of Housing and Local Government* [1965] 1 WLR 755; above, p. 437.
[89] *Thompson* v. *Randwick Cpn.* (1950) 81 CLR 87; cf. *Hanks* v. *Minister of Housing and Local Government* [1963] 1 QB 999.
[90] At p. 106.
[91] [1925] AC 338; above, p. 420.
[92] *Sadler* v. *Sheffield Cpn.* [1924] 1 Ch. 483 at 504. For other such cases see above, p. 413.
[93] *Hanks* v. *Minister of Housing and Local Government* (above); *R.* v. *Inner London Education Authority ex p. Westminster CC* (above).

are hardly ever used to mean more than that some action is found to have a lawful or unlawful purpose. It is extremely rare for public authorities to be found guilty of intentional dishonesty: normally they are found to have erred, if at all, by ignorance or misunderstanding. Yet the courts constantly accuse them of bad faith merely because they have acted unreasonably or on improper grounds. Again and again it is laid down that powers must be exercised reasonably and in good faith. But in this context 'in good faith' means merely 'for legitimate reasons'. Contrary to the natural sense of the words, they impute no moral obliquity.

A pithy statement of Lord Macnaghten to this effect has already been quoted.[94] Lord Sumner made another in *Roberts v. Hopwood*,[95] dealing with the power of a local board to pay 'such wages as they think fit':

Firstly, the final words of the section are not absolute, but are subject to an implied qualification of good faith—'as the board may bona fide think fit.'. . . Bona fide here cannot simply mean that they are not making a profit out of their office or acting in it from private spite, nor is bona fide a short way of saying that the council has acted within the ambit of its powers and therefore not contrary to law. It must mean that they are giving their minds to the comprehension and their wills to the discharge of their duty towards the public, whose money and local business they administer.

Still more pithily, Vaughan Williams LJ had said in an earlier case:[96]

You are acting mala fide if you are seeking to acquire land for a purpose not authorised by the Act.

And Lord Greene MR, in the passage already quoted, treated bad faith as interchangeable with unreasonableness and extraneous considerations.[97] Bad faith therefore scarcely has an independent existence as a distinct ground of invalidity. Any attempt to discuss it as such would merely lead back over the ground already surveyed. But a few examples will illustrate it in its customary conjunction with unreasonableness and improper purposes.

If a local authority were to use its power to erect urinals in order to place one 'in front of any gentleman's house', then 'it would be impossible to hold that to be a bona fide exercise of the powers given by the statute'.[98] If they wish to acquire land, their powers are 'to be used bona fide for the statutory purpose and for none other'.[99] If they refer numerous cases en

---

[94] Above, p. 396.

[95] [1925] AC 578 at 603.

[96] *Westminster Cpn. v. London and North Western Railway Co.* [1904] 1 Ch. 759 at 767, followed in *Webb v. Minister of Housing and Local Government* [1965] 1 WLR 755 at 784.

[97] Above, p. 408.

[98] *Biddulph v. Vestry of St. George, Hanover Square* (1863) 33 LJ Ch. 411; above, p. 409.

[99] *Denman v. Westminster Cpn.* [1906] 1 Ch. 464 at 476; above, p. 435.

masse to a rent tribunal without proper consideration, this is not 'a valid and bona fide exercise of the powers'.[1] If a liquor licence is cancelled for political reasons, the minister who brought this about is guilty of 'a departure from good faith'.[2] Such instances could be multiplied indefinitely.

Motives and malice

The courts no less frequently use the words 'good faith' in their ordinary sense, implying personal honesty and good intentions. In the licensing cases where the authorities wrongly demanded a money payment or the buying-in of suspended licences, the court in each case emphasised that the unlawful conditions were imposed in perfectly good faith, i.e. in what was genuinely thought to be in the public interest.[3] The same words were freely used in both senses in a decision condemning a district council's compulsory purchase order for land allegedly required for coast protection: at first instance the order was held to be 'an abuse of power and a flagrant invasion of private rights which the council has tried to cover up by means which do them no credit'.[4] But the Court of Appeal decided that it was not necessary to go so far as to hold the council 'guilty of bad faith'.[5] Elsewhere in this case 'mala fide' was used merely to mean 'for an unauthorised purpose'.[6] Such opprobrious terms would be more suitably restricted to the rare cases of actual dishonesty, as Megaw LJ has advocated:[7]

I would stress—for it seems to me that an unfortunate tendency has developed of looseness of language in this respect—that bad faith, or, as it is sometimes put, 'lack of good faith', means dishonesty: not necessarily for a financial motive, but still dishonesty. It always involves a grave charge. It must not be a treated as a synonym for an honest, though mistaken, taking into consideration of a factor which is in law irrelevant.

It is a pity that this good advice is not more generally accepted. The various categories of ultra vires can more fittingly be described by words which do not impute dishonesty.

---

[1] *R. v. Paddington (etc.) Rent Tribunal ex parte Bell London & Provincial Properties Ltd.* [1949] 1 KB 666; above, p. 422.

[2] *Roncarelli v. Duplessis* (1959) 6 DLR (2d) 689 at 707.

[3] *R. v. Bowman* [1898] 1 QB 663 at 667; *R. v. Birmingham Licensing Planning Committee ex p. Kennedy* [1972] 2 QB 140 at 147; above, p. 421.

[4] *Webb v. Minister of Housing and Local Government* [1964] 1 WLR 1295 at 1305.

[5] [1965] 1 WLR 755 at 777.

[6] At 784.

[7] *Cannock Chase DC v. Kelly* [1978] 1 WLR 1. See the Court of Appeal's similar protest against this 'debasement of the currency of language' in *Western Fish Products Ltd. v. Penwith DC* (1978) 38 P & CR 7 at 22, [1981] 2 All ER 204 at 215.

Where actions for damages are brought, bad faith may be described as malice. An unsuccessful plaintiff alleged that a borough corporation had rejected his building plans out of malice, because he had previously been in litigation with them.[8] The cancellation of a liquor licence on political grounds, mentioned above, was held to be malicious and therefore actionable under the law of Quebec.[9] Rand J said:

What could be more malicious than to punish this licensee for having done what he had an absolute right to do in a matter utterly irrelevant to the Alcoholic Liquor Act?

Allegations of fraud played a leading part in a decision of the House of Lords about a compulsory purchase order.[10] The question at issue was whether judicial remedies were wholly barred by statute,[11] but the House assumed that the effect of fraud (which was not in fact proved[12]) would normally be to vitiate any act or order. It was said that fraud or corruption were covered by the phrase mala fides, but that 'its effects have happily remained in the region of hypothetical cases'.[13] In a different context Denning LJ has said:[14]

No judgment of a court, no order of a Minister, can be allowed to stand if it has been obtained by fraud. Fraud unravels everything.

But in administrative law there is a dearth of material to illustrate this statement.

The House of Lords has made it clear that the court cannot question the validity of an Act of Parliament on the ground that it was obtained by misrepresentation or fraud.[15]

SUBJECTIVE LANGUAGE

A favourite device

Words such as 'if the minister is satisfied that . . .' or 'if it appears to the board that . . .' are a very common feature of statutory powers. They have an important bearing on jurisdictional questions.[16] Their evident intention

---

[8] *Davis* v. *Bromley Cpn.* [1908] 1 KB 170.
[9] *Roncarelli* v. *Duplessis*, above, p. 405.
[10] *Smith* v. *East Elloe Rural District Council* [1956] AC 736.
[11] For this see below, p. 735.
[12] *Smith* v. *Pywell*, The Times, 29 April 1959.
[13] [1956] AC at p. 770 (Lord Somervell).
[14] *Lazarus Estates Ltd.* v. *Beasley* [1956] 1 QB 702 at 712.
[15] *Pickin* v. *British Railways Board* [1974] AC 765.
[16] See above, p. 285.

is to make the minister or the board the sole judge of the existence of the conditions which make the power exercisable. They indicate that instead of judging objectively whether the conditions in fact exist, the court is merely to judge subjectively whether the requisite state of mind exists in the minister or the board. But courts have an ingrained repugnance to legislative devices for making public authorities judges of the extent of their own powers, or for exempting them from judicial control.[17] Although a number of decisions have given to such expressions a very nearly literal meaning, a number of others have developed lines of attack which have been able to penetrate behind the ostensible 'satisfaction' or 'appearance' and deal with the realities.

There is a subjective element in all discretion, and expressions such as 'if the minister is satisfied' differ only in degree from a power to act 'as he thinks fit'. The limits of that type of power have already been explained: the minister must act reasonably and in good faith, and upon proper grounds. In principle the same limits should operate however subjective the language, in order that the courts may always afford protection against an abuse of power such as the Act cannot have been supposed to authorise. But in some of the situations where such words are employed it is plain not only from the language but also from the context that the discretion granted is exceptionally wide. The most obvious example is that of emergency powers, particularly in time of war.

Emergency powers

The Emergency Powers (Defence) Act 1939 empowered His Majesty by Order in Council to make such defence regulations 'as appear to him to be necessary or expedient for securing the public safety ... and for maintaining supplies and services essential to the life of the community'. Plainly the courts were not to sit in judgment on the question of necessity or expediency or on the government's motives.[18] But if it could have been shown that a defence regulation was made for some quite extraneous purpose, for example to punish a political party which was no threat to public safety, the court in principle should have been able to intervene. Such challenges as were made fell far short of this improbable example and consequently failed. But in one case under the corresponding Canadian

---

[17] See below, p. 727.

[18] *R. v. Comptroller-General of Patents ex p. Bayer Products Ltd.* [1941] 2 KB 306; *Progressive Supply Co. v. Dalton* [1943] Ch. 54; *Point of Ayr Collieries Ltd. v. Lloyd-George* [1943] 2 All ER 547; *Carltona Ltd. v. Commissioners of Works* [1943] 2 All ER 560; *Demetriades v. Glasgow Cpn.* [1951] 1 All ER 457; *Hackett v. Lander* [1917] NZLR 947. See the discussion of emergency powers by Turner J in *Reade v. Smith* [1959] NZLR 996 at 1000.

legislation the Privy Council held that the court could intervene in a hypothetical case of bad faith or of unauthorised purposes.[19] Lord Radcliffe said:[20]

Parliament has chosen to say explicitly that [the Governor] shall do whatever things he may deem necessary or advisable. That does not allow him to do whatever he may feel inclined, for what he does must be capable of being related to one of the prescribed purposes, and the court is entitled to read the Act in this way.

The Privy Council applied this test in judging the validity of emergency regulations made in Cyprus for imposing collective fines on communities which harboured terrorists, finding that the regulations were clearly related to the prescribed purposes of securing public safety and public order for which the Governor might make 'such Regulations as appear to him to be necessary or expedient'.[21] The regulations themselves required the Commissioner to 'satisfy himself' as to certain facts. The argument that his own declaration was conclusive was rejected, since it was open to a party to show that there was no ground on which he could be satisfied. But in fact it was held that he had ample grounds.

In wartime or grave emergency it is unlikely that this theoretical judicial control will be able to come into play, since the ingredient of policy is so large by comparison with the ingredient of ascertainable and relevant fact.[22] There is some truth in the thesis of another Canadian case, that when Parliament delegates virtually unlimited powers to the executive in wartime, the powers are as large as those of Parliament itself, and scarcely more open to question in the courts; and that whatever is done must therefore be deemed to be 'necessary and advisable' for the purpose of the war.[23]

The literal approach

In ordinary legislation the requirement that the authority shall be 'satisfied' as to certain things is one of the commonest devices for conferring wide discretion. There have been times when the courts have taken it at face value and held that the authority has merely to declare itself to be satisfied in order to be free of all legal control. But this was when judicial control was at an exceptionally low ebb, so that the decisions of that time—as in the

---

[19] *A.-G. for Canada* v. *Hallett & Carey Ltd.* [1952] AC 427 at 444. See similarly *Lipton Ltd.* v. *Ford* [1917] 2 KB 647.

[20] At 450.

[21] *Ross-Clunis* v. *Papadopoullos* [1958] 1 WLR 546.

[22] In *Liversidge* v. *Anderson* [1942] AC 206 at 237 Lord Atkin commented that if the Defence Regulation had merely required the Secretary of State to be satisfied, instead of requiring him to have reasonable cause, he would have had complete discretion.

[23] *Re Chemicals Regulations (Reference as to Validity)* [1943] 1 DLR 248 at 255.

case of so many other fundamental rules—cannot be treated as sound.[24]
Both before and since the courts have, more characteristically, refused to
allow themselves to be disarmed, and for various reasons have held that the
requisite 'satisfaction' cannot exist.

Of the less characteristic cases the leading example is the Court of
Appeal's decision about the restoration of war damage at Plymouth.[25] The
minister had made an order for the compulsory purchase of a badly
damaged area of the city under an Act which empowered him to do so
'where the Minister . . . is satisfied that it is requisite, for the purpose of
dealing satisfactorily with extensive war damage, in the area of the local
planning authority, that a part or parts of their area . . . should be laid out
afresh and redeveloped as a whole'. Owners objected that what was in fact
proposed was merely restoration and repair, not redesign and redevelopment, and that 'the minister can only be "satisfied" if at the time of the
order he has before him evidence sufficient in law to entitle him to be so
"satisfied" '. This, said the court, 'imports an objective test into a matter to
which such a test is entirely inappropriate'.[26] Lord Greene MR said:[27]

How can this minister, who is entrusted by Parliament with the power to make or
not to make an executive order according to his judgment and acts bona fide (as he
must be assumed to do in the absence of evidence of the contrary), be called upon
to justify his decision by proving that he had before him materials sufficient to
support it?

Somervell LJ entered the caveat that if the application to the minister
showed on its face that the area had suffered little or no war damage, the
minister's order might be successfully attacked, quite apart from the usual
exception for bad faith.[28] But the uniform tenor of the cases of this period
was that attempts to dispute the minister's right to be 'satisfied' must be
rejected.[29]

The objective approach

Many decisions reject the literal approach, and show that the court, more
characteristically, is not content to relinquish control. An ordinance in
Singapore provided machinery for the demolition of houses without

[24] See above, p. 20.
[25] *Robinson v. Minister of Town and Country Planning* [1947] KB 702. For similarly
worded powers see *Franklin v. Minister of Town and Country Planning* [1948] AC 87; *Re
Trunk Roads Act 1936* [1939] 2 KB 515.
[26] At 714.
[27] At 717.
[28] At 724.
[29] e.g. *R. v. Ludlow ex p. Barnsley Cpn.* [1947] KB 634; *Re Beck and Pollitzer's Application*
[1948] 2 KB 339; *Land Realisation Co. Ltd. v. Postmaster-General* [1950] Ch. 435.

compensation 'whenever it appears to the Board that . . . a dwelling place . . . is in such a condition as to be unfit for human habitation'. By using an English housing standard which was not a standard of unfitness for habitation the board were held by the Privy Council to have applied a wrong and inadmissible test and to have acted beyond their powers.[30] Where a minister had power to confirm a compulsory purchase notice 'if he is satisfied that the conditions specified' in the Act are fulfilled, the court quashed his confirmation order because his stated grounds were that the land was substantially diminished in value, whereas the Act required him to be satisfied that the land was incapable of reasonably beneficial use.[31] A compulsory purchase order which could be made 'where it appears to the authority' that compulsory powers were necessary was quashed by the Court of Appeal where it was shown that it did not so appear.[32] The Privy Council similarly set aside a minister's order under an Act which empowered him to take over the management of schools in Ceylon 'where the minister is satisfied' that a school 'is being administered in contravention of any of the provisions of this Act'.[33] The minister had based his order on a past default which had been made good, whereas the Act required him to be satisfied that there was maladministration existing at the time of the order. 'There was therefore no ground on which the minister could be "satisfied" at the time of making the Order' and 'he failed to consider the right question'.

An impressive instance of subjective language being swept aside on grounds of unreasonableness was the case where purchase tax regulations were condemned by the High Court.[34] Regulations could be made by the Commissioners of Customs and Excise 'for any matter for which provision appears to them to be necessary' for the administration of the tax. The offending regulation provided that in default of a proper return they might themselves determine the tax due, and that the taxpayer should have only seven days to dispute it. This was held invalid as wholly unreasonable and wholly unprotected by the subjective words. Language of this kind is

---

[30] *Estate and Trust Agencies (1927) Ltd.* v. *Singapore Improvement Trust* [1937] AC 898 (prohibition granted).

[31] *R.* v. *Minister of Housing and Local Government ex p. Chichester Rural District Council* [1960] 1 WLR 587. See similarly *Metropolitan Life Insurance Co.* v. *International Union of Operating Engineers Local 796* (1970) 11 DLR (3d) 336 ('If the Board is satisfied' as to membership of trade union: wrong test of membership and wrong question determined); *R.* v. *Australian Stevedoring Industry Board* (1953) 88 CLR 100 ('Where the Board is satisfied' that a port employer is unfit to be registered: no basis for such finding and determination vitiated by irrelevant motive).

[32] *Webb* v. *Minister of Housing and Local Government* [1965] 1 WLR 755.

[33] *Maradana Mosque Trustees* v. *Mahmud* [1967] 1 AC 13.

[34] *Commissioners of Customs and Excise* v. *Cure & Deeley Ltd.* [1962] 1 QB 340; below, p. 869.

merely one of many devices for disarming the courts. It was described in this case as a 'drafting mechanism' employed for the exclusion of the jurisdiction of the court on the footing that 'modern drafting technique is to use words which do not exclude jurisdiction in terms but positively repose arbitrary power in a named authority.'[35] The hardening judicial attitude to this device may be compared with the attitude to clauses which oust the jurisdiction of the courts directly, which has changed similarly during the same period of time.[36]

Yet another pointer in the same direction was the statement by Lord Denning MR in a Housing Act case where there was power to modify a clearance order 'if the Minister is of opinion' that any land should not have been included. The minister's order was upheld, but Lord Denning said that the court could quash it if the minister had acted on no evidence or unreasonably or had gone wrong in law.[37] Similarly where the Act said 'Where it appears to the Secretary of State . . . that there are reasons for doubting' whether workers wished to take part in a strike, the Court of Appeal held that those words did not put his decision beyond scrutiny by the court and that it would be invalid in law if it were not one which he could reasonably reach on the facts before him—as was not, however, established in the case itself.[38] There is an obvious affinity between this class of decisions and those which have introduced the 'no evidence' principle discussed in chapter 9.

The Tameside case

The tendency just described was powerfully reinforced by the House of Lords, unanimously upholding a unanimous Court of Appeal, in the case of the Tameside schools.[39] After a local election the new council proceeded to reverse their predecessors' scheme, already in an advanced stage of execution, for introducing comprehensive schools. The Secretary of State, who favoured comprehensive schools, issued a statutory direction to the new council to carry out the original scheme. The Act empowered him to issue directions if he was 'satisfied . . . that any local authority . . . have acted or are proposing to act unreasonably' in their statutory functions.[40]

---

[35] At 364 (Sachs J).

[36] Below, p. 724.

[37] *Ashbridge Investments Ltd.* v. *Minister of Housing and Local Government* [1965] 1 WLR 1320 at 1326, quoted above, p. 324.

[38] *Secretary of State for Employment* v. *ASLEF* (No. 2) [1972] 2 QB 455.

[39] *Secretary of State for Education and Science* v. *Tameside Metropolitan Borough Council* [1977] AC 1014.

[40] Education Act 1944, s. 68. The Education Act 1976, passed after the *Tameside* case, gave wider compulsory powers to the Secretary of State.

When the new council resisted he applied for an order of mandamus to force them to comply. This was refused by the Court of Appeal and the House of Lords on the ground that he must have misdirected himself in law and misunderstood the meaning of 'unreasonable' in the Act. It was not enough that he should personally disagree with the council's policy, or even that he should genuinely think that it was unreasonable. There had to be evidence that the council was acting in a way which no reasonable council would do.[41] Since the real issue was a disagreement over policy, and the administrative difficulties were shown to be easily soluble, the Secretary of State was not legally entitled to be satisfied as the Act required, and his directions were invalid. Lord Wilberforce said:[42]

The section is framed in a 'subjective' form—if the Secretary of State 'is satisfied'. This form of section is quite well known, and at first sight might seem to exclude judicial review. Sections in this form may, no doubt, exclude judicial review on what is or has become a matter of pure judgment. But I do not think that they go further than that. If a judgment requires, before it can be made, the existence of some facts, then, although the evaluation of those facts is for the Secretary of State alone, the court must inquire whether those facts exist, and have been taken into account, whether the judgment has been made upon a proper self-direction as to those facts, whether the judgment has not been made upon other facts which ought not to have been taken into account.

Little authority was cited for this objective approach, but the House adopted it unanimously. The Privy Council has since held that an emergency power of detention exercisable 'if the Governor is satisfied' as to acts prejudicial to public safety etc., requires that the Governor should be able to show reasonable grounds, though here there was a helpful constitutional context.[43]

It does not follow that words such as 'if the minister is satisfied' are now of little significance. For it may be material whether the question for the minister is 'a matter of pure judgment', as Lord Wilberforce put it, or a matter which can be established objectively by accepted legal standards, as can unreasonableness. Lord Denning MR expressed the same thought in the Court of Appeal:[44]

Much depends on the matter about which the Secretary of State has to be satisfied. If he is to be satisfied on a matter of opinion, that is one thing. But if he has to be satisfied that some one has been guilty of some discreditable or unworthy or unreasonable conduct, that is another.

The minister may therefore be a free agent to the extent that, in the words

[41] See above, p. 407.
[42] At 1047.
[43] A.-G. of St. Christopher v. Reynolds [1980] AC 637.
[44] [1977] AC at 1025.

of Lord Greene MR, 'no objective test is possible'.[45] And even where it is a question of discreditable or unreasonable conduct the court may hold that the facts supporting the exercise of discretion are not open to review because of the nature of the legislation. The Department of Trade may investigate a company's affairs 'if it appears' to them that there are circumstances suggesting malpractice, but the department will not be put to proof of these circumstances, since summary powers are a quid pro quo for the legal privileges which limited companies enjoy.[46]

Nevertheless the *Tameside* case is undoubtedly a landmark, manifesting the same judicial resistance to statutes which attempt to confer arbitrary power as appears in the *Anisminic* case[47] and elsewhere.

Other examples

In two immigration cases where the law gave a right of entry to a Commonwealth citizen 'who satisfies an immigration officer' that he has means of support or comes for a course of study, the court treated these questions as purely objective: it quashed or upheld the immigration officer's ruling according to its own view of the law and the facts,[48] at the same time stating that it was not a court of appeal, but had to see that the Act had been administered fairly and properly construed.[49] Similarly a local authority could not lawfully be 'satisfied' that a homeless person was not 'vulnerable' when they misconstrued the latter word as requiring some substantial disability.[50]

In a case where the minister had to be satisfied by medical certificates that a person was a defective, Lord Denning said that 'satisfied' meant 'reasonably satisfied', and that if no reasonable person would have been satisfied, the minister's order would be liable to be quashed.[51] This in fact was done where a minister had power to dispense with a public inquiry into a road scheme if he was satisfied that it was unnecessary. It was held that a reasonable minister could not have been so satisfied since there were

---

[45] *Robinson* v. *Minister of Town and Country Planning* [1947] KB 702 at 713. See also *Thornloe & Clarkson Ltd.* v. *Board of Trade* [1950] 2 All ER 245; *Adegbenro* v. *Akintola* [1963] AC 614.

[46] *Norwest Holst Ltd.* v. *Secretary of State for Trade* [1978] Ch. 201.

[47] Below, p. 725.

[48] *R.* v. *Chief Immigration Officer Lympne Airport ex p. Amrik Singh* [1969] 1 QB 333 (quashed); *R.* v. *Immigration Appeals Adjudicator ex p. Khan* [1972] 1 WLR 1058 (upheld). See similarly *R.* v. *Diggines ex p. Rahmani* [1986] AC 475 (quashed).

[49] *Amrik Singh's* case (above) at p. 342.

[50] *R.* v. *Waveney DC ex p. Bowers* [1983] QB 238; and see *Kelly* v. *Monklands DC* 1986 SLT 169.

[51] *Director of Public Prosecutions* v. *Head* [1959] AC 83 at 110. cf. *Reade* v. *Smith* [1959] NZLR 996, below.

numerous objections and strongly conflicting interests.[52] These were not the first cases in which the duty to act reasonably was brought to bear upon subjective discretionary power: the same qualification had been suggested in a Housing Act case a quarter of a century earlier.[53]

The court is always likely to disregard subjective language if there is any indication that the action taken is outside the scope of the statute. Thus a council's highway order was quashed on the ground that the highway was already partly a street, although they were empowered to make the order 'where it appears to the appropriate authority that an existing highway should be converted into a new street'.[54] Where a new street already existed they were without power, and the wide subjective language could not give them final authority over 'fundamental matters such as this'. Nor will such language afford protection where the excess of power is founded on a mistake of law. A rent tribunal's rent-fixing order was accordingly quashed in so far as it was based on a premium not in fact paid by the tenant.[55] There was power to reduce the rent 'where . . . it appears to the tribunal that . . . a premium has been paid', but the payment had been made in consideration of work done by the landlord and was therefore not in law a premium, i.e. a payment in consideration of the grant of a lease. No court confronted with so patent an error is likely to allow it to stand.

Tax cases

Tax authorities are commonly invested with very wide powers, freely embellished with subjective language. Sometimes, moreover, they assume them without statutory authority, as in the case of extra-statutory concessions, already discussed.[56] Their powers of search and seizure may also be very extensive.[57] Here may be mentioned some of their more ordinary powers, as where they are empowered to call for 'such particulars as they think necessary' for specified purposes. In principle these powers are subject to the control of the court in case they may be exercised unreasonably or oppressively,[58] but in their nature they are so wide that attempts to challenge them will often fail.

---

[52] R. v. Secretary of State for the Environment ex p. Binney [1983] The Times, 8 October.

[53] Re Bowman [1932] 2 KB 621 at 634 (hypothetical case where no material, information or representation before local authority to justify clearance order). And see the Estate and Trust Agencies case of 1937, above, p. 449.

[54] Relton & Sons (Contracts) Ltd. v. Whitstable UDC (1967) 201 EG 955.

[55] R. v. Fulham &c. Rent Tribunal ex p. Philippe [1950] 2 All ER 211.

[56] Above, p. 437.

[57] See the Rossminster case, below, p. 459.

[58] Royal Bank of Canada v. Inland Revenue Commissioners [1972] Ch. 665; Clinch v. Inland Revenue Commissioners [1974] QB 76; Wilover Nominees Ltd. v. Inland Revenue Commissioners [1974] 1 WLR 1342.

Taxing Acts sometimes give the revenue authorities arbitrary powers of assessment, and the courts naturally strive to impose some control upon these. A striking example was the case where purchase tax regulations were held invalid because they allowed the taxpayer no adequate opportunity to dispute the assessment, as explained above.[59] In some cases it has been held that, however subjectively the power is worded, the authorities must at least act on evidence which could reasonably justify their assessment. A Canadian minister was empowered to disallow for tax purposes 'any expense which he in his discretion may determine to be in excess of what is reasonable or normal'. On appeal the Privy Council held that the Act made the minister 'the sole judge of the fact of reasonableness or normalcy [sic]' and that the court was not at liberty to substitute their opinion for his.[60] But they went on to refer to the familiar rule of judicial review requiring reasonableness. Although the case was in fact an appeal, the Privy Council applied the 'review' standard of reasonableness, and they set aside the minister's ruling because no evidence was produced which would reasonably justify it. They said:

The court is, in their Lordships' opinion, always entitled to examine the facts which are shown by evidence to have been before the Minister when he made his determination. If those facts are in the opinion of the court insufficient in law to support it, the determination cannot stand. In such a case the determination can only have been an arbitrary one.

This case is a remarkable contrast to *Liversidge* v. *Anderson*, discussed below.[61]

Another Privy Council case from Guyana, also on appeal, concerned a tax assessment which could be made only 'where . . . the Commissioner is of opinion that the person is liable to pay tax'. It was held that on the facts he could have formed no reasonable opinion to this effect, and the assessment was annulled.[62]

The Crown

Certain Australian decisions have created an exception in favour of the Crown's representatives, i.e. the Governor-General and State Governors.[63] According to this, subjective language of the 'if satisfied' or 'if of opinion'

---

[59] *Customs & Excise Commissioners* v. *Cure & Deeley Ltd.* [1962] 1 QB 340 (above, p. 449).

[60] *Minister of National Revenue* v. *Wrights' Canadian Ropes Ltd.* [1947] AC 109.

[61] p. 457.

[62] *Argosy Co. Ltd.* v. *Inland Revenue Commissioner* [1971] 1 WLR 514.

[63] See *Australian Communist Party* v. *The Commonwealth* (1951) 83 CLR 1 at 179–80 (Dixon J); *R.* v. *Martin* (1967) 67 SR (NSW) 404.

type renders the Crown representative's action immune from judicial review on the basis of bad faith, irrelevant considerations, misconception of the meaning of the matters to be considered, or 'some other miscarriage'. No such exception is recognised by the Privy Council, as has already been seen;[64] nor is it recognised in New Zealand. In the leading New Zealand case the Supreme Court condemned a regulation made by the Governor-General which authorised the compulsory transfer of pupils between schools and which was held to be in conflict with the principle of parental choice on which the Act was founded.[65] The Act empowered regulations which 'in the opinion of the Governor-General' were required 'for any purpose which he thinks necessary in order to secure the due administration of this Act'. The Court held that it could always inquire whether the Governor-General could reasonably have formed the necessary opinion, and whether he had acted on an untenable view of a question of law.

The exception created by the Australian decisions seems clearly contrary to principle. In a later decision the High Court of Australia has recognised this fact and has granted a declaration that a decision of a State Governor in Council violated natural justice.[66] The distinction which needs to be made has nothing to do with the empowered authority's position in the administrative hierarchy: it should be based on the nature of the matters on which it must satisfy itself. In time of war or grave emergency these are likely to be so wide and difficult of proof that it can hardly be supposed that the court will be in a position to question them.[67] In other contexts the principles of judicial review should have their normal operation. As Turner J said in the New Zealand case:[68]

Cases dealing with war regulations promulgated in time of great national danger must, in my opinion, be carefully examined before being used too hastily as a touchstone for the validity of regulations made under more normal conditions.

No case could better illustrate this truth than the decision of the House of Lords in *Liversidge* v. *Anderson*,[69] discussed below.

Formalities

It does not appear that it is essential to recite the minister's satisfaction or opinion, as the case may be, since the court is sometimes prepared to assume

[64] *A.-G. for Canada* v. *Hallett & Carey Ltd.* [1952] AC 427 at 444; above, p. 447.
[65] *Reade* v. *Smith* [1959] NZLR 996.
[66] *FAI Insurances Ltd.* v. *Winneke,* (1982) 41 ALR 1. See similarly *Re Toohey* [1981] 38 ALR 439.
[67] See *Re Chemicals Regulations* [1943] 1 DLR 248; above, p. 447.
[68] *Reade* v. *Smith* (above) at p. 1000.
[69] [1942] AC 206; below, p. 457.

it or to accept a subsequent statement.[70] In former times a full recital was required, in accordance with the old rule, now obsolete, that the order of an inferior tribunal or authority must show on its face the facts necessary to give it jurisdiction.[71] Good practice of course requires that the proper recital should be made. The House of Lords confirmed this where a judge granted warrants of search and seizure to tax officials under an Act authorising him to grant them 'if . . . satisfied' that there was reasonable ground for suspicion. The warrants did not recite that he was so satisfied, but it was held that this recital, though desirable, was not essential to their validity.[72]

STATUTORY REASONABLENESS

Objective conditions

A condition requiring some degree of reasonableness will often be prescribed by statute. If the language is objective, the authority will have to be prepared to show that the condition is fulfilled in a way which satisfies the court. If a sound building may be included in a clearance area if that is 'reasonably necessary', a minister's decision to include it will be quashed if there is no evidence of any necessity.[73] If a licensing authority has power to revoke a trader's licence if it has 'reasonable cause to believe' that the licensee has committed malpractices, the authority must show causes which the court judges to be reasonable.[74] This is simply the ordinary doctrine that empowers the court to judge whether statutory conditions are satisfied. The case is of course different if the power is worded subjectively, as where a legal aid committee may refuse aid 'if it appears unreasonable' to grant it in any case.[75] Such a subjective formula may restrict the court's control—though, as has been seen, it may be rash to count on the court accepting it at face value.[76]

In the ordinary case where the court is the judge, the standard will be the familiar legal standard of the reasonable man. But it by no means follows,

---

[70] *R. v. Comptroller-General of Patents ex p. Bayer Products Ltd.* [1941] 2 KB 306 at 314 (but the sense is doubtful); *Land Realisation Co. Ltd.* v. *Postmaster-General* [1950] Ch. 435; *Thornloe & Clarkson Ltd.* v. *Board of Trade* [1950] 2 All ER 245; *Union Motors Ltd.* v. *Motor Spirits Licensing Authority* [1964] NZLR 146. See also *Liversidge* v. *Anderson* (above) at 224. Contrast *R. v. Martin* (above).

[71] Rubinstein, *Jurisdiction and Illegality*, 170, citing *R. v. Whittles* (1849) 13 QB 248.

[72] *R. v. Inland Revenue Commissioners ex p. Rossminster Ltd.* [1980] AC 952 (Lord Salmon dissenting). No decisions on this point were mentioned in the speeches.

[73] *Coleen Properties Ltd.* v. *Minister of Housing and Local Government* [1971] 1 WLR 443.

[74] *Nakkuda Ali* v. *Jayaratne* [1951] AC 66.

[75] *R. v. Legal Aid Committee No. 1 (London) Legal Aid Area ex p. Rondel* [1967] 2 QB 482.

[76] Above, p. 448.

because the standard of reasonableness is objective, that it is also rigid. There may be a broad band of different decisions or policies all of which fall within the range of reasonableness, and two opposite policies may be equally reasonable. Under the Housing Act 1985 housing authorities 'may make such reasonable charges for the tenancy or occupation of the houses as they may determine',[77] but this leaves them at liberty either to fix their rents at flat rates which make no allowance for the tenant's personal circumstances[78] or, alternatively, to impose a scheme of differential rents which subsidises the poorer tenants at the expense of the ratepayers.[79] In the same way the authority may fix rents at overall rates which take no account of the differing costs of construction of different houses.[80] Of none of these different courses could it be said that it was 'manifestly unjust' or 'could find no justification in the minds of reasonable men' within the *Wednesbury* test previously explained.[81] The housing authority was 'applying what is, in effect, a social policy upon which reasonable men may hold different views'.[82] The degree of objectivity in the test of reasonableness can therefore vary widely with the statutory context and purpose.

'Reasonable cause to believe'

Objectivity may be reduced to vanishing point if the circumstances are strong enough—or, at least, this happened in *Liversidge* v. *Anderson*, a case of emergency powers in wartime. The Defence (General) Regulations 1939 provided: 'If the Secretary of State has reasonable cause to believe any person to be of hostile origin or associations . . . he may make an order against that person directing that he be detained'. By all accepted canons of interpretation this language required the Secretary of State to show cause which the court would adjudge to be reasonable.[83] If the Secretary of State had been intended to be the sole judge of the grounds of detention, the Regulation should have used a subjective formula such as 'the Secretary of State, if satisfied . . .'. And indeed those very words had been used in the original form of the Regulation,[84] which had been criticised in Parliament and amended into the objective form. Nevertheless, when a detainee challenged the Secretary of State's grounds, all the courts held that in the

---

[77] s. 24.
[78] *Luby* v. *Newcastle-under-Lyme Cpn.* [1964] 2 QB 64.
[79] *Smith* v. *Cardiff Cpn. (No. 2)* [1955] Ch. 159.
[80] *Summerfield* v. *Hampstead Borough Council* [1957] 1 WLR 167.
[81] Above, p. 407. See *Luby* (as above) at 71.
[82] *Luby* (as above) at 72. An obvious case of illegal abuse was *Backhouse* v. *Lambeth Borough Council*, above, p. 417.
[83] Above, p. 279.
[84] SR & O 1939 No. 978. See *Liversidge* v. *Anderson* [1942] AC 206 at 237.

circumstances of the war there could be no judicial review of the reasonableness of the Secretary of State's grounds of belief.[85]

Viscount Maugham said that despite the prima facie meaning of the vital words, they might have a different and subjective meaning where the thing to be believed was essentially something within the knowledge of the Secretary of State and a matter for his exclusive discretion. This proposition was vehemently denied by Lord Atkin in his lone dissenting speech,[86] in which he contended that 'the words have only one meaning' and 'have never been used in the sense now imputed to them'. He protested against 'a strained construction put on words with the effect of giving an uncontrolled power of imprisonment to the minister', and denied that the words 'if a man has' could ever mean 'if a man thinks he has'. His caustic remarks about judges, who 'show themselves more executive minded than the executive', arguments which 'might have been addressed acceptably to the Court of King's Bench in the time of Charles I' and Humpty Dumpty's use of a word to mean 'just what I choose it to mean' gave rise to some unusual public controversy.[87] Legal opinion was for the most part on Lord Atkin's side on the question of construction.[88] When a similar form of words came before the Privy Council in a post-war case, where the statute gave power to cancel a textile dealer's licence 'where the Controller has reasonable grounds to believe that any dealer is unfit to be allowed to continue as a dealer', the Judicial Committee held that the 'reasonable grounds' formula bore its usual objective sense, so that the Controller was required to show that his grounds were reasonable in the eyes of the court.[89] Lord Radcliffe said that it would be a very unfortunate thing if *Liversidge's* case were regarded as laying down any general rule. He added that the formula must be intended to limit an otherwise arbitrary power, but that if it was to be conclusively interpreted by the man who wielded the power, the value of the intended restraint was in effect nothing.

In 1963 Lord Reid referred dismissively to 'the very peculiar decision of this House in *Liversidge* v. *Anderson*'[90] and by then it was already clear that the decision was regarded as an aberration. It remained for Lord Diplock to say in 1979:[91]

---

[85] *Liversidge* v. *Anderson* [1942] AC 206 (action for false imprisonment); and see *Greene* v. *Home Secretary* [1942] AC 284 (habeas corpus).

[86] Another lone dissent was that of Stable J in *R.* v. *Home Secretary ex p. Budd* [1941] 2 All ER 749, affirmed [1942] 1 All ER 373 CA.

[87] For an account of this and for the case generally see (1970) 86 LQR 33, (1971) 87 LQR 161 (R. F. V. Heuston).

[88] Professor Heuston's articles (above) give a good survey.

[89] *Nakkuda Ali* v. *Jayaratne* [1951] AC 66, followed in *Registrar of Restrictive Trading Agreements* v. *W. H. Smith & Son Ltd.* [1969] 1 WLR 1460 (CA).

[90] *Ridge* v. *Baldwin* [1964] AC 40 at 73.

[91] In the *Rossminster* case (below) at 1011.

For my part I think the time has come to acknowledge openly that the majority of this House in *Liversidge* v. *Anderson* were expediently and, at that time, perhaps, excusably wrong and the dissenting speech of Lord Atkin was right.

And Lord Scarman said in the same case that the ghost of that decision need no longer haunt the law.

It will not always be the case, however, that the governmental authority can at once be put to proof of the reasonableness of its grounds. For if criminal proceedings are in prospect, the information will be protected by 'public interest immunity'[92] until the proceedings are concluded or a reasonable time has elapsed without proceedings being brought. This was the position, as the House of Lords held, where officers of the Inland Revenue had carried out an elaborate and drastic raid on the homes and offices of two tax consultants and had seized large quantities of papers. They had obtained search warrants authorising them to seize and remove anything which they had reasonable cause to believe might be required for the purposes of legal proceedings for tax offences involving fraud. Since many of the papers had been seized and removed without scrutiny, the Court of Appeal held that the tax officers could not have had reasonable cause to believe that they might be required. But the House of Lords held that this was not proved and that the issue could be litigated only after criminal proceedings were either concluded or abandoned.[93]

Statutory unreasonableness

As well as prescribing conditions in terms of reasonableness, statutes may prescribe them in terms of unreasonableness. The objective legal standard of reasonableness, as already explained, is then again the criterion, though in the negative sense. In the Tameside comprehensive school case,[94] where the Secretary of State was required to be satisfied that the local authority had acted unreasonably, the House of Lords disallowed his intervention because he had evidently misdirected himself as to the meaning of 'unreasonably': the evidence showed that the local authority's plan to restore grammar schools, though it raised difficulties, was not so impracticable that no reasonable authority could have adopted it.

[92] Explained below, p. 839.
[93] R. v. *Inland Revenue Commissioners ex p. Rossminster Ltd.* [1980] AC 952. This decision appears to have come close to another lapse from objectivity since it was presumed that a judge, who was required by the Act to be satisfied that there was reasonable ground for suspicion before he could grant search warrants, was in fact so satisfied although this was not shown by the warrants or by other evidence; but apparently this issue was not contested.
[94] Above, p. 450.

Objectivity forsaken and restored

Scarcely had the House of Lords completed the burial of *Liversidge* v. *Anderson* when they held in an immigration case that objective words might be interpreted subjectively so as to give a minister an area of discretionary power. This serious lapse and its prompt correction have been noted already,[95] but they deserve to be put alongside *Liversidge* v. *Anderson* as another example of the House of Lords forsaking the principle of objectivity and later confessing its delinquency.

Under the Immigration Act 1971 an immigration officer may detain an 'illegal entrant' who may then be removed from the country by the Home Secretary. An 'illegal entrant' is defined in the Act as a person entering or seeking to enter unlawfully. The question whether his entry was or was not unlawful ought therefore to be decided upon the objective facts. But the House of Lords held that 'the whole scheme of the Act' indicated the contrary, and that the court could intervene only if the Home Secretary was acting on no evidence or in a way in which no reasonable person could do.[96] It was said that, although there were no words such as 'in the opinion of the Secretary of State', such a formula was not necessary; and that the nature and process of the powers conferred upon immigration officers was incompatible with any requirements for the establishment of precedent objective facts which the court could verify. In less than three years, fortunately, the House reversed itself in a closely similar case, holding that 'illegal entrant' was a precedent or jurisdictional fact to be determined on all the evidence by the court, and that on the facts the Home Secretary had failed to show that one of the appellant immigrants was an illegal entrant.[97] The House restored the principle that the court must be the final judge of objectively stated facts. Why it was ever denied is even harder to understand than in *Liversidge* v. *Anderson*, since there was no situation of emergency. The explanation may be that the rapid expansion of judicial review had led judges to suppose that its rules for the review of discretionary decisions were the only operative restraints on the executive,[98] forgetting the independent and more fundamental principle of objectivity.[99]

---

[95]   Above, p. 257.

[96]   *R.* v. *Home Secretary ex p. Zamir* [1980] AC 930. The only reasoned speech was that of Lord Wilberforce. The House approved *R.* v. *Home Secretary ex p. Hussain* [1978] 1 WLR 700. See similarly *R.* v. *Home Secretary ex p. Choudhary* [1978] 1 WLR 1177, but contrast the cases cited above, p. 452. For a parallel see the Housing Act cases discussed above, p. 325.

[97]   *R.* v. *Home Secretary ex p. Khawaja* [1984] AC 74. See also *R.* v. *Home Secretary ex p. Bugdaycay* [1987] 2 WLR 606.

[98]   This seems probable from some unsound statements made in the lower courts and reviewed in the speech of Lord Wilberforce in *Khawaja*.

[99]   For which see above, p. 279.

Ambiguous language. 'Required'. 'Regulate'.

Many words take their colour from their context, and this may make the difference between objective and subjective construction. One such word is 'required'. If a public authority is empowered to take land 'required' for certain purposes, does it have to show to the court that there is a real need or is it the sole judge of the need itself? Can 'required' mean merely 'desired'? The decisions show that there is no rigid rule, even on similar words in similar Acts. Thus in one case where the question was whether a local authority was obliged to dispose of land as 'not required' for a sewage works, the judge held on the evidence that the land was likely to be required in the future and so should be retained.[1] Clearly he regarded the words as objective. And 'requisite' has been interpreted similarly.[2] But in another case it was held that it was solely for the local authority to decide whether land was 'not required' for its original purpose, so that it could be appropriated to other purposes.[3] The Court of Appeal, though not without some reluctance,[4] has declared itself in favour of the latter interpretation.[5] Russell LJ construed 'not required' as meaning 'not needed in the public interest of the locality', and said that 'the local authority is better qualified than the court to judge, assuming it to be acting bona fide and not upon a view that no reasonable local authority could possibly take'.

But just as this permissive interpretation is subject to the usual requirements of good faith and reasonableness, so it must also be subject to the rule about illegitimate purposes.[6] The Court of Appeal accordingly condemned a compulsory purchase order made by a district council for land 'required by them' for coast protection work when it appeared that a substantial part of the land was to be used for purposes of public amenity and was not needed for coast protection.[7] At first instance the order was quashed on the ground of bad faith, but on appeal the council was absolved from that charge. 'Required' was held to mean 'properly required' for the correct purpose, and since in fact the land was required for a different purpose, the order could not stand. The difference between this and the cases mentioned in the preceding paragraph is clear. The former cases are concerned only with whether land is or is not needed for an admittedly valid purpose. In this last case there is the additional feature of an

---

[1] *A.-G.* v. *Teddington Urban District Council* [1898] 1 Ch. 66. And see *Stocker* v. *Minister of Health* [1938] 1 KB 655 at 663.

[2] *R.* v. *Secretary of State for the Environment ex p. Powis* [1981] 1 WLR 584.

[3] *A.-G.* v. *Manchester Cpn.* [1931] 1 Ch. 254.

[4] Per Buckley and Lawton LJJ *Webb's* case (below) was not cited.

[5] *Dowty Boulton Paul Ltd.* v. *Wolverhampton Cpn. (No. 2)* [1976] Ch. 13.

[6] Above, p. 411.

[7] *Webb* v. *Minister of Housing and Local Government* [1965] 1 WLR 755.

illegitimate purpose, outside the powers of the Act in question. The case then becomes one of ultra vires which no court is likely to condone.

Another ambiguous word, common in administrative law, is 'regulate'. It has several times been decided that a power to regulate does not extend to a power to prohibit, the assumption being that a power to regulate implies the continued existence of what is to be regulated.[8] But the contrary has also been held where the context was suitable.[9] Power to prohibit, furthermore, may include power to regulate, as by making some activity subject to the grant of permission.[10]

[8] *Toronto Cpn.* v. *Virgo* [1896] AC 88; *Birmingham and Midland Omnibus Co.* v. *Worcestershire CC* [1967] 1 WLR 409; *Tarr* v. *Tarr* [1973] AC 254.

[9] *R.* v. *British Airports Authority ex p. Wheatley* (1983) 81 LGR 794 (control of taxicabs at airport).

[10] *Foley* v. *Padley* (1984) 54 ALR 609.

PART V
NATURAL JUSTICE

13

NATURAL JUSTICE AND LEGAL JUSTICE

Procedural justice

By developing the principles of natural justice the courts have devised a kind of code of fair administrative procedure. Just as they can control the substance of what public authorities do by means of the rules relating to reasonableness, improper purposes, and so forth, so through the principles of natural justice they can control the procedure by which they do it. It may seem less obvious that they are entitled to take this further step, thereby imposing a particular procedural technique on government departments and statutory authorities generally. Yet in doing so they have provided doctrines which are an essential part of any system of administrative justice. Natural justice plays much the same part in British law as does 'due process of law' in the Constitution of the United States. In particular, it has a very wide general application in the numerous areas of discretionary administrative power. For however wide the powers of the state and however extensive the discretion they confer, it is always possible to require them to be exercised in a manner that is procedurally fair.

Procedure is not a matter of secondary importance. As governmental powers continually grow more drastic, it is only by procedural fairness that they are rendered tolerable. The legislation which controls the use of land, for example, contains a large element of expropriation without compensation, which is for the most part accepted without public complaint. But if there is the least suggestion that a planning appeal has been handled unfairly, public complaint is loud and widespread. A judge of the United States Supreme Court has said: 'Procedural fairness and regularity are of the indispensable essence of liberty. Severe substantive laws can be endured if they are fairly and impartially applied.'[1] He went on to say that it might be preferable to live under Russian law applied by common-law procedures than under the common law enforced by Russian procedures. One of his colleagues said: 'The history of liberty has largely been the history of the observance of procedural safeguards.'[2] The work of British judges in devising procedural safeguards is the theme of this Part of the book, as also of the following Part on remedies.

Lawyers are a procedurally minded race, and it is natural that

---

[1] *Shaughnessy* v. *United States*, 345 US 206 (1953) (Jackson J).
[2] *McNabb* v. *United States*, 318 US 332 (1943) (Frankfurter J).

administrators should be tempted to regard procedural restrictions, invented by lawyers, as an obstacle to efficiency. It is true that the rules of natural justice restrict the freedom of administrative action and that their observance costs a certain amount of time and money. But time and money are likely to be well spent if they reduce friction in the machinery of government; and it is because they are essentially rules for upholding fairness and so reducing grievances that the rules of natural justice can be said to promote efficiency rather than impede it. Provided that the courts do not let them run riot, and keep them in touch with the standards which good administration demands in any case, they should be regarded as a protection not only to citizens but also to officials. A decision which is made without bias, and with proper consideration of the views of those affected by it, will not only be more acceptable; it will also be of better quality. Justice and efficiency go hand in hand, so long at least as the law does not impose excessive refinements.

Administrative justice and natural justice

In its broadest sense natural justice may mean simply 'the natural sense of what is right and wrong'[3] and even in its technical sense it is now often equated with 'fairness'.[4] It has been said that 'that romantic word "natural"' adds nothing 'except perhaps a hint of nostalgia';[5] and that 'justice is far from being a "natural" concept—the closer one goes to a state of nature, the less justice does one find'.[6]

But in administrative law natural justice is a well defined concept which comprises two fundamental rules of fair procedure: that a man may not be a judge in his own cause; and that a man's defence must always be fairly heard.[7] In courts of law and in statutory tribunals it can be taken for granted that these rules must be observed. But so universal are they, so 'natural', that they are not confined to judicial power. They apply equally to administrative power, and sometimes also to powers created by contract. It is in their application to ordinary administrative power that public authorities are prone to overlook them, for example where a police authority is dismissing a constable or a minister is confirming a housing scheme. Cases of this kind have multiplied in recent years, as the courts

---

[3] *Voinet* v. *Barrett* (1885) 55 LJQB 39 at 41 (Lord Esher MR). Lord Mansfield spoke of 'natural justice and equity' in *Moses* v. *Macferlan* (1760) 2 Burr. 1005 at 1012.

[4] Below, p. 522.

[5] *Norwest Holst Ltd.* v. *Secretary of State for Trade* [1978] Ch. 221 at 226 (Ormrod LJ).

[6] *McInnes* v. *Onslow-Fane* [1978] 1 WLR 1520 at 1530 (Megarry V-C).

[7] See Marshall, *Natural Justice*; Jackson, *Natural Justice* (2nd edn.); Flick, *Natural Justice* (2nd edn.). The two rules do not seem to have been bracketed together before the decision of the House of Lords in *Spackman* v. *Plumstead District Board of Works* (below).

have developed their rules and the range of administrative powers has increased. Natural justice has become one of the most active departments of administrative law.

There are both broad and narrow aspects to consider. The narrow aspect is that the rules of natural justice are merely a branch of the principle of ultra vires, and should really find their home in the preceding chapter. Violation of natural justice is then to be classified as one of the varieties of wrong procedure, or abuse of power, which transgress the implied conditions which Parliament is presumed to have intended. Just as a power to act 'as he thinks fit' does not allow a public authority to act unreasonably or in bad faith, so it does not allow disregard of the elementary doctrines of fair procedure. As Lord Selborne once said:[8]

There would be no decision within the meaning of the statute if there were anything of that sort done contrary to the essence of justice.

Quoting these words, the Privy Council has said that 'it has long been settled law' that a decision which offends against the principles of natural justice is outside the jurisdiction of the decision-making authority.[9] Likewise Lord Russell has said:[10]

it is to be implied, unless the contrary appears, that Parliament does not authorise by the Act the exercise of powers in breach of the principles of natural justice, and that Parliament does by the Act require, in the particular procedures, compliance with those principles.

Thus violation of natural justice makes the decision void, as in any other case of ultra vires. This effect is discussed more fully below.[11] For the moment it is enough to note that the rules of natural justice operate as implied mandatory requirements, non-observance of which invalidates the exercise of the power. The court presumes that these requirements are implied in the absence of indications to the contrary in the Act conferring the power or in the circumstances in which the Act is to be applied.

In its wider aspect the subject contains the very kernel of the problem of administrative justice: how far ought both judicial and administrative power to rest on common principles? How far is it right for the courts of law to try to impart their own standards of justice to the administration? When special powers to take action or to decide disputes are vested in administrative bodies with the very object of avoiding the forms of legal

---

[8] *Spackman* v. *Plumstead District Board of Works* (1885) 10 App. Cas. 229 at 240.

[9] *A.-G.* v. *Ryan* [1980] AC 718. Even the order of a superior court may be set aside for violation of natural justice: *Isaacs* v. *Robertson* [1985] AC 97, for which see above, p. 354.

[10] *Fairmount Investments Ltd.* v. *Secretary of State for the Environment* [1976] 1 WLR 1255 at 1263.

[11] pp. 493, 526.

process, is there yet a residuum of legal procedure which ought never to be shaken off? The judges have long been conscious of this problem, and it has prompted them to some of their more notable achievements. Rules of common law, which became in effect presumptions to be used in the interpretation of statutes, developed and refined the rules of natural justice over a period of centuries. From time to time difficult questions arose over the precise content of the rules, but their general applicability to governmental action was never doubted.

Recent vicissitudes

After the second world war natural justice suffered a setback, and the whole subject threatened to become unsettled, in a manner which is all too characteristic of case-law. This was closely connected with a parallel confusion over the remedy of certiorari.

A turning-point came in 1963 with the decision of the House of Lords in *Ridge* v. *Baldwin*.[12] This marked an important change of judicial policy, indicating that natural justice was restored to favour and would be applied on a wide basis. A spate of litigation followed in its wake, and many new questions were elucidated. The process is likely to continue, as the courts build up their code of administrative procedure and explore the implications of what they call 'fair play in action'.[13] In particular, the right to a fair hearing is capable of elaboration in many details. The citizen's right to have his case properly heard, before he suffers in some way under the official rod, can cover a whole series of procedural steps, from the initial objection to the final decision.

The litigation since 1963 has helped to make public authorities aware of the law's requirements, thereby improving administrative standards. In the courts the rules have been clarified and their enforcement has become more consistent. The legal conception of procedural justice has now a secure bridgehead in the territory of administration. Judges are no longer deterred by the disparaging remarks of some of their predecessors, such as 'the expression (natural justice) is sadly lacking in precision'[14] and 'that the judiciary should presume to impose its own methods on administrative or executive officers is a usurpation'.[15] Such comments are out of line with the current of authority which has flowed for several hundred years. In *Ridge* v. *Baldwin* Lord Reid made an apt reply:[16]

[12] [1964] AC 40.
[13] See below, p. 523.
[14] *R.* v. *Local Government Board ex p. Arlidge* [1914] 1 KB 160 at 199 (Hamilton LJ). And see *Maclean* v. *Workers' Union* [1929] 1 Ch. 602 at 604 (Maugham J).
[15] *Local Government Board* v. *Arlidge* [1915] AC 120 at 138 (Lord Shaw), followed by derogatory comments on natural justice.
[16] [1964] AC 40 at 64.

In modern times opinions have sometimes been expressed to the effect that natural justice is so vague as to be practically meaningless. But I would regard these as tainted by the perennial fallacy that because something cannot be cut and dried or nicely weighed or measured therefore it does not exist. The idea of negligence is equally insusceptible of exact definition . . . and natural justice as it has been interpreted in the courts is much more definite than that.

Another indication that natural justice is a sufficiently precise concept is that the expression has been used without further definition in Acts of Parliament.[17]

Natural justice in the common law

The rules requiring impartial adjudicators and fair hearings can be traced back to medieval precedents, and, indeed, they were not unknown in the ancient world. In their medieval guise they were regarded as part of the immutable order of things, so that in theory even the power of the legislature could not alter them. This theory lingered into the seventeenth and faintly even into the eighteenth century, though by then it was incompatible with the modern theory of parliamentary sovereignty which was supplanting the old ideas. It reached its highwater mark in *Dr. Bonham's* case (1610), where Chief Justice Coke went so far as to say that the court could declare an Act of Parliament void if it made a man judge in his own cause, or was otherwise 'against common right and reason'.[18] This was one of his grounds for disallowing the claim of the College of Physicians to fine and imprison Dr Bonham, a doctor of physic of Cambridge University, for practising in the City of London without the licence of the College of Physicians. The statute under which the College acted provided that fines should go half to the king and half to the College, so that the College had a financial interest in its own judgment and was judge in its own cause.[19]

No modern judge could repeat this exploit, for to hold an Act of Parliament void is to blaspheme against the doctrine of parliamentary sovereignty.[20] As we shall see, there are plenty of cases under modern

[17] Foreign Compensation Act 1969, s. 3(10), noted below, p. 729; Trade Union and Labour Relations Act 1974, s. 6(13), repealed as noted below, p. 502.

[18] 8 Co. Rep. 113b at 118a.

[19] In some States of the USA fines have been paid either to the judge personally or to funds in which he was politically interested; but the Supreme Court has condemned the practice: *Tumey* v. *Ohio* 273 US 510 (1927); *Ward* v. *Monroeville* 409 US 57 (1972).

[20] In *Birdi* v. *Home Secretary* (1975, unreported) Lord Denning MR said that he might hold an Act of Parliament void in so far as it conflicted with the European Convention on Human Rights, but he withdrew this remark in *R.* v. *Home Secretary ex p. Bhajan Singh* [1976] QB 198; see below, p. 498.

statutes where authorities are in a sense (sometimes even a financial sense) judges in their own affairs. Coke's opinion was by no means clear law even in his own time although it was approved by at least one contemporary Chief Justice.[21] It was also commended by another great judge, Chief Justice Holt, in 1701. Holt said that it was 'far from any extravagancy, for it is a very reasonable and true saying, that if an Act of Parliament should ordain that the same person should be party and Judge . . . it would be a void Act of Parliament'.[22] He also said that an Act of Parliament could not make adultery lawful, though it could legalise divorce and remarriage. Natural justice, natural law, the law of God and 'common right and reason' were all aspects of the old concept of fundamental and unalterable law. They no longer represent any kind of limit to the power of statute.[23] Natural justice has had to look for a new foothold, and has found it as a mode not of destroying enacted law but of fulfilling it. Its basis now is in the rules of interpretation. The courts may presume that Parliament, when it grants powers, intends them to be exercised in a right and proper way. Since Parliament is very unlikely to make provision to the contrary,[24] this allows considerable scope for the courts to devise a set of canons of fair administrative procedure, suitable to the needs of the time.

The courts also apply similar doctrines in the private sphere, in the interpretation of contracts. Members of trade unions or clubs, for example, cannot normally be expelled without being given a hearing, for their contracts of membership are held to include a duty to act fairly: by accepting them as members and receiving their subscriptions the trade union or club impliedly undertakes to treat them fairly and in accordance with the rules.[25] The same may apply to members of universities, including students. Such cases fall outside administrative law, since they are not concerned with governmental authorities, and the question at issue is not one of ultra vires but one of breach of contract. Nevertheless the principles of fair procedure may be similar to those applied in administrative law and the decisions may be helpful by analogy.

The courts are not always willing to be confined by rigid categories,

---

[21] Hobart CJ in *Day* v. *Savadge* (1614) Hobart 85, who said '. . . even an Act of Parliament made against natural equity, as to make a man judge in his own case, is void in itself, for jura naturae sunt immutabilia and they are leges legum'.

[22] *City of London* v. *Wood* [1701] 12 Mod. 669.

[23] In 1871 Willes J described the above-quoted remark of Hobart CJ as 'a warning rather than an authority to be followed': *Lee* v. *Bude & Torrington Junction Rly* (1871) LR 6 CP 576 at 582.

[24] Except in special cases, e.g. *Cheetham* v. *Manchester Cpn.* [1875] LR 10 CP 249 (demolition of dangerous buildings); *R.* v. *Herrod ex p. Leeds City District Council* [1976] QB 540 (refusal of gaming permits); *R.* v. *Dudley JJ ex p. Payne* [1979] 1 WLR 891 (offender sentenced without notice of the date of hearing).

[25] See below, p. 501.

however, and occasionally they may hold that there is a duty of procedural fairness even where there is neither statute nor contract upon which to base it. They seem to be reserving their right to control bodies which exercise important powers de facto, for example in the fields of employment, commerce, and sport. It has been held that the British Boxing Board of Control, a non-statutory body without whose licence it is in practice impossible to be a recognised promoter, trainer, or manager, must deal with applications for licences honestly and without bias or caprice, though without any obligation to disclose information held against the applicant or to give him any hearing.[26] The High Court of Australia has held also that the owner of a racecourse who admits the public has a 'moral duty' not to eject any individual arbitrarily and without hearing him fairly, and that if he does so his act is 'ultra vires and void'.[27] The Court of Appeal has held that the Panel on Take-overs and Mergers, part of the Stock Exchange's system of self-regulation which has no statutory or contractual basis, is subject to judicial review, and must observe the principles of natural justice, because it operates in the public sphere and exercises immense power de facto.[28] The same is evidently true of the Criminal Injuries Compensation Board, another non-statutory body to which judicial review has been applied.[29] Other public bodies are likely to join this company. New vistas of judicial review are thus opening, as explained later,[30] and they are sure to extend to natural justice.

Where an administrative act or decision is vitiated by a breach of natural justice, the court may award any appropriate remedies. The remedy will frequently be certiorari to quash, on the footing that the vitiated decision is void and a nullity.[31] For this same reason a declaratory judgment is equally effective, as in *Ridge* v. *Baldwin*.[32] Occasionally, where injury is done, there will be grounds for an action for damages.[33]

Traditionally natural justice has been confined to the two rules now to be

---

[26] *McInnes* v. *Onslow-Fane* [1978] 1 WLR 1520, where Megarry V-C said: 'In recent years there has been a marked expansion of the ambit of the requirements of natural justice and fairness reaching beyond statute and contract.' But the only such case cited was *Nagle* v. *Feilden* [1966] 2 QB 633, which was not concerned with natural justice but with the question whether the Jockey Club's refusal to grant a trainer's licence to a woman might be unlawful as being arbitrary and unreasonable and also contrary to public policy and to 'the right to work'; and it was no more than a decision that the statement of claim should not be struck out, no further proceedings being reported.

[27] *Forbes* v. *New South Wales Trotting Club* (1979) 25 ALR 1. Contrast *Heatley* v. *Tasmanian Racing and Gaming Commission* (1977) 14 ALR 519 at 538, holding that an owner's rights of property may be exercised without regard to natural justice.

[28] *R.* v. *Panel on Take-overs and Mergers ex p. Datafin Plc* [1987] QB 815 (not a natural justice case).

[29] See below, p. 640.   [30] See below, p. 641.   [31] See below, p. 629.

[32] [1964] AC 40.   [33] See below, p. 502.

discussed: that a man may not be judge in his own cause; and that a man's defence must always be fairly heard. It has not, as yet, included the requirement that reasons should be given for decisions.[34] On the other hand there are isolated judicial statements that natural justice requires decisions to be based on some evidence of probative value.[35] The courts are now so conscious of natural justice that they may well extend its scope in both these directions. At present, however, the materials can be grouped under the titles of the two following chapters.

Natural justice in European context

The Committee of Ministers of the Council of Europe have made recommendations in the field of administrative law based upon the law and practice of the member states. In 1977, after making a survey or procedural rights and remedies,[36] they made a formal recommendation[37] that the member states should observe five principles, which may be abbreviated as follows.

(1) The right to be heard (with argument and evidence);
(2) Access to information, before the administrative act, about the relevant factors;
(3) Assistance and representation in administrative procedure;
(4) Reasons to be stated in writing either in the act or upon request within a reasonable time;
(5) Indication of remedies and their time limits to be given.

Where exceptions need to be made for the sake of good and efficient administration, it is recommended that the procedure should achieve the highest possible degree of fairness.

In assessing how far English law succeeds in conforming to these principles it is necessary to take into account not only the rules of common law explained in the two following chapters but also the numerous statutory and administrative reforms explained in Chapters 23 and 24 in connection with the formal procedures of tribunals and inquiries.

An important provision of the European Convention on Human Rights and Fundamental Freedoms is discussed later.[38]

---

[34] See below, p. 547.   [35] See above, p. 323.
[36] Published in 1975.
[37] Resolution (77) 31 (28 September 1977).
[38] Below, p. 497.

14

THE RULE AGAINST BIAS

JUDICIAL AND ADMINISTRATIVE IMPARTIALITY

'No man a judge in his own cause'

Nemo judex in re sua. A judge is disqualified from determining any case in which he may be, or may fairly be suspected to be, biased. So important is this rule that Coke supposed, as we have seen, that it should prevail even over an Act of Parliament; and he reported a case where the Court of Chancery resolved that the equity judge in Chester was incompetent to judge a case in which he himself was a party.[1] But the classic example of an offence against this rule in the regular courts of law is that of Lord Chancellor Cottenham in 1852, who in a Chancery suit had affirmed a number of decrees made by the Vice-Chancellor in favour of a canal company in which Lord Cottenham was a shareholder to the extent of several thousand pounds. Lord Cottenham's decrees were set aside by the House of Lords on account of his pecuniary interest;[2] but the House then itself dealt with the appeal on its merits, and affirmed the decrees of the Vice-Chancellor.[3] It was not shown that Lord Cottenham's decision was in any way affected by his interests as a shareholder; in fact it was clearly not affected at all, for Lord Campbell said:[4]

No one can suppose that Lord Cottenham could be, in the remotest degree, influenced by the interest that he had in this concern; but, my Lords, it is of the last importance that the maxim, that no man is to be a judge in his own cause, should be held sacred. . . . And it will have a most salutary influence on [inferior] tribunals when it is known that this high Court of last resort, in a case in which the Lord Chancellor of England had an interest, considered that his decree was on that account a degree not according to law, and was set aside. This will be a lesson to all inferior tribunals to take care not only that in their decrees they are not influenced by their personal interest, but to avoid the appearance of labouring under such an influence.

---

[1] *Egerton* v. *Lord Derby* (1613) 12 Co. Rep. 114. In *Bridgman* v. *Holt* (1693) Shower PC 111, a King's Bench case involving the rights of Holt CJKB, he sat with his counsel and not as judge: see at 111. See also [1974] CLJ 80 (D. E. C. Yale).
[2] *Dimes* v. *Grand Junction Canal* (1852) 3 HLC 759.
[3] See 3 HLC 794.
[4] 3 HLC at 793.

A modern case, where the offending interest was of a non–pecuniary kind, has become equally well known, since it is the source of the quotation, overworked but none the less true, that 'justice should not only be done, but should manifestly and undoubtedly be seen to be done'.[5] A solicitor was acting for a client who was suing a motorist for damage caused in a road accident. The solicitor was also acting clerk to the justices before whom the same motorist was convicted of dangerous driving and he retired with them when they were considering their decision. The fact that the clerk's firm was acting against the interests of the convicted motorist in other proceedings was held to invalidate the conviction, even though it was proved that the justices had not in fact consulted the clerk and that he had scrupulously refrained from saying anything prejudicial.[6] Lord Hewart CJ expressed the essence of the rule:

The question therefore is not whether in this case the deputy clerk made any observation or offered any criticism which he might not properly have made or offered; the question is whether he was so related to the case in its civil aspect as to be unfit to act as clerk to the justices in the criminal matter. The answer to that question depends not upon what actually was done but upon what might appear to be done. Nothing is to be done which creates even a suspicion that there has been an improper interference with the course of justice.

Similarly where a prosecution for selling vegetables under weight to a local authority school was heard before a magistrate who was a member of the authority's education committee, the conviction was quashed.[7]

A line must nevertheless be drawn between genuine and fanciful cases. A justice of the peace is not disqualified, merely because he subscribes to a society for preventing cruelty to animals, from hearing a prosecution instituted by the society.[8] Where a county council had prosecuted a trader under the Food and Drugs Act, it was held no objection that the justices' clerk was a member of the council, upon proof that he was not a member of the council's Health Committee, which had in fact directed the prosecution.[9] The Court of Appeal protested against the tendency to impeach judicial decisions 'upon the flimsiest pretexts of bias', and against 'the erroneous impression that it is more important that justice should appear to be done than that it should in fact be done'.

These are examples of the rule against bias as applied in the ordinary

---

[5] [1924] 1 KB at 259. cf. Atkin LJ: 'Next to the tribunal being in fact impartial is the importance of its appearing so.' *Shrager* v. *Basil Dighton Ltd.* [1924] 1 KB 274 at 284.

[6] *R.* v. *Sussex Justices ex p. McCarthy* [1924] 1 KB 256.

[7] *R.* v. *Altrincham Justices ex p. Pennington* [1975] QB 549.

[8] *R.* v. *Deal Justices* (1881) 45 LT 439. cf. *R.* v. *Burton ex p. Young* [1897] 2 QB 468 and contrast *R.* v. *Huggins* [1895] 1 QB 563.

[9] *R.* v. *Camborne Justices ex p. Pearce* [1955] 1 QB 41. cf. *R.* v. *Minister of Agriculture and Fisheries ex p. Graham* [1955] 2 QB 140.

courts of law. The question now is how far the same rule can be applied to administrative decisions.

Administrative decisions

It was natural for the rule against bias to be applied generally to the functions of justices of the peace, whether judicial or administrative, and in this way the rule was readily adapted to administrative action. Thus in the eighteenth and nineteenth centuries, during the time when local government was mostly in the hands of the justices, many of their decisions were invalidated for bias in such matters as highway administration, poor law administration and liquor licensing. In 1705 the Court of Queen's Bench quashed a highway order because of the participation of a justice who was also the surveyor of the highway whose conduct was in question, and Holt CJ treated the case as analogous to one before a court of law.[10] In 1730 the court quashed an order for the removal of a pauper because one of the justices was an inhabitant and ratepayer of the parish from which he was to be removed: 'they said the practice could not overturn so fundamental a rule of justice, as that a party interested could not be a judge'.[11] In 1841 the same was done to a decision of Quarter Sessions allowing an appeal against a paving rate, where three of the justices were partners in a company which owned some of the rated property.[12] Lord Denman CJ said:

. . . three magistrates who were interested took part in the decision. It is enough to shew that this decision was followed by an order: and I will not enquire what the particular question was, nor how the majority was made up, nor what the result would have been if the magistrates who were interested had retired. The court was improperly instituted; and that rendered the decision invalid.

But, just as in the case of strictly judicial functions, a line had to be drawn so as not to disturb decisions where the interest in question was too slight to be appreciated. In a much-cited case[13] the court refused to quash a certificate of justices to the effect that a reservoir was duly completed, on which

[10] *Foxham Tithing Case* (1705) 2 Salk. 607.
[11] *Great Charte* v. *Kennington* (1730) 2 Str. 1173. The Justices Jurisdiction Act 1742 removed the disqualification from justices who were merely ratepayers, except at Quarter Sessions; and the Union Assessment Committee Amendment Act 1864 removed the exception: see *R.* v. *Bolingbroke* [1893] 2 QB 347.
[12] *R.* v. *Cheltenham Commissioners* (1841) 1 QB 467; and see *R.* v. *Hertfordshire Justices* (1845) 6 QB 753 (interests as creditor). Perhaps the most curious rating case was where the chairman of the magistrates, having presided in a series of decisions reducing assessments, then descended into the court and argued a similar appeal of his own. Since all the assessments had a similar basis, all were quashed on account of the chairman's interest as a litigant: *R.* v. *Great Yarmouth Justices ex p. Palmer* (1882) 8 QBD 525.
[13] *R.* v. *Rand* (1866) LR 1 QB 230.

depended the Bradford corporation's right to appropriate the water of certain streams. Two of the justices were trustees of a hospital and a friendly society which had invested in the corporation's bonds, and it was argued that the appropriated water was an asset which would improve the security of the bonds, and so dispose the justices to grant the certificate. The court held that any direct pecuniary interest, however small, would have disqualified them, for instance if they themselves had been liable for costs; and likewise if they would be likely to have a bias 'from kindred or any other cause'. But, since there was no pecuniary interest or real likelihood of bias, the certificate must stand.

Accordingly it became the rule that any direct pecuniary interest, however small, was a disqualification;[14] and this rule was applied rigorously.[15] But this is not to say that the courts were tolerant of other interests or influence which might be suspected of causing bias. As will be seen from the modern cases, pecuniary interests play a relatively small part, and the courts are vigilant to eliminate anything smacking in any way of favouritism.[16] Although it was once said that a less stringent standard should be applied to administrative than to judicial cases,[17] this suggestion has not in practice been followed.

Modern examples

Twentieth-century judges enforce the rule against bias no less strictly than their predecessors. The following are characteristic cases.

The court quashed the decision of a rural district council to allow some residential property in Hendon to be converted into a garage and restaurant. Under the planning legislation the council had power to permit this development and as matters then stood the owners of the property would have the right to compensation if their intentions were later frustrated by a planning scheme. One of the councillors, however, was the estate agent who was acting for the owners, and he was present at the meeting which approved the application. A neighbouring owner was granted certiorari to quash the permission on this ground, for it was held that the agent's interest in the business disqualified him from taking part in

---

[14] *R. v. Rand*, above; *R. v. Meyer* (1875) 1 QBD 173; *R. v. Farrant* (1887) 20 QBD 58; *R. v. Barnsley Licensing Justices ex p. Barnsley and District Licensed Victuallers' Association* [1960] 2 QB 167.

[15] See e.g. *R. v. Cambridge Recorder* (1857) 8 E & B 637. In *R. v. Farrant* (above) it was held that a magistrate who made a bet on the result of the case would be disqualified for pecuniary interest.

[16] A complaint of bias is sometimes called 'a challenge to the favour': *R. v. Rand* (above); *Maclean v. Workers' Union* [1929] 1 Ch. 602 at 625.

[17] *R. v. Huggins* [1895] 1 QB 563.

the council's consideration of it, even though the evidence was that he took no active part.[18] The mere presence of a non-member while a tribunal is deliberating is enough to invalidate their decision, and *a fortiori* if he represents one of the parties! The only exception to this rule is that the tribunal's clerk may be entitled to attend.[19]

A police sergeant was dismissed by the chief constable of Liverpool, and his appeal against dismissal was rejected by the Watch Committee. But the chief constable was present with the Watch Committee when they decided the appeal. In fact, as it was held, the police sergeant had succeeded in resigning before the purported dismissal, so that it had no legal effect, and did not prejudice his right to recover his pension contributions. But the court also granted a declaration that the presence of the chief constable, whose mind was made up in advance and who was in effect the respondent to the appeal, was fatal to the validity of the Watch Committee's decision.[20] Scott LJ said:

The risk that a respondent may influence the court is so abhorrent to English notions of justice that the possibility of it or even the appearance of such a possibility is sufficient to deprive the decision of all judicial force, and to render it a nullity.

For similar reasons the court quashed the decision of a disciplinary committee which had consulted privately with the chief fire officer who had reported a fireman for indiscipline.[21]

A rent assessment committee determined the 'fair rent' of a flat in Kensington at a figure below that asked for even by the tenant. The chairman lived elsewhere in London in a flat of which his father was tenant and of which the landlord was a company associated with the Kensington landlords; and he had advised his father and other neighbours in 'fair rent' proceedings instituted by the landlord company. The Court of Appeal quashed the Kensington determination because the chairman's position might have been thought to prejudice him against the landlords, since he was acting against their associated company elsewhere.[22] It was not contended that he was in fact biased; the question was rather whether bias might reasonably have been suspected. This is now a leading case on the

---

[18] *R. v. Hendon Rural District Council ex p. Chorley* [1933] 2 KB 696.

[19] *Barrs v. British Wool Marketing Board* 1957 SLT 153; *McDonnell, Petitioner* 1987 SLT 486.

[20] *Cooper v. Wilson* [1937] 2 KB 309. Contrast *Kilduff v. Wilson* [1939] 1 All ER 429.

[21] *R. v. Leicestershire Fire Authority ex p. Thompson* (1978) 77 LGR 373. See also *Murdoch v. New Zealand Milk Board* [1982] 2 NZLR 108. Contrast *R. v. Chief Constable of South Wales ex p. Thornhill* [1987] The Times, 1 June, accepting evidence that the matter was not mentioned.

[22] *Metropolitan Properties (F.G.C.) Ltd. v. Lannon* [1969] 1 QB 577.

question, discussed below, whether the dominant test is 'reasonable suspicion' or 'real likelihood', and on the way in which the test should be applied. In preferring the test of 'reasonable suspicion' the Court of Appeal reasserted the primary principle that justice must be seen to be done. This is an area where the appearance may be more important than the reality.

A police authority, when considering whether to retire a police officer permanently because of permanent disability, must refer the question of disablement to a qualified doctor. The Kent police authority were proceeding to retire a chief inspector compulsorily on grounds of mental health, and informed him that they would refer to a doctor who had in fact examined him during the previous year and had reported that he was suffering from mental disorder. The Court of Appeal held that the doctor to whom reference was made had a quasi-judicial duty to act fairly and in accordance with natural justice; and that he could not do so if he had committed himself to an opinion on the case in advance of the inquiry.[23] The rule against bias can apply at any stage of a statutory proceeding, e.g. to the making of a report as a preliminary step before the making of a final order.[24] This is bias by predetermination.[25]

There are other situations where previous involvement will not disqualify. Prison visitors have administrative as well as judicial functions, having the duty to supervise the administration of the prison and the treatment of prisoners, so that a visitor need not be disqualified, merely because he previously took part in considering a prisoner's application for parole, from acting as chairman when the same prisoner is charged with a disciplinary offence.[26] It is held that company inspectors investigating a company have a policing function and cannot realistically be expected to be unbiased, since they are bound to be acting on suspicion; and it is therefore no objection that the same inspectors have previously investigated a similar company under the same management.[27]

Indivisible authorities: cases of necessity

In all the cases so far mentioned the disqualified adjudicator could be dispensed with or replaced by someone to whom the objection did not apply. But there are many cases where no substitution is possible, since no one else is empowered to act. Natural justice then has to give way to

---

[23] R. v. *Kent Police Authority ex p. Godden* [1971] 2 QB 662.

[24] But a mere investigation, e.g. by Royal Commission, is not subject to the rule: *Re Copeland and McDonald* (1978) 88 DLR (3d) 724.

[25] As also where part of the decision is announced before the end of the hearing: *Ellis* v. *Ministry of Defence* [1985] ICR 257.

[26] R. v. *Frankland Prison Visitors ex p. Lewis* [1986] 1 WLR 130.

[27] R. v. *Secretary of State for Trade ex p. Perestrello* [1981] QB 19.

necessity;[28] for otherwise there is no means of deciding and the machinery of justice or administration will break down.[29]

This point made an appearance in *Dimes* v. *Grand Junction Canal*, already recounted.[30] Before the appeal could proceed from the Vice-Chancellor to the House of Lords, the Lord Chancellor had to sign an order for enrolment. But it was held that his shareholding in the company, which disqualified him from hearing the appeal, did not affect the enrolment, since no one but he had power to effect it. 'For this is a case of necessity, and where that occurs the objection of interest cannot prevail.'[31] Reference was made to a year book case of 1430 where an action was brought against all the judges of the Court of Common Pleas in a matter which lay only in that court. Comparable situations have occurred in modern cases. In one, a county court registrar was sued unsuccessfully in his own court, and had to tax costs in his own favour.[32] In another, the government of Saskatchewan called upon the court to determine whether the salaries of judges were liable to income tax; and the Privy Council confirmed that the court was right to decide it, as a matter of necessity.[33]

In administrative cases the same exigency may easily arise. Where statute empowers a particular minister[34] or official to act, he will usually be the one and only person who can do so. There is then no way of escaping the responsibility, even if he is personally interested. Transfer of responsibility is, indeed, a recognised type of ultra vires.[35] In one case it was unsuccessfully argued that the only minister competent to confirm a compulsory purchase order for land for an airport had disqualified himself by showing bias and that the local authority could only apply for a local Act of Parliament.[36] The court will naturally not allow statutory machinery to be frustrated in this way. For similar reasons a governor of a colony may validly assent to

---

[28] See [1982] PL 628 (R. R. S. Tracey).

[29] In *Great Charte* v. *Kennington* (1730) 2 Str. 1173 (above, p. 475) it was said that where there were no justices who were not ratepayers 'it might be allowed to prevent a failure of justice'.

[30] Above, p. 473.

[31] (1852) 3 HLC at 787.

[32] *Tolputt (H.) & Co. Ltd.* v. *Mole* [1911] 1 KB 836.

[33] *The Judges* v. *A.-G. for Saskatchewan* (1937) 53 TLR 464 (the Saskatchewan court's decision was adverse to the judges). Sir William Holdsworth had supposed that judges could not determine the legality of reductions in their salaries under the National Economy Act 1931: see (1932) 48 LQR 25 at 30.

[34] But if he is 'the Secretary of State', another Secretary of State can act in his stead: above, p. 52; *London and Clydeside Estates Ltd.* v. *Secretary of State for Scotland* 1987 SLT 459 at 463.

[35] See above, p. 368.

[36] *Re Manchester (Ringway Airport) Compulsory Purchase Order* (1935) 153 LT 219 (no bias was found).

an Act of indemnity for his own actions, since otherwise the Act could not be passed at all.[37] It is generally supposed, likewise, that a minister must act as best he can even in a case where he, for instance, himself owns property which will be benefited if he approves a development plan. Such cases of private and personal interest are conspicuous by their absence in the law reports. But there have been cases involving public funds. The Local Government Superannuation Act 1937 gave employees of local authorities statutory rights to pensions under certain conditions, but provided that any question concerning these rights should be decided first by the local authority, and then in case of dispute by the minister, whose decision on questions of fact was to be final. The Court of Appeal held that there was no escape from these clear provisions.[38] Scott LJ, whose enthusiasm for administrative justice used sometimes to add colour to the law reports, said of the Act:

. . . its first provision is to subject the duty to pay to the jurisdiction, not of a court, not of a lay tribunal, not even of an impartial third party, but of the debtor himself! That . . . almost converts its right into a mere discretionary privilege. At any rate the local authority is made, purely and simply, a 'judge in its own cause'. It is true that a so-called appeal is allowed to the aggrieved employee from the decision of that far from impartial judge, but to what court? To the Minister!

And he added, speaking of questions of fact such as loss of pension on the ground of fraud or misconduct:

Such an issue involves a question of character on which a wrong decision may ruin a man for life. . . . This state of affairs is not consonant with British justice or the rule of law on which British democracy depends for its very existence.

But no change was made when the next Local Government Superannuation Act was enacted in 1953.[39] There could hardly be a better example to show how remote from the modern world are the ideas expressed in Dr Bonham's case.[40]

Similarly in a New Zealand case the Privy Council held that a marketing board could not be prevented from making a zoning order allotting the milk produced by a certain district to a certain dairy company, even though the board had given the company a large loan and therefore had a pecuniary interest in its prosperity.[41] Both the power to make zoning orders and the power to make loans to dairy companies were expressly

---

[37] *Phillips v. Eyre* (1870) LR 6 QB 1.

[38] *Wilkinson v. Barking Cpn.* [1948] 1 KB 721.

[39] See s. 21. Under the Superannuation Act 1972, s. 11, a question of law can be referred to the High Court.

[40] Above, p. 469.

[41] *Jeffs* v. *New Zealand Dairy Production and Marketing Board* [1967] 1 AC 551. See likewise *NZI Financial Cpn. Ltd.* v. *New Zealand Kiwifruit Authority* [1986] 1 NZLR 159 (statutory membership of export licensing authority).

conferred by statute on the board and on no one else, so that 'although the board may find itself placed in an unenviable position', it was bound to exercise both powers if the statutory scheme was to be workable. The same doctrine should, perhaps, have been invoked in English cases where local authorities had to exercise different functions one of which could prejudice the other.[42]

Other instances where a person must necessarily act as a judge in prejudicial circumstances are the power of the Secretary of State for the Environment to make orders as to payment of his own costs at public inquiries,[43] and the duty of a public authority to rehear a case which it has already determined invalidly.[44]

Statutory dispensation

So strictly did the courts apply the rule against bias that Parliament attempted to mitigate it by granting exemption in particular cases. Difficulty arose especially in the case of justices of the peace, who often had other public functions which might disqualify them from adjudicating. An Act of 1742 allowed them to make orders in poor law cases despite the fact that they were themselves among the ratepayers who would benefit.[45] The Public Health Act 1875 allowed them to adjudicate under the Act notwithstanding membership of any local authority.[46] But the courts put a narrow interpretation upon all such provisions, holding that any departure from the universally acknowledged principle of natural justice required clear words of enactment.[47] The dispensation in the Public Health Act did not therefore prevent the court from quashing a conviction for selling bad meat where one of the justices had taken part in the meeting of the town council's committee which directed the prosecution. The Act was held to remove the disqualification which might be alleged on the ground of mere membership of a local authority, but not where the justice had actually acted in a manner inconsistent with judicial impartiality.[48]

Parliament may also adopt the somewhat contradictory policy of

[42] See below, p. 485.

[43] See below, p. 988. Compare *Rich* v. *Christchurch Girls' High School Board* [1974] 1 NZLR 1 (statutory right to attend meeting); *R.* v. *Whyalla Cpn. ex p. Kittel* (1979) 20 SASR 386 (inevitable bias of planning authority).

[44] For this see below, p. 553.

[45] Justices Jurisdiction Act 1742. See above, p. 475, n. 11.

[46] s. 258.

[47] *Mersey Docks Trustees* v. *Gibbs* (1866) LR 1 HL 93 at 110; *Frome United Breweries Co. Ltd.* v. *Bath Justices* [1926] AC 586.

[48] *R.* v. *Lee ex p. Shaw* (1882) 9 QBD 394; see similarly *R.* v. *Henley* [1892] 1 QB 504, distinguished in *R.* v. *Pwllheli Justices ex p. Soane* [1948] 2 All ER 815. And see the *Frome United Breweries* case, above.

forbidding a person to act in cases where he has some disqualifying interest
but of validating his action if he should do so. Thus the Local Government
Act 1972 makes it a criminal offence for a member of a local authority to
take part in or vote on any contract or other matter in which he has a
pecuniary interest;[49] but the Act provides in general terms that the acts of
any one elected to office and acting in that office shall be valid and effectual
notwithstanding disqualification.[50] The law of liquor licensing has a
corresponding provision on which, once again, the courts have placed a
restrictive construction. Licensing justices are subject to express statutory
disqualifications, for example in cases concerning any premises in the
profits of which they are interested or of which they are owners or
occupiers. But the Act provides that no act done by a justice so disqualified
shall be invalid by reason only of that disqualification.[51] By a subtle
interpretation the courts confine this provision to what they call 'the
technical disqualification created by the Act'.[52] They will uphold the order
if it is shown merely that one or more of the justices fell within the
disqualifying provisions; but they will quash it if, in addition, it is shown
that there was a real likelihood of bias in the particular case.[53] This
distinction may not be quite easy to explain by pure reason; but that very
fact shows how the court is concerned to prevent serious inroads upon the
principles of natural justice. If the protecting clause were allowed its full
meaning, legal questions would be determined by judges who for
fundamental reasons are incompetent to act. The Court of Appeal
confirmed the doctrine in a case where a spirits licence was granted to a co-
operative society. Six out of seven justices were members of the society and
derived small dividends from it on their purchases, so that the grant of a
licence would enable them to buy spirits at a significant discount. It was
held that this was a mere technical disqualification under the terms of the
Act and that since there was no real likelihood of bias the grant of the
licence was valid.[54]

Waiver of objection

The right to object to a disqualified adjudicator may be waived, and this
may be so even where the disqualification is statutory.[55] The court

[49] s. 94. The Secretary of State has a dispensing power: s. 97.
[50] s. 82.
[51] Licensing Act 1964, s. 193(6); and see ss. (8). Earlier Acts contained similar provisions.
[52] R. v. Tempest (1902) 86 LT 585.
[53] Likelihood here evidently means probability: see below, p. 484.
[54] R. v. Barnsley Licensing Justices ex p. Barnsley and District Licensed Victuallers' Association
[1960] 2 QB 167. Devlin LJ regarded this as 'a borderline case which comes very near the
mark'.
[55] Wakefield Local Board of Health v. West Riding and Grimsby Rly Co. (1865) 1 QB 84.

normally insists that the objection shall be taken as soon as the party prejudiced knows the facts which entitle him to object. If, after he or his advisers know of the disqualification, they let the proceedings continue without protest, they are held to have waived their objection and the determination cannot be challenged.[56] In the past this rule has been strictly applied, so much so that the practice was to refuse certiorari to quash the decision unless it was specifically shown in the affidavits that the applicant had no knowledge of the disqualifying facts at the time of the proceedings.[57] But in one case, where the litigant had appeared in person before the justices, certiorari was granted even though he knew the facts at the trial, since he did not know that he was entitled to raise his objection then, and there can be no waiver of rights of which the person entitled is unaware.[58]

'Reasonable suspicion', 'real likelihood' and 'bias in fact'

Much confusion has been caused by the concurrent use of two differently formulated tests for disqualifying bias. Many judges have laid down and applied the 'real likelihood' formula, holding that the test for disqualification is whether the facts give rise to a real likelihood of bias;[59] and this test has naturally been emphasised in cases where the allegation of bias was excessively far-fetched.[60] At the same time it was frequently emphasised that justice must be seen to be done, and that no person should adjudicate in any way if it might reasonably be thought that he ought not to act because of some personal interest.[61] In one case it was even said that the rule for judges of all kinds was that they must be free from even unreasonable suspicion of bias,[62] but that dictum is recognised as having gone too far.[63]

[56] R. v. Byles ex p. Hollidge (1912) 77 JP 40; R. v. Nailsworth Licensing Justices ex p. Bird [1953] 1 WLR 1046; R. v. Lilydale Magistrates Court ex p. Ciccone [1973] VR 122; and see R. v. Antrim Justices [1895] 2 IR 603; Tolputt (H.) & Co. Ltd. v. Mole [1911] 1 KB 836; Corrigan v. Irish Land Commission [1977] IR 317.

[57] R. v. Williams ex p. Phillips [1914] 1 KB 608; R. v. Kent Justices (1880) 44 JP 298.

[58] R. v. Essex Justices ex p. Perkins [1927] 2 KB 475.

[59] R. v. Rand (1866) LR 1 QB 230; R. v. Sunderland Justices (1901) 2 KB 357; Frome United Breweries Co. v. Bath Justices [1926] AC 586; R. v. Camborne Justices ex p. Pearce [1955] 1 QB 41; Healey v. Rauhina [1958] NZLR 945; Hannam v. Bradford Corporation [1970] 1 WLR 937.

[60] See R. v. Camborne Justices, above.

[61] The numerous decisions include R. v. Allan (1864) 4 B & S 915; R. v. Gaisford [1892] 1 QB 381; R. v. Sussex Justices ex p. McCarthy [1924] 1 KB 256; Cooper v. Wilson [1937] 2 KB 309 at 324, 344; Cottle v. Cottle [1939] 2 All ER 535; Metropolitan Properties Co. (FGC) Ltd. v. Lannon [1969] 1 QB 577; Turner v. Allison [1971] 1 NZLR 833.

[62] Eckersley v. Mersey Docks and Harbour Board [1894] 2 QB 667.

[63] See R. v. Camborne Justices ex p. Pearce [1955] 1 QB 41 at 48.

In the great majority of cases either test will lead to the same result. This might be so in all cases if 'likelihood' is given the meaning of possibility rather than probability. For if there is no real possibility of bias, no reasonable person would suspect it. But several judicial statements, more naturally, equate 'likelihood' with 'probability',[64] and then a difference emerges. In *Dimes* v. *Grand Junction Canal Co.*,[65] for example, the Lord Chancellor's shareholding in the defendant company did not create a real probability of bias, but it created a possibility which a reasonable man might have suspected. In a liquor licensing case of 1960 it was also pointed out that the two tests led to different results;[66] but in that there was the special circumstance that the statute protected the validity of acts done by disqualified justices, so that the court was not entitled to quash their order unless the facts raised a likelihood of bias over and above the technical disqualification.[67]

The courts have several times treated the two tests as different, and have felt obliged to elect between them. In 1954 a Divisional Court, after reviewing authorities, decided firmly in favour of real likelihood.[68] But in 1968 the Court of Appeal decided equally firmly in favour of reasonable suspicion,[69] although Lord Denning MR interwove this with the other test, saying that the court

does not look to see if there was a real likelihood that he would, or did, in fact favour one side at the expense of the other. The court looks at the impression which would be given to other people.

And he continued:

Nevertheless there must appear to be a real likelihood of bias. Surmise or conjecture is not enough. . . . There must be circumstances from which a reasonable man would think it likely or probable that the justice, or chairman, as the case may be, would, or did, favour one side unfairly at the expense of the other. The court will not inquire whether he did, in fact, favour one side unfairly. Suffice it that reasonable people might think he did. The reason is plain enough. Justice must be rooted in confidence: and confidence is destroyed when right-minded people go away thinking: 'the judge was biased'.

---

[64] *R.* v. *Barnsley Licensing Justices ex p. Barnsley and District Licensed Victuallers' Association* [1960] 2 QB 167 at 187 (Devlin LJ); *Metropolitan Properties (FGC) Ltd.* v. *Lannon* [1969] 1 QB 577 at 599 (Lord Denning MR).

[65] See above, p. 473.

[66] *R.* v. *Barnsley Licensing Justices* (above) at p. 198 (Devlin LJ).

[67] See above, p. 482. This feature does not seem to have been noticed in the discussion of this case by the Court of Appeal in *Metropolitan Properties (FGC) Ltd.* v. *Lannon* [1969] 1 QB 577.

[68] *R.* v. *Camborne Justices ex p. Pearce* [1955] 1 QB 41. See similarly *R.* v. *Nailsworth Licensing Justices ex p. Bird* [1953] 1 WLR 1046.

[69] *Metropolitan Properties (FGC) Ltd.* v. *Lannon* [1969] 1 QB 577; above, p. 477.

Lord Denning then applied the test of the advice which would be given by a friend if consulted: if any friend would advise against it, the justice or chairman ought not to act.[70]

This decision categorically restored 'justice must be seen to be done' as the operative principle and established, or perhaps re-established, the more stringent standard of natural justice—which, it might be said, reflected the change of judicial attitudes between 1954 and 1968.[71] But in later cases the courts do not seem to have felt that the position was clear. Sometimes they have suggested that the two tests produce the same result;[72] and sometimes that, in the 'somewhat confusing welter of authority', it suffices to say that either test is satisfied on the facts.[73]

The latest judicial suggestion is that the two tests are substantially the same, but inapplicable to policy-based decisions such as those of planning authorities, since these are radically different from those of bodies such as rent tribunals, which decide objectively according to rules. In two cases local planning authorities had made contracts with developers for the exploitation of land which the authorities themselves owned, undertaking to do their best to procure planning permission, to be granted by themselves. It was shown that in granting permission both authorities had acted fairly and without bias in fact, and both courts held that it was irrelevant that a likelihood of bias might reasonably have been suspected —as on the facts was clearly so.[74] This was put in the form that 'the reasonable man test has no application in the case of an administrative decision', as opposed to a decision 'of a judicial nature'.[75] Otherwise, it was pointed out, there might be 'an administrative impasse' in cases where the planning authority had quite properly become involved in some development.[76]

These decisions invite the comment that they might have been based more suitably on the rule of necessity, explained above, than on a distinction between judicial and administrative functions. When Parlia-

---

[70] At p. 600. Danckwerts and Edmund Davies LJJ also preferred and applied 'reasonable suspicion' as the test as opposed to 'real likelihood'.

[71] See above, p. 19.

[72] *Hannam* v. *Bradford Cpn.* [1970] 1 WLR 937 (Sachs and Cross LJJ); *R.* v. *St Edmundsbury BC* (below) (Stocker J).

[73] *Hannam* v. *Bradford Cpn.* (above) (Widgery LJ). See similarly *R.* v. *Eastern Traffic Area Licensing Authority ex p. J. Wyatt (Haulage) Ltd.* [1974] RTR 480; *R.* v. *Altrincham Justices* [1975] QB 549.

[74] *R.* v. *Amber Valley DC ex p. Jackson* [1985] 1 WLR 298; *R.* v. *St Edmundsbury BC ex p. Investors in Industry Commercial Properties Ltd.* [1985] 1 WLR 1168, following *R.* v. *Sevenoaks DC ex p. Terry* [1985] 3 All ER 226 in preference to *Steeples* v. *Derbyshire CC* [1985] 1 WLR 256 (reasonable man test applied: planning permission void).

[75] In the *St Edmundsbury* case (above) at 1193, 1194 (Stocker J).

[76] Quoted from the *Sevenoaks* case (above) (Glidewell J).

ment has empowered the same body both to undertake development and to grant planning permission, that body must perform both functions as best it can, despite the effect that one may have upon the other. That is the problem of the 'indivisible authority' already encountered.[77] But it does not mean that 'the reasonable man test' cannot apply to an administrative decision, as it has been applied in the past,[78] where it affects only particular members of a deciding body, who can be disqualified without making that body incompetent to act.

CAUSES OF PREJUDICE

Intermingling of functions

A common problem is where an adjudicator has already been concerned with the case in some other capacity. This is particularly prone to arise in the case of magistrates, who may also be members of local authorities or of other administrative bodies. Difficult questions of degree frequently arise, since the court must try to avoid impeding the work of citizens who give their services in more than one capacity, while at the same time the principle of fair and unbiased decisions must at all costs be upheld.

One class is where the adjudicator has supported the application, complaint or prosecution which comes to be adjudicated.[79] A justice who has proposed a prosecution,[80] or has voted for it,[81] as a member of a local authority is naturally disqualified; but he may act, it seems, if he was merely present at a meeting which resolved to institute proceedings, provided that he took no active part,[82] despite the fact that he may well have been influenced by things said at the meeting. In some situations mere membership, without participation, may invalidate the adjudication. Thus where a local education authority had to decide whether to prohibit the

---

[77] Above, p. 478. See especially the *Jeffs* case (p. 480).

[78] As in the *Hendon* case (above, p. 476) and many others in this chapter.

[79] *R. v. Sunderland Justices* [1901] 2 KB 357 (councillors supporting road-widening scheme sat as justices and granted liquor licence for premises involved in the scheme); *R. v. Caernarvon Licensing Justices* [1948] WN 505. Contrast *R. v. Nailsworth Licensing Justices ex p. Bird* [1953] 1 WLR 1046. See also *Thomas v. Mount St Vincent University* (1986) 28 DLR (4th) 230 (non-promotion of professor: proceedings unfair).

[80] *R. v. Gaisford* [1892] 1 QB 381. See similarly *Re French and Law Society of Upper Canada (No. 2)* (1973) 41 DLR (3d) 23.

[81] *R. v. Milledge* (1879) 4 QBD 332; *R. v. Lee ex p. Shaw* (1882) 9 QBD 394; *R. v. Henley* [1892] 1 QB 504 (justice present; resolution unanimous).

[82] *R. v. Pwllheli Justices ex p. Soane* [1948] 2 All ER 815, distinguishing *R. v. Henley*, above. But in these cases there were statutory provisions.

dismissal of a school teacher whom the governors of the school had resolved to dismiss, the Court of Appeal found objectionable bias because three members of the local authority's sub-committee, which resolved not to prohibit the dismissal, were governors; yet those members had not attended the governors' meeting which resolved upon the dismissal.[83] It was observed that members of a body such as a board of governors might be thought to have a built-in tendency to support their colleagues, and ought not therefore to sit in judgment on their decisions.[84] In a contrasting case, where a student at a teaching training college was expelled for having a man living with her in her room, the Court of Appeal upheld the expulsion even though it was effected by the board of governors who had taken it upon themselves to refer the case to the disciplinary committee which recommended expulsion.[85] Yet the procedure was strongly criticised, and had the court been sympathetic to the plaintiff it could easily have found in her favour.

Mere membership of a prosecuting body, however, raises questions of degree, and there may be a situation where a member who was inactive in the matter is not disqualified.[86] Thus a solicitor may sit as a magistrate on a prosecution brought by the Council of Law Society,[87] and a member of a society for preventing cruelty to animals may adjudicate on a prosecution brought by the society;[88] and, *a fortiori*, past membership is unobjectionable.[89]

Where functions are delegated or entrusted to committees or sub-committees, an overlap of membership may be objectionable on grounds of bias. This was plainly so where the London County Council used a committee for hearing applications for music and dancing licences and three members of the committee not only sat as members of the Council (though taking no part) when considering the committee's adverse recommendation, but also instructed lawyers to oppose the application before the Council.[90] The House of Lords followed this decision in a similar situation where justices referred a licence application to the compensation authority and instructed a lawyer to oppose it before that authority; three of the same justices not only sat but also voted as members of the

---

[83] *Hannam* v. *Bradford Cpn.* [1970] 1 WLR 937.

[84] At p. 946 (Widgery LJ).

[85] *Ward* v. *Bradford Cpn.* (1971) 70 LGR 27, not citing *Hannam* v. *Bradford Cpn.*, above. Compare *Haddow* v. *Inner London Education Authority* [1979] ICR 202.

[86] As in *R.* v. *Camborne Justices ex p. Pearce* [1955] 1 QB 41; above, p. 474.

[87] *R.* v. *Burton ex p. Young* [1897] 2 QB 468. And see *Leeson* v. *General Medical Council* (1889) 43 Ch.D. 336; *Re S. (A Barrister)* [1981] QB 683.

[88] *R.* v. *Deal Justices* (1881) 45 LT 439.

[89] *Allinson* v. *General Medical Council* [1894] 1 QB 750.

[90] *R.* v. *London County Council ex p. Akkersdyk* [1892] 1 QB 190.

compensation authority, and the decision of the authority was accordingly set aside.[91]

A particularly clear case of irregularity is where a person sits with an appellate body to hear an appeal against a decision of his own,[92] as did the chief constable in the Liverpool police case mentioned earlier.[93] Likewise a county valuation officer ought not to sit with an assessment committee while they deliberate on an objection to the valuation list.[94] Many rating cases have revealed other objectionable intermixtures of functions, for example where an employee of a town council, who took the minutes of its rating committee, acted also as a clerk to the assessment committee.[95]

It has been held that the fact that a magistrate has been subpoenaed as a witness is no ground for prohibiting him from sitting at the hearing of the same case.[96] But a witness frequently testifies on behalf of one party or another, and on general grounds also the functions of witness and judge would seem incompatible.

Other causes of prejudice

Objectionable bias may be found in a wide variety of situations and relationships. Any indication that an adjudicator has prejudged the case, or may reasonably be suspected of doing so, will normally disqualify him. This occurred where certain justices were directors and shareholders of a hotel which applied for a liquor licence; they sat with the licensing justices, who granted a licence, but before doing so they resigned their directorships and sold their shares. Even though they then had no pecuniary interest, their object from the start was to procure the grant of a licence, which was therefore quashed.[97] In another case a justice who joined in refusing a

[91] *Frome United Breweries Co. Ltd.* v. *Bath Justices* [1926] AC 586.

[92] Judges may however do this and often did so in earlier times: see *Hamlet* v. *General Municipal Boilermakers and Allied Trades Union* [1987] 1 WLR 449; *R.* v. *Lovegrove* [1951] 1 All ER 804.

[93] *Cooper* v. *Wilson* [1937] 2 KB 309; above, p. 477. See similarly *Taylor* v. *National Union of Seamen* [1967] 1 WLR 532 (trade union official who had dismissed plaintiff presided at appeal and presented case against him); *R.* v. *Barnsley Metropolitan Borough Council ex p. Hook* [1976] 1 WLR 1052 (revocation of market trader's licence: prosecuting officer sat with appeal committee). Contrast *R.* v. *Chief Constable of South Wales ex p. Thornhill* [1986] The Times, 12 May (evidence of non-involvement accepted); *Hamlet* v. *GMBATU* (above) (rules of Union required membership of both initial and appeal bodies).

[94] *R.* v. *Assessment Committee for NE Surrey ex p. F. W. Woolworth & Co. Ltd.* [1933] 1 KB 776.

[95] *R.* v. *Salford Assessment Committee ex p. Ogden* [1937] 2 KB 1.

[96] *R.* v. *Farrant* (1887) 20 QBD 58.

[97] *R.* v. *Hain* (1896) 12 TLR 323. See similarly *Meadowvale Stud Farm Ltd.* v. *Stratford CC* [1979] 1 NZLR 342 (shareholders sat on county council).

licence, and who belonged to a strict temperance sect, stated afterwards that he would have been a traitor to his position if he had voted in favour; and since this clearly indicated bias from the outset, the order of refusal was bad.[98] But a licensing justice is not disqualified by the mere fact that he is a teetotaller.[99] Nor, provided that a fair trial is given, does it matter that a justice showed from the bench that he held strong views on some relevant matter;[1] or that a member of a committee responsible for licensing sex shops had previously published his opinion that none should be allowed.[2] As was said in one licensing case, 'preconceived opinions—though it is unfortunate that a judge should have any—do not constitute such a bias, nor even the expression of such opinions, for it does not follow that the evidence will be disregarded'.[3]

Among other obvious cases of prejudice are personal friendship or hostility[4] and family relationship.[5] A justice was disqualified where he was a friend of the mother of one of the parties and that party had let it be known that the justice would be on her side;[6] but the court distinguished this sharply from cases of mere acquaintance or business contact. This type of bias is rarely alleged and authorities are scanty.

There can normally be no objection to a member of a tribunal sitting in an application by a party who has previously appeared before him on another application.[7]

Departmental or administrative bias

It is self-evident that ministerial or departmental policy cannot be regarded as disqualifying bias. One of the commonest administrative mechanisms is to give a minister power to make or confirm an order after hearing objections to it. The procedure for the hearing of objection is subject to the rules of natural justice in so far as they require a fair hearing and fair procedure generally. But the minister's decision cannot be impugned on

[98] R. v. Halifax Justices ex p. Robinson (1912) 76 JP 233; cf. Goodall v. Bilsland 1909 SC 1152. In M'Geehen v. Knox 1913 SC 688 the facts were nearly as strong, yet the order stood.

[99] R. v. Nailsworth Licensing Justices ex p. Bird [1953] 1 WLR 1046.

[1] Ex p. Wilder (1902) 66 JP 761 (justice showed prejudice against motor cars).

[2] R. v. Reading BC ex p. Quietlynn Ltd. (1986) 85 LGR 387.

[3] R. v. London County Council, re Empire Theatre (1894) 71 LT 638. See Whitford Residents Association v. Manukau City Cpn. [1974] 2 NZLR 340; R. v. Commonwealth Conciliation and Arbitration Commission ex p. Angliss Group (1969) 122 CLR 546.

[4] As in R. v. Handley (1921) 61 DLR 656; cf. White v. Kuzych [1951] AC 585. The statement to the contrary in Maclean v. Workers' Union [1929] Ch. 602 goes too far.

[5] See R. v. Rand (1866) LR 1 QB 230 at 232–3.

[6] Cottle v. Cottle [1939] 2 All ER 535.

[7] R. v. Oxford Regional Mental Health Review Tribunal ex p. Mackman [1986] The Times, 2 June. Contrast R. v. Downham Market Magistrates' Court ex p. Nudd [1988] The Times, 14 April.

the ground that he has advocated the scheme or that he is known to support it as a matter of policy. The whole object of putting the power into his hands is that he may exercise it according to government policy. Otherwise the situation might resemble the pathetic picture painted by the Committee on Ministers' Powers in their report of 1932,[8] where they suggested that a minister might be put in a dilemma where his impartiality would be in inverse ratio to his efficiency:

An easy-going and cynical Minister, rather bored with his office and sceptical of the value of his Department, would find it far easier to apply a judicial mind to purely judicial problems connected with the Department's administration than a Minister whose head and heart were in his work. . . . Parliament should be chary of imposing on Ministers the ungrateful task of giving judicial decisions in matters in which their very zeal for the public service can scarcely fail to bias them unconsciously.

As regards such 'purely judicial problems' Parliament does for the most part follow this advice, as is to be seen from the rapid multiplication in this century of independent statutory tribunals designed to take the determination of genuinely judicial cases out of ministers' hands. These, as will be seen, are nevertheless sometimes accused of departmental bias, perhaps because the clerk is an official of the ministry, or because they sit in ministry premises, or because their proceedings may have a tinge of departmental policy. The remedy for such complaints is not provided by the principles of natural justice but by the legislation on tribunals and inquiries, discussed in a later chapter.

   Attempts to represent government policy as objectionable on grounds of natural justice are usually complaints of predetermination, alleging that the effective decision was taken in advance, thus rendering the hearing futile and the result a foregone conclusion. In the case already mentioned, where the minister had confirmed a compulsory purchase order for the acquisition of land for an airport it was contended that the minister was disqualified because the Air Council, of which the minister was a member, had expressed a provisional view in favour of the scheme before objections were invited; but this was held to be perfectly proper and not prejudicial.[9] Where, before a planning application was due to come before a local authority, the members of a political party controlling the authority agreed to support the application, their political predisposition did not disqualify them, since it was 'almost inevitable, now that party politics play so large a part in local government, that the majority group on a council would

---

   [8] Cmd. 4060 (1932), p. 78.
   [9] *Re Manchester (Ringway Airport) Compulsory Purchase Order* (1935) 153 LT 219; above, p. 479.

decide on the party line'.[10] In a Scots case a Member of Parliament who had supported a constituent's objection to a proposed development later became Secretary of State and directed that an appeal by another would-be developer of the same land should be determined by himself and not by the reporter (inspector). This was held not to disqualify him in the circumstances.[11] In New Zealand members of a planning appeal board had sat in previous connected proceedings and expressed views on the best use of the land, but the court considered that such situations were inevitable where planning policy had to be administered and that they did not support allegations of bias.[12] The key to all these decisions is the fact that if Parliament gives the deciding power to a political body, no one can complain that it acts politically. The principles of natural justice still apply, but they must be adapted to the circumstances.[13]

A dramatic contest over a prior political commitment concerned the order for the new town at Stevenage.[14] Here the issue was whether the minister had truly complied with the statutory requirement that after the objections had been heard at an inquiry 'the minister shall consider the report' of the inspector. Although this issue was raised on the particular words of the Act, the substantial question was whether 'consider' meant 'consider fairly, in accordance with natural justice'.

The Minister of Town and Country Planning had determined that Stevenage should be the first of the new towns under the New Towns Act 1946. Strong objections were made and were fully heard by a ministry inspector at a public inquiry. The minister, after considering the report, confirmed the designation order. But before this procedure was set in train the minister had visited Stevenage and made a speech at a public meeting. There was heckling and jeering, and there were cries of 'dictator' and 'gestapo'. But the minister firmly stated his policy, and according to the report he said 'It is no good your jeering: it is going to be done—(applause and boos).' The objectors maintained that by this positive statement of policy the minister had in effect declared that his mind was made up in advance. He had precluded himself, they said, from 'considering' the subsequent report of the inspector fairly and without bias. This is precisely the problem of 'departmental bias'. Three courts succeeded in reaching

---

[10] R. v. Amber Valley DC ex p. Jackson [1985] 1 WLR 298 (Woolf J).

[11] London and Clydeside Estates Ltd. v. Secretary of State for Scotland 1987 SLT 459 adopting the treatment of this topic in the previous edition of this book.

[12] Turner v. Allison [1971] NZLR 833. Contrast Anderton v. Auckland CC [1978] 1 NZLR 657.

[13] See R. v. Amber Valley DC (above).

[14] Franklin v. Minister of Town and Country Planning [1948] AC 87, discussed in ' "Quasi-judicial" and its Background' (1949) 10 CLJ 216 (Wade).

three different conclusions, showing all possible variations both on the law and on the facts. The High Court held that the law required impartial consideration, and that in fact it had not been given. The Court of Appeal held that the law required impartial consideration, but that it had been given. It was left for the House of Lords to hold that the law did not require impartial consideration at all: the minister could be as biased as he liked, provided that he observed the procedure laid down by the Act.

On the facts of the case, there seems much to be said for the middle road followed by the Court of Appeal. It is a virtue in a minister to have a policy and to advocate it. He also has to face opposition and to make public speeches. If, when he does so, he lets fall a defiant remark, that is by no means inconsistent with an ability to consider, or reconsider, the whole project when later the inspector's report arrives. The law must allow for the departmental bias which he is expected and indeed required to have. The relevant question is whether the minister, when he comes to make his decision, genuinely addresses himself to the question with a mind which is open to persuasion.[15]

The decision of the House of Lords threatened to become a source of difficulty because Lord Thankerton, who delivered the only reasoned speech, appeared to throw doubt on the applicability of the rule against bias to any kind of administrative case. He said that the minister had no judicial or quasi-judicial duty and that the only question was whether he had complied with the statutory directions to appoint a person to hold the public inquiry and to consider that person's report. He made no mention of many previous cases holding that a minister considering the report of an inquiry had a quasi-judicial duty—this was, indeed, the stock example of this situation.[16] Lord Thankerton said that an example of a quasi-judicial function was that of an arbitrator, and that was only in cases of that kind that bias was relevant. But an arbitrator has a judicial as opposed to a quasi-judicial function, that is to say, he decides according to the facts and the law only, and not according to policy. It was for discretionary decisions based on policy that the term 'quasi-judicial' was introduced, so that the principles of natural justice might be applied to them so far as practicable. The House of Lords therefore unsettled the 'basic English' of administrative law, in a manner all too characteristic of that period. Forty years later, however, it can be said that the decision has been paid little more than lip-service. The need to set higher standards for inquiry procedure has been recognised by the reforms made under the Tribunals and Inquiries Act and

---

[15] *CREEDNZ* v. *Governor-General* [1981] 1 NZLR 173, where a complaint of predetermination by ministers was likewise unsuccessful. The reasoning is much superior to that in the *Franklin* case.

[16] See above, p. 47, below, p. 504.

in accordance with the Franks Committee's recommendations, so that ministers' decisions now provoke less litigation. The House of Lords has also taken a much more extensive view of what is meant by judicial and quasi-judicial functions,[17] and it is once again quite clear that the principles of natural justice apply to administrative acts generally.[18]

EFFECTS OF PREJUDICE

Void or voidable?

In the case of Lord Cottenham's judgment, cited at the outset of this discussion,[19] the judges advised the House of Lords that the disqualifying interest made the judgment not void but voidable.[20] This has sometimes been repeated as if it were true of administrative cases involving bias, thus producing the concept of a voidable administrative act, already criticised. But Lord Cottenham's case had nothing to do with administrative powers. His judgment was given in the Court of Chancery, one of the superior courts of law, and it would naturally be valid unless and until reversed on appeal. It could therefore correctly be described as voidable as opposed to being void from the beginning.

But where an administrative act or decision is subject to judicial review, as opposed to appeal, the court can intervene on two grounds only: ultra vires, and error on the face of the record. Since bias will not appear on the face of the record, the court necessarily intervenes on the basis that the vitiated act is ultra vires, i.e. wholly unauthorised by law and thus void. There is no valid analogy with an appeal from a court of law. Judgments dealing with administrative decisions therefore proceed on the footing that the presence of bias means that the tribunal is improperly constituted, so that it has no power to determine the case; and accordingly its decision must be void and a nullity.[21] Thus the reviewing court's jurisdiction fits correctly into the framework of the ultra vires principle, whereas the notion of a voidable decision does not. A long line of judges of high

---

[17] For this see below, p. 518.

[18] This statement was approved by Lord Edmund-Davies in *Bushell* v. *Secretary of State for the Environment* [1981] AC 75 at 116.

[19] Above, p. 473.

[20] *Dimes* v. *Grand Junction Canal* (1852) 3 HLC 759 at 785. Parke B. added a dictum about decisions of magistrates, but the authorities he cited did not support him: see (1968) 84 LQR at p. 108.

[21] For fuller discussion see (1968) 84 LQR at p. 104. For other aspects of 'void or voidable' see above, p. 348; below, p. 526.

authority have agreed with Lord Esher's observation that the participation of a disqualified person 'certainly rendered the decision wholly void'.[22]

This analysis is corroborated by the nature of the remedies which the courts have granted. In a police discipline case, already mentioned, the Court of Appeal granted a declaration that the officer's dismissal was a nullity.[23] But a declaratory judgment is a useless remedy where the decision is merely voidable, as has been seen already in the case of mere error on the face of the record:[24] merely to declare that a decision is voidable achieves nothing. But if it is void and a nullity, a declaration as to this is effective. Secondly there is the practice, traditional in liquor licensing cases, of sending cases back to the licensing authority by mandamus unaccompanied by certiorari:[25] this makes sense only on the footing that the initial decision was a nullity and can be ignored; yet it applies as much in cases of bias as in others.[26] Thirdly, the court will quash for bias even where there is a statutory 'no certiorari' clause;[27] but such a clause can be ignored only where the decision is ultra vires and void.[28] Fourthly, it is a well-established corollary of the principle of ultra vires that evidence outside the record can be received only to show want of jurisdiction.[29] Since bias will of course not appear on the record, it can be proved only on the hypothesis that it destroys jurisdiction altogether. Fifthly, failure to give a fair hearing undoubtedly goes to jurisdiction,[30] and it would be anomalous if the same were not true of bias.

The logic of the situation is in no way weakened by the fact that the right to object on the ground of bias can be waived in the manner already mentioned.[31] This has sometimes been supposed to show that bias must

---

[22] *Allinson* v. *General Medical Council* [1894] 1 QB 750. In agreement are *R.* v. *Cheltenham Commissioners* (1841) 1 QB 467 (decision 'invalid' despite no certiorari clause, therefore ultra vires); *R.* v. *Nat Bell Liquors Ltd.* [1922] 2 AC 128 at 160 ('without jurisdiction'); *Cooper* v. *Wilson* [1937] 2 KB 309 at 344 ('a nullity'); *R.* v. *Paddington & c. Rent Tribunal ex p. Kendal Hotels Ltd.* [1947] 1 All ER 148; *R.* v. *Paddington & c. Rent Tribunal ex p. Perry* [1956] 1 QB 229 at 237 ('no jurisdiction'); and see *Vassiliades* v. *Vassilaides* [1945] AIR 38 (Privy Council); *Ladies of the Sacred Heart of Jesus* v. *Armstrong's Point Association* (1961) 29 DLR (2d) 373; *Oscroft* v. *Benabo* [1967] 1 WLR 1087 at 1100; *Anisminic Ltd.* v. *Foreign Compensation Commission* [1969] 2 AC 147 at 171.
[23] *Cooper* v. *Wilson* [1937] 2 KB 309; above, p. 477.
[24] See above, p. 310; below, p. 601.
[25] See below, p. 658.
[26] *R.* v. *London County Council ex p. Akkersdyk* [1892] 1 QB 190.
[27] *R.* v. *Cheltenham Commissioners* (1841) 1 QB 467; *R.* v. *Hertfordshire Justices* (1845) 6 QB 753.
[28] See below, p. 722.
[29] *R.* v. *Nat Bell Liquors Ltd.* [1922] 2 AC 128 at 160; above, p. 321.
[30] Below, p. 526.
[31] Above, p. 482.

render the decision voidable only.[32] But this follows only if 'void' is given the absolute meaning criticised earlier and not the relative meaning which it ought to bear. Waiver is only one of many factors which may induce the court to refuse relief:[33] it may do so in its discretion for many reasons, however void the decision in question, and then the decision must be accepted as valid. Channell J once observed that the right to object on the ground of bias could be lost by waiver 'no matter whether the proceedings . . . are void or voidable'.[34] That question is merely irrelevant. Furthermore, there is no reason why the rule of law which says that a biased decision is void should not itself contain the qualification that it operates only if the right to object is not waived.[35]

[32] See Rubinstein, *Jurisdiction and Illegality*, 221; (1926) 42 LQR 523 (D. M. Gordon).
[33] As explained above, p. 352. See (1968) 84 LQR at 109 (Wade).
[34] *R. v. Williams ex p. Phillips* [1914] 1 KB 608.
[35] See above, p. 264 (waiver and jurisdiction).

15

THE RIGHT TO A FAIR HEARING

AUDI ALTERAM PARTEM

'Hear the other side'

It is fundamental to fair procedure that both sides should be heard: audi alteram partem, 'hear the other side'. This is the more far-reaching of the principles of natural justice, since it can embrace almost every question of fair procedure, or due process, and its implications can be worked out in great detail. It is also broad enough to include the rule against bias, since a fair hearing must be an unbiased hearing; but in deference to the traditional dichotomy, that rule has already been treated separately.

How far can this obvious principle of justice be transplanted from its native judicial soil into the territory of administration? Can the courts impose an administrative technique of their own devising by laying down standards, and are there any standards of universal validity? The answer is that the courts have succeeded in enforcing the principle very widely, broadly speaking in all cases where legal rights or status are affected by the exercise of administrative power, saving only cases where the difficulty is insuperable; and that, accordingly, natural justice has become a doctrine with a high degree of universality. It does not follow that it need be modelled strictly on court procedure: hearings need not always be oral hearings, nor need sources of evidence always be disclosed. But in general the notion of a fair hearing extends to the right to have notice of the other side's case, the right to bring evidence and the right to argue.

The right to a fair hearing has thus been used by the courts as a base on which to build a kind of code of fair administrative procedure, comparable to 'due process of law' under the Constitution of the United States. As already mentioned, there has been an outburst of such activity since 1963, when the landmark decision of the House of Lords in *Ridge* v. *Baldwin* put an end to a period of judicial backsliding. Parliament also has made many provisions for tribunals and inquiries, and, particularly since 1957, for improving these statutory procedures. These, though dealt with in separate chapters, should be viewed together with the principles of natural justice as parts of a comprehensive design for ensuring that power is exercised considerately and fairly.

As the authorities will show, the courts took their stand several centuries ago on the broad principle that bodies entrusted with legal power could not validly exercise it without first hearing the person who was going to suffer. This principle was applied very widely to administrative as well as to judicial acts, and to the acts of individual ministers and officials as well as to the acts of collective bodies such as justices and committees. The hypothesis on which the courts built up their jurisdiction was that the duty to give every victim a fair hearing was just as much a canon of good administration as of good legal procedure. Even where an order or determination is unchallengeable as regards its substance, the court can at least control the preliminary procedure so as to require fair consideration of both sides of the case. Nothing is more likely to conduce to good administration.

Since the courts have been enforcing this rule for centuries, and since it is self-evidently desirable, it might be thought that no trained professional, whether judge or administrator, would be likely to overlook it. But the stream of cases that come before British and Commonwealth courts shows that overlooking it is one of the most common legal errors to which human nature is prone. When a Lord Chief Justice,[1] an Archbishop of Canterbury,[2] and a three-judge Court of Appeal[3] have strayed from the path of rectitude, it is not surprising that it is one of the more frequent mistakes of ordinary mortals. The courts themselves must take some of the blame, for they have wavered in their decisions, particularly in the period of about fifteen years which preceded *Ridge* v. *Baldwin*.

International analogies

Under the European Convention on Human Rights and Fundamental Freedoms of 1950,[4] which is binding on the United Kingdom as a treaty and under which individuals can take proceedings before the European Commission of Human Rights, it is provided that

In the determination of his civil rights and obligations or of any criminal charge

---

[1] *Abraham* v. *Jutsun* [1963] 1 WLR 658 (Divisional Court ordered solicitor to pay costs without hearing him in his defence; order set aside by Court of Appeal as made per incuriam). See also *R.* v. *Smith* [1974] QB 531. An attempt to convict Lord Macnaghten of a breach of the rule against bias was unsuccessful: *R.* v. *Antrim Justices* [1895] 2 IR 603. But Sir William Scott, the future Lord Stowell, excommunicated an ecclesiastical offender without a hearing and was liable in damages: *Beaurain* v. *Scott* (1813) 3 Camp. 388.

[2] *R.* v. *Archbishop of Canterbury* (1859) 1 E & E 545 (Archbishop dismissed curate's appeal on consideration of his written petition of appeal only; mandamus granted).

[3] *B.* v. *W.* [1979] 1 WLR 1041 (court acted on document not disclosed to appellant). In *Hadmor Productions Ltd.* v. *Hamilton* [1983] 1 AC 191 Lord Diplock accused Lord Denning MR of violating natural justice by relying upon a speech in a debate in the House of Lords without first informing counsel. But in *Mahon* v. *Air New Zealand* [1984] AC 808 at 838 he spoke tolerantly of such judicial lapses.

[4] Cmd. 8969 (1953).

against him, everyone is entitled to a fair and public hearing within a reasonable time by an independent and impartial tribunal established by law.[5]

Although 'civil rights and obligations' may have a technical meaning which will not include administrative matters generally,[6] the European Court of Human Rights has held that these words include rights determined by an independent administrative commission.[7] It therefore seems that the right to a hearing under the European Convention may have at least some operation in the sphere of administrative law, although the requirement of a public hearing suggests that it is limited to decisions of the more formal kind.

Although the European Convention is in the form of a treaty only, and therefore not law which the courts can enforce,[8] the courts have taken it into account in several cases as an aid to interpretation of statutes or statutory rules. In one case Lord Reid said that it was hardly credible that Parliament or any government department would act contrary to it.[9] In the Court of Appeal it has several times been held that regard ought to be had to the Convention in cases where it is relevant.[10] Furthermore, the Court of Justice of the European Communities in Luxembourg takes account of the European Convention, of which all twelve EEC countries are members, as a source of law;[11] and the decisions of the Court of Justice are binding in the United Kingdom under the European Communities Act 1972. The fundamental rights declared by the Convention are therefore important in English law for two reasons: the courts themselves will have regard to them; and they may enter our law via Luxembourg.[12] It is already

---

[5] Article 6(1). See similarly Universal Declaration of Human Rights (United Nations, 1948), Article 10; [1967] PL 274 (F. C. Newman).

[6] See [1984] PL 89 (A. Boyle). And see the *Agee* case as related in [1977] 1 WLR 766 at 779.

[7] *Ringeisen* v. *Austria* (No. 1) (1971) 1 EHRR 455, holding that Article 6(1) applied to an Austrian Regional Real Property Transactions Commission's refusal to approve a contract of sale of land. See also *König* v. *Federal Republic of Germany* (1978) 2 EHRR 170; *Kaplan* v. *United Kingdom* (1980) 4 EHRR 64, where the Commission decided that Article 6(1) did not apply to the imposition of restrictions on an insurance company by the Secretary of State for Trade. But in *Pudas* v. *Sweden* and *Boden* v. *Sweden* [1987] ECHR Series A, vol. 125 (judgments of 27 October) the Court held that article applicable to the revocation of a taxi traffic licence and to an expropriation of land, neither of which was challengeable in the ordinary or administrative courts of Sweden, and awarded damages in the former case. See also [1987] PL 3 (A. W. Bradley).

[8] See *R.* v. *Home Secretary ex p. Kirkwood* [1984] 1 WLR 913.

[9] *R.* v. *Miah* [1974] 1 WLR 683 at 694.

[10] *R.* v. *Home Secretary ex p. Bhajan Singh* [1976] QB 198, referring to *Birdi* v. *Home Secretary* [1975], unreported; *R.* v. *Home Secretary ex p. Phansopkar* [1976] QB 606 (Scarman LJ, referring to *R.* v. *Home Secretary ex p. Singh* [1975], unreported); *R.* v. *Heathrow Airport Immigration Officer ex p. Bibi* [1976] 1 WLR 979.

[11] *Nold (Firma J)* v. *EC Commission* [1974] 2 CMLR 338 at 354.

[12] See (1980) 29 ICLQ 585 (P. J. Duffy). In Scotland both these reasons are rejected and account is not taken of the Convention: *Kaur* v. *Lord Advocate* 1981 SLT 322.

established that EEC law recognises 'the general rule that a person whose interests are perceptibly affected by a decision taken by a public authority must be given the opportunity to make his point of view known'; so that a condition imposed by the EEC Commission without affording a fair hearing will be annulled by the Court of Justice.[13]

The Canadian Bill of Rights of 1960 provides that in the absence of express provision to the contrary no law of Canada shall be construed or applied so as to deprive a person of the right to a fair hearing in accordance with the fundamental principles of justice for the determination of his rights and obligations.[14] In addition the Canadian Charter of Rights and Freedoms of 1982[15] confers the right not to be deprived of life, liberty, and security of the person except in accordance with the principles of fundamental justice. The Bill of Rights of 1960 remains in force and in the new constitutional climate is being interpreted more liberally than previously.[16] In the Constitution of the United States of America the fifth and fourteenth amendments, under which a person may not be deprived of life, liberty, or property without due process of law, confer a right to a fair hearing in many cases as an essential element in due process.[17]

An ancient rule

According to one picturesque judicial dictum, the first hearing in human history was given in the Garden of Eden:[18]

I remember to have heard it observed by a very learned man upon such an occasion, that even God himself did not pass sentence upon Adam, before he was called upon to make his defence. 'Adam, says God, where art thou? Hast thou not eaten of the tree, whereof I commanded thee that thou shouldst not eat?' And the same question was put to Eve also.

This was in *Bentley's* case, in which the University of Cambridge had deprived that recalcitrant scholar of his degrees on account of his misconduct in insulting the Vice-Chancellor's court; but he was reinstated on a mandamus from the Court of the King's Bench, on the ground that deprivation was unjustifiable and that, in any case, he should have received notice so that he could make his defence, as required by 'the laws of God

---

[13] *Transocean Marine Paint Association* v. *EC Commission* [1974] 2 CMLR 459 at 477. See particularly the opinion of Warner AG at 470–1.

[14] s. 2(e).

[15] s. 7, enacted as part of the Constitution Act 1982 by the Canada Act 1982.

[16] See *Re Singh and Minister of Employment and Immigration* (1985) 17 DLR (4th) 422. Contrast *Guay* v. *Lafleur* (1964) 47 DLR (2d) 226. There are also provincial bills of rights.

[17] Schwartz, Administrative Law, 2nd edn., 202.

[18] *R.* v. *University of Cambridge* (1723) 1 Str. 557 (Fortescue J).

and man'. This is a nice example of the old conception of natural justice as divine and eternal law.[19]

A century previously the same doctrine had made an appearance in an equally notorious case of contumacy, where a freeman of the borough of Plymouth had threatened and scandalised the mayor and was disfranchised. It was similarly held that the penalty was unjustified, in the absence of any special power of disfranchisement; and that even if there had been such a power, the removal would be void because it was not shown that a hearing had first been given.[20] In this case also the remedy was a mandamus for restoration. Coke's report quotes from Seneca:[21]

quicunque aliquid statuerit parte inaudita altera, aequum licet statuerit, haud aequus fuerit.

This contains the same message as does the law about bias, that where natural justice is violated it is no justification that the decision was in fact correct.[22]

The early decisions mainly concerned restoration to offices.[23] Justices of the peace, who were in those times the principal administrative authorities, were so habituated to formal hearings that they do not seem to have offended in this respect. In the first half of the nineteenth century natural justice began to affect ecclessiastical affairs. The Court of Exchequer gave a notable decision in a case where a bishop had appointed a curate, at the vicar's expense, to perform the duties of the vicar whom the bishop considered to be negligent. Statute empowered this to be done 'whenever it shall appear to the satisfaction of any bishop, either of his own knowledge, or upon proof by affidavit laid before him', that the incumbent was neglecting his duties. The bishop, acting on his own knowledge, did not call on the vicar to make any defence; and for this reason the court held the whole process to be void.[24] Whether the bishop proceeded on his own knowledge or on affidavit evidence was immaterial: in either case the exercise of his drastic power required that

---

[19] See above, p. 469.

[20] *Bagg's Case* (1615) 11 Co. Rep. 93b. The most celebrated of his misdeeds was that he 'turning the hinder part of his body in an inhuman and uncivil manner towards the aforesaid Thomas Fowens, scoffingly, contemptuously, and uncivilly, with a loud voice, said to the aforesaid Thomas Fowens, these words following, that is to say, "Come and kiss".'

[21] *Medea* 199–200, cited also in *Boswell's Case* (1606) 6 Co. Rep. 48b at 52a; *R. v. University of Cambridge* (1723) 1 Str. 557 at 561; *R. v. Archbishop of Canterbury* (1859) 1 E & E 545; Bl. Comm. ix. 283.

[22] Seneca's sentiment is exactly reproduced in *Earl* v. *Slater & Wheeler (Airlyne) Ltd.* [1973] 1 WLR 51 (dismissal without hearing held intrinsically unfair, even though fully justified).

[23] Examples are *Protector* v. *Colchester* (1655) Style 452; *Campion's Case* (1658) 2 Sid. 97.

[24] *Capel* v. *Child* (1832) 2 C & J 558. See also *Bonaker* v. *Evans* (1850) 16 QB 162; *R. v. North ex p. Oakey* [1927] 1 KB 491.

the vicar should be given the opportunity to answer the charges made against him. Bayley B said:

When the bishop proceeds on his own knowledge I am of the opinion also that it cannot possibly, and within the meaning of this Act, appear to the satisfaction of the bishop, and of his knowledge, unless he gives the party an opportunity of being heard, in answer to that which the bishop states on his own knowledge to be the foundation on which he proceeds.

It was already clear from decisions of this kind that the courts would apply the principle of natural justice to cases of an administrative character. They did so no less vigorously, as will soon appear, when the modern statutory authorities, equipped with new powers of many kinds, began to proliferate as the nineteenth century progressed. The same principle was extended beyond the sphere of administrative law, to such bodies as societies and clubs. It was held to be an implied term of each member's contract of membership that he could not be expelled without a fair hearing.[25] In a case where a member of a mutual insurance society was purportedly expelled for suspicious conduct, but without a hearing, it was held that the expulsion was absolutely void, so that he was still a member in law; and it was said:[26]

This rule is not confined to the conduct of strictly legal tribunals, but is applicable to every tribunal or body of persons invested with authority to adjudicate upon matters involving civil consequences to individuals.

Subsequently this doctrine found a fruitful field of application in protecting members and officers of trade unions from unfair expulsion or other penalties.[27] Here likewise the basis for natural justice was an implied term in the contract of membership. Denning LJ said of trade union committees:[28]

These bodies, however, which exercise a monopoly in an important sphere of human activity, with the power of depriving a man of his livelihood, must act in accordance with the elementary rules of justice. They must not condemn a man without giving him an opportunity to be heard in his own defence: and any agreement or practice to the contrary would be invalid.

---

[25] *Dawkins* v. *Antrobus* (1881) 17 Ch D 615; *Fisher* v. *Keane* (1878) 11 Ch D 853.

[26] *Wood* v. *Woad* (1874) LR 9 Ex. 190 (Kelly CB). And see *Byrne* v. *Kinematograph Renters Society Ltd.* [1958] 1 WLR 762.

[27] As in *Burn* v. *National Amalgamated Labourers' Union* [1920] 2 Ch. 364; *Abbott* v. *Sullivan* [1952] 1 KB 189 (the dissenting judgment of Denning LJ best represents the law as it stands today); *Lee* v. *Showmen's Guild* [1952] QB 329; *Annamunthodo* v. *Oilfield Workers' Trade Union* [1961] AC 945; *Lawlor* v. *Union of Post Office Workers* [1965] Ch. 712; *Leary* v. *National Union of Vehicle Builders* [1971] Ch. 34; *Edwards* v. *SOGAT* [1971] Ch. 354; *Stevenson* v. *United Road Transport Union* [1976] 3 All ER 29.

[28] *Abbott* v. *Sullivan* (above) at p. 198.

That the last ten words represent the law has now been decided definitely.[29] This extension of the general law was made the pretext for repealing the statutory requirement that trade union rules should specify the procedure for the hearing of any case in which offences against the rules were alleged and should conform to the rules of natural justice.[30]

How far the same rules apply in university disciplinary proceedings is discussed below.[31]

ADMINISTRATIVE CASES

A classic example

The numerous new administrative authorities, both local and central, which came into being in the nineteenth and twentieth centuries opened up a large new territory for the principles of natural justice. The courts saw no reason for permitting these new authorities to adopt any less fair procedure than had previously been allowed to the justices of the peace. The character of the authority was not what mattered: what mattered was the character of the power exercised. If it adversely affected legal rights or interests, it must be exercised fairly.

One case of 1863 is especially noteworthy, both because it stated the law in short judgments of great clarity, and also because it has played an important part in the recent revival of the right to be heard: *Cooper* v. *Wandsworth Board of Works*.[32] Under an Act of 1855 it was provided that no one might put up a building in London without giving seven days' notice to the local board of works; and that if any one did so, the board might have the building demolished. A builder nevertheless began to erect a house in Wandsworth without having given due notice and when his building had reached the second storey the board of works sent men late in the evening who demolished it. The board did exactly what the Act said they might do in exactly the circumstances in which the Act said they might do it. And

---

[29] *Edwards* v. *SOGAT* (above); *Enderby Town Football Club* v. *Football Association* [1971] Ch. 591 at 606. Contrast *Russell* v. *Duke of Norfolk* [1949] 1 All ER 109, where Denning LJ dissented on this point. A rule which unreasonably prevents a person from joining a trade union, even where it has a monopoly of the trade, is not contrary to natural justice: *Faramus* v. *Film Artistes' Association* [1964] AC 925.

[30] Trade Union and Labour Relations (Amendment) Act 1976, repealing Trade Union and Labour Relations Act 1974, s. 6(11), (13), which had repealed Industrial Relations Act, 1971, s. 65(8), requiring 'a full and fair hearing'.

[31] p. 568.

[32] (1863) 14 CB (NS) 180; approved in *Ridge* v. *Baldwin* [1964] AC 40; *Durayappah* v. *Fernando* [1967] 2 AC 337; *Wiseman* v. *Borneman* [1971] AC 297.

their action was, of course, purely administrative. Nevertheless, the builder brought a successful action for damages for the injury to his building, merely on the ground that the board had no power to act without first asking him what he had to say for himself. Erle CJ said:

I think the board ought to have given notice to the plaintiff and to have allowed him to be heard. The default in sending notice to the board of the intention to build, is a default which may be explained. There may be a great many excuses for the apparent default. The party may have intended to conform to the law. He may have actually conformed . . . though by accident his notice may have miscarried. . . . I cannot conceive any harm that could happen to the district board from hearing the party before they subjected him to a loss so serious as the demolition of his house; but I can conceive a great many advantages which might arise in the way of public order, in the way of doing substantial justice, and in the way of fulfilling the purposes of the statute, by the restriction which we put upon them, that they should hear the party before they inflict upon him such a heavy loss. I fully agree that the legislature intended to give the district board very large powers indeed: but the qualification I speak of is one which has been recognised to the full extent. It has been said that the principle . . . is limited to a judicial proceeding, and that a district board ordering a house to be pulled down cannot be said to be doing a judicial act. . . . I do not quite agree with that; . . . I think the appeal clause would evidently indicate that many exercises of the power of a district board would be in the nature of judicial proceedings.

Two of the other judgments in this case are important. Willes J said:

I am of the same opinion. I apprehend that a tribunal which is by law invested with power to affect the property of one of Her Majesty's subjects, is bound to give such subject an opportunity of being heard before it proceeds: and that the rule is of universal application, and founded on the plainest principles of justice. Now, is the board in the present case such a tribunal? I apprehend it clearly is. . . .

And Byles J also said:

It seems to me that the board are wrong whether they acted judicially or ministerially. I conceive they acted judicially, because they had to determine the offence, and they had to apportion the punishment as well as the remedy. That being so, a long course of decisions beginning with Dr. Bentley's case, and ending with some very recent cases, establish that, although there are no positive words in a statute, requiring that the party shall be heard, yet the justice of the common law will supply the omission of the legislature.

These last two quotations bring out clearly two especially important aspects: the universality of the principle, which make it applicable to almost the whole range of administrative powers; and the presumption that it will always apply, however, silent about it the statute may be.

How wide its application was to be is illustrated by many later decisions.

Whether the case concerned the cancellation of a Crown lease in Queensland,[33] the condemnation of a house in Manchester as unfit for human habitation,[34] the compulsory transfer of indentured labour in Trinidad,[35] or the refusal of a pension to a Canadian police officer obliged to resign,[36] the court uniformly insisted that the power could be validly exercised only after a fair hearing of the party adversely affected. In the Manchester case Lord Parker said in the House of Lords:

> The question then arises as to whether the power entrusted to the corporation is purely administrative or is a judicial power. On this point I have had considerable doubt, because there is no provision in the Act for hearing any party interested, or for receiving evidence, nor is there any provision for an appeal. But inasmuch as the order of the corporation under the section entails a penalty on persons who disregard it, I think, on the whole, that the corporation's power is in the nature of a judicial power and that consequently any party interested has a right to be heard, and, if he desires it, to adduce evidence, and in case the power is abused he could protect himself by certiorari or injunction.

Had *Cooper* v. *Wandsworth Board of Works* been cited, the doubts here expressed would have been removed. But, as will be seen, that case was forgotten and doubts increased until the law temporarily lost its confidence in its own principle.

'Judicial' and 'quasi-judicial' acts

The above quotations show very clearly how the courts justified their interventions. They held that every judicial act is subject to the procedure required by natural justice; and they then denominated the great majority of administrative acts as 'judicial' for this purpose. Instead of saying, as was in fact the truth, that natural justice must be observed in both judicial and administrative acts, the courts stretched the meaning of 'judicial' in an unnatural way. Another graphic example is a statement by Willis J in a case which in essentials was the same as *Cooper* v. *Wandsworth Board of Works*:

> In condemning a man to have his house pulled down, a judicial act is as much implied as in fining him £5; and as the local board is the only tribunal that can make such an order its act must be a judicial act, and the party to be affected should

---

[33] *Smith* v. *R.* (1878) 3 App. Cas. 614 (power to cancel in case of non-residence or abandonment: held, 'a judicial function').

[34] *Hall* v. *Manchester Cpn.* (1915) 84 LJ Ch. 732.

[35] *De Verteuil* v. *Knaggs* [1918] AC 557.

[36] *Lapointe* v. *L'Association de Bienfaisance et de Retraite de la Police de Montreal* [1906] AC 535.

have a notice given him. . . . in the present case there is nothing in the Act of Parliament to limit the natural inference as to the nature of the act.[37]

Every administrative act was thus treated as 'judicial' if it adversely affected any person's rights or, as Lord Parker put it, entailed a penalty.[38] Exactly the same abuse of language was adopted in requiring a 'duty to act judicially' as a condition of the availability of the remedies of certiorari and prohibition; and to this an unprofitable discussion must be devoted elsewhere.[39] When in time the courts came to forget the paradoxical sense which they had invented for 'judicial', they found themselves in difficulty. There seemed to be nothing but a circular argument: natural justice must be observed when the function is judicial; and the function is called judicial when natural justice ought to be observed. If every power affecting some person's rights is called 'judicial', there is virtually no meaning left for 'administrative'.

The term 'quasi-judicial' accordingly came into vogue, as an epithet for powers which, though administrative, were required to be exercised as if they were judicial, i.e. in accordance with natural justice.[40] This at least was less of a misnomer than 'judicial', and made it easier for the courts to continue the work of developing their system of fair administrative procedure. 'Quasi-judicial' was the subject of a classic discussion and definition by the Committee on Ministers' Powers,[41] who emphasised that a judicial decision consists of finding facts and applying law whereas a quasi-judicial decision consists of finding facts and applying administrative policy.[42] The latter term was much used in the housing cases, related below.

[37] *Hopkins* v. *Smethwick Local Board of Health* (1890) 24 QBD 713. See similarly *Masters* v. *Pontypool Local Government Board* (1878) 9 Ch D 677. One of the many examples is *R.* v. *London County Council ex p. Commercial Gas Company* (1895) 11 TLR 337 (report of gas examiner held 'a judicial proceeding' and quashed for failure to grant hearing).

[38] See the discussion in *Barnard* v. *National Dock Labour Board* [1953] 2 QB 18 and *Vine* v. *National Dock Labour Board* [1957] AC 488, where the removal of a dock worker from the register was held to be a judicial act, though described also as quasi-judicial.

[39] Below, p. 630, explaining that here also the duty to act 'judicially' is merely a consequence of a power to affect a person's rights, so that it arises in administrative cases generally. But it was not until Lord Reid unravelled the confusion in *Ridge* v. *Baldwin* [1964] AC 40 that this became clear.

[40] An early example of its use is in *Mersey Docks Trustees* v. *Gibbs* (1866) LR 1 HL 93 at 110.

[41] Cmd. 4060 (1932), p. 73. See above, p. 46.

[42] But judges may use the term in other senses, saying for example that a social security commissioner, who finds facts and applies law, is quasi-judicial (below, p. 900) or that an inspector at a public inquiry, who must obey the rules of natural justice, has no quasi-judicial duty (below, p. 524). A common misconception is to regard a quasi-judicial function as an inferior form of judicial function rather than as a superior form of administrative function. Judges are prone to bracket 'judicial and quasi-judicial' together and contrast them with 'administrative', without appreciating that 'quasi-judicial' means 'administrative' (see again below, p. 524).

Its utility is illustrated by a case in which the Oxford City Council had demolished two walls which a housing company had built across roads on their land. The action was held illegal on the ground (amongst others) that the company had not been given an opportunity of endeavouring to dissuade the council from this drastic step.[43] The Master of the Rolls referred to 'that most salutary principle' which laid down

that a local authority exercising such a power of demolition as this, in coming to its decision to demolish, is acting in a quasi-judicial capacity and must give the person concerned either a notice that they intend to take this matter into their consideration with a view to coming to a decision, or, if they have come to a decision, that they propose to act upon it, and give him an opportunity of showing cause why such steps should not be taken.

'Quasi-judicial' was thus being used in precisely the same sense as 'judicial' in the earlier cases.

Lord Loreburn's epitome

Of all the classical expositions of the general principle, the most frequently quoted has been from a speech of Lord Loreburn in the House of Lords in 1911. The House had to decide whether the Board of Education had properly determined a dispute between a body of school managers and the local education authority of Swansea. The local authority had refused to pay teachers in church schools at the same rate as teachers in the authority's own schools. Teachers gave notice to leave, and the managers complained that the local authority were failing to keep the schools efficient, as the Education Act required. A public inquiry was held before a barrister who made a report in favour of the managers, but the Board of Education decided in favour of the local authority. The House of Lords upheld the award of certiorari and mandamus to quash this decision and to order a proper determination of the dispute; for the Board had not dealt with the question which arose under the Act, which was whether they could legitimately discriminate between the two classes of schools.[44] But the Lord Chancellor, Lord Loreburn, spoke about the Board's duties in general terms:

Comparatively recent statutes have extended, if they have not originated, the practice of imposing upon departments or officers of State the duty of deciding or determining questions of various kinds. In the present instance, as in many others, what comes for determination is a matter to be settled by discretion, involving no

---

[43] *Urban Housing Co. Ltd.* v. *Oxford City Council* [1940] Ch. 70. The story behind this case is told in Collison, *The Cutteslowe Walls*. cf. *Quirindi Shire Council* v. *Gigli* [1985] 3 NSWLR 178 (entry by local authority to construct sewers unlawful without fair hearing).

[44] *Board of Education* v. *Rice* [1911] AC 179.

law. It will, I suppose, usually be of an administrative kind; but sometimes it will involve matter of law as well as matter of fact, or even depend upon matter of law alone. In such cases the Board of Education will have to ascertain the law and also to ascertain the facts. I need not add that in doing either they must act in good faith and listen fairly to both sides, for that is a duty lying upon every one who decides anything. But I do not think they are bound to treat such a question as though it were a trial. They have no power to administer an oath, and need not examine witnesses. They can obtain information in any way they think best, always giving a fair opportunity to those who are parties in the controversy for correcting or contradicting anything prejudicial to their view.

Although the case itself involved no breach of natural justice, Lord Loreburn's epitome of the general principle was so apt that it has been quoted with approval again and again.[45] Experience has shown that there are remarkably few true exceptions to this 'duty lying upon every one who decides anything,' at any rate anything which may adversely affect legal rights or liberties. At the same time the passage acknowledges, though not with complete accuracy,[46] the practical limitations which the administrative character of a power may impose. Practical limitations were in fact about to present the courts with some difficult dilemmas as new forms of statutory administrative procedure came into use.

STATUTORY HEARINGS

Statutory inquiries and hearings: the Arlidge case

With the extension of central government powers, particularly in the areas of health and housing, more and more use was made of the statutory procedure of the public local inquiry which the government department was either empowered or obliged to hold for the purpose of considering objections. The question then arose, how should the principles of natural justice interlock within these statutory procedures? In one sense, the court is concerned merely with statutory interpretation, in ascertaining what is meant by an 'inquiry' within the meaning of the Act and by the other steps prescribed. But, since Parliament is always presumed to intend that natural justice shall be observed, natural justice is the best guide to a true interpretation.

The House of Lords took an important stand in 1914 in *Local Government*

---

[45] The central part is also reproduced almost verbatim by Lord Denning MR in *Re Pergamon Press* [1971] Ch. 388 at 399–400.

[46] In *General Medical Council* v. *Spackman* [1943] AC 627 at 638 Lord Atkin pointed out that the Evidence Act 1851 gave power to administer oaths, and that witnesses tendered ought to be examined in many cases. On these questions see below, pp. 544, 927, 987.

Board v. *Arlidge*.[47] A public inquiry had been held on an appeal to the Local Government Board by the owner of a house against which the Hampstead Borough Council had made a closing order on the ground that it was unfit for human habitation. The owner complained to the court that the Board had dismissed his appeal without a fair hearing because he was not allowed to appear before the officer who made the decision or to see the report of the inspector who held the inquiry. That report was, of course, the principal document in the proceedings. These complaints succeeded in the Court of Appeal but failed in the House of Lords. The judges all agreed that the general importance of the case 'can scarcely be overestimated'. Where they differed was in their willingness to compromise between the procedure of courts of law and the needs of practical administration. The argument that prevailed was that by entrusting the power to a government department, Parliament must have intended that the department should act in its normal manner, and should therefore be able to take its decision without making public its papers and without having to conduct itself like a court of law. Lord Haldane, then Lord Chancellor but previously a minister with wide experience, said:

My Lords, when the duty of deciding an appeal is imposed, those whose duty it is to decide it must act judicially. They must deal with the question referred to them without bias, and they must give to each of the parties the opportunity of adequately presenting the case made. The decision must be come to in the spirit and with the sense of responsibility of a tribunal whose duty it is to mete out justice. But it does not follow that the procedure of every such tribunal must be the same. . . . The Minister at the head of the Board is directly responsible to Parliament like other ministers. The volume of work entrusted to him is very great. . . . Unlike a judge in a court, he is not only at liberty but is compelled to rely on the assistance of his staff. When, therefore, the Board is directed to dispose of an appeal, that does not mean that any particular official of the Board is to dispose of it. . . . It is said that the report of the inspector should have been disclosed. It might or might not have been useful to disclose this report, but I do not think the Board was bound to do so, any more than it would have been bound to disclose all the minutes made on the papers in the office before a decision was come to.

In attempting to reconcile the procedure of a government department with the legal standard of natural justice the House of Lords stressed the limits that must be set to the judicialisation of administrative procedure. But they missed an important opportunity in setting their faces against the disclosure of the inspector's report. It took over forty years for this mistake to be corrected, when it finally came to be understood that the supposed analogy between the report and any other departmental papers was misconceived, and in the meantime there was much public dissatisfaction at this unfairness

[47] [1915] AC 120.

in inquiry procedures. Even now the law stands where the House of Lords left it in the *Arlidge* case,[48] and the necessary reforms have been made administratively, following the report of the Franks Committee of 1957, as explained elsewhere.[49] The *Arlidge* case was therefore a turning–point, in which the law failed to keep abreast of the standard of fairness which public opinion demanded, rightly as it turned out, in the procedure of government departments. The law was, indeed, destined to fall still further behind before it returned to its old course in *Ridge* v. *Baldwin* in 1963.

Later refinements

A line of other housing cases dealt with the same dilemma, and particularly with the question how far a government department could retain its normal administrative freedom while at the same time performing its quasi-judicial function of deciding a contested issue. For example, the ministry would frequently be in close touch with the local authority promoting the housing scheme: administratively regarded, the central and local authorities ought to work in collaboration; but legally regarded, the ministry ought to hold the scales evenly between the local authority and the objectors, and not favour one party at the expense of the other. The solution devised by the courts was that the minister's freedom is unfettered up to the point where the scheme is published and objection is lodged. From that point onwards there is an issue, a *lis*, between the local authority and the objectors, and the minister is no longer free to deal with one party without due consideration of the other. It is at this point, therefore, that his quasi-judicial duty begins; and that term was applied to it throughout this series of judgments. It is also clear throughout that both the inspector holding the inquiry and the minister considering whether to confirm the order were held to be performing quasi-judicial functions and required to observe the principles of natural justice, in the light of which the statutory procedure was interpreted.[50]

The leading case is the Court of Appeal's decision on the Jarrow clearance order, *Errington* v. *Minister of Health*.[51] A public inquiry had been

[48] See *Denby (William) & Sons Ltd.* v. *Minister of Health* [1936] 1 KB 337; *Steele* v. *Minister of Housing and Local Government* (1956) 6 P & CR 386.

[49] Below, p. 915.

[50] See particularly *Marriott* v. *Minister of Health* (1935) 52 TLR 63; *Fredman* v. *Minister of Health* (1935) 154 LT 240; *Denby (William) & Sons Ltd.* v. *Minister of Health* [1936] 1 KB 337; *Errington* v. *Minister of Health* (below); *Steele's* case, above.

[51] [1935] 1 KB 249. For later decisions to the same effect see below, p. 539. Contrast *Horn* v. *Minister of Health* [1937] 1 KB 164, where the objectors failed to show that their case had in fact been discussed at a meeting held between the Ministry and the local authority. They failed similarly in *Re Manchester (Ringway Airport) Compulsory Purchase Order* (1935) 153 LT 219, where the inspector had been flown over the site in an aircraft piloted by a witness supporting the scheme, but no prejudicial communication was shown.

held but after receiving the report the ministry made efforts to persuade the Jarrow Corporation to accept a less expensive scheme. The Corporation resisted and asked the minister to receive a deputation. The minister replied that in view of his quasi-judicial function he did not think he ought to receive a deputation representing one side only. But it was arranged that an official of the ministry and also the inspector who had held the inquiry should visit Jarrow and confer with the local authority on the site. After this meeting the Corporation submitted further evidence and argument to the ministry. In the end the minister confirmed the order. But the objectors impugned it, and with success, on the ground that these dealings between the Corporation and the ministry after the public inquiry had been closed were a breach of natural justice. For at that stage issue had been joined, and evidence had been heard, yet the ministry were giving a further hearing to one party behind the back of the other. It was an example of an administrative authority failing to observe the duty enshrined in Lord Loreburn's words: 'They can obtain information in any way they think best, always giving a fair opportunity to those who are parties in the controversy for correcting anything prejudicial to their view.'

In accordance with the doctrine of the *lis*, complainants uniformly failed where they took exception only to events which had happened before their objections were lodged and the *lis* arose. The court refused to set aside orders on the ground that the ministry advised the local authority before they published their proposals,[52] or because the ministry encouraged them to suppose that their order would be likely to be confirmed.[53] Nor did natural justice require that the minister should disclose documents or advice available in his department before issue was joined, and on which his decision was based.[54] As Scott LJ said, the minister's quasi-judicial duties must always be considered in the light of his administrative duties, and Parliament must be taken to have decided deliberately that the two are compatible.[55] But the court vigilantly insisted upon the observance of natural justice once the quasi-judicial stage was reached. A compulsory purchase order for a farm was set aside because the ministry sent the owner's reasoned notice of objection to the local authority but failed to let him see the detailed reply which the local

[52] *Frost* v. *Minister of Health* [1935] 1 KB 286.
[53] *Offer* v. *Minister of Health* [1935] 1 KB 249.
[54] *Miller* v. *Minister of Health* [1946] KB 626; *Price* v. *Minister of Health* [1947] 1 All ER 47; *Summers* v. *Minister of Health* [1947] 1 All ER 184; *B. Johnson & Co. (Builders) Ltd.* v. *Minister of Health* [1947] 2 All ER 395.
[55] *Horn* v. *Minister of Health* [1937] 1 KB 164 at 186.

authority then made.[56] This was under the temporary wartime procedure by which the minister might dispense with a public local inquiry; but that did not eliminate the need for substantial natural justice. Again and again throughout these cases Lord Loreburn's broad statement of the principle was quoted with approval. Later cases where orders have been quashed on account of unfair inquiries are cited below.[57]

The problem of the lis

Although by inventing the principle of the *lis* the courts contrived to infuse a measure of natural justice into the statutory procedure at the point where it was most needed, one must admit that the mixture of administrative and judicial responsibilities makes it difficult for the ministry to fulfil their functions. As soon as an objection is lodged, they must either give up their normal dealings with the local authority, or else they must allow the objectors to intrude into the daily work of the department. This state of semi-paralysis may last for many months, from the first objection to the final decision. Once the inquiry has been held, the ministry cannot refer back to the local authority without reopening the whole operation. What makes the position seem artificial is the idea that the local authority is a party to the dispute, and that the minister is an independent judge. In fact, the two authorities are working—or should be working—hand in glove, one at the local and one at the national level. Both are wielding administrative power, and there is no real difference in the nature of their activities.[58] If the scheme had been promoted by a local office of the ministry, instead of by the local corporation, any amount of subsequent consultation might have taken place and have been passed over as ordinary departmental work. As Lord Greene MR once said: 'It is manifest that, in the operation of hybrid functions of that kind, no perfectly logical result is to be expected.'[59]

The notion of the *lis*, therefore, was not the true key to the problem.[60] It operated merely by reference to time, whereas the need was for a

---

[56] *Stafford* v. *Minister of Health* [1946] KB 621. See similarly *R.* v. *Housing Appeal Tribunal* [1920] 3 KB 334 (tribunal empowered to dispense with hearing; local authority's statement not disclosed to appellant; decision quashed); *R.* v. *Secretary of State for Wales ex p. Green* (1969) 67 LGR 560 (objector led to suppose that inquiry would be held, so made summary objections only; minister's order quashed).

[57] Below, p. 539.

[58] This comment is approved by Lloyd LJ in *R.* v. *Secretary of State for the Environment ex p. Southwark LBC* (1987) 54 P & CR 226.

[59] *B. Johnson & Co. (Builders) Ltd.* v. *Minister of Health* [1947] 2 All ER 395 at 399.

[60] It was criticised by Lord Greene MR in the *Johnson* case (preceding note), where he called it (at p. 403) a 'quasi-lis.'

distinction based on substance. Ultimately this was found in the distinction between evidence of a general character, used by the minister to guide him on policy, and evidence of the facts of the local situation investigated at the inquiry. The former may be obtained and used by the minister as he likes. The latter should be handled only quasi-judicially and in accordance with natural justice. Thus the minister is always free to consult another minister about policy.[61] But evidence about the facts of the particular case, even if obtained from the minister's own experts or from another government department, ought to be disclosed to the objectors, at whatever stage it is obtained. But this more sophisticated solution was not reached in litigation over natural justice.[62] It was reached by reforms of administrative procedure made after the report of the Franks Committee on Tribunals and Enquiries (1957). This latest episode therefore belongs to another chapter,[63] where the same problems of administrative justice are in issue.

The government made a counter-move in the Planning Act of 1947 by obtaining from Parliament an express provision that the minister might, in the case of development plans, consult the local authority or any one else at any stage without any obligation to allow further objections, or to hold any further hearing.[64] This applied only to development plans, and in all other cases the ruling in the *Jarrow* case is still respected.

Schemes originated by the deciding ministry

One particular weakness of the *lis* concept was that it could operate only in a triangular situation, where the minister was regarded (though fallaciously) as a kind of judge between some other public authority and the objector. If the minister was himself the originator of the scheme, the basis of his quasi-judicial duties disappeared—or so it was supposed. The absurdity of the resultant position was brought out in the Kingston by-pass case.[65] This concerned a trunk road, which was the responsibility of the Minister of Transport himself. A compulsory purchase order led to objections and a public inquiry. At the inquiry a ministry official read a statement of the proposals and produced documents and plans; but he called no witnesses, made no attempt to controvert the objections put forward, and declined to answer the objectors' questions about the

---

[61] *Kent CC* v. *Secretary of State for the Environment* (1976) 33 P & CR 70.

[62] But see *Darlassis* v. *Minister of Education* (1954) 52 LGR 304, discussed below, p. 982, where remarks favour the more sophisticated solution.

[63] See below, p. 980.

[64] Town and Country Planning Act 1947, s. 10(3), replaced by Town and Country Planning Act 1971, s. 9(4).

[65] *Re Trunk Roads Act 1936* [1939] 2 KB 515.

necessity for the scheme and the merits of alternative schemes. The court held that this was nevertheless a valid inquiry. The minister was 'in a somewhat peculiar position', being both the author of the scheme and the person behind the inquiry; and as a matter of public interest it was most important that he should give full information to the public and to objectors. But at the inquiry the only object was to hear the objections, not to call for evidence from the ministry. This conclusion made the public inquiry seem farcical. In 1950 a Scottish court refused to follow the Kingston decision in a case concerning the amalgamation of police forces.[66] But there the inquiry had to be held by an independent inspector, and his report had to be laid before Parliament. The need for both sides of the case to be considered was thus self-evident in the public interest, rather than in the objector's interest. Once again, the end of the story belongs to the chapter on inquiries: public opinion would not tolerate the procedure approved by the court in the Kingston case, and eventually it was accepted that elementary justice required an exposition of 'the official case' at any public inquiry.[67]

Into this category, furthermore, fell the ominous decision of the House of Lords on the Stevenage new town case, discussed earlier.[68] The language there used suggested not merely that natural justice had no part to play in a case where the minister was himself the originating authority: it suggested that a minister confirming a scheme after an inquiry had no legal duty other than to follow the procedure prescribed by the Act. The long line of decisions in which natural justice had been used to supplement and reinforce the statutory procedure was entirely ignored. And, in particular, it was said that the minister's function being 'purely administrative' was in no way quasi-judicial—though it was plain also that the House of Lords did not understand the sense in which that term had been used in the many decisions of the previous thirty years.[69] On the same day on which this decision was given, Lord Greene MR in another case[70] had set out with great clarity the well established proposition that a quasi-judicial decision was an administrative decision based on policy but required at some stage to conform to the principles of natural justice, and had quoted the familiar line of authorities. The House of Lords turned a blind eye to them all, and so missed an important opportunity to review the efforts of the lower courts to effect a marriage between natural justice and statutory procedure.

---

[66] *Ayr (Provost & c.)* v. *Lord Advocate* 1950 SC 102.

[67] See below, p. 971.

[68] *Franklin* v. *Minister of Town and Country Planning* [1948] AC 87; above, p. 491.

[69] See above, p. 492.

[70] In *B. Johnson & Co. (Builders) Ltd.* v. *Minister of Health* [1947] 2 All ER 395. This and the *Franklin* case were both decided on 24 July 1947.

The whole legal and political approach to such questions has since changed so radically that it now seems safe to treat the House of Lords' decision as of historical interest only, like the other aberrant decisions to be mentioned next.

THE RETREAT FROM NATURAL JUSTICE

The break with tradition

In the Stevenage case, as just related, the House of Lords had gone out of their way to hold, in effect, that natural justice had no part to play where an administrative decision was to be taken under a statutory procedure. This was no justification for supposing that, if no statutory procedure was prescribed, natural justice was likewise excluded. But that, extraordinary as it seems, was what the courts began to hold. This was one of the law's most mystifying lapses. Fundamentally it seemed to rest on a simple verbal confusion. It began to be said that if a function was administrative, or 'purely administrative', it could not be judicial or quasi-judicial, and was not therefore subject to the principles of natural justice. The judges seemed to forget that, as amply illustrated earlier,[71] it was essentially to administrative acts that the epithets 'judicial' and 'quasi-judicial' had been applied, in order to impose the legal standard of fair procedure on judicial and administrative conduct alike.

The first clear denial of the right to a fair hearing occurred in a case from Ceylon in which the Privy Council held that a textile trader could be deprived of his trading licence without any kind of hearing.[72] The charge against him was that his firm had falsified paying-in slips when banking coupons under the scheme of control. The Controller in fact wrote to the trader and offered him the opportunity of explaining himself and of inspecting the documents in the case; he also allowed the trader's lawyer to appear before him; and finally he arranged an inquiry before an assistant controller at which the trader and his witnesses were heard. The Supreme Court of Ceylon, following familiar English authorities, held that the circumstances demanded a fair hearing, but that it had in fact been given. Certiorari was therefore refused. The Privy Council agreed that a fair hearing had been given—but, going out of their way to raise the question, they held that it had never been necessary.

The judgment, delivered by Lord Radcliffe, stated that there was no

---

[71] Above, p. 504.
[72] *Nakkuda Ali* v. *Jayaratne* [1951] AC 66, criticised in (1951) 67 LQR 103 (Wade). As to wartime decisions, see *Ridge* v. *Baldwin* [1964] AC 40 at 73 (Lord Reid).

ground for holding that the Controller was acting judicially or quasi-judicially; that he was not determining a question but withdrawing a privilege; and that nothing in the regulations or in the conditions of his jurisdiction suggested that he need proceed by analogy to judicial rules. It said that the power 'stands by itself on the bare words of the regulation'. It assumed that there was nothing to consider beyond the bare words, and that the right to a hearing could be determined as if the question had never before arisen in an English court. No attention was paid to the long established presumption that 'the justice of the common law will supply the omission of the legislature'.[73] Nor was it remembered that licensing had long been held to be a judicial function.[74] Primary principles of law were abandoned in favour of the fallacious doctrine, devoid alike of logic, equity and authority, that a licence was a mere privilege and that therefore the holder could be deprived of his livelihood without ceremony.

Not long afterwards the Queen's Bench Division held that a London taxi-driver's licence could be revoked without a hearing.[75] The power to grant and revoke licences rested with the Metropolitan Police Commissioner. Here again, the licensing authority did not in fact act without granting a hearing: the driver was allowed to appear before the licensing committee, but the committee would not allow him to call a witness to controvert the evidence of the police. His licence was revoked and he applied for certiorari on the ground that the hearing given to him had not been full and fair. The Divisional Court replied that he was not entitled to a hearing at all. The relevant part of the London Cab Order provided for revocation by the Commissioner 'if he is satisfied . . . that the licensee is not a fit person to hold such a licence'. In language very similar to the Privy Council's, Lord Goddard CJ said that the Commissioner if he wished could summarily withdraw a licence without any sort of hearing or inquiry; that the Order did not intend that he should act as a judge or quasi-judge; and that there was no order to bring up before the court, since the Commissioner had simply decided that the applicant was not a fit person to hold a licence. He added:

He was exercising what I may call a disciplinary authority, and where a person, whether he is a military officer, a police officer, or any other person whose duty it is to act in matters of discipline, is exercising disciplinary powers, it is most

[73] Above, p. 503.

[74] Above, p. 482; below, p. 634. In *David* v. *Abdul Cader* [1963] 1 WLR 834 at 839 Lord Radcliffe expressed a view more sympathetic to judicial control of licensing functions in modern conditions.

[75] *R.* v. *Metropolitan Police Commissioner ex p. Parker* [1953] 1 WLR 1150. Contrast *R.* v. *City of Melbourne ex p. Whyte* [1949] VLR 257 (cancellation of taxi-driver's licence requires observance of natural justice).

undesirable, in my opinion, that he should be fettered by threats of orders of certiorari and so forth, because that interferes with the free and proper exercise of the disciplinary powers which he has.

These two decisions threatened to undo all the good work of earlier judges. They exposed English law to the reproach that, though a man must be heard before being expelled from his trade union or his club, he need not be heard before being deprived of his livelihood by a licensing authority.

Not the least disturbing feature of the taxi-driver's case was the novel argument that disciplinary powers should be beyond judicial control. A disciplinary power is a power to inflict punishment for an offence, and if there is one case more than another which demands fair procedure and the right of self-defence, that is it. The danger of Lord Goddard's doctrine, which he repeated in a subsequent case,[76] was that the court would deny jurisdiction altogether, so that the good and the bad cases would be rejected indiscriminately.

Commonwealth and foreign decisions

The low ebb to which natural justice appeared to have been reduced in England by the decisions of the 1950s can be appreciated by making comparison with other countries. Commonwealth countries which accepted the Privy Council as their supreme judicial authority were naturally put into difficulties by *Nakkuda Ali* v. *Jayaratne* and confusion inevitably invaded judgments which attempted to identify 'judicial' acts and to determine the status of administrative functions.[77] But the true common law tradition was preserved in Commonwealth jurisdictions overseas more effectively than it was in England. *Nakkuda Ali's* case was sometimes ignored,[78] sometimes distinguished,[79] and sometimes interpreted so as to make little difference.[80] The rule that a hearing is required, in particular, before the revocation of a licence on which the holder's livelihood depends was also upheld, as an obvious principle of legal justice,

---

[76] *Ex p. Fry* [1954] 1 WLR 730. But the Court of Appeal affirmed on different grounds.

[77] e.g. *Copithorne* v. *Calgary Power Ltd.* (1958) 16 DLR (2d) 241 (compulsory purchase—no right to hearing), a Canadian 'Nakkuda Ali'.

[78] As by the Supreme Court of Canada in *Alliance des Professeurs Catholiques de Montreal* v. *La Commission des Relations Ouvrières de la Province de Quebec* [1953] 4 DLR 161; by the High Court of Australia in *Delta Properties Pty Ltd.* v. *Brisbane City Council* (1955) 95 CLR 11; and by the Supreme Court of South Africa in *R.* v. *Ngwevela* [1954] (1) SA 123.

[79] As by the Court of Appeal of New Zealand in *New Zealand Dairy Board* v. *Okitu Co-operative Dairy Co. Ltd.* [1953] NZLR 366 and in *New Zealand Licensed Victuallers Association of Employers* v. *Price Tribunal* [1957] NZLR 167.

[80] See the judgment of Cooke J in the *New Zealand Dairy Board* case, above; *Low* v. *Earthquake and War Damage Commission* [1959] NZLR 1198.

in the United States[81] and in France[82] during the same period when it was being denied in England.

THE RIGHT TO BE HEARD REINSTATED

Ridge v. Baldwin

The tide turned once again in 1983,[83] when the House of Lords went back to the classic authorities in *Ridge* v. *Baldwin*,[84] a case which is an important landmark.

The chief constable of Brighton had been tried and acquitted on a criminal charge of conspiracy to obstruct the course of justice. Two other police officers were convicted, and the judge twice took opportunities to comment adversely on the chief constable's leadership of the force. Thereupon the Brighton Watch Committee, without giving any notice or offering any hearing to the chief constable, unanimously dismissed him from office. His solicitor then applied for a hearing and was allowed to appear before a later meeting. The Committee confirmed their previous decision, but by a vote of nine against three. The chief constable exercised his right of appeal to the Home Secretary, but his appeal was dismissed. Finally he turned to the courts of law, claiming a declaration that his dismissal was void since he had been given no notice of any charge against him and no opportunity of making his defence. This was refused by the High Court and by a unanimous Court of Appeal. But it was awarded by the House of Lords by a majority of four to one.

The initial dismissal was not only a breach of the principles of natural justice: it was contrary to the express provisions of the statutory regulations governing police discipline, which in cases of misconduct require notice of the charge and an opportunity for self-defence. They apply 'where a report

[81] *Hecht* v. *Monaghan* 307 NY 461 (1954) (taxi-driver's licence).

[82] CE 5 mai 1944, *Trompier-Gravier*, Rec. 133 (licence for newsstand). In French law the right appears to be confined to cases where there are allegations of personal deficiency or misconduct, and where the act is in the nature of a sanction as opposed to an act of policy: Vedel and Delvolvé, *Droit administratif*, 9th edn., 789; [1980] PL 288 (D. K. Allen). This restriction does not apply in England: see below, p. 532. See also *Transocean Marine Paint Association* v. *EC Commission* [1974] 2 CMLR 459 at 470 on the law of the EEC and of European countries.

[83] Favourable signs had appeared shortly beforehand: *Ceylon University* v. *Fernando* [1960] 1 WLR 223; *Kanda* v. *Government of Malaya* [1962] AC 322; *Hoggard* v. *Worsborough Urban District Council* [1962] 2 QB 93.

[84] [1964] AC 40. Academic comment on this beneficial decision was surprisingly unfavourable: (1964) 80 LQR 105 (A. L. Goodhart); [1964] CLJ 83 (A. W. Bradley). But Lord Reid, in a press interview given on his retirement after twenty-six years in the House of Lords, singled it out as the decision which he remembered with greatest satisfaction: The Times, 14 January, 1975. It will surely now be accepted as worthy of that high honour.

or allegation is received', and much intellectual effort was therefore spent on the question whether this piece of loose draftsmanship meant that the safeguards in the regulations (which justice plainly demands in any case) applied only where there was a formal 'receiving' of the complaint. A more absurd point on which to decide an important case it would be hard to find. But great benefit flowed from it, since although the dismissal was held void on this ground by the majority of four, three of them felt impelled to consider what the situation might be if the regulations did not apply. Thus they came to the question of principle, and this became the dominant theme in their opinions.

A police authority was, as the law then stood, empowered to dismiss any constable 'whom they think negligent in the discharge of his duty, or otherwise unfit for the same'.[85] Therefore in the authority's eyes the constable must be convicted of negligence or unfitness before they have power to deprive him of his office. This makes the case considerably stronger than many of the older natural justice cases, and it is certain that the judges who decided those cases would have held that no holder of a public office could be removed from it without notice of the charge and a fair hearing. For how could the committee fairly find negligence or unfitness without hearing the defence? It was on this simple and general ground that the majority upheld the chief constable's rights. Lord Morris said:[86]

My Lords, here is something which is basic to our system: the importance of upholding it far transcends the significance of any particular case.

The hearing given to the chief constable's solicitor was held to be irrelevant, since even then no notice of any specific charge was given, and natural justice was again violated.

The 'judicial' fallacy repudiated

The leading speech of Lord Reid in *Ridge* v. *Baldwin* is of the greatest significance because of its extensive review of the authorities, which inevitably exposed the fallacies into which the decisions of the 1950s had lapsed. He attacked the problem at its root by demonstrating how the term 'judicial' had been misinterpreted as requiring some superadded character-istic over and above the characteristic that the power affected some person's rights. The mere fact that the power affects rights or interests is what makes it 'judicial', and so subject to the procedures required by natural justice.[87] In other words, a power which affects rights must be exercised 'judicially', i.e.

---

[85] Municipal Corporation Act 1882, s. 191.

[86] [1964] AC at p. 114.

[87] See likewise *A.-G.* v. *Ryan* [1980] AC 718. This point is of great importance also for determining the scope of certiorari as a remedy: see below, p. 633.

fairly, and the fact that the power is administrative does not make it any the less 'judicial' for this purpose. Lord Hodson put this point very clearly:[88]

... the answer in a given case is not provided by the statement that the giver of the decision is acting in an executive or administrative capacity as if that were the antithesis of a judicial capacity. The cases seem to me to show that persons acting in a capacity which is not on the face of it judicial but rather executive or administrative have been held by the courts to be subject to the principles of natural justice.

Thus at last was verbal confusion cleared away and thus the House of Lords restored the classic doctrine of *Cooper* v. *Wandsworth Board of Works*, aptly celebrating the centenary of that case, and approving in particular the statements that the right to a hearing was 'of universal application' and that 'the justice of the common law will supply the omission of the legislature'.[89]

Lord Reid observed that 'the authorities on the applicability of the principles of natural justice are in some confusion', but that if the case had arisen thirty or forty years previously the courts would have had no difficulty in allowing the appeal; and that none of the authorities which were then so respected had ever been disapproved or doubted. It had been decided in 1937, in particular, that the principles of natural justice applied to the dismissal of police officers.[90] Lord Reid emphasised their universality: whether the cases concerned property or tenure of an office or membership of an institution, they were all governed by one principle. He also said:[91]

We do not have a developed system of administrative law—perhaps because until fairly recently we did not need it. . . . But I see nothing in that to justify our thinking that that our old methods are any less applicable today than ever they were to the older types of case. And if there are any dicta in modern authorities which point in that direction then, in my judgment, they should not be followed.

This led to the conclusion that *Nakkuda Ali* v. *Jayaratne*, holding that a licensing authority did not need to act judicially in cancelling a licence, was based on 'a serious misapprehension of the older authorities and therefore cannot be regarded as authoritative'. In a later case Lord Denning MR pithily summed up the situation:[92]

At one time it was said that the principles (sc. of natural justice) only apply to

---

[88] [1964] AC at p. 130.
[89] Above, p. 503. For further approval of *Cooper* v. *Wandsworth Board of Works* see *Wiseman* v. *Borneman* [1971] AC 297.
[90] *Cooper* v. *Wilson* [1937] 2 KB 309; above, p. 477.
[91] [1964] AC at p. 72.
[92] *R.* v. *Gaming Board for Great Britain ex p. Benaim and Khaida* [1970] 2 QB 417 at 430. See also *Pagliara* v. *A.-G.* [1974] 1 NZLR 86; *Heatley* v. *Tasmanian Racing and Gaming Commission* (1977) 14 ALR 519 (statutory ban placed on race-goer from entering public racecourse: fair hearing required).

judicial proceedings and not to administrative proceedings. That heresy was scotched in *Ridge* v. *Baldwin*. At another time it was said that the principles do not apply to the grant or revocation of licences. That too is wrong. *R.* v. *Metropolitan Police Commissioner ex p. Parker* and *Nakkuda Ali* v. *Jayaratne* are no longer authority for any such proposition.

Even more concisely, the Privy Council said:[93]

... the Minister was a person having legal authority to determine a question affecting the rights of individuals. This being so it is a necessary implication that he is required to observe the principles of natural justice when exercising that authority; and if he fails to do so, his purported decision is a nullity.

And Lord Diplock said in the House of Lords that the right of a man to be given 'a fair opportunity of hearing what is alleged against him and of presenting his own case is so fundamental to any civilised legal system that it is to be presumed that Parliament intended that a failure to observe it should render null and void any decision reached in breach of this requirement'.[94]

Legitimate expectation: positive effect

The classic situation in which the principles of natural justice apply is where some legal right, liberty or interest is affected, for instance where a building is demolished or an office-holder is dismissed or a trader's licence is revoked. But good administration demands their observance in other situations also, where the citizen may legitimately expect to be treated fairly. As Lord Bridge has explained:[95]

[93] *A.-G.* v. *Ryan* [1980] AC 718 (opinion delivered by Lord Diplock, holding that a minister in The Bahamas had failed to give a fair hearing to an applicant for registration as a citizen).

[94] *O'Reilly* v. *Mackman* [1983] 2 AC 237 at 276.

[95] *Re Westminster CC* [1986] AC 668 at 692. Lord Diplock made a formal statement in the *Council of Civil Service Unions* case (below) at 408, saying that the decision must affect some other person either

(a) by altering rights or obligations of that person which are enforceable by or against him in private law; or

(b) by depriving him of some benefit or advantage which either (i) he had in the past been permitted by the decision-maker to enjoy and which he can legitimately expect to be permitted to continue to do until there has been communicated to him some rational grounds for withdrawing it on which he has been given an opportunity to comment; or (ii) he has received assurance from the decision-maker will not be withdrawn without giving him first an opportunity of advancing reasons for contending that they should not be withdrawn.

This analysis is 'classical but certainly not exhaustive': *R.* v. *Secretary of State for the Environment ex p. Nottinghamshire CC* [1986] AC 240 at 249 (Lord Scarman). One case which does not seem to be covered is that of a first-time applicant for a licence (below, p. 559).

The courts have developed a relatively novel doctrine in public law that a duty of consultation may arise from a legitimate expectation of consultation aroused either by a promise or by an established practice of consultation.

A case of 'promise' was where the government of Hong Kong announced that certain illegal immigrants, who were liable to deportation, would be interviewed individually and treated on their merits in each case. The Privy Council quashed a deportation order where the immigrant had only been allowed to answer questions without being able to put his own case, holding that 'when a public authority has promised to follow a certain procedure, it is in the interest of good administration that it should act fairly and should implement its promise, so long as implementation does not interfere with its statutory duty'.[96] Another example was where the Court of Appeal, as explained earlier, quashed the refusal of the Home Office to admit an immigrant when this was contrary to the legitimate expectation created by one of its published circulars.[97] And where a government department encouraged a company to suppose that it would receive a grant, it could not lawfully refuse the grant without first granting a hearing.[98] A case of 'established practice' was where civil servants employed in secret work in the government communications headquarters were prohibited from belonging to trade unions. Since there was a well-established practice of consultation in such matters, but no consultation had been offered, the House of Lords held that the procedure would have been unfair and unlawful had there not been overriding considerations of national security.[99] For the same reason a local education authority acted unlawfully in proceeding with a school reorganisation without adequately consulting parents, since this was habitually done in such cases under the emphatic advice of the Secretary of State.[1]

The range of natural justice has in fact been extended beyond these two cases, and probably it ought not to be confined by rigid categories. This appears most clearly in the licensing cases, discussed later,[2] in which it has been held that a first-time applicant for a licence is entitled to an opportunity to rebut personal allegations against him and that the holder of an expiring licence may normally expect to be fairly heard before renewal

---

[96] *Attorney-General of Hong Kong* v. *Ng Yuen Shiu* [1983] 2 AC 629. Another 'promise' case, in effect one of legitimate expectation, is *R.* v. *Liverpool Cpn. ex p. Liverpool Taxi Fleet Operators' Association* [1972] 2 QB 299, for which see above, pp. 377, 380. See also *Cole* v. *Cunningham* (1983) 49 ALR 123.

[97] *R.* v. *Home Secretary ex p. Asif Mahmood Khan* [1984] 1 WLR 1337; above, p. 423.

[98] *R.* v. *Secretary of State for Transport ex p. Sherriff & Sons Ltd.* [1986] The Times, 18 December.

[99] *Council of Civil Service Unions* v. *Minister for the Civil Service* [1985] AC 374.

[1] *R.* v. *Brent LBC ex p. Gunning* (1985) 84 LGR 168.

[2] Below, p. 559.

is refused. It is held also that the protection of natural justice will extend to those affected by decisions of the Stock Exchange Take-over Panel, though they have no direct legal force.[3] In none of these cases is there either legal right or interest or promise or established practice. 'Legitimate expectation', which means reasonable expectation,[4] can equally well be invoked in any of many situations where fairness and good administration justify the right to be heard[5]—as it was when refusal of renewal of a taxi-driver's licence was quashed for failure to disclose a medical report about him.[6]

Legitimate expectation: negative effect

It was in fact for the purpose of restricting the right to be heard that 'legitimate expectation' was introduced into the law. It made its first appearance in a case where alien students of 'scientology' were refused extension of their entry permits as an act of policy by the Home Secretary, who had announced that no discretionary benefits would be granted to this sect. The Court of Appeal held that they had no legitimate expectation of extension beyond the permitted time, and so no right to a hearing, though revocation of their permits within that time would have been contrary to legitimate expectation.[7] Official statements of policy, therefore, may cancel legitimate expectation, just as they may create it, as seen above. In a different context, where car-hire drivers had habitually offended against airport byelaws, with many convictions and unpaid fines, it was held that they had no legitimate expectation of being heard before being banned by the airport authority.[8]

There is some ambiguity in the dicta about legitimate expectation, which may mean either expectation of a fair hearing or expectation of the licence or other benefit which is being sought. But the result is the same in either case: absence of legitimate expectation will absolve the public authority from affording a hearing.

'Acting fairly'

Although *Ridge* v. *Baldwin* sorted out the confusion caused by the artificial use of the word 'judicial' to describe functions which were in reality

---

[3] For this see below, p. 641.
[4] See the *Hong Kong* case (above) at 636 and the *Civil Service Unions* case (above) at 408.
[5] In *Kioa* v. *West* (1985) 60 ALJR 113 at 141 Brennan J criticised the use of legitimate expectation as a criterion, saying that it was hardly to be thought that the legislature would intend that individual interests affected by the 'myriad and complex powers conferred on the bureaucracy' should be accorded less protection than legal rights. See also *FAI Insurances Ltd.* v. *Winneke* (1982) 41 ALR 1 at 13 (Mason J).
[6] *R.* v. *Assistant Metropolitan Police Commissioner ex p. Howell* [1986] RTR 52.
[7] *Schmidt* v. *Home Secretary* [1969] 2 Ch. 149 (below, p. 577).
[8] *Cinnamond* v. *British Airports Authority* [1980] 1 WLR 582.

administrative, it did not eliminate this misnomer from the law. A means of doing so, however, appeared in a later line of cases which laid down that powers of a purely administrative character must be exercised 'fairly', meaning in accordance with natural justice—'which after all is only fair play in action'.[9] 'Natural justice is but fairness writ large and judicially.'[10] By this simple verbal short-cut the misuse of the term 'judicial' can be avoided altogether. At last we reach the result directly instead of by a devious path: administrative powers which affect rights must be exercised in accordance with natural justice.[11] As Lord Diplock has put it[12]—

Where an Act of Parliament confers upon an administrative body functions which involve its making decisions which affect to their detriment the rights of other persons or curtail their liberty to do as they please, there is a presumption that Parliament intended that the administrative body should act fairly towards those persons who will be affected by their decisions.

This development dates from a case of 1966 where an immigration officer at London Airport had refused to admit a boy from Pakistan on the ground that he appeared to be well over the age of sixteen, under which age he would have been allowed to enter with his father. Lord Parker CJ held that even if an immigration officer is not acting in a judicial or quasi-judicial capacity, he must nevertheless act fairly.[13] He added that he realised that he was overstepping the line which earlier cases had drawn, according as there was or was not a duty to act judicially or quasi-judicially. Salmon LJ likewise held that the immigration officer, acting in an administrative capacity, must act 'fairly in accordance with the ordinary principles of natural justice', although he thought that he had a quasi-judicial capacity since he had statutory power to 'make a decision affecting basic right of others'. The court did not, however, intervene, since it found on the facts that the officer had acted fairly.

Although this decision was plainly founded on a misapprehension as to the state of the law,[14] it supplied such a simple and attractive basis for natural justice that it was followed with alacrity, and it was not long before

[9] A much quoted remark of Harman LJ in *Ridge* v. *Baldwin* [1963] 1 QB 539 at 578.
[10] Lord Morris in *Furnell* v. *Whangarei High Schools Board* [1973] AC 660 at 679.
[11] On this development see (1975) 25 U. Tor. LJ 280 (D. J. Mullan); (1978) 28 U. Tor LJ 215 (M. Loughlin); [1979] S. Af. LJ 607 (L. G. Baxter).
[12] *R.* v. *Commission for Racial Equality ex p. Hillingdon LBC* [1982] AC 779.
[13] *Re H. K. (An Infant)* [1967] 2 QB 617. See similarly *R.* v. *Birmingham City Justice ex p. Chris Foreign Foods (Wholesalers) Ltd.* [1970] 1 WLR 1428.
[14] *Ridge* v. *Baldwin* was not cited and *Nakkuda Ali* v. *Jayaratne* was discussed and distinguished as if it were still good law. Judgment was not reserved.

its principle was adopted by the Court of Appeal.[15] Speaking of inspectors appointed by the Board of Trade to make a report on the affairs of a company, which might have grave consequences, Lord Denning MR said:[16]

Seeing that their work and their report may lead to such consequences, I am clearly of the opinion that the inspectors must act fairly. This is a duty which rests on them, as on many other bodies, even though they are not judicial or quasi-judicial, but only administrative.

As this and other opinions show, the courts still find difficulty in ridding themselves of the idea that if the function is administrative it is therefore not quasi-judicial. They still shrink from reverting to the traditional doctrine, that an administrative power which may gravely affect a person's position must be exercised judicially, despite 'Lord Reid's momentous speech in *Ridge* v. *Baldwin*, since which emphasis upon the distinction between judicial and non-judicial decisions is no longer good law'.[17] The fallacy that 'quasi-judicial' and 'administrative' mean two basically different things appears to be almost ineradicable.

Notwithstanding the clear statements in the original decision that 'acting fairly' was required by the rules of natural justice, judges unable to accept the logic of *Ridge* v. *Baldwin* have attempted to differentiate them, suggesting that natural justice applies only to judicial or quasi-judicial functions and 'acting fairly' to administrative or executive functions—thus compounding the old fallacy with a new one.[18] But it is now clearly settled, as is indeed self-evident, that there is no difference between natural justice and 'acting fairly', but that they are alternative names for a single but flexible doctrine whose content may vary according to the nature of the power and the circumstances of the case.[19] In the words of Lord

---

[15]   *R.* v. *Gaming Board for Great Britain ex p. Benaim and Khaida* [1970] 2 QB 417 at 430: *Re Pergamon Press* [1971] Ch. 388 at 399. See also *R.* v. *Kent Police Authority ex p. Godden* [1971] 2 QB 662; *R.* v. *Liverpool Corporation ex p. Liverpool Taxi Fleet Operators Association* [1972] 2 QB 299; *Maxwell* v. *Department of Trade and Industry* [1974] QB 523; *R.* v. *Race Relations Board ex p. Selvarajan* [1975] 1 WLR 1686; *Fraser* v. *Mudge* [1975] 1 WLR 1132.

[16]   *Re Pergamon Press* (above).

[17]   Stephen J in *Salemi* v. *Minister for Immigration* (No. 2) (1977) 14 ALR 1 at 30.

[18]   As in *Pearlberg* v. *Varty* [1972] 1 WLR 534 at 547; *Bates* v. *Lord Hailsham* [1972] 1 WLR 1373, mostly corrected in *McInnes* v. *Onslow-Fane* [1978] 1 WLR 1520 at 1530. By exploiting this supposed distinction the Supreme Court of Canada, having precluded itself from applying 'natural justice' to administrative action, has accepted the duty to 'act fairly': *Re Nicholson and Haldimand-Norfolk Police Commissioners* (1979) 88 DLR (3d) 671. See also *Flexman* v. *Franklin CC* [1979] 2 NZLR 690.

[19]   e.g. *Re Pergamon Press Ltd.* [1971] Ch. 388 at 399; *R.* v. *Home Secretary ex p. Hosenball* [1977] 1 WLR 766 at 784; *O'Reilly* v. *Mackman* [1983] 2 AC 237 at 276 (Lord Diplock); *Lloyd* v. *McMahon* [1987] 2 WLR 821 at 878 (Lord Bridge); *Salemi* v. *Minister for Immigration* (No. 2) (1977) 14 ALR 1.

Denning MR, 'the rules of natural justice—or of fairness—are not cut and dried. They vary infinitely.'[20] Attempts to represent natural justice and 'acting fairly' as two different things are a sure sign of failure to understand that *administrative* powers are subject to the principles of natural justice as explained throughout this chapter.[21] Lord Scarman has neatly combined both points in observing that the courts have extended 'the requirement of natural justice, namely the duty to act fairly, so that it is required of a purely administrative act'.[22]

The 'acting fairly' doctrine has at least proved useful as a device for evading some of the previous confusion. The courts now have two strings to their bow. An administrative act may be held to be subject to the requirements of natural justice either because it affects rights or interests and therefore involves a duty to act judicially, in accordance with the classic authorities and *Ridge* v. *Baldwin*; or it may simply be held that, 'in our modern approach',[23] it automatically involves a duty to act fairly and in accordance with natural justice, without any of the analysis which has been made into such an unnecessary obstacle.

'Acting fairly' is a phrase of such wide implications that it may ultimately extend beyond the sphere of procedure. It was suggested in one case that it included a duty of acting with substantial fairness and consistency.[24] But when Lord Denning MR said much the same thing (that not only must there be a fair hearing but 'the decision itself must be fair and reasonable') the House of Lords repudiated his opinion.[25] On the other hand, fairness may not necessarily comprise the whole domain of natural justice. Inspectors investigating the affairs of companies, who are subject to the duty to act fairly, are not required to be free from bias.[26] Yet the same phrase has been used to describe a duty to act honestly and without bias or caprice but without any need to disclose the charge or give a hearing.[27]

[20] *R.* v. *Home Secretary ex p. Santillo* [1981] QB 778.

[21] Clearly shown in Lord Pearson's statement in *Pearlberg* v. *Varty* (above) that 'where some person or body is entrusted by Parliament with administrative or executive functions there is no presumption that compliance with the principles of natural justice is required, although as "Parliament is not to be presumed to act unfairly," the courts may be able in suitable cases (perhaps always) to imply an obligation to act with fairness'. The first part of this statement contradicts *Ridge* v. *Baldwin* and the second part contradicts the first. Contrast *Twist* v. *Randwick Municipal Council* (1976) 12 ALR 379 at 382 (Barwick CJ).

[22] *Council of Civil Service Unions* v. *Minister for the Civil Service* [1985] AC 374 at 407.

[23] Lord Denning MR in the *Liverpool* case (above).

[24] *HTV Ltd.* v. *Price Commission* [1976] ICR 170 at 189 (Scarman LJ); above, p. 423.

[25] *Chief Constable of North Wales Police* v. *Evans* [1982] 1 WLR 1155, perhaps giving Lord Denning's words a wider meaning than he intended. In *Daganayasi* v. *Minister of Immigration* [1980] 2 NZLR 130 Cooke J said that 'fairness need not be treated as confined to procedural matters'. See also above, p. 423, as to unfairness amounting to abuse of power.

[26] *R.* v. *Secretary of State for Trade, ex p. Perestrello* [1981] QB 19.

[27] *McInnes* v. *Onslow-Fane* [1978] 1 WLR 1520, for which see above, p. 471.

Judges seem to be using it in a variety of different situations, so that it has no precise meaning except when used as a synonym for natural justice.

Void or voidable

Ridge v. *Baldwin* brought with it a rash of conflicting opinions about whether failure to give a fair hearing rendered the dismissal of the chief constable void or voidable.[28] In the long history of the cases on natural justice as applied to administrative action this question had never before been agitated, for the simple reason that the logic of the situation excluded it. It had always previously been held that a breach of the rules of natural justice resulted in the determination being null and void, in the same way as any other act which was ultra vires. For the duty to act fairly, just like the duty to act reasonably,[29] was enforced as an implied statutory requirement, so that failure to observe it meant that the administrative act or decision was outside the statutory power, unjustified by law, and therefore ultra vires and void. This assumption was so well understood that it was rarely spelled out in judgments.[30] As explained already,[31] there was no other basis on which the courts could intervene. The majority of the House of Lords in *Ridge* v. *Baldwin* decided entirely consistently with this hypothesis, holding expressly that the chief constable's dismissal was void. Lord Reid said:[32]

Then there was considerable argument whether in the result the watch committee's decision was void or merely voidable. Time and time again in the cases I have cited it has been stated that a decision given without regard to the principles of natural justice is void and that was expressly decided in *Wood* v. *Woad*.[33] I see no reason to doubt these authorities. The body with the power to decide cannot lawfully proceed to make a decision until it has afforded to the person affected a proper opportunity to state his case.

Lord Morris likewise held that 'the decision of the watch committee was invalid and of no effect and null and void', and could be called voidable only in the sense that unless and until the chief constable contested it, it

---

[28] For discussion see (1967) 83 LQR 499, (1968) 84 LQR 95 (Wade); (1968) 31 MLR 2, 138 (M. B. Akehurst).

[29] See above, p. 390.

[30] It was spelled out with perfect clarity in *Anisminic Ltd.* v. *Foreign Compensation Commission* [1968] 2 QB at 890 (Diplock LJ); [1969] 2 AC at 171 (Lord Reid), 195 (Lord Pearce) and 207 (Lord Wilberforce). Yet another proof is that failure to give a fair hearing renders the decision 'not within the powers of this Act' for the purposes of statutory remedies: below, p. 742. See also the quotations above, p. 467.

[31] Above, p. 41.

[32] [1964] AC at p. 80.

[33] (1874) LR 9 Ex. 190.

would stand[34] (this point is discussed elsewhere[35]). And Lord Hodson held that all authority was to the effect that a decision contrary to natural justice was void, being vitiated by 'a want of jurisdiction'.[36] For this clear decision of the majority there was an abundance of precedent.

But the dissentient judges who would have held that the chief constable had no right to a fair hearing were of opinion that the watch committee's decision was not void but voidable. As expounded by Lord Evershed in the House of Lords, the motive was a desire to enlarge judicial discretion. He argued that if the decision were merely voidable, the court need quash it only in case of 'a real substantial miscarriage of justice'.[37] This policy is open to the objection that it would introduce dangerous uncertainty—one might say, palm-tree injustice. Natural justice has for centuries been enforced as a matter of law and not of discretion. But the uncertainties of the period before *Ridge* v. *Baldwin* had seriously undermined the clear principle that used to prevail. Of the nine judges concerned in that case, five denied that there was a right to a fair hearing before deprivation of a public office. In this situation it is not discretion that is needed but consistency. The right to natural justice should be as firm as the right to personal liberty. This is a vital part of the rule of law.

No authority could be cited in support of the dissentient opinions and no authority need have been attributed to them, had they not been approved by the Privy Council, in clear preference to the views of the majority of the House of Lords, in a highly mystifying decision. The Privy Council held that a minister in Ceylon had failed to observe the requirements of natural justice in not giving a hearing to the Municipal Council of Jaffna before making an order dissolving the Council, under default powers, on the ground of its incompetence.[38] But they also held that the mayor, who had brought certiorari proceedings, was not entitled to relief since the proper plaintiff was not he but the Council itself. The question therefore was whether he was entitled to sue. Instead of answering this by reference to the rule which restricts the remedy to the person really concerned,[39] the Privy

[34] [1964] AC at p. 125.

[35] Above, p. 352.

[36] [1964] AC at p. 136. Decisions to the same effect are very numerous. One example is *R.* v. *North ex p. Oakey* [1927] 1 KB 491 at 503, 505 (Scrutton and Atkin LJJ).

[37] [1964] AC at p. 91. But *Osgood* v. *Nelson*, from which support is claimed, does not in fact support this proposition: see (1968) 84 LQR at p. 112.

[38] *Durayappah* v. *Fernando* [1967] 2 AC 337. Apart from the confusion criticised, this case contains much sound law. It upholds the broad principles of *Cooper* v. *Wandsworth Board of Works*, yet it inconsistently favours *Nakkuda Ali* v. *Jayaratne*.

[39] See below, p. 537. In *Hoffman–La Roche (F.) & Co.* v. *Secretary of State for Trade and Industry* [1975] AC 295 Lord Wilberforce adopted this explanation of the 'puzzling case' and so did Lord Diplock.

Council resorted to 'void or voidable', holding that the order was voidable only at the instance of the Council. Yet, contradicting this, they also held that if challenged by the Council it would have been held void from the outset. Misrepresenting the minority opinions in *Ridge* v. *Baldwin* as being a majority in favour of 'voidable',[40] the Privy Council interwove them with the principle of natural justice upheld by the true majority, with which they were inconsistent. The confusions in this case are inextricable; and the 'void or voidable' part of it ought to be disregarded, since both the House of Lords[41] and the Privy Council[42] have since reaffirmed that an order made contrary to natural justice is outside jurisdiction and void, and that any other terminology would be 'inconsistent with the doctrine of ultra vires as it has been developed in English law as a means of controlling abuse of power by the executive arm of government'.[43]

As pointed out elsewhere,[44] no logic can be extracted from 'void or voidable' which will assist the resolution of cases. Decisions depend upon whether the right remedy is sought by the right person in the right proceedings,[45] and on all those questions there are rules to be applied. As regards the remedy, it may be added that if a decision vitiated by breach of natural justice were merely voidable, in the sense of being intra vires at the outset, it would be impossible to remedy the situation by a merely declaratory judgment, as was done in *Ridge* v. *Baldwin*.[46] Nor is there any need for 'voidable' to explain the self-evident fact that no remedy is available until the injured party obtains it from the court. As Megarry J has said,[47]

A decision reached by a tribunal wholly outside its jurisdiction and in complete defiance of natural justice is about as void as anything can be; but if nobody who is entitled to challenge or question it chooses to do so, it remains in being. Yet to

---

[40] Lord Morris is said by the Privy Council to have decided in *Ridge* v. *Baldwin* that the decision of the watch committee was voidable and not a nullity. But this is a mistake: see (1967) 83 LQR at 513; *Hounslow London Borough Council* v. *Twickenham Garden Developments Ltd.* [1971] Ch. 233 at 258–9 (Megarry J); *Denton* v. *Auckland City* [1969] NZLR 256 (Speight J).

[41] *Anisminic Ltd.* v. *Foreign Compensation Commission* [1969] 2 AC 147; *Hoffman–La Roche (F.) & Co.* v. *Secretary of State for Trade and Industry* [1975] AC 295. Lord Denning MR has withdrawn his earlier opinions to the contrary: see above, p. 350.

[42] *A.-G.* v. *Ryan* [1980] AC 143.

[43] See the *Hoffman–La Roche* case (above) at 365 (Lord Diplock); above, p. 351.

[44] Above, p. 353.

[45] As to collateral proceedings and natural justice see above, p. 335.

[46] For this difficulty see below, p. 601. And see *Cooper* v. *Wilson* [1937] 2 KB 309; above, p. 477.

[47] *Hounslow London Borough Council* v. *Twickenham Garden Developments Ltd.* [1971] Ch. 233 at 259.

describe such a decision as being 'voidable' is to use that word in a sense that is not only very special but liable to mislead.

In natural justice cases, just as much as in the others already discussed, it is essential to remember that 'void' is not an absolute but a relative term: a decision or act may be void against one person and valid against another.[48] This is further explained below in the context of who is entitled to sue when a fair hearing is denied, and what is the position when the right to a fair hearing is waived.[49] As noted elsewhere, the possibility of waiver does not mean that there is any need for the term 'voidable'.[50]

FAIR HEARINGS—GENERAL ASPECTS

Scope and limits of the principle

Ridge v. *Baldwin* reinstated the right to a fair hearing as 'a rule of universal application' in the case of administrative acts or decisions affecting rights; and, in Lord Loreburn's oft-repeated words, the duty to afford it is 'a duty lying upon every one who decides anything'.[51] The decision gave the impetus to a surge of litigation over natural justice, in which the courts have been able to consider many of its facets and to build up something like a canon of fair administrative procedure. For the most part the numerous decisions have served only to show the correctness of the above-quoted words, sweeping though they are. Natural justice has achieved something like the status of a fundamental right.[52]

For example, the courts have repudiated earlier suggestions that the principles of natural justice do not apply to disciplinary bodies: 'they must act fairly just the same as anyone else; and are just as subject to control by the courts'.[53] Disadvantaged groups such as prisoners[54] and immigrants[55]

[48] Above, p. 353.
[49] Below, p. 537.
[50] Above, p. 494.
[51] Above, p. 506.
[52] In *Fraser* v. *State Services Commission* [1984] 1 NZLR 116 at 121. Cooke J said *obiter*, in the context of natural justice, that 'it is arguable that some common law rights may go so deep that even Parliament cannot be accepted by the courts to have destroyed them'.
[53] *Buckoke* v. *Greater London Council* [1971] Ch. 655 (Lord Denning MR).
[54] *R.* v. *Hull Prison Visitors ex p. St. Germain* [1979] QB 425, criticising the decisions of Lord Goddard CJ mentioned above, p. 515. The Court of Appeal characteristically discussed the question in terms of whether certiorari would lie to prison visitors, but the real issue was whether they were subject to the principles of natural justice. That issue was settled in *R.* v. *Hull Prison Visitors ex p. St. Germain* (No. 2) [1979] 1 WLR 1401. See also *Fraser* v. *Mudge* [1975] 1 WLR 1132; *R.* v. *Wandsworth Prison Visitors ex p. Raymond* [1985] The Times, 17 June (relief withheld in discretion); *Martineau* v. *Matsqui Institution Disciplinary Board* (No. 2) (1979) 106 DLR (3d) 385.
[55] See examples below, p. 537.

have succeeded in invalidating decisions made against them when they have not been treated fairly—though there was for a time an illogical exception in the case of prisoners, mentioned later.[56] At the other end of the spectrum of power, public authorities themselves are now given the benefit of natural justice, as illustrated at the end of this section. Basically the principle is confined by no frontiers.

On the other hand it must be a flexible principle. The judges, anxious as always to preserve some freedom of manœuvre, emphasise that 'it is not possible to lay down rigid rules as to when the principles of natural justice are to apply: nor as to their scope and extent. Everything depends on the subject-matter.'[57] 'The so-called rules of natural justice are not engraved on tablets of stone.'[58] Their application, resting as it does upon statutory implication, must always be in conformity with the scheme of the Act and with the subject-matter of the case. 'In the application of the concept of fair play there must be real flexibility.'[59] There must also have been some real prejudice to the complainant: there is no such thing as a merely technical infringement of natural justice.[60]

Sometimes urgent action may have to be taken on grounds of public health or safety, for example to seize and destroy bad meat exposed for sale[61] or to order the removal to hospital of a person with an infectious disease.[62] In such cases the normal presumption that a hearing must be given is rebutted by the circumstances of the case. So it is also, for obvious reasons, where the police have to act with urgency, e.g. in making arrests.

Even in cases not involving urgency it may be equally clear that no hearing is required. A decision to prosecute or bring legal proceedings,[63] or to carry out a search,[64] damaging though it may be to the accused, does not entitle him to be consulted or shown the evidence in advance. The same applies to a decision by the Department of Trade to appoint inspectors to investigate suspicious circumstances in the affairs of a company: it may injure the company's reputation, but that risk has to be accepted as the price of the legal privileges enjoyed by companies; and in many cases prior

---

[56] Below, p. 575.

[57] R. v. Gaming Board for Great Britain ex p. Benaim and Khaida [1970] 2 QB 417 at 439 (Lord Denning MR). For cases of national security see below, p. 574.

[58] Lloyd v. McMahon [1987] AC 625 at 702 ('so-called' because Lord Bridge prefers 'the requirements of fairness').

[59] Re Pergamon Press Ltd. [1971] Ch. 388 at 403 (Sachs LJ).

[60] George v. Secretary of State for the Environment (1979) 77 LGR 689.

[61] White v. Redfern (1879) 5 QBD 15.

[62] R. v. Davey [1899] 2 QB 301.

[63] Wiseman v. Borneman [1971] AC 297 at 308 (Lord Reid); Nicol v. Attorney-General of Victoria [1982] VR 353.

[64] R. v. Leicester Crown Court ex p. Director of Public Prosecutions [1987] The Times, 19 June.

warning would frustrate the objects of the legislation.[65] Nor need a minister offer a hearing to a local authority before calling in their local plan for his approval or consult them about objections to it received by him.[66] Another obvious case is where a minister grants to a local authority an extension of time for submitting a compulsory purchase order in connection with a slum-clearance scheme.[67] In resolving to adopt a slum-clearance scheme a local authority need not first give a hearing to an objecting landowner, since under the statutory procedure this resolution is the initial step and the Act provides amply for the hearing of objections at a statutory inquiry.[68] Sometimes a right of appeal may imply that no earlier hearing is necessary.[69] There are other situations in which an opportunity for later challenge is sufficient, as in the case of a subpoena to a witness. And it is always possible for hearings to be excluded by the scheme of the legislation.[70] But where the grant of a fair hearing is consistent with the exercise of the legal power, the law leans strongly in its favour. Judges of the highest authority have approved the epigram of Byles J, that 'the justice of the common law will supply the omission of the legislature'.[71] Nor is this presumption to be excluded merely for the sake of administrative convenience: 'convenience and justice are often not on speaking terms'.[72]

In order to preserve flexibility the courts frequently quote general statements such as the following:[73]

The requirements of natural justice must depend on the circumstances of the case, the nature of the inquiry, the rules under which the tribunal is acting, the subject-matter to be dealt with, and so forth.

To the same effect is a passage, much cited, in an opinion of the Privy Council:[74]

[65] *Norwest Holst Ltd.* v. *Secretary of State for Trade* [1978] Ch. 201. But as to the conduct of the investigation see below, p. 542.

[66] *R.* v. *Secretary of State for the Environment ex p. Southwark LBC* (1987) 54 P & CR 226 (plan rejected by minister).

[67] *Aristides* v. *Minister of Housing and Local Government* [1970] 1 All ER 195.

[68] *Fredman* v. *Minister of Health* (1935) 154 LT 240. In the case of closing orders for individual houses there is a right to be heard at the initial stage: Housing Act 1985, s. 264.

[69] Below, p. 550.

[70] As in *Commissioner of Business Franchises* v. *Borenstein* [1984] VR 375; *Building Construction Federation* v. *Minister for Industrial Relations* [1985] 1 NSWLR 197.

[71] Above, p. 503; approved in *Ridge* v. *Baldwin* [1964] AC 40; *Durayappah* v. *Fernando* [1967] 2 AC 337, *Wiseman* v. *Borneman* [1971] AC 297. But 'it is not to be used to frustrate the intention of the legislature': *Norwest Holst Ltd.* v. *Secretary of State for Trade* (above), (Ormrod LJ).

[72] *General Medical Council* v. *Spackman* [1943] AC 627 at 638 (Lord Atkin). See *R.* v. *Hull Prison Visitors ex p. St. Germain* (No. 2) [1979] 1 WLR 1401.

[73] *Russell* v. *Duke of Norfolk* [1949] 1 All ER 109 at 118 (Tucker LJ).

[74] *Durayappah* v. *Fernando* [1967] 2 AC 337 at 349 (Lord Upjohn).

In their Lordships' opinion there are three matters which must always be borne in mind when considering whether the principle should be applied or not. These three matters are: first, what is the nature of the property, the office held, status enjoyed or services to be performed by the complainant of injustice. Secondly, in what circumstances or upon what occasions is the person claiming to be entitled to exercise the measure of control entitled to intervene. Thirdly, when a right to intervene is proved what sanctions in fact is the latter entitled to impose upon the other.

This amounts to little more than saying that the whole statutory and factual context must be considered; and that is undoubtedly true. Lord Hailsham LC has observed:[75]

The doctrine of natural justice has come in for increasing consideration in recent years, and the courts generally, and your Lordships' House in particular, have, I think rightly, advanced its frontiers considerably. But at the same time they have taken an increasingly sophisticated view of what it requires in individual cases.

In other words, the courts have been working out their ideas of the procedure which fair administration requires in many different situations. Ample illustration will be found in the remainder of this chapter.

The principle is in no way limited to particular categories of cases such as interference with property, dismissal from office, and charges of personal misconduct. It applies equally to the reduction of a local authority's rate support grant,[76] to the allocation of compensation for a 'well maintained' house as between landlord and tenant,[77] and to the banning of one member of the public from local authority premises which are open to others.[78] The scope of the principle is at least as wide as it was under the old authorities cited earlier in this chapter. If anything, it is now wider, partly owing to the general administrative duty to act fairly which has now been repeatedly recognised. It is just as applicable in favour of public authorities as against them, as a series of decisions now shows. Thus a municipal council in Ceylon dissolved by the minister under his default powers was entitled to a fair hearing before the minister could legally make the order.[79] A local authority's rate support grant, as mentioned above, could not lawfully be reduced without giving them a fair hearing. A ministerial order requiring the Greater London Council to make the maximum payment to London

---

[75] *Pearlberg* v. *Varty* [1972] 1 WLR 534 at 540.

[76] See the *Brent* case, below, p. 556; *R.* v. *Secretary of State for the Environment ex p. Hammersmith and Fulham LBC* [1985] The Times, 18 May.

[77] *Hoggard* v. *Worsborough Urban District Council* [1962] 2 QB 93.

[78] *R.* v. *Brent LBC ex p. Assegai* [1987] The Independent, 12 June.

[79] *Durayappah* v. *Fernando* (above). See likewise *R.* v. *Secretary of State for the Environment ex p. Norwich City Council* [1982] QB 808. Contrast above, p. 183, n. 56.

Regional Transport was quashed for the same reason.[80] And where a mental health review tribunal discharged a patient without notifying the Secretary of State, so that he had no opportunity to be heard, the tribunal's order was set aside in 'a classic case of a failure of natural justice'.[81]

Supplementation of statutory procedures

Many cases cited in this chapter illustrate the way in which the principles of natural justice are used to supplement statutory procedures which themselves provide for a hearing or inquiry, with or without detailed regulation of the procedure. As Lord Reid said:[82]

For a long time the courts have, without objection from Parliament, supplemented procedure laid down in legislation where they have found that to be necessary for this purpose. But before this unusual kind of power is exercised it must be clear that the statutory procedure is insufficient to achieve justice and that to require additional steps would not frustrate the apparent purpose of the legislation.

Or, in the words of Lord Bridge:

In particular, it is well-established that when a statute has conferred on any body the power to make decisions affecting individuals, the courts will not only require the procedure prescribed by the statute to be followed, but will readily imply so much and no more to be introduced by way of additional procedural safeguards as will ensure the attainment of fairness.[83]

No statutory procedure is likely to cover every possibility of unfairness. Gaps may therefore be filled by resorting to 'the justice of the common law'. Thus objectors at public inquiries must be given a fair opportunity to meet adverse evidence, even though the statutory provisions do not cover the case expressly.[84]

Where a fair hearing 'would make no difference'

Procedural objections are often raised by unmeritorious parties. Judges may then be tempted to refuse relief on the ground that a fair hearing could

[80] R. v. Secretary of State for Transport ex p. Greater London Council [1986] QB 556.

[81] R. v. Oxford Regional Mental Health Review Tribunal ex p. Home Secretary [1986] 1 WLR 1180, affirmed [1988] AC 120.

[82] Wiseman v. Borneman [1971] AC 297 at 308. See also R. v. Hull Prison Visitors ex p. St. Germain [1979] 1 WLR 1401 at 1408.

[83] Lloyd v. McMahon [1987] 2 WLR 821 at 878. Several of the judgments emphasise this point.

[84] Errington v. Minister of Health [1935] 1 KB 249 and other cases cited below, p. 540. And see Steele v. Minister of Housing and Local Government (1956) 6 P & CR 386 (inspector and minister must act judicially in accordance with natural justice).

have made no difference to the result. But in principle it is vital that the procedure and the merits should be kept strictly apart, since otherwise the merits may be prejudged unfairly. Lord Wright once said:[85]

If the principles of natural jutice are violated in respect of any decision it is, indeed, immaterial whether the same decision would have been arrived at in the absence of the departure from the essential principles of justice. The decision must be declared to be no decision.

The dangers were vividly expressed by Megarry J, criticising the contention that 'the result is obvious from the start':[86]

As everybody who has anything to do with the law well knows, the path of the law is strewn with examples of open and shut cases which, somehow, were not; of unanswerable charges which, in the event, were completely answered; of inexplicable conduct which was fully explained; of fixed and unalterable determinations that, by discussion, suffered a change.

The last few words are especially apt for administrative decisions. They were adopted in a later case where the court quashed a Secretary of State's order reducing a local authority's rate support grant for failure to grant them a hearing at the proper time.[87] Even though it was 'certainly probable' that the decision would have been the same, since all the arguments had been fully rehearsed at an earlier stage, the court declined to hold that a hearing would have been a useless formality.

This question profoundly affected the course of *Ridge* v. *Baldwin*. The argument favoured by the lower courts, and in Lord Evershed's dissenting speech, was that natural justice need not be enforced in the absence of a miscarriage of justice or some probable effect on the result.[88] The House of Lords rejected this reasoning decisively, but nevertheless it has made a reappearance in several later cases. In one, a university student had been rusticated without a hearing and in breach of natural justice, but the courts refused him relief on the ground that his offence was of the kind that merited a severe penalty and the penalty inflicted on him was perfectly proper.[89] In another case, where a schoolteacher's dismissal was annulled by the House of Lords because he had not been fairly heard, it was said that a

---

[85] *General Medical Council* v. *Spackman* [1943] AC 627 at 644; and see *Annamunthodo* v. *Oilfields Workers' Trade Union* [1961] AC 945 at 956 (Lord Denning).

[86] *John* v. *Rees* [1970] Ch. 345 at 402; cf. *Fullbrook* v. *Berkshire Magistrates' Courts Committee* (1970) 69 LGR 75 at 97. And now see *R.* v. *Secretary of State for the Environment ex p. Brent LBC* [1982] 2 WLR 693 at 734, rejecting the 'no difference' argument.

[87] *R.* v. *Secretary of State for the Environment ex p. Brent LBC* [1982] QB 593.

[88] See [1963] 1 QB at 556 (contention that no hearing was required since police officer had convicted himself out of his own mouth). See also *Byrne* v. *Kinematograph Renters Society Ltd.* [1958] 1 WLR 762. For criticism see above, p. 527; [1975] PL 27 (D. H. Clark).

[89] *Glynn* v. *Keele University* [1971] 1 WLR 487; see below, p. 536.

man had no right to be admitted to state his own case unless he could show that he had a case of substance to make, since the 'court does not act in vain'; and that it need not be determined whether a hearing was required where it 'could only be a useless formality' because there was nothing that the person affected could say against the action taken.[90] Much the same was said by the Court of Appeal where car-hire drivers were banned from London airport because of repeated and persistent offences against the regulations.[91] There may be cases where it is merely futile to grant relief, as where food hawkers were refused street trading consent without being allowed to see objections which had been lodged but which, as was found when the judge inspected them, could not have affected the decision.[92]

Judges are naturally inclined to use their discretion when a plea of breach of natural justice is used as the last refuge of a claimant with a bad case. But that should not be allowed to weaken the basic principle that fair procedure comes first, and that it is only after hearing both sides that the merits can be properly considered. A distinction might perhaps be made according to the nature of the decision. In the case of a tribunal which must decide according to law, it may be justifiable to disregard a breach of natural justice where the demerits of the claim are such that it would in any case be hopeless. But in the case of a discretionary administrative decision, such as the dismissal of a teacher or the expulsion of a student, hearing his case will often soften the heart of the authority and alter their decision, even though it is clear from the outset that punitive action would be justified.[93] This is the essence of good and considerate administration, and the law should take care to preserve it.

Relief refused in discretion

Closely akin to the subject of the foregoing paragraphs, and overlapping it in some cases, is the question of the court's discretion. The remedies most used in natural justice cases—certiorari, prohibition, mandamus, injunction, declaration—are discretionary, so that the court has power to

[90] *Malloch v Aberdeen Cpn.* [1971] 1 WLR 1578 at 1595 (Lord Wilberforce), 1600 (Lord Simon), criticised by D. H. Clark (as above). For this case see below, p. 567. See also *Wislang* v. *Medical Practitioners Disciplinary Committee* [1973] 1 NZLR 29 (fact that defence was likely to be unsuccessful taken into account in refusing relief in discretion); *Stininato* v. *Auckland Boxing Association* [1978] 1 NZLR 1 (relief refused to boxer denied licence because of complaints).
[91] *Cinnamond* v. *British Airports Authority* [1980] 1 WLR 582 (Shaw and Brandon LJJ).
[92] *R.* v. *Bristol CC ex p. Pearce* (1984) 83 LGR 711.
[93] For an example see Wade, *Towards Administrative Justice*, 10. In *Ridge* v. *Baldwin* the hearing later given to the chief constable's solicitor induced three members of the watch committee to change their minds: [1964] A.C. 40 at 47; and see at 68 (Lord Reid).

withhold them if it thinks fit; and from time to time the court will do so for some special reason, even though there has been a clear violation of natural justice.[94]

In one case a magistrates' clerk was dismissed from office for misconduct and was deprived of his pension rights, in both cases without a hearing, and was subsequently imprisoned for fraudulent conversion. Later he sought declarations that the dismissal and deprivation were void, and it was held that the authorities had wrongly denied him a hearing. Nevertheless the court refused to grant relief as regards his pension rights (the other claim having been abandoned) since he had been offered a full hearing but had refused it in order to pursue legal claims which he later dropped, had given inconsistent evidence, and had brought about a situation where to grant the declaration would mean further waste of time.[95]

The House of Lords exercised discretion in an unusual way in the case of a police probationer who had been unjustly required to resign. Since he was the holder of an office, and since he was held entitled to treat himself as unlawfully dismissed, he should have been granted mandamus so as to reinstate him. The House of Lords shrank from this because 'in practice it might border on usurpation of the powers of the chief constable', and they declared the probationer entitled only to the remedies of unlawful dismissal.[96] In other words, the House were not willing to protect this particular office specifically in the circumstances of the case'[97] feeling perhaps that the chief constable's hand ought not to be forced.

Discretion has been exercised in several cases where fair hearings have not been given to university students in disciplinary proceedings. One is in the case of the rusticated student mentioned above, in which an injunction was refused.[98] In another, students who had been required to withdraw for failure in examinations ought to have been given a hearing, but they delayed for seven months before taking legal action and the court declined to grant prerogative remedies to 'those who sleep upon their rights'.[99] Academic discipline is discussed further below.[1]

---

[94] For a general statement see *Hoffman–La Roche* v. *Secretary of State for Trade and Industry* [1975] AC 295 at 320 (Lord Denning MR).

[95] *Fullbrook* v. *Berkshire Magistrates' Courts Committee* (1970) 69 LGR 75. And see *Wislang* v. *Medical Practitioners Disciplinary Committee* [1973] 1 NZLR 29.

[96] *Chief Constable of the North Wales Police* v. *Evans* [1982] 1 WLR 1155 (Lord Brightman). Lord Bridge was in favour of granting mandamus. Contrary to its title and the report (at 1157), this was an application for judicial review. For further discussion see (1983) 99 LQR 171, (1985) 101 LQR 154.

[97] For specific protection of offices see below, p. 561.

[98] *Glynn* v. *Keele University*, above.

[99] R. v. *Aston University Senate ex p. Roffey* [1969] 2 QB 538. The application for prerogative remedies was probably misconceived: see below, p. 649.

[1] p. 568.

Applicants and their advisers sometimes make mistakes or omissions which the court will be unwilling to hold against them. 'We can see that it might be permissible to quash a decision seriously affecting a person who by mistake or misunderstanding due to his own defects or those of his advisers was deprived of the opportunity of being fully heard before the decision was reached.'[2]

Judicial discretion in withholding remedies is very carefully exercised and is a good deal less dangerous than some other arguments which have been used as excuses for condoning breaches of natural justice. Nevertheless it needs to be exercised with constant regard to the dangers mentioned in the preceding section.

Who is entitled to sue?

It seems plain that denial of a fair hearing is a wrong which is personal to the party aggrieved. If he himself waives the objection and does not complain, it is not the business of other people to do so, for as against them there is nothing wrong with the decision.[3] In the above-mentioned Ceylon case, accordingly, the proper person to challenge the minister's action was the municipal council itself, which had not been lawfully dissolved.[4] Since in fact the proceedings were brought by the mayor personally, he failed as not being the proper plaintiff. The Privy Council held that this was because the minister's order was merely voidable, but the fallacy in this reasoning has already been explained. The true reason, it is submitted, is to be found by asking what is the condition to be read into the statute. That condition need not be that any order made without giving a hearing is void: it should rather be that such an order is void unless accepted by the person concerned. The same point could be expressed in terms of locus standi, but more probably it is inherent in the principle of natural justice itself.

Similarly if in *Ridge* v. *Baldwin* the chief constable had not contested his dismissal, a third party could not have contested some order made by his successor on the ground that the former chief constable's dismissal was void, so that he was still in office.[5] It would be absurd to imply into any statute a condition capable of producing that effect. Consequently there is

---

[2] *R.* v. *Immigration Appeal Tribunal ex p. Enwia* [1984] 1 WLR 117 at 130; *R.* v. *Immigration Appeal Adjudicator ex p. Rahmani* [1985] The Times, 14 January (applicants' addresses not known; appeals heard in their absence; decisions quashed).

[3] *Hoffman–La Roche & Co.* v. *Secretary of State for Trade and Industry* [1975] AC 295 at 320 (Lord Denning MR).

[4] *Durayappah* v. *Fernando* [1967] 2 AC 337; above, p. 527.

[5] As pointed out in *Durayappah* v. *Fernando*, above, at p. 353, saying that it was 'a matter of ordinary common sense'. It might also have been affected by the doctrine of officers de facto: see above, p. 336.

no contradiction in saying that a breach of natural justice can be waived but
that if it is not waived the act is void.[6]

It does not follow that no third party can ever complain of a breach of
natural justice, though this may be true as regards denial of a fair hearing. If
a biased licensing authority grants an application, this is a wrong done not
to the applicant but to interested parties and to the public interest generally.
In that case the court may suitably grant a remedy, as happened in one such
case.[7]

Where the Secretary of State calls in a local plan for decision by himself
instead of by the local planning authority, that authority has no right to be
heard since it is not sufficiently affected.[8]

The right to know the opposing case

A proper hearing must always include a 'fair opportunity to those who are
parties in the controversy for correcting or contradicting anything
prejudicial to their view'.[9] Lord Denning has added:

If the right to be heard is to be a real right which is worth anything, it must carry
with it a right in the accused man to know the case which is made against him. He
must know what evidence has been given and what statements have been made
affecting him: and then he must be given a fair opportunity to correct or contradict
them.[10]

Accordingly where a chief constable required a police probationer to resign
on account of allegations about his private life which he was given no fair
opportunity to rebut the House of Lords granted him the remedies of
unlawful dismissal.[11] The Court of Appeal likewise quashed the refusal of
renewal of a tax-driver's licence because an adverse medical report was not
disclosed to him.[12] Where a police officer was dismissed in Malaya, after a
hearing before an adjudicating officer, the Privy Council declared the
dismissal void because the adjudicating officer was in possession of a report

---

[6] See above, p. 494, and (1968) 84 LQR at 109 (Wade).

[7] *R. v. Hendon Rural District Council ex p. Chorley* [1933] 2 KB 696; above, p. 476.

[8] *R. v. Secretary of State for the Environment ex p. Southwark LBC* [1987] The Times,
11 April, holding also that there is no right to be heard before rejection of the plan, except
where a statutory inquiry is held.

[9] Above, p. 507.

[10] *Kanda* v. *Government of Malaya* [1962] AC 322. See similarly *A.-G.* v. *Ryan* [1980] AC
718 (application for citizenship refused without disclosing grounds).

[11] *Chief Constable of the North Wales Police* v. *Evans* [1982] 1 WLR 1155; see similarly *R.*
v. *Home Secretary ex p. Benwell* [1985] QB 554; *R.* v. *Chief Constable of Thames Valley Police
ex p. Stevenson* [1986] The Times, 22 April; *R.* v. *Chief Constable of Avon & Somerset ex p.
Clarke* [1986] The Independent, 27 November.

[12] *R.* v. *Assistant Metropolitan Police Commissioner ex p. Howell* [1986] RTR 52.

of a board of inquiry which made charges of misconduct but which was not available to the police officer.[13] A similar case in England led to the quashing by certiorari of a decision of an Industrial Injuries Commissioner.[14] After hearing the case the Commissioner obtained, as he was empowered to do, a report from an independent medical expert; but the parties were not notified and were therefore unable to comment on the report. The Commissioner had, in effect, taken further evidence, unknown to the parties, between the hearing and the decision.[15] The same principle applies where a party is allowed to know only part of the real charge against him, as where a minister made it clear in a later speech that he had acted partly on grounds which he had not notified to the person against whom he made his order.[16] Another case in the same class is where a tribunal decides a case on some point which has not been argued before it, without giving the party an opportunity to comment on it.[17] Another is where a rent tribunal, having inspected the property before the hearing, fails to inform the landlord of unfavourable conclusions formed at the inspection.[18] Another is where a tribunal follows some previous decision of its own without disclosing it.[19]

A group of cases concerning statutory public inquiries also falls into this class. As already explained, natural justice does not require a minister to disclose all the information about a proposed housing scheme which his department collected before any objection to the scheme was lodged.[20] Nor need he necessarily disclose other schemes in his department which might possibly affect the scheme in question.[21] But after objection is lodged he

[13] *Kanda* v. *Government of Malaya* (above); similarly *Shareef* v. *Commissioner for Registration of Indian and Pakistani Residents* [1966] AC 47. The same principle has been applied to the ejection of a housing authority's tenant: *Re Webb and Ontario Housing Cpn.* (1978) 93 DLR (3d) 187; and to the discharge of a soldier from the army: *State (Gleeson)* v. *Minister for Defence* [1976] IR 280.

[14] *R.* v. *Deputy Industrial Injuries Commissioner ex p. Jones* [1962] 2 QB 677.

[15] See similarly *Taylor* v. *National Union of Seamen* [1967] 1 WLR 532 (evidence heard in accused party's absence); *Kane* v. *University of British Columbia* (1980) 110 DLR (3d) 311.

[16] *Maradana Mosque Trustees* v. *Mahmud* [1967] 1 AC 13. See also *R.* v. *Home Secretary ex p. Awuku* [1987] The Times, 3 October (Home Secretary's decision quashed since based on facts which immigrant was given no opportunity to explain); *R.* v. *Bedfordshire CC ex p. C* (1986) 85 LGR 218 (council's refusal to return child to father quashed since based on mother's allegations not put to him).

[17] *R.* v. *Industrial Injuries Commissioner ex p. Howarth* (1968) 4 KIR 621; *Sabey (H.) & Co.* v. *Secretary of State for the Environment* [1978] 1 All ER 586 (public inquiry); *TLG Building Materials* v. *Secretary of State for the Environment* (1980) 41 P & CR 243 (public inquiry).

[18] *R.* v. *Paddington & c. Rent Tribunal ex p. Bell London Properties Ltd.* [1949] 1 KB 666.

[19] *R.* v. *Criminal Injuries Compensation Board ex p. Ince* [1973] 1 WLR 1334 at 1345.

[20] Above, p. 509.

[21] *Rea* v. *Minister of Transport* (1982) 48 P & CR 239 (claim that motorway schemes were interdependent; disclosure not required).

must not receive evidence from one party without disclosing it to the others, as is shown by the case of the Jarrow clearance order.[22] The inspector who holds the inquiry must also take care to disclose all the material facts to all concerned. Compulsory purchase orders have been quashed where the inspector during his site inspection asked the residents about their wishes and failed to inform the objectors of the answers, even though it was not clear that the answers had prejudiced the objectors' case;[23] and where the inspector based his recommendations upon what he had himself seen on his site inspection, without disclosing to the objectors that this raised questions quite different from those ventilated at the inquiry.[24] In such cases the inspector ought to give the parties a fair opportunity to comment on the new evidence.[25] Likewise the minister, when considering the inspector's report, ought not to take account of new factual evidence relating to the particular case without giving the parties an opportunity to comment on it.[26] But for this situation there are usually statutory rules, explained elsewhere.[27]

Disclosure of the charge or of the opposing case must be made in reasonable time to allow the person affected to prepare his defence or his comments.[28] He must have fair notice of any accusation against him, and this is commonly included in the right to a fair hearing by calling it the right 'to notice and hearing'. At an inquiry, for example, any person who might be affected by adverse findings should be given fair warning so that he can defend himself against them at the hearing.[29] But notice may not be indispensable as to matters where no fact is in dispute and there is no prejudice to the party charged.[30]

As several of the above-mentioned cases show, natural justice often requires the disclosure of reports and evidence in the possession of the

---

[22] *Errington* v. *Minister of Health* [1935] 1 KB 249, discussed above, p. 510, and citing other cases. See also *Lake District Special Planning Board* v. *Secretary of State for the Environment* (1975) 236 EG 417; *Reading BC* v. *Secretary of State for the Environment* (1985) 52 P & CR 385, where a planning authority was given the benefit of this rule.

[23] *Hibernian Property Co. Ltd.* v. *Secretary of State for the Environment* (1973) 27 P & CR 197.

[24] *Fairmount Investments Ltd.* v. *Secretary of State for the Environment* [1976] 1 WLR 1255 (inspector noticed signs of unsafe foundations).

[25] As to site inspections see *Winchester CC* v. *Secretary of State for the Environment* (1978) 36 P & CR 455.

[26] *Geraghty* v. *Minister for Local Government* [1976] IR 153.

[27] Below, p. 982. See also *Pfizer Co. Ltd.* v. *Deputy Minister of National Revenue* (1975) 68 DLR (3d) 9.

[28] *R.* v. *Thames Magistrates' Court ex p. Polemis* [1974] 1 WLR 1371; *Brentnall* v. *Free Presbyterian Church of Scotland* 1986 SLT 471.

[29] *Mahon* v. *Air New Zealand Ltd.* [1984] AC 808.

[30] See *Davis* v. *Carew-Pole* [1956] 1 WLR 833.

deciding authority. A licensing authority must disclose any objections lodged with it so that the applicant may reply to them.[31] Where a police officer was compulsorily retired after being examined by a medical officer chosen by the police authority, the Court of Appeal held that natural justice had been violated because the police officer's own doctor had not been allowed to see the report of an inquiry and a medical report made to the police authority, though it was also held that these need not necessarily be disclosed to the police officer himself.[32] A tribunal must disclose reports and evidence bearing upon the case before it, although it may use its own knowledge and experience as to general questions.[33] The decision of an assessment committee was therefore quashed when it failed to disclose a report by an expert valuer which made it fix a rating assessment at a figure higher than that contended for by the rating authority; and the majority of the Court of Appeal held that it made no difference whether the report was obtained before or after the assessment was objected to or whether the report was of a general or specific character.[34] In New Zealand the decision of a town planning committee was held to be void because at the hearing given to the parties the committee failed to disclose a long report from its planning officer about the case;[35] and the dismissal of a civil servant was invalid because an adverse report about him was not disclosed.[36]

Limits to the right to see adverse evidence

In some administrative situations there are limits to the broad principles stated above. The court must always consider the statutory framework within which natural justice is to operate, and a limit may sometimes necessarily be implied. What is essential is substantial fairness to the person adversely affected. But this may sometimes be adequately achieved by telling him the substance of the case he has to meet, without

[31] R. v. *Huntingdon DC ex p. Cowan* [1984] 1 WLR 501 (objections to entertainments licence not disclosed; refusal quashed).

[32] R. v. *Kent Police Authority ex p. Godden* [1971] 2 QB 662. See likewise R. v. *London County Council ex p. Commercial Gas Co.* (1895) 11 TLR 337 (reports of gas testing must be disclosed).

[33] R. v. *National Insurance Commissioner ex p. Viscusi* [1974] 1 WLR 646; *Freeland* v. *Glasgow Licensing Board* 1980 SLT 101; and see below, p. 926.

[34] R. v. *Westminster Assessment Committee ex p. Grosvenor House (Park Lane) Ltd.* [1941] 1 KB 53. Scott LJ considered that a report obtained before the objection was lodged was part of the committee's expert knowledge and need not be disclosed.

[35] *Denton* v. *Auckland City* [1969] NZLR 256.

[36] *Fraser* v. *State Services Commission* [1984] 1 NZLR 116.

THE RIGHT TO A FAIR HEARING

disclosing the precise evidence or the sources of information. The extent of the disclosure required by natural justice may have to be weighed against the prejudice to the scheme of the Act which disclosure may involve. In a leading case the Court of Appeal applied these considerations to the procedure of the Gaming Board in granting certificates of consent to persons wishing to operate gaming clubs.[37] It was the Board's duty to investigate the credentials of applicants and to obtain information from the police and other confidential sources. Such sources, it was held, need not be divulged if there were objections properly based on the public interest. The Board must, however, give the applicant an indication of the objections raised against him so that he can answer them, as fairness requires. The same doctrine was applied to the preparation of a report by inspectors appointed by the Board of Trade to investigate the affairs of a company: their duty to act fairly did not require them to disclose the names of witnesses or the transcripts of their evidence, or to show to a director any adverse passages in their proposed report in draft.[38] But, without quoting chapter and verse, they must give him a fair opportunity to contradict what is said against him, as by giving him an outline of the charge; and if their information is so confidential that they cannot reveal it even in general terms, they should not use it.[39]

In both the above cases the authorities were held to have acted properly, since they had given fair hearings on the substance of the charges. So was an immigration officer, who gave a suspected illegal immigrant a full opportunity to understand and contradict the case against him but who did not reveal reports which he had obtained when making inquiries.[40] Lord Denning MR said that 'the rules of natural justice must not be stretched too far'. But he has made it clear that the duty to act fairly applied in the same way to the investigations of the Race Relations Board (now the Commission for Racial Equality) and its committees.[41] This duty likewise obliges the Monopolies and Mergers Commission, in examining a proposed company take-over, to ensure that the parties understand the issues and arguments which will be decisive, but they need not necessarily disclose to one party every piece of evidence submitted by the other,

---

[37] R. v. Gaming Board for Great Britain ex p. Benaim and Khaida [1970] 2 QB 417.

[38] Re Pergamon Press Ltd. [1971] Ch. 388; and see Maxwell v. Department of Trade and Industry [1974] QB 523 (no duty to disclose inspectors' proposed conclusions). See also Ceylon University v. Fernando [1960] 1 WLR 223 (student suspended for cheating in examination not offered opportunity to confront accuser, but adequately informed of case to be met: student's suspension upheld); O'Rourke v. Miller (1985) 58 ALR 269.

[39] cf. Canterbury Building Society v. Baker (1979) 2 NSWLR 265. As to cases involving national security see below, p. 574.

[40] R. v. Home Secretary ex p. Mughal [1974] QB 313. And see Lim v. Minister of the Interior, Malaya [1964] 1 WLR 554; Herring v. Templeman [1973] 3 All ER 569.

[41] R. v. Race Relations Board ex p. Selvarajan [1975] 1 WLR 1686.

provided always that there is no manifest unfairness.[42] Similarly the Parole Board, in recommending that a paroled prisoner should be recalled to prison, is under a duty to act fairly but is not required to make full disclosure of all the adverse evidence in its possession.[43] The European Court of Human Rights has held that this limitation violates the prisoner's right to a proper judicial decision under the European Convention, and that the scope of judicial review is also inadequate for this purpose.[44]

Procedure generally

A 'hearing' will normally be an oral hearing.[45] But in some cases it may suffice to give an opportunity to make representations in writing, provided that any adverse material is disclosed and provided, as always, that the demands of fairness are substantially met. The House of Lords has furnished the leading example in the case of the Liverpool councillors who had failed to make a valid rate and were surcharged by the district auditor for wilful misconduct. The auditor gave them full particulars of his complaints and offered to consider their representations in writing, which they duly made without asking to be heard orally. The Court of Appeal held that this procedure fell short of fairness, since the charges were serious, they attributed bad faith, and past practice had almost invariably been to give oral hearings in surcharge cases. The House of Lords held the contrary, finding that in dealing with a group of 49 councillors acting collectively, none of whom asked to be heard orally, the auditors had adopted a procedure which was both suitable and fair in all the circumstances.[46]

In various situations it may be possible to dispense with oral hearings. It has been held that a statutory board, acting in an administrative capacity, may decide for itself whether to deal with applications by oral hearing or merely on written evidence and argument, provided that it does in substance 'hear' them;[47] and that dealing with an appeal on written communications only is not contrary to natural justice.[48] The visitor of a college may similarly deal with an appeal on written submissions only[49] and

[42] R. v. *Monopolies and Mergers Commission ex p. Matthew Brown Plc* [1987] 1 WLR 1235.

[43] R. v. *Home Secretary ex p. Gunnell* [1984] The Times, 7 November.

[44] *Weeks* v. *United Kingdom* [1987] ECHR Series A, vol. 114 (decision of 2 March).

[45] R. v. *Immigration Tribunal ex p. Mehmet* [1977] 1 WLR 795 (tribunal's decision and resulting deportation order quashed for failure to afford oral hearing).

[46] *Lloyd* v. *McMahon* [1987] AC 625.

[47] See R. v. *Local Government Board ex p. Arlidge* [1914] 1 KB 160 at 191, approved in R. v. *Immigration Appeal Tribunal ex p. Jones (Ross)* [1988] 1 WLR 477; R. v. *Amphlett (Judge)* [1915] 2 KB 223 (district wages board); *Jeffs* v. *New Zealand Dairy Board* [1967] 1 AC 551 (dairy zoning order).

[48] *Stuart* v. *Haughley Parochial Church Council* [1935] Ch. 452, affirmed [1936] Ch. 32 (lay electoral commission).

[49] R. v. *Bishop of Ely* (1794) 5 TR 475 at 477 (Buller J).

a student may be rusticated from his college without an oral hearing, if he been told the nature of the complaints against him and given a fair opportunity to state his case in writing.[50] A licensing authority may give a 'hearing' on paper,[51] provided that the applicant is allowed to reply to any objections known to the authority.[52] Some statutory tribunals have power to dispense with oral hearings;[53] but if they do so, they must be careful to give a party a fair opportunity to comment on any adverse statement submitted.[54] Large numbers of planning appeals are disposed of on paper, but in those cases the appellant previously waived his right to a statutory hearing.[55] A number of tribunals may dispense with hearings under their statutory rules in certain circumstances.[56]

Where an oral hearing is given, it has been laid down that a tribunal must (a) consider all relevant evidence which a party wishes to submit; (b) inform every party of all the evidence to be taken into account, whether derived from another party or independently; (c) allow witnesses to be questioned; (d) allow comment on the evidence and argument on the whole case.[57] Failure to allow the last two rights, which include the right of cross-examination,[58] has led to the quashing of punishments awarded by prison visitors in a series of cases. In one, the visitors refused to allow prisoners to call witnesses because of the administrative inconvenience of bringing them from distant prisons to which they had been dispersed after a riot, and for other inadequate reasons.[59] In another, a prisoner was not allowed to question his own witness or to comment on the evidence.[60] In a third, there was a witness unknown to the prisoner but known to the investigating officer, who failed to inform the visitors.[61] This last case shows

[50] *Brighton Cpn v. Parry* (1972) 70 LGR 576. See also *Ayanlowo v. Commissioners of Inland Revenue* [1975] IRLR 253 (dismissal of probationer civil servant: letter sufficient).
[51] *Kavanagh v. Chief Constable of Devon and Cornwall* [1974] QB 624. And see *British Oxygen Co. Ltd. v. Board of Trade* [1971] AC 610 at 625 (Lord Reid).
[52] *R. v. Huntingdon DC ex p. Cowan* [1984] 1 WLR 501.
[53] See below, p. 925.   [54] *R. v. Housing Appeal Tribunal* [1920] 3 KB 334.
[55] See below, p. 990. The procedure is now statutory.   [56] See below, p. 925.
[57] *R. v. Deputy Industrial Injuries Commissioner ex p. Moore* [1965] 1 QB 456 at 490 (Diplock LJ). See also *Asher v. Secretary of State for the Environment* [1974] Ch. 208 (district auditor); *R. v. Secretary of State for the Environment ex p. Stewart* (1978) 77 LGR 431 (inquiry: evidence wrongly excluded).
[58] For dicta favourable to a right of cross-examination see *Osgood v. Nelson* (1872) LR 5 HL 636 at 646; *Marriott v. Minister of Health* (1936) 154 LT 47 at 50; *R. v. Newmarket Assessment Committee ex p. Allen Newport Ltd.* [1945] 2 All ER 371 at 373.
[59] *R. v. Hull Prison Visitors ex p. St. Germain* (No. 2) [1979] 1 WLR 1401, an exemplary judgment of Geoffrey Lane LJ. See likewise *Re Cheeung and Minister of Employment and Immigration* (1981) 122 DLR (3d) 41 (adjudicator refused to allow immigration officer to be called as witness: deportation order set aside).
[60] *R. v. Gartree Prison Visitors ex p. Mealy* [1981] The Times, 14 November.
[61] *R. v. Blundeston Prison Visitors ex p. Fox-Taylor* [1982] 1 All ER 646.

that natural justice may be violated by the conduct of those who bring forward the accusation as well as by that of the tribunal—as also does a later case, where a prosecution was instigated by a detective who concealed his own criminal record.[62] Even a mistake by the applicant's own advisers, if it deprives him of the opportunity to be heard, may entitle him to relief.[63] Where there is a charge of serious misconduct it is especially important, as the Court of Appeal has emphasised,[64] that procedural fairness should be carefully observed. In various other contexts, however, it is scarcely less important.

Failure to allow cross-examination by an objector at a statutory inquiry has led to the quashing of the Secretary of State's decision,[65] though not where the objections went beyond the proper scope of the inquiry.[66] On the other hand there must be many administrative proceedings in which formal testimony and cross-examination are inappropriate, the inquiry being informal.[67] When offering a hearing after an investigation the Commission for Racial Equality need not produce witnesses for cross-examination.[68] It has been said that even the Crown Court, when acting administratively in a licensing appeal, need not allow cross-examination.[69]

It is clear that the strict legal rules of evidence need not be observed.[70] In an industrial injury case the Commissioner was therefore held entitled to take into account evidence given at a hearing of medical reports made in previous cases, although in a court of law these might have been inadmissible under the rule against hearsay.[71] But this dispensation is subject

[62] R. v. Knightsbridge Crown Court ex p. Goonatilleke [1986] QB 1 (it being a case of one man's word against another's, the conviction was quashed).

[63] R. v. Diggines ex p. Rahmani [1985] QB 1109, affirmed [1986] AC 475.

[64] In the Hull Prison case, above.

[65] Nicholson v. Secretary of State for Energy (1978) 76 LGR 693; and see Errington v. Minister of Health [1935] 1 KB 249 at 272; Wednesbury Cpn. v. Ministry of Housing and Local Government (No. 2) [1966] 2 QB 275 at 302. cf. National Companies and Securities Commission v. News Corporation Ltd. (1984) 52 ALR 417.

[66] Bushell v. Secretary of State for the Environment [1981] AC 75. For this question see below, p. 977.

[67] See Re Pergamon Press Ltd. [1971] Ch. 388 at 400; Herring v. Templeman [1973] 3 All ER 569 (no witnesses allowed); cf. Ceylon University v. Fernando [1960] 1 WLR 223 at 253 (opportunity to cross-examine not requested); O'Rourke v. Miller (1984) 58 ALR 269 (police probationer not allowed to cross-examine).

[68] R. v. Commission for Racial Equality ex p. Cottrell & Rothon [1980] 1 WLR 1580.

[69] Kavanagh v. Chief Constable of Devon and Cornwall (above).

[70] Mahon v. Air New Zealand Ltd. [1984] AC 808.

[71] R. v. Deputy Industrial Injuries Commissioner ex p. Moore (above); and see Kavanagh's case (above); Miller (T.A.) Ltd. v. Minister of Housing and Local Government [1968] 1 WLR 992 (hearsay evidence at statutory inquiry). The Supreme Court of the Irish Republic does not permit the 'laissez-faire attitude' of these decisions: Kiely v. Minister for Social Welfare [1977] IR 267.

to the overriding obligation to give a genuinely fair hearing. The admission of hearsay evidence may make it all the more necessary to allow it to be tested by cross-examination, and if that is not practicable the right course in some cases may be to exclude the evidence from consideration.[72]

It has twice been held that natural justice demands that the decision should be based on some evidence of probative value.[73] As we have seen elsewhere, the courts are now showing a strong disposition to develop 'no evidence' as a head of judicial review,[74] and if they do so it may be that natural justice will supply the peg on which to hang it.

The right to representation by a lawyer or other person may prove to be a part of natural justice in suitable cases, but this is not as yet clearly established. It probably exists in the case of a formal tribunal[75] or investigation[76] if there is no provision to the contrary;[77] but regulations excluding it have been upheld.[78] In cases concerning non-statutory domestic tribunals the Court of Appeal has favoured the right of legal representation where a serious charge was made,[79] but has held that it may be excluded by an association's rules.[80] It is also excluded, as the same Court has held, in disciplinary proceedings which demand a rapid hearing and decision, as in the case of offences committed by prisoners.[81] But prison visitors have discretion and must consider any request for representation in the light of all the circumstances, including the seriousness of the charge, the prisoner's capacity to present his case, and fairness generally; and on a charge of mutiny they cannot reasonably refuse the request.[82] There is also a

---

[72] See the Hull Prison case (above) at 1409.

[73] R. v. Deputy Industrial Injuries Commissioner ex p. Moore (above); Mahon v. Air New Zealand Ltd. [1984] AC 808. But a tribunal may accept statements agreed between the parties without violating natural justice: R. v. Oxford Local Valuation Panel ex p. Oxford CC (1981) 79 LGR 432.

[74] Above, p. 319.

[75] R. v. Assessment Committee, St. Mary Abbotts, Kensington [1891] 1 QB 378.

[76] R. v. Commissioner of Police ex p. Edwards (1977) 32 FLR 183.

[77] See below, p. 931.

[78] Maynard v. Osmond [1977] QB 240 (police discipline regulations). The Court of Appeal took account of the fact that there could be legal representation on appeal to the Home Secretary. Contrast Joplin v. Chief Constable of Vancouver (1985) 20 DLR (4th) 314 (police regulation excluding right to counsel held ultra vires on grounds of fairness).

[79] Pett v. Greyhound Racing Association [1969] 1 QB 125, not followed in (No. 2) [1970] 1 QB 46 (Lyell J).

[80] Enderby Town Football Club Ltd. v. Football Association Ltd. [1971] Ch. 591. See also London Passenger Transport Board v. Moscrop [1942] AC 332; Tait v. Central Radio Taxis (Tollcross) Ltd. 1987 SLT 506.

[81] Fraser v. Mudge [1975] 1 WLR 1132.; R. v. Maze Prison Visitors ex p. Hone [1988] 2 WLR 177 (HL) (decisions upheld).

[82] R. v. Home Secretary ex p. Tarrant [1985] QB 251 (visitors held that representation could not be allowed: decisions quashed).

right to legal assistance and representation under the European Convention on Human Rights.[83]

Wrongful refusal of an adjournment, when reasonably requested, may amount to refusal of a fair hearing, particularly where the party affected is thereby disabled from appearing at all.[84] So may the wrongful exclusion from a juvenile court of a social worker who might have assisted a boy who was convicted.[85]

Lord Denning MR has summed up the procedure in the case of an investigating body such as the Commission for Racial Equality which is under a duty to act fairly:[86]

The investigating body is, however, the master of its own procedure. It need not hold a hearing. It can do everything in writing. It need not allow lawyers. It need not put every detail of the case against a man. Suffice it if the broad grounds are given. It need not name the informants. It can give the substance only. Moreover, it need not do everything itself. It can employ secretaries and assistants to do all the preliminary work and leave much to them. But, in the end, the investigating body itself must come to its own decisions and make its own report.

Reasons for decisions

It has never been a principle of natural justice that reasons should be given for decisions.[87] There appears to be no such rule even in the courts of law themselves[88] and it has not been thought suitable to create one for administrative bodies.[89] Nevertheless there is a strong case to be made for the giving of reasons as an essential element of administrative justice. The

[83] *Campbell and Fell* v. *United Kingdom* ECHR (1984) Series A, no. 80 (prisoners' claim succeeded). See the ECHR judgment discussed in the *Maze Prison* case (above) at 187.

[84] *Priddle* v. *Fisher & Sons* [1968] 1 WLR 1478; *Re M (an infant)* [1968] 1 WLR 1897; *Rose* v. *Humbles* [1972] 1 WLR 33. Contrast *Ostreicher* v. *Secretary of State for the Environment* [1978] 1 WLR 810 (religious objection to date of inquiry).

[85] *R.* v. *Southwark Juvenile Court ex p. J.* [1973] 1 WLR 1300.

[86] *R.* v. *Race Relations Board ex p. Selvarajan* [1975] 1 WLR 1686; and see *R.* v. *Commission for Racial Equality ex p. Cottrell & Rothon* (above); same *ex p. Hillingdon LBC* [1982] AC 779.

[87] *R.* v. *Gaming Board for Great Britain ex p. Benaim and Khaida* [1970] 2 QB 417 at 431; *Payne* v. *Lord Harris* [1981] 1 WLR 754 (prisoner not entitled to reasons for refusal of parole); *R.* v. *Bristol CC ex p. Pearce* (1984) 83 LGR 711; *R.* v. *Secretary of State for Social Services ex p. Connolly* [1986] 1 WLR 421 at 431; *Public Service Board of New South Wales* v. *Osmond* (1986) 60 ALJR 209.

[88] Reasons are not normally given in applications for leave to appeal; but in any matter of importance a judge ought to give reasons: *Capital and Suburban Properties Ltd.* v. *Swycher* [1976] Ch. 319 at 325; *Hoey* v. *Hoey* [1984] 1 WLR 464.

[89] For review of authorities see *Pure Spring Co. Ltd.* v. *Minister of National Revenue* [1947] 1 DLR 501 at 534; see also (1970) 33 MLR 154 (M. Akehurst); [1978] PL 16 (G. A. Flick); *Fundamental Duties*, ch. vii (J. W. Bridge); Taggart (ed.), *Judicial Review of Administrative Action in the 1980s*, cited below.

need for it has been sharply exposed by the expanding law of judicial review, now that so many decisions are liable to be quashed or appealed against on grounds of improper purpose, irrelevant considerations and errors of law of various kinds. Unless the citizen can discover the reasoning behind the decision, he may be unable to tell whether it is reviewable or not, and so he may be deprived of the protection of the law. A right to reasons is therefore an indispensable part of a sound system of judicial review. Natural justice may provide the best rubric for it, since the giving of reasons is required by the ordinary man's sense of justice. It is also a healthy discipline for all who exercise power over others. 'No single factor has inhibited the development of English administrative law as seriously as the absence of any general obligation upon public authorities to give reasons for their decisions.'[90]

The need for this obligation was recognised both by the Committee on Ministers' Powers of 1932[91] and by the Committee on Administrative Tribunals and Enquiries of 1957;[92] and the latter's recommendation was implemented by the Tribunals and Inquiries Act 1958, as explained elsewhere,[93] which required reasons to be given on request by statutory tribunals and by ministers after statutory inquiries. American federal law has a comparable requirement.[94] In Australian federal law the right to reasons has been extended to administrative decisions generally.[95] But the High Court of Australia has emphatically reversed an attempt by the New South Wales Court of Appeal to introduce a right to reasons as a general rule of common law.[96] A more enlightened doctrine prevails in the European Economic Community, where the Council and the Commission are required to state the reasons for their regulations, directives and decisions.[97]

[90] *Administration under Law* (a JUSTICE booklet), p. 23. The Home Secretary's refusal to give reasons in cases of refusal of political asylum was criticised by Woolf LJ in *R. v. Home Secretary ex p. Singh* [1987] The Times, 8 June.

[91] Cmd. 4060 (1932), pp. 80, 100.

[92] Cmnd. 218 (1957), paras. 98, 351.

[93] Below, p. 934.

[94] Administrative Procedure Act of 1946, s. 8(*b*).

[95] Administrative Decisions (Judicial Review) Act 1977, s. 13. The Administrative Law Act 1978, s. 8, of Victoria is similar. Both Acts require reasons in writing to be given on request.

[96] *Public Service Board of New South Wales v. Osmond* (1986) 60 ALJ 209 (Board dismissed New South Wales civil servant's appeal against non-promotion and refused to state reasons). The case for the right to reasons is strongly argued by Kirby CJ in the court below, [1984] 3 NSWLR 447, and in Taggart (ed.), *Judicial Review of Administrative Action in the 1980s*, where the editor also criticises the High Court's decision.

[97] Treaty of Rome, art. 190. A regulation is invalid if reasons are not given: *REWE v. Hamptzollamt Kiel* [1982] 1 CMLR 449.

Although there is no general rule of law requiring the giving of reasons, an administrative authority may be unable to show that it has acted lawfully unless it explains itself. Thus where the Act empowered licensing justices to refuse a licence on one of several specified grounds, and they refused an application without stating any ground, mandamus was granted to make them state the ground even though they were not obliged to give their reasons for it.[98] Going still further the Privy Council held that a minister who had failed to give reasons for a special tax assessment had not shown that it was correct and that the taxpayer's appeal must be allowed.[99] And in a series of cases it has been held that statutory tribunals must give satisfactory reasons in order that the losing party may know whether he should exercise his right of appeal on a point of law.[1] In these cases there was a statutory duty to give reasons on request, but the judges spoke in such general terms that they seem to recognise that formal tribunals have an inherent duty to state their reasons, at any rate where there is a right of appeal of any kind. The same logic might be invoked for other varieties of administrative action, since there is always a right of recourse to the High Court for judicial review, which is no less important than a right of appeal. Yet a further consideration is that the House of Lords has indicated that if a minister fails to explain a decision satisfactorily, it may be condemned as arbitrary and unreasonable.[2]

A further question is how far explanation of reasons can be demanded in proceedings for judicial review. Discussing this question in a case where a local authority had refused to make a discretionary grant to a student, Sir John Donaldson MR said that though reasons need not be given for such refusals, the position was quite different once leave to apply for judicial review had been given. It was then the duty of the authority 'to make full and fair disclosure', 'to explain fully what has occured and why'. In fact the authority's evidence was little more than a bare statement that it had considered the circumstances of the case, which the Court of Appeal surprisingly accepted, though with some misgiving, as showing that there had been no abuse of discretion.[3]

Although there may be difficulties in formulating suitable rules and the

---

[98] R. v. Sykes (1875) 1 QBD 52; R. v. Thomas [1892] 1 QB 426. See likewise Flexman v. Franklin CC [1979] 2 NZLR 690; Barton v. Licensing Control Commission [1982] 1 NZLR 31.

[99] Minister of National Revenue v. Wrights' Canadian Ropes Ltd. [1947] AC 109 at 123. See likewise Giris Pty. Ltd. v. Federal Cmr. of Taxation (1969) 119 CLR 365 at 373.

[1] Norton Tool Co. Ltd. v. Tewson [1973] 1 WLR 45 and other cases cited below, p. 936. And see Pepys v. London Transport Executive [1975] 1 WLR 234.

[2] Padfield v. Minister of Agriculture, Fisheries and Food [1968] AC 997; above, p. 401.

[3] R. v. Lancashire CC ex p. Huddleston [1986] 2 All ER 941. Parker LJ emphasised the special circumstances of the case and held that a bare general statement would not normally suffice. For criticism see [1986] PL 508 (A. W. Bradley).

arguments are not all on one side, there is no doubt that the lack of a general duty to give reasons is an outstanding deficiency of administrative law.

Appeals

Natural justice does not require that there should be a right of appeal from any decision.[4] This is an inevitable corollary of the fact that there is no right of appeal against a statutory authority unless statute so provides.[5]

Whether a hearing given on appeal is an acceptable substitute for a hearing not given, or not properly given, before the initial decision is in some cases an arguable question. In principle there ought to be an observance of natural justice equally at both stages; and accordingly natural justice is violated if the true charge is put forward only at the appeal stage.[6] If natural justice is violated at the first stage, the right of appeal is not so much a true right of appeal as a corrected initial hearing: instead of a fair trial followed by appeal, the procedure is reduced to unfair trial followed by fair trial. This was pointed out by Megarry J in a trade union expulsion case, holding that, as a general rule, a failure of natural justice in the trial body cannot be cured by a sufficiency of natural justice in the appellate body.[7] He distinguished a Canadian case in which a law student had been refused leave to take a degree: he had been allowed to submit only a written statement to the faculty council, but on appeal had been given a full oral hearing and represented by counsel in a fully judicial proceeding, and the Supreme Court of Canada held that the appeal cured any earlier defect.[8] In New Zealand, also, it has been held that a fair appeal does not normally redeem a failure of natural justice at first instance, though it may be taken into account in considering the award of discretionary remedies.[9] Nor does a full hearing on appeal justify cancellation of a taxi-driver's licence[10] or dismissal of a schoolteacher[11] without an initial hearing.

[4] *Ward* v. *Bradford Cpn.* (1971) 70 LGR 27.

[5] See below, p. 937.

[6] *Annamunthodo* v. *Oilfields Workers Trade Union* [1961] AC 945.

[7] *Leary* v. *National Union of Vehicle Builders* [1971] Ch. 34. See also *R.* v. *Aston University Senate ex p. Roffey* [1969] 2 QB 538; *Glynn* v. *Keele University* [1971] 1 WLR 487; *Re Cardinal and Cornwall Police Commissioners* (1973) 42 DLR (3d) 323; *Fagan* v. *Coursing Association* (1974) 8 SASR 546 at 562; *Hall* v. *New South Wales Trotting Club* [1976] 1 NSWLR 323.

[8] *King* v. *University of Saskatchewan* (1969) 6 DLR (3d) 120. Megarry J in *Leary's* case (above) would if necessary have declined to follow this decision. See also *Pillai* v. *Singapore City Council* [1968] 1 WLR 1278, where the question was governed by rules of procedure for the dismissal of employees; *Re Clark and Ontario Securities Commission* (1966) 56 DLR (2d) 585; *Twist* v. *Randwick Municipal Council* (1976) 12 ALR 379 at 387; *Re Harelkin and University of Regina* (1979) 96 DLR (3d) 14.

[9] *Reid* v. *Rowley* [1977] 2 NZLR 472; *Wislang* v. *Medical Practitioners Disciplinary Committee* [1974] 1 NZLR 29.

[10] *Moran* v. *A.-G.* [1976] IR 400.

[11] *Pratt* v. *Wanganui Education Board* [1977] 1 NZLR 476.

According to the Privy Council, however, Megarry J's 'general rule' was too broadly stated, since in some cases members of organisations, whose rights depend upon contract, 'should be taken to have agreed to accept what in the end is a fair decision, notwithstanding some initial defect'. An appeal to the committee of the Australian Jockey Club was held, for this reason, to cure an initial decision of the stewards which failed to observe the principles of natural justice in disqualifying the owner of a horse found to have been raced improperly.[12] But the Privy Council emphasised that their reservations applied to domestic disputes which have to be settled by agreed procedure under contractual rules. Those cases fall outside administrative law, since they do not concern governmental action.

Squarely within the field of public law, however, is the case of the Liverpool councillors, in which the House of Lords followed the lead of the Privy Council. The councillors had been surcharged by the district auditor with losses resulting from their failure to make a valid rate. It was held that they had been given a fair hearing, but that, in any case, a defective hearing would have been cured by the full rehearing of their case on their appeal to the High Court.[13] It was stressed that the scope of the statutory appeal was as ample as it could be and more ample than that of judicial review;[14] and a distinction was drawn between full appeals where all the evidence may be examined and limited appeals on questions of law only or where the appellate body is bound by findings of fact.[15] It is only where the appellate body can enter into the merits and determine the issue itself that the House of Lords' reasoning applies; and in that case it is hard to deny that a fair hearing has been given, even though two fair hearings were legally due. And an appeal may have greater curative effect where the appeal tribunal has original as well as appellate jurisdiction.[16]

It is always possible that some statutory scheme may imply that an 'appeal' is to be the only opportunity of a hearing. It is surprising that this question has not been settled under the Town and Country Planning Acts. If planning permission is refused by the local planning authority the applicant may appeal to the Secretary of State who must, if requested, hold

[12] *Calvin* v. *Carr* [1980] AC 574, approving the judgment of Cooke J in *Reid* v. *Rowley* (above). See also *Murray* v. *Greyhound Racing Control Board of Queensland* [1979] Qd. R. 111.

[13] *Lloyd* v. *McMahon* [1987] AC 625. See similarly *Re Chromex Nickel Mines Ltd.* (1970) 16 DLR (3d) 273. Contrast *O'Laughlin* v. *Halifax Longshoremen's Association* (1972) 28 DLR (3d) 315; *Pollock* v. *Alberta Union of Provincial Employees* (1978) 90 DLR (3d) 506; *Colpitts* v. *Australian Telecommunications Commission* (1986) 70 ALR 554.

[14] At 884 (Lord Bridge).

[15] At 891 (Lord Templeman).

[16] As in *Clark* v. *Young* [1927] NZLR 348; *Twist* v. *Randwick Municipal Council* (1976) 12 ALR 379; *R.* v. *Marks ex p. Australian Building Federation* (1981) 35 ALR 241; *Marine Hull Insurance* v. *Hereford* (1985) 62 ALR 253.

an inquiry or hearing.[17] But does this absolve the local planning authority from giving a fair hearing before refusing the initial application? In 1952 a judge said that it did,[18] but that was at the time when judicial concern for natural justice was at its lowest ebb. In 1987, by contrast, a judge held that a planning authority was in breach of its duty to act fairly in not giving rival traders an opportunity to oppose a grant of permission for an amusement area and arcade.[19] Previously it has been assumed that the scheme of the Act does not require a fair hearing before the appeal stage; but this is questionable, as is shown by the good practice of some local planning authorities who adjourn applications which they are minded to refuse so that the applicant may first submit argument in writing. In New Zealand it has been held that the local committee must observe natural justice,[20] but that was within a different statutory framework.

The existence of a full right of appeal on the merits may be taken into account in holding that the scheme of the Act does not require a hearing for some preliminary administrative step, as where an inspector of taxes applied for leave to raise assessments outside the usual time on grounds of fraud, wilful default or neglect.[21]

The Court of Appeal on one occasion held that the exercise of a right of administrative appeal (by a police officer to the Home Secretary) deprived the appellant of his right to complain to the court of a denial of natural justice at the initial stage. Here there was clearly a confusion between a right of appeal on the merits of the case and judicial review of the legality of the whole proceedings; and the decision was duly reversed by the House of Lords.[22]

Delegated hearings

Does natural justice require that 'the one who decides must hear'?[23] In other words, may the hearing be given by one body, e.g. a committee of the deciding authority, and the decision itself by another?

Where the deciding authority is a minister or central government

---

[17] Town and Country Planning Act 1971, s. 36, replacing earlier Acts.

[18] Parker J. *obiter* in *Hanily* v. *Minister of Local Government and Planning* [1952] 2 QB 444 at 452. As to listed buildings see above, p. 193.

[19] *R.* v. *Great Yarmouth BC ex p. Botton Bros. Arcades Ltd.* [1987] The Times, 31 July. See similarly *R.* v. *Monmouth DC ex p. Jones* (1985) 53 P & CR 108 (planning permission quashed since objector not given opportunity to explain his case).

[20] *Denton* v. *Auckland City* [1969] NZLR 256.

[21] *Pearlberg* v. *Varty* [1972] 1 WLR 534; and see *Wiseman* v. *Borneman* [1971] AC 279.

[22] *Ridge* v. *Baldwin* [1963] 1 QB 539, reversed [1964] AC 40; and see *Annumunthodo* v. *Oilfields Workers Trade Union* [1961] AC 945.

[23] For this American proposition see below, p. 996.

department, it must be assumed that Parliament intends the department to operate in its usual way, so that the minister's duties may be performed by subordinate officials.[24] In other cases, the courts allow some relaxation of the normal rule which requires statutory powers to be exercised by the precise person or body on whom they are conferred and makes it impossible for them to be legally exercised by others, e.g. sub-committees.[25] The Privy Council has held that a dairy board, in making zoning orders affecting milk producers, may appoint a person or persons to receive evidence and submissions from interested parties; and that if, before deciding to make an order, the board is fully informed of the evidence and submissions, there will be no breach of natural justice.[26] In some circumstances, it was added, an accurate summary of the evidence and submissions might suffice. But since the board had merely acted on the report of a committee of inquiry which held a public hearing on its own initiative and did not report the evidence to the board, the board's order was quashed.[27] The Court of Appeal decided similarly in a licensing case where a licensing panel failed to report the applicant's submissions or the objections to them to the committee which made the decision,[28] even though delegation of the hearing was authorised by statutory rules.

There is no breach of natural justice if the deciding authority appoints a committee to investigate and report, then discloses the report to the person affected and gives him a fair hearing before itself.[29] There is here no delegation of any of the authority's powers or duties.

Hearing held after decision

What is an administrative authority to do if it has failed to give a fair hearing, so that its decision is quashed or declared void? It still has the duty to give a proper hearing and decide the case, but it has prejudiced itself by its defective decision, which it may well have defended in legal proceedings. It cannot be fair procedure to take a decision first and hear the evidence afterwards, even though the first decision is legally a nullity. But usually the only possible course is for the same authority to rehear the case.[30] For that authority will be the only authority with statutory power to

---

[24] *Local Government Board* v. *Arlidge* [1915] AC 120; see above, p. 366.

[25] See above, p. 357.

[26] *Jeffs* v. *New Zealand Dairy Production and Marketing Board* [1967] 1 AC 551.

[27] *Jeffs'* case (above); and see *Wislang* v. *Medical Practitioners Disciplinary Committee* [1974] 1 NZLR 29 (statutory requirement of 'full report' not satisfied).

[28] *R.* v. *Preston BC ex p. Quietlynn Ltd.* (1984) 83 LGR 308 (refusal of sex shop licence quashed).

[29] *Osgood* v. *Nelson* (1872) LR 5 HL 636.

[30] As in *R.* v. *Secretary of State for the Environment ex p. Hackney LBC*, below.

proceed, and there is therefore 'a case of necessity' of the kind we have already met.[31] In the case of a tribunal with variable membership the court may order the hearing to be held by a differently constituted tribunal.[32]

It was acknowledged in *Ridge* v. *Baldwin* that, if there was no such alternative, the original body would have to reconsider the case as best it could. Lord Reid said:[33]

. . . if an officer or body realises that it has acted hastily and reconsiders the whole matter afresh, after affording to the person affected a proper opportunity to present his case, then its later decision will be valid.

But in that case the hearing, when given by the watch committee, was defective in that the charges were not fully disclosed, so that the second decision was as void as the first. A Canadian case, arising out of disciplinary proceedings by the Toronto Stock Exchange, affords an example of the second decision being valid, since everything possible was done to hold a full and fair hearing on the second occasion.[34] Likewise the Secretary of State for the Environment, whose decision to reduce a local authority's rate support grant was quashed because he failed to hear their objections at the proper stage, validly came to the same decision as before after hearing the objections correctly.[35]

A different but comparable situation is where the hearing is given after action has been decided upon, but in time to prevent the decision being void. This happened in Trinidad where the Governor had power to transfer the indentures of immigrant workers from one estate to another. The Governor made an order for such a transfer without consulting the estate owner, but as soon as he heard that the owner objected he gave him a fair hearing. He then declined to cancel the order. Since the hearing was given while there was still power to cancel the order, the procedure was held valid.[36] In Canada the cancellation of a vehicle permit was upheld even though the holder was given only the opportunity to persuade the Registrar afterwards that the cancellation should be revoked.[37] Since the initial decision in such cases will almost inevitably have a prejudicial effect, the law ought to be slow to admit such dubious procedure.

---

[31] Above, p. 478.

[32] As in *Metropolitan Properties (FGC) Ltd.* v. *Lannon* [1969] 1 QB 577.

[33] [1964] AC at p. 79.

[34] *Posluns* v. *Toronto Stock Exchange* (1968) 67 DLR (2d) 165.

[35] *R.* v. *Secretary of State for the Environment ex p. Hackney LBC* [1984] 1 WLR 592.

[36] *De Verteuil* v. *Knaggs* [1918] AC 557. See similarly *Pagliara* v. *A.-G.* [1974] 1 NZLR 86. Compare *Vestry of St. James and St. John Clerkenwell* v. *Feary* (1890) 24 QBD 703.

[37] *Registrar of Motor Vehicles* v. *Canadian American Transfer Ltd.* (1972) 26 DLR (3d) 112. Contrast *Re McGavin Toastmaster Ltd.* (1972) 31 DLR (3d) 370 (Manitoba Human Rights Commission required undertakings from company before hearing it: proceedings set aside as unduly prejudicial).

FAIR HEARINGS—PARTICULAR SITUATIONS

Wide discretionary power

It is of the essence of natural justice that it should be observed generally in the exercise of discretionary power. The mere fact that the discretion conferred is wide is no reason for weakening this principle. Although it has been said that there has in the past been some correlation between wide discretionary power and absence of a duty to observe natural justice,[38] this scarcely seems to be supported except by decisions which are explicable on other grounds. At any rate, now that the frontiers of natural justice have been advanced considerably (and, as a Lord Chancellor has added, rightly[39]), there seems to be no detectable correlation of this character. All discretionary powers have limits of some kind, and whether those limits are widely or narrowly drawn, the discretion ought to be exercised fairly, just as it must also be exercised reasonably.[40]

This is corroborated, in particular, by cases in which the power has been conferred in wide subjective language. One example is the case of the bishop who was empowered to act against a vicar 'when satisfied either of his own knowledge or by affidavit' of the vicar's default.[41] Another is the case of the colonial governor empowered to act 'on sufficient ground shown to his satisfaction'.[42] Even the favourite statutory formulae which represent the ultimate in wide discretion, 'Where the Minister is satisfied'[43] and 'If it appears to the Minister',[44] which purport to make the extent of his powers depend upon his own state of mind, do not exclude the right to a fair hearing. Nor does a local authority's power to divide a payment between landlord and tenant 'in such shares as the authority think equitable in the circumstances'.[45]

---

[38] De Smith, *Judicial Review of Administrative Action*, 4th edn., 186. One of the few true examples seems to be *Re Barnett* [1967] 2 NSWR 746, but the reasoning invites criticism. Another may be the case of offices held at pleasure: see below, p. 566. Note also the *Essex County Council* case, below, p. 573.

[39] *Pearlberg* v. *Varty* [1972] 1 WLR 534 at 540 (Lord Hailsham LC).

[40] Above, p. 395.

[41] *Capel* v. *Child*, above, p. 500. But contrast *Abergavenny (Marquis)* v. *Bishop of Llandaff* (1888) 20 QBD 460.

[42] *De Verteuil* v. *Knaggs*, above, p. 504.

[43] *Maradana Mosque Trustees* v. *Mahmud* [1967] 1 AC 13.

[44] *Durayappah* v. *Fernando* [1967] 2 AC 337.

[45] *Hoggard* v. *Worsborough Urban District Council* [1962] 2 QB 93. Compare *Re Webb and Ontario Housing Corporation* (1978) 93 DLR (3d) 187 (housing authority required to act fairly in terminating lease) but contrast *Sevenoaks DC* v. *Emmett* (1979) 78 LGR 346 (council not required to give hearing or reasons when ejecting tenant).

Cases determined by policy

Closely akin to the question of wide discretionary power is the question of
policy. Policy is of course the basis of administrative discretion in a great
many cases, but this is no reason why the discretion should not be exercised
fairly *vis-à-vis* any person who will be adversely affected. The decision will
require the weighing of any such person's interests against the claims of
policy; and this cannot fairly be done without giving that person an
opportunity to be heard. The cases of slum-clearance and similar orders,
already discussed,[46] are a clear illustration of decisions based upon policy
which are nevertheless subject to the principles of natural justice.

The plainest possible case of 'pure policy' occurred where a minister
refused to meet a delegation of London borough council representatives
protesting against his decision to reduce their rate support grant on account
of their excessive spending. His policy had been fully discussed with them
and debated in Parliament before the passing of the Act empowering the
cuts. But fairness demanded that their objections should be heard at some
point between the granting of the power and its exercise, particularly since
the borough councils would otherwise have a statutory right to the normal
rate support grant. For this failure to observe natural justice, as well as for
the unlawful fettering of his discretion, the minister's decision was
quashed.[47] A similar 'pure policy' case, where also a ministerial order was
quashed, was where the minister ordered the Greater London Council to
make the maximum financial transfer to London Regional Transport
without offering any opportunity of consultation.[48]

But a statutory procedure may contain elements which do not concern
the person who will ultimately be affected, and in which therefore he is not
entitled to a hearing. Where the lord lieutenant of a county had to certify
that it was 'necessary or expedient' for defence purposes that land should be
acquired compulsorily within the county, it was held that this preliminary
step was for purposes of defence policy and general control, and that 'the
owner of the land has got nothing to do with it at all'.[49] But this was
certainly not a decision that any order could be made against him
personally without the usual right to be heard.

In some situations considerations of policy may be overriding. If
schoolteachers are dismissed because the education authority is closing
schools,[50] or taxicab licences are cancelled because there are too many
taxicabs, these are very different cases from those where some personal

---

[46] Above, p. 510.
[47] *R. v. Secretary of State for the Environment ex p. Brent LBC* [1982] QB 593.
[48] *R. v. Secretary of State for Transport ex p. Greater London Council* [1986] QB 556.
[49] *Hutton* v. *A.-G.* [1927] 1 Ch. 427. Compare *Pearlberg* v. *Varty* [1972] 1 WLR 534.
[50] For the status of schoolteachers see below, p. 600.

default has to be established before the power can be exercised. But even in cases of this class the right to be heard may be appropriate: it ought to operate in the case of loss of livelihood just as much as in the case of loss of property. However dominant policy may be, fair procedure remains the same. In cases affecting large numbers of individuals, it may be sufficient for their representatives to be heard on behalf of the whole class. In a case where a local authority proposed to increase the number of taxicab licences, contrary to the interests of the existing operators, the Court of Appeal held that the authorities, though acting purely on grounds of policy, must act fairly and afford a hearing to the operators' association.[51] Lord Denning MR said:

To apply that principle here: suppose the corporation proposed to reduce the number of taxicabs from 300 to 200, it would be their duty to hear the taxicab owners' association: because their members would be greatly affected. They would certainly be persons aggrieved. Likewise suppose the corporation propose to increase the number of taxicabs from 300 to 350 or 400 or more: it is the duty of the corporation to hear those affected before coming to a decision adverse to their interests.

Roskill LJ pointed out that this procedure should assist rather than inhibit the corporation in the performance of their licensing duties. It must be remembered that there is another side to natural justice quite apart from fairness to the individual: it helps the administrator to take a better decision if he hears the objections to his policy from those who have the strongest interest in contesting it. This may be the motive behind the statutory procedure for the compulsory amalgamations of police forces, by which their number has been greatly reduced as a matter of national policy: every police authority affected by the scheme is entitled to have its objections heard at an inquiry,[52] and the government must, as a matter of proper procedure, disclose the case to be met.[53]

Although no such questions arose in *Ridge* v. *Baldwin*, Lord Reid at one point made some problematical remarks about policy.[54] He said that where a minister was not dealing with a single isolated case, but with something like, say, a scheme for an important new road, his primary concern would be not with the damage to landowners' rights but with the fulfilment of his policy; and that it would be quite wrong to require the minister to act in the

---

[51] R. v. *Liverpool Cpn. ex p. Liverpool Taxi Fleet Operators' Association* [1972] 2 QB 299. cf. R. v. *Bristol CC ex p. Pearce* (1984) 83 LGR 711 (policy to reduce street traders; relief refused in discretion), noted above, p. 535.

[52] Police Act 1964, 3rd sched.

[53] *Ayr Magistrates* v. *Lord Advocate* [1950] SC 102.

[54] [1964] AC at 72. See also R. v. *Secretary of State for the Environment ex p. Ostler* [1977] QB 122; *Lovelock* v. *Secretary of State for Transport* (1979) 39 P & CR 468.

same sort of way as a board of works deciding whether a house should be pulled down. The passage is only a short digression and is plainly not intended to change established law. But it seems to suggest that in such a case the minister would be entitled to acquire land compulsorily without giving the owner a hearing—a suggestion which conflicts not only with decisions on natural justice[55] but with the enacted law of compulsory purchase.[56] The slum-clearance schemes in issue in the Housing Act cases involved just such acts of policy, but the courts did not hesitate to apply the rules of natural justice by quashing the minister's decision when he consulted the local authority behind the backs of the objectors.[57]

It is in just these 'policy' cases that Parliament reinforces the common law by providing for statutory inquiries, which is the best possible proof of the need for the right to be heard. The dominance of policy in no way affects the minister's duty to hear a landowner's case. What it affects is the weight that he may give to that case after he has heard it. But that is the minister's political responsibility and outside the sphere of the law.

Licensing and commercial regulation

As the preceding section has illustrated, licensing cases often contain a large element of policy, since the licensing authority will commonly be free to grant or withhold licences as it thinks best in the public interest. Very extensive licensing powers are possessed by the central government, local authorities, the police, magistrates, tribunals and other authorities, and in many cases they give what might be called powers of commercial life or death over a person's trade or livelihood.[58] Local authorities license such things as cinemas, nursing homes, road vehicles, animal boarding establishments, knackers' yards, fireworks factories, pawnbrokers and slaughterhouses. Police licensing powers cover, *inter alia*, firearms, pedlars, taxicabs, and taxi-drivers. Many of these arrangements might be thought to cry out for administrative rationalisation and procedural regularity, but before *Ridge* v. *Baldwin* only the licensing of public-houses and places of entertainment, which has been in the hands of magistrates since the sixteenth century, had made much contribution to the case-law. Although

---

[55]   Above, p. 540.

[56]   See below, p. 956.

[57]   *Errington* v. *Minister of Health* [1935] 1 KB 249; above, p. 509. The Privy Council's summary decision in *Mukta Ben* v. *Suva CC* [1980] 1 WLR 767 that there was no right to be heard before a compulsory purchase order was authorised in Fiji was evidently due to the fact that the landowner had no genuine intention of disputing the order at the relevant time.

[58]   For licensing powers see Halsbury's *Laws of England*, 3rd edn., xxiv. 140; Street, *Justice in the Welfare State*, 70; Hart, *Local Government*, 9th edn., 756; Glanville Williams (1967) 20 *Current Legal Problems*, 81.

it was firmly established that this form of licensing was a judicial function, and therefore subject to natural justice,[59] this was so far from being recognised as a general principle that the Privy Council was able to hold in 1950 that a trader's licence could be cancelled without fair procedure of any kind.[60]

Ridge v. *Baldwin* transformed the situation;[61] and in particular the courts have shown a strong disposition to bring licensing functions generally within their doctrine that administrative powers must be exercised fairly. The wide statement by Lord Denning MR as to the duty to give fair hearings by a local authority licensing taxicabs has been quoted above; it is especially notable since it extends to decisions of licensing policy which affect whole classes of licence-holders, and not merely to individual cases. Nor is the principle in any way confined to cases of cancellation or suspension on grounds of misconduct, where the claims of natural justice are obviously strongest. It is recognised that licensing is a drastic power, greatly affecting the rights and liberties of citizens, and in particular their livelihoods, and that this alone demands fair administrative procedure. Thus where a street trader, allowed to sell food under an informal arrangement with the local authority, was summarily given notice to quit, the decision was quashed because she had not first been given a hearing, even though she was a mere temporary licensee; and the court stressed the duty of fairness where livelihood is at stake.[62]

It seems, furthermore, that no distinction is drawn in principle between initial applications for the grant of licences and the revocation or non-renewal of licences already granted.[63] Subject to what was said about

[59] *Frome United Breweries Co.* v. *Bath Justices* [1926] AC 586 is a leading example. See further below, p. 635.

[60] Above, p. 514.

[61] See *Banks* v. *Transport Regulation Board (Vic.)* (1968) 119 CLR 222 at 233 (Barwick CJ); *Murdoch* v. *New Zealand Milk Board* [1982] 2 NZLR 108; (1967) 2 NZULR 282 (J. A. Farmer). As to taxi-drivers see *Moran* v. *A.G.* [1976] I R. 400 (no hearing: cancellation invalid); *R.* v. *Assistant Metropolitan Police Commissioner ex p. Howell* (below).

[62] *R.* v. *Wear Valley DC ex p. Binks* [1985] 2 All ER 699. In *R.* v. *Basildon DC ex p. Brown* (1981) 79 LGR 655, there discussed, a similar licence was validly terminated by three months' notice, written representations having first been received. Compare *R.* v. *Barnsley MC ex p. Hook* [1976] 1 WLR 1052, above, p. 488.

[63] In *McInnes* v. *Onslow-Fane* [1978] 1 WLR 1520 at 1529 Megarry V.-C. says that there is a substantial distinction between 'application cases' and 'forfeiture cases' and that this is well recognised in the case of membership of a social club. But that is a case based upon contract (above, p. 501) where a member has the protection of his contract of membership and an applicant has not. It does not follow that any such distinction applies to the exercise of statutory powers. Nor is it correct that in application cases 'in all normal circumstances there are no charges and so no requirement of an opportunity to be heard in answer to the charges'. Applicants are often prejudiced by unfavourable information possessed by the licensing authority, as in the *Gaming Board* case, below. cf. *A.-G.* v. *Ryan* [1980] AC 718 (above, p. 520).

decisions of policy,[64] a first-time applicant for a licence should normally be allowed to state his case before being refused, and in particular where the refusal is on personal grounds. It was said in a case of 1916:[65]

Persons who are called upon to exercise the functions of granting licences for carriages and omnibuses are, to a great extent, exercising judicial functions; and though they are not bound by the strict rules of evidence and procedure observed in a court of law, they are bound to act judicially. It is their duty to hear and determine according to law, and they must bring to that task a fair and unbiased mind.

In approving this passage Lord Denning MR said that according to the modern judicial vocabulary such persons act administratively but are required to act fairly.[66] He had previously laid down the same law in what was in effect a 'first application' case in which the purchasers of a gaming club applied to the Gaming Board for a certificate of consent, without which they could not apply for a licence under the Gaming Act 1968. The Court of Appeal there held that the Board must hear the applicants fairly, though subject to the limitations which have already been explained.[67] It has been held, also, that the rules of natural justice apply to an application for an entertainments licence, and although the case was in effect one of renewal, it was treated as if it were one of first application.[68]

Where a licence is due for renewal the case is still stronger, and may be reinforced by 'legitimate expectation', as in the case of the taxi-driver mentioned earlier.[69] It has been held in Canada that a new condition ought not to be attached to the renewed licence without first offering the holder an opportunity to make representations about it.[70]

On the basis of these authorities the duty to observe natural justice is now extremely wide. But it is probably safe to say that there must be many thousands of adverse licensing decisions annually in which no hearing is in

---

[64] Above, p. 556.

[65] R. v. Brighton Cpn. ex p. Thomas Tilling Ltd. (1916) 85 LJKB 1552 (Sankey J).

[66] In R. v. Liverpool Cpn. ex p. Liverpool Taxi Fleet Operators' Association [1972] 2 QB 299.

[67] R. v. Gaming Board for Great Britain ex p. Benaim and Khaida [1970] 2 QB 417; above, p. 542. See also R. v. Herrod ex p. Leeds City District Council [1976] QB 540 at 560, where Lord Denning MR said that the initial grant of a licence should be in accordance with natural justice, although natural justice was excluded by statute in the case before him.

[68] R. v. Huntingdon DC ex p. Cowan [1984] 1 WLR 501.

[69] R. v. Assistant Metropolitan Police Commissioner ex p. Howell [1986] RTR 52; above p. 522. See also R. v. Huntingdon DC ex p. Cowan (above), and Lord Diplock's statement in Council of Civil Service Unions v. Minister for the Civil Service [1985] AC 374 at 408; Smitty's Industries Ltd. v. A.-G. [1980] 1 NZLR 355; FAI Insurances Ltd. v. Winneke (1982) 41 ALR 1 (legitimate expectation of renewal of approval to provide worker's compensation insurance).

[70] Re CTV Television Network Ltd. (1980) 116 DLR (3d) 741.

fact given. These will mostly occur at the two extremes of the scale of importance: both in much petty administrative licensing by local authorities and the police; and also in the case of certain wide powers of commercial and industrial regulation under which many decisions are made from day to day and which have no statutory procedural safeguards. Examples[71] are import and export licensing, the control of insurance companies, and, before they were discontinued, foreign exchange control and the grant of industrial development certificates.[72] So far the authorities have succeeded in wielding these far-reaching powers without provoking challenge in the courts on procedural grounds. But in principle natural justice should play its normal part, subject to administrative exigencies and to any implication to the contrary that can fairly be inferred from the scheme of any particular Act of Parliament. The interests of an applicant for an import licence or for an industrial development certificate may be no less important, to put it no higher, than those of an applicant to the Gaming Board or of a taxicab-owners' association. The fact that Parliament has failed to provide any rights of hearing or appeal can hardly found an argument against natural justice, since the same is true in so many other cases, where the courts have imported it in order to 'supply the omission of the legislature'.[73]

The question whether there should be a right to be heard by a local planning authority, which is in effect a licensing authority, before refusal of planning permission has been discussed above.[74]

Offices and employments

A line has to be drawn between an office which gives its holder a status which the law will protect specifically, on the one hand, and, on the other hand, a mere employment under a contract of service. Offices used in old times to be looked upon as a form of property which could be held and recovered in specie: if the holder was wrongfully removed he could obtain restoration by mandamus; or he might be granted prohibition or an injunction. Nowadays he can also obtain a declaration that his removal was void, and that he is therefore still in office, as was done in Ridge v. Baldwin, since this remedy likewise operates specifically. In other words, he is

---

[71] Some but not all of the Department of Trade's drastic powers over insurance companies are subject to a hearing procedure: Insurance Companies Act 1974, ss. 38, 39.

[72] Lord Denning MR has said that there is no right to a hearing on the grant of industrial development certificates or the award of television programme contracts: see Cinnamond v. British Airports Authority [1980] 1 WLR 582 at 590.

[73] Above, p. 503.

[74] Above, p. 552.

removable only by a due and lawful exercise of the power of removal, failing which he remains legally in office. A servant under a mere contract of service enjoys no such protection, according to a long-established rule of law: whatever his contractual rights, he can always be dismissed and his remedy lies in damages for breach of contract.[75] In other words, there is always a power to dismiss him, even though under the contract there is no right to do so. The principle is that one man will not be compelled to employ another against his will. By contrast, the law will give specific protection to a status such as membership or office in a trade union, association or club, even though it is merely contractual; this is a less personal relationship, and an injunction or declaration may be granted so as to preserve the status.[76] A statutory status, such as that of a registered dock worker, will be protected similarly,[77] subject always to the discretion of the court in awarding remedies.[78]

The distinction is of importance for the purposes of the right to be heard. If an office-holder is removed without a hearing in a case where he has a right to one, he can recover his office specifically. But if in a similar situation a mere servant is dismissed, his dismissal remains legally effective and there is no remedy by which he can compel his employer to continue to employ him. The law then holds that the right to a fair hearing has no application in a mere relationship of master and servant. This is not because justice does not so require (for in many cases it does) but because the law will not restore the employment specifically. For this reason the Privy Council refused certiorari to a university lecturer who had been dismissed without a hearing from his post in Ceylon—though the case itself looked more like one of statutory status since the university's power to dismiss was statutory and was restricted (just as in *Ridge* v. *Baldwin*) to cases of incapacity or misconduct.[79] Lord Wilberforce has said that he could not follow this decision and has commented:[80]

A comparative list of situations in which persons have been held entitled or not entitled to a hearing, or to observation of the rules of natural justice, according to the master and servant test, looks illogical and even bizarre. A specialist surgeon is denied protection which is given to a hospital doctor; a university professor, as a

---

[75] See below, p. 599.
[76] See above, p. 501.
[77] See below, p. 600.
[78] See the *North Wales Police* case, above, p. 536.
[79] *Vidyodaya University Council* v. *Silva* [1965] 1 WLR 77, following the *Barber* case (below). Contrast *McCarthy* v. *Calgary RC School District* (1979) 101 DLR 48 (school superintendent: office).
[80] *Malloch* v. *Aberdeen Cpn.* [1971] 1 WLR 1578 at 1595, 1596, citing the *Barber, Palmer,* and *Vidyodaya* cases and *Glynn* v. *Keele University* [1971] 1 WLR 487.

servant, has been denied the right to be heard, a dock labourer and an undergraduate have been granted it; examples can be multiplied.

Although the law makes such a sharp distinction between office and service in theory, in practice it may be difficult to tell which is which. For tax purposes 'office' has long been defined as a 'subsisting, permanent substantive position which has an existence independent of the person who fills it',[81] but for the purposes of natural justice the test may not be the same.[82] Nor need an office necessarily be statutory,[83] although nearly all public offices of importance in administrative law are statutory. A statutory public authority may have many employees who are in law merely its servants, and others of higher grades who are office-holders.[84] A prison officer, holding the office of constable, has the rights of an office-holder,[85] but a nursing officer employed by a local health authority is an ordinary employee.[86] In England it has been held that a consultant surgeon employed under the national health service by a regional hospital board is a mere contractual servant, despite the 'strong statutory flavour' attaching to the contract.[87] But where, as happened in Scotland, a surgeon similarly employed was denied a hearing before the hospitals board when they decided to reject a report in the surgeon's favour by their appeals

[81] Approved by the House of Lords in *Edwards* v. *Clinch* [1981] 3 WLR 707, holding (by 3:2) that a surveyor engaged from time to time to hold public inquiries was not the holder of an office.

[82] For tax purposes 'office' has to be distinguished from 'profession', whereas for purposes of natural justice it has to be distinguished from 'employment'.

[83] See *e.g. Fisher* v. *Jackson* [1891] 2 Ch. 84 (school established under deed of trust: schoolmaster granted injunction against dismissal without hearing); *Stevenson* v. *United Road Transport Union* [1976] 3 All ER 29 (trade union officer: declaration granted).

[84] *Malloch* v. *Aberdeen Cpn.* [1971] 1 WLR 1578 at 1582 (Lord Reid). Lord Wilberforce (at 1596) defined 'pure master and servant cases' more narrowly as involving 'no element of public employment or service, no support by statute, nothing in the nature of an office or a status which is capable of protection.' By this criterion all public employees would appear to count as office-holders, but that may not have been intended. See also *Social Club (102) Ltd.* v. *Bickerton* [1977] ICR 911: *R.* v. *Brent LBC ex p. Assegai* [1987] The Times, 18 June (school governor; protected office; Lord Wilberforce's criterion applied). In Ireland the protection of natural justice has been given to a fireman (*R. (Hennessy)* v. *Department of the Environment* [1980] N. Ireland Bulletin No. 6) and an army private (*State (Gleeson)* v. *Minister for Defence* [1976] IR 280).

[85] *R.* v. *Home Secretary ex p. Benwell* [1985] QB 554.

[86] *R.* v. *East Berkshire Health Authority ex p. Walsh* [1985] QB 152. For this and the *Benwell* case see below, p. 685.

[87] *Barber* v. *Manchester Regional Hospital Board* [1958] 1 WLR 181 (declaration refused). See similarly *Francis* v. *Kuala Lumpur Councillors* (above). The *Barber* case was doubted in *Irani* v. *Southampton Health Authority* [1985] ICR 590, but in *R.* v. *Trent Regional Health Authority ex p. Jones* [1986] The Times, 19 June, a consultant surgeon in the national health service was held to be employed under an ordinary contract of service.

committee, it was held that the appeals procedure, as set out in a departmental circular, was 'an inherent condition of his contract of service' and that the breach of natural justice nullified the dismissal.[88] This case therefore departed from the usual rule that a contract of service will not be specifically enforced; and an exception to that rule has been admitted in England in abnormal circumstances.[89] Even a contractual servant may be able to have his dismissal declared void if there are statutory procedural safeguards which have not been observed, so that in effect the power to dismiss is statutory.[90]

Extended employment protection

Radical changes in the rights of contractual employees were made by the Industrial Relations Act 1971, now replaced by the Employment Protection (Consolidation) Act 1978,[91] giving protection against unfair dismissal. This new right is enforceable in industrial tribunals, which must have regard to the code of practice, now issued by ACAS, which requires formal procedure and an opportunity for the employee to state his case; and apart from the code, fairness alone will require this in most cases.[92] But the tribunal has no power to restore the employment specifically: it may recommend reinstatement or re-engagement, and if the employer refuses it may award compensation.[93] Where the dismissal was in fact justified, failure to give a fair hearing will involve no loss and therefore no compensation.[94]

The employment protection legislation, it has now been held, 'has substantially changed the position at common law so far. as dismissal is concerned', so that 'even the ordinary contract of master and servant now has many of the attributes of an office', and the court can intervene by way of injunction and declaration. An employee of the BBC, whose contract contained elaborate procedural rights of appeal, would by this decision have been protected against dismissal in breach of those rights, had she not elected to avail herself of a different procedure.[95]

---

[88] *Palmer* v. *Inverness Hospitals Board* 1963 SC 311, cited with apparent approval in *Malloch's* case, below.

[89] See below, p. 600.

[90] *Malloch* v. *Aberdeen Cpn.* [1971] 1 WLR 1578 at 1596 (Lord Wilberforce) (schoolteacher).

[91] Pt. V. As to civil servants see above, p. 71. For ACAS see below, p. 857.

[92] *Earl* v. *Slater & Wheeler (Airlyne) Ltd.* [1973] 1 WLR 51; and see *Polkey* v. *Dayton (A.E.) Services Ltd.* [1987] 3 WLR 1153.

[93] s. 106, as continued by the Act of 1974 (above).

[94] See the *Earl* case, above.

[95] *R.* v. *British Broadcasting Cpn. ex p. Lavelle* [1983] 1 WLR 23 (Woolf J). See likewise *Irani* v. *Southampton Health Authority* [1985] ICR 590 (injunction granted to protect contractual dismissal procedures).

A distinction is evidently developing between contracts containing express procedural rights, which the court now seems disposed to protect specifically, and contracts containing no such rights, where the employee has only the statutory protection. There is a clear tendency to extend the ambit of natural justice in the field of employment, as fairness undoubtedly demands. In some sense it may already be said, as in New Zealand, that the requirements of fairness apply to virtually all employment relationships, whether public or private.[96]

Suspension from office

Suspension from office, as opposed to dismissal, may be nearly as serious a matter for the employee, but the courts have wavered between two different views. One is that the employer needs a summary power to suspend without hearing or other formality as a holding operation, pending inquiries into suspicions or allegations.[97] The other is that 'suspension is merely expulsion pro tanto. Each is penal, and each deprives the member concerned of the enjoyment of his rights of membership or office.'[98] Taking the former view in a controversial decision, a majority of the Privy Council held that a schoolteacher in New Zealand need not be given a hearing before being suspended without pay pending the determination of a disciplinary charge against him on which he would be fully heard in accordance with statutory regulations.[99] Although it was recognised that suspension without pay might involve hardship and also a temporary slur on the teacher, it was held that he had accepted this possibility in the terms of his employment and that the disciplinary procedure as a whole was fair. It has been said also that a police officer need not be heard before being suspended from duty pending investigation of charges of misconduct.[1]

Favouring the opposite view, the Court of Appeal of New Zealand has

---

[96] *Marlborough Harbour Board* v. *Goulden* [1985] 2 NZLR 378. They apply to the transfer of an officer to other duties if it is made for disciplinary as opposed to administrative reasons: *Poananga* v. *State Services Commission* [1985] 2 NZLR 385. Contrast *Bullen* v. *State Services Commission* [1985] 1 NZLR 402.

[97] *Lewis* v. *Heffer* [1978] 1 WLR 1061. cf. *R.* v. *Cole* (1979) 27 ACTR 13 (suspension without hearing valid, but not as to withholding of pay).

[98] *John* v. *Rees* [1970] Ch. 345 (Megarry J). See also *R.* v. *Committee of Lloyd's ex p. Posgate* [1983] The Times, 12 January.

[99] *Furnell* v. *Whangarei High Schools Board* [1973] AC 660 (Lords Reid and Dilhorne dissenting).

[1] *Norwest Holst Ltd.* v. *Secretary of State for Trade* [1978] Ch. 201 at 224, repeated in *Cinnamond* v. *British Airports Authority* [1980] 1 WLR 582 at 590 (Lord Denning MR).

rejected the distinction between suspension and expulsion and has held that natural justice is required equally in both cases;[2] and there are similarly clear Australian decisions.[3] Suspension without pay, in particular, may be a severe penalty, and even suspension with pay may gravely injure reputation. In principle the arguments for a fair hearing are unanswerable; and if for reasons of urgency it cannot be given before action is taken, there is no reason why it should not be given as soon as possible afterwards.

Offices held at pleasure

Where the holder of an office is subject to removal 'at pleasure', as opposed to removal 'for cause' such as unfitness or neglect of duty, it has been held that he has no right to be heard before removal.[4] In *Ridge* v. *Baldwin* Lord Reid approved the decision of 1844 on which the rule rests, though admitting that it had been doubted.[5] He stated that since no reasons need be given for the removal, the court could not determine whether it would be fair to hear the officer's case. But this is circular reasoning, and it is unsatisfying on grounds of justice as well as of logic. As already explained, natural justice does not itself require the giving of reasons for decisions, but nevertheless it does require fair notice of the case to be met, and this requirement of notice is something quite different from a duty to give reasons for the decision when taken. If the officer is subject to some accusation, justice requires that he should be allowed a fair opportunity to defend himself, whatever the terms of his tenure. To deny it to him is to confuse the substance of the decision, which may be based on any reason at all, with the procedure which ought first to be followed. It is then an example of the fallacy, already mentioned, that the argument for natural justice is weaker where the discretionary power is wide.

It is therefore not surprising that Lord Hatherley LC said that he was not altogether satisfied with the reasoning of the decision of 1844,[6] and that it

---

[2] *Birss* v. *Secretary for Justice* [1984] 1 NZLR 513 (suspension of probation officer without notice or hearing declared invalid, there being no immediate urgency. The suspension was initially with pay but later without).

[3] *Dixon* v. *Commonwealth* (1981) 55 FLR 34; *Schmohl* v. *Commonwealth* (1983) 49 ACTR 24.

[4] *R.* v. *Darlington School Governors* (1844) 6 QB 682 (dismissal of schoolmaster by governors of chartered grammar school), following *R.* v. *Stratford-on-Avon (Mayor)* (1670) 1 Lev. 291. In *Tucker* v. *British Museum Trustees*, The Times, 8 December 1967, the Court of Appeal held that a senior scientific officer of the British Museum had no right to be heard before dismissal, since he held an 'office employment or service' terminable at the trustees' pleasure; whether he held an office was therefore not decided.

[5] [1964] AC at p. 66.

[6] *Dean* v. *Bennett* (1870) 6 Ch. App. 489.

has been more enthusiastically distinguished than followed.[7] Reviewing the position in 1971, the House of Lords held that a Scottish schoolteacher, who by statute held his appointment 'during the pleasure' of the school board, could not validly be dismissed without a hearing.[8] Lip-service was paid to the decision of 1844, but it was distinguished on the ground that the teacher was entitled by statute to three weeks' notice of the proposal to dismiss him, and that the only possible reason for this was to enable him to prepare his defence, which the board ought accordingly to hear. Lord Reid partly refuted the explanation which he had himself given in *Ridge* v. *Baldwin*, saying that 'it seems to me perfectly sensible for Parliament to say to a public body: you need not give formal reasons but you must hear the man before you dismiss him'.[9] Why then should this sensible provision not normally be implied, in accordance with the general presumption in favour of a fair hearing? Lord Wilberforce, though upholding the case of 1844 'as a general principle', observed that the very possibility of dismissal without reason given, which might vitally affect a man's career or pension, made it all the more important for him to be able to state his case.[10] In other words, the basis of the 'general principle' is wrong, at least if justice is the criterion. Lord Wilberforce also said that the rules of natural justice were to be excluded only where there was 'no element of public employment or service, no support by statute, nothing in the nature of an office or a status which is capable of protection'. This formula leaves no room for officers not protected by natural justice, especially when they are public and statutory. It was adopted in the case of a school governor appointed under statute by a local authority, who was held entitled to the opportunity to make representations in writing before being removed from his office.[11] The way now lies open, therefore, for the abandonment of the precedent of 1844, which is clearly out of line with the duty to act fairly as it exists to-day.

The key to the problem, it is submitted, is to be found not in the terms on which the office is held, but in the specific protection of the office. It is this which distinguishes offices on the one hand from mere contractual employment on the other. In a perfect world even a mere employee would doubtless have a right to be heard before dismissal for misconduct, and to

---

[7] See *Willis* v. *Childe* (1851) 13 Beav. 117 (schoolmaster removed by grammar school trustees; power to remove on such grounds as they deemed just held not a power to remove at pleasure).

[8] *Malloch* v. *Aberdeen Cpn.* [1971] 1 WLR 1578 (dismissal held a nullity). Cf. *Coutts* v. *Commonwealth of Australia* (1985) 59 ALR 699. If there is a statutory duty to dismiss, natural justice is excluded: *Scott* v. *Aberdeen Cpn.* 1976 SLT 141.

[9] At p. 1582.

[10] At p. 1597.

[11] *R.* v. *Brent LBC ex p. Assegai* [1987] The Times, 18 June.

some extent he now has one by statute.[12] But since the law lacks any mechanism for restoring his employment specifically, it cannot supply the remedy which is usually wanted. In the case of offices, membership, status, and so forth it is able to do so; and it would seem right therefore to protect the officer or member against wrongful deprivation of every kind and to accord him the procedural rights without which deprivation is not fair and lawful. Whether he is removable for cause or at pleasure should in principle make no difference. *

Academic discipline

The right to a fair hearing has been invoked in a number of cases by senior and junior members of universities and colleges, though not as yet with success. The courts have in general held that academic disciplinary proceedings require the observance of the principles of natural justice;[13] but equally they have refused to apply unduly strict standards, provided that the proceedings are substantially fair. Universities and colleges have in many cases established detailed disciplinary procedures under their own internal rules, often with rights of appeal. But where the case calls for the application or interpretation of internal rules, and the university or college has a visitor,[14] it will fall within the visitor's exclusive jurisdiction and the court will not entertain it. The visitor will commonly be the Crown (acting through the Lord Chancellor), unless the Crown or the founder have denominated some other visitor. The law as to visitatorial jurisdiction has recently been clarified by the House of Lords in the case of a dismissed university lecturer, holding that it extends to all questions arising out of the institution's internal rules, notwithstanding that they involve contractual relations and notwithstanding that the complainant is not a member of the institution.[15] Thus, as Megarry V-C has said, 'the extent of visitatorial jurisdiction in university life has greatly expanded in recent years'. Consequently a claim for reinstatement by a student who has failed

---

[12] Above, p. 564.

[13] For disciplinary cases generally see above, p. 529.

[14] i.e. where it was endowed by its founder, or where its charter or statutes so provide. The colleges of Oxford and Cambridge thus have visitors, but the universities themselves do not. In the *Patel* case (below) Megarry V.-C. said that in most of the modern universities the Crown appears to be the visitor.

[15] *Thomas* v. *University of Bradford* [1987] AC 795, applied in *R.* v. *Committee of the Privy Council ex p. Vijayatunga* [1988] 2 WLR 106 (holding visitor's jurisdiction not restricted to either supervisory or appellate functions) and *Oakes* v. *Sidney Sussex College, Cambridge* [1988] 1 WLR 431 (refusing to entertain action by student who failed examination). For valuable surveys of the law see (1970) 86 LQR 531 (J. W. Bridge); (1981) 97 LQR 610 and (1986) 136 NLJ 484, 519, 567 (P. M. Smith). For the rights of students generally see [1973] JSPTL 252 (A. Samuels).

examinations will be within the exclusive jurisdiction of the visitor and not cognisable in the courts.[16] There is no appeal from a visitor's decision, unless internal rules so provide, but the court can compel him to adjudicate and to keep within his jurisdiction; and, 'in the light of the modern development of administrative law', the court could quash a visitor's decision for abuse of power, doubtless including a violation of natural justice.[17]

A university lecturer was in one case held by the Privy Council to be a mere contractual employee, so that he could be dismissed without a hearing as explained in the preceding section.[18] This decision has been criticised by high authority[19] and may not now be a safe guide. But it is at least possible that academic staff of some grades may in law be mere servants. More probably holders of established posts would be regarded as office-holders and so entitled to the benefit of natural justice. Jurisdiction will be in the visitor if the case turns upon internal rules. But if it comes within the statutory law of employment protection, protecting against unfair dismissal, the statutory law is overriding.[20] To that extent Parliament has transferred the jurisdiction of the visitor to the industrial tribunals.

Students have the protection of their contracts of membership: it will be implied that in return for their fees they will be treated in accordance with the university or college rules, and natural justice will operate in the same way as with members of a trade union or association,[21] though jurisdiction will in most cases lie with the visitor as explained above. Before being expelled for failure in examinations[22] or for misconduct[23] they are entitled to be treated fairly and given a hearing—though clearly this does not apply to the conduct of examinations themselves.[24] In one case students expelled for failure in examinations succeeded in showing that they had not been treated in accordance with natural justice by the examiners, but this was

[16] *Patel* v. *Bradford University Senate* [1978] 1 WLR 1488, affirmed [1979] 1 WLR 1066; *Oakes* v. *Sidney Sussex College, Cambridge* (above).

[17] See *Thomas* v. *University of Bradford* (above) at 825; the *Vijayatunga* case (above), at 115; and below, p. 646.

[18] *Vidyodaya University* v. *Silva* [1965] 1 WLR 77; above, p. 562.

[19] Lord Wilberforce in *Malloch* v. *Aberdeen Cpn.* [1971] 1 WLR 1578 at 1596.

[20] See *Thomas* v. *University of Bradford* (above) at 824.

[21] See *Herring* v. *Templeman* [1973] 3 All ER 569 at 585. In his Report on the Sit-in at Cambridge University (1973, para. 154) Lord Devlin said that the foundation of the disciplinary power was the contract of matriculation.

[22] *R.* v. *Aston University Senate ex p. Roffey* [1969] 2 QB 538 (it was conceded that the university had no visitor: see *Patel* v. *Bradford University Senate* [1978] 1 WLR 1488 at 1501, [1979] 1 WLR 1066 at 1068); and see *Brighton Cpn.* v. *Parry* (1972) 70 LGR 576 (unsatisfactory work).

[23] *Ceylon University* v. *Fernando* [1960] 1 WLR 223; *Ward* v. *Bradford Cpn.* (1971) 70 LGR 27.

[24] See *Thorne* v. *University of London* (above).

because the examiners had themselves decided that they be asked to withdraw after taking into account personal factors as well as examination marks; and relief was refused in discretion owing to undue delay in bringing the proceedings.[25] In another case a student who had been fined and rusticated for exhibiting himself nude on the campus was able to show that the Vice-Chancellor had failed to observe the requirements of natural justice since he had given the student no hearing initially but had merely informed him that he could appeal against the penalties.[26] Once again, relief was refused in discretion, since the facts were not contested and the penalties were obviously proper; but this reasoning is dangerous,[27] and the judge himself recognised that such discretion ought to be exercised sparingly.

In cases which have gone to the court, as opposed to the visitor, the court sometimes fails to explain whether the duty to observe natural justice is based upon statute or upon contract. This may make an important difference to the remedies available. If the university or college is established by statute, it may be treated as a statutory public authority subject to remedies such as certiorari and mandamus. If it is merely incorporated by charter or privately, rights against it will depend upon contract, so that the natural remedies will be injunction, declaration or damages. These questions are discussed in the context of remedies.[28] Since administrative law is concerned with the powers and duties of governmental and statutory public authorities, a statutory university or college may fall within its scope but a private one will not.

Preliminary and advisory acts, investigations and reports

Natural justice is concerned with the exercise of power, that is to say, with acts or orders which produce legal results and in some way alter someone's legal position to his disadvantage. But preliminary steps, which in themselves may not involve immediate legal consequences, may lead to acts or orders which do so.[29] In this case the protection of fair procedure may be needed throughout, and the successive steps must be considered not only separately but also as a whole. The question must always be whether,

---

[25] R. v. *Aston University Senate ex p. Roffey* (above).

[26] *Glynn v. Keele University* [1971] 1 WLR 487; and see R. v. *Oxford University ex p. Bolchover,* The Times, 7 October 1970, quoted in *Glynn's* case.

[27] See above, p. 535.

[28] Below, p. 648.

[29] In *Peko-Wallsend Ltd. v. Minister for Arts, Heritage and Environment* (1986) 70 ALR 523 a mining company was held entitled to put its case to the cabinet before they proposed part of a national park for designation under an international convention which under Australian legislation would then empower the government to prohibit the company's operations if it so wished.

looking at the statutory procedure as a whole, each separate step is fair to persons affected.[30]

The House of Lords considered this question in an income tax case where the tax authorities, before they could take the taxpayer before the tribunal which determines whether the object of some transaction is tax avoidance, were required to show a prima facie case to the tribunal. The tribunal refused to allow the taxpayer to be represented, or to see the evidence submitted to it by the authorities, at that stage. The House of Lords upheld this ruling, since the taxpayer would have full opportunity to state his case to the tribunal in the later proceedings.[31] As Lord Reid said, every public officer who has to decide whether to prosecute ought first to decide whether there is a prima facie case, but no one supposes that he need consult the accused. There was nothing inherently unjust in the procedure, which as a whole was found to be fair in its statutory context. But the House of Lords strongly reaffirmed the general doctrine of the right to a fair hearing, and held that there was nothing about the determination of a prima facie case which automatically excluded it:[32] the procedure must pass the test of fairness at each and every stage. In another tax case the House of Lords held that the tax authorities might apply for leave to raise assessments for years beyond the normal time-limit without reference to the taxpayer, since the statutory scheme showed that leave was to be applied for ex parte.[33]

In general, however, the courts are favourable to the observance of natural justice in the making of preliminary investigations and reports which may lead to serious legal consequences to some person.[34] The Commission for Racial Equality and its committees must act fairly in making their investigations, though considerable latitude is allowed as to its procedure.[35] Inspectors investigating the affairs of a company under statutory powers must give the directors a fair opportunity to meet criticisms, even though the object is merely to make a report.[36] A police

---

[30] See (1974) 12 Osg HLJ 179 (R. D. Howe).

[31] *Wiseman* v. *Borneman* [1971] AC 297, Lord Wilberforce concurring with hesitation and holding that the tribunal must disclose the official evidence for the taxpayer's use at the hearing, and that the tribunal had a residual duty of fairness in case prejudicial evidence was introduced unfairly. See similarly *Balen* v. *Inland Revenue Cmrs* [1978] 2 All ER 1033; *Moran* v. *Lloyds* [1981] 1 Ll R 423.

[32] Contrast *Parry-Jones* v. *Law Society* [1969] 1 Ch. 1.

[33] *Pearlberg* v. *Varty* [1972] 1 WLR 534.

[34] See *R.* v. *Agricultural Dwelling-house Advisory Committee ex p. Brough* [1987] 1 EGLR 106.

[35] Above, p. 547.

[36] *Re Pergamon Press Ltd.* [1971] Ch. 388; above, p. 542; and see *State (McPolin)* v. *Minister for Transport* [1976] IR 93 (preliminary wreck inquiry: shipowner entitled to contest evidence given by crew). Contrast *Guay* v. *Lafleur* (1965) 47 DLR (2d) 226 (taxpayer not entitled to participate in inquiry into his affairs by tax authorities. The decision was later reversed by statute). For this and other Canadian cases see (1974) 12 Osg HLJ 179 (R. D. Howe).

officer threatened with compulsory retirement is entitled to have the report of a preliminary inquiry disclosed to his own doctor.[37] A gas company should be given the opportunity to comment on an adverse report by a gas tester which might lead to an order against it by the local authority.[38] These are really instances of the right to know the opposing case.[39] But an academic board considering a student's record and recommending his expulsion was not obliged to give him a hearing since it merely made a recommendation and there was adequate opportunity for his case to be heard by the governing body when considering the recommendations.[40] For similar reasons the court refused to intervene when the visitors of a hospital declined to hear the mother of a mental defective when they were preparing a report for the board of control which the board was required by statute to consider before deciding to prolong a detention order. The visitors' report was said to be a report of their opinion and 'nothing more nor less than a piece of evidence'; the body to whom the mother's representations ought to be made was the board of control itself.[41] These various cases show that procedures involving the taking of advice or the receiving of a report may turn upon the stage at which the effective determination is made. The findings of company inspectors are likely to be accepted as definitive and therefore fair procedure is required. But where a report is merely 'a piece of evidence' the situation is different.

In New Zealand, where royal commissions are statutory, their findings can be set aside for failure to observe natural justice.[42] This would not be possible in England, where royal commissions are not armed with legal powers, unless the court were to add them to the list of non-legal bodies over which it has asserted jurisdiction anomalously.[43]

EXCEPTIONS

Limitations and exceptions

Only an arbitrary boundary can be drawn between cases where the right to a fair hearing is excluded by the nature of the subject-matter and cases

[37] R. v. *Kent Police Authority ex p. Godden* [1971] 2 QB 662; above, p. 478.
[38] R. v. *London County Council ex p. Commercial Gas Co.* (1895) 11 TLR 337.
[39] Above, p. 538.
[40] *Herring* v. *Templeman* [1973] 3 All ER 569.
[41] R. v. *St. Lawrence's Hospital Statutory Visitors* [1953] 1 WLR 1158. The application for certiorari to quash the report, as distinct from the order of the board of control, may have been misconceived. The date of this case should be noted: it is reported next to the discredited case of R. v. *Metropolitan Police Commissioner ex p. Parker* (above, p. 515).
[42] As in *Mahon* v. *Air New Zealand Ltd.* (the Mount Erebus Disaster case). The Commission's order as to costs was consequently invalidated.
[43] See above, p. 245.

where there is some special exception. It has already been explained how the right may be excluded by the very nature of the power, for instance where urgent action has to be taken to safeguard public health; by the absence of 'legitimate expectation'; by the dubious doctrine that a hearing would make no difference; by the refusal of remedies in discretion; and by the rule that employees can be dismissed at pleasure.[44] On rare occasions, also it may be excluded by express legislation.[45] Here we must consider such residual exceptions as remain.

In truth the lesson of the host of cases that have been brought before the courts is that exceptions are conspicuous by their absence wherever genuine administrative power has been exercised under statute with any serious effect on a man's property, liberty or livelihood. Where a right to be fairly heard has been denied, it is more probably a case of a bad decision than of a true exception. The rule must come close to deserving the judicial tributes quoted earlier: 'a principle of universal application', 'a duty lying upon every one who decides anything'.

Legislation

There is no right to be heard before the making of legislation, whether primary or delegated, unless it is provided by statute. Accordingly an association of practising solicitors could not insist on being consulted before the Lord Chancellor made an order abolishing scale fees in conveyancing for solicitors generally—nor did it make any difference that the Act in this case specifically required consultation with the Law Society.[46] The same exception was probably the determining factor in the refusal of a hearing to a local authority which wished to dispute the siting of runways at Stansted Airport, which the government had determined to authorise by a special development order, thus avoiding the procedure of an ordinary application for planning permission.[47] It was held that the power to make such an order was 'a purely administrative or legislative power fully exercisable discretionarily' for which the minister was responsible only to Parliament. Of the three different grounds comprised in these words, the most plausible may be that the power was legislative. But it is not convincing, since a special development order is limited to specified land and is no more general than, say, a slum-clearance scheme. In a case where a local

[44] Above, pp. 530, 522, 533, 535, and 562 respectively.
[45] See above, p. 470.
[46] *Bates* v. *Lord Hailsham* [1972] 1 WLR 1373; below, p. 872. And see *R.* v. *Whalley ex p. Bordin & Co.* [1972] VR 748 (application of building regulations: legislative).
[47] *Essex County Council* v. *Ministry of Housing and Local Government* (1967) 66 LGR 23. Compare *CREEDNZ* v. *Governor-General* [1981] 1 NZLR 172, where it was held that a right to make representations would be inconsistent with the scheme of the legislation.

authority's byelaw dealt with one specified site only, the Supreme Court of Canada held that the owner was entitled to notice and a fair hearing before it was made.[48] There may always be problems in distinguishing legislative from administrative power in borderline cases,[49] but these cases hardly seem to be borderline.

Cases where statute gives a right to be heard or consulted before regulations are made are illustrated elsewhere.[50]

National security

The right to a fair hearing may have to yield to overriding considerations of national security. The House of Lords recognised this necessity where civil servants at the government communications headquarters, who had to handle secret information vital to national security, were abruptly put under new conditions of service which prohibited membership of national trade unions. Neither they nor their unions were consulted, in disregard of an established practice, and their complaint to the courts would have been upheld on grounds of natural justice, had there not been a threat to national security. The factor which ultimately prevailed was the danger that the process of consultation itself would have precipitated further strikes, walk-outs, overtime bans and disruption generally of a kind which had plagued the communications headquarters shortly beforehand and which were a threat to national security. Since national security must be paramount, natural justice must then give way.[51]

The Crown must, however, satisfy the court that national security is at risk. Despite the constantly repeated dictum that 'those who are responsible for the national security must be the sole judges of what the national security requires',[52] the court will insist upon evidence that an issue of national security arises, and only then will it accept the opinion of the Crown that it should prevail over some legal right. There is also the proviso that the opinion of the Crown should not be one which no minister could reasonably have held. 'There is no abdication of the judicial function, but there is a common sense limitation recognised by the judges as to what is justiciable.'[53]

---

[48] *Homex Realty Ltd.* v. *Village of Wyoming* (1980) 116 DLR (3d) 1, where however relief was refused in discretion on account of the applicant's conduct.

[49] Below, p. 847.

[50] Below, p. 885.

[51] *Council of Civil Service Unions* v. *Minister for the Civil Service* [1985] AC 374 (declaratory relief against minister's instructions refused).

[52] *The Zamora* [1916] 2 AC 77 at 107 (Lord Parker of Waddington).

[53] [1985] AC at 406 (Lord Scarman). The proviso as to reasonableness is the preceding sentence.

Prisoners

The benefit of the principles of natural justice has been extended to prisoners, as already noted, when they are charged with serious disciplinary offences before boards of prison visitors, who for this purpose function as an independent tribunal.[54] But in one case the Court of Appeal held that judicial review did not extend to the disciplinary decisions of prison governors in the day-to-day administration of prisons, which may impose penalties including loss of remission of sentence up to 28 days.[55] The case recalled earlier decisions, since shown to be unsound, where the court refused relief against the exercise of disciplinary powers on the ground that it would undermine disciplinary authority.[56] The House of Lords, however, has now held that a prison governor adjudicating in this way 'bears all the classic hallmarks of an authority subject to judicial review', and has overruled the earlier decision.[57] The door has thus been opened for the operation of judicial review generally and for the rules of natural justice in particular. The House of Lords has eliminated the supposed exception with a decision firmly based upon broad principle, which should ensure the full measure of procedural justice for prisoners. Non-disciplinary action, such as the transfer of a troublesome prisoner to a segregation unit, is another matter.[58]

Since procedural fairness is a fundamental matter, it may in addition be possible to claim it under another decision of the Court of Appeal which holds that judicial review is not excluded where a prison governor is alleged to be violating rights which are fundamental.[59]

Another problematical case is the revocation of parole. Where a prisoner released on licence is recalled to prison it is held that he need not first be given a hearing, at least if the reasons have been fully explained to him.[60] But the European Court of Human Rights has held the contrary in a case brought by a British prisoner.[61]

---

[54] Above, pp. 233, 529.

[55] *R. v. Camphill Prison Deputy Governor ex p. King* [1985] QB 735 (leave to appeal refused by House of Lords). In *R. v. Hull Prison Visitors ex p. St. Germain* [1979] QB 425 dicta in the Court of Appeal had been conflicting. The Court of Appeal in Northern Ireland refused to follow the *Camphill* decision: *R. v. Maze Prison Governor ex p. McKiernan* [1985] NILR Bulletin No. 6, p. 6.

[56] Above, p. 515; and see also p. 529.

[57] *Leech v. Parkhurst Prison Deputy Governor* [1988] 2 WLR 290, a natural justice case.

[58] *Williams v. Home Office* (No. 2) [1981] 1 All ER 1211 (hearing not required).

[59] *R. v. Home Secretary ex p. Herbage* (No. 2) [1987] QB 1077 (allegation that conditions of imprisonment were cruel and unusual punishment contrary to Bill of Rights 1688; leave to apply for judicial review granted).

[60] *R. v. Home Secretary ex p. Gunnell* [1983] The Times, 3 November.

[61] *Weeks v. United Kingdom* (1987) ECHR Series A, no. 114. See above, p. 235.

Aliens

The courts have shown a marked reluctance to extend to aliens the same principles of procedural protection and fair play that apply to citizens of this country. Public policy requires that the Home Secretary should have drastic powers of deportation, refusal of entry, and so forth. But there is no necessary reason why these, like drastic powers over citizens generally, should not be required to be exercised fairly, particularly since the consequences for the alien are often extremely severe.

The best possible proof is that the need for fairness is recognised both by international treaty and by domestic legislation. In 1956 the European Convention on Establishment required a higher standard of justice than did our own law, so that the Home Secretary was obliged to arrange for judicial hearings in a wide class of deportation cases, though the hearings were extra-legal and merely advisory.[62] Under European Community law (adopted in 1972) aliens of member states must be afforded the same remedies against administrative acts as are available to nationals.[63] In 1969 Parliament enacted an elaborate system of tribunals and appeals, which was extended to aliens, giving procedural rights before immigration adjudicators and the Immigration Appeal Tribunal.[64] Aliens could then appeal against exclusion, deportation, non-renewal of residence permits, conditions of residence, and other restrictions. But in 1971 the Home Secretary was given overriding powers to exclude, deport, etc., without right of appeal, in cases where he certified that his action was 'conducive to the public good'.[65] Subject to this power of last resort, the appeal system continues. Parliament has therefore moved ahead of the courts in recognizing that a civilized system of law must treat aliens fairly as well as citizens.

Prior to this legislation the law had in general declined to give aliens a right to be heard in such situations. In 1920 habeas corpus was refused to an alien resident against whom a deportation order had been made without any hearing and it was held that the Home Secretary's function was purely executive and in no way judicial since he was doing what he thought 'conducive to the public good'—though he in fact offered to hear

---

[62] See 557 HC Deb (WA) 174.

[63] Council Directive 64/221, art. 8. This is directly applicable: *Van Duyn* v. *Home Office* [1965] 1 CMLR 1. Under art. 6 there is a right to know the reasons for the decision: see *R.* v. *Home Secretary ex p. Dannenberg* [1984] QB 766 (deportation order quashed).

[64] Immigration Appeals Act 1969, extended to aliens by SI 1970 No. 151.

[65] Immigration Act 1971 (replacing the Act of 1969), ss. 13(5), 14(3), 15(4) (above, p. 227).

representations after the order was made.[66] It was also said that a right to notice and hearing might induce the alien to evade apprehension. The hollowness of these reasons is shown by the legislation mentioned above. Lord Denning has suggested that a hearing should at least be required before a deportation order is executed.[67] The Court of Appeal of New Zealand has held, without mention of the case of 1920, that the principles of natural justice must be observed in the statutory procedure for deporting an over-stayed immigrant.[68] The judgment of Cooke J firmly puts the subject into the general context of procedural fairness, instead of treating it in isolation—a lead which the High Court of Australia has followed in holding that an immigrant threatened with deportation on personal grounds is entitled to a fair opportunity to contest them as a matter of natural justice.[69] The Privy Council quashed a deportation order where an official undertaking gave rise to a legitimate expectation of a fair hearing, but they assumed, without deciding, that in the absence of such an undertaking there would be no right to be heard.[70]

At one time the government adopted a policy (since discontinued) of refusing admission to students of 'scientology', which they considered to be a socially harmful cult. The Home Secretary then refused to extend the short-term entry permits of certain alien scientology students; they were given no opportunity to make representations, though the Home Secretary later said that he was willing to consider them. The Court of Appeal struck out their claim for a declaration that the decision was void, holding that they had no right to remain and 'no legitimate expectation' of being

[66] *R.* v. *Leman Street Police Station Inspector ex p. Venicoff* [1920] 3 KB 72. See similarly *Pagliara* v. *A.-G.* [1974] 1 NZLR 86; *Tobias* v. *May* [1976] 1 NZLR 509; *Salemi* v. *Minister for Immigration* (No. 2) (1977) 14 ALR 1 (High Court of Australia equally divided); *R.* v. *Minister for Immigration ex p. Ratu* (1977) 14 ALR 317. See also *R.* v. *Home Secretary ex p. Hosenball* [1977] 1 WLR 766 at 799 (ruling of European Commission of Human Rights). In Australia deportation decisions are now reviewable by the Administrative Appeal Tribunal, which can recommend revocation of an order and judges policy for itself: *Re Georges and Minister for Immigration* [1979] 22 ALR 667; *Drake* v. *Minister for Immigration* (1979) 24 ALR 577.

[67] *R.* v. *Brixton Prison Governor ex p. Soblen* [1963] 2 QB 243. This was done in *Pagliara* v. *Attorney-General* (above) and in *Cesnovic* v. *Minister of Immigration* (1979) 27 ALR 423.

[68] *Daganayasi* v. *Minister of Immigration* [1980] 2 NZLR 130 (minister's decision invalidated for failure to disclose medical referee's report).

[69] *Kioa* v. *Minister for Immigration* (1985) 62 ALR 321 (deportation order quashed for breach of natural justice; previous decisions not followed). See likewise *Waniewska* v. *Minister for Immigration* (1986) 70 ALR 284.

[70] *Attorney-General of Hong Kong* v. *Ng Yuen Shiu* [1983] 2 AC 629; above, p. 521.

allowed to do so.[71] The absence of right or legitimate expectation is not a convincing reason for not enforcing the duty to act fairly in the making of a decision drastically affecting individuals, and Lord Denning MR held alternatively that, if the duty applied, the Home Secretary had acted fairly by offering to consider representations. Lord Denning also suggested that there should be a right to a hearing if a permit were revoked before its time limit, for then there would be 'legitimate expectation'; and Widgery LJ mentioned that a deportation order might be a very different matter.

Where the Home Secretary takes action against an alien on the ground that it is 'conducive to the public good', as mentioned above, the alien is in practice allowed a hearing before three advisers, with the assistance of a friend but without legal representation. This procedure is subject to the general duty to act fairly, so that the court could intervene if the advisers refused to consider the alien's representations.[72] But if the Home Secretary certifies that it would not be in the interests of national security to reveal details of the charges, that is conclusive. 'The rules of natural justice have to be modified in regard to foreigners here who prove themselves unwelcome and ought to be deported,' where national security is involved.[73] And where an alien has been convicted of serious crime and recommended for deportation after imprisonment, the Home Secretary, though under a duty to act fairly, need not give him a hearing on other matters taken into account, such as the fact that he was refused parole, if the case for deportation is in any case strong.[74]

Immigration is a difficult field of public policy which is no doubt better regulated by Parliament than by the courts. Nevertheless until the new legislation took over, the law was insufficiently considerate of the personal position of aliens, in comparison with the extensive protection given to citizens. One of the reasons why the right to be heard is a universal principle

---

[71] *Schmidt* v. *Home Secretary* [1969] 2 Ch. 149. Lord Denning cites the unreported case of *R.* v. *Home Secretary ex p. Avtar Singh*, in which a Commonwealth citizen was held entitled to no hearing on being refused entry, since he had no right to enter as was claimed by the boy in *Re H. K. (an Infant)* [1967] 2 QB 617 (above, p. 523). With *Schmidt* contrast *Chandra* v. *Minister of Immigration* [1978] 2 NZLR 559 (applicant for residence permit entitled to fair hearing).

[72] *R.* v. *Home Secretary ex p. Hosenball* [1977] 1 WLR 766, upholding a deportation order despite non-disclosure of particulars and sources of information.

[73] Same case at 778 (Lord Denning MR).

[74] *R.* v. *Home Secretary ex p. Santillo* [1981] QB 778. This case had been referred to the European Court of Justice on the question whether the five-year interval between conviction and decision to deport was excessive under European law; the European Court held that it might be excessive, but the Court of Appeal held that it was not so in the circumstances.

is that so little harm can be done by granting it. The fewer exceptions that are made, the sooner will all administrators learn that this is something which should never be denied or overlooked. The law should lose no opportunity to teach this lesson.

PART VI
REMEDIES AND LIABILITY

16

ORDINARY REMEDIES

RIGHTS AND REMEDIES

Rights depend upon remedies. Legal history is rich in examples of rules of
law which have been distilled from the system of remedies, as the remedies
have been extended and adapted from one class of case to another. There is
no better example than habeas corpus. This remedy, since the sixteenth
century the chief cornerstone of personal liberty, grew out of a medieval
writ which at first played an inconspicuous part in the law of procedure: it
was used to secure the appearance of a party, in particular where he was in
detention by some inferior court. It was later invoked to challenge
detention by the king and by the Council; and finally it became the
standard procedure by which the legality of any imprisonment could be
tested. The right to personal freedom was almost a by-product of the
procedural rules. A similar preoccupation with remedies is to be seen in
many cases dealing with the control of administrative powers: the courts
seem sometimes more at ease in considering 'whether certiorari will lie'
than in revealing the general principles which ought to govern judicial
intervention.[1] Principles may then become veiled in a mist of secondary
technicalities.

This tendency has both good and bad effects. It is good in that the
emphasis falls on the practical methods of enforcing any right. Efficient
remedies are of the utmost importance, and the remedies provided by
English administrative law are notably efficient. But sometimes the remedy
comes to be looked upon as a thing in itself, divorced from the legal policy
to which it ought to give expression. In the past this has led to gaps and
anomalies, and to a confusion of doctrine to which the courts have
sometimes seemed strangely indifferent.

Until not long ago anomalies were caused by the fact that the remedies
employed in administrative law belong to two different families. There is
the family of ordinary private law remedies such as damages, injunction,
and declaration; and there is a special family of public law remedies,
principally certiorari, prohibition, and mandamus, collectively known as
the prerogative remedies. There is also a third family of special statutory
remedies, which sometimes exclude all other remedies.[2] Within the

---

[1] See e.g. *R.* v. *Hull Prison Visitors ex p. St. Germain* [1979] QB 425; above, p. 529.
[2] Below, p. 733.

'ordinary' and 'prerogative' families the various remedies could be sought separately or together or in the alternative. But each family had its own distinct procedure. Damages, injunctions, and declarations were sought in an ordinary action, as in private law; but prerogative remedies had to be sought by a procedure of their own, which could not be combined with an ordinary action. It was not possible, for example, to seek certiorari and a declaratory judgment in the alternative, although this would often be a desirable course. This anomaly, though it gave rise to little difficulty in practice, was an obvious target for law reform; and in 1977 it was removed by the provision of a comprehensive procedure, 'application for judicial review', under which remedies in both families became interchangeable.[3] But this reform, useful and innocent as it looked, was fated to cause serious complications. The courts held that there must now be a dichotomy between public and private law, with mutually exclusive procedures—a retrogressive step which has caused great uncertainty and cost much time and money to litigants. It is a classic case of the remedy being worse than the disease.

In this and the following chapter the remedies themselves must first be explained individually. But in many cases they will also be affected collectively, and sometimes individually, by the procedure of application for judicial review, so that the rules discussed in both chapters will constantly need to be co-ordinated with the material of chapter 18.

All the remedies mentioned in this and the following chapters are remedies for obtaining judicial review, i.e. for invoking the inherent jurisdiction of the court. Appeals, though in some sense a form of remedy, are fundamentally different and are dealt with in chapter 23. The present chapter is concerned with the remedies of private law which play a part in public law. First come the remedies related to powers (actions for damages, injunctions, declarations and relator actions). A final section contains such remedies as private law supplies for the enforcement of duties.

ACTIONS FOR DAMAGES

The possibilities of suing governmental authorities, including the Crown, for damages for unjustified tortious injury and for breach of contract are governed by the principles of official and personal liability, explained in chapters 20 and 21. Damages as a remedy therefore need no more than a bare mention here.

Except in cases of personal injury, e.g. from highway and industrial accidents, actions for damages have in the past played a relatively small role

---

[3] Below, p. 671.

in litigation against administrative authorities. But recently the courts have been opening up new areas of liability, and there are signs that what might be called administrative torts are a subject which is on the threshold of important developments. As will be seen in due course, the remedy of damages, which has always been an essential element in the protection of the citizen against public authorities, is already gaining greater prominence as a means of ensuring that powers are exercised responsibly, in good faith and with due care.

An officer of a public authority may equally use this remedy, for instance if a sanitary inspector is wrongfully assaulted. But if he attempts to enter premises in a case where he has no power, the owner is entitled to resist him by force as he may resist any other trespasser.[4]

INJUNCTIONS

General

The injunction is the standard remedy of private law for forbidding the commission of some unlawful act, e.g. a tort or breach of contract. Its sanction is imprisonment or fine for contempt of court, or attachment of property. It is an equitable remedy, since it derives from the former Court of Chancery, and accordingly it has a discretionary character. In administrative law the most important remedies are discretionary—injunctions, declarations and certiorari, for example—but this does not greatly affect their nature since the discretion must be exercised judicially and according to settled principles.[5] The only marked effect is that there is some tendency for the court to refuse the remedy where the plaintiff has some other equally good remedy, or where he has been guilty of delay or in some other way he has forfeited the court's sympathy.

It is also possible for the court to grant a mandatory injunction, i.e. a positive order to do some act rather than a negative order to refrain. Mandatory injunctions are rare, and in particular they play little part in public law because there is a special procedure for enforcing the performance of a public duty in the prerogative remedy of mandamus, dealt with below. But where a public authority's duty is analogous to a private person's, e.g. in managing a housing estate, a mandatory injunction may be a suitable remedy.[6] There may also be more scope for mandatory

---

[4] *Stroud* v. *Bradbury* [1952] 2 All ER 76.

[5] Below, p. 709.

[6] *Parker* v. *Camden LBC* [1986] Ch. 162, holding also that the court would not usurp the local authority's duty by appointing a receiver and manager.

injunctions now that there is a dichotomy between public and private law and some duties are assigned to the latter category.[7]

Subject to certain mainly formal differences in the case of the Crown, injunctions are as readily available against public authorities as they are against private persons, and they are quite often granted to prohibit wrongful or unlawful action. There are many cases where prevention is better than cure, and where either a perpetual injunction or an interim injunction will be awarded to restrain a threatened wrong before it has taken place. And the cure itself is specific, so that a final injunction puts an end to the wrong instead of merely assessing it in money. This remedy, therefore, provides a means both of testing the legal validity of some act which still lies in the future, and also of preventing the continuance of some wrong which has already begun.

Although primarily a remedy against tort and other actionable wrongs, the injunction is also used as a remedy in public law against unauthorised action by governmental and public bodies, even though the action in question would not be a tort or breach of contract. This appears most clearly in cases where the Attorney-General, as the nominal plaintiff in a relator action, as explained below, obtains an injunction to prohibit either some breach of the criminal law or else some ultra vires act by a public authority, such as illegal local government expenditure. Injunctions have been awarded to private individuals also merely on the ground that a public authority was proposing to act ultra vires.[8]

The courts are not deterred by the fact that an injunction against a public authority is a particularly drastic step, bringing the machinery of government to a halt. They do not lend a ready ear to pleas of administrative inconvenience. 'Even if chaos should result, still the law must be obeyed.'[9] With these defiant words the Court of Appeal granted an interim injunction against a local authority's reorganisation of eight existing schools into new comprehensive schools, already approved by the Secretary of State and on the point of taking effect, since the authority had not followed the statutory procedure which required public notice and opportunity for objection.[10] The court firmly disregarded the plea that it would cause excessive disruption to reverse all these completed plans.

The necessary procedure for obtaining an injunction against a public authority is now an application for judicial review in any case assigned to the 'public law' area under the dichotomy imposed by the House of Lords. Many claims against public authorities may however fall into the 'private

---

[7] See *Cocks* v. *Thanet DC* [1983] 2 AC 286, discussed below, p. 681.
[8] Below, p. 690.
[9] Lord Denning MR in the *Bradbury* case (below).
[10] *Bradbury* v. *Enfield London Borough Council* [1967] 1 WLR 1311.

law' category, for example where an injunction is sought against a threatened tort or breach of contract. The dichotomy is explained in chapter 18.

Examples of injunctions

The injunction may be used to prevent the commission or continuance of any tort or breach of contract. Just as damages were awarded for trespass against the Wandsworth board of works when it pulled down a building without giving the owner a hearing, so in a case at Rotherham an injunction was granted to restrain the corporation from carrying out a demolition order without a proper hearing of the owner's appeal for exercise of the statutory power of postponement.[11] The only difference in the latter case was that the owner was able to act before the blow had fallen, and to prevent it from falling. The citizen is in a far stronger position if he can challenge the local authority before it has committed itself to action, and the value in this respect of the remedy by injunction need hardly be stressed. Similarly where a local authority threatened to pull down part of a school, but their byelaw was void for unreasonableness, the school governors were able to prevent this wrong by injunction.[12]

Cases of nuisance created by public authorities are suitably remedied by injunction, as illustrated in a later chapter.[13] In the Derwent pollution case, there mentioned,[14] it was argued that the corporation, since it was responsible for a vital public service, ought not to be prohibited by injunction from supplying it, but should be liable (if at all) only in damages. If this had been right, then the corporation could in effect have compulsorily expropriated the owners of the fishing rights subject to payment of damages by way of compensation. To say that the sewage-disposal arrangements were an urgent necessity for public health, while the fishing rights were relatively of minor importance, did not alter the case at all: for it still remains true that private rights can be expropriated only by statutory authority, and no such authority could be found in the statutes under which the corporation operated. Accordingly the corporation was ordered to cease from polluting the rivers within a specified time, and they were thus compelled to make new arrangements. Needless to say, a public authority can be relied upon to respect the court's order. But it is not

---

[11] *Broadbent* v. *Rotherham Cpn.* [1917] 2 Ch. 31. For the *Wandsworth* case see above, p. 502.

[12] *Repton School Governors* v. *Repton Urban District Council* [1918] 2 KB 133.

[13] Below, p. 755.

[14] *Pride of Derby and Derbyshire Angling Association Ltd.* v. *British Celanese Ltd.* [1953] Ch. 149; below, p. 756.

unknown, where an authority has been tardy in its obedience, for the courts to fine or imprison its members or officers for contempt.[15]

Injunctions are commonly used along with declarations for the purpose of protecting the tenure of public office or statutory status or employment, such as that of schoolteachers. This is dealt with under the following title on declarations.

The Crown and its servants

An injunction will not be granted against the Crown.[16] Formerly this was because the court would not make an order which it had no means of enforcing. But now the Crown Proceedings Act 1947 forbids the grant of an injunction but allows the court to make 'an order declaratory of the rights of the parties'.[17] It is no doubt safe to count on any such order being respected, so that it is a satisfactory substitute for an injunction. It has however one weakness: it has been held that the Act authorises only a definitive order, corresponding to a final injunction, and not a provisional order, corresponding to an interim injunction,[18] apparently because of the reference to 'the rights of the parties'. There seems to be no necessity for this narrow interpretation of the Act, which is contrary to its policy of putting the Crown, so far as practicable, on the same footing as a private litigant. Interim relief may be just as necessary against the Crown as against any other party. The Law Commission made a recommendation[19] for statutory reform of this 'triumph of logic over justice'.[20] Nevertheless a majority of the House of Lords have positively approved the present restriction, though Lord Diplock and a unanimous Court of Appeal deplore it.[21]

When an interim injunction is granted before trial, the party protected must give an undertaking in damages so that, if he loses at the trial, the party restrained is compensated for any loss suffered meanwhile. Formerly the court would grant an interim injunction to the Crown without any such undertaking, the doctrine being that 'the Crown does not undertake'. But the House of Lords has decided that this indulgence to the Crown is no

[15] Below, p. 650.
[16] Contrast Australia, where such relief is allowed by statute: Aronson and Franklin, *Review of Administrative Action*, 609.
[17] See below, p. 825.
[18] *International General Electric Co.* v. *Customs & Excise Commissioners* [1962] Ch. 784; *Underhill* v. *Ministry of Food* [1950] 1 All ER 591.
[19] Cmnd. 6407 (1976), para. 52. The Law Reform Commission of Canada has recommended similarly: 14th Report (1980), p. 41.
[20] Working Paper No. 40 (1971), para. 48.
[21] *R.* v. *Inland Revenue Commissioners ex p. Rossminster Ltd.* [1980] AC 952. Lords Wilberforce, Dilhorne and Scarman approved. Lord Diplock considered it 'a serious procedural defect in the English system of administrative law'.

longer justified, since the plain implication of the Crown Proceedings Act 1947 is that the Crown should so far as possible be treated like other litigants.[22] In this case at least the Act has been beneficially interpreted.

An important question is how far the special rules relating to the Crown also extend to the Crown's servants. The Act provides that no injunction or order shall issue against an officer of the Crown if the effect would be to give a remedy against the Crown which could not have been obtained in proceedings against the Crown.[23] The object of this is to prevent the Crown's immunity being stultified by substituting an individual official as the defendant. Otherwise, applying the principle that wrongs done by servants of the Crown render the servant liable personally, an injunction might be sought against the servant and thus, in effect, a specific remedy would be obtained against the Crown instead of the declaratory order which is the more seemly form of relief.

There have been cases in the past (though the examples are rare and perhaps open to doubt) where injunctions have been granted to restrain ministers of the Crown acting in their official capacity.[24] But the Act, as interpreted, appears to have taken away this possibility with one hand while giving the new declaratory order with the other. An attempt was made in 1955 to obtain a mandatory injunction against the Minister of Agriculture in order to make him withdraw a draft scheme for potato marketing which had been laid before Parliament which was alleged to be ultra vires. But it was plain that the Minister was acting in his official capacity, i.e. as a minister of the Crown; and although the Agricultural Marketing Acts provided that it was the Minister who was to make such schemes, so that the power resided in him rather than in the Crown itself, the court held that any remedy by injunction was barred by the Crown Proceedings Act.[25] This decision is contrary to principle, since ministers who have statutory powers and duties in their own names do not enjoy the immunities of the Crown and are liable to compulsory orders in the normal way;[26] and the decision has since been doubted on this ground.[27] In any case, the supposed restriction in the Crown Proceedings Act does not apply to applications for prerogative remedies,[28] which are freely obtainable

---

[22] *Hoffman–La Roche & Co.* v. *Secretary of State for Trade and Industry* [1975] AC 295.

[23] s. 21(2).

[24] e.g. *Ellis* v. *Earl Grey* (1833) 6 Sim. 214.

[25] *Merricks* v. *Heathcoat-Amory* [1955] Ch. 567.

[26] See below, p. 662 (mandamus), also p. 812 (Crown proceedings).

[27] *R.* v. *Home Secretary ex p. Herbage* [1987] QB 872, citing this criticism.

[28] Since it applies only in 'civil proceedings' and by s. 38(2) that term does not include proceedings on the Crown side of the Queen's Bench Division. This point was overlooked in *R.* v. *Home Secretary ex p. Kirkwood* [1984] 1 WLR 913 (stay of extradition proceedings refused).

against ministers and officials. It seems plain that the true intention of the Act was to protect the Crown, not ministers, against compulsory orders. Furthermore, the controversial restriction on interim relief does not operate where the procedure of application for judicial review is employed against an officer of the Crown, since the rules of court now expressly permit interim relief of any kind.[29]

Parliament

Injunctions may not be used to interfere with the processes of Parliament. As regards its proceedings within its own walls, Parliament is completely privileged from judicial intervention. Thus when the House of Commons ordered the exclusion of a member, an injunction against the Sergeant-at-Arms was refused.[30]

In extra-mural matters a line has to be drawn. The court follows the principle that it will not intervene to prevent some matter being brought before Parliament as a question of public policy, even though it may be a breach of contract to bring it forward. In one case the Wolverhampton Corporation had contracted with the Bilston Corporation that it would not oppose any application to Parliament by the Bilston Corporation for a local Act of Parliament for obtaining a water-supply from any area outside the Wolverhampton Corporation's area. The Wolverhampton Corporation did oppose such an application and were held to be in breach of their contract. The court, however, refused to restrain them by injunction, because that would have prevented Parliament from hearing all sides of the question in determining whether, as a matter of public policy, the Wolverhampton Corporation ought to be released from their obligation by statute.[31] This was a strong case, since the contract itself had been confirmed and made binding by an earlier local Act. It is not, therefore, that such contracts are void as contrary to public policy. The judges have repeatedly held that they have jurisdiction to grant an injunction in such cases, but they have invariably refused to grant it.[32] But where the court makes it a rule to refuse the only effective remedy, it would be more straightforward to admit that no remedy exists.

Where, on the other hand, a body proposes to use its funds for promoting an Act of Parliament in which it has no legitimate interest it may be restrained by injunction at the suit of the Attorney-General.[33]

---

[29] *R. v. Home Secretary ex p. Herbage* (above) where an interim order to mitigate conditions of imprisonment was refused, though there was jurisdiction to make it.

[30] *Bradlaugh v. Gossett* (1884) 12 QBD 271.

[31] *Bilston Cpn. v. Wolverhampton Cpn.* [1942] Ch. 391.

[32] Similarly with the remedy of prohibition: below, p. 628.

[33] *A.-G. v. London & Home Counties Joint Electricity Authority* [1929] 1 Ch. 513.

A dramatic case arose in 1954 which for a time seemed as if it might cause a clash between the courts and Parliament. The Boundary Commission, which had statutory powers to make schemes for the rearrangement of parliamentary constituencies, proposed some changes in the Manchester area which were opposed by local voters who would thereby be transferred. The Home Secretary had laid the Commission's report before Parliament and both Houses had approved draft Orders in Council for giving effect to it under the statutory procedure. It only remained, therefore, for the orders to be approved by the Queen in Council. The objectors, who claimed that the Commission had not complied with their statutory duties, asked for an interim injunction to restrain the Home Secretary from submitting the orders to the Queen in Council before a date which would give time for their legality to be determined. They were granted this injunction at first instance, but were deprived of it on appeal.[34] The Court of Appeal held that it could not be right for the court to intervene where the statutory procedure was subject to express parliamentary approval, and this approval had been given; and that grave constitutional questions would arise if the courts ordered ministers not to do what the two Houses of Parliament had said that they should do. But this argument has since been rejected by the House of Lords, so that the court may have jurisdiction to grant an injunction even against an order approved by both Houses.[35]

Injunctions for enforcement of statutes

An important use of the injunction, very different from those already described, is for the purpose of forbidding disobedience to statutes, for example in the case of constantly repeated offences where the statutory penalties are inadequate. Since only the Attorney-General may seek injunctions for this purpose, except where statute has provided otherwise, the practice is explained below, in the section on relator actions.[36]

Tenure of public office: injunction in nature of quo warranto

Since 1938 the injunction has been made available by statute to prohibit the usurpation of a public office, in place of the former proceedings known as quo warranto. Quo warranto was originally a prerogative writ which the

[34] *Harper v. Home Secretary* [1955] Ch. 238.
[35] *Hoffman—La Roche & Co.* v. *Secretary of State for Trade and Industry* [1975] AC 295; above, p. 29.
[36] Below, p. 610.

Crown could use to inquire into the title to any office or franchise claimed by a subject. It fell out of use in the sixteenth century and was replaced by the information in the nature of quo warranto, which in form was a criminal proceeding instituted in the name of the Crown by the Attorney-General or by a private prosecutor.[37] These informations were abolished by the Administration of Justice (Miscellaneous Provisions) Act 1938[38] (now replaced by the Supreme Court Act 1981[39]) which provided that where any person acts in an office to which he is not entitled and an information would previously have lain against him, the High Court may restrain him by injunction and may declare the office to be vacant if need be; and that no such proceedings shall be taken by a person who would not previously have been entitled to apply for an information. Consequently the old law of quo warranto is still operative, but the remedy is now by injunction and declaration. The procedure is similar to that for prerogative remedies and must now be by 'application for judicial review'.[40] But there seems to be no record of its having been used.

The old procedure by information was available to private persons but subject to the discretion of the court. A private prosecutor brought the best known modern case, in which it was unsuccessfully claimed that two foreign-born Privy Councillors were disqualified for membership, the courts holding that the Naturalisation Act 1870 had repealed the disqualification imposed by the Act of Settlement 1700.[41] The modern tendency has been to extend the remedy, subject to the discretion of the court to refuse it to a private prosecutor, for example if he has delayed unduly. A private prosecutor acting on public grounds may expect the assistance of the court.[42] He is sometimes called the relator, although he does not have to obtain the leave of the Attorney-General.

The remedy as now defined applies to usurpation of 'any substantive office of a public nature and permanent character which is held under the Crown or which has been created by any statutory provision or royal charter'.[43] But it must not be a case of 'merely the function or employment of a deputy or servant held at the will and pleasure of others'.[44] Here once again we meet the difference between office and mere contractual

---

[37] Bl. Comm. iii. 263.

[38] s. 9.

[39] s. 30.

[40] Supreme Court Act 1981, s. 31; see below, p. 671. The pre-1938 practice, as with the prerogative remedies, was to obtain a rule nisi for the information.

[41] *R.* v. *Speyer, R.* v. *Cassel* [1916] 1 KB 595, affirmed [1916] 2 KB 858. For a short history of the procedure see the judgment of Lord Reading. CJ at first instance.

[42] *R.* v. *Speyer* [1916] 1 KB at 613.

[43] Supreme Court Act 1981, s. 30.

[44] *Darley* v. *R.* (1846) 12 Cl & F 520 at 541 (Tindal CJ, advising the House of Lords).

employment.[45] The procedure was typically used to challenge the right to such offices as those of freeman or burgess of a borough, mayor, town councillor, sheriff, justice of the peace, county court judge, chief constable, or member of the General Medical Council.[46] But the alleged usurper had to be in possession of the office and to have acted in it.[47]

For challenging the qualifications of a member of a local authority there are special statutory provisions under the Local Government Act 1972.[48] Proceedings may be instituted in the High Court or a magistrates' court, but only by a local government elector for the area concerned, and only within six months of the defendant having acted as a member; if the defendant merely claims to be entitled to act, proceedings lie in the High Court only. The various remedies include declarations, injunctions and financial penalties.

DECLARATIONS

Development of this remedy

Declaratory judgments play a large part in private law and are a particularly valuable remedy for settling disputes before they reach the point where a right is infringed.[49] The essence of a declaratory judgment is that it states the rights or legal position of the parties as they stand, without changing them in any way; though it may be supplemented by other remedies in suitable cases. Typical applications are for finding the meaning of some provision in a will, or whether a statute applies to some particular case, or whether a contract has been properly performed. In administrative law there are additional advantages, as in cases where it is difficult to choose the right remedy or where the ordinary remedy is for some reason unsatisfactory.

The common law, with its insistence on compulsory remedies and its horror of maintenance and procedural abuse, long refused to countenance judgments that were merely declaratory; and so did the Court of Chancery. But they were needed inevitably in proceedings against the Crown, since in that case there was no means of enforcement, so that they were in regular use in connection with petitions of right and on the equity side of the Exchequer. Scots law had the action of declarator, which Lord

[45] See above, p. 561.

[46] Halsbury's *Laws of England*, 4th edn., vol. i, para. 171.

[47] *R. v. Tidy* [1892] 2 QB 179; Administration of Justice (Miscellaneous Provisions) Act 1938, s. 9(2).

[48] s. 92, replacing s. 84 of the Act of 1933.

[49] See generally I. Zamir, *The Declaratory Judgment* (1962) and [1977] CLP 43; P. W. Young, *Declaratory Orders* (1975).

Brougham attempted to import into England with only small success at first. Acts of 1850 and 1852 empowered the Court of Chancery to make declarations of right, but they were construed as narrowly as possible by a still mistrustful judiciary.[50] Even the Judicature Acts 1873–5 did not implant any such power generally in the remodelled judicial system. It arrived finally only with the rules of court of 1883. It must therefore be considered a statutory rather than an equitable remedy. The surprising thing is that this form of relief, indispensable in any modern system of law, should be so recent an invention.

The rules of court of 1883 provided that:

No action or proceedings shall be open to objection, on the ground that a merely declaratory judgment or order is sought thereby, and the Court may make binding declarations of right whether any consequential relief is or could be claimed, or not.[51]

This is still the rule today,[52] and the courts have grown accustomed to using it very freely. A declaratory judgment by itself merely states some existing legal situation. It requires no one to do anything and to disregard it will not be contempt of court.[53] By enabling a party to discover what his legal position is, it opens the way to the use of other remedies for giving effect to it, if that should be necessary. But it cannot be used to litigate matters which are not governed by the law and not justiciable in the courts, such as civil servants' superannuation allowances[54] or claims based upon the European Convention on Human Rights[55] or, it may be surmised, the proceedings of Royal Commissions.[56]

---

[50] Court of Chancery, England, Act 1850; Court of Chancery Procedure Act 1852. s. 50 of the latter Act was in nearly as wide a form as the later rule of court, but it was construed as allowing declaratory relief only where some other equitable relief could have been awarded: see *Dyson* v. *A.-G.* [1911] 1 KB 410 at 417, 422.

[51] RSC O. 25 r. 5, upheld as intra vires in *Guaranty Trust Co. of New York* v. *Hannay & Co.* [1915] 2 KB 536.

[52] RSC 1965, O. 15, r. 16.

[53] *Webster* v. *Southwark LBC* [1983] QB 698, where however the court approved the issue of a writ of sequestration against the property of councillors who in deliberate breach of statutory duty had refused the use of a hall for an election meeting of a National Front candidate. The court's order had been merely declaratory since it was assumed that it would be respected. Otherwise a compulsory order might have been granted. The contumaceous conduct of the defendants was a decisive factor. Nevertheless the decision seems questionable.

[54] *Nixon* v. *A.-G.* [1930] 1 Ch. 566. See also *Gouriet* v. *Union of Post Office Workers* [1978] AC 435.

[55] *Malone* v. *Metropolitan Police Commissioner* [1979] Ch. 344 (telephone tapping).

[56] In Britain royal commissions have no statutory or other powers. In New Zealand they are statutory and have power to award costs, and so are subject to judicial review: *Mahon* v. *Air New Zealand Ltd.* [1984] AC 808; and likewise in Australia: *Ross* v. *Costigan* (1982) 41 ALR 319.

The declaration is a discretionary remedy. This important characteristic probably derives not from the fact that the power to grant it was first conferred on the Court of Chancery, but from the discretionary power conferred by the rule of court. There is thus ample jurisdiction to prevent its abuse; and the court always has inherent powers to refuse relief to speculators and busybodies, those who ask hypothetical questions[57] or those who have no sufficient interest.[58] As was said by Lord Dunedin,[59]

The question must be a real and not a theoretical question; the person raising it must have a real interest to raise it; he must be able to secure a proper contradictor, that is to say, some one presently existing who has a true interest to oppose the declaration sought.

In other words, there must be a genuine legal issue between proper parties.

Declarations against public authorities

In administrative law the great merit of the declaration is that it is an efficient remedy against ultra vires action by governmental authorities of all kinds, including the Crown. If the court will declare that some action, either taken or proposed, is unauthorised by law, that concludes the point as between the plaintiff and the authority. If then his property is taken, he has his ordinary legal remedies; if an order is made against him, he can ignore it with impunity; if he has been dismissed from an office, he can insist that he still holds it.[60] All these results flow from the mere fact that the rights of the parties have been declared. This is a particularly suitable way to settle disputes with governmental authorities, since it involves no immediate threat of compulsion, yet is none the less effective.

The landmark in this use of the declaration is the famous case of *Dyson* v. *Attorney-General* (1911–12).[61] It was one of the repercussions of Lloyd George's budget proposals for a tax on land values, which the House of Lords rejected in 1909 with results so disastrous to themselves. Under the Act as finally passed in 1910 the Commissioners of Inland Revenue were empowered to demand from landowners, under threat of penalty, factual information which could be used in valuing their lands. But the demands

---

[57] As in *Re Barnato* [1949] Ch. 258; *Harrison* v. *Croydon London Borough Council* [1968] Ch. 479.

[58] See below, pp. 691, 702.

[59] *Russian Commercial and Industrial Bank* v. *British Bank for Foreign Trade Ltd.* [1921] 2 AC 438 at 448, summarising Scots law applicable in England.

[60] As in *Ridge* v. *Baldwin* [1964] AC 40; above, p. 517.

[61] [1911] 1 KB 410, holding that the procedure was admissible: [1912] 1 Ch. 158, holding that the demand was ultra vires. For a recent parallel see *R.* v. *Customs and Excise Commissioners ex p. Hedges and Butler Ltd.* [1986] 2 All ER 164 (regulation allowing demand for all records of business held excessive and ultra vires; declaration granted).

sent out (more than eight million) required in addition a statement of the annual value of the land, a demand not authorised by the Act. At the instance of a landowner, who brought proceedings against the Attorney-General, the Court of Appeal granted a declaration that the demands were wholly ineffective in law. By seeking a declaration the owner was able to take the initiative, and the court rejected the Crown's argument that his right course was to take no action and then dispute the demand when he was sued for the penalty. Fletcher Moulton LJ said:[62]

So far from thinking that this action is open to objection on that score, I think that an action thus framed is the most convenient method of enabling the subject to test the justifiability of proceedings on the part of permanent officials purporting to act under statutory provisions. Such questions are growing more and more important, and I can think of no more suitable or adequate procedure for challenging the legality of such proceedings. It would be intolerable that millions of the public should have to choose between giving information to the Commissioners which they have no right to demand and incurring a severe penalty.

On the other hand, declarations cannot be granted merely because a party prefers to attack rather than defend. If that is his only motive, the court may say to him 'Wait until you are attacked and then raise your defence', and dismiss his action.[63] Nor if a criminal prosecution has been instituted against him, can he ask for a declaration that he has committed no offence.[64] Everything therefore depends upon the merits of his motives for seeking this remedy. But *Dyson's* case gave a fair wind to the action for a declaration as a defensive weapon against the executive power.[65] As the quotation shows, the court considered that a question as to the legality of administrative action was in itself a good reason for asking for judicial intervention at the earliest possible moment. The decision is all the stronger for the fact that the Inland Revenue were not threatening any tort. They were merely making a demand which they had no power to make, and therefore no power to enforce.

Even where there is no immediate demand or threat, a declaration may be granted to settle some doubtful question of law on which an authoritative ruling is needed. One such case was where a company wished to know whether its quarrying operations required planning permission and obtained an emphatic judgment in their favour from the House of

---

[62] [1912] 1 Ch. at 168.

[63] [1911] 1 KB at 417 (Cozens-Hardy MR). And see *Smeeton* v. *A.-G.* [1920] 1Ch. 85 at 96–8. This argument was rejected in *Ealing LBC* v. *Race Relations Board* [1972] AC 342, holding that the council need not wait for the board to start proceedings but could seek a declaration that their action was lawful.

[64] *Imperial Tobacco Ltd.* v. *A.-G.* [1981] AC 718.

[65] See the strong remarks of Farwell LJ, [1911] 1 KB at 424.

Lords.[66] In two other cases the House granted declarations to settle arguments about the legality of action recommended in circulars issued by government departments, which themselves had no direct legal force. One was where nurses were stated to be allowed to perform certain functions under the Abortion Act 1967.[67] The other was where doctors were said to be entitled to give contraceptive advice to girls aged under 16 in certain circumstances without informing their parents.[68] In both cases the official advice was upheld.

Thanks to its flexibility and convenience the declaratory judgment has flourished as a general remedy in administrative law. Before the reforms of 1977 this remedy was also preferred because it had important procedural advantages as compared with certiorari, as explained later.[69] Since 1977 those advantages have disappeared, but the declaration has lost none of its popularity. Under the dichotomy ordained by the House of Lords in 1982, under which procedures in 'public law' and 'private law' have become mutually exclusive, the declaration is a primary remedy in both categories, though unfortunately it may now be difficult to know by which procedure it should be sought. This new dilemma is discussed in chapter 18.[70]

The Crown and its servants

An outstanding feature of *Dyson* v. *Attorney-General* was that the declaration was granted against the Attorney-General, as representing the Crown. As already noted, it was in proceedings against the Crown that declaratory judgments first made their appearance, as a matter of necessity, so that it could not be said that any new remedy against the Crown was being invented. A declaration is therefore a good substitute for remedies which cannot be granted against the Crown, such as injunction and mandamus. The Crown Proceedings Act 1947 has not restricted the jurisdiction in any way, but it has altered the procedure. All civil proceedings against the Crown are now subject to the standard procedure, i.e. the action must be brought against the appropriate government

---

[66] *Pyx Granite Co. Ltd.* v. *Ministry of Housing and Local Government* [1960] AC 260, for which see below, p. 716.

[67] *Royal College of Nursing* v. *Department of Health and Social Security* [1981] AC 800.

[68] *Gillick* v. *West Norfolk and Wisbech Area Health Authority* [1986] AC 112. Lord Bridge there says (at 193) that the *Royal College of Nursing* case (above) effected 'a significant extension of the court's power of judicial review'; and the *Gillick* case is so treated by Sir John Donaldson MR in *R.* v. *Panel on Take-overs and Mergers ex p. Datafin Plc* [1987] QB 815. But on this there is no clear majority view in the House of Lords. Nor is it clear why the case was not within the previous rules. For comment see (1986) 102 LQR 173 and below, p. 682.

[69] Below, p. 667.

[70] Below, p. 681.

department, and against the Attorney-General only if no appropriate department is listed.[71]

Where the power is possessed, as normally, not by the Crown itself but by some designated minister or Crown agency, a declaration is likewise available.[72] This was in fact the situation in *Dyson* v. *Attorney-General* where the power had been conferred by the Act upon the Commissioners of Inland Revenue,[73] not upon His Majesty. The same naturally applies in the case of duties.[74]

Another occasion for seeking a declaration against the Crown is for determining nationality. Thus where a prince of Hanover wished to establish his claim to British nationality under the somewhat dubious authority of an Act of Queen Anne's reign, he obtained a declaration that he was a British subject by bringing an action against the Attorney-General.[75]

Other authorities

Declarations are freely available against other authorities. A child's guardian may obtain a declaration that a county council is wrongly refusing to accept children in its schools,[76] a police officer may obtain a declaration that he has not been validly dismissed;[77] a dock worker may obtain a declaration that he has been wrongfully removed from the register, thereby preserving his right to employment under the dock labour scheme.[78] In principle, any act of a public authority may be challenged in declaratory proceedings claiming that it is ultra vires and void. Declarations have been granted against unlawful tax demands,[79] street works charges,[80] compulsory purchase orders,[81] conditions imposed on planning permission,[82] enforcement notices,[83] coast protection charges,[84]

---

[71] s. 17(3).

[72] *Pyx Granite Co. Ltd.* v. *Ministry of Housing and Local Government* [1960] AC 260; *Congreve* v. *Home Office* [1976] QB 629.

[73] As recognised by Farwell LJ, [1911] 1 KB at 422. Today the Commissioners would be the appropriate defendants.

[74] For declarations in respect of duties see below, p. 614.

[75] *A.-G.* v. *Prince Ernest Augustus of Hanover* [1957] AC 436.

[76] *Gateshead Union Guardians* v. *Durham CC* [1918] 1 Ch. 146.

[77] *Cooper* v. *Wilson* [1937] 2 KB 309; *Ridge* v. *Baldwin* [1964] AC 40.

[78] *Vine* v. *National Dock Labour Board* [1957] AC 488.

[79] *Bowles* v. *Bank of England* [1913] 1 Ch. 57; *Dyson* v. *A.-G.* [1912] 1 Ch. 159.

[80] *Elsdon* v. *Hampstead Borough Council* [1905] 2 Ch. 633.

[81] *Grice* v. *Dudley Cpn.* [1958] Ch. 329.

[82] *Hall & Co. Ltd.* v. *Shoreham-by-Sea Urban District Council* [1964] 1 WLR 240; and see *Pyx Granite Co. Ltd.* v. *Ministry of Housing and Local Government* [1960] AC 260.

[83] *Francis* v. *Yiewsley & West Drayton Urban District Council* [1958] 1 QB 478.

[84] *Cullimore* v. *Lyme Regis Cpn.* [1962] 1 QB 718.

and threats of trespass under alleged rights of way.[85] The plaintiff must have the necessary standing to sue[86] and the case must not be one where the remedy is expressly or impliedly excluded by statute.[87] But otherwise there is no limit to the variety of ultra vires acts which can be challenged by the use of this wide and flexible remedy. It has been held that the jurisdiction to grant it 'should receive as liberal a construction as possible'.[88]

Further useful applications of the declaration are for the determination of some disputed question of status;[89] for settling whether advice given in government circulars is correct in law;[90] for enabling a public authority to ascertain its own duties or powers;[91] and for the resolution of some dispute between two public authorities.[92]

A declaration may also be sought against a statutory tribunal so as to challenge the validity of its decision—and, occasionally, to tell it positively what it ought to decide.[93] Although it has been suggested that, where the tribunal has merely to make a determination which it does not itself enforce, the proper defendant is not the tribunal but the person entitled to enforce the decision,[94] declarations have in several cases been granted against tribunals and similar bodies on account of decisions which were ultra vires.[95] There would seem to be no reason why this direct challenge should not be allowed, just as it is where the remedy is certiorari.

Offices and employments

As explained earlier, the law will not specifically enforce a contract of service between master and servant: the master always has power to dismiss

---

[85] *Thornhill* v. *Weeks* [1913] 1 Ch. 438.
[86] See below, p. 688.
[87] See below, p. 716.
[88] *Guaranty Trust Co. of New York* v. *Hannay & Co.* [1915] 2 KB 536 at 572 (Bankes LJ).
[89] *A.-G.* v. *Prince Ernest Augustus of Hanover* (above).
[90] As illustrated above, p. 597.
[91] *Wimbledon & Putney Conservators* v. *Tuely* [1931] Ch. 90.
[92] e.g. *Gateshead Union Guardians* v. *Durham County Council* (above); *Surrey County Council* v. *Ministry of Education* [1953] 1 WLR 516; *R.* v. *London Transport Executive ex p. Greater London Council* [1983] QB 484 (GLC's policy of subsidising London transport fares declared lawful).
[93] As in *Barty-King* v. *Ministry of Defence* [1979] 2 All ER 80.
[94] *Anisminic Ltd.* v. *Foreign Compensation Commission* [1968] 2 QB 862 at 911 (Diplock LJ).
[95] *Taylor* v. *National Assistance Board* [1957] P. 101 at 111, affirmed [1958] AC 532; *Anisminic Ltd.* v. *Foreign Compensation Commission* [1969] 2 AC 147; and see *Lee* v. *Showmen's Guild* [1952] 2 QB 329 at 346; *Barnard* v. *National Dock Labour Board* [1953] 2 QB 18 at 41; *Punton* v. *Ministry of Pensions and National Insurance (No. 1)* [1963] 1 WLR 186; (No. 2) [1964] 1 WLR 226.

the servant, even though in breach of contract, and the servant's remedy is to sue for damages.[96] In special circumstances the court may depart from this rule,[97] but normally it is observed uniformly. Accordingly a dismissed employee cannot obtain a declaration that his dismissal was a nullity, for in that case his employment would still continue and the court would be enforcing the contract of employment specifically.[98] This does not mean that a declaration will never be granted to a dismissed employee: he may obtain a declaration that his dismissal was a breach of contract, thus establishing his right to damages.[99] But he cannot claim a declaration that will prolong his employment.

To this rule there now appears to be an exception in respect of dismissal procedures. Where a contract of employment provides rights of appeal or other procedural rights, the court may grant an injunction to prevent the employee being denied these rights.[1] This is akin to the enforcement of the principles of natural justice, in relation to which it has already been explained.[2]

An office, as opposed to mere employment, may be protected specifically, as has also been seen above; and the same applies to a statutory status, such as that of a registered dock worker.[3] This is why police officers can be removed from their posts only by a valid exercise of the statutory power of dismissal.[4] On the same principle a declaration was granted against the dismissal of a schoolteacher on 'educational grounds' (as the Act required) when no such grounds existed;[5] and against the dismissal of schoolteachers who had refused to collect money for pupils' meals, since the Education Act provided (as the court held) that teachers could not be

[96] Above, p. 562.

[97] As in *Hill* v. *Parsons* [1972] Ch. 305, where an injunction to enforce continuing employment was granted on the ground that damages were an inadequate remedy. The plaintiff had been dismissed under a closed shop policy, but might have been protected by the Industrial Relations Act 1971 coming into force within the period of notice to which he was entitled. See also *Taylor* v. *National Union of Seamen* [1976] 1 WLR 532; *Powell* v. *Brent LBC* [1987] The Times, 17 August.

[98] *Barber* v. *Manchester Regional Hospital Board* [1958] 1 WLR 181 (doubted but corroborated as mentioned above, p. 563); *Francis* v. *Kuala Lumpur Councillors* [1962] 1 WLR 1411.

[99] This appears to be the explanation of *McClelland* v. *Northern Ireland General Health Services Board* [1957] 1 WLR 594, though it is only in the dissenting speech of Lord Keith (at 609) that the point appears clearly. The report is inadequate as to the relief sought.

[1] *R.* v. *British Broadcasting Corporation ex p. Lavelle* [1983] 1 WLR 23; *Irani* v. *Southampton Health Authority* [1985] ICR 590.

[2] Above, p. 565.

[3] *Barnard* v. *National Dock Labour Board* [1953] 2 QB 18; *Vine* v. *National Dock Labour Board* [1957] AC 488.

[4] *Cooper* v. *Wilson* [1937] 2 KB 309; *Ridge* v. *Baldwin* [1964] AC 40.

[5] *Martin* v. *Eccles Cpn.* [1919] 1 Ch. 387 (a touching story).

required to act as collectors.[6] A limited statutory power of dismissal is one of the marks of a protected office or status. The ambiguous position of many public employees has been explained in the context of natural justice.[7]

In these employment cases injunctions are commonly sought and granted together with declarations and according to the same rules.[8]

Declaration in conjunction with prerogative remedies

Since 1977 the remedies of declaration and injunction have become available interchangeably with the prerogative remedies of certiorari, prohibition and mandamus under the procedure of application for judicial review.[9] The scope of declaration and injunction is therefore now coextensive with that of those remedies as explained below under their respective titles. One example of this extended scope concerns error on the fact of the record (see the following paragraphs). Another concerns non-statutory functions to which judicial review is now extended, which are discussed in the context of certiorari and prohibition[10] but for which declarations and injunctions are equally eligible, indeed sometimes more so.[11]

Error on the face of the record

It used to be a defect of the declaratory judgment that it was useless in cases of mere error on the face of the record, where the disputed determination might be intra vires but nevertheless liable to be quashed by certiorari.[12] This defect was established after a sharp conflict of opinion in the Court of Appeal, in a case where unemployment benefit was refused to some shipyard workers thrown out of work by a strike.[13] It was claimed that the

---

[6] *Price* v. *Sunderland Corporation* [1956] 1 WLR 1253; and see *Smith* v. *Macnally* [1912] 1 Ch. 816; *Sadler* v. *Sheffield Cpn.* [1924] 1 Ch. 483; *Gorse* v. *Durham County Council* [1971] 1 WLR 775; *Jones* v. *Lee* [1980] ICR 310.

[7] Above, p. 563.

[8] See cases in n. 6, above.

[9] Below, p. 672.

[10] Below, p. 640.

[11] As in the case of the *Panel on Take-overs and Mergers* (below, p. 641).

[12] For this see above, p. 308.

[13] *Punton* v. *Ministry of Pensions and National Insurance (No. 1)* [1963] 1 WLR 186 (striking out motion refused); *(No. 2)* [1964] 1 WLR 226 (declaration refused). The fact that the tribunal might have power to reconsider its decision would not appear to affect the reasoning. See also *Bousfield* v. *North Yorks CC* [1982] The Times, 4 March. For comment see (1980) 43 MLR 266 (P. Cane).

Commissioner's decision was bad for error of law on its face, and it was admitted that the applicants could have challenged it by certiorari if they had applied for that remedy in time. At a preliminary stage the Court of Appeal encouraged the action for a declaration. But in the end they held that there was no jurisdiction to grant one, since the Commissioner's decision would remain legally effective and would bar any award of unemployment benefit absolutely. In other words, merely to declare that a determination was intra vires, even though mistaken, effected nothing; whereas certiorari 'quashed' and positively removed the offending determination out of the way.

This difficulty has been eliminated by two developments. First, the introduction of the 'application for judicial review' has made the declaration and certiorari interchangeable, so that if certiorari can be sought, so also can a declaration.[14] Secondly, the doctrine that every error of law by a tribunal amounts to excess of jurisdiction, assuming that it becomes established,[15] will necessarily mean that an erroneous determination can no longer be intra vires: it must be ultra vires, and a declaration to that effect will, as usual, invalidate it.

Fitting the remedy to the case

In granting declarations, as they do so freely, the courts do not always observe that they may not fit the facts. An example was where a probationer police officer had resigned from the force under an unjustified threat of dismissal. The Court of Appeal granted him a declaration that the chief constable's decision to dismiss him was void, despite the fact that the chief constable's only legal power was to dismiss, which in fact he did not do, and he had no specific power to make a decision.[16] On appeal the House of Lords substituted a different declaration, recognising that the Court of Appeal's order could not effect the probationer's reinstatement, and that an order of mandamus was the only satisfactory remedy.[17] This case may be classed with others, explained below,[18] where there has been a misfit between the remedy and the case because it was supposed that every administrative power was a power of decision.

---

[14] See below, p. 672.

[15] See above, p. 299.

[16] *Chief Constable of North Wales Police* v. *Evans* [1982] 1 WLR 1155 (application for judicial review). There is no report of the Court of Appeal's reasons.

[17] See at 1165 (Lord Bridge) and 1176 (Lord Brightman). But mandamus was not awarded because 'it might border on usurpation of the powers of the chief constable' (at 1176, Lord Brightman). So the proper remedy was withheld in discretion.

[18] Below, p. 638.

Exclusive statutory remedy

A declaratory judgment may not be used as a substitute for an exclusive statutory remedy available from some specified court or tribunal—as for instance where a tax allowance can be claimed only by appeal to the Commissioners of Inland Revenue[19] or where a question affecting the assessment of compensation on a compulsory purchase is to be determined only by the Lands Tribunal.[20] This is a general doctrine, affecting other remedies, and is explained later.[21]

Discretionary remedy

Finally, the declaration is a discretionary remedy. The court may refuse it if it thinks fit, for example if persons who are directly interested in the proceedings are not joined as parties.[22] But this characteristic is best explained later, since injunction, declaration, and the prerogative orders are all discretionary remedies, and the same principles govern them all.[23]

The court will not normally grant a declaration in interlocutory proceedings, since this remedy is final in its nature.[24]

RELATOR ACTIONS

A hybrid procedure

A relator action is an action brought by the Attorney-General at the relation (i.e. at the instance) of some other person claiming an injunction or declaration, or both,[25] in order to prevent some breach of the law. By lending his name for this purpose the Attorney-General has enabled the injunction and declaration, which are basically remedies for the protection of private rights,[26] to be converted into remedies of public law for the protection of the public interest. They have thus acquired a hybrid character, and in this public law aspect they are comparable to the prerogative remedies.

[19] *Argosam Finance Co. Ltd.* v. *Oxby* [1965] Ch. 390.
[20] *Harrison* v. *Croydon London Borough Council* [1968] Ch. 479.
[21] Below, p. 716.
[22] *London Passenger Transport Board* v. *Moscrop* [1942] AC 332.
[23] Below, p. 709.
[24] *Meade* v. *Haringey LBC* [1979] 1 WLR 637 at 648.
[25] Most commonly an injunction. An example of declaration is *A.-G. ex rel. Tilley* v. *Wandsworth LBC* [1981] 1 WLR 854.
[26] A plaintiff may sue in his own name where interference with a public right causes him special damage: *Boyce* v. *Paddington Borough Council* [1903] 1 Ch. 109.

The foundation of this procedure is the interest of the Crown, as parens patriae, in upholding the law for the general public benefit. The Crown is concerned to see that public bodies, public trusts and charities should not exceed or abuse their powers or their funds; to abate public nuisances; and to prevent the law being flouted. The court may always restrain such abuses at the Attorney-General's instance.[27] In other words, the Crown always has standing for this purpose, whereas a private plaintiff might be refused relief on the ground that he had no more interest in the matter than any other member of the public. But in many situations the Attorney-General is willing to act on a private plaintiff's behalf, at his 'relation', thus solving the problem of standing.[28] Just as the Crown will lend its name to applicants for prerogative remedies, so the Attorney-General will lend his name to the relator.

Attorney-General's role

The Attorney-General may if he prefers act independently, ex officio.[29] But in practice he acts at the instance of the relator, whom he requires to instruct solicitor and counsel, who must certify that the statement of claim is proper for the Attorney-General's acceptance and that the relator will be responsible for costs.[30] Once the Attorney-General has accepted, 'he virtually drops out of the proceedings . . . the actual conduct of the proceedings is entirely in the hands of the relator who is responsible for the costs of the action'.[31] Having conferred the necessary standing on the relator, therefore, the Attorney-General shows no further concern with the public interest, but leaves the case to proceed like private litigation.

It has long been axiomatic that it rests entirely in the discretion of the Attorney-General to decide whether or not he will lend his name. As was said in the House of Lords:[32]

---

[27] See Edwards, *The Law Officers of the Crown*, 286. No damage or injury need be shown: *A.-G.* v. *Cockermouth Local Board* (1874) LR 18 Eq. 172.

[28] In some cases the Attorney-General requires the relator first to obtain a ruling from the court that he has no standing of his own: *Booth & Co. Ltd.* v. *National Enterprise Board* [1978] 3 All ER 624; *Barrs* v. *Bethell* [1982] Ch. 294. In the uncertain state of the law about standing this practice may require much additional litigation and its justification is not evident.

[29] The reason why this was not in practice done has been said to be that there was no satisfactory system for awarding costs prior to the Administration of Justice (Miscellaneous Provisions) Act 1933, s. 7: *Hoffman–La Roche* v. *Secretary of State for Trade & Industry* [1975] AC 295 at 363 (Lord Diplock).

[30] *A.-G. ex rel. McWhirter* v. *Independent Broadcasting Authority* [1973] QB 629 at 647 (Lord Denning MR). See *Supreme Court Practice*, notes to O. 15 r. 11. The relator may be joined as a party in suitable cases.

[31] As preceding note.

[32] *London County Council* v. *A.-G.* [1902] AC 165 at 169 (Lord Halsbury LC).

. . . the initiation of the litigation, and the determination of the question whether it is a proper case for the Attorney-General to proceed in, is a matter entirely beyond the jurisdiction of this or any other court.

But what rules, if any, the Attorney-General follows for this purpose are not known. There is no published information about his practice,[33] which can only be guessed from the reported cases in which he has consented to act. It seems that he will normally lend his name where the proceedings are against a local authority, and perhaps also where a local authority is the relator. It seems also that he never does so where the proceedings are against a minister or a department of the central government. The relator action is therefore a one-sided as well as an uncertain procedure: it is a weapon in the hands of the central government which is made available on unspecified grounds against local and other subordinate authorities, but not against the central government itself.

A relator action may be brought against a public authority that is acting, or threatening to act, ultra vires; and equally it may be brought against any private individual or body who is committing a public nuisance or otherwise violating the law.[34] The commonest defendants to relator actions are local authorities, particularly where ratepayers challenge the validity of their local authority's expenditure, suing under the Attorney-General's name. In New Zealand this procedure has been used to solve the problem of how a neighbour may challenge an invalid grant of planning permission, although as explained later he is not entitled to a declaration in his own name:[35] the Attorney-General sued on the relation of the neighbour and obtained a declaration that the permission was void and an injunction against the unauthorised use of the land.[36]

Relator actions fall outside the Crown Proceedings Act 1947, so that their scope and procedure remain unchanged.[37]

Local authorities

There is a standardised practice by which a ratepayer may dispute the validity of the local authority's expenditure in a relator action, sometimes

---

[33] The only provision in the rules of court is RSC O. 15 r. 11, requiring the relator's name to be lodged with his solicitor and filed in court. In the *McWhirter* case (above) at 656 Lawton LJ said: 'In the course of this hearing the Attorney-General gave the court information about the attitude which he and his predecessors in modern times have taken towards relator actions. . . . Much of this information is not available, as far as I know, in any of the practitioners' textbooks.'

[34] See below, p. 610.

[35] Below, p. 692.

[36] *A.-G.* v. *Codner* [1973] 1 NZLR 545.

[37] See s. 23(3).

called a 'ratepayer's action'. A typical case was where the London County Council, being empowered by statute to purchase and operate tramways, purchased a tramway company and also carried on a bus service which the company had run. The proprietors of a rival bus service, who were also ratepayers, caused the Attorney-General to sue for an injunction against the operation of buses by the Council, which was duly granted.[38] The Attorney-General appears to allow actions against local authorities with a free hand. In one case a local authority, after there had been much fire and flood damage on its housing estates, made a contract with an insurance company for the collective insurance of its tenants' effects. The staff trade union of a rival insurance company, acting apparently merely in their own interests as its employees, were allowed to bring a relator action challenging the legality of the contract—which was in fact held lawful.[39] The Court of Appeal expressed some curiosity as to these proceedings, but held that they could not question the Attorney-General's practice or the relator's standing.

Whether it was necessary for ratepayers to resort to relator actions in such cases became uncertain when in 1954 the Court of Appeal awarded a declaration to a ratepayer suing in his own name.[40] But the Court made no mention of the question of standing, and it has since been held that the decision was inadvertent and not, on this question, a precedent to be followed.[41] A ratepayer may be able to proceed unassisted under the procedure of application for judicial review, explained later, provided that he can obtain the leave of the court.[42] But whether this new avenue is open to him has not yet been established.

Local authorities have now been given a special statutory power to take action for the benefit of their areas. Formerly they could not bring proceedings for the general public benefit without the assistance of the Attorney-General, unless their own rights of property were in some way affected.[43] The courts rejected claims by local authorities, suing by themselves, for injunctions against public nuisances,[44] against obstruction of highways,[45] and against the withdrawal of bus services.[46] For such

---

[38] *London County Council v. A.-G.* [1902] AC 165. See similarly *A.-G. v. Fulham Cpn.* [1921] 1 Ch. 440 (expenditure on municipal laundry ultra vires).

[39] *A.-G. v. Crayford Urban District Council* [1962] Ch. 575.

[40] *Prescott v. Birmingham Cpn.* [1955] Ch. 210; above, p. 426. *Bradbury v. Enfield Borough Council* [1967] 1 WLR 1311 (see above, p. 586) appears to be a comparable case.

[41] *Barrs v. Bethell* [1982] Ch 294 (Warner J). And see *Collins v. Lower Hutt City Cpn.* [1961] NZLR 250; *Cowan v. Canadian Broadcasting Cpn.* (1966) 56 DLR (2d) 578.

[42] Below, p. 671.

[43] *Thorne Rural District Council v. Bunting* [1972] Ch. 470.

[44] *Prestatyn Urban District Council v. Prestatyn Raceway Ltd.* [1970] 1 WLR 33.

[45] *Hampshire County Council v. Shonleigh Nominees Ltd.* [1970] 1 WLR 865.

[46] *Sinfield v. London Transport Executive* [1970] Ch. 550.

purposes local authorities therefore needed to use relator actions, despite the provisions of the Local Government Act 1933 as follows:[47]

Where a local authority deem it expedient for the promotion or protection of the interests of the inhabitants of their area, they may prosecute or defend any legal proceedings.

The Local Government Act 1972 has substituted for the last eight words:[48]

... they may prosecute or defend or appear in any legal proceedings and, in the case of civil proceedings, may institute them in their own name.

The 1933 formula, despite an opinion of Lord Denning MR to the contrary,[49] was held not to confer any new power to sue without the Attorney-General's name.[50] But the 1972 formula has been held to remove the difficulty, so that a local authority[51] is able to obtain an injunction against unlawful Sunday trading merely in its own name.[52] As a rule, therefore, the Attorney-General's consent will no longer be needed in such cases. Local authorities can also take proceedings against statutory nuisances in their own name under the Public Health Act 1936.[53]

As regards injunctions for enforcing obedience to statute, as explained below,[54] a local authority has been held to have no power to proceed in its own name, even to enforce its own byelaws.[55] But this also may now be permitted by the Act of 1972, assuming that the enforcement of the criminal law by injunction counts as 'civil proceedings'.

Where the Attorney-General declines to act

It has been laid down by decisions of the House of Lords that if the Attorney-General declines to consent to a relator action, the court cannot question his exercise of his discretion nor can it allow a private person to sue in his own name merely in the capacity of a member of the public. In 1977

[47] s. 276.
[48] s. 222.
[49] *Warwickshire County Council* v. *British Railways Board* [1969] 1 WLR 1117 at 1122.
[50] See the *Prestatyn* and *Hampshire* cases (above).
[51] But not a local development corporation: *London Docklands Development Cpn.* v. *Rank Hovis Ltd.* (1985) 84 LGR 101.
[52] *Solihull Council* v. *Maxfern Ltd.* [1977] 1 WLR 127; *Stoke-on-Trent City Council* v. *B & Q (Retail) Ltd.* [1984] AC 754; *Barking and Dagenham LBC* v. *Essexplan Ltd.* (1982) 81 LGR 408. See likewise *Burnley BC* v. *England* (1978) 76 LGR 393 (breach of byelaw excluding dogs from parks); *Kent CC* v. *Batchelor* (No. 2) [1979] 1 WLR 213 (enforcement of tree preservation orders).
[53] s. 100.
[54] p. 536.
[55] *Devonport Cpn.* v. *Tozer* [1903] 1 Ch. 759.

the House had occasion to disapprove two dramatic decisions in which the Court of Appeal had attempted to throw open the door to the public-spirited citizen wishing to prevent a breach of the law by a public authority. In the first of these it was held that if the Attorney-General refused leave in a proper case, or his machinery worked too slowly, an offended or injured member of the public could in the last resort apply to the court himself. Lord Denning MR said that it was a matter of high constitutional principle that the court should thus assist to stop a government department or public authority transgressing the law. But these remarks were *obiter*, since before final judgment was given the Attorney-General intervened and lent his name to the proceedings. The relator's complaint was that the Independent Broadcasting Authority were about to allow the transmission of an indecent television programme, contrary to their statutory duty to see that programmes did not offend against good taste and decency.[56]

The second case was an attempt by a private citizen to restrain a threatened breach of the criminal law by trade unions, when unions of post office workers were planning to boycott communications with South Africa, despite the fact that improper interference with mails and telegrams is a statutory offence.[57] The Attorney-General declined to proceed, but Lord Denning MR held that an injunction could be granted at the suit of a private plaintiff and the other members of the court were willing to grant declaratory relief. The House of Lords reversed this decision and disapproved the remarks in the earlier case.[58] They held that to act in the public interest was the Attorney-General's exclusive right. His role was substantial and constitutional and he was free to consider the public interest generally and widely. He was therefore free to take account of any circumstances, political or otherwise.

This decision contained sweeping remarks about the Attorney-General's exclusive right to represent the public interest; and for a time it seemed that the House of Lords had administered a sharp check to the tendency towards liberality in allowing it to be vindicated by private citizens. But later events have shown otherwise. This must be explained in another place[59] as part of the law of locus standi, or standing, which the House of Lords has put upon a new and more satisfactory basis, following procedural reforms in the law of remedies. Their above-mentioned decision, it now appears, ought to be confined to its peculiar subject-matter, which is the use of civil proceedings

---

[56] *A.-G. ex rel. McWhirter* v. *Independent Broadcasting Authority* [1973] QB 629. After viewing the programme the court refused relief. See also *Wilson* v. *Independent Broadcasting Authority* (below), an interesting Scots parallel.

[57] For injunctions in aid of the criminal law see below, p. 610.

[58] *Gouriet* v. *Union of Post Office Workers* [1978] AC 435.

[59] Below, p. 692.

for the purpose of enforcing the criminal law. That is a highly abnormal procedure and there are good reasons for allowing only the Attorney-General to employ it.[60]

Observations on the relator action

The relator action is one of the useful devices, like the prerogative remedies, by which the Crown's procedural privileges have been made available to the ordinary citizen, to the advantage not only of himself but of the public interest. It imposes a measure of control on situations where otherwise any number of members of the public might attempt to bring uncoordinated actions, resulting in general confusion. Basically it is a regulated form of *actio popularis*, available to all and sundry whom the Attorney-General is willing to assist; and his practice appears to be co-operative, save only where the complaint is against the central government or where he is unwilling to act for political reasons.

Nevertheless the situation is far from logical.[61] In effect, the Attorney-General himself determines the plaintiff's standing to sue. But this is a matter which should be determined by known rules of law, and not by the undisclosed practice of a minister of the Crown. Nor is there any logic in withholding this remedy against the central government, as seems to be the present practice. The use of the relator action has therefore been an impediment to the development of satisfactory rules of law as to the ability of citizens to litigate in the general public interest. There is no such system in Scots law, which allows individuals with very general interests (e.g. as voters or members of political bodies) to sue on their own account in order to prevent breach by a public body of a duty owed by that body to the public.[62]

Now, however, the House of Lords has provided a prospect of a more uniform and liberal system under the new procedure of application for judicial review, whereby the public-spirited citizen may be enabled 'to vindicate the rule of law' in his own name, unimpeded by 'outdated technical rules of locus standi'.[63] Whether the new judicial policy will reduce the need for relator actions is one of the many questions which are now open.

---

[60] Below, p. 692.

[61] See the criticisms of Ormrod LJ in *Gouriet* v. *Union of Post Office Workers* [1977] QB 729 at 776.

[62] *Wilson* v. *Independent Broadcasting Authority* 1979 SLT 279 (interdict granted against IBA to prevent broadcasting of one-sided political programmes). Contrast *Scottish Old People's Welfare Council, Petitioners* 1987 SLT 179.

[63] See below, p. 704.

Enforcement of obedience to statute

It remains to mention a very different use of the relator action, where it operates not as a defence against the abuse of authority, but as a weapon in the hands of authority to prevent the deliberate and flagrant disregard of statute. The Attorney-General, acting on the application of a local authority or other relator, may apply for an injunction to prevent contravention of statute, or abuse of statutory rights, by any offending person. Disobedience then becomes contempt of court, punishable by fine and imprisonment in the court's discretion. The typical situation is where there are repeated offences and the statutory penalties are an adequate deterrent.[64]

In one case the defendant had often broken the provisions of the Town and Country Planning Act by using his land as a site for caravans without permission. He refused to pay fines, and was eventually sentenced to imprisonment for non-payment. But the local planning authority also moved the Attorney-General to apply for an injunction to prohibit illegal use of the land, and the injunction was granted.[65] It was held that there was jurisdiction to grant this additional remedy to prevent violation of the public policy enforced by the Act, and that the fact that the Act contained its own provisions for enforcement did not fetter the Attorney-General's discretion, as an administrative matter, to ask for an injunction either as an alternative to or in addition to the statutory penalties. The Court of Appeal similarly granted an injunction to stop flagrant disobedience of enforcement notices served for the purpose of preventing the use of green belt land as a gipsy caravan site; and they held that it was not necessary for the local planning authority to launch criminal proceedings first.[66]

In another planning case the court went even further, and granted an injunction to prevent the use of land in a manner expressly permitted by the Act.[67] This was another caravan case where the offender moved the caravans from one site to another in the same neighbourhood, making a fresh application for permission in each case and appealing to the minister on each refusal, thus taking advantage of the manifold opportunities for delay which the planning machinery provided in the days before the Caravan Sites and Control of Development Act 1960. The Attorney-General, on behalf of the local authority, was granted an injunction

---

[64] See *A.-G.* v. *Harris* [1961] 1 QB 74, where a flower-seller with over a hundred convictions for obstruction, punishable only by fine, was restrained by injunction from offending again—and offended again and was committed for contempt of court. For an account of this case see Edwards, *The Law Officers of the Crown*, 290.

[65] *A.-G.* v. *Bastow* [1957] 1 QB 514.

[66] *Runnymede BC* v. *Ball* [1986] 1 WLR 353.

[67] *A.-G.* v. *Smith* [1958] 2 QB 173.

prohibiting this person from using any land in the neighbourhood as a caravan site without first obtaining permission. The injunction was thus used as a means of supplementing the imperfect remedies provided by Parliament in the Act.

On the other hand the court has declined to use its powers over wards of court to help a local authority to enforce school attendance orders which were persistently disobeyed by a parent, on the ground that it ought not to impose more severe sanctions than those which Parliament thought suitable.[68]

The Attorney-General, acting for a local authority, was granted an injunction to restrain the use of a hotel without a certificate of fire precautions.[69] The local authority were prosecuting the owner as the Act authorised in a magistrates' court, but were concerned at a serious fire risk during the period before the charge could be heard. Lord Denning MR said:

Whenever Parliament has enacted a law and given a particular remedy for the breach of it, such remedy being in an inferior court, nevertheless the High Court always has reserve power to enforce the law so enacted by way of an injunction or declaration or other suitable remedy. The High Court has jurisdiction to ensure obedience to the law whenever it is just and convenient to do so.

It is therefore not only in the case of repeated offences that this jurisdiction may be invoked. But mere infringement of the criminal law is not enough: it must be shown that the offender is deliberately and flagrantly flouting it.[70]

Now that local authorities can bring proceedings in their own name they can dispense with the assistance of the Attorney-General, as already explained.[71]

Whether it is right to increase statutory penalties by the use of injunctions is a debatable question. The House of Lords have more than once emphasised that this remedy should be regarded as anomalous and exceptional, since it is not normally for the civil courts to enforce the criminal law, to increase statutory penalties, and to convict (in effect) on a civil standard of proof.[72] As Lord Templeman has said,[73]

Where Parliament imposes a penalty for an offence, Parliament must consider that the penalty is adequate and Parliament can increase the penalty if it proves to be

[68] *Re B (Infants)* [1962] Ch. 201.

[69] *A-G. v. Chaudry* [1971] 1 WLR 1614. And see *Stafford Borough Council v. Elkenford Ltd.* [1977] 1 WLR 324.

[70] *Stoke-on-Trent CC v. B & Q Ltd.* (above).

[71] Above, p. 607.

[72] *Gouriet v. Union of Post Office Workers* [1978] AC 435; *Stoke-on-Trent CC v. B & Q Ltd.* (above).

[73] In the *Stoke-on-Trent* case (above).

inadequate. It follows that a local authority should be reluctant to seek and the court should be reluctant to grant an injunction which if disobeyed may involve the infringer in sanctions far more onerous than the penalty imposed for the offence.

The House of Lords have also emphasised that the procedure is one which only the Attorney-General can put into motion. If he declines to act at the request of a private person, that person cannot be allowed to bring proceedings in his own name.[74] In view of the serious objections to which the whole procedure is open, it is clearly right to put it under the control of an officer of the Crown.

ENFORCEMENT OF DUTIES

Public duties

As well as illegal action, by excess or abuse of power, there may be illegal inaction, by neglect of duty. Public authorities have a great many legal duties, under which they have an obligation to act, as opposed to their legal powers, which give them discretion whether to act or not. The remedies so far investigated deal with the control of powers. The remedies for the enforcement of duties are necessarily different. The most important of them, mandamus, belongs among the prerogative remedies in the next chapter. The 'ordinary' remedies noted here play only a minor part.

Criminal prosecution

The natural way for a statute to enforce a public duty in the case of a private person is to invoke the criminal law, for example by making it an offence to fail to make an income-tax return. The common law took the same approach to the problem of making public authorities carry out their duties. Wilful neglect of a public duty was held to be an indictable offence, punishable by fine or imprisonment.[75] It was impossible, of course, to indict the Crown.[76] But the inhabitants of counties, townships and parishes were often indicted for failure to repair highways and bridges. When these duties were transferred to statutory highway authorities, it was possible to indict them also.[77] The legal basis of this procedure was that a public nuisance (a

---

[74] *Gouriet* v. *Union of Post Office Workers* (above).

[75] See *R.* v. *Hall* [1891] 1 QB 747, reviewing authorities; Holdsworth, *History of English Law*, x. 147.

[76] Nevertheless Dowdell, *A Hundred Years of Quarter Sessions*, 125, records an indictment against the King in 1670 for non-repair of Hampton Bridge; but it was 'not pressed'.

[77] Halsbury's Laws of England, 3rd edn., xix. 139.

crime) had been perpetrated. But in 1959 it was abolished in favour of statutory proceedings which any one may institute against the highway authority, with the ultimate sanction that the complainant may carry out the work himself and recover the cost from the defaulting authority.[78]

It was often laid down in the past that disobedience of a statute or neglect of the duties of a public office was a criminal offence unless Parliament had provided some other sanction or remedy.[79] This is illustrated by the decision that an indictment would lie against an overseer of the poor for not receiving a pauper under a justices' order;[80] and by the case of a magistrate who was indicted, but acquitted, for failing to take proper steps to suppress a riot.[81] Where the duty was statutory the offence was sometimes called contempt of statute. Indictment is obviously an unsatisfactory remedy, and has not often been used in recent times.[82] Modern statutes are not to be presumed to create criminal offences unless they do so clearly, and the doctrine of contempt of statute is regarded as obsolete.[83]

Private law remedies

The ordinary remedies of private law are sometimes effective in case of breach of duty by public authorities. Actions for damages play an important part where breach of statutory duty is held to be an actionable wrong, as explained in the chapter on liability of public authorities.[84]

Injunctions are in general not used. To enforce a duty requires a mandatory injunction, which the court will grant only where the duty is owed to the plaintiff personally, i.e. where he has a legal right to protect. Thus the court made a mandatory order against the police for the return of passports and other documents which were being detained unlawfully.[85] Although there is no reason in principle why a mandatory injunction should not be granted against a public authority, the prerogative remedy of mandamus is usually more suitable, particularly since the rules as to standing are there less strict. Where the duty is owed to the public generally

---

[78] Highways Act 1959, s. 59, replaced by Highways Act 1980, s. 56.
[79] Co. Inst. ii. 163; Bl. Comm. iv. 122 and other authorities cited in *R. v. Horseferry Road Justices ex p. Independent Broadcasting Authority* [1987] QB 54.
[80] *R. v. Davis* (1754) Sayer 163.
[81] *R. v. Pinney* (1832) 3 B & Ad. 947.
[82] An example is *R. v. Dytham* [1979] QB 722 (alleged failure by police officer to stop fight).
[83] *R. v. Horseferry Road Justices* (above) where the court quashed a summons issued against the IBA for breach of statutory duty in respect of a television programme. The Law Commission have recommended the abolition of the doctrine (Law Com. No. 76 (1976), p. 142).
[84] Below, p. 772.
[85] *Ghani v. Jones* [1970] 1 QB 693.

and not to the plaintiff personally an injunction to enforce performance of a duty will not be granted.[86] Formerly there was a statutory 'mandamus' which could be sought in an ordinary action and was the equivalent of a mandatory injunction, having nothing to do with the prerogative mandamus; but this redundant remedy no longer exists.[87]

In principle, also, there is no reason why the plaintiff should not seek a declaratory judgment, i.e. a declaration that a public authority has some legal duty towards him personally. This has occasionally been done successfully.[88] But in accordance with the general rule that a declaration can only declare the legal position of the plaintiff, he will have to show that it is to himself particularly that the duty is owed.[89]

General and specific duties

A *power* enables an authority to do what would otherwise be illegal or ineffective. It is always subject to legal limits, and it is safe to assume that Parliament did not intend it to be exercised beyond those limits. A *duty*, on the other hand, may or may not be legally enforceable.[90] Parliament has recently become fond of imposing duties of a kind which, since they are of a general and indefinite character, are perhaps to be considered as political duties rather than as legal duties which a court could enforce. Many such duties may be found in statutes concerned with social services and nationalisation. Thus the opening words of the National Health Service Act 1977 are

It is the Secretary of State's duty to continue the promotion in England and Wales of a comprehensive health service. . . .

The Coal Industry Nationalisation Act 1946 charges the Coal Board

---

[86] *Glossop* v. *Heston and Isleworth Local Board* (1879) 12 Ch. D. 102; *Bradbury* v. *Enfield London Borough Council* (1967) 1 WLR 1311; *Wood* v. *Ealing London Borough Council* [1967] Ch. 364 (see under default powers, below).

[87] It was introduced by the Common Law Procedure Act 1854, s. 68, in 'an attempt to engraft upon the old common law remedy a right in the nature of specific performance': *Baxter* v. *London County Council* (1890) 63 LT 767 at 771. Although rendered redundant by the Judicature Acts 1873–5, it was reproduced in RSC 1883, O. 53. It does not appear in RSC 1965, since the mandatory injunction is sufficient. The statutory mandamus could be sought along with other remedies: see e.g. *Wolstanton United Urban Council* v. *Tunstall Urban Council* [1910] 2 Ch. 347; *Watt* v. *Kesteven County Council* [1955] 1 QB 408; *Thorne* v. *University of London* [1966] 2 QB 237.

[88] As in *Gateshead Union* v. *Durham County Council* [1918] 1 Ch. 146.

[89] *Clark* v. *Epsom Rural District Council* [1929] 1 Ch. 287 and cases cited therewith below, p. 748.

[90] The Post Office's general duties are expressly made unenforceable: Post Office Act 1969, s. 9(4): above, p. 166.

with the duties of 'working and getting coal in Great Britain', 'making supplies of coal available', and so on. The Water Act 1973 allots general duties to a range of authorities: the Secretary of State and the Minister of Agriculture, Fisheries and Food are to promote jointly a national policy for water and secure its effective execution; the National Water Council is to advise on national policy, assist water authorities in research, planning and other matters, hold consultations for testing and approving water fittings, prepare education and training schemes, etc.; and water authorities are to do what they think necessary or expedient for conserving, redistributing, or augmenting water resources. Current legislation furnishes an abundance of such examples.

Only in the unlikely event of its making total default would any of the above-mentioned authorities be at risk of legal compulsion in respect of its general duties. But as soon as duties become sufficiently specific, the courts do not shrink from enforcing them. This was shown dramatically by the House of Lords and the Court of Appeal when they quashed the supplementary rate levied by the Greater London Council for the purpose of subsidising passenger transport in London.[91] The Council had power to subsidise the London Transport Executive, but they also had a duty to have regard to the Executive's own duties, which required it not to accumulate deficits and to operate with due regard to economy. The Council's general duty was to promote the provision of 'integrated, efficient and economic transport facilities' in London. But in calling upon the Executive to lower its fares, thereby accumulating a large deficit, the Council was in breach of its duty to have regard to the Executive's duties, as well as in breach of its fiduciary duty to its ratepayers.[92] The courts analysed the amalgam of general and specific duties and powers in the Transport (London) Act 1969, concluding that the Executive had a duty to minimise avoidable losses and the council a duty not to prevent them from doing so.

A very different factor which may render a statutory duty unenforceable is the rule of public policy which ordains that no one may profit from his own crime. A widow convicted of killing her husband cannot therefore claim widow's benefit under the Social Security Act 1975;[93] and a woman who has committed perjury and forgery in the course of marrying a British subject cannot compel the Home Secretary to register her as a British subject also.[94]

---

[91] *Bromley LBC* v. *Greater London Council* [1983] 1 AC 768.
[92] For the latter duty see above, p. 426.
[93] *R.* v. *Chief National Insurance Commissioner ex p. Connor* [1981] QB 758.
[94] *R.* v. *Home Secretary ex p. Puttick* [1981] QB 767.

17

PREROGATIVE REMEDIES

REMEDIES OF PUBLIC LAW

Nature of prerogative remedies

Entering now the realm of the prerogative remedies, we meet something like a system of public law. These are remedies which, if not always designed from the first for the control of governmental duties and powers, have long been in use for that purpose especially. Their hallmark is that they are granted at the suit of the Crown, as the title of every case indicates. They are 'prerogative' because they were originally available only to the Crown and not to the subject. By obtaining orders of the court in the form of mandamus, certiorari or prohibition, the Crown could ensure that public authorities carried out their duties, and that inferior tribunals kept within their proper jurisdiction. These were essentially remedies for ensuring efficiency and maintaining order in the hierarchy of courts, commissions and statutory authorities of all kinds.

By the end of the sixteenth century these remedies had become generally available to ordinary litigants (some had done so much earlier), and an applicant could begin proceedings in the Crown's name without seeking any permission or authority.[1] The Crown lent its legal prerogatives to its subjects in order that they might collaborate to ensure good and lawful government. Habeas corpus would test the legality of any prisoner's detention at his own or some friend's instance. Certiorari and prohibition were designed for controlling the machinery of justice, and were in constant use in order to enforce the performance of public duties, judicial and administrative alike. These last three remedies played a most important part in the development of administrative law. By a process of evolution characteristic of our legal history, the Crown's prerogative powers have been converted into machinery for the protection of the subject.

Nowadays all these remedies issue from the High Court and they must still be sought by a special form of procedure.[2] They are all discretionary remedies, with the exception of habeas corpus. They used to be known as the prerogative writs, but since 1938 their name has been changed to

---

[1] For the history of the prerogative remedies see Henderson, *Foundations of English Administrative Law*; de Smith, *Judicial Review of Administrative Action*, 4th edn., 584.

[2] For this see below, p. 671.

prerogative orders[3]—again with the exception of habeas corpus, which was too sacred to be tampered with, and remains a writ. The procedural peculiarities of the prerogative remedies were formerly important since they entailed certain disadvantages as compared with the remedies of private law such as declaration and injunction.[4]

There were other prerogative writs which could be used at the instance of a subject, such as scire facias for rescinding royal charters and grants, and ne exeat regno for preventing a subject from leaving the realm. The latter writ seems now to be obsolete as a weapon of the Crown, but it is still in use by ordinary litigants as a remedy to prevent a debtor from absconding; but the applicant must show that the debtor's absence from the realm would materially prejudice him.[5] The modern use of this writ is yet another instance of the conversion of the Crown's legal armoury into remedies beneficial to the subject, of which habeas corpus is the prime example.

The remedies to be discussed first are habeas corpus, certiorari and prohibition. These are grouped together since they are all remedies for the control of powers. Mandamus then follows, being the primary remedy for enforcing public duties.

HABEAS CORPUS

Utility of the writ

The writ of habeas corpus[6] plays a part, though not a large one, in administrative law, since some administrative authorities and tribunals have powers of detention. The cases most likely to arise are those where some person is detained as an illegal immigrant or in order that he may be deported, or as being of unsound mind. A writ of habeas corpus challenging the legality of the detention is then a means of challenging the validity of the administrative order which caused it. If the court orders the applicant's release, that in effect quashes the order, an additional certiorari for this purpose being unnecessary.[7]

The procedural deficiencies of the prerogative remedies, to be noticed later, were particularly acute in the case of habeas corpus. No right of

---

[3] Administration of Justice (Miscellaneous Provisions) Act 1938, s. 7, replaced by Supreme Court Act 1981, s. 29.

[4] Below, p. 665.

[5] *Felton* v. *Callis* [1969] 1 QB 200, where Megarry J explains the history and modern application of the writ. In *Parsons* v. *Burk* [1971] NZLR 244 the writ was refused to a private litigant who wished to prevent a New Zealand football team from visiting South Africa.

[6] See Sharpe, *Habeas Corpus* (1976). There is remarkably little other specialist literature on the writ.

[7] Below, p. 622.

appeal used to exist against refusal of the writ in cases of imprisonment where there was a charge of a criminal nature—a grave and irrational defect which was not remedied until 1960.[8] In criminal cases, also, there was no right to dispute the truth of facts stated in a gaoler's return to the writ, so that important questions of fact could not be investigated.[9] In the civil cases which fall within administrative law this obstacle was removed by the Habeas Corpus Act 1816 and affidavit evidence is given as to facts.[10] The famous Habeas Corpus Act 1679, designed to prevent various abuses including prolonged imprisonment on criminal charges without bail, was drawn so specifically in terms of seventeenth-century procedure that some of its safeguards were probably ineffective in modern conditions.[11] But these are matters of little significance in practice. The courts can usually be relied upon to find their way round anachronistic obstacles. The writ may be applied for by any prisoner, or by any one acting on his behalf, without regard to nationality, since 'every person within the jurisdiction enjoys the equal protection of our laws.'[12] It may be directed against the gaoler, often the appropriate prison governor, or against the authority ordering the detention, e.g. the Home Secretary.[13] It is not discretionary.[14] Nor is leave of any kind required before it can be sought: it issues as of right.[15]

It is only as an instrument of judicial review of administrative detention that habeas corpus concerns us here. It may be noted that the belief, previously held, that an applicant could renew his application for the writ on the same grounds before any number of judges successively has been rejected both by the courts[16] and by Act of Parliament;[17] that the writ will

---

[8] Administration of Justice Act 1960, s. 15.

[9] The only remedy seems to have been an action for a false return: see Wilmot's *Opinion on Habeas Corpus*, Wilm. 77 at 106; *Rutty's* case (below) at 124. For such an action in an analogous case see *Brasyer* v. *Maclean* (1875) LR 6 PC 398; below, p. 773.

[10] *R.* v. *Board of Control ex p. Rutty* [1956] 2 QB 109 at 124; *R.* v. *Home Secretary ex p. Khawaja* [1984] AC 74 at 110, where Lord Scarman quotes the Act. Even before the Act the court would sometimes admit affidavit evidence in the interests of justice: see *Goldswain's* case (1778) 2 W Bl 1207 at 1211. The Act may cut both ways, since the evidence may reveal good grounds for the detention which are not shown in the detention order: *Re Shahid Iqbal* [1979] QB 264, Boreham J forcefully dissenting.

[11] *R.* v. *Campbell* [1959] 1 WLR 646. s. 6 of the Habeas Corpus Act 1679, there discussed, was repealed by the Courts Act 1971, 11th sched., Pt. IV.

[12] *R.* v. *Home Secretary ex p. Khawaja* (above) at 112.

[13] As in cases cited below.

[14] *R.* v. *Pentonville Prison Governor ex p. Azam* [1974] AC 18 at 32.

[15] *R.* v. *Home Secretary ex p. Khawaja* (above) at 111.

[16] *Re Hastings (No. 2)* [1959] 1 QB 358; *Re Hastings (No. 3)* [1959] Ch 368. For the question of res judicata see above, p. 276.

[17] Administration of Justice Act 1960, s. 14(2), banning repeated applications on the same grounds unless supported by fresh evidence (this means evidence which could not reasonably have been put forward previously: *R.* v. *Pentonville Prison Governor ex p. Tarling* [1979] 1 WLR 1417).

not issue to Northern Ireland[18] or to a colony or foreign dominion overseas where there is a court competent to grant the writ,[19] but may issue to a protectorate;[20] and that the authority detaining the applicant carries the burden of proof of every fact described by statute as a condition of the power of detention.[21]

The procedure is governed by special rules of court.[22] It has not been affected by the rules for 'application for judicial review' introduced for other remedies in 1977. The writ may be applied for ex parte, i.e. without notice to the custodian, with the support of an affidavit made by or on behalf of the prisoner; the court will then normally adjourn the case for argument between the parties, with or without requiring the prisoner to be brought before it. The modern practice is not to require the production of the prisoner unless there are special circumstances, but to order his release if the imprisonment is found to be unlawful, whereupon the writ of habeas corpus is issued.

While habeas corpus for the most part deserves its high reputation as a bulwark of personal liberty, it has several times been weakened by unfortunate decisions, particularly in wartime and immigration cases.[23] It has also failed to measure up to the standards of the European Convention on Human Rights and Fundamental Freedoms, which entitles a detainee 'to take proceedings by which the lawfulness of his detention shall be decided speedily by a court and his release ordered if the detention is not lawful'.[24] The case concerned an inmate of a hospital for the criminally insane, whose detention was at the discretion of the Home Secretary. The European Court of Human Rights held that the scope of review on habeas corpus was inadequate, since it did not allow the court to examine whether the patient's disorder still persisted and whether the Home Secretary was entitled to think that continued detention was necessary in the interests of public safety.[25]

---

[18] *Re Keenan* [1972] 1 QB 533. It may issue to the Channel Islands and the Isle of Man: *Ex p. Brown* (1864) 5 B & S 280.

[19] Habeas Corpus Act 1862.

[20] *Ex. p. Mwenya* [1960] 1 QB 241.

[21] *R. v. Governor of Brixton Prison ex p. Ahsan* [1969] 2 QB 222; see above, p. 344.

[22] RSC 1965, O. 54.

[23] See above, pp. 307, 405, 407; also [1982] PL 89 (C. Newdick).

[24] Art. 5, para. 4.

[25] *X v. The United Kingdom* (1981) Series A, No. 46, para. 58. It seems that the court may have taken too narrow a view of the scope of review as set out in para. 19, with comment on 'the contradictory nature of the case-law'. The scope of judicial review generally was likewise held inadequate in the case of a paroled prisoner recalled to prison: *Weeks v. United Kingdom* [1987] ECHR Series A, no. 114. See also *Ireland v. United Kingdom* [1978] ECHR Series A, no. 25; Jowell and Oliver (eds.), *The Changing Constitution*, 291 (A. Lester).

Review of detention orders

Habeas corpus cannot be used as a means of appeal, but only of review.[26] In other words, the court is concerned with the question whether the order of detention is made within jurisdiction or ought to be quashed, but not with the question whether it is correct on its merits. This is the familiar distinction between appeal and review which runs right through administrative law. Accordingly habeas corpus will be granted if it can be shown that the order of detention is ultra vires on any of the normal grounds, such as a wrong finding of jurisdictional fact; or if the order is vitiated by error on the face of the record; or if (it seems) it is supported by no evidence. The House of Lords has pointed out the close similarity between the grounds for habeas corpus and the grounds for judicial review generally.[27]

Ordinary cases of ultra vires do not call for detailed discussion. One such case was where a magistrate made an order for the detention of a mental defective, which he had power to do if she was 'found neglected'. Since the evidence showed that she had not been found neglected, within the proper meaning of those words, she was released on habeas corpus.[28] This appears to have been an ordinary case of error as to jurisdictional fact. Where a Nigerian chief was deported to another part of the country and the Crown did not show that the conditions which would have justified the deportation under the local Ordinance were fulfilled, the Privy Council held that habeas corpus would be granted if these were not duly established by the Crown before the Nigerian court, for otherwise the deportation would be ultra vires.[29] The celebrated Daisy Hopkins, committed by the Vice-Chancellor of Cambridge to the Spinning-house for her presumption in 'walking with a member of the University', was released on habeas corpus on the ground that this was not an offence known to the law and the Vice-Chancellor could therefore have no jurisdiction.[30]

Review by means of habeas corpus is naturally available only where the tribunal which has made the order for detention is subject to review by the High Court. Habeas corpus will not therefore be granted on an allegation that an order for committal for contempt of court, made by one of the

---

[26] R. v. Governor of Brixton Prison ex p. Schtraks [1964] AC 556; R. v. Governor of Brixton Prison ex p. Armah [1968] AC 192.

[27] R. v. Home Secretary ex p. Khawaja (above) at 105 (Lord Wilberforce), 110 (Lord Scarman).

[28] R. v. Board of Control ex p. Rutty [1956] 2 QB 109 (Hilbery and Devlin JJ, Lord Goddard CJ concurring but evidently on grounds of 'no evidence': see below, p. 624).

[29] Eshugbayi Eleko v. Government of Nigeria [1931] AC 662.

[30] Ex p. Hopkins (1891) 61 LJ QB 640.

superior courts, was made on the authority of a judge with a disqualifying interest contrary to the principles of natural justice.[31]

Where there has been excessive delay in bringing a prisoner up for trial,[32] or in executing an order for his deportation,[33] he can use habeas corpus so as to bring himself before the court and the court will give suitable directions by declaration or otherwise. But habeas corpus will not avail to challenge the conditions of detention, provided that the detention itself is lawful.[34] A prisoner retains all his personal rights and remedies, except in so far as the law deprives him of them.[35] In case of maltreatment he can use ordinary or prerogative remedies, including certiorari and mandamus.[36] If he claims the right to be moved to another prison,[37] or to be held under better conditions[38] he can apply for judicial review, but normally the court will not interfere with the management of a prison.[39] Non-observance of the prison rules, however, will not normally entitle him to sue.[40]

Error on the face of the record

Although it has been said that in habeas corpus proceedings the court will review the detention order only to see that it was made within jurisdiction,[41] the decision of the House of Lords in the *Armah* case[42] indicates that the scope of review on habeas corpus is as wide as that on certiorari; and that, therefore, it extends to mere error on the face of the record, even though made within jurisdiction. Respectable antecedents can be found for this proposition.[43] At one time the prisoner would have had to obtain certiorari to quash the detention order at the same time as habeas corpus to secure his release, in order to succeed on this ground.[44] But to

[31] *Ex. p. Dimes* (1850) 14 QB 554 (committal for contempt for disobeying an injunction of the Court of Chancery). Compare above, p. 473.

[32] *R. v. Brixton Prison Governor ex p. Walsh* [1985] AC 154.

[33] *R. v. Durham Prison Governor ex p. Hardial Singh* [1984] 1 WLR 704.

[34] *Ex p. Rogers* (1843) 7 Jur. 992; *R. v. Wandsworth Prison Governor ex p. Silverman* (1952) 96 Sol J 853.

[35] *Raymond v. Honey* [1981] QB 874.

[36] As illustrated above, pp. 529, 575.

[37] *R. v. Home Secretary ex p. McAvoy* [1984] 1 WLR 1408 (application failed).

[38] *R. v. Home Secretary ex p. Herbage* (No. 2) [1987] QB 1077.

[39] *R. v. Home Secretary ex p. Herbage* [1986] QB 872. A change to stricter confinement, even though unjustified, gives no right to damages for false imprisonment: *R. v. Gartree Prison Visitors ex p. Sears* [1985] The Times, 20 March.

[40] See above, p. 247.

[41] See Rubinstein, *Jurisdiction and Illegality*, 107.

[42] *R. v. Governor of Brixton Prison ex p. Armah* [1968] AC 192.

[43] Sharpe, *Habeas Corpus*, 34.

[44] See Bacon's Abridgement (1768), iii. 6, cited in the *Armah* case at 234, 254. In *Ex p. Hopkins* (above) both certiorari and habeas corpus were sought and granted. Contrast *R. v. Home Secretary ex p. Mughal* [1973] 1 WLR 1133, holding that certiorari only was the proper remedy on the facts of that case.

insist upon a separate certiorari was pointless formalism, since the habeas corpus brought the whole question of the validity of the detention before the court. It therefore became the practice to receive the depositions of evidence as if there had been a certiorari and to treat them as part of the record, in the same way as used to be done in reviewing magistrates' decisions before 1848.[45] If error of law then appeared, habeas corpus would be granted and the detention order would in effect be quashed, just as it might have been quashed on certiorari.

Since the revival of the 'error on the face' in 1950,[46] the above reasoning appears to have been used for the release of the prisoner only in the *Armah* case, which is primarily one of 'no evidence' and is discussed below. But the majority of the House of Lords clearly regarded the deficiency of evidence as amounting to error of law which the court could review because it appeared on the record.[47] Lord Reid said:

If the depositions are part of the record, as they appear to be, then there would be error of law on the face of the record if the depositions were insufficient in law to support the committal.

Since the court's powers ought to be at their widest for the protection of personal liberty, it seems necessarily right that review by habeas corpus should be as ample as review by certiorari. A prisoner who is entitled to have his detention order quashed is clearly entitled to his release.

There is as yet no sign of the doctrine of error on the face being eliminated by the doctrine that all error of law is ultra vires, but that possibility remains open here as elsewhere.[48]

Evidence and proof

The somewhat uncertain status of 'no evidence' as a ground of review at the present time has already been explained.[49] In habeas corpus cases, however, it was established earlier than elsewhere, indicating that personal liberty is entitled to the benefit of every doubt. The House of Lords granted habeas corpus in the *Armah* case[50] to release a detainee whose return to Ghana had been requested by the Ghanaian government under the Fugitive Offenders Act 1881 on charges of corruption and extortion. This the magistrate was

---

[45] *Re Tivnan* (1864) 5 B & S 645.
[46] Above, p. 307.
[47] See Lord Reid at 235, Lord Pearce at 253, and Lord Upjohn at 257.
[48] See above, p. 299.
[49] Above, p. 319.
[50] Above. See also *R. v. Governor of Brixton Prison ex p. Schtraks* [1964] Ac 556, recognising the same principle but refusing habeas corpus since the evidence before the magistrate was sufficient and the court would not review his finding on the merits.

empowered to order on the production of evidence raising 'a strong or probable presumption that the fugitive committed the offence'. It was held that the court could investigate 'whether any magistrate, properly applying his mind to the question, could reasonably have come to the conclusion that a strong or probable presumption had been made out.[51] It was further held that the depositions of evidence did not satisfy this test, and that there was therefore no evidence to support the magistrate's order. Since an order based on no evidence was an error of law, and the depositions were part of the record of the magistrate's proceedings, his order could have been quashed on certiorari and habeas corpus was therefore granted.

In earlier cases of this kind the courts had consistently held that they could review for 'no evidence', but they had not put forward any consistent explanation for doing so. Sometimes they spoke as if 'no evidence' was itself a jurisdictional error[52] and sometimes as if the evidence required by the Act was a condition of the magistrate's jurisdiction, i.e. a necessary jurisdictional fact.[53] The former hypothesis raised problems which may now, however, have been solved,[54] and the latter invited the objection that the existence of the prescribed evidence is the central question which the magistrate must determine, rather than a collateral matter limiting his jurisdiction.[55] The House of Lords in the *Armah* case preferred to rely upon error of law on the record, thus avoiding jurisdictional problems; and Lord Reid, in a perplexing passage which he had to explain away on a later occasion, held that no jurisdictional question could be involved.[56] Yet, as Lord Pearce observed,[57] it could have been held that the magistrate asked himself the wrong question and applied the wrong test, and these are recognised jurisdictional errors. Furthermore, the test as formulated is really one of reasonableness, and a perverse finding, i.e. one to which no reasonable magistrate could come, can always be held to be ultra vires.[58]

A similar confusion of doctrine has been noticed already in connection

---

[51] These are the words of Lord Parker CJ in *R.* v. *Governor of Brixton Prison ex p. Mourat Mehmet* [1962] 2 QB 1 at 10, approved in the *Armah* case (above) by Lords Reid and Pearce. The Fugitive Offenders Act 1967 no longer requires a 'strong or probable presumption' but requires evidence which would justify trial in this country.

[52] e.g. Field J in *R.* v. *Maurer* (1883) 10 QBD 513 at 515: 'It is only when there is no jurisdiction, as when there is no evidence before the magistrate, that we can interfere.'

[53] e.g. Lord Russell of Killowen CJ in *Re Arton (No. 2)* [1896] 1 QB 509 at 518: 'We have only to see that he had such evidence before him as gave him authority and jurisdiction to commit.'

[54] Above, p. 326.

[55] See above, p. 284.

[56] For this and its sequel in the *Anisminic* case see above, p. 294.

[57] [1968] AC at 255.

[58] Above, p. 398.

with 'no evidence' as a general ground of review. But whereas in other contexts the present tendency appears to be towards treating this form of error as ultra vires and jurisdictional ('not within the powers of this Act'),[59] in habeas corpus cases the principle preferred seems to be error on the face of the record. It is at least clear that the courts have plenty of strings to their bow, and that they will rightly release prisoners held under unjustifiable orders.

Another possible inconsistency is that this jurisdiction to release for 'no evidence' may be confined to cases of extradition. This appears to have been suggested in the House of Lords, where it was said that it was in such cases that the error of law was 'assimilated to acting in excess of jurisdiction'.[60] But no mention was made either of error on the face of the record or of the other possible grounds available. Furthermore, Lord Goddard CJ applied the 'no evidence' principle to release a mental defective who could be detained only if she had been 'found neglected', when it was shown that there was no evidence on which a reasonable person could have held that she was so found.[61] To make findings which cannot be justified on the evidence, as opposed to findings on which opinions may reasonably differ, is an abuse which the court should always correct. But it may well be that where there are other regular procedures for its correction, the court will not allow habeas corpus to be used instead. Otherwise innumerable applications might be made by persons convicted on criminal charges and attempting to use habeas corpus as, in effect, an additional form of appeal.[62]

The law as to the burden of proof is of the greatest importance in habeas corpus cases. This has been explained already,[63] and it is now in a more creditable state than in the past.

CERTIORARI AND PROHIBITION

Common principles

Certiorari and prohibition are complementary remedies, based upon common principles, so that they can be classed together. Certiorari issues to

---

[59] Above, p. 321.

[60] R. v. *Governor of Pentonville Prison ex p. Sotiriadis* [1975] AC 1 at 30 (Lord Diplock).

[61] R. v. *Board of Control ex p. Rutty* [1956] 2 QB 109. Hilbery J held that 'found neglected' was a condition of jurisdiction which was not in fact satisfied.

[62] The Court 'cannot grant writs of habeas corpus to persons . . . who are serving sentences passed by courts of competent jurisdiction': *Re Featherstone* (1953) 37 Cr. App. R. 146 at 147 (Lord Goddard CJ).

[63] Above, p. 342.

quash a decision which is ultra vires or vitiated by error on the face of the record. Prohibition issues to forbid some act or decision which would be ultra vires. Certiorari looks to the past, prohibition to the future. In this way they are respectively comparable to the declaration and injunction in the sphere of private law remedies. Like private law remedies, they may be sought separately or together, but only by the special procedure which is common to them both. Unlike private law remedies, they have never been dependent on the applicant showing a specific personal right. Nominally they are granted to the Crown, and the Crown always has sufficient interest to call upon public bodies to act lawfully.

Certiorari and prohibition are discretionary remedies. The meaning of this is explained later.[64]

Certiorari

Certiorari is used to bring up into the High Court the decision of some inferior tribunal or authority in order that it may be investigated. If the decision does not pass the test, it is quashed—that is to say, it is declared completely invalid, so that no one need respect it.

The underlying policy is that all inferior courts and authorities have only limited jurisdiction or powers and must be kept within their legal bounds. This is the concern of the Crown, for the sake of orderly administration of justice, but it is a private complaint which sets the Crown in motion. The applicant must apply ex parte to a judge or court of the Queen's Bench Division for leave to apply for the order, and if this is granted (and if the case is contested) the judge or court will later hear argument and decide whether to grant the order. The Crown is the nominal plaintiff but is expressed to act on behalf of the applicant, so that an application by Smith to quash on order of (for instance) a rent tribunal would be entitled *R*. v. *The —— Rent Tribunal, ex parte Smith*. The court will then decide whether the tribunal's order was within its powers or showed error on the face of the record. There are normal rights of appeal both for the applicant and the tribunal.[65]

The form of the old writ was that of a royal demand to be informed (certiorari) of some matter, and in early times it was used for many different purposes.[66] It became a general remedy to bring up for review in the Court of King's Bench any decision or order of an inferior tribunal or administrative body. Its great period of development as a means of

[64] Below, p. 709.

[65] See e.g. *R*. v. *Immigration Appeal Tribunal ex p. Alexander* [1982] 1 WLR 430.

[66] Originally it issued out of the Chancery or the King's Bench: Holdsworth, *History of English Law*, i. 228, 658.

controlling administrative authorities and tribunals began in the later half of the seventeenth century, and its wide modern application was promoted particularly by Holt CJ.[67] Something was needed to fill the vacuum left by the Star Chamber, which had exerted a considerable degree of central control over justices of the peace, both in their judicial and their administrative functions, but was abolished in 1640. There was also the problem of controlling special statutory bodies, which had begun to make their appearance. The Court of King's Bench addressed itself to these tasks, and became almost the only co-ordinating authority until the modern system of local government was devised in the nineteenth century. The most useful instruments which the Court found ready to hand were the prerogative writs. But not unnaturally the control exercised was strictly legal, and no longer political. Certiorari would issue to call up the records of justices of the peace and commissioners for examination in the King's Bench and for quashing if any legal defect was found. At first there was much quashing for defects of form on the record, i.e. for error on the face. Later, as the doctrine of ultra vires developed, that became the dominant principle of control, until, as we have seen it led to the doctrine of error on the face being forgotten for a century.[68]

Failure to return the record into the High Court was punishable as contempt; in the seventeenth century commissioners of sewers several times found themselves fined and incarcerated for disobedience.[69]

Prohibition

Prohibition developed alongside certiorari as part of the system of control imposed by the Court of King's Bench.[70] It was a similar remedy, but was prospective rather than retrospective. Primarily it lay to prohibit an inferior tribunal from doing something in excess of its jurisdiction. In what might be called the jurisdictional warfare of the seventeenth century it was

[67] See the quotation below, p. 632. In *Groenvelt* v. *Burwell* (1700) 1 Ld Raym. 454 at 469 Holt CJ said: 'for it is a consequence of all jurisdictions to have their proceedings returned here by certiorari, to be examined here . . . Where any court is erected by statute a certiorari lies to it; so that if they perform not their duty, the King's Bench will grant a mandamus.'

[68] Above, p. 306.

[69] See *Hetley* v. *Boyer* (1614) Cro Jac 336; *Smith's Case* (1670) 1 Vent 66; Bacon's *Abridgement*, ii. 542.

[70] Formerly prohibition was commonly awarded on the direct application of the party rather than at the suit of the Crown: *London Corporation* v. *Cox* (1867) LR 2 HL 239 at 279. A modern example is *Turner* v. *Kingsbury Collieries Ltd.* (1921) 3 KB 169. The opinion of the judges delivered by Willes J in *London Corporation* v. *Cox* is a classic source of information on prohibition. See also Bl. Comm. iii. 113; Holdsworth, *History of English Law*, i. 228, 656. All the superior courts could grant the writ: Bl. Comm. iii. 112.

an important weapon of the King's Bench when that court struck down the pretensions of competing jurisdictions such as those of the Court of Admiralty and the ecclesiastical courts. Later, like certiorari, it developed into part of the regular mechanism of judicial control both of inferior tribunals and of administrative authorities generally. In a much cited case Atkin LJ said:[71]

I can see no difference in principle between certiorari and prohibition, except that the latter may be invoked at an earlier stage. If the proceedings establish that the body complained of is exceeding its jurisdiction by entertaining matters which would result in its final decision being subject to being brought up and quashed on certiorari, I think that prohibition will lie to restrain it from so exceeding its jurisdiction.

Typical modern examples are its use to prevent an electricity authority from proceeding with a scheme which was outside its powers;[72] to prevent the execution of a decision vitiated by a breach of the principles of natural justice;[73] to prevent a housing authority from requiring the demolition of a house which was improperly condemned;[74] to prevent a rent tribunal from proceeding with a case outside its jurisdiction;[75] and to prevent a local authority from licensing indecent films.[76] In the last-mentioned case[77] Lord Denning MR said of prohibition:

It is available to prohibit administrative authorities from exceeding their powers or misusing them. In particular, it can prohibit a licensing authority from making rules or granting licences which permit conduct which is contrary to law.

Although prohibition was originally used to prevent tribunals from meddling with cases over which they had no jurisdiction, it was equally effective, and equally often used, to prohibit the execution of some decision already taken but ultra vires. So long as the tribunal or administrative authority still had some power to exercise as a consequence of the wrongful decision, the exercise of that power could be restrained by prohibition.[78]

Certiorari and prohibition frequently go hand in hand, as where

---

[71] R. v. Electricity Commissioners ex p. London Electricity Joint Committee Co. (1920) Ltd. [1924] 1 KB 171 at 206.

[72] R. v. Electricity Commissioners (above).

[73] R. v. North ex p. Oakey [1927] 1 KB 491 (ecclesiastical court: no notice to vicar of order against him); R. v. Liverpool Cpn. ex p. Taxi Fleet Operators' Association [1972] 2 QB 299 (licensing authority not to act before giving fair hearing). Similarly a biased adjudicator may be prohibited from acting: R. v. Kent Police Authority ex p. Godden [1971] 2 QB 662.

[74] Estate and Trust Agencies (1927) Ltd. v. Singapore Improvement Trust [1937] AC 898.

[75] R. v. Tottenham and District Tribunal ex p. Northfield (Highgate) Ltd. [1957] 1 QB 103.

[76] R. v. Greater London Council ex p. Blackburn [1976] 1 WLR 550.

[77] At 559.

[78] See the Estate and Trust Agencies case (above).

certiorari is sought to quash the decision and prohibition to restrain its execution. But either remedy may be sought by itself. Where only prohibition is applied for to prevent the enforcement of an ultra vires decision, as happened in the last-cited case, the effect is the same as if certiorari had been granted to quash it; for the court necessarily declares its invalidity before prohibiting its enforcement. But where the only fault in the decision is mere error on its face, it will normally need to be quashed by certiorari before its enforcement can be forbidden by prohibition.[79] At least, this seems to follow from the fact that prohibition is a remedy strictly concerned with excess of jurisdiction.[80]

The court will not be disposed to issue prohibition if the effect will be to prevent Parliament from considering some proposal or report. If its presentation should be shown to be unlawful, the court will prefer to state the legal position by a declaratory judgment.[81]

Occasionally prohibition will lie where certiorari will not, e.g. to an ecclesiastical court. This is explained below.[82]

Disobedience of a prohibition is punishable as contempt of court.[83]

Scope of these remedies

Certiorari and prohibition are employed primarily for the control of inferior courts, tribunals, and administrative authorities. Crown courts,[84] county courts, justices of the peace, coroners, and all statutory tribunals[85] are liable to have their decisions quashed or their proceedings prohibited, except where Parliament provides otherwise—and sometimes even when it does.[86] So are all other public authorities, whether their functions are judicial or administrative.[87]

In earlier times prohibition was often used to restrict the jurisdiction of

---

[79] For an exception see below, p. 646.

[80] Rubinstein, *Jurisdiction and Illegality*, 94.

[81] *R. v. Boundary Commission for England ex p. Foot* [1983] QB 600 (report of Boundary Commission: complaint not upheld).

[82] p. 646.

[83] Bl. Comm. iii. 113.

[84] Except in matters relating to trial on indictment: Supreme Court Act 1981, s. 29(3). Jurisdiction over the Crown Court extends to quashing for error on the face of the record: *R. v. Leeds Crown Court ex p. Bradford Chief Constable* [1975] QB 314. As to ecclesiastical courts see below, p. 646.

[85] Including the Patents Appeal Tribunal, though consisting of a High Court judge: *Baldwin & Francis Ltd. v. Patents Appeal Tribunal* [1959] AC 663; and an election court: *R. v. Cripps ex p. Muldoon* [1984] QB 68, affirmed [1984] QB 686.

[86] As in the *Anisminic* case, below, p. 725.

[87] Including the Commissioners of Inland Revenue: *R. v. Inland Revenue Commissioners ex p. National Federation of Self-Employed and Small Businesses Ltd.* [1982] AC 617.

tribunals existing by virtue of common law, such as the ecclesiastical and admiralty courts. But both certiorari and prohibition, in their modern applications for the control of administrative decisions, ordinarily lie only to statutory authorities. The reason for this is that all public administrative power is statutory. Powers derived from contract are matters of private law and outside the scope of prerogative remedies.[88] In refusing to grant certiorari or prohibition against arbitrators appointed privately under a contract of apprenticeship Lord Goddard CJ said:[89]

But the bodies to which in modern times the remedies of these prerogative writs have been applied have all been statutory bodies on whom Parliament has conferred statutory powers and duties which, when exercised, may lead to the detriment of subjects who may have to submit to their jurisdiction.

Consequently the existence of statutory power may be treated as the touchstone, though the court has recently admitted some exceptions.[90]

The scope of review by these remedies has three distinct heads: they lie in cases of (a) ultra vires, i.e. excess of jurisdiction, (b) error on the face of the record, and (c) exceptional cases.[91] Under ultra vires are classified all the manifold errors described in earlier chapters which go to jurisdiction, i.e. render the decision void, such as neglect of mandatory conditions, irrelevant grounds, unlawful purposes, breach of natural justice, and fraud. 'No evidence' may be a ground for certiorari, as has been seen,[92] though the discovery of fresh evidence is not,[93] unless it raises a jurisdictional question.[94] In all cases of ultra vires the litigant may use either prerogative remedies or remedies of private law such as declaration and injunction. In the case of mere error on the face of the record, however, the only remedy is certiorari to quash, since the decision is intra vires—or so, at least, it was supposed until recently.[95]

Where the bad part of a decision is severable from the good, certiorari may be granted to quash the bad part only.[96] Severability is discussed elsewhere.[97]

A tribunal whose decision is quashed may itself appeal.[98]

---

[88] See below, p. 647.
[89] R. v. National Joint Council for Dental Technicians ex p. Neate [1953] 1 QB 704 at 707.
[90] See below, p. 639.
[91] For these see below, p. 639.
[92] Above, p. 322.
[93] Above, p. 327.
[94] See above, p. 281.
[95] See above, p. 299.
[96] As in R. v. Bournemouth Licensing Justices ex p. Maggs [1963] 1 WLR 320.
[97] Above, p. 338.
[98] As in R. v. Immigration Appeal Tribunal ex p. Manek [1978] 1 WLR 1190. Presumably it could appeal against prohibition or mandamus likewise.

'Judicial' functions

Originally certiorari and prohibition lay to control the functions of inferior courts, i.e. judicial functions. But the notion of what is a 'court' and a 'judicial function' has been greatly stretched, so that these remedies have grown to be comprehensive remedies for the control of all kinds of administrative as well as judicial acts. This is because the judges very naturally saw no reason to abdicate the control which they achieved at the zenith of their power in the eighteenth century. In that age the chief organs of local government were the justices of the peace, who in addition to their regular judicial business had many administrative functions such as the upkeep of roads and bridges, the licensing of ale-houses, and the administration of the poor law. These administrative duties were discharged in the most judicial style possible: not only were the justices themselves primarily judicial officers, whose proceedings naturally tended to follow legal patterns—they were almost completely free from central political control.[99] Maitland epitomised the position of 'the amphibious old justice who did administrative work under judicial forms'.[1]

Whatever the justice has had to do has soon become the exercise of a jurisdiction; whether he was refusing a licence or sentencing a thief, this was the exercise of jurisdiction, an application of the law to a particular case. Even if a discretionary power was allowed him, it was none the less to be exercised with a 'judicial discretion'; it was not expected of him that he should have any 'policy'; rather it was expected of him that he should not have any 'policy'.

Local administration thus had a strong tradition. When, in the nineteenth century, most of the administrative functions of the justices were transferred to elected local councils or to new statutory authorities, they carried this tradition with them. Political control was imposed, but a judicial technique was inherited. The courts had fallen into the habit of calling many administrative acts 'judicial', meaning simply that the person wielding the power was required by law to keep within his jurisdiction and to observe the elements of fair procedure, such as the principles of natural justice. For a long time this abuse of language was masked by the mixture of functions which were performed by justices of the peace. When these functions were later sorted out, the label 'judicial' still stuck to

---

[99] Thus when the government were in need of recruits under the Militia Acts during the Seven Years War they had to move the Court of King's Bench for writs of mandamus to the county authorities. This was the height of 'judicial' administration. See Holdsworth, introduction to Dowdell, *A Hundred Years of Quarter Sessions,* 1x; *History of English Law,* x. 156.

[1] *Collected Papers,* i. 478.

administrative acts. Certiorari and prohibition were still described as remedies for the control of judicial functions, and for preventing excess of jurisdiction. But 'jurisdiction' had become synonymous with 'power', and in fact certiorari and prohibition were used to control all kinds of irregular administrative acts, from those of justices to those of ministers. Their scope expanded automatically with the development of the doctrine of ultra vires.

The scope of that doctrine has been explored in earlier chapters. To discuss the scope of certiorari and prohibition is to renew that discussion, though in the context of remedy rather than of right. This cannot be avoided. Although the nature of rights ought to dictate the availability of remedies, rules of law have a stubborn habit of concealing themselves behind the technical rules of remedies, which the courts often discuss as if they were objects in themselves.

The 'Electricity Commissioners' formula

Discussion of the scope of the modern law centres round a classic statement made by Atkin LJ in 1923. The case concerned an electricity scheme for the London area, where the Electricity Commissioners had statutory power to make schemes for grouping electricity authorities into districts for the general improvement of the supply. Any scheme was subject to confirmation by the Minister of Transport, and to approval by both Houses of Parliament; it was also subject to the usual public inquiry procedure in case of objection. There was a difference of opinion between the London County Council, which wanted one district for the whole area, and the electric supply companies, who wanted two districts. The Commissioners attempted to compromise by making a scheme under which there was only one district, but the district authority was to be required to delegate its powers to two committees, so that there would be a division of the kind that the companies wanted. The companies, however, challenged the legality of the scheme, and the Court of Appeal held it ultra vires on the ground that the Act did not permit the Commissioners to set up two authorities in the form of one.[2] A writ of prohibition was granted against the Commissioners at the instance of the companies, who had applied for it only a few days after the public inquiry had opened. It was objected that the function was not judicial but executive; that the application was premature as nothing decisive had yet happened; and that in any case the court should not intervene where the scheme had to be

---

[2] R. v. Electricity Commissioners ex p. London Electricity Joint Committee Co. (1920) Ltd. [1924] 1 KB 171.

approved by Parliament.[3] All these objections were swept aside, and the court made it plain that any statutory authority acting ultra vires could be called to order by the prerogative writs—by prohibition, to prevent them proceeding further with an unauthorized scheme, and by certiorari, to declare that any decision already taken was ineffective. The judgments explained how this wide power had been exercised for centuries. It had been said in a case of 1700:[4]

For this court will examine the proceedings of all jurisdictions erected by Act of Parliament. And if they, under pretence of such Act, proceed to incroach jurisdiction to themselves greater than the Act warrants, this Court will send a certiorari to them, to have their proceedings returned here.

This was restated in modern terms by Atkin LJ in the case of 1923 in what has become the definitive statement, approved in many later cases:

Wherever any body of persons having legal authority to determine questions affecting the rights of subjects, and having the duty to act judicially, act in excess of their legal authority, they are subject to the controlling jurisdiction of the King's Bench Division exercised in these writs.[5]

Canonical though these words are, they require much interpretation. Though they overstate the true position in one respect,[6] in almost every other respect they understate it, the scope of the remedies being in reality substantially wider. For instance, the language is not apt to include review for error on the face of the record, which later became a common ground for certiorari but which the courts had forgotten when Atkin LJ spoke.[7] Nor need the power be exercised by a 'body of persons' in the plural: the principle applies equally to an individual minister.[8] The detailed anatomy which follows will show how his formula needs modification.

[3] See above, p. 29.
[4] R. v. *Glamorganshire Inhabitants* (1700) 1 Ld Raym. 580. The words are evidently those of Holt CJ. Certiorari was granted to bring up an order of justices for a rate for the repair of Cardiff bridge, despite the objection that 'it was a new jurisdiction erected by a new Act of Parliament, the trust and the execution of which is reposed in the justices, and this Court has nothing to intermeddle with it'.
[5] [1924] 1 KB at 205. Similar language was used by Brett LJ in R. v. *Local Government Board* (1882) 10 QBD 309 at 321; but since the Court of Appeal there declined to decide whether certiorari would lie to a central government department, they left a large area of doubt.
[6] Read literally they could include bodies having a contractual duty to act judicially (i.e. fairly) such as disciplinary committees of trade unions and clubs. But in their context they are confined to the area of public law. For this see below, p. 647.
[7] See above, p. 306.
[8] See below, p. 633.

Acting 'judicially'

The above quotations of 1700 and 1923, though separated by so long an interval of time, are essentially similar in meaning. But the former speaks of 'jurisdiction', the latter of persons 'having the duty to act judicially'. The former is the more accurate, since 'jurisdiction' can easily include all kinds of administrative power, whereas 'the duty to act judicially' suggests a judicial as opposed to an administrative function.[9] In reality nothing could be plainer than that the acts controlled, both in the cases themselves and in many other cases decided both before and since, were administrative acts. That was certainly true of the rate levied for the repair of Cardiff bridge, which led to the case of 1700. The *Electricity Commissioners* case concerned a scheme which was plainly administrative. Provided only that there was some determination of a question affecting or capable of affecting legal rights, certiorari would issue to quash it if it exceeded the statutory power. As it was put in a leading case,[10]

The true view of the limitation would seem to be that the term 'judicial act' is used in contrast with purely ministerial acts. To the latter the process of certiorari does not apply, as for instance to the issue of a warrant to enforce a rate, even though the rate is one which could itself be questioned by certiorari. In short, there must be the exercise of some right or duty to decide in order to provide scope for a writ of certiorari at common law.

An Irish judge summed up the position in words approved in the House of Lords,[11] saying:[12]

... a judicial act seems to be an act done by competent authority, upon consideration of facts and circumstances, imposing liability and affecting the rights of others.

In the *Electricity* case the Court of Appeal cited a long series of precedents where certiorari or prohibition, or both, had issued to administrative authorities such as the Board of Education, the Poor Law Commissioners, the Tithe Commissioners, inclosure commissioners, and licensing justices. Plenty of other authorities could be added to this list including ministers of the Crown. The truth was that certiorari and prohibition were general remedies for the judicial control of both judicial and administrative decisions, and could be invoked just as freely where a minister made an

---

[9] An administrative (or quasi-judicial) decision is a decision determined by the policy or expediency of the moment, as opposed to a judicial decision which is determined according to some rule or principle of law: see above, pp. 47, 504.

[10] R. v. *Woodhouse* [1906] 2 KB 501 at 535 (Fletcher Moulton LJ). For this case see below, p. 634.

[11] *Everett* v. *Griffiths* [1921] 1 AC 631 at 683.

[12] R. v. *Dublin Cpn.* (1878) 2 LR Ir 371 at 376 (May CJ).

invalid clearance order[13] or a local authority wrongfully granted a licence[14] or planning permission,[15] as where justices of the peace convicted without jurisdiction. But the courts failed to give candid expression to this truth. They clung to their habit of calling administrative decisions 'judicial' in order that they might seem to have a pretext for controlling them. It was as if they had never quite convinced themselves of their title to interfere with administration pure and simple, although in fact they had been doing that for centuries. They did not follow the lead given by Brett LJ when he said:[16]

My view of the power of prohibition at the present day is that the Court should not be chary of exercising it, and that wherever the legislature entrusts to any body of persons other than to the superior Courts the power of imposing an obligation upon individuals, the Courts ought to exercise as widely as they can the power of controlling those bodies of persons if those persons admittedly attempt to exercise powers beyond the powers given to them by Act of Parliament.

This admirable statement, in contrast to so many others, is entirely uncontaminated by the notion of judicial functions.

Confusions and aberrations

To misuse language is to court danger. At two different times the courts threw themselves into confusion by forgetting that in this context they had made 'judicial' a synonym for 'administrative', and by drawing the false deduction that an act which was administrative could not be judicial in the sense required. The first occasion was in the late nineteenth century, when it was suddenly held that the decisions of licensing authorities, since they were administrative, were not subject to certiorari.[17] This fallacy was soon corrected,[18] with the aid of the remarks quoted in the previous section, and

---

[13] As in R. v. Minister of Health ex p. Davis [1929] 1 KB 619 (prohibition); R. v. Minister of Health ex p. Yaffé [1930] 2 KB 98 (certiorari), reversed on other grounds [1931] AC 494. Whether certiorari lay to a minister or central government department was left open in R. v. Local Government Board (1882) 10 QBD 309; that it did so lie was accepted without argument in Board of Education v. Rice [1911] AC 179.

[14] As in R. v. London County Council ex p. Entertainment Protection Association [1931] 2 KB 215. See similarly R. v. London County Council ex p. Commercial Gas Co. (1895) 11 TLR 337 (breach of natural justice: certiorari granted); R. v. Greater London Council ex p. Blackburn [1976] 1 WLR 550 (licensing of indecent films: prohibition).

[15] R. v. Hendon Rural District Council ex p. Chorley [1933] 2 KB 696 (breach of natural justice); R. v. Hillingdon London Borough Council ex p. Royco Homes Ltd. [1974] QB 720 (permission vitiated by unreasonable conditions).

[16] R. v. Local Government Board (1882) 10 QBD 309 at 321.

[17] R. v. Sharman [1898] 1 QB 578; R. v. Bowman [1898] 1 QB 663.

[18] R. v. Woodhouse [1906] 2 KB 501, reversed on other grounds, Leeds Cpn. v. Ryder [1907] AC 420.

the House of Lords explained how licensing functions, though administrative in nature, are subject to certiorari.[19] Nevertheless the aberration left a permanent mark, for it led to the use of mandamus as a substitute for certiorari in liquor licensing cases, which still lingers on illogically.[20]

Confusion again began to reign about 1950 in other licensing cases in which the long-established course of the law was apparently overlooked completely. These were the erroneous decisions on natural justice discussed in an earlier chapter.[21] As well as temporarily damaging the law of natural justice, they shook the whole basis of the prerogative remedies. For the law of natural justice and that of certiorari and prohibition had this in common, that both applied nominally only to judicial or quasi-judicial functions. By overlooking the fact that these terms had long been used to include administrative functions, the court relapsed into a profound muddle. The Court of Appeal made heavy weather over the question whether certiorari would go to a legal aid committee which had acted ultra vires, and it was suggested that the remedy might not lie in matters determined by policy and expediency.[22] Yet the *Electricity Commissioners* case itself arose out of a question of pure policy and expediency: how best to organise the electricity companies in London. Policy and expediency play a dominant role in licensing functions, but there is abundant authority for the control of licensing authorities by certiorari.[23]

'Judicially' reinterpreted

The law was once again saved from its own backsliding in *Ridge* v. *Baldwin*,[24] where Lord Reid reinterpreted Atkin LJ's words about 'the duty to act judicially'. This was a case of a breach of natural justice remedied by a declaratory judgment, as has been seen. But Lord Reid perceived the close parallel between the part played by the term 'judicial' in cases of natural justice and in cases where certiorari and prohibition are applied for. He explained how this term had been made a stumbling-block in earlier cases which had treated it as a superadded condition.[25] In the correct analysis it was simply a corollary, the automatic consequence of the power 'to

---

[19] *Frome United Breweries Co.* v. *Bath Justices* [1926] AC 586 (Lord Sumner). Counsel contesting this proposition in 1953 was told that he was about sixty years too late: *R.* v. *Brighton Borough Justices* [1954] 1 WLR 203.

[20] *R.* v. *Cotham* [1898] 1 QB 802; see below, p. 658.

[21] Above, p. 514.

[22] *R.* v. *Manchester Legal Aid Committee ex p. R. A. Brand & Co. Ltd.* [1952] 2 QB 413.

[23] As in the *Woodhouse* and *Frome* cases, above.

[24] [1964] AC 40; above, p. 517.

[25] Notably *R.* v. *Legislative Committee of the Church of England ex p. Haynes-Smith* [1928] 1 KB 411 at 415.

determine questions affecting the rights of subjects'. Where there is any such power, there must be the duty to act judicially. In the *Electricity Commissioners* case the Court of Appeal 'inferred the judicial element from the nature of the power'. Atkin LJ might therefore have said

. . . and *accordingly* having the duty to act judicially . . .

Lord Reid explained how any other interpretation was impossible to reconcile with a long line of unquestionable authorities, including the *Electricity Commissioners* case itself,[26] and Lord Hodson criticised the fallacy of saying that 'the giver of the decision is acting in an executive or administrative capacity as if that was the antithesis of a judicial capacity'.[27]

As a result of all this effort, the law was for the second time brought back onto its course. Certiorari and prohibition were once again recognised as general remedies for the control of administrative decisions affecting rights. They simply give effect to the principle that powers of decision must be exercised lawfully. It is true that the Privy Council once made a disparaging reference to Lord Reid's analysis,[28] but that was in a decision weakened by unfathomable reasoning and factual inaccuracy.[29] Other decisions have followed Lord Reid and the long line of compelling authority on which he drew. Both Lord Widgery CJ[30] and Lord Diplock[31] have pointed out how the supposed difficulty over 'the duty to act judicially' was eliminated after Lord Reid explained it away. The courts have subsequently made no difficulty over holding that certiorari is a suitable remedy for unlawful administrative determinations of all kinds, such as the making of a rating list on wrong principles,[32] a ministerial order taking over a school for wrong reasons and in breach of natural justice,[33] refusal of permission for entry by an immigration officer on wrong grounds,[34] and refusal of a certificate of consent for a gaming club without a fair hearing;[35] and that prohibition will be granted to restrain a licensing authority from acting unfairly[36] and to prevent a local authority from licensing indecent

---

[26] [1964] AC at 75.
[27] [1964] AC at 130.
[28] In *Durayappah* v. *Fernando* [1967] 2 AC 337 at 349.
[29] See above, p. 527.
[30] *R.* v. *Hillingdon Borough Council ex p. Royco Homes Ltd.* [1974] QB 720.
[31] *O'Reilly* v. *Mackman* [1983] 2 AC 237 at 279.
[32] *R.* v. *Paddington Valuation Officer ex p. Peachey Property Corporation Ltd.* [1966] 1 QB 380 (relief refused on the facts).
[33] *Maradana Mosque Trustees* v. *Mahmud* [1967] 1 AC 13.
[34] *R.* v. *Chief Immigration Officer, Lympne Airport ex p. Amrik Singh* [1969] 1 QB 333.
[35] *R.* v. *Gaming Board for Great Britain ex p. Benaim and Khaida* [1970] 2 QB 417 (relief refused on the facts).
[36] *R.* v. *Liverpool Cpn. ex p. Liverpool Taxi Fleet Operators' Association* [1972] 2 QB 299.

films.[37] All these are purely administrative matters, mostly concerned with questions of policy, and the courts expressly recognise that as such they are reviewable by these remedies.[38]

Certiorari thus performs a function not unlike that of a declaratory judgment: by quashing the court declares that some purported decision or determination is irregular or futile and therefore of no effect in law. The result is to establish that no one need take any notice of it. The difference from a declaratory judgment is that quashing positively invalidates the offending decision or act, whereas a declaration merely leaves it exposed to other remedies if required.

Decisions and determinations

'It cannot be too clearly understood that the remedy by way of certiorari only lies to bring up to this court and quash something which is a determination or a decision.'[39] This was said in a case where the court refused to grant the remedy to quash a mere report, being the report of the visitors of a hospital as to the need for continued detention of a mental defective. The power to order continued detention rested in another body, the board of control, who were required to consider the report of the visitors before deciding. Consequently the visitors had no power to make any decision affecting the rights of any one: they could merely recommend, and their report was no more than a piece of evidence which the board of control were required to obtain.[40] Had they not obtained it, or had it not been a proper resort as required by the Act, certiorari would have issued to quash the decision of the board.

Certiorari was similarly refused against justices who had power to license cinemas but who made it their practice to approve or disapprove plans for building cinemas and then to grant or refuse licences accordingly.[41] The object was to save abortive expenditure, but the statute gave no power to approve plans. An applicant aggrieved at the refusal of his plans was therefore unable to have the refusal quashed by certiorari, nor for the same reason could he enforce consideration of his plans by mandamus.

But certiorari and prohibition will issue in respect of any exercise of

[37] R. v. *Greater London Council ex p. Blackburn* [1976] 1 WLR 550.
[38] As emphasised by Lord Denning MR in the *Greater London Council* case (above) and by Roskill LJ in the *Liverpool* case (above).
[39] R. v. *St Lawrence's Hospital Statutory Visitors ex p. Pritchard* [1953] 1 WLR 1158 at 1166 (Parker J).
[40] See also R. v. *Macfarlane* (1923) 32 CLR 518 (immigration board's recommendation for deportation not subject to certiorari or prohibition).
[41] R. v. *Barnstaple Justices ex p. Carder* [1938] 1 KB 385.

statutory power which involves a true legal decision or determination, such as the grant of a licence[42] or the issue of a search warrant.[43] They will lie where there is some preliminary decision, as opposed to a mere recommendation, which is a prescribed step in a statutory process which leads to a decision affecting rights, even though the preliminary decision does not immediately affect rights itself. Where a telegraph operator was entitled to claim compensation for telegraphist's cramp on production of a medical certificate from a medical officer specified in the Act, the refusal of a certificate by a different and unauthorised medical officer was quashed as being 'so much waste paper'.[44] The court thus removed what would otherwise have been a legal obstacle to claiming a certificate from the proper officer. In the same way certiorari was granted to quash a medical certificate stating that a boy was an imbecile and incapable of benefiting from attendance at school, when one of the signatory doctors had not himself seen the boy and the question was, in any case, for determination by the Board of Education under the Act.[45] Even a report may be quashed if it is substantially a decision rather than a mere recommendation, e.g. where the Act provides that it shall be final.[46] There is no magic in the word 'report'. The question is whether some issue is being determined to some person's prejudice in law.

The courts are accustomed to granting certiorari so freely that they sometimes do so, illogically, where it does not fit the facts and other remedies would be more suitable. In one such case, where a local authority had a statutory duty to provide accommodation for a homeless person, the Court of Appeal quashed their decision to take no action.[47] Yet this 'decision' was not made under any specific power. The local authority had merely stated its unwillingness to perform its duty, and the natural remedy was mandamus. Certiorari was also granted to quash a 'determination' of the Commission for Racial Equality to hold a formal investigation into alleged discrimination, when in fact there was no distinct power to make such a determination, but prohibition could have been granted to forbid an

---

[42] Above, p. 634.

[43] The Court of Appeal quashed search warrants in R. v. Inland Revenue Commissioners ex p. Rossminster Ltd. [1980] AC 952, though the House of Lords held that the warrants were lawful; and see R. v. Tillett ex p. Newton (1969) 14 FLR 101.

[44] R. v. Postmaster-General ex p. Carmichael [1928] 1 KB 291.

[45] R. v. Boycott ex p. Keasley [1939] 2 KB 651. The report confirming the certificate and the letter transmitting it were also quashed as being consequential to the certificate.

[46] As in R. v. London County Council ex p. Commercial Gas Co. (1895) 11 TLR 337 (gas tester's report made in breach of natural justice).

[47] R. v. Hillingdon LBC ex p. Streeting [1980] 1 WLR 1425. For criticism see (1985) 101 LQR 153. In contrast to the American 'certiorarified mandamus' (below, p. 659) this might be called 'mandamusified certiorari).

unauthorised investigation.[48] Cases of this kind are now common. So long as public authorities act in the spirit of the court's order, no problems arise. But it is obvious that to 'quash' a 'decision' that by itself has no legal effect must be an impotent remedy in case of disobedience. Perhaps it is taken for granted that some further order, such as mandamus or an injunction, will be granted if necessary.[49] If confusion and complication are to be avoided, judicial review must be accurately focused upon the actual exercise of legal power and not upon mere preliminaries.

The emphasis now given to decisions, whether or not made under a legal power of decision, is greatly extending the scope of certiorari. It appears to derive from opinions of Lord Diplock. In a case where the Act provided that a tax officer, under a power of entry and search, 'may seize and remove' anything reasonably believed to be required as evidence of tax fraud, Lord Diplock said that the seizure 'involves a decision by the officer as to what documents he may seize', and said that 'Parliament has designated a public officer as decision-maker'.[50] He then discussed the question of 'setting aside his decision', either for error on the face of the record or else as being ultra vires. Yet the Act gave no power to decide anything, and it was the act of seizure, rather than any decision, which was in dispute. Then in a later case Lord Diplock said: 'The subject matter of every judicial review is a decision made by some person (or body of persons) whom I will call the "decision-maker" or else a refusal by him to make a decision.'[51] Yet many cases of judicial review necessarily turn upon the legality of acts, as opposed to decisions, as numerous examples show. When an order is quashed, for example, it is the legality of the order itself, and not of the decision to make it, with which the law is concerned. The fact that every deliberate act is preceded by some sort of decision is legally irrelevant.

Non-statutory decisions

Judicial review is designed to prevent the excess and abuse of power by public authorities. The powers of public authorities are conferred by statute

---

[48] R. v. *Commission for Racial Equality ex p. Hillingdon LBC* [1982] QB 276. See also the Court of Appeal's order in the *North Wales Police* case (above, p. 602), which presents the same problem in the context of the declaration. Compare *Cocks* v. *Thanet DC* [1983] 2 AC 286, discussed below, p. 681, where the House of Lords split the duty to house homeless persons into a power to decide followed by a duty to act.

[49] In *Wheeler* v. *Leicester CC* [1985] AC 1054, where on judicial review the House of Lords upheld the quashing of the council's decision not to allow a club to use their football ground, instead of granting prohibition or an injunction, it was recognised (at 1079) that further relief might be needed.

[50] The *Rossminster* case (above) at 1013.

[51] *Council of Civil Service Unions* v. *Minister for the Civil Service* [1985] AC 374 at 408.

in almost all cases, so that it is usually safe to asume that statutory power is in question, as in all the examples discussed so far. But what if a public authority wields effective power without any statutory basis? The lengthening arm of judicial review has proved capable of reaching into at least three such situations.[52]

1. Crown service. The Crown's power to dismiss civil servants at pleasure, held to be an exercise of the royal prerogative, is now subject to judicial review at least in some respects, as explained earlier.[53] The same applies to the Civil Service Appeal Board,[54] which is a non-statutory body, though it might be considered quasi-statutory since it carries the Secretary of State's statutory approval.[55]

2. The Criminal Injuries Compensation Board. This Board was established for the purpose of awarding compensation to victims of criminal injury. It is now statutory.[56] It was first constituted merely administratively to make what in law were ex gratia payments out of funds put at its disposal by Parliament. The published scheme contained rules for the Board's determination of claims, and these rules were debated in Parliament and amended by the Home Secretary. The rules were therefore mere administrative instructions from the Home Secretary to the Board, made under no statutory authority. Nevertheless the courts held that certiorari would quash a decision of the Board which was not in accordance with the rules.[57] Two successful claims concerned the meaning of the provision for compensation for 'personal injury directly attributable to a crime of violence . . . or to an arrest or attempted arrest of an offender', which the Board was held to have misinterpreted, so that there was error on the face of the record. The courts have reviewed the Board's decisions

[52] A further example may be the grant of declarations to review errors of law in departmental circulars, noted above, p. 597. Another may be the judicial enforcement of the immigration rules (the Home Secretary's published instructions to immigration officers) as in *R. v. Gatwick Airport Immigration Officer ex p. Kharazzi* [1980] 1 WLR 1396 (but the status of those rules is uncertain: see below, p. 858). That there may be virtually no limit is suggested by *R. v. Ethical Committee of St Mary's Hospital* [1987] The Times, 27 October, where it was assumed that judicial review might lie to quash the advice of an informal and non-statutory committee as well as a consultant's decision to refuse fertilisation treatment to a woman.

[53] Above, p. 392.

[54] *R. v. Civil Service Appeal Board ex p. Bruce* [1987] The Times, 22 June.

[55] See above, p. 73.

[56] Criminal Justice Act 1988, Pt. VII.

[57] *R. v. Criminal Injuries Compensation Board ex p. Lain* [1967] 2 QB 864 (claim failed). Claims succeeded in *R. v. Criminal Injuries Compensation Board ex p. Schofield* [1971] 1 WLR 926; *ex p. Lawton* [1972] 1 WLR 1589; *ex p. Ince* [1973] 1 WLR 1334 (CA); *ex p. Tong* [1976] 1 WLR 1237 (CA); *ex p. Clowes* [1977] 1 WLR 1353 (mandamus also granted); contrast *ex p. Thompstone* [1984] 1 WLR 1234; *ex p. Webb* [1987] QB 74.

just as strictly as those of statutory authorities, and have quashed them even where there was room for doubt.[58] In the initial case Lord Parker CJ said that 'the exact limits of the ancient remedy by way of certiorari have never been and ought not to be specifically defined' and that they had been 'extended to meet changing conditions'.

3. The Panel on Take-overs and Mergers. This body is an unincorporated association in the City of London which monitors a code of rules, promulgated by itself, governing company take-overs and mergers. It has neither statutory nor contractual powers, nor is it governmental in character. But it wields 'immense power de facto', since violations of the code, adjudged by itself, may lead to exclusion from the stock exchange or investigation by the Department of Trade and Industry or other sanctions. The Court of Appeal has held that it must 'recognise the realities of executive power . . . in defence of the citizenry', and be prepared to grant judicial review of the panel's rulings so as to prevent abuse of 'the enormously wide discretion which it arrogates to itself'.[59] But, except for violations of natural justice, declaration will usually be a more suitable remedy than certiorari or mandamus; and even then, in view of the disruptive effect of legal proceedings on urgent commercial transactions, review should be 'historic rather than contemporaneous', so as to prevent future error and relieve against unjust penalties, but otherwise to let the instant decision stand. This illustrates 'a very special feature of public law decisions, such as those of the panel, namely that however wrong they may be, however lacking in jurisdiction they may be, they subsist and remain fully effective unless and until they are set aside by a court of competent jurisdiction'.[60] It also illustrates the flexible use of discretionary remedies to meet novel legal situations.

The dynamism of judicial review, in its present expansive phase, is vividly shown by these decisions. In the case of the take-over panel the function was, as a matter of law, entirely outside the machinery of government, though the court emphasised that, as a matter of fact, the panel performed an important public duty and the Secretary of State deliberately used it 'as the centrepiece of his regulation of that market'. Lloyd LJ held this to be 'an implied devolution of power' and held the panel to be established 'under authority of the Government', despite the

---

[58] As in the *Schofield* case (above). In *R. v. Criminal Injuries Compensation Board ex p. Webb* [1987] QB 74 the Court of Appeal suggests a more tolerant policy.

[59] *R. v. Panel on Take-overs and Mergers ex p. Datafin Plc* [1987] QB 815. The application failed on the merits. The quotations are from Sir John Donaldson MR. The decision expressly follows *R. v. Criminal Injuries Compensation Board ex p. Lain* (above). See similarly *R. v. Panel on Take-overs and Mergers ex p. Guinness Plc* [1988] The Times, 1 April (application failed). For comment see (1987) 103 LQR 323; [1987] PL 356 (C. F. Forsyth).

[60] The same point as is made above, p. 352, on 'void or voidable'.

lack of legal connection. The courts are evidently determined not to allow any powerful quasi-governmental body to contract out of the legal system, even where there may be good reasons for avoiding the law's delays and uncertainties. 'Possibly the only essential elements are what can be described as a public element, which can take many different forms, and the exclusion from the jurisdiction of bodies whose sole source of power is a consensual submission to their jurisdiction.'[61] If these are to be the only criteria, wide new vistas of judicial review are opened, and the status of many public bodies will be in question.[62]

'Questions affecting the rights of subjects'

This requirement is really correlative to the idea of legal power, the exercise of which necessarily affects some person's legal rights, status, or situation. The primary object of certiorari and prohibition is to make the machinery of government operate properly in the public interest, rather than to protect private rights. Accordingly, as will be seen below in connection with standing, the court can award these remedies to any member of the public, irrespective of his personal rights, if any. For example, certiorari will go to quash wrongful refusals by licensing authorities,[63] even though the applicant has no right to a licence whatever but merely a right to have his application fairly entertained. The requirement of a decision 'affecting rights' is not therefore a limiting factor; it is rather an automatic consequence of the fact that power is being exercised.

Had it been otherwise, the claimant's obvious lack of legal rights would have been a serious obstacle to the grant of certiorari against the Criminal Injuries Compensation Board, as explained in the last section. In the principal case it was said that 'affecting the rights of subjects' in the formula of Atkin LJ meant no more than 'affecting subjects'.[64] An alternative suggestion was that the Board's determination to make an award did not affect the recipient's rights, since it entitled him to retain the payment which would otherwise be improper and recoverable.[65] These various

---

[61] Sir John Donaldson MR (at 838).

[62] See *R. v. Independent Broadcasting Authority ex p. Rank Organisation Plc* [1986] The Times, 14 March, holding that the IBA is subject to judicial review in exercising statutory powers but not in exercising powers conferred by the applicant company's articles of association, for which the remedies of public law were not available. This distinction corresponds with the limits of certiorari as previously understood. But is there not a 'public element', in the Court of Appeal's sense, when this powerful public body refuses permission for a shareholder to exercise voting rights?

[63] See above, p. 636.

[64] [1967] 2 QB at 892 (Ashworth J).

[65] [1967] 2 QB at 888 (Diplock LJ). But it is the refusal of an award which the claimant will wish to challenge, and it is difficult to see how that can affect legal rights.

explanations show how little the court is disposed to make any technical requirement as to 'rights', and that is clearly the correct policy in dealing with remedies which belong to public law.

As to 'subjects', this word must be interpreted liberally. Aliens lawfully within the realm in time of peace have of course the same civil rights and liberties as British subjects, and the same right to prerogative remedies. Being prerogative, they are naturally available to the Crown also.[66]

Certiorari to quash nullities

Certiorari lies to quash decisions of two different kinds: decisions which are ultra vires and void, and therefore nullities in law; and decisions which are intra vires but show error on the face of the record and are merely voidable.[67] There is no need here to criticise again the judgments which have attempted to extend the term 'voidable' to acts which are ultra vires and so void.[68] But it may be noticed that something over a century ago there was a short-lived fallacy that 'certiorari will not lie to quash nullities'.[69] It seems that the court would sometimes refuse certiorari to quash a patently ineffective act, for example where an inquisition was held by a coroner's clerk instead of by the coroner himself, since new proceedings would have to be taken and the void proceedings could simply be disregarded.[70] Yet the fact remained that the matter was brought before the court and the court held that the act was a nullity. This fallacy died a natural death, since certiorari was of course constantly in use for quashing acts which were ultra vires and nullities, as is shown by most of the cases cited in the foregoing discussion of this remedy.[71]

But in two modern cases Lord Denning has said that in the case of an order which is a nullity there is 'no need for an order to quash it' and that it is 'automatically null and void without more ado'.[72] The difficulties of this proposition have already been pointed out.[73] However null and void a decision may be, there is no means by which its nullity can be established

[66] As in *R. v. Amendt* [1915] 2 KB 276; *R. v. Lewes Justices ex p. Home Secretary* [1973] AC 388 (witness summonses quashed at Home Secretary's instance).

[67] For these see above, p. 310.

[68] See above, p. 350.

[69] Rubinstein, *Jurisdiction and Illegality*, 83.

[70] *Re Daws* (1838) 8 Ad & E 936.

[71] A good example is *R. v. Postmaster-General ex p. Carmichael* [1928] 1 KB 291; above, p. 638.

[72] *Directors of Public Prosecutions* v. *Head* [1959] AC 83 at 111; *R. v. Paddington Valuation Officer ex p. Peachey Property Corporation Ltd.* [1966] 1 QB 380 at 402. For comment on these see (1967) 83 LQR at 521.

[73] Above, p. 350.

except by asking the court to say so.[74] Lord Denning's successor pointed this out very clearly in the case of the take-over panel, quoted above.[75] If for example a licensing authority refuses a licence for wrong reasons or in breach of natural justice, so that its decision is ultra vires and void, nothing will avail the applicant except a judicial decision quashing the refusal and ordering a proper determination.[76] In other situations, such as that mentioned in the preceding paragraph, it may be possible to ignore a void order provided that the public authority makes no attempt to enforce it. But unless its nullity is conceded, it will have to be established in legal proceedings, and certiorari is frequently the right remedy for this purpose.[77]

Cases where certiorari and prohibition will or will not lie

The very wide range of tribunals and administrative authorities which are subject to the control of the High Court by these remedies has already been indicated.[78] 'Any body of persons' in the formula of Atkin LJ[79] does not necessarily mean a plurality: the remedies can equally well be granted against a minister, a valuation officer, an immigration officer, or any other individual authority.[80]

Prerogative remedies do not lie against the Crown, since it is at the suit of the Crown that they are sought. But they lie against ministers, and since the practice is to give executive powers to ministers or other government agencies as such rather than to the Crown, the Crown's immunity is of no consequence. The correct remedy for use against the Crown is an action for a declaratory judgment.[81] The same is true in matters which may concern Parliament for which a declaratory judgment is more suitable than prohibition.[82]

A decision may be none the less reviewable because it is subject to approval by some other authority. The irregular proceedings in the *Electricity Commissioners* case were stopped by prohibition even though the scheme was subject to confirmation by the Minister of Transport and to

[74] As to the presumption of validity see above, p. 346.

[75] Above, p. 641.

[76] See e.g. *Quietlynn Ltd.* v. *Plymouth City Council* [1988] QB 114, where the result is correct but the dicta about collateral pleas are unsound.

[77] See especially *London & Clydeside Estates Ltd.* v. *Aberdeen DC* [1980] 1 WLR 182 at 189, where Lord Hailsham LC emphasises the need to go to the court except in extreme situations where the position is obvious to all concerned.

[78] Above, p. 628.

[79] Above, p. 632.

[80] See above, p. 633.

[81] Above, p. 597.

[82] *R.* v. *Boundary Commission for England ex p. Foot* [1983] QB 600.

approval by resolutions of both Houses of Parliament.[83] Execution of the ruling that a house was insanitary, in a case already mentioned, was restrained by prohibition even though it was subject to the approval of the Governor in Council.[84] Even where a provisional order of inclosure commissioners was to be of no legal effect until confirmed by Act of Parliament, certiorari would lie to quash it, despite the argument that the whole matter was reserved for determination by the sovereign power of the legislature, which could override any irregularity.[85]

Certiorari and prohibition will not lie to control the proceedings of a deliberative body which deals with the earlier stages of what may ultimately be legislation. These remedies were therefore refused to an applicant who wished to prevent the passage of a prayer book measure by the Legislative Committee of the Church Assembly.[86]

Delegated legislation such as byelaws seems never to have been challenged by application for prerogative orders. There is, indeed, only a difference of degree between orders such as the proposed scheme in the *Electricity Commissioners* case and delegated legislation generally. No clear line can be drawn. But for challenging byelaws and traffic orders the declaratory judgment has proved effective,[87] and it may well be that they lie beyond the scope of certiorari and prohibition.

The court will not be deterred by difficult questions turning on scientific technicalities, such as may arise in reviewing decisions of the Patents Appeal Tribunal.[88]

Prisoners may be awarded these remedies and have applied for them successfully against disciplinary decisions of prison visitors, for example where there has been a failure of natural justice.[89] The House of Lords has now abolished the former exception under which the court would not intervene against decisions of prison governors in their day-to-day management of prisons.[90] Such a departure from principle, it is held, could only be made by legislation.[91] Relief may also be granted where the governor is claimed to have infringed a fundamental right, such as the

---

[83] [1924] 1 KB 171; above, p. 631.

[84] *Estate and Trust Agencies Ltd.* v. *Singapore Improvement Trust* [1937] AC 898; above p. 627.

[85] *Church* v. *Inclosure Commissioners* (1862) 11 CB (NS) 664. Contrast *R.* v. *Hastings Local Board of Health* (1865) 6 B & S 401 (provisional order for compulsory purchase held not subject to certiorari since subject to confirmation by Act of Parliament); but on this case see Atkin LJ in the *Electricity Commissioners* case [1924] 1 KB 171 at 209.

[86] *R.* v. *Legislative Committee of the Church of England ex p. Haynes-Smith* [1928] 1 KB.

[87] See below, p. 64.

[88] *Baldwin & Francis Ltd.* v. *Patents Appeal Tribunal* [1959] AC 663.

[89] See above, p. 875.

[90] *Leech* v. *Parkhurst Prison Deputy Governor* [1988] 2 WLR 290.

[91] See at p. 312.

right not to be subjected to 'cruel and unusual punishment' contrary to the Bill of Rights 1688.[92]

It is settled that certiorari will not lie to review proceedings in an ecclesiastical court, since ecclesiastical law is a different system from the common law on which the ordinary courts will not sit in judgment.[93] But prohibition will lie, not only to restrain the ecclesiastical court from exceeding its jurisdiction,[94] but also to prevent it from executing decisions marred by error on their face, provided that the error is one which the court is competent to correct.[95] Historical reasons lie behind this distinction. It is devoid of logic, since if the court is prepared to assert control by prohibition it might as well do so by certiorari. Normally prohibition is used only in case of excess of jurisdiction, certiorari being the remedy for error on the face.[96] But in this context, having disclaimed the power to issue certiorari, the court has extended the range of prohibition, thus remedying one anomaly by another. It seems probable that the law was similar for other special jurisdictions such as those of visitors of universities, colleges and charities who have jurisdiction to determine internal disputes within those bodies;[97] but visitatorial jurisdiction has now been held to be subject to judicial review in the ordinary way.[98]

Where there is a breakdown of law and order and the ordinary courts cannot operate, and martial law is imposed by force of arms, the court cannot interfere with the actions of the military or with the proceedings of courts martial set up in such a situation. Courts martial of this kind are not judicial tribunals in any legal sense, but merely part of the methods used to repel force by force where ordinary law is in suspense. Certiorari and prohibition, like other legal remedies, are therefore inoperative.[99] The ordinary courts martial regularly established under military law in normal conditions are a different case altogether. The Courts-Martial Appeal Court is a superior court and not subject to judicial control.[1]

---

[92] *R. v. Home Secretary ex p. Herbage* (No. 2) [1987] QB 1077 (allegation of cruel conditions of imprisonment: leave to apply for mandamus granted).

[93] *R. v. St Edmundsbury and Ipswich Diocese (Chancellor) ex p. White* [1948] 1 KB 195.

[94] e.g. *R. v. North* [1927] 1 KB 491 (prohibition to Consistory Court for decision contrary to natural justice).

[95] Bl. Comm. iii. 112, giving examples; *Veley* v. *Burder* (1841) 12 Ad & E 265, esp. at 311 (prohibition to prevent ecclesiastical court enforcing irregular church rate); Rubinstein, *Jurisdiction and Illegality*, 98.

[96] Above, p. 310.

[97] Bl. Comm. iii. 112 applies this doctrine to numerous jurisdictions; and see (1970) 86 LQR 531 at 544 (J. W. Bridge).

[98] *Thomas* v. *University of Bradford* [1987] AC 795; *R. v. Judicial Committee of the Privy Council ex p. Vijayatunga* [1988] 2 WLR 106. See above, p. 568.

[99] *Re Clifford and O'Sullivan* [1921] 2 AC 570 (prohibition refused).

[1] Courts-Martial (Appeals) Act 1968, s. 1.

Domestic tribunals and disciplinary bodies

Tribunals whose jurisdiction is confined to the internal affairs of some profession or association, and which are commonly called domestic tribunals, have not until recently appeared among the numerous tribunals against which certiorari and prohibition have been granted. Where their powers are statutory, as in the case of the Disciplinary Committee of the General Medical Council[2] and the Disciplinary Committee of the Law Society,[3] there is no apparent difficulty in fitting them into Atkin LJ's formula as bodies having legal authority to determine questions affecting rights. Nevertheless in practice their decisions were reviewed by ordinary actions for injunctions and declarations until the new procedure for judicial review was introduced in 1977. Since then an application for prerogative remedies has been allowed against the General Medical Council,[4] and there have been other comparable cases.[5] A possible reason for this change of practice is suggested below.[6]

Where a disciplinary body has no statutory powers its jurisdiction will normally be based upon contract. Members of trade unions, business associations, and social clubs and also students in universities and colleges have, as we have seen, contractual rights based on their contracts of membership, with implied terms which protect them from unfair expulsion.[7] In these cases declaration and injunction are the appropriate remedies. Certiorari and prohibition are quite out of place, since the Crown's supervisory powers over public authorities are not concerned with private contracts. Certiorari will therefore not issue to a contractual arbitrator, though it may to a statutory arbitrator.[8] As Lord Parker CJ said:[9]

Private or domestic tribunals have always been outside the scope of certiorari since their authority is derived solely from contract, that is, from the agreement of the parties concerned.

On the same principle, contracts of employment are equally beyond the scope of certiorari and prohibition. Thus where a university in Ceylon

---

[2] Medical Acts, 1956–78.

[3] Solicitors Act 1974, Pt. II.

[4] R. v. *General Medical Council ex p. Gee* [1986] 1 WLR 226 at 237, also [1986] 1 WLR 1247 (CA) and [1947] 1 WLR 564 (HL).

[5] R. v. *Committee of Lloyds ex p. Posgate* [1983] The Times, 12 January; R. v. *Pharmaceutical Society of Great Britain ex p. Sokoh* [1986] The Times, 4 December.

[6] Below, p. 685.

[7] Above, pp. 470, 501, 568.

[8] See the *Dental Technicians* case [1953] 1 QB 704, quoted above, p. 629.

[9] R. v. *Criminal Injuries Compensation Board ex p. Lain* [1967] 2 QB 864 at 882. See similarly *Lee* v. *Showmen's Guild of Great Britain* [1952] 2 QB 329 at 346 (Denning LJ).

dismissed a lecturer from his post, it was held that his position was merely that of an employee under an ordinary contract of master and servant, and that in such a case certiorari would not lie.[10] There have been similar rulings on applications made by employees of a district health authority[11] and of the BBC.[12] Here again a distinction is to be drawn between a mere contract of employment and tenure of a public office. An office-holder unlawfully dismissed may have his dismissal quashed by certiorari, so that he remains in office.[13] In the past, nevertheless, public offices were in practice protected by ordinary actions for declaration and injunction.[14]

Universities and colleges may or may not have statutory powers. If they have, the court may treat them as statutory public authorities which are subject to certiorari and prohibition as well as to declaration and injunction.[15] But the mere fact that the university is established by statute does not necessarily make its powers statutory: it may engage its employees under ordinary contracts of service.[16] If there is no statutory constitution, but merely incorporation by charter, there is no basis for disciplinary rules other than contract. As Lord Devlin said in a published report about misconduct by students:[17]

Contract is the foundation of most domestic or internal systems of discipline. . . . The power to discipline should be derived from the acceptance of it by the student in the contract of matriculation.

Non-statutory discipline may therefore be controlled by the ordinary remedies for breach of contract such as injunction, declaration or damages, but not by certiorari or prohibition. But it must be remembered that any dispute over the interpretation and administration of the university's internal rules comes within the exclusive jurisdiction of the visitor, if there is one, even where there is a relationship of contract.[18]

The contractual basis of the rights of students appears to have been overlooked by the High Court in the *Aston University* case, where it was

---

[10] *Vidyodaya University Council* v. *Silva* [1965] 1 WLR 77. See similarly *R.* v. *Post Office ex p. Byrne* [1975] ICR 221.

[11] *R.* v. *East Berkshire Health Authority ex p. Walsh* [1985] QB 152.

[12] *R.* v. *British Broadcasting Corporation ex p. Lavelle* [1983] 1 WLR 23. See below, p. 684.

[13] As in *R.* v. *Home Secretary ex p. Benwell* [1985] QB 554 (prison officer).

[14] As in *Cooper* v. *Wilson* [1937] 2 KB 309 and *Ridge* v. *Baldwin* [1964] AC 40 (police officers: declarations).

[15] As in *King* v. *University of Saskatchewan* (1969) 6 DLR (3d) 120.

[16] As in the *Vidyodaya* case (above); and see *Fekete* v. *Royal Institution for the Advancement of Learning* [1969] BR 1 (Quebec), affirmed (1969) 2 DLR (3d) 129. The Universities of Oxford and Cambridge are ancient universities by prescription but have statutory power to make their own statutes. How they should be classified is uncertain.

[17] Report on the Cambridge Sit-in, 1973, para. 154.

[18] Above, p. 568.

held that the student complainants had not been treated in accordance with natural justice but that they had delayed too long to be entitled to certiorari and mandamus.[19] Since the University was founded by charter and had no statutory powers, the rights of its students presumably arose from their contracts of membership; but certiorari and mandamus are not remedies for breach of contract. This aspect of the case was later criticised by the Court of Appeal, emphasising that the relationship between the University and the students must have been contractual, and questioning whether prerogative orders could be suitable remedies.[20] It has since been made clear once again that contractual rights are outside the scope of certiorari altogether, so that this remedy is not available to a Post Office employee alleging that he was dismissed in breach of his terms of employment.[21]

MANDAMUS

Nature of this remedy

The prerogative remedy of mandamus has long provided the normal means of enforcing the performance of public duties by public authorities of all kinds. Like the other prerogative remedies, it is normally granted on the application of a private litigant, though it may equally well be used by one public authority against another. The commonest employment of mandamus is as a weapon in the hands of the ordinary citizen, when a public authority fails to do its duty by him. Certiorari and prohibition deal with wrongful action, mandamus deals with wrongful inaction. The prerogative remedies thus together cover the field of governmental powers and duties.

Mandamus reached the zenith of its utility in the eighteenth century, when as well as protecting the citizen it played a conspicuous part in the machinery of government. It proved to be one of the few effective instruments of public policy in the era between the abolition of the Star Chamber in 1640 and the creation of the modern system of local government in the nineteenth century. During that interregnum the business of administration was mainly in the hands of local magistrates and other authorities who enjoyed an extraordinary measure of independence. A mandamus from the King's Bench was virtually the only effective means of forcing some such body to carry out its duties under common law or

[19] R. v. Aston University Senate ex p. Roffey [1969] 2 QB 538 (Divisional Court) above, p. 569. For discussion see (1969) 85 LQR 468, (1974) 90 LQR 157 (Wade); 90 LQR 6 (J. F. Garner); (1970) 86 LQR 531 (J. W. Bridge).

[20] Herring v. Templeman [1973] 3 All ER 569 at 585.

[21] R. v. Post Office ex p. Byrne [1975] ICR 221, repeating the above criticism.

Acts of Parliament. We have already seen an example of its use in that heyday of the rule of law.[22]

The essence of mandamus is that it is a royal command, issued in the name of the Crown from the Court of King's Bench (now the Queen's Bench Division of the High Court), ordering the performance of a public legal duty. It is a discretionary remedy, and the Court has full discretion to withhold it in unsuitable cases. It has never lost the wide scope which the courts gave it in the eighteenth and early nineteenth centuries, when it was so vital a part of the mechanism of the state. But in the highly organized administrative system of the modern state it has no longer this prominent role to play. Governmental bodies today respond more naturally to the political stimulus, and the ultimate legal sanction has to be invoked only in a handful of stubborn cases.

Disobedience to a mandamus is a contempt of court, punishable by fine or imprisonment.[23] A mandamus is therefore very like a mandatory injunction: both are commands from the court that some legal duty be performed. But the two remedies have different spheres. The injunction is an equitable remedy, and it is very rare to find mandatory injunctions outside private law. Mandamus is a common law remedy, based on royal authority, which is used only in public law.

Changing scope

Originally the writ of mandamus was merely an administrative order from the sovereign to his subordinates. But from early times it was made generally available through the Court of King's Bench, as was natural when the central government had little administrative machinery of its own. The writ would issue to enforce the terms of royal charters and by the seventeenth century it was in common use to compel the admission or restoration of freemen or burgesses to their offices or rights in borough corporations.[24] Another early use for it was to enforce the rights of members of universities;[25] and Lord Mansfield said that he had seen a report

[22] Above, p. 630, n. 99.
[23] See R. v. Poplar Borough Council ex p. London County Council (No. 2) [1922] 1 KB 95, granting a mandamus under which members of the defaulting council were imprisoned. Enforcement against a corporate body is against its members personally as individuals. For the political background, a story of great interest, see [1962] Public Law 52 (B. Keith-Lucas).
[24] The landmark here was Bagg's Case (1615) 11 Co Rep 93b, recounted above, p. 500, but there were fifteenth- and sixteenth-century precedents: see Middleton's Case (1574) 3 Dyer 332b.
[25] As in R. v. St John's College, Cambridge (1693) 4 Mod. 233; R. v. University of Cambridge (1723) 1 Str 557; R. v. Vice-Chancellor of Cambridge (1765) 3 Burr. 1647; R. v. Chancellor of Cambridge (1794) 6 TR 89; Tapping on Mandamus (1848) 267. But this is subject to the exclusive jurisdiction of any visitor: see below.

of a mandamus in the time of Edward III commanding the University of Oxford to restore a member who had been banished.[26] Lord Holt and Lord Mansfield favoured the free use of the writ for the enforcement of public duties of all kinds, for instance against inferior tribunals which refused to exercise their jurisdiction or against municipal corporations which did not duly hold elections, meetings, courts, and so forth. Lord Mansfield said in sweeping terms:[27]

It was introduced, to prevent disorder from a failure of justice, and defect of police. Therefore it ought to be used upon all occasions where the law has established no specific remedy, and where in justice and good government there ought to be one. . . . The value of the matter, or the degree of its importance to the public police, is not scrupulously weighed. If there be a right, and no other specific remedy, this should not be denied. Writs of mandamus have been granted, to admit lecturers, clerks, sextons, and scavengers, &c., to restore an alderman to precedency, an attorney to practice in an inferior court, &c.

This was in a case where a writ issued for the admission of a presbyterian preacher whose only title was under a trust deed, showing that the duty enforced need be neither statutory nor under royal charter.[28] Furthermore, the duty was public only in the sense that it was a duty to execute a charitable trust. Mandamus used to be employed for enforcing the admission of copyholders in manors, where it was a matter of private duty only.[29]

An example of mandamus enforcing a duty existing at common law is *Bentley's* case,[30] mentioned elsewhere, where the writ was granted to restore him to his degrees which had been unlawfully taken away by the Vice-Chancellor's court of Cambridge University. Where a university or college has a visitor, mandamus may be granted to require the visitor to act, and to hear the parties fairly,[31] but the court will not otherwise interfere with his exercise of his jurisdiction, provided that he keeps within it.[32] There was much litigation on such questions in the eighteenth century.

Although the older authorities have not been invalidated, mandamus has

[26] *R. v. Askew* (1768) 4 Burr 2185 at 2189. Oxford University was ordered by mandamus in 1396 to expel Lollards: Tapping on Mandamus, 269.

[27] *R. v. Barker* (1762) 3 Burr. 1265 at 1267.

[28] It may also show Lord Mansfield's leaning towards incorporating equity into the common law.

[29] See *R. v. Powell* (1841) 1 QB 352; *R. v. Garland* (1879) LR 5 QB 269.

[30] *R. v. University of Cambridge* (1723) 1 Str. 557; above, p. 499. The University's charters had been confirmed by statute, but the duty to restore was evidently at common law. The court held that it could intervene because the University did not claim to have a visitor.

[31] *R. v. Bishop of Lincoln* (1785) 2 TR 338 n.

[32] For university visitors see above, p. 568.

in practice acquired a more precise scope than that which Lord Mansfield advocated. Modern government is based almost exclusively on statutory powers and duties vested in public bodies, and mandamus is the regular method of enforcing the duties. The plethora of ancient and customary jurisdictions no longer exists. The introduction in the nineteenth century of the modern system of local government, and the provision by the state in the twentieth century of social services and benefits which were previously a matter for private charity, have sharpened the distinction between bodies and activities which are governmental and those which are not. As the picture has come into focus, the proper sphere of mandamus has become clearer. Mandamus now belongs essentially to public law. It seems safe to say that it would not be granted today to enforce the duties of trustees, even where these are statutory, since for this there are sufficient remedies in private law. Nor will it be granted to enforce the private rights of shareholders against companies,[33] though courts entertained such cases previously.[34] The distinction between public and private rights became easier to draw after the Judicature Acts 1873–5, since there was no longer the temptation to use mandamus in order to save resorting to proceedings in Chancery.[35]

Today the majority of applications for mandamus are made at the instance of private litigants complaining of some breach of duty by some public authority. But public authorities themselves may still use the remedy, as they did in the past, to enforce duties owed to them by subordinate authorities. When the borough council of Poplar refused to pay their statutory contribution to the London County Council for rates, the county council obtained a mandamus ordering the proper payments to be made;[36] and when they were not made, the county council obtained writs of attachment for the imprisonment of the disobedient councillors.[37] Statutes also may provide for mandamus as a remedy for one public authority against another, as observed later in the case of default powers.[38]

Within the field of public law the scope of mandamus is still wide and the court may use it freely to prevent breach of duty and injustice:

Instead of being astute to discover reasons for not applying this great constitutional

---

[33] *Davies* v. *Gas Light and Coke Co.* [1909] 1 Ch 708, holding that the proper remedy was injunction.

[34] See *R.* v. *London and St. Katherine's Docks Co.* (1874) 44 LJQB 4.

[35] For a case where it was pleaded that all beneficiaries would be dead before relief could be had in Chancery, see Tapping on Mandamus 63–4. A mandatory order of the Court of Chancery was sometimes called a mandamus, and this must be distinguished from the prerogative mandamus in the Queen's Bench.

[36] *R.* v. *Poplar Borough Council ex p. London County Council* (No. 1) [1922] KB 72.

[37] Same (No. 2) [1922] 1 KB 95.

[38] Below, p. 747.

remedy for error and misgovernment, we think it our duty to be vigilant to apply it in every case to which, by any reasonable construction, it can be made applicable.[39]

For the sake of this principle technical difficulties may be overcome. The court can, for example, order the fulfilment of a duty even though a statutory time limit for its performance has expired;[40] and if the defaulting officer has been replaced by a successor, the latter may be ordered to make good his predecessor's default.[41]

Discretionary remedy

Like certiorari and prohibition, mandamus is a discretionary remedy.[42] What this means is explained later.[43] It may therefore be refused to an applicant who has been guilty of undue delay, as where nine years were allowed to elapse before claiming a refund of tax.[44] It may also be refused where a public authority has done all that it reasonably can to fulfil its duty,[45] or where the remedy is unnecessary, as where a tribunal undertakes to rehear the case according to law after its decision has been quashed.[46] In the case of the police, to whom mandamus may issue if they refuse to perform their duty, the court may prefer to explain their duty to them in general terms and leave them to act on their own responsibility in any particular situation.[47] The court always retains discretion to withhold the remedy where it would not be in the interests of justice to grant it.[48] But where no such question arises the remedy will be granted, and the court may even deny that discretion exists.[49]

Modern statutory duties

Typical applications of mandamus in modern cases are to enforce statutory duties of public authorities to make a rate,[50] to refer a complaint to a

[39] *R. v. Hanley Revising Barrister* [1912] 3 KB 518 at 529 (Darling J).
[40] *R. v. Farquhar* (1870) LR 9 QB 258; *R. v. Hanley Revising Barrister* (above); *R. v. Woodbury Licensing Justices* [1960] 1 WLR 461.
[41] *R. v. Hanley Revising Barrister* (above).
[42] *R. v. Churchwardens of All Saints, Wigan* (1876) 1 App Cas 611 at 622.
[43] Below, p. 709.
[44] *Broughton* v. *Commissioner of Stamp Duties* [1899] AC 251. An extreme case is *R.* v. *Leeds to Liverpool Canal Co.* (1840) 11 A & E 316 (sixty-five-year delay fatal).
[45] *R. v. Bristol Cpn. ex p. Hendy* [1974] 1 WLR at 503 (duty to rehouse tenant).
[46] *R. v. Northumberland Compensation Appeal Tribunal ex p. Shaw* [1952] 1 KB 338 at 357.
[47] *R. v. Metropolitan Police Cmr ex p. Blackburn* [1968] 2 QB 118; *R. v. Devon and Cornwall Chief Constable ex p. Central Electricity Generating Board* [1982] QB 458.
[48] As in *R. v. Garland* (1879) LR 5 QB 269.
[49] *R. v. Bishop of Sarum* [1916] 1 KB 466 at 470.
[50] *R. v. Poplar Borough Council* (No. 1) [1922] 1 KB 72.

statutory committee,[51] to decide a dispute between education authorities on proper grounds,[52] to determine an application for a licence,[53] to reconsider an application for a licence on proper grounds,[54] to appoint an inspector of a company,[55] to adjudicate between landlord and tenant,[56] to approve building plans,[57] to pay college lecturers,[58] to pay a police pension,[59] and to improve conditions of imprisonment.[60] Where the duty is to reach a decision the order will usually be 'to hear and determine according to law', the law being indicated by the court.[61] In other cases the order will be to act according to law, with or without further details and instructions which the court may add. Occasionally mandamus may be sought to enforce a non-statutory duty, such as the duty of the police to prosecute offenders against the law,[62] or the duty of a local authority to produce documents which a councillor reasonably needs for the proper performance of his duties as such.[63]

A statutory duty must be performed without unreasonable delay, and this may be enforced by mandamus. Mandamus was granted on this ground against the Home Secretary when the Home Office insisted that a would-be immigrant who was legally entitled to enter the country 'without let or hindrance' should wait for over a year in the queue of applicants for entry certificates.[64]

Statutory duties are by no means always imposed by mandatory language with words such as 'shall' or 'must'. Sometimes they will be the implied counterparts of rights, as where a person 'may appeal' to a tribunal and the tribunal has a correlative duty to hear and determine the appeal.[65] Sometimes also language which is apparently merely permissive is construed as imposing a duty, as where 'may' is interpreted to mean 'shall'.[66]

---

[51] *Padfield* v. *Minister of Agriculture, Fisheries and Food* [1968] AC 997.
[52] *Board of Education* v. *Rice* [1911] AC 179.
[53] *R.* v. *Tower Hamlets London Borough Council ex p. Kayne-Levenson* [1975] QB 431.
[54] *R.* v. *London County Council ex p. Corrie* [1918] 1 KB 68; and see the liquor licensing cases cited below, p. 658.
[55] *R.* v. *Board of Trade ex p. St. Martin's Preserving Co. Ltd.* [1965] 1 QB 603.
[56] *R.* v. *Pugh (Judge)* [1951] 2 KB 623 (mandamus to require county court to hear case).
[57] *R.* v. *Tynemouth Rural District Council* [1896] 2 QB 219 (the conditions for approval being satisfied).
[58] *R.* v. *Liverpool CC ex p. Coade* [1986] The Times, 10 October.
[59] *R.* v. *Leigh (Lord)* [1897] 1 QB 132.
[60] *R.* v. *Home Secretary ex p. Herbage* (No. 2) [1987] QB 1077.
[61] As in (e.g.) *R.* v. *St. Pancras Vestry* (1890) 24 QBD 371.
[62] See below, p. 699.
[63] See *R.* v. *Barnes Borough Council ex p. Conlan* [1938] 3 All ER 226 and cases there cited.
[64] *R.* v. *Home Secretary ex p. Phansopkar* [1976] QB 606; above, p. 439.
[65] See below: 'Duty to exercise jurisdiction'.
[66] For this see above, p. 258.

Even though no compulsory words are used, the scheme of the Act may imply a duty.

Having developed from a piece of purely administrative machinery, mandamus was never subject to the misguided notion which afflicted its less fortunate relative certiorari, that it could apply only to 'judicial' functions. Administrative or ministerial duties of every description could be enforced by mandamus. It was, indeed, sometimes said that this remedy did not apply to judicial functions,[67] meaning that where a public authority was given power to determine some matter, mandamus would not lie to compel it to reach some particular decision. The law as to this is explained below under 'Duty to exercise jurisdiction'.

The fact that the statutory duty is directory as opposed to mandatory, so that default will not invalidate some other action or decision,[68] is no reason for not enforcing it by mandamus.[69]

Contractual duties distinguished

A distinction which needs to be clarified is that between public duties enforceable by mandamus, which are usually statutory, and duties arising merely from contract. Contractual duties are enforceable as matters of private law by the ordinary contractual remedies, such as damages, injunction, specific performance and declaration. They are not enforceable by mandamus, which in the first place is confined to public duties and secondly is not granted where there are other adequate remedies.[70] This difference is brought out by the relief granted in cases of ultra vires. If for example a minister or a licensing authority acts contrary to the principles of natural justice, certiorari and mandamus are standard remedies. But if a trade union disciplinary committee acts in the same way, these remedies are inapplicable: the rights of its members depend upon their contract of membership, and are to be protected by declaration and injunction, which accordingly are the remedies employed in such cases.[71]

But occasionally the courts appear to have overlooked the distinction. Lord Campbell CJ once said that 'a legal obligation, which is the proper substratum of a mandamus, can arise only from common law, from statute, or from contract',[72] a loose dictum which need not necessarily mean that Lord Cambell thought that mandamus was a remedy for breach of contract. In a university disciplinary case, already mentioned, the High

---

[67] As in *R. v. London Justices* [1895] 1 QB 214, 616.
[68] For this distinction see above, p. 245.
[69] *Brayhead (Ascot) Ltd.* v. *Berkshire County Council* [1964] 2 QB 303 at 313–14.
[70] See below, p. 660.
[71] As in the cases cited above, p. 647.
[72] *Ex p. Napier* (1852) 18 QB 692 at 695.

Court proceeded as if the rights of students to be treated in accordance with natural justice could be enforced by mandamus, although the university had no statutory powers and the rights of its student members were evidently contractual.[73] The authority of this case has been shaken as regards the appropriate remedies, which should have been injunction and declaration.[74] It is possible that mandamus would lie to enforce rights flowing directly from the charter of a university or college for which there was no other remedy.[75] But rights flowing merely from a contract of membership should not be within the scope of mandamus.

For similar reasons mandamus will not issue to a private arbitrator appointed under an arbitration clause in a contract, for such an arbitrator has no public function or statutory duty. This is equally true where a statutory tribunal is appointed as arbitrator if the appointment is made under the terms of a contract and the tribunal is used in the same way as a private arbitrator, acting voluntarily.[76] For here also there is no statutory duty.

Duty to exercise jurisdiction

A court or tribunal has a public duty to hear and decide any case within its jurisdiction which is properly brought before it. Mandamus is frequently granted to enforce this duty on the part of inferior courts and statutory tribunals, which will be ordered to hear and determine according to law. Thus magistrates, licensing justices, county courts, statutory tribunals, and other jurisdictions subject to the High Court can be prevented from refusing jurisdiction wrongfully. A county court judge, who mistakenly declined to hear an action for possession by mortgagees on the ground that the county court had no jurisdiction, was ordered to hear and determine the case on a mandamus from the Queen's Bench Division.[77] The same occurred where a county court judge refused to investigate the correctness of jurisdictional facts on which the validity of a rent tribunal's decision depended, and which were properly disputed before him.[78] Refusal to receive evidence on some relevant point may also amount to refusal of

---

[73] R. v. Aston University Senate ex p. Roffey (1969) 2 QB 538; above, p. 648.

[74] Herring v. Templeman [1973] 3 All ER 569 at 585; above, p. 649.

[75] See above, p. 568.

[76] R. v. Industrial Court ex p. ASSET [1965] 1 QB 377 (complaint that supplier of spectacles to Ministry of Health was in breach of Fair Wages Resolution of House of Commons: matter referred by Ministry to Industrial Court under arbitration clause in contract). Compare R. v. National Joint Council for Dental Technicians ex p. Neate [1953] 1 QB 704 (certiorari and prohibition likewise inapplicable).

[77] R. v. Briant (Judge) [1957] 2 QB 497.

[78] R. v. Pugh (Judge) [1951] 2 KB 623.

jurisdiction, so that mandamus will go to compel a magistrate to receive it; though this has to be distinguished from a decision by the magistrate, within the scope of his discretion, that the evidence is irrelevant.[79] Refusal to consider a party's case also has to be distinguished from refusal to accept his argument. As Lord Goddard CJ said:[80]

... to allow an order of mandamus to go there must be a refusal to exercise the jurisdiction. The line may be a very fine one between a wrong decision and a declining to exercise jurisdiction; that is to say, between finding that a litigant has not made out a case, and refusing to consider whether there is a case.

If the inferior court or tribunal merely makes a wrong decision within its jurisdiction, as opposed to refusing to exercise it, mandamus cannot be employed to make it change its conclusion.[81] This is merely the familiar rule that the court cannot interfere with action which is intra vires.

An instance of mandamus to a statutory tribunal was where a housing appeal tribunal dismissed an appeal by a company wishing to build a picture house without giving them a hearing as required by law. This was a breach of an implied statutory duty; the decision was accordingly quashed by certiorari and mandamus issued to require the tribunal to exercise its jurisdiction properly.[82] The same remedies were likewise granted where an immigration tribunal wrongly refused leave to appeal.[83]

The basis of all such cases is that the court or tribunal has a legal duty to hear and determine the case which is correlative to a statutory right of some person to apply or appeal to it. But now that the High Court will grant certiorari to quash decisions of the Criminal Injuries Compensation Board, which has no statutory constitution and therefore no statutory duties, it seems that it will also grant mandamus to require the Board to hear and determine—though it might be difficult to add the usual words 'according to law'. The anomaly of granting legal remedies to enforce mere administrative directions has already been pointed out. But since it is already established, it is only logical to extend it to mandamus, thus completing the system of judicial control over a non-statutory body.[84]

Mandamus has also been granted anomalously, as it would appear, to enforce what the court called 'a rule of practice'. Magistrates had refused to authorise legal aid by counsel for a man charged with murder; and though

[79] R. v. Marsham [1892] 1 QB 371 (mandamus granted). For this question see above, p. 326.
[80] R. v. Goods Vehicles Licensing Authority ex p. Barnett Ltd. [1949] 2 KB 17 at 22.
[81] R. v. London Justices [1895] 1 QB 616 at 637; Smith v. Chorley Rural Council [1897] 1 QB 678; R. v. Goods Vehicles Licensing Authority (above).
[82] R. v. Housing Appeal Tribunal [1920] 3 KB 334.
[83] R. v. Immigration Appeal Tribunal ex p. Shezada [1975] Imm. AR 26.
[84] See above, p. 640.

the statute gave them discretion as to the type of aid to be granted, it was held that there was a practice of allowing counsel in trials for murder, and that the practice was obligatory.[85] But perhaps this case ought to be regarded as one of an unreasonable decision, or of a duty implied in the statute, in which case certiorari and mandamus would be normal remedies.

The position where there is a duty to hear and determine, but discretion as to the correct determination, must be distinguished from that where there is a discretion not to act in the matter at all. The Parliamentary Commissioner for Administration, who 'may investigate' complaints of maladministration, and is expressly given discretion whether to initiate any investigation,[86] cannot therefore be ordered by mandamus to entertain a complaint, since this is a matter of discretion and not of duty.[87]

Mandamus and certiorari

Mandamus is often used as an adjunct to certiorari. If a tribunal or authority acts in a matter where it has no power to act at all, certiorari will quash the decision and prohibition will prevent further unlawful proceedings. If there is power to act, but the power is abused (as by breach of natural justice or error on the face of the record), certiorari will quash and mandamus may issue simultaneously to require a proper rehearing. An example is *Board of Education* v. *Rice*, cited elsewhere:[88] the Board's decision was ultra vires since they had addressed their minds to the wrong question; consequently it was quashed by certiorari and the Board were commanded by mandamus to determine the matter according to law, i.e. within the limits indicated by the House of Lords.

But either remedy may be used by itself. Defective decisions are frequently quashed by certiorari without any accompanying mandamus. Once the decision has thus been annulled, the deciding authority will recognise that it must begin again and in practice there will be no need for mandamus. If on the other hand mandamus is granted without certiorari, the necessary implication is that the defective decision is a nullity, for it is only on this assumption that the mandamus can operate. A simple mandamus therefore does the work of certiorari automatically. Normally mandamus is not used by itself in this elliptical way. But, by a curious practice, this use of it has become habitual in liquor licensing cases, so that the standard remedy for judicial control of licensing justices' decisions is

---

[85] *R.* v. *Derby Justices ex p. Kooner* [1971] 1 QB 147.

[86] Parliamentary Commissioner Act 1967, s. 5(1), (5). See above, p. 93.

[87] *Re Fletcher* [1970] 2 All ER 527. Compare *Environmental Defence Society Inc.* v. *Agricultural Chemicals Board* [1973] 2 NZLR 758 (power rather than duty).

[88] [1911] AC 179; above, p. 506.

mandamus rather than certiorari.[89] This is because it was those cases which were first bedevilled by illogical doubts as to whether licensing was a judicial function for the purposes of certiorari;[90] and though the doubts were long ago swept away, the habit lives on.

In the *Paddington* rating case, where the validity of the whole rating list was attacked (though unsuccessfully), Lord Denning MR suggested that, in order to avoid administrative inconvenience, an invalid rating list might be kept in operation by withholding certiorari for the time being, and that meanwhile mandamus might issue against the rating authority to enforce the preparation of a valid list.[91] But this was on the hypothesis that an invalid list was voidable rather than void, a heresy criticised elsewhere.[92] As Salmon LJ more logically observed, mandamus could not be granted if there was a valid valuation list in being; it could be granted only on the footing that a legal list had never been made at all.[93] In an earlier case Lord Denning himself had said:[94]

The cases on mandamus are clear enough: and if mandamus will go to a tribunal for such a cause, then it must follow that certiorari will go also: for when a mandamus is issued to the tribunal, it must hear and determine the case afresh, and it cannot well do this if its previous order is still standing. The previous order must either be quashed on certiorari or ignored: and it is better for it to be quashed.

Although both certiorari and mandamus are discretionary remedies, the court's discretion must be limited by the basic rules of judicial control. Unless the rating list disputed in the *Paddington* case had been void, the court would have had no power to intervene.

Requirement of demand and refusal

It has been said to be an 'imperative rule' that an applicant for mandamus must have first made an express demand to the defaulting authority, calling

---

[89] Examples are *R.* v. *Weymouth Licensing Justices ex p. Sleep* [1942] 1 KB 465; *R.* v. *Flintshire County Licensing Committee ex p. Barrett* [1957] 1 QB 350 (licence refused on irrelevant grounds); *R.* v. *Birmingham Licensing Planning Committee ex p. Kennedy* [1972] 2 QB 140 (similar); *Fletcher* v. *London (Metropolis) Licensing Planning Committee* [1976] AC 150 (similar). The first such case was *R.* v. *Cotham* [1898] 1 QB 802. In some American States, where the fallacy over judicial functions persists, mandamus has taken the place of certiorari and is known as 'certiorarified mandamus'; see below, p. 667.

[90] See above, p. 634.

[91] *R.* v. *Paddington Valuation Officer ex p. Peachey Property Co. Ltd.* [1966] 1 QB 380 at 402; above p. 350.

[92] Above, p. 351.

[93] In the *Paddington* case (above) at 419.

[94] *Baldwin & Francis Ltd.* v. *Patents Appeal Tribunal* [1959] AC 663 at 693–4.

upon it to perform its duty, and that the authority must have refused.[95] But these formalities are usually fulfilled by the conduct of the parties prior to the application, and refusal to perform the duty is readily implied from conduct.[96] The substantial requirement is that the public authority should have been clearly informed as to what the applicant expected it to do, so that it might decide at its own option whether to act or not.[97]

The court does not insist upon this condition where it is unsuitable. As Channell J said:[98]

The requirement that before the court will issue a mandamus there must be demand to perform the act sought to be enforced and a refusal to perform it is a very useful one, but it cannot be applicable to all possible cases. Obviously it cannot apply where a person has by inadvertence omitted to do some act which he was under a duty to do and where the time within which he can do it has passed.

An obvious case where no demand need be made is where mandamus is used as a substitute for certiorari to quash a decision, as explained in the preceding section.

Effect of alternative remedies

The prerogative order of mandamus is not to be granted where the law provides some other adequate remedy. At one time this rule was very strictly applied, in conformity with the doctrine that mandamus was a supplementary remedy, to be invoked where there was no specific remedy for enforcing some right.[99] Mandamus was thus refused where there was a possibility of obtaining a tax refund by way of petition of right.[1] An extreme instance, criticised later, was where the House of Lords held that ministerial default powers were an adequate remedy for an individual aggrieved by the failure of a local authority to provide sewers as required by law.[2] This view of mandamus was expounded by Bowen LJ:[3]

A writ of mandamus, as everybody knows, is a high prerogative writ, invented for the purpose of supplying defects of justice. By Magna Charta the Crown is bound

---

[95] Tapping on Mandamus, 282.

[96] See *The State (Modern Homes Ltd.)* v. *Dublin Corporation* [1953] IR 202.

[97] *R.* v. *Brecknock & Abergavenny Canal Co.* (1835) 3 Ad & E 217 (mandamus refused on this ground); *R.* v. *Commissioners of Public Utilities ex p. Halifax Transit Corpn* (1970) 15 DLR (3d) 720.

[98] *R.* v. *Hanley Revising Barrister* [1912] 3 KB 518 at 531.

[99] Above, p. 651. See e.g. *R.* v. *Gamble* (1839) 11 A & E 69.

[1] *Re Nathan* (1884) 12 QBD 461 (but it was also held that no duty to the applicant existed).

[2] *Pasmore* v. *Oswaldtwistle Urban District Council* [1898] AC 387; below, p. 748.

[3] *Re Nathan* (above) at 478.

neither to deny justice to anybody, nor to delay anybody in obtaining justice. If, therefore, there is no other means of obtaining justice, the writ of mandamus is granted to enable justice to be done. The proceeding, however, by mandamus, is most cumbrous and most expensive; and from time immemorial accordingly the courts have never granted the writ of mandamus where there was another more convenient, or feasible remedy within the reach of the subject.

Mandamus may therefore be refused where there is an adequate right of appeal. Where the statute provides a right of appeal or other remedy, it may well be held that the statutory remedy is intended to be exclusive, so that mandamus is inapplicable.[4] But where licensing justices had rejected an application without giving reasons as the statute required, with the consequence that the applicant could not tell upon what grounds he might appeal, mandamus was granted to require the justices to hear and determine according to law.[5] The Court of Appeal has held that ratepayers may challenge the validity of the local authority's rating list as a whole, despite the existence of a right of appeal against any particular assessment.[6] This once again illustrates that the court will not require an applicant to exercise a right of appeal on the merits when his complaint is of lack of jurisdiction or ultra vires.

Today mandamus has largely lost the character of a residual remedy. As noted earlier, it has become the regular remedy for enforcing the statutory duties of public authorities, and its procedure is no longer 'cumbrous and expensive'. Accordingly the courts have grown accustomed to awarding it more freely, even where some other remedy exists. Thus the Local Government Board obtained mandamus against a local authority which refused to appoint a vaccination officer, even though the Act empowered the board, in case of default, to make the appointment themselves.[7] Similarly the London County Council were granted mandamus to compel the Poplar Borough Council to pay a precept for rates, even though the Act provided that they might enforce their claim by levying distress—a wholly inadequate remedy, as the court held.[8]

It is expressly provided that the new remedies introduced by the Crown Proceedings Act 1947 shall not limit the discretion of the court to grant mandamus.[9]

[4] R. v. City of London Assessment Committee [1907] 2 KB 764; R. v. Thomas [1892] 1 QB 426 at 429; Stepney Borough v. Walker & Sons Ltd. [1934] AC 365.
[5] R. v. Thomas [1892] 1 QB 426.
[6] R. v. Paddington Valuation Officer ex p. Peachey Property Corporation Ltd. [1966] 1 QB 380.
[7] R. v. Leicester Guardians [1899] 2 QB 632; see below, p. 749.
[8] R. v. Poplar Borough Council ex p. London County Council (No. 1) [1922] 1 KB 72.
[9] Crown Proceedings Act 1947, s. 40(5).

Statutory protection

Mandamus has been given the same protection as certiorari against statutes passed before 1 August 1958 which purport to exclude the powers of the High Court to question orders or determinations.[10] This provision must be explained later.

The Crown and its servants

It is inherent in the nature of the prerogative remedies that, since they emanate from the Crown, they cannot lie against the Crown itself.

That there can be no mandamus to the Sovereign, there can be no doubt, both because there would be an incongruity in the Queen commanding herself to do an act, and also because disobedience to the writ of mandamus is to be enforced by attachment.[11]

This is no impediment in the case of certiorari and prohibition, since they lie to control inferior jurisdictions and they apply to all the ministers of the Crown and other public authorities upon whom powers are conferred by Parliament in their own names. But it is serious in the case of mandamus, since the Crown itself has public duties. How is their performance to be enforced?

There is a clear distinction as to the duties of Crown servants. Where the Crown servant is merely the instrument selected by the Crown for the discharge of the Crown's duty, any complaint of default must be made against the Crown and not against the servant. No mandamus can then lie. For example, an army officer disputed the terms of his retiring pay and compensation, which had to be determined under the terms of a royal warrant (a prerogative instrument making regulations as to terms of service in the army), and sought a mandamus against the Secretary of State for War in order to enforce what he thought were his rights under the royal warrant. In fact the royal warrant imposed no legal obligation on the Crown. But even if it did, the action could not succeed, since the Secretary of State was merely one of the Crown's servants who owed no legal duty as such to any individual affected by the warrant.[12] Similarly no mandamus will issue to the Treasury to pay moneys appropriated by Parliament for a given purpose, since the money is granted to the Crown, and even though it is in the hands of the Treasury, they are merely the instrument of the Crown for handling the money.[13]

---

[10] Tribunals and Inquiries Act 1971, s. 14; below, p. 729.
[11] R. v. Powell (1841) 1 QB 352 at 361.
[12] R. v. Secretary of State for War [1891] 2 QB 326.
[13] R. v. Lords Commissioners of the Treasury (1872) LR 7 QB 387.

On the other hand, where Parliament has imposed a duty on particular persons acting in some particular capacity, mandamus will issue notwithstanding that those persons are servants of the Crown and acting on the Crown's behalf. This is because the legal duty is cast upon them personally, and no orders given to them by the Crown will be any defence. If therefore the Act requires 'the Minister' to do something, mandamus will lie to compel the minister to act.[14] Similarly mandamus was granted against the Special Commissioners of Income Tax, acting as servants of the Crown, commanding them to authorise repayment to a taxpayer where the Act said that 'the . . . Commissioners shall issue an order for the repayment, etc.'.[15] Although the Crown Proceedings Act 1947 prevents the grant of a mandatory injunction in such cases, it does nothing to impede the use of mandamus as in the past.[16]

Nevertheless it should make no difference in principle whether the duty is cast upon the Crown as such or upon some government department or other agency of the Crown. It is a pity that this untidy situation was left unaltered by the Crown Proceedings Act 1947, which in other respects put the Crown effectively onto the same footing as a private person. Logically the Act ought to have empowered the court to make a declaratory order against the Crown in lieu of mandamus. There would seem to be no reason why the court should not itself fill this lacuna by exercising its ordinary jurisdiction to grant declaratory relief, for it is established that this jurisdiction is effective against the Crown.[17] The reason why the question has not arisen is probably that the statutory duties of the Crown, as opposed to those of specific ministers and government departments, are very few. If they were numerous and important, some remedy for their enforcement would be indispensable.

The Privy Council have suggested another solution to this problem of royal immunity, saying that mandamus could be awarded against cabinet ministers requiring them to advise the Crown to perform its duty. This was in the context of the proclamation of a security area in Malaysia which the Crown had power to revoke and also, according to the Privy Council, a duty to revoke if its continuance could no longer be considered necessary, i.e. if failure to revoke it would be an abuse of

[14] As in *Padfield* v. *Minister of Agriculture Fisheries and Food* [1968] AC 997; *R.* v. *Home Secretary ex p. Phansopkar* [1976] QB 606. In the case of 'the Secretary of State' the mandamus will evidently issue to the person responsible in practice. For doubts suggested by the *Town Investment* case see above, p. 52.

[15] *R.* v. *Special Commissioners of Income Tax* (1888) 21 QBD 313. See similarly *R.* v. *Special Commissioners of Income Tax ex p. Dr. Barnardo's Homes* [1920] 1 KB 26; *R.* v. *Commissioners of Customs and Excise ex p. Cook* [1970] 1 WLR 450 at 455.

[16] See below, p. 825.

[17] Above, p. 597.

discretion.[18] But the facts of the case provided no occasion for applying this interesting theory.

The Crown or a government department may itself be granted mandamus, for example for compelling a local authority to levy a rate to finance a payment due to the Treasury.[19]

Procedure

Mandamus must be sought by 'application for judicial review' in the same way as certiorari and prohibition, as described in the next chapter. Leave to apply for the order must therefore be obtained *ex parte* before the application itself can be heard, and evidence is normally taken by affidavit. Undue delay is a ground for withholding the remedy in discretion, subject to the same qualifications as regards hardship, prejudice to rights, and detriment to good administration as apply in the case of certiorari and prohibition.[20] No action may be instituted against anyone in respect of anything done in obedience to a mandamus.[21] Disobedience to a mandamus is punishable as a contempt of court, by fine or imprisonment.[22] Without prejudice to its power to punish disobedience as contempt, the court may direct that the default be made good by the party who obtained the mandamus at the cost of the disobedient party.[23]

[18] *Teh Cheng Poh v. Public Prosecutor* [1980] AC 458. The Constitution of Malaysia (Art. 40) requires the Yang di-Pertuan Agong to act in accordance with ministerial advice in most matters.

[19] *R. v. Maidenhead Cpn.* (1882) 9 QBD 494.

[20] O. 53 r. 4.

[21] O. 53 r. 10.

[22] *R. v. Poplar Borough Council ex p. London County Council* (No. 2) [1922] 1 KB 95; above, p. 650. In the case of a corporation, which cannot be imprisoned, the members responsible should be named in the writs of attachment; but in the *Poplar* case this requirement was held to be waived by members who appeared and persisted in disobedience.

18

THE NEW PROCEDURAL SYSTEM

DEFECTS OF PREROGATIVE REMEDIES

Procedural peculiarities

For a long time the prerogative remedies as a body suffered from hereditary procedural defects. They had escaped the radical reforms of the nineteenth century in which the old forms of action, with their exclusive character and their multifarious peculiarities, were swept away. The prerogative remedies were left on one side, so that they remained as isolated survivors from the old era. They thus retained their own special procedure, which was of a summary and limited character and could not be combined with applications for other remedies. Before 1933 the applicant had to 'obtain a rule', i.e. an order of the court calling upon the other party to show cause why the prerogative writ should not issue; if this was done successfully at the hearing, the rule was discharged, otherwise it was made absolute and the remedy was granted.

In 1933 a new system was introduced[1] for certiorari, prohibition and mandamus which required a motion to be made to the High Court asking for leave to apply for the remedy. The motion was made ex parte, i.e. without notice to the respondent public authority. Refusal was subject to appeal, and the Court of Appeal might then dispose of the whole case itself.[2] The rules of court prescribed a time-limit of six months for seeking certiorari, though the court had discretion to extend it.[3] And even within this time limit the remedy might be refused if the applicant had been guilty of delay and so caused hardship to the other party.[4] In 1938 formalities were simplified by replacing the 'writs' of certiorari, prohibition and mandamus by 'orders' of similar title and scope.[5]

---

[1] Administration of Justice (Miscellaneous Provisions) Act 1933, s. 5.

[2] *R. v. Industrial Injuries Commissioner ex p. Amalgamated Engineering Union* [1966] 2 QB 21.

[3] RSC 1965, O. 3 r. 5. There is also a wide inherent jurisdiction to extend time limits: *R. v. Bloomsbury County Court ex p. Villerwest Ltd.* [1976] 1 WLR 362. The time limit derived historically from an Act of 1740 (13 Geo 2, c. 18, s. 5) which provided that no certiorari should issue for the removal of orders of justices after six months. The court had no discretion to extend this time: *R. v. Anglesea Justices* (1846) 10 Jur 817. For a discussion of the Act see *R. v. Tillett ex p. Newton* (1969) 14 FLR 101. It was repealed by the Statute Law Revision Act 1888.

[4] See below, p. 709.

[5] Administration of Justice (Miscellaneous Provisions) Act 1938, s. 7, replaced by Supreme Court Act 1981, s. 29.

None of these changes cured the two major deficiencies. The first of these was the procedural incompatibility which made it impossible to seek certiorari and a declaration (for example) in one proceeding.[6] The second deficiency was the lack of interlocutory facilities: prerogative remedy procedure made no provision for obtaining discovery of relevant documents by the other side[7] or for serving interrogatories, which were normal facilities in an ordinary action and were therefore available in ordinary proceedings for injunctions or declarations. These incongruities were unjustifiable survivals, especially when judicial review was developing so rapidly after about 1960.

A feature of prerogative remedy procedure which remains unaltered is that evidence is taken on affidavit, i.e. by sworn statements in writing rather than orally. It is possible, but exceptional, for the court to allow cross-examination on the affidavits.[8] The court's only means of deciding disputed issues of fact in the normal manner is to direct a special issue to be tried; but that is a roundabout procedure, and the court may dismiss the application rather than resort to it. If the case turns upon a conflict of evidence,[9] certiorari and prohibition may therefore involve difficulties. It was said of them[10] that they

afford speedy and effective remedy to a person aggrieved by a clear excess of jurisdiction by an inferior tribunal. But they are not designed to raise issues of fact for the High Court to determine de novo . . . Where the question of jurisdiction turns solely on a disputed point of law, it is obviously convenient that the court should determine it there and then. But where the dispute turns on a question of fact, about which there is a conflict of evidence, the court will generally decline to interfere.

The Crown has a privileged position for obtaining its own prerogative remedies. Where the Attorney-General applies for certiorari on the Crown's behalf, he does not require leave to apply, and there is no time

---

[6] For attempts to mitigate this by allowing amendment of the proceedings see *Metropolitan Properties Ltd.* v. *Lannon* [1968] 1 WLR 815, reversed [1969] 1 QB 577; *Chapman* v. *Earl* [1968] 1 WLR 1315.

[7] *Barnard* v. *National Dock Labour Board* [1953] 2 QB 18 at 43 (Denning LJ). Under RSC 1965, O. 24 r. 3, the court may order discovery in any cause or matter. But in practice there was no discovery in prerogative order procedure.

[8] When this was allowed for special reasons in *R.* v. *Stokesley, Yorkshire, Justices ex p. Bartram* [1956] 1 WLR 254 Lord Goddard CJ said that it was probably 'the first case in recent history,' and that no one knew of a precedent. See also *George* v. *Secretary of State for the Environment* (1979) 77 LGR 689.

[9] As it may well do in a case of jurisdictional fact or breach of natural justice.

[10] *R.* v. *Fulham & c. Rent Tribunal ex p. Zerek* [1951] 2 KB 1 at 11 (Devlin J). See likewise *R.* v. *Pugh (Judge)* [1951] 2 KB 623; above, p. 291.

limit.[11] But the court retains all its normal control over the merits of the case.[12] Likewise the Crown may obtain prohibition in case of an excess of jurisdiction, even though the party affected cannot do so because his conduct has disentitled him to the remedy.[13]

Certiorari versus declaratory judgment

One result of these procedural handicaps and incompatibilities was that a kind of rivalry developed between certiorari (and prohibition) on the one hand and the declaratory judgment on the other. This is worth brief notice because it formed the background to the subsequent reforms.

The story goes back about thirty years, to a time when it seemed that certiorari and prohibition might almost be put out of business by the rapidly developing remedy of declaration, aided where necessary by injunction. In legal history a shift of this kind from inferior to superior remedies is a familiar method of progress. In the United States declarations and injunctions have taken the place of certiorari to quash in federal administrative law for over sixty years. In 1913 the Supreme Court fell into profound confusion over the question what was a 'judicial' function—just the same question which plagued the English courts until half a century later[14]—and so destroyed the utility of certiorari.[15] There have been signs that a similar change might take place in England, where likewise the evolution of remedies is governed by the survival of the fittest.

The advantages of the declaration were brought into prominence in 1953 in *Barnard* v. *National Dock Labour Board*.[16] Dock workers in London had been dismissed for refusing to operate a new system for the unloading of raw sugar, and began actions for declarations that their dismissal was illegal. When they obtained discovery of documents they found that the vital order had been made not by the local board but by the port manager, who had no power to make it. Thus they won their case. But had they

---

[11] *R.* v. *Amendt* [1915] 2 KB 276; *Re Application for Certiorari* [1965] NI 67. The Act of 1740 (above, p. 665) did not bind the Crown, and presumably the Supreme Court Act 1981 (below, p. 675) does not do so either.

[12] *R.* v. *Amendt* (above).

[13] *Board* v. *Perkins* (1888) 21 QBD 533 at 535.

[14] Above, p. 634.

[15] *Degge* v. *Hitchcock*, 229 US 162 (1913). Professor Jaffe of Harvard has commented: 'One can only wonder whether so grossly flagrant a misreading of history was deliberate.' And he calls the case 'reminiscent of recent English decisions': [1956] *Public Law*, 230. The confusion spread to many State courts, some of which circumvented it by allowing mandamus to be used in place of certiorari—a remedy which became known as 'certiorarified mandamus'. See above, p. 659.

[16] [1953] 2 QB 18.

applied for certiorari they would probably have been unable to discover the irregularity[17] and they would have been out of time, more than six months having expired. The Court of Appeal observed that certiorari was 'hedged round by limitations' and that it was right to grant declarations and injunctions in order to prevent statutory tribunals from disregarding the law.

This policy of encouraging litigants to circumvent the limitations of certiorari was twice approved by the House of Lords in later cases. One concerned a dock worker who had been invalidly dismissed, to whom the House granted a declaration which had been refused by the Court of Appeal.[18] In the other case the question was whether planning permission was needed for quarrying operations in the Malvern Hills, and, if so, whether conditions imposed by the minister were valid.[19] The time limit for certiorari had expired and the quarrying company asked instead for declarations as to its rights. These were granted by the House of Lords, and the minister's argument that the right remedy, if any, was certiorari was rejected on the ground that the two remedies are in no way mutually exclusive.

But then it was found that the declaration had its own deficiencies. It lacked the 'public' character of the prerogative remedies, so that it might be refused to a plaintiff on the ground that he had not the necessary personal standing. It also had the serious (at that time) weakness that it was useless in cases of error on the face of the record. It began to be realised that the prerogative remedies represented the nucleus of a system of public law, operating in the name of the Crown, whose importance might be as great in the future as it had been in the past. Two contrasting statements by Lord Denning will illustrate the swing of opinion. In 1949 he said in a public lecture:[20]

Just as the pick and shovel is no longer suitable for the winning of coal, so the procedure of mandamus, certiorari and actions on the case are not suitable for the winning of freedom in the new age. They must be replaced by new and up-to-date machinery, by declarations, injunctions and actions for negligence. . . . The courts must do this. Of all the great tasks that lie ahead, this is the greatest.

But in 1959 he said judicially:[21]

There is nothing more important, to my mind, than that the vast number of tribunals now in being should be subject to the supervision of the Queen's courts.

[17] This was true also of *Anisminic Ltd.* v. *Foreign Compensation Commission* [1969] 2 AC 147 as related by Lord Diplock in *O'Reilly* v. *Mackman* [1983] 2 AC 237 at 278.
[18] *Vine* v. *National Dock Labour Board* [1957] AC 488.
[19] *Pyx Granite Co. Ltd.* v. *Ministry of Housing and Local Government* [1960] AC 260.
[20] *Freedom under the Law*, 126.
[21] *Baldwin & Francis Ltd.* v. *Patents Appeal Tribunal* [1959] AC 663 at 697.

This can only be done if the remedy by certiorari is maintained in the full scope which the great judges of the past gave to it. . . . this historic remedy has still a valuable part to play: or at any rate, it should have, if we wish any longer to ensure that the rights of the people are determined according to law.

The solution, then, was evidently to be found by preserving all the various remedies but making them interchangeable under a unified system of procedure, the 'application for judicial review'.

THE REFORMS OF 1977–1981

Proposals and reforms

By about 1970 it had become obvious that the dilemmas and anomalies which disfigured the law of remedies could be eliminated by simple procedural reforms under which the virtues of each separate remedy could be preserved. The pioneering measures were enacted in Ontario in 1971[22] and in New Zealand in 1972.[23] Their central feature was to provide for a single form of application to the court under which the court might award any one or more of the remedies of certiorari, prohibition, mandamus, declaration or injunction. There was supplementary provision for a uniform interlocutory process by which discovery of documents, interrogatories, etc., were available, regardless of the remedies sought. Later legislation has gone still further: the Administrative Decisions (Judicial Review) Act 1977 of Australia not only provided these procedural facilities but also enumerated the grounds of judicial review and strengthened it in various ways.[24]

For England the Law Commission in 1971 tentatively proposed a much more drastic plan.[25] Here again there was to be a new remedy called 'application for review', under which the court could award any of the remedies of private or public law and which would have full procedural facilities. But this was to be 'an exclusive remedy not only where an administrative act or order is challenged directly, but also where it is challenged collaterally in an action for tort or contract and in other cases which essentially involve the exercise of public powers'. To establish an exclusive remedy for the purposes of administrative law would have required a statutory definition of its scope, probably in terms of the bodies

---

[22] Judicial Review Procedure Act 1971. This was recommended by a Royal Commission (the McRuer Commission) whose report (5 vols., 1968–71) resulted also in the Statutory Powers Procedure Act 1971 and the Public Inquiries Act 1971.

[23] Judicature Amendment Act 1972.

[24] Compare also the Administrative Law Act 1979 of Victoria.

[25] Remedies in Administrative Law (published working paper no. 40, 1971).

against which it would lie. Any such definition would certainly have been imperfect, and would probably have presented litigants with more problems than before. It was criticised[26] for aiming to create a dichotomy between public and private law, despite the fact that in the British system these are closely interlocked. Any attempt to unscramble them would have run counter to the whole trend of modern procedural development, as it has evolved since the first Common Law Procedure Act of 1852. The policy has been, and should always be, to eliminate exclusive forms of action, since clear and simple dividing lines are usually impossible to draw, with the inevitable risk of good cases being lost by choice of the wrong procedure. In comparison with the simple and effective law reforms made in Ontario and New Zealand, the proposals seemed over-elaborate and in some ways retrogressive.

In 1976, however, the Law Commission put forward a much simpler and less problematical scheme,[27] basically similar to the Ontario and New Zealand reforms. All proposals for exclusive remedies were dropped—and, ironically, no one foresaw that the House of Lords would later enforce the very policy that the Law Commission for good reason abandoned. It was recommended simply that by an 'application for judicial review', made in accordance with rules of court, an applicant might seek any one or more of the five remedies of mandamus, certiorari, prohibition, declaration or injunction. This and accompanying proposals as to interlocutory procedure and other matters were incorporated in a draft Bill, but it proved possible to put them into effect without an Act of Parliament, since changes in 'practice and procedure' can be made by the Rule Committee of the Supreme Court. The Commission's Bill accordingly provided the basis of the rules of court adopted in 1977, some of which have since been incorporated in the Supreme Court Act 1981. Analogous reforms were made in Scotland in 1985.[28]

The reforms of 1977 were effected by radical amendment of Order 53 of the Rules of the Supreme Court.[29] The Act of 1981 gave statutory force to a number of the primary provisions, so removing any doubt that they might

---

[26] By the author in an unpublished memorandum of December 1971, expressing fears which were largely fulfilled by *O'Reilly* v. *Mackman* (below).

[27] Report on Remedies in Administrative Law (Law Com. No. 73), 1976, Cmnd. 6407.

[28] Act of Sederunt (Rules of Court Amendment No. 2) (Judicial Review) 1985, SI No. 500, requiring 'application for judicial review' to be used in any application for 'the supervisory jurisdiction of the court', thus establishing an exclusive procedure. See *The Laws of Scotland* (Stair Memorial Encyclopedia) vol. i, para. 345; [1987] PL 313 (A. W. Bradley). The Encyclopedia contains a valuable account of administrative law in Scotland by Professor Bradley.

[29] SI 1977 No. 1955. For a statistical survey and comment on the new procedure see (1987) 50 MLR 432 (M. Sunkin).

have been beyond the powers of the Rule Committee. Except where thus replaced by the Act, Order 53 remains in force.

Application for judicial review

The basis of the reformed procedure is laid down in section 31 of the Supreme Court Act 1981 in the two following subsections.

(1) An application to the High Court for one or more of the following forms of relief, namely—

(a) an order of mandamus, prohibition or certiorari;

(b) a declaration or injunction under subsection (2); or

(c) an injunction under section 30 restraining a person not entitled to do so from acting in an office to which that section applies,[30]

shall be made in accordance with rules of court by a procedure to be known as an application for judicial review.

(2) A declaration may be made or an injunction granted under this subsection in any case where an application for judicial review, seeking that relief, has been made and the High Court considers that, having regard to—

(a) the nature of the matters in respect of which relief may be granted by orders of mandamus, prohibition or certiorari;

(b) the nature of the persons and bodies against whom relief may be granted by such orders; and

(c) all the circumstances of the case,

it would be just and convenient for the declaration to be made or the injunction to be granted, as the case may be.

The object of the 'having regard' provisions is to confine the new procedure to the sphere of judicial review, i.e. the control of governmental powers and duties. That is the sphere within which the prerogative remedies themselves operate. It must be remembered that application for judicial review is not itself a remedy, but is a procedure for seeking one or more of the long-established remedies, which still have their own limits. It follows that the scope of judicial review is still determined by the rules which govern the various remedies rather than by the procedure for obtaining them. 'The purpose of section 31 is to regulate procedure in relation to judicial review, not to extend the jurisdiction of the court.'[31] It

---

[30] For this see above, p. 591.

[31] *Law* v. *National Greyhound Racing Club Ltd.* [1983] 1 WLR 1302 (Lawton LJ); and see *R.* v. *Inland Revenue Commissioners ex parte National Federation of Self-Employed and Small Businesses Ltd.* [1982] AC 617 at 639, 648; *R.* v. *British Broadcasting Corporation ex p. Lavelle* [1983] 1 WLR 23; *Davy* v. *Spelthorne BC* [1984] AC 262 at 278.

would be just as unsuitable, for example, to apply for judicial review in seeking an injunction against a tort of breach or contract by a public authority as it would be to seek prohibition for the same purpose.

All the remedies mentioned are made interchangeable by being made available 'as an alternative or in addition' to any of them.[32] In addition, the court may award damages if they are claimed in the application and if they could have been awarded in an action at the same time.[33] But neither declaration nor injunction nor damages can be claimed unless one of the prerogative remedies could have been sought.[34] Even where no prerogative remedy is sought, the application is usually entitled in the name of the Queen.[35]

Uniform interlocutory facilities are made available, extending to discovery of documents, interrogatories, and cross-examination.[36] In fact it is still exceptional for these facilities to be allowed, and in most cases evidence continues to be taken by affidavit only.[37] Judges still regard the procedure of judicial review as unsuitable for trying questions of fact.[38] Lord Diplock has argued, though not very convincingly,[39] that facts can seldom be a matter of relevant dispute in an application for judicial review; but at the same time he held that cross-examination on affidavits should be allowed whenever the justice of the case so requires.[40] Questions of fact may easily be crucial, for example where the case turns on jurisdictional fact or (as Lord Diplock recognised) procedural error or violation of natural justice. The law will be very defective if there is no proper procedure for trying such issues.

Where prohibition or certiorari are sought, the court may direct a stay of the challenged proceedings, and where other remedies are sought it may

---

[32] O. 53 r. 2.

[33] Supreme Court Act 1981, s. 31(4).

[34] *Davy* v. *Spelthorne BC* (above) at 277–8.

[35] As in *R.* v. *London Transport Executive ex p. Greater London Council* [1983] QB 484. Contrast *Chief Constable of North Wales* v. *Evans* [1982] 1 WLR 1155; *Council of Civil Service Unions* v. *Minister for the Civil Service* [1985] AC 374.

[36] O. 53 r. 8.

[37] See O. 53 rr. 3, 5, 6 and *George* v. *Secretary of State for the Environment* (1979) 77 LGR 689. Discovery was ordered in *R.* v. *Home Secretary ex p. Herbage* (No. 2) [1987] QB 1077. The court may direct the trial of an issue of fact: *Irlam Brick Co.* v. *Warrington BC* [1982] The Times, 5 February.

[38] See *R.* v. *Jenner* [1983] 1 WLR 873.

[39] Lord Diplock argues that the court has only limited power to review findings of fact in accordance with *Edwards* v. *Bairstow* [1956] AC 14. But that case, for which see below, p. 941, was concerned with appeal, not review. Review used to be limited as described above, p. 292. But one objective of the 1977 reforms was to remove those limitations by providing full facilities for trying disputed facts.

[40] *O'Reilly* v. *Mackman* [1983] 2 AC 237 at 282–3. Cross-examination was allowed in *R.* v. *Waltham Forest LBC ex p. Baxter* [1988] 2 WLR 257.

grant interim relief as in an ordinary action. Beneficial effects have flowed from this provision.[41]

A necessary first step is to obtain the leave of the court,[42] which will be granted only if an arguable case is shown.[43] The application for leave is made ex parte (i.e. without involving the other party), though the court may direct that the other party be notified and adjourn the application for argument inter partes. This application is made normally to a single judge who need not hold a hearing unless requested and need not sit in open court.[44] If refused ex parte the application may be renewed,[45] and it may be further renewed before the Court of Appeal.[46] After a hearing inter partes there is a right of appeal to the Court of Appeal,[47] but not to the House of Lords.[48] If the Court of Appeal grants leave, and does not order otherwise, the substantive application is then made to a Divisional Court.[49]

The requirement of leave, which formerly applied only to the prerogative remedies, has thus been extended to declarations and injunctions when sought for the purpose of judicial review, its justification being that it enables many unmeritorious cases to be disposed of summarily if an arguable case cannot be shown.[50] In principle it seems wrong to impose this special requirement on proceedings against public authorities, who ought not to be treated more favourably than other litigants.[51] It

[41] O. 53 r. 3(10). See R. v. Home Secretary ex p. Herbage [1987] QB 872, noted above, p. 589.

[42] Supreme Court Act 1981, s. 31(3).

[43] See e.g. R. v. Income Tax Special Commissioner ex p. Stipplechoice Ltd. [1985] 2 All ER 465.

[44] O. 53 r. 3, as amended by SI 1980 No. 2000.

[45] SI 1980 No. 2000, para. 2, amending O. 53 r. 3, requiring renewed applications to be made to a single judge or, if the court so directs, to a Divisional Court.

[46] In the Stipplechoice case (above) leave was refused without hearing by Nolan J, refused after hearing by Woolf J, but granted by the Court of Appeal; all these proceedings were ex parte. See also R. v. Home Secretary ex p. Swati [1986] 1 WLR 477.

[47] Supreme Court Act 1981, s. 16. This also applies to ex parte refusals of leave but the right practice then is to renew the application: see WEA Records Ltd. v. Visions Channel 4 Ltd. [1983] 1 WLR 721 at 727. See also R. v. Home Secretary ex p. Turkoglu [1987] 3 WLR 992.

[48] Re Poh [1983] 1 WLR 2; and see Bland v. Chief Supplementary Benefit Officer [1983] 1 WLR 262.

[49] Practice Direction [1982] 1 WLR 1375. Previously the Court of Appeal would normally decide the case, and occasionally it may still do so, as in R. v. Panel on Take-overs and Mergers ex p. Datafin Plc. [1987] QB 815.

[50] See Law Com. No. 73 (as above), para. 37.

[51] In Scotland there is no requirement of leave: see [1987] PL at 315 (A. W. Bradley). In Australia, where there is also no requirement of leave, the Administrative Review Council has concluded that the requirement is wrong for 'sound reasons of both principle and pragmatism': Report No. 26, 1986, para. 66.

would be open to grave objection if the applicant did not enjoy the right of appeal against refusal of leave.[52]

When quashing on certiorari the court may remit the case to the tribunal or deciding body with a direction to decide in accordance with the court's findings.[53] This removes the need for an order of mandamus in addition.

The court may order that an application should proceed as if it were an action begun by writ if it seeks a declaration, injunction or damages and the court considers it ineligible for judicial review but eligible for proceedings by writ.[54] The court may thus transfer the proceedings from the public law to the private law channel, but not vice versa.[55] 'This is an anti-technicality rule',[56] evidently designed for the rescue of misconceived applications if it emerges that the complaint relates to private law rather than public law rights.[57] But in one case it has been held that no order of this kind can be made unless the application also contains an arguable complaint in public law—a pro-technicality conclusion which might often frustrate the purpose of the provision.[58]

Delayed applications

Order 53, as remade in 1977, empowered the court to refuse preliminary leave, and also to refuse any remedy, where there had been undue delay in making the application—but only if, in the court's opinion, granting the remedy would be likely to cause substantial hardship to, or substantially prejudice the rights of, any person or would be detrimental to good administration; and in the case of certiorari three months was equivalent to undue delay. This rule, which seemed likely to present the courts with awkward problems, was replaced in 1980 by a simpler one, which appeared to be an improvement:[59]

---

[52] In the Administration of Justice Bill 1985, clause 43, the government proposed to abolish this right of appeal, but after much protest the clause was dropped. The reports show that many applications succeed on appeal after refusal of leave. See e.g. the *Stipplechoice* case (above), where the court expresses its concern at the Bill of 1985; *R. v. Panel on Take-overs and Mergers ex p. Datafin Plc* (above); *R. v. Stratford-on-Avon DC ex p. Jackson* [1985] 1 WLR 1319.

[53] Supreme Court Act 1981, s. 31(5).

[54] O. 53 r. 9(5). An example is *R. v. British Broadcasting Corporation ex p. Lavelle* [1983] 1 WLR 23. Contrast *R. v. East Berkshire Health Authority ex p. Walsh* [1985] QB 152 (order refused since only certiorari and prohibition were claimed in the application).

[55] See *O'Reilly v. Mackman* [1983] 2 AC 237 at 284.

[56] *R. v. East Berkshire Health Authority ex p. Walsh* [1985] QB 152 at 166 (Sir John Donaldson MR).

[57] See *O'Reilly v. Mackman* (above) at 283–4 (Lord Diplock).

[58] *R. v. Home Secretary ex p. Dew* [1987] 1 WLR 881.

[59] Rule 4, as amended by SI 1980 No. 2000.

An application for judicial review shall be made promptly and in any event within three months from the date when grounds for the application first arose unless the court considers that there is good reason for extending the period within which the application shall be made.

But the existence of this amendment was apparently overlooked when section 31 of the Supreme Court Act 1981 was drafted, since the Act contained the following subsections:

(6) Where the High Court considers that there has been undue delay in making an application for judicial review, the court may refuse to grant—

(a) leave for the making of the application; or

(b) any relief sought on the application,

if it considers that the granting of the relief sought would be likely to cause substantial hardship to, or substantially prejudice the rights of, any person or would be detrimental to good administration.

(7) Subsection (6) is without prejudice to any enactment or rule of court which has the effect of limiting the time within which an application for judicial review may be made.

The rule thus reverted to its less satisfactory 1977 form. But since the amendment of 1980 was not repealed, its three-months time limit (subject to extension) continues to apply by virtue of subsection (7).[60] A proposal to remedy this confusing situation in 1985 unfortunately came to nothing.[61] As they now stand, the Act and the Order do not dovetail together, and they are not well drafted.

Confronted with this tangle, the Court of Appeal has held that 'An application for judicial review' in the Order must mean an application for leave, and not the substantive application, since it makes no sense otherwise; and that even where the court for good reason extends the period, it retains discretion to refuse either leave or the relief sought if it apprehends personal hardship or prejudice or detriment to good administration as mentioned in the Act.[62] Contradictory though this seems, it is the only way in which effect can be given to those provisions of the Act—which ought, in fact, to have been repealed in 1985.

It was held in the same case that even though made within three months

[60] See *R. v. Hillingdon LBC ex p. Thomas* [1987] The Independent, 22 January (five months' delay fatal).

[61] Clause 43 of the Administration of Justice Bill 1985 proposed to repeal the conflicting provisions of the Act. But when the clause was dropped (see n. 52, above), this provision fell with it, though for no evident reason.

[62] *R. v. Stratford-on-Avon DC ex p. Jackson* [1985] 1 WLR 1319 granting extension of time on account of time taken to ask the Secretary of State to call in a planning application and to obtain legal aid.

an application for leave is not necessarily made 'promptly' so as to satisfy the Order.[63] Nor does the grant of leave preclude the later dismissal of the application on account of undue delay.[64]

Standing

The application for leave required by Order 53 was subject to a provision about standing, reproduced in the Act as follows:[65]

the court shall not grant leave to make such an application unless it considers that the applicant has a sufficient interest in the matter to which the application relates.

The Law Commission had recommended this 'sufficient interest' formula in order to allow further development of the law about standing, which they recognised was changing to meet new situations.[66] The wisdom of this advice was shown by the decision of the House of Lords in the *Inland Revenue Commissioners* case, in which the House made use of the new rule to remodel the law radically. That subject must be reserved for later discussion in the context of the whole law about standing.[67]

THE DIVORCE OF PUBLIC AND PRIVATE LAW

An exclusive procedure?

In preparing the ground for the new procedure adopted in 1977 the Law Commission emphasised that they did not intend it to be exclusive. They were clearly of opinion that ordinary actions for a declaration or injunction, as contrasted with applications for prerogative orders, and also public law issues raised collaterally in ordinary actions or criminal proceedings, should remain unaffected.[68] Their object was to remove the procedural disadvantages of the prerogative remedies and to allow declarations and injunctions to be sought along with them, but not to deprive the litigant of the choice of procedures which he had enjoyed previously and which the courts had for several decades encouraged him to exploit to the full.

This policy, however, contained a fatal flaw. Before 1977 there was only one procedure by which any one remedy could be sought. After 1977,

---

[63] As in *R. v. Lewes Magistrates Court ex p. Oldfield* [1987] The Times, 6 May.
[64] *R. v. General Commissioners of Income Tax for Tavistock* (1985) TC leaflet No. 3039.
[65] Supreme Court Act 1981, s. 31(3).
[66] Cmnd. 6407 (1976), para. 48.
[67] Below, p. 700.
[68] Law Com. No. 73 (as above), para. 34.

according to the Law Commission's plan, there would have been two quite different procedures by which declaration and injunction could be sought in the public law field, one under Order 53 and the other by ordinary action. Between these two procedures there were sharp contrasts. The former was subject to obtaining leave of the court and to a very short time limit extendable only at the court's discretion, and its facilities for disputing questions of fact were in practice limited. The latter was free from all these restraints. How then could it make sense to allow a choice of procedures for obtaining the same remedies under which the restrictions of one could simply be evaded by recourse to the other? As soon as judges were confronted with this contradiction they began to hold that they should no longer grant declarations and injunctions in cases falling within Order 53 except in accordance with that Order.[69] They could no longer claim, as they had done before the reforms, that it was reasonable to allow the defects of the ancient prerogative remedies to be evaded by the use of ordinary actions. For those defects had now been remedied, or at least reviewed, and the new procedure had been sanctified by a deliberate act of policy. It was now quite a different matter for the courts to allow its evasion at the litigant's option. This was the reasoning which led to the decision of the House of Lords in *O'Reilly* v. *Mackman*, in which the divorce of public and private law was proclaimed in categorical terms. Judicial review by declaration and injunction in an ordinary action, which the courts had encouraged with great success for many years, was suddenly held to be an abuse of the process of the court. Yet in the changed circumstances, and for the reasons just explained, some such result was probably inevitable.

Under the former law the prerogative remedies had, indeed, represented a separate system of public law since they were confined to the sphere of governmental powers and duties. But that system was not exclusive, and much benefit resulted from the availability of declaratory judgments in ordinary actions begun by writ or originating summons, which the courts in their discretion allowed freely. It was the availability of the alternative procedure of private law for public law purposes which made it unnecessary for the sphere of public law to be rigidly defined. Now, however, it is ordained that public and private law procedures are mutually exclusive; and since the dividing line between them is impossible to draw with certainty, a great deal of fruitless litigation has resulted and will probably continue. The former open frontier has been closed.

The rigid dichotomy which has been imposed, and which must now be

[69] e.g. *Heywood* v. *Hull Prison Visitors* [1980] 1 WLR 1386; *Re Tillmire Common, Heslington* [1982] 2 All ER 615 (originating summons seeking declaration as to error of law by commons registration authority disallowed). Contrast *Steeples* v. *Derbyshire CC* [1985] 1 WLR 256 (decided in 1981), the last reported example of the former procedure.

explained, must be accounted a serious setback for administrative law. It has caused many cases, which on their merits might have succeeded, to fail merely because of choice of the wrong form of action. It is a step back towards the time of the old forms of action which were so deservedly buried in 1852. It has produced great uncertainty, which seems likely to continue, as to the boundary between public and private law, since these terms have no clear or settled meaning. Procedural law, which caused very little difficulty before 1977, is now full of doubts and pitfalls. Nor are these in any way necessary, as may be seen from a comparison with judicial review legislation in Australia, New Zealand and Canada, where exclusive procedures have been avoided. Nor do there appear to be countervailing benefits in the English reforms. The time limit, formerly six months for certiorari only, is reduced to a minimal three months and extended to all the remedies of judicial review. There are the new interlocutory facilities (discovery, interrogatories, cross-examination) but the courts are reluctant to employ them. As will be seen, the House of Lords has expounded the new law as designed for the protection of public authorities rather than of the citizen. Such are the misfortunes which can flow from the best-intentioned reforms.

O'Reilly v. Mackman[70]

The sole issue in this case was whether the court could grant declaratory relief in ordinary actions begun by writ or originating summons at the instance of prisoners disputing the validity of punishments awarded by a board of prison visitors. The plaintiffs were four inmates of Hull prison, who sued (three by writ and one by originating summons) for declarations that the visitors' awards were void for breach of the prison rules and for violation of natural justice. They chose the ordinary forms of action because they expected substantial disputes on questions of fact and wanted to be sure that they could call oral evidence. As the trial judge said, this was clearly a rational choice.[71] The House of Lords held that in view of the new Order 53 the proceedings should be struck out as an abuse of the process of the court;[72] and that the only available procedure in such a case, since it was a matter of public law, was application for judicial review.

---

[70] [1983] 2 AC 237, noted in (1983) 99 LQR 166 and discussed in (1985) 101 LQR 180. In the Court of Appeal Lord Denning MR decided in the same sense as the House of Lords, but Ackner and O'Connor LJJ held that although an ordinary action could not be used to dispute awards of prison visitors, it might be allowed in some other cases at the court's discretion.

[71] [1983] 2 AC at 249 (Peter Pain J).

[72] They were 'blatant attempts to avoid the protections for the defendants for which Order 53 provides' (at 285).

Lord Diplock's speech, in which the whole House concurred summarily, is an outstanding feat of analysis and synthesis, ranging widely over the landmarks of administrative law. Observing that the distinction between private law and public law 'has itself been a latecomer to the English legal system', he attributed its arrival to the expansion of judicial review over the previous thirty years, beginning with the *Northumberland* case,[73] reinforced by the Tribunals and Inquiries Act 1958,[74] and culminating in the *Anisminic* case.[75] He took the opportunity to restate his doctrine of jurisdictional error and to broaden Atkin LJ's *Electricity Commissioners* formula[76] by eliminating the 'duty to act judicially' in accordance with Lord Reid's speech in *Ridge* v. *Baldwin*.[77] He pointed out that *Anisminic* was an action by writ for a declaration where the vital facts had been obtained only upon discovery of documents, so that certiorari would have been useless. In the most striking part of the speech he then presented the restrictions of prerogative remedy procedure, both before and after 1977, as designed to protect public authorities against irresponsible and protracted litigation, emphasising the following:

1. The need to obtain leave to apply.
2. The need to file affidavits from the outset, so that the case has to be stated on oath and with the utmost good faith, 'an important safeguard against groundless or unmeritorious claims', in contrast with the unsworn pleadings of an ordinary action.
3. The court's power on granting leave to impose terms as to costs or security.
4. Very speedy procedure, 'available in urgent cases within a matter of days rather than months'.
5. The time limit, now reduced to three months and extended to all forms of relief.

'The public interest in good administration', Lord Diplock explained, 'requires that public authorities and third parties should not be kept in suspense as to the legal validity of a decision' disputed by a litigant.

The remainder of the speech is concerned with the availability of declaratory relief before and after 1977. Lord Diplock accepted that the disadvantages of prerogative writ procedure, particularly the absolute bar on discovery of documents, justified the use of ordinary actions for declarations before 1977, as the House of Lords had allowed in *Ridge* v. *Baldwin*, *Anisminic* and other cases, even though the safeguards imposed in the public interest were thereby evaded. But those disadvantages had now

---

[73] Above, p. 307.
[74] Below, p. 915.
[75] Below, p. 725.
[76] Above, p. 631.
[77] Above, p. 518.

all been removed by the new Order 53. Discovery of documents, interrogatories and cross-examination were now allowable wherever the justice of the case required, though cross-examination would be needed only on rare occasions, since issues of fact would seldom be crucial because of the court's limited function on review.[78] To allow ordinary actions for public law remedies might subject public authorities to lengthy delays which would defeat the policy of the reforms and the interests of good administration. To do so, therefore, was as a general rule contrary to public policy and an abuse of the process of the court. There might be exceptions, such as collateral pleas of public law issues in private law litigation, or cases where none of the parties objected to ordinary procedure. But the classes of cases where the new procedure was mandatory, and any further exceptions, should be left for future decision on a case-to-case basis.

The need for a single procedure

It is undoubtedly right that public authorities should not be harassed by vexatious legal procedures and that disputes about their powers and duties should be settled expeditiously. But it is questionable whether the logic of *O'Reilly* v. *Mackman* is as compelling as Lord Diplock maintains. For several decades before 1977 the courts were actively encouraging ordinary actions for declarations in order to evade the handicaps of certiorari, yet it did not appear that public authorities were lacking any protection which they could properly claim. In the case of baseless actions they could, like other litigants, apply for pleadings to be struck out, and they often did so. Points of law could be tried as preliminary issues, often saving trial of the facts. Public authorities did not appear to feel the need of the procedural privileges on which the House of Lords laid such stress. The Public Authorities Protection Act had been repealed in 1954[79] with general approval. Despite some incongruities, public and private law worked harmoniously together without any need for exclusive forms of action, and the system of remedies efficiently supported the great expansion of administrative law during those years.

The last decade, on the other hand, has been one of unprofitable litigation about which of two exclusive procedures a litigant should use. The decisions are summarised below and they show that plenty of problems remain. The need for law reform is clearly greater now than it was before 1977. The first necessity is to abandon mutually exclusive procedures and institute a single comprehensive procedure, which ought to be the ordinary procedure of private law. Instead of putting declaration and

---

[78] For criticism see above, p. 672.
[79] See below, p. 786.

injunction into the group of the prerogative remedies, as was in effect done in 1977, the prerogative remedies ought to be grouped, for procedural purposes, with ordinary remedies. If it is really thought necessary to give special privileges to public authorities,[80] it could be provided that on any question of excess or abuse of their powers or neglect of their duties they could apply for expedited procedure, sworn statements, and dismissal of the claim on the ground of undue delay. If judicial review and other relief were both sought in one action, the various claims could be sorted out and directed into the right channels at the interlocutory stage. Cases of judicial review should still have a prerogative-style title with the Queen as the nominal plaintiff, in order to preserve the important public interest element. No case could then be lost by choice of the wrong procedure before it ever came before the court. The law would no longer be disfigured by the primitive feature of rigidly exclusive forms of action, and it would then again be worthy of the twentieth century.

Problems of dichotomy

As soon as O'Reilly v. Mackman was decided the courts had to undertake surgical operations in order to sever public from private law.[81] Never having had to do this previously, and now being called upon to do it with precision, they naturally encountered difficulty.

Their work made a mystifying start in a decision of the House of Lords delivered on the same day as O'Reilly v. Mackman and co-ordinated with that case.[82] Proceedings had been started in the county court for a declaration that a district council was in breach of its duty to provide permanent accommodation for the plaintiff under the Housing (Homeless Persons) Act 1977.[83] He found himself taken to the House of Lords on the preliminary issue whether he should have sought judicial review in the High Court. The House of Lords held that there was now 'a dichotomy between a housing authority's public and private law functions': their decision[84] whether they were satisfied that the plaintiff fulfilled the statutory conditions was a matter of public law, but their obligation to provide housing, if so satisfied, was a matter of private law enforceable by

---

[80] 'We are in danger of creating an incomplete system of "public law" which operates more as a shield for public authorities than as a protection for the rights of individuals': [1984] PL 46 at 68 (A. Lester QC).

[81] For discussion see (1987) 103 LQR 34 (J. Beatson); [1985] CLJ 415 (C. F. Forsyth).

[82] Cocks v. Thanet DC [1983] 2 AC 286. See comment in (1983) 99 LQR at 169 and [1984] PL at 20 (P. Cane).

[83] Now Part III of the Housing Act 1985.

[84] For such 'decisions' see above, p. 638.

injunction and damages. Since the plaintiff was challenging the decision of the housing authority, he could proceed only by judicial review in accordance with *O'Reilly* v. *Mackman*. The difficulty in this case is to understand how a single statutory duty (to provide housing in certain circumstances) can be dichotomised into both public and private law. A duty of that kind has always previously been enforceable by mandamus, which is now available only by way of judicial review. But it is also enforceable by an action for damages,[85] which is now held to be a matter of private law.[86] It is therefore not so much the duty as the procedures for enforcing it that are dichotomised. Nor is it clear why the whole proceeding in such a case should not belong to public law, since a claim to damages is allowed to be joined with an application for judicial review,[87] and the public character of the duty is obvious.

Another such case was similarly resolved by the Court of Appeal when a candidate in a local government election sued to enforce the local authority's statutory duty to provide him with a room for an election meeting. The local authority claimed that he should have applied for judicial review, but it was held to be a matter of private law suitable for an action by writ claiming a declaration and injunction.[88] Here again the duty was clearly of a public character and the natural remedy would previously have been mandamus, for which a mandatory injunction is evidently now to be substituted.

The difficulty of dividing public and private law cleanly is illustrated by another case where the House of Lords gave a variety of different reasons for allowing an action by writ for a declaration to be brought against a government department. The department had issued a circular to local health authorities to the effect that doctors could in some circumstances give contraceptive advice and treatment to girls under 16 without parental consent. Mrs Gillick, a mother of five young girls, sued by writ for a declaration that to act on this advice would infringe her parental rights. Her claim failed on the merits, but the House of Lords approved the procedure used.[89] Of the various reasons given[90] the simplest was that the defendants raised no objection—an exception expressly recognised in *O'Reilly* v.

---

[85] See below, p. 774.
[86] See below, p. 684.
[87] Supreme Court Act 1981, s. 31(4).
[88] *Ettridge* v. *Morrell* [1986] The Times, 5 May.
[89] *Gillick* v. *West Norfolk and Wisbech Area Health Authority* [1986] AC 112. The effective defendant was the Department of Health and Social Security. For comment see (1986) 102 LQR 173. On the question whether the scope of judicial review has been extended to include such cases see above, p. 597.
[90] Others were that it was a pre-*O'Reilly* case (Lord Fraser, *contra* Lord Scarman) and that it was a collateral issue (Lord Scarman).

Mackman,[91] presumably on the ground that if a public authority chooses to waive its procedural privileges, the logic of that decision no longer applies. Another reason, put forward by Lord Scarman, was that 'the private law content of her claim was so great as to make her case an exception to the general rule': and, abandoning the mutual exclusivity of *O'Reilly*, he held that she was entitled to proceed either by ordinary action or by judicial review. It might, indeed, be expected that she could bring an ordinary action for a declaration as to her personal legal rights without being caught in the *O'Reilly* entanglement, as has for so long been allowed in classic cases such as *Dyson*[92] and *Pyx Granite*.[93] No mention was made of those authorities in the *Gillick* case and it is not clear how they now stand.[94] But it does seem that the House of Lords is avoiding a collision course and is disinclined to press the logic of *O'Reilly* to its limit.

The evils of rigid demarcation were aptly observed by Lord Wilberforce two years earlier:[95]

The expressions 'private law' and 'public law' have recently been imported into the law of England from countries which, unlike our own, have separate systems concerning public law and private law. In this country they must be used with caution, for, typically, English law fastens, not upon principles but upon remedies. . . . Before the expression 'public law' can be used to deny a subject a right of action in the court of his choice it must be related to a positive prescription of law, by statute or by statutory rules. We have not yet reached the point at which mere characterisation of a claim as a claim in public law is sufficient to exclude it from consideration by the ordinary courts: to permit this would be to create a dual system of law with the rigidity and procedural hardship for plaintiffs which it was the purpose of the recent reforms to remove.

Since that, in fact, was what was in effect permitted in *O'Reilly* v. *Mackman* and other cases here discussed, Lord Wilberforce's words have a hollow ring. But Mrs Gillick's case suggests that they might yet be heeded.

Tort, contract, employment and offices

Claims to remedies for tort or breach of contract are based on the infringement of private law rights and are in principle ineligible for judicial

---

[91] [1983] 2 AC at 285. This may also explain *R.* v. *Doncaster MBC ex p. Braim* [1986] 85 LGR 233 (declaration that land was statutory 'open space' granted on judicial review).

[92] *Dyson* v. *Attorney-General* [1911] 1 KB 410 (above, p. 595).

[93] *Pyx Granite Co. Ltd.* v. *Ministry of Housing and Local Government* [1960] AC 260 (above, p. 596).

[94] Perhaps *Dyson* would now require judicial review since the validity of a departmental demand was challenged but *Pyx Granite* would not since no administrative action was disputed. On the latter point see *O'Reilly* at 281. See also *R.* v. *Bromley LBC ex p. Lambeth LBC* [1984] The Times, 16 June (declaration that local authorities might lawfully subscribe to association of London authorities granted on judicial review).

[95] *Davy* v. *Spelthorne BC* [1984] AC 262 at 278.

review, even though brought against public authorities. An action for damages for negligence, for example, must be brought against a public authority by the same procedure as against a private defendant. The House of Lords made this clear in a planning case where the plaintiff sued by writ for damages for negligent official advice which had prevented him from appealing in time against an enforcement notice, and also claimed, in the alternative, an injunction against its enforcement and an order to set it aside on the ground that it was invalid. It was held that the first claim could proceed but that the second and third claims must be struck out, since they could be raised only by judicial review.[96] The claim to damages raised no issue of public law since it assumed the validity of the enforcement notices, whereas the other claims impugned it. A litigant wishing to pursue alternative claims is thus compelled by the dichotomy to institute different proceedings and to face resultant complications. It is hard to understand how such a system can be tolerable.

Despite the House of Lords' ruling, the High Court later dismissed as an abuse of process an action for damages and breach of statutory duty brought against a local authority for alleged failure to make proper provision for a child in their care. Since it was claimed that the degree of negligence was such as to render their conduct ultra vires,[97] this was held to be 'a substantial public law element' which made judicial review the only available procedure, even though public and private law rights were intermingled.[98] If this decision is right, litigants are faced with even more insoluble dilemmas.

Contracts of employment are held to be enforceable by ordinary action and not by judicial review. An employee of the BBC failed in her application for certiorari to quash her dismissal by the Corporation since the ordinary obligations of master and servant had never been within the scope of the prerogative remedies, which had not been extended by Order 53 and the Supreme Court Act 1981.[99] The Court of Appeal

[96] *Davy* v. *Spelthorne BC* [1984] AC 262. See also *An Bord Bainne Co-operative Ltd.* v. *Milk Marketing Board* [1984] 2 CMLR 584 where the Court of Appeal held that an action for damages and an injunction against the Board for price discrimination contrary to EEC law was properly brought by ordinary action rather than by judicial review; *Garden Cottage Foods Ltd.* v. *Milk Marketing Board* [1984] AC 130 at 144, where the House of Lords ruled similarly; and *Bourgoin SA* v. *Ministry of Agriculture, Fisheries and Food* [1986] QB 716 (dicta in Court of Appeal). See also *Shears Court (West Mersey) Management Co. Ltd.* v. *Essex CC* (1986) 85 LGR 479 (landowner can sue in trespass to contest county council's determination as to public right of way).

[97] For this point see below, p. 765.

[98] *Guevara* v. *Hounslow LBC* [1987] The Times, 17 April. In general wardship proceedings are preferable in the case of children in care: *R.* v. *Newham LBC ex p. McL.* [1987] The Times, 25 July.

[99] *R.* v. *British Broadcasting Corporation ex p. Lavelle* [1983] 1 WLR 23 (decided before *O'Reilly* v. *Mackman*). Leave to continue as if by writ was granted.

similarly rejected an application for certiorari to quash the dismissal of a male nurse by a health authority.[1] The Master of the Rolls said that 'employment by a public authority does not *per se* inject any element of public law'. It could be different if there were statutory 'underpinning' of the employment such as statutory restrictions on dismissal, which would support a claim of ultra vires, or a statutory duty to incorporate certain conditions in the terms of employment, which could be enforced by mandamus. A sufficient 'statutory underpinning' was found immediately afterwards in a case where the Home Secretary's decision to dismiss a prison officer was quashed for violation of natural justice.[2] Unlike the male nurse, he was not under a contract of employment but was appointed to an office and subject to a statutory code of discipline which had not been fairly applied. His dismissal was therefore ultra vires, and judicial review was the right way to contest it.

Private law also regulates associations and bodies whose relations with their members are governed by contract, however powerful their licensing and disciplinary powers may in fact be. Where a greyhound trainer disputed the suspension of his trainer's licence and sued by originating summons for declarations, the national association's objection that he should have proceeded by judicial review was disallowed by the Court of Appeal, which emphasised that the new rules did not extend public law remedies to private law relationships.[3] The same is presumably true in the case of trade unions.[4] But where disciplinary powers are statutory, judicial review now seems to be favoured, even in the case of professional associations which, being outside the sphere of government, were formerly outside the scope of the prerogative remedies.[5] A possible reason for this change may be that, in the uncertainty created by *O'Reilly* v. *Mackman*, it is

---

[1] R. v. *East Berkshire Health Authority ex p. Walsh* [1985] QB 152. Leave to continue as if by writ was refused. See similarly R. v. *Trent Regional Health Authority ex p. Jones* [1986] The Times, 19 June (consultant surgeon: no sufficient 'statutory underpinning'); *Connor* v. *Strathclyde Regional Council* 1986 SLT 530 (teacher's non-statutory appointment by local education authority: private law). Contrast R. v. *Salford Health Authority ex p. Janaway* [1988] 2 WLR 442 (dismissal of secretary by health authority: judicial review).

[2] R. v. *Home Secretary ex p. Benwell* [1985] QB 554.

[3] *Law* v. *National Greyhound Racing Club Ltd.* [1983] 1 WLR 1302.

[4] See R. v. *Inland Revenue Commissioners ex p. National Federation of Self-employed and Small Businesses Ltd.* [1982] AC 617 at 639 (Lord Diplock).

[5] As in R. v. *Committee of Lloyd's ex p. Posgate* [1983] The Times, 12 January; R. v. *Pharmaceutical Society of Great Britain ex p. Sokoh* [1986] The Times, 4 December; R. v. *General Medical Council ex p. Gee* [1987] 1 WLR 564. See above, p. 647. Perhaps the same may happen with public utilities. In R. v. *Midlands Electricity Board ex p. Busby* [1987] The Times, 28 October, the court entertained an (unsuccessful) application for judicial review against a 'decision' of the Board to require a domestic customer to pay in advance for electricity under his agreement with the Board.

safer to seek judicial review, which in case of mistake can be converted into a private law proceeding as if by writ, than to begin by writ when the reverse process is not allowed.[6]

Defensive and collateral pleas

Issues of public law may be raised by way of defence, or as collateral issues, in proceedings of any kind. On a rigorous interpretation of *O'Reilly* v. *Mackman* it might be thought that a defendant who wished to attack the validity of some official act or order should do so by separate proceedings for judicial review,[7] and apply for an adjournment of the main proceedings meanwhile. But the House of Lords, once again refraining from the extreme course, has held that it would be wrong to deprive a defendant of the opportunity to raise any available defence as a matter of right. The question arose when a tenant of a local authority refused to pay an increase of rent on the ground that the local authority's decision raising the rent from £12.06 to £18.53 was void for unreasonableness. The local authority applied to strike out this defence to its action in the county court for the rent, and for possession, claiming that the issue could be raised only by application for judicial review; and it took the tenant to the House of Lords on this preliminary question alone. The House held that it could not be an abuse of the process of the court to raise the familiar defence of ultra vires when the defendant was not able to select the procedure adopted.[8] 'In any event,' Lord Fraser said, 'the arguments for protecting public authorities against unmeritorious or dilatory challenges to their decisions have to be set against the arguments for preserving the ordinary rights of private citizens to defend themselves against unfounded claims.' A defendant is entitled to make his defence as a matter of right, whereas judicial review proceedings are subject to the discretion of the court.

This principle has since been held by the Court of Appeal to be confined to persons who are 'seeking to raise a true defence'; and it was denied to gipsies resisting a local authority's eviction action because they did not deny that they were trespassers but contended that the local authority was in breach of its statutory duty to provide sites for them and so was acting

---

[6] See above, p. 674.

[7] This was the opinion of Ackner LJ in the *Wandsworth* case (below) and also of the county court judge, who had granted a stay so that judicial review might be sought, but the High Court refused leave. For a similar view see [1986] PL at 234 (Woolf LJ).

[8] *Wandsworth LBC* v. *Winder* [1985] AC 461. For the law on such collateral pleas see above, p. 331. Contrast *Aspin* v. *Estill* [1987] The Times, 10 November, where the Court of Appeal held that the General Commissioners of Income Tax could not consider a plea by a taxpayer that the Inland Revenue had misled him and abused their power.

unreasonably.[9] Having no 'defence on the merits', they could make their complaint only by application for judicial review. But it seems impossible to draw any logical line between this defence and that which was allowed by the House of Lords[10]. Here then is yet another trap for the litigant.

The House of Lords' principle will at least apply where the defence is raised against a criminal charge. On a prosecution for violation of a byelaw the crown court or a magistrates' court must decide upon the validity of the byelaw if this is raised by way of defence.[11] On the other hand a firm prosecuted for operating a sex shop without a licence cannot escape by pleading that its application for a licence had been wrongfully refused, since this cannot alter the fact of the offence.[12] Nor can gipsies escape conviction for disregarding planning enforcement notices by pleading that the local authority was in breach of its duty to provide sites for them, since that cannot alter the fact that they had no planning permission.

[9] *Avon CC* v. *Buscott* [1988] 2 WLR 788, approving *Waverley BC* v. *Hilden* (below). Compare *West Glamorgan CC* v. *Rafferty* [1987] 1 WLR 457, where a gipsy sought judicial review successfully on similar grounds.

[10] See above, p. 400.

[11] *R.* v. *Reading Crown Court ex p. Hutchinson* [1987] 3 WLR 1062; and see *R.* v. *Jenner* [1943] 1 WLR 873, where however the defence was not the invalidity but the inapplicability of a stop notice.

[12] *Quietlynn Ltd.* v. *Plymouth City Council* [1988] QB 114, where the result is correct but the decision that such defences cannot now be raised in criminal proceedings is erroneous: see the *Reading Crown Court* case (above).

[13] *Waverley BC* v. *Hilden* [1988] 1 WLR 246, holding that this plea could be made only by way of judicial review and refusing, on the merits, to grant a stay for that purpose.

19

RESTRICTION OF REMEDIES

THE OLD LAW OF STANDING

The problem of standing

It has always been an important limitation on the availability of remedies that they are awarded only to litigants who have sufficient locus standi, or standing.[1] The law starts from the position that remedies are correlative with rights, and that only those whose own rights are at stake are eligible to be awarded remedies. No one else will have the necessary standing before the court.

In private law that principle can be applied with some strictness. But in public law it is inadequate, for it ignores the dimension of the public interest. Where some particular person is the object of administrative action, that person is naturally entitled to dispute its legality and other persons are not. But public authorities have many powers and duties which affect the public generally rather than particular individuals. If a local authority grants planning permission improperly, or licenses indecent films for exhibition, it does a wrong to the public interest but no wrong to any one in particular. If no one has standing to call it to account, it can disregard the law with impunity—a result which would 'make an ass of the law'.[2] An efficient system of administrative law must find some answer to this problem, otherwise the rule of law breaks down.

Having grown to a considerable extent out of private law, administrative law has traditionally contained a number of restrictive rules about

---

[1] Monographs on standing are L. Stein (ed.), *Locus Standi*; S. M. Thio, *Locus Standi and Judicial Review*; J. Vining, *Legal Identity* (discussing United States law); P. Van Dijk, *Judicial Review of Government Action and the Requirement of Interest to Sue* (discussing Anglo-American, European and international law). See particularly *Standing in Public Interest Litigation* (1985, Report No. 27), Law Reform Commission, Australia—an extensive study); Eleventh Report (1978), Public and Administrative Law Reform Committee, New Zealand.

[2] *Steeples* v. *Derbyshire CC* [1985] 1 WLR 256 at 296 (Webster J). See also *Minister of Justice* v. *Borowski* (1982) 130 DLR (3d) 588.

standing. But as governmental powers and duties have increased, and as public interest has gained prominence at the expense of private right, more liberal principles have emerged. The prerogative remedies, in particular, have shown their worth, since they exist for public as well as private purposes and provide the nucleus of a system of public law. The Attorney-General also can act in the public interest and will sometimes, though not always, do so. The resources of the legal system are adequate to solve the problems, which are basically problems of judicial policy.

Judges have in the past had an instinctive reluctance to relax the rules about standing. They fear that they may 'open the floodgates' so that the courts will be swamped with litigation. They fear also that cases will not be best argued by parties whose personal rights are not in issue. But recently these instincts have been giving way before the feeling that the law must somehow find a place for the disinterested, or less directly interested, citizen in order to prevent illegalities in government which otherwise no one would be competent to challenge.

The law in transition

The law about standing has been passing through a transitional stage which makes it complicated to expound. Until recently there were different rules for different remedies, as might be expected in a system which operates with a mixture of private law and public law remedies. The private law remedies of injunction and declaration were for the most part available only to parties whose own rights were in issue. The prerogative remedies, on the other hand, were nominally sought by the Queen and might be awarded at the instance of any one whom the court considered to be deserving. The strict rules as to injunction and declaration could sometimes be evaded with the assistance of the Attorney-General. The generous rules for the prerogative remedies, on the other hand, were tightened in an illogical way by making them stricter for mandamus than for certiorari and prohibition. So long as the two groups of remedies had to be sought by mutually exclusive procedures the rules about standing had to be explained separately in the account of each remedy, as was done in the previous edition of this book.

The situation was transformed by the introduction in 1977 of the application for judicial review.[3] The remedies in both groups then became available in a single proceeding and it became obvious (as indeed it had been beforehand) that a uniform rule about standing ought to apply to them all. The provision in the rules of court, now embodied in the Courts Act 1981, appeared to leave this question open. But when it came before

---

[3] Above, p. 671.

the House of Lords in the *Inland Revenue Commissioners* case[4] the majority opinion was that a uniform rule had been established. The decision contains elements of uncertainty owing to the different approaches of different members of the House. A major reassessment has been effected, but precisely what it means remains in some respects uncertain.

In this state of affairs it is premature to consign to oblivion the rules which made distinctions between the various remedies previously. 'We should be unwise in our enthusiasm for liberation from procedural fetters to discard reasoned authorities which illustrate this.'[5] Those authorities will retain importance both as a background and as showing how the courts analysed many different situations, and some at least of the former rules will remain valid. An abbreviated account of them is therefore given in the following sections. After that we will see how the House of Lords has remoulded them under the new procedure, and how the law has since developed.

Injunction

Any person whose own legal rights are under threat from a public authority naturally has standing to seek an injunction. If a public right is under threat, a private person may seek an injunction in two cases: if some private right of his is interfered with at the same time (e.g. by obstruction of the highway which also obstructs access to his land); and where he suffers special damage peculiar to himself from the interference with the public right.[6] In other cases it was held that only the Attorney-General could vindicate a public right.[7] If for example a public authority created a public nuisance which did no special damage to any private person, only the Attorney-General could apply for an injunction. It was a 'fundamental rule' that 'the court will only grant an injunction at the suit of a private individual to support a legal right'.[8] But there are many situations where a person has a special interest without any specific legal right, and there has

---

[4] *R. v. Inland Revenue Commissioners ex p. National Federation of Self-Employed and Small Businesses Ltd.* [1982] AC 617, explained below, p. 701.

[5] [1982] AC at 631E (Lord Wilberforce); and see at 646A (Lord Fraser).

[6] *Boyce v. Paddington BC* [1930] 1 Ch. 109, summarising earlier cases.

[7] *Gouriet v. Union of Post Office Workers* [1978] AC 435, following *London Passenger Transport Board v. Moscrop* [1942] AC 332. For the *Gouriet* case see the following section on declaration. An earlier classic statement is that of Lord Chelmsford LC in *Ware v. Regent's Canal Co.* (1858) 3 De G & J 212 at 228: 'Where there has been an excess of the powers given by an Act of Parliament, but no injury has been occasioned to any individual, or is imminent and of irreparable consequences, I apprehend that no one but the Attorney-General on behalf of the public has a right to apply to this Court to check the exorbitance of the party in the exercise of the powers confided to him by the Legislature.'

[8] *Thorne v. British Broadcasting Corporation* [1967] 1 WLR 1104 (Lord Denning MR).

been a tendency for the courts to grant injunctions on the strength of the special interest only. In one of the Enfield comprehensive school cases, where it was shown that the local education authority's scheme did not comply with the Act, the court granted an injunction at the instance of a governor of one of the affected schools, holding that he had a sufficient interest in the observance of the law in relation to that school.[9] It was also said that a ratepayer or parent[10] might equally have standing, but this point was left open. In another of the Enfield cases an injunction was granted at the instance of ratepayers who should have been given an opportunity to object if the statutory procedure had been followed correctly, but who would have suffered no actionable wrong if the unlawful scheme had been carried out.[11] Similarly where a comprehensive school scheme in Lambeth was vitiated by discrepancies between the proposals, the public notice, and the Secretary of State's approval, parents were held to be entitled to an injunction merely because the scheme was ultra vires.[12] But in neither of the last two cases did the court mention the question of standing, and it may be that the decisions conflict with restrictive remarks made later in the House of Lords.[13] Several of the cases discussed earlier in connection with the Crown and Parliament were attempts to obtain injunctions in support of interests rather than rights.[14]

Local authorities, as already explained,[15] have statutory powers to bring proceedings in the public interest and they usually seek injunctions.

Declaration

An applicant for a declaration does not need to have a subsisting cause of action or a right to some other relief, but some legal right of his own must be in issue, actually or contingently. Unless this is the case, there is nothing relating to his legal position which the court can declare. As Lord Diplock has said:[16]

But the jurisdiction of the court is not to declare the law generally or to give

---

[9] Lee v. Enfield London Borough Council (1967) 66 LGR 195 at 208.

[10] A parent has standing to seek remedies, including injunctions, on behalf of his children: see below, p. 750.

[11] Bradbury v. Enfield London Borough Council (1967) 1 WLR 1311.

[12] Legg v. Inner London Education Authority [1972] 1 WLR 1245.

[13] In Gouriet v. Union of Post Office Workers [1978] AC 435 at 484 Lord Wilberforce said that only the Attorney-General could apply in the civil courts for injunctive relief against threatened breaches of the law. But in its context this probably means breaches of the criminal law.

[14] Above, p. 588.

[15] Above, p. 606.

[16] Gouriet v. Union of Post Office Workers [1978] AC 435 at 501.

advisory opinions; it is confined to declaring contested legal rights, subsisting or future, of the parties represented in the litigation before it and not those of any one else.

The law as thus laid down confined the declaration, much like the injunction, to the character of a private law remedy. If the applicant had no personal right at stake, he could succeed only if the Attorney-General would assist him by allowing a relator action. This position was emphatically confirmed by the House of Lords in a case where a member of the public, whom the Attorney-General had refused to assist, failed in a claim for a declaration that the calling of a strike by Post Office Workers would be a criminal offence as provided in the Post Office Act 1953.[17] Lord Wilberforce said:

It can be properly be said to be a fundamental principle of English law that private rights can be asserted by individuals, but that public rights can only be asserted by the Attorney-General as representing the public.

This principle was held to rule out injunction and declaration alike. It is equally applicable even where the plaintiff has some special concern with the matter in hand. Thus where it was a criminal offence to refuse to supply information to inspectors holding an inquiry into the affairs of a housing association, the inspectors themselves failed in their action for a compulsory order against the defaulters. Only the Attorney-General could employ civil proceedings to enforce the criminal law.[18] A ratepayer, likewise, must obtain the aid of the Attorney-General in the traditional form of a relator action if he wishes to contest the legality of expenditure by his local authority.[19] An apparently inadvertent decision of the Court of Appeal to the contrary[20] is not taken to have changed the law.

The requirement of a legal right has restricted the utility of the declaration in planning cases, owing to the fact that the planning legislation gives no rights to neighbours and other third parties. If, for instance, a planning authority grants permission for the building of a school but fails to follow the statutory procedure, a neighbour who objects to the school has been held unable to obtain a declaration that the permission is invalid.[21] What a man may do on his own land is a matter between him and the planning authority, and is not legally the business of anyone else. A mere neighbour has no right or status in the matter which the court can declare,

---

[17] *Gouriet* v. *Union of Post Office Workers* (above); and see above, p. 608.

[18] *Ashby* v. *Ebdon* [1985] Ch. 394.

[19] *Barrs* v. *Bethell* [1982] Ch 294. But he may be able to make an application for judicial review.

[20] *Prescott* v. *Birmingham Cpn.* [1955] Ch. 210; above, p. 426.

[21] *Gregory* v. *Camden London Borough Council* [1966] 1 WLR 899; *Bray* v. *Faber* [1978] 1 NSWLR 335.

unless some nuisance or other wrong is committed or threatened against him. Yet it is possible that he may be granted certiorari,[22] or allowed to bring a relator action.[23]

Where the plaintiff's legal position is prejudiced it does not matter that he is one of many people equally affected.[24] This opens the way for challenging legislative acts such as byelaws, without having to wait for penal proceedings for infringement. Accordingly a farmer obtained a declaration against an invalid byelaw prohibiting auction sales in a market[25] and a hotel owner was granted a declaration against an invalid order for a one-way street.[26]

Before the House of Lords temporarily shut the door on declaratory relief for disinterested citizens Lord Denning MR had twice said that he would not object on grounds of standing to actions for declarations brought by private citizens, disputing the exercise of the treaty-making power of the Crown, and he rejected the plaintiffs' claims solely on their merits.[27] There were also signs of relaxation of doctrine in other jurisdictions. The Supreme Court of Canada, in an important decision, laid down the principle that the rule requiring personal standing applies to legislation of a regulatory character which affects particular persons or classes; but that where no particular persons or classes are affected more than others, where the issue is justiciable and where the nature of the case is suitable, the court may grant declaratory relief to any citizen in its discretion.[28] A taxpayer was accordingly held able to dispute the constitutional validity of the Official Languages Act in Canada. Drawing an analogy from the generous rules for the prerogative remedies Laskin J said:

It is not the alleged waste of public funds alone that will support standing but rather

[22] See below, p. 695.

[23] As to this see above, p. 603; and *A.-G.* v. *Codner* [1973] 1 NZLR 545; *A.-G. ex rel Benfield* v. *Wellington CC* [1979] 2 NZLR 385; *A.-G.* v. *Taff-Ely BC* (1981) 42 P & CR 1.

[24] *Dyson* v. *A.-G.* [1911] 1 KB 410; *Gouriet* v. *Union of Post Office Workers* (above) at 483, 506.

[25] *Nicholls* v. *Tavistock UDC* [1923] 2 Ch. 18. See also *London Association of Shipowners and Brokers* v. *London and India Docks Joint Committee* [1892] 3 Ch. 242.

[26] *Brownsea Haven Properties Ltd.* v. *Poole Cpn.* [1958] Ch. 574. See Zamir, *The Declaratory Judgment*, 278.

[27] *Blackburn* v. *A.-G.* [1971] 1 WLR 1037; *McWhirter* v. *Attorney-General* [1972] CMLR 882 (note contrary opinion of Cairns LJ). These were unsuccessful challenges to the legality of joining the European Economic Community. See also *Booth & Co. Ltd.* v. *National Enterprise Board* [1978] 3 All ER 624 (commercial competitor's action for declaration allowed to proceed); *Wilson* v. *IBA* 1979 SLT 279 (above, p. 609).

[28] *Thorson* v. *A.-G. of Canada* (No. 2) (1974) 43 DLR (3d) 1. This decision did not deal with the merits. See similarly *Nova Scotia Board of Censors* v. *McNeil* (1975) 55 DLR (3d) 632; *Benjamin* v. *Downs* [1976] 2 NSWLR 199.

the right of the citizenry to constitutional behaviour by Parliament where the issue in such behaviour is justiciable as a legal question.

In the United States also, a federal taxpayer has been awarded a declaration and injunction against federal expenditure which was unconstitutional.[29] But the federal courts, despite some liberal decisions,[30] have insisted that the applicant show actual injury to his personal interest as opposed to mere concern.[31] Similar rules used to prevail in Australia[32] and New Zealand.[33]

Certiorari and prohibition

The prerogative remedies, being of a 'public' character as emphasised earlier, have always had more liberal rules about standing than the remedies of private law.[34] Prerogative remedies are granted at the suit of the Crown, as the titles of the cases show; and the Crown always has standing to take action against public authorities, including its own ministers, who act or threaten to act unlawfully. As Devlin J said:[35] 'Orders of certiorari and prohibition are concerned principally with public order, it being the duty of the High Court to see that inferior courts confine themselves to their own limited sphere.' In the same sense Brett J had said in an earlier case[36] that the question in granting prohibition 'is not whether the individual suitor has or has not suffered damage, but is, whether the royal prerogative has been encroached upon by reason of the prescribed order of administration of justice having been disobeyed'. Consequently the court is prepared to act at the instance of a mere stranger, though it retains discretion to refuse to do so if it considers that no good would be done to the public.[37] Every citizen has standing to invite the court to prevent some

[29] *Flast* v. *Cohen* 392 US 83 (1968).

[30] Schwartz and Wade, *Legal Control of Government*, 290. It must however be noted that in federal administrative law the declaration has to do the work of the prerogative remedies, which it has superseded.

[31] *Sierra Club* v. *Morton* 405 US 727 (1972), 348 F Supp 219 (1972); *Simon* v. *Eastern Kentucky Welfare Rights Organisation* 426 US 26 (1975). But slight and hypothetical injury may suffice: *United States* v. *Students Challenging Regulatory Agency Procedures* 412 US 669 (1973). The American rules have been greatly relaxed.

[32] *Australian Conservation Foundation* v. *Commonwealth* (1979) 28 ALR 257 (conservation society denied standing for declaration and injunction against ministerial permission for development of tourist resort).

[33] See below, p. 699, n. 64.

[34] See (1955) 71 LQR 388, (1956) 72 LQR 36 (D. C. M. Yardley); (1955) 71 LQR 483 (D. M. Gordon).

[35] *R.* v. *Fulham & c. Rent Tribunal ex p. Zerek* [1951] 2 KB 1 at 11.

[36] *Worthington* v. *Jeffries* (1875) LR 10 CP 379 at 382.

[37] *Re Forster* (1863) 4 B & S 187; *London Cpn.* v. *Cox* (1867) LR 2 HL 239 at 279; *R.* v. *Surrey Justices* (1870) LR 5 QB 466; *R.* v. *Speyer* [1916] 1 KB 595 at 613.

abuse of power, and in doing so he may claim to be regarded not as a meddlesome busybody but as a public benefactor. Parker LJ thus stated the law as to certiorari:

Anybody can apply for it—a member of the public who has been inconvenienced, or a particular party or person who has a particular grievance of his own. If the application is made by what for convenience one may call a stranger, the remedy is purely discretionary. Where, however, it is made by a person who has a particular grievance of his own, whether as a party or otherwise, then the remedy lies *ex debito justitiae* . . .[38]

This was a case where a newsvendor obtained certiorari to quash the allocation of a street trader's pitch to a vendor of jellied eels, the magistrates having assigned the pitch without jurisdiction. Although the newsvendor was a mere rival for the pitch, and had not been a party to the proceedings before the magistrates, it was held that he was a person with a particular grievance and not a mere stranger. The same was held in the case of a local inhabitant who obtained the quashing of a highway order made without proper notice.[39] A ratepayer, likewise, has a particular grievance if the rating list is invalidly made, even though the defects will make no difference to him financially.[40] In licensing cases a mere commercial rival who objects to the granting of the licence to another person has a particular grievance.[41] So also has a neighbour who objects to a grant of planning permission.[42] The extreme case, perhaps, is that of newspapers who are held to be persons aggrieved by magistrates' orders affecting the rights of the press to report criminal proceedings.[43]

When the remedy lies *ex debito justitiae*, as in these cases, this means that the court will normally exercise its discretion in the applicant's favour; it does not mean that the court has no discretion to withhold the remedy, for

[38] R. v. Thames Magistrates' Court ex p. Greenbaum (1957) 55 LGR 129. The law as thus stated was not mentioned in Durayappah v. Fernando [1967] 2 AC 337, where the Privy Council denied certiorari to a mayor who had lost office when the municipal council was dissolved by a ministerial order made in breach of natural justice. The decision may be justified on the ground that failure to give a hearing is a wrong which is strictly personal to the party entitled to be heard: see above, p. 537. The Privy Council's confused reasoning (see above, p. 527) does not refer to the ordinary rules as to standing.
[39] R. v. Surrey Justices (above); and see R. v. Bradford-on-Avon Urban District Council ex p. Boulton [1964] 1 WLR 1136.
[40] R. v. Paddington Valuation Officer ex p. Peachey Property Corporation Ltd. [1966] 1 QB 380 at 400.
[41] R. v. Richmond Confirming Authority ex p. Howitt [1921] 1 KB 248. The police may also intervene: R. v. Berwyn JJ ex p. Edwards [1980] 1 WLR 1045.
[42] See the Hendon case and others noted below.
[43] R. v. Russell ex p. Beaverbrook Newspapers Ltd. [1969] 1 QB 342.

example, where there has been undue delay.[44] In the case of prohibition, it has been held that there is no discretion to withhold the remedy where there is a patent defect of jurisdiction on the face of the proceedings, however unmeritorious the applicant and however remote his interest;[45] but this refinement may perhaps be obsolete since similar rules should govern certiorari and prohibition alike.

The meaning of 'particular grievance' being so wide, there are few examples of certiorari or prohibition being granted to total strangers. But the Court of Appeal supplied one by holding that prohibition might issue at the instance of a private citizen, applying primarily from motives of public interest, to prevent the Greater London Council from licensing indecent films by applying an unduly indulgent test of obscenity.[46] As Lord Denning MR said, 'if he has not sufficient interest, no other citizen has'. Unless any citizen has standing, therefore, there is often no means of keeping public authorities within the law unless the Attorney-General will act—which frequently he will not. That private persons should be able to obtain some remedy was therefore 'a matter of high constitutional principle'.[47] Lord Denning added: 'The court would not listen, of course, to a mere busybody who was interfering in things which did not concern him. But it will listen to any one whose interests are affected by what has been done.'[48] The same tendency is illustrated by the courts' willingness to grant certiorari to a trade union acting on behalf of one of its members.[49]

The broad principle which almost eliminates the requirement of standing for these remedies shows how far the law has gone in the direction of admitting an element of *actio popularis* on grounds of public interest, just as it has done with mandamus and with the relator action. By such means, therefore, a remedy may be found for the citizen who is genuinely aggrieved but who has no grievance in the eye of the law. He may, for

---

[44] *R. v. Stafford Justices ex p. Stafford Corporation* [1940] 2 KB 33; *R. v. Herrod ex p. Leeds City Council* [1976] QB 540; but see [1978] AC 403.

[45] *London Cpn.* v. *Cox* (1867) LR 2 HL 239 at 278, 285; *Ellis* v. *Fleming* (1876) 1 CPD 237; *Farquharson* v. *Morgan* [1894] 1 QB 552. Contrast *Chambers* v. *Green* (1875) 20 Eq 552, where Jessel MR held that the court always had discretion to refuse prohibition to a stranger. Decisions on this question conflicted freely.

[46] *R. v. Greater London Council ex p. Blackburn* [1976] 1 WLR 550. The applicant's wife and co-applicant was a ratepayer and they had children who might have been harmed by indecent films, but that interest was not decisive. Issue of the prohibition was suspended to give the Council 'time to mend their ways.' See similarly *Benjamin* v. *Downs* [1976] 2 NSWLR 199.

[47] This revised version of Lord Denning's principle, unlike its predecessor (above, p. 608), earned the approval of the House of Lords: see below, p. 704).

[48] *R. v. Paddington Valuation Officer* (above) at 401 (Lord Denning MR).

[49] As in *Minister of Social Security* v. *Amalgamated Engineering Union* [1967] AC 725. This practice is now common.

example, object strongly to a building for which his neighbour has been granted planning permission, although legally this is no concern of his. If he can show that the permission is void, for example because the principles of natural justice have been violated, he may have it quashed by certiorari[50] even though he could not have obtained a declaratory judgment because of his lack of personal legal right.[51]

Mandamus: restrictions and contradictions

In principle the law as to the standing of an applicant for mandamus should be no more exacting than it is in the case of other prerogative remedies. It should recognise that public authorities should be compellable to perform their duties, as a matter of public interest, at the instance of any person genuinely concerned, subject always to the discretion of the court. That this is now the position under the new law of standing is explained below. The following paragraphs summarise the evolution of the earlier case-law, which may retain some importance for reasons already mentioned.

A line of restrictive decisions was started by a case (now overruled[52]) where a local sanitary authority unsuccessfully sought mandamus against the guardians of a poor law union on the ground that they were neglecting their statutory duty to enforce the Vaccination Acts.[53] It was laid down that an applicant for mandamus 'must first of all show that he has a legal specific right to ask for the interference of the court'. Citing this decision with approval, later cases added that the court proceeds 'on a very strict basis',[54] and must apply 'a far more stringent test' than in applications for certiorari.[55] None of the cases indicated any reason for this differentiation:[56] it was merely repeated mechanically.

[50] As in *R. v. Hendon RDC ex p. Chorley* [1933] 2 KB 696; *R. (Bryson) v. Ministry of Development* [1967] NI 180; *Re Prince Edward Island Land Use Commission and Beatson* (1979) 101 DLR (3d) 404. Although the *Hendon* case was treated with some doubt in the *Gregory* case (below), it was followed with approval in *R. v. Hillingdon LBC ex p. Royco Homes Ltd.* [1974] QB 720. See also *Murphy (J.) & Sons Ltd. v. Secretary of State for the Environment* [1973] 1 WLR 560 (where however the neighbour's standing appears to have been taken for granted); *R. v. Sheffield CC ex p. Mansfield* (1978) 77 LGR 126.

[51] *Gregory v. Camden London Borough Council* [1966] 1 WLR 899; above, p. 692.

[52] By *R. v. Inland Revenue Commissioners* (below).

[53] *R. v. Lewisham Union Guardians* (1897) 1 QB 498.

[54] *R. v. Commissioners of Customs and Excise ex p. Cook* [1970] 1 WLR 450.

[55] *R. v. Hereford Cpn. ex p. Harrower* [1970] 1 WLR 1424; and see *R. v. Russell ex p. Beaverbrook Newspapers Ltd.* [1969] 1 QB 342.

[56] Possibly it derives from the well-known remark of Lord Ellenborough in *R. v. Archbishop of Canterbury* (1812) 15 East 117 at 136 that mandamus is 'the suppletory means of substantial justice in every case where there is no other specific legal remedy for a legal right'. This in turn derives from Lord Mansfield: see above, p. 651.

The result was to encourage government departments to break the law. In one case[57] the Commissioners of Customs and Excise were allowing bookmakers to pay betting duty in monthly instalments, as an administrative concession, instead of in half-yearly instalments as required by the Act. The court refused mandamus to other bookmakers who wanted the Act enforced against their competitors. In theory mandamus might have been sought by the Attorney-General, who always has standing to enforce the law: but his practice, as it appears, is not to apply for mandamus and never to proceed against the central government.[58] So the Commissioners were able to defy the law with impunity.

In many other cases, however, the courts applied a more liberal test, while paying lip-service to the supposed requirement of specific legal right. Ratepayers, in particular, were allowed to apply for mandamus to require their local authority to fulfil its duties, as to make a proper rating list[59] or to act in accordance with their standing orders,[60] as required by statute, in letting contracts. In the latter case it was said that ratepayers had a sufficient 'specific legal right', though this was plainly a contradiction in terms; and that contractors on the local authority's approved list had no standing as such to require observance of the standing orders, but had standing as ratepayers, though plainly they had a more direct interest in the former capacity than in the latter. The courts were led into contradictory positions by not appearing to recognise that mandamus was a remedy of public law, which ought to be available on the same basis as certiorari. To restrict it to cases of personal legal right was in effect to make it a private law remedy.

Mandamus: private and public interests

Against the statements that an applicant for mandamus must show a specific legal right could be set decisions merely requiring the applicant to have 'a sufficient interest', i.e. some genuine interest greater than that of the public at large. One way to show such an interest was to become a party to some sort of legal process. An insurance company was granted a mandamus to compel the Manchester Corporation to make a byelaw as required by a

[57] *R. v. Commissioners of Customs and Excise* (above). This decision was held to be wrong by Lord Denning MR but was not criticised by the House of Lords in *R. v. Inland Revenue Commissioners ex p. National Federation of Self-Employed and Small Businesses Ltd.* [1982] AC 617.
[58] See above, p. 605.
[59] *R. v. Paddington Valuation Officer ex p. Peachey Property Co. Ltd.* [1966] 1 QB 380 (application failed on the facts).
[60] *R. v. Hereford Cpn. ex p. Harrower* [1970] 1 WLR 1424; *R. (McKee) v. Belfast Cpn.* [1954] NI 122. In *R. v. Peterborough (Mayor)* 1875 44 LJQB 85 mandamus was refused to a ratepayer, apparently on the ground that he was not genuinely acting as such.

local Act, since the company had procured the provision in question and that gave them an interest superior to that of the general public.[61] In a case where justices had improperly allowed the transfer of a liquor licence a clergyman obtained a mandamus to direct them to hear and determine the case correctly,[62] merely on the ground that he had appeared as an objector to the application for the transfer. The case was still clearer where the applicant had suffered loss personally. Thus the Irish High Court granted mandamus against the Dublin Corporation for failing to make a planning scheme and submit it to the minister 'with all convenient speed', so injuring the interests of the applicant, a property company, which could not obtain planning permissions.[63]

Furthermore, the courts were preparing the way for allowing standing to an applicant whose interest was no greater than that of other people generally, and who might come before the court in the guise of a public-spirited citizen concerned to see that the law was obeyed in the interests of all. The Court of Appeal showed itself clearly in favour of this use of mandamus in the proceedings brought against the police in which it was sought to compel them to take more effective action to enforce the law against gaming clubs and pornography.[64] The applicant had no special interest other than his concern as a citizen that the police should fulfil their legal duty to enforce the law. Yet so far from objecting to his lack of standing, the court in both cases emphasised that he had performed a public service in bringing the proceedings. Lord Denning MR said of them in a later case:[65]

Take the recent cases when Mr Raymond Blackburn applied to the court on the ground that the Commissioner of Police was not doing his duty in regard to gaming or pornography. Mr Blackburn had a sufficient interest even though it was shared with thousands of others. I doubt whether the Attorney-General would have given him leave to use his name. . . . But we heard Mr Blackburn in his own name. His intervention was both timely and useful.

Public authorities have many such duties of a general character, enforceable

---

[61] R. v. Manchester Cpn. [1911] 1 KB 560.

[62] R. v. Cotham [1898] 1 QB 802 (see at 804).

[63] The State (Modern Homes Ltd) v. Dublin Cpn. [1953] IR 202.

[64] R. v. Metropolitan Police Commissioner ex p. Blackburn [1968] 2 QB 118; Same (No. 3) [1973] 1 QB 241. Above, p. 403. See also Adams v. Metropolitan Police Cmr [1980] RTR 289 (local residents may require police to prosecute traffic offenders). It was held in Environmental Defence Society Inc. v. Agricultural Chemicals Board [1973] 2 NZLR 758 that an amenity society had no standing to ask for mandamus to require a public board to prevent the use of injurious chemicals; but it appeared that the board had discretionary power and no specific duty.

[65] A.-G. ex rel. McWhirter v. Independent Broadcasting Authority [1973] QB 629. Compare Wilson v. IBA 1979 SLT 279 (above, p. 609).

by no one unless by the ordinary citizen. The Attorney-General does not appear to concern himself with them. If the private citizen could not do so, there would be a serious gap in the system of public law.

The House of Lords, with a reference to these last words,[66] have now decisively put mandamus onto the same bias as certiorari and prohibition, as will shortly be seen.

Statutory remedies

Many statutes exclude all the remedies hitherto discussed and instead allow 'any person aggrieved' to apply to the court for the quashing or suspension of the order. Standing is then determined by the interpretation of those words, and here too there is conflict between restrictive and liberal interpretations. This is best explained later along with the special statutory remedies themselves.[67]

THE NEW LAW OF STANDING

The reformed procedure

When the application for judicial review was introduced in 1977 the prerogative remedies, declaration and injunction all became available in a single form of proceeding, in which the first step was to obtain the court's leave to apply. The rules of court provided:[68]

The Court shall not grant leave unless it considers that the applicant has a sufficient interest in the matter to which the application relates.

This provision has since been incorporated in the Supreme Court Act 1981.[69]

Standing for the purposes of this procedure is thus first of all made a 'threshold question', to be determined at the stage of the initial application for leave, which is made ex parte. At this point the court can reject 'simple cases in which it can be seen at the earliest stage that the person applying for judicial review has no interest at all, or no sufficient interest',[70] and so 'prevent abuse by busybodies, cranks and other mischief-makers'.[71] The

---

[66] [1982] AC at 654 (Lord Scarman).
[67] Below, p. 641.
[68] O. 53 r. 3(5).
[69] s. 31(3).
[70] [1982] AC at 630C (Lord Wilberforce).
[71] [1982] AC at 653G (Lord Scarman).

Law Commission had recommended that the test of standing should apply to the grant of relief, not to the grant of leave,[72] and the rule as enacted suggests that the test is to be a broad one, designed to turn away futile or frivolous applications only.

By requiring the interest to be 'in the *matter* to which the application relates' the rule suggests also that standing is to be related to the facts of the case rather than (as previously) to the particular remedy sought, so that one uniform test should apply to all the remedies alike. Extrajudicially Lord Denning MR has expressed the view that the rule 'lays down one simple test' and gives standing to 'an ordinary citizen who comes asking that the law should be declared and enforced'.[73] The House of Lords has now indicated that this may indeed be its result. It is no longer a problem to explain how such changes in the law can be effected by rules of court,[74] since the new rule now has full statutory effect in the Supreme Court Act 1981.

The Inland Revenue Commissioners case

The House of Lords gave a new and liberal but somewhat uncertain character to the law of standing in the *Inland Revenue Commissioners* case.[75] This decision was to some extent a result of the above-mentioned procedural reforms. But in fact the rules gave the House a wide choice of solutions and their decision is an act of judicial policy which is clear in its general thrust if not in all particulars. In general it may be said to crystallise the elements of a generous and public-oriented doctrine of standing which had previously been sporadic and uncoordinated.

Application for judicial review was made by an association of taxpayers who resented the fact that the Inland Revenue had agreed to waive large arrears of income tax due from some 6,000 workers in the newspaper printing industry who for some years had collected pay under false names and defrauded the revenue. The applicants complained that the Inland Revenue had failed in their duty to administer the tax laws fairly as between different classes of taxpayers and that they had been unduly influenced by the fact that the printing workers might cause serious disruption by striking if their co-operation could not be obtained. The

[72] Cmnd. 6407 (1976), p. 32.

[73] *The Discipline of Law*, 133.

[74] Rules of Court must deal with 'practice and procedure'. In the *Inland Revenue Commissioners* case (below), decided before the rule became statutory, Lord Diplock held that standing was a matter of practice in the exercise of the court's discretion: [1982] AC at 638B.

[75] R. v. *Inland Revenue Cmrs ex p. National Federation of Self-Employed and Small Businesses Ltd.* [1982] AC 617. For comment see [1981] PL 322 (P. Cane).

remedies sought were a declaration that the Inland Revenue had acted unlawfully and an order of mandamus requiring them to collect the arrears of tax. The Divisional Court granted leave ex parte but upon hearing both parties held, as a preliminary matter, that the applicants had not 'sufficient interest'. The Court of Appeal reversed them and the House of Lords reversed the Court of Appeal. The House of Lords' decision may be summarised as follows.

1. It was right to grant leave on the ex parte application.[76]

2. It was wrong to treat standing as a preliminary issue for determination independently of the merits of the complaint. 'In other words, the question of sufficient interest can not, in such cases, be considered in the abstract, or as an isolated point: it must be taken together with the legal and factual context.'[77] It 'is not simply a point of law to be determined in the abstract or upon assumed facts—but upon the due appraisal of many different factors revealed by the evidence produced by the parties, few if any of which will be able to be wholly isolated from the others'.[78]

3. On the facts (not considered by the lower courts), the applicants had failed to show any breach of duty by the Inland Revenue. Their wide managerial powers allowed them to make 'special arrangements' of the kind in question, despite their legal duty to act fairly as between one taxpayer and another.[79]

4. But if it had been shown that the Inland Revenue had yielded to improper pressure, or had committed a breach of duty of sufficient gravity, the applicants might have succeeded.[80] Such rare cases apart, the assessment of one taxpayer is not the business of another, individual assessments being confidential.[81] Rating assessments are another matter.[82]

5. The law as to standing is now the same for all the remedies available under Order 53. Mandamus is not subject to stricter rules than certiorari.[83] Injunction and declaration are available where certiorari would be available.[84]

The testing of an applicant's standing is thus made a two-stage process.[85]

[76] Decided unanimously.
[77] [1982] AC at 630D (Lord Wilberforce). Lords Diplock and Scarman agreed, Lord Fraser disagreed, as also does Scots law: *Scottish Old People's Welfare Council, Petitioners* 1987 SLT 179, holding that 'the matter of locus standi is logically prior to and conceptually distinct from the merits of the case'; but in fact the court decided the merits first.
[78] At 656D (Lord Roskill).
[79] Decided unanimously.
[80] Decided unanimously.
[81] At 633C (Lord Wilberforce), 646E (Lord Fraser), 663A (Lord Roskill).
[82] At 632H (Lord Wilberforce); 646D (Lord Fraser); *Arsenal Football Club Ltd.* v. *Ende* [1979] AC 1, explained below, p. 743.
[83] At 640D (Lord Diplock), 646A (Lord Fraser—probably), 653C (Lord Scarman), 656G (Lord Roskill). See also *R.* v. *Metropolitan Police Cmr ex p. Blackburn* [1980] The Times, 7 March.
[84] At 639D (Lord Diplock), 646A (Lord Fraser—possibly), 648A (Lord Scarman), 656G (Lord Roskill—probably).
[85] See at 630C (Lord Wilberforce), 642E (Lord Diplock), 645E (Lord Fraser).

On the application for leave (stage one) the test is designed to turn away hopeless or meddlesome applications only. But when the matter comes to be argued (stage two), the test is whether the applicant can show a strong enough case on the merits, judged in relation to his own concern with it. As Lord Scarman put it:[86] 'The federation, having failed to show any grounds for believing that the revenue has failed to do its statutory duty, have not, in my view, shown an interest sufficient in law to justify any further proceedings by the court on its application.' He added that had reasonable grounds for supposing an abuse been shown, he would have agreed that the federation had shown a sufficient interest to proceed further.

The novel aspect of the second-stage test, as thus formulated, is that it does not appear to be a test of standing but rather a test of the merits of the complaint. The essence of standing, as a distinct concept, is that an applicant with a good case on the merits may have insufficient interest to be allowed to pursue it. The House of Lords' new criterion would seem virtually to abolish the requirement of standing in this sense. However remote the applicant's interest, even if he is merely one taxpayer objecting to the assessment of another, he may still succeed if he shows a clear case of default or abuse. The law will now focus upon public policy rather than private interest.

Another, though minor, curiosity is that the House of Lords repeatedly spoke of the formula of Order 53 ('a sufficient interest in the matter to which the application relates') as the second-stage test whereas the Order makes it the first-stage test. Since they are substantially different tests, the same formula will hardly do for both. This may be another indication that the second-stage test is not in fact based upon a distinct concept of standing. This, again, is tantamount to saying that standing has been abolished as a restrictive principle of public law.

A citizen's action?

A recurrent theme of the speeches in the *Inland Revenue Commissioners* case is the 'change in legal policy'[87] which has greatly relaxed the rules about standing in recent years. This was put at its highest by Lord Diplock, who related it to 'that progress towards a comprehensive system of administrative law that I regard as having been the greatest achievement of the English courts in my judicial lifetime'.[88] He spoke of 'a virtual abandonment of the former restrictive rules as to the locus standi' of applicants for prerogative orders[89] and he approved the widest implications of the award of

---

[86] At 654H; likewise at 644D (Lord Diplock).
[87] At 656G (Lord Roskill).
[88] At 641C.
[89] At 640C.

prohibition to a citizen seeking to prevent a local authority from licensing indecent films.[90] He also approved the eloquent words of Lord Denning MR in the same case:

I regard it as a matter of high constitutional principle that if there is good ground for supposing that a government department or a public authority is transgressing the law, or is about to transgress it, in a way which offends or injures thousands of Her Majesty's subjects, then any one of those offended or injured can draw it to the attention of the court of law and seek to have the law enforced, and the courts *in their discretion*[91] can grant whatever remedy is appropriate.

Lord Diplock expressed the same point in his own words:[92]

It would, in my view, be a grave lacuna in our system of public law if a pressure group, like the federation, or even a single public-spirited taxpayer, were prevented by outdated technical rules of locus standi from bringing the matter to the attention of the court to vindicate the rule of law and get the unlawful conduct stopped.

Although Lord Diplock's speech was the most far-reaching in its terms, it is fully consistent with the majority view that the real question is whether the applicant can show some substantial default or abuse, and not whether his personal rights or interests are involved.

In effect, therefore, a citizen's action, or *actio popularis*, is in principle allowable in suitable cases. Whether the case is suitable will depend upon the whole factual and statutory context, including any implications that can fairly be drawn from the statute as to who are the right persons to apply for remedies.[93] In fact the possibility of a citizen's action has long existed in the case of the prerogative remedies; but now the court may, in its discretion, grant a declaration or an injunction also. Although the House of Lords had laid it down in 1977 that only the Attorney-General could sue on behalf of the public for the purpose of preventing public wrongs, and that declarations could be granted only to litigants whose own legal position was in issue,[94] the House held that these sweeping statements were inapplicable to judicial review of governmental powers, to the prerogative remedies and to declarations and injunctions available in the same procedure under Order 53.[95] Lord Diplock pointed out that neither the Attorney-General's practices, nor the doctrine of ministerial responsibility to Parliament, were adequate to fill the 'grave lacuna' which would exist

---

[90] *R. v. Greater London Council ex p. Blackburn* [1976] 1 WLR 550; above, p. 696.
[91] Lord Diplock's italics.
[92] At 644E.
[93] At 646C (Lord Fraser).
[94] *Gouriet* v. *Union of Post Office Workers* [1978] AC 435; above, p. 690.
[95] [1981] AC at 639A (Lord Diplock), 649F (Lord Scarman), 657H (Lord Roskill). Compare the liberal Scots doctrine in *Wilson* v. *IBA* 1979 SLT 279 (above, p. 609).

otherwise.[96] It would seem, *a fortiori*, that under Order 53 a ratepayer will now have standing to challenge the legality of his local authority's actions without needing to enlist the aid of the Attorney-General, provided only that he can show a good case.[97]

Uniformity of rules under Order 53

The House of Lords has made it clear that Order 53 signalises a rationalising and simplifying of the tangle of different rules which used to complicate the subject of remedies. The changes were, as Lord Roskill said, 'intended to be far-reaching'.[98] He continued:

They were designed to stop the technical procedural arguments which had too often arisen and thus marred the true administration of justice, whether a particular applicant had pursued his claim for relief correctly, whether he should have sought mandamus rather than certiorari, or certiorari rather than mandamus, whether an injunction or prohibition, or prohibition rather than an injunction, or whether relief by way of declaration should have been sought rather than relief by way of prerogative order. All these and the like technical niceties were to be things of the past. All relevant relief could be claimed under the head of 'judicial review', and the form of judicial review sought or granted (if at all) was to be entirely flexible according to the needs of the particular case. The claims for relief could be cumulative or alternative under rule 2 as might be most appropriate.

Not all the law lords were willing to go so far and to hold that the old technical rules could now be forgotten,[99] and as already mentioned, it is probably premature to treat them merely as history. There was a similar difference of opinion as to the discretion which the court may exercise.[1] But the House of Lords is clearly now determined to prevent technicalities from impeding judicial review so as to protect illegalities and derelictions committed by public authorities. The law about standing has moved forward, and the more progressive interpretations of it are probably the more likely to prove right in the future.[2]

Later decisions on standing

Since the decision of the House of Lords the law has continued to reflect the liberal character of their ruling. Their condemnation of the practice of

[96] At 644E.
[97] See *Barrs* v. *Bethell* [1982] Ch. 294 and *Steeples* v. *Derbyshire CC* (since reported: [1985] 1 WLR 256) there discussed.
[98] At 657E.
[99] See at 631E (Lord Wilberforce), 646A (Lord Fraser), Lord Diplock (at 640A), and Lord Roskill (at 656E) said that decisions earlier than 1950 were no longer to be relied upon.
[1] Contrast Lord Diplock's 'unfettered discretion' (at 642E) with Lord Fraser's rejection of 'uncontrolled discretion' (at 646A).
[2] For a full study see the Australian Law Reform Commission's report No. 27 (1985).

treating standing as a preliminary issue has inclined the courts to decide on the merits of the case, taking standing for granted, where this offers an easier route to the solution. The Court of Appeal dealt in this way with challenges made by the Leader of the Opposition and three local authorities to proposals published by the Boundary Commission for the reorganisation of parliamentary constituencies; the alleged illegalities were clearly not made out, so that there was no need for the court to express any opinion about standing.[3]

Lord Diplock's 'single public-spirited taxpayer' has also received encouragement. In the capacity merely of a taxpayer and elector an individual was able to dispute (though unsuccessfully) the legality of the government's undertaking to pay its contribution of some £121 million to the European Community, claiming that the draft Order in Council laid before Parliament was ultra vires.[4] Quoting the House of Lords' decision, Slade LJ referred to the 'change in legal policy' and to the 'virtual abandonment' of the old restrictive rules. 'If only in his capacity as a taxpayer', he said, the applicant should have standing, and on the serious question raised the right of challenge should not belong to the Attorney-General alone. Another taxpayer, public-spirited no doubt but also self-interested, achieved standing on the same question as in the *Inland Revenue Commissioners* case, namely whether one taxpayer could complain that the Inland Revenue had treated another taxpayer too leniently.[5] The applicant was a chemical company which contended that the Inland Revenue had accepted from competitor companies an unduly low valuation of ethane contrary to the Oil Taxation Act 1975. Although this was 'one of the rare cases' where one taxpayer could complain of the treatment of another, it would seem that such an applicant with a genuine and substantial complaint is likely to be accorded standing. And on this occasion the complaint was upheld.

Other individual applicants have had mixed fortunes, but on the whole have fared well. A journalist, in the capacity of a public-spirited citizen, has been able to obtain a declaration that it was unlawful for a magistrates' court to conceal the identity of the justices as a matter of policy.[6] The press, 'as guardian and watchdog of the public interest', was entitled to raise this 'matter of national importance'. It is held that every holder of a television

---

[3] *R. v. Boundary Commission for England ex p. Foot* [1983] QB 600.

[4] *R. v. Her Majesty's Treasury ex p. Smedley* [1985] QB 657 (Sir John Donaldson MR not deciding positively).

[5] *R. v. Attorney-General ex p. Imperial Chemical Industries Plc* [1987] 1 CMLR 72 (partial report).

[6] *R. v. Felixstowe Justices ex p. Leigh* [1987] QB 582 (mandamus in respect of a particular decision was refused since the journalist could show no sufficient interest in the identity of the justices).

licence has an interest in the quality of the programmes, so that a breach by the Independent Broadcasting Authority of its duty to monitor controversial programmes effectively was remedied by a declaration at the instance of a lady offended by the film *Scum*.[7] On the other hand an opponent of cigarette smoking was denied standing to seek to restrain the BBC from broadcasting a snooker championship sponsored by a tobacco company, since he was no more affected than anybody else and so could proceed only with the aid of the Attorney-General.[8] The apparent inconsistency of these decisions may be due to the fact that standing is no longer a matter separate from the merits of the complaint. A public duty may amount to a sufficient interest to confer standing, so that a chief constable's duty to secure the restoration of stolen property can justify his application for an injunction to prevent its dissipation in a third party's hands.[9] In Canada a citizen was allowed to complain that statutory provisions about abortion conflicted with the right to life in the Canadian Bill of Rights;[10] but in New Zealand a doctor was not allowed to challenge a duly certified abortion with which he had no connection.[11]

If a personal right or interest is in issue the case is still stronger. A gipsy living on a caravan site may apply for an order that the Secretary of State should direct the local authority to fulfil its statutory duty to provide an adequate site.[12] No objection was raised to the standing of a mother of five young girls who sued a government department for a declaration that contraceptive advice given to her daughters without her knowledge, as proposed in a departmental circular, would infringe her rights as a parent, even though no such advice had been given and she was in no different position from any similar parent.[13] The holder of a gaming licence who objects to the grant of a licence to another company may challenge it by judicial review.[14]

Amenity societies and other representative groups have profited from the relaxation of the former restrictions. Where a government department had failed to review cases of benefits wrongfully refused, contrary to social

---

[7] R. v. *Independent Broadcasting Authority ex p. Whitehouse* [1984] The Times, 14 April. In *Ogle* v. *Strickland* (1987) 71 ALR 41 priests were allowed standing to oppose registration of an allegedly blasphemous film, their vocation giving them a special interest.

[8] *Holmes* v. *Checkland* [1987] The Times, 15 April.

[9] *Chief Constable of Kent* v. *V.* [1983] QB 34.

[10] *Minister of Justice* v. *Borowski* (1981) 130 DLR (3d) 588.

[11] *Wall* v. *Livingstone* [1982] 1 NZLR 734.

[12] R. v. *Secretary of State for the Environment ex p. Ward* [1984] 1 WLR 834.

[13] *Gillick* v. *West Norfolk and Wisbech Area Health Authority* [1986] AC 112 (the active defendant was the DHSS).

[14] *Patmor Ltd.* v. *City of Edinburgh District Licensing Board* 1987 SLT 492.

security regulations, because the administrative cost far outweighed the amount at stake, standing was accorded to the Child Poverty Action Group, acting in the interests of claimants; but at the same time standing was refused to the Greater London Council who were held not to have a sufficient interest.[15] In the same way the National Union of Mineworkers had standing to represent one of its members, but the Trades Union Congress had not.[16] The Royal College of Nursing was entitled to sue a government department in order to settle a doubtful question as to the legality of nurses performing certain functions in terminating pregnancy.[17] A local action group were able to proceed against a district council in an attempt to force them into action to prevent the demolition of listed buildings.[18] An environmental defence society in New Zealand had standing to oppose (though unsuccessfully) the construction of an aluminium smelter by disputing the validity both of the government's order[19] and of the company's planning application.[20] Australian aborigines were also able to oppose plans for a similar smelter in Victoria, having a special interest in the land concerned.[21]

The problem of the standing of neighbours and third parties alleging the illegality of a planning permission[22] may now be close to resolution. In one case, where the grant of permission for a 'leisure centre' was held to be vitiated by bias, a neighbour was able to sue both because his land adjoined the proposed development and, apparently, because he was a ratepayer.[23] A hostile precedent of 1966[24] was obviated by the 'considerable development in the field of administrative law' and the new law of judicial review. In another case, where a number of rival companies had applied for permission to build a supermarket, an unsuccessful applicant challenged the

---

[15] *R. v. Secretary of State for Social Services ex p. Greater London Council* [1984] The Times, 16 August. Compare *Scottish Old People's Welfare Council, Petitioners* 1987 SLT 179 (standing refused to welfare organisation disputing legality of circular on social security payment for severe weather).

[16] *R. v. Chief Adjudication Officer ex p. Bland* [1985] The Times, 6 February.

[17] *Royal College of Nursing v. Department of Health and Social Security* [1981] AC 800.

[18] *R. v. Stroud DC ex p. Goodenough* (1980) 43 P & CR 59 (no relief granted).

[19] *Environmental Defence Society Inc. v. South Pacific Aluminium Ltd.* (No. 3) [1981] 1 NZLR 216.

[20] Same (No. 4) [1981] 1 NZLR 530. Contrast *Everyone v. Tasmania* (1983) 49 ALR 381, where the High Court of Australia held that 'mere intellectual or emotional concern' was not enough.

[21] *Onus v. Alcoa of Australia Ltd.* (1981) 149 CLR 27.

[22] For this see above, p. 692.

[23] *Steeples v. Derbyshire CC* [1985] 1 WLR 256 (decided in 1981, before the House of Lords' decisions in the *Inland Revenue Commissioners* case and *O'Reilly v. Mackman*).

[24] The *Gregory* case, above, p. 692.

legality of the permission eventually granted without their standing being questioned.[25]

In none of these cases has it been suggested that there is any remaining difference as regards standing between the various remedies available by way of judicial review.

DISCRETION, EXHAUSTION, IMPLIED EXCLUSION

Discretion and its consequences

The most important remedies discussed in this book—declaration, injunction, certiorari, prohibition,[26] mandamus—are discretionary and the court may therefore withhold them if it thinks fit. In other words, the court may find some act to be unlawful but may nevertheless decline to intervene.

Such a discretionary power may make inroads upon the rule of law, and must therefore be exercised with the greatest care. In any normal case the remedy accompanies the right. But the fact that a person aggrieved is entitled to certiorari *ex debito justitiae* does not alter the fact that the court has power to exercise its discretion against him, as it may in the case of any discretionary remedy. This means that he may have to submit to some administrative act which is ex hypothesi unlawful. For, as has been observed earlier, a void act is in effect a valid act if the court will not grant relief against it.[27]

Nevertheless distinctions may have to be drawn according to the nature of the remedy sought, and according to the differences between public and private law remedies. Certiorari and prohibition have as their primary purpose the preservation of order in the legal system by preventing excess and abuse of power, rather than the final determination of private rights.[28] If certiorari is refused in discretion, the applicant is not prevented from disputing the legality of the administrative decision in other proceedings, e.g. by suing his tenant for the original rent after a rent tribunal has ordered a reduction and an application for certiorari has failed.[29] In other words, he cannot be met with a plea of res judicata, and he may always show, if he

---

[25] R. v. *St Edmundsbury BC ex p. Investors in Industry Commercial Properties Ltd.* [1985] 1 WLR 1168 (complaint not upheld). cf. *Consumers Co-operative Society (Manawatu) Ltd.* v. *Palmerston North CC* [1984] 1 NZLR 1 (standing allowed to commercial rival).

[26] For the former rule that prohibition could not be refused to a party aggrieved where the case was clear see above, p. 696.

[27] Above, p. 352.

[28] Above, p. 694.

[29] See above, p. 264.

can, that the tribunal has no jurisdiction.[30] It would be logical to extend the same doctrine to all the remedies now obtainable by judicial review.

Examples of refusal of relief

An applicant may lose his claim to relief because his own conduct has been unmeritorious[31] or unreasonable.[32] Examples of this have already been given in the context of natural justice.[33] An applicant may also have raised his objection too late.[34] If a party appearing before a tribunal knows that it is improperly constituted because one of the members has an interest in the case, but raises no objection at the time, he may be refused certiorari.[35] He is treated, in effect, as having waived the objection by accepting the tribunal's jurisdiction. It is a general rule that the court will not intervene in favour of an applicant who has allowed a court or authority to proceed to a decision without setting up an objection of which he was aware at the time—'except perhaps upon an irresistible case, and an excuse for the delay, such as disability, malpractice, or matter newly come to the knowledge of the applicant'.[36]

The court may also withhold remedies for objective reasons—a tendency which has come to the fore with the widening ambit of judicial review. The Court of Appeal gave a notable example in a case where a take-over bid had been referred to the Monopolies and Mergers Commission.[37] The chairman of the Commission, being satisfied by assurances from the bidding company, decided that the controversial part of the proposals had been abandoned, and obtained the Secretary of State's consent to discontinuing the reference. But under the statutory procedure

[30] For res judicata in relation to prerogative remedies see above, p. 276.

[31] As in *R. v. Kensington General Commissioners of Income Tax ex p. Polignac* [1917] 1 KB 486 (material facts suppressed in affidavit); *White v. Kuzych* [1951] AC 585 (breach of contract); *Windsor and Maidenhead RBC v. Brandrose Investments Ltd.* [1983] 1 WLR 509 (council ought not to have litigated); *R. v. Secretary of State for Education and Science ex p. Birmingham CC* (1984) 83 LGR 79 (council changed its mind about school closure and pleaded its own procedural error to nullify Secretary of State's confirmation order); *Hill v. Wellington Transport District Licensing Authority* [1984] 2 NZLR 314 (taxi owner threatened with revocation of licence boycotted hearing and later pleaded defect in hearing procedure).

[32] As in *ex. p. Fry* [1954] 1 WLR 730 (above, p. 516); *Fulbrook v. Berkshire Magistrates Courts Committee* (1970) 69 LGR 75 (above, p. 536).

[33] Above, p. 536.

[34] As in *R. v. Stafford Justices ex p. Stafford Corporation* [1940] 2 KB 33; *R. v. Aston University Senate ex p. Roffey* [1969] 2 QB 538; *R. v. Herrod ex p. Leeds City Council* [1976] QB 540, but see [1978] AC 403.

[35] *R. v. Williams ex p. Phillips* [1914] 1 KB 608; above, p. 483.

[36] *London Cpn. v. Cox* (1867) LR 2 HL 239 at 283; *Broad v. Perkins* (1888) 21 QBD 533.

[37] *R. v. Monopolies and Mergers Commission ex p. Argyll Group Plc* [1986] 1 WLR 763.

it should have been the Commission itself, and not the chairman alone, who decided the question of abandonment. It was therefore a case of ultra vires delegation. But a rival company, also a bidder, was refused certiorari to quash the discontinuance of the reference. The court considered that the Commission would have reached the same conclusion as the chairman and that account should be taken of the demands of good public administration. These were that substance should prevail over form; that there should be speed of decision, especially in the financial field; that the Secretary of State could protect the public interest; that the statutory scheme was not intended to benefit rival companies; and that decisiveness and finality were vital. The result was that the reference stood discontinued, despite the procedural illegality.

Another striking case was where the court declined to quash unlawful regulations.[38] Before making regulations for the housing benefits scheme the Secretary of State had a mandatory duty to consult organisations representing housing authorities, but his consultation with them was so inadequate both as to time and as to substance that he was held to have failed to consult. The court granted a declaration to this effect but refused to quash the regulations by certiorari or to declare them void, since they had already been acted upon by local authorities and had been consolidated into new regulations which had not been challenged. Since the applicants did not object to the substance of the regulations, there was no point in invalidating them. So, unlawful though they were, they took effect.

The freedom with which the court can use its discretion to mould its remedies to suit special situations is shown by two decisions already encountered. One was the case where the House of Lords refused mandamus to a police probationer wrongly induced to resign, although he made out a good case for that remedy, in order not to usurp the powers of the chief constable, and instead granted him an unusual form of declaration to the effect that he was entitled to the remedies of unlawful removal from office except for reinstatement.[39] The other was the case of the Take-over Panel, where in fact no relief was granted but the Court of Appeal explained the novel way in which remedies should be employed in future cases, with the emphasis on declaration rather than certiorari and on 'historic rather than contemporaneous' relief.[40]

The court may also exercise a discretion not to interfere with the internal discipline of forces such as the police and fire brigades.[41] Where time is

---

[38] R. v. Secretary of State for Social Services ex p. Association of Metropolitan Authorities [1986] 1 WLR 1.
[39] Chief Constable of North Wales Police v. Evans [1982] 1 WLR 1155 (above, p. 536).
[40] R. v. Panel on Take-overs and Mergers ex p. Datafin Plc. [1987] QB 815 (above, p. 641).
[41] Ex p. Fry (above); Buckoke v. Greater London Council [1970] 1 WLR 1092.

needed for making arrangements to comply with the court's judgment, an order of prohibition may be withheld in discretion, with liberty to apply for it again later.[42]

Exhaustion of remedies—(a) the established rule

First principles dictate that there should be no rule requiring the exhaustion of administrative remedies before judicial review can be granted. A vital aspect of the rule of law is that illegal administrative action can be challenged in the court as soon as it is taken or threatened. There is therefore no need first to pursue any administrative procedure or appeal in order to see whether the action will in the end be taken or not.[43] An administrative appeal on the merits of the case is something quite different from judicial determination of the legality of the whole matter. This is merely to restate the essential difference between review and appeal, which has already been emphasised. The only qualification is that there may occasionally be special reasons which induce the court to withhold discretionary remedies where the suitable procedure is appeal,[44] for example where an appeal is already in progress,[45] or the object is to raise a test case on a point of law.[46] But that course is questionable in principle, particularly where the appeal is to an administrative authority or tribunal, which may not be well qualified to investigate questions of ultra vires, error of law, etc.

In the *Electricity Commissioners* case, accordingly, even though the minister might in the end not have confirmed the scheme, the proceedings were halted by prohibition as soon as it was shown that the scheme would be invalid.[47] Where a police officer, invalidly dismissed by a watch committee, did not exercise his statutory right of appeal to the Home Secretary, this was held no bar to his obtaining a declaration from the

---

[42] *R. v. Greater London Council ex p. Blackburn* [1976] 1 WLR 550.

[43] Where there is a right of appeal within a time limit, RSC O. 53 r. 3(6) empowers the court to adjourn an application for certiorari until the appeal is determined or the time limit has expired. But this does not affect the principle here discussed.

[44] *R. v. Gatwick Airport Immigration Officer ex p. Kharrazi* [1980] 1 WLR 1396 at 1403. See also *R. v. Special Commissioners of Income Tax* (1972) 48 Tax C. 46; *R. v. Oxford University ex p. Bolchover* [1970] The Times, 7 October; *R. v. Traffic Cmrs. ex p. British Railways Board* [1977] RTR 179; *Minford Properties Ltd.* v. *Hammersmith LBC* (1978) 247 EG 561; *R. v. Oxford Local Valuation panel ex p. Oxford CC* (1981) 79 LGR 432. In Scotland the practice appears to be to refuse review where appeal lies: *Bellway Ltd.* v. *Strathclyde Regional Council* 1980 SLT 66; *Nahar* v. *Strathclyde Regional Council* 1986 SLT 570.

[45] As in *R. v. Civil Service Appeal Board ex p. Bruce* [1987] The Times, 22 June; *Nahar* v. *Strathclyde Regional Council* (above).

[46] *R. v. Chief Adjudication Officer ex p. Bland* [1985] The Times, 6 February.

[47] [1924] 1 KB 171; above, p. 631.

court.[48] Similar decisions have many times been given.[49] A redundant vestry clerk was not obliged to pursue his right of appeal to the Treasury before obtaining mandamus to require the local authority to compute his compensation correctly.[50] A vicar did not have to appeal to the Court of the Arches before obtaining prohibition against a Consistory Court which had not given him a hearing.[51] A planning permission vitiated by unreasonable conditions may be quashed at once on certiorari, even though there is a right of appeal to the Secretary of State and a further appeal to the High Court on a question of law.[52] In this last case Lord Widgery CJ explained the court's policy of awarding the most expeditious remedy against an illegal act, and said:

An application for certiorari has however this advantage: that it is speedier and cheaper than the other methods, and in a proper case, therefore, it may well be right to allow it to be used in preference to them. I would however define a proper case as being one where the decision is liable to be upset as a matter of law because on its face[53] it is clearly made without jurisdiction or in consequence of an error of law.

These decisions confirm what was said on one of the classic cases: 'A party is not concluded by not appealing against a nullity.'[54] If the order is one which the applicant is entitled for any reason to have quashed as a matter of law, it is pointless to require him first to pursue an administrative appeal on the merits.

The same principle applies in habeas corpus cases, so that a detained immigrant need not go through the procedure of immigration appeals before he can apply for his release on the ground that he is detained

---

[48] *Cooper* v. *Wilson* [1937] 2 KB 309.

[49] See e.g. *Burder* v. *Veley* (1841) 12 Ad & E 263; *White* v. *Steele* (1862) 12 CBNS 383 at 409; *London Cpn.* v. *Cox* (1867) LR 2 HL 239 at 278; *R.* v. *Comptroller-General of Patents ex p. Parke Davis & Co* (1953) 1 All ER. 862 at 865 (affirmed on other grounds, [1954] AC 321); *R.* v. *Wimbledon Justices ex p. Derwent* [1953] 1 All ER 390; *Graddage* v. *Haringey London Borough Council* [1975] 1 WLR 241; *R.* v. *Galvin* (1949) 77 CLR 432; *Bell* v. *Ontario Human Rights Commission* (1971) 18 DLR (3d) 1.

[50] *R.* v. *Stepney Cpn.* [1902] 1 KB 317.

[51] *R.* v. *North ex p. Oakey* [1927] 1 KB 491, citing earlier cases.

[52] *R.* v. *Hillingdon Borough Council ex p. Royco Homes Ltd.* [1974] 1 QB 720. Compare *Munnich* v. *Godstone Rural District Council* [1966] 1 WLR 427.

[53] In the previous paragraph of his judgment (at 729) Lord Widgery CJ also says that certiorari is limited to errors on the face of the order. Perhaps this and the paragraph quoted are incorrectly reported, since certiorari of course lies for all decisions made without jurisdiction, whether this appears on the face or not: see above, p. 629. The judgment discusses one example of certiorari for non-apparent error: *R.* v. *Hendon Rural District Council ex p. Chorley* [1933] 2 KB 696.

[54] *Bunbury* v. *Fuller* (1853) 9 Ex 111 at 135.

illegally.[55] Domestic tribunals such as trade union disciplinary committees are also subject to the same rule,[56] even though their jurisdiction is based upon contract and even though the terms of the contract expressly purport to exclude the jurisdiction of the court[57]—for this the court will not allow.

An opposite contention, occasionally put forward, is that the exercise of an administrative appeal implies a waiver of judicial remedies. In *Ridge* v. *Baldwin* the Court of Appeal held that since the chief constable had appealed to the Home Secretary unsuccessfully he had thereby waived his right to seek a declaration from the court that his dismissal was legally invalid.[58] The House of Lords reversed this decision, which rests on an obvious confusion between appeal on the merits of the case and judicial review of the legality of the whole proceeding. Since these are quite different things, it would be an illogical trap if they were mutually exclusive. Administrative remedies are highly desirable and people should be encouraged to use them. But to allow unlawful action to stand, merely because it has been appealed against on its merits, is indefensible.

Exhaustion of remedies—(b) conflicting dicta

Recently the case-law has produced a crop of judicial statements which conflict with the rule just explained. It has been said that, where there is some right of appeal, judicial review will not be granted 'save in the most exceptional circumstances'; and that the normal rule is that the applicant 'should first exhaust whatever other rights he has by way of appeal'.[59] This novel attitude, which does not appear to be based on authority, may be due to the increasing pressure of applications for judicial review, which are now so numerous. It has not, as yet, resulted in judicial review being denied merely because a right of appeal has not been exercised. But that may occur before long if these formidable dicta are taken at face value.

In a tax case, where the complainant had failed to show abuse of power by the commissioners, Lord Scarman said that it was 'a proposition of great importance' that 'a remedy by way of judicial review is not to be made

---

[55] *R.* v. *Governor of Pentonville Prison ex p. Azam* [1974] AC 18 at 31, 41.

[56] *Lawlor* v. *Union of Post Office Workers* [1965] Ch 712; *Leigh* v. *National Union of Railwaymen* [1970] Ch 326.

[57] *Leigh* v. *National Union of Railwaymen* (above). Contrast *White* v. *Kuzych* [1951] AC 585, decided when the attitude of the courts was different.

[58] *Ridge* v. *Baldwin* [1963] 1 QB 539, reversed [1964] AC 40. See also *Annamunthodo* v. *Oilfield Workers' Trade Union* [1961] AC 945. For a sound statement see *Ackroyd* v. *Whitehouse* [1985] 2 NSWLR 239 at 248 (Kirby P).

[59] *R.* v. *Chief Constable of Merseyside Police ex p. Calveley* [1986] QB 424 at 435 (May LJ). In Scotland the rules of court require resort to appeal if available: see *O'Neill* v. *Scottish Joint Negotiating Committee for Teaching Staff* 1987 SLT 648.

available where an alternative remedy exists', and that 'it will only be very rarely that the courts will allow the collateral process of judicial review to be used to attack an appealable decision'.[60] But he at once went on to say that judicial review would be available had the commissioners done something equivalent to an abuse of power. Lord Templeman said that 'judicial review should not be granted where an alternative remedy is available', but almost in the same breath he neatly epitomised the familiar grounds which in such a case would allow review;[61] and he added, significantly, that the case in hand was exceptional in that the appeal procedure could not operate if the conduct of the commissioners was unlawful.[62] In another tax case Sir John Donaldson MR said that 'it is a cardinal principle that, save in the most exceptional circumstances, [the judicial review] jurisdiction will not be exercised where other remedies were available and have not been used'.[63] He repeated these words when in fact granting judicial review to police officers who had been unfairly dismissed in a typical natural justice case which had nothing exceptional about it at all.[64] The police officers had already lodged notice of appeal to the Home Secretary but had then sought judicial review. The established rule is therefore still working, but behind a camouflage of discouraging language. It has also been said that the choice of remedy should depend upon whether the statutory remedy would resolve the question fully, whether it would be quicker or slower, or whether it demands special knowledge.[65] Applicants would then be presented with yet further dilemmas and uncertainties.

None of these dicta appear to recognise that appeal and review have radically different purposes; that appeal is concerned with merits, while review is concerned with legality; that review is the primary mechanism for enforcing the rule of law under the inherent jurisdiction of the court, while appeal is a statutory adjunct with no such fundamental role. If an

---

[60] R. v. *Inland Revenue Commissioners ex p. Preston* [1985] AC 835 at 852 (allegations of unfairness and abuse of power not upheld). See likewise R. v. *Inland Revenue Commissioners ex p. Opman International UK* [1986] 1 All ER 328.

[61] 'Where a decision-making authority exceeds its powers, commits an error of law, commits a breach of natural justice, reaches a decision which no reasonable tribunal could have reached, or abuses its powers.'

[62] At 862. For this supposed difficulty see below, p. 946.

[63] R. v. *Epping and Harlow General Commissioners ex p. Goldstraw* [1983] 3 All ER 257 at 262 (no case for judicial review shown).

[64] R. v. *Chief Constable of Merseyside Police ex p. Calveley* (above) at 433, May and Glidewell LJJ concurring. See similarly R. v. *Inspector of Taxes ex p. Kissane* [1986] 2 All ER 37 (allegation of improper decision by tax inspector: judicial review granted despite availability of appeal). Contrast R. v. *Home Secretary ex p. Swati* [1986] 1 WLR 477, where however no arguable case was shown.

[65] *Ex parte Waldron* [1986] QB 824 at 852 (Glidewell LJ).

applicant can show illegality, it is wrong in principle to require him to exercise a right of appeal. Illegal action should be stopped in its tracks as soon as it is shown. It has to be recognised, however, that review and appeal may overlap, particularly in the area of errors of fact and law,[66] and that within this area there may be certain classes of cases, such as tax cases and employment cases, for which specialised tribunals exist, where the court may reasonably hold that recourse to the tribunal is the normal remedy, subject always to the grant of review in case of excess or abuse of power, breach of natural justice, and so forth. What does not seem right is to insist that there is something exceptional about judicial review, that remedies given for other purposes must be exhausted first, and that the choice of remedies depends upon convenience, speed, and other factors which, as well as being imponderable, are in principle irrelevant. If the fundamental difference between review and appeal is borne in mind, the correct choice will in most cases be obvious, and the court will have clear grounds for refusing unsuitable applications for review.

In reality the courts are better than their word. When genuine grounds for judicial review are alleged, it is the refusal rather than the grant of review which is the exceptional course.[67]

A diametrically opposite judicial heresy, namely that jurisdictional questions ought not to be raised by way of appeal, is discussed in a later place.[68]

Does a statutory remedy exclude ordinary remedies?

Many statutory schemes contain their own system of remedies, e.g. by way of appeal to a tribunal or to a minister. There may then be a choice of alternative remedies either under the Act or according to the ordinary law. On the other hand it may be held that the statutory scheme impliedly excludes the ordinary remedies. If its language is clear enough it may exclude them expressly.[69]

As a general rule, the courts are reluctant to hold that ordinary remedies are impliedly excluded, particularly where the statutory remedy is in the hands of an administrative body. The House of Lords adopted this policy in granting a declaration that certain quarrying operations did not need planning permission, even though the Act provided that application might be made to the local planning authority to determine whether planning

---

[66] If it proves to be right that all error of law is reviewable (above, p. 299) the overlap is extensive.
[67] As illustrated above, p. 710.
[68] Below, p. 946.
[69] Below, p. 733.

permission was required in any case.[70] Here the plaintiff was merely seeking to establish that the planning legislation did not affect his ordinary legal liberties, which the ordinary courts protect. Lord Simonds said:[71]

It is a principle not by any means to be whittled down that the subject's recourse to Her Majesty's courts for the determination of his rights is not to be excluded except by clear words. That is . . . a 'fundamental rule' from which I would not for my part sanction any departure. It must be asked, then, what is there in the Act of 1947 which bars such recourse. The answer is that there is nothing except the fact that the Act provides him with another remedy. Is it, then, an alternative or an exclusive remedy? There is nothing in the Act to suggest that, while a new remedy, perhaps cheap and expeditious, is given, the old and, as we like to call it, the inalienable remedy of Her Majesty's subjects to seek redress in her courts is taken away.

The difference between this case and the cases mentioned in the previous section on non-exhaustion of administrative remedies is as follows. In the non-exhaustion cases the statutory remedy exists for a different purpose from the ordinary remedy, being usually an appeal on the merits whereas the ordinary remedy is for the prevention of illegality. In the present context, on the other hand, the overlapping remedies exist for identical purposes, and the question is whether the statutory remedy is exclusive or concurrent.

The court's interpretation may be determined by convenience. Certiorari and mandamus will not be granted to a ratepayer wishing to challenge the correctness of a rating assessment, since the rating legislation provides a detailed procedure for that purpose which impliedly excludes other remedies.[72] But if the validity of the whole rating list is challenged, certiorari and mandamus may be sought, since to challenge every one of the many thousands of assessments would be excessively inconvenient.[73] It is not, however, clear why this distinction should not rest simply on that between legality and correctness, irrespective of convenience, since the

---

[70] *Pyx Granite Estates Ltd.* v. *Ministry of Housing and Local Government* [1960] AC 260. See also *Slough Estates* v. *Slough Borough Council* [1968] Ch 299 (appeal to minister and action for declaration pursued concurrently on question whether planning permission effective: conditions as to costs imposed by court); *Ealing LBC* v. *Race Relations Board* [1972] AC 342 (statutory procedure for legal proceedings by the board held no bar to action for declaration against the board).

[71] At 286.

[72] *Stepney Cpn.* v. *John Walker & Sons Ltd.* [1934] AC 365. See similarly *British Railways Board* v. *Glasgow Cpn.* 1975 SLT 45.

[73] *R.* v. *Paddington Valuation Officer ex p. Peachey Property Co. Ltd.* [1966] 1 QB 380 at 399. See also the remarks as to convenience in *R.* v. *Hillingdon London Borough Council ex p. Royco Homes Ltd.* [1974] QB 720 at 728, though that case belongs properly to the previous section: above, p. 713.

ordinary jurisdiction of the High Court to quash illegal acts will not be excluded by the existence of an administrative appeal on the merits, as the decisions in the previous sections show.

On the other hand there are situations where the statutory remedy is the only remedy. For example, where a taxing statute gives a right of appeal to the Commissioners of Inland Revenue on a disputed assessment, the court will not grant a declaration that the taxpayer is entitled to certain allowances,[74] or that he is not the owner of the property assessed.[75] Similarly where a river authority is given a statutory right to recover certain expenses in a magistrates' court, it cannot obtain a declaration from the High Court that its claim is good;[76] and where Trinity House were empowered to grant pilotage certificates, with a provision for complaint to the Board of Trade if they failed to do so without reasonable cause, disappointed applicants could not complain to the court.[77] These are cases where the right given by the statute does not exist at common law, and can be enforced only in the way provided by the statute. 'The right and the remedy are given *uno flatu*, and the one cannot be dissociated from the other.'[78]

A still clearer case is where the power of determination is expressly conferred by the Act on a named authority. The court could not entertain an action for a declaration that a claimant to superannuation benefits under the National Health Service Act 1946 was a 'mental health officer' since the Act and regulations validly made under it provided that 'any question arising under these regulations as to the rights or liabilities of an officer . . . shall be determined by the Minister'.[79] Strong judicial comments have been made on enactments of this kind where the minister might have an interest in the result;[80] and a narrow construction has sometimes been put upon them in order to preserve the court's control over the limits of any act which is ultra vires.[81]

---

[74] *Argosam Finance Co. Ltd.* v. *Oxby* [1965] Ch 390. Compare *Harrison* v. *Croydon London Borough Council* [1968] Ch 479.

[75] *Re Vandervell* [1971] AC 912. Contrast *Thorne Rural District Council* v. *Bunting* [1972] Ch 470.

[76] *Barraclough* v. *Brown* [1897] AC 615. See the *Pyx Granite* case (above) at 286, 300. See also *Cook* v. *Ipswich Local Board of Health* (1871) LR 6 QB 451; *Wake* v. *Sheffield Corporation* (1883) 12 QBD 142; *Vestry of St James and St John, Clerkenwell* v. *Feary* (1890) 24 QBD 703; *Re Al-Fin Corporation's Patent* [1970] Ch 160; *Wilkes* v. *Gee* [1973] 1 WLR 742.

[77] *Jensen* v. *Trinity House* [1982] 2 Ll R 14. But if the Board of Trade 'should misdirect itself in law or in fact', judicial review could be granted (Lord Denning MR).

[78] *Barraclough* v. *Brown* (above) at 622. See also *Turner* v. *Kingsbury Collieries Ltd.* [1921] 3 KB 169.

[79] *Healey* v. *Minister of Health* [1955] 1 QB 221.

[80] *Wilkinson* v. *Barking Cpn.* [1948] 1 KB 721 at 728; above, p. 480.

[81] *Martin* v. *Eccles Cpn.* [1919] 1 Ch 387, and cases there cited.

In any case of excess or abuse of power the court may intervene in the usual way.[82]

Difficult cases may arise out of ministerial 'default powers', i.e. special powers under which ministers may take steps to compel local authorities to carry out their functions properly. Since these are special statutory remedies, they are discussed later. But it may be noted that the existence of the minister's default power is sometimes held to imply the exclusion of other remedies, and that this interpretation is open to criticism.[83] Where there is ultra vires action as well as failure to perform a duty, the two may have to be disentangled. This was done by the Court of Appeal where a local education authority had both ceased to maintain existing schools and had also established new schools, in both cases in ways not permitted by the Act.[84] In the first case they were acting contrary to an express statutory prohibition and the court granted an injunction to the plaintiff ratepayers and parents; but in the second case there was merely a failure to perform a duty, for which the only remedy, it was held, was by means of the minister's default power.

PROTECTIVE AND PRECLUSIVE CLAUSES

Presumption in favour of judicial review

Acts of Parliament frequently contain provisions aimed at restricting, and sometimes at eliminating, judicial review, and various forms of these provisions must now be investigated. But first it must be stressed that there is a presumption against any restriction of the supervisory powers of the court. Denning LJ said in one case:[85]

I find it very well settled that the remedy by certiorari is never to be taken away by any statute except by the most clear and explicit words.

The Court of Appeal has re-emphasised this rule in interpreting the provision of the Mental Health Act 1983 which prohibits the bringing of civil proceedings for anything done without bad faith or negligence in executing the Act. It was held that this language was unsuitable to include judicial review, so that a mental patient could proceed with her application

---

[82] *Healey* v. *Minister of Health* (above) at 227. Ouster clauses in contracts are void as against public policy in so far as they attempt to exclude the courts from deciding questions of law, e.g. where the rules of an association give its council exclusive and final power to interpret its rules: see *Baker* v. *Jones* [1954] 1 WLR 1005; compare *Leigh* v. *National Union of Railwaymen* [1970] Ch 326.

[83] See below, p. 748.

[84] *Bradbury* v. *Enfield Borough Council* [1967] 1 WLR 1311; above, p. 691.

[85] *R.* v. *Medical Appeal Tribunal ex p. Gilmore* [1957] 1 QB 574 at 583.

for certiorari and declaration contesting the legality of her admission to hospital.[86]

'Final and conclusive' and similar clauses

Many statutes provide that some decision shall be final. That provision is a bar to any appeal.[87] But the courts refuse to allow it to hamper the operation of judicial review. As will be seen in this and the following sections, there is a firm judicial policy against allowing the rule of law to be undermined by weakening the powers of the court. Statutory restrictions on judicial remedies are given the narrowest possible construction, sometimes even against the plain meaning of the words.[88] This is a sound policy, since otherwise administrative authorities and tribunals would be given uncontrollable power and could violate the law at will. 'Finality is a good thing but justice is a better.'[89]

If a statute says that some decision or order[90] 'shall be final' or 'shall be final and conclusive[91] to all intents and purposes' this is held to mean merely that there is no appeal: judicial control of legality is unimpaired. 'Parliament only gives the impress of finality to the decisions of the tribunal on condition that they are reached in accordance with the law.'[92] This has been the consistent doctrine for three hundred years.[93] It safeguards the whole area of judicial review, including error on the face of the record as well as ultra vires. In the leading modern case the Court of Appeal granted certiorari to quash the decision of a medical appeal tribunal which had, by misconstruction of the complex 'paired organ' regulations, miscalculated the rate of disablement benefit payable to a colliery pick sharpener whose one good eye had been injured.[94] The Act provided that the tribunal's

---

[86] *Ex parte Waldron* [1986] QB 824. This accords with the definition of 'civil proceedings' in the Crown Proceedings Act 1947: see above, p. 589. Contrast *Hutchins* v. *Broadcasting Corporation* [1981] 2 NZLR 593 (protection against 'civil proceedings' restricts judicial review).

[87] It precludes the Court of Appeal's jurisdiction 'however expressed': Supreme Court Act 1981, s. 18(1)(c).

[88] See (1956) 3 U. of Queensland LJ 103 (D. C. M. Yardley).

[89] *Ras Behari Lal* v. *King-Emperor* (1933) 60 IA 354 at 361 (Lord Atkin).

[90] *Pollway Nominees Ltd.* v. *Croydon LBC* [1987] AC 79 (repairs notice under Housing Act 1969 served on wrong party: held a nullity despite provision making it 'final and conclusive').

[91] The words 'and conclusive' add nothing: *Hockey* v. *Yelland* (below).

[92] *Gilmore's* case (below) at 585 (Denning LJ).

[93] *R.* v. *Smith* (1670) 1 Mod. 44; *R.* v. *Plowright* (1686) 3 Mod. 94. See *R.* v. *Nat Bell Liquors Ltd.* [1922] 2 AC 128 at 159–60; *Gilmore's* case (below) at 584.

[94] *R.* v. *Medical Appeal Tribunal ex p. Gilmore* [1957] 1 QB 574. See also *R.* v. *Berkley and Bragge* (1754) 1 Keny. 80 at 100; *Tehrani* v. *Rostron* [1972] 1 QB 182; *Hockey* v. *Yelland* (1984) 56 ALR 215.

decision 'shall be final', but the court would not allow this to impede its normal powers in respect of patent error of law.[95] In cases where the decision is ultra vires the court may equally grant a declaration.[96]

The normal effect of a finality clause is therefore to prevent any appeal. There is no right of appeal in any case unless it is given by statute. But where there is a general provision for appeals, for example from quarter sessions to the High Court by case stated, a subsequent Act making the decision of quarter sessions final on some specific matter will prevent an appeal.[97] But in one case the Court of Appeal has deprived a finality clause of part even of this modest content, holding that a question which can be resolved by certiorari or declaration can equally well be the subject of a case stated, since this is only a matter of machinery.[98] This does not open the door to appeals generally, but only to appeals by case stated on matters which could equally well be dealt with by certiorari or declaration, i.e. matters subject to judicial review.

A provision for finality may be important in other contexts, for example when the question is whether the finding of one tribunal may be reopened before another,[99] or whether an interlocutory order is open to appeal,[1] or whether an action in tort will lie.[1a]

A provision that a determination 'shall be conclusive for all purposes' or that a certificate 'shall be conclusive evidence' of something might be expected to be interpreted in the same way as a finality clause, so as not to restrict judicial review. But this is not always the case, as will be seen below in the context of the Tribunals and Inquiries Act 1971.[2]

---

[95] Contrast *R. v. Minister of Health* [1939] 1 KB 232, decided when these powers were in abeyance.

[96] *Pyx Granite Co. Ltd.* v. *Ministry of Housing and Local Government* [1960] AC 261; *Ridge v. Baldwin* [1964] AC 40.

[97] *Kydd v. Watch Committee of Liverpool* [1908] AC 327; *Piper v. St Marylebone Justices* (above).

[98] *Tehrani v. Rostron* [1972] 1 QB 182. Although nowadays treated as a mode of appeal, the procedure by case stated used to require a certiorari to bring up the case, until this requirement was removed by Summary Jurisdiction Act 1857, s. 10: see *R. v. Chantrell* (1875) LR 10 QB 587; *Walsall Overseers* v. *L & NW Rly* (1878) 4 App Cas 30; *R. v. Northumberland Compensation Appeal Tribunal ex p. Shaw* [1952] 1 KB 338 at 349–50. Historically therefore a case stated is a form of review for error on the face. The High Court now brings up cases by mandamus: Supreme Court Act 1981, s. 29(4).

[99] As in *R. v. National Insurance Commissioners ex p. Hudson* [1972] AC 944 (decisions of national insurance local tribunals held final as against medical boards and tribunals later assessing disablement. A special House of Lords of seven was divided by four to three. The majority decision was reversed by National Insurance Act 1972, s. 5).

[1] *R. v. Lands Tribunal ex p. London Cpn.* [1981] 1 WLR 985 (order for disclosure of documents held appealable).

[1a] *Jones v. Department of Employment* [1988] 2 WLR 493 (action for negligence barred).

[2] See below, p. 730, and *Piper v. St Marylebone Justices* [1928] 2 KB 221.

'No certiorari' clauses

An even bolder, though equally justifiable, judicial policy was that
certiorari would be granted to quash an act or decision which was ultra
vires even in the face of a statute saying expressly that no certiorari should
issue in such a case. When in the seventeenth century the court began to use
certiorari in the modern way, it was excessively prone to quash the
decisions of justices for trivial defects of form. As one statute recited, orders
or judgments were 'quashed or set aside upon exceptions or objections to
the form of the order or judgment, irrespective of the truth and merits of
the matters in question'.[3] Parliament retaliated by providing in many
statutes that no certiorari should issue to remove or quash decisions made
under the Act. The court said of such a clause:[4]

The doctrine of defects and variances in the examinations and grounds of removal
before the trial of appeals had been mischievous; and the statute in question was a
most beneficial alteration of the law, designed to check a practice which had
introduced lamentable and disgraceful technicalities.

But, while giving full effect to these clauses for their proper purposes, the
court refused to allow them to interfere with the court's control over excess
of jurisdiction; for otherwise (once again) subordinate tribunals would
have become a law unto themselves. In any case of ultra vires, therefore, the
court continued to grant certiorari regardless of the 'no certiorari' clause. In
an early case the Commissioners of Sewers claimed the benefit of a statute
of 1571, providing that they should not be compellable to make any return
of their actions, and disobeyed writs of certiorari from the King's Bench;
but since they had rated lands outside their jurisdiction, they were fined and
imprisoned for contempt, Kelynge CJ saying that the court would take
care not to allow uncontrollable jurisdictions.[5] In 1759 Lord Kenyon CJ
disregarded an express no certiorari clause in an Act of 1690 where justices
made an order outside their jurisdiction,[6] and a long succession of similar
cases followed.[7] Denning LJ said of them:[8]

---

[3] Quarter Sessions Act 1849 (12 & 13 Vict. c. 45), s. 7.
[4] R. v. Ruyton (Inhabitants) (1861) 1 B & S 534 at 545.
[5] Smith's case (1670) 1 Vent 66; compare 1 Mod 44; R. v. Plowright (1686) 3 Mod. 94.
[6] R. v. Derbyshire Justices (1759) 2 Ld Kenyon 299.
[7] e.g. R. v. West Riding of Yorkshire Justices (1794) 5 TR 629; R. v. Cheltenham
Commissioners (1841) 1 QB 467 (breach of natural justice); R. v. Gillyard (1848) 12 QB 527;
Colonial Bank of Australasia v. Willan (1874) LR 5 PC 417; Ex p. Bradlaugh (1878) 3 QBD
509; R. v. Hurst ex p. Smith [1960] 2 QB 133; compare R. v. Worthington-Evans ex p. Madan
[1959] 2 QB 145.
[8] R. v. Medical Appeal Tribunal ex p. Gilmore [1957] 1 QB 574 at 586. See also R. v.
Northumberland Compensation Appeal Tribunal ex p. Shaw [1951] 1 KB 711 at 716 (Lord
Goddard CJ) affirmed [1952] 1 KB 338.

In stopping this abuse the statutes proved very beneficial, but the court never allowed those statutes to be used as a cover for wrongdoing by tribunals. If tribunals were to be at liberty to exceed their jurisdiction without any check by the courts, the rule of law would be at an end.

This epitomises the court's determination to preserve regularity in the legal system, and to construe every Act of Parliament as intended to uphold it. 'The consequence of holding otherwise', it was said in one case, 'would be that a Metropolitan magistrate could make any order he pleased without question.'[9]

Control for mere error on the face of the record, however, could not be maintained in the face of express no certiorari clauses, for it was precisely this control, and the abuse of it, that these enactments were intended to stop. Otherwise they would have been of no effect whatever. Although a judge pointed out that an exception might well have been made for substantial questions of law, which ought to be determined by the court, he felt obliged to refuse certiorari for this purpose.[10]

No certiorari clauses were extremely common until about a century ago,[11] and indeed may have been used too freely.[12] They are of relatively rare occurrence today since Parliament uses other devices, to be explained shortly. But one or two examples are still to be found in modern statutes, such as the County Courts Act 1959.[13] By enacting them repeatedly in similar form Parliament made it clear that it was content with the construction put upon them by the courts.

All such clauses enacted before August 1958 are now subject to the provision, explained below, which restores the full powers of the court to grant certiorari and mandamus.[14] No such clause will therefore any longer prevent the quashing of an order or decision for error on the face of the record.

'As if enacted' clauses

Another form of protective clause is to the effect that a statutory order shall 'have effect as if enacted in this Act' and that confirmation by the minister

[9] Ex p. Bradlaugh (above).
[10] R. v. Chantrell (1875) LR 10 QB 587 (Field J) (certiorari refused to bring up a case stated). It seems that the parties could by consent evade this obstacle: R. v. Dickenson (1857) 7 E & B 831. In Metropolitan Life Assurance Co. v. International Union of Operating Engineers (1970) 11 DLR (3d) 366 the headnote states that certiorari was granted, despite a no certiorari clause, for error of law on the face of the record; but it is clear that it was a case of excess of jurisdiction.
[11] See under Certiorari in index to Ruffhead's Statutes at Large, ix. 232. A typical example is Highway Act 1835, s. 107.
[12] See R. v. Chantrell (above).
[13] s. 107. On this see R. v. Hurst, R. v. Worthington-Evans (above).
[14] Tribunals and Inquiries Act 1971, s. 14; below, p. 729.

shall be 'conclusive evidence that the requirements of this Act have been complied with, and that the order has been duly made and is within the powers of this Act'.[15] Even this formula should not protect a flagrant case of ultra vires,[16] despite a judicial ruling that it makes an order unchallengeable.[17] The House of Lords has held that the 'as if enacted in this Act' formula applies only to orders which themselves conform to the Act, since it is only such orders that the Act contemplates.[18] Thus the court could still control procedural or other legal errors, and the exclusion clause would be virtually meaningless. This type of clause came into use in the nineteenth century. But it is now in disuse, since Parliament has resorted to a different formula which, instead of attempting to give statutory validity to defective acts, protects them by removing judicial remedies. To this we must turn next.

More about 'as if enacted' clauses will be found in the chapter on delegated legislation.[19]

'Shall not be questioned' clauses

Modern legislation has adapted itself to the wide variety of remedies available in administrative law, and has evolved a comprehensive provision that the order or determination[20] to be protected 'shall not be questioned in any legal proceedings whatsoever'. Sometimes this has been combined with the older form of no certiorari clause, but more commonly it is used on its own. Most commonly of all it is framed so as to take effect only after a time limit, before which remedies may be sought. But that type of provision raises different problems and needs separate discussion. Wide enactments designed to oust the jurisdiction of the courts entirely in respect of all remedies have come to be known as 'ouster clauses'. However they are worded, they are interpreted according to the same principle.

The law as now settled by the House of Lords is that these ouster clauses are subject to exactly the same doctrine as the older no certiorari clauses, namely, that they do not prevent the court from intervening in the case of excess of jurisdiction. Violation of the principles of natural justice, for example, amounts to excess of jurisdiction, so that where a minister refused

[15] e.g. Smallholdings and Allotments Act 1908, s. 39(3); Housing Act 1925, 3rd sched. para. (2).

[16] See Report of the Committee on Ministers' Powers, Cmd. 4060 (1932), p. 40.

[17] Certiorari to quash a compulsory purchase order protected by this formula was refused in *Ex p. Ringer* [1909] 73 JP 436; and see *Reddaway* v. *Lancashire County Council* (1925) 41 TLR 422.

[18] *Minister of Health* v. *R. ex p. Yaffé* [1931] AC 494.

[19] Below, p. 876.

[20] Sometimes even anything 'which purports to be' an order to determination: below, p. 729 n. 40.

an application for citizenship without giving the applicant a fair hearing the Privy Council invalidated his decision notwithstanding a statute providing that it 'shall not be subject to appeal or review in any court'.[21]

Wide as the doctrine of ultra vires is, the House of Lords has made it even wider for the purpose of minimising the effect of ouster clauses. This they did in the leading case of *Anisminic Ltd.* v. *Foreign Compensation Commission.*[22] That case was a high-water mark of judicial control. But for judges in later cases it presented an acute dilemma.

The crucial words were the provision of the Foreign Compensation Act 1950 that a determination of the Commission 'shall not be called in question in any court of law'.[23] Yet a determination of the Commission was questioned for five years before successive courts, and in the end the House of Lords granted a declaration that it was ultra vires and a nullity. The House held

(a) (unanimously) that the ouster clause did not protect a determination which was outside jurisdiction; and

(b) (by a majority) that misconstruction of the Order in Council which the Commission had to apply involved an excess of jurisdiction, since they based their decision 'on a ground which they had no right to take into account',[24] and sought 'to impose another condition, not warranted by the order'.[25]

Question (b) has been considered elsewhere already, in the context of ultra vires action.[26] But it is significant here also, since it shows clearly the great determination of the courts to uphold their long-standing policy of resisting attempts by Parliament to disarm them by enacting provisions which, if interpreted literally, would confer uncontrollable power upon subordinate tribunals.

Anisminic and after

The Foreign Compensation Commission, which has to adjudicate claims for compensation against funds paid by foreign governments to the British

[21] *A.-G.* v. *Ryan* [1980] AC 718. Whether the same reasoning applies to an ouster clause in a Commonwealth country's constitution was left an open question in *Harrikissoon* v. *A.-G. of Trinidad and Tobago* [1980] AC 265. See also *McDaid* v. *Clydebank DC* 1984 SLT 162 (planning enforcement notice not served and so a nullity; time for appeal expired; ouster clause held no bar to judicial review); *Renfrew DC* v. *McGourlick* 1987 SLT 538 (housing order ultra vires; ouster clause no bar).

[22] [1969] 2 AC 147, restoring a notable judgment of Browne J, for which see [1969] 2 AC at 223, [1969] CLJ 230. The case is discussed in (1969) 85 LQR 198 (Wade). For an American parallel see *Lindahl* v. *Office of Personnel Management* 105 S Ct 1620 (1985) explained in context with *Anisminic* in 38 *Administrative Law Review* 33 (B. Schwartz).

[23] s. 4(4).

[24] [1969] 2 AC at 175 (Lord Reid).

[25] [1969] 2 AC at 214 (Lord Wilberforce).

[26] Above, p. 299.

government for the expropriation of British property abroad, had rejected a claim for some £4m. in respect of a manganese mine in the Sinai peninsula after the Suez hostilities of 1956. The reason was that the claimants had sold their undertaking to the United Arab Republic before the date of the treaty of 1959 under which the compensation fund was established, and that they did not therefore comply with a provision of the Order in Council, duly made under the Act, requiring that claimants and their successors in title should be British nationals at that date. But it was held that the Commission were misled by 'unfortunate telescopic drafting',[27] and that the requirement about the nationality of successors in title did not apply where the original owner was the claimant. This meant that the Commission had entered into matters which it had no jurisdiction to consider and had imposed a condition which it had no jurisdiction to impose. Consequently it had exceeded its jurisdiction, and the ouster clause was no impediment to intervention by the court.

Under this decision the only effect of a 'shall not be questioned' clause was to prevent judicial review for mere error on the face of the record within jurisdiction.[28] This was the same doctrine as had for so long been applied to no certiorari clauses, so that the House of Lords' decision on question (a) represented no change of judicial policy. The remarkable feature of the case was the decision of the majority on question (b), which made a jurisdictional error out of what might have been considered to be a mere error of law (misconstruction) within jurisdiction.

The House of Lords had in fact extended their concept of jurisdictional error to such an extreme point that judges were driven to conclude that the basic distinction between jurisdictional and non-jurisdictional error, upon which the *Anisminic* judgment purported to be founded, had been rendered unintelligible. All error of law now appeared to fall within the definition of jurisdictional error, so that the decision of any administrative tribunal or authority could be quashed for such error, regardless of its nature. It has already been explained how this deduction was drawn in the *Pearlman* and *Racal* cases, although they themselves were concerned with decisions of courts of law rather than of tribunals; and how, on the other hand, the basic jurisdictional distinction is still upheld in the Privy Council.[29]

---

[27] [1969] 2 AC at 214 (Lord Wilberforce).

[28] As in *A.-G. v. Car Haulaways (NZ) Ltd.* [1974] 2 NZLR 331.

[29] Above, p. 299. In *Pearlman v. Harrow School Governors* [1979] QB 56 the Court of Appeal quashed a county court judge's decision that the installation of central heating by the tenant of a dwelling-house was not a 'structural alteration'. Judicial review was ousted by s. 107 of the County Courts Act 1959 and the normal right of appeal was barred by Housing Act 1974, 8th sched., para. 2(2). In *Re Racal Communications Ltd.*, reported as *Re a Company* [1981] AC 374, the House of Lords held that there could be no appeal against a decision of a High Court judge under the Companies Act 1948 which by s. 441(3) 'shall not be appealable'. For Lord Diplock's opinion as to ouster clauses see above, p. 301.

According to the logic of *Pearlman* and *Racal*, 'shall not be questioned' clauses must now be totally ineffective. Every error of law is jurisdictional; and error of fact, if not jurisdictional, is unreviewable anyway.[30] So there is no situation in which these clauses can have any effect. The policy of the courts thus becomes one of total disobedience to Parliament. Under the basic distinction which formerly obtained, and which the House of Lords supposed that they were upholding in the *Anisminic* case, judges could at least say that they were obeying Parliament in some situations, while construing ouster clauses as not applicable in others. But now they seem to have lost sight of the reasons which justified their attitude originally.

Wider considerations

The *Anisminic* case and its sequels were the culmination of the judicial insistence, so often emphasised in this work, that administrative agencies and tribunals must at all costs be prevented from being sole judges of the validity of their own acts. If this were allowed, to quote Denning LJ again, 'the rule of law would be at an end'.[31] Lord Wilberforce expressed the same idea in different words:[32]

What would be the purpose of defining by statute the limit of a tribunal's powers if, by means of a clause inserted in the instrument of definition, those limits could safely be passed?

This is the identical point that was made so clearly by Farwell LJ in the *Shoreditch* case, quoted earlier, when he said that subjection to the jurisdictional control of the High Court was 'a necessary and inseparable incident to all tribunals of limited jurisdiction'.[33] That passage was quoted with approval in the *Anisminic* case as correctly expressing the fundamental principle which maintains a coherent and orderly legal system.

In order to preserve this vital policy the courts have been forced to rebel against Parliament. The object of the ouster clause in question in the *Anisminic* case was to keep the distribution of compensation outside the courts altogether,[34] since the proved claims will normally exceed the

---

[30] Above, p. 282. If alternatively, the courts will now review for error of material fact (above, p. 328), this will be a branch of the ultra vires doctrine and thus another form of jurisdictional error.

[31] Above, p. 723.

[32] [1969] 2 AC at 208.

[33] R. v. *Shoreditch Assessment Committee ex p. Morgan* [1910] 2 KB 859 at 880; above, p. 297. This was cited by Browne J (see [1969] 2 AC at 233) with reference to (1966) 82 LQR 226 and was approved in the House of Lords by Lords Pearce and Wilberforce in the *Anisminic* case at 197, 209.

[34] Witness the specific exemption of the Commission from s. 11 of the Tribunals and Inquiries Act 1958: below, p. 730.

available compensation and they must all be finally settled before the claimants can be paid their dividend. In the *Pearlman* case the object of the legislation was to make the county court's decision final, so as to save further litigation between landlord and tenant. The intention of Parliament was clear in both cases. In refusing to enforce it the court was applying a presumption which may override even their constitutional obedience, namely that jurisdictional limits must be legally effective. This is tantamount to saying that judicial review is a constitutional fundamental which even the sovereign Parliament cannot abolish.[35] But Parliament has not abandoned the attempt. Its latest formula is: 'The decisions of the Tribunal (including any decisions as to their jurisdiction) shall not be subject to appeal or liable to be questioned in any court.'[36] This is scarcely different from the clause which failed in the *Anisminic* case, but it may be at this point that the judges will accept the unambiguous instructions of Parliament.

Parliament is mostly concerned with short-term considerations and is strangely indifferent to the paradox of enacting law and then preventing the courts from enforcing it. The judges, with their eye on the long term and the rule of law, have made it their business to preserve a deeper constitutional logic, based on their repugnance to allowing any subordinate authority to obtain uncontrollable power. Needless to say, they have maintained throughout that they are correctly interpreting Parliament's true intentions. In the *Anisminic* case they did so behind a dense screen of technicalities about jurisdiction and nullity; and Lord Wilberforce bravely said:[37]

In each task they are carrying out the intention of the legislature, and it would be misdescription to state it in terms of a struggle between the courts and the executive.

That this is fair comment, at least at the most sophisticated level of legal thought, is shown by the fact that the policy of the judges has been wisely tolerated by Parliament. The restricted meaning given to no certiorari clauses was never made the object of a legislative counter-attack. After the *Anisminic* decision the government did indeed propose a more elaborate ouster clause to empower the Foreign Compensation Commission to

[35] See Wade, *Constitutional Fundamentals*, 66. Yet a 'conclusive evidence' clause has proved to be proof against the *Anisminic* doctrine: see *R. v. Registrar of Companies ex p. Central Bank of India* [1986] QB 1114, explained below, p. 730.

[36] Interception of Communications Act 1985, s. 7(8). The tribunal investigates complaints of telephone tapping etc. and itself applies the principles of judicial review (s. 7(4)). But the complainant is not allowed to know the facts discovered by the tribunal and the purpose of s. 7(8) is to preserve secrecy.

[37] [1969] 2 AC at 208.

interpret the Orders in Council for itself and making its interpretations unquestionable. But after criticism both in and out of Parliament[38] this proposal was dropped, and instead provision was made for a right of appeal direct to the Court of Appeal, but no further, on any question as to the jurisdiction of the Commission or the interpretation of the Orders in Council; and all restriction of remedies was removed as regards breaches of natural justice.[39] So far, therefore, from joining issue with the courts over their recalcitrance, Parliament to a large extent restored the judicial remedies which the ouster clause had vainly attempted to take away, and which the courts had insisted on preserving.[40]

Encouraged perhaps by these successes, the courts have now gone to the length of making ouster clauses meaningless, inconsistent though this is with the constitutional position of the judiciary.[41] There can surely be no more striking illustration of the potentialities of judicial review.

Statutory reform

Just as the judges have opposed ouster clauses which attempt to restrict judicial control, so lawyers generally are hostile to them as opening the door to dictatorial power. The Committee on Ministers' Powers recommended in 1932 that they 'should be abandoned in all but the most exceptional cases',[42] and in 1957 the Franks Committee recommended that no statute should contain words purporting to oust the prerogative remedies.[43] The Tribunals and Inquiries Act 1971, replacing the Act of 1958, has done something towards fulfilling the latter recommendation. Section 14 provides that

any provision in an Act passed before 1st August 1958 that any order or determination shall not be called into question in any court, or any provision in such an Act which by similar words excludes any of the powers of the High Court, shall not have effect so as to prevent the removal of the proceedings into the High

[38] 776 HC Deb col 568; 299 HL Deb cols 640; letters in The Times, 1 and 4 February 1969.
[39] Foreign Compensation Act 1969, s. 3(2), (10). Since breach of natural justice goes to jurisdiction (above, p. 467), questions of natural justice can apparently be taken either to the Court of Appeal direct or else raised in ordinary proceedings with unrestricted rights of appeal. In view of the specific provision, it might be held that only the latter course was open.
[40] It should be noted that the Act of 1969 in other respects protects 'anything which purports to be a determination' of the Commission from question in any court of law: s. 3(3), (9).
[41] Though see Wade, *Constitutional Fundamentals*, 66.
[42] Cmd. 4060 (1932), p. 65.
[43] Cmnd. 218 (1957), para. 117.

Court by order of certiorari or to prejudice the powers of the High Court to make orders of mandamus.

In the Act of 1958 the Foreign Compensation Commission was specifically excepted;[44] and there is an important exception still in force, for time-limited ouster clauses, as explained in the next section. Further exceptions were any order or determination of a court of law; and discretionary decisions on questions of nationality under the British Nationality Act 1948.[45]

The remedy of certiorari has therefore been restored, along with mandamus, in cases governed by pre-1958 ouster clauses which fall within the section. It seems also that a post-1958 clause which substantially re-enacts a pre-1958 clause will be treated as pre-1958 for this purpose. For the Court of Appeal has held that the provision that any determination of a supplementary benefit appeal tribunal 'shall be conclusive for all purposes' does not exclude review by certiorari, although contained in the Supplementary Benefit Act 1966[46] which replaced the National Assistance Act 1948,[47] and this was held to be due to the above-cited section of the Tribunals and Inquiries Act 1971.[48] Another possibility might be that 'shall be conclusive' clauses are to be construed in the same way as 'final and conclusive' clauses, discussed above. The Court of Appeal's decision also makes it clear that review by certiorari extends to review for error on the face of the record. But, without referring to it, the Court of Appeal has since held that a pre-1958 provision making a registrar's certificate 'conclusive evidence' of compliance with statutory registration require-ments is unaffected by the Act of 1971.[49] There is thus a conflict of authorities as to what are 'similar words' for the purposes of section 14.

This last decision also holds that a 'conclusive evidence' clause is equally unaffected by the *Anisminic* principle, i.e. that it effectively precludes judicial review.[50] This produces the paradox that the strongest form of

---

[44] s. 11(3), now repealed in view of the Foreign Compensation Act 1969 (above).

[45] For the exceptions see Tribunals and Inquiries Act 1971, s. 14(3).

[46] ss. 18(3), 26(2). This is the same as the Ministry of Social Security Act 1966: see Social Security Act 1973, s. 99(18).

[47] s. 14(4).

[48] *R. v. Preston Supplementary Benefits Appeal Tribunal ex p. Moore* [1975] 1 WLR 624 at 628.

[49] *R. v. Registrar of Companies ex p. Central Bank of India* [1986] QB 1114 at 1182. The *Preston* case was cited in argument but not in the judgments.

[50] See particularly at 1175–6 (Slade LJ), stressing that the *Anisminic* principle rests on a presumption which is rebuttable. The European Court of Justice holds that a clause of this kind is unlawful in a case where, as in sex discrimination cases, European Community law requires an effective judicial remedy: *Johnston* v. *Chief Constable of the Royal Ulster Constabulary* [1987] QB 129.

ouster clause may fail to protect some ultra vires decision or act whereas the weaker one may succeed in doing so.

For no apparent reason section 14 of the Act of 1971 assumed that certiorari and mandamus were the only relevant remedies in England, ignoring declaratory judgments and injunctions, though it may now be possible to obtain those remedies under the Supreme Court Act 1981, since that Act has made them interchangeable with certiorari and mandamus.[51] There is no such discrimination in Scotland, where the Act safeguards the whole jurisdiction of the Court of Session over the validity of any decision, without reference to particular remedies.[52]

Partial ouster clauses

Instead of providing that an act or order may not be questioned at all, statute may provide that it shall not be questioned on certain specified grounds. Thus under the Town and Country Planning Act 1971 the validity of an enforcement notice may not be questioned in any proceedings whatsoever, except by way of appeal under the Act on certain grounds, including (for example) that there has been no breach of planning control.[53] Since the statutory appeal procedure is in any case more convenient, and provides for an appeal to the court on a point of law, the court will enforce the statute according to its terms.[54]

Such an enactment is scarcely to be distinguished from a provision that all questions of a certain kind shall be determined in the manner provided by the Act and not otherwise. Such provisions are enforced without judicial resistance,[55] as already noticed,[56] since they do not purport to protect any excess or abuse of power.

Canadian and Australian variations

Canadian and Australian legislation has made free use of ouster clauses, sometimes in the 'no certiorari' form, sometimes in the 'shall not be questioned' form, and sometimes in both forms combined.[57] Particularly

---

[51] In *Ridge v. Baldwin* [1964] AC 40 at 120–1 Lord Morris expressed the opinion that the Act protected the declaratory judgment in the same way as certiorari. In *O'Reilly* v. *Mackman* [1983] 2 AC 237 at 278 Lord Diplock said that the Act of 1971 suggested a parliamentary preference for certiorari.

[52] Tribunals and Inquiries Act 1971, s. 14(2).

[53] s. 243, replacing earlier provisions to the same effect.

[54] *Square Meals Frozen Foods Ltd.* v. *Dunstable Corporation* [1974] 1 WLR 59.

[55] e.g. *Healey* v. *Minister of Health* [1955] 1 QB 221.

[56] Above, p. 718.

[57] For the law in Canada, Australia and New Zealand see [1982] PL 451 (G. L. Pieris).

drastic formulae have been employed in the attempt to prevent the courts
from interfering with labour boards and similar bodies administering
industrial legislation. The Supreme Court of Canada has in several labour
law cases followed the English policy of refusing to allow provisions of this
kind to take away its powers of review for jurisdictional error;[58] and they
have penetrated the area of non-jurisdictional error to the extent of holding
that a 'patently unreasonable' error will destroy jurisdiction.[59] But in other
contexts the Court has bowed to novel forms of ouster clauses. It has held
that judicial review is altogether excluded by a clause giving to an
immigration appeal board 'sole and exclusive jurisdiction to hear and
determine all questions of fact and law, including questions of
jurisdiction'.[60] and by a provision that 'any determination of the Minister
made under this subsection is hereby ratified and confirmed and is binding
on all persons', where the minister had power to determine whether a
beneficiary under a will was a charitable organisation.[61]

The High Court of Australia has made interesting attempts to steer a
middle course. Its solution is to retain power to quash for plain excess of
jurisdiction,[62] however strong the ouster clause, but not to intervene
'where the tribunal has made a bona fide attempt to exercise its authority in
a matter relating to the subject with which the legislation deals and capable
reasonably of being referred to the power possessed by the tribunal'.[63] On
this principle it refused relief where a tribunal was said to have exceeded its
jurisdiction by misconstruing 'lock-out'.[64] But it granted prohibition,
despite express ouster of that remedy, where a board sat without the
statutory quorum required for it to function validly,[65] and where a board
made an error of jurisdictional fact in finding that workers were eligible for

[58]   *Toronto Newspaper Guild* v. *Globe Printing Co.* [1953] 3 DLR 561; *Metropolitan Life
Insurance Co.* v. *International Union of Operating Engineers* (1970) 11 DLR (3d) 336; (1952) 30
Can BR 986 (B. Laskin). See likewise *New Zealand Engineering Union* v. *Court of Arbitration*
[1976] 2 NZLR 283.
[59]   *Blanchard* v. *Control Data Canada Ltd.* (1984) 14 DLR (4th) 289; *Re Ontario Public
Service Employees' Union and Forer* (1985) 23 DLR (4th) 97. See Jones and de Villars,
Principles of Administrative Law, 283.
[60]   *Pringle* v. *Fraser* (1972) 26 DLR (3d) 28. See also *Re Robertson and British Columbia
Securities Commission* (1973) 42 DLR (3d) 135.
[61]   *Woodward's Estate (Executors)* v. *Minister of Finance* (1972) 27 DLR (3d) 608.
[62]   But not for mere error of law: *Houssein* v. *Under Secretary, Department of Industrial
Relations* (1982) 38 ALR 577.
[63]   *R.* v. *Murray ex p. Proctor* (1949) 77 CLR 387. This doctrine appears to derive from the
reference to 'manifest defect of jurisdiction' in *Colonial Bank of Australasia* v. *Willan* (1874)
LR 5 PC 417 at 442.
[64]   *Coal Miners Union of Western Australia* v. *Amalgamated Collieries Ltd.* (1960) 104 CLR
437.
[65]   *R.* v. *Murray* (above). The Act provided that the decision was not to be challenged,
quashed or called in question in any court on any account whatever.

membership of a particular union.[66] This distinction is plainly difficult to apply in borderline cases. But the court's compromise is a brave endeavour to strike some sort of balance between legislative intention and constitutional logic.

EXCLUSIVE STATUTORY REMEDIES

Statutory review provisions

A prominent feature of many modern statutes is a provision which allows judicial review to be sought only within a short period of time, usually six weeks, and which thereafter bars it completely. These provisions have become common, particularly in statutes dealing with the compulsory acquisition and control of land. They are therefore of great importance in administrative law. Their primary object is to make it safe for public money to be spent, for example on housing schemes, hospitals, or motorways, without the danger that the order acquiring the land might later be invalidated.[67] If the six weeks elapse without legal proceedings being started, the public authority can go ahead with its plans in the knowledge that they cannot be upset subsequently. Where any statutory scheme depends upon the authority being able to acquire a secure title to land, a preclusive clause of this kind plays a key role.

But these clauses do not merely cut off remedies after the period of six weeks. They also prescribe how judicial review may be sought within that period, and upon what grounds. Except as provided by the Act itself, the order is not to be questioned in any legal proceedings whatsoever. The whole basis of judicial review is therefore changed. Instead of depending, as it normally does, upon the inherent powers of the court at common law, it depends upon the terms of the Act. These clauses have therefore introduced a form of statutory review which, though in general similar to review at common law, may reveal important differences, according to the interpretation adopted by the courts.

The standard formula

The first example of this type of review clause was provided by the Housing Act 1930.[68] Later Acts have not altered the formula in any

---

[66] R. v. Coldham ex p. Australian Workers Union (1983) 49 ALR 259. See similarly R. v. Hickman ex p. Fox (1945) 70 CLR 598.

[67] Sometimes private expenditure is also protected, as by preventing challenge to the validity of planning permission after six weeks: Town and Country Planning Act 1971, ss. 242, 245.

[68] s. 11.

important respect, so that it may be taken as the type. It provides that with respect to clearance orders and compulsory purchase orders made under the Act the following provisions shall have effect.

(3) If any person aggrieved by an order desires to question its validity on the ground that it is not within the powers of this Act or that any requirement of this Act has not been complied with, he may, within six weeks after the publication of the notice of confirmation, make an application for the purpose to the High Court, and where any such application is duly made the court—

    (i)   may by interim order suspend the operation of the order either generally or in so far as it affects any property of the applicant until the final determination of the proceedings; and

   (ii) if satisfied upon the hearing of the application that the order is not within the powers of this Act or that the interests of the applicant have been substantially prejudiced by any requirement of this Act not having been complied with, may quash the order either generally or in so far as it affects any property of the applicant.

(4) Subject to the provisions of the last preceding subsection, an order shall not, either before or after its confirmation, be questioned by prohibition or certiorari or in any legal proceedings whatsoever, and shall become operative on the expiration of six weeks from the date on which notice of its confirmation is published in accordance with the provisions of subsection (2) of this section.

Later versions, such as that in the Acquisition of Land Act 1981[69] (dating from 1946), which governs a great many compulsory purchase orders, omit the reference to prohibition or certiorari and use the generalised form of ouster clause: 'shall not, either before or after it has been confirmed, made, or given, be questioned in any legal proceedings whatsoever.'[70] The final words include criminal proceedings, thus ruling out a collateral plea in defence to a criminal charge.[71] It has been suggested that they do not include appeals to the Secretary of State under the planning legislation,[72] but the contrary seems equally possible.

Similar provisions are found in numerous statutes, primarily but not exclusively[73] in connection with compulsory acquisition and control of the use of land. The Town and Country Planning legislation contains a complex series of sections which apply the usual formula to a wide variety

---

[69] s. 25.

[70] These words do not restrict judicial review of a local authority's resolution to make a compulsory purchase order (*R.* v. *Camden LBC ex p. Comyn Ching & Co.* (1983) 47 P & CR 417) or of a minister's decision refusing confirmation (*Islington LBC* v. *Secretary of State for the Environment* (1980) 43 P & CR 300).

[71] *R.* v. *Smith* (1984) 48 P & CR 392.

[72] *Westminster CC* v. *Secretary of State for the Environment* [1984] JPL 27.

[73] e.g. Medicines Act 1968, s. 107 (licensing system for control of medicines).

of orders and decisions.[74] It is not applied to the decisions of local planning authorities on applications for planning permission, which may therefore be challenged by ordinary procedures,[75] but it applies to the Secretary of State's decisions on planning appeals and to cases which he calls in for his own initial decision and to a long list of other matters; and there are special provisions restricting challenge to enforcement notices on a number of specified grounds which can be raised only by way of appeal.[76]

In all the clauses now under discussion it is enacted that the court 'may' suspend or quash the offending order. This indicates that the statutory remedy is discretionary,[77] like the other principal remedies of administrative law.[78] But if the statutory conditions are fulfilled the court will normally quash, unless the error is merely technical.[79] There is no provision for declaration or injunction.

If application is made to the High Court within the six weeks, the normal rights of appeal to the higher courts may be exercised without restriction as to time.

The statutory formula has generated many problems,[80] of which three in particular stand out.

1. Is judicial review absolutely cut off after six weeks?
2. What is the scope of review if the action is duly brought within the six weeks?
3. What is the meaning of 'any person aggrieved'?

In addition there are a number of other questions of construction, such as the meaning of 'substantially prejudiced'.

Effect of expiry of the six weeks

In cases decided prior to the *Anisminic* case it was held that after the expiry of the period of six weeks judicial review of the validity of the order was absolutely cut off. In *Smith* v. *East Elloe Rural District Council*,[81] where it was alleged that a local authority had taken land for housing under a

---

[74] Town and Country Planning Act 1971, ss. 242–5, replacing earlier Acts.
[75] As in *R.* v. *Hillingdon Borough Council ex p. Royco Homes Ltd.* [1974] QB 720.
[76] s. 243.
[77] *Errington* v. *Minister of Health* [1935] 1 KB 249 at 279; *Miller* v. *Weymouth Cpn.* (1974) 27 P & CR 498; *Kent CC* v. *Secretary of State for the Environment* (1976) 75 LGR 452.
[78] Above, p. 709.
[79] *Peak Park Joint Planning Board* v. *Secretary of State for the Environment* (1980) 39 P & CR 361.
[80] See (1975) 38 MLR 274 (J. Alder).
[81] [1956] AC 736. The House allowed an action for a declaration of wrongful action to proceed against the clerk to the council on the footing that the validity of the order was not questioned: for this see below, p. 779.

compulsory purchase order made wrongfully and in bad faith, the House of Lords refused to allow the action to proceed since it was brought more than six weeks after publication of the notice of confirmation. This was a majority decision,[82] but in an earlier case the Court of Appeal had decided similarly where a minister's certificate that requisitioned land should be retained, which the Act required to be treated as a compulsory purchase order, was challenged on the ground that it had been confirmed by an irregularly appointed tribunal.[83] The only exception was a case where an order confirming a coast protection scheme, which was not to be questioned in any proceedings whatsoever after six weeks, was followed by a compulsory purchase order for the land required, and the legal proceedings were started within six weeks of the compulsory purchase order but more than six weeks after the confirmation order.[84] The validity of the compulsory purchase order depended upon the validity of the confirmation order, and for the purpose of challenging the compulsory purchase order, which was quashed, the Court of Appeal allowed proof of the invalidity of the confirmation order, which was vitiated by failure to comply with the requirements of the Act. This is the one example of the court insisting on its powers of review after the expiry of the six weeks, in a case where it felt that an order had been improperly made.

In the cases in which the 'shall not be questioned' provision was applied literally, no reference was made to the long-established policy of preserving judicial review, or to the earlier authorities on no certiorari clauses which the House of Lords reactivated in the *Anisminic* case.[85] Furthermore, the *East Elloe* case was for this reason criticised in the *Anisminic* case, Lord Reid and Lord Pearce saying that they did not regard it as a binding authority, and Lord Wilberforce saying that he could not regard it as a reliable solvent of any similar case.[86] The House of Lords did not suggest that there was any fundamental difference between absolute ouster clauses and ouster clauses which operated only after a prescribed time: if anything they tended to emphasise their similarity.[87] The question

---

[82] Lords Reid and Somervell dissented.

[83] *Woollett* v. *Minister of Agriculture and Fisheries* [1955] 1 QB 103; and see similarly *Cartwright* v. *Ministry of Housing and Local Government* (1967) 65 LGR 384 (grant of planning permission and compulsory purchase order for ring road).

[84] *Webb* v. *Minister of Housing and Local Government* (1965) 1 WLR 755 (scheme under Coast Protection Act 1949 included land not genuinely 'required' and did not require compulsory purchase).

[85] [1969] 2 AC 147; above, p. 725.

[86] [1969] 2 AC at 171, 200, 210. In the *East Elloe* case no reference was made to the decisions about no certiorari clauses and bad faith such as *R.* v. *Gillyard* (1848) 12 QB 527; *Colonial Bank of Australasia* v. *Willan* (1874) LR 5 PC 417.

[87] See [1969] 2 AC at 170 (Lord Reid), 200 (Lord Pearce), 210 (Lord Wilberforce).

therefore is whether an order protected by a time-limited ouster clause can be challenged in proceedings brought after the expiry of the time limit on any of the grounds which would render it ultra vires, such as bad faith, wrong grounds, or violation of natural justice, in accordance with the principle of the *Anisminic* case.

Both reason and authority dictate a negative answer. Public authorities would be in an impossible position if their compulsory purchase, housing, planning and similar orders were exposed to invalidation by the court after they had invested much public money, for example in building on land compulsorily purchased. It is true that the remedy is discretionary,[88] and that the court might therefore confine it to cases where this objection did not apply. But more probably the court would, despite the *Anisminic* dicta, make a radical distinction between absolute ouster clauses and time-limited ouster clauses. The latter might well be regarded not as ousting the jurisdiction of the court but merely as confining the time within which it can be invoked. In other words, clauses of this type might be regarded as analogous to statutes of limitation, setting limits of time within which action must be brought. There is no judicial criticism of statutes of limitation as 'ousting the jurisdiction of the court', though this is exactly what they do; and the courts formerly made no difficulties about enforcing the Public Authorities Protection Act 1893 (repealed in 1954[89]) which set a time limit of six months, later extended to a year,[90] on actions against public authorities acting in execution or intended execution of any Act of Parliament. On this basis the *East Elloe* and *Anisminic* decisions can be reconciled.

At least two decisions have adopted this solution. In 1972 a Scots court rejected a challenge made more than six weeks after a compulsory purchase order, distinguishing the *Anisminic* case since the statute there made no provision for questioning the order at any stage;[91] and in another such case challenge was held to be barred even where the order had not been served on the owner of the land and an innocent purchaser was deceived.[92] The Court of Appeal has decided similarly in a case where breach of natural justice and bad faith were alleged in the case of compulsory purchase orders for a trunk road scheme, under which much work had already been done but which the complainant had not challenged within the six weeks because he had not known of the supplementary plans which would affect

---

[88] See above, p. 735.
[89] Law Reform (Limitation of Actions, etc) Act 1954.
[90] Limitation Act 1939, s. 21.
[91] *Hamilton* v. *Secretary of State for Scotland* 1972 SLT 233 (averment of receipt of new evidence after inquiry and failure to consult objectors).
[92] *Martin* v. *Bearsden and Milngavie DC* 1987 SLT 300.

his property.[93] Lord Denning MR expressly mentioned the analogy with a limitation period and pointed also to the public interest in imposing finality where action had already been taken under the disputed orders. And the House of Lords refused leave to appeal. Other decisions have pointed in the same direction.[94]

The time limit

The real question, in the case of time-limited ouster clauses, should be whether the time limit is reasonable. In the *East Elloe* case Lord Radcliffe described six weeks as 'pitifully inadequate'.[95] In 1932 the Committee on Ministers' Powers recommended that the period should be at least three months and preferably six months.[96] In 1971 the Law Commission, in suggesting that there should be a general time limit of one year for actions seeking judicial review of administrative acts, proposed that an examination should be made of all special statutory limitation periods to see whether a shorter period than one year was really justifiable.[97] But in their formal report on remedies in 1976 they abandoned this proposal.[98] A general view of the kind suggested in 1971 is in fact what is required, since too many time limits have been enacted in too severe terms and with too little attention to the right overall policy.

The time to be allowed ought to be a fair compromise between the expedition needed for proceeding with public works and development of land and the time reasonably required for legal advice and investigation by the citizen whose property is being taken or whose interests are affected. The danger is that Parliament pays little attention to these provisions in Bills and enacts them sometimes too freely at the instance of government departments. In one case, where the Council on Tribunals protested, a

---

[93] *R. v. Secretary of State for the Environment ex p. Ostler* [1977] QB 122. Lord Denning MR suggested a variety of reasons including one based on void or voidable, which he later recanted: see above, p. 350. Goff LJ found difficulty in the analogy of a limitation period, but in effect adopted it by holding that literal construction was easier where the order was one which needed to be acted upon promptly.

[94] *Jeary v. Chailey Rural District Council* (1973) 26 P & CR 280 (following *East Elloe*, distinguishing *Anisminic*); *Routh v. Reading Corporation* (1971) 217 EG 37 (following *East Elloe*, not mentioning *Anisminic*); *Westminster CC v. Secretary of State for the Environment* [1984] JPL 27 (following *Ostler*). See also (1975) 38 MLR 274 (J. Alder); (1980) 43 MLR 173 (N. P. Gravells).

[95] [1956] AC at 769.

[96] Cmd. 4060 (1932), p. 62.

[97] Law Com. Working Paper No. 40, 1971, para. 123.

[98] Cmnd. 6407 (1976) (Law Com. No. 73), para. 7. For the proposals generally see above, p. 669.

period of six weeks in a Bill was extended to three months in the Act.[99] In the Town and Country Planning legislation, where the cutting off of legal remedies for various purposes after six weeks is effected by complicated provisions which are probably excessively wide,[1] one case has been omitted, apparently by mistake, so that no statutory remedy is available for quashing an improper order,[2] but in any such case ordinary remedies should be available.

The period of six weeks begins to run from the date on which the decision letter or order was signed and dated, not from the date when it was posted, and there is apparently no obligation as to its notification.[3]

Scope of review: 'powers', 'requirements' and 'substantial prejudice'

It is important to ascertain the scope of judicial review provided by the standard time-limited ouster clause where the action is duly brought within the six weeks or other prescribed period. Ordinary review at common law is replaced by a statutory formula specifying two grounds on which the court may quash: (a) that the order is 'not within the powers of this Act'; and (b) 'that any requirement of this Act has not been complied with'. These are evidently intended to be distinct, because for ground (b) there is the additional requirement that 'the interests of the applicant have been substantially prejudiced'. This last requirement does not apply to ground (a).[4]

It has been held that a breach of natural justice, brought about by improper consultation or receipt of evidence after a formal inquiry, renders the order liable to be quashed on both grounds, there being substantial prejudice to the objecting party for the purposes of ground (b)[5] The power

[99] Medicines Act 1968, s. 107; Council on Tribunals, Annual Report, 1967, para. 34.
[1] It is not apparent, for instance, why a tree preservation order should not be challengeable after six weeks: s. 242(2)(c).
[2] The case is that of the Secretary of State's power to call in an application for approval required under a development order, under Town and Country Planning Act 1971, s. 35(1); s. 242(3)(a) has not been extended to include this case, as evidently it should have been. The mistake dates from 1968. See Turner v. Secretary of State for the Environment (1973) 28 P & CR 123.
[3] Griffiths v. Secretary of State for the Environment [1983] 2 AC 51.
[4] The contrary was held in Re Manchester (Ringway Airport) Compulsory Purchase Order (1935) 153 LT 219, but probably wrongly.
[5] Errington v. Minister of Health [1935] 1 KB 249 at 268 (Greer LJ: not within powers of Act), 279 (Maugham LJ: non-compliance with requirement and substantial prejudice), 282 (Roche LJ agreeing with Maugham LJ); Hibernian Property Co. Ltd. v. Secretary of State for the Environment (1973) 27 P & CR 197 (Browne J: both grounds); Fairmount Investments Ltd. v. Secretary of State for the Environment [1976] 1 WLR 1255 (House of Lords; both grounds). See also R. v. Secretary of State for the Environment ex p. Ostler [1977] QB 122; Lithgow v. S. of S. for Scotland 1973 SLT 81.

to quash on ground (*a*) follows from the fact that a breach of natural justice is an ultra vires act which makes the decision void and a nullity.[6] The same applies to a decision vitiated by failure to take account of some relevant consideration,[7] or by error of law, since that is now also ultra vires.[8] But where the only objection was that a statutory report was defective in form,[9] or that owing to a slip a minister's confirmation order did not agree with the decision letter stating his reasons for extending the time within which a use of land had to be discontinued,[10] it was held that these flaws were merely non-compliance with the requirements of the respective Acts; and that since the objectors had not been misled in any way and had suffered no substantial prejudice, the court had no power to quash the orders. These decisions suggest that the court may attempt to differentiate grounds (*a*) and (*b*) by a distinction between substantial breaches of the law and minor irregularities.[11]

Substantial prejudice was found to have been caused where a local authority served an invalid improvement notice in respect of a cottage,[12] and where a minister advertised his intention to take land for road improvements but misdescribed the land so that persons who would have wished to object were not informed of their opportunity to do so.[13] But where notice of a compulsory order was served upon one only of two joint owners, who were husband and wife, and both were in fact fully aware of the order, there was no prejudice at all.[14]

Since judges have commented on the difficulty of distinguishing between ground (*a*) and ground (*b*),[15] and have favoured a narrow

---

[6] Above, p. 467.

[7] *Eckersley* v. *Secretary of State for the Environment* [1977] 34 P & CR 124; *North Surrey Water Co.* v. *Same* [1976] 34 P & CR 140; *Spackman* v. *Same* [1977] 1 All ER 257.

[8] Following the *Pearlman* and *Racal* cases (above, p. 300); *Peak Park Joint Planning Board* v. *Secretary of State for the Environment* (1979) 39 P & CR 361.

[9] *Gordondale Investments Ltd.* v. *Secretary of State for the Environment* (1971) 70 LGR 158.

[10] *Miller* v. *Weymouth Cpn.* (1974) 27 P & CR 468. See also *Re Bowman* [1932] 2 KB 621 (minor formal defect in clearance order: no substantial prejudice); *Steele* v. *Minister of Housing and Local Government* (1956) 6 P & CR 386 (clearance order containing redundant statement: no substantial prejudice).

[11] See the *Gordondale* case (above) at 167 (Megaw LJ).

[12] *De Rothschild* v. *Wing Rural District Council* [1967] 1 WLR 740 (in this case the requirement of substantial prejudice was made applicable to invalid improvement notices: Housing Act 1964, s. 27(3)).

[13] *Wilson* v. *Secretary of State for the Environment* [1973] 1 WLR 1083.

[14] *George* v. *Secretary of State for the Environment* (1979) 77 LGR 689.

[15] See the *Gordondale* case (above) at 167 (Megaw LJ); *Miller's* case (above) at 478 (Kerr J). In *George* v. *Secretary of State for the Environment* (above) Lord Denning MR suggests that where the defect is a breach of natural justice the two grounds are almost indistinguishable, since an actionable breach of natural justice must involve substantial prejudice.

construction of ground (*a*) in order to find some meaning for ground (*b*),[16] it may be suggested that the difficulty would disappear if they were construed with reference to the well-known distinction between statutory requirements which are mandatory and those which are directory. Neglect of a mandatory requirement renders an order ultra vires and void, whereas neglect of a directory requirement has no invalidating effect at all.[17] Neglect of a mandatory requirement therefore makes an order 'not within the powers of this Act,' just as much as does bad faith or a breach of natural justice. There is no need to confine such cases to ground (*b*) merely because they are cases of non-compliance with some requirement. Ground (*b*) may well be intended for the case of neglect of merely directory requirements. Although such neglect does not affect the validity of the order, and therefore does not fall within ground (*a*), it would be reasonable to empower the court to quash the order where an irregularity of this class has in fact caused substantial prejudice to the aggrieved person. The scope of judicial review under ground (*b*) would then go further than at common law, though always subject to proof of substantial prejudice and subject also to the discretion of the court. The forms of words used in the standard clause suggest that precisely this may have been the legislative intention. If that were established, the distinction between grounds (*a*) and (*b*) would then be a familiar one, and their combined effect would be eminently reasonable.

Scope of review: the East Elloe *case*

In the foregoing commentary it is assumed that, as both the words of the Acts and the decisions indicate, 'not within the powers of this Act' means ultra vires for any of the normal reasons, e.g. bad faith or unreasonableness or breach of natural justice. But in the *East Elloe* case a remarkable variety of opinions were expressed on the meaning of these innocent-looking words. It was treated as a case where, as Lord Simonds said, 'plain words must be given their plain meaning'.[18] But there was little agreement about what the plain meaning might be.

Lord Reid was of opinion that the whole area of bad faith and unreasonableness fell outside the statutory clause altogether, and remained an available ground of challenge even after the six weeks;[19] and Lord Somervell held that fraud was not a matter of ultra vires at all, and could be

---

[16] As in *Hamilton* v. *Secretary of State for Scotland* 1972 SLT 223 at 240. See also *Hamilton* v. *Roxburgh County Council* 1971 SLT 2 for another case of narrow construction.

[17] As explained above, p. 246.

[18] *Smith* v. *East Elloe RDC* [1956] AC 736 at 751.

[19] At 763.

alleged at any time likewise.[20] Lord Simonds, Morton and Radcliffe opposed these views, holding that challenge for fraud, as for any other reason, was barred after the six weeks. But Lord Morton also held that the Act allowed challenge only for violation of express statutory requirements,[21] so that many kinds of unlawful action would not be challengeable even within the six weeks. This extraordinary conclusion would allow uncontrollable abuse of statutory power and cannot conceivably have been intended by Parliament. The case shows what paradoxes can result from using literal verbal interpretation as a substitute for legal principle.

Later decisions have sensibly turned a blind eye to this source of confusion, though Lord Denning MR[22] has expressed his preference for the opinion of Lord Radcliffe,[23] that the words 'not empowered to be granted under this Act' (equivalent to 'not within the powers of this Act') embraced the whole range of the varieties of ultra vires, without any need 'to pick and choose'. Lord Denning also said that the differing voices in the House of Lords gave no clear guidance, or at least none that was binding. Since then he has himself given a particularly wide meaning to 'not within the powers of this Act', as explained in the next section.

The key to the true interpretation of these statutory clauses must surely be to presume, following Lord Radcliffe and Lord Denning, that Parliament did not intend to authorise any of the abuses normally controlled by the courts of law, but intended only to set a short time limit within which proceedings must be initiated. 'Not within the powers of this Act' is simply a draftsman's translation of 'ultra vires' comprising all its varieties such as bad faith, breach of natural justice, irrelevant considerations and, now, error of law.[24] The other parts of the clause then fall easily into place if interpreted as suggested above. The draftsman may have been rash to attempt to express the whole subject of judicial review in a statutory formula; but he could scarcely have foreseen the fate that was in store for it.

Scope of review: error on the face; no evidence

The statutory formula does not, it will be noticed, provide for error on the face of the record. Since at common law the court can quash a decision vitiated by such error, even though it is intra vires, it would seem that the statutory review power is in this one respect narrower than that at common law. The natural explanation is that the statutory formula came into use

---

[20] At 772.

[21] At 755.

[22] In *Webb* v. *Minister of Housing and Local Government* [1965] 1 WLR 755 at 770.

[23] [1956] AC at 708.

[24] Above, p. 300. This interpretation was adopted in *Peak Park Planning Board* v. *Secretary of State for the Environment* (1980) 39 P & CR 361.

during the time when review for mere error on the face was in its period of eclipse.[25]

But, as already explained elsewhere, the Court of Appeal has in several cases given a widely extended meaning to 'not within the powers of this Act', holding that it authorises judicial review not only for unreasonableness and irrelevant considerations but also for misinterpretation of statute, or other error of law, and for acting on no evidence.[26] And in any case, the law as to error on the face of the record has now become redundant, as explained earlier. Every error of law will now be 'not within the powers of this Act' and the face of the record will cease to be relevant.[27] If this should be the result, the scope of review under time-limited ouster clauses may be slightly wider than that at common law. It is likely, however, that review for mere error of law would be restricted to error on the face of the record, for the sake of conformity with the common law. No such case has yet occurred, and as regards error on the face the Court of Appeal's doctrine has the status of dictum only. As regards 'no evidence', it has once been positively applied by Lord Denning MR.[28]

Standing. 'Any person aggrieved'

The statutory remedy may be invoked by 'any person aggrieved'. This is the same phrase as is used at common law to define standing for obtaining certiorari and prohibition, and as has been seen it bears a very wide meaning in that context, so that virtually any one concerned in any way personally falls within it.[29] It has also been used in many statutes, where its meaning ought to be equally wide; for in earlier times the usual phrase was 'any person who feels aggrieved' or 'any person who thinks himself aggrieved', which made it clear that the grievance was purely subjective.[30]

---

[25] Above, p. 306.

[26] *Ashbridge Investments Ltd.* v. *Minister of Housing and Local Government* [1965] 1 WLR 1320; *Coleen Properties Ltd.* v. *Same* [1971] 1 WLR 433; *Gordondale Investments Ltd.* v. *Secretary of State for the Environment* (1971) 70 LGR 158; *R.* v. *Secretary of State for the Environment ex p. Ostler* [1977] QB 122, holding that the formula of the *Ashbridge* case is the accepted interpretation, but omitting to mention error of law. The key passage is quoted above, p. 324, where the cases are discussed.

[27] See n. 24, above.

[28] In the *Coleen* case (above); but not by the other judges: above, p. 325.

[29] Above, p. 694.

[30] e.g. Highway Act 1835, s. 72 ('if any person shall think himself aggrieved'); Public Health Act 1875, s. 268 ('deems himself aggrieved'). The National Insurance Act 1911, s. 66(1) referred to 'any person who feels aggrieved'. In the National Insurance Act 1965, s. 65(3) this had become 'any person aggrieved'. The phraseology evolved similarly in rating law: see *Arsenal Football Club Ltd.* v. *Ende* [1979] AC 1 at 15. Even the 'feels aggrieved' formula can be restrictively interpreted: see *R.* v. *Ipswich Justices ex p. Robson* [1971] 2 QB 340.

When this was abbreviated to 'any person aggrieved' the meaning should have remained the same, as indeed is the natural sense of the words,[31] corroborated by at least one statute.[32]

But in some cases the courts interpreted this apparently guileless phrase as expressing a requirement of standing, and treated it as meaning 'any person affected'.[33] In particular, they were reluctant to hold that a public authority was a person aggrieved for the purpose of a statutory right of appeal, so that a local planning authority was not allowed to appeal against the quashing of its own enforcement notice;[34] only if the decision imposed some liability upon the authority was it held to be aggrieved in law.[35] By glossing the natural meaning of the words the courts introduced so much ambiguity that judges vainly appealed to Parliament to rescue them from their own confusion.[36] Meanwhile they could only take refuge in the proposition that the meaning of the expression in one Act was no guide to its meaning in another.[37]

The question arose on the statutory six-weeks formula of the Town and Country Planning Act 1959 in a case where a landowner had objected to an application for permission to work chalkpits on neighbouring land, alleging that the minister had rejected his inspector's findings on the basis of evidence taken after the inquiry and not disclosed. He brought his action within the six weeks, but it was held that, genuinely aggrieved though he was, he was not a person aggrieved within the meaning of the Act.[38] As a mere neighbour he had no rights under the Act, since the question whether permission should be granted is one between the applicant and the planning authority, and the grant of permission affects no one's legal rights adversely. He could have applied for the quashing of the order only if he had been one of the specified classes of persons having a statutory right to have their representations considered by the minister. Since then, however, statutory rules of procedure for planning inquiries have been made[39] which

---

[31] R. v. *Surrey Assessment Committee* [1948] 1 All ER 856.

[32] Parliamentary Commissioner Act 1967, s. 12(1), defining 'person aggrieved' as the person 'who claims or is alleged' to have sustained injustice.

[33] See *Ex p. Sidebotham* (1879) 14 Ch D 458 at 465.

[34] *Ealing Cpn.* v. *Jones* [1959] 1 QB 384. Contrast *Attorney-General of the Gambia* v. *N'Jie* [1961] AC 617.

[35] R. v. *Nottingham Quarter Sessions ex p. Harlow* [1952] 2 QB 601 (obligation to provide dustbin); *Phillips* v. *Berkshire County Council* [1967] 2 QB 991; but a mere order for costs does not count for this purpose: R. v. *Dorset Quarter Sessions Appeals Committee ex p. Weymouth Cpn.* [1960] 2 QB 230.

[36] In the *Ealing* case (above) and the *Buxton* case (below).

[37] *Sevenoaks Urban District Council* v. *Twynam* [1929] 2 KB 440.

[38] *Buxton* v. *Minister of Housing and Local Government* [1961] 1 QB 278. Compare *Simpson* v. *Edinburgh Cpn.* 1960 SC 313 (neighbour unable to dispute planning permission).

[39] For these rules see below, p. 986.

confer this status on persons allowed to appear at the inquiry at the inspector's discretion. This has made an important difference, and members of a local preservation society, allowed by the inspector to appear at the inquiry, have been held to be persons aggrieved and so entitled to challenge the validity of the order.[40] In any case, since a neighbour is a person aggrieved for the purpose of obtaining certiorari (when not barred by statute) to quash a planning decision,[41] it is hard to understand why these identical words should be held to debar him from the corresponding remedy under the Act.

The root of the problem is that the common statutory formula contains no other provision about standing, but allows 'any person aggrieved' to apply to the court. Judges have therefore felt that any question of standing must be resolved by interpreting these words restrictively. Since standing depends upon indefinable factors which vary from one case to another, the interpretations have become inconsistent. There has evidently been some confusion of two different questions: whether a person is at liberty to apply to the court; and whether, having done so, he has shown sufficient standing to be entitled to a remedy. There seems to be no reason to hold that, because he passes the first test, he necessarily passes the second. In any case, the statutory formula expressly makes the remedy discretionary, thus giving ample scope for withholding remedies from applicants with inadequate standing. Thus in a planning case it should be possible to hold that a neighbour is a 'person aggrieved', even though he may be denied a remedy because of the implication of the planning legislation that a neighbour has no standing to challenge a grant of planning permission. By disentangling the two questions the court could avoid laying down a restrictive general rule.

As already observed in the case of other remedies, the current tendency is to relax requirements as to standing, and this is in accordance with an enlightened system of public law.[42] The House of Lords has given the

---

[40] *Turner* v. *Secretary of State for the Environment* (1973) 28 P & CR 123; and see *Sevenoaks UDC* v. *Twynam*, above (objector without special personal interest held to be person aggrieved); *Wilson* v. *Secretary of State for the Environment* [1973] 1 WLR 1083 (objectors conceded to be persons aggrieved). If the Act requires the Secretary of State to 'consider all objections' all objectors may be persons aggrieved: *Nicholson* v. *Secretary of State for Energy* (1978) 76 LGR 693; *Lovelock* v. *Minister of Transport* (1980) 40 P & CR 336. See also *Environmental Defence Society Inc.* v. *South Pacific Aluminium Ltd.* (No. 3) [1981] 1 NZLR 216 and contrast *Burke* v. *Minister of Housing and Local Government* (1957) 8 P & CR 25. A technical change of legal personality may not matter: *R.* v. *Hammersmith and Fulham LBC ex p. People Before Profit Ltd.* (1981) 45 P & CR 364.

[41] *R.* v. *Hendon Rural District Council ex p. Chorley* [1933] 2 KB 696; *R. (Bryson)* v. *Ministry of Development* [1967] NI 180; above, p. 697.

[42] Above, p. 688.

subject a new and broader basis in the *Inland Revenue Commissioners* case,[43] and the principles of that decision should be applicable also to special statutory remedies. In several cases the courts had already favoured a generous interpretation of 'person aggrieved' and it is now less likely that these words will be made an obstacle to any person who may reasonably consider himself aggrieved. Judicial statements suggest that they are likely to cover any person who has a genuine grievance of whatever kind—and that is tantamount to any person who reasonably wishes to bring proceedings.[44] The House of Lords construed them liberally in a rating case, holding that a ratepayer had standing to object to the under-assessment of another property in the same area, but that the interest of a taxpayer would be too remote.[45]

Interim suspension order

One noteworthy element in the common form of time-limited statutory remedy is that it empowers the court to make an interim order suspending the operation of the order challenged, pending the result of the proceedings. In principle this should be a useful power which ought to be available as an adjunct to all remedies by which unlawful orders can be set aside. To a limited extent it may be available (though it does not seem to be used) in conjunction with prohibition and certiorari;[46] but the lack of it in other areas has been remarked upon in the House of Lords.[47] If the court had a general power to suspend the operation of an administrative order until its validity could be determined, this could be used in suitable cases to protect persons affected who would otherwise have to obey the order in the meantime, thereby perhaps suffering irreparable loss.[48]

In fact, however, it does not appear that the courts have availed themselves of this power, any more than in the case of prohibition and certiorari. The reason probably is that where the validity of an order is in dispute, a public authority cannot safely proceed to do anything, in case it should turn out that the order was void and its acts were ultra vires, perhaps

---

[43] Above, p. 701.

[44] See the remarks of Lord Denning in *A.-G. of the Gambia* v. *N'Jie* [1961] AC 617 at 634 and *Maurice* v. *London County Council* [1964] 2 QB 362 at 377 (where the statute said 'who may deem himself aggrieved'). In the latter case the interpretation in the *Buxton* case (above) was disapproved.

[45] *Arsenal Football Club Ltd.* v. *Ende* [1979] AC 1. But the law of rating provided a special context.

[46] See RSC (Amendment No. 3) 1977, O. 53 r. 3(10).

[47] *Hoffman–La Roche & Co.* v. *Secretary of State for Trade and Industry* [1975] AC 25 at 359 (Lord Wilberforce).

[48] See above, p. 346.

with consequent liabilities in tort. Interim suspension of disputed orders, therefore, is virtually automatic in many situations, at any rate in cases involving the compulsory taking of land, which form so large a proportion of those covered by time-limited statutory remedies.

DEFAULT POWERS

Default powers: exclusive effect

It is common for ministers to be given statutory powers to compel local authorities to fulfil their duties, together with power for the minister to step in and remedy the default himself.[49] Thus the Education Act 1944 provides that if the minister is satisfied, on complaint by any interested person or otherwise, that a local authority has failed to discharge any duty under the Act, the minister may by order declare them to be in default and give them such directions as he thinks expedient for performing the duty; and that any such directions may be enforced by mandamus on the minister's application.[50] Under the Public Health Act 1936 the minister may cause a local inquiry to be held if complaint is made to him, or he is himself of opinion, that a local authority have failed to discharge their functions under the Act; he may then, if satisfied as to the failure, give them directions for making good the default; and if they do not, he may by order transfer any of their functions to a county council or to himself, the expense being charged to the defaulting authority.[51] Similar default powers are conferred by The National Health Service Act 1977.[52] The Town and Country Planning Act 1971 contains more limited powers which the Secretary of State may enforce by mandamus.[53] A number of the more sweeping default powers have been repealed, such as those formerly conferred by the Housing Act 1957[54] and the Housing Finance Act 1972;[55] but the Housing Act 1985 empowers the Secretary of State to act as he may think necessary or expedient for enforcing tenants' 'right to buy' from local authorities, if difficulties are put in their way,[56] and the Local Government Act 1985

---

[49] For a list of default powers to which local authorities are subject see 58 HC Deb (WA) 249 (11 April 1984); [1984] PL 485.

[50] s. 99. Private persons are given certain default powers against highway authorities: above, p. 613.

[51] s. 322. The Public Health Act 1875, s. 299 was the prototype of these powers.

[52] s. 85.

[53] s. 276.

[54] ss. 171 (conferring such powers on county councils), 173.

[55] s. 95.

[56] s. 164. See R. v. *Secretary of State for the Environment ex p. Norwich CC* [1982] QB 808.

contains default powers in case local planning authorities fail in their duty to make unitary development plans.[57]

Powers of this kind are a standard administrative mechanism for enabling the central government to deal with an inefficient or recalcitrant local authority. The mere fact of their existence puts a powerful lever in the minister's hands. In principle they should be powers of last resort and rarely used. But in recent years the tensions between central and local government have called them into play more frequently.[58] Ministers have sometimes been armed with such a complex battery of default powers that they have misunderstood them and acted unlawfully.[59]

One legal effect of these default powers is that the courts are prone to treat them as exclusive remedies, impliedly excluding other remedies for the enforcement of the duty. The principle is the same as that already explained in connection with powers, but in the case of duties the courts seem less disposed to allow ordinary remedies to be used as alternatives. A learned judge once said:

Where an Act creates an obligation and enforces the performance in a specified manner, we take it to be a general rule that performance cannot be enforced in any other manner.[60]

The House of Lords approved this proposition in a case where the owner of a paper mill was trying to force the local authority to build sewers adequate to the discharge of effluent from his mill.[61] Under the Public Health Act 1875 the local authority had the duty to provide such sewers as might be necessary for effectually draining their district. The Act also provided that if complaint was made to the Local Government Board about failure to provide sewers, the Board after duly inquiring into the case might order performance of the duty within a fixed time, and might enforce their order by mandamus, or else appoint some person to perform the duty. This scheme of enforcement was held to bar the right of a private person to seek mandamus on his own account, since the Act implied that his right course

---

[57] 1st sched., para. 13.

[58] Notably when more than twenty local authorities refused to implement the Housing Finance Act 1972; see *Asher* v. *Secretary of State for the Environment* [1974] Ch 208. The Act was replaced by the Rent Act 1974 and most of the councillors were discharged from personal liability to district auditors' surcharges by the Housing Finance (Special Provisions) Act 1975. See [1985] PL 283 at 289 (G. Zellick).

[59] As in *Lambeth LBC* v. *Secretary of State for Social Services* (1908) 79 LGR 61; *R.* v. *Secretary of State for Transport ex p. Greater London Council* [1985] The Times, 31 October (discretionary power mistaken for duty).

[60] *Doe* v. *Bridges* (1831) 1 B &Ad 847 at 859 (Lord Tenterden CJ).

[61] *Pasmore* v. *Oswaldtwistle Urban District Council* [1898] AC 387. See also *Clark* v. *Epsom Rural District Council* [1929] 1 Ch 287 (sewers); *R.* v. *Kensington LBC ex p. Birdwood* (1976) 74 LGR 424 (refuse).

was to complain to the Board. The same principle has several times been applied in proceedings for injunctions[62] or declarations[63] against local education authorities in connection with the provision or administration of schools, the courts holding that their obligations in these matters were remediable only by means of the Secretary of State's default power. That was also the only remedy where a local authority was accused of failing to provide temporary accommodation for persons in urgent need under the National Assistance Act 1948.[64]

Default powers: non-exclusive effect

On the face of it it is strange that the courts should thus regard default powers as a substitute for ordinary legal remedies. A default power is an administrative device of last resort which is rarely used and which has as its object the internal efficiency of the executive machinery of the state. It is suitable for dealing with a general breakdown of some public service caused by a local authority' default, but it is quite unsuitable as a remedy for defaults in individual cases. As a judge once said, a power of this kind is not really a legal remedy at all, and certainly not an equally convenient and beneficial remedy for an individual so as to exclude the remedy of mandamus.[65] Scots law also rejects the English doctrine.[66] A better explanation of the cases mentioned above is probably that the nature of the duty made it unsuitable for enforcement by private action or that, in other words, Parliament did not intend to make it a duty owed to individuals personally. Thus in the case of the sewers Lord Halsbury LC said that

it would be extremely inconvenient that each suitor in turn should be permitted to apply for a specific remedy against the body charged with the care of the health of the inhabitants of the district in respect of drainage.

In the case under the National Assistance Act Lord Denning MR likewise said:[67]

---

[62] *Bradbury* v. *Enfield London Borough Council* [1967] 1 WLR 1311 (failure to submit plans and obtain approval before establishing new schools); *Wood* v. *Ealing London Borough Council* [1967] Ch 364 (duty to provide sufficient schools). Contrast *Meade* v. *Haringey LBC* [1979] 1 WLR 637 (duty to keep schools open enforceable by parents).

[63] *Cumings* v. *Birkenhead Cpn.* [1972] Ch 12 (duty to provide sufficient schools); *Watt* v. *Kesteven County Council* [1955] 1 QB 408 (duty to have regard to wishes of parents); and see *R.* v. *Northampton CC ex p. Gray* [1986] The Times, 10 June (choice of parent governors).

[64] *Southwark London Borough Council* v. *Williams* [1971] Ch 734. See similarly *Roberts* v. *Dorset CC* (1976) 75 LGR 79; *Wyatt* v. *Hillingdon LBC* (1978) 76 LGR 727.

[65] *R.* v. *Leicester Guardians* [1899] 2 QB 632 at 639 (Darling J).

[66] *Docherty (T.) Ltd.* v. *Burgh of Monifieth* 1971 SLT 13 (local authority ordered to construct sewers); *Walker* v. *Strathclyde Regional Council* (No. 1) 1986 SLT 523; and see *Wilson* v. *Independent Broadcasting Authority* 1979 SLT 279.

[67] *Southwark London Borough Council* v. *Williams* [1971] Ch 734 at 743.

It cannot have been intended by Parliament that every person who was in need of temporary accommodation should be able to sue the local authority for it.

It is reasonable to suppose that the general obligations of public authorities in the areas of health, education and welfare are not intended to be enforceable at the suit of individuals. It is unrealistic to suppose that ministerial default powers supply an adequate alternative remedy.

This last point is recognised by the courts in a number of situations. They will not accept default powers as a substitute for ordinary remedies in a case of breach of statutory duty causing personal injury;[68] or where something is done which is positively forbidden by the Act;[69] or where something is done which is ultra vires.[70] In these situations it would plainly be wrong to deprive an injured or affected person of his ordinary legal rights. Furthermore, the duty of a body such as a local education authority may sometimes be owed to an individual and therefore enforceable by him. Parents who are obliged to send their children to school under criminal penalties have a legal right to have them accepted by the local education authority in accordance with their statutory duty. Consequently where an authority refused to accept poor children in its schools without a special payment which it was not entitled to demand, the guardians of the children were granted a declaration that the children must be accepted.[71] Where an authority closed schools which it had a duty to keep open, it was held by the Court of Appeal that the minister's default power was not exclusive but left open all the established remedies for breach of statutory duty.[72] In a relator action brought on behalf of a member of the public for an injunction against the broadcasting of an indecent television programme, contrary to the statutory duty of the broadcasting authority, the same court rejected the argument that the complainant's only remedy was to apply for a ministerial intervention under the Television Act 1964.[73]

[68] *Ching* v. *Surrey CC* [1910] 1 KB 736; *Reffell* v. *Surrey County Council* [1964] 1 WLR 358 (failure to keep school buildings safe; pupil injured).

[69] *Bradbury* v. *Enfield London Borough Council* [1967] 1 WLR 1311 (ceasing to maintain school without giving opportunity for objection).

[70] *Cumings* v. *Birkenhead Cpn.* [1972] Ch 12 (Lord Denning MR); *Meade* v. *Haringey LBC* [1979] 1 WLR 637. See also *R.* v. *Secretary of State for the Environment ex p. Ward* [1984] 1 WLR 834.

[71] *Gateshead Union* v. *Durham County Council* [1918] 1 Ch 146. The court would have granted an injunction also if necessary.

[72] *Meade* v. *Haringey LBC* (above).

[73] *A.-G. ex rel. McWhirter* v. *Independent Broadcasting Authority* [1973] QB 629 at 649 (no breach of duty was found).

20

LIABILITY OF PUBLIC AUTHORITIES

Categories of liability

Any attempt to describe the liability of public authorities to pay monetary damages or compensation runs at once into difficulties of classification. In the first place, there is the problem of the Crown. Crown liability for torts such as trespass and negligence has a very different history from the liability of local authorities and other governmental bodies. But since the Crown Proceedings Act 1947 the Crown has in principle been put on the same footing as public authorities generally. To treat the Crown in an entirely separate compartment would therefore mean segregating materials and illustrations which are best grouped together; but to deal adequately with the Crown in one single discussion would require too many digressions. The course which will be followed here will be to treat matters involving the Crown as part of the general law so far as they rest on the same principles; but the history and peculiarities of Crown proceedings, together with certain connected matters, must be relegated to the next chapter.

Inevitably, also, there will be overlap with the chapter on remedies. The law of liability can never be cleanly detached from the law of remedies, so that reference back may be needed from time to time. The present chapter is concerned primarily with liability to pay damages or compensation in money, though the injunction is also an important remedy in actions for nuisance and for breach of contract.

LIABILITY IN TORT GENERALLY

General principles[1]

Public authorities, including ministers of the Crown,[2] enjoy no dispensation from the ordinary law of tort and contract, except in so far as statute gives it to them. Unless acting within their powers, they are liable like any other person for trespass, nuisance, negligence, and so forth. This is an

---

[1] See Street, *Governmental Liability*, ch. II: Hogg, *Liability of the Crown*, ch. 4; Harlow, *Compensation and Government Torts*; Aronson and Whitmore, *Public Torts and Contracts*; (1980) 96 LQR 413 (P. P. Craig).

[2] See below, p. 812.

important aspect of the rule of law. Similarly they are subject to the ordinary law of master and servant, by which the employer is liable for torts committed by the employee in the course of his employment, the employee also being personally liable. Examples are furnished by many classic cases. In *Cooper* v. *Wandsworth Board of Works*[3] the board was held liable in damages in an ordinary action of trespass: as has been seen, it was acting outside its powers because it caused its workmen to demolish a building without first giving the owner a fair hearing; therefore it had no defence to an action for damages for trespass. The famous cases which centred round John Wilkes in the eighteenth century, and which denied the power of ministers to issue general warrants of arrest and search, took the form of actions for damages against the particular servants who did the deeds, who were sued in trespass just as if they were private individuals.[4] The Governor of Jamaica, who had ordered the seizure of a ship chartered to the plaintiff and could show no legal justification, was held personally liable in damages for trespass.[5] Before 1948 the Crown itself was not legally liable for its servants' misdeeds, but the Crown would be the natural defendant today.[6] The plaintiff may sue the master or the servant or both, since both are jointly liable, but in most cases he will naturally choose to sue the master. He must, however, be able to show some recognised legal wrong. Thus there was no remedy at common law for tapping of telephones, which was held not to be a tort,[7] though compensation may now be payable under the Interception of Communications Act 1985.[8]

There are some situations where an officer of central or local government has an independent statutory liability by virtue of his office, because the statute imposes duties upon him as a designated officer rather than on the public authority which appoints him. In that case the employee only will be liable. Thus an action failed against a local authority when their inspector of animals had seized supposedly infected sheep in a market, since the statutory order empowered the inspector but not the local authority to seize infected animals; and it made no difference that the local authority had a statutory duty to appoint the inspector and power to dismiss him.[9] But if the duties of the designated officer are in fact carried out by employees of the local authority, that authority may be liable in the same way as for its

---

[3] (1863) 14 CB (NS) 180; above, p. 503.
[4] *Entick* v. *Carrington* (1765) 19 St. Tr. 1030; *Leach* v. *Money* (1765) 19 St. Tr. 2002; *Wilkes* v. *Wood* (1763) 19 St. Tr. 1153.
[5] *Musgrave* v. *Pulido* (1879) 5 App. Cas. 102. Similarly *Mostyn* v. *Fabrigas* (1774) 1 Cowp. 161.
[6] Below, p. 814.
[7] *Malone* v. *Metropolitan Police Commissioner* [1980] QB 49.
[8] Above, p. 167.
[9] *Stanbury* v. *Exeter Cpn.* [1905] 2 KB 838.

other employees. This last proposition was applied by the Court of Appeal where a junior employee of a local authority negligently certified that no local land charges were registered against land which was being sold, so that an incumbrancer lost a charge over the land, although the statutory duty of issuing certificates rested specifically upon the local authority's clerk as registrar.[10] In cases where the designated officer alone is liable, his employer (whether the Crown or a local authority) will normally indemnify him; but this is only a matter of grace.[11]

Another rule which emerged in the course of Wilkes's legal adventures was that oppressive or unconstitutional action by servants of the government could justify an award of exemplary or punitive damages, i.e. damages which take into account the outrageous conduct of the defendant and not merely the actual loss to the plaintiff. This is one of the special cases in which exemplary damages are allowed, according to the law as declared by the House of Lords.[12] So the position here is that the law is sterner with the government than with the citizen.

Inevitable injury

What is duly done under statutory authority is lawful action of which no one is entitled to complain. A public authority will therefore not be liable in tort where the injury is the inevitable consequence of what Parliament has authorised, as is the nuisance caused by the running of trains on a railway authorised to be operated on a particular line,[13] or by the erection of a barrier on a pavement.[14] But it is important to ascertain precisely what the statute authorises. The principle worked out in the railway cases in the last century was that if the empowering Act expressly authorised the use of locomotives and trains,[15] no action could lie for such nuisance as their use inevitably involved;[16] but that if the Act merely authorised the construction of the railway, without expressly providing for the use of trains, any nuisance caused by trains was actionable in the normal way.[17]

---

[10] *Ministry of Housing and Local Government* v. *Sharp* [1970] 2 QB 223. For this case see below, p. 761.

[11] Same case, at 269, 275. See Town and Country Planning Act 1971, s. 4(6).

[12] *Rookes* v. *Barnard* [1964] AC 1129 at 1226; and see *Ashby* v. *White* (1703) 2 Ld Raym. 938 at 956; *Broome* v. *Cassell & Co. Ltd.* [1972] AC 1027; *A.-G. of St Christopher* v. *Reynolds* [1980] AC 637. For awards of exemplary damages against the police see *George* v. *Commissioner of Metropolitan Police* [1984] The Times, 31 March; *Connor* v. *Chief Constable of Cambridgeshire* [1984] The Times, 11 April.

[13] *Hammersmith Rly. Co.* v. *Brand* (1869) LR 4 HL 171. A claim for statutory compensation was also rejected: see below, p. 802.

[14] *Dormer* v. *Newcastle upon Tyne Cpn.* [1940] 2 KB 204.

[15] As did the Railway Clauses Consolidation Act 1845, s. 86.

[16] *Vaughan* v. *Taff Vale Rly Co.* (1960) 5 H & N 679.

[17] *Jones* v. *Festiniog Rly Co.* (1868) LR 3 QB 733.

The basis of the latter proposition was that the Act left the railway company at liberty to use trains, but without any privilege to commit nuisances.

This principle was invoked by the Court of Appeal where an oil company had obtained an Act of Parliament authorising the acquisition of specific land for a refinery.[18] The Act also authorised the construction and use of ancillary works, such as railways, with provision for compensation in case of damage. But, although it clearly contemplated the operation of the refinery, it did not authorise that expressly. Lord Denning MR made a persuasive case for applying the principle of the railway cases, holding that the absence of express authority was a deliberate omission, indicating an intention that the company was not to be exempted from the law of nuisance. But the House of Lords reversed, holding that the Act at least by necessary implication authorised the operation of the refinery and that neighbours who complained of excessive smell, vibration and noise would have no remedy in so far as the nuisance was the inevitable result of the authorised operation. The House made no mention of the principle of the railway cases[19] and their decision seems to have weakened, if not removed, the protection which it gave to persons injured by the operations of public authorities and bodies with statutory powers. As is pointed out later,[20] this is an injustice which Parliament has felt bound to remedy.

Rights over property are similarly overridden where a public authority acquires land which is subject to some third party right such as a right of way or a restrictive covenant. No such right can prevent the authority from exercising its statutory powers;[21] and to the extent that the right is expropriated, there is, as mentioned below, a statutory claim to compensation.[22] But the right is not extinguished, and may be enforced in any situation where it does not conflict with action based on statutory authority. For example, the Air Ministry may set up an aerodrome on land compulsorily purchased, even though the land is subject to a covenant that it shall be used only for agriculture; but if the Ministry let the aerodrome to a company for commercial flying, the company may be restrained by injunction from breaking the covenant.[23]

---

[18] *Allen* v. *Gulf Oil Refining Ltd.* [1980] QB 156 (reversed [1981] AC 1001).

[19] Except in Lord Keith's dissenting speech.

[20] Below, p. 802. Lord Denning also proposed that it should be remedied by holding in future that Acts authorising the use of such works should not be construed as taking away the right of action for nuisance at common law, since the injustice was comparable to expropriation without compensation: *Allen* v. *Gulf Oil Refining Ltd.* (above).

[21] *Kirby* v. *Harrogate School Board* [1896] 1 Ch. 437; *Re Simeon and Isle of Wight RDC* [1937] Ch. 525; *Marten* v. *Flight Refuelling Ltd.* [1962] Ch. 115.

[22] Below, p. 802.

[23] *Marten* v. *Flight Refuelling Ltd.*, (above).

These are cases where private interests must suffer inevitably. But in many situations there is no such inevitability. If there is a choice of sites or methods, some of which will injure private rights and some of which will not, a public authority may have a duty to choose the latter. In each case the court has to consider whether Parliament presumably intended to permit the infringement. The presumption is that infringement is to be avoided unless reasonably necessary, and the onus of proving necessity is on the public authority.[24] In an early case where paving commissioners were empowered to carry out paving works as they should think fit, damages were awarded against them for raising a street so as to obstruct doors and windows, since they had acted, as Blackstone J said, 'arbitrarily and tyrannically'.[25]

A leading case was decided by the House of Lords under an Act which gave power to build hospitals in London for the benefit of the poor. A hospital was built at Hampstead for smallpox and other contagious diseases, and neighbouring residents obtained an injunction against it on the ground that, sited where it was, it was a nuisance.[26] The District Managers were unable to show that such a hospital in such a place was expressly or impliedly authorised by the Act: the Act gave no compulsory powers, it made no provision for compensation, and the inference was that it was not designed to permit interference with private rights. This principle may also apply even where the Act authorises a specific undertaking on a specific site. The Manchester Corporation was empowered to build and operate an electric power station on certain land outside the city, but this did not prevent a farmer from obtaining an injunction and damages on the ground that the Corporation had not used all reasonable diligence to prevent the creation of a nuisance by sulphurous fumes and contamination of grass.[27] Furthermore, the House of Lords held that the degree of nuisance which might have to be accepted as inevitable would vary with the state of scientific knowledge from time to time, so that the Corporation would have to keep abreast of the best current practice in this respect in order to discharge the onus lying upon them. Lord Dunedin said:[28]

When Parliament has authorised a certain thing to be made or done in a certain place, there can be no action for nuisance caused by the making or doing of that

---

[24] See *Manchester Cpn.* v. *Farnworth*, below.
[25] *Leader* v. *Moxton* (1773) 3 Wils. KB 461.
[26] *Metropolitan Asylum District* v. *Hill* (1881) 6 App. Cas. 193; similarly *Fletcher* v. *Birkenhead Corporation* [1907] 1 KB 205 (local authority's waterworks pumped out silt from beneath plaintiff's house, causing subsidence); *Tate & Lyle Ltd.* v. *Greater London Council* [1983] 2 AC 509 (power to construct ferry terminal does not justify adoption of a design which diverts silt to plaintiffs' jetty).
[27] *Manchester Cpn.* v. *Farnworth* [1930] AC 171.
[28] At p. 183.

thing if the nuisance is the inevitable result of the making or doing so authorised. The onus of proving that the result is inevitable is on those who wish to escape liability for nuisance, but the criterion of inevitability is not what is theoretically possible but what is possible according to the state of scientific knowledge at the time, having also in view a certain common sense appreciation, which cannot be rigidly defined, of practical feasibility in view of situation and of expense.

This 'criterion of inevitability' will depend in each case on the true implications of the empowering statute, and this may pose difficult questions of construction. A contrasting case concerned a river authority which, in dredging a river, deposited the spoil along the banks and thus raised their height. This prevented the river, when in flood, from overflowing into its usual flood channels, and the diversion of flood waters caused the collapse of a bridge belonging to the plaintiff. But the plaintiff failed in an action for nuisance, since it was held that the injury 'was clearly of a kind contemplated by the Act'.[29] The depositing of soil along river banks was a normal accompaniment of dredging, and if any owner of land which would be injured thereby could obtain an injunction, the river authority could in many cases be prevented from exercising its powers.[30] It was said also that there was an important distinction between powers to execute particular works (such as the building of power stations or hospitals) and powers to execute a variety of works of specified descriptions (such as river drainage works); and that the principle of avoiding injury to private rights, except where demonstrably necessary, applied only to the former.[31] But the decisive point was probably that the Land Drainage Act 1930 gave a right to compensation for injury done, with the implication that this was intended to be in substitution for the ordinary remedies of private law.

If a public authority commits an unauthorised nuisance, it is no defence that it is taking the most reasonable action possible in the public interest, or that the injury done is relatively unimportant in relation to the benefit to the public. Thus an injunction was granted at the instance of an angling club whose fishing rights in the river Derwent were injured by pollution from the sewage works of the Derby Corporation.[32] The Corporation had

[29] *Marriage* v. *East Norfolk Rivers Catchment Board* [1950] 1 KB 284. cf. *Lagan Navigation Co.* v. *Lambeg Bleaching etc. Co.* [1927] AC 226.
[30] This argument, which recurs through the cases (e.g. in *Allen* v. *Gulf Oil Refining Ltd.* above), may be fallacious, since injunction is a discretionary remedy which need not necessarily be granted in an action for damages at common law. See [1982] CLJ 87 (S. R. Tromans).
[31] At p. 307 (Jenkins LJ).
[32] *Pride of Derby and Derbyshire Angling Association Ltd.* v. *British Celanese Ltd.* [1953] Ch. 149.

a statutory duty to provide a sewerage system and had originally provided an adequate one. But the growth of the city had overloaded it, and the Corporation had taken to discharging inadequately treated sewage into the river. It was clear from the Acts of Parliament in question that there was no intention to give power to do this—indeed, it appeared that it was prohibited. The Court of Appeal rejected the argument that an injunction ought not to be granted to interfere with the Corporation's actions as sewage authority because, having initially provided a satisfactory plant, they could not be blamed for its subsequent operation under conditions of overload. They also rejected the argument that the Corporation's duty to act in the public interest gave it some sort of immunity from injunctions. The court did, however, suspend the operation of the injunction for sixteen months so as to give the Corporation reasonable time to make better arrangements.

In the *Derby* case the Corporation itself caused the nuisance by discharging the effluent from its own plant. If it had reached the river merely by overflowing from the sewers, without any action on the Corporation's part, the Corporation would have done nothing to incur liability. This situation arose at Ilford through sewage overflowing through a manhole, due to the growth of the population and the overloading of what was previously an adequate sewerage system. A householder whose premises were flooded failed in an action for nuisance, since the Corporation themselves had committed no unlawful act.[33] This has nothing to do with the distinction between misfeasance and nonfeasance, mentioned below.[34] The point is simply that the cause of the injury is not any act of the Corporation but the use of the sewers by other people whom the Corporation has no power to prevent. If the overflow had been caused by a housing estate built by the Corporation, the result might have been different.[35] The Corporation would also have been liable if they had diverted the overflow from one man's land to another's, even though that minimised the injury.[36] For their failure to provide a more adequate sewage system there is only the statutory remedy of complaint to the minister.[37] The Public Health Act 1936 provides for compensation for injury caused by the exercise of powers of this kind;[38] but the exercise of some power must be the cause of the injury.

That Act, like many other Acts, also contains an express 'nuisance clause'

---

[33] *Smeaton* v. *Ilford Cpn.* [1954] Ch. 450.
[34] Below, p. 769.
[35] See the *Smeaton* case at 463.
[36] See at 465.
[37] See above, p. 748.
[38] s. 278.

providing that the local authority shall not create a nuisance.[39] Clauses of this kind may be interpreted as excluding strict liability, i.e. liability without fault, under the rule in *Rylands* v. *Fletcher* in case of accidents caused by the escape of noxious things such as sewage or gas,[40] if indeed that rule applies at all to statutory authorities providing public services (see below). A provision that an authority shall not create a nuisance, or shall not be exonerated from liability for nuisance, does not affect its non-liability for nuisances inevitably resulting from the performance of its duties and the exercise of its powers.[41]

A public authority which itself deliberately creates a nuisance cannot escape liability by pleading that it was acting outside its powers.[42] But unauthorised action by its servants or agents, if outside the powers of the authority, might well be outside the scope of their employment. The principle of vicarious liability, explained below with reference to negligence, applies equally to nuisance and other torts.

The grant of planning permission, for example to build a factory, under the Town and Country Planning Acts confers no right to commit nuisances or to infringe private rights in any way.[43] It confers no special power to carry out the permitted operation. It merely removes the statutory impediment, and thus *pro tanto* restores to the successful applicant the liberty to develop his own property, subject to the rights of his neighbours, which he would otherwise enjoy at common law.

A local authority may be liable in nuisance for failing to remove gipsies from its land[44] and for allowing trees in the highway to cause the subsidence of a neighbouring house.[45]

NEGLIGENCE AND STRICT LIABILITY

Negligence—ordinary cases

Unlike nuisance, negligence is never inevitable. No statute can be expected to authorise works to be carried out negligently, and the ordinary law of

---

[39] s. 31. Another example is Gas Act 1948, 3rd sched., para. 42. And see *Radstock Co-operative Society Ltd.* v. *Norton-Radstock Urban District Council* [1968] Ch. 605.

[40] See *Smeaton* v. *Ilford Cpn.* (above) and cases there cited. For the rule in *Rylands* v. *Fletcher* see below, p. 770.

[41] See Public Utilities Street Works Act 1950 as applied in *Department of Transport* v. *North West Water Authority* [1984] AC 336.

[42] *Campbell* v. *Paddington Cpn.* [1911] 1 KB 869.

[43] See *Buxton* v. *Minister of Housing and Local Government* [1961] 1 QB 278.

[44] *Page Motors Ltd.* v. *Epsom BC* (1981) 80 LGR 337.

[45] *Russell* v. *Barnet LBC* (1984) 83 LGR 152.

liability therefore has full scope. Discretionary decisions are another matter, as will be seen below.

The liability of statutory bodies for the negligence of their servants and agents, acting within the scope of their employment, was firmly established by the House of Lords in 1866. The plaintiff's ship had been damaged by hitting a mudbank which the harbour board's employees had negligently allowed to block the entrance of one of the docks. It was held that public bodies created by statute must in principle bear the same liabilities for the torts of their servants as were borne by private employers, subject only to any contrary statute.[46] The fact that the public body was acting solely for the public benefit and for no profit was immaterial. Nor was there any room for the defence that employer and employee were all alike holders of public offices with no vicarious liability. This argument exonerates an intermediate employee in a hierarchy such as the civil service.[47] But it cannot exonerate the true employer. In a later case the broad principle of liability was stated by Lord Blackburn:[48]

It is now thoroughly well established that no action will lie for doing that which the legislature has authorised, if it be done without negligence, although it does occasion damage to anyone; but an action does lie for doing what the legislature has authorised, if it be done negligently.

This was a case where a reservoir company had statutory power to make use of a certain stream but neglected to clean it out, so that their use of it caused flooding and made them liable.

Actions for negligence against government departments, local authorities, etc., are accordingly very common. Traffic accidents are one large class, but there are many others. The following are examples where liability was established and compensated in damages.

Post Office workmen left a manhole open in a street, covered with a tent and surrounded with warning lights. A child, tempted to investigate, knocked a lamp into the manhole causing an explosion which injured him.[49]

A district council built an air-raid shelter in a road but left it unlit at night, so that a motorist was injured.[50]

A small boy ran out from a county council's nursery school onto the road, and a lorry-driver, trying to avoid him, was killed.[51]

---

[46] *Mersey Docks and Harbour Board Trustees* v. *Gibbs* (1866) LR 1 HL 93.

[47] See below, p. 812.

[48] *Geddis* v. *Proprietors of Bann Reservoir* (1873) 3 App. Cas. 430 at 455.

[49] *Hughes* v. *Lord Advocate* [1963] AC 837.

[50] *Fisher* v. *Ruislip-Northwood UDC* [1945] KB 584; cf. *Morrison* v. *Sheffield Cpn.* [1917] 2 KB 866; *Baldock* v. *Westminster CC* (1918) 120 LT 470.

[51] *Carmarthenshire CC* v. *Lewis* [1955] AC 549.

Local councils failed to repair a dangerous step in one requisitioned house and a dangerous ceiling in another, whereby the occupiers were injured.[52]

Surgeons and medical staff of a hospital, for whom the Ministry of Health were responsible, treated a patient's hand in such a way as to render it useless.[53]

A water board, supplying water through old lead pipes, neglected to warn or protect consumers who suffered lead poisoning.[54]

Public authorities are similarly liable for any injury caused by failure to take due care for the safety of persons coming onto their premises under the Occupiers' Liability Act 1957.

The court construes statutes, wherever possible, so as to preserve the general liability for negligence. It is not reduced merely because the authority also has more limited statutory duties.[55] Nor is it affected by a statutory provision which has been widely applied to local health and sanitary authorities and which protects them and their members from liability for anything done by them or their officers or servants if done bona fide for the purpose of executing the Act.[56] The court construes 'bona fide' as meaning 'bona fide and without negligence'.[57] An alternative construction is that protection is given only against personal and not against corporate liability.[58] But if a statute specifically authorises some dangerous activity, that by itself cannot create liability. In one case a railway company obtained an Act allowing it to maintain gateposts which had been erected in a public highway, but was held not liable for damage to a taxi-cab which collided with them, even though it had taken no steps to light them.[59]

In this last case Lord Parker restated the general rule:

. . . it is undoubtedly a well-settled principle of law that when statutory powers are conferred they must be exercised with reasonable care, so that if those who exercise them could by reasonable precaution have prevented an injury which has been occasioned, and was likely to be occasioned, by their exercise, damages for negligence may be recovered.

---

[52] *Hawkins v. Coulsdon & Purley UDC* [1954] 1 QB 319; *Greene v. Chelsea BC* [1954] 2 QB 127.

[53] *Cassidy v. Ministry of Health* [1951] 2 KB 343.

[54] *Barnes v. Irwell Valley Water Board* [1938] 1 KB 21. See also *Read v. Croydon Cpn.* [1938] 4 All ER 631 (typhoid).

[55] *Barnes v. Irwell Valley Water Board* (above); *Read v. Croydon Cpn.* (above).

[56] Public Health Acts 1875, s. 265; 1936, s. 305; National Health Service Act 1977, s. 125.

[57] *Bullard v. Croydon Hospital Management Committee* [1953] 1 QB 511.

[58] *Southampton and Itchen Bridge Co. v. Local Board of Southampton* (1858) 8 E &B 801.

[59] *Great Central Railway Co. v. Hewlett* [1916] 2 AC 511. Contrast *Fisher v. Ruislip-Northwood UDC* [1945] KB 584 (above).

Negligence—special situations

There are infinite varieties of actionable negligence, an account of which belongs to the law of tort. But the courts have extended the principle of liability to certain acts of public authorities which are of a peculiarly governmental character and which require notice.[60]

In 1970 the House of Lords held the Crown (the Home Office) liable for damage done by escaping Borstal boys. These were boys with criminal records who had been taken out on a training exercise in charge of Borstal officers who had instructions to keep them in custody but who neglected to do so; they escaped and damaged a yacht, the owner of which was the successful plaintiff.[61] Despite the novel nature of the claim, and the contention that there was no liability for the acts of persons other than servants or agents, it was held that the custody of these dangerous boys imposed a duty to take reasonable care that they could not injure the public. This was an application of the doctrine of the law of tort that a duty of care arises from a relationship of proximity where the damage done is the natural and probable result of the breach of duty. The required degree of proximity may exist, on the facts of such a case, only in the vicinity of the place of detention, so that liability may be limited to damage done locally in the course of the escape.[62] Crimes committed later and further afield would come within the principle that the loss resulting from criminal acts normally lies where it falls.[63] Nevertheless in this decision the House of Lords has taken a noteworthy step towards spreading over the whole community the price that has to be paid for experimental penal policies, rather than requiring it to be borne by the individual victim[63]. In the same way a local authority was held liable for negligent custody of a boy, known to be an incendiary, who escaped and burned down a church.[64]

Liability for negligence in administrative office work is illustrated by a planning case in which a government department successfully sued a local authority for damages.[65] A clerk of the local authority had negligently overlooked a compensation notice entered in the local land charges register, so that it failed to operate against a later purchaser of the land affected; and accordingly, when planning permission was granted and the

[60] See [1973] PL 84 (G. Ganz); (1976) 92 LQR 213, (1978) 94 LQR 428 (P. P. Craig).

[61] *Dorset Yacht Co. Ltd.* v. *Home Office* [1970] AC 1004 (discussed further below). On the comparable French law, which now extends to prisoners released on licence, see (1969) 27 CLJ 273 (C. J. Hamson) and [1987] PL 465.

[62] See at p. 1070 (Lord Diplock).

[63] Contrast the Court of Appeals attitude (below, p. 771).

[64] *Writtle (Vicar)* v. *Essex CC* (1979) 77 LGR 656.

[65] *Ministry of Housing and Local Government* v. *Sharp* [1970] 2 QB 223. But an official whose decisions are subject to appeal owes no duty of care: *Jones* v. *Department of Employment* [1988] 2 WLR 493 (social security adjudication officer).

compensation paid for a previous refusal should have been repayable, the ministry were unable to recover it. The Court of Appeal discussed the possibility that the local registrar, though an employee of the district council, might have been the party liable, as an independent statutory authority, rather than the council itself, but in fact the council accepted legal liability for his functions.

It is not clear whether this last case should be considered an example of the recently recognised tort of negligent misstatement.[66] That tort is now proving important as a head of government liability, particularly in connection with misleading official advice, the problems of which were explained earlier.[67] It has enabled a firm to recover damages from a government department which wrongly advised them that they were covered by export credit insurance against default by a foreign company;[68] and purchasers of land to recover damages from local authorities who overlooked proposals for a subway[69] and for road widening[70] in answering planning enquiries. The principle has been extended to planning authorities who negligently grant invalid planning permissions under which the developer later suffers loss,[71] or valid permissions where the right to object is negligently denied to a neighbour.[72] At this point the cases merge with those of negligent discretionary decisions, discussed in the following section. They may be noted also as examples of actionable negligence causing economic loss only.[73]

[66] Recognised by the House of Lords in *Hedley Byrne & Co. Ltd.* v. *Heller & Partners Ltd.* [1964] AC 465 and applied by the Court of Appeal in *Esso Petroleum Co. Ltd.* v. *Mardon* [1976] QB 801.   [67] Above, p. 381.

[68] *Culford Metal Industries Ltd.* v. *Export Credits Guarantee Dept.* [1981] The Times, 25 March. Other examples are *Windsor Motors Ltd.* v. *District of Powell River* (1969) 4 DLR (3d) 155 (municipality liable for negligence of inspector who recommended a car dealer to rent a site on which his business was forbidden by zoning byelaws); *Jung* v. *District of Burnaby* (1978) 91 DLR (3d) 592 (negligent misstatement about fire regulations); *Christchurch Drainage Board* v. *Brown* [1987] The Times, 26 October (drainage board failed to warn applicant for building permit of flood danger); *Meates* v. *Attorney-General* [1983] NZLR 308 (government liable for negligent assurances about future subsidies to industry). A disclaimer of liability may be effective: *Hadden* v. *Glasgow DC* 1986 SLT 557; *Vaughan* v. *Edinburgh DC* 1988 SLT 191.

[69] *Coats Patons (Retail) Ltd.* v. *Birmingham Cpn.* (1971) 69 LGR 356 (disclaimer of liability held ineffective).

[70] *Shaddock & Associates Pty Ltd.* v. *Parramatta CC* (1981) 36 ALR 385, where Gibbs CJ and Stephen J held that the duty of care extends to public bodies which make a practice of supplying information. See likewise *Bell* v. *City of Sarnia* (1987) 37 DLR (4th) 438.

[71] *Hull* v. *Canterbury MC* [1974] 1 NSWLR 300; *Knight Holdings* v. *Warringah Shire Council* [1975] 2 NSWLR 796; *Port Underwood Forests Ltd.* v. *Marlborough CC* [1982] 1 NZLR 343. Contrast *Dunlop* v. *Woollahra MC* [1982] AC 158 (above, p. 347).

[72] *Craig* v. *East Coast Bays CC* [1986] 1 NZLR 99 (breach of authority's duty, based on proximity, to notify neighbour whose view was spoiled: damages awarded).

[73] See the comments of Megarry V.-C. in *Ross* v. *Caunters* [1980] Ch. 297.

A remarkable extension of the law of official liability, which 'opened up a whole new area of actionable negligence',[74] was made by the Court of Appeal in holding a local authority answerable in damages for the negligent inspection and passing of the foundations of a house, at the instance of a later purchaser.[75] The foundations were partly on the site of an old rubbish tip and should not have been passed by the council's inspector. The builder sold the house to a purchaser who then sold it to the plaintiff, who found that it subsided badly. The builder was held to have been equally liable, but the action was pursued against the local authority only. Lord Denning MR said:[76]

Never before has an action of this kind been brought before our courts. Nor, as far as we can discover, before the courts of any other countries which follow the common law . . . In the end it will be found to be a question of policy, which we, as judges, have to decide.

Lord Denning concluded that there was no reason why the local authority should not be held liable for the negligence of their inspector. Under the Public Health Act 1936 it was their duty to see that their byelaws were complied with, and their byelaws required foundations to be inspected and passed, the object of inspection being to protect purchasers and occupiers of houses.

The House of Lords approved this epoch-making decision in a closely similar case, where a block of flats developed cracks because it had been built on inadequate foundations.[77] The questions raised, as preliminary issues, were whether the local authority owed a duty of care to tenants of the flats for not ensuring that the foundations conformed to the plans originally approved, for failing to inspect the foundations during building, and (alternatively) for inspecting them negligently. As regards negligent inspection the House affirmed the earlier decision of the Court of Appeal, holding that there was a duty to the tenants to exercise reasonable care. As

[74] *Sparham-Souter* v. *Town & Country Developments Ltd.* [1976] QB 858 at 880 (Lane LJ). It is 'the high water mark of a trend in the development of the law of negligence': *Curran* v. *Northern Ireland Co-ownership Housing Association Ltd.* (below) (Lord Bridge).

[75] *Dutton* v. *Bognor Regis Urban District Council* [1972] 1 QB 373. At 391 Lord Denning says that the 'power or duty' dichotomy is not complete, and that 'there is a middle term', 'control', which imposes liability. But there is no reason to suppose that a mere power does not have to be exercised with reasonable care: see the preceding section.

[76] At 390; and see the *Dorset Yacht* case (above) at 1039 (Lord Morris preferring the criterion of 'fair and reasonable' to that of 'policy') and 1058 (Lord Diplock).

[77] *Anns* v. *Merton LBC* [1978] AC 728. The decision is followed in Canada (*Kamloops* v. *Nielsen* [1984] 10 DLR (4th) 641, S. Ct.) and New Zealand (*Morton* v. *Douglas Homes Ltd.* [1984] 2 NZLR 239; *Stieller* v. *Porirua CC* [1986] 1 NZLR 84) but not in Australia (*Sutherland Shire Council* v. *Heyman* (1985) 60 ALR 1). For criticism see (1983) 46 MLR 147 (J. C. Smith and P. Burns); *Rawling* v. *Takaro Properties Ltd.* [1988] 2 WLR 418 at 430.

regards failure to inspect the foundations at all, there was a duty to consider properly whether to inspect or not. This was a discretionary power, due to be considered in the next section. As regards the non-conformity of the works with the plans, it was held that there was no duty: the duty was to take reasonable care to secure that the foundations were in accordance with the building byelaws. The cause of action, it was held also, would arise not at the time of the breach of duty but at the time when there was present or imminent danger to health or safety,[78] so that it would not be barred six years after the act of negligence.

The wide duties of care unexpectedly thrust upon local authorities by these decisions have been brought within limits in a series of later cases. The building laws 'are public health measures', whose purpose is to protect the health and safety of occupiers, and of the public generally; it is not to safeguard building developers, or anyone else, against economic loss.[79] Consequently when an inspector neglected to take action after discovering that, contrary to the approved plans, rigid drains had been laid instead of flexible drains, the House of Lords held that the local authority were not liable to the developers for the cost of reconstructing the defective drains two years later.[80] The original owner, furthermore, is normally owed no duty of care by the local authority, since he himself has a duty to comply with the building laws;[81] and even if he acts on expert advice without personal carelessness, the local authority is not liable because that is neither just nor reasonable.[82] A later occupier, when danger to health or safety arises, may be entitled to carry out repairs and claim the cost from the local authority.[83] But a public authority which merely requires to be satisfied with the building before making an improvement grant is under no liability when the building proves unsound.[84] Nor will

[78] See also *Pirelli General Cable Works Ltd.* v. *Oscar Faber & Partners* [1983] 2 AC 1, holding that time runs from the date when the damage comes into existence, and continues to run against successive owners. Lord Fraser's suggestion (at 16) that there might be an exception in the case of a building 'doomed from the start' has not been adopted: *Ketteman* v. *Hansel Properties Ltd.* [1987] AC 189. The law has now been changed by the Latent Damage Act 1986, which allows an alternative period of three years running from the discovery of the cause of action or the time when it might reasonably have been expected to be discovered, with an overriding limit of fifteen years from the act of negligence.
[79] See the *Peabody* case (below) at 241 and the *Investors in Industry* case (below) at 1062.
[80] *Peabody Donation Fund Governors* v. *Sir Lindsay Parkinson & Co. Ltd.* [1985] AC 210, overruling *Acrecrest Ltd.* v. *W. S. Hattrell & Partners* [1983] QB 260.
[81] *Investors in Industry Commercial Properties Ltd.* v. *South Bedfordshire DC* [1986] QB 1034, treating *Dennis* v. *Charnwood BC* [1983] QB 409, where the original owner succeeded, as a decision explained by its own special facts.
[82] See at 1062, where the Court of Appeal sums up the law in five propositions.
[83] As in *Jones* v. *Stroud DC* [1986] 1 WLR 1141.
[84] *Curran* v. *Northern Ireland Co-ownership Housing Association Ltd.* [1987] AC 718. See also *Harris* v. *Wyre Forest DC* (below); *Vaughan* v. *Edinburgh DC* (above).

there be liability if it is expressly and clearly disclaimed as a condition of the transaction.[85]

Public authorities must now accept important duties of care in the discharge of their statutory duties and powers.[86] Throughout this group of cases the courts have consciously extended governmental liability, along with that of other persons,[87] so as to match, to some extent at least, the great extension of governmental functions and the increasing need for them to be exercised with the responsibility that good administration demands.

Negligent discretionary decisions

In holding the Home Office liable for the negligent custody of Borstal boys, as explained above, the House of Lords related the degree of negligence to the degree of unreasonableness which will render a discretionary decision ultra vires. Lord Reid put this as follows:[88]

> When Parliament confers a discretion . . . there may, and almost certainly will, be errors of judgment in exercising such a discretion and Parliament cannot have intended that members of the public should be entitled to sue in respect of such errors. But there must come a stage when the discretion is exercised so carelessly or unreasonably that there has been no real exercise of the discretion which Parliament has conferred. The person exercising the discretion has acted in abuse or excess of his power. Parliament cannot be supposed to have granted immunity to persons who do that. The present case does not raise the issue because no discretion was given to these Borstal officers. They were given orders which they negligently failed to carry out.

In other words, liability for negligence in a discretionary decision is a corollary of the principle of ultra vires. This is merely to restate the point that what is done within the limits of statutory authority is not actionable.[89]

In the case of discretionary decisions there is accordingly a relationship between ultra vires and liability in tort.[90] This was confirmed by the House

---

[85] *Harris* v. *Wyre Forest DC* [1988] 2 WLR 1173 (effective disclaimer of liability for negligent mortgage valuation). A claim for negligent mortgage valuation succeeded in *Westlake* v. *Bracknell DC* [1987] 1 EGLR 161.

[86] For the question whether this type of liability is more extensive in the case of public authorities than of other defendants see (1976) 92 LQR 213 at 227 (P. P. Craig).

[87] Lord Wilberforce's wide proposition in the *Anns* case (above) at 751, that the duty of care based upon 'proximity or neighbourhood' may operate in any factual situation unless there is some consideration that should exclude it, was not approved by the Privy Council in *Yuen Kun Yeu* v. *Attorney-General of Hong Kong* [1988] AC 175, following the criticism of Brennan J in the *Sutherland* case (above).

[88] At p. 1031. See also pp. 1068–9 (Lord Diplock); 1037 (Lord Morris). And see the *Writtle* case, above, p. 761.

[89] Above, p. 753; and see Lord Morris (preceding note).

[90] See *Fellowes* v. *Rother DC* [1983] 1 All ER 513 (possible liability for damage caused by coast protection works if shown to be outside the council's statutory powers).

of Lords in their decision about the duty of care to inspect foundations, Lord Wilberforce saying that 'in the case of a power, liability cannot exist unless the act complained of lies outside the ambit of the power'.[91] He made a distinction between 'the area of policy or discretion', where there is a choice of courses of action, and 'the operational area' where a chosen course of action is carried out, saying that 'the more "operational" a power or duty may be, the easier it is to superimpose upon it a common law duty of care'.[92] Taking an apt example from an American case, he pointed to the difference between a decision whether or not to build a lighthouse and a failure, after one had been built, to keep the light in working order.[93] Lord Grieve in the Court of Session said similarly that the duty of care in exercising a statutory power 'does not arise until the discretionary stage of its exercise has ceased and the executive stage has begun'.[94] Two cases well illustrate these different stages. A chief constable was held not liable in negligence for not equipping his force with a particular CS gas device which might have avoided damage to the plaintiff's shop; but he was liable for failing to have fire-fighting equipment on hand when the use of a more dangerous CS gas device set the shop on fire.[95] On a motion to strike out pleadings it was held that the government could not be liable for adopting a policy of immunisation against whooping cough, but could be liable for negligent or misleading advice about the performance of innoculations.[96] As a pendant may be mentioned the predictable failure of an action by the mother of a girl murdered by the 'Yorkshire Ripper', based on allegations of negligence in the efforts of the police to capture him.[97]

But even at the 'policy' end of the spectrum there is the possibility of actionable negligence. Lord Wilberforce has held that a local authority which has power to inspect foundations has at least a duty to give proper

---

[91] *Anns* v. *Merton LBC* (above).

[92] For criticism see [1986] CLJ 430 (S. H. Bailey and M. J. Bowman).

[93] *Indian Towing Co.* v. *US* (1955) 350 US 61.

[94] *Bonthrone* v. *Secretary of State for Scotland* (1981) reported in 1987 SLT 34 (no liability for alleged official negligence in encouraging vaccination of infants without adequate warning of risk).

[95] *Rigby* v. *Chief Constable of Northamptonshire* [1985] 1 WLR 1242 (police siege of gunsmith's shop occupied by violent psychopath). See similarly *Minister for Administering Environmental Planning* v. *San Sebastian Pty Ltd.* [1983] 2 NSWLR 268 (no state liability for negligently prepared development plan); *Sasin* v. *Commonwealth of Australia* (1984) 52 ALR 299 (government not liable for approval of design of aircraft seat belt). Contrast *Bruce* v. *Housing Corporation of New Zealand* [1982] 2 NZLR 28 (Corporation liable for approving faulty design of house).

[96] *Department of Health and Social Security* v. *Kinnear* [1984] The Times, 7 July.

[97] *Hill* v. *Chief Constable of West Yorkshire* [1988] 2 WLR 1049 (HL).

consideration to the question whether they should inspect or not, and that their immunity 'though great is not absolute'. He added:

A plaintiff complaining of negligence must prove, the burden being on him, that action taken was not within the limits of a discretion bona fide exercised, before he can begin to rely upon a common law duty of care. But if he can do this, he should, in principle, be able to sue.

A similar doctrine was adopted by the New Zealand Court of Appeal in deciding that a minister's refusal of consent to a financial transaction rendered him liable in negligence in a situation where he plainly should have taken legal advice as to the extent of his power and by neglecting to do so made an unlawful decision on an irrelevant ground which caused heavy loss to a company.[98] But the Privy Council reversed them, holding that the minister had not acted negligently in the circumstances, that he could reasonably have taken account of the factor which the New Zealand courts had held to be irrelevant, and that, in any case, it was questionable whether liability for negligence ought to be imposed in such cases in addition to the existing liability for acting in bad faith.[99]

It is not every careless decision, therefore, which will involve liability, even if damage is caused. A statutory power of decision may include power to decide wrongly and even negligently. A minister or official making a decision is allowed a margin of error which is not allowed, for example, to the driver of a motor vehicle. The distinction between the 'policy' and 'operational' areas is evident, although the Privy Council were sceptical of its value as a touchstone of liability. They inclined rather to suggest that ministers' decisions on such matters as the allocation of scarce resources or the distribution of risks were altogether unsuitable for actions in negligence.[1]

Although important questions remain to be answered, there is a clear tendency, in England at least, against applying the ordinary law of negligence to discretionary administrative decisions. The decisions of licensing authorities, for example, may be held ultra vires and quashed if proper attention is not given to the case. But there is no indication that actions for damages will lie for any resulting loss, merely because negligence can be shown. The Court of Appeal has held that there is no liability in tort for the negligent handling of a planning application, even

---

[98] *Takaro Properties Ltd.* v. *Rowling* [1986] 1 NZLR 22. The minister had refused consent for the sale of the company's shares to a Japanese firm on the ground that its undertaking (a high class tourist lodge) ought not to pass into foreign ownership. This ground was held to be irrelevant to the minister's statutory power: [1975] 2 NZLR 62.

[99] *Rowling* v. *Takaro Properties Ltd.* [1988], 2 WLR 418.

[1] Citing Craig, *Administrative Law*, 534–538.

though this is plainly in the 'operational' class.[2] So far the English courts have progressed no further than suggesting that an action may succeed if a licence or permission is refused maliciously, i.e. if it is a case of misfeasance.[3] Legislative functions probably impose no duty of care at all, being essentially 'policy'.[4]

The immunity which operates in the case of judicial functions is explained later.[5]

Non-exercise of powers

It used to be a familiar proposition that mere failure to exercise a power was not actionable. A sharp contrast was thus made between exercising a power negligently and not exercising it at all, however negligent the latter course might in fact be. There was a corresponding contrast between failure to exercise a power and failure to perform a duty. The former by itself was not actionable, but the latter might be.[6] But the decisions discussed in the preceding section show that these contrasts are no longer so sharp. Failure to exercise a discretionary power, if sufficiently negligent, may involve breach of a duty of care and consequent liability. The House of Lords has categorically rejected the notion of 'an absolute distinction in the law between statutory duty and statutory power—the former giving rise to possible liability, the latter not, or at least not doing so unless the exercise of the power involves some positive act creating some fresh or additional damage'.[7]

Accidents in ill-lit streets formerly provided many illustrations of the 'absolute distinction' which used to be made. If the local authority had a statutory duty to provide lighting, and failed to do so negligently, an injured wayfarer might obtain damages.[8] But if it had a mere power, there

---

[2] *Strable* v. *Dartford BC* [1984] JPL 329. Contrast the New Zealand planning cases cited above, p. 762. See also *Jones* v. *Department of Employment* [1987] The Times, 27 November (no liability for negligent decision of social security adjudication officer). In *Revesz* v. *Commonwealth of Australia* (1951) 51 SR (NSW) 63 an importer was held to have no remedy for the negligent loss and delay of an import licence which should have been issued to him by the customs department, with the result that he later had to pay higher rates of import duty. For the duty to deal with applications fairly and in a reasonable time, see above, p. 762.
[3] See below, p. 780.
[4] *Wellbridge Holdings Ltd.* v. *Greater Winnipeg* [1970] 22 DLR (3d) 470 (city not liable in negligence for procedural mistakes invalidating planning byelaw in reliance on which builder expended money and suffered loss.)
[5] Below, p. 783.
[6] See below, p. 772.
[7] *Anns* v. *Merton LBC*, above (Lord Wilberforce).
[8] *Carpenter* v. *Finsbury Borough Council* [1920] 2 KB 195.

was no remedy. Thus the injured plaintiff failed in a case where the Act said merely that the local authority 'may provide' such lighting 'as they may think necessary', even though the authority was in fact in the habit of providing lighting at the dangerous place during certain hours.[9] But permissive words such as 'may' were not an infallible guide, since what appeared to be a mere power might be held to involve duty, as explained elsewhere.[10]

The House of Lords has now reassessed one of its decisions which turned upon the former distinction between power and duty.[11] A river catchment board had taken an excessive time to repair a sea-wall, so that land which need only have been flooded for fourteen days remained flooded for 178 days. The board had merely a power to repair sea-walls, so that had they done nothing they could not (under the former law) have been held liable. The House of Lords held that the true cause of the loss was the flood, and that the board were not liable for their slowness because this was mere inaction. But Lord Atkin, dissenting, held that, once the board had undertaken the repair, they were under the ordinary duty of care which a man owes to his neighbour, and that their breach of this duty was the cause of the damage. The present House of Lords has made it clear that it approves Lord Atkin's analysis and that, in any case, there is no longer an absolute immunity for failure to exercise a power.[12]

Nonfeasance and misfeasance in highway cases

Although the principal ingredient of negligence is usually mere inaction, the courts refused to allow the liability of public authorities to be undermined by the distinction between misfeasance and nonfeasance which was a long-standing anomaly of the law of highways. The old law was that the public highway was repairable by the parish; and that since the duty was owed to the public, non-repair should be enforced by criminal prosecution of the inhabitants at large and not by civil action by any individual.[13] But an individual had a remedy in damages against any one who caused him injury by creating a danger on the highway. These rules crystallised into the illogical distinction between misfeasance and nonfeasance which expressed the liability of the local authorities to which

---

[9] *Sheppard* v. *Glossop Cpn.* [1921] 3 KB 132.

[10] Above, p. 258.

[11] *East Suffolk Rivers Catchment Board* v. *Kent* [1941] AC 74.

[12] *Anns* v. *Merton LBC* (above). Lord Wilberforce thought that the full effect of *Donoghue* v. *Stevenson* [1932] AC 562 had not then been fully recognised. Lord Salmon expressed his agreement with Lord Atkin.

[13] *Russell* v. *Men of Devon* (1788) 2 Term Rep. 667.

responsibility for highways was transferred by statute.[14] If they merely neglected the highway (nonfeasance), an injured traveller had no remedy.[15] But if they opened a manhole or dug a trench and left it inadequately protected (misfeasance), they were liable for any injury.[16] This distinction would have been correct if the highway authority had merely a power; but in fact it was a case of duty. The courts confined the immunity for nonfeasance to the narrowest possible area,[17] and rejected arguments for extending it into other areas so as to create a general defence of inactivity.[18]

The immunity for non-feasance was abolished in 1961 (with effect from 1964), since when highway authorities have been made equally liable for the exercise or non-exercise of their powers, and for neglect of their duties, subject to a statutory defence of showing that they have used reasonable care in all the circumstances.[19] Although their duty to maintain the highway is absolute[20] (as in the case with statutory duties generally[21]), the statutory defence makes it in effect a liability for negligence only; and in any case there is no breach of the duty if the highway authority could not, in a difficult situation, be blamed for non-performance.[22]

Strict liability—Rylands v. Fletcher

Even in the absence of negligence the law of tort imposes liability on those who create situations of special danger. This strict liability is imposed by the rule in *Rylands* v. *Fletcher*[23] on 'the person who for his own purposes brings

---

[14] The Highways Act 1959 finally abolished the duty of the inhabitants at large to repair and imposed on highway authorities a duty to maintain public highways (above, p. 612). Duties had been imposed from the Highway Act 1835 onwards.

[15] *Cowley* v. *Newmarket Local Board* [1892] AC 345.

[16] *Newsome* v. *Darton UDC* [1938] 3 All ER 93.

[17] See e.g. *Skilton* v. *Epsom & Ewell UDC* [1937] 1 KB 112; *A.-G.* v. *St Ives RDC* [1961] 1 QB 366.

[18] *Pride of Derby and Derbyshire Angling Association Ltd.* v. *British Celanese Ltd.* [1953] Ch. 149.

[19] Highways (Miscellaneous Provisions) Act 1961, s. 1. See now Highways Act 1980, s. 58.

[20] *Griffiths* v. *Liverpool Cpn.* [1967] 1 QB 374.

[21] Below, p. 772.

[22] *Haydon* v. *Kent CC* [1978] QB 343, where the statutory defence was not pleaded. The majority of the Court of Appeal held that 'maintain' went further than 'repair', so as to impose liability for failure to remove snow and ice; but Lord Denning MR held that the Act of 1961 removed the former immunity for non-repair only, so that there was no liability in damages for non-maintenance in other respects. No culpable breach of duty was proved, and a claim for injury from a fall on an icy footpath failed. So for the same reason did a claim by the widow of a driver killed on icy roads which the defendant's workers, being on strike, refused to grit: *Bartlett* v. *Department of Transport* (1984) 83 LGR 579.

[23] (1868) LR 3 HL 330.

on his lands and collects and keeps there anything likely to do mischief if it escapes', if the operation involves abnormal risk; and this rule has been held to cover many situations where damage has been done by such things as chemicals, fire and electricity.[24] Considering how many dangerous operations are undertaken by public authorities, it is curious that few cases under this rubric have been reported. Statute has made special provision in a number of cases, as in the Gas Act 1965,[25] the Nuclear Installations Act 1965[26] and the Deposit of Poisonous Waste Act 1972.[27]

The Court of Appeal has held that a public authority, since it acts for the public benefit, does not act 'for its own purposes' within the meaning of the above rule, and is therefore not liable in the absence of negligence.[28] This is an unfortunate example of literal verbal interpretation, treating the rule like a clause in an Act of Parliament rather than as a statement of principle. What happened was that a leaky water main washed away the soil supporting a gas main, which then broke and caused an explosion. It was said that the provision of services such as gas, water, and electricity, being well-nigh necessities of modern life, ought not to impose liability without fault on suppliers acting under powers approved by Parliament.[29] But where the suppliers are acting for the benefit of the community, it would be altogether fairer to require them to bear liability for accidents irrespective of fault, for then the cost would be spread equitably over the users of the service instead of being charged wholly upon the unfortunate person injured. French law long ago achieved this socially just result,[30] which accords with the requirement of the rule of law that public authorities should bear the same legal responsibilities as ordinary citizens

[24] See Salmond on Torts, 16th edn., ch. 13.
[25] s. 14 (underground storage of gas).
[26] s. 12, as amended by Nuclear Installations Act 1969.
[27] s. 2.
[28] *Dunne* v. *North Western Gas Board* [1964] 2 QB 806; *Pearson* v. *North Western Gas Board* [1968] 2 All ER 669, suggesting that the House of Lords might have other views; *Lloyde* v. *West Midlands Gas Board* [1971] 2 All ER 1240. *Lowery* v. *Vickers Armstrong Ltd.* [1969] 8 KIR 603 at 606 suggests the possibility of liability in nuisance without negligence but *RHM Bakeries (Scotland) Ltd.* v. *Strathclyde Regional Council* 1985 SLT 214 (HL) denies it. In the Aberfan Disaster report (1966, HC 553, para. 74) Edmund-Davies LJ treated *Rylands* v. *Fletcher* as incontestably applicable to the National Coal Board.
[29] The Law Commission's Report No. 32 (1970), para. 15, attributes the decision to the fact that the gas board were acting under statutory duty and not mere power. But the decision probably rested upon broader grounds. The Royal Commission on Civil Liability recommended a statutory code for dangerous operations (Cmnd. 7054–1 (1978), paras. 1641. See also (1980) 96 LQR 419 (P. P. Craig).
[30] See CE 28 mars 1919, *Regnault-Desroziers,* Rec. 329; CE 22 nov. 1946, *Commune de Saint-Priest-La Plaine,* Rec. 279; Vedel and Delvolvé, *Droit administratif,* 9th edn., 503; [1985] CLP 330 (R. Errara).

unless dispensed by statute. The argument that a statutory 'nuisance clause' implies no liability without fault is also unconvincing.[31] The anomaly is all the more glaring in that the Crown has, it seems, been duly made liable to the rule in *Rylands* v. *Fletcher* under the Crown Proceedings Act 1947.[32]

There are signs that Parliament is alive to this injustice, even if the courts are not. The Water Act 1981[33] makes water authorities liable without fault for damage caused by the escape of water from their mains and pipes, subject to the ordinary law about contributory negligence and limitation of actions and except where the damage is wholly the fault of the injured party. There ought to be general legislation on the same lines.

BREACH OF DUTY AND MISFEASANCE

Breach of statutory duty

Where a statute imposes a duty, it is sometimes to be inferred that any person injured as the result of breach of the duty shall have a remedy in damages, even in the absence of negligence.[34] This is therefore another form of strict liability. It applies in private law to employers who fail to fulfil statutory duties to fence dangerous machinery or to maintain factory floors, gangways, etc. in a safe condition. Where a motor car is used without the third-party insurance required by statute, an injured person may recover damages against the owner of the car who has allowed an uninsured person to drive it.[35] But everything depends upon the true intent of the statute, which will often be difficult to divine when it says nothing.[36] Some guidance may be obtained from the nature of the duty, which may be intended for the benefit of the public generally or for the benefit of particular persons. The court is usually sympathetic to an action for damages if the statute has no scheme of its own for penalties and enforcement: 'for, if it were not so, the statute would be but a pious aspiration'.[37] But where the statute provides penalties, there is prima facie no civil remedy, for otherwise crimes would too freely be turned into torts.

[31] Above, p. 757.
[32] Below, p. 814.
[33] s. 6.
[34] See Salmond on Torts, 16th edn., ch. 10; Craies, *Statute Law*, 7th edn., 229. For a valuable discussion see (1984) 100 LQR 204 (R. A. Buckley).
[35] *Monk* v. *Warbey* [1935] 1 KB 75. Contrast *Phillips* v. *Britannia Hygienic Laundry Co. Ltd.* [1923] 2 KB 832 (motor car used when in dangerous condition: no civil action).
[36] Lord Denning MR has called the dividing line 'so blurred and so ill-defined that you might as well toss a coin to decide it': *Ex p. Island Records Ltd.* [1978] Ch. 122.
[37] *Cutler* v. *Wandsworth Stadium Ltd.* [1949] AC 398 (Lord Simonds). See *Thornton* v. *Kirklees BC* [1979] QB 626 at 639; *Booth* v. *National Enterprise Board* [1978] 3 All ER 624.

Thus a bookmaker failed in an action against the proprietors of a dog-racing track for failure to provide him with facilities as required by the Betting and Lotteries Act 1934, which made this an offence punishable with fine and imprisonment.[38]

In public law there is a clearer principle of liability, which depends not upon statutory interpretation but upon a general rule of law. It was stated as follows by the House of Lords in 1842:[39]

When a person has an important duty to perform, he is bound to perform that duty; and if he neglects or refuses to do so, and an individual in consequence sustains injury, that lays the foundation for an action to recover damages by way of compensation for the injury that he has so sustained.

Similarly in 1873 Bovill CJ said:[40]

It is a general rule of law that, when a ministerial duty is imposed, an action lies for breach of it, without malice or negligence.

In this case the Court of Common Pleas held that a candidate who lost a municipal election because the officer in charge of the polling station failed to provide proper ballot papers had a right of action against the officer for damages, irrespective of negligence or malice. This was breach of an implied statutory duty under the Ballot Act 1872. Under the general rule damages were awarded in many cases, as where a postmaster failed to deliver letters for ten days,[41] where the managers of a statutory lottery failed to declare the right winner,[42] where a customs officer refused to clear goods except on payment of excessive duty,[43] and where a local authority failed to remove refuse from a workhouse.[44] The liability in damages of a gaoler who made a false return to a writ of habeas corpus may rest on the same principle.[45] A 'ministerial duty' meant simply an administrative duty

---

[38] *Cutler's* case (above).

[39] *Ferguson* v. *Kinnoul (Earl)* (1842) 9 Cl. & F. 251 at 280 (Lord Lyndhurst LC). Lords Brougham and Campbell concurring (at 289, 310) (Scots presbytery liable in damages for refusal to accept presentee to a church). For early antecedents see *Couch* v. *Steel* (1854) 3 E & B 402 at 411; Coke's note in 12 Co. Rep. 100; Holt's note in 6 Mod. 27; *Turner* v. *Sterling* (1672) 2 Vent. 25.

[40] *Pickering* v. *James* (1873) LR 8 CP 489 at 503 (see also Brett J at 509).

[41] *Rowning* v. *Goodchild* (1773) 2 W. Black. 906 (misfeasance in a 'great public trust').

[42] *Schinotti* v. *Bumstead* (1796) 6 TR 646.

[43] *Barry* v. *Arnaud* (1839) 10 Ad. & E 646 (Lord Denman CJ at 671 restates the general rule).

[44] *Holborn Union* v. *Vestry of St Leonard Shoreditch* (1876) 2 QBD 145.

[45] See *Brasyer* v. *Maclean* (1875) LR 6 PC 398, where the sheriff of New South Wales made a false return on a writ of capias ad respondendum without malice or want of probable cause, so that the plaintiff was committed for contempt. Held: he was liable in damages for misfeasance in the exercise of his powers and the discharge of his duty as a public ministerial officer. The gist of the action seems to have been the misfeasance rather than the imprisonment.

which was not discretionary or judicial.[46] Failure to perform the duty was commonly called nonfeasance or misfeasance.

On this principle the Court of Appeal awarded damages for misfeasance against a local authority which failed to mark the site of a fireplug accurately, so that the delay in finding it caused the loss of the plaintiff's building. Farwell LJ said:[47]

The breach of a statutory duty created for the benefit of an individual or a class is a tortious act, entitling any one who suffers special damage therefrom to recover such damages against the tortfeasor. . . . The breach of the statute is sufficient cause of action, because the tortious act, being done in breach of the statute, becomes by legal intendment an act done with intent to cause wrongful injury, just as a false and libellous statement is by legal intendment made maliciously. The act done or omitted may, apart from the statute, be innocent, or its omission may be not actionable, but the enactment makes it actionable.

In fact the jury had found that there was negligence, and that would probably be the basis of the action today.[48] The extensive modern tort of negligence may disguise the face that behind it lies the liability for mere breach of statutory duty, without either malice or negligence.

That stricter liability is still, however, enforceable. A child injured by an unsafe glass door in a school was awarded damages on the footing of the county council's absolute liability for breach of the safety regulations.[49] A county borough council was liable in damages for breach of its duty to supply pure water to a householder who caught typhoid fever.[50] A local authority may be liable in damages for failing to provide accommodation for a homeless person with a priority need under the Housing (Homeless Persons) Act 1977 (now the Housing Act 1985).[51] If it closes schools, contrary to its duty under the Education Act 1944 to make them available, it may be liable in damages to parents whose children thereby suffer.[52]

---

[46] *Ferguson* v. *Kinnoul* (above) at 290 (Lord Brougham); *Tozer* v. *Child* (1857) 7 E. & B. 377 at 382; *Partridge* v. *General Medical Council* (1890) 25 QBD 90.

[47] *Dawson & Co.* v. *Bingley Urban District Council* [1911] 2 KB 149 at 156, distinguishing (at 159) *Atkinson* v. *Newcastle Cpn. Waterworks Co.* (1887) 2 Ex.D 441 (company failed to maintain water pressure required by statute; plaintiff's house burnt down; no liability).

[48] As in *Carpenter* v. *Finsbury Borough Council* [1920] 2 KB 195; above, p. 768. This case was based on both breach of duty and negligence and the two categories will often overlap.

[49] *Reffell* v. *Surrey County Council* [1964] 1 WLR 358. Negligence was also found, but as an alternative basis of liability. See similarly *Ching* v. *Surrey CC* [1910] 1 KB 736.

[50] *Read* v. *Croydon Cpn.* [1938] 4 All ER 631, finding also actionable negligence but rejecting a claim in contract.

[51] *Thornton* v. *Kirklees BC* [1979] QB 626; *De Falco* v. *Crawley BC* [1980] QB 460; *Mallon* v. *Monklands DC* 1986 SLT 347, where damages were awarded for resultant psychiatric illness.

[52] *Meade* v. *Haringey LBC* [1979] 1 WLR 637 (Lord Denning MR).

Subject to any contrary intention expressed or implied in the statute, the presumption is in favour of liability.

It is not, however, clear where the limits of this liability lie. Almost all administrative duties are statutory, but not every default entails liability in damages, as is illustrated by the cases on misfeasance, and on European Community law, explained below. There is also the possibility that statutory duties may be held to be merely directory, so that there is no liability for disregard of them.[53]

An exception to the rule of strict liability is the case of judges and others entitled to judicial immunity.[54] There are also statutory exceptions. Thus persons performing functions under the Mental Health Act 1983 are protected unless they act in bad faith or without reasonable care, and an action lies only with leave of the court.[55]

Other remedies for the non-performance of duties, such as mandamus, are discussed in chapter 18.

Statutory duties under European Community law

Member states of the European Communities and their public authorities have many duties under the Treaty of Rome and subordinate Community legislation. These duties are to be given legal effect in the United Kingdom, and enforced by the courts, under the European Communities Act 1972.[56] In a general sense, therefore, all these duties are statutory. But how far they are subject to the rules just explained, and how far they may be enforceable by actions for damages in the courts, is as yet uncertain, since the question has so far arisen only in preliminary proceedings; and, in any case, the answer will probably depend upon the nature of the particular duty.

The House of Lords has held that the duty imposed by Article 86 (not to abuse a dominant position) is to be categorised in English law as a statutory duty and has given a strong hint that breach of it should be remediable in damages.[57] The Court of Appeal, however, has held that a minister's duty under Article 30 (not to impose restrictions on imports) is not a statutory duty under Lord Diplock's analysis, and that an invalid restriction imposed

---

[53] As in the case of the Prison Act 1952 and the prison rules (above, p. 247).

[54] Below, p. 783.

[55] s. 139. See *Winch* v. *Jones* [1986] QB 296.

[56] s. 2(1).

[57] *Garden Cottage Foods Ltd.* v. *Milk Marketing Board* [1984] AC 130 (allegation of discriminatory supply of bulk butter; application for interim injunction failed since damages, if obtainable, would be an adequate remedy. Lord Wilberforce dissented, holding that the remedy might be injunction but not damages). See also *An Bord Bainne* v. *Milk Marketing Board* [1984] 2 CMLR 584 (above, p. 684).

by the minister should be classified as 'a simple excess of power'.[58] As such it is discussed below under the heading of misfeasance in public office.

The conflicting opinions of the two courts are likely to be reconciled by recognising that there is no inherent reason why breach of any and every EEC duty should found an action for damages. To bracket them all together simply because they are given effect by the Act of 1972 involves an obvious fallacy.[59] Some will be suitable for a remedy in damages and some will not, and the courts should be at liberty to distinguish them accordingly. EEC law requires national courts to enforce rights under the Treaty by remedies not less favourable than those available for similar rights under domestic law. But that is no reason why the same remedies need be provided for different situations.

Liability for subordinates

Public officers may also be responsible for their subordinates. Lord Denning MR has thus described their position, speaking of a registrar of local land charges:[60]

He is a public officer and comes within the settled principle of English law that, when an official duty is laid on a public officer, by statute or by common law, then he is *personally* responsible for seeing that the duty is carried out. He may, and often does, get a clerk or minor official to do the duty for him, but if so he is answerable for the transgression of the subordinate: see *Sanderson* v. *Baker*,[61] where Blackstone J states the position of the sheriff. Sometimes it is an *absolute* duty, in which case he must see that it is performed *absolutely*: see the instances given by Holt CJ in *Lane* v. *Cotton*.[62] At other times it is only a duty to use *diligence*, in which case he must see that due diligence is used: see the celebrated judgment of Best CJ in *Henly* v. *Lyme Corporation*.[63] But, in any event, if the duty is broken, and injury done thereby to one of the public, then the public officer is answerable. The injured

[58] *Bourgoin SA* v. *Ministry of Agriculture Fisheries and Food* [1986] QB 716 (Ministry's order prohibiting import of French turkeys held unlawful by European Court. Plaintiff's claim to damages held to show a cause of action for misfeasance in public office but not for breach of statutory duty. Oliver LJ dissented on the latter point, agreeing with Mann J at first instance).

[59] See Lord Wilberforce's dissent in the *Garden Cottage* case (above), pointing out that Lord Diplock's wide proposition is 'a conclusionary statement concealing a vital and unexpressed step', and does not necessarily determine the remedy. The same is true of Lord Denning MR's statement in *Application des Gaz SA* v. *Falks Veritas Ltd.* [1974] Ch 381 at 396 that article 85 and 86 'create new torts or wrongs'; many questions remain before that can be said: see the *Garden Cottage* case at 145.

[60] *Ministry of Housing and Local Government* v. *Sharp* [1970] 2 QB at 266.

[61] (1772) 3 Wils. 309, 317.

[62] (1701) 1 Ld. Raym. 646, 651 (postmaster general held not liable for packet lost by subordinate, Holt CJ dissenting; subordinate held liable).

[63] (1828) 5 Bing. 91, 107–9 (corporation liable to repair sea-walls under crown grant liable in damages for non-repair).

person can sue him in the civil courts for compensation. . . . Our English law does not allow a public officer to shelter behind a droit administratif.

Lord Denning held that the registrar of local land charges had an absolute duty, so as to make him liable for a subordinate clerk's negligent search of the register, which caused loss to a purchaser of land; Salmon and Cross LJJ held that the registrar had no such absolute duty.

Misfeasance in public office

Even where there is no ministerial duty as above, and even where no recognised tort such as trespass, nuisance, or negligence is committed, public authorities or officers may be liable in damages for malicious, deliberate or injurious wrong-doing.[64] There is thus a tort which has been called misfeasance in public office, and which includes malicious abuse of power, deliberate maladministration, and perhaps also other unlawful acts causing injury. To the credit of public authorities it must be said that there are remarkably few reported English decisions on this form of malpractice.

The famous case of *Ashby* v. *White* (1703)[65] is the best known of the English examples, arising as it did from the disputed Aylesbury election which brought the two Houses of Parliament and the courts of law into such sharp conflicts that they were resolved only by the dissolution of Parliament.[66] The plaintiff was one of the electors who was wrongfully prevented from voting and who sued the borough constables in charge of the poll for £200 damages, pleading their fraud and malicious intent. There seems to have been no breach of ministerial duty.[67] The plaintiff failed in the Court of King's Bench, Holt CJ vigorously dissenting; but the House of Lords (involved as it was in the controversy, on the plaintiff's side) reversed the judgment by a majority of fifty to sixteen. Holt CJ's opinion is a classic instance of invoking the principle *ubi jus, ibi remedium*:

> If the plaintiff has a right, he must of necessity have a means to vindicate and maintain it, and a remedy if he is injured in the exercise or enjoyment of it, and indeed it is a vain thing to imagine a right without a remedy; for want of right and want of remedy are reciprocal.[68]

---

[64] See [1964] CLJ 4 (A. W. Bradley); [1964] PL 367 (G. Ganz); (1972) 5 NZULR 105 (B. C. Gould); [1979] CLJ 323 (J. McBride); 14th Report of the Public and Administrative Law Reform Committee, New Zealand (1980). There may also be criminal liability: *R* v. *Llewellyn-Jones* [1968] 1 QB 429.

[65] (1703) 2 Ld Raym. 938, 3 Ld Raym. 320; 1 Smith's Leading Cases, 13th edn., 253, with notes supplementing the defective reports.

[66] The events are summarised in Smith's Leading Cases, 13th edn., at 281.

[67] See *Tozer* v. *Child* (below) at 382.

[68] 2 Ld. Raym. at 953. Compare Denning LJ (dissenting) in *Abbott* v. *Sullivan* [1952] 1 KB 189 at 200: 'I should be sorry to think that, if a wrong has been done, the plaintiff is to go without a remedy simply because no one can find a peg to hang it on.'

But the true gist of the action for damages was later held to have been malice, and similar actions failed where malice could not be established.[69] Otherwise, it was said, 'the officer could not discharge his duty without great peril and apprehension, if, in consequence of a mistake, he became liable to an action'.[70] Actions for damages for breach of official duty at elections were abolished by statute in 1949, since when there are only criminal penalties.[71] But the principle of *Ashby* v. *White* might be applied in many other situations.

Almost equally celebrated among modern cases is that in which the Supreme Court of Canada awarded damages against the Prime Minister of Quebec personally for directing the cancellation of a restaurant-owner's liquor licence solely because the licensee provided bail on many occasions for fellow-members of the sect of Jehovah's Witnesses, which was then unpopular with the authorities.[72] The Prime Minister had no legal power to interfere with the liquor commission which on his directions nevertheless cancelled the licence, and the cancellation was an abuse of discretion based on irrelevant and illegal grounds. It was indeed said that an allegation of good faith would be no defence for such a flagrant abuse of power, there being in fact no power at all; but it seems right to regard the case as one of malicious abuse of power because of the deliberate intent to injure without legal justification. Rand J said:[73]

What could be more malicious than to punish this licensee for having done what he had an absolute right to do in a matter utterly irrelevant to the Alcoholic Liquor Act? Malice in the proper sense is simply acting for a reason and purpose knowingly foreign to the administration, to which was added here the element of intentional punishment by what was virtually vocation outlawry.

But in an earlier case the same court had taken a step further, holding that the wrongful withdrawal of a pilot's licence by a port authority entitled him to damages:[74] there was no malice in the above sense, but there was a deliberate withdrawal of the licence on grounds of neglect and incompetence, without legal justification and in breach of natural justice—in other words, a plain case of ultra vires.

[69] *Cullen* v. *Morris* (1819) 2 Stark. 577; *Tozer* v. *Child* (1857) 7 E. & B. 377; and see *Drewe* v. *Coulton* (1787) 1 East 563, note.
[70] *Cullen* v. *Morris* (above) at 587.
[71] Representation of the People Act 1949, s. 50.
[72] *Roncarelli* v. *Duplessis* (1959) 16 DLR (2d) 689 (damages of $33,123 awarded).
[73] At 706.
[74] *McGillivray* v. *Kimber* (1915) 26 DLR 164. In *Polley* v. *Fordham* [1904] 2 KB 345 at 348 Wills J said: 'No such thing was ever heard of as an action for making an order against a person without jurisdiction. If the order is not followed by consequences against the individual, it comes to nothing.' But the meaning of this is obscure: see *Farrington* v. *Thomson* (below).

According to the nearest comparable English authority, such an action will succeed only on proof of malice. The Court of Appeal so held in dismissing an action by a dentist who had been struck off the register without being given a hearing but without malice.[75] In a later case, where it was alleged that a local authority had refused to pass building plans out of spite towards the applicant, with whom they had been in litigation, it was even held that no action for damages would lie for malice, and that the only remedies were mandamus or certiorari.[76] But that unsatisfactory decision was not followed by the Privy Council, which decided that an action might lie for the malicious refusal of a licence for a cinema in Ceylon.[77] Likewise the House of Lords has held that an action for damages might proceed against the clerk of a local authority personally on the ground that he had procured the compulsory purchase of the plaintiff's property wrongfully and in bad faith;[78] but in the event the allegations were not substantiated.[79]

'Misfeasance in public office' is the name now given to the tort of deliberate abuse of power. It has been mostly discussed in cases where claims have failed, but a rare illustration of the award of damages comes from the Supreme Court of Victoria.[80] Purporting to exercise a power which they knew they did not possess, a licensing inspector and a police officer ordered the plaintiff to close his hotel and cease supplying liquor. He obeyed, and sued for the resultant loss.[81] In awarding damages Smith J referred to a wide statement by Best CJ in 1828:[82]

Now I take it to be perfectly clear, that if a public officer abuses his office, either by an act of omission or commission, and the consequence of that is an injury to an individual, an action may be maintained against such public officer. The instances of this are so numerous, that it would be a waste of time to refer to them.

This and other authorities, including the last-mentioned decision of the

[75] *Partridge* v. *General Medical Council* (1890) 25 QBD 90. The plaintiff had been restored to the register by mandamus.

[76] *Davis* v. *Bromley Cpn.* [1908] 1 KB 170 (CA. No authority cited). And see *Bassett* v. *Godschall* (1770) 3 Wils. KB 121, another example of the fallacy that because there is no right to be granted a licence there is therefore no right to a proper determination of the application—the same fallacy as in *Nakkuda Ali* v. *Jayaratne* (below).

[77] *David* v. *Abdul Cader* [1963] 1 WLR 834. See similarly *Ballantyne* v. *City of Glasgow Licensing Board* 1987 SLT 745 (action for wrongful refusal of liquor licenses; malice not alleged; action dismissed).

[78] *Smith* v. *East Elloe Rural District Council* [1956] AC 736.

[79] *Smith* v. *Pyewell*, The Times, 29 April 1959. See also *R.* v. *Secretary of State for the Environment ex p. Ostler* [1977] QB 122.

[80] *Farrington* v. *Thomson* [1959] VR 286.

[81] No regard was paid to the argument that a void order need not be obeyed: above, p. 347.

[82] *Henly* v. *Lyme Cpn.* (1858) 5 Bing. 91 at 107.

House of Lords, were held to establish that the tort of misfeasance in public office goes at least to the length of imposing liability on a public officer who does an act which to his knowledge amounts to an abuse of his office and which causes damage. There was also discussion of a shadowy English decision which may go even further.[83] A dairy-farmer's manageress contracted typhoid fever and the local authority served notices forbidding him to sell milk, except under certain conditions. These notices were void, and the farmer was awarded damages on the ground that the notices were invalid and that the plaintiff was entitled to damages for misfeasance.[84] It was expressly found that the defendants had acted from the best motives, and an allegation that they well knew that their powers did not apply to the facts of the case was apparently not made out. This decision therefore appears to make a tort out of mere ultra vires action not otherwise tortious (not being trespass, negligence, etc.) and vitiated neither by malice nor by deliberate abuse of power.[85] But the Court of Appeal said nothing about the basis of liability, which had been conceded, and concerned itself only with the measure of damages; and of the judgment below there is no adequate record.

There are now clear indications that the courts will not award damages against public authorities merely because they have made some order which turns out to be ultra vires, unless there is malice or conscious abuse. Where an Australian local authority had passed resolutions restricting building on a particular site without giving notice and fair hearing to the landowner and also in conflict with the planning ordinance, the Privy Council rejected the owner's claim for damages for depreciation of his land in the interval before the resolutions were held to be invalid.[86] 'The well-established sort of misfeasance by a public officer', it was held, required as a necessary element either malice or knowledge by the council of the invalidity of its resolutions. In New Zealand, also, a company failed in a claim for damages resulting from a minister's refusal of permission for

[83] *Wood* v. *Blair*, The Times, 3, 4, 5 July 1957 (Hallett J and Court of Appeal). See the account of this case in *Farrington* v. *Thomson* (above).

[84] Supreme Court Library, transcript no. 209, 1957. Parker LJ said: 'But at the trial before Hallett J an amendment was made raising a new cause of action in this way. It was said that the notices, to which I have referred, were invalid, and that the plaintiff was entitled to recover against the defendants for misfeasance. The learned judge held that subject to proof of damage, such a claim was sustainable. . . . and there is no cross claim by the respondents to that ruling of the learned judge.'

[85] Other possible examples are *Brayser* v. *Maclean* (above, p. 773), though there the misfeasance led to false imprisonment, a recognised tort; *Whitelegg* v. *Richards* (1823) 2 B. & C. 45 (wrongful discharge of debtor by clerk of court).

[86] *Dunlop* v. *Woollahra Municipal Council* [1982] AC 158. As to the invalidity of the resolutions see [1975] 2 NSWLR 446.

it to obtain finance from a Japanese concern.[87] The minister's refusal was quashed as ultra vires, but it was held that this alone was not a cause of action.[88] Nor does it appear that claims of this kind can be strengthened by pleading breach of statutory duty.[89]

The Court of Appeal has reinforced these decisions in an important case under European Community law.[90] A ministerial order had prohibited the import of turkey meat from France and was held unlawful by the European Court as being in breach of Article 30 of the Treaty of Rome, which is binding in British law under the European Communities Act 1972. Traders who had suffered losses under the ban then sued the ministry for damages. On preliminary issues it was held that they had no cause of action merely for breach of statutory duty, as already related.[91] Likewise there was no cause of action merely because the minister's order was unlawful: it could be quashed or declared unlawful on judicial review, but there was no remedy in damages.[92] There would be such a remedy, however, if it could be shown that the minister had abused his power, well knowing that his order was a breach of Article 30 and would injure the plaintiffs' business.[93] It was alleged that his conscious purpose was to protect English turkey producers rather than to prevent the spread of disease, and that he knew that this made his order unlawful. The element of bad faith, or malice as judges have often called it, seems now to be established as the decisive factor. This was emphasised also in Scotland when ship-owners sued the Shetland Islands Council for attempting to ban their ship from entering a harbour by denying mooring and other facilities which the Council could not lawfully deny for this purpose. Since it was found that the Council and

---

[87] *Takaro Properties Ltd.* v. *Rowling* [1978] 2 NZLR 314. The Court of Appeal (NZ) later awarded damages for negligence but was reversed by the Privy Council: above, p. 767.

[88] The so-called *Beaudesert* principle, that there is liability in tort for 'unlawful, intentional and positive acts', laid down by the High Court of Australia in *Beaudesert Shire Council* v. *Smith* (1966) 120 CLR 145 but never applied since, was doubted in both the foregoing cases and rejected by the House of Lords in *Lonhro Ltd.* v. *Shell Petroleum Co. Ltd.* [1982] AC 173. See 40 ALJ 296, 347.

[89] *R.* v. *Secretary of State for the Environment ex p. Hackney LBC* [1983] 1 WLR 524 at 539, affirmed [1984] 1 WLR 592; *Bourgoin SA* v. *Ministry of Agriculture, Fisheries and Food* (below).

[90] *Bourgoin SA* v. *Ministry of Agriculture, Fisheries and Food* [1986] QB 716. Article 30 prohibits quantitative restrictions on imports. See also *An Bord Bainne Co-operative Ltd.* v. *Milk Marketing Board* [1987] The Times, 20 November, where the Court of Appeal held that there was no remedy in damages for alleged failure by the minister to ensure the due observance of Community law.

[91] Above, p. 775.

[92] Parker and Nourse LJJ treated this as a self-evident proposition, without citing authority. Oliver LJ dissented.

[93] This was agreed by all the judges. The authorities were reviewed by Mann J at first instance and partially by Oliver LJ, both citing this book.

the harbourmaster had acted in good faith and without malice, the claim necessarily failed.[94]

It has been held that an action for damages will not lie against magistrates in respect of payments made by a husband to a wife under a maintenance order made in good faith but outside jurisdiction;[95] but it might have been otherwise if malice could have been shown.[96] The gist of the decision appears to be that it is not a tort for A to cause B to pay money to C when both A and B are under a common mistake of law.[97] It is certainly not an authority applying to invalid administrative orders generally, being concerned in any case with a judicial order.

These various authorities, together with those on breach of duty discussed previously, are still in need of exposition and synthesis, particularly in relation to European Community law. But the main principles of liability seem now to be emerging clearly. It can be said that administrative action which is ultra vires but not actionable merely as a breach of duty will found an action for damages in any of the following situations:

1. if it involves the commission of a recognised tort such as trespass, false imprisonment or negligence;[98]
2. if it is actuated by malice, e.g. personal spite or a desire to injure for improper reasons;[99]
3. if the authority knows that it does not possess the power to take the action in question.[1]

The decisions suggest that there is unlikely to be liability in the absence of all these elements, for example where a licensing authority cancels a licence in good faith but invalidly, perhaps in breach of natural justice or for irrelevant reasons. Since loss of livelihood by cancellation of a licence is just as serious an injury as many forms of trespass or other torts, it may seem illogical and unjust that it should not be equally actionable; and in *obiter dicta* in a dissenting judgment Denning LJ once suggested that it was.[2] Some cases of this kind may involve breach of statutory duty, where there

---

[94] *Micosta SA* v. *Shetland Islands Council* 1986 SLT 193, noted in [1986] PL 380 (C. T. Reid).

[95] *O'Connor* v. *Isaacs* [1956] 2 QB 288. Compare *Stott* v. *Gamble* [1916] 2 KB 504.

[96] See at 313 (Diplock J), 352 (Singleton LJ).

[97] See above, p. 347.

[98] Above, p. 751.

[99] *Ashby* v. *White, Roncarelli* v. *Duplessis, Smith* v. *East Elloe Rural District Council, David* v. *Abdul Cader* (above); and see the review of authorities in *Takaro Properties Ltd.* v. *Rowling* (above).

[1] *Farrington* v. *Thomson* (above); the *Bourgoin* case (above).

[2] *Abbott* v. *Sullivan* [1952] 1 KB 189 at 202; and see *Davis* v. *Carew-Pole* [1956] 1 WLR 833. Contrast *Hlookoff* v. *Vancouver City* (1968) 67 DLR (3d) 119.

is the broad principle of liability discussed above.[3] But where there is no such breach it seems probable that public authorities will be held to be free from liability so long as they exercise their discretionary powers in good faith and with reasonable care. Losses caused by bona fide but mistaken acts of government may have to be suffered just as much when they are invalid as when they are valid.

A comparable doctrine prevails in the European Court, based upon 'the general principles common to the laws of the member states'.[4] It is held that the mere illegality of regulations made by the Council of the EEC gives no cause of action to traders who have suffered loss by obeying them;[5] but that damages must be paid if an EEC authority has 'manifestly and gravely disregarded the limits on the exercise of its powers', with resultant loss.[6] The non-liability for mere illegality is justified by 'the exercise of a wide discretion essential for the implementation of the common agricultural policy'—a ground reminiscent of the House of Lords' 'policy or operational' distinction in the law of negligence, where 'policy' also restricts liability.[7]

IMMUNITIES AND TIME LIMITS

Judicial immunity

Judges in courts of law enjoy special immunity from actions in tort. The object is to strengthen their independence, so that their decisions may not be warped by fear of personal liability.

It is a principle of our law that no action will lie against a judge of one of the superior courts for a judicial act though it be alleged to have been done maliciously and corruptly.[8]

The fact that the judge may have exceeded his jurisdiction is irrelevant. But a judge may be liable in damages, like any other judicial officer, if in bad faith he does what he knows he has no power to do. Lord Bridge has said:[9]

---

[3] Above, p. 772.

[4] Treaty of Rome, Art. 215.

[5] *Bayerische HNL Vermehrungsbetriebe* v. *Council and Commission* [1978] 3 CMLR 566; *Koninklijke Scholten Honig NV* v. *Council and Commission of the European Communities* [1982] 2 CMLR 590.

[6] As in *Deutsche Getreideverwertung* v. *Council and Commission*, case 241/78, judgment of 4 October 1979.

[7] Above, p. 766.

[8] *Fray* v. *Blackburn* (1863) 3 B. & S. 576 at 578 (Crompton J) (unsuccessful action against Blackburn J). See also *Anderson* v. *Gorrie* [1895] 1 QB 668. A judge wrongfully refusing a writ of habeas corpus was by statute made personally liable for a penalty of £500.

[9] *Re McC.* [1985] AC 528 at 540.

If the Lord Chief Justice himself, on the acquittal of a defendant charged before him with a criminal offence, were to say: 'That is a perverse verdict', and thereupon proceed to pass a sentence of imprisonment, he could be sued for trespass.

In the case of judges of inferior courts, meaning courts which were subject to control by mandamus, certiorari and prohibition,[10] it used to be the law that they were liable if they acted maliciously and without reasonable and probable cause, even though within their jurisdiction.[11] For acts done outside their jurisdiction they had no protection at all, and were liable in damages for any injury so caused.[12]

The House of Lords has recently reaffirmed the latter rule, though not the former, in a case where justices of the peace were sued for false imprisonment and trespass for ordering a juvenile to be detained without informing him of his right to apply for legal aid so that he could have legal representation.[13] Neglect of this statutory requirement was fundamental and the justices acted without jurisdiction. The House rejected an earlier decision of the Court of Appeal which had held that in respect of acts outside jurisdiction the rule was nowadays the same for inferior as for superior judges.[14] In a full review of the law Lord Bridge explained the legislation which has to some extent modified and restricted the liability of justices of the peace and provided for them to be indemnified at public expense where they have acted reasonably and in good faith.[15] As regards acts within jurisdiction, the House by a majority held that the former rule was obsolete and that magistrates were entitled to the same immunity as superior judges.

In this context 'jurisdiction' is used in a wider sense than for the purposes of the ultra vires doctrine, where errors of many kinds may destroy jurisdiction. It requires something like 'some gross and obvious irregularity of procedure, as for example if one justice absented himself for part of the

---

[10] This includes the Crown Court except in relation to trial on indictment: Supreme Court Act 1981, s. 29(3); *Sirros* v. *Moore* (below).

[11] The authorities seem to be *obiter dicta*, e.g. *Cave* v. *Mountain* (1840) 1 M. & G. 257 at 263.

[12] Examples concerning magistrates are *Jones* v. *Gurdon* (1842) 2 QB 600; *Clark* v. *Woods* (1848) 2 Ex. 395; *R.* v. *Manchester Magistrates' Court ex p. Davies* [1988] 1 WLR 667; and see *Beaurain* v. *Scott* (above, p. 497). But honest mistake of fact was a defence: *Pease* v. *Chaytor* (1861) 1 B. & S. 658; *London Corporation* v. *Cox* (1867) LR 2 HL 239 at 263.

[13] *Re McC.* (above), decided on the preliminary question whether the action lay.

[14] *Sirros* v. *Moore* [1975] QB 118, now explained on the ground that the judge of the Crown Court, who had caused an appellant to be arrested by irregular procedure, had made only a procedural and not a jurisdictional error: see *Re McC.* (above) at 551.

[15] Justices of the Peace Act 1979, ss. 44–54, replacing Justices Protection Act 1848 and other legislation. See *R.* v. *Manchester City Justices ex p. Davies* (above).

hearing and relied on another to tell him what had happened during his absence', or a flagrant breach of the rules of natural justice, as opposed to 'some narrow technical ground' such as an error of jurisdictional fact[16] or a minor violation of natural justice.[17] Earlier examples of inferior courts exceeding jurisdiction in this sense were where the judge of the Court of the Marshalsea, having jurisdiction over members of the king's household, imprisoned someone who was not a member of it;[18] where a county court judge in Lancashire committed for contempt a party in Cambridgeshire who was outside the judge's territorial jurisdiction;[19] and where a revising barrister wrongly expelled a plaintiff from his court.[20] In all these cases the judges were held personally liable in damages for the false imprisonment and assault, even where they had acted in good faith; and officers executing their judgments were liable similarly.[21]

The rules of common law which benefit magistrates ought also to benefit statutory tribunals which operate like courts, by finding facts and applying law, as do for example national insurance tribunals and industrial tribunals. At the other end of the scale, it seems obvious that judicial immunity will not extend to an administrative authority merely because its function is denominated judicial or quasi-judicial for the purposes of the rules of natural justice or of control by certiorari;[22] for in those cases the function is basically administrative. Thus no immunity should be enjoyed by an inspector holding a public inquiry. The same might apply to licensing agencies such as planning authorities.[23] Such bodies have only limited opportunities for committing torts, since they possess no powers of arrest or detention. Mental health review tribunals possess such powers, but their members have statutory protection provided that they act in good faith and with reasonable care.[24] Where there is neither judicial immunity nor statutory protection, tribunals will have the same liability as other administrative authorities, as explained in the preceding sections.[25]

A principle which might prove important was propounded in the House of Lords in 1921 in a case where it was held that there could be no liability for negligence on the part of a justice of the peace or guardian in making an

[16] See *Pease* v. *Chaytor* (above).

[17] *Re McC.* (above) at 546–7. But see the *Manchester City Justices* case (above) holding that failure to consider a statutory requirement was actionable.

[18] *Marshalsea Case* (1613) 10 Co. Rep. 68b.

[19] *Houlden* v. *Smith* (1850) 14 QB 841.

[20] *Willis* v. *Maclachlan* (1876) 1 Ex. D. 376.

[21] *Marshalsea Case* (above); *London Cpn.* v. *Cox* (above).

[22] See e.g. *Cooper* v. *Wandsworth Board of Works* (1863) 14 CB (NS) 180 (above, p. 503).

[23] Licensing justices appear to have the protection of the Justices of the Peace Act 1979 (above). They are not liable for the exercise of their discretion (s. 47).

[24] See above, p. 775.

[25] For the position of arbitrators and valuers see *Arenson* v. *Arenson* [1977] AC 405.

order for the detention of a lunatic, provided that the justice or guardian was honestly satisfied that it was a proper case for the order.[26] Lord Moulton said:[27]

If a man is required in the discharge of a public duty to make a decision which affects, by its legal consequences, the liberty or property of others, and he performs that duty and makes that decision honestly and in good faith, it is, in my opinion, a fundamental principle of our law that he is protected.

This wide statement ought probably to be confined to decisions made within jurisdiction, since at the time it was made there was undoubtedly liability for interference with personal liability or property where there was no jurisdiction.[28] It probably means no more than that members of a tribunal which acts within its jurisdiction and in good faith are not personally liable to actions for negligence or for acting on no evidence.[29] In this case the House of Lords were aware of the need to define judicial immunity with reference to the growing adjudicatory powers of administrative authorities, 'a fresh legal problem of far-reaching importance';[30] but they did not attempt to do so.

Time limits for actions in tort

Until 1954 there were specially short statutory periods within which actions against public authorities (including the Crown) had to be brought. A limitation period of six months was laid down by the Public Authorities Protection Act 1893[31] (replacing many earlier enactments) for 'any action, prosecution, or other proceeding' against any person for

any act done in pursuance, or execution, or intended execution of any Act of Parliament, or of any public duty or authority, or in respect of any alleged neglect or default in the execution of any such Act, duty, or authority.

This gave public authorities very favourable treatment in comparison with private persons, against whom actions in tort were not barred for six years. In 1939 the period under the Act of 1893 was extended to one year,[32] and in 1954 the legislation was repealed.[33] Actions in tort against public authorities and their servants or agents are now governed by the ordinary period of

[26] *Everett* v. *Griffiths* [1921] AC 631. Compare *Welbridge Holdings Ltd.* v. *Greater Winnipeg Cpn.* (1970) 22 DLR (3d) 470 at 476.
[27] At 695.
[28] See above, p. 784.
[29] See *Cave* v. *Mountain* (1840) 1 M. & G. 257.
[30] [1921] AC at 659 (Lord Haldane).
[31] s. 1. See Preston and Newsom, *Limitation of Actions*, 3rd edn., 192; *Bradford Corporation* v. *Myers* [1916] 1 AC 242; *Griffiths* v. *Smith* [1941] AC 170.
[32] Limitation Act 1939, s. 21.
[33] Law Reform (Limitation of Actions, etc.) Act, 1954, s. 1. See *Arnold* v. *Central Electricity Generating Board* [1987] 3 WLR 1009 (no revival of claims previously barred).

limitation for actions in tort generally, which is three years for actions based on personal injury and six years in other cases,[34] with an alternative, in the case of latent damage, of three years from its manifestation.[35] Discrimination in favour of public authorities was thus abolished, in conformity with the policy of making them subject to the ordinary law—the same policy which was embodied in the Crown Proceedings Act 1947. At the same time the Act of 1954 abolished special three-year periods of limitation which had been enacted in favour of nationalised industries such as coal, electricity, gas, and transport.[36]

For the purposes of computing the time limit where a public authority has acted in some way outside its powers, time runs from the tortious act committed, e.g. entry on land (trespass), detention of a person (false imprisonment), or seizure of goods (trespass), rather than from the time of any invalid determination or order under which the action was taken. This is because an invalid determination or order by itself inflicts no injury: the right of action necessarily accrues only when there is some injurious result which the invalid determination or order does not excuse. In one case Wills J said:[37]

No such thing was ever heard of as an action for making an order against a person without jurisdiction. If the order is not followed by consequences against the individual, it comes to nothing.

He therefore held that an action for illegal distress on non-payment of a fine was not statute-barred since time ran from the taking of the goods and not from the order of conviction.

LIABILITY IN CONTRACT

Ordinary law applies

English law, unlike that of France and other countries,[38] has no special system of rules governing contracts made by public authorities.[39] Formerly the Crown had a special legal position, and to some extent it still has; but, as explained in the following chapter, it has for most practical purposes been put into the same position as an ordinary litigant by the Crown Proceedings Act 1947. Central government departments normally make

---

[34] Limitation Act 1980, ss. 2, 11.

[35] Latent Damage Act 1986 (above, p. 764).

[36] Act of 1954, sched.

[37] *Polley* v. *Fordham* [1904] 2 KB 345; above, p. 778.

[38] For the French regime, which applies to certain kinds of contracts only according to complicated rules, see Brown and Garner, *French Administrative Law*, 3nd edn., 125.

[39] See J. D. B. Mitchell, *The Contracts of Public Authorities* (1954), dealing also with the USA and France; Colin Turpin, *Government Contracts* (1972).

contracts in their own names but as agents of the Crown, so that the enforcement of such contracts is governed by the Act. Other governmental bodies such as local authorities are subject to the ordinary law of contract which applies to them in the same way as to private individuals and corporations. They are, as also are government departments, restricted in certain ways by rules of administrative law, such as the rules which prevent their contracts from fettering their discretionary powers[40] and from creating estoppels in some cases.[41] But there is no special body of law governing their contracts other than that which governs contracts generally. A local authority building houses, for example, will generally use a standard form of contract approved by the Royal Institute of British Architects and other professional bodies, which apart from a few variations is similar to that used in private business. This has the advantage for contractors that they work under much the same terms in both public and private sectors of industry.

For the purposes of administrative law, therefore, only the Crown's position needs separate discussion. Nevertheless, in practice, as opposed to law, there are many special aspects of public authorities' contracts which, though interpreted and enforced according to the ordinary law, may therefore be regarded as the subject of a distinct body of rules. Rates of profit on central government contracts are subject to review, either upwards or downwards, and either generally or for particular contracts, by the Review Board for Government Contracts. This independent body was set up in 1969 by agreement between the Treasury and the Confederation of British Industries, after revelations of exorbitant profits made in defence and health service contracts. Common form clauses such as the 'Standard Conditions of Government Contracts for Stores Purchases'[42] and 'General Conditions of Government Contracts for Building and Civil Engineering Works'[43] are employed by government departments so as to produce a high degree of uniformity in contracts for procurement and public works.

Contracts may also be used as an administrative device in order to enforce some policy.[44] It is by this means that the government regulates tobacco advertising, by agreement with traders' representative bodies,[45] and secures compensation for the victims of accidents caused by uninsured drivers, by agreement with the Motor Insurers' Bureau.[46] Government

---

[40] Above, p. 375.

[41] Above, p. 261.

[42] Form of GC/Stores/1.

[43] Form CCC/Wks/1.

[44] See Colin Turpin, *British Government and the Constitution*, 337.

[45] See 29 HC Deb 437 (WA) (27 October 1982).

[46] See *Hardy* v. *Motor Insurers' Bureau* [1964] 2 QB 745, where the defence that a third party could not enforce the contract was deliberately not pleaded and the claimant succeeded.

contracts formerly incorporated the Fair Wages Resolution of the House of Commons, designed to prevent government contractors from under-cutting wages and exploiting 'sweated labour'. The first such resolution was adopted in 1891 and the last in 1946, by agreement between the government and representatives of employers and trade unions.[47] It provided primarily that rates of wages should not be less favourable than those established by negotiating machinery or arbitration for the trade or industry in the district where the work was carried out; and it required that workpeople be free to join trade unions. As a mere resolution it could have no legislative force: it was effective only as a term of the contract in which it was incorporated. This system of control was abandoned in 1982, when the resolution was rescinded.[48]

Another example of the use of government contracts to enforce a policy is the 'pay control clause' which the government inserted into its standard forms of contract in the period 1975–8, when it was attempting to control wages without recourse to legislation. This clause took various forms, but basically it was an undertaking to comply with the government's guidelines on wages, backed by a power of cancellation if the minister was not satisfied. The government's commercial business is now so vast that it is easily tempted to use it for ulterior purposes, as mentioned earlier.[49] It has been suggested that this is a kind of 'new prerogative'.[50]

Local authorities also make use of their statutory contract powers for ulterior purposes of policy. In the planning field, in particular, they have wide powers to enter into agreements for 'restricting or regulating' the development or use of land.[51] They are often able to induce applicants for planning permission to agree to concessions which they would have no power to impose by way of statutory conditions. Their bargaining power *vis-à-vis* an applicant usually is strong, so by agreement they can do what the courts forbid them to do otherwise. The agreement may require the developer to dedicate an open space or incorporate offices or houses in his scheme or provide a public right of way or even put up buildings. Subject to the familiar rule that the authority cannot by such an agreement fetter its own powers,[52] there is scarcely any limit to what can be achieved by this

[47] 427 HC Deb col. 619 (14 October 1946). See *R.* v. *Industrial Court ex p. ASSET* [1965] 1 QB 377; *Racal Communications Ltd.* v. *Pay Board* [1974] 1 WLR 1149.
[48] 34 HC Deb 499 (16 December 1982).
[49] Above, p. 416.
[50] [1979] CLP 41 (T. C. Daintith).
[51] Town and Country Planning Act 1971, s. 52. See e.g. *Avon CC* v. *Millard* (1985) 83 LGR 597; [1977] CLP 63 (J. Jowell); above, p. 433.
[52] Above, p. 375. See *Windsor and Maidenhead RBC* v. *Brandrose Investments Ltd.* [1983] 1 WLR 509.

device. But the legality of some of its uses has been questioned in the Court of Appeal on the ground that consent cannot empower a planning authority to impose conditions which are ultra vires.[53]

Local authorities' contracts make less use of standard clauses and are more likely to be drawn up by the authorities themselves, though they are represented on the Joint Contracts Tribunal, an unofficial body which settles the terms of the commonly-used RIBA form. This latter form incorporates a version of the Fair Wages Resolution which may be adopted in other local authority contracts, usually in accordance with the authority's standing orders which lay down its rules for obtaining tenders and so forth.[54] Administrative collaboration between local authorities and other public bodies may be arranged by contract, so that one may perform services on behalf of another, and powers for this purpose are conferred by the Local Authorities (Goods and Services) Act 1970 and the Local Government Act 1972.[55]

Contracts of service with public authorities rest on the same 'ordinary law' basis as other contracts, except in the case of the Crown.

At common law a contract could be made by a corporate body, such as a local authority, only under its common seal. No binding obligation could arise for either party from the mere resolution of a meeting or from an agent's transaction, unless ratified under seal.[56] The inconvenience of this rule was mitigated by somewhat ill-defined exceptions in favour of the contracts of trading companies and contracts of minor importance.[57] Limited companies were also freed from it by statute in 1948.[58] Finally it was abolished by the Corporate Bodies Contracts Act 1960, which allowed corporate bodies of all kinds to make binding contracts under the same rules as to formalities which apply to ordinary individuals, provided that the contract was made after 29 July 1960.

LIABILITY TO MAKE RESTITUTION

Payments exacted unlawfully

If a public authority demands a payment, perhaps by imposing a tax or rate which is ultra vires, can a person who pays it later recover his money when

[53] *Bradford City MC* v. *Secretary of State for the Environment* (1986) 53 P & CR 55 (above, pp. 265, 433). Perhaps, however, s. 52 supplies the 'vires'.

[54] See *R.* v. *Hereford Cpn. ex p. Harrower* [1970] 1 WLR 1424.

[55] s. 101.

[56] *Oxford Cpn.* v. *Crow* [1893] 3 Ch. 535; *Wright (A. R.) & Sons Ltd.* v. *Romford Borough Council* [1957] 1 QB 431.

[57] There were also many statutory exceptions, e.g. under Companies Clauses Consolidation Act 1845, s. 97.

[58] Companies Act 1948, s. 32.

the demand later turns out to have been illegal? The reason why this question has not been much discussed in works on administrative law is that it has been treated as merely a matter of the ordinary law which governs private transactions.[59] There have been no special rules for public authorities.[60] Furthermore, there have been few reported cases of much importance, strange though this seems. The explanation may be partly that public authorities are often willing to make restitution voluntarily when they have acted unlawfully, as witness the case of the television licences where the Home Office mounted an elaborate operation to repay all the surcharges which they had wrongly levied.[61] Nevertheless the position in public law certainly deserves attention,[62] and all the more so in the light of the House of Lords' decision in 1981 that a rate of over £100m levied by the Greater London Council was ultra vires.[63]

The law of restitution (formerly called quasi-contract) is in fact basically unfavourable to the recovery of money paid in such circumstances. The primary rule is that there can be no recovery of money paid voluntarily under a mistake of law, as opposed to a mistake of fact.[64] In general this is a sound rule, since otherwise innumerable transactions might be reopened by parties who later discover that they might have acted more advantageously.[65] It has been applied in favour of public authorities in a number of cases, for example where a taxpayer established in litigation with the inland revenue that the tax was not due, but was unable to recover earlier payments made under similar assessments;[66] and where a local authority miscalculated a water rate and was overpaid.[67] Rates overpaid to local authorities were as a rule not recoverable, but they could be set off against later demands.[68] Where the validity of the demand is a matter of law, any voluntary payment will count as made under a mistake of law, unreasonable though it may be to expect the payer to know the true legal position.

[59] For which see Goff and Jones, *The Law of Restitution*, 3rd edn., chs. 3, 4, 9; Stoljar, *The Law of Quasi-Contract*, chs. 2, 3. Formerly claims against the Crown lay by petition of right and now they lie under Crown Proceedings Act 1947, s. 1: Street, *Government Liability*, 125.

[60] *Twyford* v. *Manchester Cpn.* [1946] Ch 236 at 241.

[61] See above, p. 406.

[62] Attention is drawn to it by articles in [1980] CLP 191 (P. B. H. Birks); (1980) 96 LQR at 428 (P. P. Craig).

[63] Above, p. 426.

[64] Goff and Jones (as above), 117.

[65] See *Rogers* v. *Ingham* (1876) 3 Ch D 351 at 357 (Mellish LJ).

[66] *William Whiteley Ltd.* v. *R.* (1909) 101 LT 741 (tax on male servants), criticised by Stoljar (as above) 65. See similarly *National Pari-Mutuel Association Ltd.* v. *R.* (1930) 47 TLR 110 (betting tax).

[67] *Slater* v. *Burnley Cpn.* (1888) 59 LT 636. See similarly *Hydro Electric Commission of Nepean* v. *Ontario Hydro* (1982) 132 DLR (3d) 193 (overcharge for supply of electricity).

[68] See *R.* v. *Tower Hamlets LBC ex p. Chetnik Development Ltd.* [1988] 2 WLR 654.

Rigid application of the primary rule may produce inequitable results,[69] and judges have sought escape from it by two different routes. One, always a judicial favourite, is to represent mistakes of law as mistakes of fact.[70] The other is to exploit the doctrine of 'duress'. That doctrine holds that the payment does not count as voluntary, and is therefore recoverable, if it in fact has to be made to secure the performance of some duty or service due to or sought by the payer, such as the return of property[71] or the grant of a licence or permission.[72] But it has been carried to the point of protecting the payer where he is not upon equal terms or not equally to blame (in pari delicto) with the recipient for any reason, such as where the latter declines to grant him a lease unless he pays an unlawful premium.[73] Abbott CJ stated the principle when allowing recovery of money wrongfully required for the grant of a liquor licence:[74]

But if one party has the power of saying to the other, 'that which you require shall not be done except upon the conditions which I choose to impose,' no person can contend that they stand upon anything like an equal footing.

On the other hand, the mere threat to sue for the payment is not duress, even when it is backed by a statutory penalty clause, provided that there is no collateral withholding (actual or threatened) of something from the payer.[75] Nor does it help the payer that he pays under protest.[76]

---

[69] The rule has been abolished in New Zealand and in parts of Australia and the United States: Goff and Jones (as above), 118.

[70] As in *Cooper* v. *Phibbs* (1867) LR 2 HL 149; *George Jacobs Enterprises Ltd.* v. *City of Regina* (1964) 44 DLR (2d) 179 (mistake as to validity of byelaw held mistake of fact); Goff and Jones (as above), 124. Compare below, p. 938.

[71] *Irving* v. *Wilson* (1791) 4 TR 485.

[72] *Morgan* v. *Palmer* (1824) 2 B. & C. 729 (liquor licence); *Brocklebank Ltd.* v. *R.* [1925] 1 KB 52 (licence to sell ship); *South of Scotland Electricity Board* v. *British Oxygen Co. Ltd.* [1959] 1 WLR 587 (electricity supply) (a 'duress' case: see Lord Merriman at 607); *Eadie* v. *Township of Brantford* (1967) 63 DLR (2d) 561 (payment exacted for planning permission under byelaw later held invalid); *Bell Bros. Pty. Ltd.* v. *Shire of Serpentine-Jarrahdale* (1969) 121 CLR 137 (quarrying fees paid under invalid byelaw). *Hooper* v. *Exeter Cpn.* (1887) 56 LJQB 457 (unjustified harbour dues) evidently belongs to this class, since the payment was held to be involuntary. So does *Mason* v. *New South Wales* (1959) 102 CLR 108, where the High Court of Australia allowed restitution to a carrier who had to buy permits for his business under an Act later held unconstitutional. So would *A.-G.* v. *Wilts United Dairies Ltd.* (1921) 37 TLR 884 if, as Atkin LJ said, the payments were recoverable, since it was a licensing case.

[73] *Kirri Cotton Co. Ltd.* v. *Dewani* [1960] AC 192, where the Privy Council (Lord Denning) emphasised that the legislation was intended to protect tenants from exploitation by landlords, so that the parties were not in pari delicto. It should have been sufficient to hold that the tenant in fact was obliged to pay the premium in order to obtain his lease.

[74] *Morgan* v. *Palmer* (above) at 733.

[75] *William Whiteley Ltd.* v. *R.* (above); *Mason* v. *New South Wales* (above).

[76] *William Whiteley Ltd.* v. *R.* (above); *Twyford* v. *Manchester Cpn.* (above). Contrast *Glidurray Holdings Ltd.* v. *Village of Qualicum Beach* (1980) 118 DLR (3d) 33.

Unresolved problems

The doctrine of duress, extended far beyond the natural meaning of the term, has enabled the courts to soften the rigour of the 'mistake of law' principle in many cases where justice seemed to demand restitution. But it fails to deal with the simplest class of cases, where there is no withholding of any service or facility by the recipient. So, as already mentioned, taxpayers have been unable to recover tax unlawfully demanded, unconscionable as this may appear.[77] Yet there is only an arbitrary distinction to be drawn between the two cases, for it seems just as inequitable to deny restitution of an unlawful tax as of an unlawful licence fee. The constitutional impropriety of unlawful taxation should make the case for restitution all the stronger. It hardly seems reasonable to tell the citizen, on the one hand, that administrative acts must be presumed valid until a court holds otherwise[78] and, on the other hand, that if he acts on this presumption he may have to submit to unlawful taxation. Moreover, the government has an absolute right to recover unauthorised payments out of the exchequer (the consolidated fund),[79] and this rule ought to work both ways.

At least in some situations, however, there may be legal remedies. Taxes administered by the Board of Inland Revenue under the Taxes Management Act 1970 are subject to a provision requiring that in respect of error or mistake in a tax return or associated statement the board shall make such repayment 'as is reasonable and just'.[80] This provision appears to cover mistake of law,[81] but a proviso excludes it in cases where the prevailing revenue practice is correctly observed at the time but later turns out to be wrong. Where a local authority levies an illegal rate, or refuses to refund an overpayment, the ratepayer should find succour in two familiar legal doctrines. One is that discretionary powers must not be exercised so as to frustrate the intention of Parliament. Under the General Rate Act 1967 a rating authority may, in their discretion, repay rates overpaid.[82] This power was conferred upon them in order to remedy cases of injustice, and if they refuse a refund where it is equitable to grant it, the court may quash the decision and order it to be reconsidered according to law.[83] Secondly

---

[77] See the comments of Vaisey J in *Sebel Products Ltd.* v. *Customs & Excise Cmrs* [1949] Ch. 409 and of Spence J in *Eadie* v. *Township of Brantford* (above) at 570.

[78] See above, p. 346.

[79] *Auckland Harbour Board* v. *R.* [1924] AC 318 at 326.

[80] s. 33(2).

[81] Goff and Jones (as above), 135.

[82] s. 9, providing for various cases, including that where the person paying was not liable to make the payment.

[83] *R.* v. *Tower Hamlets LBC ex p. Chetnik Developments Ltd.* [1988] 2 WLR 654 (council's plea of mistake of law rejected; certiorari and mandamus granted); *R.* v. *Rochdale MBC ex p. Cromer Ring Mill Ltd.* [1982] 3 All ER 761.

there is the doctrine, confirmed by the House of Lords,[84] that a local authority has a fiduciary duty towards its ratepayers. Payment of a rate levied in breach of that duty, as was the rate condemned by the House of Lords, ought to be recoverable on the footing that no body should be able to take advantage of a mistake of law induced by breach of its own fiduciary obligations to the payer.[85] Plainly the parties are not then in pari delicto. Nor would it be tolerable if, in such a case, ratepayers who had delayed payment were exempt while those who had paid promptly were penalised.

The argument against allowing the recovery of unjustified tax and similar payments is that public authorities need to know where they stand and must, like other people, rely on the principle that uncontested transactions are final. As Isaacs J said in an Australian case,[86]

After several years, questions might be raised which, on some suddenly discovered interpretation of a taxing act, whether internal revenue or customs, would unexpectedly require the return of enormous sums of money, and quite disorganise the public treasury.

But that argument carries little weight where, as in the case of the Greater London Council, a new and controversial tax is promptly disputed. Considerations of that kind underlay the specially short period of limitation within which, until 1954, actions against public authorities had to be brought.[87] Such a restriction 'prevents one generation of ratepayers from being saddled with the obligations of another, and secures steadiness in municipal and local accounting'.[88] That law was repealed because it favoured public authorities unfairly. But it might be said that no less unfairness is to be found in the present distinction between 'duress' cases and others. There is certainly a difficult dilemma. There are obvious objections to allowing the reopening of innumerable tax transactions every time that a court holds that some accepted interpretation of the law was wrong. As against this, unlawful taxation is a constitutional abuse for which amends ought to be made, as was acknowledged in the television licence case, which was itself clearly in the 'duress' category. Perhaps the solution is suggested by the above-cited provision of the Taxes Management Act 1970, that restitution should normally be made where it

---

[84]   Above, p. 426.

[85]   In *Eadie* v. *Township of Brantford* (above) the Supreme Court of Canada held (at 572) that the municipality was under a duty to its taxpayers and that when it demanded payment under an invalid byelaw made by itself the parties were not in pari delicto. See similarly *Conin Construction Ltd.* v. *Borough of Scarborough* (1981) 122 DLR (3d) 291.

[86]   *Sargood Bros.* v. *The Commonwealth* (1911) 11 CLR 258 at 303.

[87]   See above, p. 786.

[88]   *Bradford Cpn.* v. *Myers* [1916] 1 AC 242 at 260 (Lord Shaw).

is justly due, but not where the payment was made in accordance with a settled practice generally accepted at the time. In addition, payments levied in breach of fiduciary obligation should be no less recoverable than payments levied under 'duress'.

LIABILITY TO PAY COMPENSATION

Compensation and expropriation

Compensation will often have to be paid by a public authority even though it has committed no tort or breach of contract, for instance where it takes land by compulsory purchase. The duty to pay is normally imposed by statute, but this is not invariably so. In 1964 the House of Lords held that the government had a duty at common law to pay compensation to an oil company for the destruction in 1942 of its installations in Burma, then about to fall to the Japanese; this was carried out on the orders of the Crown in the lawful exercise of its prerogative power to provide for the defence of British territory.[89] It was held that there was no common law right to compensation for damage inflicted by the Crown's forces while actually fighting the enemy; but that destruction of property for the purpose of denying its use to the enemy did give rise to such a right. In other words, there was a general rule that seizure or destruction of property within the realm under prerogative powers, even in grave national emergency, could be done only on the footing that compensation was payable. This had been so with the ancient prerogative rights of purveyance and angary,[90] which respectively empowered the requisition of supplies for the royal household and of neutral property such as ships in time of war. Today prerogative powers of this kind are confined to time of war, and even then they have for the most part been replaced by statute. When provision has to be made for mobilizing the whole resources of the country for wartime purposes, statutes and regulations naturally cover virtually everything.[91]

The House of Lords' decision, reached by a narrow majority, was immediately nullified by the War Damage Act 1965, which prevented the payment of compensation in that or any similar case. It provided in sweeping terms that no compensation should be payable at common law for damage or destruction of property caused by acts lawfully done by or

---

[89] *Burmah Oil Co. Ltd.* v. *Lord Advocate* [1965] AC 75. On the pleadings it had to be assumed that the Crown was acting lawfully under the prerogative. Contrast *In re a Petition of Right* [1915] 3 KB 649, now no longer good law.

[90] See the above case at 102 (Lord Reid). Purveyance was also used to obtain military supplies: see the *Saltpere* Case (1606) 12 Co. Rep. 12.

[91] See *A.-G.* v. *De Keyser's Royal Hotel Ltd.* [1920] AC 508.

on the authority of the Crown during or in contemplation of war, whether before or after the Act. By this unusual measure of retaliation Parliament demonstrated that it can, when it wishes, expropriate without compensation and in violation of existing legal right, in a manner not permitted in some other countries which enjoy the protection of written constitutions and bills of rights.[92] A further example was the Leasehold Reform Act 1967, which gave no compensation to the expropriated owners of reversionary rights in houses let on long leases at ground rents, the tenants being empowered to purchase the property compulsorily at site value only. In this case the expropriation can scarcely be said to have been for public purposes, since its object was merely to enrich certain tenants at the expense of their landlords. The article in the European Convention on Human Rights, which provides that 'no one shall be deprived of his possessions except in the public interest',[93] was held by the European Court of Human Rights, nevertheless, to allow the government sufficiently wide discretion to justify the legislation.[94]

Presumption in favour of compensation

Despite occasional departures of the kind just illustrated, Parliament has in the past usually respected the principle that compensation should be paid. It has accordingly become an established presumption that 'an intention to take away the property of a subject without giving him a legal right to compensation for the loss of it is not to be imputed to the Legislature unless that intention is expressed in unequivocal terms'.[95] On this ground the House of Lords invalidated a government scheme for assessing compensation on an ex gratia basis for property taken under wartime regulations, holding that there was a legal right to have compensation assessed in the ordinary way under the Lands Clauses Act 1845.[96] For the same reason the Privy Council held that an Australian statute vesting Melbourne Harbour in commissioners did not override private rights which had been acquired over part of the land.[97] Where there are no provisions for compensation, therefore, it may be presumed that existing rights are not to be infringed.

---

[92] e.g. United States of America (fifth amendment, also fourteenth amendment as interpreted); Federal Republic of Germany (art. 14). Both constitutions also require that expropriation shall be for public purposes only.

[93] First Protocol (1952), art. 1.

[94] *James* v. *United Kingdom* ECHR Series A, vol. 98 (judgment of 21 February 1986).

[95] *Central Control Board* v. *Cannon Brewery Co. Ltd.* [1919] AC 744 (Lord Atkinson). See also *Manitoba Fisheries* v. *R.* (1978) 88 DLR (3d) 462.

[96] Same case.

[97] *Colonial Sugar Refining Co. Ltd.* v. *Melbourne Harbour Trust Commissioners* [1927] AC 343.

The House of Lords applied this principle in a planning case where the local authority, in granting permission for the use of a caravan site, had imposed conditions which materially cut down the pre-existing rights of the owner.[98] Although the local authority were empowered to impose such conditions as they thought fit, it was presumed that Parliament could not have intended to infringe rights already existing, particularly since there were other powers under which this could be done, subject to payment of compensation.

This presumption does not, however, empower the court to award compensation for administrative acts authorised by Act of Parliament, unless the Act itself so provides. The planning legislation as a whole is in effect an extensive system of expropriation without compensation, since no compensation is payable in the great majority of cases where permission to develop land is refused, even though the land is then greatly reduced in value.[99] The most that can be done with the aid of the presumption is to place a narrower interpretation on administrative powers where no compensation is provided for interference with rights of property. The French Conseil d'État has in some cases spontaneously awarded compensation for lawful interference under statutory powers;[1] but no such power is known in Britain.

Compensation on compulsory purchase

The machinery for making, confirming and executing orders for the compulsory purchase of land was explained in outline earlier.[2] Compensation has to be assessed after the service of the notice to treat and in accordance with the Land Compensation Acts 1961 and 1973. Any dispute over compensation is decided by the Lands Tribunal, from which appeal lies direct to the Court of Appeal. Compensation used to be assessed as at the date of the notice to treat, but the unfairness of this rule when there has been delay and a fall in the value of money has led the House of Lords to hold that the correct time is when the compensation is assessed or when possession is taken.[3]

[98] *Hartnell* v. *Minister of Housing and Local Government* [1965] AC 1134; see above, p. 432.

[99] But this is regulation rather than 'taking' of property: *Belfast Corporation* v. *O.D. Cars Ltd.* [1960] AC 490 (a decision that planning restrictions did not conflict with s. 5 of the Government of Ireland Act 1920, prohibiting legislation for the taking of property without compensation).

[1] As in CE 14 janv. 1938, Société La Fleurette, Rec. 25 (compensation awarded to manufacturers of synthetic cream put out of business by legislation); CE 25 janv. 1963, Bovero Rec. 53 (compensation awarded to landlord for loss caused by regulation giving security of tenure to soldiers serving in Algeria). See [1985] CLP 157 (R. Errera).

[2] Above, p. 172.

[3] *West Midland Baptist Association* v. *Birmingham Cpn.* [1970] AC 874; and see *Chilton* v. *Telford Development Corporation* [1987] 1 WLR 872.

Before 1845 each Act contained its own provisions for assessing compensation, as did for instance the Defence Act 1842. The Lands Clauses Act 1845 introduced a standardised system, though with such vague provisions that the courts were able to interpret them generously in the interests of landowners, taking the full value to the owner as the basis and making additions as compensation for disturbance[4] and for the compulsory nature of the transaction, the latter usually being assessed at ten per cent.[5] The Acquisition of Land (Assessment of Compensation) Act 1919 forbade this last addition and established the basis of assessment as open market value with a willing seller, subject to certain qualifications; where there was no ascertainable market, because of the purpose for which the land was used, compensation might (and still may) be assessed on the basis of the reasonable cost of equivalent reinstatement.[6]

Radical changes were made by the Town and Country Planning Act 1947, which substituted a new basis of existing use value, i.e. a value which took no account of possibilities of development. The theory of that legislation was that the value of development rights was in future to be the property of the community, all development rights then existing being extinguished by a once-for-all payment of compensation. This system was modified in 1954 and abandoned in 1959, when the basis of open market value was restored by the Town and Country Planning Act 1959. But since it was impossible in many cases to assess the open market value without knowing what development might be permitted by the planning authorities, rules were laid down as to the assumptions to be made. In certain cases application might be made to the local planning authority (with a right of appeal to the minister) for a 'certificate of appropriate alternative development' specifying what planning permission 'might reasonably have been expected to be granted', and it might be assumed that additional permission would be granted where this was reasonable. The Community Land Act 1975 changed the formula to cases where permission 'would have been granted',[7] thus excluding hypothetical assumptions which might be unrealistic. Value which would have been added by the acquiring authority's own scheme had to be left out of account; but it was to be assumed that planning permission would be granted for such development as that scheme would involve.

During this phase, therefore, the owner was given the benefit of the development to be carried out on the land acquired from him, but not of the rest of the scheme, e.g. the development of a new town on the

---

[4] As explained in *Palatine Graphic Arts Co. Ltd.* v. *Liverpool CC* [1986] QB 335.
[5] Cripps, *Compulsory Acquisition of Land,* 11th edn., 695.
[6] See now Land Compensation Act 1961, s. 5(4), and the *West Midland* case (above).
[7] s. 47, re-enacted by Local Government, Planning and Land Act 1980, s. 121.

surrounding land.[8] The statutory rules were consolidated in the Land Compensation Act 1961. The system remained based on open market value, but with allowance for the fact that the owner, like all other owners, might suffer from uncompensated planning restrictions. A large part of the benefit of development value is now taken away by the Development Land Tax Act 1976, so that this element in the compensation is once again partially expropriated.

Community Land and Development Land Tax

Yet another attempt (the fifth in this century[9]) to expropriate development value for the benefit of the community was made by the Community Land Act 1975 (now repealed[10]) and the Development Land Tax Act 1976 (still in force). The scheme of the Act of 1975 was as already explained, that local authorities should acquire all land required for development of many kinds, buying the land at current use value and disposing of it, before or after development, at full market value.[11] The local authority would thus make a profit equal to the development value, part of which they would keep, part of which would be paid to the central government, and part of which would be transferred to a fund for the benefit of local authorities generally. But acquisition at current use value was not to be the rule until the 'second appointed day' under the Act of 1975, which never arrived. Meanwhile the Act of 1976 imposed a tax of 80 per cent[12] on realised development value in excess of £10,000 in any one year, subject to certain rebates in the period up to 31 March 1979.[13] The tax did not apply to public authorities or to disposal of private residences;[14] and there were certain exemptions and concessions for charities.[15]

Before the second appointed day public authorities acquiring land were entitled to deduct development land tax from the compensation.[16] Thus they could acquire land net of the tax, so that in many cases they could obtain most of the development value. After the second appointed day all compensation in respect of compulsory purchase was to be assessed on the footing that no planning permission would be granted except for

---

[8] See *Myers* v. *Milton Keynes Development Cpn.* [1974] 1 WLR 696, where the rules are explained by Lord Denning MR.

[9] See *Inland Revenue Commissioners* v. *Metrolands Ltd.* [1981] 1 WLR 637.

[10] By Local Government, Planning and Land Act 1980, s. 101, except as regards Wales.

[11] Above, p. 180.

[12] Reduced in 1980 to 60 per cent.

[13] ss. 1, 12, 13.

[14] ss. 11, 14.

[15] ss. 24, 25.

[16] Act of 1976, s. 39.

development which was normally permitted anyway.[17] In other words, compensation was then to revert to current use value. There were certain exemptions for charities where the land had been held for a specified qualifying period and had not been used otherwise than for charitable purposes.[18] It was recognised that the Act would cause hardship where land was taken which the owner had bought at a price including development value, and in deserving cases additional compensation might be awarded by 'financial hardship tribunals' to be constituted under regulations.

The principle that development value is the property of the community remains accepted, despite the repeal of the Act of 1975. It was given partial effect through the continuance of the levy on development gains imposed by the Act of 1976; but that levy was abolished in 1985.[19]

Additional rules

Where land in a clearance area, i.e. an area of houses unfit for human habitation, is purchased compulsorily by a local authority for clearance under the Housing Act 1985, compensation is limited to 'cleared site value', being the value of the site cleared of buildings and available for development,[20] and disregarding any increase which might flow from the clearance of adjacent land.[21] But since this value may easily exceed the previous open market value of the land (with bad houses and protected tenants), compensation is limited also to the latter value, if it is in fact the lower.[22] The Secretary of State may require the local authority to make an additional payment if he is satisfied, after inspection, that a house within the clearance area has been well maintained.[23] The local authority must also pay compensation in respect of well-maintained houses which are required to be demolished under demolition or clearance orders or which are purchased compulsorily as unfit for human habitation.[24] In certain conditions also compensation is payable in respect of the house in any event, in order that owner-occupiers and others may not suffer undue loss.[25]

On a compulsory purchase the owner is also entitled to compensation for

---

[17] Community Land Act 1975, s. 25, referring to 1st sched., para. 1 and to Town and Country Planning Act 1971, 8th sched.

[18] s. 25(5), (6).

[19] Finance Act 1985, s. 93.

[20] s. 585.

[21] See *Davy* v. *Leeds Corporation* [1965] 1 WLR 445.

[22] Land Compensation Act 1961, s. 10 and 2nd sched.

[23] Housing Act 1985, sched. 23.

[24] Housing Act 1985, sched. 23. For these orders see above, p. 202.

[25] Housing Act 1985, sched. 24.

'injurious affection' of his remaining land, if its value is impaired by severance or by the use made of the land taken from him.[26] If part of his land is taken for a motorway, for example, he may claim compensation for any fall in the value of his adjacent land caused by the noise and disturbance of traffic. Formerly, however, compensation under this head was limited to the proportion of the noise, etc., attributable to the land actually taken from him, so that if only a small piece of his land was taken the compensation might be little or nothing.[27] This restriction was removed by the Land Compensation Act 1973, in accordance with its policy as explained below. Injurious affection of retained land is now assessed by reference to the whole of the works causing it.

Compensation for nuisance and disturbance

It used to be the general rule that no compensation was payable to a person from whom no land was taken, however injuriously affected his property might be as a consequence of public works lawfully executed and operated, e.g. a motorway or an airport. An action for nuisance at common law is of no avail against the lawful exercise of statutory powers.[28] In addition, there is the unrealistic rule that ordinary user of the highway is not a nuisance,[29] and aircraft are exempted by legislation.[30] There was therefore an artificial contrast between those from whom part of their land was taken, and who were compensated for the injury to the remainder, and those from whom nothing was taken but who might suffer heavy uncompensated loss. This was an inducement to many people to resist projects for roads, airports and other public works by every possible means, thus causing many lengthy public inquiries into objections. Parliament made repeated attempts to secure for the community the increase of land values created by social development.[31] But the loss of land values inflicted for the benefit of the community had to be borne in a great many cases by the owners upon whom it happened to fall, 'for the greater good of the greater number'.[32] In

---

[26] Compulsory Purchase Act 1965, ss. 7, 10, replacing provisions of the Lands Clauses Consolidation Act 1845, as interpreted in *Buccleugh (Duke)* v. *Metropolitan Board of Works* (1872) LR 5 HL 418. The same applies on purchase by agreement: *Kirby* v. *Harrogate School Board* [1896] 1 Ch. 437. The principle covers subsidiary rights such as rights of way and restrictive covenants: *Re Simeon and Isle of Wight Rural District Council* [1937] Ch. 525.

[27] *Edwards* v. *Minister of Transport* [1964] 2 QB 134. It was assessed 'by some alchemy which I do not understand' (Harman LJ).

[28] Above, p. 753.

[29] *Hammersmith Railway Co.* v. *Brand* (1869) LR 4 HL 171 at 196.

[30] Civil Aviation Act 1949, ss. 40, 41.

[31] See below (planning restrictions).

[32] *Edwards* v. *Minister of Transport* (above), at 144 (Harman LJ).

a leading case of 1869 the House of Lords held that the owner of a house beside a new railway, from whom no land was taken, had no right to compensation for damage caused by vibration from the trains.[33] The legislation in question was so obscure[34] that there was ample room for the issue of personal sacrifice versus public benefit to be considered. It was said that the common law contained the principle of sacrifice, since any landowner could dedicate a highway beside his neighbour's land, and ordinary user of the highway was not a nuisance. With this unconvincing analogy the House of Lords paved the way for technological progress at the expense of individual rights. Nor does their attitude appear to be different today.[35]

Not until a century later did Parliament take steps to remedy the injustice. Under the Land Compensation Act 1973 compensation is now payable by public authorities and other bodies where the value of an interest in land is depreciated by 'physical factors caused by the use of public works', whether highways, aerodromes, or other works on land provided or used under statutory powers.[36] The 'physical factors' in question are noise, smell, fumes, smoke, artificial lighting, and the discharge of any substance onto the land. The 'interest in land' must be that of a freeholder or of a leaseholder with at least three years of his term unexpired (both may claim simultaneously); but if the land is not a dwelling, the interest must be that of an owner-occupier and, unless agricultural, its rateable value must not exceed a prescribed sum.[37] No claim may be made until twelve months after the nuisance began (this is the 'settling down' period) and then it must be made within the ensuing six years.[38] The Act is retrospective in that the nuisance may have begun on or after 17 October 1969, and retrospective claims could be made until 23 June 1975.[39] A claimant must have acquired

---

[33] *Hammersmith Rly Co.* v. *Brand* (above). This fundamental question was decided by two votes to one and against the advice of the majority of the judges.

[34] The amalgam of statutory obscurity and judicial elucidation, deriving from Lands Clauses Consolidation Act 1845 and Railway Clauses Consolidation Act 1845, was deliberately preserved: see Compulsory Purchase Act 1965, ss. 7, 10, especially s. 10(2).

[35] See *Allen* v. *Gulf Oil Refining Ltd.* [1981] AC 1001; above, p. 754.

[36] s. 1. See (1974) 90 LQR 361 (K. Davies).

[37] s. 2. The sum is the same as that prescribed under s. 192(4) (*a*) of the Town and Country Planning Act 1971 for claims based on 'planning blight', at present £750 in the case of old valuations (made before April 1973) and £2,250 in the case of new valuations.

[38] Under the Act of 1973 this period was two years. After many complaints and criticism by the Parliamentary Commissioner for Administration the Local Government, Planning and Land Act 1980, s. 112, adopted the normal period for statutory claims, i.e. six years (Limitation Act 1980, s. 9). By s. 113 special provision is made for the revival of time-barred claims in respect of roads managed by the central government where the right to claim was given inadequate publicity.

[39] ss. 1(8), 14.

his interest before the nuisance began[40] (as opposed to 'coming to the nuisance') unless he took it by inheritance from someone who so acquired it.[41] Similar rules apply in cases where the nuisance arises from alterations or changes of use in public works, but in the case of aerodrome alterations only where a runway or apron is altered.[42] Compensation is assessed at prices current on the first day when a claim could be made and is the whole amount of the depreciation, subject to certain assumptions about planning permission[43] and to provisions about overlapping compensation and other matters.[44] No compensation is payable if the amount does not exceed £50,[45] or in respect of highway or aircraft accidents.[46] Disputed claims are adjudicated by the Lands Tribunal.

The same Act made provision, inter alia, for 'home loss payments',[47] 'farm loss payments' and 'disturbance payments',[48] as well as for higher compensation in some cases of compulsory purchase. It has therefore done much to shift the true social cost of public works and developments from the shoulders of individual victims onto the broader shoulders of the community at large. But there are still cases where the social cost may fall heavily on individuals, for example where a business is ruined because a through road is turned into a cul-de-sac.[49]

Planning restrictions

Compensation is sometimes payable to a landowner for restrictions imposed by the Town and Country Planning Acts on his liberty to use his land as he wishes.[50] The rules are highly involved, and have been subject to sharp changes arising from Parliament's repeated attempts to find a workable method of expropriating for the benefit of the community the development rights in land held in private ownership.

The Town and Country Planning Act 1947 was the first of these attempts. It required virtually all important development or change of use of land to be authorised by planning permission, which could be refused in discretion by the local planning authority, subject to appeal to the minister. The general rule was that no compensation was payable for refusal of

[40] s. 2(1).
[41] s. 11.
[42] s. 9.
[43] s. 5.
[44] ss. 4, 5, 6.
[45] s. 7.
[46] s. 1(7).
[47] An example is *Greater London Council* v. *Holmes* [1986] QB 989.
[48] An example is *Prasad* v. *Wolverhampton BC* [1983] Ch. 333.
[49] As in *Jolliffe* v. *Exeter Cpn.* [1967] 1 WLR 993.
[50] For this legislation see above, p. 178.

permission, even though this might greatly depreciate the land. But a fund of £300m. was provided for compensating the owners of all development rights existing on 1 July 1948 who made their claims within the ensuing year. From 1948 onwards development rights were to be the property of the community, and this was secured by levying a 'development charge' on those to whom planning permission was granted, representing the full difference between the existing use value and the value with the benefit of the permission. But before any payments had in fact been made from the £300 million fund, radical changes were made by the Town and Country Planning Acts 1953 and 1954. Development charge was abolished as from 18 November 1952. Claims against the fund, instead of being paid outright, were turned into a kind of credit balance, to be drawn upon only when the planning law actually caused loss. Against this credit, development charges already paid could be recovered, as could be also the development value of land compulsorily purchased at existing use value. The remainder of the credit was carried forward as 'unexpended balance of established development value', to be drawn upon if permission for certain types of development was refused in future, or in case of compulsory purchase before the return to open market value in 1959. Thus established claims to the 'once-for-all' compensation may still be lingering on, and may become payable at some future time on a refusal of planning permission if the case falls within the rules, which are complicated and restrictive.[51]

Apart from such remnants of the original scheme for buying out development value, there is in general no right to compensation for refusal of planning permission. To a large extent, therefore, the planning legislation is a system of expropriation without compensation, the element expropriated being the development value of the land. This principle has been maintained continuously since it was introduced by the Act of 1947, even during the period (1958–75) when compensation upon compulsory purchase was based upon open market value—nor was this contradictory, since open market value was assessed only with the benefit of such planning permission as was reasonably probable. For forty years it has been recognised that the value of land to the owner is subject to social policy, which may restrict it severely.

Nevertheless there are a few cases of particularly stringent control in which the law provides for compensation.[52] The most important instances

---

[51] Town and Country Planning Act 1971, Pt. VII. The compensation is payable by the Secretary of State. It is repayable if planning permission is subsequently given and this obligation is registrable as a local land charge against future owners: s. 158(5). See *Ministry of Housing and Local Government* v. *Sharp* [1970] 2 QB 223.

[52] Same, Pt. VIII.

are where a planning authority exercises its overriding powers of requiring some lawful use of land to be discontinued or some building to be removed or of revoking[53] or modifying a planning permission already given (drastic powers of interference with vested rights which are normally exercisable only with the consent of the Secretary of State),[54] and where permission is refused (or is restricted by conditions) for what is called 'existing use development', i.e. relatively small development which is normally permitted under the General Development Order[55] such as addition to a house within a 15 per cent limit, building or other operations needed for agriculture or forestry, or a change of use which falls within certain interchangeable classes.[56] Other cases are where abnormally strict control is enforced over buildings listed as being of special architectural or historic interest and under tree preservation orders.[57] Any available right of appeal to the Secretary of State must first be exercised.

Since the collapse of the development charge system in 1952 Parliament has from time to time resorted to taxation as a means of asserting the principle that the community should benefit from the exploitation of development value.[58] A 'betterment levy' was imposed by the Land Commission Act 1967 at a rate of 40 per cent of realised development value, payable by the person who realised it (as opposed to the 1947 development charge levied at 100 per cent on the person carrying out the development); this was charged both on sales and leases and also on the commencement of any development within the Act. But the Act was repealed in 1971. The next move came with the Finance Act 1974, which introduced 'development gains tax', payable on gains resulting from disposals of land where the price or rent represented a value above the current use value plus 10 per cent, with allowance made also for additional costs of acquisition and improvement; this was charged at income tax rates on the person realising the gain. It has now in its turn been replaced by

---

[53] See e.g. *Pennine Raceway Ltd.* v. *Kirklees LBC* [1983] QB 382 (licensee entitled to claim).

[54] Town and Country Planning Act, 1971, ss. 45, 51; above, p. 187. In this case the compensation is payable by the local planning authority, and is repayable and registrable as noted above: ss 166(5), 168.

[55] See Act of 1971, s. 169 and 8th sched., Pt. II. For the General Development Order see above, p. 185.

[56] See Act of 1971, 8th sched. Compensation is allowed in these cases because such relatively minor development was not taken into account for compensation under the original 1947 scheme, so falls outside the general expropriation of development rights. It is accordingly payable by the local planning authority.

[57] Town and Country Planning Act 1971, ss. 171–5.

[58] The first such tax was that on 'increment value', otherwise known as 'unearned increment', under the Finance (1909–1910) Act 1910. For an episode in its eventful history see above, p. 595. It was abolished by the Finance Act 1920.

development land tax under the Development Land Tax Act 1976, briefly explained above in connection with the short-lived Community Land Act 1975.

Compulsory sale to public authorities

There are certain situations in which the owner of land can turn the tables on a public authority and make a compulsory sale to them. In effect this is a form of compensation for the blighting effect of planning schemes and controls, generally known as 'planning blight'. The procedure is sometimes called compulsory purchase in reverse. One such situation is where land has become 'incapable of reasonably beneficial use in its existing state' after the refusal, revocation or modification of planning permission or after an order requiring discontinuance of an existing use or the removal of a building.[59] The owner may then serve a notice calling on the local authority to purchase the land, subject to confirmation by the Secretary of State if the local authority resists. If the notice is confirmed, compulsory purchase by the local authority is deemed to be authorised, and a notice to treat is deemed to have been served.[60] As noted elsewhere, the owner may then compel the local authority to complete the purchase.[61] This procedure may also be invoked where a building listed as of special architectural or historic interest is similarly blighted by refusal, revocation or modification of permission.[62] All these provisions apply equally in the case of restrictive conditions attached to a permission, as they do in the case of refusal.

'Planning blight' has now become the statutory name for the special kind of injury which can be inflicted by the mere existence of overall plans for some area, quite apart from questions of planning permission. If, for example, a structure plan or local plan shows the land as being intended for a new road, or a municipal car park, there is likely to be no market for it. Owners of land affected in such ways may serve a 'blight notice' on the potential acquiring authority, which will be the Department of the Environment in the case of a trunk road or motorway and the local authority in the case of the car park.[63] The owner must show that he has made reasonable endeavours to sell his interest since the blight occured and has been unable to do so except at a substantial loss. If he satisfies the various statutory conditions, which are numerous and technical, he may then

---

[59] Town and Country Planning Act 1971, ss. 180, 188, 189. See e.g. *Plymouth Cpn.* v. *Secretary of State for the Environment* [1972] 1 WLR 1347.
[60] Same, s. 186.
[61] Above, p. 176.
[62] Town and Country Planning Act, 1971, s. 190.
[63] Same, ss. 192–207.

compel the appropriate authority to acquire his interest at its unblighted
value. The authority may object on a number of specified grounds, which
if disputed are adjudicated by the Lands Tribunal. The authority may stave
off the compulsory purchase altogether by giving notice that they do not
intend to acquire the land or, in a group of cases including land earmarked
for governmental authorities and highways, by declaring that they do not
propose to proceed within fifteen years.[64] The Land Compensation Act
1973[65] extended the scope of this system in various ways, for example by
including blight inflicted by plans not yet in force and compulsory
purchase orders advertised but not confirmed.

[64] Same, s. 194(2)(b), (d).
[65] Pt. V, extended to urban development areas by Local Government, Planning and Land
Act 1980, s. 147.

21

CROWN PROCEEDINGS

THE CROWN IN LITIGATION

Legal status of the Crown

It is fundamental to the rule of law that the Crown, like other public authorities, should bear its fair share of legal liability and be answerable for wrongs done to its subjects. The immense expansion of governmental activity from the latter part of the nineteenth century onwards made it intolerable for the government, in the name of the Crown, to enjoy exemption from the ordinary law. For a long time the government contrived, in the manner dear to the official heart, to meet the demands of the time by administrative measures, while preserving the Crown's ancient legal immunity. But the law caught up with the practice when finally the Crown Proceedings Act was passed in 1947. In principle the Crown is now in the position of an ordinary litigant. But the history and development of the law of Crown proceedings, together with some important surviving peculiarities, make it essential to explain this subject separately.

The position of the Crown causes little difficulty in the law which governs judicial control of powers, since statutory powers are in the vast majority of cases conferred upon designated ministers or public authorities rather than upon the Crown itself[1] and the same is true of duties. Ministers and public authorities acting in their own names enjoy none of the immunities of the Crown, as many examples have already been illustrated.[2] Where the Crown's position becomes important is in the law of tort and contract, since the Crown itself is legally the employer of the central government's officials and is legally the contracting party in many central government contracts. Consequently this chapter may be regarded as an extension of the preceding one, continuing the discussion of the liability of public authorities in one special aspect.[3]

Discussion of the Act of 1947 requires, as an essential prologue, some account of the traditional position of the Crown as litigant at common law.

---

[1] See above, p. 52, where the *Town Investments* case is criticised.
[2] See e.g. above, pp. 401, 761.
[3] See generally Glanville Williams, *Crown Proceedings*; Street, *Government Liability*; Hogg, *Liability of the Crown*.

'The king can do no wrong'

English law has always clung to the theory that the king is subject to law and, accordingly, can break the law. There is no more famous statement of this ideal than Bracton's, made 700 years ago: 'rex non debet esse sub homine sed sub deo et sub lege, quia lex facit regem.'[4] But in practice rights depend upon remedies, and the theory broke down—as Bracton's words suggest that it would—because there was no human agency to enforce the law against the king. The courts were the king's courts, and like other feudal lords the king could not be sued in his own court. He could be plaintiff—and as plaintiff he had important prerogatives in the law of procedure[5]—but he could not be defendant. No form of writ or execution would issue against him, for there was no way of compelling his submission to it. Even today, when most of the obstacles to justice have been removed, it has been found necessary to make important modifications of the law of procedure and execution in the Crown's favour.

The maxim that 'the king can do no wrong' does not in fact have much to do with this procedural immunity. Its true meaning is that the king has no legal power to do wrong. His legal position, the powers and prerogatives which distinguish him from an ordinary subject, is given to him by the law, and the law gives him no authority to transgress. This also is implicit in Bracton's statement, and it provided the justification, such as it was, for the rule that the Crown could not be sued in tort in a representative capacity, as the employer of its servants. But the king had a personal as well as a political capacity, and in his personal capacity he was just as capable of acting illegally as was any one else—and there were special temptations in his path. But the procedural obstacles were the same in either capacity. English law never succeeded in distinguishing effectively between the king's two capacities. One of the best illustrations of this is that, despite mystical theories that the Crown is a corporation and that 'the king never dies', the death of the king caused great trouble even in relatively modern times: Parliament was dissolved; all litigation had to be begun again; and all offices of state (even all commissions in the army) had to be regranted. Until numerous Acts of Parliament had come to the rescue the powers of government appeared wholly personal, and it

---

[4] 'The king must not be under man but under God and under the law, because it is the law that makes the king': Bracton, De legibus et consuetudinibus Angliae. fo. 5b (S. E. Thorne's edn., p. 32); cited by Coke, Prohibitions del Roy (1608) 12 Co. Rep. 63 at 65. For later instances of this principle see Holdsworth, History of English Law, ii. 435; v. 348.

[5] Thus costs could not be awarded against the king and lapse of time could not prejudice his claims.

could truly be said that 'on a demise of the Crown we see all the wheels of the state stopping or even running backwards'.[6]

The petition of right

Justice had somehow to be done, despite the Crown's peculiarities, and out of the streams of petitions which flowed in upon medieval monarchs came the procedure known as petition of right.[7] This held the field until the new system began in 1948, and many of the vagaries of its early procedure were rationalised by the Petitions of Right Act 1860, which provided a simplified form of petition and made provision for awarding costs on either side. In essence the petition of right was a petition by a subject which the Crown referred voluntarily to the decision of a court of law. The Crown's consent was signified by endorsing the petition 'Let Right be Done' (fiat justitia), so that after obtaining this fiat the plaintiff could obtain the judgment of one of the regular courts. Employed originally for the recovery of land or other property, this remedy made an important stride (as was to be expected) after the Revolution of 1688, when it was agreed by the judges that it would lie to enforce a debt. This was in the *Bankers' case* (1690–1700),[8] in which various bankers attempted to sue the Crown for payments due on loans to Charles II on which that king had defaulted. It was, in fact, by other means that the bankers finally obtained their judgment—though not their money, for the problem of enforcement was as intractable as ever. No further case of importance arose until 1874, when an inventor of a new kind of heavy artillery sued for a reward promised to him by the War Office.[9] This case finally settled the point that judgment could be given against the Crown on a petition of right for breach of contract made by the Crown's agent. Since in any normal case the Crown would grant the fiat[10] and respect the judgment, there was now a reasonably effective remedy in contract.

A claim made by petition of right was judged in accordance with the ordinary law, under which the Crown enjoyed no special advantages. A case of 1865 was at one time thought to lay down that monetary liability of the Crown in contract was contingent upon funds being voted by Parliament.[11] But the contract in question expressly provided that

---

[6] Maitland, *Collected Papers*, iii. 253.

[7] For the form of the petition of right see below, p. 821 n. 63.

[8] 14 How St Tr 1.

[9] *Thomas* v. *The Queen* (1874) LR 10 QB 31.

[10] The fiat could not properly be refused where the claim was arguable: *Dyson* v. *Attorney-General* [1911] 1 KB 410 at 422.

[11] *Churchward* v. *R.* (1865) LR 1 QB 173, especially at 209 (Shee J.). On this question see Mitchell, *The Contracts of Public Authorities*, 68.

payments (for the carriage of mails) were to be made out of moneys to be provided by Parliament, and no such moneys were voted. The notion of contingent liability as a general rule was rejected in a strong decision of the High Court of Australia[12] and may be regarded as exploded. If Parliament refuses to vote the money for the due performance of a Crown contract, payment cannot properly be made. But there is no reason why the other contracting party should not recover damages for the breach.[13] Nor is there any sign that the Crown would wish to assert the contrary.

No liability in tort

Meanwhile the judges had set their faces against any remedy in tort. This was an unfortunate by-product of the law of master and servant as it was understood in the nineteenth century. For obvious reasons it had become necessary that employers should be liable for the torts—most commonly negligence—committed by their employees in the course of their employment. But in seeking a legal basis for this, judges at first tended to say that it depended on the implied authority given by the master to the servant, or that the fault was the master's for not choosing his servants more carefully. Neither line of thought would bring liability home to the Crown, for as we have seen the theory has always been that the Crown's powers cannot be exercised wrongly. Thus 'the king can do no wrong' meant that the Crown was not liable in tort—even though a breach of contract is just as much a 'wrong' as a tort, and even though the social necessity for a remedy against the Crown as employer was just as great as, if not greater than, the need for a remedy in contract. The first important case was an unsuccessful petition of right by Viscount Canterbury in 1842.[14] He had been Speaker of the House of Commons in 1834 when some workmen in the employ of the Crown, being told to burn the piles of old tallies from the Exchequer, succeeded in burning down both Houses of Parliament and the Speaker's house in addition. But the Speaker's claim against the Crown for the value of his household goods foundered on the objection that the negligence of the workmen could not be imputed to the Crown either directly or indirectly. Similarly, where a British naval commander, suppressing the slave trade off the coast of Africa, seized and burnt an allegedly innocent ship from Liverpool, the owner's petition of right was

[12] *New South Wales* v. *Bardolph* (1934) 52 CLR 455, upholding a notable judgment of Evatt J. and considering inconclusive decisions of the House of Lords and Privy Council.
[13] This proposition seems clearly supported by Cockburn C.J. in *Churchward's* case (above) at 200 and by Lord Haldane in *A.-G.* v. *Great Southern and Eastern Rly Co. of Ireland* [1925] AC 754 at 771: see *Bardolph's* case (above) at 514 (Dixon J.).
[14] *Canterbury (Viscount)* v. *A.-G.* (1842) 1 Ph 306.

rejected.[15] It was later recognized that employer's liability is quite independent of fault on the part of the master, and depends rather on the fact that it is for the master's benefit that the servant acts and that the master, having put the servant in a position where he can do damage, must accept the responsibility. But it was then too late to challenge the doctrine that the Crown could have no liability in tort, which was an unshakeable dogma until Parliament abolished it in 1947. But for any claim which did not 'sound in tort'—such as for breach of contract, recovery of property, or for statutory compensation—a petition of right would lie.

Personal liability of Crown servants

The Crown's immunity in tort never extended to its servants personally. It was, and is, a principle of the first importance that ministers and officials of all kinds, high or low, are personally liable for any injury for which they cannot produce legal authority. The orders of the Crown are not legal authority unless it is one of the rare acts which the prerogative justifies, such as the detention of an enemy alien in time of war. Thus although in past times the Crown was not liable in tort, the injured party could always sue the particular Crown servant who did the deed, including any minister or superior officer who ordered him to do it or otherwise caused it directly.[16] A superior officer cannot be liable merely as such, for it is not he but the Crown who is the employer;[17] but if he takes part in the wrongful act he is no less liable than any other participant. Superior orders can never be a defence, since neither the Crown nor its servants have power to authorise wrong. The ordinary law of master and servant makes the master and the servant jointly and severally liable for torts committed in course of the employment. Before 1948, therefore, some one negligently injured by an army lorry could sue the driver of the lorry but not the commander-in-chief or the war minister or the Crown. Had the lorry been owned by a private employer, the action would have lain both against the driver and against the employer, although, of course, the damages could have been recovered only once.

The personal liability of officials was not only one of the great bulwarks of the rule of law: it also provided a peg on which a remedial official practice was hung. The Crown did in fact assume the liability which could not lie upon it in law by regularly defending actions brought against its

---

[15] *Tobin* v. *The Queen* (1864) 16 CBNS 310. Similarly *Feather* v. *The Queen* (1865) 6 B & S 257.

[16] See *Raleigh* v. *Goschen* [1898] 1 Ch 73; *Roncarelli* v. *Duplessis* (1959) 16 DLR (2d) 689 (above, p. 405).

[17] *Bainbridge* v. *Postmaster-General* [1906] 1 KB 178.

servants for torts committed by them in their official capacities. The legal process was issued solely against the individual servant, but his defence was in practice conducted by the Crown, and if damages were awarded they were paid out of public funds. Government departments did their best to be helpful in making this practice work smoothly, and if there was any doubt as to which servant to sue they would supply the name of a suggested defendant, known as a 'nominated defendant'.[18]

Breakdown of the fiction

For many years the practice of supplying nominated defendants provided a satisfactory antidote to the shortcomings of the law. But ultimately two fatal flaws appeared. One was in a case where it was clear that some Crown servant was liable but the evidence did not make it clear which. A representative defendant might then be nominated merely in order that the action might in substance proceed against the Crown, but this practice was condemned by the House of Lords in 1946.[19] The other difficulty was that there can be torts (such as failure to maintain a safe system of work in a factory) which render only the employer liable, so that there could be no one to nominate in, say, a government-owned factory where the occupier was in law the Crown.[20] These two cases exposed the weaknesses of the makeshift practice of suing the Crown indirectly through a nominated defendant. The favourite argument that juries would award extravagant damages against government departments had also lost its force, since juries were no longer used in most civil cases. The Minister of Transport had been made liable for his department in tort (as also in contract) since 1919.[21] The time had at last come—and was, indeed, overdue—for abolishing the general immunity in tort which had been an anomaly of the Crown's legal position for more than a hundred years. This was the genesis of the Crown Proceedings Act 1947. To some extent the Act followed the proposals of a committee which had reported in 1927, but whose report was shelved until the extra-legal machinery had begun to show clear signs of breakdown. The Committee on Ministers' Powers, in their report of 1932,[22] had also emphasised this 'lacuna in the rule of law'. But reform had to wait for a more favourable climate which followed the second world war, when the above-mentioned cases supplied the immediate stimulus.

The law as it now stands under the Act may be divided under four

[18] This device was adopted by statute and still operates for criminal liability for traffic offences: Road Traffic Act 1972, s. 188 (8); *Barnett* v. *French* [1981] 1 WLR 848, where the court pointed out problems and suggested that 'John Doe' be nominated in future.

[19] *Adams* v. *Naylor* [1946] AC 543.

[20] *Royster* v. *Cavey* [1947] KB 204.

[21] Ministry of Transport Act 1919, s. 26.

[22] Cmd. 4060 (1932), p. 112.

headings: 1. Tort; 2. Contract; 3. Procedure and other matters; 4. Statutes affecting the Crown.

LIABILITY IN TORT

General rules

The Act subjects the Crown to the same general liability in tort which it would bear 'if it were a private person of full age and capacity'.[23] The general policy, therefore, is to put the Crown into the shoes of an ordinary defendant. Furthermore, the Act leaves untouched the personal liability of Crown servants, which was the mainstay of the old law, except in certain cases concerning the armed forces (and formerly the Post Office), to be mentioned presently. The principle of the new law is that where a servant of the Crown commits a tort in the course of his employment, the servant and the Crown are jointly and severally liable. This corresponds to the ordinary law of master and servant.

The Act[24] specifically makes the Crown liable for:

(a) torts committed by its servant or agents;
(b) breach of duties which a person owes to his servants or agents at common law by reason of being their employer; and
(c) breach of duties attaching at common law to the ownership, occupation, possession, or control of property.

Head (a) is subject to the proviso that the Crown shall not be liable unless the servant or agent would himself have been liable. This proviso gives the Crown a dispensation which a private employer does not enjoy in occasional cases where the servant has some defence but the employer is still liable as such; for the doctrine is that personal defences belonging to the servant do not extend to the employer unless he also is entitled to them personally, and they may not prevent the servant's act from being a tort even though he personally is not liable. But in other respects it seems that the three heads are comprehensive. Head (c) subjects the Crown to the normal rule of strict liability for dangerous operations (*Rylands* v. *Fletcher*), so that the position is more satisfactory than in the case of other public authorities.[25]

The Crown is also given the benefit of any statutory restriction on the

---

[23] s. 2(1). There is no liability in tort outside the Act: *Trawnik* v. *Lennox* [1985] 1 WLR 532.
[24] s. 2(1).
[25] See above, p. 771. But if the same meaning as there mentioned is given to 'its own purposes', the Crown also might escape liability anomalously.

liability of any government department or officer.[26] A number of statutes contain such limitations of liability, for example the Mental Health Act 1983 which protects those who detain mental patients under the Act unless they act in bad faith or without reasonable care,[27] and the Land Registration Act 1925, which frees officials of the Land Registry from liability for acts or omissions made in good faith in the exercise or supposed exercise of their functions under the Act.[28]

Statutory duties

Statutory duties can give rise to liability in tort, as already explained. The Act therefore subjects the Crown to the same liabilities as a private person in any case where the Crown is bound by a statutory duty which is binding also upon other persons.[29] The Act makes no change in the general rule that statutes do not bind the Crown unless an intention to do so is expressed or implied,[30] so the Crown will normally be liable only where the statute in question says so. This rule might well be the other way round, so that (so to speak) the Crown would have to contract out instead of having to contract in. But many important statutes do expressly bind the Crown, such as the Road Traffic Act 1960, the Factories Act 1961, and the Occupiers' Liability Act 1957. Under the last of these Acts, for instance, the Crown becomes liable in the same way as any other occupier of premises for not taking reasonable care for the safety of visitors invited or permitted to be there. A visitor to a government office or workshop who was injured by a negligently maintained roof or staircase would be able to sue the Crown for the tort. So far as concerns the occupation of land, the Crown shares both the common law and statutory liabilities of its subjects.

The Act does not allow the Crown to shelter behind the fact that powers may be given (either by common law or statute) to a minister or other servant of the Crown directly, and not to the Crown itself. In such cases the Crown is made liable as if the minister or servant were acting on the Crown's own instructions.[31]

---

[26] s. 2(4).

[27] 139. See *R. v. Bracknell Justices ex p. Griffiths* [1976] AC 314.

[28] s. 131.

[29] s. 2(2). In *Ministry of Housing and Local Government v. Sharp* [1970] 2 QB 233 at 268 Lord Denning M.R. says that the Crown is not liable for mistakes in the Land Registry by virtue of s. 23(3)(*f*) of the Crown Proceedings Act 1947. That provision however applies only to Part II of the Act (Jurisdiction and Procedure) and does not exclude Crown liability under s. 2(3). But Land Registry officials acting in good faith are not liable: see above.

[30] s. 40(2)(*f*); below, p. 827.

[31] s. 2(3).

These primary rules for imposing liability in tort may be said, in general, to achieve their object well. The Crown occasionally claims that public policy should entitle it to exemption in respect of its governmental functions. But this claim is now, as in the past, rejected by the courts. Thus where boys escaped from an 'open Borstal' and damaged a yacht, the Home Office was held to have no defence if negligent custody could be established, despite its claims to immunity on grounds of public policy.[32]

Who is a Crown servant?

In broaching the question who is a servant of the Crown, it must be remembered that the Crown is liable to the same extent as a private person for torts committed by its servants *or agents*, and that 'agent' includes an independent contractor.[33] The general principle in tort is that the employer is liable for the misdeeds of his servant or agent done in the course of the employer's business but not for the misdeeds of independent contractors, who bear their own responsibility. Where the employer can control what the employee does and how he does it, the relationship is likely to be that of master and servant, so that they are liable jointly. The same is true when an agent is employed. But an agent has to be distinguished from an independent contractor, for whose tortious acts the employer is not liable at all. For example, a person who takes his car for repair to an apparently competent garage is not liable if, because of careless work by the garage, a wheel comes off and injures some one.[34] Yet there are some special cases where there is liability even for independent contractors, for example where the work is particularly dangerous. Thus a householder had to share the liability when she called in workmen to thaw out frozen pipes and by using blowlamps they set fire both to her house and her neighbour's.[35] If this had happened on Crown land, the Crown would have been equally liable under the Act because of its general liability for the torts of its agents.

But in the case of *servants* the Act sets up a special criterion based on appointment and pay. It says that the Crown shall not be liable for the torts of any officer of the Crown 'unless that officer has been directly or indirectly appointed by the Crown' and was at the material time paid wholly out of moneys provided by Parliament or out of certain funds (which in case of doubt may be certified by the Treasury), or would

---

[32] *Dorset Yacht Co. Ltd.* v. *Home Office* [1970] AC 1044; above, p. 761.

[33] s. 38(2).

[34] Compare *Phillips* v. *Britannia Hygienic Laundry* [1923] 2 KB 823, where the plaintiff failed to circumvent this principle by pleading breach of statutory duty (above, p. 772).

[35] *Balfour v Barty-King* [1957] 1 QB 496.

normally be so paid.[36] The final words cover the case of voluntary office-holders, such as ministers acting without salary. But the principal importance of this provision is that it prevents the Crown becoming answerable for the police. It can be said, as explained earlier,[37] that in some of their functions at least the police act as officers of the Crown. Yet since the police, both in London and in the provinces, are partly paid out of local rates, and in the provinces are appointed by local authorities, they are all excluded by the Act.[38] This left an unsatisfactory situation until the Police Act 1964 remedied it by placing representative liability on the chief constable as explained previously.[39]

Nor do there seem to be any other plausible complaints against the restriction. It has been suggested that it frees the Crown from responsibility for the acts of 'borrowed' servants—as where the servant of A is told to work at B's orders, so that B may be liable for his negligence—but the answer to this may be that if the Crown borrows A's servant, A's servant is not for that reason an 'officer of the Crown', so that the exclusion clause does not operate. There is also some doubt as to the Crown's liability for the servants of certain public corporations. It is clear that the nationalised industries and the BBC are independent bodies and not servants or agents of the Crown. But the less industrial and more governmental corporations, such as the New Town Development Corporations and the Regional and Area Health Authorities, stand in much closer relationship with the Crown, and whether they and their servants can render the Crown liable must depend on careful examination of their constituent Acts as was explained earlier.[40] But this is unlikely to afford the Crown any exemption to which it would not be entitled on ordinary legal principles. What matters in practice is that there should be an employer with a long enough purse to satisfy a judgment, and there is no doubt of the capacity of public corporations on that score.

Judicial functions

The Crown has one general immunity in tort which is a matter of constitutional propriety. The Act provides against Crown liability in tort for any person discharging judicial functions or executing judicial process.[41] This expresses the essential separation of powers between

[36] s. 2(6).
[37] Above, p. 145.
[38] Above, p. 141.
[39] Above, p. 148.
[40] Above, p. 170.
[41] s. 2(5).

executive and judiciary. Judges and magistrates are appointed by the Crown or by ministers. They are paid (if at all) out of public funds, and so may be said to be servants of the Crown in a broad sense[42]—a sense that was brought home to them when their salaries were reduced as 'persons in His Majesty's service' under the National Economy Act 1931.[43] But the relationship between the Crown and the judges is entirely unlike the relationship of employer and employee on which liability in tort is based. The master can tell his servant not only what to do but how to do it. The Crown has had no such authority over the judges since the days of Coke's conflicts with James I.[44] The master can terminate his servant's employment, but the superior judges are protected by legislation, dating from 1700, against dismissal except at the instance of both Houses of Parliament.[45] Their independence is sacrosanct, and if they are independent no one else can be vicariously answerable for any wrong that they may do.

It is virtually impossible for judges of the Supreme Court to commit torts in their official capacity, since they are clothed with absolute privilege, and this privilege has now been extended to lower judges, such as magistrates, if acting within their jurisdiction.[46] But the Act comprehensively protects the Crown in the case of any one 'discharging or purporting to discharge' judicial functions. In this context the word 'judicial' ought naturally to cover members of independent statutory tribunals, e.g. rent tribunals, even when they are whole-time employees of the Crown as are some of the Special Commissioners of Income Tax.[47] A contrasting case is that of independent authorities such as social security adjudication officers, whose functions are basically administrative.[48] Nor would the functions of inspectors holding public inquiries seem not to be 'judicial' in this sense, though they are so denominated for other purposes. The same question arises here as has already been discussed in the context of personal liability. If there is no personal liability, the Crown cannot be liable in the capacity of employer.[49]

---

[42] See above, p. 75.

[43] See (1932) 48 LQR 35 (W. S. Holdsworth).

[44] *Prohibitions del Roy* (1608) 12 Co Rep 63.

[45] See above, p. 75.

[46] See above, p. 784.

[47] See *Slaney* v. *Kean* [1970] Ch 243. But see also above, p. 46. Note the questionable reasoning of the majority of the Judicial Committee of the Privy Council in *Ranaweera* v. *Ramachandran* [1970] AC 951, holding that for the purposes of the constitution of Ceylon members of the income tax Board of Review did not exercise judicial functions and were not servants of the Crown.

[48] *Jones* v. *Department of Employment* [1988] 2 WLR 493.

[49] There would be no basis of liability at common law and in any case the proviso to s. 2(1) of the Act would exclude liability.

The Post Office and armed forces

Both the Post Office and its employees were given remarkably wide dispensations by the Act.[50] But since the Post Office is no longer a Crown service, they are discussed elsewhere.[51]

In the case of the armed forces there were provisions (now repealed) designed to prevent the taxpayer from paying twice over for accidents in the services, once by way of damages and once more by way of disability pension to the injured person or his dependants. The dispensation therefore applied only where the injury was attributable to service for pension purposes, and it could not affect the right of plaintiffs outside the armed forces. The main provision was that, provided that pensionability was certified, neither the Crown nor the tortfeasor was liable for death or personal injury caused by one member of the armed forces,[52] while on duty as such, to another member of the armed forces who was either on duty as such or was on any land, premises, ship, aircraft, or vehicle for the time being used for service purposes.[53] Similarly the Crown and its servants as owners or occupiers of any such land, etc., were exempted if a certificate of pensionability was given and the injured party was a member of the forces. Ministers were empowered to give certificates to settle the question whether any person was or was not on duty, or whether any land, etc., was in use by the forces at the relevant time.

Although these provisions were supposed to produce equitable results, they were too restrictive and caused injustice.[54] In one case a territorial reservist was accidently killed by the firing of a live shell, and the death was duly certified as attributable to service for pension purposes; but the award was nil, since his parents, who were his nearest surviving relatives, did not themselves qualify under the pension scheme.[55] Thus the sole result was to deprive the parents of their remedy in damages, as their son's personal representatives, for his death. Protest at this injustice has brought about the

[50] s. 9, replaced by Post Office Act 1969, ss. 29–30.

[51] Above, p. 165.

[52] In *Pearce* v. *Secretary of State for Defence* [1988] 2 WLR 144, where the plaintiff claimed to have been injured by the negligence of employees of the Atomic Energy Authority while on duty on Christmas Island in connection with tests of nuclear weapons, the transfer to the Secretary of State of the A.E.A.'s liabilities, effected by statute, did not enable the Secretary of State to claim exemption. The Court of Appeal, upholding Caulfield J., declined to apply *Town Investments Ltd.* v. *Department of the Environment* [1978] AC 359, criticised above, p. 52; the House of Lords affirmed, overruling the *Bell* case (below).

[53] s. 10. In *Bell* v. *Secretary of State for Defence* [1986] QB 322, where a fatally injured soldier in Germany was sent to a civilian hospital, the Court of Appeal were divided on the question where the alleged injury took place (the claim failed).

[54] See [1985] PL at 287 (G. Zellick).

[55] *Adams* v. *War Office* [1955] 1 WLR 1116.

repeal of the whole provision for exemption in respect of the armed forces.[56] But the Secretary of State is empowered to revive it by statutory instrument in case of imminent national danger or great emergency or warlike operations outside the United Kingdom.

LIABILITY IN CONTRACT

General principles

The Crown's liability for breach of contract was, as previously explained, acknowledged in principle long before the Crown Proceedings Act 1947, but was subject to the ancient procedure of petition of right. There were also a few special cases where statute had provided other remedies. The Minister of Transport was expressly made liable in contract by the Ministry of Transport Act 1919,[57] and could be sued by ordinary procedure. Other departments were incorporated by statute (such as the former Office of Works), and it was held that this rendered them liable on their contracts. Some ministers or departments were by statute made able 'to sue and be sued', which was held to render them liable in contract, though not in tort.[58]

The Crown Proceedings Act 1947 modernized and simplified the procedure, without altering the general principle of Crown liability. The petition of right is abolished, together with a number of old forms of procedure. Also abolished are the special provisions as to the Ministry of Transport and as to departments able to sue and be sued. Instead, all actions in contract are brought against the appropriate government department, or against the Attorney-General, under the standard procedure laid down in the Act. Proceedings both in contract and in tort are thus covered by the same set of rules, which are explained in the next section.

The principal provision of the Act is that any claim against the Crown which might have been enforced, subject to the fiat, by petition of right or under any of the statutory liabilities repealed by the Act, may now be enforced as of right and without the fiat in proceedings under the Act.[59] Thus the scope of the Act depends upon the scope of the petition of right and the other old procedures, and the old law relating to them will still be of importance if the Crown ever resists a claim on the ground that it falls outside the area of Crown liability. But apart from tort and certain cases

---

[56] Crown Proceedings (Armed Forces) Act 1987.
[57] Above, p. 813.
[58] *Minister of Supply* v. *British Thompson-Houston Co. Ltd.* [1943] 1 KB 478.
[59] s. 1.

such as actions by servants of the Crown (discussed elsewhere),[60] and the special case of salvage (now covered by the Act),[61] the scope of the old actions was probably comprehensive. The petition of right, for instance, appears to have been available for recovery of money from the Crown where an ordinary subject would have been liable in quasi-contract, a head of liability which is not truly contractual; and, as already noted, the petition of right could be used to recover money due from the Crown under statute. The substance of these remedies is thus infused into the new statutory scheme, and there are no obvious gaps.

The Act applies to proceedings by or against the Crown, however, only in respect of the United Kingdom government.[62] Except where local legislation provides otherwise, therefore, claimants attempting to enforce Crown liabilities in respect of other territories must fall back on the old pre-1947 procedures. Such claimants have even been deprived of the benefits of the Petitions of Right Act 1860, since it has been held that the repeal of that Act by the Crown Proceedings Act 1947 is total.[63] This inconvenient conclusion does not seem to be necessary, since the Act of 1947 merely provides that nothing in it shall affect proceedings against the Crown in respect of non-United Kingdom claims, and this saving should qualify the repeal of the Act of 1860 as much as any other provision of the Act of 1947.

Personal liability of the sovereign

The Act of 1947 may have created a lacuna, though of more theoretical than practical importance, as regards actions against the sovereign personally. A petition of right used to lie, and the Petitions of Right Act 1860 provided for payments from the privy purse. But now the Crown Proceedings Act both abolishes the petition of right and provides that 'nothing in this Act shall apply to' proceedings by or against the sovereign in his private capacity, or authorise proceedings in tort against him.[64] Is the Crown then no longer personally liable in contract? It seems possible, following the words of the Act, that the petition of right is not abolished to

---

[60] Above, p. 66.

[61] s. 8.

[62] s. 40(2)(*b*), (*c*). See *Trawnrik* v. *Lennox* [1985] 1 WLR 532 (no Crown liability for nuisance created by British forces in Germany).

[63] *Franklin* v. *A.-G.* [1974] 1 QB 185 at 201, where the reasoning of Lawson J. is not explained. The pre-1860 procedure was however simplified by agreement of the Crown: see at 202, where the form of petition is given. But under the pre-1860 procedure there may be difficulty as to costs: see above, p. 809. This was one of a series of claims by holders of Rhodesian stocks: see also *Franklin* v. *The Queen (No. 2)* [1974] 1 QB 205; *Barclays Bank Ltd.* v. *The Queen* [1974] 1 QB 823. In none of these cases was there any order as to costs.

[64] s. 40(1).

that extent,[65] so that it still survives for claims against the Crown in person, which remain under the old law, with or without the benefit of the Act of 1860.[66] This result would be far from ideal, but at least it would preserve the remedy in some form.

Agents in contract

The Crown servant or agent who actually makes the contract—for example, a War Office official who orders boots for the army—is not in law a party to the contract, and is not liable on it personally. He is merely the Crown's agent, and the ordinary law is that where a contract is made through an authorised agent, the principal is liable but the agent is not. The agent is merely a mechanism for bringing about a contract between his principal and the other contracting party. Thus if the boots are ordered from a manufacturing company, the parties to the contract are the Crown and the company. If a minister in his official capacity takes a lease of land, the parties to the contract are the lessor and the Crown, and the Crown becomes the tenant.[67] The agents on either side are not personally liable on the contract. It has long been clear that Crown servants, acting in their official capacity, are as immune as any other agents: in 1786 it was decided that the Governor of Quebec could not be sued on promises made by him to pay for supplies for the army in Canada.[68] This immunity of the agent must be contrasted with the position in tort, where master and servant are both fully liable personally for torts committed by the servant in the course of his employment, and where the personal liability of Crown servants is an important safeguard—though not quite so important as it was in the era before the Crown itself became liable in tort.

Where a contract is made through an agent duly authorised,[69] the

---

[65] The petition of right is listed in the 1st schedule among 'Proceedings abolished by this Act'; but the Act itself contains no other provision for abolition: it merely substitutes the new procedure under s. 1. Where that does not apply, therefore, the petition of right may survive.

[66] See the comment on the *Franklin* case, above.

[67] *Town Investments Ltd.* v. *Department of the Environment* [1978] AC 359, where the House of Lords held that a special principle of public law equates the government, i.e. ministers and officials, with the Crown. No special rule is needed to make the Crown the contracting party, but without a special rule the grant of a lease to a minister could not make some other person tenant. For the importance of the distinction between the Crown and ministers see above. p. 52.

[68] *Macbeath* v. *Haldimand* (1786) 1 TR 172.

[69] Actual or ostensible authority is determined according to the ordinary law of agency (subject to doubts created by the *Town Investments* case, above, p. 52): *Verrault* v. *A.-G. for Quebec* (1975) 57 DLR (3d) 403; *Meates* v. *A.-G.* [1979] 1 NZLR 415 (Prime Minister held not authorised to contract on behalf of the Crown).

principal is liable but not the agent. Where the agent is unauthorised, the agent is liable but not the principal. This latter result is achieved by allowing the other party an action against the agent for breach of warranty of authority. This is a contractual remedy, for a contract is implied by law to the effect that the agent promises, in consideration of the party agreeing to deal with him, that he had the authority of his principal. Thus the law finds a means of making agents responsible for any loss which they may cause by exceeding their authority. But it is doubtful whether this remedy is available against agents of the Crown. The Court of Appeal has upheld a judgment to the effect that a Crown servant acting in his official capacity is, on grounds of public policy, not liable to actions for breach of warranty of authority. 'No action lies against a public servant upon any contract which he makes in that capacity, and an action will only lie on an express personal contract.'[70] There seem to be two distinct strands of argument, one that public policy requires Crown agents to be able to contract free of personal liability, and the other that in such cases the implied contract of warranty is unjustified on the facts. Public policy should weigh less heavily now that the Crown Proceedings Act has gone so far towards assimilating the Crown's prerogatives with the ordinary law of the land. The other argument is also of dubious validity. Since the case was one arising out of a contract of employment, where (as explained elsewhere[71]) the principles underlying the case-law are confused, it is sometimes regarded as a less formidable obstacle than it appears at first sight. There were also other alternative grounds for the decision in the Court of Appeal. Nevertheless, while this authority stands, Crown agents appear to have a privileged position and to enjoy an anomalous personal immunity in making contracts on behalf of the Crown. If they exceed their authority, therefore, neither the Crown nor its agent is liable, and the law fails to provide the remedy which justice demands.

Difficulty also arises over subjecting the Crown to the normal rule that the principal may be liable for an unauthorised contract made by the agent if the principal has given the agent ostensible authority, as by putting him in a position where the other contracting party might reasonably assume that the agent was duly authorised. This rule in effect rests on the principle of estoppel; and as has been explained previously there are problems in applying this principle to governmental powers exercised in the public interest, so that officers of the Crown cannot be safely assumed to have the powers which they purport to exercise.[72] Consequently the fact that a customs officer would appear to have authority to sell unclaimed goods

[70] *Dunn v. Macdonald* [1897] 1 QB 401, 555.
[71] Above, p. 68.
[72] Above, p. 382.

from a customs warehouse will not give a good title to the buyer if in fact the sale was outside his statutory powers.[73] This does not mean that the Crown cannot be made liable in contract by way of an estoppel. In one case a supplier of ships' stores made an oral contract with an Admiralty officer and next day wrote to the Admiralty confirming the agreed terms as he understood them. When the Admiralty later disputed the terms, the supplier succeeded in enforcing them because the Admiralty had not replied to his letter and had consequently induced him to believe that his version was correct, thereby estopping the Crown from maintaining otherwise.[74] This ruling, however, did not turn on any question of agency.

REMEDIES, PROCEDURE AND OTHER MATTERS

The statutory procedure

The Crown Proceedings Act 1947 has much to say about procedure. The general policy is that the ordinary procedure in civil actions shall apply so far as possible to actions by and against the Crown, both in the High Court and in the County Court. But inevitably there must be modifications in detail. The Crown is not nominally a party to proceedings under the Act: where the Crown is suing, the plaintiff is a government department or the Attorney-General; where the Crown is being sued, it is represented similarly.[75] The Treasury is required to issue a list of the departments which can sue and be sued under the Act, and if there is no suitable department or if there is doubt in any particular case the Attorney-General will fill the gap.[76] It is a departure from ordinary legal notions that departments which are not juristic persons (for some departments are not incorporated) should be able to be parties to actions, but all things are possible by Act of Parliament.[77]

  The Act also exempts the Crown from the compulsory machinery of law enforcement. This is not in order to enable the Crown to flout the law, but because it would be unseemly if, for example, a sheriff's execution could be issued against a government department which failed to satisfy a judgment. The Crown must be treated as an honest man, and the ordinary

---

  [73] *A.-G. for Ceylong* v. *A.D. Silva* [1953] AC 461, quoted above, p. 385. See [1957] PL at 337 (G. H. Treitel).
  [74] *Orient Steam Navigation Co. Ltd.* v. *The Crown* (1952) 21 Ll LR 301 (successful petition of right); see Turpin, *Government Contracts*, 31.
  [75] s. 17.
  [76] s. 17.
  [77] An example in common law is the case of the prerogative remedies, where the respondent is often a tribunal.

laws must have their teeth drawn. Therefore the Act provides that no execution or attachment or process shall issue for enforcing payment by the Crown.[78] Nor can the Crown be made the object of any injunction or order for specific performance or order for the delivery up of property. Instead of these remedies the court merely makes a declaratory order so that the plaintiff's rights are recognised but not enforced.[79]

A special provision prohibits any injunction or order against an officer of the Crown where the effect would be to grant relief against the Crown which could not be obtained in proceedings against the Crown.[80] This has been held in questionable decisions, explained and criticized earlier,[81] to protect ministers in cases where the statute empowers the minister specifically and not the Crown, thus conflicting with the principle that the law of Crown proceedings does not apply to ministers on whom statutory powers and duties are conferred directly in their own names.[82] Ministers as such are subject to the ordinary law, and can therefore be subjected to compulsory orders such as mandamus—with the normal penalties of imprisonment or fine in case of disobedience.[83]

The remedy most often desired is the payment of money. Here the court's order will state the amount payable, whether by way of damages, or costs, or otherwise, and the Act provides that the appropriate government department shall pay that amount to the person entitled.[84] It is also provided that payments made under the Act shall be defrayed out of moneys provided by Parliament.[85] A successful plaintiff against the Crown must thus be content with a declaration of his rights or with a mandatory order for payment. The statutory duty to pay, being cast upon the department rather than the Crown, should be enforceable, if necessary, by mandamus.[86]

The Act in no way affects the prerogative remedies, e.g. certiorari and mandamus, which are outside its definition of 'civil proceedings'[87] and which in any case do not lie against the Crown.[88]

---

[78] s. 25(4).

[79] s. 21(1). For the problem of interim injunctive orders and undertakings in damages see above, p. 588.

[80] s. 21(2).

[81] Above, p. 589.

[82] Above, p. 808.

[83] For cases of mandamus granted against ministers see above, p. 663. That remedy is unaffected by the Act, as noted below.

[84] s. 25(3).

[85] s. 37.

[86] See above, p. 663. s. 21(2) is inapplicable owing to the definition of 'civil proceedings' (below).

[87] s. 38(2).

[88] See above, p. 644.

In his or her private capacity the sovereign stands wholly outside the Act and under the older law.[89] Nor does the Act apply in respect of matters arising outside the government of the United Kingdom.[90]

The ordinary legal rules as to indemnity and contribution now apply in Crown proceedings.[91] The rule most likely to come into play is that which allows an employer, who has to pay damages for his servant's wrongful act, to recover the amount from the servant. This illustrates the general principle that where there are joint tortfeasors—and master and servant are in law joint tortfeasors—the tortfeasor who is innocent may claim contribution from the tortfeasor who is to blame. Thus if a government driver knocks down and injures some one negligently, and the injured man sues the Crown and obtains damages, the Crown has a legal right as employer to make the driver indemnify it.[92] Since the salaries of Crown servants are in any case, legally speaking, at the Crown's mercy,[93] the Crown is in a strong position to enforce this right, though like many employers it may not wish to do so.

The Act now provides one uniform procedure for all actions against the Crown, including interlocutory matters such as discovery of documents and interrogatories.[94] The Act has therefore abolished the petition of right and various other antiquated forms of procedure.[95] But, as already noticed, a petition of right may still have to be used in cases not covered by the Act, such as proceedings in respect of overseas territories.[96]

Other Crown privileges

The Crown has various advantages under the general law, which fall outside the scope of this book. Under the law of limitation of actions the Crown's title to land is not barred until the land has been in adverse possession for thirty years,[97] whereas the normal period in ordinary cases is twelve years. Formerly the Crown and its servants shared with other public authorities the privilege of a short limitation period for wrongful acts, until the legislation was repealed in 1954.[98]

---

[89] s. 41; see above, p. 821.

[90] s. 40(2).

[91] s. 4.

[92] See *Lister* v. *Romford Ice and Cold Storage Co. Ltd.* [1957] AC 555.

[93] Above, p. 69, subject now to doubt.

[94] s. 28.

[95] s. 23 and 1st sched. For an example of a 'latin information' see *Attorney-General* v. *Valle-Jones* [1935] 2 KB 209.

[96] Above, p. 821.

[97] Limitation Act 1980, 1st sched., Pt. II.

[98] See above, p. 786.

STATUTES AFFECTING THE CROWN

Presumption against Crown liability

An Act of Parliament is presumed not to bind the Crown in the absence of express provision or necessary implication.[99] This is a long-standing rule of interpretation,[1] which has nothing to do with the royal prerogative.[2] The Crown Proceedings Act 1947 expressly refrains from altering the position.[3] In this respect, contrary to its general policy, the Act does not impose on the Crown the same liability as lies upon other people.

In fact it is frequently necessary that statutes should bind the Crown, and in such cases each statute makes the necessary provision. Thus the speed limits now in force under the Road Traffic Act 1960 are expressly made applicable to the Crown by the Act itself, which makes detailed provision for these and other traffic rules to apply to vehicles and persons in the public service of the Crown.[4] Sometimes the Act will provide for its partial application to the Crown: thus the Crown is bound by the Equal Pay Act 1970[5] and the Sex Discrimination Act 1975[6] in respect of the civil service but not in respect of the armed forces.

Other statutes which have been held not to bind the Crown, because of the absence of any provision, are the Town and Country Planning Act 1971 and the Contracts of Employment Act 1972. Accordingly the Crown does not need planning permission for developing Crown land,[7] and a Crown employee is not entitled to a written statement of the terms of his employment.[8] But the Crown's exemption, according to a Scots decision,

[99] Examples are *Province of Bombay* v. *Municipal Corporation of Bombay* [1947] AC 58; *Attorney-General for Ceylon* v. *A.D. Silva* [1953] AC 461; *Madras Electric Supply Co. Ltd.* v. *Boarland* [1955] AC 667; *China Ocean Shipping Co.* v. *South Australia* (1979) 27 ALR 1. For the rule generally see Hogg, *Liability of the Crown*, 166.

[1] In earlier times the Crown was more readily held bound, it being said that it was bound by statutes passed for the public good, the relief of the poor, the advancement of learning, religion and justice, and the prevention of fraud, injury and wrong: *Willion* v. *Berkeley* (1561) 1 Plowd. 223; *Magdalen College Case* (1615) 11 Co Rep 66b; *R.* v. *Archbishop of Armagh* (1711) 1 Str 516; Chitty, *Prerogatives of the Crown*, 382. But these exceptions are no longer admitted: see the *Province of Bombay* case (above).

[2] *Madras Electric Supply Corporation Ltd.* v. *Boarland* [1955] AC 667 at 684–5. But 'prerogative' is sometimes used in a loose sense (see above, p. 241) in connection with this rule: *Coomber* v. *Berkshire Justices* (1883) 9 App Cas 61 at 66, 71, 77; and see the *Madras* case (above) at 687.

[3] s. 40(2)(*f*).

[4] s. 250. Other examples are Social Security Act 1975, ss. 127, 128; Race Relations Act 1976, s. 75, applying the procedure of Crown Proceedings Act 1947.

[5] s. 1(8).

[6] s. 85.

[7] *Ministry of Agriculture* v. *Jenkins* [1963] 2 QB 317.

[8] *Wood* v. *Leeds Area Health Authority* [1974] ICR 535.

is confined to cases where the statute encroaches upon the Crown's own rights or interests. Thus the Ministry of Defence was liable under highway and planning legislation when it fenced off part of a main road in which the Crown claimed no proprietary or other right.[9]

Whether the Crown can commit a criminal offence under a statute made binding upon it was discussed in one case by the High Court of Australia.[10]

Crown may claim benefit of statutes

It has been maintained consistently for centuries that the Crown, although not bound by the obligations of a statute, might take the benefit of it in the same way as other persons.[11] Accordingly the Crown was able to claim the benefit of statutes of limitation which prevented actions being brought after a fixed time.[12] Although the historical justification for this one-sided arrangement has been treated as an open question,[13] there can be little doubt that it represents the law. There is no reason why the Crown's exemption from the burden of a statute should prevent its taking the benefit, since the exemption was originally a limited rule for the protection of the Crown's executive powers and prerogatives rather than a rule that statutes did not concern the Crown. On the other hand, the Crown cannot pick out the parts of a statute which benefit it without taking account of qualifications: if it claims some statutory right, it must take that right subject to its own statutory limitations, whether imposed by the original Act or otherwise.[14]

The Crown's common law rights are confirmed by the Crown Proceedings Act 1947, which provides that the Act shall not prejudice 'the

---

[9] *Lord Advocate* v. *Strathclyde Regional Council* [1988] The Times, 17 March (Inner House, Court of Session).

[10] *Cain v*. *Doyle* (1946) 72 CLR 409. The question was raised on the prosecution of a Commonwealth munition factory manager for aiding and abetting an offence by the Crown in wrongfully dismissing an ex-serviceman. The majority opinion was that an offence could be committed, but the accused was acquitted.

[11] *Case of the King's Fine* (1605) 7 Co Rep 32a; *Magdalen College Case* (1615) 11 Co Rep 66b at 68b; *R*. v. *Cruise* (1852) 2 Ir Ch Rep 65; Bl Comm i. 262; Chitty, *Prerogatives of the Crown*, 382; Hogg, *Liability of the Crown*, 181. See also *Town Investments Ltd.* v. *Department of the Environment* [1978] AC 359.

[12] *A.-G.* v. *Tomline* (1880) 15 Ch D 150; *Cayzer Irvine & Co. Ltd.* v. *Board of Trade* [1927] 1 KB 269 at 274 (Rowlatt J.).

[13] By Scrutton L.J. in the *Cayzer Irvine* case (above) at 294.

[14] *R. and Buckberd's Case* (1594) 1 Leon 149; *Crooke's Case* (1691) 1 Show KB 208; *Nisbet Shipping Co.* v. *The Queen* [1955] 1 WLR 1031; *Housing Commission of New South Wales* v. *Panayides* (1963) 63 SR (NSW) 1; Hogg (as above).

right of the Crown to take advantage of the provisions of an Act of Parliament although not named therein', and that in any civil proceedings against the Crown the Crown may rely upon any defence which would be available if the proceedings were between subjects.[15] The Crown is thus amply entitled to claim statutory rights and defences.

LIMITATIONS OF STATE LIABILITY

Political action: tort

A line has to be drawn between governmental acts which can give rise to legal liability because they are analogous to the acts of ordinary persons, and acts which give rise to no such liability because the analogy breaks down. There is a certain sphere of activity where the state is outside the law, and where actions against the Crown and its servants will not lie. The rule of law demands that this sphere should be as narrow as possible. In English law the only available examples relate in one way or another to foreign affairs.

In tort, the Crown and its servants can sometimes plead the defence of act of state. But this plea is only available for acts performed abroad. It would subvert the rights of the citizen entirely if it would justify acts done within the jurisdiction, for it would be the same as the defence of state necessity, which has always been rejected. But acts of force committed by the Crown in foreign countries are no concern of the English courts. In the time of the naval campaign against the slave trade, for example, a Spanish slave trader failed in an action for damages against a British naval commander who destroyed one of his establishments in West Africa.[16] It is by this fundamental rule that acts of violence in foreign affairs, including acts of war, if committed abroad, cannot be questioned in English courts. It also casts a complete immunity over all acts of the Crown done in the course of annexing or administering foreign territory.

A British protectorate was in principle considered to be a foreign territory, so that a person arrested by the government's orders had no remedy.[17] But where, as used to happen in practice, a protectorate was in fact completely 'under the subjection of the Crown' and was ruled as if it were a colony, the courts asserted their jurisdiction and the Crown was

---

[15] s. 31(1). It may be that 'therein' refers to 'provisions' rather than to 'Act', so that mention of the Crown elsewhere in the Act is immaterial.
[16] *Buron v. Denman* (1848) 2 Ex 167.
[17] *R. v. Crewe (Earl) ex p. Sekgome* [1910] 2 KB 576.

required to act according to law.[18] The boundaries of the area within which the rule is upheld may thus sometimes be difficult to draw. But it is clear that within that area the Crown cannot extend its limited legal power by plea of act of state. Another naval case will illustrate this. The British and French governments had made an arrangement for the control of lobster fishing in Newfoundland, by which no new lobster factory was to be established there without joint consent. A factory was in fact established by the plaintiff, contrary to the terms of the inter-governmental agreement, and the defendant, a naval captain acting under Admiralty orders, seized it. The plaintiff was a British subject and his factory was within British territory. The Crown's attempt to justify the seizure as an act of state therefore failed, and the plaintiff was awarded damages against the responsible Crown officer.[19] Today, under the Crown Proceedings Act, the Crown would also be liable directly. The enforcement of treaties, so far as it affects the rights of persons within the jurisdiction, must be authorised by Act of Parliament. The Crown has no paramount powers.

It is often said that act of state cannot be pleaded against a British subject. No such rule was laid down in the lobster-fishing case; but the case was treated as an illustration of some such rule in a number of *obiter dicta* in a later case in the House of Lords.[20] This is weighty authority, but even so there are grounds for thinking that the proposition may be too wide. All the cases in question were cases where the acts took place within the jurisdiction—and within the jurisdiction the rights of an alien (not being an enemy alien) are similar to those of a subject. If in British territory an alien has his property taken, or is detained, in any way not justified by law, he has full legal protection[21]—not because of his nationality, but because he is within the area where the government must show legal warrant for its acts. Conversely, if a British subject chooses to live outside the jurisdiction, it is hard to believe that he can thereby fetter the Crown's freedom of action in foreign affairs. If the house of a British subject living in Egypt had been damaged by British bombs in the operations against the Suez Canal in 1956, would its owner really have been able to recover damages in an English court?

An affirmative answer indeed appears to be given by Lord Reid in a later case where a British subject claimed compensation from the Crown for injury done to his hotel in Cyprus (a foreign country) when it was in the

---

[18] *Ex p. Mwenya* [1960] 1 QB 241 (Northern Rhodesia, now Zambia).

[19] *Walker* v. *Baird* [1892] AC 491.

[20] *Johnstone* v. *Pedlar* [1921] 2 AC 262 (successful action by American citizen resident in Ireland for recovery of money taken from him by the police: plea of act of state rejected by the House of Lords).

[21] *Johnstone* v. *Pedlar* (above); *Kuchenmeister* v. *Home Office* [1958] 1 QB 496; *R.* v. *Home Secretary ex p. Khawaja* [1984] AC 74 at 111.

occupation of a 'truce force' of British troops.[22] But the other Lords of Appeal left this question open, holding that there was in fact no act of state. In any case, the gist of the action allowed was for use and occupation of the land and for breach of contract, and act of state is no defence to contractual or quasi-contractual claims as opposed to claims in tort. A different answer is suggested by another case in which British subjects lost valuable concessions granted by the paramount chief of Pondoland when that territory was annexed by the Crown. The Crown refused to recognise the concessions and pleaded act of state successfully.[23]

The latter case perhaps gives the right lead. Generalities about the immunity of British subjects ought probably to be confined to (a) acts done within the realm, and (b) acts against British subjects abroad which are not in themselves acts of international policy, such as the above-mentioned injury to the hotel in Cyprus. A logical basis for 'act of state' then emerges. It is not so much a matter of nationality as of geography—that is to say, the Crown enjoys no dispensation for acts done within the jurisdiction, whether the plaintiff be British or foreign; but foreign parts are beyond the pale (in Kipling's words, 'without the law'), and there the Crown has a free hand, whether the plaintiff be foreign or British.

Political action: contract

In contract there are also cases where ordinary business must be distinguished from political acts. It has been laid down that 'it is not competent for the Government to fetter its future executive action, which must necessarily be determined by the needs of the community when the question arises'.[24] But this was an isolated decision, and its scope is by no means clear. It concerned a Swedish ship which was detained in England in 1918 after its owners had been given an assurance through the British Legation in Stockholm, on behalf of the British government, that the ship would be given clearance if she brought (as she did) an approved cargo. The owners sued the Crown by petition of right for damages for breach of contract. The court held that this was not a contract at all—so far from being a commercial transaction, it was merely a statement by the government that it intended to act in a particular way in a certain event. Up to this point there is no difficulty, for plainly a boundary must be drawn

---

[22] *Nissan* v. *A.-G.* [1970] AC 179. The fact that the 'truce force' was for some time part of a United Nations peace-keeping force was held to make no difference to the Crown's responsibility. On the questions raised by this case see [1968] CLJ 102 (J. C. Collier).

[23] *Cook* v. *Sprigg* [1899] QC 572; and see *Winfat Enterprise (HK) Co. Ltd.* v. *Attorney-General of Hong Kong* [1985] AC 733.

[24] *Rederiaktiebolaget 'Amphitrite'* v. *The King* [1921] 3 KB 500. See Mitchell, *The Contracts of Public Authorities*, 27; Turpin, *Government Contracts*, 19.

between legal contracts and mere administrative assurances. That is a question of fact. But the judge went on to say that the Crown not merely *had* not made such a contract but *could* not make such a contract, because it could not hamper its freedom of action in matters which concerned the welfare of the state; and he argued *a fortiori* from the doctrine that Crown servants are always dismissible at will, which is discussed elsewhere.[25]

The rule thus laid down is very dubious; it rests on no authority, and it has been criticized judicially.[26] Very many contracts made by the Crown must fetter its future executive action to some extent. If the Admiralty makes a contract for the sale of a surplus warship, that fetters the Crown's future executive action in that the ship will have to be surrendered or damages will have to be paid. Yet there ought to be a remedy against the Crown for breach of contract in that case as much as in any other.[27] The only concession that need be made to public policy is that the remedy should be in damages rather than by way of specific performance or injunction. But that is achieved by the Crown Proceedings Act 1947, and in any case the court would use its discretion.

Another case which falls outside the ordinary law of contract is that of treaties. No English court will enforce a treaty, that is to say an agreement made between states rather than between individuals. 'The transactions of independent states between each other are governed by other laws than those which municipal courts administer.'[28] In the days when much of India was governed by the East India Company this principle was often invoked by English courts in order to disclaim jurisdiction over transactions between the Company, acting in effect as a sovereign power, and the native rulers of India. For the same reason the Company was given the benefit of the doctrine of act of state, so that it could commit acts of force with no legal responsibility.[29] Its commercial and its governmental activities had to be separated, so that while liable for the one it was not liable for the other. Similarly, where money is paid to the Crown under a treaty as compensation for injury inflicted on British subjects, those subjects cannot sue the Crown to recover the money, for the transaction is on the plane of international affairs out of which no justiciable rights arise.[30] The ordinary principles of trust or agency are no more suitable to the case than the law of contract is suitable for the enforcement of treaties.

[25] Above, p. 67.
[26] In *Robertson* v. *Minister of Pensions* [1949] 1 KB 227 and *Howell* v. *Falmouth Boat Co.* [1951] AC 837, for which see above, p. 382.
[27] Compare the problems of contracts which fetter statutory powers: above, p. 375.
[28] *Secretary of State for India* v. *Kamachee Boye Sahaba* (1859) 13 Moo PC 22.
[29] *Salaman* v. *Secretary of State for India* [1906] 1 KB 613.
[30] *Rustomjee* v. *The Queen* (1876) 2 QBD 69; *Civilian War Claimants Association* v. *The King* [1932] AC 14. The principle is not changed by the Foreign Compensation Acts 1950–69.

SUPPRESSION OF EVIDENCE IN THE PUBLIC INTEREST

'Crown privilege'

A dilemma arises in cases where it would be injurious to the public interest to disclose evidence which a litigant wishes to use. The public interest requires that justice should be done, but it may also require that the necessary evidence should be suppressed. In many cases the Crown has successfully intervened to prevent evidence being revealed, both in cases where it was a party and in cases where it was not. To hear the evidence in camera is no solution, since to reveal it to the parties and their advisers may be as dangerous as to reveal it to the public generally. The Crown's object must therefore be to suppress it altogether, even at the cost of depriving the litigant of his rights.

It was for long supposed that only the Crown could make application to the court for this purpose, and its right to do so was known as 'Crown privilege'. But in 1972 the House of Lords disapproved this expression, and held that any one may make such an application. The turning-point in the history of the subject had come in 1968, when in *Conway* v. *Rimmer*[31] the House held that the court should investigate the Crown's claims and disallow them if on balance the need for secrecy was less than the need to do justice to the litigant. This was the culmination of a classic story of undue indulgence by the courts to executive discretion, followed by executive abuse, leading ultimately to a radical reform achieved by the courts themselves. Since the struggle was one between the Crown and litigants, it belongs properly to this chapter, even though the House of Lords has now thrown open the door to all comers.

The Crown's claims had caused so much discontent that important administrative concessions were made in 1956, and judicial rebellion began in the Court of Appeal in 1964. The initial wrong turning had been made in 1942, when the House of Lords, departing from the current of earlier authority, declared in wide terms that a ministerial claim of privilege must be accepted without question by the court. This meant that the court was obliged to refuse to receive any evidence if a minister swore an affidavit stating that he objected to the production of the evidence since in his opinion its disclosure would be contrary to the public interest. The power thus given to the Crown was dangerous since, unlike other governmental powers, it was exempt from judicial control. The law must of course protect genuine secrets of state. But 'Crown privilege' was also used for suppressing whole classes of relatively innocuous documents, thereby

---

[31] [1968] AC 910; below, p. 838.

sometimes depriving litigants of the ability to enforce their legal rights. This was, in effect, expropriation without compensation. It revealed the truth of the United States Supreme Court's statement in the same context, that 'a complete abandonment of judicial control would lead to intolerable abuses'.[32]

The Crown Proceedings Act 1947 made no attempt to resolve the difficulty. It applied to Crown proceedings the ordinary procedure for obtaining discovery of documents and answers to interrogatories.[33] The Crown may therefore be required to authorise the disclosure of official information, which would otherwise be an offence under the Official Secrets Act 1911. But the Crown Proceedings Act also provides that this shall not prejudice any rule of law which authorises or requires the withholding of any document or the refusal to answer any question on the ground that disclosure would be injurious to the public interest.[34]

Duncan v. Cammell, Laird & Co. Ltd.[35]

This case of 1942 was for long a source of trouble because the House of Lords laid down the law in terms far wider than were required by the question before them. In 1939 the submarine *Thetis* sank during her trials with the loss of ninety-nine men. Many of their dependants brought actions for negligence against the contractors who had built the submarine, and this was a test case. The plaintiffs called on the contractors to produce certain important papers, including the contract with the Admiralty for the hull and machinery and salvage reports made after the accident. But the First Lord of the Admiralty swore an affidavit that disclosure would be against the public interest. The House of Lords held that this affidavit could not be questioned, so that the plaintiffs inevitably lost their case. After the war it was divulged that the *Thetis* class of submarines had a new type of torpedo tube which in 1942 was still secret. The case is a good example of the most genuine type, where it seems plain that the interests of litigants must be sacrificed in order to preserve secrets of state. Diplomatic secrets and methods for the detection of crime might demand similar protection.

But the House of Lords unanimously laid down a sweeping rule that the court could not question a claim of Crown privilege made in proper form, regardless of the nature of the document. Thus the Crown was given legal power to override the rights of litigants not only in cases of genuine necessity but in any cases where a government department thought fit. This

[32] *U.S.* v. *Reynolds* 345 US 1 (1953).
[33] s. 28.
[34] s. 28.
[35] [1942] AC 624.

had not been the law previously. In several English cases judges had called for and inspected documents for which privilege was claimed in order to satisfy themselves that the claim was justified. In 1931 the Privy Council held that the court could examine such a claim, and remitted a case to Australia with directions to examine the documents and strong hints that the claim of privilege should be disallowed.[36] In that case the plaintiff was suing a State government for faulty storage of his wheat, and the Privy Council did not see how the public interest could require non-disclosure of the documents showing how it had been allowed to go bad or how mice had got into it. An English court had actually disallowed a claim of privilege in one case, and the document (quite innocuous) may be seen in the report.[37]

'Class' claims

The principal danger of the *Thetis* doctrine was that it enabled privilege to be claimed merely on the ground that documents belonged to a class which the public interest required to be withheld from production, i.e. not because the particular documents were themselves secret but merely because it was thought that all documents of that kind should be confidential. A favourite argument—and one to which courts of law have given approval[38]—was that official reports of many kinds would not be made fearlessly and candidly if there was any possibility that they might later be made public. Once this unsound argument gained currency, free rein was given to the tendency to secrecy which is inherent in the public service. It is not surprising that the Crown, having been given a blank cheque, yielded to the temptation to overdraw.

Two cases illustrate excessive 'class' claims. In one, the Home Office claimed privilege for police and medical reports on a prisoner who violently assaulted a man awaiting trial in Winchester prison. Without these reports the injured man could not show whether the prison authorities knew that the prisoner was dangerous and were negligent.[39] In the other, the Secretary of State for War intervened in a soldier's divorce case so as to prevent disclosure of reports of a marriage conciliator. The court felt obliged to allow the claim, but it rejected a further claim that the conciliator should not be called as a witness.[40] It was held that the Crown could not render a witness totally incompetent, but could only object to

---

[36] *Robinson* v. *South Australia* (No. 2) [1931] AC 704.
[37] *Spiegelman* v. *Hocker* (1933) 50 TLR 87 (statement to police after accident).
[38] *Smith* v. *East India Co.* (1841) 1 Ph 50; *Hennessy* v. *Wright* (1888) 21 QBD 509.
[39] *Ellis* v. *Home Office* [1953] 2 QB 135.
[40] *Broome* v. *Broome* [1955] P 190.

evidence being given on specific matters. In fact the witness gave evidence without in any way jeopardising the public interest.

Official concessions

The next event was that the government made important concessions administratively. The Lord Chancellor announced in 1956 that privilege would no longer be claimed for reports of witnesses of accidents on the road, or on government premises, or involving government employees; for ordinary medical reports on the health of civilian employees; for medical reports (including those of prison doctors) where the Crown or the doctor was sued for negligence; for papers needed for defence against a criminal charge; for witnesses' ordinary statements to the police; and for reports on matters of fact (as distinct from comment or advice) relating to liability in contract.[41] These heads, which were defined in more detail in the statement, were said to comprise the majority of cases which came before the courts. It will be noted that they included medical reports on prisoners of the kind that the Crown refused to produce in the Winchester prison case. Privilege would still be claimed in cases of inspectors' reports into accidents not involving the Crown (such as factory inspectors' reports), though the inspector would not be prevented from giving evidence; for medical reports and records in the fighting services and in prisons in cases not involving negligence; and for departmental minutes and memoranda. These were said to be the cases where freedom and candour of communication with and within the public service would be imperilled if there were to be the slightest risk of disclosure at a later date. Supplementary announcements were made in 1962 and 1964.[42]

After these concessions it became all the harder to accept the argument about 'freedom and candour of communication with and within the public service'. Lord Radcliffe said in the House of Lords: 'I should myself have supposed Crown servants to be made of sterner stuff', and he criticised the insidious tendency to suppress 'everything however commonplace that has passed between one civil servant and another behind the departmental screen'.[43] More recently, and on a different note, Lord Wilberforce has said that it seems fashionable to decry 'the need for candour in communication between those concerned with policy making'; but that 'if as a ground it may at one time have been exaggerated, it has now, in my opinion,

---

[41] 197 HL Deb col 741 (6 June 1956).

[42] 237 HL Deb 1191 (8 March 1962), referring to this book (proceedings against police and statements made to police); 261 HL Deb 423 (12 November 1964) (claims based on national security).

[43] *Glasgow Cpn.* v. *Central Land Board* 1956 SC 1 at 20, 19.

received an excessive dose of cold water'.[44] But in the same case Lord Keith gave it a deluge:[45]

The notion that any competent or conscientious public servant would be inhibited at all in the candour of his writings by consideration of the off-chance that they might have to be produced in litigation is in my opinion grotesque. To represent that the possibility of it might significantly impair the public service is even more so . . . the candour argument is an utterly insubstantial ground for denying [the citizen] access to relevant documents.

When this favourite argument was later deployed by the Home Office to justify withholding top-level departmental documents about prison policy McNeill J. rejected it out of hand.[46]

The judicial rebellion

The concessions helped legal opinion to mobilise for the overthrow of the extreme doctrine of the *Thetis* case and the unrestricted use of 'class' privilege. In 1956 the House of Lords held that in Scotland the court had power to disallow a claim by the Crown, and that in the *Thetis* case the House had failed to consider a long line of authority.[47] In 1964 the Court of Appeal, noting the superior law of Scotland, Canada, Australia, New Zealand, and the United States,[48] held that the same was true of England and asserted (though without exercising) its own power to inspect the documents in a 'class' case and order their production.[49] In fact privilege continued to be claimed on a wide basis by the Crown. 'It is not unnatural that its servants fight trench by trench to preserve the citadel of immunity which the years have built up for them.'[50] Moreover, the Court of Appeal changed its mind in 1967 and relapsed into the unqualified *Thetis* doctrine.[51]

Finally in 1968 the House of Lords was given the opportunity to lay

---

[44] *Burmah Oil Co. Ltd.* v. *Bank of England* [1980] AC 1090 (dissenting).

[45] Lord Keith also said that to expose the workings of government might be positively beneficial.

[46] *Williams* v. *Home Office* [1981] 1 All ER 1151.

[47] *Glasgow Cpn.* case (above). For a case of a claim disallowed see *Whitehall* v. *Whitehall* 1957 SC 30.

[48] As in *R.* v. *Snider* (1953) 2 DLR (2d) 9; *Corbett* v. *Social Security Commission* [1962] NZLR 878; *Bruce* v. *Waldron* [1963] VR 3. Later cases rejecting claims of privilege are *U.S.* v. *Nixon* (1974) 418 US 683; *Konia* v. *Morley* (1976) 1 NZLR 455; *Sankey* v. *Whitlam* (1978) 21 ALR 505.

[49] *Re Grosvenor Hotel (No. 2)* [1965] Ch 1210.

[50] *Wednesbury Cpn.* v. *Ministry of Housing and Local Government* [1965] 1 WLR 261 at 273 (Harman L.J.).

[51] *Conway* v. *Rimmer* [1967] 1 WLR 1031, Lord Denning M.R. strongly dissenting.

down more acceptable law. In *Conway* v. *Rimmer*[52] the House unanimously reversed what it unanimously stated in 1942, it shattered the basis of
the unrestricted 'class' privilege, and it successfully ordered the production
of documents against the objections of the Crown. These documents were
reports by his superiors on a probationer police constable who was
prosecuted by the police for theft of an electric torch and decisively
acquitted. He sued the prosecutor for damages for malicious prosecution,
and applied for discovery of five reports about himself which were in the
police records and which were important as evidence on the question of
malice. Both parties wished this evidence to be produced, but the Home
Secretary interposed with a wide claim of 'class' privilege, asserting that
confidential reports on the conduct of the police officers were a class of
documents the production of which would be injurious to the public
interest.

The House of Lords heaped withering criticism on the overworked
argument that whole classes of official documents should be withheld, at
whatever cost to the interests of litigants, for the sake of 'freedom and
candour of communication with and within the public service'. The Court
of Appeal has since held that 'the candour argument has not survived the
decision of the House of Lords in *Conway* v. *Rimmer*,'[53] and in the House of
Lords Lord Salmon has said that he could not accept it.[54] But Lord
Wilberforce's remark about 'an excessive dose of cold water'[55] may
indicate that it has not yet been given decent burial.

In *Conway* v. *Rimmer* the House of Lords also concluded that the earlier
authorities had been misinterpreted in the *Thetis* case as regards England as
well as Scotland. On the other hand they made it clear that the court would
seldom dispute a claim based upon the specific contents of a document
concerning, for example, decisions of the cabinet,[56] criminal investigations,
national defence, or foreign affairs. But in every case the court had the
power and the duty to weigh the public interest of justice to litigants
against the public interest asserted by the government. In many cases this

---

[52] [1968] AC 910. Little mention was made of the precedents in the Court of Appeal and
in other countries of the Commonwealth which prepared the way for this reform. Lord
Denning M.R. in *Air Canada* v. *Secretary of State for Trade* [1983] 2 AC 394 at 408 gave a
spirited and dramatised account of the deeds of the 'Three Musketeers' who shot down
earlier claims, of how he was 'taken prisoner' by a different Court of Appeal, and how 'from
over the hill there came, most unexpectedly, a relief force. It was the House of Lords
themselves'.
[53] *Campbell* v. *Tameside M.B.C.* [1982] QB 1065 (O'Connor LJ, in agreement with
Ackner LJ).
[54] *Science Research Council* v. *Nassé* [1980] AC 1028 at 1070.
[55] Above, p. 836.
[56] As to cabinet decisions and papers see below, p. 841.

could be done only by inspecting the documents, which could properly be shown to the court, but not to the parties, before the court decided whether to order production.

At a later date the House itself inspected the five documents in question, held that their disclosure would not prejudice the public interest, and ordered them to be produced to the plaintiff.[57]

Thus did the House of Lords bring back a dangerous executive power into legal custody. Some of the earlier decisions, and the official concessions in administrative practice, will remain of importance. But the legal foundation of excessive 'class' claims has been destroyed.

'Crown privilege' replaced by 'public interest immunity'

The House of Lords once again put the law onto a fresh basis in a case where a would-be gaming club proprietor took proceedings for criminal libel against a police officer who had supplied the Gaming Board with unfavourable information about him.[58] The Home Secretary asked the court to quash orders requiring the police and the board to produce the correspondence, and the board itself applied similarly. Lord Reid said:[59]

The ground put forward has been said to be Crown privilege. I think that that expression is wrong and may be misleading. There is no question of any privilege in any ordinary sense of the word. The real question is whether the public interest requires that the letter shall not be produced and whether that public interest is so strong as to override the ordinary right and interest of a litigant that he shall be able to lay before a court of justice all relevant evidence. A Minister of the Crown is always an appropriate and often the most appropriate person to assert this public interest, and the evidence or advice which he gives the court is always valuable and may sometimes be indispensable. But, in my view, it must always be open to any person interested to raise the question and there may be cases where the trial judge should himself raise the question if no-one else has done so.

The House of Lords then allowed not only the Home Secretary's claim but also the claim made independently by the board. It was held that the board would be seriously hampered in its statutory duty of making stringent

---

[57] See [1968] AC 996.

[58] R. v. Lewes Justices ex p. Home Secretary [1973] AC 388.

[59] At 400. Lords Pearson, Simon and Salmon also criticised the expression 'Crown privilege'. Lord Salmon said (at 412) that in such cases as cabinet minutes, dealings between heads of government departments, despatches from ambassadors and police sources of information the law had long recognised their immunity from disclosure and that 'the affidavit or certificate of a Minister is hardly necessary'. In Buttes Gas & Oil Co. v. Hammer (No. 3) [1981] QB 223 the Court of Appeal recognised a public interest in non-disclosure of certain kinds of information relating to foreign states, but the interest is that of this country not that of foreign states.

inquiries into the character of applicants if information obtained from the police or from sources 'of dubious character' was liable to be disclosed; and that in weighing the opposing claims in the balance the risk of a gaming club getting into the wrong hands should outweigh the risk of a licence being denied to a respectable applicant.[60] The social evils which had attended gaming clubs before the Gaming Act 1968, and the obvious necessity for the board to be able to make confidential inquiries in order to fulfil its duties, tilted the balance against disclosure.

'Public interest immunity' may now be claimed by any party or witness in any proceedings without using ministerial certificates, affidavits, or special formalities.[61] As with the old 'Crown privilege' there may be 'class' cases in which whole classes of documents ought to be protected in the public interest, and several of the examples which follow are of this kind. The doctrine extends beyond the sphere of central government and, indeed, beyond the sphere of government altogether.

Weighing the public interest

The operation of balancing the public interest against the interests of a litigant may or may not require the inspection of the documents. There will be no need for inspection where the preponderance is clear one way or the other. In a case where a company sued the Bank of England for the recovery of a large holding of securities, and the Attorney-General intervened to resist disclosure of papers about government policy and confidential matters, a majority of the House of Lords decided that inspection was necessary. But, having inspected, the House upheld the claim of immunity, largely on the ground that the evidential value of the papers was insufficient to outweigh the objections to disclosure.[62] The relevance and cogency of the evidence may thus be weighed in the balance along with other matters.

In confirming this last proposition the House has since held that in the case of a 'class' claim the court should not inspect documents unless satisfied that they are likely to give substantial support to the applicant's case, and that he is not merely undertaking a 'fishing expedition'.[63] The House for this reason declined to authorise inspection of ministerial papers about

---

[60] See at 412 (Lord Salmon).

[61] As to waiver of the immunity see *Hehir* v. *Metropolitan Police Cmr.* [1982] 1 WLR 715.

[62] *Burmah Oil Co. Ltd.* v. *Bank of England* [1980] AC 1090.

[63] *Air Canada* v. *Secretary of State for Trade* [1983] 2 AC 394. Contrast *Fowler & Roderique Ltd.* v. *Attorney-General* [1981] 2 NZLR 728 (correspondence between minister and official advisers about grant of licences inspected and ordered to be disclosed). Disclosure was also ordered in *Brightwell* v. *Accident Compensation Commission* [1985] 1 NZLR 132. See (1985) 101 LQR 200 (T. R. S. Allan).

decisions of policy, and also correspondence between senior civil servants, of which a group of airlines sought disclosure in attempting to show that the government had unlawfully compelled the British Airports Authority to make a large increase in their charges. Since it was not contended that the government had other motives than those published in their white paper, there was nothing to outweigh the consideration that high-level documents about policy should not normally be disclosed.

As regards cabinet documents Lord Fraser said:

I do not think that even Cabinet minutes are completely immune from disclosure in a case where, for example, the issue in a litigation involves serious misconduct by a Cabinet minister.

He cited such cases in Australia[64] and the United States[65] where claims of immunity had been disallowed. But he made it clear that cabinet documents were entitled to 'a high degree of protection against disclosure'. In previous cases dicta in the House of Lords have been conflicting, some favouring absolute immunity and others not.[66]

Confidential information

Information is not protected from disclosure merely because it has been supplied in confidence. The House of Lords made this clear in another case in which they accepted a Crown claim to withhold documents on the ground that disclosure would be harmful to the efficient working of an Act of Parliament.[67] The customs and excise authorities objected to disclosing details which they had obtained in confidence from traders about dealings in amusement machines supplied by a manufacturer whose liability to purchase tax was in dispute. It was held that, much as traders might resent disclosure of such details, 'confidentiality' was not a separate head of

---

[64] *Sankey* v. *Whitlam* (1978) 21 ALR 505.

[65] *United States* v. *Nixon* 418 US 683 (1974).

[66] See the *Lewes Justices* and *Burmah Oil* cases (above). See also *A.-G.* v. *Jonathan Cape Ltd.* [1976] QB 752 (Attorney-General's application for injunction against publication of the Crossman Diaries refused since the cabinet materials contained in them were about ten years old and no longer required protection in the public interest); *Lanyon Pty. Ltd.* v. *Commonwealth of Australia* (1974) 3 ALR 58 (discovery of cabinet and cabinet committee papers refused); *Environmental Defence Society Inc.* v. *South Pacific Aluminium Ltd.* (No. 2) [1981] 1 NZLR 153 (cabinet papers inspected but production not ordered); [1980] PL 263 (I. G. Eagles).

[67] *Alfred Crompton Amusement Machines Ltd.* v. *Customs and Excise Commissioners* (No. 2) [1974] AC 405. The Court of Appeal had inspected the documents (see at 426). See also *Science Research Council* v. *Nassé* [1980] AC 1028; *British Steel Cpn.* v. *Granada Television Ltd.* [1981] AC 1096.

immunity, though it might be very material in the balancing of the public interest against the interest of justice to the litigant.[68] Lord Cross also said:[69]

In a case where the considerations for and against disclosure appear to be fairly evenly balance the courts should I think uphold a claim to privilege on the grounds of public interest and trust to the head of the department concerned to do whatever he can to mitigate the effects of non-disclosure.

Although the case against disclosure was apparently not very strong, and although some of the documents were of a routine character, the House of Lords decided on this basis that the confidential character of these particular inquiries should be protected. But since the taxpayers' liability was to be decided by arbitration, and the documents withheld would not be available for use by either side, the case for disclosure was also not strong. By contrast, a plea by the Home Office to protect top-level departmental documents about prison policy did not avail when a prisoner brought an action against them, and after inspection several were ordered to be disclosed.[70] Where a local authority pleaded confidentiality in resisting a claim for preliminary discovery of their records about a violent schoolboy who had severely injured a teacher, the Court of Appeal ordered discovery after inspecting the documents.[71]

The House of Lords have also held that the anonymity of informers should be protected where the public interest so demands.[72] This applies both to police informers[73] and also to those who report maltreatment of children to a local authority or protection society. The Court of Appeal has refused to order production of a local authority's records of children in their care, holding that confidentiality was essential for the proper functioning of the child care service and this public interest outweighed that of facilitating an action for negligence by a former child in care.[74] For the same reasons the same court refused to assist a plaintiff in an action for

[68] Or, where there is no public interest, in deciding whether discovery is really necessary for disposing fairly of the proceedings: *Science Research Council* v. *Nassé* (above).

[69] At 434.

[70] *Williams* v. *Home Office* [1981] 1 All ER 1151, taking into account that documents so disclosed may not be used for other purposes.

[71] *Campbell* v. *Tameside M.B.C.* [1982] QB 1065 (the teacher was the prospective plaintiff, applying under Administration of Justice Act 1970, s. 31. Contrast *Ellis* v. *Home Office*, above, p. 835.

[72] *D.* v. *National Society for the Prevention of Cruelty to Children* [1978] AC 171. And see *R.* v. *Cheltenham Justices ex p. Secretary of State for Trade* [1977] 1 WLR 95; *Buckley* v. *The Law Society* (No. 2) [1984] 1 WLR 1101.

[73] As in *Friel, Petitioner* 1981 SLR 113. See also *R.* v. *Rankine* [1986] QB 861 (police not required to disclose location of observation post).

[74] *Gaskin* v. *Liverpool C.C.* [1980] 1 WLR 1549. Contrast *Waugh* v. *British Railways Board* [1980] AC 521 (railway accident report: disclosure ordered).

damages against the police for trespass, false imprisonment, etc., when he sought to obtain the records of the police investigation into his complaint.[75] In both cases the records were protected on a broad 'class' basis of public interest, and the court declined to inspect them, holding that this should rarely be done in such cases. Where, on the other hand, the police investigation concerned a violent death, and a possible charge of serious crime, the public interest in clearing up the matter outweighed the claim to secrecy.[76]

A continuing dilemma

That the courts have not reverted to undue tenderness to Crown claims is shown by a decision that the customs and excise authorities may not, in the absence of a strong public interest, withhold information which is vital to the enforcement of a person's rights.[77] The owners of a patent for a chemical compound found that it was being infringed by unknown importers and they applied for orders to make the customs authorities disclose the importers' names, in accordance with the duty of persons possessing information about legal wrongs to make it available to the party wronged. This duty was held by the House of Lords to prevail over the Crown's objection that disclosure of the information might cause importers to use false names and so hamper the customs administration; and the 'candour' argument was once again rejected.[78] There was in fact no head of public policy to set against the rights of the owners of the patent.

Nothing will eliminate the conflict between public interest and private right which arises in situations such as these. But it is clear that a much fairer balance between them is being struck, now that the courts have asserted their control and are willing to weigh all claims in the scales of justice.

---

[75] *Neilson* v. *Lougharne* [1981] QB 736. Similarly in *Evans* v. *Chief Constable of Surrey* [1988] The Times, 21 January, the court refused to order disclosure of police reports made to the Director of Public Prosecutions.

[76] *Peach* v. *Commissioner of Metropolitan Police* [1986] QB 1064 (action for damages by mother and administratrix of man killed during disturbance: discovery ordered).

[77] *Norwich Pharmacal Co.* v. *Customs and Excise Commissioners* [1974] AC 133. The same principle was applied in *British Steel Cpn.* v. *Granada Television Ltd.* [1981] AC 1096.

[78] See at 190 (Lord Dilhorne).

PART VII
ADMINISTRATIVE LEGISLATION AND
ADJUDICATION

22

DELEGATED LEGISLATION

NECESSITY OF DELEGATED LEGISLATION

Administrative legislation

There is no more characteristic administrative activity than legislation.[1] Measured merely by volume, more legislation is produced by the executive government than by the legislature. All the orders, rules, and regulations made by ministers, departments and other bodies owe their legal force to Acts of Parliament, except in the few cases where the Crown retains original prerogative power.[2] Parliament is obliged to delegate very extensive law-making power over matters of detail and to content itself with providing a framework of more or less permanent statutes. Law-making power is also vested in local authorities,[3] in water authorities,[4] and some of the nationalised industries,[5] which have power to make byelaws. Outside the sphere of government it is also conferred upon professional bodies such as the Law Society, and various other bodies authorised by Parliament to make statutes or regulations for their own government.[6]

Administrative legislation is traditionally looked upon as a necessary evil, an unfortunate but inevitable infringement of the separation of powers. But this is an old-fashioned view, for in reality it is no more difficult to justify it in theory than it is possible to do without it in practice. There is only a hazy borderline between legislation and administration, and the assumption that they are two fundamentally different forms of power is misleading. There are some obvious general differences. But the idea that a clean division can be made (as it can be more readily in the case of the judicial power) is a legacy from an older era of political theory. It is easy to

---

[1] Valuable works on this subject are Allen, *Law and Orders*, 3rd edn.; Carr, *Delegated Legislation* and *Concerning English Administrative Law*, ch. 2. A classic survey is sect. II of the *Report of the Committee on Ministers' Powers*, Cmd. 4060 (1932). See also Pearce, *Delegated Legislation in Australia and New Zealand*.

[2] Above, p. 240.

[3] Local Government Act 1972, s. 235; above, p. 131.

[4] Under Water Act 1973, 7th sched., Pt. 2, subject to ministerial confirmation.

[5] e.g. British Railways Board under Transport Act 1962, s. 67, subject to ministerial confirmation.

[6] e.g. Oxford and Cambridge Universities under Universities of Oxford and Cambridge Act 1923, s. 7, subject to approval by the Privy Council.

see that legislative power is the power to lay down the law for people in general, whereas administrative power is the power to lay down the law for them, or apply the law to them, in some particular situation. In the case of the scheme for centralising the electricity supply undertakings in London, which has been instanced already as a matter of administrative power,[7] it might be said that the power was just as much legislative. The same might be said of ministerial orders establishing new towns or airports[8] or approving county councils' structure plans, which are specific in character but lay down the law for large numbers of people. And what of 'directions of a general character' given by a minister to a nationalised industry?[9] Are these various orders legislative or administrative? Probably the only correct answer is that they are both, and that there is an infinite series of gradations, with a large area of overlap, between what is plainly legislation and what is plainly administration. Nevertheless a distinction must be maintained to some extent. For one thing, it is a general principle that legislative acts should be public; for another, the distinction may sometimes affect legal rights.[10]

For the most part, however, administrative legislation is governed by the same legal principles that govern administrative action generally. For the purposes of judicial control, statutory interpretation and the doctrine of ultra vires there is common ground throughout both subjects. Both involve the grant of wide discretionary powers to the government. Much that has already been said about the legal control of powers can be taken for granted in this chapter, which is concerned only with the special features of the administrative power to legislate.

If we look at the practical side, it is at once plain that administration must involve a great deal of general law-making, and that no theory which demands segregation of these functions can be sound. Parliament can lay down that cars must carry suitable lights, or that the price of eggs shall be fixed, or that there shall be a free health service, or that national insurance benefit shall be payable in certain cases. But where, as happens so frequently, such legislation can be properly administered only by constantly adjusting it to the needs of the situation, discretion has to be allowed. This is the work of administration, in the clearest sense of the term, and the fact that it may also be said to be legislation is of no relevance. Flexibility is essential, and it is one of the advantages of rules and

---

[7] Above, p. 631.

[8] The development order for Stansted Airport was judicially described as 'purely administrative or legislative': see above, p. 573.

[9] Above, p. 159.

[10] e.g. the right to a fair hearing (above, p. 572). For discussion of the distinction see *Yates (Arthur) & Co. Pty. Ltd.* v. *Vegetable Seeds Committee* (1945) 72 CLR 37; *Attorney-General of Canada* v. *Inuit Tapirisat of Canada* (1980) 115 DLR (3d) 1 at 19.

regulations that they can be altered much more quickly and easily than can Acts of Parliament.

As Parliament thrusts ever greater responsibilities onto the executive, and social and other regulatory services are constantly multiplying, delegated legislation is increasing simply as a function of the growth of discretionary power. The true constitutional problem presented by delegated legislation is not that it exists, but that its enormous growth has made it difficult for Parliament to watch over it.

A new dimension has been added to these problems by membership of the European Communities. Community law contains its own administrative law, which is outside the scope of this book. But the arrangements for parliamentary scrutiny of Community legislation are mentioned at the end of this chapter.

The growth of a problem

Uneasiness at the extent of delegated legislation began to be evident towards the end of the nineteenth century. It was not a new device, but the scale on which it began to be used in what Dicey called 'The Period of Collectivism'[11] was a symptom of a new era. Perhaps the most striking piece of delegation ever effected by Parliament was the Statute of Proclamations 1539 (repealed in 1547), by which Henry VIII was given wide power to legislate by proclamation. In 1531 the Statute of Sewers delegated legislative powers to the Commissioners of Sewers, who were empowered to make drainage schemes and levy rates on landowners. These were early examples of a technique which Parliament has always felt able to use. But the flow of these powers was no more than a trickle until the age of reform arrived in the nineteenth century. Then very sweeping powers began to be conferred. The Poor Law Act 1834 gave to the Poor Law Commissioners, who had no responsibility to Parliament, power to make rules and orders for 'the management of the poor'. This power, which lasted for over a century (though responsibility to Parliament was established in 1847), remained a leading example of delegation which put not merely the detailed execution but also the formulation of policy into executive hands.[12]

But this was part of a particular experiment in bureaucratic government. As a thing in itself, delegated legislation did not begin to provoke criticism until later in the century. The publication of all delegated legislation in a

---

[11] Law and Opinion in England, p. 64.

[12] See Report of the Committee on Ministers' Powers (1932) Cmd. 4060, p. 31. For the development of delegated legislation see the Report, p. 21; Holdsworth, History of English Law, xiv. 100.

uniform series under the title of Statutory Rules and Orders (since 1947, Statutory Instruments) began in 1890, and in 1893 the Rules Publication Act made provision (as will be explained) for systematic printing, publication and numbering, and for advance publicity. These measures brought the proportions of the problem to public notice. In 1891, for instance, the Statutory Rules and Orders were more than twice as extensive as the statutes enacted by Parliament. The first world war inevitably brought a great increase, as the government assumed almost unbounded emergency powers under the Defence of the Realm Act 1914. In 1920, when the wartime surfeit had not yet worn off, rules and orders were five times as bulky as the statutes. Delegated legislation therefore became a target when the outcry against the growth of administrative powers developed in the 1920s. It formed the first of the matters referred to the Committee on Ministers' Powers, whose Report was published in 1932.[13] Since that time, although delegated legislation has continued to grow in bulk and importance, it has not been such a subject of controversy. The second world war brought another flood of regulations, which hardly abated at first when the war was succeeded by the welfare state. But, apart from the question of publication,[14] it was no longer felt that rules and regulations represented a problem about which anything could be done. Some people wanted more of them, and others less, but that they must continue in their accustomed form was assumed with resignation. A committee of the House of Commons which made a general review in 1953 was unable to recommend any important changes.[15]

SCOPE OF ADMINISTRATIVE LEGISLATION

Wide general powers

A standard argument for delegated legislation is that it is necessary for cases where Parliament cannot attend to small matters of detail. But, quite apart from emergency powers (considered below), Parliament sometimes delegates law-making power that is quite general. The provision of the Poor Law Acts 1834–1930 empowering regulations for 'the management of the poor' was exceptional for peacetime legislation of its period. But it was far surpassed by the powers conferred in the heyday of state controls after the second world war. Under the Supplies and Services (Extended Purposes) Act 1947 controls authorised by many regulations already in force were extended for the following additional purposes:

[13] As preceding note.
[14] See below, p. 878.
[15] See below, p. 888.

(a) for promoting the productivity of industry, commerce, and agriculture;

(b) for fostering and directing exports and reducing imports, or imports of any classes, from all or any countries and for redressing the balance of trade; and

(c) generally for ensuring that the whole resources of the community are available for use, and are used, in a manner best calculated to serve the interests of the community.

This was much more than 'emergency' legislation, in any fair sense of that overworked word. Subject to one single reservation for the sake of freedom of the press, the whole economic life of the community was subjected to executive power. The time seemed to have come to which a former minister had looked forward in the Report of 1932, when protesting against the view that delegated legislation was a necessary evil:

I feel that in the conditions of the modern state, which not only has to undertake immense new social services, but which before long may be responsible for the greater part of the industrial and commercial activities of the country, the practice of parliament delegating legislation and the power to make regulations, instead of being grudgingly conceded, ought to be widely extended, and new ways devised to facilitate the process.[16]

These sweeping economic controls were for the most part removed, but statutory social services have inevitably extended the permanent field of delegated legislation. Some of the regulatory powers are wide, for instance the power in the National Health Service Act 1977 (replacing the National Health Service Act 1946) for the Secretary of State to control the medical services to be provided, to secure that adequate personal care and attendance is given, and so on. An example of skeleton legislation which relied heavily on regulations was the Community Land Act 1975 (since repealed). Acts of this kind do little more than provide an outline, and the only effective control left to Parliament is through the subsequent political responsibility of the Minister.

Some of the most indefinite powers ever conferred are those of the European Communities Act 1972, under which Orders in Council and departmental regulations can give effect to the law of the Communities and do anything that could be done by Act of Parliament, subject to the reservations mentioned below.[17]

Taxation

Even the tender subject of taxation, so jealously guarded by the House of Commons, has been invaded to a considerable extent. Under the Import Duties Act 1958 the Treasury was authorised to specify the classes of goods

---

[16] Miss Ellen Wilkinson in Cmd. 4060 (1932), p. 137.

[17] Below, p. 892.

chargeable and the rates of duty, subject to affirmative approval by the House of Commons where duty was imposed or increased; and under the European Communities Act 1972[18] the Treasury was given similar powers, subject to Community obligations. The rate of value added tax is variable within limits by Treasury order under the Finance Act 1972, but again subject to an affirmative vote of the House of Commons if the tax is increased. Many Acts give power to prescribe charges for services rendered, for example by the Post Office or by water authorities or under the National Health Service. Perhaps the most notable delegated taxing power is the power of local authorities to levy rates under the General Rate Act 1967.

Sometimes a power to make charges for services is given in such wide terms that it is in effect a taxing power. The House of Lords has criticised the provision of the Water Act 1973 which empowers water authorities to levy such charges as they think fit for services performed, facilities provided or rights made available, holding that such wide language must be given a limited construction, so that sewerage charges cannot be imposed on properties not served by sewers.[19]

Power to vary Acts of Parliament

It is quite possible for Parliament to delegate a power to amend statutes. This used to be regarded as incongruous, and the clause by which it was done was nicknamed 'the Henry VIII clause'—because, said the Committee of 1932, 'that King is regarded popularly as the impersonation of executive autocracy'. The usual object was to assist in bringing a new Act into effect, particularly where previous legislation had been complicated, or where there might be local Acts of Parliament which some centralised scheme had to be made to fit. A well known example—well known because it was said that the Act could not otherwise have been carried through at the time when Parliament was favourable to it—is the National Insurance Act of 1911, which provided that if any difficulty arose in bringing one part of the Act into operation, the Insurance Commissioners with the consent of the Treasury might do anything that they thought necessary or expedient for that purpose, and might modify the provisions of the Act, provided that they acted before the end of 1913. Such clauses were not uncommon, and sometimes they gave power to amend other Acts as well; but the Committee of 1932 criticised them as constituting a temptation to slipshod work in the preparation of bills, and said that they

---

[18] s. 5.
[19] *Daymond v. Plymouth City Council* [1976] AC 609.

should be used only where they were justified before Parliament on compelling grounds.[20]

But in fact, as the intricacy of legislation grows steadily more formidable, some power to adjust or reconcile statutory provisions has to be tolerated. If there is to be delegated legislation at all, it is inevitable that it should affect statute law as well as common law. Although such clauses may no longer be cast in such striking terms, substantially similar devices have been even more in vogue since the Report than before it. One need look no further than the Statutory Instruments Act 1946 itself to find an example: the King in Council may direct that certain provisions about laying statutory instruments before Parliament shall not apply to instruments made under pre-existing Acts if those provisions are deemed inexpedient. Under the Factories Act 1961 there is wide power to modify or extend the provisions of the Act dealing with health or safety. Under the Sex Discrimination Act 1975 there is again wide power to vary the Act by order. Under the Land Commission (Dissolution) Act 1971 the Secretary of State was empowered to amend or repeal any other Acts, as might appear to him to be appropriate. Many more examples could be given.[21] Among these none would be more remarkable than the provision of the European Communities Act 1972, which gives power to make Orders in Council and regulations for giving effect to Community law which are to prevail over all Acts of Parliament, whether past or future, subject to safeguards against increased taxation, retrospective operation and excessive penalties.[22]

It is common for statutes to come into operation on a date to be fixed by ministerial order. Cases have occurred where the commencement order deliberately omitted some provision of the Act, thereby in effect repealing it administratively.[23]

Emergency powers

The common law contains a doctrine of last resort under which, if war or insurrection should prevent the ordinary courts from operating, the actions of the military authority in restoring order are legally unchallengeable. When the courts are thus reduced to silence, martial law (truly said to be 'no law at all') prevails. This principle has had to be called into play in

[20] Cmd. 4060 (1932), p. 61.
[21] For a case of modification of an Act by regulations see *Britt* v. *Buckinghamshire C.C.* [1964] 1 QB 77.
[22] s. 2(2), (4), and 2nd sched.
[23] See *R.* v. *Home Secretary ex p. Anosike* [1971] 1 WLR 1136 (right of appeal under Immigration Appeals Act 1969 not brought into force).

Ireland as late as 1921, but it lies outside our subject.[24] All other emergency powers derive from Parliament by delegation. The executive has no inherent *pouvoir réglementaire*, as it has in France.

The one standing provision for peacetime emergencies is the Emergency Powers Act 1920,[25] which is designed to protect the public from the effects of serious strikes. It was invoked in 1921, 1924, 1926 (the general strike), 1948 and 1949 (dock strikes), 1955 (rail strike), 1966 (seamen's strike), 1970 (dock strike), 1972 and 1973 (coal strikes). The Crown may by proclamation declare an emergency on account of any threat to the supply and distribution of food, water, fuel, or light, or to the means of locomotion, if it appears that the community, or any substantial part of it, will be deprived of 'the essentials of life'. While the proclamation is in force the Crown may by Order in Council make regulations 'for securing the essentials of life to the community', and may confer on ministers or others any powers and duties deemed necessary for a wide variety of purposes connected with public safety and the life of the community. But there are some limits. No form of compulsory military service or industrial conscription may be imposed. Nor can it be made an offence to take part in a strike. Nor, thirdly, can there be any alteration of criminal procedure, or any right to inflict fine or imprisonment without trial. Trial by courts of summary jurisdiction may be authorised, subject to maximum penalties of three months' imprisonment and a fine of £100. A proclamation of emergency must at once be communicated to Parliament, which must be summoned if necessary; the regulations must be laid before Parliament as soon as possible, and will expire in seven days from the time when they are so laid, unless both Houses approve them by resolution. The proclamation itself expires in a month, but without prejudice to a further proclamation.

The powers granted in wartime are naturally much wider, and are too extensive to describe in detail. In 1914 the Defence of the Realm Act, in a single short section, gave power to the King in Council to make regulations 'for securing the public safety and the defence of the realm', including trial by court martial in wide classes of cases. The courts found the formula to be subject to a number of implied restrictions, for instance as regards taxation, expropriation and access to the courts.[26] By the end of the war many things of questionable legality had been done, and it was thought necessary to pass the Indemnity Act 1920 and the War Charges Validity Act 1925. Profiting by this lesson, Parliament granted more elaborate and specific powers in the Emergency Powers (Defence) Act 1939. The King in Council was

---

[24] See Wade (ECS) and Phillips, *Constitutional Law*, 10th edn., 551.

[25] As amended by the Emergency Powers Act 1964. See [1979] PL 317 (G. S. Morris) where a full list of the emergencies is given.

[26] Below, p. 866.

empowered to make defence regulations, being such regulations 'as appear to him to be necessary or expedient for securing the public safety, the defence of the realm, the maintenance of public order and the efficient prosecution of any war in which His Majesty may be engaged, and for maintaining supplies and services essential to the life of the community'. A series of specific powers was then added, providing for such things as detention of persons and requisitioning of property, for amending, modifying or suspending any statute, and for delegating any of the powers to other authorities. The Treasury was given power to make orders imposing charges in connection with any scheme of control under the regulations, subject to affirmative resolution by the House of Commons within twenty-eight days. In 1940 a further Act provided that defence regulations might require persons 'to place themselves, their services, and their property at the disposal of His Majesty' if it appeared to him to be necessary or expedient for public safety, the defence of the realm, etc. Under these virtually unlimited powers the government undertook the close control of industrial employment as well as of very many other matters. So extensive were the powers that no Indemnity Act was found necessary. Powers which for some purposes were even wider were continued in the post-war decade by a succession of Acts of Parliament which adapted the wartime governmental machine to peacetime control of economic activity, and under which rationing schemes continued to be administered.[27] Although the number of operative controls was much reduced from 1951 onwards, it took a long time to dispose of the framework of 'emergency' laws.[28]

LEGAL FORMS AND CHARACTERISTICS

Regulations, rules, orders, etc.

Parliament follows no particular policy in choosing the forms of delegated legislation, and there is a wide range of varieties and nomenclature. An Act may empower an authority to make regulations, rules, or byelaws, to make orders, or to give directions. Acts often empower the Crown to make Orders in Council, as for example under the Emergency Powers Act 1920, and particularly where the subject-matter falls within the province of no designated minister.[29] Such orders must be distinguished from Orders in Council made in the exercise of the royal prerogative:[30] the former are

---

[27] Above, p. 850.
[28] A few powers lingered on under the Emergency Laws (Re-enactments and Repeals) Act 1964.
[29] Above, p. 52.
[30] Above, p. 240.

valid only in so far as they conform to the power conferred by Parliament; the latter are valid only in so far as they fall within the Crown's remaining prerogative powers at common law.

The Committee on Ministers' Powers recommended that the expressions 'regulation', 'rule', and 'order' should not be used indiscriminately, but that 'rule' should be confined to provisions about procedure and that 'order' should be used only for executive acts and legal decisions.[31] But the nomenclature in practice honours these distinctions nearly as much in the breach as in the observance. Thus under the Fishing Vessels (Safety Provisions) Act 1970 the detailed precautions are prescribed by 'rules'.[32] Import duties, contrariwise, though their character is purely that of general legislation, are prescribed by 'orders'.[33] Untidy though the language is, it makes no legal difference. 'Byelaws', for example, are subject to no special rules merely because they are given this title.

'Directions' are also used for general legislation. Under the Town and Country Planning Act 1971 the Secretary of State for the Environment may make development orders of a specific or general character;[34] the general development order provides that he may give directions to local planning authorities;[35] and under this he has issued a formal direction as to the procedure for dealing with planning applications which are inconsistent with the development plan.[36] The Act itself says nothing about 'directions' but the wide powers which it confers have been used to create this species of legislation. But many Acts expressly authorise ministers to give directions. Directions play a large part in the administration of the National Health Service,[37] and in ministerial control over nationalised industries.[38] Other Acts empower a minister to give 'guidance', the observance of which may or may not be mandatory, according as the Act provides. It was mandatory under the Civil Aviation Act 1971,[39] where the Secretary of State for Trade gave written 'guidance' to the Civil Aviation authority, subject to express approval by each House of Parliament. The

---

[31] Cmd. 4060 (1932), p. 64.

[32] Fishing Vessels (Safety Provisions) Rules 1975, SI No. 330.

[33] Import Duties (General) (No. 5) Order 1975, SI No. 1744. 'Order' is a word of wide meaning: R. v. Clarke [1969] 2 QB 91; R. v. Oxford Recorder ex p. Brasenose College [1970] 1 QB 109.

[34] s. 24.

[35] SI 1973 No. 31, art. 10.

[36] Town and Country Planning (Development Plans) Direction 1975, contained in Circular 96/75 of the Department of the Environment.

[37] National Health Service Act 1977, ss. 13, 17. Some directions are required to be made by regulations: s. 18.

[38] Above, p. 159.

[39] s. 3(2) (repealed by Civil Aviation Act 1980, s. 12). See Laker Airways Ltd. v. Department of Trade [1977] QB 643, holding guidance ultra vires.

National Enterprise Board operates under a variety of directions, guidelines and requirements imposed by the Secretary of State under the Industry Act 1975.[40] This is now a common technique of government.

There is scarcely a limit to the varieties of legislative provisions which may exist under different names. The statutory 'code of practice' is now in constant use, and since this has, or may have, legal effects in certain circumstances it ranks as legislation of a kind.[41] Under the Employment Protection Act 1975 the Advisory Conciliation and Arbitration Service issues a code of practice, giving guidance for the purpose of promoting good industrial relations.[42] Its legal effect is that it is admissible in evidence before the industrial tribunals which adjudicate employment cases, and is to be taken into account on any question to which the tribunal thinks it relevant.[43] The ministerial code of guidance to which local authorities must 'have regard' in administering the Housing (Homeless Persons) Act 1977 (now the Housing Act 1985) is statutory but not absolutely binding since 'have regard' does not mean 'comply'.[44] By contrast, the code of practice which the Secretary of State has published explaining the arrangements for the 'examination in public' of structure plans is not statutory in any way: it is merely a statement of administrative policy.[45] In fact the Town and Country Planning Act 1971 empowers the Secretary of State to make regulations for the procedure at these examinations,[46] but instead of doing so he has published the code of practice, with the object of promoting informality and flexibility.

Codes of practice, guidance, and so forth have proliferated in a disorderly way reminiscent of delegated legislation at the time of the Committee on Ministers' Powers. There is now a jungle of quasi-legislation of this kind, some codes having legal effect and others not and some, though only a minority, being subject to parliamentary approval.[47]

---

[40] See *Booth & Co. Ltd.* v. *NEB* [1978] 3 All ER 624.

[41] See Ganz, *Quasi-legislation,* discussing many examples from the Highway Code of 1930 onwards. The great majority of these codes are recent. See also [1986] PL 239 (R. Baldwin and J. Houghton) for a detailed survey and comment.

[42] The Secretary of State may do the same (with overriding effect) under Employment Act 1980, s. 3.

[43] s. 6, replacing Trade Union and Labour Relations Act 1974, 1st sched.

[44] *De Falco* v. *Crawley BC* [1980] 460. See similarly *R.* v. *Police Complaints Board ex p. Madden* [1983] 1 WLR 447.

[45] Department of Environment booklet: Structure Plans—The Examination in Public. So likewise was the 'memorandum of guidance' issued to health authorities and yet judicially reviewed in *Gillick* v. *West Norfolk and Wisbech Area Health Authority* [1986] AC 112.

[46] s. 9, as amended by Town and Country Planning (Amendment) Act 1972, s. 3.

[47] Some require affirmative resolution, e.g. under Employment Protection Act 1975, s. 6(5).

In a debate upon them[48] the House of Lords deplored the general confusion, the lack of parliamentary control, the lack of rules for publication and numbering, and other deficiencies; and a code of practice on codes of practice was suggested.[49] Informal codes offer a way of escape from the rules governing statutory instruments and this is being freely exploited.

Administrative rules

Mere administrative rules, for example as to the allocation of business within the civil service, or for extra-statutory concessions to taxpayers,[50] are not legislation of any kind. The same applies to statements of policy and of practice and to many other pronouncements of government departments, whether published or otherwise. But the clear line which ought to divide legislative from administrative rules is blurred by ambiguous categories. Statutory rules which are undoubtedly legislation may be held to be merely regulatory and not legally enforceable. This is the case with the prison rules, made under the Prison Act 1952, which have sometimes been held to be regulatory directions only and not enforceable at the suit of prisoners, but at other times are held to be mandatory in law and fully enforceable.[51] On the other hand non-statutory rules may be treated as if they were statutory. As explained elsewhere, the High Court has assumed jurisdiction to quash decisions of the Criminal Injuries Compensation Board, the Civil Service Appeal Board and the Panel on Take-overs and Mergers[52] if they do not accord with their published rules, even though the rules rest upon no statutory authority. The last of these cases is especially striking, since the rules of the Panel are not made by a minister or other agency of government, and thus have no constitutional or democratic basis. Yet rules which the court will enforce must be admitted to be genuine legislation, anomalous though this is in the absence of any statutory warrant.

Another dubious case is that of the immigration rules, which are made by the Home Secretary under the Immigration Act 1971, subject to parliamentary disapproval, and which explain how his wide discretionary powers over visitors from overseas and immigrants are to be exercised.[53] Thses rules have repeatedly been held to be rules of administrative practice merely, not rules of law and not delegated legislation,[54] and the House of

---

[48] 469 HL Deb 1075 (15 January 1986).

[49] Col. 1086 (Lord Renton).

[50] For these see above, p. 437.

[51] See above, p. 247.

[52] For these cases see above, p. 640.

[53] See above, p. 225. The rules are published as House of Commons papers, not as statutory instruments. The current rules are HC 169 (1982–3).

[54] *R. v. Home Secretary ex p. Hosenball* [1977] 1 WLR 766 and cases cited below.

Lords has held that they have 'no statutory force'.[55] Breach of them by an immigrant does not therefore make him an illegal immigrant under the Act,[56] though breach of them by an immigration officer may show that he had no authority to grant admission, thus making the immigrant illegal.[57] The rules undoubtedly have statutory force to some extent, in that an immigrant's appeal must be allowed if the adjudicator considers that the immigration officer's decision was not in accordance with them.[58] Furthermore, the courts have several times quashed immigration decisions for misconstruction or misapplication of the rules, for example where admission was wrongly refused to a boy coming to this country for education,[59] or where a rule was invalid for unreasonableness.[60] The courts did not explain whether they were treating the rules as having statutory force, or whether they were enforcing non-statutory rules as in the case of the Criminal Injuries Compensation Board. It is not surprising that the rules have been called 'very difficult to categorise or classify', being 'a curious amalgam of information and description of executive procedures'.[61] Lord Bridge has said that they are 'quite unlike ordinary delegated legislation', that they 'do not purport to enact a precise code having statutory force', and that they are 'discursive in style and, on their face, frequently offer no more than broad guidance as to how discretion is to be exercised'.[62] Roskill LJ, on the other hand, has said that they are 'just as much a part of the law of England as the Act itself'.[63]

In the United States the assimilation of different categories has been carried further,[64] and the courts have enforced administrative rules and practices merely because they have been followed in fact rather than because they have statutory backing.[65] The dismissal of a civil servant has

---

[55] R. v. Home Secretary ex p. Zamir [1980] AC 930; R. v. Entry Clearance Officer, Bombay ex p. Amin [1983] 2 AC 818.

[56] R. v. Home Secretary ex p. Mangoo Khan [1980] 1 WLR 569.

[57] R. v. Home Secretary ex p. Choudhary [1978] 1 WLR 1177.

[58] Immigration Act 1971, s. 19.

[59] R. v. Gatwick Airport Immigration Officer ex p. Kharrazi [1980] 1 WLR 1396, holding that the immigration officer had erred in 'law' and so acted ultra vires under the doctrine of the Racal case (above, p. 300). See similarly R. v. Immigration Appeal Tribunal ex p. Shaikh [1981] 1 WLR 1107, quashing the tribunal's decision for misapplication of the rules; R. v. Immigration Appeal Tribunal ex p. Swaran Singh [1987] 1 WLR 1394 (similar).

[60] R. v. Immigration Appeal Tribunal ex p. Begum Manshoora [1986] The Times, 24 July.

[61] Lane and Cumming-Bruce LJJ respectively in the Hosenball case, above.

[62] R. v. Immigration Appeal Tribunal ex p. Bakhtaur Singh [1986] 1 WLR 910.

[63] R. v. Chief Immigration Officer, Heathrow Airport, ex p. Bibi [1976] 1 WLR 979.

[64] The definition of 'rule' in the federal Administrative Procedure Act of 1946 includes statements of policy, organisation, procedure, or practice made by government agencies.

[65] Schwartz and Wade, Legal Control of Government, 92. But this practice may discourage public authorities from publicising their procedures.

thus been set aside because the department's internal rules were not observed;[66] and a regulatory commission has been held bound to follow its own 'usual practice' when this was known to and relied upon by the public.[67] 'He that takes the procedural sword shall perish with that sword', said Mr Justice Frankfurter.[68] English judges have confined themselves to cases where formal rules have been promulgated, as in the case of the Criminal Injuries Compensation Board and other cases mentioned below,[69] and to cases where an established practice creates a legitimate expectation of a fair hearing.[70] So they also have made a breach in the legal barrier, and this may be exploited further.

Circulars

Departmental circulars are a common form of administrative document by which instructions are disseminated, e.g. from a department in Whitehall to its local offices or to local authorities over which it exercises control. Many such circulars are identified by serial numbers and published, and many of them contain general statements of policy, for instance as to the Secretary of State's practices in dealing with planning appeals. They are therefore of great importance to the public, giving much guidance about governmental organisation and the exercise of discretionary powers. In themselves they have no legal effect whatever, having no statutory authority.[71] But they may be used as a vehicle for conveying instructions to which some statute gives legal force, such as directions to local planning authorities under the Town and Country Planning Act 1971.[72] They may also contain legal advice of which the courts will take notice.[73]

   Much confusion has been caused by the failure to distinguish between the legal and the non-legal elements in circulars. A leading example is *Blackpool Corporation* v. *Locker*.[74] Under wartime regulations, continued in force, the Minister of Health was empowered to take possession of land for any purpose and to delegate that power, subject to such restrictions as he

   [66] *Vitarelli* v. *Seaton*, 359 US 535 (1959).
   [67] *Sangamon Valley Television Corporation* v. *United States,* 269 F. 2d 221 (1959).
   [68] In *Vitarelli* v. *Seaton* (above) at 547.
   [69] Below, p. 863.
   [70] Above, p. 520.
   [71] See e.g. *Colman (JJ) Ltd.* v. *Commissioners of Customs and Excise* [1968] 1 WLR 1286 at 1291 (Commissioners' 'notices' cannot alter law).
   [72] Above, p. 856.
   [73] As in the *Gillick* case, below.
   [74] [1948] 1 KB 349. See similarly *Patchett* v. *Leathem* (1949) 65 TLR 69; *Acton Borough Council* v. *Morris* [1953] 1 WLR 1228. Scott LJ's legal analysis was criticised in *Lewisham BC* v. *Roberts* [1949] 2 KB 608.

thought proper. He delegated the power to local authorities by a series of circulars sent out from his department, which contained numerous instructions. Two of these instructions were that there should be no requisitioning of furniture, or of any house which the owner himself wished to occupy. Both these were disregarded in an attempted requisition of the plaintiff's house. The question then was, were the instructions in the circulars legal conditions restricting the delegated power, or were they merely administrative directions as to how that power, delegated in all its plenitude, should in practice be exercised? On this vital point the circulars were entirely ambiguous. The Court of Appeal held that the instructions were legal restrictions limiting the delegated power and that the requisition was therefore invalid. But the local authority and the ministry had acted on the opposite view: they had refused to disclose the terms of the circulars, and had even at first resisted disclosing them to the court on grounds of privilege.[75] Thus they had 'radically misunderstood their own legal rights and duties', and had refused to let the plaintiff see the very legislation by which his rights were determined. A judgment notable for its forceful language, as well as for its awareness of the wide constitutional implications, was delivered by Scott LJ who had formerly been chairman of the Committee on Ministers' Powers and was inclined to deplore the failure to implement its report. He described some of the events as 'an example of the very worst kind of bureaucracy'. But the root of the trouble may well have been the difficulty of telling where legislation began and ended.

In a case of the same kind, where the requisition was held invalid for non-observance of the condition in the circular requiring notice to be given to the owner, Streatfeild J said:[76]

Whereas ordinary legislation, by passing through both Houses of Parliament or, at least, lying on the table of both Houses, is thus twice blessed, this type of so-called legislation is at least four times cursed. First, it has seen neither House of Parliament; secondly, it is unpublished and is inaccessible even to those whose valuable rights of property may be affected; thirdly, it is a jumble of provisions, legislative, administrative, or directive in character, and sometimes difficult to disentangle one from the other; and, fourthly, it is expressed not in the precise language of an Act of Parliament or an Order in Council but in the more colloquial language of correspondence, which is not always susceptible of the ordinary canons of construction.

Contradictory opinions as to the legal status of a circular were expressed in the House of Lords in a case where a departmental 'memorandum of guidance', issued to local health authorities, was alleged to contain

[75] For privilege see above, p. 833.
[76] *Patchett* v. *Leathem* (above) at 70.

erroneous legal advice as to the counselling of young girls about contraception.[77] Lords Fraser and Scarman held that the error would be ultra vires, thus treating the circular as having legal effect. Lords Bridge and Templeman held that it could have no legal effect but was subject to judicial review, as explained earlier.[78] Lord Brandon expressed no opinion. The source of this confusion was the National Health Service Act 1977, which gave the Secretary of State a duty 'to meet all reasonable requirements' for providing contraceptive advice, so that the question whether the circular was issued under specific statutory authority was arguable either way.

It is now the practice to publish circulars which are of any importance to the public and for a long time there has been no judicial criticism of the use made of them.

Amendment, revocation, dispensation

In addition to providing that statutory powers and duties may be exercised and performed from time to time as occasion requires,[79] the Interpretation Act 1978 also lays down that a statutory power to make 'rules, regulations or byelaws' or statutory instruments shall be construed as including a power to revoke, amend, or re-enact them, subject to the same conditions as applied to the making of them.[80] This is to be done, of course, only in so far as no contrary intention appears in the empowering Act.

When an Act is repealed, any rules or regulations made under it cease to have effect,[81] despite the statutory saving clause for things done while the Act was in force.[82] But where an Act is repealed and replaced, with or without modification, rules, etc. made under it are treated as if made under the new Act in so far as that Act gives power to make them.[83] Rules also continue in force notwithstanding any change in the person or body constituting the rule-making authority.[84]

So long as its rules stand, a public authority has no power to grant dispensation from them, either generally or in particular cases.[85] Whether

---

[77] Gillick v. West Norfolk and Wisbech Area Health Authority [1986] AC 112. For comment see (1986) 102 LQR 173.

[78] Above, p. 682.

[79] s. 12; above, p. 254.

[80] s. 14. But note the need for consistency: above, p. 423.

[81] Watson v. Winch [1916] 1 KB 688.

[82] Interpretation Act 1978, s. 16.

[83] s. 17.

[84] Wiseman v. Canterbury Bye-Products Co. Ltd. [1983] 2 AC 685.

[85] Yabbicom v. King [1899] 1 QB 444; Bean (William) & Sons v. Flaxton Rural District Council [1929] 1 KB 450; above, p. 268.

there may be an exception to this rule in the case of formal or procedural irregularities is controversial. This has already been discussed in the context of waiver.[86]

JUDICIAL REVIEW

Control by the courts

In Britain the executive has no inherent legislative power.[87] It cannot, as can the French government, resort to a constitutional *pouvoir réglementaire* when it is necessary to make regulations for purposes of public order or in emergencies. Statutory authority is indispensable, and it follows that rules and regulations not duly made under Act of Parliament are legally ineffective. Exceptions have been made, it is true, in the cases of the Criminal Injuries Compensation Board, the Civil Service Appeal Board and the Panel on Take-overs and Mergers.[88] But they do not alter the fact that the courts must determine the validity of delegated legislation by applying the test of ultra vires, just as they do in other contexts. It is axiomatic that delegated legislation no way partakes of the immunity which Acts of Parliament enjoy from challenge in the courts, for there is a fundamental difference between a sovereign and a subordinate law-making power. Acts of Parliament have sovereign force, but legislation made under delegated power can be valid only if it conforms exactly to the power granted. Even where, as is often the case, a regulation is required to be approved by resolutions of both Houses of Parliament, it still falls on the 'subordinate' side of the line, so that the court may determine its validity.[89] Only an Act of Queen, Lords and Commons is immune from judicial review.[90]

The court has to look for the true intent of the empowering Act in the usual way. A local authority's power to make byelaws, for example, will

---

[86] Above, p. 265.

[87] Except where the law breaks down and martial law is in force (above, p. 853). The Crown's prerogative power to legislate for colonies acquired by cession or conquest is also an exception, but it has been superseded by the British Settlement Acts 1887–1945 and the Foreign Jurisdiction Acts 1890–1913.

[88] For the judicial enforcement of the non-statutory rules of these bodies see above, p. 640.

[89] See above, pp. 29, 411; below, p. 870.

[90] For judicial control over legislation by non-sovereign legislatures in countries of the Commonwealth see *A.-G. for New South Wales* v. *Trethowan* [1932] AC 526; *Clayton* v. *Heffron* (1960) 105 CLR 214; *Rediffusion (Hong Kong) Ltd.* v. *A.-G. of Hong Kong* [1970] AC 1136; *Cormack* v. *Cope* (1974) 131 CLR 433. There are many more such authorities in the sphere of constitutional law.

not extend to allow it to modify Acts of Parliament. A county council's byelaw was accordingly void when it forbade betting in public places altogether whereas the applicable Act of Parliament allowed it under certain conditions.[91] A straightforward example of the ultra vires principle was where the House of Lords invalidated an order of the Minister of Labour which would have imposed industrial training levy on clubs which were not within the Industrial Training Act 1964.[92] Another was where the Secretary of State for Trade prescribed unauthorised requirements for Jewish shops wishing to be closed on Saturdays and open on Sundays.[93] Another was where the Secretary of State for Social Services made regulations to enable him to reduce and regulate payment of supplementary benefit in cases which by statute were for adjudication officers to determine.[94] And another was where the Inland Revenue made regulations taxing dividends and interest paid by building societies on which tax had already been paid.[95]

The strict conformity which the courts require is illustrated by an Australian case where the Privy Council held a regulation to be ultra vires and void.[96] A statute allowed regulations to be made relating to excavation work, both as to 'the manner of carrying out' such work and as to 'safeguards and measures' to protect workers engaged in it. A regulation requiring tunnels to be 'securely protected and made safe for persons employed therein' was held to be outside the authority of the statute, since it attempted to impose an absolute duty to make tunnels safe, whereas the statute gave power only to prescribe particular methods of work and specific precautions. A worker injured in tunnelling in the Snowy Mountains scheme was thus unable to rely on this regulation in suing for damages.

The judicial attitude is also illustrated by a decision of the House of Lords on the validity of emergency regulations in Northern Ireland.[97] Under an Act of 1922 the government of Northern Ireland had very wide powers to make regulations 'for preserving the peace and maintaining order', subject to a proviso that the ordinary avocations of life were to be interfered with as little as possible. The disputed regulation made it a criminal offence to be

---

[91] *Powell* v. *May* [1946] 1 KB 330.

[92] *Hotel & Catering Industry Training Board* v. *Automobile Pty. Ltd.* [1969] 1 WLR 697.

[93] R. v. *London Committee of Deputies of British Jews ex p. Helmcourt Ltd.* [1981] The Times, 2 May.

[94] R. v. *Secretary of State for Social Services ex p. Cotton* [1985] The Times, 14 December.

[95] R. v. *Inland Revenue Commissioner ex p. Woolwich Equitable Building Society* [1987] The Times, 3 September (the society recovered £57m.).

[96] *Utah Construction and Engineering Pty. Ltd.* v. *Pataky* [1966] AC 629. Another example is *Reade* v. *Smith* [1959] NZLR 996 (above, p. 455).

[97] *McEldowney* v. *Forde* [1971] AC 632.

a member of an organisation describing itself as a 'republican club' or of 'any like organization howsoever described'. The appellant was convicted of membership of such a club, but there was no evidence that there was any threat to public order. The House of Lords upheld the conviction; but two of its members agreed with the Chief Justice of Northern Ireland that the regulation was too wide to fall within the powers of the Act and too vague in its meaning to be enforceable.[98] Only by the narrowest margin did the regulation escape being condemned as ultra vires and void for uncertainty.[99]

An example of voidness for uncertainty was a local authority's byelaw which ordained that 'no person shall wilfully annoy passengers in the streets'.[1] This was one of a group of byelaws, the rest of which prohibited various specified annoyances, and left it uncertain what the general prohibition was intended to cover. Another example was a byelaw forbidding the flying of gliders in a pleasure ground, which was excessively uncertain in its application to hang gliders.[2]

Despite their strict standards, the courts will lean in favour of upholding a regulation which forms part of a statutory scheme and which has long been relied upon in property transactions.[3]

Constitutional principles

It is axiomatic that primary constitutional statutes such as the Bill of Rights 1688 and the Act of Settlement 1700 are just as subject to repeal or amendment as any others, since constitutional guarantees are inconsistent with the unlimited sovereignty of Parliament. Safeguards like those provided in the constitution of the United States, or in 'entrenched provisions' in some Commonwealth countries, are unknown in this country. Faced with an Act of Parliament, the court can do no more than make certain presumptions, for example that property will not be taken without compensation[4] and that the European Convention on Human Rights will be respected.[5]

---

[98] As was part of a regulation in *Transport Ministry* v. *Alexander* [1978] 1 NZLR 306.

[99] Furthermore, one of the majority misdirected himself (at 643) by saying that he could find no example of challenge to a statutory instrument since 1917, and that any challenger therefore had a heavy task. The House had itself held a statutory instrument to be void in the previous month (in the *Hotel & Catering Industry* case, above) and any book on administrative law would have furnished other examples.

[1] *Nash* v. *Finlay* (1901) 85 LT 682.

[2] *Staden* v. *Tarjanyi* (1980) 78 LGR 614.

[3] As in *Ministry of Housing and Local Government* v. *Sharp* [1970] 2 QB 223.

[4] Above, p. 796.

[5] Above, p. 498.

But in the case of delegated power the judges have sometimes treated fundamental rights as exempt from infringement unless Parliament has expressed itself with unmistakable clarity. An example occurred in 1921 under the Defence of the Realm Regulations, which gave the Food Controller power to make regulations for controlling the sale, purchase, consumption, transport, etc., of food, and to control prices. The Controller gave a dairy company a licence to deal in milk, but on condition that they paid a charge of twopence per gallon, as part of a scheme for regulating prices and controlling distribution. The company expressly agreed to accept this condition, but later refused to pay the charge. It was held by the House of Lords that the condition infringed the famous provision of the Bill of Rights 1688, that no money may be levied to the use of the Crown without consent of Parliament; and that even the company's own written consent could not legalise what the statute made illegal.[6] The argument that the general power to impose controls impliedly included the power to tax was rejected. Atkin LJ said:

The circumstances would be remarkable indeed which would induce the courts to believe that the Legislature had sacrificed all the well-known checks and precautions, and, not in express words, but merely by implication, had entrusted a Minister of the Crown with undefined and unlimited powers of imposing charges upon the subject for purposes connected with his department.

In the second world war the statute itself silenced all such arguments by supplementing its general provision with a battery of specific powers.[7] But in a case from the earlier war a regulation was held invalid because it purported to authorise requisitioning of property without fair compensation at market value, and without any right to dispute the value in a court of law.[8]

The right of access to the courts is a matter that the courts themselves guard strictly,[9] and that has led to the overthrow of both wartime and peacetime regulations. In 1920 a Defence of the Realm Regulation was held ultra vires because, in order to prevent disturbance of munition workers, it provided that no one might sue for possession of a munition worker's house without the permission of the Minister.[10] So extreme a disability, it was held, could only be imposed by express enactment; and it could not really be said to be relevant to the public safety or the defence of

---

[6] *A.-G.* v. *Wilts United Dairies Ltd.* (1921) 39 TLR 781, (1922) 127 LT 822. But contrast *Institute of Patent Agents* v. *Lockwood* [1894] AC 347.

[7] Above, p. 854.

[8] *Newcastle Breweries* v. *The King* [1920] 1 KB 854.

[9] As by resisting attempts to oust their jurisdiction: above, p. 725.

[10] *Chester* v. *Bateson* [1920] 1 KB 829; and see *Raymond* v. *Honey* [1982] 2 WLR 465.

the realm. In 1937 a byelaw made by the Wheat Commission, which had power to make byelaws for the settlement by arbitration of disputes under the Wheat Act 1932, was invalidated in the House of Lords because it purported to exclude the Arbitration Act 1889 from applying to any such arbitration, and thus it purported to exclude the right to carry a point of law to the High Court.[11] In 1961 a purchase tax regulation was held invalid because it purported to give the Commissioners of Customs and Excise power to determine conclusively what tax was due from a taxpayer, thereby attempting to oust the jurisdiction of the court to determine the matter on appeal.[12]

But in wartime constitutional presumptions have not availed to protect the most fundamental right of all, personal liberty. In the first world war the House of Lords held that the power to make regulations 'for securing the public safety and the defence of the realm' justified a regulation for the compulsory internment of persons of hostile origin or associations.[13] In the second world war regulations for detention were expressly authorised by the primary legislation. As explained earlier,[14] a profound difference of judicial opinion was provoked by the defence regulation actually made, which took power to detain 'if the Secretary of State has reasonable cause to believe any person to be of hostile origin or associations', leaving it obscure whether the Home Secretary had to show reasonable grounds for his belief.

Whether delegated legislation can have retrospective operation without express parliamentary sanction is a question upon which there is scant authority.[15] It is natural to presume that Parliament is unlikely to confer a power which it uses only most sparingly itself. The creation of retrospective criminal offences is contrary to the European Convention on Human Rights, and there is a strong presumption that legislation will not authorise a breach of the Convention.[16] The Convention specifically forbids what English courts several times upheld during the war, the imposition by regulation of a heavier penalty than existed at the time when the offence was committed.[17] The Select Committee on Statutory Instruments has from time to time drawn the attention of the House of

---

[11] R. v. W. Paul Ltd. v. The Wheat Commission [1937] AC 139.

[12] Commissioners of Customs and Excise v. Cure and Deeley Ltd. [1962] 1 QB 340. See below, p. 869.

[13] R. v. Halliday [1917] AC 260.

[14] Above, p. 457.

[15] Malloch v. Aberdeen Cpn. (No. 2) 1974 SLT 5 is perhaps an instance (regulations invalid retrospectively); below, p. 891.

[16] See R. v. Miah [1974] 1 WLR 683 at 694 (Lord Reid), where the prosecution appears to have been in breach of the Convention and counsel for the Crown stated that there was no argument which he could properly submit to the House of Lords (see at 694).

[17] Art. 7. See e.g. R. v. Oliver [1944] KB 68; Allen, Law and Orders, 3rd edn., 205.

Commons to orders purporting to have retrospective operation,[18] but they have not been tested in the courts.

Unreasonableness

Just as with other kinds of administrative action, the courts must sometimes condemn rules or regulations for unreasonableness.[19] In interpreting statutes it is natural to make the assumption that Parliament could not have intended powers of delegated legislation to be exercised unreasonably, so that the legality of the regulations becomes dependent upon their content.

This assumption has often been called into play in the case of local authorities' byelaws, which they are empowered to make for the good rule and government of their area and for the suppression of nuisances.[20] In the leading case, where in fact the court upheld a byelaw against singing within fifty yeards of a dwelling-house, it was said:[21]

If, for instance [byelaws] were found to be partial and unequal in their operation as between different classes; if they were manifestly unjust; if they disclosed bad faith; if they involved such oppressive or gratuitous interference with the rights of those subject to them as could find no justification in the minds of reasonable men, the Court might well say, 'Parliament never intended to give authority to make such rules; they are unreasonable and ultra vires.' But . . . a byelaw is not unreasonable merely because particular judges may think that it goes further than is prudent or necessary or convenient . . .

But a byelaw which forbade playing music, singing, or preaching in any street, except under express licence from the mayor, was held void as being plainly arbitrary and unreasonable.[22] The same fate befell a byelaw which prohibited selling cockles on the beach at Bournemouth without the agreement of the Corporation[23] and a byelaw which restricted sales by action in a public market.[24] The Supreme Court of Canada upholds 'the rule of administrative law that the power to make byelaws does not include

---

[18] See Allen (as above). Another example is the Trustee Savings Bank (Increase of Pensions) Order 1959, reported in HC (1959–60) 18—II.

[19] Above, p. 388. See (1973) 36 MLR 611 (A. Wharam).

[20] Local Government Act 1972, s. 235. The doctrine was developed originally for the byelaws or regulations made by chartered corporations and other institutions under common law powers: *Slattery* v. *Naylor* (1888) 13 App. Cas 446 at 452.

[21] *Kruse* v. *Johnson* [1898] 2 QB 91 (Lord Russell CJ).

[22] *Munro* v. *Watson* (1887) 57 LT 366.

[23] *Parker* v. *Bournemouth Cpn.* (1902) 66 JP 440; and see *Moorman* v. *Tordoff* (1908) 98 LT 416.

[24] *Nicholls* v. *Tavistock UDC* [1923] 2 Ch 18.

a power to enact discriminatory provisions.'[25] This is 'a principle of fundamental freedom'.

Byelaws have often failed to pass the test of reasonableness, which in some respects is strict in relation to the wide words of the statutory power. Clear examples of unreasonable byelaws were where landlords of lodging-houses were required to clean them annually under penalty, yet would in many cases have no right of access against their lodgers;[26] and where a building byelaw required an open space to be left at the rear of every new building, so that in many cases it became impossible to build new extensions to existing buildings.[27] But the court normally construes byelaws benevolently and upholds them if possible.[28]

The same doctrine applies to rules and regulations as well as to byelaws. It is true that where the power is granted to a minister responsible to Parliament, the court is less willing to suppose that Parliament intended his discretion to be limited; and this attitude is further reinforced if the regulations themselves must be laid before Parliament. On these grounds the Ministry of Transport's regulations for pedestrian crossings were upheld in 1943, despite the argument that to give the right of way to pedestrians was unreasonable during the nightly wartime blackout.[29] But in a later case a purchase tax regulation made by the Commissioners of Customs and Excise, and duly laid before Parliament, was held invalid.[30] The Commissioners had power to make regulations 'for any matter for which provision appears to them to be necessary' for the purpose of collecting purchase tax. Their regulation provided that where a proper return was not made they might themselves determine the tax due and that the amount so determined should be deemed to be the proper tax payable. This was held ultra vires as an attempt to take arbitrary power to determine a tax liability which was properly to be determined according to the Act with a right of appeal to the court, and as an attempt to oust the court's

[25] *Re City of Montreal and Arcade Amusements Inc.* (1985) 18 DLR (4th) 161, holding invalid a byelaw prohibiting minors from entering amusement halls or using amusement machines. Challenge to the validity of byelaws is particularly common in Canada.

[26] *Arlidge v. Mayor &c. of Islington* [1909] 2 KB 127.

[27] *Repton School Governors v. Repton RDC* [1918] 2 KB 133. See also *A.-G. v. Denby* [1925] 1 Ch 596 (building byelaw uncertain and unreasonable); *London Passenger Transport Board v. Sumner* (1935) 154 LT 108 (byelaw penalising non-payment of fare unreasonable); *Cassidy v. Minister for Industry and Commerce* [1978] IR 297 (unreasonable price control order).

[28] *Kruse v. Johnson* (above); *Townsend (Builders) Ltd. v. Cinema News and Property Management Ltd.* [1959] 1 WLR 119; *Cinnamond v. British Airports Authority* [1980] 1 WLR 582.

[29] *Sparks v. Edward Ash Ltd.* [1943] KB 223.

[30] *Commissioners of Customs and Excise v. Cure and Deeley Ltd.* [1962] 1 QB 340 (Sachs J); above, p. 449. The Crown did not appeal.

jurisdiction. The court regarded the regulation as an arbitrary and unreasonable exercise of the power conferred. This case well shows how even the widest power will admit judicial review. So does another case from the same department where a Customs and Excise regulation was held to be ultra vires because it purported to empower the authorities to inspect all the records of a business, instead of being limited to records of dutiable goods.[31]

One of the Home Secretary's immigration rules, which restricted the admission of dependent relatives to those 'having a standard of living substantially below that of their own country', was 'manifestly unjust and unreasonable' and also 'partial and unequal in its operation as between different classes', and therefore invalid.[32] The court held that this unreasonable requirement could be severed from the remainder of the rule which was unobjectionable. It had been laid before Parliament.

As these cases show, judicial review is in no way inhibited by the fact that rules or regulations have been laid before Parliament and approved, despite the ruling of the House of Lords that the test of unreasonableness should not then operate in its normal way.[33] The Court of Appeal has emphasised that in the case of subordinate legislation such as an Order in Council approved in draft by both Houses, 'the courts would without doubt be competent to consider whether or not the Order was properly made in the sense of being intra vires'.[34]

Subjective language

The purchase tax case also illustrates the court's refusal to be disarmed by language which appears to make the legislating authority the sole judge of the extent of its power or of the purposes for which it may be used. Even where the Act says that the minister may make regulations 'if he is satisfied' that they are required, the court can enquire whether he could reasonably have been satisfied in the circumstances. A number of instances of the application of this principle to subordinate legislation have been given in an earlier chapter[35] and need not be repeated here.

[31] R. v. Customs and Excise Commissioners ex p. Hedges and Butler Ltd. [1986] 2 All ER 164, holding that the power to provide for 'incidental or supplementary' matters did not assist.

[32] R. v. Immigration Appeal Tribunal ex p. Begum Manshoora [1986] The Times, 24 July (tribunal's decision quashed). The phrases quoted are from Kruse v. Johnson, above. The rule had been laid before Parliament.

[33] See above, p. 29.

[34] R. v. HM Treasury ex p. Smedley [1985] QB 657 (unsuccessful challenge to proposal to pay British contribution to the European Communities without specific statutory authority). See also R. v. Secretary of State for the Environment ex p. Greater London Council (3 April 1985, unreported) discussed in 1985 SLT at 373 (C. M. G. Himsworth).

[35] Above, pp. 449, 455.

Wrong purposes and bad faith

An Act of Parliament is immune from challenge on the ground of improper motives or bad faith, even in the case of a private Act allegedly obtained by fraud.[36] In the federal countries of the Commonwealth the same is true of Acts of provincial and state legislatures, provided that they do not violate constitutional restrictions. In the United States of America the doctrine even protects the legislative acts of bodies such as municipalities.[37]

'But in English law', as Dixon J once observed, 'the position is not quite the same.'[38] An Act of Parliament is the only form of sovereign legislation, and all other legislation is subordinate. Subordination necessarily means subjection to the principle of ultra vires. Since delegated powers of legislation are nearly always given for specific purposes, their use for other purposes will be unlawful. Here again we can refer back to an earlier chapter for such illustrations as there are. One clear case of legislation being condemned for improper purposes was the Western Australian decision that regulations prescribing bus routes were invalid since their object was to protect the state-owned trains from competition.[39] In Canada municipal byelaws have been set aside where they were made with the object of restricting or penalising some individual owner of property rather than for the general benefit.[40] The Privy Council has clearly approved the same principle,[41] and hints to the same effect have been dropped in the House of Lords.[42]

Natural justice

One context in which legislative and administrative functions must be distinguished is that of natural justice.[43] This was made clear in a case arising out of the abolition of the scale fees formerly charged by solicitors in

[36] *Pickin* v. *British Railways Board* [1974] AC 765.

[37] *Yates (Arthur) & Co. Pty. Ltd.* v. *Vegetable Seeds Committee* (1945) 72 CLR 37 at 80 (Dixon J). This case contains a valuable discussion of the law applicable to legislative and administrative acts, holding the regulations restricting dealings in seeds would be invalid if intended to promote the Committee's own trade rather than to ensure the supply of seeds in the market.

[38] Same case, at 81.

[39] *Bailey* v. *Conole* (1931) 34 WALR 18, above, p. 421.

[40] *Boyd Builders Ltd.* v. *City of Ottowa* (1964) 45 DLR (2d) 211; *Re Burns and Township of Haldimand* (1965) 52 DLR (2d) 101.

[41] *A.-G. for Canada* v. *Hallett & Carey Ltd.* [1952] AC 427 at 444; above, p. 455.

[42] *Scott* v. *Glasgow Cpn.* [1899] AC 470 at 492; and see *Baird (Robert) Ltd.* v. *Glasgow Cpn.* [1936] AC 32 at 42.

[43] Above, p. 573, citing additional cases.

conveyancing business. Under the Solicitors Act 1957[44] solicitors' charges were regulated by a statutory committee, which had to submit its orders in draft to the Law Society and allow them a month for comment. This procedure was followed in the case of the draft order of 1972 abolishing scale fees. But a member of another association of solicitors, which was not consulted, sought a declaration and injunction in order to postpone the making of the order and to allow wider consultation. Refusing these remedies Megarry J said:[45]

Let me accept that in the sphere of the so-called quasi-judicial the rules of natural justice run, and that in the administrative or executive field there is a general duty of fairness. Nevertheless, these considerations do not seem to me to affect the process of legislation, whether primary or delegated. Many of those affected by delegated legislation, and affected very substantially, are never consulted in the process of enacting that legislation; and yet they have no remedy. . . . I do not know of any implied right to be consulted or make objections, or any principle upon which the courts may enjoin the legislative process at the suit of those who contend that insufficient time for consultation and consideration has been given.

Since it was plain that the proposed order was legislative rather than executive, there was no room for the principle that persons affected must be given a fair hearing.

Difficult problems may therefore lie ahead in the wide area in which legislative and administrative functions overlap. But although the law gives no general right to be consulted, a duty of consultation is widely acknowledged in practice and sometimes also by statute, as was the duty to consult the Law Society in the above case. This system is explained below.[46]

With reference to the other principle of natural justice, that no man may be judge in his own cause, it has been held that a regulation empowering an insurance commission to decide claims against its own insurance fund is not for this reason invalid, at any rate where the power delegated is wide.[47]

The right to reasoned decisions under the Tribunals and Inquiries Act 1971 is expressly excluded in the case of rules, orders or schemes 'of a legislative and not an executive character'.[48]

Procedural errors

Innumerable statutes empower delegated legislation by various procedures, some requiring the laying of drafts before Parliament or the laying

[44] Since replaced by the Solicitors Act 1974.
[45] *Bates* v. *Lord Hailsham* [1972] 1 WLR 1373 at 1378. For comment on the first sentence see above, p. 524.
[46] Below, p. 884.
[47] *Low* v. *Earthquake and War Damage Commission* [1959] NZLR 1198.
[48] s. 12(2).

of orders before Parliament when made, others prescribing consultation with advisory bodies or with persons affected. There is thus ample scope for false steps in procedure. Errors of this kind will invalidate the legislation if the statutory procedure is mandatory, but not if it is merely directory. Once again, the principle is the same as in the case of other administrative action.[49]

A statutory duty to consult is a matter of importance and so normally mandatory. In one case a minister was required, before making an industrial training order, to consult associations appearing to him to be representative of those concerned. He invited numerous organisations to consult with him about an order for the agricultural industries, but in one case the letter miscarried so that the mushroom growers' association was not consulted. Members of the association, it was held, were not bound by the order, since a mandatory requirement had not been observed.[50]

From time to time there are serious oversights in procedure which demand legislation to put matters right. It came to light in 1944 that numerous regulations made under the Fire Services (Emergency Provisions) Act 1941 had never been laid before Parliament as the Act required; an Indemnity Act was passed to prevent this lapse from having any legal consequences, and to validate the regulations.[51] In fact it was not entirely clear that they were invalid, for it is possible that statutory requirements of this kind are mere directions, and not mandatory conditions,[52] and do not affect the validity of the regulations themselves. But this point has never come before the courts. In 1954, however, the government were obliged to concede, in an unreported case, that the Post Office had for many years collected charges for wireless transmitting and receiving licences without legal authority, and therefore presumably contrary to the Bill of Rights. The Wireless Telegraphy Act 1904 empowered the Postmaster-General to make regulations for collecting the fees, but no regulations had ever been made. Retrospective legislation was at once enacted by Parliament to cure the default.[53] In 1972 it was necessary to validate national insurance regulations which had not been made by the correct authority.[54]

How far the validity of regulations may be affected by failure to follow the prescribed procedure for publishing them is separately dealt with below.[55]

---

[49] Above, p. 245.
[50] *Agricultural (etc.) Training Board* v. *Aylesbury Mushrooms Ltd.* [1972] 1 WLR 190.
[51] National Fire Service Regulations (Indemnity) Act 1944.
[52] Above, p. 247.
[53] Wireless Telegraphy (Validation of Charges) Act 1954.
[54] National Insurance Regulations (Validation) Act 1972.
[55] Below, p. 881.

Sub-delegation

The general rule against sub-delegation of statutory powers, encountered once already, turns upon statutory construction.[56] If Parliament confers power under A, the evident intention is that it shall be exercised by A and not by B. But where power is conferred upon a minister, it is (as we have seen[57]) taken for granted that his officials may exercise it in his name, since that is the normal way in which executive business is done. This is as true of legislative as of administrative powers.[58] Many ministerial regulations, though made in the minister's name, are validly signed by officials, with or without the minister's official seal.[59]

Delegation to some different authority is another matter. In accordance with general principle, and with the few available authorities,[60] it seems safe to presume that unless Parliament expresses or implies a dispensation, legislative power must be exercised by those to whom it is given, and not by further delegates. But this presumption is subject to circumstances, and may be greatly weakened in time of emergency. Power to make regulations was freely delegated in the first world war, although the Defence of the Realm Act did not authorise it expressly. No case came before the courts to show whether delegation was lawful. But in the second world war the Supreme Court of Canada held that the Governor-General's emergency powers entitled him without express authorization to delegate the power to make regulations.[61] In Britain the Emergency Powers (Defence) Act 1939 itself gave express powers to delegate, so that an elaborate pyramid of regulations was constructed, delegated, sub-delegated, sub-sub-delegated, and so on.

Partial invalidity

As several cases already cited illustrate, it is possible for delegated legislation to be partially good and partially bad.[62] In the mushroom growers' case, where the minister was required to consult certain representative associations, it was held that the industrial training order was valid as

---

[56] Above, p. 357.

[57] Above, p. 366.

[58] See *Lewisham BC* v. *Roberts* (above, p. 367).

[59] *R.* v. *Skinner* [1968] 2 QB 700.

[60] There is a clear line of New Zealand authorities from *Geraghty* v. *Porter* [1917] NZLR 554 to *Hawke's Bay Raw Milk Products Co-operative Ltd.* v. *New Zealand Milk Board* [1961] NZLR 218; and see *King-Emperor* v. *Benoari Lal Sarma* [1945] AC 14 at 24.

[61] *Re Chemicals Regulations* [1943] SCR 1; above, p. 365.

[62] See above, p. 338.

regards the organisations consulted and invalid as to those not consulted.[63] In the case of water authorities' sewerage charges the House of Lords held that the statutory instrument fixing the charges was invalid as regards properties connected to a public sewer and invalid as to others.[64] Since legislation by definition consists of general rules affecting large numbers of people, it is easy for such situations to arise, and there is no necessary reason for condemning what is good along with what is bad. The general rule is:[65]

Unless the invalid part is inextricably interconnected with the valid, a court is entitled to set aside or disregard the invalid part, leaving the rest intact.

On this principle an order prohibiting herring fishery, which purported to extend slightly beyond the waters covered by the Act, was held ultra vires as to the excess only, and enforceable in respect of the remainder;[66] and a provision of the immigration rules, held void for unreasonableness, could be severed from the rest without affecting their validity.[67]

Remedies

The commonest method of resisting an invalid regulation or byelaw is to plead its invalidity in defence to a prosecution or enforcement proceedings.[68] The court may also grant an injunction, for example where a local authority is threatening demolition of a building;[69] and if unjustified demolition were carried out, an action for damages would lie. Any proceedings against a central government department are subject to the Crown Proceedings Act 1947, as explained in an earlier chapter.

In several cases also the courts have granted declarations to the effect that some general order or byelaw was invalid.[70] Nor has there been any indication that this remedy will be refused on account of any lack of locus

---

[63] *Agricultural Horticultural and Forestry Industrial Training Board* v. *Aylesbury Mushrooms Ltd.* [1972] 1 WLR 190.

[64] *Daymond* v. *Plymouth City Council* [1976] AC 609; above, p. 852. See also *Malloch* v. *Aberdeen Cpn.* (No. 2) 1974 SLT 5 (regulations requiring registration of teachers void as regards teachers already employed); *Cassidy* v. *Minister for Industry and Commerce* [1978] IR 297 (order unreasonable for some purposes, but not others); *Burke* v. *Minister for Labour* [1979] IR 354 (similar); *Transport Ministry* v. *Alexander* [1978] 1 NZLR 306 (regulation partially invalid for uncertainty).

[65] Halsbury's Laws of England, 4th edn., vol. i, para. 26.

[66] *Dunkley* v. *Evans* [1981] 1 WLR 1522, rejecting the so-called 'blue pencil' test under which amendment may be made only by textual deletion.

[67] *R.* v. *Immigration Appeal Tribunal ex p. Begum Manshoora* [1986] The Times, 24 July.

[68] As in the purchase tax case, above, p. 869.

[69] As in the *Repton* case, above, p. 869.

[70] This was done in both the cases of partial invalidity mentioned above; and see above, p. 693.

standi on the plaintiff's part.[71] The rule that the declaration is a discretionary remedy is a sufficient protection against plaintiffs who are not genuinely concerned.

Certiorari and prohibition apply to 'judicial' rather than legislative action, but the dividing line is far from distinct. It is at least clear that they are not used to challenge such plainly legislative instruments as regulations or byelaws. But mandamus, which has no such limitations, has been used to compel the making of a byelaw.[72]

Statutory restriction of judicial review

Just as with administrative powers,[73] Parliament may make delegated legislation virtually judge-proof. Normally this is done by granting very wide powers rather than by clauses restricting the jurisdiction of the courts. 'Modern drafting technique is to use words which do not exclude jurisdiction in terms but positively repose arbitrary power in a named authority.'[74] But, as already emphasized, it is almost impossible to find language wide enough to exclude judicial control entirely, when the courts are determined to preserve it.[75] All subordinate power must have legal limits somewhere.

In the past Parliament has experimented with protective clauses of varying degrees of severity. It has been enacted that regulations purporting to be made under the Act shall be deemed to be within the powers of the Act, and shall have effect as if enacted by the Act.[76] Only slightly less drastic was the provision that confirmation of an order by the minister should be conclusive evidence that it was duly made and within the powers of the Act.[77] Such naked attempts to create uncontrolled power were condemned by the Committee on Ministers' Powers[78] and are not nowadays acceptable.[79] The formula which has been more used is a simple one, as, for example, in the Emergency Powers Act 1920: 'The regulations so made shall have effect as if enacted in this Act.' The evident intention of this form

---

[71] Zamir, *The Declaratory Judgment*, 279.

[72] See the *Manchester* case, above, p. 698.

[73] Above, p. 719.

[74] *Customs and Excise Commissioners* v. *Cure & Deeley Ltd.* [1962] 1 QB 340 at 364 (Sachs J).

[75] Above, p. 727.

[76] e.g. Foreign Marriage Act 1892, s. 21(2). Compare above, p. 729 n. 40.

[77] For this see above, p. 730.

[78] Cmd. 4060 (1932), p. 41.

[79] But see London Government Act 1963, s. 1(2): charter purporting to be granted under the Act to be deemed valid and within the powers of the Act and not to be questioned in any legal proceeding whatever. A charter, however, can create only rights, not liabilities.

of words is that regulations duly and properly made shall have full legal effect. But in 1894 a majority of the House of Lords, preferring literal verbal construction to legal principle, declared that it made the regulations as unquestionable by a court of law as if they were actually incorporated in the Act.[80] Any conflict between the regulations and the Act must, it was said, be solved by interpretation as in any other case of conflicting provisions in the same statute. In other words, the regulations were to be treated as sovereign rather than subordinate legislation[81] and thus as exempt from judicial control. On this view, arbitrary executive power would reign.[82]

But in 1931 the House found a more reasonable solution in a case under the Housing Act 1925, where the Minister of Health had power to confirm a housing scheme and the Act said that his order when made 'shall have effect as if enacted in this Act'. The minister, it was held, was empowered to confirm only schemes which conformed to the Act; if the scheme itself conflicted with the Act, the order was not an order within the meaning of the Act, and was not saved by the clause.[83] Lord Dunedin said:[84]

It is evident that it is inconceivable that the protection should extend without limit. If the Minister went out of his province altogether . . . it is repugnant to common sense that the order would be protected, although, if there were an Act of Parliament to that effect, it could not be touched.

Although in fact the House upheld the order on its merits, they drew the teeth of the 'as if enacted' clause—which, as the Ministers' Powers Committee recommended,[85] has now fallen into disuse.

These decisions exhibit the same dilemma that has already been pointed out in relation to statutes which take away judicial remedies. Such provisions must either be held to make lawful action which ought to be

[80] *Institute of Patent Agents* v. *Lockwood* [1894] AC 347, followed in *Insurance Committee for Glasgow* v. *Scottish Insurance Commissioners* 1915 SC 504.

[81] In *Re Dances Way, Hayling Island* [1962] Ch 490 at 508 Diplock LJ said that such regulations were 'not subordinate legislation'. But in that case the validity of the regulation was not in question.

[82] This interpretation may be compared with the pre-*Anisminic* decisions on 'shall not be questioned' clauses, which would have allowed powers to be freely abused: above, p. 724. It might also have led to difficulties over amending regulations, since the power given by the Interpretation Act 1978, s. 14 (above, p. 862) might be excluded by contrary intention.

[83] *Minister of Health* v. *R. ex p. Yaffe* [1931] AC 494. The minister modified the scheme so as to make it conform to the Act. See likewise *McEwen's Trustees* v. *Church of Scotland General Trustees* 1940 SLT 357. Other cases involving clauses of this kind are *R.* v. *Electricity Commissioners ex p. London Electricity Joint Committee Co.* [1924] 1 KB 171; *R.* v. *Minister of Health ex p. Davis* [1929] 1 KB 619; *London Parochial Charities Trustees* v. *A.-G.* [1955] 1 WLR 42; *Foster* v. *Aloni* [1951] VLR 481.

[84] At 501.

[85] Above, p. 876.

unlawful, or else they must be virtually meaningless. The long-established policy of the courts is to resist all attempts to confer unlimited executive power, and to uphold the ultra vires principle at all costs. This has been amply illustrated elsewhere.

The Ministers' Powers Committee recognised the same principle in a general recommendation about delegated legislation:[86]

The use of clauses designed to exclude the jurisdiction of the courts to enquire into the legality of a regulation or order should be abandoned in all but the most exceptional cases, and should not be permitted by Parliament except upon special grounds stated in the ministerial memorandum attached to the Bill.

What has since happened in practice is that government draftsmen have preferred to put their faith in clauses which confer the widest possible discretionary power rather than in clauses which attempt to exclude the jurisdiction of the court—as was observed in the opening paragraph of this section. But generally speaking the Committee's recommendation has been observed. In one case Parliament has conscientiously provided that national insurance regulations which were incorporated in a subsequent Act should remain open to challenge in the same way as if they were still merely regulations.[87]

PUBLICATION

Arrangements for publication

The maxim that ignorance of the law does not excuse any subject represents the working hypothesis on which the rule of law rests in British democracy. . . . But the very justification for that basic maxim is that the whole of our law, written or unwritten, is accessible to the public—in the sense, of course, that, at any rate, its legal advisers have access to it, at any moment, as of right.

The theory so stated in *Blackpool Corporation* v. *Locker*[88] is of the greatest importance, but as that case itself showed, it may break down occasionally. It was long ago realised that the first remedial measure demanded by the growing stream of delegated legislation was a systematic scheme for publication and reference. The first statute was the Rules Publication Act 1893, which regulated the publication of *Statutory Rules and Orders*, begun in 1890. The statute now in force is the Statutory Instruments Act 1946, under which the title of the series has been changed to Statutory Instruments.

---

[86] Cmd. 4040 (1932), p. 65.
[87] National Insurance Act 1965, s. 116(2).
[88] Above, p. 860.

The Act of 1893 had two different objects. The first was, in the case of rules which had to be laid before Parliament, to give them (with some exceptions) *antecedent* publicity by requiring notice of them to be published and copies to be provided on demand. Any representations made in writing by 'a public body' had then to be considered before the rules were finally made and laid before Parliament. But these safeguards could be evaded on plea of urgency or special reasons, and provisional orders could (and sometimes did) remain in force indefinitely.

The second object was to secure publication of all statutory rules (whether or not to be laid before Parliament) *after* they were made, by requiring them to be sent to the Queen's printer to be numbered, printed and sold. Statutory rules were comprehensively defined as including rules made under any Act of Parliament, by Order in Council, or by any minister or government department. But the Treasury were given power to alter the effect of the definition by regulations, and a number of exceptions were so made for special cases—for example rules of a local and personal nature—and the definition was confined to cases 'of a legislative and not an executive character'.[89] The great bulk of delegated legislation became subject to an orderly system of publication, and this was a great gain. The Ministers' Powers Committee in 1932 made no complaint that delegated legislation was not accessible, and said that the Act had worked well within its sphere. They did, however, suggest widening the provisions for antecedent publicity, and they advocated a new and more comprehensive Act.[90] This eventually appeared in the form of the Act of 1946, in time to deal with the flood tide of rules and regulations which arrived with the welfare state.

The Act of 1946

The Statutory Instruments Act of 1946 came into force in 1948, repealing and replacing the Act of 1893. Its definition of 'statutory instrument' covers three categories of 'subordinate legislation' made (or confirmed or approved) under the authority of some statute:[91]

(i) Orders in Council;
(ii) Ministerial powers stated in the statute to be exercisable by statutory instrument; and
(iii) future rules made under past statutes to which the Act of 1893 applied.

As regards (iii), regulations under the Act continue the requirement that

[89] SR & O 1894 No. 734 (Treasury Regulations).
[90] Cmd. 4060 (1932), pp. 62, 66.
[91] s. 1.

such rules shall be 'of a legislative and not an executive character'.[92] But as regards (ii), though it applies only to 'legislation', the real test is that it will only apply where Parliament provides, as it now normally does in each statute, that 'regulations made under this Act shall be made by statutory instrument'. Parliament has abandoned the attempt to define subordinate legislation by its substance, since this could never achieve precision. It now relies on itself to prescribe on each occasion that the provisions for publication, etc., shall apply. For statutes made after 1947, therefore, there is a clear-cut but mechanical definition. For statutes made before 1948, the older, vaguer, but more ambitious definition continues. The Act again gives power to control the scope of the old definition by Treasury regulations.[93] And Treasury regulations may exempt any classes of statutory instruments from the requirements of being printed and sold. Exemption has been given to local instruments,[94] and also to instruments regularly printed in some other series. Subject to this, all statutory instruments must be sent to the Queen's printer as soon as made, and must be numbered, printed, and sold.[95] A Reference Committee is empowered to deal with points of difficulty as to numbering, printing, classification, and so on.[96]

Reference to statutory instruments and other delegated legislation on any subject is facilitated by an official index, the Index to Government Orders in Force, published biennially.

Sub-delegated legislation

The Acts of 1893 and 1946 have been accused of a serious shortcoming, namely, that they do not extend to sub-delegated legislation. A positive opinion was expressed by Scott LJ in *Blackpool Corporation* v. *Locker:*[97]

They are both expressly limited to such delegated legislation as is made under powers conferred by Act of Parliament, whether on HM in Council or on a minister of the Crown. Such primary delegated legislation has now (and had under the Act of 1893) to be printed forthwith by the King's Printer and published as a statutory rule or order, etc.: but for delegated legislation made under powers conferred by a regulation or other legislative instrument not being itself an Act of Parliament, there is no general statutory requirement of publicity in force today.

[92] SI 1947 No. 1.
[93] s. 8.
[94] This exemption renders inaccessible many orders, for example those made in the Clay Cross case, mentioned in *Asher* v. *Secretary of State for the Environment* [1974] Ch 208.
[95] s. 2.
[96] By regulations under s. 8(1)(e).
[97] [1948] 1 KB 349 at 369; above, p. 860. See likewise *Patchett* v. *Leathem* (1949) 65 TLR 69, quoted above, p. 861.

... The modern extent of sub-delegated legislation is almost boundless: and it seems to me vital to the whole English theory of the liberty of the subject, that the affected person should be able at any time to ascertain what legislation affecting his rights has been passed under sub-delegated powers.

In another case Scott LJ spoke feelingly of the unfairness to the public when 'administration is mixed up with sub-delegated legislation and none of the mixture is made public'.[98] But, as to the extent of the statutory definitions, it is not clear that either Act is deficient in the manner supposed. If the question were fully argued—as it has not yet been—it might be found that at least some kinds of sub-delegated legislation were included. But since sub-delegated legislation is a product of emergency powers, this problem is unlikely to present itself in normal times.

Effect of non-publication on validity

Another question is whether the validity of rules and regulations is affected by failure to obey the statutory requirements for publication. It may be that these requirements are merely directory—that is to say, that they embody Parliament's directions, but without imposing any penalty for disobedience.[99] In one case a minister was empowered by statute to control the use of explosives in mines by order, 'of which notice shall be given in such manner as he may direct', and though he failed to give any notice, his order was upheld on the ground that the condition was directory only.[1] It would seem *a fortiori* that neglect of a general statute requiring publication would be less serious. It was, indeed, held in 1918 that an order made by the Food Controller did not take effect until it was published: *A* had sold 1,000 bags of beans to *B* on 16 May 1917, and on that same day an order was made requisitioning all such beans, but it was not published until the following day; *B* tried to recover his money from *A* but failed, since the order was held to take effect only when it was made known.[2] But the true explanation is probably that the order, as construed by the court, was intended to take effect only at that time.

This hypothesis is impliedly supported by a provision of the Statutory Instruments Act 1946. It requires the Stationery Office to publish lists showing the dates on which they issue statutory instruments, and in any

[98] *Jackson Stansfield & Sons Ltd.* v. *Butterworth* [1948] 2 All ER 558.

[99] See above, p. 245. For discussion and criticism see (1974) 37 MLR 510 (D. J. Lanham); [1982] PL 569 (A. I. L. Campbell); [1983] PL 385 (D. J. Lanham).

[1] *Jones* v. *Robson* [1901] 1 QB 673; and see *Duncan* v. *Knill* (1907) 96 LT 911 (order valid although statutory notice not given). But see the views expressed by the High Court of Australia in *Watson* v. *Lee* (1979) 26 ALR 461.

[2] *Johnson* v. *Sargant & Sons* [1918] 1 KB 101.

proceedings against any person for offending under such statutory instruments

it shall be a defence to prove that the instrument had not been issued by His Majesty's Stationery Office at the date of the alleged contravention unless it is proved that at that date reasonable steps had been taken for the purpose of bringing the purport of the instrument to the notice of the public, or of persons likely to be affected by it, or of the person charged.[3]

It seems to be assumed that non-publication would not by itself be a sufficient defence, and since the provision deals only with criminal liability, it suggests that non-publication would not affect the validity of a statutory instrument altering civil rights. This was the construction adopted in a case of 1954, where a company were prosecuted for infringing an Iron and Steel Prices Order. The order had been printed, but not the schedules for it, which were extensive and bulky. The judge decided that non-publication of the schedules did not invalidate the order, because the Act made an obvious distinction between the making of the instrument and the issue of it, and the provisions for printing and publication were merely procedural.[4] The making of the instrument was complete, in his opinion, when it was made by the minister and (if so required by the empowering statute) laid before Parliament. Since the prosecution were able to prove that reasonable steps had been taken for notification by other channels, a conviction followed. The judge's suggestion that validity might depend upon laying before Parliament is in conflict with at least two previous judicial opinions;[5] and it may be held that even that requirement, important though it is, would be held to be directory merely, as being essentially a form of supervision *ex post facto*. As we have seen, Acts of Indemnity have been used to prevent the question arising.[6]

Rules required to be laid before Parliament

We have already noticed how the Rules Publication Act 1893 provided for advance publication of regulations which had to be laid before Parliament. Laying before Parliament is commonly required by the statute under which the regulations are made, as explained below. The Statutory Instruments Act 1946 has the same objective as the Act of 1893, but

---

[3] s. 3(2).

[4] *The Queen* v. *Sheer Metalcraft Ltd.* [1954] 1 QB 586.

[5] *Bailey* v. *Williamson* (1873) LR 8 QB 118; *Starey* v. *Graham* [1899] 1 QB 406 at 412. But much depends upon the precise statutory language.

[6] Above, p. 873.

prescribes a different procedure. It requires the laying to take place before the instrument comes into operation.[7] If, however, it is essential that it should come into operation before it can be laid, it may do so; but a reasoned notification must be sent to both Houses. There will obviously be occasions, especially when Parliament is not sitting, when orders may have to be brought into force urgently. The forty-day period provided by the Act of 1893 has gone, but it gave rise to so many 'provisional orders' ('provisional' merely for the purpose of avoiding it) that the Act of 1946 makes a more realistic compromise.

But even under the latter Act it was found inconvenient to make special explanations for every order brought into force at times when Parliament was not sitting. The Laying of Documents (Interpretation) Act 1948 accordingly allowed each House to give its own meaning to 'laying' for the purposes of the Act;[8] the Houses then made standing orders to the effect that delivery of copies to their offices should count as 'laying' at any time when a Parliament was legally in being, even though it was prorogued or adjourned at the time. The safeguards designed in 1893 have been progressively whittled down as the weight of delegated legislation has grown greater and greater.

The timetable for 'laying' has also been made more uniform by the Statutory Instruments Act 1946 in two classes of cases:

(i) instruments which are subject to annulment on an adverse resolution of either House, and

(ii) instruments which must be laid before Parliament in draft, but which may later be made if no hostile resolution is carried.

The first class is much more common than the second. In order to escape from the provisions of numerous Acts which had laid down different timetables, and in order to provide one timetable for the future, it is now provided that instruments of class (i) shall be duly laid and shall be subject to annulment for forty days, and that instruments of class (ii) shall not be made within forty days of being laid. In counting the forty days, no account is taken of periods when Parliament is dissolved or prorogued, or adjourned for more than four days. It will be observed that no provision is made for regulations which expire within a time-limit unless expressly confirmed by Parliament (of which we have already met examples)[9] or for regulations which do not take effect at all unless so confirmed. In those cases the

---

[7] s. 4.

[8] 'Laying' has no technical meaning: see *R. v. Immigration Tribunal ex p. Joyles* [1972] 1 WLR 1390 (unsuccessful challenge to validity of the immigration rules of 1970 on the ground that they were presented to Parliament but not 'laid').

[9] Above, p. 854.

timetable is usually of intrinsic importance to the subject-matter, and is best left as it is.

PRELIMINARY CONSULTATION

Hearing of objections

In the case of rules and orders which are clearly legislative as opposed to administrative, there is no room for the principle of natural justice which entitles persons affected to a fair hearing in advance.[10] But orders for such things as housing and planning schemes, although they may affect numerous people, are for this purpose treated by Parliament, and also by the courts, as matters of administration and not of legislation. They are subject to the procedure of preliminary public inquiry under various Acts, and also to the principles of natural justice, as we have seen.[11] The right to reasoned decisions given by the Tribunals and Inquiries Act 1971 is expressly excluded in the case of rules, orders or schemes 'of a legislative and not an executive character'.[12] But it may be presumed that the right extends to all orders and schemes of the kind just mentioned.

In the true sphere of delegated legislation, a limited legal duty to consider objections was imposed by the provision of the Rules Publication Act 1893 that the rule-making authority must consider any written representations made within the forty-day period of preliminary publicity. But, as we saw, this proved of little benefit, and was repealed by the Act of 1946. A few statutes however provide for a right to make objection to draft regulations and for a right to a public inquiry in some circumstances. Examples are the Factories Act 1961 and the Offices Shops and Railways Premises Act 1963.[13] Under these Acts certain 'special regulations' must be published in draft and written objections lodged by persons affected must be considered by the minister. If a majority of persons affected lodge a 'general objection' they are entitled to a public inquiry. But apart from these exceptional cases no one has a right to a hearing before regulations are made.

In this respect English law has moved in the opposite direction from American law.[14] The Federal Administrative Procedure Act of 1946[15] gives a right to 'interested persons' to 'participate in the rule-making through submission of written data, views or arguments', and in some cases

---

[10] Above, p. 573.
[11] Above, p. 507.
[12] s. 12(2).
[13] 4th and 1st schedules respectively.
[14] For comparative discussion see (1983) 3 OJLS 253 (M. Asimow).
[15] s. 4. See Schwartz and Wade, *Legal Control of Government*, 87.

Congress has prescribed a formal hearing. Hearings preliminary to rule-making have thus become an important part of the administrative process in the United States. But there is often no right to an oral hearing and there is a wide exception where the authority finds 'for good cause' 'that notice and public procedure thereon are impracticable, unnecessary or contrary to the public interest'.

In Britain the practice counts for more than the law. Consultation with interests and organisations likely to be affected by rules and regulations is one of the firmest and most carefully observed conventions.[16] It is not a matter of legal right, any more than it is with Parliament's own legislation. But it is so well settled a practice that it is most unusual to hear complaint.[17] It may be that consultation which is not subject to statutory procedure is more effective than formal hearing, which may produce legalism and artificiality. The duty to consult is recognised in every sense except the legal one. The Committee on Ministers' Powers were told: 'No minister in his senses, with the fear of Parliament before his eyes, would ever think of making regulations without (where practicable) giving the persons who will be affected thereby (or their representatives) an opportunity of saying what they think about the proposal.'[18] But it is for the department to decide whom it will consult, and more attention is likely to be given to official and representative bodies than to individuals. The consultation of local authorities, professional bodies, trade unions, etc., is often on a very wide scale, and may involve reference to dozens of different organisations.[19]

Consultation before rule-making, even when not required by law, is in fact one of the major industries of government. It is doubtful whether anything would be gained by imposing general legal obligations and formal procedures. At least, there appears to be no demand for any such reform.

Statutory consultation and advisory bodies

Particular Acts often require particular interests to be consulted. Some provide for schemes of control to be formulated by the persons affected themselves. Another device which is often used is that of an advisory committee or council, which is set up under the Act and which must be consulted. The council will usually be constituted so as to represent various interests, and so as to be independent of ministerial control. And, in its turn, it may often consult other persons. Thus many regulations made under the

[16] See [1964] PL 105 (J. F. Garner); [1978] PL 290 (A. D. Jergesen).
[17] A rare exception was *Bates* v. *Lord Hailsham* [1972] 1 WLR 1373; above, p. 871.
[18] *Minutes of Evidence*, p. 35.
[19] See [1964] PL at 116–18 (J. F. Garner).

Social Security Acts must be submitted to the Social Security Advisory Committee, and the Committee's report must be laid before Parliament by the minister along with the regulations.[20] Similarly the Home Secretary is required to consult the Police Council or a Police Advisory Board before making certain regulations governing the police;[21] and procedural rules for statutory tribunals may be made only after consultation with the Council on Tribunals.[22] In these cases there is no statutory procedure for consulting other interests such as there is with the Social Security Advisory Committee. But these councils may consult other people and hear evidence if they wish, and frequently they do so.

A statutory duty to consult requires that the person or body consulted should be given a reasonably ample and sufficient opportunity to state their views[23] 'before the mind of the executive becomes unduly fixed'.[24] It is not satisfied if it is treated as a mere opportunity to make ineffective representations.[25] Failure to consult will normally render the order void, as for neglect of a mandatory requirement.[26]

PARLIAMENTARY SUPERVISION

The trend of the times

One of the features of the twentieth century has been a shift of the constitutional centre of gravity, away from Parliament and towards the executive. Mr Lloyd George once said: 'Parliament has really no control over the Executive; it is a pure fiction.'[27] Party discipline gives the government a tight control over Parliament in all but the last resort; and the electoral system, tending as it does to eliminate minority parties, normally gives the government a solid basis for its power. But, in addition, the sheer volume of legislation and other government work is so great that the parliamentary machine is unequal to it. This is itself one of the principal reasons for delegated legislation. It is also the reason why it is difficult for Parliament to supervise it effectively. To treat the subject of parliamentary

[20] Social Security Act 1980, s. 10.
[21] Police Act 1964, ss. 45, 46.
[22] See below, p. 916.
[23] *Port Louis Corporation* v. *Attorney-General of Mauritius* [1965] AC 1111. See also *Rollo* v. *Minister of Town and Country Planning* [1948] 1 All ER 13; *Re Union of Benefices of Whippingham and East Cowes, St. James* [1954] AC 245.
[24] *Sinfield* v. *London Transport Executive* [1970] Ch 550 at 558.
[25] *Sinfield* (as above) at 558. Compare the question of 'blowing off steam' below, p. 966.
[26] Above, p. 247.
[27] Quoted by Sir Carleton Allen, *Law and Orders*, 3rd edn., 161.

control in any detail would take us beyond administrative law. But mention may be made of a few matters of special interest.[28]

Laying before Parliament

An Act of Parliament will normally require that rules or regulations made under the Act shall be laid before both Houses of Parliament.[29] Parliament can then keep its eye upon them and provide opportunities for criticism. Rules or regulations laid before Parliament may be attacked on any ground. The object of the system is to keep them under general political control, so that criticism in Parliament is frequently on grounds of policy. The legislation concerning 'laying' has already been explained.[30]

Laying before Parliament is done in a number of different ways.[31] The regulations may merely have to be laid; or they may be subject to negative resolution within forty days; or they may expire unless confirmed by affirmative resolution; or they may have to be laid in draft. Occasionally they do not have to be laid at all, because Parliament has omitted to make any provision.[32] The prescribed procedure corresponds in a general way to the importance of the subject-matter—but only in a general way, for the vagaries in legislative practice have been called by a leading authority 'extraordinary'.[33]

Nevertheless there are two clear categories into which the majority of cases fall. Either the regulations will be of no effect unless confirmed by resolution of each House (or, if financial, of the House of Commons only[34]); or else they will take effect without further formality in Parliament, but subject to annulment in pursuance of a resolution of either House (with some exceptions). These are known as the 'affirmative' and 'negative' procedures respectively. The affirmative procedure is normal for regulations which increase taxes or charges.[35] The negative procedure is normal in the great majority of other cases. Sometimes an Act will employ

[28] See generally Allen (as above), ch. 5; [1956] PL 200 (Sir C. Carr).
[29] Congressional control (the 'legislative veto') is held unconstitutional in the United States: *Immigration and Naturalisation Service* v. *Chadha*, 462 US 919 (1983).
[30] Above, p. 881.
[31] Documents referred to in the regulations but not forming part of them do not have to be laid: *R.* v. *Secretary of State for Social Services ex p. Camden LBC* [1987] 1 WLR 819.
[32] e.g. regulations for Rent Tribunals under the Furnished Houses (Rent Control) Act 1946, s. 8. The omission is inexplicable.
[33] Allen (as above), 130.
[34] If the Act says 'Parliament' in such a case, this may mean the House of Commons only: *R.* v. *Secretary of State for the Environment ex p. Leicester CC* [1985] The Times, 1 February.
[35] e.g. under Customs and Excise Duties (General Reliefs) Act 1979, s. 17 (4); Income and Corporation Taxes Act 1988, s. 788 (10).

both procedures[36] and it may even allow a choice between them.[37] But whatever course is adopted, the regulations are either approved or disapproved. Parliament cannot itself amend them.

Opportunities for challenge

Where regulations have merely to be laid, there is no special opportunity for control, and the laying does no more than advertise the regulations to members, who may then put questions to ministers. At the other extreme, where an affirmative resolution is necessary, the government must find time for a motion and debate, so that there is full scope for criticism. In the intermediate and commonest case, where the regulations are subject to annulment, the procedure of the House of Commons allows them to be challenged by any member at the end of the day's business. He must move a 'prayer', because the method of annulment is by Order in Council (as provided by the Statutory Instruments Act 1946),[38] and the motion is for a humble prayer to the Crown that the regulations be annulled. Provided that the necessary quorum of forty can be kept in the House, the annulment procedure ensures an opportunity for debate at the instance of any member. Every member may therefore 'watch and pray'.[39] But the House could not possibly debate all the annullable regulations laid before it. In 1951, when the Labour government's majority had fallen to 8, there was suddenly a great increase in 'praying'. On many successive nights—for prayers are necessarily nocturnal—resolutions were moved against various statutory instruments, as it was alleged, 'for no other reason than the exhaustion of honourable members and Ministers of the Crown'.[40] Although the question here was not exactly that of controlling delegated legislation, the opportunity was taken to ask a Select Committee of the House to consider 'the existing procedures by which the control of this House over delegated legislation is exercised'. The Committee carried out a wide review and considered many possible reforms—for example, that there should be a Standing Committee to hear prayers, and that objectors should be given some sort of formal hearing.[41] But all such ideas were rejected, for various reasons, and the only immediate outcome was a

---

[36] e.g. Census Act 1920, s. 1(2).

[37] As does the European Communities Act 1972, 2nd sched., para. 2(2).

[38] s. 5.

[39] Allen (as above), 123.

[40] See Allen (as above), 162.

[41] Report of the Select Committee on Delegated Legislation, HC 310, 1952–3. For later reviews see Reports of the Joint Committee on Delegated Legislation, HC 475, 1971–2; HC 407 and 468, 1972–3.

change of procedure to prevent debates on prayers running on far into the night: they must be closed or (in the Speaker's discretion) adjourned at half past eleven. In other respects the House appeared to be satisfied with the machinery of control.

In 1973, however, the House of Commons established a 'merits committee' to consider statutory instruments requiring affirmative resolutions and other cases where there was a prayer for annulment or other hostile motion before the House.[42] But this could be done only on the motion of a minister, and only if twenty members did not object. The purpose of this innovation was to enable the committee to discuss the merits of the instrument, as opposed to its technical propriety—as to which see the following section.

The Scrutiny Committee and the Joint Committee

One successful innovation, which was already part of the machinery with which the Committee of 1953 declared itself satisfied, was the House of Commons' Select Committee on Statutory Instruments, commonly called the Scrutiny Committee. A committee of this kind had been recommended in 1932 by the Ministers' Powers Committee, which thought that it should deal both with Bills proposing new delegated legislation and with all rules and regulations as they were made. But not until 1944 was the Committee appointed, and then only for the second of these purposes. Since then it has been in continuous existence and has done valuable work, contrary to a good deal of expert and official opinion to the effect that its tasks were impracticable, undesirable, and so forth.

In 1973, following the Report of a joint committee of Lords and Commons,[43] the two Houses formed the Joint Committee on Statutory Instruments.[44] In this were merged both the Scrutiny Committee and the House of Lords' Special Orders Committee, which had been in existence since 1924 but which dealt only with cases where an affirmative resolution was required. The Joint Committee has seven members from each House. The Commons' members sit by themselves as a select committee in the case of financial instruments which are laid before the House of Commons only.

The Joint Committee, like its predecessors, is not concerned with policy but with the manner, form and technique of the exercise of rule-making powers. Consequently it can do its work without party strife, with the single object of keeping statutory instruments up to a satisfactory

[42] 853 HC Deb col. 680 (22 March 1973). This is a standing committee under Standing Order 73A.
[43] See preceding note.
[44] See 850 HC Deb col. 1217 (13 February 1973).

administrative standard. Its chairman is normally a member of the Opposition in the House of Commons, thus signifying that it exists in order to criticise.

The Joint Committee is required to consider every statutory instrument, rule, order or scheme laid or laid in draft before each House if proceedings may be taken upon it in either House under any statute. The Committee has to decide whether to bring it to the attention of the House on any of the following grounds:[45]

   (i) that it imposes a charge on the public revenues, or imposes or prescribes charges for any licence, consent, or service from any public authority;

   (ii) that it is made under a statute which preludes challenge in the courts;

   (iii) that it purports to have retrospective effect, without statutory authorisation;

   (iv) that publication or laying before Parliament appear to have been unjustifiably delayed;

   (v) that notification to the Speaker appears to have been unjustifiably delayed, in cases where the Statutory Instruments Act 1946 requires it;[46]

   (vi) that there is doubt whether it is intra vires or that it appears to make 'some unusual or unexpected use' of the powers conferred;

   (vii) 'that for any special reason its form or purport calls for elucidation',

   (viii) 'that its drafting appears to be defective'.

But the Committee may also act 'on any other ground which does not impinge on its merits or on the policy behind it.' They therefore have a free rein for non-political comment.

Under this final head, for example, the Committee reported that there was inadequate scrutiny of many orders in Northern Ireland, since those that were subject to annulment by the Northern Ireland Assembly ceased to be laid before any legislature when the Assembly was dissolved by the Northern Ireland Act 1974.[47] A case of 'unexpected use of the powers' was where the power to prescribe forms was used to enforce metric measurement of the height of stallions instead of the traditional measurement by hands and inches.[48] Another was where rules made for the Employment Appeal Tribunal allowed the tribunal to depart from the rules at its own discretion.[49] The need for elucidation is illustrated by an order under the Sex Discrimination Act 1975 which was not clear and

---

  [45] HC 18—iii (1980–1).

  [46] Above, p. 883.

  [47] HC 54—xxvii (1975–6).

  [48] HC 55—iii (1975–6) criticising Horse Breeding (Amendment) Rules 1975, SI No. 1777.

  [49] HC 54—xxi (1975–6) criticising Employment Appeal Tribunal Rules 1976 SI No. 322.

whose explanatory note was misleading.[50] Defective drafting was found in an order designating bodies able to grant permits for the use of minibuses.[51] These are examples taken at random from a very large number of reports. Much the commonest reasons for reporting an order are that it requires elucidation, or makes an unexpected use of powers, or is marred by defective drafting.

Before reporting an instrument to the two Houses, the Committee must hear the government department's explanations. Contrary to the proposals of 1932, their reports will often not reach the Houses within the forty-day period, if applicable. But where an affirmative resolution is required, the rule in the House of Lords is that the Committee's report must first be made available. There is no such rule in the House of Commons.

The Committee also makes general reports. It has criticised lax departmental practices such as the laying of instruments before Parliament 'in a scruffy form with manuscript amendments, and the omission of necessary details so as to confer wide discretion on ministers and thus bypass Parliament'.[52]

Probably the most important result of the Committee's vigilance is not that it brings regulations to debate in Parliament (though there have been some notable examples of this happening), but that it gives government departments a lively consciousness that critical eyes are kept upon them. The fact that 2 per cent or less of the instruments scrutinised are reported to the House is in part a measure of the Committee's success in establishing a standard. Its work is another example of the value of a standing body as opposed to periodical inquests by ad hoc committees.

In particular, the successive committees have been able to secure more satisfactory explanatory notes, which now accompany statutory instruments as a matter of course and are particularly useful when the instrument is complicated. Obscurities have often been criticised, and also the practices of legislating by reference, sub-delegation on dubious authority, and (occasionally) retrospective operation. The terms of reference expressly allow a point of ultra vires to be raised, as is done from time to time. The Scrutiny Committee was able to secure consolidation of various scattered regulations, and it helped to provide the impetus for the Statutory Instruments Act 1946. A few regulations escape scrutiny, since statutes sometimes omit to provide for them to be laid. But the system extends to much the greater part of delegated legislation which is of national as

[50] HC 54—iv (1975–6) criticising Sex Discrimination (Designated Educational Establishments) Order 1975, SI No. 1902.

[51] HC 33—xv (1978–9), criticising Minibus (Designated Bodies) (Amendment) Order 1978, SI No. 1930.

[52] HC 169 (1977–8).

opposed to local effect. It may be said to be the one successful result of the efforts of reformers to impose discipline on all this legislative activity.

The Ministers' Powers Committee originally recommended that both Houses should have scrutiny committees with similar terms of reference. But the House of Lords did not follow the House of Commons' lead until the Joint Committee was established. The combined committee saves duplication of effort over a wide and technical field, with a gain in efficiency. It reports on every instrument within its terms of reference, even if only to say that it has no comment to make. The fruits of its labours are not to be counted in motions carried against the government, but in the improvements in departmental practice which its vigilance has secured. In this respect its work may be compared with that of the Parliamentary Commissioner for Administration—another example of the value of non-political scrutiny of administrative action. The impartial character of the Committee's reports means that they do not have to face the steam-roller of the ruling majority.

Legislation of the European Communities

New problems of parliamentary supervision of regulations arose when the United Kingdom became a member of the European Communities and the European Communities Act 1972 gave the force of law to Community legislation. Under this Act Parliament has renounced, or at least attempted to renounce, its power to legislate contrary to the law of the Communities, as laid down in the case of the European Economic Community by the Council and the Commission in accordance with the Treaty of Rome.[53] So long as this self-denying ordinance is observed, Parliament has no control over Community legislation, even though it automatically becomes part of the law of this country.

Most Community legislation is made by the Council on proposals from the Commission. Each House of Parliament has established a select committee to scrutinise these proposals. Although the Houses have no direct powers, they can call ministers to account for what they do as members of the Council. The object of the two select committees is to keep Parliament informed of Community legislation due to come before the Council, so that pressure can be brought to bear on ministers before they consider it in the Council; and the government undertake to arrange debates for this purpose.[54] Both Committees make regular reports to their Houses.

The House of Lords' Committee is called the Select Committee on the

[53] European Communities Act 1972, s. 2(4).
[54] See Erskine May, Parliamentary Practice, 19th edn., 842.

European Communities; it has six sub-committees dealing with different areas of policy. The House of Commons' Committee is called the Select Committee on European Legislation. Community legislation must of course be distinguished from orders and regulations made under the European Communities Act 1972 for enforcing Community law, which are subject to affirmative resolution or annulment in Parliament as already mentioned.[55]

[55] Above, p. 887.

23

STATUTORY TRIBUNALS

THE TRIBUNAL SYSTEM

Special tribunals

A prominent feature of the governmental scene is the multitude of special tribunals created by Act of Parliament.[1] Each of these is designed to be part of some scheme of administration, and collectively they are sometimes called administrative tribunals.

A host of these tribunals has arisen under the welfare state, such as the local tribunals which decide disputed claims to benefit under the social security legislation, and industrial tribunals which decide many disputes involving employers and employees and often involving the state also. Other tribunals deal with taxation, property rights, immigration, mental health, allocation of pupils to schools. A vast range of controversies is committed to the jurisdiction of these bodies, which is by no means confined to claims against public authorities. Can A resist a notice to quit from his landlord or get his rent reduced? Can B claim unemployment benefit or a retirement pension or a redundancy payment? Should C, a Pakistani, be refused admission to the country? Ought Dr D to be removed from the health service? Should E be forbidden to conduct an independent school? These are samples of the many questions which may come before statutory tribunals. The ordinary law-abiding citizen is more likely to find himself concerned with them than with the regular courts of law.

Tribunals are conspicuous in administrative law because each of them has a limited jurisdiction and its errors are subject to judicial review in the High Court to the extent already described. In this chapter we are concerned rather with the organisation and normal operation of the tribunal system. This is an important aspect of the machinery of administrative justice, as was recognised in 1958 by the enactment of the

---

[1] For tribunals see *Report of the Committee of Adminstrative Tribunals and Enquiries* (the Franks Report), Cmnd 218 (1957); Wraith and Hutchesson, *Administrative Tribunals* (1973); Farmer, *Tribunals and Government*; Bell, *Tribunals in the Social Services*; Van Dyk, *Tribunals and Inquiries*; Jackson, *The Machinery of Justice in England*, 7th edn., ch. 3. The Annual Reports of the Council on Tribunals are an important source. For the situation before the Franks Committee's report see Allen, *Administrative Jurisdiction* (1956); Robson, *Justice and Administrative Law* (3rd edn., 1951).

Tribunals and Inquiries Act, now replaced by the Tribunals and Inquiries Act 1971. The more satisfactory the tribunals are, the less judicial review will be required. Legal technicalities therefore play a relatively small part in this chapter: the problems which arise are mainly of legal policy and organisation. Tribunals exist in order to provide simpler, speedier, cheaper, and more accessible justice than do the ordinary courts. The question which runs through the subject is how far the standards set by the courts can be reconciled with the needs of administration. It may be taken for granted that the principles of natural justice must be observed, as illustrated in earlier chapters.[2] These supply the essential minimum of fairness in administration and adjudication alike. But should there be rights of appeal to other tribunals? Or to the courts? Ought reasons always to be given for decisions? Should legal representation always be allowed? And are there too many different tribunals? There is no shortage of problems of this kind.

The Tribunals and Inquiries Act 1958 was preceded by the Report of the Committee on Administrative Tribunals and Enquiries (the Franks Committee).[3] This report made a full review of the subject and was the turning-point in its development. Previously tribunals had become too isolated from the rest of the legal system and the standard of justice had suffered. Implementation of the report did much to restore the situation. It has since been recognised that statutory tribunals are an integral part of the machinery of justice in the state, and not merely administrative devices for disposing of claims and arguments conveniently.

Historical antecedents

Tribunals are mainly a twentieth-century phenomenon, for it was long part of the conception of the rule of law that the determination of questions of law—that is to say, questions which require the finding of facts and the application of definite legal rules or principles—belonged to the courts exclusively. The first breaches of this principle were made for the purpose of efficient collection of revenue. The Commissioners of Customs and Excise were given judicial powers by statutes dating from 1660;[4] but though these were criticised by Blackstone[5] and execrated in the definition of 'excise' in Johnson's Dictionary,[6] they were the forerunners of many

---

[2] Tribunals figure in many of the cases cited in chapters 14 and 15.
[3] Cmnd. 218 (1957).
[4] 12 Charles II, c. 23, s. 31, giving a right of appeal to justices of the peace.
[5] Bl. Comm. iv. 281. See *Report of the Committee on Ministers' Powers*, Cmd. 4060 (1932), p. 11.
[6] 'A hateful tax levied upon commodities, and adjudged not by the common judges of property, but wretches hired by those to whom excise is paid.'

such powers, such as those of the Land Tax Commissioners who in 1799 were succeeded by the General Commissioners of Income Tax, a tribunal which still exists. Although the Board of Railway Commissioners (1846) and the Railway and Canal Commission (1873) are often cited as examples of early tribunals, their powers were in many respects administrative rather than judicial since much of their work was governed by policy rather than by law.[7] This anomalous feature of tribunals concerned with transport is still to be observed.[8]

The type of tribunal so familiar today, and so prominent in the administration of the welfare state, arrived on the scene with the Old Age Pensions Act of 1908 and the National Insurance Act 1911. The Act of 1908 established local pensions committees to decide disputes, with a right of appeal to the Local Government Board. The Act of 1911, which in important ways was the prototype of modern social legislation, provided for appeals concerning unemployment insurance to go to a court of referees with a further right of appeal to an umpire. Although this agreeable terminology, with its flavour of football and cricket, has long been dropped, the referees and the umpire were the recognisable predecessors of the present-day social security tribunals and commissioners. In particular, the courts of referees contained lay members drawn from panels representative of employers and employees respectively, as do industrial tribunals today. But the decision of health insurance claims under the Act of 1911 was a matter for the friendly societies through which that part of the scheme was administered in association with insurance companies, though on some matters appeal lay to insurance commissioners with further appeal to the courts. In this period a number of different techniques were being tried, in an attempt to avoid the excessive litigation produced by reliance on insurance companies and the courts under the Workmen's Compensation Acts 1897–1945.

Thus four different methods of settling disputes were conceived within a decade. Workmen's compensation became the province of county court judges, old-age pensions were handed over to local authorities for administration, unemployment insurance fostered a new set of tribunals, and national health insurance was largely administered through existing friendly societies or industrial insurance firms.[9]

It was soon found that the unemployment insurance system was the most successful. As will be seen, it has served as the model for tribunals in other fields. But later developments have modified it in one important respect. It made no provision for reference to the courts of any questions of any kind.

---

[7] Wraith and Hutchesson, *Administrative Tribunals*, 25.
[8] Below, p. 901.
[9] Wraith and Hutchesson, *Administrative Tribunals*, 35.

The normal rule today is that there is a right of appeal from a tribunal to the High Court on a question of law.

Advantages of tribunals

One reason for the appointment of special tribunals, such as those concerned with railway regulation, was that they had to deal with questions of commercial policy rather than of law, which were unsuitable for the ordinary courts. But the social legislation of the twentieth century demanded tribunals for purely administrative reasons: they could offer speedier, cheaper and more accessible justice, essential for the administration of welfare schemes involving large numbers of small claims. The process of the courts of law is elaborate, slow and costly. Its defects are those of its merits, for the object is to provide the highest standard of justice; generally speaking, the public wants the best possible article, and is prepared to pay for it. But in administering social services the aim is different. The object is not the best article at any price but the best article that is consistent with efficient administration. Disputes must be disposed of quickly and cheaply, for the benefit of the public purse as well as for that of the claimant. The whole system is based on compromise, and it is from the dilemma of weighing quality against convenience that many of its problems arise.

A classic illustration is the case of compensation for industrial injuries. Under the Workmen's Compensation Acts, as already mentioned, disputed cases went to the courts of law and the system generated much unproductive litigation, usually financed by insurance companies, particularly on the question whether the injury was suffered in the course of the employment. In 1946 the system of commercial insurance was replaced by one of state insurance, under which disputes were remitted to statutory tribunals with no right of appeal to the courts. For the purposes of social administration the new scheme was far more suitable; and although it has since become possible for questions of law, including 'course of employment' questions, to be brought to the High Court,[10] there is far less waste of time and money in litigation. In 1966 the industrial injuries tribunals were merged with the national insurance tribunals, later renamed social security tribunals. The resultant hierarchy of tribunals and appeal tribunals is described below.

An accompanying advantage is that of expertise. Under the industrial injuries scheme, for instance, disablement questions are referred to an 'adjudicating medical practitioner', with a right of appeal to a medical appeal tribunal, while other questions go to the ordinary lay tribunals.

[10] See below, p. 908.

Qualified surveyors sit on the Lands Tribunal and experts in tax law sit as Special Commissioners of Income Tax. Specialised tribunals can deal both more expertly and more rapidly with special classes of cases, whereas in the High Court counsel may take a day or more to explain to the judge how some statutory scheme is designed to operate. Even without technical expertise, a specialised tribunal quickly builds up expertise in its own field. Where there is a continuous flow of claims of a particular class, there is every advantage in a specialised jurisdiction.

Other characteristics

The system of tribunals has now long been an essential part of the machinery of government. The supplementary network of adjudicatory bodies has grown up side by side with the traditional courts of law. There is a close relationship between the two systems, both because under the ordinary law the tribunals are subject to control by the courts and also because Parliament has in the majority of cases provided a right of appeal from the tribunals to the courts on any question of law. A case which starts, say, in a social security or industrial local tribunal may therefore end in the House of Lords, having passed through four or five stages of litigation.[11] This is a rare event, since otherwise the tribunal system would be self-defeating. But the tribunals must in some way be integrated with the machinery of justice generally. As will be seen, it has proved necessary to increase the supervisory powers of the courts, as well as to extend rights of appeal.

   Tribunals are subject to a law of evolution which fosters diversity of species. Each one is devised for the purposes of some particular statute and is therefore, so to speak, tailor-made. When any new scheme of social welfare or regulation is introduced the line of least resistance is always to set up new ad hoc tribunals rather than reorganise those already existing. For a long time there were two distinct tribunals dealing with rents, several tribunals dealing with taxes, and numerous tribunals dealing with social security benefits. Uncontrolled growth has produced over fifty different types of tribunal falling within the Tribunals and Inquiries Act 1971. When all their local subdivisions are aggregated the total (including Scotland) exceeds 2,000. They range from extremely busy tribunals such as those dealing with social security, industrial affairs, rating appeals, and rent control to tribunals which have no business at all and have therefore never been appointed, such

---

[11] As in *R. v. National Insurance Commissioner ex p. Hudson* [1972] AC 944, where a special House of seven Law Lords was divided by four to three on an important question of the respective jurisdictions of local tribunals and medical boards in industrial injury cases. The decision of the majority was thereupon reversed by National Insurance Act 1972, s. 5.

as the mines and quarries tribunals. In 1986 social security appeal tribunals disposed of over 90,000 appeals, local valuation courts disposed of over 48,000 rating appeals, and rent tribunals determined over 15,000 cases. A detailed catalogue of the tribunals falling within the Act will be found at the end of this chapter, showing also the number of cases disposed of by each in a single year.

The responsibilities of tribunals are in general no less important than those of courts of law. Large awards of money may be made by tribunals, for example, in cases of industrial injuries. Mental Health Review Tribunals[12] determine whether a patient ought to be compulsorily detained, and so lose his personal liberty, whereas the administration of his property is a matter for the courts of law.

The name 'tribunal' is used in a confusing way for some bodies which have the status of superior courts of law. Examples are the Employment Appeal Tribunal and the Patents Appeal Tribunal, over which High Court judges preside. They are to be regarded as courts and not as tribunals of the kind discussed in this chapter.

'Administrative tribunals'

The designation 'administrative tribunals' is misleading in a number of ways. In the first place, no tribunal can be given power to determine legal questions except by Act of Parliament. Normally a tribunal is constituted directly by the Act itself. Sometimes, however, the power to constitute a tribunal may be delegated by the Act to a minister, but in such cases the Act will make it clear that a tribunal is intended.[13] The statute will give power to the relevant minister (or, for some purposes, to the Lord Chancellor) to appoint the members, clerks, and so forth, and to provide facilities, and usually to make procedural rules for the tribunal.

Secondly, the decisions of most tribunals are in truth judicial rather than administrative, in the sense that the tribunal has to find facts and then apply legal rules to them impartially, without regard to executive policy. Such tribunals have in substance the same functions as courts of law. When, for example, unemployment benefit is awarded by a social security tribunal, its

---

[12] The tribunals have power to direct the discharge of the patient. Formerly in criminal cases they could only give advice to the Home Secretary, but this restriction was held to violate Art. 5 of the European Convention on Human Rights, which requires access to a court for persons deprived of liberty: *X. v. United Kingdom*, ECHR Series A, No. 46 (5 November 1981). The restriction was removed by Mental Health (Amendment) Act 1982, s. 28(4), since replaced by Mental Health Act 1983, s. 79.

[13] e.g. industrial tribunals (Industrial Training Act 1964, s. 12; Employment Protection (Consolidation) Act 1978, s. 128); NHS service committees (National Health Service Act 1977, s. 16); vaccine damage tribunals (Vaccine Damage Payments Act 1979, s. 4).

decision is as objective as that of any court of law.[14] Only two elements
enter into it: the facts as they are proved, and the statutory rules which have
to be applied. The rules may sometimes give the tribunal a measure of
discretion. But discretion is given to be used objectively, and no more alters
the nature of the decision than does the 'judicial discretion' which is familiar
in courts of law. These tribunals therefore have the character of courts, even
though they are enmeshed in the administrative machinery of the state.[15]
They are 'administrative' only because they are part of an administrative
scheme for which a minister is responsible to Parliament, and because the
reasons for preferring them to the ordinary courts are administrative
reasons.

Thirdly, tribunals are not concerned exclusively with cases to which
government departments are parties. Rent assessment committees and
agricultural land tribunals, for example, adjudicate disputes between
landlords and tenants without any departmental intervention.

Fourthly, and most important of all, tribunals are independent. They are
in no way subject to administrative interference as to how they decide any
particular case. No minister can be held responsible for any tribunal's
decision. Nor are tribunals composed of officials or of people who owe
obedience to the administration. It would be as improper for a minister to
try to influence a tribunal's decision as it would be in the case of a court of
law. More will be said about this after tribunals have been distinguished
from inquiries.

Tribunals and inquiries contrasted

In principle there is a clear contrast between the function of a statutory
tribunal and that of a statutory inquiry of the kind discussed in the next
chapter. The typical tribunal finds facts and decides the case by applying
legal rules laid down by statute or regulation. The typical inquiry hears
evidence and finds facts, but the person conducting it finally makes a

---

[14] In R. v. Deputy Industrial Injuries Commissioners ex p. Jones [1962] 2 QB 677 at 685 Lord
Parker C.J. called the Commissioner 'a quasi-judicial tribunal' and so did Lord Diplock in
R. v. Deputy Industrial Injuries Commissioner ex p. Moore [1965] 1 QB 456 at 486. But a quasi-
judicial tribunal is concerned with questions of policy (above, pp. 46, 504) whereas the
Commissioner is concerned only with questions of fact and law. Compare Slaney v. Kean
[1972] Ch. 243 at 251 (General Commissioners of Income Tax judicial 'or at least quasi-
judicial' in determining tax appeals). In A.-G. v. British Broadcasting Corporation [1981] AC
303 the House of Lords held that the functions of a local valuation court are 'administrative
not judicial' (at 340) although that court is concerned solely with questions of fact and law
and Lord Widgery C.J. called it 'one of the clearest examples of an inferior court that we
meet in the field of administrative justice' ([1978] 1 WLR at 483). See further below, p. 929.

[15] It does not follow that they will be classified as courts for particular purposes such as
contempt of court: see below, p. 929.

recommendation to a minister as to how the minister should act on some question of policy, e.g. whether he should grant planning permission for some development scheme. The tribunal need look no further than the facts and the law, for the issue before it is self-contained. The inquiry is concerned with the local aspects of what will usually be a large issue involving public policy which cannot, when it comes to the final decision, be resolved merely by applying law. Tribunals are normally employed where cases can be decided according to rules and there is no reason for the minister to be responsible for the decision. Inquiries are employed where the decision will turn upon what the minister thinks is in the public interest, but where the minister, before he decides, needs to be fully informed and to give fair consideration to objections. In other words, tribunals make judicial decisions, but inquiries are preliminary to administrative or political decisions, often described as quasi-judicial decisions.

But Parliament has experimented with many different bodies and procedures and has in some cases set up tribunals where one would expect to find inquiries and vice versa. Transport licensing, in particular, has been affected by the tradition of employing independent tribunals for deciding what are really questions of policy. The Railway Commission (1873), the Railway and Canal Commission (1888), the Railway Rates Tribunal (1921) and the Transport Tribunal (1947) were successively empowered to control railway rates and charges. This was essentially a commercial and political matter, yet an independent tribunal was employed. Rate control for railways ceased to be necessary when railways ceased to be profitable, and was abolished in 1962.[16] Similarly the licensing of commercial road services was formerly entrusted to tribunals, the Traffic Commissioners; appeals lay from them to the Transport Tribunal in respect of goods vehicle licensing and to the Secretary of State for Transport in respect of passenger services.[17] The logic of these arrangements was not evident, but they survived several investigations.[18] Road service licensing has since been abolished, but the Commissioners remain responsible for public service vehicle operators' licensing, and those appeals now go to the tribunal.[19] But the Secretary of State still takes appeals against traffic regulation conditions attached to licences by traffic commissioners and against refusal of London local service licences.[20] Air transport licensing, which was introduced in 1960 to control the allocation of routes and the scales of charges, is assigned

[16] Transport Act 1962, s. 43.
[17] Transport Act 1968, s. 70 (goods); Public Passenger Vehicles Act 1981, s. 50 (passengers).
[18] See Report of the Committee on Tribunals and Enquiries, Cmnd. 218 (1957), para. 229.
[19] Transport Act 1985, s. 31.
[20] ss. 9, 42.

to the Civil Aviation Authority (formerly the Air Transport Licensing Board) from which appeal lies to the Secretary of State.[21] The Secretary of State formerly had power to give mandatory guidance to the Authority,[22] indicating that this was a licensing system dominated by government policy; but that power was withdrawn in 1980.[23]

Where an appeal has to be decided by a minister, he must necessarily appoint some one to hear the case and advise him. The procedure is therefore that of an inquiry,[24] even though the subject-matter seems more suitable to a tribunal. This is the situation where ministers have to decide questions of fact and law, for example under the social security scheme where certain important questions in claims for benefit are 'Secretary of State's questions', subject to a right of appeal to the court on a point of law.[25] The same is true of appeals to the Secretary of State from the Civil Aviation Authority, mentioned above, and of appeals to the Secretary of State for Trade by disqualified estate agents.[26] In the latter case the appeal is from the Director General of Fair Trading who for this purpose is a statutory tribunal, so that the procedure consists of tribunal followed by inquiry.

Independence

An essential feature of tribunals, as mentioned already, is that they make their own decisions independently and are free from political influence. In the abnormal cases where appeal lies only to a minister it is true that the minister's policy may influence the tribunal through the minister's appellate decisions; but then this is what Parliament intended. In all other cases tribunals are completely free from political control, since Parliament has put the power of decision into the hands of the tribunal and of no one else. A decision taken under any sort of external influence would be invalid.[27]

In order to make this independence a reality, it is fundamental that members of tribunals shall be independent persons, not civil servants.[28] Tribunals have more the character of people's courts than of bureaucratic

---

[21] Civil Aviation Act 1971, ss. 21, 24(6).

[22] s. 3(2). This was subject to approval by both Houses of Parliament.

[23] Civil Aviation Act 1980, s. 12. See the *Laker Airways* case, above, p. 418.

[24] The Tribunals and Inquiries Act 1971 and the jurisdiction of the Council on Tribunals will apply only when the inquiry is obligatory: see below, p. 988.

[25] Social Security Act 1986, 5th sched., Pt. II. Compare *Healey* v. *Minister of Health* [1955] 1 QB 221 (minister's power to decide category of employment).

[26] Estate Agents Act 1979, s. 7; SI 1981 No. 1518.

[27] See above, p. 368.

[28] For two exceptional cases see below, p. 905.

boards. The Lord Chancellor or the relevant minister will appoint the chairmen and members, but people outside the government service will be chosen. Various devices are employed for insulating tribunals from any possibility of influence by ministers. Often there will be a panel system by which the names on the panel are approved by the Lord Chancellor or the minister but the selection for any one sitting is made by the chairman. The Lord Chancellor is usually made responsible where legal qualifications are required, but he is also sometimes responsible for non-legal members.[29] Rent assessment committees are made up from panels of names supplied both by the Lord Chancellor and by the Secretary of State for the Environment; the chairman must be a 'Lord Chancellor's man', and the other members may or may not be.[30] An elaborate panel governs the membership of independent schools tribunals: chairmen are selected from a Lord Chancellor's panel and members from a panel appointed by the Lord President of the Council,[31] the former being legally qualified and the latter being experienced in education. In order to emphasise independence even further, members of social security appeal tribunals are no longer appointed by the Secretary of State but are appointed by the President of those tribunals.[32] Their chairmen are selected from a Lord Chancellor's panel.[33]

The public by no means always gives tribunals credit for their impartiality, often because of minor factors which arouse suspicion. A typical tribunal will have a civil servant as its clerk, who will tell the appellant how to proceed and require him to fill up forms. The tribunal may sit in the department's premises, and the part played by the official representing the department before the tribunal, as well as the position of the clerk, may give an impression of influence. But the truth is to the contrary. Where a large number of more or less routine decisions have to be given in rapid succession, it can sometimes appear that the tribunal and the clerk are working hand in glove and in favour of the ministry. Good chairmen take trouble to guard against this misleading impression, and in general they succeed.

Another fundamental feature of the tribunal system is that procedure is adversary, not inquisitorial. In other words, the business of the tribunal is to

---

[29] e.g. surveyors as members of the Lands Tribunal (Lands Tribunal Act 1949, s. 2) and medical members of medical appeal tribunals (Tribunals and Inquiries Act 1971, s. 7) and of mental health review tribunals (Mental Health Act 1983, 2nd sched.).

[30] Rent Act 1977, 10th sched.

[31] Education Act 1944, 6th sched. But these tribunals are quiescent.

[32] Health and Social Security Act 1984, s. 16, abolishing also the former panel of trade union representatives, one of whom was required to sit in every case. Trade union nominations had proved difficult to obtain.

[33] Tribunals and Inquiries Act 1971, s. 7.

judge between two opposing contentions, as does a court of law, rather than to conduct the case and call for testimony itself. This aspect of the procedure is explained below.

Membership

The personnel of tribunals varies greatly in accordance with the character of their business. A form frequently adopted is the 'balanced tribunal', consisting of an independent chairman, usually legally qualified and appointed by the Lord Chancellor, and two members representing opposed interests. These two members may be chosen from two different panels of persons willing to serve, not themselves in the employment of the ministry but appointed by the minister as representatives of, for example, employers' organisations on one panel and trade unions on the other. Thus an industrial tribunal will consist of a chairman from a Lord Chancellor's panel, and one member from each of the Secretary of State's panels. Similarly an agricultural land tribunal will have a legally qualified chairman assisted by members chosen as representatives of organisations representing property-owners and tenants. Experience has shown that members selected in this way seldom show bias in favour of the interest they are supposed to represent. The principal purpose of the system is to assure every party before the tribunal that at least one member will understand his interests. In tribunals of this kind the chairman will usually be paid, but the members will sometimes be unpaid, giving their time as a public service in the same way as magistrates.

In other cases expert qualifications are indispensable. The law which tribunals have to apply is often of great complexity, sometimes to a degree which perplexes the courts themselves,[34] and tribunals such as social security tribunals, industrial tribunals, the Lands Tribunal, and taxation tribunals may be confronted with formidable legal problems. Accordingly the Social Security Commissioners, who hear appeals from the local tribunals, are highly qualified lawyers holding full-time appointments;[35] and industrial injury and pensions cases involving personal injury are adjudicated by qualified doctors where the issue requires medical diagnosis. The members of the Lands Tribunal, which adjudicates compensation on compulsory purchase of land, rating appeals, and questions concerning the discharge of restrictive covenants, must be qualified lawyers or surveyors.

---

[34] See e.g. R. v. *Industrial Injuries Commissioner ex p. Cable* [1968] 1 QB 729 (difficulties of the 'paired organ' regulations in industrial injury cases); R. v. *National Insurance Commissioner ex p. Hudson* [1972] AC 944 (above, p. 898); Sir R. Micklethwait, *The National Insurance Commissioners*, chs. 8–9.

[35] For valuable information and comment on the work of the commissioners and the law which they administer see Sir R. Micklethwait, *The National Insurance Commissioners*.

The Special Commissioners of Income Tax are revenue experts and, exceptionally, some of them are government officials; they are however acknowledged to be wholly independent in practice—if this were not so, officials would have to be disqualified from membership. Since 1984 they are appointed and administered by the Lord Chancellor.[36] Exceptionally, also, officials may be members of family practitioner committees in the national health service, which are statutory tribunals for some purposes.[37] Another, though different, special case is the Patents Appeal Tribunal, which consists of a High Court judge and is a tribunal only in name.[38]

Some of the more specialised tribunals are organised on a presidential system, the president being the chief adjudicator and also having general responsibility for the working of the tribunals. The President of Industrial Tribunals,[39] the Chief Social Security Commissioner,[40] the President of Social Security Appeal Tribunals and Medical Appeal Tribunals,[41] and the President of Value Added Tax Tribunals[42] thus preside over groups of tribunals, as in effect does the President of the Lands Tribunal.[43] The value added tax tribunals are organised under a president who decides how many of them there shall be and when and where they shall sit.[44] In the social security, industrial and value added tax systems there are also regional chairmen.[45] These arrangements promote efficiency in the organisation of business, and guard against the neglect in which some tribunals may be left. Government departments are so respectful of the principle of non-interference with judicial functions that their tribunals may languish in isolation if no one is responsible for general superintendence.

Tribunals' clerks have an important function and can much assist parties by explaining procedure and other matters. In most cases they are civil servants supplied by the ministry under which the tribunal falls. Originally rent tribunals had to appoint and employ their own clerks, who accordingly had no civil service status, but this disadvantage was removed in 1965.[46]

---

[36] Finance Act 1984, 22nd sched.

[37] Below, p. 907.

[38] It is therefore not subject to the Tribunals and Inquiries Act 1971.

[39] Appointed by the Lord Chancellor under SI 1965 No. 1101, reg. 3. He has power to determine the number of industrial tribunals.

[40] Appointed by the Crown under Social Security Act 1975, s. 97(3).

[41] Appointed by the Lord Chancellor under Health and Social Services and Social Security Adjudications Act 1983, 8th sched., para. 8.

[42] Appointed by the Lord Chancellor under Value Added Tax Act 1983, 8th sched.

[43] Appointed by the Lord Chancellor under the Lands Tribunal Act 1949.

[44] Finance Act 1972, 6th sched.

[45] Appointed by the Lord Chancellor under Health and Social Services and Social Security Adjudications Act 1983, 8th sched., para. 8.

[46] Annual Report of the Council on Tribunals for 1965, para. 27.

Types of appeal

There are numerous different avenues of appeal from tribunals. No right of appeal exists unless conferred by statute,[47] but Parliament, though it has created so many appellate procedures, has followed no consistent pattern. Appeal may lie from one tribunal to another; from a tribunal to a minister; from a tribunal to a court of law; from a minister to a court of law; from a minister to a tribunal; or no appeal may lie at all. An appeal may be on questions of law or fact or both, or on questions of law only. The position for any given tribunal may be seen from the table at the end of this chapter.

(i) *Inter-tribunal appeals*

Social and regulatory legislation sometimes contains its own built-in appeal structure at more than one level. A good example is the social security system.[48] Claims to benefit are first determined by the local social security officer, a departmental official who is not a tribunal, though he has his own statutory status and duties. From his decision there is an appeal to a social security appeal tribunal, consisting of a chairman appointed by the Secretary of State and two members drawn from a panel appointed by the President. From the appeal tribunal appeal lies to a social security commissioner,[49] who is appointed by the Crown and a barrister or solicitor of at least ten years' standing; but appeal lies only on a point of law and only with leave of the chairman or the commissioner.[50] Formerly there was a parallel structure of industrial injuries local appeal tribunals and industrial injuries commissioners for dealing with claims to industrial injury benefit; but that system was merged with national insurance (now social security) in 1966.[51] Claims to disablement benefit (which as opposed to injury benefit requires medical assessment of the degree of disablement[52]) do not go to the social security officer but are referred directly to medical adjudicators, from whom there is an appeal to a medical appeal tribunal, with appeal on a

---

[47] *A.-G.* v. *Sillem* (1864) 10 HLC 704; *R.* v. *Special Commissioners of Income Tax* (1888) 21 QBD 313 at 319.
[48] For the adjudicating authorities see Social Security Act 1975, s. 97 and 10th sched., as amended by Health and Social Services and Social Security Adjudications Act 1983, 8th sched.
[49] For the further appeal to the Court of Appeal see under (iii), below.
[50] Social Security Act 1986, 5th sched., para. 7.
[51] National Insurance Act 1966, s. 8.
[52] Above, p. 220.

point of law only to a social security commissioner.[53] In addition there is an attendance allowance board which determines claims to that benefit, from which appeal lies on a point of law only to a social security commissioner.[54] Formerly there were separate referees for claims to family allowances (now child benefit), but the national insurance (now social security) tribunals took over that work in 1959.[55]

The national health service has an elaborate appeal structure which in some cases allows appeal from one tribunal to another. Complaints by patients against health service practitioners are heard in the first place by the service committees of the family practitioner committees established by area health authorities.[56] The family practitioner committees are primarily administrative bodies, but for this purpose they and their service committees are tribunals and subject to the Tribunals and Inquiries Act 1971.[57] If the family practitioner committee decides that a practitioner should be removed from the health service, he has a right of appeal to the National Health Service Tribunal and he (but no one else) has a further right of appeal to the Secretary of State.[58] This unilateral appeal is regarded as a kind of prerogative of mercy. Where the committee decides on a lesser penalty, such as deduction from remuneration, the practitioner may appeal only the the Secretary of State.[59]

The two-tier system is also provided for immigration cases. Appeals against refusal of leave to enter, conditions imposed, and deportation and similar orders may be made to an adjudicator appointed by the Home Secretary; and from the adjudicator appeal lies to the Immigration Appeal Tribunal, whose members are appointed by the Lord Chancellor.[60]

Appeals from industrial tribunals to the Employment Appeal Tribunal are classified under head (iii) below.

All these rights of appeal, except where otherwise mentioned, extend to questions of both fact and law. In a number of cases it is necessary to obtain leave to appeal. An appeal to a social security commissioner may be made only with leave of the tribunal or of the Commissioner.[61] An appeal to the

[53] Social Security Act 1975, ss. 107–13.

[54] Same Act, ss. 105, 106.

[55] Family Allowances Act 1959, s. 1.

[56] National Health Service Act 1977, s. 15, 5th sched. Pt. II; SI 1974 No. 455. See *R. v. Ministry of Health ex p. Ellis* [1968] 1 QB 84, refusing the right of appeal to a successful complainant who thought that a fine of £5 was too lenient. Appeals are available only to unsuccessful parties.

[57] Same Act, 4th sched., para. 134.

[58] National Health Service Act 1977, s. 46.

[59] SI 1974 No. 455, reg. 11.

[60] Immigration Act 1971, Pt. II. For exceptions see above, p. 228.

[61] SI 1987 No. 214, reg. 3.

Immigration Appeal Tribunal requires leave either of the adjudicator or of the Tribunal.[62] If leave is wrongfully refused, for example where an adjudicator has misdirected himself in law, judicial review is available.[63]

The title 'appeal tribunal' by no means always indicates that the tribunal hears appeals from a lower tribunal. Social security appeal tribunals and betting levy appeal tribunals, for example, are tribunals of first instance only, hearing appeals against rulings made administratively by officials.

(ii) *Appeals from tribunals to ministers*

This class has always been an object of legal criticism, but it survives in several areas, particularly in two which are rich in anomalies: transport licensing and the national health service. The ministerial appeals provided in the fields of passenger road services and civil aviation have already been mentioned,[64] and those available in the national health service have just been explained under 'inter-tribunal appeals'. Under the Estate Agents Act 1979 an appeal lies from the Director General of Fair Trading, who for this purpose is a tribunal, to the Secretary of State for Trade.

(iii) *Appeals from tribunals to courts of law*

It is now the generally accepted principle that there should be a right of appeal from a tribunal to the High Court on a point of law, in order that the law may be correctly and uniformly applied. In the period before this need was recognised different local tribunals might be applying the same law in contradictory ways, though this danger was mitigated by the extension of judicial review of errors of law.[65]

The Tribunals and Inquiries Act 1971,[66] following the Act of 1958, confers the right of appeal on a point of law in the case of a number of tribunals such as the National Health Service Tribunal, and rent assessment committees; and the statutory catalogue can be extended by order.[67] In other cases the appeal on a point of law may lie direct to the Court of Appeal, as it does from a Social Security Commissioner,[68] the Lands Tribunal[69] and the Transport Tribunal.[70] In others, again, an appeal to the

---

[62] SI 1984 No. 2041, rule 14.
[63] *R. v. Immigration Appeal Tribunal ex p. Kumar* [1986] The Times, 13 August.
[64] Above, p. 901.
[65] Below, p. 910.
[66] s. 13.
[67] s. 15(3). Thus VAT tribunals were added by SI 1972 No. 1210.
[68] Social Security Act 1980, s. 14.
[69] Lands Tribunal Act 1949, s. 3(3).
[70] Transport Act 1985, 4th sched.

High Court on a point of law is provided by legislation outside the Tribunals and Inquiries Act, as in the case of the Special Commissioners of Income Tax[71] and the agricultural land tribunals.[72] Occasionally the appeal is not as of a right, but only if the tribunal or the court in its discretion so directs.[73] From industrial tribunals appeal lies in certain cases to the High Court on a point of law under the Tribunals and Inquiries Act 1971. But in employment protection, equal pay, and discrimination cases appeal lies to the Employment Appeal Tribunal under the Employment Protection (Consolidation) Act 1978, in most cases on a question of law only, but in certain cases (including trade union membership[74]) also on a question of fact.[75] The Employment Appeal Tribunal is equivalent to the High Court, and therefore not subject to the Act of 1971, although in addition to judges it contains experts on industrial relations appointed by the Lord Chancellor and the Secretary of State jointly, two of whom sit with a single judge.[76] It has the remarkable feature that the two lay members can (and occasionally do) overrule the judge's opinion on a question of law.

Except as above mentioned, these appeals are confined to points of law. What this means, and how the appeal operates, is discussed below.[77]

(iv) *Appeals from ministers to courts of law*

The appeal to the court on a point of law is sometimes given from a minister's decision, e.g. from decisions on 'Secretary of State's questions' under the social security system, already mentioned,[78] from certain Secretary of State's decisions under planning law;[79] and, formerly, from Secretary of State's decisions on passenger road service appeals.[80]

(v) *Appeals from ministers to tribunals*

This is an unusual avenue of appeal, but it can be illustrated from the Immigration Act 1971 under which, as explained elsewhere,[81] appeal

---

[71] Taxes Management Act 1970, s. 56.

[72] Agriculture (Miscellaneous Provisions) Act 1954, s. 6.

[73] As from Mental Health Review Tribunals to the High Court under Mental Health Act 1983, s. 78(8); and from the Industry Arbitration Tribunal to the Court of Appeal under Industry Act 1975, 3rd sched.

[74] Unreasonable exclusion or expulsion from trade unions is a matter for industrial tribunals under Employment Act 1980, s. 4.

[75] s. 136. From the tribunal appeal lies to the Court of Appeal on a question of law.

[76] s. 135 and 11th sched.

[77] Below, p. 937.

[78] Above, p. 902.

[79] Above, p. 189.

[80] Tribunals and Inquiries Act 1971, s. 13(5).

[81] Above, p. 228.

sometimes lies from Secretary of State's decisions in immigration and deportation cases to an adjudicator and to the Immigration Appeal Tribunal.

(vi) *No right of appeal*

In a number of cases there is no right of appeal: instances are the National Health Service Tribunal, the Immigration Appeal Tribunal, and the Betting Levy Appeal Tribunal. Supplementary Benefit (now Social Security) Appeal Tribunals and National Insurance (now Social Security) Commissioners were in the same category until 1977 and 1980 respectively, representing the earlier welfare state philosophy which aimed at cutting tribunals off from the legal system so far as possible, and which has now been much modified. The situation changed radically in 1952, when the Court of Appeal revived judicial review for error on the face of the record,[82] and in 1958 when the first Tribunals and Inquiries Act gave a right to reasoned decisions on which the revived judicial review could operate.[83] Since a decision containing an error of law could thenceforward be quashed on certiorari, the provision of a right of appeal on a point of law no longer seemed necessary. The existence of this broad ground of judicial review, which has since grown even broader,[84] has been used as an argument for not providing a right of appeal in addition.[85]

Whatever rights of appeal may or may not have been provided by statute, therefore, it is always necessary to remember that the court has extensive powers of review which may cover much the same ground. The effect of these developments in the case of the national insurance (social security) system has been mentioned elsewhere.[86] Similarly the High Court was able to quash decisions of supplementary benefit appeal tribunals, at a time when no appeal lay from them, if they revealed error of law, e.g. by misinterpreting regulations.[87] Now, however, appeals lie to the courts of law in social security matters as explained under (iii) above. The importance of this right has at last been generally recognised.

[82] Above, p. 307.

[83] Below, p. 934.

[84] Above, p. 308.

[85] As the Council on Tribunals found in the case of the Immigration Appeal Tribunal: Annual Report of the Council on Tribunals, 1972–3, p. 16.

[86] Above, p. 319.

[87] *R. v. Greater Birmingham Appeal Tribunal ex p. Simper* [1974] QB 543 (certiorari granted); *R. v. West London Supplementary Benefits Appeal Tribunal ex p. Taylor* [1975] 1 WLR 1048 (certiorari and mandamus granted). On these tribunals see Bell, *Research Study on Supplementary Benefit Appeal Tribunals* (HMSO); Adler and Bradley, *Justice, Discretion and Poverty*; Herman, *Administrative Justice and Supplementary Benefits*.

PROBLEMS OF TRIBUNALS. THE FRANKS COMMITTEE

Errors and complaints

The intensive social legislation which followed World War II not only put great trust in tribunals: it was based on an attitude of positive hostility to the courts of law. This was the era when a minister could speak of 'judicial sabotage of socialist legislation'.[88] The policy was to administer social services in the greatest possible detachment from the ordinary legal system, and to dispense with the refined techniques of procedure and decision which the courts had developed over the centuries.

It soon became evident that the price to be paid for this policy was more than the public would endure. During the following decade a swelling chorus of complaint forced a reappraisal of the philosophy of the tribunal system. It was found that legal standards and principles had been disregarded in too cavalier a manner. Steps had to be taken to bring the tribunals back into touch with the regular courts, to improve the standard of justice meted out by them, and to impose order and discipline generally. The spadework was done by the Committee on Administrative Tribunals and Enquiries (the Franks Committee). The necessary reforms were made by the Tribunals and Inquiries Act 1958 and by administrative changes which accompanied it. It may now be said generally that tribunals have found their place in the legal system, and that they operate harmoniously with it instead of in opposition.

Anomalies and injustices

Many of the complaints made before 1958 were caused by the lack of rights of appeal and by procedural anomalies. Some tribunals sat in public, others sat in private. Some allowed unrestricted legal representation, others allowed none. Some followed the legal rules of evidence, others disregarded them. Some allowed full examination and cross-examination of witnesses, others allowed witnesses to be questioned only through the chairman. Some took evidence on oath, others did not. Some gave reasoned decisions, others did not. The social security tribunals (as they are now called) well illustrated some of these diversities. National insurance local tribunals sat in private and allowed representation by any one except a qualified lawyer.[89] Industrial injuries local tribunals sat in public, unless they decided otherwise, and would permit legal representation with the chairman's consent for special reasons.

---

[88] 425 HC Deb 1983 (27 July 1946. Mr A. Bevan).
[89] SI 1948 No. 1144, reg. 13.

Some of these discrepancies had good reasons behind them originally. Tribunals which inquire into the intimate personal circumstances of poor people, such as supplementary benefit appeal tribunals, ought to sit in private. And where a patient under the national health service wishes to make a complaint against a doctor, the whole procedure may fail to work if the complainant knows that he will have to face a hostile lawyer. But in other tribunals a rule that allows representation by any one except a lawyer is as unreasonable as a rule that any one may prescribe medicine except a doctor. Rules designed to produce cheapness and informality of procedure, which were suitable for some tribunals, were being applied indiscriminately.

As a sample of the kind of complaint made by people whose livelihoods were greatly affected by tribunals' decisions may be cited the following comments on rent tribunals which were made to the Franks Committee by the Justice for Landladies Association.

1. There is no appeal against the tribunal's decision. Tremendous power, which can ruin a person's life, has been put into the hands of three men. Yet there is no higher court in which their decisions can be tested.
2. The three on the bench of the tribunal need have no proper legal qualifications. A court of no appeal has been put into the hands of men who are generally neither qualified lawyers, magistrates or judges.
3. There is no evidence on oath, and therefore can be no proper cross-examination as in a court of law. Statements are made on both sides, but the time-honoured method of getting to the truth cannot be used.
4. Procedure is as the tribunal shall determine. No rules have been laid down as to the procedure at a tribunal hearing. Witnesses may be heard or not heard at their pleasure.

The Committee on Administrative Tribunals and Enquiries

The Committee presided over by Sir Oliver Franks (as he then was) was commissioned by the Lord Chancellor in 1955 as an immediate, though illogical, result of the *Crichel Down* case of 1954.[90] That case really had nothing to do with tribunals and inquiries, but was a manifestation of public concern over the way in which government departments had handled a landowner's request (based on no legal right) to have land which had been compulsorily acquired returned after the war. This was a purely departmental matter. It was what might be called, with due apology to the civil service, ordinary maladministration. The correct remedy for this was the ombudsman, but the time for him was not yet ripe. Meanwhile the public outcry was to some extent appeased by commissioning the review of

[90] Report of the Inquiry by Sir Andrew Clarke Q.C., Cmd. 9176 (1954).

tribunals and inquiries. The Committee was not primarily a legal body, though it had strong legal membership.

The Committee had to make a fundamental choice between two conflicting attitudes, the legal and the administrative. The legal attitude was that tribunals must be regarded as part of the machinery of justice and organised accordingly. The administrative attitude was that tribunals were primarily part of the machinery of administration. The head of the Lord Chancellor's Department and the Treasury Solicitor, being both lawyers and administrators, were able to appreciate both viewpoints, but other government departments strongly pressed the 'administrative view'. Witnesses from the universities put forward suggestions for a permanent body of some kind to concern itself with tribunal procedure, to supervise the making of procedural rules, and to make sure that the elements of legal justice were observed throughout the whole system with as much uniformity as was practicable.

The Committee's Report

In its Report (1957)[91] the Committee first acknowledged the undoubted need for tribunals as a supplementary system of judicature. No general transfer of functions from tribunals to courts of law was suggested. On the other hand, the Committee firmly adopted the legal view as to tribunals' status. They said:[92]

Much of the official evidence, including that of the Joint Permanent Secretary to the Treasury, appeared to reflect the view that tribunals should properly be regarded as part of the machinery of administration, for which the government must retain a close and continuing responsibility. Thus, for example, tribunals in the social service field would be regarded as adjuncts to the administration of the services themselves. We do not accept this view. We consider that tribunals should properly be regarded as machinery provided by Parliament for adjudication rather than as part of the machinery of administration. The essential point is that in all these cases Parliament has deliberately provided for a decision independent of the Department concerned . . . and the intention of Parliament to provide for the independence of tribunals is clear and unmistakable.

To make tribunals conform to the standard which Parliament thus had in mind, three fundamental objectives were proclaimed: openness, fairness and impartiality.

In the field of tribunals openness appears to us to require the publicity of proceedings and knowledge of the essential reasoning underlying the decisions; fairness to require the adoption of a clear procedure which enables parties to know

---

[91] Cmnd. 218 (1957).
[92] Para. 40.

their rights, to present their case fully and to know the case which they have to meet; and impartiality to require the freedom of tribunals from the influence, real or apparent, of Departments concerned with the subject-matter of their decisions.

The Council on Tribunals

The Committee's central proposal was that there should be a permanent Council on Tribunals in order to provide some standing machinery for the general supervision of tribunal organisation and procedure. It was to consist of both legal and lay members, with lay members in the majority—thus manifesting the spirit which runs all through the Report, that tribunal reform was to be based on general public opinion, and was not a kind of lawyers' counter-revolution against modern methods of government and the welfare state. Such a body, it was hoped, would provide the focal point which had previously been lacking. It was to be appointed by the Lord Chancellor and to report to him, so that the Lord Chancellor would undertake a general responsibility for the well-being of tribunals, in somewhat the same way as he already did for the courts of law. This reflects the Committee's conception of tribunals as one branch of the judicial system. It also reflects dissatisfaction with ad hoc inquiries such as the Ministers' Powers Committee of 1932 and the Franks Committee itself. A body is needed which can deal with complaints as they arise, instead of leaving them to build up into a volume of public discontent which, every twenty-five years or so, discharges itself in a special but temporary inquest by a committee which merely reports once and then dissolves.

Other recommendations

The following are a selection from the Committee's other recommendations on tribunals.

1. Chairmen of tribunals should be appointed and removed by the Lord Chancellor; members should be appointed by the Council and removed by the Lord Chancellor.
2. Chairmen should ordinarily have legal qualifications—and always in the case of appellate tribunals.
3. Remuneration for service on tribunals should be reviewed by the Council on Tribunals.
4. Procedure for each tribunal, based on common principles but suited to its needs, should be formulated by the Council.
5. The citizen should be helped to know in good time the case he will have to meet.
6. Hearings should be in public, except only in cases involving (i) public security, (ii) intimate personal or financial circumstances, or (iii) professional reputation, where there is a preliminary investigation.

7. Legal representation should always be allowed, save only in most exceptional circumstances. In the case of national insurance tribunals the Committee were content to make legal representation subject to the chairman's consent.

8. Tribunals should have power to take evidence on oath, to subpoena witnesses and to award costs. Parties should be free to question witnesses directly.

9. Decisions should be reasoned, as full as possible, and made available to the parties in writing. Final appellate tribunals should publish and circulate selected decisions.

10. There should be a right of appeal on fact, law and merits to an appeal tribunal, except where the lower tribunal is exceptionally strong.

11. There should also be an appeal on a point of law to the courts; and judicial control by the remedies of certiorari, prohibition and mandamus should never be barred by statute.

12. The Council should advise, and report quickly, on the application of all these principles to the various tribunals, and should advise on any proposal to establish a new tribunal.

In addition there were numerous recommendations about particular tribunals.

THE REFORMS OF 1958

The Tribunals and Inquiries Act

The Tribunals and Inquiries Act 1958 gave effect to the policy of the Franks Committee's report, though with some variations in detail. The Act was short and did not present the whole picture, since important reforms were also made by changes of administrative regulations and practice. It has now been replaced by the Tribunals and Inquiries Act 1971, a consolidating Act which makes no change of substance.

The Act of 1958 provided first for the Council on Tribunals.[93] It has a maximum membership of sixteen;[94] but there is special provision for a Scottish Committee of the Council, consisting partly of persons not members of the Council itself. The Council emerged as a purely advisory body, without the function of appointing tribunal members, but with general oversight over tribunals and inquiries. The tribunals under its superintendence were listed in a schedule, which included the great majority of those considered by the Committee. It was probably right that such a body, which is intended to be a watch-dog and independent of ministerial control, should not be given executive functions; it was

[93] ss. 1–3.
[94] Including the Parliamentary Commissioner for Administration: above, p. 96.

designed to bark but not to bite. It is not therefore a court of appeal, or a council of state on the French or Italian model. But it has to keep under review the 'constitution and working' of the listed tribunals, and report on any other tribunal questions which the government may refer to it. In practice it receives complaints from individuals and invites testimony from witnesses. It is also frequently consulted by government departments in the ordinary course of their work. Its annual report must be laid before Parliament. It is specifically empowered to make *general* recommendations as to the membership of the listed tribunals, and it must be consulted before any new procedural rules for them are made.[95] Some particulars of the Council's work will be found below.

As the Franks Committee had recommended, the Council on Tribunals consists partly of lawyers and partly of lay members, the lay members being in the majority. The purpose of the lay majority is to make sure that the Council's guiding principle shall be the ordinary man's sense of justice and fair play, freed so far as possible from legal technicality. The membership comprises wide experience in industrial, commercial and trade union affairs, as well as administrative experience contributed by eminent retired civil servants. This structure has both advantages and disadvantages.[96] Although much of the Council's work, such as the vetting of Bills in Parliament and procedural regulations, requires the aid of lawyers, its policy is to evolve and maintain the standards which the public demands of tribunals, rather than to copy the practices of the established courts of law.[97] But naturally the elements of substantial justice are to a large extent the same in both systems.

Other reforms made by the Act of 1958

The Tribunals and Inquiries Act 1958 also made the following provisions.

1. Chairmen of rent tribunals[98] and of tribunals dealing with national insurance, industrial injuries, national assistance, and national service were to be selected by their ministries from panels nominated by the Lord Chancellor.[99]
2. Membership of any of the listed tribunals, or of a panel connected with it, could be terminated only with the Lord Chancellor's consent.[1]

---

[95] Act of 1971, ss. 5, 10.

[96] See below, p. 920.

[97] For accounts of the Council's work see its Annual Reports; 1960 PL 351 (Wade); 1965 PL 321 (J. F. Garner); [1984] *PL* 73 (D. G. T. Williams); Schwartz and Wade, *Legal Control of Government*, 174–80; Jackson, *The Machinery of Justice in England*, 7th edn., 166.

[98] As to rent assessment committees, which now do the work of rent tribunals, see above, p. 903.

[99] Tribunals and Inquiries Act 1971, s. 7.

[1] Act of 1971, s. 8.

3. No procedural rules or regulations for the listed tribunals might be made without consultation with the Council on Tribunals.[2]
4. A right of appeal to the High Court on a point of law was given in the case of a number of specified tribunals, including rent tribunals,[3] and tribunals dealing with children, employment, schools, nurses, and mines.[4] In various other cases this right already existed, as explained earlier.
5. Other tribunals could be brought within the Act by ministerial order.[5] Since Parliament has continued to create new tribunals as fast as ever, many additions have been made to the schedule, including mental health review tribunals, betting levy appeal tribunals, industrial tribunals, rent assessment committees, immigration tribunals, VAT tribunals, school allocation appeal committees, the data protection tribunal, and the financial services tribunal.
6. Judicial control by means of certain remedies (certiorari and mandamus) was safeguarded. This is discussed elsewhere.[6]
7. The Act gave a legal right to a reasoned decision from any of the listed tribunals, provided this was requested on or before the giving or notification of the decision. This is discussed below.[7]
8. The ministers responsible under the Act, and to whom the Council on Tribunals was to report, were the Lord Chancellor and the Secretary of State for Scotland (replaced for this purpose in 1973 by the Lord Advocate[8]).[9]

The Act fell short of the Committee's recommendations in certain respects, for instance in its arrangements as to the appointment of chairmen and members of tribunals. Perhaps the most notable divergence was in the failure to provide for appeals on questions of fact and merits. The Committee recommended a right of appeal on 'fact, law and merits', but the Act provided only a right of appeal on a question of law. Thus the Committee's proposal that there should be a right of appeal from rent tribunals to county courts remained unfulfilled, and no right of appeal was given, except on a point of law, from the rent assessment committees set up by the Rent Act 1965. Nor has the Council on Tribunals recommended any change: it has investigated the question of appeals from rent tribunals and concluded that the balance of advantage is in preserving the finality of the tribunals' decisions on matters of fact.[10] Jurisdictional facts are of course reviewable independently.[11]

---

[2] Act of 1971, s. 10.
[3] Rent assessment committees were added by the Act of 1971, s. 13.
[4] Act of 1971, s. 13.
[5] Act of 1971, s. 15.
[6] Above, p. 729.
[7] Below, p. 934.
[8] SI 1972 No. 2002.
[9] Act of 1971, ss. 2, 4.
[10] Annual Report for 1962, para. 50.
[11] Above, p. 280.

The schedule of tribunals covered by the Act includes almost all tribunals. But where they have executive as well as judicial functions, the Act does not apply to the former.[12] Exceptional cases to which the Act does not apply at all are medical boards,[13] attendance allowance boards,[14] and housing benefit review boards[15] (components of the social security system); rent scrutiny boards, which formerly fixed 'fair rents' for houses provided by local authorities;[16] boards of prison visitors who adjudicate disciplinary offences by prisoners;[17] medical practices committees which deal with the allocation of practices under the National Health Service;[18] the tribunal constituted under the Interception of Communications Act 1985;[19] and 'tribunals' of High Court status, such as the Employment Appeal Tribunal[20] and the Patents Appeal Tribunal.[21] The Foreign Compensation Commission, which assesses claims for loss of foreign property, was excluded originally but is now included.[22] The Act was not concerned with domestic tribunals, as they are often called, even when established by statute, e.g. the Disciplinary Committee of the Law Society, or the General Medical Council; or with non-statutory bodies such as trade unions and their disciplinary committees, or with professional associations, universities and colleges. Such bodies fall outside administrative law since they form no part of the machinery of government.

Administrative reforms

The Tribunals and Inquiries Act 1958 was accompanied by many administrative reforms which did not require legislation. The inconsistencies in national insurance and industrial injuries tribunals as regards sitting in public and the right of legal representation were removed by order.[23]

---

[12] Act of 1971, s. 19(4).
[13] Now replaced by adjudicating medical practitioners. Appeal lies to a medical appeal tribunal, to which the Act applies.
[14] From an attendance allowance board appeal lies on a point of law to a social security commissioner, to whom the Act applies.
[15] Constituted under S.I. 1982 No. 1124.
[16] Housing Finance Act 1972, s. 51. No appeal was provided.
[17] Prison Act 1952. s. 6.
[18] National Health Service Act 1946, s. 34(2); 1977, s. 7. The appeal bodies dealing with refusal of certificates of medical experience, constituted by S.I. 1979 No. 1644, were also not brought within the Act.
[19] s. 7.
[20] Employment Protection (Consolidation) Act 1978, s. 135.
[21] Patents Act 1949, s. 85.
[22] SI 1984 No. 1247.
[23] SI 1958 Nos. 701, 702.

These tribunals (amalgamated in 1966[24] and now known as social security appeal tribunals[25]) sit in public unless the tribunal otherwise directs, and the right to representation (legal or otherwise) is unrestricted. Administrative steps were also taken to ensure that most chairmen of tribunals should have legal qualifications.

The extent to which the various recommendations of the Franks Committee were implemented may be seen from a survey published by the Council on Tribunals in 1964.[26]

Work of the Council on Tribunals

The work of the Council on Tribunals is explained in its annual reports and, in particular, in its special report on its functions published in 1980.[27]

Although the Council has no legal right to be consulted about Bills in Parliament constituting or affecting tribunals, it is in practice consulted as the Franks Committee intended. The Council comments on Bills in much the same way as it does on procedural rules, and in particular it attempts to help departments drafting provisions for new tribunals. In this way it has been able, for example, to secure a statutory right to be heard for a licence-holder threatened with cancellation of his licence.

In some cases the Council has not been satisfied with the reception of its suggestions about Bills, which are sometimes too far advanced before the Council is consulted. The Council has also proposed that there should be some procedure for making its views publicly known when Bills are debated, since otherwise Parliament may be unaware that important questions of tribunal policy arise. Formal representations were made on these matters to the Lord Chancellor,[28] but in vain.

Confronted with these and other impediments, the Council in 1980 made a special report[29] on its functions, reviewing its constitution, staffing, responsibilities and effectiveness. It recommended, inter alia, that it should be concerned with the whole area of administrative adjudication, that it should have a statutory right to be consulted on draft legislation, that its comments on draft legislation and regulations should be laid before Parliament at the time, and that it should have statutory power to deal with complaints and call for papers. The government rejected all these recommendations, though accepting that the arrangements for consul-

---

[24] National Insurance Act 1966, s. 8.
[25] Health and Social Services and Social Security Adjudications Act 1983, s. 1.
[26] Annual Report for 1963, Appendix A.
[27] Cmnd. 7805.
[28] Council on Tribunals, Annual Report for 1970–1, p. 4 and Appendix A.
[29] Cmnd. 7805.

tation about procedural rules should be clarified and that informal guidelines might be formulated for consultation about draft Bills.[30] The Council later drew up a code of practice for consultation which it asked government departments to follow.[31]

The Council has had most impact in a miscellany of relatively minor matters. It has secured many amendments to draft Bills, rules and regulations. It has made various studies, for example of rent tribunals[32] and supplementary benefit appeal tribunals.[33] It has investigated various complaints made to it by dissatisfied parties, and in some cases has been able to reform tribunals' practices. It has secured improvements in tribunals' accommodation by following up complaints, and also as a result of its members' visits to tribunal hearings. It has thus acted as a kind of ombudsman in the sphere of tribunals, as also in that of inquiries. For some years now the flow of complaints about tribunals has been much reduced. This may be in some degree a measure of the success of the reforms of 1958 and the improvements effected subsequently by government departments, stimulated in some cases by the Council.

The Council remains handicapped by its weak political position and its scanty resources.[34] By comparison with the Parliamentary Commissioner for Administration, who is equipped with effective powers and a large staff, the Council has proved relatively impotent in securing attention for its recommendations except in minor matters. It has not succeeded in establishing any connection with Parliament of the kind which gives such strength to the Parliamentary Commissioner, having failed to secure that its views about tribunal organisation should be made available publicly in connection with Bills. It therefore remains an inconspicuous advisory committee. Its heterogeneous membership, furthermore, is not well suited to its work, much of which requires the ability to handle technical legal material and also some systematic knowledge of administrative law. Compared with the Australian Administrative Review Council,[35] which is concerned with the whole field of judicial review as well as with the organisation and procedure of tribunals, the Council of Tribunals is confined within narrow limits. But at least its provides a permanent body which can study and advise on some important problems of administrative justice as they arise, and which can comment and criticise from an independent standpoint.

---

[30] 419 HL Deb 118 (27 April 1981).
[31] Annual Report for 1981–2, Appendix C.
[32] Annual Report for 1962, Pt. IV.
[33] Special Report on Functions of the Council (above), Appendix 3.
[34] Annual Report for 1985–6, para. 3, 73.
[35] Constituted by the Administrative Appeals Tribunal Act 1975, s. 51.

REORGANISATION OF TRIBUNALS

Danger of proliferation

The tribunal system has an inherent resistance to uniformity and simplicity. When legislation is in preparation the line of least resistance is usually to create new tribunals rather than to reorganise those already existing. This tendency, if unchecked, leads to a jungle of different jurisdictions which are as inconvenient to the citizen as they are bewildering. Just as in the nineteenth century the accumulation of traditional courts of law with their awkward jurisdictional divisions had to be swept away by the Judicature Acts 1873–5, so in the twentieth century the network of specialised tribunals needs reorganisation from time to time.

The policy, therefore, should be to constitute fewer and stronger tribunals by amalgamating or grouping the existing tribunals according to their functions, as by unifying those concerned with social security benefits, those concerned with land, those concerned with national health service, and so on. Thus the multifarious jurisdictions which new legislation is constantly augmenting would be rationalised. The Franks Committee saw little scope for this at the time of their report. But subsequently the local tribunals dealing with family allowances and industrial injuries were merged in the national insurance tribunals.[36] An important unifying tendency has been the use of industrial tribunals for a number of different purposes. But the simplification of the national health service system that the Franks Committee favoured has not been carried out: the proposal was that the National Health Service Tribunal should be the final tribunal of appeal and that appeals to the minister should be abolished; but all the professional associations opposed the suggestion and the Council of Tribunals felt unable to press it.[37]

A clear case for amalgamation, which the Council pressed strongly, arose when rent assessment committees were set up by the Rent Act 1965.[38] Rent tribunals dating from 1946 were already in existence and would have been improved by revision of their arrangements. But instead of constituting one type of tribunal for dealing with all rents, or empowering the minister to do so later, the Act of 1965 created rent assessment committees alongside but distinct from the existing rent tribunals, with an awkward jurisdictional division between them

[36] Family Allowances Act 1959, s. 1; National Insurance Act 1966, s. 8.
[37] Annual Report for 1964, para. 47. The arrangements are regarded as a kind of treaty between the medical profession and the government, and change is difficult to achieve.
[38] Annual Report for 1965, para. 20.

depending on whether the premises were furnished or unfurnished.[39] The desirability of amalgamation was admitted in Parliament and minor provision was made for overlap of membership. But the Act was passed in such haste that the opportunity was lost. The Council on Tribunals made emphatic representations to the Lord Chancellor about the dangers of proliferation of this kind.[40] It was not until 1980 that the residual functions of rent tribunals were finally transferred to rent assessment committees and the tribunals were abolished.[41]

Beneficial amalgamations were also made when national insurance local tribunals and supplementary benefits appeal tribunals were merged into the social security appeal tribunals[42] and when registered homes tribunals took charge of the various appeals concerning residential homes, nursing homes and children's homes.[43]

Industrial tribunals provide a good example of the groupings of a number of different jurisdictions in one strong tribunal. These tribunals have grown greatly in importance and have developed into labour courts with wide jurisdiction and a heavy case-load. After they were first constituted for the sole purpose of hearing industrial training levy appeals,[44] they were called upon to deal with redundancy payments,[45] selective employment tax (now abolished),[46] certain compensation appeals,[47] and disputes about statements of terms of employment[48] and about 'dock work'.[49] In addition they have been given extensive jurisdiction over employment questions, including unfair dismissal,[50] equal pay,[51] sex[52] and race[53] discrimination, and unreasonable exclusion or expulsion from trade unions.[54] As mentioned earlier, these tribunals are organised under a presidential system, as also are the social security tribunals.

[39] See e.g. *Thomas* v. *Pascal* [1969] 1 WLR 1475. Under the Rent Act 1974, s. 1, the criterion is whether the landlord resides on the premises: Megarry and Wade, *Real Property*, 5th edn., 1107.
[40] Annual Report for 1970–1, Appendix A.
[41] Housing Act 1980, s. 72, providing however that when performing those functions the Committee shall be known as a rent tribunal.
[42] Health and Social Services and Social Security Adjudications Act 1983, ss. 1, 2.
[43] Same Act, 4th sched.
[44] Industrial Training Act 1964, s. 12.
[45] Employment Protection (Consolidation) Act 1978, s. 91.
[46] Selective Employment Payments Act 1966, s. 7.
[47] Employment Protection (Consolidation) Act 1978, s. 130.
[48] Employment Protection (Consolidation) Act 1978, s. 11.
[49] Docks and Harbours Act 1966, s. 51.
[50] Employment Protection (Consolidation) Act 1978, s. 67.
[51] Equal Pay Act 1970, s. 2.
[52] Sex Discrimination Act 1975, s. 63.
[53] Race Relations Act 1976, s. 54.
[54] Employment Act 1980, s. 4.

PROCEDURE OF TRIBUNALS

Adversary procedure

It is fundamental that the procedure before a tribunal, like that in a court of law, should be adversary and not inquisitorial.[55] The tribunal should have both sides of the case presented to it and should judge between them, without itself having to conduct an inquiry of its own motion, enter into the controversy, and call evidence for or against either party. It if allows itself to become involved in the investigation and argument, parties will quickly lose confidence in its impartiality, however fair-minded it may be. This principle is observed throughout the tribunal system, even in the adjudging of small claims before social security local tribunals and supplementary benefit appeal tribunals by a departmental officer. Naturally this does not mean that the tribunal should not tactfully assist an applicant to develop his case, particulary when he has no representative to speak for him, just as a judge will do with an unrepresented litigant.

In 1965 the Council on Tribunals discovered that the tribunal constituted under the Prevention of Fraud (Investments) Act 1958 was conducted inquisitorially. Although called a 'tribunal of inquiry', this tribunal had in fact a judicial function in that it had to judge whether charges of misconduct against dealers in securities were well founded, before reporting to the Board of Trade. The Board of Trade merely referred the charges to the tribunal, which at the hearing had to inquire into them itself without any one appearing for (so to speak) the prosecution. The dealer whose livelihood was at stake would naturally conclude that the tribunal was predisposed against him. The procedure was changed as soon as the objections to it were pointed out, and evidence for the charges was presented by the Department of Trade in the normal adversary way.[56] Yet tribunals concerned with financial business continue to be given investigatory functions. Two recent examples are the Financial Services Tribunal,[57] which has replaced the tribunal established by the Act of 1958, and the Insolvency Practitioners Tribunal.[58]

Tribunal procedures ought to be simple and not legalistic, but this ideal is difficult to attain when the statutes and regulations to be applied are

---

[55] It does not follow that a party can always withdraw: *Hanson* v. *Church Commissioners* [1978] QB 823.

[56] Council on Tribunals, Annual Report for 1965, para. 45.

[57] Financial Services Act 1986, s. 98.

[58] Insolvency Act 1985, s. 8, criticised by the Council on Tribunals, Annual Report for 1985–6, para. 4.19. Another example, for which there are special reasons, is the tribunal established by the Interception of Communications Act 1985, s. 7 (with which the Council on Tribunals is not concerned).

extremely complex, as they are most conspicuously in the field of social security. The Royal Commission on Legal Services has called for a general review by the Council on Tribunals, so that applicants may be able to conduct their own cases whenever possible.[59]

Procedural rules

Experience has shown that published rules of procedure are highly desirable. Although the Council on Tribunals does not itself draw up procedural rules as the Franks Committee recommended, it has to be consulted before rules are made for any of the tribunals under its supervision.[60] The usual practice is for each type of tribunal to be equipped with its own set of rules by ministerial order. The Council therefore considers all rules for new tribunals, and any revised or amending rules for other tribunals. In the course of its first ten years the Council considered about a hundred sets of rules. A general account of this work is given in one of its reports,[61] and its annual reports contain details. References to the rules for the various tribunals are given in the table at the end of this chapter.

In scrutinising procedural rules the Council endeavours to promote simplicity, intelligibility and consistency, with particular attention to matters such as publicity of hearings, the right of representation and the right of cross-examination. A great many amendments in draft rules have been secured with the co-operation of government departments, providing for example for the disclosure to both sides of information given to the tribunal, for freedom from the legal rules of evidence, and for unrestricted rights of representation. A number of draft rules have been criticised as being ultra vires and have been withdrawn.[62]

Tribunals are so diverse in their nature that, although considerable progress has been made towards procedural uniformity, there is nothing as yet resembling a common code of procedure, and there are exceptions to almost every rule.[63] Even the rules that legal representation should be allowed, and that reasons should be given for decisions, are subject to exceptions in the respective cases of complaints against health service practitioners and mental health adjudications, as noted below.

It is therefore all the more necessary for every set of procedural rules to

---

[59] Cmnd. 7648 (1979), i. 170.

[60] Tribunals and Inquiries Act 1971, s. 10.

[61] Annual Report for 1964, Pt. II.

[62] The power to make 'rules of procedure' may be exceeded if the rules infringe procedural rights required by the principles of natural justice: R. v. *Housing Appeal Tribunal* [1920] 3 KB 334 at 342, 343, 346.

[63] See (1970) 4 NZULR 105 (J. A. Farmer).

be judged on its own merits, and this work constantly occupies the Council on Tribunals. Examples of amendments made in special situations are the provisions in the Plant Breeders Rights Regulations 1965 allowing licensees to contest the cancellation of breeders' rights in which they may have purchased important interests, and in the Betting Levy Appeal Tribunal Rules 1963 allowing a bookmaker to object to having his accounts automatically investigated by an auditor if he appeals to the tribunal.[64]

Hearings. Evidence. Precedent

The great majority of tribunals give oral hearings, and probably have a legal duty to do so.[65] But there are some exceptions.[66] Appeals to the Secretary of State from the Civil Aviation Authority may be made in writing only[67] and so may appeals to the Immigration Appeals Tribunal, if the appellant is neither in this country nor has a representative in it, or if, in certain cases, the Tribunal is satisfied that a hearing is not warranted.[68] The social security commissioners have power to dispense with oral hearings and decide many cases without them,[69] though not without giving the appellant an opportunity to contest the case against him.[70] The Lands Tribunal has a similar power.[71] The social security appeal tribunals, though obliged to give oral hearings if desired, in practice dispose of numerous appeals on paper. Where an oral hearing is given, it must be in accordance with the principles of natural justice which, as explained elsewhere, require the reception of relevant evidence, its disclosure to all parties, the opportunity to question witnesses and the opportunity for argument.[72] Natural justice therefore provides a broad basis for fair tribunal procedure. Statutory rules of procedure also commonly provide for the right to call, examine and cross-examine witnesses.

A statutory tribunal is not normally bound by the legal rules of evidence.

[64] Annual Report for 1964, para. 30.
[65] See R. v. Immigration Tribunal ex p. Mehmet (below).
[66] See the criticisms of the Council on Tribunals, Annual Report, 1971–2, pp. 14, 18.
[67] SI 1983 No. 550, reg. 21.
[68] SI 1984 No. 2041, rule 20, upheld as intra vires in R. v. Immigration Appeal Tribunal ex p. Jones (Ross) [1988] 1 WLR 477. See also R. v. Immigration Appeal Tribunal ex p. Enwia [1984] 1 WLR 117. An appellant in this country should be given an oral hearing: R. v. Diggines ex p. Rahmani [1986] AC 475.
[69] S.I. 1984 No. 451, reg. 26. See R. v. Deputy Industrial Injuries Commissioner ex p. Jones [1962] 2 QB 677.
[70] Sir R. Micklethwait, The National Insurance Commissioners, 48.
[71] S.I. 1977 No. 1820.
[72] Above, p. 544.

It may therefore receive hearsay evidence, provided always that the party affected is given a fair opportunity to contest it, as natural justice requires.[73] Thus in an industrial injury case the commissioner was entitled to receive evidence at the hearing about previous medical reports which technically would have been inadmissible as hearsay.[74] Even a court of law, when acting in an administrative capacity in hearing licensing appeals, is not bound by the legal rules;[75] for otherwise it might have to decide on different evidence from that which was before the licensing officer. Nor need a tribunal's decision be based exclusively on the evidence given before it: it may rely on its own general knowledge and experience, since one of the reasons for specialised tribunals is that they may be able to do so.[76] But this does not entitle it to make use of its members' specialised knowledge,[77] or an independent expert's report,[78] without disclosing it so that the parties can comment. An appeal tribunal may refuse to receive evidence not given in the proceedings at first instance.[79]

Some tribunals are equipped with compulsory powers to summon witnesses and to order production of documents. In the case of industrial tribunals disobedience is a punishable offence[80] and in the case of the Lands Tribunal it may be penalised in costs.[81] In other cases a party may be able to use a High Court subpoena, as explained below.

A statutory tribunal has inherent power to control its own procedure. It

[73] R. v. Hull Prison Visitors ex p. St. Germain (No. 2) [1979] 1 WLR 1401 (prisoners' punishments quashed for failure to allow them to call witnesses to contravene hearsay evidence).

[74] R. v. Deputy Industrial Injuries Commissioner ex p. Moore [1965] 1 QB 456.

[75] Kavanagh v. Chief Constable of Devon and Cornwall [1974] QB 624 (licensing of firearms); R. v. Aylesbury Crown Court ex p. Farrer [1988] The Times, 9 March (similar).

[76] R. v. City of Westminster Assessment Committee ex p. Grosvenor House (Park Lane) Ltd. [1941] 1 KB 53; R. v. Brighton and Area Rent Tribunal, ex p. Marine Parade Estates (1936) Ltd. [1950] 2 KB 410; Crofton Investment Trust Ltd. v. Greater London Investment Committee [1967] 1 QB 955; Metropolitan Properties Ltd. v. Lannon [1969] 1 QB 577. See [1975] PL 65 (J. A. Smillie).

[77] Hammington v. Berker Sportcraft Ltd. [1980] ICR 248; Dagg v. Lovett [1980] Est Gaz Dig. 27.

[78] R. v. City of Westminster Assessment Committee (above); R. v. Deputy Industrial Injuries Commissioner ex p. Jones (above); and see above, p. 539.

[79] National Graphical Association v. Howard [1985] ICR 97. An immigration adjudicator has no power to take account of facts occurring after the Secretary of State's initial decision: R. v. Immigration Appeal Tribunal ex p. Weerasuriya [1983] 1 All ER 195; nor may he or the appeal tribunal take account of facts existing but unknown at the time of that decision: R. v. Immigration Appeal Tribunal ex p. Nashouki [1985] The Times, 17 October. See also Brady v. Group Lotus Car Plc [1987] 2 All ER 674 (tax case remitted to special commissioners; new evidence not admissible).

[80] Employment Protection (Consolidation) Act 1978, sched. 9; S.I. 1985 No. 16, rule 4.

[81] SI 1975 No. 299, rules 40, 41.

has power to require evidence to be given on oath,[82] but most tribunal proceedings are conducted informally without requiring witnesses to be sworn.[83]

Pre-hearing assessments or reviews are provided for in the rules of some tribunals, so that the nature of the case can be assessed in advance and time saved at the hearing itself.[84]

In the use of its own precedents a tribunal is, as explained earlier,[85] in a radically different position from a court of law. Its duty is to reach the right decision in the circumstances of the moment, any discretion must be genuinely exercised, and there must be no blind following of its previous decisions. This does not mean that discretion cannot be exercised according to some reasonable and consistent principle. Nor does it mean that no regard may be had to previous decisions. It is most desirable that the principles followed by tribunals should be known to the public, and for this purpose selected decisions of the more important tribunals are published.[86]

Sittings. Publicity. Membership

Tribunals being part of the machinery of justice, they ought in principle to sit in public. In many cases this is so, and the anomalies that prevailed before 1958 have been removed.[87] But where tribunals have to inquire into intimate personal circumstances, private sittings are naturally preferred by most applicants and tribunal rules provide accordingly. Tribunals which sit in private are the General and Special Commissioners of Income Tax,[88] Betting Levy Appeal Tribunals,[89] Mental Health Review Tribunals,[90] Family Practitioner Committees and their Service Committees in the National Health Service,[91] agricultural arbitrators[92] and social security

[82] The Evidence Act 1851, s. 16, confers this power on every person authorised by law or by consent of parties to receive evidence. See *General Medical Council* v. *Spackman* [1943] AC 627 at 638 (Lord Atkin), correcting *Board of Education* v. *Rice* (above, p. 507). The Act was also overlooked in *R.* v. *Fulham etc. Rent Tribunal ex p. Zerek* [1951] 2 KB 1 at 7. Sometimes the power is conferred expressly, e.g. on Mental Health Review Tribunals by SI 1983 No. 942, rule 14.

[83] See the Franks Report, Cmnd. 218 (1957), para. 91.

[84] SI 1985 No. 16, rule 6 (industrial tribunals); SI 1981 No. 105, rule 4 (Lands Tribunal).

[85] Above, p. 371.

[86] Government departments published selected social security commissioners' decisions (the practice goes back to 1914), industrial tribunal reports, and value added tax tribunal reports. Many decisions of the Land Tribunal are reported in the Property and Compensation Reports, the Estates Gazette and elsewhere.

[87] Above, p. 918.

[88] Though the Taxes Management Act 1970, s. 50, so provides only by implication.

[89] Unless the appellant requests otherwise: S.I. 1963 No. 748, rule 7.

[90] SI 1983 No. 942, rule 21 (the tribunal may direct otherwise).

[91] SI 1974 No. 455, regs. 8, 54.

[92] Agricultural Holdings Act 1986, 11th sched.

adjudicating authorities where the claimant so requests or where, in a hearing by a Commissioner, intimate person circumstances or public security are involved.[93] The rules make provision for members of the Council on Tribunals to attend private hearings in the course of their supervisory duties, and sometimes also for research workers[94] and others to whom the tribunal may give leave. On an appeal to the High Court the right of privacy is lost, as may be seen from the details of tax cases and supplementary benefit cases in the law reports.

Many applications, particularly if of a preliminary or subsidiary character, may be disposed of without any sitting at all: the papers may be circulated to the members, who may express their opinions in writing to the chairman.[95] The majority of social security cases, including appeals to a Commissioner, are in practice disposed of in this way.[96]

Where a tribunal consists of a fixed number of members it is necessary that all should participate;[97] but if timely objection is not made it may be held to have been waived.[98] In one case of ambiguity the statute was construed as creating, in effect, a panel, so that a lesser number sufficed.[99] The same members must give the decision who heard the evidence.[1] Where a tribunal has power to use an assessor, and does so at an oral hearing, the assessor must sit with the tribunal throughout that part of the hearing in which the evidence is given on which his assistance is required.[2] Administrative or investigatory functions are another matter: all the members of a board or committee need not then participate.[3]

A tribunal may itself make an inspection, e.g. of a site or building, though it should do so with the knowledge of the parties[4] and preferably in their presence.[5] It must always be careful not to take evidence without disclosing it to all of them,[6] and it must remember that to make an inspection is to take evidence.[7]

---

[93] SI 1984 No. 451, rule 4.

[94] e.g. as n. 88, above.

[95] See *Howard* v. *Borneman* (No. 2) [1975] Ch. 201 (determination of prima facie case of tax avoidance).

[96] Above, p. 925.

[97] *R.* v. *Race Relations Board ex p. Selvarajan* [1975] 1 WLR 1686 at 1695.

[98] *Turner* v. *Allison* [1971] NZLR 833.

[99] *Howard* v. *Borneman* (above). As to non-members see above, p. 357.

[1] *Irish Land Commission* v. *Hession* [1978] ICR 297.

[2] *R.* v. *Deputy Industrial Injuries Commissioner ex p. Jones* [1962] 2 QB 677.

[3] *R.* v. *Race Relations Board ex p. Selvarajan* (above).

[4] *Hickmott* v. *Dorset C.C.* (1977) 35 P & CR 195.

[5] See *Salsbury* v. *Woodland* [1970] 1 AB 324. Rent Assessment Committees may make inspections at any stage of the proceedings but must allow the parties to attend: S.I. 1971 No. 1065, reg. 7.

[6] See above, p. 538, also *Wilcox* v. *H.G.S.* [1976] ICR 306.

[7] *Gould* v. *Evans & Co.* [1951] 2 TLR 1189.

Contempt of court. Subpoena

The High Court will sometimes use its own inherent powers in order to aid and protect inferior courts which do not themselves possess the power to punish for contempt of court. It used to be thought that this protection was available to tribunals also, since they are part of the machinery of justice, so that the High Court might punish someone who insulted the tribunal or disrupted its proceedings or otherwise committed contempt.[8] But the House of Lords has decided that the great majority of statutory tribunals are not courts for this purpose, even if so named; and the House refused to intervene where it was claimed that a television programme about a religious sect might prejudice its claim for exemption from rates which was about to be heard by a local valuation court (a tribunal subject to the Tribunals and Inquiries Act 1971).[9] Only where a tribunal is expressly given the status of a court, like the Transport Tribunal and the Iron and Steel Arbitration Tribunal,[10] or where it has a distinct legal status, like the Lands Tribunal,[11] will it qualify for the protection of the High Court, it seems.[12] Otherwise it will not be regarded, for this purpose at least, as exercising 'the judicial power of the state' which resides in courts properly so called.[13] If its proceedings are disrupted by misconduct, that is a matter for the criminal law.[14] If they are subjected to prejudicial comment, that is within the right of free speech.[15] Since most tribunals have judicial functions, in the sense of a duty to find facts and apply law objectively,[16] and since it is in the public interest that they should do justice, it might be thought that they deserve at least some protection against prejudice of their proceedings.

[8] See *R. v. Daily Herald ex p. Bishop of Norwich* [1932] 2 KB 402 and cases there cited and the Court of Appeal's decision in the *BBC* case, below.

[9] *A.-G. v. British Broadcasting Corporation* [1981] AC 303. Lord Salmon reserved the question whether the High Court might protect such tribunals in case of obstruction of their proceedings. But the majority held that protection was not available at all; and three of them held that the local valuation court's functions were administrative, despite the fact that it had to determine whether the sect's premises were exempt from rating as 'places of public religious worship' within the meaning of General Rate Act 1967, s. 39. For comment see [1982] PL 418 (N. V. Lowe and H. F. Rawlings).

[10] Both made courts of record by their constituent statutes.

[11] Yet the Lands Tribunal is often composed of a single non-lawyer, thus not meeting the requirement suggested by Lord Denning M.R. in the *BBC* case (above) at 314. The reasons for singling it out from other tribunals do not appear.

[12] See the *BBC* case at 338 (Lord Dilhorne).

[13] At 359 (Lord Scarman). There is likewise no protection for commissions or committees of inquiry: *Badry v. Director of Public Prosecutions* [1983] 2 AC 297.

[14] At 362 (Lord Scarman).

[15] At 342 (Lord Salmon).

[16] See above, p. 899.

'The judicial power of the state' was adopted as a definition in the Contempt of Court Act 1981,[17] which inter alia tempered the rule of strict liability for prejudicial publications. 'Court' for the purposes of the Act, 'includes any tribunal or body exercising the judicial power of the State.' The Act confers limited contempt powers upon magistrates but none upon tribunals, so the position of the latter is still as laid down by the House of Lords.[18]

The High Court's powers are available to tribunals on a more generous basis for the purpose of enforcing the attendance of witnesses and the production of documents by subpoena. High Court subpoenas are obtainable without restriction by parties appearing before tribunals, so that they have the same facilities for this purpose as before courts of law.[19] In principle subpoenas are available in aid of any tribunal discharging judicial or quasi-judicial functions, for example a disciplinary hearing held under the Police (Discipline) Regulations 1977.[20] The recipient of a subpoena may apply to the court for it to be set aside and he has a right of appeal to the court.

The Council on Tribunals preferred this system to the recommendation of the Franks Committee that tribunals themselves should have powers of subpoena, since that would give tribunals inquisitorial functions in appearance at least.[21]

Immunity and privilege

Whether members of tribunals, and parties and witnesses who appear before them, are entitled to the same personal immunities as apply in courts of law[22] is a doubtful question. The problem of the liability of members will rarely arise; the only tribunals with power to affect personal liberty are immigration tribunals and mental health review tribunals, and members of the latter are given statutory protection while acting in good faith and with reasonable care.[23] It has been held in New Zealand that a witness at a tribunal may claim the usual privilege against self-incrimination, provided that it does not stultify the statutory scheme.[24]

---

[17] s. 19.
[18] See Annual Report of the Council on Tribunals, 1980–1, s. 3.8.
[19] *Soul* v. *Inland Revenue Commissioners* [1963] 1 WLR 112.
[20] *Currie* v. *Chief Constable of Surrey* [1982] 1 WLR 215. Contrast *Re Sterritt* [1980] N. Ireland Bulletin No. 11 (police complaint investigation: subpoenas set aside).
[21] See Council on Tribunals, Annual Reports, 1960, p. 15; 1964, p. 12; 1979–80, p. 5.
[22] For which see above, p. 783.
[23] Mental Health Act 1983, s. 139. Actions may be brought only with leave of the High Court. See *Winch* v. *Jones* [1986] QB 296.
[24] *Taylor* v. *New Zealand Poultry Board* [1984] 1 NZLR 394.

Witnesses before tribunals appear to enjoy absolute privilege, so that they cannot be made personally liable if their evidence is defamatory. This follows *a fortiori* from the House of Lords' decision that witnesses at inquiries enjoy this protection.[25]

Legal representation. Legal aid. Costs

As a general rule, any party before a tribunal may be represented by a lawyer or by any one else. Whether this is a legal right is not at all clear. It is not certain that it is covered by the principles of natural justice.[26] In practice the position is that representation is freely permitted except in rare cases where it is restricted by regulation. The procedural rules of many tribunals give an unrestricted right of representation, which the Council on Tribunals encourages.[27] Representation by an experienced trade union representative or social worker may often be the most effective, and this is very common before social security tribunals and comparable bodies.[28]

In an earlier period there were irrational restrictions on representation by qualified lawyers, but these were removed in 1958 as already related.[29] One restriction which survived was that enforced in service committees of family practitioner committees (formerly executive councils) in the national health service, where it was thought that patients making complaints against their doctors ought not to be confronted with a professional lawyer defending the doctor. The rule in its earlier form prohibited paid advocates and also barristers and solicitors, whether or not paid and whether or not in practice.[30] But an amendment restricted the prohibition to persons acting in the capacity of paid advocate, so that a barrister or solicitor, if unpaid, may now assist a party in the capacity of a friend.[31]

In courts of law there is a legal right for a party appearing in person to have the assistance of some one to give advice and take notes,[32] and this right presumably applies equally before tribunals, at any rate when they sit

---

[25] See below, p. 987.
[26] Above, p. 546.
[27] See Council on Tribunals, Annual Report, 1964, pp. 10, 16.
[28] See [1972] PL 278 (J. E. Alder).
[29] Above, p. 911.
[30] SI 1974 No. 455, reg. 7.
[31] SI 1974 No. 907.
[32] *McKenzie* v. *McKenzie* [1971] P 33. This right does not exist in proceedings before boards of prison visitors unless the board in its discretion grants it: *R.* v. *Home Secretary ex p. Tarrant* [1985] QB 251, holding that the right exists only where the hearing is in public.

in public. Legal aid (as opposed to advice and assistance) is at present available for four tribunals only, the Lands Tribunal, the Employment Appeal Tribunal, Mental Health Review Tribunals and the Commons Commissioners.[33] In practice the proceedings in many tribunals are inexpensive and informal, particularly where trade unions and social workers provide assistance and representation, so that legal representation is often not a necessity. But difficult problems of law and fact are always prone to occur, particularly under complicated regulations. The Royal Commission on Legal Services found that there was some need for legal aid in all tribunals and recommended that it be made available.[34] The same recommendation has often been made before, but never with success.[35] But legal advice and assistance (though not representation) is available for tribunal proceedings,[36] and the adviser may assist the client at the hearing though he may not take part in it otherwise. The Lord Chancellor has been empowered to extend 'assistance' to include representation before tribunals and inquiries, but he has not as yet done so.[37] The machinery of legal aid is shortly to be reorganised, but it does not seem that it is to be any more liberally provided in tribunals than before.[38]

Few tribunals have powers to award costs, so that parties usually bear their own in cases involving expense. The Lands Tribunal however possesses this power, and normally exercises it in favour of the successful party in the same way as a court of law.[39] An industrial tribunal will not normally award costs, but may do so against a party who acts unreasonably.[40]

Tribunals normally have no power to award interest on delayed payments of compensation.[41] Judges presiding over the Employment Appeal Tribunal have called this a blot on the administration of justice where, for example, redundancy payments have been long delayed.[42]

---

[33] Council on Tribunals Annual Report for 1986–7, p. 13.

[34] Cmnd. 7648 (1979), in 172.

[35] Council on Tribunals, Annual Report, 1976–7, p. 6; Legal Aid Advisory Committee's Report, HC 160 (1979–80), p. 97 (mental health review tribunals).

[36] Legal Aid Act 1974, s. 2. The '£25 scheme' (s. 3) has been raised to £50 (£90 in some matrimonial cases).

[37] Legal Aid Act 1979; S.I. 1980 No. 1898 authorises representation in magistrates' courts only.

[38] See Cm. 118 (1987).

[39] Lands Tribunal Act 1949, s. 3(5). See *Pepys* v. *London Transport Executive* [1975] 1 WLR 235.

[40] SI 1985 No. 16, rule 11.

[41] The Lands Tribunal can award interest on claims in the nature of debt or damages under Law Reform (Miscellaneous Provisions) Act 1934, s. 3(1): *Knibb* v. *National Coal Board* (1986) 52 P & CR 354.

[42] See *Caledonian Mining Co.* v. *Bassett* [1987] ICR 425.

Decisions

The general rule is that a tribunal, like a court of law, may decide by a majority of its members and need not be unanimous.[43] In addition its rules of procedure may provide for majority decisions; but even where they do not, the general rule will apply in the absence of contrary intent in the statute. It has been held that a rent assessment committee may decide by majority in accordance with the general rule.[44] It does not appear to make any difference that the tribunal may be composed of members chosen from panels representative of opposed interests; or that two lay members overrule a legal chairman on a question of law.[45] In two earlier cases it had been held that the decisions of pensions appeal tribunals must be unanimous[46] but these were treated as special cases and their correctness must be doubted.

Once a tribunal has announced its decision it has, as a general rule, no power to reconsider it or to reopen the case,[47] unless of course its decision is quashed by the High Court. This applies equally where one of the parties later discovers fresh evidence which might well alter the decision, and in such a case the court has no power to assist by quashing.[48] But there is an exception where the tribunal's decision is given in ignorance that something has gone wrong, e.g. that a notice sent to one of the parties has miscarried. In that case the tribunal may and indeed should reopen the case, provided it is satisfied that the party prejudiced by the mistake has a real and reasonable excuse.[49] There are also important statutory exceptions. Social

[43] *Picea Holdings Ltd.* v. *London Rent Assessment Panel* [1971] 2 QB 216. For the principle see *Grindley* v. *Barker* (1798) 1 B & P 229. If a member dies, the others can still give a majority decision: *R.* v. *Greater Manchester Valuation Panel ex p. Shell Chemicals Ltd.* [1982] QB 255 (local valuation court). If there is no clear majority decision the tribunal may refer the case to a differently constituted tribunal, where that is possible: *R.* v. *Industrial Tribunal ex p. Cotswold Collotype Ltd.* [1979] ICR 190.

[44] Same case, approving *Atkinson* v. *Brown* [1963] NZLR 755 and referring to *Grindley* v. *Barker* (1798) 1 B & P 229. This is now confirmed by procedural regulations: SI 1971 No. 1965, reg. 10.

[45] As in *President of the Methodist Conference* v. *Parfitt* [1984] ICR 176; but the Court of Appeal reversed them: [1984] QB 368.

[46] *Brain* v. *Minister of Pensions* [1947] KB 625; *Minister of Pensions* v. *Horsey* [1949] 2 KB 526.

[47] Above, p. 253.

[48] Above, p. 327. See also *Jones* v. *Douglas Ltd.* [1979] ICR 278 (new point requiring evidence not entertained by Employment Appeal Tribunal).

[49] *R.* v. *Kensington & Chelsea Rent Tribunal ex p. MacFarlane* [1974] 1 WLR 1486; and see *Charman* v. *Palmers Ltd.* [1979] ICR 335 (power to order rehearing).

security tribunals have been given wide power to review their own decisions,[50] and so have industrial tribunals.[51]

A binding decision by a tribunal is res judicata and cannot be relitigated by the same parties.[52]

Reasons for decisions are the subject of the following section.

Reasons for decisions

Perhaps the most important of all the Franks Committee's achievements in the sphere of tribunal procedure is the rule which gives a right to a reasoned decision. Reasoned decisions are not only vital for the purpose of showing the citizen that he is receiving justice: they are also a valuable discipline for the tribunal itself. Curiously enough, the courts of law are not subject to any rule requiring reasons,[53] nor are reasons commonly given for findings of fact. But for decisions generally a statement of reasons is one of the essentials of justice.

The Tribunals and Inquiries Act 1971, replacing the provision of 1958, requires the tribunals listed in the Act

to furnish a statement, either written or oral, of the reasons for the decision if requested, on or before the given or notification of the decision, to state the reasons.[54]

A request therefore has to be made before the right to a reasoned decision arises. It has been held that the word 'on' is capable of 'an elastic meaning' in such a context,[55] so that a reasonably prompt request made after receipt of a tribunal's decision ought to satisfy the Act. In fact the policy of the Council on Tribunals has been to require that procedural rules for particular tribunals should incorporate an unqualified duty to give reasoned decisions, and this has been done in many cases.[56]

One important feature of the Act is the provision that reasons, when given, 'shall be taken to form part of the decision and accordingly to be

[50] Social Security Act 1975, s. 104; Health and Social Services and Social Security Adjudications Act 1983, 8th sched., para. 3; Social Security Act 1986, 5th sched., paras. 10–14.
[51] S.I. 1985 No. 16, 1st sched., rule 10. See Flint v. Eastern Electricity Board [1975] ICR 395; Acrow (Engineers) Ltd. v. Hathaway [1981] 2 All ER 161.
[52] Above, p. 270.
[53] Above, p. 547.
[54] Act of 1971, s. 12; Act of 1958, s. 12. See (1970) 33 MLR 154 (M. Akehurst).
[55] Scott v. Scott [1921] P. 107. See also R. v. Special Commissioners of Income Tax (1888) 21 QBD 313.
[56] See e.g. SI 1984 No. 451, regs. 19 (Social Security Appeal Tribunals), 34 (Medical Appeal Tribunals); SI 1985 No. 16, rule 9 (Industrial Tribunals). But the need for a request was restored in the case of Rent Assessment Committees by S.I. 1981 No. 1783.

incorporated in the record'.[57] This is a warrant of parliamentary approval for the court's jurisdiction to quash decisions of tribunals for error on the face of the record. It must, apparently, apply even where the reasons are stated orally, despite the incongruity of an oral 'record'.[58]

The Act contains a number of exceptions. It does not apply to decisions in connection with a scheme or order 'of a legislative and not an executive character'. Reasons may also be withheld or restricted on grounds of national security; and they may be withheld from a person not primarily concerned where to furnish them would be contrary to the interests of any person primarily concerned. Nor does the Act apply where any other Act or regulation governs the giving of reasons. Thus under the Mental Health Act 1959 reasons need not necessarily be given by Mental Health Review Tribunals,[59] for in some cases this may be contrary to the interests of the patient.

There is also power to dispense tribunals from the duty to give reasons where the Lord Chancellor is of opinion that the giving of reasons is 'unnecessary or impracticable', subject to consultation with the Council on Tribunals.[60] One exemption granted under this provision has been in favour of certain tax tribunals, not because they should not give reasons but because there are other statutory provisions under which they can be required to do so.[61] Social security commissioners are not required to give reasons for decisions refusing leave to appeal.[62] But no general use of the escape clause has been made. On the other hand there are many cases where extensive reasons cannot be given, for example where the tribunal merely finds facts on evidence. No tribunal can be expected to give fuller reasons than the nature of the case admits.[63] For this reason an application for dispensation of agricultural arbitrators was rejected by the government, on the advice of the Council on Tribunals.[64] Although in many cases these arbitrators will merely form an expert opinion of the value of farmland or of agricultural buildings, for which elaborate reasons can hardly be given, this does not mean that reasons cannot be shortly stated. Such cases do not therefore qualify for exemption.

---

[57] s. 12(3). For this see above, p. 315.

[58] See above, p. 313, for this question.

[59] Mental Health Act 1983, s. 78(2)(i).

[60] Tribunals and Inquiries Act 1971, s. 12(6).

[61] Council on Tribunals, Annual Report, 1959, paras. 61–4.

[62] SI 1987 No. 214, reg. 22. See R. v. Secretary of State for Social Services ex p. Connolly [1986] 1 WLR 421.

[63] See Metropolitan Property Holdings Ltd. v. Lauter (1974) 29 P & CR 172; Guppy's (Bridport) Ltd. v. Sandoe [1975] 30 P & CR 69; Elliott v. Southwark LBC [1976] 1 WLR 499 (two-line reason for demolition rather than rehabilitation upheld by Court of Appeal); Westminster C.C. v. Great Portland Estates Plc. [1985] AC 661.

[64] Council on Tribunals, Annual Report, 1959, para. 68.

In some cases formal and exiguous reasons may be held adequate, as where an immigration officer stated simply that 'I am not satisfied that you are genuinely seeking entry only for this limited period'.[65] But the Master of the Rolls indicated that the court would intervene if it appeared that such a formula was used merely as a 'ritual incantation'. A case of that kind was where the court allowed an appeal from a mental health review tribunal which had merely recited the statutory words which empowered it to refuse to discharge a patient.[66]

The duty to state reasons is now so generally accepted that the Industrial Relations Court held that it applied to an industrial tribunal in the same way as it applied to that court itself, since otherwise parties would be deprived of their right of appeal on questions of law.[67] No mention was made of the Tribunals and Inquiries Act or of any need for a request.

The Court of Appeal has emphasised that the statutory duty to give reasons 'is a responsible one and cannot be discharged by the use of vague general words'.[68] It requires, as the High Court has held, 'proper, adequate reasons', being 'reasons which will not only be intelligible but which deal with the substantial points which have been raised'. In the same case the court treated inadequacy of reasons as error on the face of the record, so that an inadequately reasoned decision could be quashed, even if the duty to give reasons was not mandatory.[69] This case concerned an agricultural arbitrator who found that a notice to quit was justified because the tenant had not done sufficient work to make good dilapidations which the landlord had specified under numerous different heads. It was held that the reasons given were too vague and the award was set aside. As noted above, agricultural arbitrators were specifically refused dispensation from the duty to give reasons.

Sir John Donaldson has said that 'in the absence of reasons it is impossible to determine whether or not there has been an error of law. Failure to give reasons therefore amounts to a denial of justice and is itself an error of law.'[70] Lord Lane CJ, while not wishing to go so far, has held that a

[65] R. v. Home Secretary ex p. Swati [1986] 1 WLR 477.
[66] Bone v. Mental Health Review Tribunal [1985] 3 All ER 330; and see R. v. Mental Health Review Tribunal ex p. Chatworthy [1985] 3 All ER 699.
[67] Norton Tool Co. Ltd. v. Tewson [1973] 1 WLR 45. See also Alexander Machinery (Dudley) Ltd. v. Crabtree [1974] ICR 120; Beardmore v. Westinghouse Brake Co. [1976] ICR 49; Green v. Waterhouse [1977] ICR 759; Albyn Properties Ltd. v. Kuox 1977 SC 108; Caims (R. W.) Ltd. v. Busby Session 1985 SLT 493.
[68] Elliott v. Southwark LBC (above). See similarly Dagg v. Lovett [1980] Est Gaz Dig 27.
[69] Re Poyser and Mills' Arbitration [1964] 2 QB 467. See likewise R. v. Industrial Injuries Commissioner ex p. Howarth (1968) 4 KIR 621 (ambiguous reasons: decision quashed); Elliott v. University Computing Co. [1977] ICR 147 (adequate findings required).
[70] In the Alexander Machinery case (above) at 122.

statement of reasons must show that the tribunal has considered the point at issue between the parties and must indicate the evidence for its conclusion.[71] Where there is a conflict of evidence, the tribunal ought to state its findings.[72]

As explained earlier, the duty to state reasons is normally held to be mandatory, so that a decision not supported by adequate reasons will be quashed or remitted to the deciding authority.[73]

APPEALS ON QUESTIONS OF LAW AND DISCRETION

Appeal on a point of law

Where statute gives a right of appeal from a tribunal to a court of law, it is usually confined to a right of appeal on a point of law. The wide extension of this right as part of the reform of the tribunal system has already been noted.[74] It is of great importance that it should be generally available, so that the courts may give guidance on the proper interpretation of the law and so that there may not be inconsistent rulings by tribunals in different localities.[75] It is through appeals that the courts and the tribunals are kept in touch, so that the tribunals are integrated into the machinery of justice. Difficult questions of law can if necessary be carried to the appellate courts, and thus they may reach the House of Lords.[76]

The Tribunals and Inquiries Act 1971[77] gives a right of appeal to a party 'dissatisfied in point of law' with a decision of one of the tribunals specified, and the party may appeal to the High Court, or require a case to be stated to the High Court, as rules of court may provide. In fact the rules of court provide for both procedures.[78] The Act also gives power for the tribunal itself to state a case to the High Court on any question of law arising in the course of its proceedings.[79] Other Acts sometimes provide for appeals to go straight to the Court of Appeal.[80]

The Act of 1971 and the rules of court also authorise the High Court, on

[71] R. v. Immigration Appeal Tribunal ex p. Khan (Mahmud) [1983] QB 790.
[72] Levy v. Marrable & Co. Ltd. [1984] ICR 583.
[73] Above, p. 251.
[74] Above, p. 908.
[75] See Pearlman v. Harrow School Governors [1979] QB 56.
[76] Supplementary benefit appeals reached the House of Lords in Supplementary Benefits Commission v. Jull [1981] AC 1025.
[77] s. 13. See Esso Petroleum Co. Ltd. v. Ministry of Labour [1969] 1 QB 98 at 110 for a suggested but questionable restriction on raising new points of appeal.
[78] RSC O 94 rr. 8, 9. See Hoser v. Minister of Town and Country Planning [1963] Ch. 428.
[79] s. 13(2); RSC O 94 r. 9A. As to appeals on interlocutory decisions see R. v. Lands Tribunal ex p. City of London Cpn. [1982] 1 WLR 258.
[80] See above, p. 908.

any such appeal, to give any decision which might have been given by the tribunal, to remit the case for rehearing or determination by the tribunal in accordance with the court's opinion, and to give directions to the tribunal.[81] The case should be remitted to the tribunal where a question of fact has been decided under a misconception as to the law, since questions of fact are for the tribunal alone, unless the tribunal's decision is unarguably right.[82]

To find facts based on no evidence is, by a well–established rule, an error of law. In principle, therefore, a tribunal's findings of fact can be challenged by way of appeal on a point of law if they are based on no evidence, within the meaning of the rule discussed in an earlier chapter.[83] But in the case of many tribunals this rule is severely qualified by their liberty to act on their own knowledge and experience. Thus if no evidence of facts bearing on the right level of rent is given before a rent tribunal or rent assessment committee, the tribunal must nevertheless determine the statutory rent as best it can, and its determination cannot be challenged on the basis of lack of evidence.[84] Furthermore, the courts are inclined to be tolerant in reviewing the decisions of specialised tribunals, provided that they have not misdirected themselves on the facts or gone wrong in law.[85]

Since appellate courts are concerned almost exclusively with questions of law, there should be little difference in practice between an unrestricted right of appeal and a right of appeal on a point of law only. But the definition of 'law' for this purpose is liable to be narrowed artificially, so that many questions of legal interpretation which appellate courts can suitably resolve are not regarded as questions of law and are therefore not appealable.

What is 'law'?

Questions of law must be distinguished from questions of fact, but this has always been one of the situations where the rules have taken different forms under judicial manipulation.[86] The House of Lords has made determined efforts to clarify them, but two rival doctrines are still contending for supremacy.

The simpler and more logical doctrine has been recognised in many

---

[81] s. 13(3); RSC O 55 r. 7.

[82] *Dobie* v. *Burns International Security Services Ltd.* [1985] 1 WLR 43.

[83] Above, p. 319.

[84] See above, p. 926 n. 76, and especially the discussion in the *Crofton Investment Trust* case.

[85] *Retarded Children's Aid Society Ltd.* v. *Day* [1978] ICR 437; and see above, p. 317.

[86] See Emery and Smythe, *Judicial Review*, ch. 2, 3; (1987) 104 LQR 264 (C. T. Emery); (1984) 100 LQR 612 (C. T. Emery and B. Smythe).

judgments.[87] This is that matters of fact are the primary facts of the particular case which have to be established before the law can be applied, the 'facts which are observed by the witnesses and proved by testimony',[88] to which should be added any facts of common knowledge of which the court will take notice without proof. Whether these facts, once established, satisfy some legal definition or requirement must be a question of law, for the question then is how to interpret and apply the law to those established facts.[89] If the question is whether some building is a 'house' within the meaning of the Housing Acts, its location, condition, purpose of use, and so forth are questions of fact. But once these facts are established, the question whether it counts as a house within the meaning of the Act is a question of law.[90] The facts themselves not being in dispute, the conclusion is a matter of legal inference.

It follows that such questions as 'is the building a house?', or 'did the defendant cause the accident?' cannot be characterised as questions of fact or questions of law without knowing what is in issue. If the question is whether the defendant's act was part of the chain of events, that is a question of fact. But if the question is whether it was sufficiently proximate to amount in law to the real cause, that is a question of law.[91] Where both questions are in dispute the question is sometimes called a mixed question of law and fact, or a question of mixed law and fact. The former expression is the more accurate, since law and fact are two different things which ought not to be mixed. As Sir John Donaldson MR has said, 'the appeal tribunal has no jurisdiction to consider any question of mixed fact and law until it has purified or distilled the mixture and extracted a question of pure law'.[92]

According to this analysis, an appeal on a point of law should be available on every question of legal interpretation arising after the primary facts have

---

[87] One of the earliest and clearest is *Johnstone* v. *Sutton* (1785) 1 TR 510 at 545 (Lords Mansfield and Loughborough): 'The question of probable cause is a mixed proposition of law and fact. Whether the circumstances alleged to show it probable, or not probable, are true and existed, is a matter of fact; but whether, supposing them true, they amount to a probable cause, is a question of law.' Other examples are cited below.

[88] *Bracegirdle* v. *Oxley* [1947] KB 349 (Denning J.).

[89] See below, p. 942.

[90] *Re Butler* [1939] 1 KB 570; *Quiltotex Co. Ltd.* v. *Minister of Housing and Local Government* [1966] 1 QB 704; *Lake* v. *Bennett* [1970] 1 QB 663; *Tandon* v. *Trustees of Spurgeon's Homes* [1982] 2 WLR 735; *R.* v. *Camden L.B.C. ex p. Rowton Ltd.* (1983) 82 LGR 614.

[91] On causation see *Hoveringham Gravels Ltd.* v. *Secretary of State for the Environment* [1975] QB 754.

[92] *O'Kelly* v. *Trusthouse Forte Plc* [1984] QB 90. In fact the Court of Appeal followed *Edwards* v. *Bairstow* (below), holding that the Employment Appeal Tribunal was not entitled to interfere with an industrial tribunal's reasonable findings on whether applicants were 'employees' under a 'contract of employment'.

been established. It ought to cover all legal inferences of the kind mentioned above. But although judges have frequently acted upon this principle, and still do so, the reigning rule today is more sophisticated and less logical. It is designed to give greater latitude to tribunals where there is room for difference of opinion. The rule is, in effect, that the application of a legal definition or principle to ascertained facts is erroneous in point of law only if the conclusion reached by the tribunal is unreasonable. If it is within the range of interpretations within which different persons might reasonably reach different conclusions, the court will hold that there is no error of law. In his above-quoted judgment the Master of the Rolls thus explained the limited function of the appellate court or tribunal:

Unpalatable though it may be on occasion, it must loyally accept the conclusions of fact with which it is presented and, accepting those conclusions, it must be satisfied that there *must* have been a misdirection on a question of law before it can intervene. Unless the direction of law has been expressed it can only be so satisfied if, in its opinion, no reasonable tribunal, properly directing itself on the relevant questions of law, could have reached the conclusions under appeal. This is a heavy burden on the appellant.

An alternative but substantially similar doctrine is that 'the meaning of an ordinary word in the English language is not a question of law', unless the tribunal's interpretation is unreasonable; but that where the word is used 'in an unusual sense' the appellate court will determine the meaning.[93]

The truth is, however, that there can hardly be a subject on which the courts act with such total lack of consistency as the difference between fact and law. The House of Lords has indeed laid down the rule explained in the following paragraphs, but it is commonplace to find courts proceeding in complete disregard of it. It may be that judges instinctively agree with an American comment:[94]

No two terms of legal science have rendered better service than 'law' and 'fact'. . . . They are the creations of centuries. What judge has not found refuge in them? The man who could succeed in defining them would be a public enemy.

The House of Lords' attempts at definition have had, as will be seen, only partial success.

Leading cases on 'law'

The House of Lords has expounded the law authoritatively in two tax cases, where appeal lay from the inland revenue commissioners to the High

---

[93] *Cozens* v. *Brutus* [1973] AC 854 at 861 (Lord Reid), not followed in *A.C.T. Construction Ltd.* v. *Customs & Excise Cmrs* [1979] 1 WLR 870, affirmed [1981] 1 WLR 1542. Compare *Inland Revenue Commissioners* v. *Lysaght* [1928] AC 235 at 246, 247.
[94] Leon Green, *Judge and Jury*, 270.

Court only on a point of law. The question was whether transactions amounted to 'trade' for tax purposes. In the first case[95] there had been a purchase and sale of machinery as an isolated transaction, and the facts themselves were not in dispute. All the lower courts nevertheless held that the question whether this amounted legally to 'trade' was 'purely a question of fact'. The House of Lords held that it was a question of law, since on the particular facts no reasonable person could fail to conclude that the transaction was 'trade' within the meaning of the Act. Lord Radcliffe said:

If the Case contains anything ex facie which is bad law and which bears on the determination, it is, obviously, erroneous in point of law. But without any such misconception appearing ex facie, it may be that the facts found are such that no person acting judicially and properly instructed as to the relevant law could have come to the determination under appeal. In these circumstances, too, the court must intervene. It has no option but to assume that there has been some misconception of the law, and that this has been responsible for the determination. So there too, there has been an error in point of law. I do not think it much matters whether this state of affairs is described as one in which there is no evidence to support the determination, or as one in which the evidence is inconsistent with, and contradictory of, the determination, or as one in which the true and only reasonable conclusion contradicts the determination. Rightly understood, each phrase propounds the same test. For my part, I prefer the last of the three . . .

Lord Radcliffe emphasised, however, that there were many combinations of circumstances in which it could not be said to be wrong to arrive at a conclusion one way or the other on the same facts. And he added:

All these cases in which the facts warrant a determination either way can be described as questions of degree and, therefore, as questions of fact.

This last statement is the basis of the expression 'questions of fact and degree'[96] which is often applied to conclusions which fall within the permitted range of reasonableness and which the court holds to be ineligible for appeal on a point of law.

In the second case,[97] where the House of Lords held that on the facts it

---

[95] *Edwards* v. *Bairstow* [1956] AC 14. See (1946) 62 LQR 248, (1955) 71 LQR 467 (A. Farnsworth).

[96] See e.g. *Birmingham Cpn.* v. *Habib Ullah* [1964] 1 QB 178; *Marriott* v. *Oxford & District Co-operative Society Ltd.* [1969] 1 WLR 254; *Global Plant Ltd.* v. *Secretary of State for Health and Social Security* [1972] 1 QB 139. Earlier decisions equating questions of degree with questions of fact are *Currie* v. *I.R.C.* [1921] 2 KB 332; *Inland Revenue Commissioners* v. *Lysaght* [1928] AC 234.

[97] *Ransom* v. *Higgs* [1974] 1 WLR 1594. See also *Taylor* v. *Good* [1974] 1 WLR 556; *Central Electricity Generating Board* v. *Clwyd County Council* [1976] 1 WLR 151; *Furniss* v. *Dawson* [1984] AC 474.

could not reasonably be concluded that there was 'trade', Lord Wilberforce similarly said:

Sometimes the question whether an activity is to be found to be a trade becomes a matter of degree, of frequency, of organisation, even of intention, and in such cases it is for the fact-finding body to decide on the evidence whether a line is passed. The present is not such a case: it involves the question as one of recognition whether the characteristics of trade are sufficiently present.

Lord Simon also explained how the facts may fall into three categories: if they plainly amount to trade, or plainly do not, the court must reverse any decision to the contrary as erroneous in law; but between these extremes is the third category which depends on the evaluation of the facts, and is suitably called on of 'fact and degree'.

Logic versus legal policy

The House of Lords' third or intermediate category, as defined above, may be vulnerable to logical analysis in that, once the facts of the case are established, the application to them of some legal definition or test is in its nature a matter of law. Law and fact are two different things, and a question of law should not become one of fact merely because it is one on which opinions may reasonably differ. Questions of degree are not 'therefore' questions of fact. In one case, where the question was whether there had been a 'transfer' of a business, two industrial tribunals came to different conclusions on the same established facts: one of them must therefore have erred in law, and the court naturally entertained an appeal on 'law'.[98] Citing this in a similar case, Lord Denning MR held that if a tribunal drew a wrong conclusion from the primary facts, thus misinterpreting the statute, they went wrong in law.[99] The House of Lords' doctrine that the error must be one which a reasonable tribunal could not make is frequently disregarded,[1] and judges willingly revert to the simpler and more logical doctrine as stated in a typical income tax case of 1915 by Lord Parker:[2]

My Lords, it may not always be easy to distinguish between questions of fact and questions of law . . . The views from time to time expressed in this House have been far from unanimous, but in my humble judgment where all the material facts are fully found, and the only question is whether the facts are such as to bring the

---

[98] *Huggins* v. *Gordon (A.J.) Ltd.* (1971) 6 ITR 164.

[99] *Woodhouse* v. *Brotherhood Ltd.* [1972] 2 QB 520 at 536, rejecting the 'fact and degree' category; see similarly *British Railways Board* v. *Customs and Excise Commissioners* [1971] 1 WLR 588.

[1] In the *Huggins* case (above) both decisions might have been reasonable.

[2] *Farmer* v. *Cotton's Trustees* [1915] AC 922 at 932. See similarly *R.* v. *Port of London Authority* [1920] AC 1 at 31; *Great Western Rly.* v. *Bater* [1923] AC 1 at 22.

case within the provisions properly construed of some statutory enactment, the question is one of law only.

There have been many similar statements and they show no sign of ceasing.[3] Where a tribunal has misconstrued and misapplied the law the urge to intervene is often more than an appellate court can resist, whether or not there is room for reasonable difference of opinion.

The House of Lords' 'fact and degree' doctrine, on the other hand, provides a more tolerant and flexible rule for appeals than would exist under a rigid dichotomy where the court was obliged to substitute its own opinion in every borderline case of legal interpretation. Courts are in any case reluctant to reverse the conclusions of expert tribunals on matters falling peculiarly within their province, for example where an industrial tribunal has to apply the complicated classification of industrial operations.[4] The principle expounded by Lord Radcliffe, as quoted above, has obvious affinities both with the doctrine of reasonableness[5] and with the doctrine of review for 'no evidence'.[6] Here, as elsewhere, the courts have been working towards a broad power to review unjustifiable decisions while always leaving to the administrative authority or tribunal a reasonable margin of error. American administrative law has taken a similar direction in evolving the substantial evidence rule for testing the reasonableness of findings of fact and the 'reasonable basis' rule for testing determinations of law.[7]

The courts ought, however, to guard against any artificial narrowing of the right of appeal on a point of law, which is clearly intended to be a wide and beneficial remedy. Very difficult questions of law have to be determined by many tribunals and for the sake of consistency and fairness it is important that the guidance of the courts should be available. On an appeal from an industrial tribunal in a redundancy payment case, where the question was whether a certain term could be implied in the claimants' contracts of employment, the Queen's Bench Divisional Court held that this was a question of fact, so that the appeal was incompetent; but the Court of Appeal reversed them, holding that it was clearly a question of

[3] e.g. *British Launderers' Research Association* v. *Hendon Rating Authority* [1949] 1 KB 462 at 471; *Morren* v. *Swindon B.C.* [1965] 1 WLR 576 at 583; *R.* v. *Kelly* [1970] 1 WLR 1050; *Woodhouse* v. *Peter Brotherhood Ltd.* [1972] 2 QB 520 at 536; *Pearlman* v. *Harrow School Governors* [1979] QB 56; *A.C.T. Construction Ltd.* v. *Customs & Excise Cmrs* [1981] 1 WLR 49, affirmed *ibid.*, 1547.

[4] As in *Maurice (C.) & Co. Ltd.* v. *Ministry of Labour* [1969] 2 AC 346; *Esso Petroleum Co. Ltd.* v. *Ministry of Labour* [1969] 1 QB 98. Compare *Libman* v. *General Medical Council* [1972] AC 217.

[5] Above, p. 395. See *Griffiths* v. *J. P. Harrison (Watford) Ltd.* [1963] AC 1 at 15–16.

[6] Above, p. 319.

[7] See Schwartz and Wade, *Legal Control of Government*, 228.

law, and allowed the appeals.[8] In another case, where it was held that an official referee had exercised his discretion wrongly in striking out a claim for want of prosecution, Lord Denning M.R. said:[9]

There are many tribunals from which an appeal lies only on a 'point of law': and we always interpret the provision widely and liberally.

The extension in recent years of the right of appeal on questions of law has, as already noted, done much to assist the integration of the tribunal system with the general machinery of justice. Judicial policy ought to reinforce this beneficial trend.

Appeals against discretionary decisions

Where appeal lies only on a point of law, an appeal against an exercise of discretion by a tribunal should succeed, in theory at least, only where the decision is vitiated by unreasonableness, self-misdirection, irrelevant considerations, or some other legal error. For otherwise no point of law arises.[10] But in fact the court may allow such an appeal if it appears that the tribunal's decision produces 'manifest injustice'[11] or is 'plainly wrong'.[12] In any case, unreasonableness, self-misdirection, and so forth are grounds which are 'so many and so various that it virtually means that an erroneous exercise of discretion is nearly always due to an error in point of law'.[13]

It is where the right of appeal is unrestricted, paradoxically, that judges are inclined to restrict it. It has many times been said in the House of Lords that the appellate court ought to interfere with an exercise of discretion by a lower court or tribunal only where there has been disregard of some legal principle and not merely where it would itself exercise the discretion differently.[14] In addition, an appellate court is naturally disinclined to intervene where the tribunal's decision is based on its own observance of witnesses and its assessment of oral evidence.[15] Where, on the other hand, the evidence is entirely documentary the appellate court is in an equally good position to exercise the discretion.[16] The same may be true of

---

[8] *O'Brien* v. *Associated Fire Alarms Ltd.* [1969] 1 WLR 1916.

[9] *Instrumatic Ltd.* v. *Supabrase Ltd.* [1969] 1 WLR 519.

[10] *Nelsovil Ltd.* v. *Minister of Housing and Local Government* [1962] 1 WLR 404.

[11] *Wootton* v. *Central Land Board* [1957] 1 WLR 424 at 432.

[12] *Instrumatic Ltd.* v. *Supabrase Ltd.* (above).

[13] *Re DJMS* [1977] 3 All ER 582 at 589 (Lord Denning MR). See e.g. *Priddle* v. *Fisher & Sons* [1968] 1 WLR 1478; *Hadmor Productions Ltd.* v. *Hamilton* [1983] 1 AC 191.

[14] *Zacharia* v. *Republic of Cyprus* [1963] AC 634 at 661; *Shiloh Spinners Ltd.* v. *Harding* [1973] AC 691 at 727; *Duport Steels Ltd.* v. *Sirs* [1980] 1 WLR 142 at 171; *Customs and Excise Cmrs* v. *J. H. Corbitt (Numismatics) Ltd.* [1981] AC 22 at 52.

[15] *Blunt* v. *Blunt* [1943] AC 517 at 526–7.

[16] *Osenton (Charles)* v. *Johnston* [1942] AC 130; *Blunt* v. *Blunt* (above).

interlocutory orders made before any evidence has been heard.[17] Although there are different nuances in the judicial statements, which mostly concern appeals from courts of law, the correct position is probably as explained by Lord Atkin:[18]

I conceive it to be a mistake to hold . . . that the jurisdiction of the Court of Appeal on appeal from such an order is limited so that . . . the Court of Appeal have no power to interfere with [the judge's] exercise of discretion unless we think that he acted upon some wrong principle of law. Appellate jurisdiction is always statutory: there is in the statute no restriction on the jurisdiction of the Court of Appeal; and while the appellate court in the exercise of its appellate power is no doubt entirely justified in saying that normally it will not interfere with the exercise of the judge's discretion except on grounds of law, yet if it sees that on other grounds the decision will result in injustice being done it has both the power and the duty to remedy it.

Appellate courts therefore keep their options open, and in practice they are likely to allow an appeal when they think that a substantial mistake has been made. Much may depend upon the legal context. In appeals against refusal of leave to apply for judicial review,[19] for example, the Court of Appeal uses its own discretion freely.

Unappealable discretion

Where a right of appeal is subject to leave from a court or tribunal, there is no right of appeal from a refusal of leave[20] or from a refusal to extend the time for appeal,[21] unless it is expressly conferred in those cases. Otherwise appeals would be multiplied in situations where it is thought necessary to restrict them.[22]

Appeal in relation to review

The existence of a statutory right of appeal does not deprive the High Court of its ordinary powers of quashing a tribunal's decision which is ultra vires or erroneous on its face. It has been noticed already that the law often

[17] *British Library* v. *Palyza* [1984] ICR 504 (industrial tribunal's order for discovery of documents held fully reviewable on appeal).
[18] *Evans* v. *Bartlam* [1937] AC 473 at 480. See similarly Lord Wright's speech. See also *Tsai* v. *Woodworth* [1983] The Times, 30 November, holding that the right of appeal would be nugatory unless Lord Atkin's principle was accepted.
[19] Above, p. 673.
[20] *Re Poh* [1983] 1 WLR 2 (immigration appeal); *Bland* v. *Chief Supplementary Benefit Officer* [1983] 1 WLR 262.
[21] *White* v. *Chief Adjudication Officer* [1983] 1 WLR 262 (social security pension appeal).
[22] See authorities cited in *Bland* v. *Supplementary Benefit Officer* (above).

allows alternative remedies, and a decision which is open to appeal may nevertheless be quashed on certiorari.[23]

Appeal and review are in principle two distinct procedures, appeal being concerned with merits and review being concerned with legality.[24] But in practice an appellant will often wish to raise questions which strictly are questions of legality, such as violation of natural justice or some objection to the tribunal's jurisdiction. It is important that this should be freely allowed, since otherwise many cases could not be fully disposed of on appeal.

But in several appeals under the Tribunals and Inquiries Act 1958 the court has acted as if jurisdictional questions could not be decided on appeal, and has permitted conversion of the proceedings into review by certiorari.[25] This would restrict the right of appeal for purely technical reasons and would make unnecessary difficulties for appellants wishing to appeal both on the merits and on some question of jurisdiction. There is abundant authority to the effect that jurisdictional questions can be raised by way of appeal,[26] and the implication of the Act is to the same effect, since the appellant need only be 'dissatisfied in point of law'. And now that it is held that a tribunal exceeds its jurisdiction if it makes any error of law,[27] there would be virtually no scope for appeals if jurisdictional questions could not be raised.

It is true that judges have occasionally professed themselves puzzled as to how, if a tribunal's decision is held to be a nullity, that there can be an appeal against it.[28] One ingenious answer is that the tribunal's decision implies a decision that it has jurisdiction, that this is a question of law which the tribunal necessarily has jurisdiction to determine (though not

[23] Above, p. 712.

[24] Above, p. 36.

[25] *Metropolitan Properties Ltd.* v. *Lannon* [1968] 1 WLR 815 at 822, reversed on the merits, [1969] 1 QB 577; *Chapman* v. *Earl* [1968] 1 WLR 1315; *Picea Holdings Ltd.* v. *London Rent Assessment Panel* [1971] 2 QB 216 at 218. See also *Henry Moss Ltd.* v. *Customs and Excise Commissioners* [1981] 2 All ER 86, where Lord Denning MR suggested the same restriction, but refrained from enforcing it. In *Hanson* v. *London Rent Assessment Committee* [1978] QB 823 an appeal and an application for certiorari were heard together; certiorari was granted.

[26] In *R.* v. *Inland Revenue Commissioners ex p. Preston* [1985] AC 835 at 862 Lord Templeman expressly states that on appeal the High Court can correct all kinds of errors of law including errors which might otherwise be the subject of judicial review. Other similar examples are plentiful, e.g. *R.* v. *Minister of Housing and Local Government ex p. Finchley Borough Council* [1955] 1 WLR 29 at 35; *Re Purkiss' Application* [1962] 1 WLR 902 at 914; *Essex C.C.* v. *Essex Incorporated Church Union* [1963] AC 808; *Shell* v. *Unity Finance Co. Ltd.* [1964] 2 QB 203; *Arsenal Football Club* v. *Ende* [1977] QB 100 at 116.

[27] Above, p. 299.

[28] *Harman* v. *Official Receiver* [1934] AC 245 at 251 (Lord Tomlin); *McPherson* v. *McPherson* [1936] AC at 177 at 189 (Lord Macmillan); *White* v. *Kuzych* [1951] AC 585 (PC).

conclusively),[29] and that an appeal therefore lies against the determination.[30] A more direct path to the same result is to hold that the 'decision' from which the statute gives an appeal need not be a valid decision, since 'otherwise the statute would be futile and unworkable'. This was said by the Privy Council in holding that a committee of the Australian Jockey Club could validly determine an appeal from a decision of the stewards which was claimed to be void for breach of natural justice.[31] It was pointed out that the decision was in fact effective unless and until challenged, and that to hold it legally non-existent would be wholly unreal. The judgment corroborates the point made earlier, that 'void' has a relative rather than an absolute meaning.[32] Its evident good sense has been endorsed by the House of Lords.[33]

[29] Above, p. 283.

[30] *Re Padstow Total Loss Assurance Association* (1882) 51 LJ Ch. 344 at 348 (Jessel MR).; *Re Purkiss' Application* (above) at 914 (Diplock LJ). See Rubinstein, *Jurisdiction and Illegality*, 50–2.

[31] *Calvin* v. *Carr* [1980] AC 574. Although the right of appeal was given by statute, it was held that the jurisdiction of the committee was 'founded on consensual acceptance', i.e. based upon contract. But in contractual cases the question is whether there has been a breach of contract. It is not easy to see what 'void' can mean in this context or how the supposed difficulty about appeal can arise.

[32] Above, p. 351.

[33] *London & Clydeside Estates Ltd.* v. *Aberdeen D.C.* [1980] 1 WLR for which see above, p. 352.

TABLE OF TRIBUNALS

This table is based on that appended to the Annual Report of the Council on Tribunals for 1986–7, with the kind permission of the Council, whose secretariat have been most helpful. Columns have been added to show procedural regulations and rights of appeal. New tribunals have been added and some of the titles have been rearranged. Scotland is excluded.

Where procedural regulations have been amended, the latest amending order is shown in brackets. 'C. Act' means the tribunal's constituent Act, as shown under its title; 'T. & I. Act' means Tribunals and Inquiries Act 1971, s. 13, as extended by order under s. 15; '(law)' means that the appeal is on a point of law only.

Tribunal and constituent Act	Procedural regulations (mostly SI Nos.)	Body to which appeal lies	Number of tribunals constituted	Number of cases decided in 1986
Agriculture and Food				
Agricultural Land Tribunals (Agriculture Act 1947, s.73)	1978/259 1984/1301	High Court (law) (Ag. (Misc. P.) A.	8	134
Arbitrators (Agricultural Holdings Act 1986, sched. 11)	C. Act, sched 11	1954, s. 6)	192	72
Dairy Produce Quota Tribunal (SI 1986/470)	1986/470	None	1	79
Milk and Dairies Tribunals (Food Act 1984)	1986/723	None	5	2
Aircraft and Shipbuilding				
Arbitration Tribunal (Aircraft and Shipbuilding Industries Act 1977, s. 42)	1977/1022	Court of Appeal (C. Act, sched. 7)	1	0
Banking				
Banking Act Tribunal (Banking Act 1987, s. 28)	1987/1299	High Court (law) (C. Act, sched 7)	1	Not available
Betting Levy				
Betting Levy Appeal Tribunal (Betting, Gaming and Lotteries Act 1963, s. 29)	1963/748 (1982/270)	None	1	11
Building Societies				
Building Societies Tribunal (Building Societies Act 1986, s. 47)	1987/891	High Court (law) (C. Act, s. 49)	1	Not available

Tribunal and constituent Act	Procedural regulations (mostly SI Nos.)	Body to which appeal lies	Number of tribunals constituted	Number of cases decided in 1986
Civil Aviation				
Civil Aviation Authority (Civil Aviation Act 1982, s. 2)	1983/550 (1987/379)	Sec. of State (C. Act, s. 24)	1	1, 151
Commons				
Commons Commissioners and Assessors (Commons Registration Act 1965, s. 17)	1971/1727	High Court (law) (C. Act, s. 18)	4	224
Consumer Credit				
Director General of Fair Trading (Consumer Credit Act 1974, s. 3)	1976/837	Sec. of State, then High Court (law) (C. Act, ss. 41, 42)	5	250
Copyright and Patents				
Comptroller-General of Patents, Designs and Trade Marks (Patents and Designs Act 1907, s. 63)	1982/717 (1987/288) 1984/1989 (1987/287) 1986/1319	Patents Court (High Court)	3	6, 803
Copyright Tribunal (Copyright, Designs and Patents Act 1988, ch. VIII)	None yet	High Court (C. Act, ch. VIII)	None yet	Not in operation
Criminal Injuries				
Criminal Injuries Compensation Board (Criminal Justice Act 1988, pt. VII)		None	1	Act not in force
Data Protection				
Data Protection Registrar	None	Data Protection Tribunal	1	100, 718
Data Protection Tribunal (Data Protection Act 1984)	1985/1568	High Court (law) (C. Act, s. 14)	1	
Education				
Independent Schools Tribunals (Education Act 1944, s. 72)	1958/519 (1975/1298)	High Court (law) (T. & I. Act)	As required	1
Education Appeal Committees (Education Act 1980, sched. 2)	C. Act, sched. 2	None		Not available
Estate Agents				
Director General of Fair Trading (Estate Agents Act 1979, s. 3)	1981/1518	Sec. of State (C. Act, s. 7)	5	46

Tribunal and constituent Act	Procedural regulations (mostly SI Nos.)	Body to which appeal lies	Number of tribunals constituted	Number of cases decided in 1986
Financial Services				
Financial Services Tribunal (Financial Services Act 1986, s. 96)	None yet	High Court (law) (C. Act, sched. 6)		Not in operation
Foreign Compensation				
Foreign Compensation Commission (Foreign Compensation Act 1950, s. 1)	1956/962 (1968/164)	Court of Appeal (law) (Foreign Compensation Act 1969, s. 3)	1	647
Forestry				
Reference Committees (Forestry Act 1967, ss. 20, 21)	None	None	As required	0
Immigration				
Immigration Adjudicators	1984/2040	Immig. App. Tribunal	84	6, 664
Immigration Appeal Tribunal (Immigration Act 1971, s. 12)	1984/2041	None	4 divisions	592
Industry and Employment				
Industry Arbitration Tribunal (Industry Act 1975, s. 20)	C. Act, sched. 3	Court of Appeal (law) (C. Act, sched. 3)	None	0
Industrial Training Referees (Industrial Training Act 1982, s. 14)	1974/1335	None	1	4
Industrial Tribunals (Employment Protection (Consolidation) Act 1978, s. 128) for appeals etc. under—			14 regional offices	11, 532 (all heads)
(a) C. Act;	1985/16	Employment		
(b) Equal Pay Act 1970;	1985/16	Appeal Tribunal		
(c) Sex Discrimination Act 1975;	1977/1094	(mostly law)		
(d) Race Relations Act 1976;	1977/1094	(C. Act, s. 136)		
(e) Health and Safety at Work etc. Act 1974; S.I. 1977/500 reg. 11;	1974/1925	High Court (law) (T. & I. Act)		
(f) Industrial Training Act 1982;	1965/1101 (1967/302)	do.		
(g) Docks and Harbours Act 1966;	1985/16	do.		
(h) Dock Work Regulation Act 1976.	1985/16	do.		

Tribunal and constituent Act	Procedural regulations (mostly SI Nos.)	Body to which appeal lies	Number of tribunals constituted	Number of cases decided in 1986
Insolvency				
Insolvency Practitioners Tribunal (Insolvency Acts 1985, s. 8; 1986, s. 396)	1986/952	High Court (law) (Act of 1985, sched. 1)	1	0
Iron and Steel				
Iron and Steel Arbitration Tribunal (Iron and Steel Act 1982, s. 25)	1965/1415	Court of Appeal (C. Act, s. 26)	1	0
Justices and Clerks Indemnification	1965/1367	None	None	0
Appointed person (Justices of the Peace Act 1979, s. 53)				
Land				
The Lands Tribunal (Lands Tribunal Act 1949, s. 1) *see also* Commons, Rents	1975/299 (1986/1322)	Court of Appeal (law) (C. Act, s. 3)	1	647
London Building Acts				
Appeal Tribunal (London Building Acts (Amendment) Act 1939, s. 109)	1953, July (not SI)	High Court (law) (C. Act, s. 116)	As required	0
Mental Health				
Mental Health Review Tribunals (Mental Health Act 1983, s. 65)	1983/942	High Court (law) (C. Act, s. 78)	2, 920	
Mines and Quarries				
Mines and Quarries Tribunals (Mines and Quarries Act 1954, s. 150)	C. Act, sched. 3	High Court (law) (T. & I. Act)	None	0
Misuse of Drugs				
Misuse of Drugs Tribunal (Misuse of Drugs Act 1972, sched. 3)	1974/85	None	2	
National Health Service				
Family Practitioner Committees and Service Committees (National Health Service Act 1977, s. 10 and SI 1974 No. 455)	1974/455 (1974/907)	N.H.S. Tribunal or Sec. of State (SI 1974/455)	90 360	2, 312

Tribunal and constituent Act	Procedural regulations (mostly SI Nos.)	Body to which appeal lies	Number of tribunals constituted	Number of cases decided in 1986
National Health Service Tribunal (National Health Service Act s. 1977, s. 46)	1974/455 (1974/907)	High Court (law) (T. & I. Act) and Sec. of State (SI 1974/455)	2	7
Pensions				
Occupational Pensions Board (Social Security Act 1973, s. 66)	1973/1776 1976/185	High Court (law) (C. Act, s. 86)	1	0
Pensions Appeal Tribunals (Pensions Appeal Tribunals Act 1943)	1980/1120 (1986/366)	High Court (law) (C. Act, s. 6)	Ad hoc	1, 861
Police Pensions Tribunals (SI 1987/257, reg. H6)	None	High Court (law) (C. reg.)	None	0
Performing Rights				
Performing Right Tribunal[1] (Copyright Act 1956, s. 23)	1965/1506 (1971/636)	High Court (law) (C. Act, s. 30)	2	4
Plant Varieties and Seeds				
Controller of Plant Variety Rights	1978/294 (1982/1101)	Tribunal (C. Act, s. 7 (11))	2	0
Plant Varieties and Seeds Tribunal (Plant Varieties and Seeds Act 1964, ss. 10, 11(5); European Communities Act 1972, sched. 4, para. 5(5))	1974/1136	High Court (law) (C. Act, s. 10(2))	4	0
Rates and Community Charge				
Local Valuation Courts (General Rate Act 1967, s. 88)	1956/632	Lands Tribunal (C. Act, s. 77)	64 panels	48,335
Valuation and Community Charge Tribunals (Local Government Finance Act 1988)	None yet		None yet	Not in operation
Registered Homes				
Registered Homes Tribunals (Registered Homes Act 1984, s. 41) for appeals under (a) C. Act; (b) Nursing Homes Act 1975;	1984/1346	High Court (law) (HSSSSA Act[2] 1983, sched. 9)	Ad hoc	39

[1]   This tribunal will disappear when the Copyright Act 1988 comes into force.
[2]   Health and Social Services and Social Security Adjudications Act.

Tribunal and constituent Act	Procedural regulations (mostly SI Nos.)	Body to which appeal lies	Number of tribunals constituted	Number of cases decided in 1986
(c) Child Care Act 1980;				
(d) Residential Homes Act 1980;				
(e) Children's Homes Act 1982.				
Rents and Enfranchisement				
Rent Tribunals	1980/1700	High Court (law)	Ad hoc	3,653
(Housing Act 1980, s. 72)	(1981/1493)	(T. & I. Act)	from	
Rent Assessment Committees	1971/1065	High Court (law)	13 Panels	15,346
(Rent Act 1977, 10th sched.)	(1981/1783)	(T. & I. Act)		
Leasehold Valuation Tribunals	1981/271	Lands Tribunal	As above	Not
(Housing Act 1980, s. 142)		(C. Act, sched. 22)		available
Revenue				
General Commissioners of Income Tax	C. Act, s. 48	High Court (law) (C. Act, s. 56)	429	565, 995
(Taxes Management Act 1970, s. 2)				
Special Commissioners of Income Tax	C. Act, s. 48	High Court (law) (C. Act, s. 56) or Court of Appeal (SI 1987/1422)	6 Commrs. quorum of 2	
(Taxes Management Act 1970, s. 4)				
Tax Avoidance Tribunal	None	High Court (law) (C. Act, s. 462)	1	2
(Income and Corporation Taxes Act 1970, s. 463)				
Value Added Tax Tribunals	1986/590	High Court (law)	7 centres	547
(V.A.T. Act 1983, sched. 8)	(1986/2290)	(SI 1972/1210)		
Social Security				
Social Security Appeal Tribunals	1986/2218	S.S. Commissioner	181	34, 624
(HSSSSA Act 1983,[3] sched. 8)	(1987/1424)	(S.S. Act 1975, s. 101)		
Medical Appeal Tribunals	1986/2218	S.S. Commissioner	22	9, 764
(S.S. Act 1975, sched. 12)	(1987/335)	(law) (S.S. Act 1975, s. 112)		
Social Security Commissioners	1987/214	Court of Appeal	15	3, 702
(S.S. Act 1975, s. 97)		(law) (S.S. Act 1980, s. 14)		
Tax Tribunals: *See* Revenue				
Transport (road)				
Traffic Commissioners	1980/1354	Sec. of State	9	8, 496
(Transport Act 1985, s. 3)	(1986/1668)	(C. Act, ss. 9, 42) Transport Tribunal (C. Act, s. 31)		

[3]   See note 2, above.

Tribunal and constituent Act	Procedural regulations (mostly SI Nos.)	Body to which appeal lies	Number of tribunals constituted	Number of cases decided in 1986
Transport Tribunal (Transport Act 1985, sched. 4)	1986/1547	Court of Appeal (law)[4] (C. Act, sched. 4)	1	23
Vaccine Damage				
Vaccine Damage Tribunals (Vaccine Damage Payments Act 1979, s. 4)	1979/432	None	6	26
Wireless Telegraphy				
Wireless Telegraphy Tribunal (Wireless Telegraphy Act 1949, s. 9)	Rules, 1953 (not SI)	High Court (law) (T. & I. Act)	1	0

[4] No appeal lies on questions of fact or locus standi: C. Act, sched. 4, para. 14(2).

24

STATUTORY INQUIRIES

THE SYSTEM OF INQUIRIES

An administrative technique

The statutory inquiry is the standard device for giving a fair hearing to objectors before the final decision is made on some question of government policy affecting citizens' rights or interests.[1] Any project such as the compulsory acquisition of land, the making of a slum-clearance order, the siting of a power station or an airport, or the building of a motorway will provide for a public inquiry as a preliminary to the decision; and the same applies to some very common procedures such as planning appeals. People who wish to object have important procedural rights, derived partly from statute and partly from the principles of natural justice and regulated in some respects by the Tribunals and Inquiries Act 1971.

The inquiry system is a prominent feature of British administrative law in comparison with that of other countries. In France and some countries where there are special administrative courts, there are sometimes more generous principles of compensation for loss caused by official action, whether rightful or wrongful; but there is less procedural protection before the action is taken. The English system makes elaborate provision for preliminary inquiries, on the principle that prevention is better than cure. The primary objectives are to make sure that the best possible decision is made in the public interest, and that the citizen has his objections fairly considered. There is no conflict between these objectives: the best way to assess the merits of an administrative scheme or order is to give full consideration to the arguments of the potential victims.

The distinction between tribunals and inquiries, explained in the previous chapter,[2] is based on the difference between judicial and administrative power. Inquiries are part of the procedure for ensuring that administrative power is fairly and reasonably exercised, so that they have the same purpose as the legal principles of natural justice. Although an official act cannot be challenged if it is good on its face and within the powers conferred, rules can still be laid down for ensuring that the elements

---

[1] For a detailed treatment of public inquiries and their problems see Wraith and Lamb, *Public Inquiries as an Instrument of Government*. See also Ganz, *Administrative Procedures*, 39.

[2] Above, p. 900.

of fair procedure are followed before the moment of decision. On the one hand there is the common law rule requiring a fair hearing, *audi alteram partem*. On the other hand there are many statutes which themselves provide for inquiries or hearings and which lay down a mandatory procedure for dealing with objections. The statutory procedure is only a framework, within which the principles of natural justice operate to fill in details.[3] Each Act contains its own rudimentary code, usually in a schedule at the end of the Act; but the provisions have become stereotyped and may be discussed without much differentiation.

Although a main object of these inquiries is to assuage the feelings of the citizen, and to give his objections the fairest possible consideration, they have given rise to many complaints. They are a hybrid legal-and-administrative process, and for the very reason that they have been made to look as much as possible like a judicial proceeding, people grumble at the fact that they fall short of it. They were reviewed both by the Ministers' Powers Committee of 1932 and by the Committee on Tribunals and Enquiries (the Franks Committee) of 1957. The first report had little practical effect; but the government's acceptance of the Franks Committee's principal recommendations marked a turning-point at which repeated criticisms at last achieved results.

Statutory inquiries are now so common that it is unusual to find a statute concerned with planning control or with the acquisition of land, or indeed with any important scheme of administrative control, which does not provide this machinery for one or more purposes. Acts concerned with housing, town and country planning, new towns, road, agriculture, health, transport, aviation, rivers, police, local government—these are merely a few examples to show the range of subjects covered by what has now become a standard technique. Many inquiries have to be held in cases of compulsory acquisition, as, for example, where land is taken for roads, schools, hospitals, airfields, housing estates, town development, open spaces and playing fields, swimming-baths, cemeteries, children's homes, markets, slaughter-houses, smallholdings. Planning inquiries are the most numerous class, since they are held not only before the adoption of planning schemes of a general character but also in many cases of individual appeals against refusal of planning permission or against conditions imposed by a local planning authority. The Department of the Environment, which arranges inquiries concerning local authorities and some central departments, as well as all its own cases of housing and planning, has in England a corps of some 380 inspectors[4] responsible for about 3,000 inquiries a year.

[3] Above, p. 533.
[4] Including about 90 independent consultant inspectors and about 115 part-time inspectors.

Relation of law and policy

In the vast majority of cases in which statutory inquiry procedures are employed the ultimate decision is one of policy, and commonly it is taken by a minister. It is essentially for such decisions that the technique of inquiries has been developed. Should the minister confirm a scheme for the motorway? Should he approve a slum-clearance scheme? Should he confirm a compulsory purchase order? Should he allow an appeal against refusal of planning permission by the local authority? The answers will depend on what he decides is expedient in the public interest. They cannot be found by applying rules of law, and the problems are therefore unsuitable for independent tribunals.

There are exceptional cases, as noted in the previous chapter, where ministers have to decide questions of law or fact which do not depend upon policy and are therefore judicial, such as the questions reserved to the Secretary of State in the award of social security benefits.[5] Here also the minister will appoint some person to hear the case and report to him, much in the manner of an inquiry; for unless he is to adjudicate in person there is no other way for him to have the case heard. He will not, of course, take part personally in the great majority of his decisions, whether political or otherwise; his officials will issue a decision in his name in the normal way.[6] But any case of special importance may reach him, and in one which gave rise to public controversy he told the House of Commons that a crucial part of the decision letter was drafted 'in my own fair hand'.[7]

The inquiries which matter most in administrative law are those which are required by statute before the minister may lawfully make some order. This is the situation in most of the examples discussed in this book. If some part of the statutory procedure has not been properly followed, or there has been a breach of natural justice, there will have been no valid inquiry and any order made in consequence, if challenged within any statutory time limit, can be quashed by the court.[8] Legal irregularity here has a clear legal result. But inquiries are set up by ministers in many other situations where they have no effect on the validity of any particular act or order. An Act will often give power for the minister to hold an inquiry, if he thinks fit, into any matter connected with his functions under the Act, as for instance do the National Health Service Act 1977,[9] the Town and Country

---

[5] Above, p. 902.
[6] Above, p. 366.
[7] 725 HC Deb col 1370 (2 March 1966). This was the *Islington* case mentioned below, p. 995.
[8] For examples see above, p. 539.
[9] s. 84.

Planning Act 1971[10] and the Local Government Act 1972.[11] There are also many specific cases where the Act makes the holding of the inquiry discretionary. Some attention must be paid to discretionary inquiries since many of them have been brought within the Tribunals and Inquiries Act 1971.[12] Furthermore, it would be rash to say that irregularity in an inquiry of this class could never affect the validity of a ministerial order, even though the minister could have dispensed with the inquiry altogether had he wished.

Evolution of the inquiry system

'A scholarly treatise on the history of public inquiries would perhaps start with the Domesday surveys.'[13] But the statutory inquiries which are the subject of this chapter need not be traced back to any remote origin. Like so many other features of administrative law, they came into prominence along with the expansion of central and local government powers in the nineteenth century. When it became impossible to provide for all the details of government by Act of Parliament, inquiries were adopted as a kind of substitute, in the administrative sphere, for the parliamentary process which accompanied legislation. Parliament was accustomed to a great deal of private and local bill legislation, in the course of which parliamentary committees gave full hearings to persons affected, who were often represented by counsel who called and examined witnesses before the committees, much as they would do before a court of law. When more expeditious procedures had to be found, an administrative inquiry was the natural way to give effect to the right to be heard.

The first step in this direction was the introduction of Provisional Order procedure. An Act granting powers to some statutory authority would authorise it to make a provisional order, which could not be made until the authority had held an inquiry and considered objections, and which would not take effect until confirmed by Act of Parliament. An early example was the General Inclosure Act 1845, which required inclosure commissioners to publish inclosure schemes and to hold 'meetings to hear objections'; they might then make a provisional order, which would take effect when a Provisional Order Confirmation Act (usually confirming a multitude of such orders) was passed. Many important Acts such as the Public Health Acts 1848, 1875 and 1936 and the Local Government Acts from 1858 to

---

[10] s. 282.

[11] s. 250.

[12] Below, p. 988.

[13] Wraith and Lamb, *Public Inquiries as an Instrument of Government*, 17, relating in greater detail the history here summarised.

1933 adopted this procedure. Its advantage was that the objections were considered locally, more conveniently and less expensively,[14] by the promoting authority itself before the parliamentary stage. But its disadvantage was that if the inclusion of the order in the Confirmation Bill was petitioned against in Parliament, objectors were entitled to further hearings as in the case of a private Bill. For the most part the initial inquiry obviated further objection at the parliamentary stage, and the procedure remained in general use for a century. Ultimately a further simplification was made by the Statutory Orders (Special Procedure) Act 1945, which dispensed with confirmation by Act of Parliament where any Act made an order 'subject to special parliamentary procedure', substituting a system whereby the order took effect automatically[15] in the absence of opposition, though it was annullable by either House and petitions could be examined by a joint committee.[16] This Act in no way weakened the system of initial inquiries, nor did it abolish provisional order procedure in all cases.[17]

A more drastic simplification was to empower a minister himself to confirm provisional orders such as compulsory purchase orders made by local authorities. This innovation was made by the Local Government Act 1894[18] under which county councils might acquire land on behalf of parish councils. The county council had first to hold a public inquiry before submitting the order, and the Local Government Board had to hold a further local inquiry if a memorial of opposition was then presented to them; but if no memorial was presented, the order was to be confirmed by the Board itself. An inquiry by the Board, as by any other public authority, was held before an inspector appointed by them. Doubts which arose about the validity of the Board of Trade's inquiries held in this way were set at rest by the Board of Trade Inquiries Act 1872.[19] Meanwhile general powers to

[14] See *R. v. Hastings Local Board of Health* (1865) 6 B & S 401 (the court's ruling that an irregular order could not be quashed by certiorari seems out of line with later authority: see above, p. 632).

[15] After fourteen days, extended to twenty-one days by Statutory Orders (Special Procedure) Act 1965.

[16] An example is the Acquisition of Land Act 1981, ss. 17–20, requiring special parliamentary procedure for compulsory purchase of land belonging to a local authority, statutory undertakers, or the National Trust: above, p. 175.

[17] The new procedure could be applied by order to earlier Acts: it was applied to the Public Health, Local Government, and Housing Acts by SI 1949 No. 2393; but provisional order procedure was partially restored by SI 1962 No. 409. See Allen, *Law and Orders*, 3rd edn., 79, 81. For provisional orders and special procedure orders in local government see Local Government Act 1972, s. 240.

[18] s. 9.

[19] The Board of Trade had to conduct many inquiries, e.g. accident inquiries and inquiries under the Telegraph Act 1863 and the Electric Lighting Act 1882 connected with the laying of lines.

hold inquiries into any matter arising under an Act were conferred by the Education Act 1870 and the Public Health Act 1875.

In fact the familiar combination of public inquiry followed by departmental order, made without reference to Parliament, was in use well before the Local Government Act 1894. It was employed by the Charity Commissioners in reorganising obsolete charities under the Charitable Trusts Act 1853 and by the Education Department in setting up school boards under the compulsory powers of the Education Act 1870. The latter Act, like a number of others of its period, contained detailed provisions about the inquiries which it authorised or required for various purposes. Most of the elements of the modern inquiry system could therefore be observed in practice more than a century ago.

Specimen procedure (slum clearance)

The procedure of statutory inquiries has now become standardised. No single statute lays down the procedure, but the numerous modern statutes which prescribe inquiries follow a common pattern, with only a few significant variations. Inquiries held under the Housing Acts provide a typical example. Several cases arising out of earlier Housing Acts have illustrated inquiries in relation to natural justice.[20] The Housing Act 1957, formerly the principal statute, contained four separate sets of detailed rules for inquiries among its schedules. The Housing Act 1985 has simplified matters by adopting the procedure of the Acquisition of Land Act 1981 except in the case of compulsory purchase for slum clearance. It is this latter procedure, as scheduled to the Act of 1985,[21] that is summarised in the following paragraphs. These orders are made on the initiative of local authorities for the acquisition of areas of bad housing for the purpose of their wholesale demolition and clearance (commonly called slum clearance), as explained earlier.[22]

The first step is for the local authority to pass a resolution defining the clearance area, which they are obliged to do if satisfied as to certain facts. The resolution is only a preliminary step to prepare the way for either a compulsory purchase order or else a purchase by agreement. A compulsory purchase order requires the consent of the Secretary of State before it can become effective, and the time for making objections is between the making of the order and the Secretary of State's decision upon it. Before the local authority may submit a clearance order to the Secretary of State they must make it available for inspection and advertise it in the local press.

[20] Above, p. 507.
[21] 22nd sched.
[22] Above, p. 201.

They must also notify owners, occupiers and mortgagees of the land, and inform them of their opportunities for making objections. If no objection is made, the Secretary of State may confirm the order with or without modification. But the important provision is to the following effect:[23]

If any objection duly made is not withdrawn, the Secretary of State shall, before confirming the order, either cause a public local inquiry to be held or afford to any person by whom an objection has been duly made and not withdrawn an opportunity of appearing before and being heard by a person appointed for the purpose, and, after considering any objection not withdrawn and the report of the person who held the inquiry or was so appointed, may confirm the order with or without modification.

It has been held that the final words empower the Secretary of State to modify an invalid order so as to make it a valid one, at least in cases where the flaw is not of a fundamental character;[24] and that an order of this two-stage type is legally 'made' when it is confirmed by the Secretary of State, since before then it has no operative force in law.[25]

If the order is confirmed, the local authority must against advertise it and inform objectors. A period of six weeks is then allowed within which any one who wishes to challenge the order on legal grounds (e.g. ultra vires) must apply to the High Court. Subject to any legal dispute, the order becomes operative at the end of the six weeks, and thereafter 'shall not be questioned in any legal proceedings whatsoever'. The significance of this drastic clause is explained elsewhere.[26] Standardised provisions of the same kind are found in the legislation governing the compulsory purchase of land both under the general statute, the Acquisition of Land Act 1981,[27] and a variety of other Acts such as the Water Resources Act 1963, the Forestry Act 1967 and the New Towns Act 1981.

Hearing, report and decision

Where there is opposition to the order, the usual sequence of events is that objection is formally lodged and a public local inquiry is held. In fact the statutory formula allows the Secretary of State to hold either a public local inquiry or a hearing, which suggests that a hearing need not be public. But

---

[23] This states the combined effect of paras. 4(1) and 5(1) of the 22nd sched., slightly paraphrased.

[24] *Minister of Health* v. *The King ex p. Yaffé* [1931] AC 494. See also *Re Bowman* [1932] 2 KB 621; *Legg* v. *Inner London Education Authority* [1972] 1 WLR 1245 (Secretary of State's power to approve with 'modifications' exceeded).

[25] *Iveagh (Earl)* v. *Minister of Housing and Local Government* [1964] 1 QB 395 (historic building preservation order).

[26] Above, p. 724.

[27] See above, p. 174.

other statutes speak merely of a 'local inquiry',[28] and it is not clear how this is intended to differ from a hearing, although the words seem to indicate an investigation going beyond a hearing of those who have lodged formal objections.[29] It may be that the word 'public' is omitted in order to prevent the validity of the inquiry being questioned if the public, or members of it, are excluded, for instance where they try to disrupt the inquiry by misbehaviour. The regular practice, in any case, is to hold public inquiries rather than hearings,[30] thus giving the public an opportunity to participate and giving the minister the benefit of all points of view. The Tribunals and Inquiries Act 1971 will apply in either case,[31] but in other statutes there may be differences.[32]

The person appointed by the Secretary of State to hold the inquiry or hearing is in most cases a departmental inspector. The 'case' is thus 'heard' before an official of the department concerned. But the local authority and the objectors may be legally represented, and an important inquiry will have some of the atmosphere of a trial. The inspector may conduct the inquiry as he wishes, subject in some cases to procedural regulations. The objectors will call witnesses and examine them, and the local authority's representatives may cross-examine them. The authority will also frequently call witnesses of its own. The inspector, like a judge, will often take very little part in the argument; his task is to hear the objections and the arguments and then give advice to the minister. Despite the implications of 'inquiry', the procedure is basically adversary, i.e. between opposing parties, and not inquisitorial.

In due course the inquiry is closed, and the inspector makes his report. Until 1958 the normal practice was to refuse disclosure of this report to the objectors: it was treated as an official document like any other paper on the department's files, and like any other report from a civil servant to his department, it was treated as confidential.[33] Eventually the minister's decision would be given; but often under the old practice it would be unaccompanied by reasons, unless, exceptionally, the statute required

---

[28] e.g. Town and Country Planning Act 1971, s. 282; Local Government Act 1972, s. 250; Highways Act 1980, 1st sched., para. 7. 'Public local inquiries' are required in compulsory purchase cases under the Acquisition of Land Act 1981, s. 13 and 1st sched., para. 4.

[29] See below, p. 975. Where there are statutory rules of procedure (below, p. 984) they normally apply to both inquiries and hearings.

[30] A hearing rather than an inquiry is now exceptional: Parliamentary Commissioner for Adminstration, Annual Report for 1974 (HC 1974–5 No. 126), p. 7. See also Wraith and Lamb, *Public Inquiries as an Instrument of Government*, 159.

[31] Below, p. 969.

[32] As in the matter of costs: below, p. 988.

[33] Above, p. 508.

reasons to be given.[34] The failure to disclose the report and to state reasons was the source of much of the dissatisfaction with inquires before the reforms of 1958. Although the controversies which raged round these questions have now passed into history, they provide a classic illustration of the clash between the legal and administrative points of view.

Statutory inquiries and natural justice

A statutory inquiry is a parliamentary and formalised version of the fair hearing which is required by the common law according to the principles of natural justice. It does not displace natural justice:[35] it should be regarded rather as a framework within which natural justice can operate and supply missing details. The common law's presumption that Parliament intends power to be exercised fairly is all the stronger where Parliament itself has provided for a hearing.

We have already seen how the statutory and common law procedures interacted in the Housing Act cases. In the *Arlidge* case the House of Lords imposed restrictions that were thought to be necessary in the interests of departmental efficiency but which proved to be wrong in principle.[36] In the *Errington* case the Court of Appeal filled a gap in the statutory procedure by invalidating the minister's order where he consulted one party behind the back of the other, thus violating natural justice.[37] The minister's quasi-judicial duty was discussed on the footing that the statutory inquiry made no material difference. Lord Loreburn's famous formula[38] was taken as the rubric, and the minister's function was held to be quasi-judicial—as the inspector's had been held to be also.[39] Natural justice has in fact been applied in a long series of cases to the whole procedure of a public inquiry, comprising the inspector's and the minister's functions alike.[40] The principle of these cases was that the law could not be content with seeing merely that the form of the statutory procedure had been followed. The same applies to the statutory rules of procedure which have been made for many inquiries, as explained later.[41]

---

[34] As did the Housing Act 1957 in certain cases: see 5th sched., para. 5(4) (minister to give reasons, if requested, for treating a building as unfit for human habitation if disputed by owner at the inquiry).

[35] In *Bushell* v. *Secretary of State for the Environment* [1981] AC 75 at 95 Lord Diplock preferred the terminology of 'fairness', which has come into vogue since the earlier decisions.

[36] Above, p. 508.

[37] Above, p. 509.

[38] Above, p. 506.

[39] *Denby (William) & Sons Ltd.* v. *Minister of Health* [1936] 1 KB 337.

[40] Above, p. 510.

[41] See the cases on compulsory purchase and planning cited above, p. 539.

This principle may now be taken to be correct, despite unsound dicta in the House of Lords suggesting that the minister need do nothing beyond what is specified in the statute,[42] and that natural justice has no part to play where ministers have to attach importance to their policy.[43] The advantages of a statutory inquiry should be additional to the basic procedural fairness which natural justice supplies.

COMPLAINTS AND REFORMS

Lawyers' criticisms

Lord Hewart spoke for many lawyers when he made his attack on the then prevailing procedures in his book *The New Despotism*, published in 1929 when he was Lord Chief Justice. He wrote:[44]

The departmental policy of secrecy, which is inveterate, is in itself sufficient to condemn the system under which the public departments act as tribunals to decide disputes of a judicial nature. This secrecy naturally leads to the conclusion that the departments are afraid of their proceedings being made public, and tends to destroy confidence in the fairness of their decisions. How is it to be expected that a party against whom a decision has been given in a hole-and-corner fashion, and without any grounds being specified, should believe that he has had justice? Even the party in whose favour a dispute is decided must, in such circumstances, be tempted to look upon the result as a mere piece of luck.

Turning then to inquiries specifically, he continued:[45]

It is sometimes enacted that, before the Minister comes to a decision, he shall hold a public inquiry, at which interested parties are entitled to adduce evidence and be heard. But that provision is no real safeguard, because the person who has the power of deciding is in no way bound by the report or the recommendations of the person who holds the inquiry, and may entirely ignore the evidence which the inquiry brought to light. He can, and in practice sometimes does, give a decision wholly inconsistent with the report, the recommendations, and the evidence, which are not published or disclosed to interested individuals. In any case, as the official who decides has not seen or heard the witnesses, he is as a rule quite incapable of estimating the value of their evidence . . . the requirement of a public inquiry is in practice nugatory. . . . It seems absurd that one official should hold a public inquiry into the merits of a proposal, and that another official should be entitled, disregarding the report of the first, to give a decision on the merits.

---

[42] Criticised above, p. 491.
[43] Criticised above, p. 556.
[44] p. 48.
[45] p. 51.

The essential compromise

The fact that these criticisms failed to face was that where the decision is one of policy there is no reason why the final decision should be based exclusively on evidence given at the inquiry—and often it will not be. Suppose, to take the case of the new town at Stevenage,[46] that the local residents oppose the scheme for a new town on the grounds that there will be serious difficulties of water supply and sewage disposal. The objections are merely one factor which must be weighed by the minister and his advisers against the demands of national policy. It may be that these objections apply to all the other eligible sites for the new town. It may be, also, that the need to develop new towns is so great that the expense of overcoming serious physical obstacles will justify itself. It may be, again, that the other advantages of the site outweigh the objections. These are eminently the sort of matters upon which the final decision will turn. But it is impossible to bring them all to a head at a public inquiry in the same way in which a legal issue can be brought to a head in a court of law.[47] For the question before a court of law is self-contained: the evidence on matters of fact and the argument on matters of law provide the judge with all the material for his decision. If fed with the right data he should deliver the right answer.

A minister's decision on a planning scheme or a clearance scheme or a new town order is a different kind of mental exercise, for there is the whole exterior world of political motive.[48] Even if the minister sends representatives to explain questions of policy before the inspector, as is often now required, this does not solve the problem. For it is fundamental that political decisions should be taken by a minister responsible to Parliament, and that the political responsibility should rest entirely upon him and not upon his officials or advisers. Furthermore, the place where policy should be explained is Parliament, where the responsibility lies. Nothing, therefore, can prevent the ultimate responsibility lying outside the forum of an inquiry, whereas it must lie inside the forum of a court of law.

Nevertheless there are exceptional cases. Courts of law may appear to take decisions of policy and ministers may decide particular cases into which policy does not seem to enter. For reasons of convenience inspectors hearing planning appeals have been empowered to decide a great many of

---

[46] Above, p. 491.

[47] The minister may naturally use knowledge acquired elsewhere: *Price* v. *Minister of Health* (1947) 116 LJR 291. This is subject to the limits indicated below, p. 982. For the position generally see above, p. 508.

[48] See *Johnson (B.) & Co. Ltd.* v. *Minister of Health* [1947] 2 All ER 395 at 399 (Lord Greene MR).

the cases themselves.[49] This does not alter the fact that legal decisions and political decisions are different things and require different procedures.

'Blowing off steam'

The realities sometimes leave objectors with a sense of frustration, feeling that they are fighting a phantom opponent, and that they have no assurance of coming to grips with the real issues which are going to decide the case. In the *Stevenage* case the judge of first instance said:[50]

To take any other view [sc. than that the minister must have reasonable grounds for his decision] would reduce the provisions for objections, the holding of a local public inquiry, the report of the officer who holds it, and the consideration of that report by the Minister to an absurdity, because when all has been said and done the Minister could disregard the whole proceedings and do just as he pleased. The Attorney-General argued that that was, indeed, the position, and that the sole use of the liberty to make objections was that the objectors (I am quoting his words) might 'blow off steam' and so rally public opinion to which alone the Minister might bow.

But as is obvious, and as the appellate courts held,[51] the minister's decision cannot be dictated to him by the inspector's conclusions from the inquiry.

To conclude from this that the inquiry is merely an opportunity to blow off steam is cynical and unrealistic. It assumes that a government department will take no notice of its inspector's report unless it is legally obliged to do so, and that is obviously wrong. The important thing is not that the decision should be dictated by the report but that the objectors' case should be fairly heard and should be fairly taken into account. The law can ensure that their case is heard. But it cannot ensure that any particular weight is given to it.[52] That, after all, is precisely the basis on which the judges have developed the principles of natural justice. In imposing the general rule that a man is entitled to be heard in his defence before his property or his livelihood can be taken from him, the law has never required that there must be any rational connection between the defence put forward and the final order made. It is enough to assume that a responsible official will pay due regard to the other side of the case once his mind is directed to it. The real risk is not that he will perversely disregard the evidence but that he will be tempted to act before he has discovered that there is another side to the case. The same applies to public inquiries, which

---

[49] Above, p. 189. for rules of procedure in these cases see SI 1974 No. 420.
[50] [1947] 1 All ER at 398.
[51] Above, p. 492.
[52] Subject to the rules as to judicial review for unreasonableness, etc.: above, p. 395.

are merely a statutory and formal method of giving effect to the same principle of justice which the judges developed by case-law.

The running fire of adverse comment from the legal profession was not therefore always directed at the right target. The statutory inquiry has proved to be an essential piece of mechanism and the committees who have reported upon it have been unable to suggest anything better. It is incessantly in use, and it is now as familiar as any other governmental procedure. After the reforms and improvements which it received from 1958 onwards it may be fairly called one of the more successful institutions in the sphere of administrative procedure.

The Ministers' Powers Committee (1932)

The first general report on the system of inquiries was made by the Committee on Ministers' Powers of 1932.[53] The whole tenor of its approach was that the statutory procedure was a vehicle for the principles of natural justice, and it was recommended that those principles should go further than they did. Natural justice ought, it was suggested, to include a right to have reasons for the decision, and perhaps also a right to see the report of the inspector. The Committee concluded that in any case, regardless of natural justice, the right solution to the dilemma of inspectors' reports was to publish them. The right to a hearing should also include the right for the objector to know in good time the case which he had to meet.

None of these recommendations resulted in any change in the law or in departmental practice, and twenty-five years were to pass before the same questions were taken up with greater success by the Franks Committee. Meanwhile complaint continued unabated, especially on the non-disclosure of inspectors' reports. Discontent was aggravated by comparison with the enlightened practices of departments such as the Ministry of Transport which already employed independent inspectors, published their reports, and gave reasons for their decisions.

The Franks Committee (1957)

The Committee on Tribunals and Inquiries (the Franks Committee) surveyed the whole ground again in its report of 1957.[54] This was a more extensive, factual, and practical report than the report of 1932; and it caught a favouring tide of public opinion. Although there was a recommendation (not accepted) that inspectors should be put under the control of the Lord Chancellor, no real attempt was made to follow the

[53] Cmd. 4060 (1932).
[54] Cmnd. 218 (1957).

American lead in separating the functions of 'prosecutor' and 'judge'.[55] The value of the Committee's work lay rather in its proposals for improving the existing system, which have achieved considerable success and have greatly reduced the volume of public complaint. Of outstanding importance were the recommendations (accepted) that inspectors' reports should be published and that objectors should be able to know as early as possible what case they had to meet.

Just as in the case of tribunals,[56] the Committee contrasted 'two strongly opposed views': the 'administrative' and the 'judicial' views.[57] The administrative view, which had been dominant previously, stressed that the minister was responsible to Parliament and to Parliament only for his decision, and that it could not in any way be governed by rules. The judicial view held that an inquiry was something like a trial before a judge and that the decision should be based wholly and directly on the evidence. Both these extremes were rejected—and this involved rejecting the established philosophy that was supposed to justify non-disclosure of the government's case and non-disclosure of the inspector's report. The Committee said:[58]

If the administrative view is dominant the public enquiry cannot play its full part in the total process, and there is a danger that the rights and interests of the individual citizens affected will not be sufficiently protected. In these cases it is idle to argue that Parliament can be relied upon to protect the citizen, save exceptionally. . . . If the judicial view is dominant there is a danger that people will regard the person before whom they state their case as a kind of judge provisionally deciding the matter, subject to an appeal to the Minister. This view overlooks the true nature of the proceedings, the form of which is necessitated by the fact that the Minister himself, who is responsible to Parliament for the ultimate decision, cannot conduct the enquiry in person.

The Committee rejected the notion that objectors could not expect the same standard of justice when the scheme was initiated by the same minister who had ultimately to decide its fate rather than by some other authority. This misconception had gained currency because of the difficulty of finding any other explanation for what was said by the House of Lords in one case.[59] But one anomaly does not justify another. The Committee put fallacious distinctions firmly aside:[60]

These and other possible distinctions are useful in considering detailed aspects of

[55] Below, p. 996.
[56] Above, p. 913.
[57] Para. 262.
[58] Paras. 273–4.
[59] *Franklin* v. *Minister of Town and Country Planning* [1948] AC 87; above, p. 491.
[60] Para. 267.

the various procedures, but they are misleading when what has to be considered is their general nature. Not only is the impact of these various procedures the same so far as the individual citizen is concerned, for he is at issue with a public authority in all of them, but they also have basic common features of importance when regarded from a wider point of view. All involve the weighing of proposals or decisions, or provisional proposals or decisions, made by a public authority on the one hand against the views and interests of individuals affected by them on the other. All culminate in a ministerial decision, in the making of which there is a wide discretion and which is final.

The plan of reform

Two primary recommendations were that there should be a permanent and independent body, the Council on Tribunals, and that the Council should formulate rules of procedure for inquiries which would have statutory force. The Council on Tribunals was constituted by the Tribunals and Inquiries Act 1958 (now replaced by the Act of 1971) but as a purely advisory body. As regards inquiries, it has to consider and report on such matters as may be referred to it by the Lord Chancellor, or as it may itself determine to be of special importance, concerning 'administrative procedures involving, or which may involve, the holding by or on behalf of a Minister of a statutory inquiry'.[61] A statutory inquiry is defined as 'an inquiry or hearing held or to be held in pursuance of a duty imposed by any statutory provision'—that is to say, an inquiry which the minister is obliged to hold—with the addition of such other inquiries or hearings as may be designated by order.[62] This latter limb of the definition dates from 1966 and is explained below.[63]

Standing machinery is thus provided for dealing with the problems of inquiries as and when they arise. The work of the Council will be illustrated under a number of different headings. As it has developed, the Council has entertained complaints from members of the public. Thus the Council has, in its limited sphere of operation, undertaken the work of an ombudsman. Its constitution and other activities have been explained in the previous chapter.

Power to make procedural rules for inquiries was given by an Act of 1959, which added a new section to the Tribunals and Inquiries Act.[64] The power is conferred on the Lord Chancellor, acting by statutory instrument and after consultation with the Council on Tribunals. Rules have been

---

[61] s. 1(1)(c).
[62] Tribunals and Inquiries Act 1971, s. 19(1).
[63] Below, p. 989.
[64] s. 7A, added by Town and Country Planning Act 1959, s. 33, now replaced by Tribunals and Inquiries Act 1971, s. 11.

made for a number of the commoner types of inquiries, as explained below.[65] In Scottish affairs the Lord Advocate acts in place of the Lord Chancellor.[66]

Of the Committee's detailed recommendations about inquiries the following were the most noteworthy.

1. A public authority initiating a scheme or order should be required to make available, in good time before the inquiry, a written statement giving full particulars of its case.
2. The minister who will ultimately decide the case should, whenever possible, make available before the inquiry a statement of the policy relevant to the particular case; but he should be free to direct that the statement be wholly or partly excluded from discussion at the inquiry.
3. If the policy changes after the inquiry, the letter conveying the minister's decision should explain the change and its relation to the decision.
4. The main body of inspectors should be placed under the control of the Lord Chancellor.
5. The initiating authority (including a minister) should explain its proposals fully at the inquiry and support them by oral evidence.
6. Statutory codes of procedure should be formulated by the Council on Tribunals.
7. Public inquiries are preferable to private hearings in cases of compulsory acquisition of land, development plans, planning appeals, and clearance schemes.
8. The inspector should have power to administer the oath and subpoena witnesses.
9. Costs should be more generally awarded and the Council on Tribunals should keep the subject under review.
10. The inspector's report should be divided into two parts: (i) summary of evidence, findings of fact, and inferences of fact; and (ii) reasoning from facts including application of policy and (normally) recommendations.
11. The complete text of the report should accompany the minister's letter of decision and also be available on request centrally and locally.
12. If any of the parties wish for an opportunity to propose corrections of fact, the first part of the report should, as soon as possible after the inquiry, be sent both to the authority and to the objectors. They should have fourteen days in which to propose corrections.
13. The minister should be required to submit to the parties for their observations any new factual evidence, including expert evidence, obtained after the inquiry.
14. The minister's letter of decision should set out in full his findings and inferences of fact and the reasons for the decision.

---

[65] Below, p. 984.

[66] SI 1972 No. 2002, substituting the Lord Advocate for the Secretary of State for Scotland.

The great majority of these recommendations were accepted and put into effect. Only numbers 2 and 4 were rejected outright, though numbers 9 and 12 were reserved for further consideration. The remainder were declared to be 'wholly or partly acceptable'—a form of acceptance which left open a way of retreat, as appeared later in connection with number 13.[67]

The necessary changes were effected more by administrative directions than by alteration of the law. The Tribunals and Inquiries Act 1958 constituted the Council on Tribunals with authority to consider and report on questions referred to it under the Act, or determined by itself to be of special importance, 'with respect to administrative procedures involving, or which may involve, the holding by or on behalf of a Minister of a statutory inquiry'. The Act also provided for reasons to be given for decisions. The statutory rules of procedure which have now been made for some inquiries also give legal force to some of the other improvements. These various matters are explained below. But the chief instrument of reform has been the ministerial circular, a document which has no legal operation but which 'invites' local authorities and other bodies to make arrangements suggested by the minister, or else explains the minister's own departmental practice. Many important reforms, such as the publication of inspectors' reports and the giving of reasoned decisions, could be made merely by changes of practice and without any alteration of the law. These changes were therefore explained in circulars, which were published documents freely available to all concerned.

The action taken on the various recommendations of the Franks Committee was set out in an appendix to the annual report of the Council of Tribunals for 1963.

LAW AND PRACTICE TODAY

The right to know the opposing case

One important requirement of natural justice is that the objector should have the opportunity to know and meet the case against him.[68] 'The case against him', in the context of an inquiry, will be some scheme or order proposed by some public authority, such as a compulsory purchase order, or some adverse decision such as the refusal of planning permission. The Franks Committee stressed that the reasons behind, say, a compulsory purchase order for the acquisition of land are capable of explanation to an objector and should be explained in advance of the inquiry, so that he has time to prepare his case.

[67] See below, p. 981.
[68] Above, p. 538.

Ministerial instructions therefore ask local authorities to prepare written statements setting out the reasons for their proposals and to make these available to objectors in good time before the inquiry. This has now become standard practice. In the cases where the rules of procedure now apply, they require the authority to serve on the objector, usually at least twenty-eight days before the inquiry, a written statement (known as the 'policy statement') of their reasons for seeking confirmation of their order or else a written statement of the submissions which they will make at the inquiry. If directions or opinions of other government departments are to be relied upon, they must be disclosed in advance. Facilities must be given for inspection and copying of relevant documents and plans. Where the minister is himself the originating authority, he will act similarly.

Although the government rejected the recommendation that the deciding minister, as opposed to the initiating authority, should provide a statement of policy before the inquiry, there has been an improvement in the issue of explanatory material, particularly from the Department of the Environment, which helps policy to be understood.

Inspectors' reports

None of the reforms achieved by the Franks Committee was of greater importance than the successful conclusion of the long struggle to secure publication of inspectors' reports. Before the Committee there was strong official opposition to the proposal. The Ministry of Housing and Local Government testified that publication would embarrass the minister, would be administratively impracticable, would require many more inspectors, would impaire frankness, would put inspectors under an 'enormous strain' in polishing up their reports for publication, would do no good, would bewilder the objectors, and so forth. Another witness objected that the inspector would be unduly worried about his grammar and spelling. Yet the official case was not so weak as might be thought from some of these arguments used to defend it. It had been accepted by the House of Lords in the *Arlidge* case[69] and treated with respect by the Ministers' Powers Committee. But no argument could alter the overriding fact that it was impossible to persuade people that they had received justice if they were not allowed to see the document which conveyed their objections to the minister. If inquiries were to be acceptable to public opinion, the 'administrative view' had to make concessions.

Since 1958 it has been the standard practice for a copy of the report to accompany the minister's letter of decision. Where statutory rules apply, they require this specifically. Where they do not, there is no legal right to disclosure of the report, but in practice it is supplied. None of the evils that

[69] Above, p. 508.

were feared seem to have resulted. Inspectors gained in public respect, since it could be seen how fairly they handled cases. It was not long before the Chief Inspector of the Ministry of Housing and Local Government stated publicly that the disclosure of reports had led to markedly better public relations. At the same time it is easier for objectors to tell whether legal remedies may be open to them or whether there is cause for complaint to the Council on Tribunals. The public's sense of grievance has been assuaged. Good administration and the principles of justice have once again proved to be friends, not enemies. The departments that were most tenacious of secrecy have found that it has done them good to abandon it.

The government however rejected the recommendation that the first part of the report, dealing with the evidence and findings of fact, should be disclosed in time for the parties to suggest corrections before the decision. In Scotland this practice is not only followed but is legally mandatory;[70] and ideally England ought to follow suit.[71] But in England the delays caused by intricate procedures, particularly for development plans and planning appeals, are so serious that any increase in the time taken by an inquiry is unacceptable. Administrative congestion has here affected procedural fairness. Inspectors' findings of fact are a rare subject of complaint; but a decision may be quashed if the inspector omits to report evidence of importance.[72]

The minister is in no way bound to follow the recommendations of the report: his duty is to decide according to his own independent view,[73] taking account of all relevant information.[74] It is not necessary that the inspector should always make recommendations[75] or that he should make findings on all the issues raised.[76]

Reasons for decisions

The Tribunals and Inquiries Act 1971,[77] repeating the Act of 1958, provides for the giving of reasons for decisions. This is a matter of great importance.

[70] See e.g. Town and Country Planning Appeals (Inquiry Procedure) (Scotland) Rules 1964, SI No. 181, rule 10(1) and *Kirkpatrick (J. & A.)* v. *Lord Advocate* 1967 SLT. (Notes) 27 (decision of Secretary of State quashed for failure to observe this rule); similarly *Paterson* v. *Secretary of State for Scotland* 1971 SC 1; *Wordie Property Co. Ltd.* v. *Secretary of State for Scotland* 1984 SLT 345.

[71] But there is no such obligation in law: *Steele* v. *Minister of Housing and Local Government* (1956) 6 P & CR 386.

[72] *East Hampshire D.C.* v. *Secretary of State for the Environment* [1979] Est Gaz Dig 1048.

[73] *Nelsovil Ltd.* v. *Minister of Housing and Local Government* [1962] 1 WLR 404.

[74] See *Prest* v. *Secretary of State for Wales* (1982) 81 LGR 193, allowing the use of evidence which was not available at the inquiry.

[75] *R.* v. *Secretary of State for Transport ex p. Gwent CC* [1987] 2 WLR 961.

[76] *London & Clydeside Estates Ltd.* v. *Aberdeen D.C.* 1984 SLT 50.

[77] s. 12.

It enables the citizen to understand the connection between the inspector's report and the minister's decision. It also enables the court to quash the decision if the reasons are not adequately given,[78] thus making a notable extension of judicial control over inquiry procedures.

As regards inquiries the Act applies where

any minister notifies any decision taken by him after the holding by him or on his behalf of a statutory inquiry, or taken by him in a case in which a person concerned could (whether by objecting or otherwise) have required the holding as aforesaid of a statutory inquiry.

The meaning of 'statutory inquiry' is explained below.[79] The second limb of the provision covers cases where a party may waive his right to a formal hearing, as is common in planning appeals.[80]

The terms and qualifications of the Act were explained in the chapter on tribunals, where it is noted that the reasons may be written or oral, and that the statutory duty applies only where reasons are requested.[81] But in practice a reasoned decision letter is now sent out as a matter of course. Where procedural rules have been made (as explained below[82]), they impose an unqualified duty to give reasons, so that there is no need to make any request.

It has been held that reasons given under the rules must be as full and as adequate as reasons given under the Act, though if they are clear and adequate they may be briefly stated.[83] Where a bad decision letter leaves real and substantial doubt as to the minister's reasons,[84] or fails to deal with a substantial objection,[85] or does not explain a departure from the development plan[86] or the minister's published policy,[87] or is misleading,[87a] the decision may be quashed on the same grounds as apply in the case of tribunals. In another case[88] Lord Denning MR said:

---

[78] See above, p. 251.   [79] p. 988.
[80] See below, p. 990.   [81] Above, p. 934.
[82] p. 984.
[83] *Westminster CC* v. *Great Portland Estates Plc* [1985] AC 661. As to structure plans see below, p. 980.
[84] *Givaudan & Co. Ltd* v. *Minister of Housing and Local Government* [1967] 1 WLR 250 (obscurely worded decision quashed under Town and Country Planning Act 1962, s. 179, applying the reasoning of *Re Poyser and Mills' Arbitration* [1964] 2 QB 467, above, p. 936). See similarly *French Kier Developments Ltd.* v. *Secretary of State for the Environment* [1977] 1 All ER 296; *Niarchos* v. *Secretary of State for the Environment* [1977] 76 LGR 480; *Strathclyde Passenger Executive* v. *McGill Bus Service* 1984 SLT 377.
[85] *Barnham* v. *Secretary of State for the Environment* (1985) 52 P & CR 10 (structure plan).
[86] *Reading BC* v. *Secretary of State for the Environment* (1985) 52 P & CR 385.
[87] See the *Barnham* case (above).
[87a] *London Residency Body* v. *Secretary of State for the Environment* [1988] The Times, 30 March.
[88] *Iveagh (Earl)* v. *Minister of Housing and Local Government* [1964] 1 QB 395.

Section 12(1) of the Tribunals and Inquiries Act 1958 says that the minister must give his reasons, and that his reasons are to form part of the record. The whole purpose of that enactment is to enable the parties and the courts to see what matters he has taken into consideration and what view he has reached on the points of fact and law which arise. If he does not deal with the points that arise, he fails in his duty, and the court can order him to make good the omission.

In a transport licensing case in the Court of Appeal, where the decision letter merely made 'bald assertions' that the Secretary of State was not satisfied as to various facts, Lord Lane CJ said:[89]

Such decision letters are unfair to the parties. The parties are unable to challenge the reasoning or the reasons, if any, which lay behind the decision. They are particularly reprehensible where the Secretary of State is differing from the commissioners and from the inspector who heard the appeal on matters of fact, as was the case here.

The courts' insistence on adequate decision letters shows how far the law has progressed from the time when the objector saw neither the inspector's report nor the reasons for the action taken upon it.

The Act has been made applicable also to inspectors who decide planning appeals themselves.[90] But otherwise it has no application where the inquiry is held by or on behalf of someone other than a minister or a board presided over by a minister.[91]

The right to participate

A 'public local inquiry', and likewise a 'local inquiry', implies that there will be a right of audience for all persons in the locality who are genuinely concerned for good reasons, and not merely for those who have legal rights at stake. In the *Arlidge* case Lord Moulton said:[92]

The inquiry is termed a 'public local inquiry'. Although it appears to be novel to speak of a 'public' local inquiry being held by the Local Government Board, yet local inquiries have for many years been held by them in connection with the exercise of other functions of the Board, and such inquiries were commonly held in public. The effect of the insertion of the word 'public' appears to me to be that every member of the public would have a locus standi to bring before the inquiry any matters relevant thereto so as to ensure that everything bearing on the rights of the owner or occupier of the house affected, or the interests of the public in general, or of the public living in the neighbourhood in particular, would be brought to the

[89] *R. v. Secretary of State for Transport ex p. Cumbria CC* [1983] RTR 129.
[90] Town and Country Planning Act 1971, 9th sched., para. 7.
[91] Tribunals and Inquiries Act 1971, s. 19(1).
[91] *Local Government Board v. Arlidge* [1915] AC 120 at 147; above, p. 508.

knowledge of the Local Government Board for the purpose of enabling it to discharge its duties in connection with the appeal.

Diplock L.J. expressed a similar opinion about a 'local inquiry':[93]

I agree with the judge that a 'local inquiry . . . into the objections'—which may be contrasted with 'an opportunity of appearing before and being heard by a person appointed by the Minister' . . .—involves that the person appointed to hold the inquiry should listen not merely to representations by the objector but also to representations by other persons who have an interest in the subject matter of the objections whether in support of the objections or against them.

He added that these other persons should be allowed to give evidence and cross-examine opposing witnesses, though the inspector had a wide discretion to curb irrelevance and repetition, and to control the proceedings generally.

But the statutory procedural rules which have been made for certain classes of inquiries confer the right of appearance and participation only upon parties who have legal rights which are in some way in issue, and allow other members of the public to appear only in the inspector's discretion. In so far as these restrictions conflict with the judicial statements just quoted, their validity may be open to question, since the power to make procedural rules can hardly avail to cut down rights of participation granted by Act of Parliament. But the question has not yet arisen before a court, since in practice public inquiries and local inquiries, including planning appeals, are open freely to all comers.[94] This is good administration, since neighbours, amenity societies and other third parties may often be able to make important contributions, and the object is to enable the best decision to be made in the public interest. This does not mean that third parties have in practice all the advantages of those whose legal rights are affected. They may sometimes be unable to challenge the validity of the proceedings as 'persons aggrieved'[95] and they have a number of disadvantages in cases covered by procedural rules, as explained below.[96]

Scope of inquiries: the problem of policy

The parties who participate in an inquiry, whether as of right or otherwise, are entitled to a fair hearing of their cases or objections. For this purpose statutory rights and the principles of natural justice operate in conjunction,

[93] *Wednesbury Corporation v. Ministry of Housing and Local Government* (No. 2) [1966] 2 QB 275 at 302.

[94] On the position of third parties see Wraith and Lamb, *Public Inquiries as an Instrument of Government*, 253.

[95] Above, p. 744.

[96] Below, p. 985.

as explained elsewhere.[97] But these rights cannot be used to carry the inquiry beyond its proper scope. Even where the Act says that the minister 'shall consider all objections' he need not consider objections which do not fairly and reasonably relate to the true purpose of the inquiry or which merely repeat objections made more suitably at an earlier inquiry.[98]

The central difficulty is to know how far matters of general policy should be open to question. The place for debating general policy is Parliament, and at an inquiry there should be no 'useless discussion of policy in the wrong forum'.[99] The purpose of a local inquiry is to provide the minister with information about local objections so that he can weigh the harm to local interests and private persons against the public benefit to be achieved by the scheme.[1] The policy behind the scheme, as opposed to its local impact, should therefore be taken for granted. The Franks Committee consequently recommended that the minister should be entitled to direct that any policy statement issued by him should be wholly or partly excluded from discussion at the inquiry; and statutory rules of procedure normally provide that the inspector shall disallow questions directed to the merits of government policy.[2]

But the line between general policy and its local application may not be easy to draw, and it is often the underlying policy which objectors wish to attack. In practice inspectors tend to be indulgent, allowing objectors to criticise policy and reporting such objections to the minister. Where this is done the inquiry is likely to be fairer to all concerned, since it is unrealistic to suppose that objectors have any effective voice to criticise policy in Parliament. The latitude allowed to them may vary according to the subject matter, and they may more reasonably claim to attack the policy underlying a development plan (for example) than that underlying the need for a power station or an airport.

This issue came to a head before the House of Lords in a case where objectors wished to dispute the need for a motorway. In advance of the inquiry into the schemes for two sections of the motorway the minister announced that the government's policy to build the motorways would not be open to debate at the inquiry, but that objectors could contest the lines proposed. The inspector in fact allowed the objectors to call evidence questioning the need for the motorway as a whole, but he refused to allow

---

[97] Above, p. 533.

[98] *Lovelock v. Minister of Transport* (1980) 40 P & CR 336 (objection disputing need for motorway held out of order).

[99] Franks Report, Cmnd 218 (1957), para. 288.

[1] *Bushell v. Secretary of State for the Environment* [1981] AC 75 at 94 (Lord Diplock). See also *Lovelock v. Vespra Township* (1981) 123 DLR (3d) 530 (right to cross-examine on policy statement upheld by Supreme Court of Canada).

[2] e.g. SI 1967 No. 720, rule 6(2) (compulsory purchase by ministers).

cross-examination of departmental witnesses about the methods used for predicting traffic flow for roads generally, which the objectors maintained were faulty. Upholding this refusal as fair in the circumstances, the House of Lords held that traffic prediction technique was a part of general policy and beyond the true scope of a local inquiry.[3] In admitting evidence about need the inspector had made a concession beyond what was required by law, and it was for him to say where the concession should stop. Lord Diplock observed that it would be a rash inspector who felt able to make recommendations on such a matter merely on evidence from one particular inquiry and that it would be an unwise minister who acted on it. Lord Lane also pointed out that it would be no help to the minister to receive differing recommendations about need from a series of local inquiries dealing with separate sections of the route.

The problem of distinguishing between general policy and its local application will appear again in connection with extrinsic evidence, discussed below.

There are strong practical reasons for not allowing local inquiries to be carried too far beyond their proper range. It is not unusual for a major inquiry to take a hundred days or more. The inquiry into the Greater London development plan in 1970–2 sat for 237 days to deal with over 28,000 objections and led to a 1,200 page report. The inquiry of 1977 into the nuclear reprocessing plant at Windscale sat for 100 days and the report extended to 689 pages. The Sizewell B nuclear power station inquiry of 1985–7 held 340 sittings and produced a 3,000 page report. In the weighing of conflicting public and private interests some account must be taken of expenditure of time and money.

Scope of inquiries: statutory restriction

The scope of some inquiries is restricted. The normal enactment requires the minister to hold an inquiry and to consider the inspector's report. But some Acts say that the inquiry shall be merely an inquiry into the objection. Thus the formula in the New Towns Act 1981 provides for an inquiry to be held 'with respect to the objection'.[4] Another instance to the Police Act 1964, which deliberately makes the same restriction is the case of police amalgamation schemes. Its intention is to prevent discussion of the merits of the scheme as opposed to the merits of the objection, and to nullify the Scottish decision requiring both sides of the case to be expounded.[5] Where

---

[3] *Bushell* v. *Secretary of State for the Environment* (above).

[4] 1st sched., para. 3. This (in its 1946 form) was the provision in question in the *Franklin* case, above, p. 491.

[5] See above, p. 512. This change was recommended by the Royal Commission on the Police, 1962, Cmnd 1728, para. 289.

there was an inquiry 'into the objection' to proposals for the reorganisation of local authorities the minister was held to be entitled to refuse to disclose the terms of reference of the inspectors (under a plea of Crown privilege) and to direct them to make no recommendations but merely to report about the objections.[6] But more liberal arrangements now obtain under the Local Government Act 1972.[7]

An inquiry 'into the objection' merely is fundamentally inadequate, for as the Franks Committee observed, 'an objection cannot reasonably be considered as a thing in itself, in isolation from what is objected to'.[8] The restriction is a crude and imperfect attempt to make the distinction between general policy and its local application explained above. In fact it is questionable whether an inquiry 'into the objection' is really restricted in any significant way, since it is easy to frame an objection so as to put in issue the whole policy behind the scheme. In any case, to repeat the point made by Lord Diplock,[9] the subject-matter of a local inquiry is the objections which have been received by the minister and its purpose is to provide him with as much information about them as will ensure that in reaching his decision he will have adequately weighed local interest against public benefit.

A more effective restriction is the power which some statutes give to the minister to disregard objections of certain kinds. For example, under the Acquisition of Land Act 1981[10] the minister may call upon the objector to a compulsory purchase order to state his grounds of objection, and he may disregard the objection if he is satisfied that it can be dealt with in the assessment of compensation. The Community Land Act 1975[11] (now repealed) greatly extended this power, though only for its own purposes, by allowing the minister to disregard an objection if satisfied that it was made on the ground that the acquisition was unnecessary or inexpedient. In the case of certain road schemes under the Highways Act 1980[12] the minister may dispense with an inquiry if he is satisfied that it is unnecessary, though he cannot invoke this power against some classes of objectors, such as public authorities. Objections to compulsory purchase orders which in substance amount to objections to approved road schemes of certain kinds may be disregarded under the same Act, which also allows the minister to

---

[6] *Wednesbury Cpn.* v. *Minister of Housing and Local Government* (No. 2) [1966] 2 QB 275.
[7] ss. 60, 61, 250 establish a consultative procedure with power to hold unrestricted inquiries.
[8] Cmnd. 218 (1957), para. 271. This paragraph erroneously assumes that the standard form of inquiry is into objections only.
[9] In the *Bushell* case (above).
[10] s. 13 and 1st sched., para. 4.
[11] 4th sched., para. 2.
[12] 1st sched., paras. 7, 14.

call for particulars of objections advocating alternative routes or new roads and to disregard such objections not notified in advance of the inquiry.[13] The Town and Country Planning Act 1971[14] allows the minister to disregard objections to compulsory purchase orders which amount in substance to objections to development plans.

A special case where the scope of the inquiry may be drastically limited is that of the 'examination in public' of structure plans submitted to the Secretary of State by local planning authorities. He is required to consider all objections duly made, but the 'examination in public' (the work 'inquiry' is avoided) is restricted to 'such matters affecting his consideration of the plan as he considers ought to be so examined'; and one decision holds that an objector is not entitled to so full a hearing as he could claim at an inquiry.[15] The Council on Tribunals may concern itself with this peculiar procedure; but otherwise the Tribunals and Inquiries Act 1971 does not apply.[16] The Secretary of State need only give 'such statement as he considers appropriate' of the reasons for his decision; but it has been held that the reasons must be adequate and intelligible, no less than in other cases.[17] He makes procedural regulations after consultation with the Lord Chancellor but not necessarily with the Council on Tribunals.[18]

Extrinsic evidence: the problem

Acute difficulty can arise where the minister bases his decision on facts which he obtains otherwise than through the inquiry. This is another case where the mixture of semi-legal procedure and political decision readily causes misunderstanding. If the objector finds that the minister has taken account of facts which there was no opportunity of contesting at the inquiry, he may feel that the inquiry is a waste of time and money. But, as has been emphasised already, it is inherent in most inquiry procedures that in the end the minister takes a decision of policy, and that the inquiry provides him with only part of the material for his decision. *Ex hypothesi* he may take account of other material. But of what sort of other material?

Controversy centred upon this question in the case of the Essex chalkpit

---

[13] 1st sched., Pt. III.

[14] s. 132(1).

[15] *Bradley (Edwin H.) & Sons Ltd.* v. *Secretary of State for the Environment* (1982) 47 P & CR 374.

[16] Town and Country Planning (Amendment) Act 1972, s. 3, adding s. 9(6) to the Act of 1971.

[17] *Bradley (Edwin H.)* v. *Secretary of State for the Environment* (above); *Barnham* v. *Secretary of State for the Environment* (1985) 52 P & CR 10.

[18] SI 1974 No. 1486, not reciting consultation with the Council.

in 1961.[19] A company had been refused planning permission to dig and work chalk on their own land. They appealed to the minister and the usual local inquiry was held. Neighbouring landowners appeared at the inquiry and opposed the appeal, giving evidence that the dust from chalk-working would be injurious to their land and their livestock. On these grounds the inspector recommended that the appeal be dismissed. But the minister rejected the inspector's recommendation and granted permission after consulting the Ministry of Agriculture whose experts advised that there was no likelihood of serious injury if a particular process ('kibbling') was used and if other conditions were imposed as to fencing of stockpiles and other matters. This evidence was not before the inquiry and the minister did not give the objectors an opportunity to comment on it before making his decision. It appeared that the government had not fully accepted the Franks Committee's recommendation that the minister ought to invite comment on 'new factual evidence', including 'expert opinion on matters of fact', obtained after the inquiry.[20] This was the substance of the objectors' grievance. After an unsuccessful attempt to obtain a legal remedy,[21] they complained to the Council on Tribunals. The Council took up the question with government departments and made a special report to the Lord Chancellor. There were also several debates in Parliament and much public comment.

The Council on Tribunals criticised the rejection by the minister of his inspector's recommendation in cases where (i) the rejection was based on ministerial policy which could and should have been made clear at the inquiry or (ii) the minister took advice after the inquiry from persons who neither heard the evidence nor saw the site, but yet controverted the inspector's findings as to the facts of the local situation. These final words contain the heart of the matter. The minister's policy may be formed on the basis of all kinds of facts, reports and advice which have nothing to do with the local situation which is the subject of the inquiry, and which therefore need not necessarily be known to the objectors or investigated at the inquiry. But the facts of the local situation are in a different category, and there is bound to be complaint if due respect is not paid to the inspector's findings. In the chalkpit case the government's explanations were not clear on this vital question: was the advice given by the Ministry of Agriculture general advice, to the effect that a certain mode of chalk-working was incapable of creating excessive dust; or was it really advice about the local situation, to the effect that chalk-working in that particular

---

[19] See Annual Reports of the Council on Tribunals, 1960, para. 111; 1961, para. 56.

[20] Para. 350; above, p. 970, item 13. The Committee had also recommended that the duty should be statutory.

[21] Above, p. 744 (the *Buxton* case).

pit would be innocuous? It was the possibility that the advice was of the latter character that justified the complaint.

Extrinsic evidence: the solution

The Council on Tribunals recommended that there should be a rule for future cases providing that the minister, if differing from the inspector's recommendation on a finding or a fact or on account of fresh evidence (including expert opinion) or a fresh issue (not being a matter of government policy), should first notify the parties and allow them to comment in writing; and that they should be entitled to have the inquiry reopened if fresh evidence or a fresh issue emerged. The proposed rule was accepted and has since been followed in practice. It is also embodied in the statutory rules of procedure which have been made for various classes of inquiries including planning appeals.[22] Failure to observe it has led to the quashing or remitting of a number of decisions.[23]

In some situations it may be difficult to tell what is a finding of fact and what is a matter of opinion. The rule was held not to apply where the minister rejected his inspector's finding that a house in a particular place would be unobjectionable, since the minister was held not to be differing from the inspector on the facts but forming a different opinion of them on the 'planning merits' and enforcing a general policy of not permitting building outside the village boundaries.[24]

The same principle may be seen in a case of 1954 in which an objector unsuccessfully challenged a compulsory purchase order for the acquisition of land for a school.[25] At the inquiry the owner persuaded the inspector that

[22] See next section. For planning appeals see SI 1974 No. 419, rule 12(2). A technical defect is that the rule does not apply where the inspector makes no recommendation: see *Westminster Bank Ltd.* v. *Beverley Borough Council* [1971] AC 508. Violation of the rule was found in *Hamilton* v. *Roxburgh County Council* 1971 SC 2 but no remedy was held to be available because of defective statutory drafting. It appears that the Parliamentary Commissioner for Administration is willing to investigate complaints of breach of the rule, despite the obvious legal remedy: see his Annual Report for 1969 (HC 138, 1969–70) at p. 169 (Case C.54/L).

[23] *French Kier Developments Ltd.* v. *Secretary of State for the Environment* [1977] 1 All ER 296; *Penwith DC* v. *Secretary of State for the Environment* (1977) 34 P & CR 269 (erroneously citing the Tribunals and Inquiries Act instead of the inquiry rules); *Pyrford Properties Ltd.* v. *Secretary of State for the Environment* (1977) 36 P & CR 28; *Pollock* v. *Secretary of State for the Environment* (1979) 40 P & CR 94.

[24] *Luke (Lord)* v. *Minister of Housing and Local Government* [1968] 1 QB 172. See similarly *Vale Estates Ltd.* v. *Secretary of State for the Environment* (1970) 69 LGR 543; *Murphy & Sons Ltd.* v. *Secretary of State for the Environment* [1973] 1 WLR 560; *Brown* v. *Secretary of State for the Environment* (1978) 40 P & CR 285.

[25] *Darlassis* v. *Minister of Education* (1954) 52 LGR 304; see similarly *Summers* v. *Minister of Health* [1947] 1 All ER 184; *Lithgow* v. *Secretary of State for Scotland* 1973 SLT 81.

another piece of land would be a better site. But that land was already in course of development as a municipal housing estate. The Minister of Education therefore asked the Minister of Housing and Local Government whether the land could be released, and was told that it could not be since the development was far too advanced. The court held that this was a matter of policy on which one minister was always at liberty to consult another between the inquiry and the decision. But, the court added, the situation would have been wholly different if the Minister of Housing had replied that the land was not wanted because it was waterlogged or otherwise unsuitable for building. Information of that kind, concerning the relative merits of the two sites, should be disclosed to an objector so that its accuracy could be challenged. This decision, given before the reforms of 1958, suggests that the principles of natural justice might have achieved substantially the same results as the rule recommended by the Council on Tribunals. So also does a later case, in which a decision of the Secretary of State was quashed because he based it upon his own information about the local effects of a new road which natural justice required him to give the parties an opportunity of contesting.[26]

It is fully established that the principles of natural justice do not permit the minister, any more than the inspector, to receive evidence as to the local situation from one of the parties concerned in the inquiry, without disclosing it to the others and allowing them to comment. To take evidence from one party behind the backs of the others vitiates the whole inquiry and renders the minister's order liable to be quashed.[27] To take evidence or advice from other sources raises cognate but different questions which the courts have not yet fully explored. It is clear that the inspector must not himself obtain local evidence without disclosing it to the parties,[28] and in principle the minister should be subject to the same restriction. In one case Lord Denning MR said:[29]

The minister on his part must also act judicially. He must only consider the report and the material properly before him. He must not act on extrinsic information which the houseowner has had no opportunity of contradicting. Thus far have the courts gone . . .

But this 'extrinsic information' should be limited to information about the

---

[26] *Burwoods (Caterers) Ltd.* v. *Secretary of State for the Environment* (1972) Est Gaz Dig 1007. The brief report makes no mention of the statutory rule, which would appear to have been applicable.

[27] As in the cases cited above, p. 539.

[28] As in *Hibernian Property Co. Ltd.* v. *Secretary of State for the Environment* (1973) 27 P & CR 197 and *Fairmount Investments Ltd.* v. *Secretary of State for the Environment* [1976] 1 WLR 1255 (above, p. 540).

[29] *Steele* v. *Minister of Housing and Local Government* (1956) 6 P & CR 386 at 392.

local situation in the particular case. It can hardly extend to information relating only to general policy, which the minister should always be able to obtain and use with complete freedom.[30]

Procedural rules

The Tribunals and Inquiries Act 1971,[31] dating in this respect from 1959,[32] empowers the Lord Chancellor to make rules of procedure for statutory inquiries, or classes of inquiries, held by or on behalf of ministers. The rules may provide for preliminary matters; they must be made by statutory instrument; and the Council on Tribunals must be consulted.

Various types of inquiry[33] have been furnished with rules made under this power, including three large classes: compulsory purchase inquiries held under the Acquisition of Land Act 1981 (formerly 1946);[34] planning appeals, applications and enforcement;[35] and inquiries into schemes for trunk roads and motorways.[36] Rules have also been made for inquiries connected with the underground storage of gas,[37] electricity supply[38] and pipe-lines.[39] But after 1967 the business of making inquiry rules in new areas was allowed to come to a halt. It was only outbreaks of disorder at trunk road and motorway inquiries that caused rules to be made for them belatedly in 1976,[40] followed by a review promising numerous administrative improvements in 1978.[41] Rules for drought order inquiries were made in 1984.[42] In the remaining types of inquiries not yet covered by rules, it is the practice to follow the Lord Chancellor's rules by analogy so far as possible, since many of them are capable of general application. Positive procedural rules are of great help to all concerned with inquiries.

The Act has a flaw in it that it applies only when rules are made by the Lord Chancellor. Other ministers are sometimes empowered to make rules

---

[30] See *Bushell* v. *Secretary of State for the Environment* [1981] AC 75, discussed above, p. 977.

[31] s. 11.

[32] Town and Country Planning Act 1959, s. 33.

[33] The rules normally apply also to hearings (see above, p. 969).

[34] SI 1967 No. 720 (compulsory purchase by ministers); SI 1976 No. 746 (compulsory purchase by public authorities). But it is anomalous that there are no rules for other cases, such as compulsory purchase by new town development corporations.

[35] SI 1974 Nos. 419, 420; 1981 No. 1743; for minor amendments see 1986 No. 420.

[36] SI 1976 No. 721.

[37] SI 1966 No. 1375.

[38] SI 1967 No. 450; 1981 No. 1841; 1987 No. 2182.

[39] SI 1967 No. 1769.

[40] SI 1976 No. 721.

[41] Cmnd 7133 (White Paper).

[42] SI 1984 No. 999.

for inquiries, but in practice they consult the Council on Tribunals, and their rules may be made in similar form.[43]

Among the more important provisions of the Lord Chancellor's rules are those dealing with:

the timetable for the various steps and formalities, e.g. requiring at least forty-two days' notice to the parties legally entitled to appear;[44]

the written statement of its case by the initiating or opposing authority,[45] usually to be supplied at least forty-two days before the inquiry;

the persons entitled to appear at the inquiry;

the right of representation;

evidence of government departments concerned with the proposal;

the right to call evidence and cross-examine departmental representatives and witnesses (though not to ask questions directed to the merits of government policy);

procedure for site inspections;

evidence obtained after the inquiry;[46]

notification of the decision, with reasons;[47]

the right to obtain a copy of the inspector's report.[48]

The persons entitled to appear as of right under the rules are those who have some statutory standing in the matter. In compulsory purchase cases this means any owner, lessee or occupier of the land who is entitled to have notice of the compulsory purchase order and has made formal objections, and also the acquiring authority.[49] In planning appeals it means the appellant, the local planning authority, certain other local authorities in some cases, certain other persons with legal rights in the land affected, persons who have made formal objection in cases where advertisement of the application is required, and any person on whom the Secretary of State has required notice of it to be served.[50] The rules then provide that any other person may appear at the inspector's discretion, and in practice appearances by neighbours, amenity societies and others are freely

[43] Examples are SI 1967 No. 449 (licensing of port employers); 1968 No. 1062 (ports welfare amenities). Less similar examples are SI 1965 No. 618 (police appeals); 1965 No. 1360 (offices, shops, and railway premises); 1969 No. 86 (driving instruction). See Council on Tribunals, Annual Report for 1967, pp. 12, 14. All appeals to ministers involve inquiries (above, p. 902) and where rules are made by the minister they are likewise outside the Act.

[44] In *Ostreicher* v. *Secretary of State for the Environment* [1978] 1 WLR 810 a complaint that the objector could not attend on the specified date for religious reasons was disallowed.

[45] Above, p. 971.

[46] Above, p. 982.

[47] Above, p. 973.

[48] Above, p. 972.

[49] SI 1976 No. 746, rule 5.

[50] SI 1974 No. 419, rule 7; No. 420, rule 9; 1981 No. 1743, rule 8; all as amended by 1986 No. 420.

allowed. The question whether there is really any legal power to exclude them has been mentioned above.[51] At any rate, they do not under the statutory rules enjoy the full rights of a party. They are not entitled to be sent the statement of the initiating or opposing authority's case; and they are not entitled to the benefit of the rule, discussed above, about disclosure of evidence from sources other than the inquiry. The Council on Tribunals was unsuccessful in asking for an assurance that the benefit of the latter rule should in practice be extended to them.[52] Their only protection is that they will usually have similar interests to one of the statutory parties, who will be officially encouraged to keep them informed.[53]

This difficulty illustrates the paradox which underlies many inquiries where an issue which in law lies between particular parties is in practice thrown open to the public at large. The principal legal advantage that has so far been won by third party objectors is that an objector who under the rules has been given leave to appear at the inquiry thereby acquires the character of a 'person aggrieved' for the purpose of challenging the legality of the decision under statutory procedure.[54] This improvement in his position is held to flow from the existence of the rules, though they do not in fact alter the previous practice in this respect. He may also benefit from the progressive relaxation of the rules about the standing of third party objectors, of which examples have been given earlier.[55]

An objector's right of representation is unrestricted, so that he may appear by a lawyer or by any other person, as well as by himself.

The Department of the Environment has published a code of practice for major inquiries, designed primarily to improve procedure in the pre-inquiry stages.

Public or private hearings

The rules contain no requirement that the proceedings should be held in public. Although public hearings have always been the rule, the inspector was able (as in a court of law) to exclude the public and even other parties where the evidence to be given was confidential, for example a secret commercial process. In such cases there is an irreconcilable conflict between the objectors' rights to know the case against them and to cross-examine witnesses and, on the other hand, the need for secrecy in genuine cases. A partial solution occasionally adopted was that the objectors' legal representatives were allowed to be present, since they were bound by their

[51] Above, p. 976.
[52] Annual Report for 1962, para. 37.
[53] Same report, para. 39.
[54] See above, p. 745.
[55] Above, p. 744.

professional standards of conduct and could be expected to respect confidences.[56] But complaints led the government to announce in 1972 that in future the policy would be that inspectors should not hear evidence in private at planning inquiries;[57] and in 1982 this rule was made statutory, subject only to exceptions where the national interest required secrecy in order to protect national security or to safeguard measures taken for the security of premises or property.[58]

Procedure, evidence, costs

The inspector is master of the procedure at an inquiry, always provided that the principles of natural justice and the statutory rules, if any, are properly observed.[59] He may adjourn it if this is reasonable,[60] and he may exclude any one who disrupts the proceedings.[61] The legal rules of evidence do not apply, so that hearsay may be admitted, if relevant, without vitiating the proceedings, whether or not the evidence is taken on oath.[62] Cross-examination is allowed by procedural rules[63] and evidently also by the rules of natural justice,[64] if it is within the proper scope of the inquiry. The House of Lords has decided that witnesses enjoy absolute privilege against actions for defamation.[65]

Powers to take evidence on oath[66] or affirmation, and also to require persons to attend and produce documents, are conferred on the inspector in many classes of inquiries, including planning and compulsory purchase inquiries.[67]

[56] See Parliamentary Commissioner for Administration, Annual Report for 1969 (HC 138, 1969–70), p. 55.

[57] 836 HC Deb, written answers, col. 199 (4 May 1972).

[58] Planning Inquiries (Attendance of Public) Act 1982.

[59] See *Miller (T.A.) Ltd.* v. *Minister of Housing and Local Government* [1968] 1 WLR 992; *Winchester CC* v. *Secretary of State for the Environment* (1979) 39 P & CR 1 (inspector rightly refused to hear expert witness).

[60] *Ostreicher* v. *Secretary of State for the Environment* [1978] 1 WLR 810; *Greycoat Commercial Estates Ltd.* v. *Radmore* (1981) The Times, 14 July (3 months adjournment upheld).

[61] *Lovelock* v. *Secretary of State for Transport* (1979) 39 P & CR 468 (disrupters removed by police; disrupter excluded from the inquiry cannot complain of breach of natural justice).

[62] *Marriott* v. *Minister of Health* (1935) 154 LT 47; *Miller (T.A.) Ltd.* v. *MHLC* (above).

[63] Above, p. 985.

[64] Above, p. 544.

[65] *Trapp* v. *Mackie* [1979] 1 WLR 377 (Secretary of State's inquiry into reasons for dismissal of headmaster), holding that it is not necessary for the inspector to have the power of decision. See [1982] PL at 432 (N. V. Low and H. F. Rawlings).

[66] This power exists in any case: Evidence Act 1851, s. 16; above, p. 927.

[67] e.g. Acquisition of Land Act 1981, s. 5(2); Town and Country Planning Act 1971, s. 282; both applying (as is usual) the powers of Local Government Act 1972, s. 250 (as it now is).

Legal representation is always allowed in practice, as well as under procedural rules, and is probably a matter of natural justice. Legal advice and assistance, but not legal aid, are available in connection with statutory inquiries on the same basis as in the case of tribunals.[68]

Ministers have power in numerous cases, again including planning and compulsory purchase, to make orders for the recovery of costs incurred in connection with inquiries either by the department or by local authorities or by other parties.[69] These powers were rarely exercised before 1964, when the Council on Tribunals made a special report.[70] The principal recommendations were that the power should be extended to cover all inquiries and hearings; that it should be exercised more freely, particularly against any party who behaves unreasonably and vexatiously, including a public authority; that a higher standard of behaviour should be expected from a public authority than from the citizen; that costs should normally be awarded to successful objectors in compulsory purchase and similar cases; and that inspectors should always make recommendations as to costs in their reports.

The recommendation in favour of successful objectors was accepted and put into force administratively, together with other recommended changes.[71] After a long interval legislation has extended the power to award costs to hearings in addition to inquiries and also to planning appeals decided on written representations.[72] Inspectors have also been empowered to award costs on the same basis as the Secretary of State.[73] That basis is now very wide, since it may extend to 'the entire administrative cost of the inquiry' including staff costs and overheads.[74] Since these costs can only be computed by the department, and in any case the department acts as judge in its own cause when costs are awarded in its favour, the arrangements seem far from satisfactory in principle.

Discretionary inquiries

The Tribunals and Inquiries Act 1971 defines a 'statutory inquiry' as an inquiry or hearing held under a statutory duty.[75] The jurisdiction of the Council on Tribunals and the other provisions of the Act therefore apply

[68] Above, p. 932.
[69] As n. 67 above.
[70] Cmnd. 2471 (1964).
[71] Ministry of Housing and Local Government circular 73/65.
[72] Housing and Planning Act 1986, 11th sched, para. 9. Before this Act, nevertheless, the Parliamentary Commissioner for Administration had obtained an award of costs of a hearing for a complainant: Annual Report for 1974 (HC 1874–5 No. 126), p. 7.
[73] Act of 1986 (above), 11th sched., para. 8.
[74] Act of 1986, s. 42. This applies even where the inquiry does not take place.
[75] Above, p. 969.

where an Act provides that the minister *shall* hold an inquiry, but do not apply where the provision is merely that the minister *may* hold an inquiry. There are many discretionary inquiries of the latter class, and it is no less important that they should be brought within the Act. It is also sometimes difficult, where the statute is ambiguous, to tell whether there is a duty or a discretion. Examples of discretionary inquiries are those held under the Local Government Act 1972, where departments have a general power to hold inquiries in connection with their functions under the Act,[76] inquiries into objections to compulsory purchase orders for defence purposes,[77] and inquiries held under the general powers of the Education Act 1944,[78] the National Health Service Act 1977[79] and the Highways Act 1980.[80] A new class was added by the Community Land Act 1975,[81] which made inquiries discretionary in certain cases of compulsory purchase under the Act, but it has now been repealed.[82]

The Tribunals and Inquiries Act 1966 dealt with this problem by giving power to the Lord Chancellor to make orders designating particular classes of inquiries as subject to the relevant parts of the Tribunals and Inquiries Act 1958, relating to supervision by the Council on Tribunals and the making of procedural rules.[83] The duty to give reasons for decisions could also be made applicable, but this required express direction in the order.[84] The first order, made in 1967, applied the Act to sixty-five varieties of inquiries, including those held under the Local Government Act 1972 and the provisions of the Education, National Health Service and Highways Acts mentioned above; and it directed that all of them should be subject to the duty to give reasons.[85] The current order, made in 1975, has extended the list to seventy-nine classes where reasons must be given, and has added thirty-five additional classes where reasons need not be given.[86] In this latter group are, amongst others, certain accident inquiries,[87] certain cases where inquiries may be held into any matter arising under an Act,[88] and also decisions on 'Secretary of State's questions' in social security matters.[89]

[76] s. 250.
[77] See Council on Tribunals, Annual Report for 1961, para. 79.
[78] s. 93.
[79] s. 84.
[80] s. 302.
[81] 4th sched., para. 2.
[82] Local Government, Planning and Land Act 1980, s. 101.
[83] See now Tribunals and Inquiries Act 1971, s. 19, making the designated inquiries subject to the Act generally, except as regards reasons for decisions.
[84] Same Act, s. 12(3).
[85] SI 1967 No. 451.
[86] SI 1975 No. 1379, as amended by 1976 No. 293, 1983 No. 1287.
[87] Below, p. 999.
[88] e.g. Electricity Act 1947, s.66; Police Act 1964, s. 32.
[89] Under Social Security Act 1975, s. 93(3). For these questions see above, p. 902.

Informal procedures

Since any inquiry into anything may always be held administratively, ministers sometimes prefer to avoid statutory procedures altogether and to hold non-statutory inquiries. The first inquiry into the development of Stansted Airport (1965–6), which might well have been held under the planning legislation (as was the second inquiry of 1981–2), was in fact held as a mere administrative inquiry after which the government proposed to authorise the development by special order. Similarly the minister may ask regional hospital boards to hold non-statutory inquiries into complaints against hospitals instead of using his statutory powers under the National Health Service Act 1977. In such cases objectors have no procedural rights (apart from the principles of natural justice), their complaints cannot be taken up by the Council on Tribunals, and the safeguards intended by the Act of 1966 cannot operate. The Council on Tribunals has publicly criticised this practice.[90] Where an 'enterprise zone' is established,[91] important and controversial developments may take place without any inquiry at all.

   An informal inquiry procedure, which proved so useful that it was made statutory in 1986, was that by which appellants in planning appeals were invited by the department to agree to have their appeals decided on written representations only, without an inquiry or hearing.[92] The attraction of this voluntary alternative was that it saved time and expense and was frequently satisfactory—so much so that the great majority of all planning appeals came to be decided by inspectors after an exchange of written representations and a site visit.[93] In 1986 this simplified appeal system was given a statutory basis and procedural regulations were made.[94] The inspector's report and the Secretary of State's decision (if any) are now made available and there is the usual right to a reasoned decision on request. But this procedure makes no provision for the views of third party objectors such as neighbours and amenity societies.

Major inquiries

Big projects for such things as major airports and power stations often raise difficult questions about alternative sites and other problems of more than

[90] Annual Reports for 1967, p. 27; for 1968, p. 14.   [91] See above, p. 188.
[92] Council on Tribunals, Annual Reports for 1964, para. 76; for 1966, para. 89.
[93] In the first half of 1986 the median processing time under this procedure had been reduced to 18 weeks, and it was hoped to reduce it to 11 weeks by 1988: Council on Tribunals, Annual Report for 1985–6, p. 63.
[94] Housing and Planning Act 1986, 11th sched., para. 10; SI 1987 No. 701. See also Department of the Environment Circulars 18/86 and 11/87. Costs may be awarded: above, p. 988. Reason must be adequate: *South Bedfordshire DC* v. *Secretary of State for the Environment* [1987] JPL 507.

local character which cannot well be handled at an ordinary local inquiry.[95] Sometimes they are of gigantic proportions, such as the inquiries concerned with the Greater London Development Plan (1970), which sat on 240 days, and the Sizewell B nuclear power station (1983–5), which sat on 340 days. In the hope of improving the procedure for exceptionally complicated inquiries special provision was made by the Town and Country Planning Act 1971, under which the minister might refer applications and appeals, and also the government's own proposals, to a 'planning inquiry commission' consisting of from three to five persons.[96] The commission must then proceed in two stages: first, it must conduct a general investigation; secondly, it must hear objectors at a local inquiry before one or more of its members. It is only the second stage which is subject to the Tribunals and Inquiries Act 1971 and to the usual safeguards. The first stage is to be an unrestricted investigation comparable to an inquiry by a royal commission, and the only formal requirement is that notice of the reference to the commission shall be published and served on certain parties. The right to object to a specific proposal at the second stage is, as in other cases, confined to persons with a statutory status; but it will no doubt be the practice, as also in other cases, to allow anyone genuinely concerned to be heard.

But no planning inquiry commission has yet been constituted. Attention has turned rather to informal pre-inquiry procedures designed to secure the fullest possible exchange of information, and also public participation, before the formal and adversarial proceedings begin. The government has published a draft code of practice for the preliminary stages of major inquiries and these proposals have found more favour than did those for planning inquiry commissions.[97]

Decisions by inspectors

The large number of planning appeals, now in the order of 18,000 a year, and their over-centralisation in the Department of the Environment, inevitably led to severe delays. In order to reduce the time-lag the Secretary of State was empowered in 1968 to prescribe classes of appeals to be decided by the inspector himself without reference to the Department, subject to the Secretary of State's option to require any particular case to be referred.[98]

---

[95] See above, p. 977.

[96] ss. 47, 48, replacing the Act of 1968, ss. 61–3.

[97] See White Paper, Cm. 43 (1986), Appendix II, Annex 2, published in response to proposals by the House of Commons Select Committee on the Environment, HC 181–1 (1985–6).

[98] Now Town and Country Planning Act 1971, 9th sched.

The prescribed classes have now been extended to cover the great majority of planning appeals.[99] The Tribunals and Inquiries Act 1971 applies in all respects,[1] and rules of procedure of the usual kind have been made.[2] Furthermore, there is provision for the parties to waive their right to an oral hearing, so that in these cases the procedure for determining appeals on written representations only has acquired a statutory basis and is subject to the general law governing inquiries.[3]

This procedure has in general worked well, despite the abnormal expedient of putting final decisions on matters of policy into the hands of officials not responsible to Parliament. It has done something, though not enough, to reduce delays.[4]

The Secretary of State has experimented with 'informal hearings' which he may offer in selected 'inspector's decision' cases where the appellant and the local planning authority agree. The timetable is accelerated[5] and the hearing takes the form of a discussion led by the inspector, sitting with the parties and their advisers round the same table. Evidence is circulated in advance and is not read out at the hearing, and cross-examination is by informal questioning. The inspector gives his decision in writing soon after the hearing and the formal decision letter follows later. These are statutory hearings and the normal rules of procedure apply with minor adjustments, and with the aid of a code of practice. They have proved to be a popular and efficient alternative to a formal local inquiry.[6]

Inspectors generally

All the evidence before the Franks Committee of 1955–7 was to the effect that the inspectors were competent, patient and open to very little criticism as to the manner in which they controlled the proceedings. Their reputation was strengthened still further by the practice of publishing their reports. But certain questions of principle remain. What should the inspector's status be? Is it right that he should be a permanent official of the ministry concerned with the scheme? Or should he be an independent person, with a position more like that of a judge? The 'administrative' and the 'judicial' views can both be supported by an appeal to precedent.

---

[99] SI 1981 No. 804. See above, p. 189.

[1] 9th sched. (as above), para. 7.

[2] SI 1974 No. 420, amended by 1986 No. 420.

[3] 9th sched. (as above), para. 2(2).

[4] In 1985 the median figures for England were as follows: Secretary of State's appeals: on written representations, 34 weeks; after inquiry, 49 weeks. Inspectors' appeals: on written representations, 18 weeks; after inquiry, 33 weeks. For these and other details see the annual reports of the Chief Planning Inspector, Department of the Environment.

[5] In 1985 the median overall time was 25 weeks for 380 hearings.

[6] Chief Planning Inspector's annual report, 1986, para. 18.

The Ministry of Housing and Local Government, the predecessor of the Department of the Environment, which held more inquiries than any other ministry, had a permanent staff of inspectors for housing and planning inquiries. These men were its own officials, and usually served as inspectors for the rest of their careers once they had been assigned to that work. Certain other ministries, notably the Ministry of Transport, and all the Scottish departments, normally employed independent persons such as surveyors, lawyers, or retired officials. Now that the Ministry of Transport is absorbed in the Department of the Environment, a single inspectorate has been established which however contains two different classes of inspectors: full-time salaried departmental inspectors; and a panel of part-time fee-paid independent inspectors, some of them drawn from private practice,[7] appointed by the Lord Chancellor. The policy is to allocate inspectors according to the nature and degree of the Department's interest or prior involvement in the question at issue.[8] Where, as in the majority of cases, the Secretary of State plays the part of umpire or arbiter between a local authority and the citizen, a departmental inspector is employed. But where the Department has itself initiated the proposals, for example in the case of motorways, trunk roads and new towns, the inquiry is normally held before an independent inspector chosen from the panel. In addition, an independent inspector may always be employed if the case has special features or is particularly controversial. In a number of important inquiries a Queen's Counsel has been engaged to act as inspector, sometimes assisted by an assessor.[9]

Sometimes an inquiry is held by two inspectors, one or both of whom may have technical qualifications. Thus a major proposal for an atomic power station or an overhead electricity line may be held before a planning inspector and an engineering inspector sitting together. Alternatively technical assessors may sit with an inspector to assist him.[10] But the most common situation in England is that the inquiry is presided over by a single government inspector.

The advantage of the departmental inspector is that he will usually be in closer touch with the department's policy. It is obviously easier to entrust the case to an independent inspector if it is a decision which will turn more on local facts than on national policy, such as a decision to acquire one site rather than another for a school, or to acquire land for road widening. An

---

[7] See 997 HC Deb 524 (29 January 1981).

[8] Council on Tribunals, Annual Report for 1972–3, para. 96.

[9] See *Sovmots Investments Ltd.* v. *Secretary of State for the Environment* [1979] AC 144.

[10] See *General Poster and Publicity Co. Ltd.* v. *Secretary of State for Scotland* 1960 SC 266, holding that no specific power to appoint an assessor was needed and that there was no obligation to disclose his assessment of the evidence for comment by the parties before the inspector made his report, provided that it did not introduce new facts.

important planning scheme, depending on the degree to which private interests ought to be overriden, obviously lies more in the sphere of policy; and when the general public interest has to be weighed against private interests the inspector's recommendations will need to be based on an accurate appreciation of the prevailing policy.

The ideal would be for the Minister himself to hold the enquiry and thus hear the evidence at first hand, but since this is clearly out of the question the next best course is for one of his own officers, who can be kept in touch with developments in policy, to perform this function.[11]

Yet, paradoxically, it is in the largest and most controversial cases that independent inspectors such as Queen's Counsel are now often employed.

Another argument for the departmental inspector is that an independent inspector may positively mislead the objectors into supposing that the process is judicial, and that the decision will be based entirely on the evidence heard at the inquiry. Then, when they find in the end that this is not so, they are all the more dissatisfied. At some stage or other the objector must face the fact that he is the object of an administrative, not a judicial, process, and that policy must often play a large part.

The Franks Committee's conclusion on this dilemma was that inspectors should be placed under the control of the Lord Chancellor, so that they would no longer be identified in the minds of the objectors with the department of the deciding minister.[12] But the government thought it essential that the corps of professional inspectors, whose lives are spent in an endless succession of inquiries, should remain an integral part of the departmental organisation. The pleas made in Parliament that the inspectors should become 'Lord Chancellor's men' achieved nothing initially, but led eventually to the Lord Chancellor's panel of independent inspectors, mentioned above. The use of departmental inspectors has in fact ceased to be controversial. The Council on Tribunals has received at least one complaint, on the other hand, that an independent inspector was not sufficiently expert.

The Council on Tribunals

Various complaints reach the Council on Tribunals from people dissatisfied with inquiries. These complaints are taken up with government departments when they seem to have merit, and a number of improvements in practice have resulted.

In most of these cases no legal right has been infringed, but the

---

[11] *The Franks Committee's Report.* Cmnd. 218 (1957), para. 293.
[12] Para. 303.

complainant alleges some injustice. In one case a London borough council had put forward a scheme for a large housing estate which involved demolishing an area of old houses. An inquiry was held at which local landowners objected the scheme and argued that the best plan was that the old houses should be rehabilitated. The minister dismissed the appeal, apparently on the ground that the objectors had made out their case. But the borough council prepared a modified scheme and after negotiations with the minister, who had meanwhile become the authority to whom application for permission had to be made, they obtained permission for it. From these negotiations the objectors were excluded. They had no right to take part, nor had they any legal right to take part in the original inquiry. But after their successful opposition to the first scheme it seemed less than fair to exclude them from the consideration of the modified scheme, since the two were so closely connected. The Council on Tribunals issued a special report criticising the handling of this case, and it was debated in Parliament.[13]

Another notable case which arose out of complaints to the Council on Tribunals was that of Stansted Airport in 1968.[14] After holding a non-statutory inquiry, as already mentioned,[15] the government decided to alter the alignment of the runways and to proceed without further inquiry. This decision prompted strong complaints from those who would have suffered from the new alignment but not from the original proposals. The Council on Tribunals made a special report to the Lord Chancellor saying that, as a matter of justice, all persons likely to be seriously affected ought to be allowed to object at a statutory inquiry. The day after this report was made the government announced that a new inquiry would be held on a much wider basis into the siting of the third airport for London—an inquiry which ultimately led to the abandonment of the whole project.

In handling such complaints the Council on Tribunals performs an 'ombudsman' function like that of the Parliamentary Commissioner for Administration.[16] The Parliamentary Commissioner is also himself an ex officio member of the Council.[17] It was apparently the intention of this arrangement that their respective functions should be determined by informal agreement, since the Commissioner has discretion to decide whether to take up any case. But, as pointed out earlier, the Commissioner's policy is to investigate all eligible complaints, even though they

[13] Annual Report for 1965, para. 77 (Packington Estate, Islington).
[14] Annual Report for 1967, pp. 26–9, explaining the basis of the Council's jurisdiction in this case.
[15] Above, p. 990.
[16] Above, p. 81.
[17] Parliamentary Commissioner Act 1967, s. 1(5).

may also fall within the sphere of the Council, so that there are now two alternative avenues in cases connected with inquiries where the two jurisdictions overlap.[18] Thus the Parliamentary Commissioner has investigated complaints about delays in planning appeals, evidence heard *in camera* at an inquiry, costs and similar matters. This overlap, though untidy, is advantageous to complainants, since the Parliamentary Commissioner's powers of investigation and of obtaining satisfaction are much greater than those of the Council.[19]

OTHER INQUIRY PROCEDURES

Experiments in the United States

An attempt to 'judicialise' departmental procedure, much in the manner the House of Lords refused to approve in the *Arlidge* case,[20] has led the law of the United States through some interesting gyrations. In a famous case of 1936, which concerned the Secretary of Agriculture's power to fix prices for sales of livestock after a public hearing, the Supreme Court invalidated a price-fixing order merely on the ground that the Secretary himself had not personally heard or read any of the evidence or considered the arguments submitted, but had decided the matter solely on the advice of his officials in consultations at which the objectors were not present.[21] A heroic decision! The opinion given by Chief Justice Hughes rejected the very essence of administrative practice by refusing to allow that 'one official may examine evidence, and another official who has not considered the evidence may make the findings and order'. He said:

That duty [sc. of decision] cannot be performed by one who has not considered evidence or argument. It is not an impersonal obligation. It is akin to that of a judge. The one who decides must hear.

One may well imagine the comments of civil servants, on both sides of the Atlantic, upon this doctrine. It has since been made subject to severe qualification, including statutory modification, as indeed was inevitable if it was not to bring government business to a standstill. The facts of administrative life make it impossible for a minister personally to peruse all the evidence, even assuming that he can attend to the case at all. Nor can it be right to subpoena him in every case and demand to know his exact state

---

[18] Above, p. 96.
[19] Above, p. 920.
[20] Above, p. 507.
[21] *Morgan v. United States*, 298 US 468 (1936). See Schwartz and Wade, *Legal Control of Government*, 250; Schwartz, *Administrative Law*, 2nd edn., 384ff.

of mind and how much of his homework he did before he signed the order.[22] Obviously the work of holding the inquiry and reporting on the evidence must be delegated to officials, and so in many cases must be the substantive decision itself. But what the Supreme Court of the United States continued to require was that the decision should be the personal decision of the minister in the sense that he sees the record and exercises his personal judgment upon it. The case may be predigested for him in his department, but he is the one who is required to decide. He must therefore 'hear' in the sense of applying his mind to both sides of the case. He may not simply ratify a decision taken by his subordinates, as he may in England.[23]

The Federal Administrative Procedure Act

Congress adopted a new line of attack in the Administrative Procedure Act of 1946. This Act is an ambitious attempt to deal with some of the problems discussed in this book.[24] It does, indeed, adopt the ideal 'the one who decides must hear' for the inquiries to which it applies, meaning obligatory statutory inquiries held by agencies of the federal government and decided 'on the record'. But instead of attempting to control the final decision of the minister or agency, and postponing the substantial decision until the last possible moment, it allows a substantial decision to be taken by the official who holds the hearing. The object is to meet the complaint that hearing officers may be—or at any rate appear to be—too much the puppets of their agencies. The position of these officers is therefore strengthened under the American statute, which endeavours to give them a position of independence and responsibility almost like that of a judge of first instance. Hearing officers are formed into something like a special corps, and are removable only for good cause established before the Civil Service Commission; and their salaries and conditions of service are controlled by the Commission rather than by their own agencies. Having given them a status of greater independence, the Act then provides that, unless they submit the whole record to the agency, they shall decide the case, and not merely make a recommendation to the agency. The Act says:[25]

In cases in which the agency has not presided at the reception of the evidence, the

---

[22] United States v. Morgan 313 US 409 (1941); see also Morgan v. United States, 304 US 1 (1938).

[23] Above, p. 366. In Steel v. Minister of Housing and Local Government (1956) 6 P & CR 386 at 392 Denning LJ said, dealing with a Housing Act inquiry, that in a judicial matter such as that it was 'infinitely better' that the man who heard the evidence and arguments should decide; but he added that Parliament had prescribed otherwise: 'one man hears, another decides'.

[24] See Schwartz and Wade, Legal Control of Government, 108; Schwartz (as above), 401.

[25] s. 8.

officer who presided . . . shall initially decide the case or the agency shall require (in specific cases or by general rule) the entire record to be certified to it for initial decision. Whenever such officers make the initial decision and in the absence of either an appeal to the agency or review upon motion of the agency within time provided by the rule, such decision shall without further proceedings then become the decision of the agency.

Thus the ideal has become: 'The one who hears must decide'. If the case is heard on the lower level, the parties will obtain a decision from the hearing officer himself, subject to appeal to the agency. Reasons must be given for the decision, and also for any further decision by the agency, so that the agency's appellate function is much less free from constraint than it would be if it were taking an initial decision on an unpublished report from its hearing officer.

Would this 'judicialised' procedure improve the system of statutory inquiries in Britain? The Franks Committee in their report of 1957 did not think so: it was fallacious, they said, to regard the inspector as 'a kind of judge provisionally deciding the matter, subject to an appeal to the minister'.[26] This is undoubtedly correct in the cases for which statutory inquiries are primarily designed: the cases where the decision is likely to be dominated by ministerial policy. It is a mistake to suppose that the person in the best position to decide on the site of an atomic power station or of a new town is the inspector who held the inquiry. The inquiry can determine the local aspects, but it cannot determine the national aspects.

But in cases where policy is stereotyped or easy to ascertain, the position may be otherwise. These are the cases for which the American procedure is designed; and it reflects the American feeling that policy ought to be crystallised in rules and formulae rather than left at large.[27] This class of cases is not so extensive in Britain, where many powers of regulation are either purely political (like control of nationalised industries) or commercial (like those of the Independent Broadcasting Authority) or else are allotted to special tribunals. But something like the American system is to be found in some parts of the British system of road passenger transport and air transport licensing, where the initial decision is made by an independent tribunal, but is subject to an appeal to the minister.[28] And something like it applies to the classes of planning appeals which are decided by the inspector, subject only to intervention by the minister in special cases.[29] But what appears to be the standard case in the United States is likely to remain the exceptional case in Britain.

---

[26] Cmnd. 218 (1957), para. 274.
[27] This is discussed in (1965) 81 LQR 357.
[28] See above, p. 901.
[29] Above, p. 991.

Administrative procedure is now the concern of the Administrative Conference of the United States, an advisory body which was set up in 1968.[30] The Conference is in some respects comparable to the Council on Tribunals, though it is much larger in size and contains many official members. Less than half its membership (of over eighty) are persons independent of the government.

Accident inquiries

Railway accidents, shipwrecks, air crashes, factory accidents, and so forth often have to be inquired into, and in general the familiar form of the public inquiry is followed.[31] But under the various statutes providing for such inquiries the practice varies a good deal. It is obviously of great importance that it should be satisfactory, since the reputation and livelihood of drivers, pilots and others—not to mention the safety of their passengers—will often depend upon the findings. The Franks Committee did not investigate them, confining itself to the more controversial inquiries affecting land.

Taking the ordinary railway accident inquiry[32] as an example, we find that although the inquiry is statutory and a report is made by the railway inspectorate of the Department of the Environment,[33] there are no rules of procedure, no right to legal representation, no right of cross-examination, and no right of appeal. The Secretary of State has, indeed, power to direct a formal inquiry by a county court judge, magistrate or other person, which must be held in open court with power to summon witnesses, administer oaths and enter premises. But there are no procedural rules, and in any case this power has been used only once since the Tay Bridge disaster of 1879.[34] Shipping casualty inquiries,[35] on the other hand, where there is power to cancel a mariner's licence, are much more formal and judicial: they are held by a court of summary jurisdiction or a wreck commissioner, there are statutory rules of procedure,[36] rights of calling witnesses and cross-examination, and a right of appeal to the High Court.[37] For aircraft

---

[30] Schwartz and Wade, *Legal Control of Government*, 180.

[31] On accident inquiries see Wraith and Lamb, *Public Inquiries as an Instrument of Government*, 146.

[32] Held under the Railway Regulation Act 1871, s. 7.

[33] See *Waugh* v. *British Railways Board* [1980] AC 521, where the House of Lords ordered the report to be disclosed to a railwayman's widow in an action for negligence.

[34] In the Hixon level crossing disaster case, where a Queen's Counsel and two assessors held the inquiry: Cmnd. 3706 (1968).

[35] Held under Merchant Shipping Act 1894, s. 466. Less formal preliminary inquiries can be held under s. 465.

[36] SR & O 1923 No. 752.

[37] Merchant Shipping Act 1894, s. 475(3).

accidents an up-to-date procedure is provided.[38] An inspector first makes a private investigation, but must invite representations from anyone whom he proposes to criticise in his report. Any such person is entitled to have his case reviewed by a review board appointed by the Lord Chancellor, which normally sits in public and affords full procedural rights. In important cases the Secretary of State for Trade and Industry may alternatively order a formal public inquiry, which takes place before a commissioner (an experienced barrister) and at least two skilled assessors, all appointed by the Lord Chancellor. The case is then presented under the control of the Attorney-General. The reports of inspectors, review boards and commissioners are normally to be published. Investigations and reviews may be reopened on the directions of the Secretary of State.

Accident inquiries raise very difficult questions and their procedure needs to be kept under review no less than that of other inquiries. Steps towards this end have only recently begun to be taken. Accident inquiries were excluded from the order of 1967 which brought numerous discretionary inquiries within the Tribunals and Inquiries Acts.[39] On the other hand, the Council on Tribunals were consulted about, and secured amendments in, the procedure introduced in 1969 for aircraft accident inquiries.[40] They pointed out that the Review Board was an obligatory inquiry and therefore automatically came within the Tribunals and Inquiries Act 1958, so that the Council could deal with complaints; but that the other inquiries provided for were discretionary and would not be subject to the Act unless brought under it by order. The second discretionary inquiries order, made in 1975, accordingly included aircraft accident inquiries, along with road accident inquiries, shipping casualty inquiries, and formal investigations into boiler explosions.[41] But it omitted other cases, e.g. railway accident inquiries. To a substantial extent, however, it is now recognized that accident inquiries need supervision and attention.

Tribunals of Inquiry

A special form of inquiry, which from time to time becomes a focus of public attention, is the inquiry which Parliament may at any time authorise

---

[38] SI 1983 No. 551, made under the Civil Aviation Act 1982, ss. 75, 102.
[39] SI 1967 No. 451. Item 49 of the schedule specifically excluded road accident inquiries.
[40] Council on Tribunals, Annual Report for 1969–70, para. 99.
[41] SI 1975 No. 1379 (above, p. 989). See 1st sched., items 75–7 (shipping, diving and hovercraft), 78 (boiler explosions), 82–3 (aircraft). Road accident inquiries are covered by item 40, no longer being excluded. Since item 40, unlike the others, is in Part I of the schedule, the duty to give reasons applies.

under the Tribunals of Inquiry (Evidence) Act 1921.[42] This has no particular connection with administrative powers or with administrative law; for though it has often been used to investigate allegations of administrative misdeeds by ministers of the Crown, civil servants, local authorities, or the police, it is not confined to such matters. An inquiry of this kind is a procedure of last resort, to be used when nothing else will serve to allay public disquiet, usually based on sensational allegations, rumours, or disasters. There have been some twenty such occasions since the Act was passed, including cases of improper gifts to ministers,[43] disclosure of budget secrets by ministers,[44] a leak of information about bank rate,[45] accusations of brutality against the police,[46] the supervision of an insurance company by ministers and civil servants,[47] disorders in Northern Ireland,[48] and the Aberfan landslide disaster,[49] involving the National Coal Board.

These inquiries are fundamentally extra-legal, being commissioned by the government which can always set up an inquiry into anything. But the Act of 1921 clothes Tribunals of Inquiry with the powers of the High Court to summon witnesses, send for documents, administer oaths, and so forth, reinforced by the sanction of citing cases of disobedience or contempt before the High Court, which can then punish offenders as for contempt of court. The tribunal must sit in public unless in its opinion this is inexpedient in the public interest; and it may allow or refuse legal representation to any one involved. There are no other rules of procedure. In order to bring the Act into play both Houses of Parliament must resolve that a tribunal shall investigate some matter described as being 'of urgent public importance'. The tribunal is then appointed by the Crown or a Secretary of State in a document reciting that the Act is to apply. The parliamentary resolutions serve to differentiate tribunals of inquiry from ordinary administrative inquiries or investigations, such as royal commissions and departmental committees, which have no statutory authority or special powers.

Experience of tribunals of inquiry has revealed the dangers to which a procedure of this kind is naturally prone. The inquiry is inquisitorial in character, and usually takes place in a blaze of publicity. Very damaging allegations may be made against persons who may have little opportunity of defending themselves and against whom no legal charge is preferred.

[42] For a general account see Keeton, *Trial by Tribunal.*
[43] Cmd. 7616 (1948)
[44] Cmd. 5184 (1936).
[45] Cmnd. 350 (1957).
[46] Cmd. 3147 (1928); Cmnd. 718 (1959).
[47] HC 133, February 1972.
[48] Cmd. 566 (NI), April 1972; HC 220, April 1972.
[49] HC 553, July 1967.

The tribunal is usually presided over by an eminent judge, who can be relied upon to mitigate these dangers so far as possible. But an inquisitorial public inquiry is not always easily controllable, and its evils would be grave if its use were not infrequent.

A royal commission reviewed the whole procedure in 1966 and made fifty recommendations.[50] It rejected various alternatives which had been suggested and it emphasised that some powerful and unrestricted means of inquiry must be 'available for use in emergencies. Basically therefore it approved the existing system of tribunals of inquiry. But it also emphasised that they were justifiable only on exceptional occasions when there was something like a nation-wide crisis of confidence. In order to minimise the risk of injustice to individuals it was recommended that the tribunal should satisfy itself that each witness was really involved, that he should be informed in advance of any allegations and evidence against him, that he should have legal advice and representation (normally to be paid for from public funds), that he should be able to state his case in public and cross-examine witnesses whose testimony affected him,[51] and that his own testimony should not be used against him in later civil or criminal proceedings. Some of the recommendations would require amendment of the Act of 1921, for example to confer a right to legal representation, to confer immunity on members of the tribunal, counsel, solicitors and witnesses, and to give power to inform the tribunal of witnesses' previous convictions. The proposed immunity would encourage witnesses to speak freely without fear of civil or criminal prosecution, and all the more so because it would cancel the normal privilege against self-incrimination. A supplementary report from a committee dealt separately with the question of contempt of the tribunal by prejudicial comment in the press and elsewhere, which arose for the first time in connection with the Aberfan disaster, shortly after the royal commission's report,[52] when it was suggested that the tribunal's contempt powers might be used to stifle public comment. The committee recommended principally that there should be no restriction of comment on the subject matter of the inquiry at any time, but that after a tribunal was appointed it should be a contempt to do anything likely to suppress or pervert evidence; that specially vulnerable individuals should be protected by the chairman asking that no interview with them should be published (though without legal penalty); and that the Act of 1921 should be amended and clarified accordingly. Strong emphasis

---

[50] Cmnd. 3121 (1966, chairman Salmon LJ).

[51] Compare *Mahon* v. *Air New Zealand* [1984] AC 808 at 820–1, where Lord Diplock states the principles of natural justice applicable to a statutory royal commission in New Zealand.

[52] Cmnd. 4078 (1969, chairman Salmon LJ).

was put upon the importance of the maximum freedom of discussion in matters of acute public concern.

In 1973 the government published its comments on these various recommendations, accepting the greater part of them but rejecting the committee's proposals for amendment of the Act of 1921 in the matter of contempt.[53] It said that legislation would be brought forward to make other amendments which would be necessary, but this has not been done.

One problem which engaged the royal commission was how evidence should be presented before an inquisitorial tribunal where there was no plaintiff, appellant or similar originating party. The practice has been for the Attorney-General to undertake this task, even when it has involved making charges against his ministerial colleagues and conducting hostile cross-examinations of them.[54] This is a remarkable example of the Attorney-General's ability to detach himself from his political and personal ties when he has to act in his capacity of guardian of the law and of the public interest. Creditable though this ability is, it is not easily understood by the public and there is no convincing reason why it should be called for. The royal commission therefore recommended that the practice should cease, and that the tribunal should appoint its own counsel, none of whom should be law officers of the Crown.[55] But the government considered that the tribunal in appointing its counsel should be free to include a law officer if it thought fit and to limit his role if that seemed desirable.[56] In subsequent cases the tribunal has in fact appointed the Attorney-General as one of its counsel, though it has arranged for evidence which might involve ministers or government departments to be prepared and presented by others.[57]

---

[53] Cmnd. 5313 (1973, White Paper).

[54] The classic case was the conduct by Sir Hartley Shawcross A.-G. of the 'prosecution' before the tribunal of inquiry into 'bribery of ministers of the Crown or other public servants in connection with the grant of licences, etc.', Cmd. 7616 (1948).

[55] Cmnd. 3121 (1966), para. 96.

[56] Cmnd. 5313 (1973), para. 16.

[57] This was done, for example, by the tribunal of inquiry into the collapse of the Vehicle and General Insurance Co., HC 133 (February 1972).

APPENDIX

The Justice – All Souls Review

(see Preface)

In 1969 the Government declined to act on the recommendation of the Law Commission that a Royal Commission should undertake a comprehensive examination of administrative law (see above, p. 13). In 1978, shortly after the procedural reforms which established the application for judicial review, this task was undertaken by an independent and unofficial committee constituted by JUSTICE, the British section of the International Commission of Jurists, in collaboration with All Souls College, Oxford. The Committee was composed of fifteen eminent persons of wide knowledge and experience under the chairmanship of Sir Patrick Neill QC. A Scottish working group and an advisory panel were also formed.

The Committee's report (*Administrative Justice – Some Necessary Reforms*) was published in 1988, too late for proper treatment here. It is a volume of 450 pages, rich in detail and replete with judicious recommendations, some of which correspond with criticisms already made in this book. The following much abbreviated summary of a few of them will give a general idea of the scope and content of this important and well argued report.

1. *Principles of Good Administration*
   A non-statutory statement of principles should be drawn up, preferably by the Parliamentary Commissioner for Administration. It should be based upon the recommendations of the Committee of Ministers of the Council of Europe (above, p. 472, also 388).

2. *Reasons for Decisions*
   Administrators should have a statutory general duty to give reasons for their decisions on demand, together with findings on material questions of fact. Exceptions should be made for the purpose of protecting national security, confidential information, staff appointments and certain other matters.

3. *Administrative Review Commission*
   Under this name should be constituted a permanent body, independent of the Government, with the duty of overseeing all aspects of administrative justice, drawing attention to defects and proposing reforms. It should be statutory, should report annually to Parliament, and have Parliamentary links.

4. *Ombudsmen*
   Direct access to the Parliamentary Commissioner for Administration should be allowed. There is no need for legal machinery to enforce his

recommendations, but it should be provided to enforce recommendations of the Local Commissioners by way of application to the County Court.

5. *Application for Judicial Review*
   (a) *O'Reilly* v. *Mackman* [1983] 2 AC 237 should be reconsidered by the House of Lords at an early opportunity. Parliament should decide whether applicants should be obliged to use the Order 53 procedure exclusively.
   (b) The term 'public law' should cease to be used as the key to identifying cases for the Order 53 procedure.
   (c) The requirement of leave for proceeding under Order 53 should be abandoned.
   (d) The three months' time limit should be repealed.
   (e) The grounds for judicial review should be made statutory, following the model of the Australian Administrative Decisions (Judicial Review) Act 1977.
   (f) The court should be able to order that proceedings wrongly commenced by writ should continue as if under Order 53.

6. *Misleading Official Advice*
   There should be a remedy for loss caused by erroneous or misleading official advice without the need to prove negligence. A compulsory purchase order procured by fraud should be liable to set aside notwithstanding the expiry of the statutory six-week period.

7. *Error of Law*
   The rule requiring error of law to appear on the face of the record should be abolished.

8. *Standing*
   The need to obtain the Attorney General's assistance in relator actions should be eliminated and the question of standing should be decided by the court. Among other factors the court should take account of any public interest indicating that the question at issue should be determined. The Supreme Court Act 1981, s. 31 (3) should be amended accordingly.

9. *Tribunals*
   All tribunals should be placed under the supervision of the Council on Tribunals, which should be given adequate resources and support. Representation before tribunals should be provided more liberally.

10. *Inquiries*
    Participants should be able to question the policy behind development plans and also questions of need generally. There should be a right of appeal against the grant of planning permission. Third-party participation should sometimes be supported financially. Inquiries into proposed rule-making need consideration.

11. *Compensation*

There should be a remedy for loss suffered as a result of wrongful administrative action not involving negligence, including delay. Claims in restitution should be provided for by legislation. Members of courts and tribunals should be exempted.

INDEX